D0255068

FROMMER'S
DOLLARWISE GUIDE TO GERMANY

by Darwin Porter
Assisted by Danforth Prince

1986-87 Edition

020A   171
PRICE   11.95
M 6A 0214

Sponsored by

Lufthansa

Copyright © 1972, 1974, 1976, 1978, 1980, 1982, 1984, 1986

All rights reserved
including the right of reproduction
in whole or in part in any form

Published by Frommer/Pasmantier Publishers
A Division of Simon & Schuster, Inc.
1230 Avenue of the Americas
New York, N.Y. 10020

ISBN 0–671–55599-5

Manufactured in the United States of America

*Lufthansa German Airlines shall not be responsible for any errors,
faulty information, and/or printing errors of any sort.*

CONTENTS

MAPS

To Stanley Haggart

Acknowledgment

The author of this book acknowledges the generous contributions of Margaret Foresman.

A DISCLAIMER: Although every effort was made to ensure the accuracy of the prices and travel information appearing in this book, it should be kept in mind that prices do fluctuate in the course of time, and that information does change under the impact of the varied and volatile factors that affect the travel industry. Readers should also note that the establishments described under Readers' Selections or Suggestions have not in many cases been inspected by the author and that the opinions expressed there are those of the individual reader(s) only. They do not in any way represent the opinions of the publisher or author of this guide.

INFLATION ALERT: I don't have to tell you that inflation has hit Germany as it has everywhere else. In researching this book I have made every effort to obtain up-to-the-minute prices, but even the most conscientious researcher cannot keep up with the current pace of inflation. As the guide goes to press, I believe I have obtained the most reliable data possible. Nonetheless, in the lifetime of this edition—particularly its second year (1987)—the wise traveler will add 15% to 20% to the prices quoted throughout these pages.

Introduction

A DOLLARWISE GUIDE TO GERMANY

The Reason Why

A NEW, WEALTHY, industrial, yet beautiful, Germany awaits you.

Many of its medieval treasures were lost during the war, but much remains and much has been rebuilt in the old style. Natural scenery, particularly such places as the Black Forest, the Mosel Valley, and the Bavarian Alps, was and is a potent lure for any prospective traveler to Germany.

The people of the Federal Republic of Germany are complex, the descendants of widely varied cultural backgrounds. Distinguishing differences can be noted among the Westphalians, the Lower Saxonians, the Bavarians, and the Rhinelanders. Don't expect to find a nation of happy, laughing beer drinkers running around in lederhosen with feather-topped hunting caps resting jauntily on their heads. However, enough of these tradition-minded souls exist to reinforce the stereotype.

In capsule fashion, here's a running impression of Germany:

Bavarian baroque . . . cow bells . . . white-capped Alps . . . crystal-blue lakes . . . golden old cities on the banks of the Danube . . . green hills and castles along the majestic Rhine . . . the fragrance of a new harvest in the wine towns . . . the dark pines of the Black Forest . . . sailors and strippers after dark in the port of Hamburg . . . the canaries of the Harz Mountains . . . half-timbered buildings in medieval villages . . . bold, courageous modern architecture rising in industrial cities . . . operas, theaters, fairs, and festivals . . . soaring Gothic cathedrals . . . wine drinking and dancing . . . the good regional cuisine in a typical ratskeller . . . the finger-sized sausages of Nürnberg . . . the health spas with their kur baths and roulette wheels.

All in all, it's a land that knows how to harmonize contrasts.

THE BEST OF GERMANY: I have set for myself the formidable task of seeking out Germany at its best and condensing that between the covers of this book. The best includes not only descriptions of important cities, towns, villages, and sightseeing attractions, but recommendations of hotels, restaurants, bars, cafés, and nightspots as well.

This book is based on the premise that the best need not be the most expensive. Hence, my ultimate aim, beyond that of familiarizing you with the offerings of Germany, is to stretch your dollar power, to reveal that you need not always pay scalper's prices for charm, top-grade comfort, and first-rate food.

I'll devote a great deal of attention to the tourist meccas: Munich, Frankfurt, Hamburg, and Berlin, focusing on both obvious and hidden treasures. But important as they are, they do not reflect completely the widely diverse and complicated country that is Germany.

To seek out the wonders of this often perplexing land, you must also go to the Bavarian Alps, Lake Constance, the Rhine and Mosel Valleys, and the coast of the North Sea, to name only a few areas.

It may be presumptuous to give you reasons why to go to Germany. Dozens may have already occurred to you. I'll merely add a few, beginning with . . .

(1) To live in a castle like royalty

If this has been a long-suppressed desire, Germany offers an opportunity to fulfill it. More chances, in fact, to spend the night in a real castle than you'll find in any other country of Europe. Picture yourself perched high in the clouds (1800 feet altitude), the window of your bedchamber opening onto a wall of fortress-like houses. At night, under a full moon, the Middle Ages come alive.

(2) To take "the cure" at a spa

Regardless of your ailment, hypochondriacal or otherwise, a German spa claims a cure. No country in Europe has more health resorts. Ever since the Romans came this way 2000 years ago, "taking the waters" has been a long-established rejuvenation process throughout the land. Once the spa was the exclusive domain of royalty and the aristocracy, but today it has become a firmly entrenched middle-class institution. Of course, Germans like to take the cure in style, even—or especially—if nothing is wrong with them. Therefore the spa dining table is the best in the country. The major resorts have gambling casinos, with dancing and entertainment in the evening. It's no surprise then that some spa devotees come just to have fun, spending their daytime hours golfing and horseback riding. Others take the treatment more seriously, immersing themselves in thermal pools, even taking sand baths. The curative spring is the therapeutic beverage to many Germans, as the eternal search for the fountain of youth goes on.

(3) To get the biggest hangover of the year at Munich's annual Oktoberfest

Even if you don't like to drink, you can get bombed just walking through Munich's Oktoberfest meadow when it's in full swing, filled to the brim with beer-drinking revelers. Lasting for 16 days, the festival begins late in September. Barn-like beer halls are assembled on the Theresienwiese. Beer wagons, drawn by horses, bring in kegs of the golden brew that eternally delights the Bavarians, who seem to hold all sorts of world records for beer consumption. All the famous breweries are represented, including Löwenbräu and Pschorrbräu. You'll think you're reliving the days of the Roman Empire when you see oxen roasting, beer being guzzled, screaming girls being hoisted into the air and twirled around, and throngs of merrymakers in corny hats, making the festival an eternal New Year's Eve party. Enough pork sausage is consumed "to girdle Munich," as the saying goes. However, for those who have imbibed too heavily, tents are set up which dispense coffee. Gone is the "oompah" band in these rehabilitation centers for the boozed out. Rather, the quiet, melodious sound of the zither is heard. Many of the "patients" are often successfully rejuvenated enough by the music to try their luck once again!

(4) To see if the Reeperbahn of Hamburg lives up to its reputation

If you grew up in the Bible Belt and were tantalized by sermons on the evils of Sodom and Gomorrah and have been searching for those cities ever since, you may find their spirit on the streets of Hamburg's Reeperbahn. This so-called sin strip is a genuine Teutonic sex circus. Mere topless or bottomless is never enough. It's a voyeuristic delight as dozens of girlie joints vie for the marks of the visiting sailor or the local businessman looking for some divertissement. The parade, or rather the posture, of erotic adventuring continues throughout the evening and into the early hours. A bit of comedy, a touch of perversity—all in all, a bold adventure!

DOLLARWISE—WHAT IT MEANS: In brief, this is a guidebook giving specific, practical details (including prices) about Germany's hotels, restaurants, sightseeing attractions, and nightlife. Establishments in all price ranges have been documented and described, from the extravagant chambers of the Vier Jahreszeiten (Four Seasons) in Hamburg to a moderately priced, 12th-century knight's castle commanding a spectacular view of the Harz Mountains.

In all cases, establishments have been judged by the strict yardstick of value. If they measured up, they were included in this book, regardless of price classification. The uniqueness of this book, I think, lies in the fact that it could be used by a matron ("We always stay at the Bayerischer Hof in Munich"), or by a mark-mindful collegian ("There's this great little restaurant in Berlin that serves you a complete dinner for 15 DM").

But the major focus of the book is centered neither on the impecunious nor on the affluent. Rather, my chief concern is the average, middle-income-bracket voyager who'd like to patronize the almost wholly undocumented establishments of Germany that offer maximum value.

SOME "VORSPEISEN" OF BARGAINS: Borrowing the word in this heading from the array of tempting beginnings to the German meal, I'll preview some of the most delectable establishments awaiting you. In my journeys through every province of Germany, through its large cities and small villages, I have discovered surprising luxury offered for little cost, or establishments where the home-made or creative touch of their proprietors lifted them far above the ordinary. For a truer understanding of what dollarwise means, I'll now recall only a few as examples. You'll find dozens more in the pages ahead—and perhaps discover others on your own when you actually go to Germany.

In the Mosel Valley at **Traben-Trarbach,** you can stay at Clauss-Feist, a heavily Germanic structure right on the banks of the river. It was created in an ornamental style around 1900, with elaborate timberwork, a domed tower, a highly pitched roof, gables, and dormers. Warmly decorated double rooms without bath cost from 58 DM ($19.14) to 68 DM ($22.44).

Or on Germany's famed Romantic Road, in the medieval town of **Dinkelsbühl,** still surrounded by ancient walls, you can stay in the Deutsches Haus, an inn whose fascinating carved and painted facade dates from 1440. In the individually furnished bedrooms, you're likely to find a ceramic stove in one room, a Biedermeier desk in another. For this you'll pay 65 DM ($21.45) in a bathless double.

What about restaurants? In the Bavarian capital is the Weinstadl, reportedly the oldest house in **Munich,** tracing its history back to 1468. But in spite of its antique look, it's no museum. Waitresses in regional dress hurry across the natural brick floor, serving up hearty Bavarian fare at scrubbed wooden tables lit by candles. Typical main dishes include pork cutlet with vegetables and a salad. A complete, filling meal costs from 18 DM ($5.94) to 38 DM ($12.54).

In the large Black Forest city of **Freiburg,** you can dine in the Oberkirchs Weinstuben, where you can saturate yourself with the food and flavor of the old town. The restaurant's situation is picture-postcardy, on a little square, with step-gabled roof houses. An old wrought-iron sign hangs over the restaurant's entrance, and red and white tables are set out front for wine sampling or meals. A memorable lunch in the dark-paneled weinstube costs as little as 25 DM ($8.25).

THE ORGANIZATION OF THIS BOOK: Here's how *Dollarwise Guide to Germany* sets forth its information:

Chapter I, directly ahead, deals with getting to Germany (the most natural choice is by air, of course). Then it deals with various modes of transportation within the country. The chapter also includes some vital data on the ABCs of life in Germany that will help ease your adjustment into that country.

Chapter II focuses on Frankfurt am Main, the country's seventh-largest city but its most important transportation center. It is likely to be your gateway to Germany. Hotels in all categories are documented first, followed by restaurants, sights, and nightlife attractions. (This will be the pattern followed in Germany's other leading cities such as Munich and Berlin.)

Chapter III turns the spotlight on the major tourist city of Germany—Munich, the capital of Bavaria. This thick chapter is packed with information on hotels, restaurants, sightseeing attractions (both in the city proper and in its environs), shopping suggestions, nightlife attractions, and much other useful information, ranging from previews of beer gardens to a trip to Olympic City.

After all this high living, you may be ready for a treatment at a spa. **Chapter IV** visits ten of the leading spas of Germany, ranging from Wiesbaden to Bad Homburg. Known since Roman times, the "healing waters" of these spas have attracted everybody from royalty to workaday Germans. A wide range of hotels and restaurants is described.

Chapter V visits the Rhineland, the most legendary attraction of Germany. The Rhine is the home of many of the country's largest and most modern cities, such as Cologne and Düsseldorf, but the reader will also want to follow along as we visit the small towns and villages where Bacchus reigns supreme.

Quiet university towns and ancient castle ruins are found along the Neckar Valley, explored in **Chapter VI,** which begins in one of Germany's most visited tourist cities, Heidelberg, of *The Student Prince* fame. In this chapter we'll also visit Stuttgart, the home of the Mercedes and Porsche automobiles.

Germany has another great "river of wine," the Mosel, explored in **Chapter VII,** which weaves its snake-like path through the mountains west of the Rhineland.

In southwestern Germany, the fabled Black Forest (called Schwarzwald in German) is the subject of **Chapter VIII.** Roughly 90 miles long and 25 miles wide, it is a land of cuckoo clocks and toys. Freiburg is the capital, Baden-Baden its most famous spa.

In **Chapter IX** we sail across Lake Constance (Bodensee in German) where three nations—Austria, Germany, and Switzerland—share a 162-mile shoreline.

The Romantic Road is traveled in **Chapter X,** a strasse cutting through central Bavaria, with its medieval villages and 2000-year-old towns. The route stretches for 180 miles between the cities of Würzburg in the north, and Füssen, in the foothills of the Bavarian Alps, the latter a good base for exploring the castles of "Mad Ludwig."

Along the German-Austrian frontier, the Bavarian Alps in **Chapter XI** is considered the most scenic attraction of Germany. In both summer and winter this part of southern Germany is a playground, where the action centers around such resorts as Garmisch-Partenkirchen. More of Ludwig's castles are previewed in this chapter, along with scenic belvederes and sylvan lakeside retreats.

In northern Bavaria, the hillsides and medieval castles, churches, and monasteries of Franconia beckon in **Chapter XII.** A land of culture and history, Franconia takes in such stopovers as history-rich Nürnberg, but perhaps you'll find your most mellow times sailing along the German Danube.

Lower Saxony and North Hesse, between Frankfurt and Hamburg, much less known than the areas previously considered, are given their moment in **Chapter XII,** as our trail heads for the Harz Mountains. But along the way we'll visit the old Hanseatic city of Bremen, stately Hannover, and everyplace from the Pied Piper town of Hameln to the Upper Weser Valley, Germany's "fairytale country," setting for *The Sleeping Beauty* and characters in the tales of the Grimm Brothers.

Chapters XIV and XV might be called a "sampler" of the highlights of northern Germany, of which Hamburg is the major attraction. This section takes in such historic cities as Lübeck, but also visits such offshore resorts in the North Sea as Sylt.

Our tour of West Germany concluded, we blaze a new trail in **Chapter XVI,** taking in the old city of West Berlin, which has emerged from the rubble of war's defeat to become a symbol of freedom, even though it is literally surrounded by Soviet-occupied territory. A wide range of attractions is described in this section, including nightlife and sights. A full range of eating places and hotels is also documented.

Chapter XVII, the conclusion of this guide, is billed as a "side trip," as it's to another country entirely, East Germany, called the GDR. The tenth leading industrial power of the world, this little-known country is visited in detail, beginning with East Berlin, but going on to such famed places as Potsdam, Leipzig, Dresden, and Meissen, along with Weimar. Such dark places as Buchenwald are visited, but the spirit is lifted once more on a motor trip through the Harz Mountains, with a final stopover at some Baltic Sea resorts. Because visiting this country can be difficult, detailed instructions are given.

THE DEUTSCHES MARK AND THE DOLLAR: The unit of German currency is the **Deutsches Mark (DM),** which is subdivided into **pfennigs.** What the Deutsches Mark is worth in terms of U.S. money is a tricky question, the answer to which you determine the same way you determine what your stock holdings are worth: by consulting the daily market quotations from day to day, in this case the money market.

The best advice is to consult a broker immediately before you leave or upon arrival to determine the most up-to-the-minute rate of exchange.

Still, some idea of what you'll be spending will be useful as you read these pages, so I've prepared a DM-to-dollar chart to be used *only as a gauge.* It is based on an exchange rate of approximately 3.05 DM to $1 U.S.

DM	U.S.$	DM	U.S.$
0.25 (25 pfennigs)	.08	20	6.60
0.50 (50 pfennigs)	.17	25	8.25
1	.33	50	16.50
2	.66	75	24.75
5	1.65	100	33.00
7.50	2.48	125	41.25
10	3.30	150	49.50
15	4.95	200	66.00

WHERE TO GO: Most visitors begin their tour of West Germany in Frankfurt, which is a convenient center because you can branch out in all directions, including on one of the most popular tours, a cruise of the Rhineland. This can be done by an organized boat excursion or independently in your own private car. After flying to Frankfurt, you'll need a day to recover from the flight, another day to tour Frankfurt itself.

On your third day, you can head west from Frankfurt, paying visits at two famous stopovers along the way: Mainz and Wiesbaden, each on opposite banks of the Rhine. Mainz, 24 miles from Frankfurt, is a 2000-year-old city founded by the Romans (Gutenberg invented moveable type here in 1440). Wiesbaden, on the opposite bank, eight miles north from Mainz, is one of the world's leading belle époque spas. From Wiesbaden it is a 64-mile drive northwest to Koblenz, which stands at the confluence of the Rhine and Mosel Rivers. On the way there you can go through the famous Rheingau, whose little wine towns such as Rüdesheim are known around the world. Koblenz doesn't have all that much to recommend it, but because of its strategic position it makes a suitable base for an overnight stop.

On the morning of your fourth day, you can explore the enchanting Mosel Valley, which many visitors find more appealing than the Rhineland. Your final destination, a distance of some 77 miles, might be Trier, considered the oldest city in Germany, lying some six miles from the Luxembourg border.

You can also take boat trips on the Mosel (see Chapter VII). The most intriguing stopovers along the way include Zell, Traben-Trarbach, Bernkastel-Kues, Belstein, Cochem, and Eltz Castle. Of course, many motorists spend a week or more exploring the Mosel. But on a rushed schedule, you may have to confine it to a day.

On the fifth day, I suggest that you return to Koblenz (exploring whichever riverbank of the Mosel you missed the preceding day). From Koblenz it is but a 55-mile trip north to Cologne. Along the route you can stop at the capital of West Germany, Bonn, only 17 miles south of Cologne.

Cologne with its cathedral is the largest city in the Rhineland, and also one of the premier attractions of Germany. Following our "slow" route, you will need to spend at least a day getting to Cologne, so figure on a two-night stopover there, the second day spent discovering the city itself.

On the seventh day, which will have made for a total week of touring, you can press north to Düsseldorf, a city of haute couture and culture, lying 24 miles north of Cologne, or else you can return to Frankfurt, where yet another exciting tour is recommended.

If you'd like to take a "Grand Tour," beginning in Frankfurt and working your way eventually to Munich, via Heidelberg, the Black Forest, the Romantic Road, and the Bavarian Alps, you can motor along the following suggested route. Count on spending at least eight nights before you reach Munich. Even so, you'll only have skimmed the highlights, but modern time schedules have to be dealt with realistically.

Most of the run between Frankfurt and Heidelberg can be made by auto-bahn. There are a lot more scenic routes you can take, but if your desire is to spend as much time in Heidelberg as possible, you can be there in about an hour and a half, covering a distance of some 60 miles.

Spend your first night in Heidelberg exploring its castle of *Student Prince* fame and visiting one of the student drinking taverns in the evening. Leave the next day along the autobahn heading south toward Basel (Switzerland). If you have time, stop off for a visit to the internationally famous spa at Baden-Baden, with its casino and baths. Visitors anchor in here for days or weeks, but, again, if time is very limited you can continue along the autobahn until you reach Frei-burg, the capital of the Black Forest, a distance of 70 miles from Baden-Baden. Filled with charming inns and cozy wine taverns, Freiburg makes an ideal stop-over.

The next day, your third, you can travel northeast to Stuttgart, a distance of 129 miles with some stopovers along the way. The first morning visit might be to Triberg, home of the cuckoo clock, lying 38 miles from Freiburg. Here you can visit the highest waterfall in all of Germany. From Triberg, you can head east to Schwenningen where you can take a major artery north to Tübingen, an old university town on the upper Neckar River, which is often compared to Heidelberg. If it's running late, you can spend the night here; otherwise, motorists can press on to Stuttgart, 29 miles to the north-east.

After a night in Stuttgart, continue northeast to Würzburg, stopping off for lunch at either Schwäbisch Hall or Bad Mergentheim. Würzburg, lying some 102 miles from Stuttgart, is one of the loveliest baroque cities of Germany. It lies about 60 miles from Frankfurt.

After a night there, you can begin on your fifth day to explore the Roman-tische Strasse or Romantic Road, which stretches for 180 miles between Würz-burg in the north and Füssen at the foothills of the Bavarian Alps.

Some motorists cover this route in just one day, but to do so you will be able to see mainly the sights passing in review from your car window. It's better to head first for Rothenburg, which is considered one of the finest medieval cit-ies in Europe, some say *the* finest. It lies 40 miles south of Würzburg. After time spent there, you might settle in for the rest of the day and evening or head in-stead to the picture-book towns of Dinkelsbühl or Nördlingen, both of which are considered irresistible stopovers along the Romantic Road. Each has old-fashioned inns.

To begin your sixth day, I'd leave either Dinkelsbühl or Nördlingen, paying a morning visit to the old city of Augsburg, which, incidentally, is only 42 miles from Munich if you've run out of time. Otherwise you can continue along the Romantic Road south to Füssen. At this point you'll be near the Austrian fron-tier.

In the morning of your seventh day you can explore the royal castles of Bavaria, including Hohenschwangau (built by Ludwig's father, Maximilian II) and Neuschwanstein, the fairytale castle of the "mad king."

For accommodations that evening, it's an easy drive east to Garmisch-Partenkirchen, Germany's leading alpine resort and the largest city of the Ba-varian Alps. I suggest two nights there. First, the visit to the royal castles will have eaten up your first day, and Garmisch deserves the minimum of a day to itself. Not only that, but you may be tempted to visit Berchtesgaden, which is set below the summits of the Watzmann Mountain. You can drive from Berchtesga-den to Obersalzberg, one of the most scenic routes in Bavaria, which Hitler used as a retreat.

On the morning of the ninth day, you can head north to Munich, a distance of 55 miles, where you'll want to spend at least three days—much more if you can afford the time.

What about Berlin? West Berlin, as covered in Chapter XVI, is a destination unto itself.

By taking this tour I've outlined, you will not have seen Germany, but you will have seen a good part of it, at least the section that tourists have praised for centuries. Other cities, such as Hamburg and Nürnberg, are outlined in detail in the chapters ahead for those with more time; and other areas, such as the famed Harz Mountains, await exploration by the visitor with more time to venture into the less trampled parts of Germany.

To be frank, chances are you can't do Germany in one visit—so you may want to return again and again.

SOME DISCLAIMERS: No restaurant, inn, hotel, gasthaus, shop, tour agency, or nightclub paid to be mentioned in this book. What you read are entirely personal recommendations. In many cases, proprietors never knew their establishments were being visited or investigated for inclusion in a travel guide.

A word of warning: Unfortunately, costs change—and they rarely go down. All prices quoted in this book are subject to change.

Always, when checking into a hotel, inquire about the price. This policy can save much embarrassment and disappointment when the time comes to settle your bill. You cannot insist on being charged the precise prices quoted in this guide, although much effort has been made to secure accurate tariffs as they were foreseeable.

An additional note: The price quoted for double or twin hotel rooms is the rate for two persons, unless otherwise indicated.

AN INVITATION TO READERS: Like its sister Dollarwise books, *Dollarwise Guide to Germany* hopes to maintain a continuing dialogue between its writer and its readers. All of us share a common aim—to travel as widely and as well as possible, at the best value for our money. In achieving that aim, your comments and suggestions can be of aid to other visitors. Therefore if you come across an appealing hotel, restaurant, nightclub, shopping bargain, sightseeing attraction, please don't keep it to yourself. And the letters need not only apply to new establishments, but to hotels and restaurants already recommended in this guide. The fact that a listing appears in this edition doesn't give it squatter's rights in future publications. If its services have deteriorated, its chef grown stale, its room prices risen unfairly, whatever, these failings need to be known. Even if you enjoyed every place and found every description accurate, a letter letting me know that too can cheer many a gray day. Send your comments to Darwin Porter, c/o Frommer/Pasmantier Publishers, 1230 Avenue of the Americas, New York, NY 10020.

TIME OUT FOR A COMMERCIAL: The very fact that you've purchased a guide to Germany (both East and West) puts you in a special, sophisticated category of traveler—that is, those who want to explore and get to know a single country or two, as opposed to the "Grand Tour" individual who wants to do not only Belgium on Tuesday, but Rome on Wednesday, and perhaps the North Cape by Friday.

Even so, in your tour of Germany you come to the very doorstep of major attractions in other countries which you may want to explore. Since I had to set some limitations on the number of pages in this book, it was impossible to devote separate chapters to neighboring attractions.

I'll cite only an example or two to prove my point. As you tour Bavaria, you'll be on the doorstep of Switzerland, Liechtenstein, and Austria, with sunny Italy just a short drive away. As you tour along the western section of West Germany you'll be by-passing the old provinces of Alsace and Lorraine, and may want to explore some of eastern France. North from Hamburg, as you go through Schleswig-Holstein, you'll be near the border of Denmark, with all of Scandinavia opening up to you.

Because of the geography of Germany, and depending on which sections of the country you plan to travel in, you may want to take along some of our sister guides as traveling companions. Specific ones that might appeal to you include:

Dollarwise Guide to Switzerland and Liechtenstein
Dollarwise Guide to Austria and Hungary
Dollarwise Guide to Italy
Dollarwise Guide to France
Scandinavia on $35 a Day

The $25-a-Day Travel Club—How to Save Money on All Your Travels

In this book we'll be looking at how to get your money's worth in Germany but there is a "device" for saving money and determining value on *all* your trips. It's the popular, international $25-a-Day Travel Club, now in its 23rd successful year of operation. The Club was formed at the urging of numerous readers of the $$$-a-Day and Dollarwise Guides, who felt that such an organization could provide continuing travel information and a sense of community to value-minded travelers in all parts of the world. And so it does!

In keeping with the budget concept, the annual membership fee is low and is immediately exceeded by the value of your benefits. Upon receipt of $18 (U.S. residents), or $20 U.S. by check drawn on a U.S. bank or via international postal money order in U.S. funds (Canadian, Mexican, and other foreign residents) to cover one year's membership, we will send all new members the following items.

(1) *Any two* of the following books

Please designate in your letter which two you wish to receive:

Europe on $25 a Day
Australia on $25 a Day
England on $35 a Day
Greece including Istanbul and Turkey's Aegean Coast on $25 a Day
Hawaii on $35 a Day
Ireland on $25 a Day
India on $15 & $25 a Day
Israel on $30 & $35 a Day
Mexico on $20 a Day
New York on $45 a Day
New Zealand on $20 & $25 a Day
Scandinavia on $35 a Day
Scotland and Wales on $35 a Day
South America on $25 a Day
Spain and Morocco (plus the Canary Is.) on $35 a Day
Washington, D.C. on $40 a Day

Dollarwise Guide to Austria and Hungary
Dollarwise Guide to Bermuda & The Bahamas

> **Dollarwise Guide to Canada**
> **Dollarwise Guide to the Caribbean**
> **Dollarwise Guide to Egypt**
> **Dollarwise Guide to England and Scotland**
> **Dollarwise Guide to France**
> **Dollarwise Guide to Germany**
> **Dollarwise Guide to Italy**
> **Dollarwise Guide to Japan & Hong Kong**
> **Dollarwise Guide to Portugal (plus Madeira and the Azores)**
> **Dollarwise Guide to Switzerland and Liechtenstein**
> **Dollarwise Guide to California and Las Vegas**
> **Dollarwise Guide to Florida**
> **Dollarwise Guide to New England**
> **Dollarwise Guide to the Northwest**
> **Dollarwise Guide to the Southeast and New Orleans**
> **Dollarwise Guide to the Southwest**

(Dollarwise Guides discuss accommodations and facilities in all price ranges, with emphasis on the medium-priced.)

A Guide for the Disabled Traveler
(A guide to the best destinations for wheelchair travelers and other disabled vacationers in Europe, the United States, and Canada by an experienced wheelchair traveler. Includes detailed information about accommodations, restaurants, sights, transportation, and their accessibility.)

A Shopper's Guide to Best Buys in England, Scotland, and Wales
(Describes in detail hundreds of places to shop—department stores, factory outlets, street markets, and craft centers—for great quality British bargains.)

Bed & Breakfast—North America
(This guide contains a directory of over 150 organizations that offer bed & breakfast referrals and reservations throughout North America. The scenic attractions, businesses, and major colleges and universities near the homes of each are also listed.)

Dollarwise Guide to Cruises
(This complete guide covers all the basics of cruising—ports of call, costs, fly-cruise package bargains, cabin selection, booking, locations of embarkation and debarkation and describes in detail over 60 or so ships cruising in Alaska, the Caribbean, Mexico, Hawaii, Panama, Canada, and the United States.)

Dollarwise Guide to Skiing USA—East
(Rates and describes the many resorts in Massachusetts, Vermont, New Hampshire, Connecticut, Maine, Quebec, New York, Pennsylvania, plus new areas in North Carolina, the Virginias, and Maryland. (Includes detailed information about lodging, dining, and non-skier activities.)

Dollarwise Guide to Skiing USA—West
(All the diverse ski resorts of the West—in California, Colorado, Idaho, New Mexico, Montana, Oregon, and Wyoming—are fully described and rated. Lodging, dining, and non-skier activities are also included.)

Frommer's Travel Diary and Record Book
(A 72-page diary for personal travel notes plus a section for such vital data as

passport and traveler's check numbers, itinerary, postcard list, special people and places to visit, and a reference section with temperature and conversion charts, and world maps with distance zones.)

How to Beat the High Cost of Travel
(This practical guide details how to save money on absolutely all travel items—accommodations, transportation, dining, sightseeing, shopping, taxes, and more. Includes special budget information for seniors, students, singles, and families.)

Marilyn Wood's Wonderful Weekends
(This very selective guide covers the best mini-vacation destinations within a 175-mile radius of New York City. It describes special country inns and other accommodations, restaurants, picnic spots, sights, and activities—all the information needed for a two- or three-day stay.)

Museums in New York
(A complete guide to all the museums, historic houses, gardens, zoos, and more in the five boroughs. Illustrated with over 200 photographs.)

Swap and Go—Home Exchanging Made Easy
(Two veteran home exchangers explain in detail all the money-saving benefits of a home exchange, and then describe precisely how to do it. Also includes information on home rentals and many tips on low-cost travel.)

The Fast 'n' Easy Phrase Book
(The four most useful languages—French, German, Spanish, and Italian—all in one convenient, easy-to-use phrase guide.)

The New York Urban Athlete
(The ultimate guide to all the sport facilities in New York City for jocks and novices.)

Where to Stay USA
(By the Council on International Educational Exchange, this extraordinary guide is the first to list accommodations in all 50 states that cost anywhere from $3 to $25 per night.)

(2) A one-year subscription to *The Wonderful World of Budget Travel*

This quarterly eight-page tabloid newspaper keeps you up to date on fast-breaking developments in low-cost travel in all parts of the world bringing you the latest money-saving information—the kind of information you'd have to pay $25 a year to obtain elsewhere. This consumer-conscious publication also features columns of special interest to readers: **Hospitality Exchange** (members all over the world who are willing to provide hospitality to other members as they pass through their home cities); **Share-a-Trip** (offers and requests from members for travel companions who can share costs and help avoid the burdensome single supplement); and **Readers Ask . . . Readers Reply** (travel questions from members to which other members reply with authentic firsthand information).

(3) A Copy of *Arthur Frommer's Guide to New York*

This is a pocket-size guide to hotels, restaurants, nightspots, and sightseeing attractions in all price ranges throughout the New York area.

(4) Your personal membership card

Membership entitles you to purchase through the Club all Arthur Frommer publications for a third to a half off their regular retail prices during the term of your membership.

So why not join this hardy band of international budgeteers and participate in its exchange of travel information and hospitality? Simply send your name and address, together with your annual membership fee of $18 (U.S. residents) or $20 U.S. (Canadian, Mexican, and other foreign residents), by check drawn on a U.S. bank or via international postal money order in U.S. funds to: $25-A-Day Travel Club, Inc., Frommer/Pasmantier Publishers, 1230 Avenue of the Americas, New York, NY 10020. And please remember to specify which *two* of the books in section (1) above you wish to receive in your initial package of members' benefits. Or, if you prefer, use the last page of this book, simply checking off the two books you select and enclosing $18 or $20 in U.S. currency.

Once you are a member, there is no obligation to buy additional books. No books will be mailed to you without your specific order.

Chapter I

GETTING THERE

1. Traveling to Germany
2. Traveling Within Germany
3. The Facts of Life

YOU COULDN'T CHOOSE a more central place than Germany to start your European experience. Germany is in the heartland of Europe. Not only is it jam-packed with atmosphere, nightlife, and sightseeing interests, but it's a perfect gateway to the rest of Europe. The Eastern European countries beckon with increasing accessibility, while to the south are storybook Austria and Switzerland, as well as tantalizing Italy. Directly to the west is France, to the north the Scandinavian countries. You can use Germany as your starting point to explore any of these countries with comparative ease.

Moreover, in planning a trip to Germany, there are several available methods of cutting your air transportation costs, previewed here.

1. Traveling to Germany

PLANE ECONOMICS: For flights between Germany and the United States, Lufthansa has introduced a fare package which will suit a large number of travelers, whether they go in tourist, business, or first class.

For convenience, I will list fares in each category from various U. S. cities to Germany. The basic conditions that apply to each fare category are also given. When you know your exact travel plans, it's best to check with your travel agent or with Lufthansa.

In all the charts that follow the fares are effective as of November 1, 1985. The fares quoted to Frankfurt apply also to Bonn, Cologne, Düsseldorf, Hamburg, and Stuttgart; those to Munich apply also to Berlin, Bremen, Hannover, Münster, Nürnberg, Saarbrücken, Bayreuth, and Hof. All these fares are subject to change without notice.

We'll begin with Lufthansa's most attractive bargain, the special Holiday Fare.

The Holiday Fare

This special fare permits no stopovers, has advance purchase and minimum/maximum stay requirements, and also carries a penalty for cancellation that must be complied with. Tickets must be purchased 21 days in advance and are valid for 7 to 90 days. *Basic season* is November 1 to December 8 and

December 25 to April 30; *shoulder season* runs from May 1 to 31, September 15 to October 31, and December 12 to 24; *peak season* applies from June 1 to September 14. These dates are for eastbound and westbound travel.

As mentioned before, the fares to Frankfurt and to Munich also apply to a number of other German cities (enumerated above). Please note that the fares quoted are for roundtrip.

7 to 90-Day Holiday Fare (Roundtrip)

From:	To:	Basic Midweek	Basic Weekend	Shoulder Midweek	Shoulder Weekend	Peak Midweek	Peak Weekend
New York	F*	$ 498	$ 548	$ 652	$ 702	$ 734	$ 784
	M	538	588	692	742	787	837
Anchorage	F	1001	1051	1062	1112	1236	1286
	M	1040	1090	1102	1152	1288	1338
Atlanta	F	585	635	715	765	815	865
	M	624	674	755	805	867	917
Boston	F	498	548	647	697	734	784
	M	538	588	687	737	787	837
Chicago	F	565	565	719	769	823	873
	M	604	604	759	809	876	926
Dallas/Ft. Worth	F	670	670	764	814	870	920
	M	709	709	804	854	923	973
Houston	F	670	670	815	865	923	973
	M	709	709	855	905	975	1025
Los Angeles	F	720	720	876	926	994	1044
	M	759	759	916	966	1047	1097
Miami	F	585	635	730	780	836	886
	M	624	674	769	819	888	938
Philadelphia	F	518	568	668	718	771	821
	M	558	608	708	758	823	873
San Francisco	F	720	720	876	926	994	1044
	M	759	759	916	966	1047	1097

* F = Frankfurt   M = Munich

Tourist Class

This is a more economical fare than first class or business class, but it allows no stopovers.

Again, the fares to Frankfurt apply also to Bonn, Cologne, Düsseldorf, Hamburg, and Stuttgart, and the fares to Munich apply also to Berlin, Bremen, Hannover, Münster, Nürnberg, Saarbrücken, Bayreuth, and Hof.

Basic season is eastbound September 15 to May 14, and westbound October 15 to June 14. Peak season is eastbound May 15 to September 14, and westbound June 15 to October 15. Fares quoted are for roundtrip.

Tourist Class (Roundtrip)

From:	To:	Basic Midweek	Basic Weekend	Peak Midweek	Peak Weekend
New York	F*	$ 941	$ 991	$ 1161	$ 1211
	M	972	1022	1193	1243
Anchorage	F	1504	1554	1826	1876
	M	1535	1585	1857	1907

Atlanta	F	1073	1123	1328	1378
	M	1104	1154	1359	1409
Boston	F	931	981	1151	1201
	M	962	1012	1183	1233
Chicago	F	1034	1084	1269	1319
	M	1065	1115	1300	1350
Dallas/Ft. Worth	F	1063	1113	1300	1350
	M	1094	1144	1331	1381
Houston	F	1057	1107	1303	1353
	M	1083	1133	1333	1383
Los Angeles	F	1248	1298	1508	1558
	M	1279	1329	1539	1589
Miami	F	1049	1099	1286	1336
	M	1079	1129	1317	1367
Philadelphia	F	965	1015	1197	1247
	M	996	1046	1228	1278
San Francisco	F	1248	1298	1508	1558
	M	1279	1329	1539	1589

* F = Frankfurt   M = Munich

First-Class and Business-Class Fares

First-class and business-class fares to Germany are applicable all year and are for one-way travel. The prices listed for Frankfurt and Munich apply to a number of other German cities—in most cases, unlimited stopovers are allowed, although with certain restrictions. For accurate and up-to-date information, you should contact your travel agent or Lufthansa. Please keep in mind that fares are *subject to change without notice.*

Note: Passengers traveling in business class will be seated in a separate section of the aircraft. They will have separate check-in facilities as well as complimentary alcoholic beverages and headsets. They are also allowed the same baggage allowance as holders of first-class tickets.

The fares quoted apply all year and are for one-way travel only. Please note that they are subject to change without notice. Again, you can fly to a number of other German cities (listed previously in "Plane Economics") for the same prices quoted below.

First Class / Business Class (One Way)

From:	To:	First-Class One Way	Business Class One Way
New York	F*	$1590	$ 837
	M	1609	862
Anchorage	F	2041	1135
	M	2060	1160
Atlanta	F	1590	931
	M	1609	956
Boston	F	1581	832
	M	1600	857
Chicago	F	1785	1014
	M	1803	1039

Dallas/Ft. Worth	F	1785	1045
	M	1803	1070
Houston	F	1762	1040
	M	1780	1065
Los Angeles	F	2060	1135
	M	2079	1160
Miami	F	1723	1035
	M	1742	1060
Philadelphia	F	1670	892
	M	1689	917
San Francisco	F	2060	1135
	M	2079	1160

* F = Frankfurt   M = Munich

A Warning

All fares, rules, and regulations are subject to change.

THE CHOICE OF AIRLINE: To get a head start on your German travel adventure, it seems only appropriate to fly the German airline, **Lufthansa.** It makes good sense from a practical standpoint too. True to Germanic tradition, Lufthansa emphasizes punctual, efficient, yet warm and friendly service. The worldwide Lufthansa system, with one of the most modern fleets in commercial aviation, offers more flights to Germany than any other airline.

For the convenience of travelers from the U.S. and Canada, Lufthansa now serves 16 gateway cities: New York, Chicago, Boston, Philadelphia, Los Angeles, Atlanta, Miami, San Francisco, Dallas/Ft. Worth, Houston, San Juan (Puerto Rico), Anchorage, Toronto, Montréal, Calgary, and Vancouver. Lufthansa provides fast, frequent service to such major German cities as Frankfurt, Munich, Düsseldorf, and Hamburg. Nearly any other city in Germany you may wish to go to can easily be reached by Lufthansa's convenient connecting flights.

If you plan to extend your vacation trip beyond Germany, you will find that Lufthansa also offers excellent connecting services from Frankfurt to cities throughout Europe, the Middle East, Far East, and Africa. Frankfurt Airport, Lufthansa's home base, has a reputation among seasoned travelers as the most efficient connecting point in Europe.

· To get an idea just how much Lufthansa can do for the vacation traveler, ask your travel agent for *The Lufthansa Holiday Collection* brochure—a handsome travel book featuring selected German and Central European vacation programs. Great care has been taken to include only those tour operators, hotels, resorts, and transportation companies whose standards of quality and reliability measure up to Lufthansa's.

Besides escorted motorcoach tours, the brochure contains money-saving Lufthansa/Avis Classics car-rental rates and hotel plans for do-it-yourself travelers. Vacation packages offered in the Lufthansa Holiday Collections depart from all of Lufthansa's 12 U.S. gateway cities. Any of the programs can be booked in conjunction with the Lufthansa Holiday Fare—the airline's lowest airfare from the U.S. to Germany (see "Holiday Fare" above) Similiar vacation packages are available from the four Lufthansa gateways in Canada.

A unique Lufthansa service that many tourist travelers enjoy is the Lufthansa Airport Express. A high-speed train that follows the scenic route between Frankfurt and Düsseldorf Airports, it stops at Bonn, Cologne, and Düsseldorf city centers en route. An optional alternative to flying for those who wish to make a connection between Frankfurt and one of the other cities, it can be reserved in the same way as your Lufthansa flight, and included in your transatlantic airfare. The Lufthansa Airport Express gives the passenger a splendid opportunity to view the romantic beauty of the Rhine Valley in luxurious comfort.

2. Traveling Within Germany

GERMAN FEDERAL RAILROAD: Whether you travel first or second class, GermanRail's trains deserve their good reputation for comfort, cleanliness, and punctuality. They are modern and fast, running smoothly over welded tracks. Both first- and second-class trains carry smoker and nonsmoker compartments. A snackbar or a dining car serving German dishes and international cuisine, as well as good wines and beers, will usually be on your train (unless you're taking a "local"), and you can enjoy the landscape through picture windows.

Actually, GermanRail's customer service begins long before you board the train. Special features of major rail stations include information desks and ticket offices, pictorial directional signs (eliminating language problems), and posted timetables listing departures and arrivals of trains chronologically. In addition, each car carries signs, inside and out, describing its routing, point of origin, destination, and important stops en route. Restaurants, snackbars, post and money-exchange offices, newsstands and bookstores, flower shops, beauty parlors, pharmacies, and often a cinema are just some of the facilities major railroad stations offer. And they're usually located right in the center of the city.

For city sightseeing, you can leave your baggage in a locker or check it at the station's baggage counter. In many cities GermanRail provides door-to-door baggage service, allowing passengers to have their luggage picked up at or delivered to their hotels. Accompanying baggage can be checked for an economical fee. Suitcases, plus baby carriages, skis, bicycles, or a steamer trunk, are permitted as baggage. Insurance policies of various kinds, even a travel medical plan, may be obtained in addition to your ticket (inside Europe only).

About 20,000 passenger trains per day comprise the network of first-class Intercity (IC) trains offering express service every hour among 48 major German cities. IC trains carry first as well as coach class. These trains, as well as the Trans Europe Express (TEE) trains, require a surcharge (but not from holders of the Eurailpass and the first-class GermanRail Tourist Card). Seat reservations on TEEs are obligatory when crossing international borders, but should be made regardless. The luxurious interiors of IC trains match the quality of the TEE. Cushioned, adjustable seats and individual reading lights are just samples of the features you can expect. Business travelers appreciate the telephone and secretarial services offered on most of these trains. Bars, lounges, and dining rooms are available too.

Sound sleep is almost guaranteed on GermanRail's smoothly running trains. You can make selections from different types of accommodations. Many prefer a private compartment (some even contain showers); others share bunk-type couchette compartments with five other passengers. Advance reservations for sleeping accommodations are necessary. Travelers wanting to avoid the fatigue of long-distance driving can reach their destination on special car-sleeper trains (Auto Trains). Some daytime automobile trains are also operated.

Children below the age of 4, provided they do not require a separate seat, travel free; those between the ages of 4 and 12 pay half fare.

In several countries outside Europe, Eurailtariff tickets may be purchased either at a GermanRail office or at authorized travel agencies. Eurail tickets are valid for six months and allow unlimited stopovers en route. With a Eurail ticket, you just board the train, avoiding lines at ticket counters and currency problems.

These tickets are interchangeable for travel on many bus lines in Germany. You may, for example, take the Europabus along the Romantic Road from Frankfurt am Main via Würzburg to Füssen and Munich, or along the Castle Road from Heidelberg to Rothenburg to Nürnberg. If your ticket is valid for the railroad portions, Mainz-Cologne and Koblenz-Trier, the payment of a small supplement entitles you to the corresponding boat passage on the Rhine and Mosel steamers operated by Köln-Düsseldorfer Deutsche Rheinschiffahrt AG.

For group travel the Eurailtariff allows substantial reductions. Groups of 10 to 24 members pay 25% to 30% less than the normal fare; groups of 25 or more members pay almost 50% less. Free transportation is offered to one member of a group consisting of 15 to 20 paying passengers. For youth groups of at least ten members (age below 21), the price reductions amount to 50%. Reservations for groups have to be made at least six weeks in advance.

The Eurailpass and the Eurail Youthpass are well-known travel bargains. These passes are valid in 15 Western European countries, excluding Great Britain and Yugoslavia.

But before I go into specifics about these passes, I should certainly mention that GermanRail runs trains directly from the Düsseldorf and Frankfurt Airports to the Düsseldorf and Frankfurt am Main Hauptbahnhof (railroad station), Wiesbaden, and Mainz. Travel time is all of 30 minutes, and the usual hassle of getting yourself from airport to town is considerably lessened.

GERMANRAIL TOURIST CARD: This rail pass offers unlimited travel within the Federal Republic of Germany, plus many bonuses, either free or with substantial reductions. GermanRail Tourist Cards are available for first- and coach-class travel. The card is available for 9 or 16 days. A 9-day coach-class card costs less than $14 a day, and the 16-day coach-class card comes to under $10 a day, quite a bargain. More specifically, a 9-day coach ticket sells for $120, going up to $155 for 16 days. A first-class, 9-day pass is $165, rising to $215 for 16 days. Children from 4 to 11 pay half these fares. The many bonuses include a reduced-fare round-trip rail ticket to Berlin, which also provides a free city sightseeing tour. Also included are free bus transportation on specified routes and reduced-rate steamer excursions on the Rhine between Cologne and Mainz or on the Mosel River between Koblenz and Trier.

The GermanRail Tourist Card is now also available for four days: first class, $100 (U.S.); coach class, $70. There is a Junior Tourist Card version for persons under 26 years of age available in coach class for 9 days at $70 and 16 days at $90, for unlimited rail service.

INSIDE GERMANY ONLY: In addition to these travel plans, GermanRail offers various other programs which can be purchased at railroad ticket offices and authorized travel agencies—but within Germany only.

Physical fitness enthusiasts, overworked managers, and nature lovers have long heeded GermanRail's advice to take the train to the countryside and enjoy the landscape "bike-back." More than 300 railroad stations in scenic areas participate in the "Bicycle at the Station" plan. The cost per day, including insurance, is 10 DM ($3.33). If you arrive by rail, it's only 5 DM ($1.65). There is no charge for holders of the GermanRail Tourist Card. Together with your bike ticket, you receive an area map with tour suggestions, telling you where to stop and visit a baroque church, a historical site, or some other attraction. You do not have to return the bicycle to the starting station—you can leave it at another station (after having made certain that its baggage counter is still open).

Other travel plans include programs for senior citizens as well as "junior citizens," city-to-city weekend tours, and district tickets. In addition, German-Rail offers reduced fares for mini-groups, holiday tickets (Vorzugskarte), conference compartments in IC trains, or even conference cars.

Before leaving for Germany, you can get complete details about the GFR and the many plans it offers at the following offices:

German Federal Railroad
747 Third Ave.
New York, NY 10017
(tel. 212/308-3100)

German Federal Railroad
625 Statler Office Building
Boston, MA 02116
(tel. 617/542-0577)

German Federal Railroad
104 So. Michigan Ave.
Chicago, IL 60603
(tel. 312/263-2958)

German Federal Railroad
8000 E. Girard Ave., Suite 518
South Denver, CO 80231
(tel. 303/695-7715)

German Federal Railroad
1 Hallidie Plaza, Suite 250
San Francisco, CA 94102
(tel. 415/981-5548)

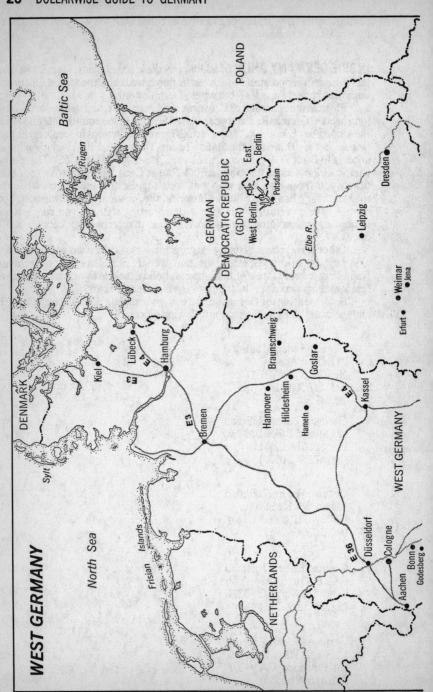

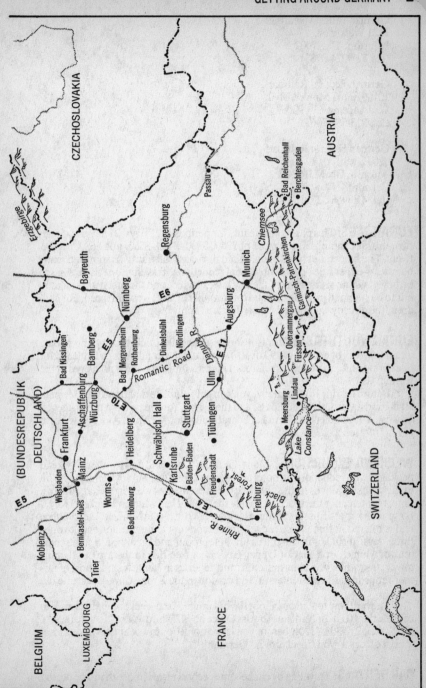

nan Federal Railroad
Walker St.
Houston, TX 77002
(tel. 713/224-8781)

German Federal Railroad
10100 Santa Monica Blvd.
Los Angeles, CA 90067
(tel. 213/553-7063)

German Federal Railroad
520 Bay St.
Toronto, ON M5R 2C3
Canada
(tel. 416/968-3272)

EURAILPASS: This pass is obtainable for periods of 15 days, 21 days, and one, two, or three months at the price of $260, $330, $410, $560, and $680, respectively. The holder is entitled to unlimited first-class rail transportation and many bonuses—either free or with substantial reductions. Traveling on this pass has to be begun within six months of the day it was issued, and the first day of validity has to be stamped in at the railroad station where travel is commenced. For children, the already-mentioned rate reductions apply.

EURAIL YOUTHPASS: This is a single, convenient ticket for young people under 26 years of age. For $290 or $370, unlimited second-class rail mileage for one- or two-month periods is offered. This pass offers the same privileges as the Eurailpass.

Before leaving for Germany, you can get complete details on the German-Rail Tourist Card, the Eurailpass, and the Eurail Youthpass from travel agents. You can also contact the German Federal Railroad, 747 Third Ave., New York, NY 10017 (tel. 212/308-3100).

WEEKEND EXCURSIONS: Many German cities and towns offer weekend packages with reductions on hotel accommodations, restaurants, and admission to nightclubs and museums. The list of such excursions is extensive, and I have, unfortunately, not the space to review them all. The "Munich Weekend Key," however, is a particularly exciting example. It's run by the Munich Tourist Office and is offered in three price ranges, from economy to deluxe, for one, two, or three days. Included in the prices are hotel room and breakfast, a sightseeing tour of Munich or a tour of Upper Bavaria, a free ride to the top of Olympia tower, free admission to all museums and galleries in Munich, and a host of further reductions (on car rentals and admission to the Krone Circus, to name but two).

The best way to find out about the full range of the weekend excursions is to consult the **German National Tourist Office** at 747 Third Ave., New York, NY 10017 (tel. 212/308-3100), before you leave home, or to ask at the various local tourist offices as you travel around Germany.

CAR RENTALS: Traveling by car becomes economical if more than one person goes along for the ride. When four share expenses, it makes for a particularly dollarwise bargain. American car-rental organizations provide rental services, or else you might rent from one of the big German companies.

For example, of all the big U.S. firms, including Hertz and Avis, Budget has the least expensive rates. Budget maintains rental facilities in 29 West German cities, including locations at each of the country's major airports. The official name of Budget's German subsidiary is **Sixt-Budget,** whose distinctive black, white, and orange sign is prominently posted.

Additional information can be gathered and reservations made by calling Budget's toll-free information center in Dallas (tel. 800/527-0700).

To give you an idea of price guidelines (likely to change from season to season), you can usually rent a Fiat Panda, holding two passengers and with manual shift, for $77 (U.S.) per week; each extra day goes for another $11. This is the cheapest car in Budget's German fleet. However, a slightly bigger car, a Ford Fiesta, carries four passengers comfortably and has a manual shift, all for $84 weekly and $12 per extra day.

The famous German-made VW Rabbit, a four-passenger car with manual shift, costs $119 weekly, plus another $17 for each extra day.

If a passenger requires an automatic, the price jumps to $175 per week and $25 for each extra day. For visitors wanting to travel with more luxury, Budget can provide a Mercedes 190 sedan, suitable for five passengers, at a cost of $199 weekly. Even the lowest cost cars are equipped with radios and cassette players.

Budget charges $1.50 per day or $10 per week for personal accident insurance. This covers the driver and his or her passengers while driving. Renters are responsible for a certain monetary value of any accident they might have. This varies, depending on the value of the car, from $300 to $500. A CDW (collision damage waiver) will negate this. It costs $7 per day or $35 per week.

Drivers must be 21 years of age or older to rent a car, and must have a valid driver's license. An imprint of a credit card is taken, unless a cash deposit is made instead. This ranges from a minimum of $65.60 up to the estimated total value of the car rental.

Ski racks are available at no extra charge, but they must be reserved in advance.

If you're keeping costs really low, you might want to rent a motor home from **Executive Motorhomes,** 28 Opelstrasse, D 6082 Moerfelden (tel. 06105/ 3037). It offers brand-new vehicles, airport pickup and return, and reserve vehicles in case of a breakdown. The dinnerware in the little kitchens is Rosenthal china. Established in 1964, this is the oldest and largest camper and motor-home rental company in Europe. Their location is only 15 kilometers from the Frankfurt airport. Depending on the camper desired, rates range from 170 DM ($56.10) to 220 DM ($72.60) daily, plus 14% VAT. Off-season reductions are granted, and there are extra charges made for such things as cooking gas and cleaning.

3. The Facts of Life

The experience for the first-time visitor of plunging madly into the traffic of the autobahn can be maddening. However, being armed with some "facts of life" about how to cope can ease your adjustment not only into such major destinations as Frankfurt and Munich, but into the fascinating countryside of Germany itself.

Such problems as tipping must be faced even before you check into your hotel room. There are any number of situations that might mar your trip. Included in this is a medical emergency, of course. I don't promise to answer all your needs in a small section of this guide, but there is a variety of services available in Germany that you need to know about.

The concierge of your hotel, incidentally, is usually a reliable dispenser of information, getting theater tickets, arranging tours, whatever. At least this is true in the bigger establishments. In many of the smaller third-class hotels and pensions listed in this guide, you're pretty much on your own, as the proprietor is generally overworked. Therefore the following summary of pertinent facts may prove helpful.

Many "practical facts," such as transportation within Munich, the address of a local U.S. consulate, or the location of the local American Express, are given under the individual chapter headings.

AIR SERVICES: More than 60 international airlines serve the Federal Republic of Germany, but the most frequent connections to and from the greatest number of destinations are operated by **Lufthansa.** Its globe-spanning network links more than 130 cities throughout the world with the Federal Republic of Germany.

Germany's international airports are at West Berlin, Bremen, Cologne/Bonn, Düsseldorf, Frankfurt/Main, Hamburg, Hannover, Munich, Nürnberg, Stuttgart, and Saarbrücken. The commercial airports of West Germany are linked with one another by scheduled Lufthansa services and other carriers. For example, from Frankfurt/Main, all Lufthansa destinations in Germany can be reached in an average of 50 minutes with at least four flights daily. Contact your Lufthansa travel agency or Lufthansa town office for the most economical current offers.

All German cities with commercial airports have their own **airport shuttle service,** offering reduced fares and fast connections between the city and the airport. Departure points are usually the airlines' town offices and the main railway terminal. Luggage can be turned in at the DB (GermanRail) baggage counter at the airport for delivery to all railroad stations throughout Germany.

BANKS AND EXCHANGES: Banks are open weekdays from 8:30 a.m. to 1 p.m. and 2:30 to 4 p.m. (Thursday until 5:30 p.m.). They are closed Saturday, Sunday, and holidays. Money exchanges at airports and border-crossing points are generally open from 6 a.m. to 10 p.m. daily. Exchanges at border railroad stations are kept open for arrivals of all international trains.

CAMPING AND CARAVANING: Some 2100 German camping sites, located in the most beautiful and popular resort districts, and with all the necessary facilities, welcome visitors from abroad. Blue signs bearing the international camping symbol—a black tent on a white background—make it easy to find camping sites. Some 400 camping sites are kept open during the winter. Information on camping matters and camping sites is available on request from the **Allgemeine Deutscher Automobil-Club (ADAC),** 8 Am Westpark, D-8000 München 70, and the **Deutscher Camping-Club (DCC),** 28 Mandlstrasse, D-8000 München 23.

CAR REGULATIONS: Car operators arriving from most European countries only need their national driving license and permit. Otherwise, an international license and permit must be obtained. Anyone with a green insurance card (except from EEC member countries) must take out short-term, third-party insurance at the border, costing about 100 DM ($33) for 14 days. In Germany, drive on the right-hand side of the road.

CASINOS: Roulette and baccarat are just some of the international games that can be played at the spa resorts of Germany, the most famous of which is Baden-Baden in the Black Forest. It was from Bad Homburg, close to Frankfurt, that roulette was "exported" to Monte Carlo. Other famous casinos are at Wiesbaden and at Garmisch-Partenkirchen, south of Munich. Admission tickets are available to persons over 21 years of age upon presentation of a valid passport.

CLIMATE: It can be very cold in winter, especially in January, and very warm in summer, and even in July and August there may be days when it's cool and rainy. You have to dress for "all occasions." For example, on the same trip you can be chilled on a Bavarian Alp, yet the next day be running around in a bikini at Lake Constance. Winters tend to be mild, springs "stretched out," and summers most agreeable. In fact, I've enjoyed many a Bavarian-style "Indian summer" until late in October when it starts to get chilly. The most popular tourist months are May until October, although winter travel to Germany is becoming increasingly popular, obviously to the ski areas in the Alps.

CLOTHING: There are no dress regulations to speak of. Collars, ties, and jackets are expected to be worn in the evening in first-class bars and restaurants.

CLOTHING SIZES: It should be pointed out that German clothing and footwear sizes often vary slightly from international standards, especially in some shops. Sometimes the sizes are quite different. Therefore you should always try on or at least ask for the appropriate international size.

CRIME: As in all the industrialized nations of Western Europe, crime is on the increase. That section between the railway terminal in Frankfurt (called the Hauptbahnhof) and the Inner Ring is considered one of the most dangerous in the country, particularly at night. Otherwise, if you act discreetly and protect your valuables, you should encounter little problem.

CURRENCY: Refer to "The Deutsches Mark and the Dollar," in the Introduction.

CROSSING POINTS: The border-crossing points into the Federal Republic are open day and night, including those to West Berlin. In the case of West Berlin, foreign visitors always need a passport and a transit visa, which are issued at the border. This costs nothing for coach and rail travelers, but tourists going by car are charged 10 DM ($3.30) for the return journey. Short-term third-party insurance must also be taken out at the border-crossing point for all foreign cars. Visitors arriving by air merely require the documents necessary for travel to the Federal Republic.

CUSTOMS: In general, items required for your personal and professional use or consumption may be brought in duty free. No duty is levied for your private car, provided that it is reexported. Gifts are duty free up to a total value of 620 DM ($204.60), to include a maximum of 115 DM ($37.95) in items from non-Common Market countries. This limitation covers all commodities, including food, imported as gifts or for your personal use or consumption.

The following items are permitted into West Germany duty free (imports from Common Market countries in parentheses): 200 (300) cigarettes or 100 (150) cigarillos, or 50 (75) cigars, or 250 (400) grams of tobacco. Americans or Canadians not residing in Europe may import double the tobacco allowance. You are also allowed 1 (1.5) liters of liquor above 44 proof, or 2 (3) liters of liquor less than 44 proof, or 2 (3) liters of sparkling wines and 2 (4) liters of other wines; 50 (75) grams of perfume and .25 (.375) liters of eau de cologne; 250 (750) grams of coffee, 100 (150) grams of tea. The duty-free tobacco and alcoholic beverage allowances are authorized for persons age 17 and above only, the coffee quota for persons age 15 and above only. All duty-free allowances are authorized only when the items are carried in the traveler's personal baggage.

On returning to the United States, American citizens who have been out of the country for at least 48 hours or more are allowed to bring back to their home country $400 worth of merchandise duty free—that is, if they haven't claimed a similar exemption within the past 30 days. Beyond this free allowance, the next $1000 worth of merchandise is assessed at a flat rate of 10% duty. If you make purchases in Germany, it is important to keep your receipts. The duty-free limit on gifts sent from abroad has been increased to $50.

DOCUMENTS FOR ENTRY: U.S. and Canadian citizens need only a valid passport to enter the Federal Republic of Germany and West Berlin.

DRINK: Nowhere else are there so many good and different kinds of **beer.** Nowadays, many inns brew their own. The world's oldest brewery is, it is true, in Bavaria, but the Bavarians are not the only ones who know about beer, which in Germany, incidentally, comes straight from the barrel. Export beers and the rather more bitter "Pils," the most popular kinds, are also produced in Berlin, Hamburg, the Ruhr, Hesse, and Stuttgart. "Altbier," a very early product of the brewer's art, is today to be found all over Germany. "Berliner Weisse" is another kind of beer (made from wheat, like a Bavarian white beer), but with a dash of raspberry or woodruff syrup. Malt beer is dark and sweet and contains hardly any alcohol, whereas "March beer" is also dark but considerably stronger.

There is now an even greater number of German **wines** to choose from— and not just Liebfraumilch! The fruity, sparkling white wines from the Rhine and Mosel are famed throughout the world. Connoisseurs, of course, will distinguish between wines from the larger and more celebrated Rheingau, those from the small Central Rhine area, and the delicate wines from Rheinhessen. Red wine is rarer but is also produced, notably in the Ahr Valley south of Cologne, Germany's northernmost wine-growing belt. Toward the French border, along the Saar and Ruwer Rivers, wines are similar to those from the nearby Mosel.

In the Rhineland Palatinate there are strong red and white varieties. In Franconia, the dry, sharp wine comes in peculiar "squat" bottles, while in

Württemberg and Swabia there are wines that the vintners prefer to keep
their own consumption. And in Baden, on the Black Forest hillsides, around
Kaiserstuhl and Lake Constance, where there is plenty of sunshine, there ar
strong, vigorous varieties, mostly obtainable there only direct from the growers.

And what about the hard stuff? A clear corn **brandy** and juniper **schnaps**
are made in North Germany and Westphalia and are often served in earthenware bottles. From the Black Forest come clear fruit brandies and delicate herb
liqueurs, often produced in places where, centuries ago, they were invented by
monastery friars.

DRUGSTORES: Don't go to a drugstore in Germany for a banana split! They
come mainly in two types, the *Apotheke* selling pharmaceuticals, and the *Dro-
gerie* which sells cosmetics and standard drugs. German pharmacies are open
during regular business hours. All post lists of pharmacies that are open nights,
on Sunday, and holidays.

ELECTRICAL APPLIANCES: In most places the electrical current is 220 volts
AC, 50 cycles. Therefore adapters will be needed for your U.S. appliances.
Many of the leading hotels will supply you with an adapter if you ask for one.

EMBASSIES: The **U.S. Embassy** is on Mehlemer Avenue (tel. 33-91) in Bad
Godesberg, and the **Canadian Embassy** is at 18 Friedrich-Wilhelmstrasse (tel.
23-10-61) in Bonn. (U.S. consulate addresses appear in various city listings.)

EMERGENCY: For a police emergency or rescue service, you can dial 110 in
more than 95% of German telephone exchanges. The telephone numbers of
individual police stations can also be obtained by dialing "Auskunft" 118 or
0118.

FILM: German film is among the best in the world, and is readily available in all
cities and small towns. If you want color, as most visitors do, the price is tripled.
Caution: Be extremely careful about snapping pictures on the border between
East and West Germany. You could get shot!

FOOD: Nouvelle cuisine has invaded Germany with a vengeance. If you still
think you'll eat nothing but sausage and sauerkraut, maybe a dumpling or two,
you are very mistaken. Young chefs, trained in Switzerland, France, or Italy,
are returning to Germany in droves and opening continental restaurants. Ital-
ians, many who came originally to Germany as "guest workers," have stayed to
open up trattorie.

Aside from the continental influence, you can also get German cookery as
well. Every region has its own specialties, ranging from A (aalsuppe, or eel
soup) to Z (zwiebelbrot, or onion bread). You might begin with a Hamburg
herring dish, then follow with red wine soup from the Palatinate, and for a main
course, Berlin liver with Bavarian potato dumplings, then some Allgäu cheese,
with some zwetschkuchen (plumcake) for dessert, rounded off by a glass of
cherry brandy from the Black Forest.

Fish comes from two seas in the north and also from the south. All regions
share a love for a variety of bread and many kinds of sausages, the latter exported all over the world. The smoked sausages from Westphalia and the Black
Forest are particularly notable.

There is sauerbraten, for example (roasted, marinated beef from the

...abian roast beef, Bavarian apple strudel, saddle of venison, ...k Forest cherry gâteau. And let's also mention Aachen spicy ...ingerbread, Black Forest ham, and pumpernickel from ...ng in Germany becomes part of your enjoyment of your holi-

...AS: Gas is readily available throughout the Federal Republic, and service stations appear frequently along the autobahns. As of this writing, the average cost for gasoline or petrol is about 1.50 DM (50¢) per liter (about $1.90 per gallon).

GOVERNMENT: The country is a federal republic, with a legislative body of two houses.

HIKING: In the German uplands, a network of marked hiking trails (approximately 132,000 kilometers) is serviced by regional hiking associations organized under the **German Hiking and Climbing Association** (Verband Deutscher Gebirgs-und-Wandervereine), 21 B Hospitalstrasse, D-7000 Stuttgart 1. The associations provide information about trails, shelters, huts, whatever, in their respective regions. A directory of local hiking associations may be requested by writing the above address.

HITCHHIKING: West Germany offers some of the best hitchhiking possibilities in Europe. Seemingly every West German owns an auto, and there is a splendid network of autobahns. "Der Weg-Wanderer," as hitchhikers are known, aren't frowned upon here, as they are in some countries. However, you should never hitch a ride on an autobahn or freeway. It is also illegal to hitch a ride near an exit or entrance to a freeway. Therefore you'll have to stand far enough away so you won't get picked up by the police. You'd better have a sign (always use the German name for a city, not the American one—for example, Köln instead of Cologne).

HOLIDAYS: Public holidays are January 1; Easter (Good Friday through Easter Monday); May 1 (Labor Day); Ascension Day (ten days before Whitsunday); Corpus Christi (ten days after Whitsunday); June 17 (Unity Day); November 1 (All Saints Day), mid-November (day of prayer and repentance), and Christmas (lasting through December 26).

INFORMATION: Nearly all major towns and certainly all cities in the Federal Republic have tourist offices. The headquarters of the **German National Tourist Board** is at 69 Beethovenstrasse, D-6000 Frankfurt am Main (tel. 0611/7-57-21). Before you go, you'll find the German National Tourist Office at 747 Third Ave., New York, NY 10017 (tel. 212/308-3300); in Los Angeles at 444 So. Flower St., Los Angeles, CA 90017 (tel. 213/688-7332), and in Montréal at 2 Fundy, Place Bonaventure, Montréal, PQ H5A 1B8 (tel. 514/878-9885).

LANGUAGE: The official language, of course, is German, but English is commonly spoken, at least at major hotels and restaurants and in the principal tourist areas.

LAUNDRY: Upper-bracket hotels have facilities for getting your clothes laundered, but the service is very expensive. To cut costs, you can use a laundromat, available in all major cities and towns. They are called Wäscherei in the telephone directories. Coin laundries are called Münzwäscherei.

MAIL DELIVERY: General delivery—mark it "poste restante"—can be used in any major town or city in the Federal Republic. Your mail may be picked up upon presentation of a valid identity card or passport.

MEDICAL: Most major hotels in West Germany have a doctor on staff or on call. If you can't get hold of a doctor, the best thing to do is to dial the emergency service, which is open day and night. The number is listed in every telephone directory under the heading of **Ärztlicher Notdienst** (emergency medical service). The Red Cross can also help in cases of illness or accident. Medical and hospital services in the Federal Republic and West Berlin aren't free. It is therefore advisable, before departure, to take out appropriate insurance or at least inquire from your own sick-fund organization or insurance company.

METRIC MEASURES: Here's your chance to learn metric measures before they're introduced to America.

U.S.	Germany	U.S.	Germany
1 ounce	28.3 grams	1 inch	2.54 centimeters
1 pound	454 grams	1 foot	0.3 meters
2.2 pounds	1 kilo (1000 grams)	1 yard	0.91 meters
1 pint	0.47 liter	1.09 yards	1 meter
1 quart	0.94 liter	1 mile	1.61 kilometers
1 gallon	3.78 liters	0.62 mile	1 kilometer
		1 acre	0.40 hectare
		2.47 acres	1 hectare

MOUNTAIN CLIMBING: The **German Alpine Association** (Deutscher Alpenverein, Praterinsel 5, D-8000 München 22), owns and operates 252 huts in the uplands and in the Alps that are open to all mountaineers. In addition to the huts, the association maintains a 15,000-kilometer network of alpine trails.

NEWSPAPERS: The *International Herald Tribune* is widely distributed throughout the Federal Republic. News magazines such as *Time* and *Newsweek* are sold at major newsstands in the big cities.

PETS: Keep Fido or Morris at home. Germany has rigid controls on pets. If you're traveling with a pet, you must have proof of a rabies vaccination.

POSTAGE: Airmail letters up to 20 grams take 1.40 DM (46¢) to the U.S. or Canada; postcards, .90 DM (28¢). Domestic letters up to 20 grams cost .80 DM (26¢); postcards, .70 DM (23¢). These rates are subject to change of course, and should be verified on the spot in case there is a postal increase by the time of your visit. Post offices are generally open from 8 a.m. to 6 p.m. Monday to Friday and from 8 a.m. to noon on Saturday. Railway terminal post offices, found in all principal cities, are open weekdays until late evening.

RAILWAY INFORMATION: Please refer to "Traveling within Germany," Section 2 in this chapter.

RELIGIOUS SERVICES: Roman Catholic and Protestant churches are found throughout Germany. Your hotel should be a helpful source in locating a church near you.

REST ROOMS: Women's toilets are usually marked with an "F," meaning Frauen, and men's toilets are marked with an "H" for Herren. Germany, frankly, doesn't have enough public toilets, except in terminal areas. The locals have to rely on bars, cafés, or restaurants, which in some cases isn't always appreciated unless you're a paying customer. In a public toilet, tipping is customary, usually .30 DM (9¢). If you need soap and towel, give something extra.

ROMANTIK HOTELS: Throughout Germany you'll encounter hotels with a "Romantik" in their name. This is not a chain, but a voluntary association of small inns and guest houses that have only one element in common: they are usually old and charming, romantic in architecture. If you like a traditional ambience as opposed to bandbox modern, then a Romantik Hotel might be for you. The requirement is that they must be in a historic building (or at least of vintage date), and personally managed by the owner. Usually you get a regional cuisine, and good, personal service, along with an old-fashioned setting and cozy charm. Whenever possible, I always book myself into one, savoring a life known to travelers years ago. Sometimes the plumbing could be better, and standards of comfort vary widely, but all of them have been preinspected. Therefore there should be no Dracula's dungeon or cobwebs waiting by the time of your visit.

SHOPPING AND SOUVENIRS: No one wants to return home without an attractive or useful souvenir, and small "typically German" articles can be obtained on the spot at reasonable prices. And as you travel throughout the country, you can often buy direct from the manufacturer: jewelry in Idar-Oberstein, china in the Bavarian Forest, stoneware in Westerwald, woodcarvings in Upper Bavaria, cuckoo clocks in the Black Forest, and wine from the growers.

In large cities you'll find the sign "tax-free" in some shops. In these shops, you can get a form which later entitles you, on leaving the country, to claim back part of the price (approximately 10%).

SHOPPING HOURS: These can vary slightly from state to state. Shops are generally open from 9 a.m. to 6:30 p.m. Monday to Friday and from 9 a.m. to 2 p.m. on Saturday (except the first Saturday of the month when they remain open till 4 p.m.).

SPAS: Some 250 registered spas and health resorts are found in Germany. They feature the most modern therapeutic facilities and provide numerous treatments, amusements, and sports for rest and recuperation. Information on spas and health resorts may be obtained by writing **Deutscher Bäderverband e.V.,** 111 Schumannstrasse, D-5300 Bonn. Also refer to Chapter IV in this guide, "Leading Spa Resorts."

SWIMMING: Nearly every town, especially the popular tourist resorts, has one or more outdoor and indoor pools (some heated). More and more hotels also have their own facilities for guests. German beaches are found along the North and Baltic Seas. Thermal- and mineral-water swimming pools may be found in a great number of health resorts and spas.

TAXES: As a member of the European Common Market, the Federal Republic imposes a tax on most goods and services—currently 14%. It is a "value added tax."

TELEGRAMS: The post office runs the telegraph service. You can go directly to a post office or else file a telegram at your hotel desk. Charges to the States are about 1.20 DM (40¢) per word.

TELEPHONES: Local and long-distance calls may be placed from all post offices and coin-operated public telephone booths. The unit charge is .30 DM (9¢) or three 10-pfenning coins. All towns and cities in the Federal Republic may be dialed directly by using the prefix listed in the telephone directory above each local heading. Telephone calls made through hotel switchboards can double, triple, or *whatever* the charge. Therefore try to confine your calls to outside where you are staying. Confused? Call 118 or 0118 for information.

TELEX: These most often are sent through your hotel.

TIME: West Germany is six hours ahead of Eastern Standard Time in the United States. Germany operates on Central European Time, which places it one hour ahead of Greenwich Mean Time. However, confusion occurs in the summer months, since the spring of 1980 when the Federal Republic went on East European Summer Time. Clocks are changed until the end of September. German time is changed after England reverts to summer time and before America goes on Daylight Saving Time. Rail timetables and most everything else can be thrown off during this transition period. Before the East Coast U.S. goes on Daylight Saving Time, and after Germany changes over, there is for a short period a difference of seven hours between the two countries. That confusion occurs again in the fall as countries make a time change again. Always check carefully if you're traveling in those time zones and, say, plan to catch a plane.

TIPPING: Bills always include VAT and a service charge. There is generally no need to give extra, unless the service has been satisfactory. Then it is customary that the total amount of the bill be rounded upward. Porters and bellhops usually get 2 DM (66¢) per bag, as does the doorman at your hotel, restaurant, or nightclub. Maids aren't tipped in Germany, but a concierge is, providing he or she did some special favor such as obtaining hard-to-get theater or opera tickets. Cab drivers aren't usually tipped, except for a loose coin or two. The reason for this is that taxi fares are lethal in the Federal Republic. Tip hairdressers or barbers 5% to 10%. Many Germans leave nothing.

TRAFFIC SIGNS: Easy-to-understand international road signs are used throughout Germany.

WINTER SPORTS: More than 300 winter sports resorts are found in the German Alps and such wooded hill country as the Harz Mountains, the Black Forest, and the Bavarian Forest at altitudes of up to 1500 meters. In addition to outstanding ski slopes, trails, lifts, and jumps, toboggan slides, and skating rinks, many of the larger resorts also offer ice hockey, ice boating, and bobsledding. Curling is very popular, especially in Upper Bavaria. The Olympic sports facilities at Garmisch-Partenkirchen enjoy international renown, as do the ski jumps of Oberstdorf and the artificial-ice speed-skating rink at Inzell. More than 250 ski lifts are found in such places as the German Alps, the Black Forest, and the Harz Mountains. Information on winter sports facilities is available from local tourist bureaus and the offices of the German National Tourist Board.

YOUTH HOSTELS: Germany has some of the finest youth hostels in the world. There are about 580 of them, many in old castles in bucolic situations. Young people up to 24 years of age pay 6.30 DM ($2.08) to 7.30 DM ($2.41) per night. Adults over 24, provided there is room, are charged 8.30 DM ($2.74) to 9.30 DM ($3.07). Space allowing, adults are given a bed only after 6 p.m. In Bavaria, adults over 27 may not stay in youth hostels. For young people up to age 24, a junior membership card is issued for 10 DM ($3.30); the adult membership costs 18 DM ($5.94). Membership cards stamped for families go for 18 DM also. These are annual dues.

Membership cards of associations affiliated to the International Youth Hostel Federation are regarded as the equivalent of German membership cards. Foreigners who are not members of an association affiliated to the IYHF, and who are only temporarily in Germany, must obtain an international guest card at 30 DM ($9.90). The average price for a meal in one of these hostels is between 3 DM (99¢) and 6 DM ($1.98). Application should be made in writing to **Deutsches Jugendherbergswerk,** which is the German Youth Hostel Association, 26 Bülowstrasse, 4930 Detmold 1, or to the American Youth Hostel Association, 132 Spring St., New York, NY 10012 (tel. 212/431-7100).

Chapter II

FRANKFURT AM MAIN AND ENVIRONS

1. Hotels
2. Restaurants
3. Sights
4. Frankfurt After Dark
5. Exploring the Environs

YOUR FIRST GLIMPSE of Germany will very likely be this thriving industrial metropolis. It's only the country's seventh-largest city, but Frankfurt is Germany's most important transportation center. Its huge *flughafen* welcomes every major international airline. More than 1200 trains run in and out of its massive 19th-century station, the largest in Germany, and some of these trains run from the station right to the airport to transport arriving passengers back to town.

As the home of the Bundesbank (Federal Bank), Frankfurt is also the financial center of the Federal Republic. Since the Rothschilds opened their first bank here in their hometown in 1798, it has been a major banking city, currently containing more than 220 banks and the third-largest stock exchange in the country. It is also a heavily industrial city, with more than 2450 factories operating around the ford *(furt)* on the Main where the Frankish tribes once settled.

Frankfurt has also been the home of Germany's most important trade fairs since way back around A.D. 1200. The International Frankfurt Fairs in spring and autumn bring some 1.2 million visitors to the city, causing a logjam in its hotels. Fairs include the Motor Show, the Chemical Industries, the Cookery Fair, and the Book Fair. Of these, the International Book Fair is perhaps the best known, drawing some 5500 publishers from nearly 100 countries. The occasion is the most important meeting place in the world for the acquisition and sale of book rights and translations.

But in spite of its commerce and industry, it is also a tourist city, offering numerous attractions to its many visitors. One out of 11 persons in Frankfurt on any given day is actually a stranger to the city.

For shoppers, Frankfurt has everything—the specialty shops are so much like those back in the States that most visitors from America will feel right at home. The Zeil is the major shopping district, with its huge department stores lining both sides of the street, offering everything from raincoats to rock records in a wide range of prices.

GETTING AROUND: The best way to go from the airport into Frankfurt and vice versa is by the airport train. A taxi will charge from 30 DM ($9.90), maybe more, but the train costs only $2 for a 15-minute ride. Tickets for the train must be purchased in advance at automatic ticket-vending machines. Every ten minutes a district train (S-Bahn) heads for the Hauptbahnhof, Frankfurt's main railway station, and every 20 minutes for the Hauptwache in the city center. Travel time is between 11 and 15 minutes, making this far faster than other means of transport. Every 15 to 30 minutes a no. 61 city bus runs between the airport and the Sudbahnhof in Frankfurt Sachsenhausen. One-way fare for train or bus is 4 DM ($1.32) in peak hours, 3.10 DM ($1.02) at other times. To and from the airport, there are direct connections with 14 other S-Bahn stations in the direction of Mainz and Wiesbaden and also direct intercity connections with 64 main stations between Amsterdam and Munich as well as the special Lufthansa "Airport Express" to Bonn, Cologne, and the Düsseldorf airport.

Between the airport at Frankfurt am Main and the city's main railway station, all trains stop at F-Sportfield and F-Niederrad. All S14 line trains come in at the Hauptbahnhof underground and then continue to Taunusanlage, to the Hauptwache in the city center, and to Konstablerwache at the end of the line, one minute on from the Hauptwache. All S15 lines pull in on platform 21 above ground at the Hauptbahnhof (on platform 18 after 8 p.m.) and are therefore better suited for passengers with lots of luggage who wish to take a taxi or make further rail connections. All the S15 trains travel underground from the Konstablerwache (one minute earlier than the Hauptwache) to the main railway subway station. Minutes after they arrive at the airport, they go on to Rüsselsheim, the Mainz main station, and Wiesbaden. All S15 line trains start above ground on platform 21 at the main railway station (on platform 18 after 8 p.m.) and are therefore more suitable for passengers with heavy luggage.

The city of Frankfurt and its surrounding area, up to a radius of 24 miles, is connected by a number of fast, modern means of transport, under the Frankfurt Transport Federation (FVV). City and overland buses, trams, subways, and district trains can be used within fare zones at one price, including transfers. Tickets are obtained at *blue* coin-operated automatic machines labeled *Fahrscheine*. These machines will change up to 5 DM ($1.65). Fares vary depending on the time of day, dropping from 2 DM (66¢) in rush hours to 1.50 DM (50¢) at other times. A 24-hour ticket with unlimited travel costs 7 DM ($2.31), half price for children. Zone charts and additional information in six languages are displayed on all the automatic machines. Be sure to buy your ticket before you board the transport conveyance. If you are caught traveling without the proper card, you are subject to a fine of about 40 DM ($13.20).

Bicycles can be taken on the S1 to S6, the S14, the S15, and the U1–4 on weekends, public holidays, and during school vacation, as well as Monday to Friday between 8 a.m. and 3 p.m. and after 7 p.m. on regular work days. An additional ticket, costing 2 DM (66¢) must be purchased and the bicycle must be placed in a specially marked section of the train for safety.

Tickets for the German Railway (Bundesbahn) within a 30-mile radius of Frankfurt, plus necessary additional tickets, may be obtained from the *red* coin-operated automatic machines in the main station foyer in front of the platforms. The machines return your change.

If for some reason public transport is not feasible, you'll have to rely on taxi service. Radio taxis are on call day and night, either at marked taxi stands or by calling 25-00-01, 23-00-33, or 54-50-11. There is no extra charge for pickup. The meter drops at 3.60 DM ($1.19), and an additional 1.60 DM (53¢) is charged per kilometer. Waiting time is 20 DM ($6.60) per hour. The fare is charged per trip, not per passenger or per piece of luggage transported. From the airport to the main railway station (Hauptbahnhof) the basic charge is 26 DM ($8.58); to the Hauptwache it's 28 DM ($9.24); and from the main railway station to the Hauptwache, 9 DM ($2.97). The fares are the same day and night.

PRACTICAL FACTS: To exchange dollars into marks, go to **Deutsche Verkehrs-Kredit Bank** (tel. 2-64-82-01), at the main station between 6:30 a.m. and 10 p.m., or the branch at the airport (tel. 6-90-35-06), which is open from 7:30 a.m. to 9 p.m.

The offices of the **American Express** are centrally located at 5 Steinweg (tel. 2-10-51), open weekdays from 8:30 a.m. to 5:30 p.m. (on Saturday from 9 a.m. to noon). Unless you have an American Express card (either green or gold), you'll be assessed a 2-DM (66¢) surcharge for using its mail services.

If you lose a passport or have some such emergency, get in touch with the **U.S. Consulate,** 21 Siesmayerstrasse (tel. 74-00-71).

The official tourist office, dispensing information for all the country, is the **German National Tourist Board,** 69 Beethovenstrasse (tel. 75-72-1). (For other information bureaus, refer to the section on hotels, below.)

Frankfurt has several **emergency numbers** that might come in handy. Among them are: 110—accident; 112—fire; 112—first aid; 7-92-02-00 for emergency medical service; and 6-60-72-71 for emergency dental service.

The **central post office** in Frankfurt is 108–110 Zeil, near the Hauptwache, which is open from 8 a.m. to 9 p.m. Go here to pick up general delivery mail (called "poste restante" in Europe). There is also a post office in the main railway station which is open both day and night.

If you're planning to tour the country, you might want to check with **ADAC** for membership possibilities. This is the major automobile club of the country, and can be most useful if you have breakdowns or experience other difficulties on the road. Its main offices are at 4 Schumannstrasse (tel. 74-30-1).

1. Hotels

If you arrive during a busy trade fair, you may find many of the better hotels full. Rooms in Frankfurt are rather expensive. You can generally find a room on the spot by going to the tourist office in the railway station, near Track 23. There you will find an office of **Verkehrsamt Frankfurt am Main,** Im Hauptbahnhof, Nordseite (tel. 212-88-49). In summer, hours are 8 a.m. to 10 p.m. (on Sunday from 9:30 a.m. to 8 p.m.). In the off-season, hours are more limited: from 8 a.m. to 9 p.m. (on Sunday from noon to 8 p.m.). During a particularly busy season you may have to take a room as far as two or three miles from the city's center. The cost for staying in a hotel or pension starts at $15 (U.S.) to $25, plus another $3 charged for a continental breakfast. The center charges 3 DM (99¢) for its services.

Another tourist information center is at the Hauptwache, on the B level (tel. 212-87-08), open weekdays from 9 a.m. to 6 p.m. and on Saturday from 9 a.m. to 2 p.m.

THE TOP CHOICES: Steigenberger Hotel Frankfurter Hof, am Kaiserplatz (tel. 2-02-51), run by the Steigenberger chain, is the grand hotel of Frankfurt. This massively restored structure is the number one choice of traditionalists. Its position in the center of the city is ideal for visitors and business people alike, as it's just a few short blocks from the main railway station and near the sights of the Altstadt (Old Town).

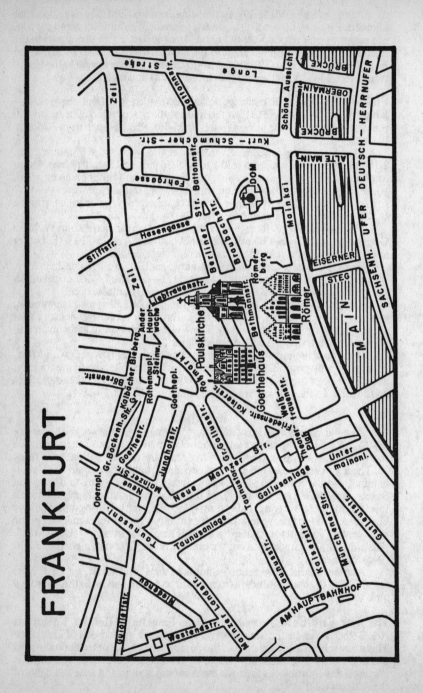

Behind a 100-year-old, neobaroque facade, the Frankfurter Hof has successfully combined the classic and the modern. Its art collection, particularly its Gobelin tapestries, is outstanding. In spite of its size—you and your friends could stay here for a month without running into one another—this comfortably furnished hotel offers a personalized atmosphere. The rooms are well maintained, furnished in restrained and dignified modern. The cost varies with size and location of your room: a single begins at 225 DM ($74.25). Doubles begin at 320 ($105.60) for a moderate chamber. All have well-equipped baths. An American breakfast is included in all room prices.

In keeping with the management's belief that a fine hotel is "more than just a place to sleep," the Frankfurter Hof boasts several fine attractions. There is the Restaurant Français, decorated in Empire style, and the thatch-roofed Grill Restaurant has fine grilled meats. The Kaiserbrunnen offers light meals and the finest of wines and champagne in a cozy setting with a Biedermeier decor. The hotel's Lipizzaner Bar is now regarded by discerning visitors as the most elegant in the city (see my nightlife recommendations). The favorite spot in the hotel is the provincial-style Frankfurt Stubb, recommended in the upcoming restaurant section.

Hotel Frankfurt Intercontinental, 43 Wilhelm-Leuschner (tel. 23-05-61), is West Germany's largest hotel. It has everything: you may find no reason whatsoever to leave its precincts. Right on the Main River, the south wing (21 stories) and the north wing (18 stories) offer 800 bedrooms of quiet comfort and dignity. Singles in price from 240 DM ($79.20) to a peak of 360 DM ($118.80); doubles are anywhere from 300 DM ($99) to 420 DM ($138.60).

The public rooms are mammoth, including a ballroom that can stuff in nearly 1000 Frankfurters. The general tone of the decor is quiet, but you get a feeling of warmth from the rich basic colors. The Rôtisserie is a favorite spot for dining, as is the Brasserie. The hotel's Bierstube is among the best in the city. There are two bars, a swimming pool, a sauna, massage facilities, and a solarium.

Parkhotel Frankfurt, 28–38 Wiesenhüttenplatz (tel. 2-69-70), is considered by many discriminating guests the finest hotel in Frankfurt. It provides not only warmth but personal attention as well for each of its guests. Near the station, it opens onto a quiet square, offering parking (the underground garage has additional space for 50 cars). The hotel has been built in two sections—an ornately decorated 19th-century building right alongside a sleek 1970s wing. The decor is rich in autumnal tones, making for a soft, mellow atmosphere throughout. A single room with either shower or complete private bath ranges in price from 180 DM ($59.40) to 310 DM ($102.30); a double with bath is anywhere from 280 DM ($92.40) to 520 DM ($171.60). The hotel's gourmet restaurant, La Truffe, dishes out some of the best hors d'oeuvres in Frankfurt and has one of Germany's best wine cartes, recognized by the Deutsche Sommelier Union. The restaurant, Die Parkstube, offers German cuisine, buffets for breakfast, lunch, and splendid pastries. The Casablanca Bar, inspired by the Bogart film (a part Ronald Reagan turned down), offers a live piano with artists from overseas and Europe. Furthermore, the Parkhotel Frankfurt has a wine and gourmet shop, Die Trüffelei; a beer pub, Königsbrunnen; and a wine garden, Weinlaube.

Incidentally, my most trusted and discriminating friends in Frankfurt patronize La Truffe on special occasions, considering its dining room the premier place in the city for an elegant repast. To challenge that local assertion, you'd have to stick around Frankfurt for a long time and do a lot of dining.

Hessicher Hof, 40 Friedrich-Ebert-Anlage (tel. 7-54-00), is a private, traditional hotel with an elegant atmosphere. All 160 rooms are comfortably furnished, often with frilly decorator touches and all with private bathrooms. Always bearing in mind the well-being of its guests, the Hessischer Hof has chosen one of Goethe's quotations as its slogan: "Here I feel like a human being." The furnishings in the public rooms give the hotel character: gilt-framed oil paintings and a museum-level collection of Sèvres porcelain in the dining room.

Singles range from 240 DM ($79.20) to 400 DM ($132); twin-bedded rooms, from 320 DM ($105.60) to 460 DM ($151.80). Breakfast is extra, and suites are more expensive, of course.

CP Frankfurt Plaza, 2–10 Hamburger Allee (tel. 77-07-21), stands across from the Messegelände (fairgrounds), and during the Book and Trade Fairs of Frankfurt it is packed to the rafters. Prices then are whatever the market will bear. Top publishers book rooms years in advance.

However, in the likely possibility that you'll arrive at other times, this Canadian Pacific hotel is an inviting and appealing selection. It's within walking distance to the heart of town, as well as to the famous Palmengarten (botanical garden) and the well-known Senckenberg Museum around the corner.

Its rooms are sandwiched between the 26th and 44th floors, and are equipped with radio, color TV, phone with direct outside lines, mini-bar, private bath, and adjustable air conditioning. Traffic noise is left far below, and you can look out over the city and the surrounding countryside, framed against a backdrop of the Taunus Mountains.

The hotel offers two restaurants, the luxuriously appointed Geheimratsstube, and the Bäckerei, where you can watch the hotel's bakers turn out fresh bread and rolls each morning. (The bar, Biblio-Theke, and the hotel's disco, Blue Infinitum, are previewed in the nightlife section.)

Singles range in price from 190 DM ($62.70) to 310 DM ($102.30), and doubles run from 240 DM ($79.20) to 380 DM ($125.40), plus the cost of breakfast which can be either continental or buffet style. Several more expensive suites are also offered.

Hotel National, 50 Baseler Strasse (tel. 23-48-41), has long been my "home in Frankfurt." It has an appealing and winning quality for the traditionalist, with an ambience unmatched by the larger, more impersonal sleek hotels of Frankfurt. Leitung J. Steier is an engaging and efficient host, who generally takes a personal interest in the comfort of his guests. Much of the patronage is from an older, more affluent crowd.

An IHA first-class hotel, the 130-bed hostelry lies only two minutes from the central station, from which the Rhine-Main airport can be reached in just 12 minutes by electric train. The fairgrounds are also near the hotel.

The hotel is made richer by its use of antiques or handsome reproductions in both its public and private chambers. Many of the rooms are spacious and not overly decorated, the atmosphere enhanced by Oriental carpeting. Singles come in a wide range, with little or no plumbing at a rock-bottom 80 DM ($26.40), going up to 135 DM ($44.55) and 155 DM ($51.15) with private shower and bath. Bathless two-bedded rooms cost 180 DM ($59.40), rising to 225 DM ($74.25) with shower and peaking at 250 DM ($82.50) with twin beds and private bath. All rates include a complete buffet breakfast.

If you don't want to venture out into the station area at night, you might want to dine at the hotel, in a beautifully appointed room where an international menu features a 40-DM ($13.20) dinner. There are à la carte selections as well.

Frankfurt Savoy Hotel, 42 Wiesenhüttenstrasse (tel. 23-05-11). With a name like "Savoy," you expect luxury. What you get here is a big 150-room sleek, modern, and commercial hotel lying only 300 yards from the main railway terminal. The big feature of the place is a tenth-floor heated swimming pool with a jetstream, massage, sauna, solarium, and sun terrace. Rooms are not super-spacious, but they are pleasingly furnished, each with private bath and shower, radio, soundproof windows (a godsend in this part of the city), automatic alarm clock, mini-bar, and TV that includes U.S. programs.

Singles begin at 135 DM ($44.55), going up to 165 DM ($54.45), and twin-bedded units cost from 225 DM ($74.25). If you don't like to dine around, you might ask for the half-board rate when checking in. Tariffs already include a continental breakfast, service, and tax, but for another 35 DM ($11.55) you'll get a set dinner as well.

The place is quite lively, drawing loyal patronage from the business community of Frankfurt, those attracted to its Savoy Grill, smart and fashionable with its separate grill dining bar, and the rustic-style Chalet Savoie with its view of the city. The Savoy Bar and Le Tourbillon, a disco, also lure the visitors as well as the locals. There is also a hairdressing salon for both men and women.

Hotel Gravenbruch-Kempinski-Frankfurt, 2 Neu-Isenburg (tel. 06102/50-50), lies in the suburbs, a 20-minute haul from the center of Frankfurt, and as such is recommended for guests wanting to escape the bustle of a commercial city. The location is only ten minutes from the Frankfurt airport. The hotel is set back from Highway 459, nestled on 37 acres of parkland. The grounds are complete with a lake. Limousine transfer service brings guests free to and from the hotel to the airport and city center.

The structure was built on the foundation and old walls of a former manor house dating from 1568. Luxury is combined with rural charm. More modern residential wings were positioned along the lakeshore, harmoniously blending with the environment. Some touches of the old country-mansion character remain, as exemplified by the large atrium-style courtyards.

Today the hotel provides sleep-inducing bedrooms, each attractively furnished and styled. Amenities include color TV, mini-bar, phone, radio, and adjustable air conditioning. Singles with bath cost 290 DM ($95.70) to 310 DM ($102.30); twins, from 340 DM ($112.20) to 380 DM ($125.40).

Many in-the-know Frankfurters journey down here just to sample the savory viands of this cozy place as the menu offers a choice from nouvelle cuisine to local dishes to continental specialties. My favorite is the Forst-schänke, a 15th-century hunting lodge, with tables set on a stone-slab floor in the rustic style. Draft beer at the bar comes straight from a keg barrel. In summer, food and drink are served on the tree-shaded terrace.

With its view of the park, the Restaurant Forsthaus is more elegant. It was converted from a 16th-century hunting lodge and serves meals costing from 50 DM ($16.50) to 85 DM ($28.05). And better still is the Gourmet-Restaurant, seating only 40 diners and serving dinners that begin at 65 DM ($21.45), ranging up to 135 DM ($44.55). The Torschaenke, with a stone-slab floor and draft beer from a barrel, is housed in what were horse stables in the 16th century. The hotel bar offers dancing to music from international trios and entertainers.

Other facilities include heated indoor and outdoor swimming pools, a fitness center, a sauna, a solarium, tennis courts, boutiques, and a hairdressing salon; golf and horseback riding are available nearby. A beauty and fitness farm was opened in 1984.

THE MODERATE RANGE: Hotel Continental, 56 Basseler Strasse (tel. 23-03-41), is generally conceded to be the leader among the middle-bracket hotels standing in the vicinity of the railway station. At the turn of the century (founded in 1889) it was a leading choice in the city, enjoying its heyday in the belle-époque era. From the ashes of World War II it was reconstructed in 1952, and has been attracting raii travelers and others ever since.

Around the corner are lively bars, but serenity prevails inside this hotel.

The housekeepers have decent standards, and some of its chambers, especially those with more modern plumbing, are most comfortable. Windows, mercifully, have been soundproofed to keep out the traffic din. A single ranges in price from 108 DM ($35.64) to 120 DM ($39.60); a double costs 165 DM ($54.45) to 210 DM ($69.30). The Continental is the choice of many business people, including Japanese clients.

It also has a pleasant restaurant with an international cuisine. À la carte orders can be very expensive. However, a table d'hôte is a potent bait, costing only 35 DM ($11.55).

Savigny Hotel, 14–16 Savignystrasse (tel. 7-53-30), in the general vicinity of the railway station, often attracts the business client with its meeting rooms, but it's also geared to receive the international tourist. The staff here will house you in one of 120 rooms, with balcony, bath, shower, toilet, mini-bar, TV, radio, and phone.

Some of the rooms are very tiny, seemingly as compact as an ocean liner and decorated in a severe modern style, while others draw for inspiration upon the more mellow past. At least the bedchambers aren't uniform in style and decor. A single costs 140 DM ($46.20) to 200 DM ($66), rising to 200 DM ($66) to 310 DM ($102.30) in a double. The tariffs include a buffet-style breakfast, service, and tax. If you're traveling with a child, an extra bed will be put in the room for 50 DM ($16.50).

The atmosphere is most definitely international. On my last inspection the hotel was filled, seemingly, with guests from all the continents of the world. They convene in the restaurant, where menus are priced at 24 DM ($7.92) and 75 DM ($24.75), later—or before—enjoying mugs of chilled beer in the Pilsstube.

Mozart, 17 Parkstrasse (tel. 55-08-31), is a honey, perhaps the best of the small hotels in Frankfurt. It stands on the periphery of the Botanical Gardens, overlooking the U.S. Army building where Eisenhower headquartered himself in Frankfurt. Right off the busy Fürstenbergerstrasse, the hotel is recognized by its cold marble facade, softened by blue panels and the filmy curtains at the windows. Everything inside—walls, furniture, bed coverings—is gleaming white, with the small exception of the rosebuds at the breakfast table. The breakfast room, incidentally, could easily pass for a salon with its crystal chandeliers and Louis XV-style chairs. The cheaper rooms are those with shower and toilet; the more expensive offer a bidet, separate toilet, and tub with shower. All have TV sets. A single ranges in price from 130 DM ($42.90) to 150 DM ($49.50); a double goes for 210 DM ($69.30). Members of the staff are polite and helpful.

Turm Hotel, 20 Eschersheimer Landstrasse (tel. 55-00-01), is a six-story structure, with 75 compact, boxy rooms where, as the Germans say, *"Der Komfort ist gut."* The lines in the bedrooms are sleek and uncluttered, in a spartan taste. A single with bath or shower costs from 102 DM ($33.66), a double with bath goes for 160 DM ($52.80), and a three-bedded room peaks at 190 DM ($62.70), these rates including breakfast, service, and VAT.

Innkeeper Gerard Sedlmeyer has employed an efficient, helpful staff to run this centrally located structure. The most winning part of the hotel is its restaurant, Sudpfanne, which attracts a local business of city folk (not just residents). It's done in a rustic style, and features dishes from an international kitchen. At the hotel, parking is also available.

Hotel An der Messe, 102 Westendstrasse (tel. 74-79-79), is small and special, even though its facade is boxy. The lobby and public rooms are more inviting, not a decorator's paradise, but not cold either. There are only 46 bedrooms, each with private bath or shower (also a toilet), phone, small refrigerator, radio, and TV on request. The staff does much to make you feel comfortable.

Half the rooms have been completely refurnished, and there are inviting little thoughtful touches to make everything seem more home-like. Only half a dozen singles are rented, at 130 DM ($42.90) each, and they're hard to come by unless reserved well in advance. Doubles cost around 180 DM ($59.40). Tariffs include breakfast, served in a light, airy room. The hotel stands about five minutes from the exhibition grounds, the university, the rail terminal, and the banking district. A porch overlooks the greenery, and there is also an underground garage.

Hotel Jaguar, 17–19 Theobald-Christ-Strasse (tel. 43-93-01), is an elegant name for an elegant animal, suggesting grace and style. Don't get your hopes up too much, but what you get here isn't bad. At least the management feels with some justification that this is the "leading hotel garni in the city" (garni refers to the fact that no meals other than breakfast are offered). The location is near the zoo.

The decor is bright and cheerful throughout, especially in the breakfast room. The staff is pleasant and helpful. The price is attractive too: a single without bath costs only 70 DM ($23.10), rising to 106 DM ($34.98) with complete bath. Doubles, all with private bath, range in price from 118 DM ($38.94) to 136 DM ($44.88). Rooms are compact. The TV and reading room is inviting, and you can store your car in an underground garage.

Hotel Falk, 38a Falkstrasse (tel. 70-80-94), is stark outside, but there is much to recommend it once you go inside. The innkeeper likes it bright and modern, but with enough traditional touches of the past to make it warm and cozy. The hotel opened in 1972, and it's been a success ever since. It rents out only 50 bedrooms, small, compact, and uncluttered. They're also well maintained, as the staff likes a spotless hotel. A single with shower costs 90 DM ($29.70) to 100 DM ($33), and a double goes for 150 DM ($49.50) to 170 DM ($56.10). These prices include tax, service, and breakfast. My favorite spot is the rustic hotel bar with Spanish tiles and hanging lights. It's called the Toledo-Stil.

Hotel Ebel, 26 Taunusstrasse (tel. 23-07-56), is a good, 55-bed hotel where innkeeper Gerlinde Kreh has set a policy of welcoming families with children. The hotel lies only 100 yards from the central station. Its rooms come in a variety of shapes and sizes, but they have been modernized with good plumbing and soundproof windows. Each unit is equipped with radio and color TV which is fitted to receive AFN, the TV program of the American Forces network. Depending on the plumbing, singles begin at 75 DM ($24.75) and climb to 100 DM ($33); doubles start at 104 DM ($34.32), going up to 140 DM ($46.20) for the best units in the house. A triple room with bath costs 178 DM ($58.74) to 190 DM ($62.70). A big array of food, including the inevitable cornflakes, is placed out for your breakfast the next morning, and it's all been included in the prices quoted. There's a pleasant little nook with greenery where guests gather for drinks.

Frankfurt Luxor Hotel, 2–4 Allerheiligen (tel. 29-30-67), is modern and reliable, offering good middle-class comfort right in the heart of the city. A Golden Tulip Hotel, it has a quiet urbanity that appeals to many. The staff gives you personal attention, and shelters you in tiny, severely modern rooms, 46 in all, each with private bath, self-dial phone, color TV, and radio, and in some cases a mini-bar. A double costs 195 DM ($64.35), while a single rents for 150 DM ($49.50), including breakfast. Of course during fair periods prices climb, as they do all over Frankfurt. The hotel also has a cozy bar with a plaid design and a TV lounge. A tram stops right in front of the Luxor. If you arrange it in advance, the hotel will have you picked up at either the airport or the railway station.

Hotel Monopol, 11–13 Mannheimer Strasse (tel. 23-01-71), lies opposite the railway station, near the city center. It has a distinguished atmosphere, attracting the individual client. The use of mahogany furniture in the 100 bedrooms makes for a more inviting, traditional ambience.

Units have phone, radio, and color TV on request. Some of the rooms are still bathless, and naturally these cost less—from 135 DM ($44.55) in a single, from 190 DM ($62.70) in a double. A single with bath rents for 150 DM ($49.50), rising to 220 DM ($72.60) in a double with bath. These tariffs include an American breakfast from the buffet table, tax, and service. The Monopol has a first-class restaurant and cocktail lounge.

THE BUDGET HOTELS: Hotel am Zoo, 6 Alfred-Brehm-Platz (tel. 49-07-71), is a modern little hotel with a nice restaurant just across from the entrance to the zoo gardens. The rooms are extremely clean, furnished in simple but comfortable modern pieces. Singles with showers and toilets rent for 60 DM ($19.80) to 85 DM ($28.05); doubles with bath, 95 DM ($31.35) to 130 DM ($42.90). The breakfast room on the street level is the hotel's most charming feature, with its linen-covered tables and attractive stained-glass windows. Parking facilities are available behind the hotel. The tram stops just across the street for convenient shopping and sightseeing trips.

Admiral, 25 Hölderlinstrasse (tel. 44-80-21), is often favored by families, including many connected with the U.S. military forces in Germany. Perhaps they like its location near the Zoologischer Garten, a short haul from the center of Frankfurt. Beyond its gunmetal-gray facade, the hotel serves breakfast only. It rents 52 bedrooms, each plainly furnished but adequately comfortable, and containing a TV set. Much use is made of natural wood, in the style of one of the Nordic countries. Units come equipped with private bath (often shower) and rent for 80 DM ($26.40) to 95 DM ($31.35) in a single, from 120 DM ($39.60) to 150 DM ($49.50) in a double.

Schwille, 50 Grosse Bockenheimerstrasse (tel. 28-30-54), is a 90-bed establishment with a charming café that is popular and well known for its pastries. Guests of the hotel sit in the charming, first-floor breakfast room facing the trees of the pedestrian zone. All rooms are quiet despite the fact that the hotel is in the center of the city. There is a private hotel parking place holding about 20 cars. Single accommodations without bath are 35 DM ($11.55), increasing to 85 DM ($28.05) to 115 DM ($37.95) with bath or shower and toilet in completely renovated, well-furnished rooms with radios. A bathless twin-bedded room costs 100 DM ($33), going up to 115 DM ($37.95) to 175 DM ($57.75) with private bath and toilet. The underground is a one-minute walk from the hotel.

Hotel Niedenau, 5 Niedenau (tel. 72-25-36), is a family-style little hotel of only ten rooms, run by Kurt Grün. But it's a find. The atmosphere is intimate, and the well-furnished rooms are individualized to make them more inviting. The establishment is immaculately kept, for scrubbing and polishing go on daily. Singles without bath go for 55 DM ($18.15), rising to 90 DM ($29.70) with bath. Bathless doubles cost 100 DM ($33), peaking at 110 DM ($36.30) with private bath; a continental breakfast with one egg and sausage is included in the tariffs. In the vicinity of the railway station, the Niedenau is near two other suitable hotels, the Württemberger Hof and the Haus Hübner.

Neue Kräme, 23 Neue Kräme (tel. 28-40-46), stands on a street of the same name in the heart of the pedestrian area, right off Berlinerstrasse, not far from Römerberg. It is modest and strictly functional and serves breakfast only, but many visitors like it because of its strategic location. Admittedly, you save a lot of money on public transport by staying here. If you lodge here, you can cover on foot much of the shopping area and a lot of the sightseeing attractions as well. Rooms are modernized and are pleasantly (not spectacularly) decorated. Nearly two dozen chambers are rented, ranging in cost from 90 DM ($29.70) in a single to a high of 130 DM ($42.90) in a double. A continental breakfast buffet is included.

Diana, 83–85 Westendstrasse (tel. 74-70-07), is spotless and homey. A leader in its price class, it is a copy of a private villa, with a drawing room and an intimate breakfast salon. In the West End, it is set on a pleasant residential street and maintains a tone of quiet dignity. The Diana is a postwar building, but the surrounding neighborhood contains many 19th-century houses at least partially spared from bombings. The rooms at the Diana are quite comfortable. Singles with private bath or shower range in price from 60 DM ($19.80) to 72 DM ($23.76), the latter equipped with toilet as well. Doubles with complete bath are 105 DM ($34.65) to 150 DM ($49.50), the latter the price of a suite.

Pension Uebe, 3 Grüneburgweg (tel. 59-12-09), is a mother-daughter venture—and a successful one at that. Both the mother, Elizabeth Kern, and her daughter, Andrea, speak English and are artistic and color conscious, having named and decorated each room after a European city, such as Munich or Vienna. Prints and decorative objects carry out the motif of the particular city. Reached by elevator, the pension occupies three floors over a grocery store and is entered through a covered passageway with window displays for an adjoining clothing store. The rooms are quiet, having windows insulated against noise. Of the 18 bedrooms, nine have shower (two with bath and toilet), and the rest have hot and cold water in the room with a bath and toilet available on the same floor. Some large rooms can be used as triples. Singles rent for 46 DM ($15.18) without shower, 62 DM ($20.46) with shower or bath, and 68 DM ($22.44) with shower and toilet. Doubles cost 75 DM ($24.75) with shower, 104 DM ($34.32) with shower and toilet. A large selection is offered in the country-style breakfast room. The pension is for those seeking a gentle, warm, home-like atmosphere. It is centrally located, with a subway station and taxi stand across the street. A garage and parking spaces are available in the courtyard.

Hotel-Pension Palmengarten, 8 Palmengartenstrasse (tel. 75-20-41), is a quiet little hotel within an apartment building just opposite the entrance to the famous Palmengarten. Run by Frau Hoffman, it's ideal particularly for American women traveling alone. The units are fairly large, always fresh and clean, and have sitting room areas with chairs or sofas. Everything is comfortable and homey. Most rooms are on the second floor, and there is an elevator. The hotel has no public lounges other than the cozy breakfast room. The price structure depends on the plumbing. Rooms are available without bath or with shower or bathtub. Singles begin at 55 DM ($18.15), going up to 105 DM ($34.65). Doubles range from 105 DM ($34.65) to 150 DM ($49.50). Breakfast is included. An added attraction—on Sunday in summer you can hear the music of the concerts in the Palmengarten without leaving your room.

Hotel am Kurfürstenplatz, 38 Kurfürstenplatz (tel. 77-78-16). Frau Petzel, the English-speaking owner, has decorated the hotel in a mixture of styles, perking up each room with bright, cheerful colors, filmy curtains, and boxes of plants at the windows. The combination breakfast room and lounge sparkles with sunny, bright colors. The front rooms face a park complete with fountain, church spire, and lots of baby carriages. The hotel provides one bath and toilet for every three rooms. Singles rent for 50 DM ($16.50), doubles go for 80 DM ($26.40), and triples run 100 DM ($33). There's an additional charge of 5 DM ($1.65) for use of the bath. There are some rooms with shower, and for these a single pays 65 DM ($21.45); a double, 95 DM ($31.35). Rates include breakfast, tax, and service.

Hotel Pension West, 81 Gräfstrasse (tel. 77-80-11), occupies part of an old house just off a busy street opposite the university. The atmosphere is like that of a private home. Managers Herr and Frau Operhalski see that everything is clean and orderly here. Single rooms with shower cost 75 DM ($24.75). Doubles with shower are priced at 104 DM ($34.32). Breakfast, included in the rates, is served in a room on the ground floor. There are no parking facilities, but metered parking is usually available on the nearby streets.

Hotel Haus Hübner, 23 Westendstrasse (tel. 74-60-44), is solid and modern, lying about 500 yards from the main railroad station. However, the house is placed on a one-way street, and at night all is very quiet here, noises sometimes absorbed by the small gardens of the neighboring houses. The yard of the hotel offers space for cars. The little hotel is well run and guests are made to feel welcome. All the pleasantly comfortable rooms have hot and cold running water, and a few have complete plumbing. A single without bath costs 48 DM ($15.84), rising to 65 DM ($21.45) to 88 DM ($29.04) with shower or bath and toilet. A double with shower only goes for 102 DM ($33.66), increasing to 120 DM ($39.60) with bath and toilet. These rates include a continental breakfast. Rooms, reached by elevator, contain phones as well. Although in theory the hotel serves only breakfast, drinks can be ordered at any time, and if a guest so desires, he or she can request a small snack in the evening.

Württemberger Hof, 14 Karlstrasse (tel. 23-31-06), has the family style of a Germanic gasthof, even though it's on a busy commercial street close to the main station. The bedrooms, 67 in all, are functional and modern. Those overlooking the street are equipped with special soundproof windows. Tariffs, including a continental breakfast, are as follows: a single without bath costs 52 DM ($17.16), and increases to 85 DM ($28.05) with bath. In a double without bath the tariff is 85 DM ($28.05), going up to 120 DM ($39.60) with bath. This is a good, standard overnight stop.

Hotel Westfälinger Hof, 10 Düsseldorfer Strasse (tel. 23-47-48), has been the same family's property for some 60 years. It is a 60-room, 85-bed, stark-modern hotel in the vicinity of the rail station. Rooms are comfortable but cramped, and they're all neat and clean. A single room without bath but with direct-dial phone rents for 58 DM ($19.14), the cost rising to 85 DM ($28.05) with complete bath. Twin-bedded or double rooms, with complete bath and phones, cost 125 DM ($41.25). On the premises is Panda, a Chinese restaurant (tel. 25-12-90), serving good and reasonably priced fare from 11:30 a.m. to midnight. Meals begin at 35 DM ($11.55).

Corona Hotel, 48 Hamburger Allee (tel. 77-90-77), is a hotel garni (a breakfast-only hostelry) directed by Mr. and Mrs. Zimmerman. The location is in the vicinity of the railway station. Most bedrooms have been freshened up and are light, homey, and well kept. None are particularly spacious, but the prices are good. A double costs 110 DM ($36.30) to 135 DM ($44.55), and a single rents for 65 DM ($21.45) to 80 DM ($26.40). The tariffs include breakfast, served in a little room with separate tables.

Kolpinghaus, 26 Lange Strasse (tel. 28-85-41), is a modern 65-bed hotel, whose most winning feature is the little garden out back where café tables are placed in fair weather. The rooms are teeny in dimension, and some of them reminded me of those available in a modern American university dormitory. Nevertheless, they are well maintained and cared for, and the sheets are nice, crisp, and white. Both singles and doubles come with almost no plumbing, or a shower and toilet, or a complete bath. Singles range from 55 DM ($18.15) to 80 DM ($26.40); doubles go from 85 DM ($28.05) to 110 DM ($36.30). The location is within walking distance of the famous Frankfurt Zoo.

A LEFT BANK CHOICE: Hotel Maingau, 38 Schifferstrasse (tel. 61-70-01), is just right for those who want to live among the Frankfurters rather than with their fellow visitors on the right bank. The hotel opens onto a small park in the colorful apple wine district, just across the Main from the Old Town. Plenty of blond wood and plastic make up the Nordic furnishings in both the old building and the annex. Bathless singles rent for 58 DM ($19.14), increasing to 90 DM ($29.70) with private shower or bath. Bathless doubles cost 75 DM ($24.75), and one with private bath will run a high of 113 DM ($37.29). The Maingau is a good point from which to launch a nighttime pub crawl of the apple wine district, beginning at the friendly restaurant and bierstube next door.

READER'S HOTEL SELECTION: "I recommend the **Hotel Schiff**, 33 Triftstrasse (tel. 67-70-12), a well-run, modern hotel on the left bank of the River Main. A single room costs 90 DM ($29.70) and a double runs 150 DM ($49.50), in well-appointed accommodations with a shower and toilet. Breakfast is included and features a buffet containing various meats, cereals, juices, yogurts, and cheeses, as well as the usual rolls and coffee, and there is no extra charge. The hotel caters to large numbers of German business and professional women traveling alone. This shows that they consider it to be well run and safe. Service is excellent, and the desk personnel show a great deal of concern for the guests" (Christopher Blake, San Diego, Calif.).

2. Restaurants

At the crossroads of European travel, Frankfurt's restaurants reflect a sophisticated international flavor. You can find everything here, from haute cuisine to nouvelle cuisine, to great French and Italian restaurants, to the city's sausage namesake. The best wines are also readily available, but many Frankfurters still prefer to wash their food down with beer and apfelwein.

THE TOP RESTAURANTS: Restaurant Français, Steigenberger Hotel Frankfurter Hof, Kaiserplatz (tel. 2-02-51). If you don't like to dine in hotel restaurants as a general rule, you might make a mistake to ignore this citadel of haute cuisine on the main floor of the already-recommended Frankfurter Hof. It is by far the most outstanding restaurant in Frankfurt today. As the name suggests, the cuisine is French, more haute than nouvelle. The stress, in the main, is on cookery from Lyon and Provence (Lyon, the gastronomic capital of France, you anticipate, while Provence might come as a bit of a surprise).

Bernhard Stumpf is a perfectionist, insisting that dish after dish reflect not only professionalism but enthusiasm. One of my favorite dishes presented here is a filet of turbot with zucchini and a delicate puree of watercress. You might begin your meal with a velvety-smooth cream of wild mushroom soup or a gâteau of mostelle, a delicately flavored fish found mainly in the Mediterranean. The fish (which used to have to be eaten where it was caught, since it deteriorates so rapidly) is covered with orange butter.

Breast of chicken is served with a truffle butter sauce, and a magret of duckling is prepared with blackcurrants and a confit of onions. Try also the Angus beef grille Villette or roast pork "like your grandmother used to make" (not my grandmother!). In season, game is a specialty.

The chairs in the restaurant are Louis-Philippe in style, with peach-colored upholstery and vivid forest-green walls with impeccably white trim. For lunch, costing from 60 DM ($19.80), plus wine, the place largely fills up with business people. Dinner, averaging around 135 DM ($44.55), plus wine, is more romantic. The restaurant is open from noon to 2:30 p.m. and 7 until 11:30 p.m., except on Sunday when it is closed.

Weinhaus Brückenkeller, 6 Schützenstrasse (tel. 28-42-38), is also a leading restaurant in Frankfurt, perhaps the favorite watering spot of North American visitors to that city. In the heart of the Old Town, you dine under medieval-looking arches at candlelit tables. Strolling musicians encourage singing and gaiety. Franconian carvings adorn the alcoves, and huge wooden barrels are decorated with scenes from Goethe's *Faust* and from the life of Martin Luther. The food is well prepared, a happy mix of German and French cuisine. A typical meal might begin with cream of sorrel soup or a more substantial goose liver terrine, and follow with saddle of venison or saddle of young lamb. For a perfect finish, you might order a soufflé of strawberries with vanilla. Their tafelspitz (prime cut of boiled beef) is the best in town, as good as any you might have in Vienna. It's served with a sauce made with herbs and fresh vegetables such as spinach. Count on parting with 90 DM ($29.70) for an evening repast. Homemade sourdough bread is served with the meal. The wine cellar holds an excellent collection of German wines, some 180 in all, including the best from the Rhineland. The Brückenkeller is invariably crowded, so reservations are imperative. Personal attention and efficient service are hallmarks here. It's open for dinner only, from 6 p.m. to 1 a.m.

Frankfurter Stubb, Kaiserplatz (tel. 21-56-79), in the Steigenberger Hotel Frankfurter Hof, takes a giant step backward to the simple German cooking of the past century. The food here is straightforward and honest. The ambience is that of an elegant wine cellar, with cozy dining nooks. Colorful fabrics soften the wood and stucco look. The attentive English-speaking waitresses in regional garb are most helpful in translating the difficult German menu. For openers, try the excellent lentil soup with frankfurters. One of the house specialties is boiled beef (tafelspitz) with Frankfurt green sauce, served with potatoes cooked in bouillon. The featured dessert is rote grüte, a jelly of fresh fruit served with either vanilla sauce or cream. Expect to spend from 30 DM ($9.90) to 60 DM ($19.80) for a complete meal here. The Stubb is a favorite with North Americans, who can visit from noon to 11:30 p.m. daily except Sunday.

The **Grill Restaurant,** in the Steigenberger Hotel Frankfurther Hof, Kaiserplatz (tel. 2-02-51), completes the dining trio in this deluxe hotel. We've already visited the Restaurant Français and the Frankfurter Stubb, but many in-the-know local stockbrokers insist that "the Grill" decorated in the rustic style, dishes up the most savory viands in the city. It offers specialties from an open grill along with an international cuisine.

A luncheon buffet, costing 40 DM ($13.20) is served from noon to 2 p.m. on Sunday only. The regular dinner menu is from 6:30 to 10 p.m., when it's likely to cost from 65 DM ($21.45). Always look to see what's offered on the specialty menu. It might feature, as an appetizer, parfait of tomatoes on avocado mousse with chopped salmon. On my latest visit I was served seasonal mushrooms in a herb broth, followed by rib-eye steak gratinée with a beef marrow ragoût and glazed turnips, topped by rhubarb ice cream with mangoes. The Grill is shuttered on Saturday.

Erno's Bistro, 15 Liebigstrasse (tel. 72-19-97), is my personal favorite in Frankfurt. It's a chic rendezvous, right in midtown between the Old Opera House and the Palmengarten. This fashionable oasis draws everybody from visiting film stars to OPEC executives in full Arab attire. Fine service and appointments, plus a commendable French cuisine, are hallmarks of this fast-rising establishment where you must never show up without a reservation or else you'll be turned away. The place is much favored by an international community that convenes in Frankfurt.

For more than a decade the chef has been Erno W. Schmitt, a real Frankfurter who's already a legend in this part of the world. To prove how famous he is, I once, on a dare, sent him a letter marked Erno's Bistro, West Germany (not even Frankfurt)—and he got it!

For such a big reputation, his bistro is a little place where the staff speaks English. The menu is trilingual.

Erno learned his craft at some of the greatest French restaurants and at the École Cuisinière at Strasbourg. He changes his menu daily, and this is one of those rare places where the cooking seems to improve year by year.

He serves only the fish brought fresh from Paris by airplane or from European coasts. He offers both nouvelle cuisine and what he calls "cuisine formidable." The most exciting—and also the most expensive—appetizer is his foie gras natural à l'ombre. For a main course, I'd suggest the grilled brill, whose flesh is very delicate and light, served with a very special, rare type of mushroom. Also sample his vegetable terrine in lobster sauce, or his noisettes d'agneau (lamb) flavored with sprigs of fresh tarragon.

Actually, it may be best to let one of the efficient waiters or "Madame Erno" herself serve you the "surprise." This chef's special dinner will be tailored to your individual tastes as they are perceived by the staff, and will include the best dishes of the day. Chances are, you won't be disappointed. This nine-course gourmet dinner is a real highlight of the Frankfurt culinary scene.

You'll also find what is probably the best wine list in town. I think you'd prefer to skip over some of the $250 choices and settle instead for one of the fine Rhine or Mosel wines. The list has more than 280 selected wines and more than 30 champagnes. For his wine carte, Erno was honored with a golden diploma from the French Academie du Vin in Paris. House wines, served in carafes, are also excellent, and you can leave the 1953 Château Latour to those who actually come from an oil kingdom.

At lunch the bistro serves a plat du jour for 25 DM ($8.25) or a business lunch for 60 DM ($19.80). If you dine à la carte, expect to spend from 80 DM ($26.40) to 120 DM ($39.60) or even a lot more. The restaurant is closed from mid-June to mid-July, and between Christmas and New Years, and on Saturday and Sunday, except during the great international fairs.

Jacques Offenbach, 1 Opernplatz (tel. 28-48-20), is the perfect place for an after-theater supper, in the midst of a setting that Offenbach himself might have found stimulating. Surely the composer of *Tales of Hoffmann* would gravitate to the dusty-pink and beige walls with globe lights, the brass belle-époque lighting fixtures, and the comfortably upholstered oval-backed chairs that look like a Renoir painting.

Both a classical and a nouvelle cuisine are served here, the elegant service matching the elegant decor. Visitors gaze at Frankfurt's music lovers, their fellow diners, across the long expanse of the large room. Head chef Claus Fischer has a brigade of talent in the kitchen, turning out such delicacies as cream of broccoli soup, a perfectly done tournedos with roquefort sauce, loin of veal with fresh cabbage, scallops with fennel, and frog leg salad in the style of Camargue in Provence. A gourmet supper costs from 55 DM ($18.15) to 80 DM ($26.40) and the menu is in both French and German. Hours are daily from 6 p.m. to midnight (the restaurant closes in July every year).

Bistrot 77, 1 Ziegelhüttenweg (tel. 61-40-40), is one of the chicest restaurants in Frankfurt. The overall impression is one of lots of light, glass, and white. You get French cookery with a flair, the nouvelle cuisine and high prices of Dominique and Guy Mosbach, two French citizens who have made a name for themselves in Frankfurt. Their co-proprietor is Chester Sauri, also French, who was the founder of the restaurant and is now its general manager. A black-and-white tiled floor, with an airy latticework ceiling, is the setting, along with white bentwood chairs and pink-and-white table linen. For one of the dozen tables, you must reserve in advance. The food here is a frequently changing array of imaginatively prepared fish and meat dishes, along with intriguing appetizers and desserts. The bill of fare depends on the shopping of the day. The

Bistrot is open from noon to 3 p.m. and from 6 p.m. to midnight (dinner only on Saturday). It is closed on Sunday. A seven-course menu here costs from 110 DM ($36.30). A set menu is offered at 55 DM ($18.15).

Henninger-Turm, 60-64 Hainer Weg (tel. 606-36-00), is a revolving restaurant spectacle in a silo, housing barely enough for 200 million glasses of beer. The pride of Henninger Brewery, it's not only the largest brewery silo in the world, but the site of a revolving restaurant, Frankfurter Museums-Stubb. To go up in the elevator costs 3 DM (99¢) if you're just sightseeing. On the upper part is a lookout platform with a panoramic sweep of the city from a position across the Main in Sachsenhausen.

Hessian specialties are featured here, 357 feet above ground. The menu offers such typical fare as a rumpsteak or veal schnitzel, with mushrooms. The soup of the day is usually good and filling, especially the lentil. Expect to spend from 30 DM ($9.90) to 65 DM ($21.45) for an average meal. Look also for local seasonal specialties such as medallions of hare in a juniper cream sauce. Desserts include fresh strawberries in season. There are also places for beer drinking, and you might also hear a band. The Frankfurter Brauerei Museum contains artifacts of the beer industry.

Mövenpick am Opernplatz, 2 Opernplatz (tel. 28-78-57), is the spot where the Swiss have invaded Frankfurt and have given Hesse cuisine a real challenge in the doing. Having long enjoyed an outstanding reputation for cooking in their own country, the Mövenpick interests have created dramatic dining in this German city, especially in the main restaurant, Baron de la Mouette (a second Mövenpick at Wiesbaden is too remote for the casual visitor). In this restaurant, the roast rib of Angus beef with horseradish cream, Warwick mustard sauce, beef pan gravy, and baked potato is the daily specialty. More seductive dishes of the French and international cuisine include scampi in a tarragon sauce and entrecôte Bordelaise. Many Frankfurters prefer the Mövenpick's pub, Rob Roy, named after the Scottish rebel. It's open from 11:30 a.m. to 3 p.m. and 5 p.m. to 1 a.m., and serves apéritifs, liquors, steaks, warm snacks, seafoods, and salads. Specialties include a crayfish cocktail and Angus entrecôte. Scotch whiskey, the national drink of Scotland, is the favored beverage, of course. Meals come in a wide price range here, from 30 DM ($9.90) for a simple business lunch all the way to 60 DM ($19.80) for a big dinner. Waitresses and tartan-vested waiters place the savory dishes before you.

Börsenkeller, 11 Schillerstrasse (tel. 28-11-15), is an oasis in the austere metropolis, concealing its old-world atmosphere behind a deceptively modern exterior. It is a favorite choice for stockbrokers and bankers. Dining is on the lower level, where you'll find arched cellar rooms and lots of nooks and recessed areas. During the evening, accordion music is played. The restaurant begins serving its savory viands around noon. Specialties include rumpsteak Rothschild with croquettes and pork chops in the Swiss style. Tabs begin at 30 DM ($9.90), ranging upward to 70 DM ($23.10). If you've just arrived in Germany, a memorable meal at the Börsenkeller will whet your appetite for exploring the countryside. Closed Sunday.

Firenze, 30 Berger Strasse (tel. 43-39-56), is the leading Italian restaurant of Frankfurt, having outclassed a lot of others that have opened in recent months, many by cooks who originally came to Frankfurt as workers. The fine restaurant serves Tuscan specialties, and is noted mainly for its antipasti. It's very popular for late dining, attracting a thriving local trade. Fish is a specialty, and the pasta dishes are homemade and good. A favorite specialty of mine is saltimbocca (literally, "jump-in-your-mouth") à la Romana. Try also the filet steak à la chef with gorgonzola. The table wines are good, and the bottled red ones excellent. Expect to part with anywhere from 35 DM ($11.55) to 65 DM

($21.45) for the privilege of dining here. It's open daily except Monday from noon to 2:30 p.m. and 6 to 11 p.m.

Heyland's Weinstuben, 7 Kaiserhofstrasse (tel. 28-48-40). What is astonishing is the number of dishes a relatively small restaurant can offer. There are only two dozen tables but some 140 menu choices, with an emphasis on fish, shrimp, and lobster. The lobsters, by the way, are kept alive until the last minute in a tank in the kitchen. A favorite of editors and publishers, the weinstuben has a tasteful interior. The wine list is intelligent and classy. The chef cooks unassisted. His name is Karlo Heyland, and he keeps very long and hard hours (noon to midnight). This dedicated professional charges from 30 DM ($9.90) to 65 DM ($21.45) for a meal. He closes on Sunday for a much-needed day of rest.

MEDIUM-PRICED DINING: Rheinpfalz-Weinstuben, 1 Gutleutstrasse (tel. 23-38-70), stands directly across the street from the new theater. During the summer, lunch is served in the canopy-covered wine garden. It's a typical wine tavern atmosphere, with good food in hearty portions and excellent wines. Hesse cookery is available until midnight. Main dishes include rumpsteak with roast onions, Pfalzer topf, a choice of three pieces of meat with mushrooms, or schweinhaxe. Dessert will leave you satisfied and fatter. Every month you may select a new wine. Count on spending 35 DM ($11.55) for a complete meal. The restaurant is open every day all year. Dinners are served daily.

Sudpfanne, 20 Eschersheimer Landstrasse (tel. 55-21-22), is a pleasantly rustic restaurant with rough-hewn tables and chairs. The decor is not the only rural aspect of the establishment: many of the well-prepared specialties are made with forest-fresh mushrooms and served directly at the table from the pan in which they were cooked. Trout, done several different ways, is one of the house favorites. The à la carte items change seasonally, according to the local ingredients available, but there's always an ample selection. However, many guests prefer to order one of the daily menus, priced at 9 DM ($2.97) to 21 DM ($6.93) depending on how elaborate they are. The ambience here is fairly intimate, since there are only about 20 tables. The restaurant is open daily from 11:30 a.m. to 2:30 p.m. and 5 p.m. to midnight.

Zur Stadt Wien, 13-15 Weckmarkt (tel. 28-82-87), behind the cathedral, is a bit of Old Vienna in Old Frankfurt. The innkeeper, Herr Jerepp, is a wine expert who shares his interest with his patrons. More than 80 wines from 12 different countries are stored in the wine cellar. The best and most traditional wine is the Grinzig. The restaurant is softly lit, with a rather schmaltzy but fun decor. A zither, accordion, or violin is usually playing Viennese melodies. The food is good, concentrating on German-Austrian specialties such as wienerschnitzel. Tasty wiener goulaschsuppe is a most filling appetizer, and the Salzburger nockerl "made with nine egg whites and seven egg yolks" is a knockout. Meals begin at 35 DM ($11.55), plus wine.

Churrasco, 6 Domplatz (tel. 28-48-04), is where Frankfurters go for succulent Argentine beef steaks. The black sign with the steer outside marks the spot of this dimly lit tavern, just next door to the cathedral. The Argentine beef filet comes in two sizes: 180 grams or 250 grams. Cheaper orders of rumpsteak are also available. All cuts are charcoal-grilled to your specifications. Rounding out the menu are a typical Argentine gazpacho and a limited list of desserts. A steak and salad luncheon goes for 20 DM ($6.60) and up; a complete dinner begins at around 40 DM ($13.20).

You will find Churrasco restaurants in Berlin (two locations), Bonn, Bremen, Dortmund, Düsseldorf (two), Essen, Hamburg, Hannover, Karlsruhe,

Cologne (four), Mannheim, Munich (two), Münster, Stuttgart, and Wiesbaden.

THE BUDGET APFELWEINSTUBEN:

For your best bargains in dining, head across the Main to a district known for its apple wine taverns or apfelweinstuben. These taverns—there are dozens of them—are in the **Alt-Sachsenhausen** section of the Left Bank. Here you drink local apple wine which some Frankfurters enjoy and some foreigners consider a cousin to vinegar. My verdict: an acquired taste. Tradition says that you won't like the apple wine until you've had three big steins. After that, what does taste matter?

You can go on a tavern crawl, stopping off at the **Zum Grauen Bock,** 30-54 Grosse Rittergasse (tel. 61-80-26), which is run by the Elsässer family. It's open only from 5 p.m. till 1 a.m. (closed Sunday). A hearty gemütlich atmosphere prevails in this smoke-filled tavern. Sometimes the communal singing is so robust it's necessary to slide back the roof on a summer night. A six-foot-six accordionist stumbles over pretzel vendors as he goes from table to table, involving everyone in his song. Contact is made, instant friendships formed, at least for the evening.

Featured on the menu is something known as handkäs mit musik (cheese with vinegar, oil, and onions). You may want to let the locals enjoy the subtle pleasures of this repast, selecing instead a Germanic specialty known as schweinhaxen, a huge pork shank with sauerkraut and boiled potatoes. A good beginning is the Frankfurter bohnensuppe (bean soup). A simple menu begins at only 15 DM ($4.95).

Zum Gemalten Haus, 67 Schweizerstrasse (tel. 61-45-59). Don't bother to call—no one takes reservations around here. You simply arrive and chances are you'll share a table with some of the other patrons, perhaps in the garden if the weather is fair. Both of you will have the same aim: ample portions of good Hessian cooking. If your taste dictates sauerbraten with red cabbage and potato dumplings or perhaps knackwurst, you won't be disappointed. The smoked pork chops, washed down with the local apple wine, is the cook's specialty. The apple wine is homemade, and the patrons of the restaurant love it. Not only are the portions gigantic, but the sauces are heavy, making this place a hazardous spot for the diet-minded. You might begin your feast with herring or chopped chicken livers, then follow with lentil soup or various types of sausage. Perhaps flanken or veal goulash will interest you as a main course. Sauerkraut and home-fried potatoes are regularly featured as side dishes. An entire repast is likely to cost no more than 25 DM ($8.25), a great bargain. Your hosts are Rigo and Ingrid Hanauske. Hours are 10 a.m. to midnight.

A RUSTIC INN ON THE OUTSKIRTS:

Gutsschänke Neuhof, between Neu Isenburg and Götzenhain, 20 minutes south of Frankfurt (tel. 06102/32-14), is a dining adventure. Surrounded by woods, meadows, and fields of flowers, the inn is part of a huge farm estate (Hofgut Neuhof) dating from 1499. In summer, tables are set out on the wide terrace overlooking the pond. Inside, the former manor farmhouse is a maze of connecting rooms for dining. It's a totally rustic atmosphere, with pewter candlesticks and fresh-cut field flowers on the tables. On the walls hang antlers, maps, swords, rifles, and old prints. You'll sit in hefty captain's chairs while English-speaking waiters in red waistcoats proffer excellent service. The food is exceptional, beginning with the vorspeise Neuhof, an assortment of hors d'oeuvres including such delicacies as fresh crayfish with dill. Served at your table from a cart, the array of appetizers is priced by size. If you prefer a different appetizer, try the herring salad or the Hungarian goulash soup. Venison is a popular main course in season, and two house specialties are gespickte rehkeule Hubertus (leg of venison) and roast duck.

Vegetarians will enjoy the pichelsteiner gemüseeintopf, a vegetable stew made from produce grown on the estate. The owner of Neuhof supplements the excellent wine cellar with wines from his own local vineyards. Expect to spend from 35 DM ($11.55) to 65 DM ($21.45) for a complete meal. Gutsschänke Neuhof is open every day, serving lunch from noon to 3 p.m. and dinner from 6 to 9:45 p.m. Live music is played in the evening on Thursday, Saturday, and Sunday.

While you're visiting Neuhof, stop in and browse in the gift shop on the premises, which sells pottery and linens as well as homemade sausages, candy, applecakes, and aromatic breads.

THE CAFÉS: Not as firmly entrenched in the Frankfurter's daily life as it is in Vienna, the café is still a pleasant place for people-watching, light (or full) meals, and drinks, along with pastries, of course.

The one nearly everybody finds without any guidance is **Zur Hauptwacht,** an der Hauptwache (tel. 28-53-38), which is historic, dating from 250 years ago. It stands in the strategic heart of Frankfurt. The present building was reconstructed after World War II bombings. Helmut Scheuermann, the owner, welcomes guests to his restaurant/café/snackbar on three levels, offering partial and full-course meals throughout the day and evening. The menu appears in English among other languages. On a warm evening the street level, attracting coffee-drinkers and pastry-eaters, is a delight. The pedestrian zone has been completed, making it more pleasant for a stroll. The atmosphere is casual, and many a lonely traveler has found a companion for the evening. Don't fail to ask for the special beer, Römer Pilsner. Four types of draft beer are available, beginning at 1.60 DM (53¢) per glass, and daily menus range from 7.50 DM ($2.48) to 12 DM ($3.96).

If you have a sweet tooth, head for the **Café Schwille,** 50 Grosse Bockenheimer Strasse (tel. 28-30-54), the most famous place in Frankfurt for pastries and sweets. The hotel there was already recommended. Light snacks begin at 7 DM ($2.31).

3. Sights

When the bombs rained on Frankfurt in 1944, nearly all the oldest historical buildings were leveled to mere piles of rubble. Visitors to the city today wouldn't sense this, however, except in the lack of some of the old-timbered buildings in the Old Town. For in what must have been a record reconstruction, the Frankfurters have not only built up their city into a fine melange of modern and traditional architecture, but they have faithfully restored some of their most prized old buildings as well.

The **Goethe House,** 23 Grosser Hirschgraben (tel. 28-28-24), is among them. It's been a shrine for Goethe enthusiasts since it was opened to the public in 1863. Originally built about 1755, when two 16th-century Gothic houses were joined, the red sandstone and masonry structure was faithfully restored after it was destroyed in 1944. Today the house appears much as it did when Goethe lived here, until he joined the Weimar court in 1755. One critic wrote that the restoration was carried out "with loving care and damn-the-expense craftsmanship."

Reflecting the fashion trends of the 18th century, the house illustrates three successive periods of style. The dining room and most of the first floor are in baroque, but the second floor, at the top of the elaborate wrought-iron balustraded staircase, is a rococo world. The second and third floors are more classical, and contain the library where Goethe's father worked and often watched the street for the return of his son. A portrait of the severe-looking gentleman hangs behind the door of his wife's room.

On the second floor is an unusual astronomical clock built about 1749 and repaired in 1949 to run again for another 200 years. One room also contains a picture gallery with paintings collected by Goethe's father. Most of them painted by contemporary Frankfurt artists, these works influenced Goethe's artistic views for a great part of his life. The poet's rooms contain a puppet theater which was one of Goethe's most important childhood possessions and which played a significant role in his *Wilhelm Meister*.

Annexed to the house is the **Frankfürter Goethe Museum,** built since the war on the site of its predecessor. The museum contains a library of 120,000 volumes and a collection of about 30,000 manuscripts, as well as 15,000 graphic artworks and 400 paintings associated in some way with Goethe and his works. The house and museum are open from April to September on weekdays from 9 a.m. to 6 p.m. (otherwise, from 9 a.m. to 4 p.m.); on Sunday from 10 a.m. to 1 p.m. Admission is 3 DM (99¢).

The **Altstadt (Old Town)** centers around three Gothic buildings with stepped gables, known collectively as the **Römer.** These houses were originally built in 1305 and bought by the city a century later for use as city hall. For more than 500 years Frankfurters had their own "Bridge of Sighs" to cross the Main to pay their taxes at the town hall in these burghers' houses. The second floor of the center house is the **Imperial Hall** (Kaisersaal), lined with the rather romanticized portraits of 52 emperors. Thirteen of the emperors depicted celebrated their coronation banquets here. You can visit this hall any weekday from 9 a.m. to 1 p.m. and 1:30 to 5 p.m., on Sunday from 10 a.m. to 4 p.m. Tickets can be purchased at the entrance to the Römer building. The cost is 1 DM (33¢).

The elaborate facade of the Römer, with its ornate balcony and statues of four emperors, overlooks the **Römerberg Square.** On festive occasions in days gone by, the square was the scene of roasting oxen and flowing wine. Today, unfortunately, the Justitia fountain only pours forth water, but oxen are still roasted on special occasions.

Towering over the opposite side of the square is the belfry of St. Nicholas, but the dominating feature of the Old Town is the 15th-century red-sandstone tower of the **cathedral,** 14 Domplatz (tel. 28-43-24), in whose chapel German emperors were elected and crowned for nearly 300 years.

The architecture of many buildings in the Old Town has changed over the centuries, through enlargement or reconstruction, and since the war many buildings have been rebuilt along more modern lines. The oldest structure left unscathed by the bombings of 1944 was the 12th-century chapel of the Saalhof, constructed as a palace for Frederick Barbarossa. The Goethe House, described above, also in the Altstadt, has been carefully reproduced. The Carmelite Convent and 13th-century St. Leonard's Church have a few modifications in their restorations.

At the northern edge of the Old Town is the **Hauptwache,** an old guard house, which is the heart of modern Frankfurt. Under it is the main subway station with a modern shopping promenade, but the Hauptwache remains serene in spite of the traffic whirling around and underneath.

Städel Museum, 63 Schaumainkai (tel. 61-70-92), on the south bank of the Main opposite the Old Town, is Frankfurt's most important art gallery, containing a fine representative collection of most European schools and periods of paintings. The French impressionists are represented on the first floor by Renoir and Monet, mixed in with the best German painters of the 19th and 20th centuries. One of the best of these is Ernst Ludwig Kirchner (1880–1938). See in particular his *Nude Woman with Hat.* Also on the first floor is Johann Heinrich

Wilhelm Tischbein's portrait of Goethe in the Campagna in Italy. If you're short on time, however, go directly to the second floor to view the outstanding collection of Dutch primitives, Dutch paintings from the 17th century, and German masters of the 16th century. Works by Dürer, Hans Memling, Hans Holbein, Mantegna, Elsheimer, Rembrandt, Vermeer, Claude Lorrain, Tiepolo, and many others have been brought together here. One of the most impressive paintings is Jan Van Eyck's *Madonna* (1433). Lucas Cranach is represented in several works, including a large winged altarpiece and his rather impish nude *Venus.* The museum also includes a display of works from the Italian school, including a *Madonna* by Bellini. There is also a department of prints and drawings containing 25,000 drawings and 65,000 prints of European schools. Recent acquisitions include Jean Antoine Watteau's *L'Île de Cythère* (1709). In the Department of Modern Art are works by Bacon, Dubuffet, Tapiès, and Yves Klein. The museum is open (except Monday) from 10 a.m. to 5 p.m.; on Wednesday until 8 p.m. Admission is 2 DM (66¢); Sunday is free.

Liebieghaus, 71 Schaumainkai (tel. 63-89-07), contains the city's largest collection of sculpture, spanning thousands of years, from ancient Egyptian to baroque. One of the most impressive works is a bas relief by Andrea della Robbia. Outside of the Bargello in Florence, this museum is considered to be one of the most important museums of sculpture in Europe. The museum is open daily, except Monday, from 10 a.m. to 5 p.m., on Wednesday from 10 a.m. to 8 p.m. Admission is free. The house was built at the turn of the century, and it's surrounded by a garden. At a tiny café on the premises you can order tasty little fruit pies baked by the woman caretaker.

The Frankfurt **Zoo** (tel. 212-37-71) is a multifaceted institution, intent more on education than entertainment, and because of this, it is unique and interesting for both young and old. Most of the animals wander about in exhibits enough like their native habitats to make them feel at home. One of the best examples of this is the African Veldt Enclosure, landscaped with hills and bushes so that the animals living there can avoid encounters with other breeds. In this single exhibit, gazelles, antelopes, and ostriches roam freely. In the Exotarium, fish and various reptiles live under special climatic conditions. In an artificially cooled polar landscape, King and gentoo penguins swim and dive. Half-hour radio-guided tours are available throughout the day at the Exotarium. In keeping with its educational policy, the zoo has, in addition to many typical animal exhibits, a nursery were young apes are cared for by zookeepers (this is done only when the mother cannot care for the baby properly), and a breeding aviary, where you can watch birds preparing unusual nests. A building for small mammals with a nocturnal section opened in 1978. It is one of the largest and most diversified of its kind in the world and also contains many educational facilities. The zoo is open from 8 a.m. to 5 p.m. in winter, to 7 p.m. in summer. The Exotarium is open until 10 p.m. Admission to the zoo and Exotarium is 8.50 DM ($2.81) for adults, 4 DM ($1.32) for children aged 2 to 17; for the Exotarium alone (after closing hours of the zoo) 3.50 DM ($1.16) for adults, 1.50 DM (50¢) for children. A special permit costing .50 DM (17¢) per day is required to take photographs.

The **Palmengarten,** 61 Siesmayerstrasse (tel. 212-33-81), is more than just a botanical garden; it is a pleasure ground throughout the year for relaxation and music. All year the gardens flourish with flowers of all kinds of annuals and perennials, such as tulips, daffodils, iris, day lilies, and bed plants of the seasons, rose gardens, alpine gardens, and various species of trees. The northern part of the garden was reestablished during the last few years. Flower shows and exhibitions of flowering pod plants are held from the end of February until Christmas in the gallery around the old palm house, which is connected to the Gesellschaftshaus, a restaurant with ballrooms. Conservatories contain a huge collection of succulents and cacti as well as plants from the Mediterranean regions. In others, you can see a rain forest, a monsoon forest, a mountain cloud forest, a mangrove stand, a bromeliarium, a semidesert, thorn woods, and a savannah. Collections of orchids, waterlilies, insectivorous plants, and many different palm trees are shown. In summer, daily concerts are given in the bandshell. Once a week in the evening there's open-air dancing and jazz. The fountains are lit at night. Admission is 4 DM ($1.32).

ORGANIZED TOURS: In addition to seeing the sights of Frankfurt on foot or by tram, you can enjoy many attractions from a comfortable coach seat on one of the two daily tours sponsored by the tourist office. Thd 2½-hour tours depart in season from the tourist office in front of the **main railway station** at 10 a.m. and 2 p.m. From November 1 to February 28, the tours depart at 2 p.m. on Saturday and 10 a.m. on Sunday. The English-speaking guide provides a running commentary as you drive through old and new Frankfurt. You'll get brief glimpses of the Old Town, some of the more interesting modern buildings, and a stop at Goethe's House and the Palmengarten. If you prefer a longer or more detailed look at any of the major sights, you'll have to visit them on your own, however. But the tour provides a good general look at Frankfurt for 30 DM ($9.90), half price for children.

Bus tours are made to the **Bad Homburg** and **Weisbaden gambling casinos.** An express bus leaves Baseler Platz at 2:15 p.m. for Bad Homburg, and then every hour on the hour until 11 p.m. The last bus leaves from the Savigny Hotel at 12:45 a.m. and from opposite the fairgrounds at the Hotel Frankfurt Plaza about five minutes later. Return trips are from 3 p.m. to midnight every hour on the hour, and also after the casino closing at 2 or 3 a.m. The price is 6 DM ($1.98), which includes the 5-DM ($1.65) admission to the casino.

The bus to the Wiesbaden casino leaves Baseler Platz and the main railway station, south side (corner of Karlsruher Strasse), at 2, 4, 6, 8, and 10 p.m. and at 12:20 a.m. From Savignystrasse (Esso station) and opposite the fairgrounds at the Hotel Frankfurt Plaza about five minutes later. Return trips are at 3, 5, 7, 9, and 11:30 p.m. and 2 a.m. (3 a.m. on Saturday). The price is 5 DM ($1.65), which includes admission to the casino. However, you must pay a cover charge of 5 DM ($1.65), which is returned to you in chips.

Tram tours, organized by Stadtwerke Frankfurt am Main, 3 Rathenauplatz (tel. 13-68-24-25), are offered aboard the **Apple Wine Express,** a colorful, old-fashioned streetcar. Regular trips start from the railway station east (Ostbanhof, Danziger Platz) or the zoo on the half hour from 1:35 to 5:40 p.m. on Saturday and Sunday. You can get on at any of the tram stops. It passes through the city center and Sachsenhausen, celebrated for its apple wine (cider) taverns. The tour costs 3 DM (99¢), which includes a glass of apple wine or juice and pretzels. Children ages 4 to 14 pay 2 DM (66¢).

A trip on a **historic steam train** is offered by **Historische Eisenbahn Frankfurt e.V.,** 140 Eschborner Landstrasse, F 90 (tel. 7-89-43-10). The train runs along the banks of the River Main, on the tracks of the Frankfurt Harbor Railway, from Eiserner Steg (Mainkail) west to Frankfurt-Griesheim or east to Frankfurt-Main-kur and back. Schedules vary, so for complete information, get in touch with the historic train group cited above.

4. Frankfurt After Dark

For robust Teutonic antics after dark, business visitors and GIs head for a 16-square-block area in front of the railway station, the Hauptbahnhof. This is the mail rail station of the city, bisected by Kaiserstrasse and Münchner Strasse.

Here you'll find a rowdy—and very dangerous—district which the Germans call *erotische Spiele*. Doormen will practically pull you inside to view porno movies, sex shows, sex shops, even discos teaming with prostitutes.

A more romantic setting is found at **St. John's Inn,** 20 Grosser Hirschgraben (tel. 29-25-18), across from Goethe's House, a short walk from an der Hauptwache. Its cozy, old-world ambience is created in part by its large brick and timbered fireplace with its raised hearth, Windsor chairs, and candlelit tables. It's possible to drop in just for drinks, but you may order food as well. The house specialty is a pot of Irish stew. The peppersteak is prepared to taste. Light meals cost 50 DM ($16.50) and up. John Paris, the owner, sings every night in various languages. Often it's so crowded you can't get in. It's open every night at 8, but never on Sunday.

Jimmy's, in the cellar of the Hessischer Hof, 40 Friedrich-Ebert-Anlage (tel. 74-55-07), is popular with a crowd in their 20s and 30s. Sometimes there is live music or perhaps dancing to records. There's no minimum, no cover—just the standard drink prices. Whisky is around 12 DM ($3.96). It's a good place to take a date or find one. The bar opens at 7 p.m., but the action doesn't begin till much later. Parking is free, and the bar is closed on Sunday.

Frankfurt is one of the leading jazz centers of Europe, and it's certainly a leader in West Germany. Here the style ranges from traditional Basin Street blues to the modern, trendy stuff. One of the leading centers is **Jazz-Keller,** 18 Kleine Bockenheimer Strasse (tel. 28-85-37). This club stands right on the Jazz Alley of Frankfurt, and since I first discovered it a long, long time ago, it's been host to some of the best known names in jazz, including the American geniuses. It's a cellar atmosphere, with a sort of "smoke-gets-in-your-eyes" ambience.

If you don't take to this place, check out **Jazz-Haus,** right down the way at 12 Kleine Bockenheimer Strasse (tel. 28-71-94). This is a cozy, tall, and narrow building that evokes the 1500s, except for the sounds coming from it.

Another good possibility is **Jazz-Kneipe,** 70 Berlinstrasse (tel. 28-71-73), which has some lively jam sessions. It's considered the number one place in Frankfurt for traditional swing. It's open from 8 p.m. to 4 a.m., with live music from 10 p.m. to 3 a.m. Most of these places are red hot and full of action. You'll never escape for less than $6 at any of them.

A real Teutonic nightlife choice is the **Paradieshof,** Paradiesgasse (tel. 62-40-53), a Henninger Bräu house in the apple wine district. Upstairs it's a beer hall, with singing and dancing. Downstairs, Frankfurt teenagers flock to the **Nachteule** (Night Owl), where the entrance fee is 5 DM ($1.65). The price of the local brew is the same in the beer hall upstairs or the disco below, 5 DM ($1.65). You can have a cheap evening here with lots of fun.

If you like music (and who doesn't?), one of the best known places in Frankfurt is **Sinkkasten,** 5 Brönnerstrasse (tel. 28-03-85). Here you can hear on any given night a wide range of international bands playing everything from reggae to rock. Admission is $3.50.

Maier Gustl's Bayrisch Zell, 57 Münchener Strasse (tel. 23-20-92). Many of the musical acts that perform here are so laden with Bavarian schmaltz and mountain folksiness that you can practically see the heavily timbered ceiling begin to sprout leaves. The place is perfect for a checkered tablecloth kind of Teutonic nostalgia in a heavily timbered recreation of a mountain chalet. Sometimes the musicians lean slightly toward an updated version of modern pop or rock. However, a yodeler will quickly return you to folkloric enjoyment. More than 1500 revelers can fit in here between the mugs of foaming suds tapped at the bars near three dance floors. Some of the tables have private phones for electronic assignations with a person you fancy.

Beer, depending on the size, costs between 4 DM ($1.32) and 10 DM

($3.30). Meals, costing from 25 DM ($8.25), include a limited but flavorful menu of steaks, soups, salads, and grills. The place is animated until closing at 4 a.m. on weekdays and 5 a.m. on Friday and Saturday. The lights begin to twinkle and the oom-pah-pah begins every evening at 7.

Frankfurt is one city where the hotels have some of the best—and safest—nightlife possibilities. Take the **CP Frankfurt Plaza,** 2-10 Hamburger Allee (tel. 77-07-21), for example. An evening here might begin in the luxuriously appointed **Biblio-Theke,** where, if it's a slow evening, you could remove a book from one of the shelves. There are 1000 original works in all. It's not only the library that's fully stocked, but the bar as well. A happy place to meet business associates (during the Book Fair, it's packed), it makes for a pleasant, relaxing, even seductive interlude before venturing over to the **Blue Infinitum,** a disco on the first floor of the hotel. One of Frankfurt's favorite nightspots, with a heavy patronage of locals (a good sign), this active joint was clearly inspired by the New York scene. Disco music is played every day from 9:30 p.m. (much too early for anybody to be seen here), lasting until 4 a.m. Drinks begin at $4.50. A selection of hot and cold dishes is served until the early hours.

The **Lipizzaner Bar,** in the Steigenberger Hotel Frankfurter Hof, am Kaiserplatz (tel. 2-02-51), is regarded as the most elegant bar in town, with crystal mirrors, petrol-green wood panels, and international drinks and cocktails. There is nightly live entertainment by a pianist. A disco that enjoys wide popularity is **Dorian Grey** on the O level of Section C at the Frankfurt Airport (tel. 69-15-21). (It's not to be confused with "Dorian Gay," a self-styled "gaymen sexshop" in another part of the city.) Dorian Grey is reached fom the heart of the city in about 15 minutes aboard the S-train. Trains depart from the Hauptbahnhof every 20 minutes or so. This exclusive disco, drawing a fashionable crowd, opens at 9 in the evening, but most clients go much later of course. You're charged about $6 for admission, and once inside, the bartenders will serve you a wide range of drinks. Beer is the cheapest, of course.

If you're still caught up in the disco nostalgia of the '70s, you'll find several good ones still going strong in Frankfurt other than Dorian Grey. One of the best asks the provocative question, **Why Not?** It's at 4 am Salzhaus (tel. 28-71-94), right near the museum and house devoted to Goethe memorabilia. This place has loud, raucous music until at least 3 a.m. (maybe later) every morning. In all of these places, you're staring at a $6 check just to get you going good.

Instead of discos, if you've returned to cheek-to-cheek dancing, your best bet is to head for the 21st floor of the **Hotel Intercontinental** (tel. 23-05-61). There, on the rooftop of this supper club, you can dance most often to a lively Latin combo every night except Monday. The fare is in the supper-club tradition, and the view is spectacular. Drinks average around 15 DM ($4.95).

Another good bet in the same vein is the nightclub **Le Tourbillon,** an elegantly decorated choice at the Frankfurt Savoy, 42 Wiesenhüttenstrasse (tel. 23-05-11). Drinks begin at 15 DM ($4.95), and there's music for dancing as well, some mood pieces, but also disco too.

Cultural Frankfurt

On the cultural scene, Frankfurt has one of the most ultramodern and prestigious municipal arts complexes in Europe. It's the **Städtische Bühnen** on Theaterplatz. The center houses an opera house (tel. 25-62-335) with a magnificent repertoire; a spacious theater (tel. 25-62-434), and a more intimate theater (tel. 25-62-395) for productions on a smaller scale.

The **Alt Oper** (old opera house), Opernplatz (tel. 13-40-400), is still going, with frequent symphonics and choral group concerts.

Likewise, **Hessische-Rundfunk,** 8 Bertramstrasse (tel. 1551), has a changing repertoire of musical events, including chamber music concerts. Music, of course, has a universal language.

But most German theater is limited only to those readers who speak German. There are some two dozen or so theaters in Germany. The most important ones are in the municipal complex already cited. Others include the **Fritz Rémond Theater** im Zoo at the Frankfurt Zoo, 76 Alfred Brehm Platz (tel. 43-51-66), which often stages Stateside and British productions in German.

Light comedy—often called "boulevard theater"—is presented at **Die Kömodie,** Theaterplatz at 18 Neue Mainzer Strasse (tel. 28-45-80).

Dramatic productions are also presented at the **Theater am Turm,** 1 Oederweg (tel. 15-45-100).

You can purchase tickets at the tourist office for many of these major cultural presentations, or at the theater box offices.

5. Exploring the Environs

Unless you're rushed beyond reason, you should allow an extra day or two in Frankfurt to take a look at some of the attractions of the surrounding countryside. Here you'll stumble over little medieval towns, or you'll be awed by the sophisticated spas of the Taunus. I'll highlight some of the best attractions below.

THE TAUNUS: These wooded hills north of Frankfurt include the highest peaks of the ancient mountain range cut by the Rhine and its tributaries. The geological formations have created a number of mineral springs along the periphery of the range. Entrepreneurs have developed these springs into spas. Two of the most active Taunus spas, Bad Homburg and Bad Nauheim, are described separately in Chapter IV. From the Taunus's highest peak, the **Grosser Feldberg,** the towers of Frankfurt, 15 miles away, become part of the panoramic view. Because of its altitude, this peak is an important telecommunications post for the German post office. A few miles south of the Grosser Feldberg is one of the Taunus's most popular landmarks.

Kronberg im Taunus

The **Schloss Hotel Kronberg,** 25 Hainstrasse (tel. 06173/70-11), comes as close as one can get to living in a royal castle. Actually, a royal prince does live in a more modest place on the grounds. Architecturally, the hotel is Wagnerian in scope, with towers, turrets, and stone terraces overlooking the vast forest (where there is an 18-hole golf course, used by Eisenhower when he was a general). The Schloss attracts everyone from presidents to kings to international bankers and industrialists, including on one occasion Nixon and Constantine of Greece.

The former castle of Queen Victoria's eldest daughter, the German Empress Frederika, was turned into a hotel in 1954, after serving as a casino for U.S. officers after World War II. Throughout the salons, drawing rooms, and dining halls, there are abundant antiques and a number of valuable tapestries. Guests enjoy the English library and the petite salon. Everywhere you turn, even in the intimate drinking lounge, you'll see paintings worthy of a museum. The hotel boasts the only bar in the world with originals by Turner, Sir Thomas Lawrence, and Sir Joshua Reynolds.

The hotel's 54 rooms, five of which are suites, all contain private bath. In 1967 the castle was swept by a devastating fire and during the restoration, 20 rooms and some modern furnishings were added. Some rooms still have real antiques, however. The price of a single room, including breakfast and taxes, ranges from 150 DM ($49.50) to 195 DM ($64.35). Doubles go for a whopping 275 DM ($90.75) to 350 DM ($115.50). Rates include a continental breakfast, the service charge, and government tax. The hotel is open all year.

The hotel's dining room serves good food and the service is superb, almost courtly. Since space is limited, it is imperative to telephone in advance for reservations. The menu is à la carte, a dinner costing from 55 DM ($18.15) to 110 DM ($36.30).

In all, the Schloss Hotel Kronberg provides pampered care in a country estate.

A Quiet Hotel on the Southern Slopes

Sonnenhof Königstein, 7 Falkensteinerstrasse, Königstein im Taunus (tel. 30-51), surrounded by fields of wildflowers and wooded hills, is ideal for nature visitors seeking a peaceful interlude. If you're just passing through Königstein on a tour of the Taunus, you may want to stop here for dinner after viewing the feudal ruins of the Königstein fortress overlooking the town. The hotel's menu is an international one, with German specialties as well. For appetizers, try pâté of salmon and sole in a lobster sauce. Roast dishes are a specialty (for example, a haunch of stag in cream) and there are a number of seafood items on the menu, including shrimp soufflé in a champagne sauce. Try also marinated filet of beef with lemon sauce. Meals cost from 35 DM ($11.55) to 75 DM ($24.75).

If you do plan to stay over, the hotel offers 80 comfortable rooms, all overlooking the Main Valley and Taunus hills. Full-board terms are quoted for a minimum of three days. Otherwise, a bathless single goes for 82 DM ($27.06), increasing to 128 DM ($42.24) and up with bath. Bathless doubles are in the 113-DM ($37.29) bracket, and you'll pay from 185 DM ($61.05) with a complete bath, breakfast included. But whether you're staying for dinner or for the night, you'll find the whole staff attentive and the atmosphere one of relaxed elegance. A swimming pool is an additional attraction, plus a sauna and tennis.

THE ODENWALD: Odin, chief of the Nordic gods, could probably still identify his forest today. Many of the landmarks in this farm country south of Frankfurt date back to legendary beginnings. For instance, the well in the forest where Siegfried met his death at the hand of Hagen stands today in a tiny village on the Siegfriedstrasse, one of the best roads for exploring the Odenwald.

The climate here is among the warmest in Germany, owing to the shelter of the surrounding mountains. Blossoms appear early on trees and vines, and abundant harvests are celebrated in the otherwise quiet little German towns. To reach the Odenwald, drive south from Frankfurt to Darmstadt, then take the Bergstrasse (Rte. 3) running toward Heidelberg. This scenic route leads along the western slopes of the mountains to the old town of . . .

Bensheim

Just 30 miles south of Frankfurt, Bensheim could be an inspired place for a short flying visit from Frankfurt if you're between planes and want to sample or preview a typical German town. Here the old timbered and plastered buildings, clustered about the tiny squares and fountains, look as if they've been removed from a Christmas card. The vineyards around the town indicate that this, like the Rhine Valley, is wine country. Each September, Bensheim is the scene of the most exuberant wine festival in the Odenwald, the Bergstrasse Wine Festival.

Just west of Bensheim is its major sightseeing attraction, the ruins of the great abbey at **Lorch,** at the edge of the Rhineland Palatinate. The monastery was built in Carolingian style in the eighth century, with a massive Königshalle (King's Hall), adorned with huge columns and walls covered with mosaics.

The best place to stay in the area is the **Parkhotel Krone,** 168 Darmstädter Strasse (tel. 7-30-81), which is the center of social life and business conferences in the area. Since 1655 there has been an inn on this spot, and wayfarers to Frankfurt have often stopped here before venturing on to the big Hessian city. Today it is not done up as an antique, but is completely modernized and updated, its bedrooms streamlined, perhaps graced with an occasional Oriental carpet. Single rooms rent for 90 DM ($29.70) nightly, and doubles go for 125 DM ($41.25). In addition to its comfort, special features of the Krone include an indoor pool, sauna, and fitness room. The hotel's restaurant, Die Ente, is the best in the area. If featured, try the duck breast in a cream sauce laced with Calvados, a specialty of Normandy. Meals cost from 10 DM ($3.30) to 50 DM ($16.50), depending on what you order.

After a satisfying stopover, a drive eastward from the town through the Odenwald leads to . . .

Erbach im Odenwald

This town's "reason for being" seems to be the magnificent baroque palace of the ruling Erbach-Erbach family, **Schloss Erbach.** The present structure, dating from 1736, was built on the site of an earlier 14th-century castle, of which only an ancient round watch tower has survived. The palace is a museum, with its huge knight's hall, endless corridors, and Gothic painted windows. But even more remarkable are the collections exhibited within the castle halls: art treasures of the Erbach-Erbach family, including medieval sculpture and ivory displays.

Concerts are given in the Erbacher Festhalle, the modern town hall. The castle and its museums are open March 1 to October 31 from 8:30 a.m. to 11 a.m. and 1:30 to 4 p.m., charging 5 DM ($1.65) for admission.

Just three miles north of Erbach, and 30 miles east of Bensheim, is yet another medieval town . . .

Michelstadt

In a valley of the Odenwald, Michelstadt reflects a more prosperous and commercial medieval town than most of the neighboring communities. Around the marketplace are old houses and the 15th-century town hall, a half-timbered structure with oriel windows and a pointed roof supported by wooden pillars.

Just outside the town is the ancient fortified **Fürstenau Castle,** built in the 14th century for the archbishopric of Mainz. In the 16th century it was expanded into a Renaissance palace with an unusual archway connecting it to the courtyard. The castle sits in a huge English-style park which dates from 1756. The courtyard can be visited by the public. Visiting hours are 9 a.m. to noon and 1 to around 5:30 p.m. (closes at 4 p.m. in winter).

For meals or lodgings in Michelstadt, the inn described below is the most logical choice.

Drei Hasen, 5 Braunstrasse (tel. 6-14), is a glamorized tavern, established in 1830. Glittering with copper, it is rich in the old Germanic tradition. From his post at the cash register, the innkeeper makes frequent appearances at the tables to wish his guests "bon appétit." Here you get a good accommodation in rooms that are furnished in a Directoire style. Singles without bath cost 45 DM ($14.85), rising to 50 DM ($16.50) with bath. A double without bath is 65 DM ($21.45) nightly, increasing to 100 DM ($33) with bath, including breakfast. The best rooms have a view of the market square. In the true inn fashion, the meals are more of a source of revenue than the beds. Be sure to sample the specialty, original Nürnberger rostbratwüste. Other recommended and featured items include schweinhaxe and Holsteiner schnitzel. Menus cost from 15 DM ($4.95) to 30 DM ($9.90).

THE SPESSART: Separated from the Odenwald by the snake-like Main River, the Spessart Mountains are much more rugged than the rolling hills to the west. The oak-covered mountains are broken here and there to make room for an old village or castle, and then the trees seem to join together again to cover the land. Most of the towns in the Spessart lie along the Main, their link to the outside world. At the confluence of the Main and the Tauber stands . . .

Wertheim

Towering over the medieval town are the ruins of the ancient castle of the feudal counts of Wertheim. The town is much better preserved than the castle, with a marketplace dating from the 16th century and narrow brick streets sheltered by overhanging timbered houses. Beside the Tauber stands the ancient city gate of Wertheim, the Kittstein Tower, a reminder of the days when Wertheim was an important 14th-century city and not the sleepy community of today.

The **Hotel Schwan,** 23 Main Platz (tel. 12-78), is an enchanting little inn, part of it incorporating the already-mentioned medieval stone tower. The inn is colorful and well decorated, a friendly oasis. Only a roadway separates it from the river, and in true inn fashion less attention is paid to lounges than to dining rooms. The upstairs accommodations are comfortable. Doubles with bath rent for 100 DM ($33) to 140 DM ($46.20). Singles with bath range in price from 70 DM ($23.10) to 95 DM ($31.35). The innkeeper, Rolf Wiessler, has considerably upgraded the Schwan, in more contemporary taste. The plumbing is updated, and the welcome's still as warm as ever.

Set lunches start at 16 DM ($5.28), going up to 45 DM ($14.85). Specialties on the à la carte menu range from fresh French chicken with tarragon, filet of pork provençale, saddle of lamb, eel in dill gravy, and filet of rabbit. The Schwan is easy to spot, with its ornate wrought-iron sign projecting over the front dining terrace.

In the environs, in-the-know Frankfurters flock to the **Hotel Schweizer Stuben,** 11 Geiselbrunnweg (tel. 43-51), at Bettingen, which has some of the finest food in the area—in fact this gourmet mecca is one of the best restaurants of Germany. Country elegance is the byword here. The chef, Dieter Müller, turns nouvelle cuisine into his own delightful expression. He heads an 18-man brigade of cooks, who with grace and style produce the region's best cuisine.

Appetizers could include terrines and mousselines, followed by a variety of homemade pastas, dressed with sauces "according to the season." From October to May clients may want to try mussels cooked in Noilly Prat or liver in a sauce flavored with raspberry vinegar. Have you ever had a soufflé of frog legs in a cream sauce made with truffles? Game is another seasonal delicacy.

All portions are served on exquisite bone-white china, and the service by the well-trained staff is impeccable. Service is from noon to 2 p.m. and 7 to 10 p.m. It is closed on Sunday, for Monday lunch, and for the first three weeks in January. Daily fixed-price menus range from 125 DM ($41.25) to 175 DM ($57.75). Always call for a reservation.

The hotel has a few rooms to rent, nine in all, each a double costing from 120 DM ($39.60) to 220 DM ($72.60). All of them are individualized in decor, and quiet and tranquil. The furnishings are wooden and tasteful, and there is a beautiful garden near this villa, which is the core of the complex. Tennis courts are found near the terrace, where the excellent French meals are served. On the balconies of this modern landhaus are window boxes filled with masses of flowers, with a row of international flags on the walkway leading to the main house.

Set farther back from the Main, among the thick forests of the mountains, is the tiny village of . . .

Mespelbrunn

Just three miles from the Weibersbrunn exit of the Frankfurt–Würzburg autobahn, the little village of Mespelbrunn seems far removed from the reality of 20th-century living. The chief attraction of the town is the well-preserved Renaissance castle of the Counts von Ingelheim. The **Schloss Mespelbrunn** is a lake palace, more common in France than in Germany, completely surrounded by water, and still the property of nobility today. The rooms are open to the public daily from 9 a.m. to 6 p.m., March to November. The price is 5 DM ($1.65). Included is a museum devoted to the history of the ruling family, and those for whom beauty is not food enough can visit a nearby restaurant.

The best one close at hand is **Schlossgaststätte**, 25 Schlossallee (tel. 2-56), run by Ludwig Büger. Lots of natural stone graces the facade of this hotel, which is run with discreet care and attention. It has a garden terrace and a café, serving good, reasonably priced food. Fixed-price menus range from 15 DM ($4.95) to 35 DM ($11.55), or else you can order from a more expensive à la carte menu. The hotel also has some good and pleasantly furnished bedrooms, costing 40 DM ($13.20) to 46 DM ($15.18) in a single and 65 DM ($21.45) to 80 DM ($26.40) in a double. Many of these tranquil units open onto a lovely view of the forest, only 55 yards from the hotel, which is closed from November until the first of March.

Chapter III

MUNICH

1. Hotels
2. Restaurants
3. Sights
4. Munich After Dark
5. Some Notes on Shopping

TO MÜNCHNERS, BEER has been the core of existence for centuries. Songs were written in praise of the brew, festivals were organized in its honor, and beer halls were the scenes of all major events.

The people of Munich don't need much of a reason for celebrating. If you arrive here in late September, you'll find them in the middle of a festival in honor of Ludwig I's engagement to Princess Theresa—and that took place in 1810! The **Oktoberfest** starts on a Saturday, lasts 16 days, and ends the first Sunday in October. Although this great Oktoberfest, where beer flows as freely as water, is the most famous of Munich's festivals, the city is actually less inhibited and more individualistic in the pre-Lenten Carnival (**Fasching**). Even the most reserved Germans are caught up in this whirl of colorful parades, masked balls, and revelry.

Between these two festival seasons, Munich remains lively all year—fairs and holidays seem to follow one on top of the other. But no "oom-pah-pah" town this. You'll find the most sophisticated clubs, the best theaters, and the finest concert halls as well. Don't go to Munich to rest—it's a city in which you can really let yourself go.

TRANSPORTATION IN THE CITY: The city has a rapid-transit system. The **subway** is much preferred to streetcars and certainly a high-priced taxi, which costs from $6 to $7 for an average ride. However, in an emergency you might want to take one. They are radio-dispatched by calling 2-1611.

The underground network contains many convenient electronic devices, and the rides are relatively soundless. The same ticket entitles you to ride the "U" railways and the "S" railways, streetcars, and buses. The U-Bahn or Untergrundbahn is the line you will use most frequently, as the S-Bahn or Stadtbahn services suburban locations.

At the Marienplatz, 135 services of the U-Bahn and S-Bahn crisscross each other. It's possible to use your Eurailpass on S-Bahn journeys, as it's a state-owned railway. Otherwise, you must purchase a single-trip ticket or a strip ticket for several journeys at one of the blue vending machines positioned at the entryways to the underground stations. These tickets entitle you to ride both the "S" and "U" railway lines, and are also good for rides on streetcars/buses as well. If you're only making one trip, a single ticket will average about 1.80 DM (59¢).

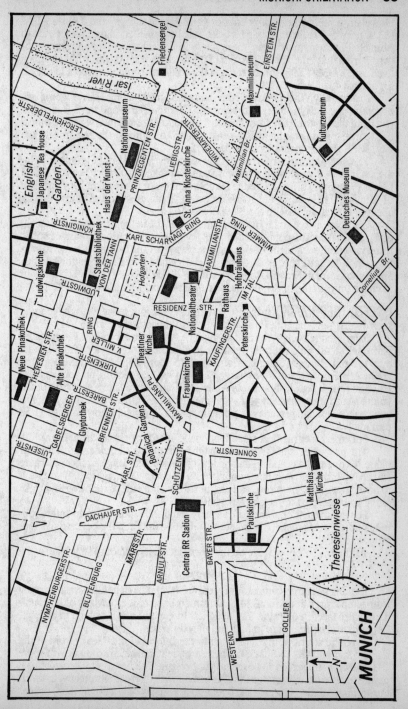

However, a *Mehrfahrtenkarte* entitles you to several trips, and it costs 9 DM ($2.97). Two parts of this six-part ticket will be absorbed in an average ride in Munich. For the network area, there are 24-hour tickets valid for any number of trips during that time. These cost 6.50 DM ($2.15) for most trips within Munich itself, or 12 DM ($3.96) for journeys in the environs, a radius that could extend for at least 45 miles.

Incidentally, the U-Bahn runs across Munich from Harras going via Schwabing to the Nürnberg autobahn and Olympia Park, and the S-Bahn lines (six from the west and five from the east) run under the city in a two-track tunnel between the main station and the east station to combine the region with the city. For S-Bahn information, dial 55-75-75.

The **international airport** is at Riem, some five miles from the heart of Munich. Once you've cleared Customs, you can take an airport bus for 7 DM ($2.31) which will bring you to the Hauptbahnhof, or the main railway terminal of Munich. These buses depart about every 18 minutes, and of course are far cheaper than the cabs with their lethal prices.

Once you arrive at the **Hauptbahnhof,** you'll be in the very core of Munich, and from that central point you can avail yourself of the various means of public transportation, such as the U-Bahn (the subway), or the S-Bahn (the metropolitan railway), that I've already discussed. For general train information (that is, about the German Federal Railway), call 59-29-91 or 59-33-21. And if you want to check on your flight, the number to call at Airport Munich-Riem is 92-11-21.

USEFUL INFORMATION: In case you should lose your passport, or have some such emergency, the **U.S. Consulate** is at 5 Königinstrasse (tel. 2-30-11).

Your lifeline back to the States might be **American Express,** 3 Promenadeplatz (tel. 22-81-66), which is open for mail pickup and check cashing from 9 a.m. to 5 p.m. (also on Saturday from 9 a.m. to noon). Unless you have a gold or green Am Ex card, you'll be charged 2 DM (78¢) for picking up your mail. If you don't have a card, show them American Express traveler's checks to prove you're a customer; that way you avoid the surcharge. On a weekend or at night, you can also **exchange money** at the main railway terminal from 6 a.m. to 11:30 p.m. daily.

For **emergency medical aid,** telephone 55-86-61; or phone the **police** at 110.

The **post office** stands across from the main railway terminal at 1 Bahnhofplatz. It's open all day and night, and you can also make long-distance calls here (far cheaper than at your hotel where you'll be charged for service). If you want to have your mail sent to you, mark it "poste restante" for general delivery (take along your passport to reclaim any mail).

For an international **drugstore** where English is spoken, go to **Internationale Ludwig's Apotheke,** 8 Neuhauser (tel. 260-30-21), in the pedestrian shopping zone.

And now, before we take on the town, let's find a place to stay.

1. Hotels

Finding a room is comparatively easy. The choice of hotels is vast, ranging from simple prewar pensions to sleek, streamlined modern. Many older candidates were facelifted for the '72 Olympics. In general, the tabs tend to be high. Bargains are few and hard to find, but they do exist.

If you're stranded in Munich, go to the **Information Office** in front of the railway station (tel. 239-12-58). There a patient Bavarian woman with some 20,000 listings in her file will come to your rescue. Tell her what you can afford, pay a fee, and get a receipt, as well as a map with instructions on how to reach the accommodation in which she books you. You pay only a 2-DM (66¢) fee per room. Keep your receipt. If you dislike the room to which you've been sent, return to the same desk and the woman will try to find another room at no extra charge. The emergency room-booking office is open daily from 8 a.m. to 11 p.m., and in the Airport Arrivals Hall (tel. 90-72-56), Monday through Saturday from 9 a.m. to 10 p.m., on Sunday from 11 a.m. to 7 p.m.

The number to call for general information—that is, the main headquarters of the **Munich Tourist Office**—is 2-39-11, which is the number at their central office at 5 Rindermarkt.

DELUXE HOTELS: Bayerischer Hof and Palais Montgelas, 2-6 Promenadeplatz (tel. 2-12-00), are considered by many travelers a Bavarian version of the Waldorf-Astoria. The location is swank, across from American Express, opening onto a little tree-filled square. The tastefully decorated central lounge, with English and French reproductions and Oriental rugs, is practically the living room of Munich. "Meet you in the lounge of the Bayerischer Hof" is heard often. The Palais Montgelas, sumptuously decorated, was integrated into the hotel with deluxe suites and double rooms and a number of conference and banqueting rooms.

The major dining room evokes the grandeur of a small palace, with ornate ceiling, crystal chandeliers, and French provincial chairs. Generous drinks and charcoal specialties from the rôtisserie are served in the club-like bar, where the tables are lit by candlelight and the reflected glow from the octagonally paned stained-glass windows.

Some of the best looking women in Bavaria are found lounging on the bricked sun terrace alongside the rooftop swimming pool and garden. Other facilities include the Kleine Komödie Theatre, a sauna, massage rooms, a Trader Vic's, and the best nightclub in Munich. Bedrooms are priced according to size, bath facilities, and view. A single goes for 155 DM ($51.15) with shower, 220 DM ($72.60) with complete bath. Doubles with complete bath cost 220 DM ($72.60) to 350 DM ($115.50), including breakfast.

Grand Hotel Continental, 5 Max-Joseph-Strasse (tel. 55-79-71), is exceptional, perhaps the nicest in Munich if you appreciate a stylish, antique-filled hotel run in a personal manner (its owner is Herman Prinz von Sachsen). Just five minutes from the railway station, it's a delight for one or 150 nights. The formal lounge, with an overscale tapestry, sets the tone. The grill room is furnished as a country inn, with pine walls, crude tables, shelves of pewter plates, and antler horns. The more formal dining room is also provincial, with a wooden beamed ceiling, an open château fireplace, and high antique cupboards. That the Continental deserves its "Grand" appellation is reflected everywhere: in the French provincial coffee and card room; in the formal sitting salon, with ornate Louis XVI–style furniture, brocaded walls, and baroque doors; in the garden room, with its arbor, vines, and planters of red geraniums. In fair weather guests seek the inner garden for dining. Breakfast is served at tables near the fish pond, splashing fountain, and ivy-covered wall. Each of the bedrooms, no matter what you pay, has style. A single with shower costs 190 DM ($62.70); with a complete bath, from 190 DM ($62.70) to 290 DM ($95.70). A double with shower goes for 240 DM ($79.20), peaking at 260 DM ($85.80) to 310 DM ($102.30) with complete bath.

Vier Jahreszeiten, 17 Maximilianstrasse (tel. 23-03-90). Whenever you see this name Four Seasons in Germany, you're almost assured of a good hotel. In addition to the famed hotel in Munich, one of the best hotels in the north of Germany, the prestigious Vier Jahreszeiten in Hamburg also uses this name. A substantial, quiet dignity prevails at Munich's front-ranking hotel. The tone is set as your taxi drives up to the covered entryway, where a liveried doorman greets you warmly.

Inside, you may feel as if you've arrived at an exclusive country club. One writer found that its rooms "radiated the atmosphere of the Wittelsbach era." The bedrooms are what you'd expect: immaculate comfort in spacious, well-appointed surroundings. The prices are from 225 DM ($80.85) to 260 DM ($85.80) for single rooms with bath. Doubles with bath rent for anywhere from 320 DM ($105.60) to 420 DM ($138.60). Unquestionably, the Vier Jahreszeiten offers the finest hotel dining in the Bavarian capital. In fact, it has won its fame for its gastronomic excellence. The cuisine generates from the Walterspiel Restaurant.

München Hilton, 7 am Tucherpark (tel. 34-00-51), is a modern, 15-story hotel between the Isar River and the English Garden. Built in 1972 in the center of the former Tivoli park, it's about a ten-minute ride from the downtown shopping areas. The hotel's 481 bedrooms contain floor-to-ceiling picture windows, plus a balcony affording a distant view of the Alps. Chambers are contemporary yet elegant, with dark Macassar wood furniture, a perfect foil for the autumnal colors used throughout. Each accommodation is equipped with color TV and a self-service refrigerator bar, plus air conditioning and direct-dial phone. Depending on the floor and location, singles range from 170 DM ($56.10) to 235 DM ($77.50); doubles, from 200 DM ($66) to 315 DM ($103.95).

Overlooking the pool is the hotel's popular-priced restaurant, which offers a buffet and an à la carte menu. In summer the restaurant opens out onto the hotel's garden, where you can enjoy the best of Bavarian beer and specialties. International and creative dishes are offered in the grill on the ground floor. Scottish rib of beef is a specialty. Before dinner, you can have a "Mass" of good beer in the Piano Bar with its wood paneling. The bar features an intern pianist and the best martinis in town. In Club Bavaria, there's a lively weekly program, and you can grill your own meat on hot stones.

A special feature is a Medicur Revitalization Center offering several therapies to restore and preserve health and productivity. You can also relax in the health club facing the English Garden, with a heated indoor swimming pool, sauna, and solarium. Luxury cars such as Rolls-Royce, Lamborghini, or Maserati can be hired through the new Royal Rent concession in the shopping gallery.

München Sheraton, 6 Arrabellastrasse (tel. 92-40-11). If you're in Munich on a convention, chances are good that you'll be housed here. East of the heart of Munich, the 22-story structure, with 650 attractively furnished bedrooms, opens onto the English Garden. All rooms, many quite large, contain bath, toilet, air conditioning, TV, radio, and automatic phone. A single ranges in price from 160 DM ($52.80) to 310 DM ($102.30); a double goes for 190 DM ($62.70) to 310 DM ($102.30).

The hotel places a strong emphasis on keeping fit. In addition to a health club, they have a 20-meter swimming pool, a solarium, a fitness room, a sauna, and a massage parlor (strictly legit). The Sheraton is almost a world unto itself, as if it wants to keep the business all within its premises. With that purpose in mind, it offers three bars, three restaurants, a coffeeshop, nightclub, shopping arcade, car-rental agency, and a 260-car garage. Die Mühle (The Mill) is a favorite spot for breakfast, and in the Alt Bayern Stube Bavarian specialties are served. In the nightclub, Vibraphon, international bands and disco music entertain until 4 a.m. The Sheraton even has a beer garden.

So with all this action it's hardly necessary to leave. But if you do, you'll find bus and tram connections nearby. You should be in town in no less than 10 to 15 minutes.

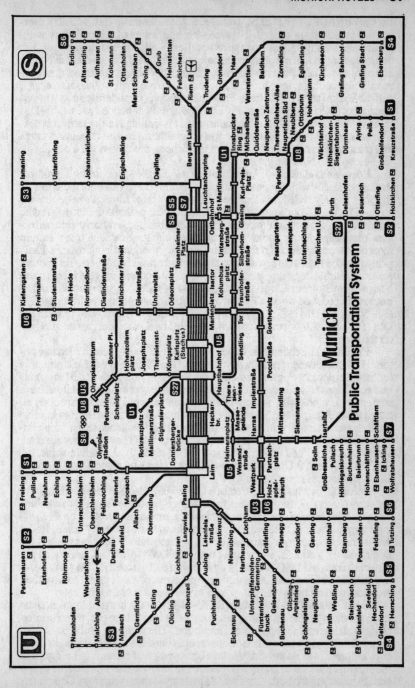

UPPER BRACKET HOTELS: Arabella, 5 Arabellastrasse (tel. 9-23-21), is excellent, but distantly located. The free-wheeling design of Arabella is contemporary, with many dramatic public rooms. Best of all is the swimming pool. The bedrooms are modern, with private balcony, tiled bath, direct-dial telephone, and mini-bar. The accommodations seem more like chic living rooms than bedrooms. For example, lime-green walls, with overscale chalk-white sofas, chairs, and tables, are style pacesetters. Prices are sensible, considering what you get. Singles cost 145 DM ($47.85) to 210 DM ($69.30); twin-bedded rooms, 200 DM ($66) to 280 DM ($92.40). A breakfast buffet is included in the tariffs quoted. The bars and restaurant have their own special flair. Guests can relax in sauna and massage rooms. Three miles from the airport, this city within a city lies off the autobahn to Nürnberg.

Eden-Wolff-Hotel, 4-8 Arnulfstrasse (tel. 55-82-81), opposite the railway station, misleads with its sedate exterior. The interior is not only more attractive, but warmly styled, making the Eden-Wolff one of Munich's better hotels. Each of its main-floor lounges is richly traditional; perhaps the most intimate and sophisticated is the old-world wood-paneled bar. A Bavarian theme permeates the main dining room—natural pine ceiling, gleaming brass lantern sconces, tavern chairs, and thick stone arches. Another dining room is like a richly paneled men's club, with oil paintings and brass chandeliers. Yet another contains murals depicting pastoral scenes. Quite consistently, the bedrooms borrow heavily from Bavarian styling. Most of them are substantial and lustrous, with polished woods, TV set, and radio. Single rooms cost from 150 DM ($49.50) to 240 DM ($79.20), and twin-bedded units go for 200 DM ($66) to 310 DM ($102.30). All prices include a buffet breakfast. An underground garage is on the premises.

Excelsior, 11 Schützengasse (tel. 55-79-06), is one of Munich's leading hotels. Halfway between the railway station and the Stachus, it was built primarily for business people. For that reason it is used less on weekends and often grants rate reductions from Friday evening through Monday morning. The hotel has a contemporary look with a stamp of elegance in its public rooms. Especially attractive is the multitiered St. Hubertus restaurant, with its bas relief of hunting scenes, open charcoal grill, wood paneling, and excellent cuisine, featuring Bavarian game specialties. Adjoining is an intimate bar. The bedrooms are modern. Singles go for 160 DM ($52.80) to 190 DM ($62.70); doubles or twins, 190 DM ($62.70) to 220 DM ($72.60), according to size and placement. The hotel also offers several suites on the roof.

Splendid, 54 Maximilianstrasse (tel. 29-66-06), is one of the most attractive old-world hotels in Munich. Every room reflects the owner's ability to combine antiques with good reproductions, achieving harmony and style. The small living rooms, as well as the bedrooms, evoke the aura of a country home. Room prices are scaled according to size, furnishings, and bath. A bathless single is 120 DM ($39.60); a double, also without bath, 205 DM ($67.65). A single with private bath costs 185 DM ($61.05); a double with bath, from 275 DM ($90.75). A tasty breakfast is included. On sunny mornings many guests prefer to have their morning meal on the paved patio, with its trellis and bubbling fountain.

Der Königshof, 25 Karlsplatz (tel. 55-84-12), in the heart of Munich, overlooks the famous Stachus (Karlsplatz) and the old part of the city, wherein interesting walking and shopping areas are found. The pedigree of the place goes back to 1862 when a baronal mansion was built outside the medieval walls of the city. Before it was destroyed, the hotel enjoyed great renown in its day. The proprietors, the Geisel family, have done much to see that it maintains its legend. In fact it's much better than when I first stayed there years ago. Completely facelifted for the 1972 Olympics, the hotel offers traditional comfort with up-to-date facilities. It's not only a commercial hotel, but attracts many visitors. All of its sleekly styled rooms have private bath, are air-conditioned and soundproof, and feature TV sets and picture windows. Doubles or twins go for anywhere from 190 DM ($62.70) to 220 DM ($72.60). Singles are in the 170-DM ($56.10) to 190-DM ($62.70) range. On the second floor is a well-known terrace restaurant, serving a French and international cuisine. The lobby houses an intimate club bar, the Königshof-Bar. An underground garage shelters 200 cars.

Hotel Metropol, 43 Bayerstrasse (tel. 53-07-64), is a modern business person's hotel, in a "you-can't-miss-it" location, directly across from the main railway station in the heart of Munich. English-speaking receptionists have literally rolled out the red carpet in the cavernous reception and lobby. Sleek, contemporary lines and styling attract those who are tired of the rustic and traditional.

Bedrooms are furnished in a "sober" style, nothing grand in any way, but nothing overlooked either. In high season, a double with complete bath costs 155 DM ($51.15), dropping to 135 DM ($44.55) with a shower and toilet. The cheapest single has a shower—no toilet—costing 85 DM ($28.05) nightly, rising to 110 DM ($36.30) with complete bath. The windows are soundproofed, and each unit has a phone and radio and some contain TV. In all, the Metropol at peak capacity can shelter 370 guests. In addition, a garage holds 200 cars. The hotel also has a restaurant if you (wisely) don't want to venture out into the railway station area at night.

The **München Penta Hotel,** 3 Hochstrasse (tel. 448-55-55), lies near the city center, a ten-minute walk from the Marienplatz. The S-Bahn railway which stops within the hotel complex (station: Rosenheimer Platz) whisks visitors to the heart of the city in three minutes. The München Penta has 583 completely air-conditioned modern-style guest rooms, with private bath, shower, and toilet, direct-dial telephone, radio, mini-bar, and color TV. An indoor pool, a sauna, three restaurants, and a shopping center are in the complex. A single room ranges in price from 175 DM ($57.75) to 185 DM ($61.05), and a double costs 220 DM ($72.60) to 410 DM ($135.20), including service and VAT.

Drei Löwen (Three Lions), 8 Schillerstrasse (tel. 59-55-21), is better than ever, a trim, attractive, and tasteful 130-bedroom hotel adjacent to the railway station. It attracts clients who like a quality setting where they can entertain a bit. Its dignified lounge is more like a library. Other little sitting rooms have the same sedate character—even the dining room, with its wood-paneled dado and scenic murals. The bedrooms are half traditional, half modern, all nicely styled, with complete mini-bar, direct-dial phone, radio, color TV, and private bath. A single ranges in price from 112 DM ($39.60) to 128 DM ($42.24), and a double costs from 175 DM ($57.75) to 194 DM ($64.02), including a buffet breakfast. A supplementary bed can be added for 32 DM ($10.56).

Hotel Preysing, 1 Preysingstrasse (tel. 48-10-11). If you don't mind the inconvenience of a hotel on the outskirts, one of the best places to stay in Munich today is the Preysing. It has already attracted the patronage of some of the most discriminating clients in the world, who seem to want to keep its whereabouts a secret. A short train ride will whisk you into the center of the city, and you can leave your car safely in their underground garage.

When you first view the building, a seven-story modern structure that won't win any architectural design contests, you may feel I've misled you. However, if you've gone this far—on the other side of the Isar, near the German Museum—venture inside for an amazing surprise.

The family who runs it has one of the most thoughtful staffs in Munich. Not only the service, but the friendly smiles will warm your day. Furthermore, the style of the hotel is most agreeable, filled with dozens of little extras to provide home-like comfort. Fresh flowers are placed about, and the traditional furnishings combined with modern were thoughtfully selected. Each room has a private bath, costing from 150 DM ($49.50) to 225 DM ($74.25) in a single and from 250 DM ($82.50) in a double. Not only that, but the location is quiet, far removed from the increasingly noisy downtown section of Munich. The 60 rooms are also all air-conditioned, and contain such extras as a radio, self-dial phone, color TV, and a well-stocked refrigerator. A grand breakfast is included in the tariffs. Facilities include an indoor swimming pool with a sauna, solarium, and hot whirlpool. If you're still not tempted to cross over the river, know that its restaurant is one of the finest dining rooms in Munich (we'll call on it in the restaurant section to follow).

MIDDLE-BRACKET HOTELS: **Deutscher Kaiser,** 2 Arnulfstrasse (tel. 55-83-21) is a mini-skyscraper opposite the railway station. Its 15th-floor dining room provides both a panoramic view of the city and a relaxed opportunity to get your geographic bearings. In addition, the fourth-floor terrace contains a restaurant and cozy wood-paneled bar. The bedrooms feature built-in contemporary designs and room-wide picture windows. The accommodations are generously sized, combining sitting and sleeping areas. Singles with toilet and hot and cold running water rent for 112 DM ($36.96), increasing to 125 DM ($41.25) with full bath. Doubles with sink and toilet cost 195 DM ($64.35), or 205 DM ($67.65) with full bath. A buffet breakfast is included.

Ambassador Hotel, 4 Mozartstrasse (tel. 53-08-40), can become your pied-à-terre in Munich, where you can have your own home-like setup, perfect for entertaining friends. For a reasonable outlay of marks you get a studio apartment decorated in functional Nordic style, including a complete sitting room, with sofa, coffee table, reading lamp, armchairs, desk, TV, and three-channel radio. Silk draperies draw across a bed recess, with night light and telephone. In a corridor leading to an all-tile bathroom is your own little bar and refrigerator (stocked with basic materials). Singles run from 115 DM ($37.95) to 150 DM ($49.50); doubles, from 210 DM ($69.30) to 240 DM ($79.20). In addition to all this, there's an intimate lounge-bar on the lower level, plus a dignified wood-paneled dining room. Another asset: The Ambassador lies a few blocks south of the railway station. Garage space is available.

Hotel Reinbold, 11 Adolf-Kolping-Strasse (tel. 59-79-45), is a no-nonsense, no-frills hotel that delivers what it promises: a clean, decent room and quiet, efficient, and polite service. If that's what you're after, then you'll find it right in the heartbeat of Munich, about a three-minute walk from the main rail terminal and only a five-minute stroll from the fair and exhibition site. All its compact, comfortably (but not lavishly) furnished rooms contain a variety of plumbing, a refrigerator-bar, TV, and air-conditioning. A single with hot and cold running water and toilet is 85 DM ($28.05), going up to 135 DM ($44.55) with shower. Likewise, the low double rate starts at 145 DM ($47.85), rising to 200 DM ($66) with complete private bath. Tariffs include a continental breakfast, and for only 12 DM ($3.96) you can use the underground garage.

Hotel an der Oper, 10 Falkenturmstrasse (tel. 22-87-11), stands just off the Maximilianstrasse, in the vicinity of Marienplatz. It's superb either for sightseeing or shopping in the traffic-free malls. In spite of its basic, clean-cut modernity, there is a touch of elegance. The little reception area has a salon look with crystal chandeliers and trim leather chairs. The luxurious cellar bar, the Opern-Taverne, is richly decorated with wood paneling and lots of crystal. Adjoining is one of the most prestigious restaurants of Munich, the Bouillabaisse. The bedrooms aren't super-chic, but they do offer first-class amenities, each with a private bath, phone, refrigerator, and small sitting areas with armchairs and tables for breakfast. Traditional elements have been combined with a severe modern. Including breakfast, a single rents for 90 DM ($29.70) to 105 DM ($34.65) nightly, a double for 130 DM ($42.90) to 165 DM ($54.45).

Adria, 8a Liebigstrasse (tel. 29-30-81), is a completely revamped hotel, offering many special appointments to remove it from the ordinary. With redshaded lamps, global map behind the reception desk, wood panels, planters of greenery, and Oriental rugs, the lobby sets the stylish contemporary look. Some of the 53 rooms have a TV as well as a refrigerator filled with cold drinks. Armchairs or sofas and small desks add to the comfort. Singles without bath range in price from 60 DM ($19.80), increasing to 125 DM ($41.25) with bath. Bathless twin-bedded rooms go from 90 DM ($29.70); with private bath, from 180 DM ($59.40). Breakfast, included in the room rate, is the only meal served in the garden room—brightly decorated in red and white, with wrought-iron furniture.

Germania, 28 Schwanthalerstrasse (tel. 5-16-80), is conservative and sedate on the outside, but has many winning touches of design inside. Special features include .automatic air conditioning, soundproofing, a separate private entrance, a box for shoes in the vestibule, and bathrooms lined either with pearl gray, black, or blue tiles or Venetian glass mosaic. Usually there is a sitting room adjoining the bedroom, with original paintings, etchings, Oriental rugs, and fruitwood furnishings. Large windows let in plenty of light. A single with bath costs 155 DM ($51.15), and a double with bath is 175 DM ($57.75). All these rates include breakfast, service charge, and taxes.

Hotel Mark, 12 Senfelderstrasse (tel. 59-28-01). This 141-bed hotel, near the south exit of the railway station, should be considered for its comfort and moderate prices. Rebuilt in 1956, it offers either a shower or tub bath, plus toilet, in most rooms. The beds are good, the furnishings sleekly modern, and everything is undeniably serviceable. Included in the rates are taxes, service, and breakfast. A single with basin and toilet costs 70 DM ($23.10), increasing to 110 DM ($36.30) with bath. Doubles with shower rent for 120 DM ($39.60); with bath, from 150 DM ($49.50). Many rooms have TV. You can park your car in an underground garage. The charming, tavern-style dining room has good food.

Hotel Habis, 2a Maria-Theresa-Strasse (tel. 47-05-071), wins my respect as a special small hotel of character. The location is across from Isarpark overlooking the river. Across the bridge are some of the leading museums of Munich. The renovated hotel is built on a corner with five floors of individualized bedrooms. The top floor has the old Munich architectural styling, and in general is well conceived. On the premises is a wine restaurant which combines old-style furnishings set in nooks and has a mezzanine of rough white plaster and arches. Also on the premises is the unusual Komödientheater where shows are presented nightly except Monday. The general decor of the hotel, especially the entrance with its gracious, curving staircase, is a moderate art nouveau style. The bedrooms have strong earth colors, with painted built-in pieces, trim beds, casual wicker armchairs, and balloon lights. All rooms have private bath. Singles range in price from 80 DM ($26.40) to 100 DM ($33), and doubles go for 120 DM ($39.60) to 140 DM ($46.20), including a buffet breakfast.

THE BEST FOR VALUE: **Bundesbahn-Hotel,** im Hauptbahnhof (tel. 55-85-71), is part of the railway station complex (right inside it). However, it shuts out that dreary world as soon as you enter its doors. A dignified, traditional lounge, with contemporary flair, greets you. In the snug little leather-coated bar you can drown your troubles, or enjoy good Germanic cooking in the Bavarian restaurant. More important, however, are the fresh bedrooms. Most of the accommodations combine French and art nouveau designs; romanticists will gravitate to the top-floor rooms, with their dormer windows and built-in furniture (curved posts as headboards, painted armoires). Each room seems to have its own personality. The prices differ, depending on bath arrangement and size. Bathless singles cost 80 DM ($26.40) to 89 DM ($29.37). A bathless twin-bedded room costs 130 DM ($42.90) to 144 DM ($47.52), 158 DM ($52.14) to 168 DM ($55.44) with bath and toilet.

Europäischer Hof, 31 Bayerstrasse (tel. 55-46-21), is a nine-floor hotel opposite the railway station, which was originally built by a group of Catholic sisters and is now run by the Stürzer family. There's even a chapel on the premises. It's one of the best buys in Munich. Many of the accommodations overlook an inner courtyard, with a subterranean parking area. Singles cost 65 DM ($21.45) bathless, 100 DM ($33) with full bath. Twin-bedded rooms go for 108 DM ($35.64) bathless, 158 DM ($52.14) with full bath. These rates include a generous breakfast buffet. Despite its dreary station location, the hotel couldn't be more immaculate: the constantly dusting, polishing, buffing, and waxing maids make spring cleaning a year-round activity here. Most of the rooms are of fair size, with built-in headboards, three-channel radios, a desk table, sofa, a pair of armchairs, coffee table, luggage racks, and an entry hall wardrobe.

Hotel-Pension Am Markt, 6 Heiliggeiststrasse (tel. 22-50-14), is a Bavarian-style hotel with a regional gingerbread trim that stands in the heart of the Old Town. It's not that easy to get in here, but it's worth a try. The hotel is not luxurious, but it has many decorative trappings reflecting the glory of another era. The owner, Harald Herrler, has wisely maintained an interesting, nostalgic decor in the dining room and entrance lobby. Behind his reception desk is a wall of photographs of friends or former guests of the hotel, including the late Viennese chanteuse Greta Keller. As Mr. Herrler points out, when you have breakfast here, you are likely to find yourself surrounded by opera and concert artists who like to stay here because they're close to the houses in which they perform. The bedrooms are basic modern, quite small, but trim and neat. A few rooms have private bath, and all of the units have hot and cold running water, with free use of the corridor baths and toilets. The cost in a single is 52 DM ($17.16). In a bathless double the rate is 86 DM ($28.38), rising to 96 DM ($31.68) with shower. Breakfast is included in the tariffs quoted.

Kraft Hotel, 49 Schillerstrasse (tel. 59-48-23), is a neat little modern hotel that is especially attractive. Set back from a busy street, about five minutes from the railway station, it has just enough space in front to park four cars. The reception lounge is inviting, but you guessed it—absolutely tiny. An adjoining breakfast room is well decorated. The emphasis, however, is mostly on the streamlined bedrooms, which are well kept and up-to-date, with many built-in units. Depending on the bath facilities you get, singles range in price from 90 DM ($29.70) to 120 DM ($39.60); doubles, from 120 DM ($39.60) to 150 DM ($49.50). Included in these tariffs are taxes, service, and breakfast.

Haberstock, 4 Schillerstrasse (tel. 55-78-55), was reconstructed in 1952. It is close to the railway station and priced reasonably. Singles without bath rent for 48 DM ($15.84), from 90 DM ($29.70) with shower bath. Bathless doubles are 88 DM ($29.04); with bath or shower, from 150 DM ($49.50). These prices include breakfast. The dining room is old-fashioned, the bedrooms all modern. Everything is clean and serviceable.

Hotel Ariston, 10 Unsöldstrasse (tel. 22-26-91), stands bleakly modern in the center of Munich, not too far from the Haus der Kunst and the National Museum. It's a straightforward, no-frills type of place, with 60 rooms in all, furnished in a very simple, modern style. In every room, however, you'll find a private bath or shower, toilet, radio, and direct-dial phone. Singles range in price from 95 DM ($31.35) to 125 DM ($41.25), and doubles go for 110 DM ($36.30) to 150 DM ($49.50). These tariffs include the standard buffet breakfast. A small entryway to all units allows for greater quietness and privacy.

City Hotel, 3a Schillerstrasse (tel. 55-80-91), lies just a few minutes from the main railway terminal, the Stachus, and the exhibition ground. It likes to think of itself as your "cozy home in Munich," and for many travelers it's just that. Rooms are compact, with all the necessities and a decorative touch or two to soften the severity. A single rents for 128 DM ($42.24) per day and a double costs 188 DM ($62.04), these tariffs including a buffet, breakfast, service, and taxes. All units contain a private bath, toilet, radio, phone, mini-bar, TV, and air conditioning.

Hotel Arnulf, 12-14 Arnulfstrasse (tel. 59-86-41), is another midcity hotel with impersonal architecture, but not an impersonal reception. It's near the main railway station and close to Munich's fine private transport system. For what you get, its prices are reasonable: from 75 DM ($24.75) to 120 DM ($39.60) in a single with phone, shower, and toilet, rising to 105 DM ($34.65) to 170 DM ($56.10) in a double with much the same equipment (except, in many cases, a private tub bath is included as well). Guests can choose among three different furnishing styles. The hotel rents 76 singles (much preferred by business people) and 60 double rooms, with (thank God) soundproofing. The breakfast room is warmly decorated, and your morning meal is included in the rates quoted. You can park your car in their underground station.

Hotel Torbräu, 37 Tal (tel. 22-50-16), is an inviting choice. A totally renovated hotel, it's owned by the Kirchlechner family, who also run it. The Torbräu stands in the center of Old Munich, near the old Istartor subway station, and only 300 yards from the city hall and the pedestrian shopping mall, within easy reach of the Deutsches Museum, the Residence, and the Opera. It's much more charming and warmly decorated than some of the bandbox modern hotels we've been considering so far. The staff rents out 165 beds, all with private bath and toilet. Rooms are traditionally furnished. The single rate with a continental breakfast included ranges from 120 DM ($39.60) to 170 DM ($56.10), from 190 DM ($62.70) to 210 DM ($69.30) in a double, and from 210 DM ($69.30) to 225 DM ($74.25) in a triple. The restaurant is bright and festive, serving Bavarian specialties, and there's also a Café-Conditorei on the premises.

Hotel Königswache, 7 Steinhellstrasse (tel. 52-20-01), is not as regal as its name, yet it has much to recommend it. The location is about a ten-minute ride to the train station, and only two minutes from the technical university. It lies between the Stachus and Schwabing, and this section of Munich is preferred by many clients who find the railway station area dangerous, especially at night. An 80-bed hotel, the place is warmly decorated, and the staff are hospitable and speak English. The rooms are modern and comfortable, very well done, with private bath, color TV, radio, mini-bar, and a little writing desk with a self-dial phone. For the privilege of staying here, a single pays from 130 DM ($42.90) to 165 DM ($54.45); a double costs from 175 DM ($57.75) to 205 DM ($67.65), and a triple, from 205 DM ($67.65) to 245 DM ($80.85). These tariffs include a buffet breakfast with champagne. The restaurant is attractively decorated and serves Korean food, offered by a Korean staff. The hotel bar is decorated in a cozy, rustic style.

Hotel Domus, 31 St.-Anna-Strasse (tel. 22-17-04), may sound like a university dormitory, but it isn't. Sleekly modern, it's a contemporary hotel, lying near the English Garden and the Haus der Kunst. The hotel is about a 10-minute ride from the main railway terminal and a 20-minute haul from the airport. The staff is to be congratulated, one of the most helpful and efficient I've discovered in

Munich. After a hectic day of sightseeing, you return here to comfort, as you would in a private home, even though it's a good-size hotel. A single room with a private bath costs 140 DM ($46.20) a night, rising to 180 DM ($59.40) if a private terrace is attached. Doubles with bath and terrace go for 180 DM ($59.40), jumping up to 220 DM ($72.60) in an apartment with bath, toilet, and terrace. Tariffs include breakfast, color TV, service charge, and taxes.

The hotel pays special attention to decreasing noise, in its carpeting and doors. The aim is to give you a peaceful, undisturbed night's rest. The hotel will serve you breakfast in your room or else downstairs. If you can't find a place to park your car in front of the hotel, there's also an underground garage.

Hotel Wapler, 8 Schwanthalerstrasse (tel. 5-91-664), is almost like a Bavarian inn, with compact, snug bedrooms that may not be a decorator's showcase, but are warm and inviting. The management is friendly and cooperative, and filled with suggestions about touring or "survival" in Munich. For a single room with bath and breakfast, expect to pay from 125 DM ($41.25) to 180 DM ($59.40), the rate going up to 155 DM ($51.15) to 220 DM ($72.60) in a double room.

Hotel Concorde, 38 Hernstrasse (tel. 22-45-15), has always seemed a little dark to me, but it's a suitable oasis for those seeking an intimate hotel in the center of Munich. It's not very well known, and perhaps it should be. The location on a side street is obscure, yet it's only a few minutes of walking to some of the major sightseeing attractions of the Bavarian capital. The staff was friendly and hospitable on my visit. They rent 50 guest rooms with large and comfortable beds, along with such amenities as private bath, direct-dial phone, color TV, radio, and mini-bar. A single room with shower rents for 120 DM ($39.60), the price rising to 170 DM ($56.10) with private bath. A double room with shower goes for 140 DM ($46.20), increasing to 200 DM ($66) in a twin-bedded room with bath.

Central Hotel, 111 Schwanthalerstrasse (tel. 50-60-81), managed by the Arabella conglomerate, is called in German *Das kleine Grosstadthotel* or the "little metropolitan hotel." A hotel garni (meaning it serves only breakfast), it lies only five minutes from Messegelände (exhibition grounds) and the Oktoberfest grounds, a distance of one kilometer from the main railroad station. Everything is modern, often attractively so, here. The 130-bed hotel was designed for modern convenience, and each unit is equipped with a private bath, balcony, radio, mini-bar, alarm clock, and self-dial phone along with a color TV set. A single room rents for 120 DM ($39.60) to 145 DM ($47.85) nightly; a double goes for 145 DM ($47.85) to 185 DM ($61.05). Some apartments are also available, and tariffs include a breakfast buffet, service, and tax.

THE PICK OF THE PENSIONS: Mariandl, 51 Goethestrasse (tel. 53-41-08), is one of the best pensions in Munich, having taken over the Pension Tirol in the same building. The pension is sheltered in a prewar building on a tree-shaded street, just an eight-minute walk from the railway station. It's run with efficiency by English-speaking Hans Brugger. The rooms are modestly furnished but well kept, and the price includes a buffet breakfast consisting of cold cuts, cheese, bread, butter, and jelly, as well as coffee. Genuine hospitality is offered to overseas guests. A double ranges in price from 85 DM ($28.05) to 100 DM ($33), and a triple-bedded accommodation costs from 115 DM ($37.95) to 130 DM ($42.90). Some of the accommodations contain a total of four beds, going for 150 DM ($49.50) a night. Donwstairs you'll find an old Bavarian restaurant, also managed by Mr. Brugger. Live classical music is played during the dinner hour.

Hotel Uhland Garni, 1 Uhlandstrasse (tel. 53-92-77), is a stately, dignified town mansion, standing in its own small garden, just three blocks from the

Bahnhof. A well-run family hotel, it offers good accommodations at fair prices and could easily become your home in Munich. The owners enjoy North American visitors. They have a sliding price scale, based on the location and size of your room. The pension has been considerably upgraded, and accommodations contain private shower with toilet, as well as mini-bar and color TV. The charge in a single ranges from 80 DM ($26.40) to 100 DM ($33), while doubles go for 105 DM ($34.65) to 140 DM ($46.20).

Pension Westfalia, 23 Mozartstrasse (tel. 53-03-77), stands only two blocks from the meadow where the annual Oktoberfest takes place. This four-story town house is near Goethe Platz, and is reached by taking tram no. 17; it's one of the best pensions in Munich. The rooms are immaculately maintained. Bathless doubles cost 70 DM ($23.10) to 75 DM ($24.75); bathless singles, 50 DM ($16.50). With a shower a single costs 75 DM ($24.75), rising to 95 DM ($31.35) in a double with complete bath. Rates include breakfast, service, and tax. The owner, Herr Bertram Hoos, speaks English and was trained at the Hilton in Berlin.

Karl-Friedrich, 13 Mozartstrasse (tel. 53-40-78), is a family pension that, in the words of its owner, is a "good place in these days when money is scarce and not everybody is a millionaire." The host, Eugene Kranovitz-Köváry, adds, "It's suitable for those who like to live in a small house where they speak English, French, and Spanish." The rooms are comfortably and pleasantly furnished. The price is 80 DM ($26.40) in a double, 55 DM ($18.15) in a single, with a good breakfast included. The bathrooms are shared. The location is fairly central—three minutes by subway to the heart of Munich.

Hotel Penison Utzelmann, 6 Pettenkoferstrasse (tel. 59-48-89), is an impersonal building, but the atmosphere inside is family-like. Its owner, Mrs. Hermann Ernst, has freshened everything with furniture, carpeting, and modern toilets. The large accommodations are well kept, airy, and bright. Singles range in price from 40 DM ($13.20) to 50 DM ($16.50); doubles, 80 DM ($26.40) to 85 DM ($28.05). A bathroom is conveniently placed on each floor.

HOTELS IN SCHWABING: Residence, 4 Artur-Kutscher-Platz (tel. 38-17-80),
provides a breath of fresh modernity in Schwabing. A corner honeycomb structure, it contains eight floors of rooms, most of which have balconies. The lounge is most attractive, its vibrant colors intermixed with chalk white and wood paneling. There's even a sauna-style swimming pool, with a wall and ceiling of natural pine, subtropical plants, and lounge chairs. Color and style are also notable features of the spacious bedrooms. Prices are set according to the floor you're assigned—those nearer the ground are cheaper. All rooms have private bath, balcony, refrigerator, and radio. Singles cost 188 DM ($62.04), going up to 258 DM ($85.14) in a double. Breakfast is extra. An underground garage is available. You can dine here at the elegant Le Pavillon restaurant, with glass globe lighting, bentwood chairs, and filmy white curtains; patronize the cozy, post-coach-like bar-restaurant, Die Kutsche (air-conditioned), or meet for drinks in the wood-paneled bar.

Holiday Inn, 200 Leopoldstrasse (tel. 34-09-71), acquainted Munich with this American motel chain. And this one's quite a glamorous introduction. Long a leading Munich hotel, it was created originally to lure business for the year of the Olympics, offering a lot in modern living from the beginning. Every one of its rooms—it contains a total of 700 beds—is air-conditioned, with private bath and shower, queen-sized bed (two in doubles), TV set, as well as direct-dial telephone. The decor is streamlined, with upholstered furniture, natural woods, and picture windows. Singles are 170 DM ($56.10) to 210 DM ($69.30); doubles, 200 DM ($66) to 280 DM ($92.40). A copious buffet breakfast is included. A distinctive plus is the no-cost policy for children under 12 who occupy the same room as their parents. Guests are invited to use the marble-edged inside swimming pool, the Old Munich cocktail bar, the restaurants Omas Küche and Almstuben-Grill, or the Aquarius nightclub. The inn is in Schwabing, near the Olympic area, right at the Autobahn Nürnberg/Berlin and Frankfurt.

International Hotel Auer, 5 Hohenzollernstrasse (tel. 33-30-43), is one of the best run little hotels of Schwabing, a first-class selection, with 70 rooms. The owners have created a friendly, hospitable environment, with up-to-date comfort. Rooms are completely modern with all the comforts for a good night's rest. Each has a private bath, shower, toilet, radio, direct-dial phone, TV, and carpeting, along with a little balcony. A single rents for 170 DM ($56.10), and a double costs 220 DM ($72.60). Children up to 12 years of age sharing a room with their parents stay free. The location is only a few steps away from the Leopoldstrasse and very near the English Gardens which we'll visit later. A two-minute walk from the hotel leads to the underground station. A cozy café provides informal dining, and in summer, tables are placed out on the sidewalk. Or you can ask the mangement to direct you to a rustic-style restaurant nearby which serves very good Bavarian food.

Hotel Biederstein, 18 Keferstrasse (tel. 39-50-72), is small and has a loyal clientele. Lying only a few minutes' walk from the park and a lake, it is fairly new, containing enough space for 39 beds. In spite of its deceiving outward appearance, it has somewhat the style of a country house inside. Warming touches include the Bavarian antiques occasionally used. All the well-furnished rooms have baths, costing from 95 DM ($31.35) in a single, from 120 DM ($39.60) to 155 DM ($51.15) in a double, including a continental breakfast. The underground is just 500 yards away, and a garage nearby costs only 10 DM ($3.30) to lodge your car for the night. The manager is most helpful.

The Consul, 10 Viktoriastrasse (tel. 33-40-35), is a bright, welcoming hotel whose innkeeper has employed a particularly fine staff. The public areas have nice, warming touches such as Oriental carpets and "comfy" chairs, and the bedrooms often have little sitting areas. Decorative accessories help avoid the impersonal look. The hotel has a bar and a cozy little breakfast room. To save marks, you can ask for a single without shower for 110 DM ($36.30), the price rising to 170 DM ($56.10) should you want a private shower. Doubles contain private showers and rent for 120 DM ($39.60), the cost rising to 170 DM ($56.10) with complete bath and a phone thrown in. These tariffs include a continental breakfast.

Tourotel, 26 Domagkstrasse (tel. 36-00-10), in north Munich, is slightly outside the Schwabing district, close to the Olympic stadium. The nearby Mittlerer Ring makes it quick and easy to reach the airport and the motorway. The hotel is big, 230 well-furnished rooms in all, and each has a full private bath, phone, color TV, mini-bar, and radio. A single ranges from 109 DM ($35.97 to 129 DM ($42.57), and a twin rents for 140 DM ($46.20) to 160 DM ($52.80), including a buffet breakfast, service, and taxes. As an added attraction, the hotel has plenty of health facilities, including an indoor swimming pool and sauna. There's also a garage as well as outdoor parking. Bavarian food and Munich beer are served in the Schmankerin restaurant, along with international dishes. All day long you can order snacks or full meals in their own Wienerwald.

Leopold, 119 Leopoldstrasse (tel. 36-70-61), is a unique hotel in Schwabing, run by the Kiefer family. A 1924 villa, it offers a modern annex behind its garden, connected by a glassed-in passageway. Passing the hotel is the exit road of the superhighway Nürnberg–Würzberg–Berlin. Think of the Leopold as a kind of motel, with plentiful parking. Two subway stations are 250 yards from the hotel; a bus and tram stop is in front of the door, taking you into the center in about ten minutes. Finally, the English Garden is only a few minutes away by foot. Most of the public rooms are furnished in a Bavarian style, with wooden wing chairs and pine dado. The bedrooms are nicely designed, many with built-in beds, end tables, and all with armchairs or sofas. Bathless doubles are 140 DM ($46.20), 170 DM ($56.10) with private bath. Bathless singles go for 110 DM ($36.30) peaking at 145 DM ($47.85) with bath, breakfast included. Whether in the old or new wing (which has an elevator), you'll have a telephone and double-soundproofed doors.

Hotel Gebhardt, 38 Goethestrasse (tel. 53-94-46), lies only three minutes from the main rail station, right in the center of town. Frau Gebhardt, the warm, friendly owner, is helpful to her guests. Her rooms are pleasantly and attractively furnished, usually in autumnal colors. In a bathless single the rate is 60 DM ($19.80), rising to 80 DM ($26.40) with shower. Bathless doubles cost 88 DM ($29.04), but 110 DM ($36.30) with shower. Some units, ideal for families, are rented as triples and quadruples.

AT OLYMPIA PARK: Olympiapark Hotel, 12 Helene-Mayer-Ring (tel. 351-60-71), stands right at Europe's biggest sports and recreation center. The hotel is near the stadium, which is the site of so many major sports events. For those fitness-minded souls who want to be near all the action, the Olympiapark Hotel is very appealing. Its rooms are among the most modern and well kept in the city, and sports heroes, both European and American, casually stroll through the lobby. They are housed in one of 200 beds, which rent for 120 DM ($39.60) to 150 DM ($49.50) in a single, from 150 DM ($49.50) to 190 DM ($62.70) in a double. These units contain complete bath, color TV, and toilet, and a breakfast buffet is included in the tariffs. There's also plenty of free parking, and there's no need to drive into the city center. The U-bahn will whisk you there in minutes. The airport is about 20 minutes away, maybe more, depending on traffic conditions. If you want to unwind after a tough night in the beer houses, you'll find a refreshing swimming pool, sauna, and massage room.

A BAVARIAN INN ON THE OUTSKIRTS: Brauereigasthof Hotel Aying, 80-11 Aying bei München (tel. 08-09-5/705), is a country inn owned by the famous Aying Brewery. It's all hearts-and-flowers alpine. Everything is traditional, except for the excellent bathrooms and 20th-century comfort. The beds are as large as Ping-Pong tables, and the colors are coordinated. Large double accommodations rent for 180 DM ($59.40), including breakfast. Some smaller doubles are offered for 155 DM ($51.15).

The dining room pleases both the palate and the eye. On chilly days a fire burns in the fireplace, and soft candles light the meals. A well-cooked dinner might cost from 25 DM ($8.25) to 65 DM ($21.45), including a simple but pure consommé, grilled veal steak with potatoes, a seasonal green salad with fresh lemon dressing, and a goodly amount of beer, followed by apple pie.

Directions: Take the autobahn toward Salzburg, leaving it at the second exit. Aying is about 18 miles from the center of Munich.

2. Restaurants

It is said that the good people of Munich consume more beer and food than the people in any other city of Germany. If the cuisine isn't exactly delicate, it's certainly plentiful, and if you haven't already noticed, every housewife here seems destined to give her husband a bulging waistline before he's 30. So if you like food, and plenty of it, you've come to the right city.

In many restaurants, especially the beer halls, you'll find that the gemütlich atmosphere prevails until the early hours of the morning. Stamina is needed if you're going to live life as the natives do. Bernd Boehle once wrote: "If a man really belongs to Munich he drinks beer at all times of the day, at breakfast, at midday, at teatime; and in the evening, of course, he just never stops."

Some of the local fare may frighten the timid: minced liver, dumplings, "spleen" wurst, calf feet, pig trotters, and pork and liver "cheese." But if your palate requires careful attention, you needn't fear. Many of the restaurants of Munich, admittedly the upper-bracket ones, feature an international cuisine, with emphasis on French dishes. A number of specialty restaurants exist. The most classic dish of Munich, however, is "weisswürste." These are herb-flavored white veal sausages that have been blanched in water. Traditionally, they are consumed early in the morning.

Munich is definitely the place to practice *Edelfresswelle* ("high-class gluttony").

But our main interest is lunch and dinner, and here are the spots where you'll find the best meals for the best value in Munich:

THE TOP RESTAURANTS: Aubergine, 5 Maximilianplatz (tel. 59-81-71), is discreet and distinguished, a citadel of fine taste, good food, impeccable service, and lethal tariffs. It's chic, elegant, and fashionable. The owner-chef, Austria-born Eckart Witzigmann, has studied with the famous Paul Bocuse of Lyon, France. His cuisine is a mixture of classic dishes along with some nouvelle cuisine offerings. At lunch you can order a set menu for 105 DM ($34.65), although the cost of the table d'hôte dinner rises to 165 DM ($54.45).

One food expert has divided West Germany's gastronomic history into two parts—"before Witzigmann and after." The extraordinary chef has been called a "culinary messiah." There are many experts who consider the Aubergine the finest restaurant in West Germany today. The great chef told Craig Claiborne of the *New York Times* that "the important things are slow cooking and patience and freshness of ingredients." Sometimes his guests at the Aubergine are very special indeed, as when he prepared a private banquet for King Carl XVI Gustaf of Sweden and his queen.

The set menu is almost invariably good, and it contains an array of widely varying specialties, including a sorbet served in between to clear your palate. Menus change every day, and can't be written until the owner returns from the market after having decided what was fresh and good that day. Fresh ingredients and top-quality produce are keys to the success of the Aubergine (eggplant).

You can also order à la carte, selecting such tempting treats as sole filet in a champagne sauce or crab salad with broccoli in vinaigrette. Many specialties are for two persons, such as venison with wild berries. Hours are noon to 2 p.m. and 7 to 11 p.m. It is closed on Sunday and usually for the first three weeks in August.

Tantris, 7 Johann-Fichte-Strasse (tel. 36-20-61), in Schwabing, serves some of the best food in Munich—and it's French. In an unlikely setting, near the Holiday Inn, the restaurant stands near an Esso gasoline station. But once you've gone down the street and inside the restaurant's doors, you're transported into an ultramodern atmosphere with fine service.

Incidentally, don't arrive without reservations, as many of the leading members of Munich's business colony like to entertain here, not only their families and friends, but foreign associates as well.

The food, as presented, is a treat to the eye as well as the palate. The soups are especially interesting. Among the main courses, I'd recommend the roast lamb with herbs. You also might enjoy suprême de turbot Marguery or a salmon soufflé. One way to dine here is to order a set menu which might include a mousseline de crab aux avocats, salmis de chevreuil aux girolles, and purée de persil, as well as sole à la sauce estragon, climaxed by sorbet de Johannisberg. The head chef is Heinz Winkler, who was the former sous chef for Eckart Witzigmann, now at his own Aubergine. Like Mr. Witzigmann, Mr. Winkler is Austrian, and he learned to cook outside of Germany, mainly in France. A seven-course menu which changes daily is offered for about 175 DM ($57.75). At noon, a table d'hôte consists of five courses for 100 DM ($33).

The choice of dishes is wisely limited, and everything is served and prepared with the utmost care. The cooking is both subtle and original, the beautiful interior adding to one's enjoyment.

Tantris is open from noon to 2:30 p.m. and 6:30 p.m. to midnight daily, except on Monday and Saturday when it only serves dinner.

Sabitzer, 21 Reitmorstrasse (tel. 29-85-84), ranks among the top three gourmet citadels of the city. Like Aubergine and Tantris, it is a devotee of the nouvelle cuisine with classical specialties as well. The Austrian head chef, Herwig Sabitzer, made his debut on the Munich restaurant scene in 1981, and within months he was the "talk of the town." The restaurant is in a baroque setting, with white stucco and furnishings from the era. Mr. Sabitzer is assisted by his wife, Dorothea. Together they offer seasonal specialties and only the freshest of products, based on the shopping of the day. The menu changes so frequently one hesitates to recomend a specific specialty. However, turbot is often cooked in paupiette and salmon in a saffron sauce. The restaurant is open from noon to 2 p.m. and 6:30 p.m. till 1 a.m. Warm food, however, is only available from noon to 2 p.m. and 6:30 to 11 p.m. The restaurant is closed on Saturday and Sunday. A fixed-price menu is likely to cost around 110 DM ($36.30).

Restaurant Le Gourmet, 46 Ligsalzstrasse (tel. 50-35-97), is an evening restaurant, open from 6 p.m. till 1:30 a.m., specializing in nouvelle cuisine. The decor is classical and elegant, with a tasteful and restful combination of burgundies and beiges below a white ceiling. Antiques are used profusely. The head chef and owner, Otto Kochs, is the motivating force behind the success of this place. He graciously circulates in the restaurant, attending to the well-being and desires of his guests.

I'd recommend the special 11-course "degustations-menu" at 170 DM ($56.10), if you have the appetite for it. Each course is light, and made all the more so when accompanied by French wine and champagne. Your meal might have such outstanding specialties as marinated loup de mer (sea bass) with pink peppercorns or filet of fresh salmon steamed in a tarragon broth. The least expensive dining tab here is likely to cost from 82 DM ($27.06), but chances are you'll spend far, far more, of course. Reservations are absolutely essential.

Walterspiel, 17 Maximilianstrasse, in the Hotel Vier Jahreszeiten (tel. 23-03-90), is named after two brothers who entertained and catered to the tastes of kings. The atmosphere is dignified and refined, the service extremely competent, and the food prepared along classic lines, although with many imaginatively original variations.

The cuisine is rich and filling, as you'll quickly realize merely by reading a list of the appetizers offered, including some of the following suggestions: homemade goose liver terrine, warmed pigeon breast with truffles and bean salad, lamb salad with thinly sliced raw beef filet, and green asparagus tips with smoked salmon in sorrel cream. Or as an alternative opening to a fine repast, you might try the scallop cream soup; consommé with spinach, sliced ham, and croutons; homemade noodles in cream sauce with fresh truffles; or soufflé of smoked salmon with morels.

For a main course, try, if featured, medallions of lamb with fresh herbs and assorted vegetables, venison suprême with roasted yellow mushrooms in a savory sauce, or veal sweetbreads with crayfish and artichokes in roquefort cream sauce.

Desserts include marinated fruits with poppy ice cream, chocolate mousse rendezvous, and a warm cherry soufflé. Lunch is served from noon to 3 p.m. and dinner from 6 p.m. to midnight, costing from 100 DM ($33) to 150 DM ($49.50).

Maximilianstuben, 27 Maximilianstrasse (tel. 22-90-44), serves elegant dishes in a traditional setting, as befits its location near the Vier Jahreszeiten Hotel. Behind filmy curtains, while seated at candlelit tables, you must make the difficult decision of what to order. The many offerings are all just so tantalizing, running the gamut of favorite international dishes with a decided French and Italian influence. A good beginning might be homemade pastries of fish, game, or poultry, but many patrons prefer noodles Alfredo, before going on to a fish or meat entree. Fresh Norwegian salmon in a tantalizing sauce is the chef's specialty, as is his sirloin steak bordelaise (a red-wine sauce). A rumtopf parfait with home-preserved fruit in rum is one of the best desserts. Everything is under the direction of Erich Bischof. Hours are daily except Saturday from noon to 3 p.m. and 6 p.m. to 1 a.m. Count on spending 40 DM ($13.20) to 100 DM ($33) for a meal here.

Käfer-Schänke, 1 Schumannstrasse (tel. 41-68-1), is famous for its cookery. You have to reserve if you want a seat here. It's crowded and popular, with good reason. In one room on the main floor is a deluxe gourmet shop. The decor suggests the home of a wealthy countryman, with a few farm-style antiques placed here and there. You select your own hors d'oeuvres, the most handsome and dazzling display in Munich, and are billed according to how many pâtés or croûtes you made off with. The main dishes are served by waiters. Often Käfer-Schänke features a week devoted to a particular country's cuisine. On my latest rounds it was France. I enjoyed the classic loup with fennel as it is presented on the French Riviera.

The salads here have what one reviewer called "rococo splendor." From a cold table, you can select such temptations as smoked salmon or smoked eel. Venison, quail, and guinea hen are regularly featured, as are quiches made of sweetbreads. You've surely had beef Wellington, but have you tried veal Wellington? And the wild duck in truffle sauce is definitely worth writing home about. Service is daily from 11:30 a.m. to midnight except Sunday. Menus begin at 35 DM ($11.55), going up to 55 DM ($18.15) or maybe a lot more.

Alois Dallmayr, 14 Dienerstrasse (tel. 21-35-100), is the Fauchon's of Munich, tracing its history back to 1700. Near the City Hall, it is perhaps the most famous delicatessen in Germany and actually is one of the most renowned in the world. After walking through it, looking at its tempting array of delicacies from all around the globe, you'll think you're lost in a millionaire's supermarket. Here you'll find the most elegant consumers in all of Munich, looking for that "tinned treasure," perhaps Scottish salmon, foie gras, English biscuits, wines and spirits, as well as fashionably out-of-season fresh produce.

It's possible to dine upstairs. The food is a subtle German version of the continental cuisine, owing a heavy influence to France. Dallmayr has been a purveyor to many of the royal courts, and the food array is dazzling, ranging from the best herring and sausages I've ever tasted, to such rare treats as perfectly vine-ripened tomatoes flown in from Morocco to papayas from Brazil. The famous French poulet de Bresse, believed by many gourmets to be the finest in the world, is also shipped in. The smoked fish such as eel is particularly outstanding. The soups are superb (especially one made with shrimp I recently ordered). Your bill is likely to be *anything* here, depending on your selection. Count on at least 18 DM ($5.94) for a light snack, 60 DM ($19.80) for a big meal. If you're dining alone, you might prefer to anchor at the counter instead of a table. The bustling restaurant is usually crowded at lunchtime. Hours Monday to Friday are 9 a.m. to midnight (on Saturday from 9 a.m. to 3 p.m.; closed Sunday).

Schwarzwälders Naturweinhaus, 8 Hartmannstrasse (tel. 22-72-16), is an Old Munich wine restaurant. Loyal habitués come here to order meals accompanied by fine German wines. From the moment you enter, the atmosphere evokes a warm and hospitable charm that sets the mood for a fine meal. You can select almost any wine you might desire from the extensive wine list. The menu is international, reflected in such main dishes as peppersteak with cognac, but in season game is the specialty, and it's prepared with flair by the chef. House specialties also include pikant hirschgoulash with noodles and berries. For dessert you might prefer the ice bombé moka and kirsch. Meals begin at 35 DM ($11.55) and can easily climb to 100 DM ($33). The restaurant is only a short walk from the Bayerischer Hof and American Express, both of which open onto the Promenadeplatz. Hours are daily from noon to 3 p.m. and from 6 p.m. to midnight.

Der Königshof, 25 Karlsplatz (am Stachus) (tel. 55-84-12). Münchners have become increasingly sophisticated in their taste for food, and the owners of this deluxe hotel, already surveyed, want Der Königshof to surface near the top in culinary delights. The Geisel family has made major renovations to the dining room, with its oyster-white panels of oak, bronze chandeliers gleamingly polished, silver candelabra, sandstone, and porcelain worthy of a country like Germany. The black-jacketed waiters in long white aprons are among the most polite and skilled in the city.

They wisely hired Wolfgang Abrell as chef, for he's one of the most inventive and creative in Germany today. His "culinary masterpieces" depend on his whim of the moment and, almost as important, upon what is available in season. Whenever possible, he likes extremely fresh ingredients, and the food here reflects his passion.

Perhaps you'll get to try his foie gras with sauterne, a lobster soufflé, loin of lamb with fine herbes, lobster with vanilla butter, or sea bass suprême. Meals begin at 50 DM ($16.50). If you go for the more expensive selections, your bill could easily climb up to 110 DM ($36.30). Hours are noon to 3 p.m. and 6:30 to 11:30 p.m.

Preysing-Keller, 6 Innere-Wiener-Strasse (tel. 48-10-15), in many ways was the highlight of my most recent swing through Munich. It's a "find," but you have to cross over the Isar to discover its superb cookery and wines. It's connected to the hotel which was already surveyed. Go only for dinner, served from 6 p.m. to 1 a.m., and be sure to make a reservation.

You dine in a 300-year-old cellar, with massive beams and high masonry arches over a modern tiled floor. The decor, other than architectural essentials, is simple, with wooden tables and chairs.

The head chef is Gottfried Lenz, and he's a good one. Under his direction, daily excursions to the market are made by the staff who are told to select only the freshest ingredients. The fish and seafood served here are stored in aquariums on the premises prior to cooking.

The goose-liver pâté is a specialty, as is lobster in butter sauce and a steak tartare of venison. Pigeons in basil sauce with lettuce might be on your menu, perhaps beef filet in beaujolais with artichoke hearts. In addition to a wise selection of original recipes, the chef also prepares old-fashioned Bavarian dishes as well. Meals begin at 40 DM ($13.20). A seven-course menu is offered for 110 DM ($36.30).

Bouillabaisse, 10 Falkenturmstrasse, in the Hotel An der Oper (tel. 29-79-09), is highly rated in local gourmet circles. The restaurant does beautiful food in a lovely setting near the Hofbräuhaus and across from Harry's Bar. The peppersteak is served Madagascar style here, but the chef's specialty is bouillabaisse, honoring the name of the restaurant. You can have a small plate as an appetizer or a large order. An unusual hors d'oeuvre for Munich is the specially prepared squid. The menu generally remains the same from day to day, and somehow the kitchen manages to secure some of the finest sole in Munich. The chef prepares the fish in several ways. Scampi is another specialty prepared in several different ways too, according to your choice. A more classic offering is the veal schnitzel Cordon Bleu. For dessert, I suggest the peach Melba. Meals begin at 40 DM ($13.20), averaging around 60 DM ($19.80). Hours are noon to 2:30 p.m. and 6 to 11:30 p.m. The restaurant is closed in August and on Sunday, plus Monday for lunch.

A. Boettner, 8 Theatinerstrasse, off the Marienplatz (tel. 22-12-10), is one of the choicest specialty restaurants in Munich. It's tiny and totally intimate, and at times everybody seems to know everybody else. Here you're assured of some of the most savory viands in Munich. You'll do well sticking to such international fare as saddle of venison and fried goose liver on green beans. Lobster is a specialty. For dessert, the chocolate mousse makes a particularly velvety choice. Menus begin at 50 DM ($16.50), going up to 115 DM ($37.95), and beyond that if you should go crazy with the caviar and the lobster. The restaurant is open from 11 a.m. to midnight Monday to Friday, 11 a.m. to 3 p.m. on Saturday; closed Sunday. The wine cellar is excellent, the relatively unadorned surroundings pleasant, and the service polite and skilled. For the discriminating gourmet only! Reservations are imperative.

BEST ALL-AROUND RESTAURANTS: Mövenpick Restaurant, im Künstlerhaus, 8 Lenbachplatz, (tel. 55-78-65). All the Swiss gastronomic know-how has been poured into this cluster of five different spots to dine in under one roof, making Mövenpick a success with Munich residents, whatever their budgets. The Mövenpick chain chose a historic building for its restaurants, in what used to be called "the house of the artists," where the literary elite would gather for coffee. Posted at the door is a menu bulletin for each of the restaurants, allowing you to select in advance. In summer the terrace, seating 250 patrons, is one of the most popular rendezvous places in Munich. Depending on which restaurant you select, meals can cost from 18 DM ($5.94) to 45 DM ($14.85).

The **Rob Roy** bar on the downstairs floor is dimly lit, with hanging mugs and plaid carpeting. The waiters serve authentic British ale in mugs. You can also get your favorite drink along with a Pickburger at 12 DM ($3.96), a toast Armstrong, or a wienerschnitzel.

Möpi Square is a nice outdoor section overlooking busy Lenbachplatz, where you can order a light lunch or a snack at any time. Try Salisbury steak. Baked potatoes are served with different sauces.

The palazzo-style **Venezia** is more suitable for quick lunches, with already-prepared main dishes, such as spaghetti Mexicaine or pork Waikiki. A specialty is shrimp Daniel.

At **Pastorale** on the second floor, excellent Swiss and international dishes are served. The salad buffet is self-service—as much as you like on your plate. A special dish, depending on seasonal marketing, is featured each week. The outstanding Züricher geschnetzeltes is a good choice, as is the entrecôte Züricher Art.

Finally, the **Long Horn Corner** features Angus steaks in a western ranch setting, replete with saddles, horns, stirrups, and cowhides. Specialties include fresh homemade goose liver, a tender roast, ribeye, lamb chops Bretagne, and scampi Montagnani.

THE FOREIGN COLONY: La Belle Époque, 29 Maximilianstrasse (tel. 29-33-11), rides the crest of the wave of the French food craze that long ago overtook Munich. Returning to the nostalgic style of the turn of the century, Hilmar Schweigart has a restaurant where the atmosphere is low-key, the cuisine first class, and the service deft and efficient. Hours are Monday to Sunday from 6 p.m. to midnight, and he's also open Monday to Friday for lunch from noon to 2 p.m. Every year he closes for the first two weeks in January and from around mid-August until the end of the month.

The menu changes daily, but a satisfactory table d'hôte is offered for 90 DM ($29.70). This is likely to include an appetizer, followed by a small soufflé, then a tiny dish or palate-cleansing sorbet au champagne, and then the main course, topped by a dessert, often delicate crêpes. A simplified menu, including, say, the pâté maison, a main course, followed by a sorbet or melon for dessert, is featured for 35 DM ($11.55). There is also a limited, but select, à la carte menu that might include gazpacho, sea bass, veal medallions, or peppersteak. Always call for a reservation.

El Toulà, 5 Sparkassenstrasse (tel. 29-28-69). Whenever you see this name, know that you will be in a showcase of the haute cuisine. This Munich restaurant is one of the finest links in a chain that stretches from Rome to Cortina to Sardinia. This place attracts some of the favorite flowers of the international set. The place itself is elegant, decorated somewhat in a turn-of-the-century style, with wickered bentwood and chairs, simple and warm. Featured prominently in the restaurant is a work of the well-known artist Dudovic, called *Woman with Hound.*

The menu in both German and Italian has many worthy selections. All pasta is homemade on the premises, and the fish and meat specialties use only the finest, freshest ingredients. The style of cookery ranges across Italy from the Piedmont to Lombardy, with a stopover in Venice. Care is taken with the vegetables as well, and desserts are luscious in the Italian tradition. Prices are also a bit luscious as well, as it costs from 50 DM ($16.50) to 70 DM ($23.10) or a lot more to dine here, which you can do from noon to 2:30 p.m. and 7 p.m. till 1 a.m. It's closed for lunch on Sunday and all day Monday (also closes down for the first three weeks in August).

Restaurant Tivoli, 52 Widenmayerstrasse (tel. 22-12-74), is one of the leading Italian restaurants of Munich. The cookery here is dependably enjoyable, and service is attentive and professional. It is open daily except Sunday from noon to 2 p.m. and 6:30 to 11 p.m. charging from 30 DM ($9.90) to 70 DM ($23.10) for a well-prepared meal. One part of the menu is devoted to the specials of the day, which might include such intriguing selections as asparagus prepared in the Milanese style or linguine as the Sicilians prefer it. On my recent visit I found the risotto alla milanese a delightful selection.

There is also a large à la carte menu with an intriguing selection of both hot and cold antipasti, ranging from the classic melon with prosciutto to spaghetti alla carbonara. Or you may prefer the soup of the Roman kitchen, stracciatella. Main courses are intriguing, again relying on such classic Italian standards as liver in the style of Venice and the famous veal-and-ham dish of Rome, saltimbocca all romana. In season they serve my favorite salad, radicchio, the red lettuce grown in Italy. Desserts include a velvety zabaglione al marsala, prepared for two persons.

Chesa Rüegg, 18 Wurzerstrasse (tel. 29-71-14), beside the Vier Jahreszeiten, has rough white plaster walls, a crude beamed ceiling, and a collection of large cow bells. Red-shaded kerosene lamps on the tables, plus vases of red roses and an overscale peppermill, further enhance the alpine-tavern theme. The star of this intimate dining theater is the Swiss chef. From start to finish, your meal is carefully planned and served. A meal here might consist of a rich-tasting soup, followed by crab with lobster sauce or perhaps a venison steak. A complete meal here could easily top 45 DM ($14.85). The restaurant is closed Saturday, Sunday, and holidays. Hours are noon to 3 p.m. and 6 p.m. to 1 a.m.

Goldene Stadt, 44 Oberanger (tel. 26-43-82). Come here for the finest Bohemian specialties in Bavaria. The setting is sedate, much like the ground floor of a town house. You're given a choice of three dining rooms (the central one is the most often reserved). Against a background of scenic etchings and a mural depicting scenes of Czechoslovakia, the savory cuisine from Germany's neighboring country is served. Beer is usually drunk with the meals, and the more you eat of the rock salt rolls, the more you'll want to drink. A friendly and gracious English-speaking host takes your order. Borscht is the classic beginning, but not the type you're served in New York. Bohemian specialties include roast goose and duckling. After dinner it's customary to order apricot brandy, served in a glass that looks like a bud vase. A complete meal will cost from 28 DM ($9.24) to 50 DM ($16.50) per person. Hours are 11:30 a.m. to 3 p.m. and 6 p.m to midnight. The restaurant is closed on Sunday.

At the **Csarda Piroschka,** 1 Prinzregentenstrasse (tel. 29-54-25), the Hungarian cuisine is absolutely first rate. The location is decidedly offbeat: occupying the ground floor of the Haus der Kunst art museum, a long taxi haul from the center. The service is as smooth as the food is good, while violin music and candlelight create a romantic ambience. The menu is placed before you by one of the most gracious proprietors in Munich who is the epitome of Hungarian charm. The house specialty, served to two persons only, is called Husarenspiess flambiert. Another good dish is the Hungarian farmer's steak. A fine beginning is the bohnensuppe (bean soup) jókai. A bottle of the Hungarian wine, Tokaji, rounds it out nicely. Count on spending 35 DM ($11.55) to 70 DM ($23.10) for a complete meal. The place is closed Sunday. Go in the evening from 6 p.m. to 1:30 a.m., and be sure to reserve a table in advance.

Ochs'n Willi, 54 Sendingerstrasse (tel. 26-58-43). Verna Richert of Morgan Hill, California, suggested I check out this place. She said she discovered it when "my stomach finally rebelled against sausages, Hungarian goulaschuppe, and wienerschnitzel. Under a ceiling of time-darkened beams, you get familiar Stateside fare. They'll even cook you up a "mess of spare ribs." Just like "back home," you can get steaks as you like them along with baked potatoes. Fresh salads are offered, along with homemade and tasty soups, topped off by creamy desserts—all for a cost of 40 DM ($13.20) and up for a good dinner.

BUDGET BAVARIAN RESTAURANTS: **Nürnberger am Dom,** 9 Frauenplatz (tel. 22-03-85), is the coziest and warmest of Munich's local restaurants. You sit in carved chairs that look as if they came from some little carver's shop in the Black Forest. Country-like tablecloths add to the regional atmosphere, and the collection of memorabilia is wide ranging, including, among other things, pictures, prints, pewter, and beer steins. Upstairs, reached through a hidden stairway, is a dining room devoted to Dürer. Open from 9 a.m. to midnight, the restaurant has a strict policy of shared tables. The homesick Nürnberger comes here for just one dish: Nürnberger stadtwurst mit kraut, those delectable little sausages. Other main dishes include steak tartare and a pork cutlet salad. A robust meal here will cost from 25 DM ($8.25) to 35 DM ($11.55). The service is on tin plates. A short walk from the Marienplatz, the restaurant faces the cathedral of Munich.

Weinstadl, 5 Burgstrasse (tel. 22-10-47), has been a wine house since 1850. Luckily, it survived World War II, and it is now reportedly the oldest house in Munich, tracing its history back to 1468. But it's no museum, even though first appearances would lead you to think so. Real old-world charm is to be found here: vaulted ceilings, coats-of-arms, a trompe l'oeil facade, and wrought-iron sconces. Dining is on three levels. Waitresses in regional dress hurry across the natural brick floor, serving up hearty Bavarian food at candlelit wooden tables. Especially hearty is the bean soup with ham. A typical main dish is pork cutlet with vegetable and salad. A typical dinner will cost from 18 DM ($5.94) to 38 DM ($12.54). Hours are 11 a.m. to midnight.

Restaurant zum Bürgerhaus, 1 Pettenkoferstrasse (tel. 59-79-09), dates from 1827 and has furnishings typical of that era. Little known to North American visitors, it has a loyal German patronage attracted to its good home-style cookery from the Bavarian region. There are about two dozen or so tables, but this place can really fill up, seating around 65 hungry diners who select one of the fixed-price menus, costing from 30 DM ($9.90) to 70 DM ($23.10), the latter too big for the average appetite. It is open daily from 10 a.m. to midnight but closed weekends and holidays.

Haxnbauer, 5 Münzstrasse, at Sparkassenstrasse (tel. 22-19-22), could get by on atmosphere alone. One of the most colorful and typical of all Bavarian restaurants in Munich, it offers the patron a choice of dining rooms. More than 100 years in the same family, it has a devoted following. Soups are rich tasting and hearty. A specialty is radi mit hausgeräuchertem schinken—razor-thin slices of ham with white radishes and chive bread, an excellent appetizer. Other specialties of the house are schweinhaxn and kalbshaxn (pork or veal shank), priced according to weight. You can also order truthahnhaxn or turkey shank. Both are spit roasted, the skin cooked a crusty brown. The meat or poultry is guaranteed fresh, as the restaurant has its own butcher. For dessert, the chef's pride is apfelkucherl flambé. You can easily spend 25 DM ($8.25) to 45 DM ($14.85) here for complete meal, served until midnight.

Spatenhaus, 12 Residenzstrasse (tel. 22-78-41), is one of the best known beer restaurants in Munich. Its wide windows overlook the Opera House on Max-Joseph-Platz. Of course, to be loyal, you'll accompany your meal with the restaurant's own beer, called Spaten-Franziskaner-Bier. You can choose to sit in the intimate, cozy semiprivate dining nooks or at a big table in the beer-garden-like atmosphere. The Spatenhaus has old traditions, offering typical Bavarian food. It is known for its generous portions and reasonable prices. The cost range is from 25 DM ($8.25) to 50 DM ($16.50).

Donisl, 1 Weinstrasse (tel. 22-01-84), is reputedly the oldest beer hall in Munich, dating from 1715 and now run by Toni Gartner. Some readers praise this typical Munich "lokal" full of getmütlichkeit; others prefer newer and more hygienic retreats. In summer you can eat and drink in front of the Donisl, enjoying the hum and bustle of the Marienplatz. The beer hall also has a large interior courtyard with a gallery, offering a view of the spires of Munich's cathedral. English is spoken, and the menu is changed daily. But you can always count on certain fare to be available. Specialties include weisswürste, the delectable little white sausages served here that have been a tradition of this place for decades. Others order the Bavarian meat loaf (leberkäs) and fried sausages, all from their own butcher. Waiters and waitresses in original Bavarian costumes bring out dumplings as big as baseballs. Select beers from the Hacker-Pschorr Brewery in Munich are served. The walls are hung with pictures by well-known artists. Some depict roly-poly Bavarians, not unlike some of the present clientele. An average meal will cost from 25 DM ($8.25). In the morning a genuine Bavarian yodeler will sing for your entertainment, and music is also offered by a zither player or an accordionist. The Donisl is open daily from 8 a.m. to 1 a.m., and hot meals are served at all times.

Badische Weinstuben, 5 Marsstrasse (tel. 59-83-94), in the Württemberger Hof Hotel, two blocks from the railroad station, is nicely decorated with old-style prints on crude white walls. Small wooden tables with chairs and benches covered with fabric give a warm ambience. The fare is country Bavarian—blood sausages, dumpling soup, and the like—as well as international menus. The wine carte offers a choice of 60 sorts of wine from Baden. Meals begin at 25 DM ($8.25).

St. Georg Weinhaus, Prinzregentenplatz (tel. 47-30-38). Here you dine under the massive beams of a 500-year-old farmhouse, in one of five vaulted cellar rooms in the Upper Bavarian style. As you enter, a bar is on the left. To the right are candlelit tables with colorful napkins. The restaurant is owned by a former wine merchant, Herr Hummert, who stocks the finest Rhine, Franconia, and Mosel bottles. This family-run winehouse has been going for more than a quarter of a century, and is noted for its simple yet tasty dishes. Try the lentil soup with bacon. Set dinners range in price from 9 DM ($2.97) to 25 DM ($8.25). It's open daily from 7 p.m.

Ratskeller, im Rathaus, Marienplatz (tel. 22-03-13). Many visitors discover the tradition of the German "ratskeller" in Munich. Throughout Germany you'll find these customary cellar restaurants in the basements of town halls, serving inexpensive good food and wine. Although not as celebrated as some of its sisters (the one at Bremen, for example), the Munich Ratskeller holds its own. Bavarian background music adds to the ambience. The decor is much what you'd expect, with lots of dark wood and carved chairs. The most interesting tables, and the ones staked out first by the in-the-know locals, are at the rear, resting under vaulted, painted ceilings. One mural depicts a Bavarian choking a dragon to make the monster swallow poison. The ideal table is a cozy, semiprivate dining nook in the rear. A large wine vat suggests that Bavarians don't drink only beer.

The menu is a showcase of regional fare, but it also includes some international dishes. A freshly made soup of the day is always featured, and you can help yourself from the salad bar. Specialties include ragoût of venison in red wine, served with juniper berries, and a sausageplatter, with four homemade broiled sausages of beef, veal, and pork, served with mashed potatoes and sauerkraut. Good desserts are the chocolate Bavarian cream tart and the Black Forest tart. The chef has prepared an English menu especially for North American guests offering typical German dishes. Complete dinners cost from 15 DM ($4.95) and include soup or dessert and a choice of four typical meals. The waiters are helpful, and most of them speak English. Ice water is served at the beginning of your meal—unusual in Europe unless specifically requested.

Weinhaus Neuner, 8 Herzogspitalstrasse (tel. 260-39-54), is an "Altestes Weinhaus Münchens," where the food is good and the setting mellow. Between the Karlsplatz (Stachus) and Marienplatz, the wine house has been such since 1852, but originally it was the site of a Jesuit monastery. Two large dining rooms, paneled in wood, suggest an old Tyrolean atmosphere. The wine list is quite good, but many diners tenaciously stick to their favorite beer. A traditional beginning for a meal is the goulaschsuppe. The chef specializes in steaks, juicy and tender. Each day a different specialty is offered, including Irish stew on my most recent visit. A meal begins at 30 DM ($9.90).

DINING IN SCHWABING: This district of Munich, which back in the stone age used to be called "Bohemian," overflows with restaurants, many of them cheap, attracting a youthful patronage. It has a few exceptional choices, which we'll dine at, should you decide to make the most recommended trek up here. Nighttime is more fun.

La Mer, 24 Schraudolphstrasse (tel. 272-24-39), deserves its well-earned reputation. A French restaurant, it offers only the freshest of fish and seafood, as its name would suggest. It's very expensive, a set daily menu costing from 95 DM ($31.35) per person. You can also order à la carte a meal costing from 50 DM ($16.50). Go only for dinner from 7 to 11:30 p.m. except on Sunday and Monday. La Mer attracts *tout München*.

A decorator went wild here, with gilt mirrors, crystal chandeliers, candelabra, flowers, ceramics—no surface untouched by adornment. Gilt on the lily never bothered him. If you can take your eye off the trappings long enough to order, you'll find a truly superb cuisine (my sole was perfect, for example). Obviously, the menu must be composed of what the catch was that day. Specialties are turbot in champagne and duck liver mousse. A *menu dégustation* is a regular feature of the place. Service and reception are first class. The restaurant closes from the middle of July until the middle of August, and also shuts down for one week at Christmas.

Walliser Stuben, 33 Leopoldstrasse (tel. 34-80-00), is like a Hollywood version of a Swiss tavern. Because of its skill with the Helvetian cuisine, it attracts many visitors to Schwabing. It not only serves some of the best food in the area, but is one of the leading Swiss-style restaurants in Germany. The atmosphere is an inviting one, with an open fireplace, lots of copper pans about, and carved wooden chairs. But the master chef, Adi Holzmuller, doesn't just rely on these old-world touches. Rather, he enchants his patrons with such classic dishes as fondue bourguignonne. Very popular and very good are the flambé desserts. The price of an average meal will range from 30 DM ($9.90) to 65 DM ($21.45). The Swiss House in Schwabing is closed on Sunday but open otherwise from 5 p.m. to 1 a.m.

Bistro Terrine, 89 Amalienstrasse (tel. 28-17-80), has an inviting outdoor terrace where you might like to sit in warm weather. Locals, however, request a freshly set table in the art nouveau interior, even in summer. This is a warmly decorated, popular bistro where small tables are set between high-ceilinged walls festooned with old mirrors, hanging tassel-bottomed lamps, and cozy, turn-of-the-century bric-a-brac. Yves Decker, the chef, turns the freshest possible ingredients into nouvelle cuisine concoctions. Menu items vary, but they might include a soufflé of dorade with pike mousse in a saffron-flavored sauce made from fresh mussels. A main course may sate your hunger without benefit of an appetizer, but few guests are able to resist one of the tempting light desserts, such as rhubarb and ginger ale soufflé. A fixed-price noon meal, costing around 28 DM ($9.24), represents good value. An à la carte dinner is likely to cost from 65 DM ($21.45). Lunch is served from noon to 2:30 p.m. and dinner from 6:30 p.m. to 1 a.m., to accommodate the after-theater crowd. The bistro is closed Saturday at lunch and all day Sunday and Monday.

Weinbauer, 5 Fendstrasse (tel. 39-81-55), off Leopoldstrasse, is one of the most preferred budget favorites in the area. It's a rather small gaststätte full of students and smoke. No bright accessories are found here, just wood tables and passable food, and plenty of it. To keep costs trimmed, order from one of the daily menus, costing from 8.50 DM ($2.81) to 15 DM ($4.95). The restaurant is closed on Wednesday.

THE BEER GARDENS: If you're in Munich anytime between the first sunny spring day and the last fading light of a Bavarian-style Indian summer in autumn, head for one of the city's celebrated beer gardens *(biergarten)*. These so-called gardens are opposed to the beer halls explored in the nightlife section. Hopefully, you will have learned the words to the famous German drinking song, "Ein Prosit," before heading to one. These beer gardens are literally "soaked with suds" throughout the long Bavarian summer.

It is estimated that today Munich has at least 400 beer gardens and cellars. My favorite one, however, is in the capital's best known park, the English Garden *(Englischer Garten)*, that pleasure garden on the northeast fringe of Munich's center, lying between the Isar River and Munich's Greenwich Village district of Schwabing.

The park, the largest city-owned park in Europe, has several beer gardens, of which the **Chinesischer Turm** (tel. 39-50-28) is preferred. It takes its name from its location at the foot of a pagoda-like Chinese tower, a landmark that is easy to find.

Traditionally, a beer garden had to have tables placed under chestnut trees. That comes from an old tradition of planting chestnuts above the storage cellars to keep the beer cool in summer. People, naturally, started to drink close to the source of their pleasure, and the tradition has remained. The lids on the beer, incidentally, originally stemmed from an attempt to keep the flies out. Beer and Bavarian food, and plenty of it, is what you get here. A large glass or mug of beer (ask for *eine Mass Bier)*, enough to bathe in, costs 7 DM ($2.31). It will likely be slammed down still foaming from a big Brunhilde who is carrying 12 other tall steins as well. Food is very cheap too, a simple meal costing around 15 DM ($4.95). Homemade noodles are often a specialty, as are all kinds of tasty sausages. Oom-pah bands often play, and it's most festive.

Sometimes you can get a first-rate schweinbraten, which is Bavaria's answer to the better known sauerbraten of the north (a braised loin of pork served with a bread dumpling and rich, brown gravy). Leberknödl is classic, served in a broth with fresh chives. Huge baskets of pumpernickel are passed around, and the bread is sometimes eaten with radi, a large, tasty white radish famous in these parts.

Space is too tight to allow me to document and describe too many beer gardens of Munich. However, I'll cite a few more favorites. Know that the food and drink and the atmosphere all have much in common; likewise the price structure is about the same.

If you're going to the zoo, which I'll recommend later, you might want to stop over for fun and food at the **Gaststätte zum Flaucher,** 1 Isarauen (tel. 72-32-677), which is close by. Gaststätte tells you that it's a typical Bavarian inn. This one is mellow and traditional, with tables set out in a tree-shaded garden overlooking the river. Here you can order that local specialty, Leberkäse, which many foreigners mistakenly think is "liver cheese." It's neither—rather, a large loaf of sausage eaten with black bread and plenty of mustard, a deli-delight.

If you're motoring, you might visit a hunting lodge that was once owned by the kings of Bavaria. It's **Zum Aumeister,** 1 Sondermeierstrasse (tel. 32-52-24), which lies off the Frankfurter Ring at Munich-Freimann. It offers a daily list of seasonal specialties, and you might end up with cream of cauliflower soup or perhaps a rich oxtail. Meals cost from 25 DM ($8.25).

Another one to try is **Hirschgarten,** 1 Hirschgarten (tel. 17-25-91), in the Nymphenburg Park sector of the city, near one of Munich's leading sightseeing attractions, Schloss Nymphenburg, west of the heart of the town. It is part of a nearly 500-acre park with hunting lodges and lakes. Try to go here on any day except Monday so you can visit the palace as well. This is the largest open-air restaurant in Munich, seating some 6500 beer drinkers and Bavarian merrymakers. To reach it, take the tram to Romanplatz or the S-Bahn to the Laim station.

AT OLYMPIC CITY: The **Olympia Tower** (tel. 308-10-39) offers a choice of dining experiences. You can either take your pie in the sky or ground your chicken at the base. The television tower is 950 feet in height, and it costs 3 DM (99¢) for adults, 1.50 DM (50¢) for children, to take the speediest elevator on the continent to its summit. Parking is 2 DM (66¢).

The most expensive dining spot in the tower is the **Tower Restaurant,** featuring a selection of international dishes. Food is served from 11 a.m. to 10:30 p.m., a complete meal costing from 35 DM ($11.55) to 50 DM ($16.50). While you're sampling your entrecôte, why not think about this important statistic: you're in the "tallest reinforced concrete structure in Western Europe." Before or after dinner you'll want to take in the view, including the alpine mountain chain. Four observation platforms look out over the Olympic grounds. The Tower Restaurant revolves around its axis at the rate of 36, 53, or 70 minutes, giving the guests who linger longer a changing vista of the entire Olympic grounds.

At the base of the tower is the **Am Olympiasee,** serving genuine Bavarian specialties. Favored items include half a roast chicken and hearty soups. Meals cost from 25 DM ($8.25). The decor is in a warm Bavarian motif.

On the observation deck is a cafeteria, serving low-cost snacks and würst (sausage) costing from 6 DM ($1.98) and washed down with draft beer.

THE CHAINS AND FAST FOOD: The **Wienerwalds,** a chain of restaurants, are the most popular in Germany. Adopting the romantic name of the Vienna Woods, these are stylized rustic restaurants, where a gemütlich atmosphere prevails. Even though they're busy and bustling, there are still many quiet corners for relaxed dining. Soups are regional and filling, and service is by dirndl-clad waitresses. Prices are standard in all the restaurants, 10 DM ($3.30) for a satisfying meal. The house specialty is half a chicken, but other main courses are offered. The most popular Wienerwald is at 44 Leopoldstrasse in Schwabing, but there are others at 12 Karlsplatz, 6 Odeonsplatz, and 23 Amalienstrasse. Their main phone number is 5-79-61.

Tchibo or **Frielo** coffee stores are found throughout Munich. You can only drink coffee at .90 DM (30¢) a cup, and eat pastries at 2 DM ($66¢) and up, at most of them, but there is one restaurant. It's the **Tchibo-Höflinger,** 85 Schleissheimerstrasse (tel. 56-73-59), and it's a bargain. Ordering from the daily menu, you can eat here for a total cost of 15 DM ($4.95). They feature a soup as a beginning course, followed by a main dish of either fish or meat, served with vegetables, a salad, and dessert. The decoration is rather appealing, with large tables and leather benches. A lamp hanging over each table provides bright light.

McDonald's, 26 Martin-Luther-Strasse (tel. 39-81-55). Actually it seems quite authentic. It even looks like this popular chain back in the States. Naturally, you can get a hamburger here, a Big Mac German style, and of course mama's own apple pie. For 15 DM ($4.95) you should be able to order a light meal.

In most department stores in German cities, you have two choices for eating—top-floor restaurants with scenic views or stand-up counters in the basement. The prices are widely varied. The two leading candidates in Munich are

Herties Department Store (tel. 55-79-46), across from the railroad station, and **Kaufhof Department Store,** at Karlsplatz (tel. 55-84-01). They all have good, filling soups and bratwurst, along with main-course selections such as pork cutlets and half a roast chicken. Nearly all of them have creamy desserts. If you eat downstairs, you can compose a simple meal for about 13 DM ($4.29), but it will cost twice as much upstairs where the food and view are much better.

CAFÉS AND PASTRIES: About 10:30 a.m. or before (to make sure you have a good seat), head for the **Café Glockenspiel,** 28 Marienplatz (26-42-56), right in the heart of Munich. There you'll have a good perch for watching the miniature tournament staged each day by the little enameled copper figures on the Rathaus (Town Hall) facade. In addition to its view, the café has good coffee and pastries, which cost from 3.50 DM ($1.16).

The **Luitpold,** 11 Brienner Strasse (tel. 29-28-65), doesn't have the heartbeat position of the Café Glockenspiel, yet it's even better known. Before the war it attracted such notables as Emil Jannings of *The Blue Angel* and great musicians, authors, artists, and the literati. A string orchestra performed, in fact. Destroyed by the bombs that rained down on Munich, the café has long been rebuilt, with sidewalk tables and a grill room turning out tasty specialties. It's a favorite rendezvous point with Münchners, who enjoy its whipped-cream-laden pastries, costing from 4 DM ($1.32). Coffee goes for around 3 DM (99¢).

3. Sights

Munich is stocked with so many treasures and sights, the visitor who plans to "do" the city in one or two days makes a mistake. Not only will such a person miss many of the highlights, but will also fail to grasp the spirit of Munich and to absorb fully its special flavor, unique among the cities of the world. But faced with an enormous list of important attractions and a time clock running out, the visitor may have to limit sightseeing to a few of the more vital attractions, especially in the area of museums and galleries, with which Munich is endowed. After a quick trip through the Old Town with its numerous sights, I'll survey the most important of Munich's museums and churches, and then add a few interesting excursions from the city.

THE OLD TOWN: Try to arrive at the **Marienplatz** before 11 a.m. This square, dedicated to the patron of the city, whose statue stands on a huge column in the center, is the heart of the Old Town. On its north side is the **New Town Hall,** built in 19th-century Gothic. At 11 a.m. each day the glockenspiel on the facade performs a miniature tournament, with little enameled copper figures moving in and out of the archways.

Since you're already at the Town Hall, you may wish to climb the 55 steps to the top of its tower (an elevator is available if you're conserving your energy) for a good overall view of the Old Town. To the south of the square you can see the oldest church in Munich, **St. Peter's.** To the north lies **Odeonsplatz,** Munich's most beautiful square, surrounded by the Royal Palace (Residenz) and the Theatinerkirche. Adjoining the Residenz is the restored National Theater, home of the acclaimed Bavarian State Opera.

Running westward from the Odeonsplatz is the wide shopping avenue, Briennerstrasse, leading to the **Königsplatz** (King's Square). Flanking this large Grecian square are three classical buildings constructed by Ludwig I—the Propyläen, the Glyptothek, and the Antikensammlungen. Returning to the Odeonsplatz, take the busy Ludwigstrasse north to the section of Munich known as **Schwabing**. This is the Greenwich Village, Latin Quarter, or Chelsea of Munich, proud of its artist and writer element, numbering among its own such literati as Ibsen and Rilke. Painters from all over Germany found their way here. In fact the "Blue Rider" group which so influenced abstract art in the early 20th century was originated here by Kandinsky, along with Marc and Klee. Today it still retains a frankly offbeat flavor, with racks of handmade jewelry for sale along the streets and sidewalk tables filled with young people from all over the world.

Bordering Schwabing on the east and extending almost to the Isar River is Munich's city park, the 18th-century **Englischer Garten** (English Garden), laid out by Sir Benjamin Thompson. Here you can wander for hours along the walks and among trees and flowers, even stopping for tea on the plaza near the Chinese pagoda.

MUSEUMS AND GALLERIES: Thus far, seeing Munich has been a walking experience, looking mainly at the outsides of buildings and admiring parks and squares which have been around for centuries. Now, to see some of its biggest attractions, we will have to go indoors to the museums and galleries where the city has preserved some of the finest and most varied collections of art found anywhere. If you have time to visit only one of these during your stay, it definitely should be:

Alte Pinakothek

Art lovers come to Munich just to gaze at the hundreds of famous works exhibited in this huge classicistic building at 27 Barerstrasse (tel. 23-80-52-16) (tram no. 18, U-Bahn no. 8, or bus no. 53). The nearly 900 paintings on display (many thousands more are gathering dust in the basement) represent the greatest European artists of the 14th through the 18th centuries. Begun as a small court collection of the royal Wittelsbach family in the early 1500s, the gallery is now the largest and most important in Germany. There are only two floors with exhibits, but the museum is immense, and I do not recommend that you try to cover all the galleries in one day. If you have only a few hours to spend here, however, some works definitely merit your time.

The landscape painter par excellence of the Danube school, Albrecht Altdorfer, is represented by no fewer than six monumental works.

The works of Albrecht Dürer include his greatest—and final—self-portrait (1500). Here the artist has portrayed himself with almost Christ-like solemnity. Also displayed is the last great painting of the artist, his two-paneled work, *The Four Apostles* (1526).

Several of the galleries in the main branch are given over to the works of the Dutch and Flemish masters. The *St. Columba Altarpiece* (1460–1462), by Roger van der Weyden, is one of the greatest of these, in size as well as importance. Measuring nearly ten feet across, this triptych is a triumph of van der Weyden's subtle linear style, and one of his last works (he died in 1464).

Several galleries display a number of works by three of the Dutch and Flemish masters, Rembrandt, Rubens, and van Dyck. Included are a series of religious panels painted by Rembrandt for Prince Frederick Hendrick of the Netherlands. A variety of French, Spanish, and Italian artists are displayed in both the larger galleries and the small rooms lining the outer wall. The Italian masters are well represented by Fra Filippo Lippi, Giotto, Botticelli, Raphael (his *Holy Family),* and Titian.

You'll also find a *Madonna* by Da Vinci, a famous self-portrait of the young

Rembrandt (1629), and a number of works by Lucas Cranach, one of Germany's Renaissance painters. Cranach's *Venus* is also displayed. Pieter Bruegel's *Land of Cockaigne,* where nothing has to be done and where food simply falls into one's mouth, is on view too. Bruegel has taken the popular subject of European folk literature and satirized it in this painting. Note the little egg on legs running up to be eaten, and the plucked and cooked chicken laying its neck on a plate. In the background you'll see a knight lying under a roof with his mouth open, waiting for the pies to slip off the eaves over his head.

Important works are always on display, but exhibits are changed in two rooms on the first floor. To save yourself a fruitless search for one work, you'd be wise to buy the 1.50-DM (50¢) map of the gallery which will guide you through the dozens of rooms. The museum is open daily from 9 a.m. to 4:30 p.m., with additional hours on Tuesday and Thursday evenings from 7 to 9 p.m. Closed Monday. Admission is 3.50 DM ($1.16); free on Sunday.

Neue Pinakothek

Neue Pinakothek offers a survey in the main of 19th-century art. Across the Theresienstrasse from the just-previewed Alte Pinakothek, the $44-million museum at 29 Barerstrasse (tel. 23-80-5195) was reconstructed after its destruction in World War II, reopening again in 1981. Closed Monday, it may be visited daily from 9 a.m. to 4:30 p.m. (on Tuesday it is also open in the evening from 7 to 9 p.m.). Admission is 3.50 DM ($1.16); free on Sunday.

Natural light from the ceilings helps illuminate the paintings in the galleries below. As a reflection of the times when Munich was one of the great centers of world art, the museum has a collection of art, notably German, that has been hailed by critics. You'll also find strong representation from the schools of England, Spain, and France as well.

You go from Gainsborough and Wilson to Goya and David, eventually "working your way" to Manet, van Gogh, and Monet. Among the more popular German artists represented is Wilhelm Leibl, and you should encounter a host of others whose art is less well known.

Placed throughout the gallery are sculptures, mainly in bronze, by German artists, with a Degas and Rodin here and there. I've enjoyed the French paintings that include several Cézannes, Corots, Gauguins, and Renoirs.

Deutsches Museum (German Museum)

On an island in the Isar River, the Deutsches Museum of science and technology (tel. 2-17-91) is a world unto itself, with five floors of exhibits, including the Zeiss Planetarium in the dome above the entrance hall. The exhibits consist of original pieces of historical apparatus and machinery, as well as scale working models and even complete reconstruction of workshops and mines.

The basement level of the museum is devoted to mineral resources and mining. Here you can see everything from a replica of an old Bavarian coal mine to exhibits of drilling equipment from 1844 to the present. On the floor above, working models show how the ore from metal and coal mines is converted into usable material.

One of the most popular exhibits is in the department of aeronautics and astronautics. Models of airships designed by Zeppelin and an 1895 glider help the visitor understand more about the development of aircraft and space material. Equally popular, but more complicated to the casual observer, are the departments of physics and chemistry (on the same level).

Besides the purely scientific departments, you can also visit rooms devoted to musical instruments, printing and writing, and an exhibit of old automobiles. Each exhibit is designed to be understood and appreciated by every visitor—

whether he or she is a scientist, a student, or simply a casual sightseer. The museum is open every day from 9 a.m. to 5 p.m. Admission is 5 DM ($1.65), 2 DM ($66¢) for students and children. Guided tours are available if ordered in advance. A restaurant is on the premises.

The Residenz

When a member of the royal Bavarian family said he was going to the castle, he could have meant any number of places, especially if he was Ludwig II. But if he said he was going home, it could only be the Residenz to which he referred. This enormous palace, with a history almost as long as that of the Wittelsbach family, was the official residence of the rulers of Bavaria from 1384 to 1918. Added to and rebuilt over the centuries, this complex of buildings is a conglomerate of various styles of art and architecture. Depending on the direction from which you approach the Residenz, your impression can be one of a German Renaissance hall (the western facade), a Palladian palace (on the north), or a Florentine Renaissance palace (on the south facing Max-Joseph-Platz).

The Residenz has been completely restored since its almost total destruction in World War II and now houses the Residenz Museum, a concert hall, the Cuvilliés Theatre, and the Residenz Treasury.

The **Residenz Museum** (tel. 22-46-41) takes up the whole southwestern section of the palace, some 100 rooms of art and furnishings collected by centuries of Wittelsbachs. To see the entire collection, you'll have to take two tours, one in the morning and the other in the afternoon. You may also visit the rooms on your own.

The Ancestors' Gallery is designed almost like a hall of mirrors with one important difference: where the mirrors would normally be, there are portraits of the members of the royal family, set into gilded, carved paneling. The largest room in the museum section of the palace is the Hall of Antiquities, possibly the finest example of interior Renaissance styling in Germany (outside of churches, that is). Frescoes seemingly adorn every inch of space on the walls and ceilings alike, painted by dozens of 16th- and 17th-century artists. The room is broken into sections by wall pillars and niches, each with its own bust of a Roman emperor or a Greek hero. The hall contains pieces of furniture dating from the 16th century as well, but the center of attraction is the two-story chimney-piece of red stucco-marble. Completed in 1600, it is adorned with Tuscan pillars and a large coat of arms of the dukes of Bavaria.

On the second floor of the palace, directly over the Hall of Antiquities, the museum has gathered its enormous collection of Far Eastern porcelain. Note also the fine assemblage of Oriental rugs in the long narrow Porcelain Gallery.

Many of the rooms have been organized as exhibit salons with glass cases and pedestals, and some have been furnished as they were when the palace was actually a residence. The best example is the Elector's bedroom on the second floor. Several tapestries adorn the walls, and the room is lit by carved and gilded sconces as well as by the massive cut-glass chandelier. The focal point is the ornate bed (1750) enclosed by a balustrade.

Entrance to the museum, open from 10 a.m. to 4:30 p.m. Tuesday through Saturday (on Sunday from 10 a.m. to 1 p.m.), costs 2.50 DM (83¢). You'll have to pay another 2.50 DM to visit the **Schatzkammer** (Treasure House) of the Residenz, open the same hours. If you've time to see only one item here, it should be the Renaissance statue of *St. George Slaying the Dragon* (16th century). The equestrian statue is made of gold, but you can barely see the precious metal for the thousands of diamonds, rubies, emeralds, sapphires, and semiprecious stones imbedded in it.

Room 4 is devoted to sacred objects, including several icons and numerous crucifixes, carved in ivory, ebony, or hammered in gold. The Wittelsbach equivalent to the Crown Jewels is in Room 5, with sceptres and royal orbs. The crown of the realm is also on display.

Both the Residenz Museum and the Treasury are entered from Max-Joseph-Platz on the south side of the palace. From the museum, for another 1.50 DM (50¢), you can visit the **Cuvilliés Theatre,** whose rococo tiers of boxes are supported by nymphs and angels. Directly over the huge center box, where the royal family sat, is a crest in white and gold topped by a jewel-bedecked crown of Bavaria held in place by a group of cherubs in flight. In summer this theater is the scene of frequent Mozart concerts.

Bavarian National Museum

King Maximilian II in 1855 began an ever-growing institution that today presents the largest and richest display of the artistic and historical riches of Bavaria. So rapidly has its collection grown in the past 100 years that the museum has had to move into larger quarters several times. Its current building, at 3 Prinzregentenstrasse (tel. 22-25-91), near the Haus der Kunst, contains three vast floors of sculpture, painting, folk art, ceramics, furniture, and textiles, as well as clocks and scientific instruments.

Entering the museum, turn to the right and go into the first large gallery (called the Wessobrunn Room). Devoted to early church art, from the 5th through the 13th centuries, this room holds some of the oldest and most valuable works. The desk case contains ancient and medieval ivories, including the so-called Munich ivory, from about A.D. 400. The carving shows the women weeping at the tomb of Christ while the resurrected Lord is gingerly stepping up the clouds and into heaven. The adjoining room is named for the stone figure of the *Virgin with the Rose Bush,* from Straubing (c. 1300). This is one of the few old Bavarian pieces of church art to be influenced by the spirit of mysticism.

The Riemenschneider Room (no. 16) is devoted almost entirely to a Gothic contemporary of Dürer. Characteristic of the sculptor's works is the natural, unpainted look of his carvings and statuary. Note especially the 12 apostles from the Marienkapelle in Würzburg (1510), St. Mary Magdalene, central group of the high altar in the parish church of Münnerstadt (1490–1492), and the figure of St. Sebastian (1490). Also on display, in Rooms 18 and 19, are famous collections of arms and armories from the 16th to the 18th centuries.

Other salons on the main floor are devoted to various periods of German and northern Italian art (which is closely tied to the cultural evolution of Bavaria). One gallery (no. 47) is occupied by scale models of important Bavarian towns as they looked in the 16th century.

The second floor contains a fine collection of stained and painted glass—an art in which medieval Germany excelled. Other rooms on this floor include historic glassware, Meissen porcelain, and ceramics. One of the novelty additions to the museum is the collection of antique clocks (Rooms 58 and 59), dating from as early as the 16th century.

In the east wing of the basement level are some Christmas Cribs, not only from Germany, but from Austria, Italy, Moravia, and Sicily as well. The variety of materials competes with the styles themselves—wood, amber, gold, terracotta, and even wax were used in making these nativity scenes. Also on this level is a display of Bavarian folk art, including many examples of woodcarving.

From April 1 to September 30 the Bavarian National Museum is open daily, except Monday, from 9:30 a.m. to 4:30 p.m. (from 10 a.m. to 4 p.m. on Sunday). Admission is 3 DM (99¢). Reductions are granted for children and students. It's free on Sunday. From October 1 to March 31, hours are Tuesday to Friday from 9 a.m. to 4 p.m. (on Saturday and Sunday from 10 a.m. to 4 p.m.).

Munich Antikensammlungen

After 100 years of floating from one museum to another, the Museum of Antiquities finally found a home in the 19th-century neoclassical hall on the south side of the Königsplatz, A no. 1 (tel. 59-83-59). The collection grew up around the vase collection of Ludwig I and the Royal Antiquarium, both of which were incorporated after World War I into a loosely defined group called the Museum Antiker Kleinkunst (Museum of Small Works of Ancient Art). Many of the pieces may be small in size, but never in value or artistic significance.

Entering the museum, you find yourself in the large central hall. On your left near the stairs you'll see a marble bust of King Ludwig I, who was responsible for the three classic buildings around the Grecian-style square. The five halls of the main floor house more than 650 Greek vases, collected from all parts of the Mediterranean. The pottery has been restored to a near-perfect condition, although most of it dates as far back as 500 B.C. The oldest piece is "the goddess from Aegina," dating from 3000 B.C. Technically not pottery, this pre-Mycenaean figure, carved from a mussel shell, is on display along with the Mycenaean pottery exhibits in Room I. The upper level of the Central Hall is devoted to large Greek vases discovered in Sicily and to the art of the Etruscans.

Returning to the Central Hall, take the stairs down to the lower level to see the collection of Greek, Roman, and Etruscan jewelry. Note the similarities of today's fashions in design. Included on this level as well are rooms devoted to ancient colored glass, Etruscan bronzes, and Greek terracottas.

The **Glyptothek,** 3 Königsplatz (tel. 28-61-00), is the ideal neighbor for the Museum of Antiquities. It supplements the pottery and smaller pieces of the main museum with an excellent collection of ancient Greek and Roman sculpture, e.g., the Archaic Kouroi. Included are the famous pediments from the temple of Aegina. Both the Glyptothek and the Antikensammlungen are open Tuesday through Sunday from 10 a.m. to 4:30 p.m. On Wednesday the Antikensammlungen and on Thursday the Glyptothek are open from noon to 8 p.m. A 4-DM ($1.32) ticket admits you to both. Students are admitted free, and everybody gets in free on Sunday.

Staatsgalerie Moderner Kunst

Munich's State Gallery of Modern Art, at 1 Prinzregentenstrasse, in the Haus der Kunst (tel. 29-27-10), is considered one of the dozen finest repositories of modern art in the world, everybody from Warhol to Picasso. The "House of Art," as it is known, is a complex of two galleries. The west wing of the building charges 3 DM (99¢) for admission (free on Sunday) and displays around 400 works of art, dating from the turn of the century to the 1980s. Naturally, the largest selection is devoted to German art. You'll see paintings by Klee, Marc, Kirchner (my favorite), and Beckmann. Italian art with such stars as Marino Marini, American abstract expressionism, and a host of celebrated artists, Bacon to Braque, de Chirico to Dali, Dubuffet to Giacometti, Matisse to Mondrian, round out the collection.

Picasso is especially honored, with 14 works, the earliest dating from 1903. You'll also see examples of Fauvism and surrealism.

Haus der Kunst in the east wing is entered separately and also requires a separate ticket, costing 5 DM ($1.65). It is devoted to changing exhibits. You never know what to expect, from displays of Nazi and Communist propaganda posters to American patriotic banners, or even covers from *Harper's*. The works of young artists are nearly always exhibited, and many of them can be purchased at moderate prices.

Opening times are Tuesday to Sunday from 9 a.m. to 4:30 p.m. and on Thursday from 7 to 9 p.m. It's closed on Monday and on all important holidays. The underground station to head for is Odeonplatz. Bus no. 53 or 55 will take you there from the main station. These buses stop right in front of the gallery.

Münchner Stadtmuseum (Municipal Museum)

Munich's Municipal Museum is to the city what the Bavarian National Museum is to the whole of the province. In what was once the armory building at 1 St. Jakobsplatz (tel. 233-23-70), its collections give you an insight into the history and daily lives of the people of this unique community. A wooden model shows how Munich looked in 1572. Special exhibitions about popular arts and traditions are frequently presented.

The extensive collection of furnishings is changed annually so that visitors will have a chance to see various periods from the vast storehouse.

The museum's main exhibit is its *Moorish Dancers* (Moriskentänzer) on the ground floor. These ten figures, each two feet high, carved in wood and painted in bright colors by Erasmus Grasser in 1480, are among the best examples of secular Gothic art in medieval Germany. In the large Gothic hall on the ground floor you can admire an important collection of armor and weapons from the 14th to the 18th centuries.

You are invited to the photo museum on the second floor. This department traces the early history of the camera technique, going back to 1733. Cabinet after cabinet of early cameras, many from about 1915, line the walls. Every day the film museum shows a film at 8 and again at 9 p.m. from its wide archives.

On the third floor is an array of puppets from around the world, but naturally the puppeteer's art in Munich gets star billing. The comical and grotesque figures include marionettes and hand puppets. Like a Lilliputian version of the world of the stage, the collection also includes detailed puppet theaters, miniature scenery, and one stage where visitors can practice puppeteering.

One salon is devoted to the replica of an old brewery, with effective models, vats, and other equipment. The adjacent room contrasts the modern technique of bottling, depicting with large photo murals and other exhibits, right down to the beer cans.

Some readers have found the collection on the fourth floor even more impressive. The display of musical instruments is one of the greatest of its kind in the world. For example, this historical collection shows examples of the harp and violin from earliest times. In addition, an ethnological collection displays instruments in use in Africa, Oceania, the Americas, the Orient, the Middle East, Byzantium, and Europe.

Enter the Municipal Museum through the main courtyard. It is open daily except Monday from 9 a.m. to 4:30 p.m. On Sunday it is open till 6 p.m. Admission is 3 DM (99¢) daily but free on Sunday and holidays.

Städtische Galerie

The ancient villa of Franz von Lenbach, this gallery exhibits works by that 19th-century artist (1836–1904). Entering the gold-colored mansion at 33 Luisenstrasse (tel. 52-10-41) through the gardens, you'll be greeted with a large collection of early works by Paul Klee (1879–1940)—mainly those predating World War I. There's also an outstanding representation of works by Kandinsky, leader of the "Blue Rider" movement in early 20th-century art. There are many other 19th-century paintings throughout the villa, along with a few works from the 15th through the 18th centuries. The enclosed patio is pleasant for a coffee break. The gallery is open daily, except Monday, from 10 a.m. to 6 p.m. Admission is 3 DM (99¢).

CHURCHES OF MUNICH: As Germany's largest Catholic city, Munich naturally contains a number of outstanding churches. For those interested in ecclesiastical art and architecture, I offer a trio of the finest.

Frauenkirche (Cathedral of Our Lady)

When the smoke cleared from the bombings of 1945, only a fragile shell remained of Munich's largest church. Workmen and architects who restored the 15th-century Gothic cathedral used whatever remains they could find in the rubble, supplementing it with several modern innovations. The overall effect of the rebuilt Frauenkirche is strikingly simple, yet dignified.

The twin towers (which remained intact), with their strangely un-Gothic onion-shaped domes, have been the city's landmark since 1525. However, the red-brick exterior of the cathedral proper has retained its Gothic appearance. Instead of the typical flying buttresses, the edifice is supported by huge props on the inside which separate the side chapels. The Gothic vaulting over the nave and chancel is borne by 22 simple octagonal pillars.

Entering the main doors at the west end of the cathedral, you first notice that there are no windows (they are actually hidden, except for the tall chancel window, by the enormous pillars). According to legend, the devil thought so too, and you can still see the strange foot-like mark called "the devil's step" in the entrance hall where he stamped in glee at the stupidity of the architect. As you enter the left aisle of the three-aisled nave, you'll see photographs showing the cathedral as it looked after it was destroyed in the air raids of World War II. Many of the works of art formerly housed in the church were safely put away at that time, and are displayed in the chapels along the nave and behind the chancel.

In the chapel directly behind the high altar is the most interesting painting in the cathedral: *The Protecting Cloak,* a 1510 work by Jan Polack, showing the Virgin holding out her majestic robes symbolically to shelter all of mankind. The collection of tiny figures beneath the cloak includes everyone from pope to peasants. At the entrance to the vestry, just to the left of the choir, is a huge painting of *The Ascension of the Virgin Mary* by Peter Candid. In the south chapel adjoining the Chapel of the Holy Sacrament is one of the modern works, *The Immaculate Virgin,* a graceful bronze statue (1959) hung over a simple altar.

The Baptistry, to the right of the choir, contains the cathedral's oldest work, a stone sculpture of the suffering Christ, dating from 1380.

Returning to the entrance via the south nave, you'll pass the mausoleum of Emperor Ludwig IV, built in 1622. The elaborately carved tomb is guarded at each corner by armored soldiers with banners of the realm. In the front stands a sculpted likeness of the emperor, sword in hand.

St. Peter's Church

Munich's oldest church (1180) has turned over a new leaf, and it's a gold one at that. The white and gray interior has been decorated with painted medallions of puce and lots of gilded baroque. It contains a series of murals by Johann Baptist Zimmermann, but nothing tops the attraction of the bizarre relic in the second chapel on the left: a gilt-covered and gem-studded skeleton staring at you with two false eyes in its head, which rests on a cushion. Jewels cover the mouth of rotten teeth, quite a contrast to the fresh roses usually kept in front of the black and silver coffin.

Near the Town Hall, St. Peter's, known locally as Old Peter, also has a high steeple, although you may be discouraged from going up it by the lack of an elevator. The colored circles on the lower platform will tell you whether the climb is worthwhile, however. If the circle is white, you can be assured of a spectacular view as far as the Alps.

Theatinerkirche

Named for a small group of Roman Catholic clergy (the Theatines) and not for the Residenz Theatre just across the Odeonsplatz, this church is the finest example of Italian baroque in Munich. Dedicated to the scholar-saint Cajetan, it was begun in the mid-17th century by two Italian architects, Barelli and Zucalli. It was completed in 1768 by the son of the dwarf court jester-cum-architect, François Cuvilliés. The facade and the interior are both studded with cherubs. Some of them are quite mischievous, especially the "Angel of Silence," which points the way to the interior with one hand while he holds the other to his lips to form an obvious "shh."

The arched ceiling of the nave is supported by fluted columns lining the center aisle. Above the transept dividing the nave from the choir, the ceiling breaks into an open dome with an ornate gallery decorated with large but graceful statues. Nothing seems to detract from the whiteness of the interior, except the dark wooden pews and the canopied pulpit.

ON THE OUTSKIRTS—SCHLOSS NYMPHENBURG: When the call of spring made city life unbearable, the Wittelsbachs would pack up their bags and head for their country house. But they were hardly getting away from it all. The summer residence at Nymphenburg was, if anything, a more complete, more sophisticated palace than the Residenz in Munich. Begun in the style of an Italian villa in 1664 by Elector Ferdinand Maria, Nymphenburg took more than 150 years and several architectural changes before it was completed in 1823. The final plan of the palace was due mainly to Elector Max Emanuel, who in 1702 decided to enlarge the villa by adding four large pavilions connected by arcaded passageways. Gradually, the French style took over, and today the facade is a subdued baroque.

The interior of the palace is less subtle, however. Upon entering the main building, you're in the Great Hall, decorated in rococo colors and stuccos. The frescoes by Zimmermann (1756) depict incidents from mythology, especially those dealing with Flora, goddess of the nymphs, for whom the palace was named. This hall was used for both banquet and concerts during the reign of Max Joseph III, elector during the mid-18th century. Concerts are still presented here in summer. The smaller rooms are devoted to tapestries, paintings, and period furniture.

From the main building, turn left and head for the arcaded gallery connecting the northern pavilions. The first room in the arcade is the Great Gallery of Beauties, painted for Elector Max Emanuel in 1710, containing portraits of five of the loveliest ladies in the court of Louis XIV. More provocative, however, is King Ludwig I's Gallery of Beauties in the south pavilion (the apartments of Queen Caroline). Ludwig commissioned no fewer than 36 portraits of the most beautiful women of his day. The paintings by J. Stieler (painted from 1827 to 1850) include the *Schöne Münchnerin* (lovely Munich girl), and the dancer Lola Montez, whose "friendship" with Ludwig I caused such a scandal that she was considered a factor in the Revolution of 1848, which resulted in the abdication of the king.

To the south of the palace buildings, in the rectangular block of low structures that once housed the court stables, is the **Marstallmuseum,** containing carriages, coaches, sleighs, and riding accessories from the 18th and 19th centuries. As soon as you enter the first hall, look for the Coronation Coach of Elector Karl Albrecht. Built in Paris in 1740, this so-called glass coach is ornamented with everything from acanthus leaves to dolphins. The few flat panels on the side of the coach are filled with oil paintings of Justitia, Bellona, and Ecclesia. From the same period is the hunting sleigh of Electress Amalia, with the statue of Diana, goddess of the hunt. Even the runners of the sleigh are decorated with shellwork and hunting trophies.

The coaches and sleighs of Ludwig II are displayed in the third hall. In keeping with his constant longing for the grandeur of the past, his State Coach was ornately designed for his marriage to Duchess Sophie of Bavaria, a royal wedding that never came off. The fairytale coach wasn't wasted, however, since Ludwig often rode off to one of his many castles in it, creating quite a picture through the countryside. The coach is completely gilded, inside and out. Rococo carvings cover every inch of space except for the panels, faced with paintings on copper of the French Louis XV period. In winter the king would use his State Sleigh, nearly as elaborate as the Cinderella Coach.

Returning outdoors, you find Nymphenburg's greatest attraction, the park. Stretching for 500 acres in front of the palace, it is divided into two sections by the canal that runs from the pool at the foot of the staircase to the cascade at the far end of the gardens. From the palace steps, you can see the formal design of the gardens, laid out in an English style, with lakes, greenery, and beds of flowers.

Within the park are several pavilions. On the guided tour, you begin with **Amalienburg,** whose plain exterior belies the rococo decoration inside. Built as a hunting lodge for Electress Amalia (1734), the pavilion carries the hunting theme through the first few rooms and then bursts into salons of flamboyant colors, rich carvings, and wall paintings. The most impressive room is the "Hall of Mirrors," a symphony of silver ornaments on a faintly blue ground.

The **Badenburg Pavilion** sits at the edge of the large lake of the same name. As its name implies, it was built as a bathing pavilion, although it's difficult to visualize little Ludwig dashing in from the water with swimming suit dripping on those elegant floors. A trip to the basement, however, will help you appreciate the pavilion's practical side. Here you'll see the unique bath, surrounded by blue and white Dutch tiles. The ceiling is painted with several frescoes of bathing scenes from mythology.

The **Pagodenburg,** on the smaller lake on the opposite side of the canal, is octagonal and looks little like a Chinese pagoda from the outside. The interior, however, is decorated with pseudo-Chinese motifs, often using Dutch tiles in place of the Oriental ones.

The **Magdalenenklause** may look like a ruin, but it was intended that way when it was built in 1725. Also called the Hermitage, it was planned as a retreat for prayer and solitude. The four main rooms of the one-story structure are all paneled with uncarved, stained oak. All the furnishings are simple and the few paintings religious. It's really a drastic change from the frequent gaudiness of the other buildings.

You can park your car beside the main building and walk through the palace and gardens. Those arriving by tram (no. 17 or 21) can get off at Auffahrtsallee and go along the small canal to the palace. If you have the better part of a day, buy the 5-DM ($1.65) ticket to the palace, carriage museum, and the pavilions in the park. Otherwise, you can pay 3 DM (99¢) to be admitted to the three main attractions, including the castle, Marstallmuseum, and Amalienburg. Hours are generally the same for all sights except the Marstallmuseum. The palace and pavilions are open daily except Monday from 9 a.m. to 12:15 p.m. and 1 to 5 p.m. in summer; in winter, from 10 a.m. to 12:15 p.m. and 1 to 4 p.m. The Carriage Museum is open the same hours as those above in summer. The museum is closed on Monday. For information, call 1-20-81.

OTHER SIGHTS: The **Hellabrunn Zoo** or Munich Zoo, as Americans call it, stands in the Tierpark Hellabrunn entered from Siebenbrunnerstrasse (tel. 66-10-21), about four miles south of the Bavarian capital. It is one of the largest zoos in the world, and may be visited daily from 8 a.m. to 6 p.m. (off-season, from 9 a.m. until 5 p.m.), for an admission of 4.50 DM ($1.49) for adults and 2.50 DM (83¢) for children. To reach the park, you can take a bus leaving from Marienplatz, no. 52. Hundreds of animals roam in a natural habitat. A walk through the park is so attractive it's recommended even if you're not a zoo buff. The zoo also has a big children's zoo where your kids are allowed to pet the animals (the harmless ones, of course). There's also a large aviary whose inhabitants are allowed "free flight" (relatively speaking).

The **Viktualienmarkt,** right in the heart of Munich, is the Covent Garden of Bavaria. Since 1807 this has been the gathering place of Munich where citizens go not only to buy fruits and vegetables, but to gossip, browse, and snack as well. The location is off the Marienplatz, just around the corner of St. Peter's Church. Many of the vendors are old Bavarian farm women, selling their white asparagus and their fresh strawberries in season.

If you've got the munchies, this is the place to sample the wares, any day except Sunday. One stand will specialize in cactus, another in countless varieties of honey. Game birds and wild game are also displayed, sometimes rather unattractively so. Cheese shops abound. Try one of Munich's sour pickles or the famous weisswürst, with spicy, sweet mustard. Thick soups are also sold, along with liver dumplings and beer, lots of beer.

For a closer look at what has been called "the lifeblood of Munich," you can go on a tour of the **Spaten Brewery,** 46 Marsstrasse (tel. 51-22 for reservations). A guide who speaks English will take you on a 30- to 40-minute walk of the brewery, informing you of such astonishing statistics that the average Münchner polishes off about 450 pints of beer a year. Actually the city has five large working breweries where you can arrange tours, but surely one will be enough to satisfy your curiosity and/or thirst. The brewery still follows that "purity decree" issued by Duke Wilhelm IV in 1516, stating that beer could only be made from "barley, hops, and water." The man didn't mean additives!

EXCURSION TO DACHAU: In 1933 what had once been a quiet little artists' community just ten miles from Munich became a tragic symbol of the Nazi era. Himmler and the SS set up the first German concentration camp in March of that year, on the grounds of a former ammunition factory. Dachau saw countless prisoners arrive between 1933 and 1945. Although the files show a registry of more than 206,000, the exact number of people imprisoned here is unknown.

Entering the camp today, you are faced by three memorial chapels—Catholic, Protestant, and Jewish—built in the early 1960s. Immediately behind the Catholic chapel is the "Lagerstrasse," the main camp road lined with poplar trees, once flanked by the 30 barracks, each housing 208 prisoners who had to share two washrooms and lavatories. Two of these barracks have been rebuilt to give visitors an insight into the horrible conditions endured by the prisoners.

The museum is housed in the large building that once contained the kitchen, laundry, and shower baths where prisoners were often brought for torture by the SS. Photographs and documents show the rise of the Nazi regime, the super-power of the SS, as well as exhibits depicting the persecution of Jews and other prisoners. Every effort has been made to present the facts truthfully.

The tour of Dachau is heartbreaking, a truly moving experience. You can get to the camp by taking the frequent S-Bahn trains (train S-2) from Munich to the Dachau station for 6 DM ($1.98), and then bus 722 from the station to the camp. The entrance-free camp is open every day except Monday from 9 a.m. to 5 p.m. The English version of a documentary film, *KZ-Dachau,* is shown daily at 11:30 a.m. and 3:30 p.m. All documents are translated in the catalogue that is available at the entrance of the museum.

OLYMPIC CITY: The center of the Olympiads, site of the 1972 World Olympics, is a 740-acre plot of land at the northern edge of the city. More than 15,000 workers from 18 countries transformed the site into a park-like setting of nearly 5000 trees, 27 miles of roads, 32 bridges, and a lake.

Olympic City has its own railway station, subway line, mayor, post office, churches, even an elementary school. It broke the skyline of Munich by the addition of a 960-foot television tower in the center of the park.

The showpiece of the city is a huge stadium, capable of seating 80,000 spectators, and topped by the largest roof in the world—nearly 90,000 square yards of tinted acryl glass. The supports for the stadium are anchored by two huge blocks, each capable of resisting 4000 tons under stress. The roof serves the additional purposes of collecting rainwater and draining it into the nearby Olympic lake.

Nearly 5000 apartments and cottages were built on the grounds to house members of the Olympic staffs and teams. After the games were over, these were turned into modern housing projects for some 10,000 residents.

Smaller halls throughout the park are used for exhibitions and such competitive events as wrestling, judo, fencing, and weight lifting. The covered swimming stadium, with four large pools, is now a municipal enterprise open to the public.

4. Munich After Dark

Munich is a city with a lively and quite inexpensive nightlife. It won't take you long to realize that most of it centers around . . .

THE BEER HALLS: **Hofbräuhaus,** 9 Platzl (tel. 22-08-59), is a legend among beer halls, the most famous in the world. Visitors with only one night in Munich usually target the haus as their number one nighttime destination. Owned by the state, Hofbräuhaus was built in 1897 and restored by the government recently to the tune of $1.2 million. The first Hofbräuhaus grew up on this spot 175 years ago. Back in 1864 it attracted artists, students, civil servants, whatever. It was called the blue hall, because of its dim lights and smoky atmosphere. They were the mug-swinging clientele.

When it grew too small to contain everybody, architects designed another one in 1897. This was the one that was the 1920 setting for the first mass meeting of Hitler's newly launched party, the German Workers Party. Fistfights erupted as the Nazis battled their Bavarian enemies right in the beer palace.

Today that unhappy memory is gone, and 4000 beer drinkers can crowd in here on a given night. They eat about 10,000 meals a day, and consume nearly 3000 gallons of beer (as the traffic back and forth from the rest rooms clearly reveals).

There are several rooms spread over three floors, including one on the top floor for dancing on certain nights of the week. But with its brass band (which starts playing in the afternoon), the ground-floor Zur Schwemme is most typical of what you always expected of a beer hall—here it's the eternal Oktoberfest. At the second-floor restaurant, strolling musicians, including an accordion player and a violinist, entertain you. Waitresses in dirndls place mugs of beer at your table between sing-alongs. For a half liter, expect to pay 3 DM (99¢); meals are in the 10-DM ($3.30) to 25-DM ($8.25) range.

In season, from mid-March to the end of October, the Hofbräuhaus presents a typical Bavarian show in its fest-hall every evening, starting at 7 and lasting till midnight. The entrance fee is 5 DM ($1.65), and the food is the same as that served in the other parts of the beer palace. Beer here will be more expensive, costing around 7 DM ($2.31) for a half liter.

Augustinerbräu, 16 Neuhauserstrasse (tel. 260-41-06), stands on the principal pedestrian-only street of Munich, and is handy for many, as it offers generous helpings of food, good beer, and mellow atmosphere. Dark-wood panels and ceilings in carved plaster make the place look even older than it is. It's been around for less than a century, but beer was first brewed on this spot in 1328, or so the printed literature about the establishment claims. Waitresses in dirndls will hand you the menus, which change daily. The menu is long, and the cuisine is not for dieters, as it's hearty, heavy, and definitely starchy, but that's what the customers want. Meals begin at 25 DM ($8.25).

Platzl, am Platzl, 8 Münzstrasse (tel. 29-31-01), faces its more famous competitor, the Hofbräuhaus. It presents a Bavarian folk program nightly in the large beer hall area.

The women dancers wear the dirndl (a skirt and blouse popular with many Bavarian girls); the men dress in lederhosen (leather shorts), worn with a Loden jacket and a felt hat with a badger's tail. Together they perform the *schuhplattler,* the thigh-slapping folk dance of the Bavarian Alps. The entrance charge is 10 DM ($3.30). The inn offers fine Bavarian food and sausages, and Platzl draft beer in a keg is placed at the table.

Mathäser Bierstadt, 5 Bayerstrasse (tel. 59-28-96), is a beer city, filled both afternoons and evenings with happy imbibers. To reach the bierhalle, walk through to the back, then go upstairs. Featured is a brass band oompahing away. The largest of all Bavarian taverns, the Bierstadt contains tables and tables of drinkers joining in the songs. Even at midafternoon the place is often packed, making you wonder if anybody is working in the entire city. In addition to the main hall, there is a downstairs tavern and a rooftop garden. Here Löwenbräu kegs spill out onto the sidewalk for stand-up sausage and kraut nibblers. Specialties of the house include knuckles of veal and pork. Be sure to try leberkäs. The most favored dish is the half a roast chicken. At certain times of the year you can order soups made with fresh white asparagus. Meals cost around 25 DM ($8.25).

"During the spring 'Strong Beer Season,' two weeks after the end of Fasching, and during Oktoberfest, the beer house holds a special typical Bavarian program with a big brass band and yodeling," writes reader A. L. Witmer of South Haven, Michigan. "The Mathäser is also famous for its Bavarian breakfasts with weisswürste and beer."

Zum Pschorrbräu, 11 Neuhauserstrasse (tel. 260-30-01), is the showcase of the Pschorrbräu interests. It's a good place for both food and entertainment. Live music is played in the wine cellar, St. Michael, from 7 p.m. until midnight. The wine list provides 60 different varieties, and hot food is served until closing. Actually, the Pschorrbräu offers a more toned-down introduction to a Bavarian beer restaurant than does, say, the Hofbräuhaus. The atmosphere is in a typical Bavarian motif, and the food is better than usually found in such places—and it's not expensively priced. For example, set lunches range from 15 DM ($4.95) to 25 DM ($8.25).

Löwenbräukeller, 2 Nymphenburgerstrasse (tel. 52-00-1). This beer hall should be better known. Admittedly it's somewhat removed from the center of town, yet it offers one of the best gemütlich evenings in Munich. On the à la carte menu, a typical main dish would be sauerbraten with dumplings and red cabbage. In summer, such Bavarian specialties are served in the open-air beer garden. A simple meal might cost 15 DM ($4.95), but you could spend a lot more of course, from 25 DM ($8.25) and beyond. The Löwenbräukeller is especially known for its individual Bavarian evenings and royal Bavarian nights when live entertainment is offered.

A MEDIEVAL FEAST: Welser Kuche, 27 Residenzstrasse (tel. 29-69-73), offers hearty medieval feasts nightly from 6 p.m. to midnight. Guests can come early (but no later than 8 p.m.), and they must be prepared to stick around for three hours, as they are served by "mägde" and "knechte" (or wenches and knaves) in 16th-century costumes, as was the custom 450 years ago. In many ways this is like a take-off on one of the many medieval Tudor banquets that enjoy such popularity in London. Food is served in hand-thrown pottery, and guests eat these medieval delicacies with their fingers, aided only by a stiletto-like dagger (later it's used for cleaning your teeth, but I don't recommend this).

You can order a six- or a ten-course menu, called a Welser feast, costing between 55 DM ($18.15) and 75 DM ($24.75). For smaller appetites, four-course meals are also served, beginning at 28 DM ($9.24). Many of the recipes served here were found in a cookbook that belonged to Freiin von Zinnenburg, the wife of the Habsburg Archduke Ferdinand II. Discovered in 1970, the cookbook serves as a culinary guide for some of the dishes. Most of the guests accompany their meals with a special dark beer. The place can be good fun if you're in the mood, but because it is likely to be overflowing, reservations are recommended way, way in advance. For reservations, don't use the restaurant's direct number. Instead call 089/29-65-65.

THE TOP NIGHTCLUBS: The **Bayerischer Hof,** 2-6 Promenadeplatz (tel. 2-12-00). The ground-floor cellar nightclub of this deluxe hotel offers the most gilt-edged entertainment in Munich. The orchestras are the smoothest in town, and so is the clientele. Dancing goes on in front of the bandstand (the combo wisely varies the pace from fast to slow); some of the tables are placed above the dance floors, others are right in the center of the action. Large drinks are served, and most whiskies average around 15 DM ($4.95) to 20 DM ($6.60) a drink. The club opens at 8 p.m., then the action builds until it probably rocks the rice in the adjoining Trader Vic's.

Club Bavaria, Hilton International München, 7 am Tucherpark (tel. 34-00-51), is a rustic Bavarian parlor with a cozy and elegant atmosphere for dancing, dining, and drinking with the local international set the whole night through. Either stick to old favorite drinks or order a typical Bavarian cocktail. You can dance to nostalgic sounds of the '50s, '60s, and '70s, or else ask the disc jockey to play the tune of your choice.

FAVORITE BARS: **Boccaccio,** 10 Briennerstrasse, is dark and cozy. The choice of drinks is wide, and so are the prices. Most libations are in the 12-DM ($3.96) to 22-DM ($7.26) range. A small combo plays every night. You'll meet a really nice crowd of professional people here.

Harry's New York Bar, 9 Falkenturmstrasse (tel. 22-27-00), lies in the heart of Munich, near the Hofbräuhaus. All the members of the "International Bar Flies" of the world pay an obligatory visit here when in Munich. The establishment, which is managed by its owner, Bill Deck, takes its name from the first American bar in Paris on "Sank Roo Doe Noo." The German bar continues the tradition of mixing very fortifying drinks which feature concoctions based on the original recipes. They include the Sidecar cocktail, created in 1931, and the Monkey's Gland, created in 1930. Attentive waiters will bring you simple food items as well, including chili con carne, tomato cream soup with vodka, and a "BLT" (bacon, lettuce, and tomato sandwich). The roast beef sandwich is another popular item. Beer is also available on tap at 6.50 DM ($2.15). The bar shuts down on Sunday, but opens otherwise at 4 p.m.

WINE DRINKING: Weinschencke am Markt, 1 Dreifaltkeitplatz (tel. 22-61-33), is an ancient wine house which Münchners have patronized since around 1400. At the edge of the city's huge outside vegetable and fruit market, the Viktuellenmarkt, the wine house has arched ceilings and hand-painted country furnishings. One of the dirndl-clad waitresses will bring your order. You can have cheese, Black Forest ham, and herb bread to accompany one of the Austrian, French, or German wines, which cost around 9 DM ($2.97) a glass.

JAZZ: domicile, 19 Leopoldstrasse, in the Schwabing district, is the main spot for jazz in Munich—in fact, it is one of perhaps three clubs in Europe that has jazz all year long. It also features rock music. The best artists seem to perform there from late April through early October. Everything or everyone from big bands to solo performers can be seen until 4 a.m. Students and artists are drawn to the place, a typical jazz cellar, its walls decorated with enlarged transparencies of many performing jazz artists, the work of Josef Werkmeister, a rich German who photographs for pleasure. Whiskies go for around 8 DM ($2.64) to 12 DM ($3.96), or open wine for the same price.

CABARETS: In Munich when you "come to the cabaret," you may end up at the **Rationaltheatre,** 18 Hesseloherstrasse (tel. 33-50-40), which many consider the most important in Germany. It has existed since 1963, and is a political cabaret, having already overthrown one president, Heinrich Lübke. The show is performed every day except Monday, starting at 8:30 p.m. Tickets must be reserved by phone beginning at 2 p.m. Prices range from 18 DM ($5.94) to 25 DM ($8.25).

Nearby, **Schwabinger Podium,** 1 Wagnerstrasse (tel. 39-94-82), offers different entertainment nightly. A lot of "rockers" appear here. Some nights are devoted to jazz, and on other occasions I've been entertained by Dixieland as well as rock. Hours are 8 p.m. to 1 a.m., and beer is priced at 6.50 DM ($2.15); whisky costs from 10 DM ($3.30).

DISCOS: East Side, 30 Rosenheimerstrasse (tel. 48-48-58), is the most popular disco in Munich and one of the best. Near the München Penta Hotel, the disco has some of the finest and most effective lights and sounds in Germany. The club caters to a select clientele, and on most nights the patrons are fairly well dressed. There's a policy, for example, against wearing jeans to the club. Your first drink is expensively priced at 15 DM ($4.95), and there are no reductions for your second or third libation. The setting is modern in the extreme.

Aquarius, Holiday Inn, 200 Leopoldstrasse (tel. 34-09-71), is the latest incarnation of the famous old Yellow Submarine, for years and years a favorite on the Schwabing after-dark circuit. It's like discoing within a gigantic aquarium, except the sharks are now gone. If you like your disco underwater, this is the place, with drinks costing around 15 DM ($4.95).

Pl, in the Haus der Kunst, 1 Prinzregentenstrasse (tel. 29-42-52), near the English Gardens. At first you'll think you're arriving at a museum, and you are —the Staatsgalerie Moderner Kunst, which we've already visited, with its display of modern artists ranging from Picasso to Warhol. The walls of this club are also decorated with modern art by young Germans, and it might even be for sale. Painters and authors (usually unpublished ones) go to this popular nighttime rendezvous which stays open until 3 a.m. or even later in the morning. You talk, you dance, you drink. Food is served, but I've never sampled it. A whisky begins at around 12 DM ($3.96), and you can also order beer at 6.50 DM ($2.15).

OLD MUNICH: Alter Simpl, 57 Türkenstrasse (tel. 272-30-83), was once a literary café, taking its name from a satirical revue in 1903. There is no one around anymore who remembers that revue, but Alter Simpl remained on the scene and was made famous by its mistress, Kathi Kobus. She went on to become a legend, but even she is no longer with it. Once Lale Andersen, who made "Lili Marlene" famous in World War II, frequented the café whenever she was in Munich. Today it attracts actors, journalists, painters, and students. Whisky ranges in price from 8 DM ($2.64) to 12.50 DM ($4.13). The cook's special soup is linsensoup and gulaschsoup, costing from 5 DM ($1.65) to 6 DM ($1.98). Hours are 9 p.m. to 3 a.m., and on Friday and Saturday they stay open until 4 a.m. They're closed on Sunday. Ms. Toni Netzle is the owner.

THE CASINO BLITZ: Although it may seem contradictory after recommending so much nightlife, you can spend your best evening in Bavaria just by taking the Casino Blitz bus to the fashionable alpine resort of Garmisch-Partenkirchen. (For a detailed description of the attractions of this southern Bavarian town, see Chapter IX.)

The Blitz Bus leaves from a side of the railway station (facing the station, it'll be on your right). The bus stop is more or less opposite the Hotel Deutscher Kaiser. It departs Monday through Friday at 5:15 p.m., returning to Munich at 11 p.m. On weekends and holidays the departure time is 2 p.m. and the return time is the same. The round-trip fare is 10 DM ($3.30).

The bus takes you to the Casino at Garmisch-Partenkirchen, where you're under no obligation to play the roulette tables. Rather, you can explore the town, have dinner, and do some shopping. But at some point in your trip you must make an appearance at the Casino to have your ticket validated. The Casino, incidentally, opens at 3 p.m. You must be 21 years old to enter, and able to prove it with a passport.

THEATERS, OPERA, AND CONCERTS: Perhaps nowhere else in Europe, other than London and Paris, will you find so many orchestras and artists performing. And the good news is the low cost of the seats—so count on indulging yourself and going to concerts several times. You'll get good tickets if you're willing to pay anywhere from 12 DM ($3.96) to 50 DM ($16.50). Finally, you may want to consider standing room, around 6 DM ($1.98).

Practically any night of the year you'll find a performance at the **National Theater,** on Max-Joseph-Platz (tel. 21-85-1), the home of the Bavarian State Opera. The Germans give their hearts, perhaps their souls, to opera. Productions are beautifully mounted and presented. Hard-to-get tickets may be purchased weekdays from 10 a.m. to 12:30 p.m. and 3:30 to 5:30 p.m., and one hour before each performance (during the weekend, only on Saturday from 10 a.m. to 1 p.m.). For ticket information, telephone 22-13-16.

The regular season of the **Deutsches Theatre,** 13 Schwanthalerstrasse (tel. 59-33-01), lasts from March to June and July to December. Musicals are popular, but operettas and classical plays are performed as well. It's the only theater in Germany that is both a theater and a ballroom. During the "Carnival Season" in January and February the seats are removed and stored away, replaced by tables and chairs for more than 3000 guests. Handmade decorations by artists combined with lighting effects create an enchanting ambience. Waiters serve wine, champagne, and food. There are costume balls and official black-tie festivals, famous throughout Europe.

Staatstheater am Gärtnerplatz, 3 Gärtnerplatz (tel. 201-67-67), is yet another theater where the presentations are varied and entertaining. The program includes anything from ballet to opera, operettas, and musicals. The ticket office is open during the same hours as those of the National Theater.

Altes Residenztheater (Cuvilliés Theater), in the Residenz (entrance at 1 Residenzstrasse; tel. 29-68-36), is a sightseeing attraction in its own right. The Bavarian State Opera and the Bayerisches Staatsschauspiel perform smaller works here in keeping with the more intimate character of the unique baroque architecture of the tiny theater. Ticket hours are the same as those for the National Theater.

Nearby, the **Residenz Theater,** 1 Max-Joseph-Platz (tel. 22-57-54), features plays, comedies, and dramas in its Bayerisches Staatsschauspiel. The price of seats ranges from 12 DM ($3.96) to 50 DM ($16.50).

If you speak German, you'll find at least 20 theaters offering plays of every description: classic dramas, comedies, experimental, contemporary—take your pick. The best way to find what current productions might interest you is to go to a theater ticket agency. The most convenient one is at the railway station, opposite Track 21. You'll see theater, concert, and opera posters on the wall, and can save time and energy by purchasing your tickets here.

Special mention should be made of a few unusual theaters: **Theater Rechts der Isar,** 9 Wörthstrasse (tel. 45-58-13), which might show a production by Peter Handke one day, one by Bertolt Brecht the next; and the **Münchner Marionetten Theater,** 29a Blumenstrasse (tel. 26-57-12), where you can attend puppet shows and the théâtre de marionnettes. Adults as well as children are delighted with these productions.

Finally, not to be ignored is the **Circus Krone,** 43 Marstrasse (tel. 55-81-66). It might be compared to London's Albert Hall, its productions are so varied. One night, a jazz festival; the next night, a hard rock concert; yet another night, gospel singers; and December 25 to March 31, a circus show every night.

5. Some Notes on Shopping

The most interesting shops are concentrated on Munich's pedestrians-only street, lying between Karlsplatz and Marienplatz at the Rathaus. In general, Munich is the most varied shopping city in Germany, with merchandise-loaded shops lining many intriguing streets.

Rosenthal, 8 Theatinerstrasse (tel. 22-04-22), near the City Hall, attracts everybody from the pope to Queen Juliana of the Netherlands. Ask for Dr. or Mrs. Hans Zoellner. Several factories in Bavaria combine to produce this high-quality china, such as Rosenthal with its Classic Rose collection, the Studio Linie, and the collection of Hutschenreuther. In this Munich outlet you will also find matching crystal, cutlery, and many gift items. You'll save about 50% of what you would at home by shopping at this fashionable Munich store. Traditional dinner sets begin at $75 and can go up into the thousands. Dr. Zoellner's china export store also does a lot of mail-order business and sends gift parcels all over the world.

In optical goods, Germany has been known since the birth of that industry. For contact lenses and other eye aids, I suggest you patronize **Söhnges,** 7 Briennerstrasse and 34 Kaufingerstrasse. For information, telephone 2-12-31.

Germany's cameras are magnificent, and Leica is perhaps the most famous name. The shop of **Kohlroser,** 14 Maffeistrasse (tel. 29-52-50), carries a good assortment of cameras and equipment. The location is within an easy walk of the Hotel Bayerischer Hof and American Express. Look also for the Minox cameras (sometimes referred to humorously as "spy cameras"). The staff is friendly and so democratic they even carry Japanese cameras as well. They have another shop in the major shopping center, Luitpoldblock, on 10 Maximilian-splatz, just a five-minute walk from the parent store.

Dirndl Ecke, 4 am Platzl (tel. 22-01-63), across from the famous Hofbräu-haus, gets my unreserved recommendation as a stylish shop specializing in high-grade dirndls, feathered alpine hats, and all clothing associated with the alpine regions. Everything sold here is of fine quality—there is no tourist junk. The chic Salzburg dirndls sell for around 500 DM ($165); blouses with regional designs, around 100 DM ($33). Wide-brimmed felt hats begin at 150 DM ($49.50), and for plumage you'll pay another 100 DM ($33). Other merchandise includes needlework hats, beaded belts, and pleated shirts for men. You may also be attracted to the stylish capes, the silver jewelry in old Bavarian style, the shoes in leather, or the linen and cotton combinations, such as skirts with blouses and jackets. The shop is open weekdays from 9 a.m. to 6 p.m. (on Saturday to 1 p.m.).

For folk art and handicrafts, **Wallach,** 3 Residenzstrasse (tel. 22-08-71), is preferred. In fact I consider it the finest place in Germany to obtain handcrafts, both newly made and antique. It can save much time in your search for a memorable object which will remind you of your trip to Germany. You'll find such items as antique churns, old kitchen ware, brass hunting horns, rag rug lengths sold by the yard, paintings on glass, charmingly hand-painted wooden boxes and trays, milking stools, painted porcelain clocks, wooden wall clocks, doilies, napkins, and towels.

Kunsthandlung Timberg, 15 Maximilianstrasse (tel. 29-52-35), in the central shopping mall, has the best collection of new and antique Meissen and Dresden porcelain. It's almost a miniature museum. Look for both an old or new Meissener coffee set with the blue-and-white onion design. The shop has outlets to Dresden porcelain denied to other retail stores. Important: Any purchase here can be packed and shipped safely. They've had a lot of experience in doing just that.

Ludwig Beck am Rathauseck, am Marienplatz (tel. 22-82-64), is a four-floor shopping bazaar selling handmade crafts from all over Germany, both old and new. You'll find it a feast of tasteful, colorful items to purchase. Items offered for sale include decorative pottery and dishes, beer steins and vases of etched glass, painted wall plaques depicting rural scenes, or decorative flower arrangements. There is much unusual kitchenware, colored flatware, calico hot pads and towels, plus a stunning collection of leather-trimmed canvas purses that are chicly casual.

Chapter IV

LEADING SPA RESORTS

1. Bad Pyrmont
2. Bad Wildungen
3. Wiesbaden
4. Bad Nauheim
5. Bad Homburg
6. Bad Wiessee
7. Bad Reichenhall
8. Bad Neuenahr
9. Bad Oeynhausen
10. Bad Kissingen

EVEN IF YOU WANDER into the most out-of-the-way places in Germany, you'll never get away from the greatest of all Teutonic institutions, the spa. With dozens of them spread throughout the country, these resorts have been as much a part of German life as beer and sausages. Some of the spas have been known since Roman times, while others are of much more recent vintage, but they all have one thing in common—"healing" waters.

These waters vary much more than just hot or cold. From seawater to thermal or radioactive springs, the Germans have learned to make the best use of all types of water for all types of ailments. The Kneipp treatment, commonly called hydrotherapy, was formulated by a Bavarian pastor, and through his man-made water treatment, natural mineral springs are no longer a prerequisite for the establishment of a spa. Thus spas exist in every imaginable location, from seaside resorts to mountaintops in the Bavarian Alps.

But Germans vacation in the spas for more than just taking the waters. Between mud baths and hydrotherapy, they have a wide range of activities and facilities from which to choose. From the casinos in Baden-Baden, Bad Homburg, and Westerland, to golf courses and horse racing, there's never a dull moment during the busy summer spa season. Some of the larger spas are active all year.

In this chapter, I'll sample some of the variety to be found among the spas —it really would take a massive volume devoted solely to spas to cover the whole subject. In addition to the ten spas detailed, you'll find other important German resorts, such as Baden-Baden, Bad Godesberg, and Westerland, in separate chapters of this book.

1. Bad Pyrmont

This attractive spa has enjoyed a notable reputation for more than 2000 years. Its springs are of different kinds, from the brine variety in the fields to the medicinal iron waters on the southern side of the valley of the Weser Hills. In the center of town you can drink a medicinal cocktail from the fountain at the Hyllige Born spring. Another popular pastime is taking mud baths. But Bad Pyrmont is a good place to vacation even if you don't come just to take the waters. Horseback riding in the hills, hiking, tennis, and swimming, as well as concerts and live shows, make the resort a lively place, a sort of German Tunbridge Wells.

The spa gardens are among the most beautiful in Germany, with little temples, flowering trees, and even a palm garden, an unusual touch in the temperate climate. The concert house in the Kurpark produces live shows during the busy summer. At night the central promenade is glamorously lit, giving the spa a festive air, while guests sit out at sidewalk tables drinking beer.

FOOD AND LODGING: Several fine possibilities exist in Bad Pyrmont, some with real historic atmosphere.

Bergkurpark, 11 Ockelstrasse (tel. 40-01), is the most distinguished hotel at the spa, certainly the most glamorous architecturally. Its entryway has a thatched roof, covering a combination hewn-stone and stucco facade with half-rounded picture windows—most dramatic. The effect is enhanced by a Louis XVI-style lamppost. After checking in, you're shown your room, which might be in a modern block with private terraces overlooking a park. The hotel has 45 single rooms, costing from 50 DM ($16.50) with toilet and wash basin, rising to 110 DM ($36.30) with complete bath. Twin-bedded units with bath or shower begin at 122 DM ($40.26), climbing to 175 DM ($57.75) for the best in the house.

The hotel has its own park, a forest, a heated swimming pool, and a cheerful terrace with sun parasols overlooking the garden. There are also exercise rooms and a sauna. Its restaurant serves the best food at the spa (see below). The hotel has an elegant café, Sanssouci, and the rustic-style Wilhelm Busch-Stube where beer, wine, and good food are served. The hotel is closed in November.

Kurhotel-Kurhaus, 4 Heilengenangerstrasse (tel. 1-51), is the most active hotel in town, as it houses the Spielcasino. The building itself has much architectural style, constructed with graceful lines, and its garden terrace is a summer lure. Rooms are furnished in a sleek, modern style (the fresh flowers help a lot). In high season, a single begins at 120 DM ($39.60), rising to 160 DM ($52.80) with more complete plumbing. A twin-bedded room sans bath begins at 200 DM ($66), going up to 275 DM ($90.80) with complete bath. Many guests check in here to enjoy the hotel's thermal baths.

Park-Hotel Rasmussen, 8 Kirschstrasse (tel. 44-85), is a completely renovated 12-room villa right in the heart of Bad Pyrmont, on the traffic-free promenade mall. The spacious rooms are well furnished, beds are comfortable, and many rooms have balconies overlooking the promenade. Prices are 120 DM ($39.60) for a double with bath, 80 DM ($26.40) for a single with bath. The staff of the hotel is pleasant, although a wee bit formal for some tastes.

The hotel's restaurant offers set lunches in the quiet dining room overlooking the mall, costing from 35 DM ($11.55). In the evening, diners are offered a more expensive array of dishes, including trout au bleu and wild game for two. The bar adjoining the dining room has a club-like atmosphere.

Next to the Rasmussen is the **Café Konditorei,** In Hauptallee, a social gathering point in town. It has attractive outside tables on the mall and offers set lunches for 18 DM ($5.94) to 35 DM ($11.55). The cookery is traditionally German.

Hotel Bad Pyrmonter Hof, 32 Brunnenstrasse (tel. 60-93-03), is a 70-bed hotel which provides a personal atmosphere, friendly service, and comfort. The place has been considerably modernized, especially the bedrooms, which are immaculate and restful. Plumbing comes in a variety of styles. A single ranges from a low of 65 DM ($21.45) to a high of 70 DM ($23.10), the latter with complete private bath. A twin-bedded room with private bath goes for 110 DM ($36.30) to 130 DM ($42.90). A continental breakfast is included in the tariffs quoted. All units contain color TV and a self-dial phone.

Hotel-Pension Westfalen, 1 Altenauplatz (tel. 37-55), is one of the best bargains of the resort. An attractive, tile-roofed villa, it has front rooms with terraces overlooking a fountain. Overflow guests are housed in its annex, Haus Kersten. Many of the rooms often have elegant touches, such as half-tester beds and reproductions of antiques. A homey atmosphere prevails. Even if you don't like the style, it's not impersonal, and service is good. It's best to stay here on half-board terms, costing 85 DM ($28.05) to 95 DM ($31.35) daily in a single, and from 145 DM ($47.85) to 165 DM ($54.45) in a double, also including breakfast and dinner. All units contain shower or bath as well as a toilet.

Hotel Kaiserhof, 1-2 Kirchstrasse (tel. 1-81-20), is like an overscale villa, a pinkish structure with elegant multipaned windows on a tree-shaded street not far from the Kurpark and almost directly across the street from the Casino. The coffeehouse on the ground floor is the best known one at the spa. At the breakfast buffet, guests serve themselves from a large table loaded with goodies. The interior is, in large part, beige and pink, and everything is clean and comfortable, especially in the well-furnished private rooms, each with bath or shower, plus phone. Many units have balconies opening onto the promenade. Singles rent from 70 DM ($23.10) to 95 DM ($31.35), and doubles cost from 110 DM ($36.30) to 150 DM ($49.50). For half-board terms, add another 20 DM ($6.60) per person. The owner, Wolfgang Schene, does everything he can to make a guest comfortable.

Restaurant Separée, in Hotel Bergkurpark, 11 Ockelstrasse (tel. 40-01), is part of the finest hotel in town, already previewed. In summer many diners, both foreign and domestic, like to eat on the beautifully decorated terrace. Otherwise, food is served in this elegantly decorated restaurant, with large, comfortable chairs. On my tour of the kitchen I was impressed by its size and cleanliness. An array of international specialties is turned out, and trout and lobster are kept alive until the last moment in the hotel's aquarium. The restaurant is not as expensive as it looks, offering eight different fixed-price menus, costing between 22 DM ($7.26) and 35 DM ($11.55). Service is from noon till 2:30 p.m. and 6 to 10 p.m.

2. Bad Wildungen

The healing mineral springs of Bad Wildungen have long attracted northern Europeans to the rolling hills and deep forests of the Waldeck region southwest of Kassel. Thousands of visitors flock here annually, seeking treatment for kidney and gall bladder disorders, or simply for the rest and relaxation combined with the spa's numerous cultural activities.

The spa gardens are well planned, augmenting the natural wooded surroundings with carefully planted flowers from all parts of the world, and several attractive buildings, including two bandshells where frequent outdoor concerts are given. The modern horseshoe-shaped arcade houses the Georg-Viktor spring, as well as several exclusive shops and a small auditorium. Lawn chairs are placed throughout the grounds for the convenience and comfort of the strollers. Admission to the Kurpark is 3 DM (99¢) daily.

Bad Wildungen is more than 700 years old. Rising above the Old Town (Altstadt) is the massive tower of the 14th-century church, **Stadtkirche,** the most impressive structure, and the oldest, in the town. The highlight of the church is not its interesting hallenkirch architecture, however, as much as its remarkable *Niederwildungen Altarpiece,* one of the best examples of early German painting. The wing-paneled altarpiece, painted in 1403 by Master Konrad von Soest, contains a large dramatic scene of the Crucifixion, flanked by six smaller scenes, depicting the birth, passion, and resurrection of Christ. The work shows an obvious French influence in the use of delicate colors and figures, made even more dramatic by the use of actual gold. The colors seem more striking in contrast to the simple drab interior of the church.

FOOD AND LODGING: Staatliches Badehotel, in the Kurpark (tel. 8-60), has the most enviable position for a spa hotel—right at the entrance to the gardens, in the center of the clinical and cultural activities. Evoking the grandeur of another era, the Badehotel is large and rambling, branching out in two great wings from the circular domed entrance. Aside from the standard conveniences of a fine hotel, it has its own private clinic and sanitorium, providing diagnostic and therapeutic devices, including carbon dioxide baths, massages, and complete medical attention by a fine professional staff.

The hotel's 74 rooms (43 more in the sanitorium) are large, sunlit, and airy, all with views of the Waldeck woodlands and spa gardens. The furnishings are sleek, comfortable, modern, and kept spotless by an efficient staff. Prices of rooms vary according to size and location. Bathless singles are 95 DM ($31.35); with bath, 120 DM ($39.60). Bathless doubles cost 140 DM ($46.20), rising to 220 DM ($72.60) with complete bath. Room rates include breakfast, service, tax, and use of the large indoor heated pool. Garage facilities are available.

The hotel's restaurant is just what the doctor ordered—that is, if you're not worried about calories. Special diets are available, but the menu offers such a tempting array that nearly everyone cheats at least once. Veal dishes are the specialty, and the kalbsschnitzel (veal scallops) cooked with herbs is a tasty choice. Other dishes include trout au bleu, filet of sole, and nasi-goreng. A carafe of Mosel Valley wine is good with most meals, which cost from 30 DM ($9.90) to 60 DM ($19.80).

Hotel-Pension Die Hardtmühle, 5-7 im Urfftal (tel. 7-41), at Bergfreiheit, is my favorite spot in the area, and it's most suitable for motorists. The Rieger family, who run it, are the finest hosts I've ever encountered in Bad Wildungen or its environs. Their family hotel places a strong accent on sports, including swimming (with both indoor and outdoor pools), tennis, and other activities. The setting is in the countryside, with lazy cows grazing the pastureland. A single room with shower or bath rents for 50 DM ($16.50) daily, a double with the same plumbing costing about the same per person. Many family rooms are also rented, suitable for three to five persons.

Your meals are an extra 30 DM ($9.90) per person, and they are good ones. Sometimes a buffet is set out, or the cook may grill meals and have a barbecue. Rooms are cozy and warmly inviting, most often furnished as in a private home. The place is very special and not everyone fits in, but hopefully you will. Some English is spoken, but of course most of your fellow guests will be German-speaking. This place is so popular in summer that reservations should be made well in advance.

Hotel Am Golfplatz, 17 Talquellenweg (tel. 20-92), is aggressively modern.

However, for those who want to combine golfing with their holiday, it's ideal. Rooms are streamlined, nothing cluttered. Singles cost 53 DM ($17.49) to 63 DM ($20.79) and doubles run from 88 DM ($29.04) to 98 DM ($32.34). The restaurant is only for hotel guests who take full-board terms, costing from 76 DM ($25.08) to 85 DM ($28.05) per person daily. In back, lawn chairs are spread out in the yard, where you can join fellow guests in enjoying the sun. Terraces overlook the greenery.

Hotel-Café Schwarze, 42 Brunnenallee (tel. 40-64), was founded in 1876, and for decades it has been one of the most popular rendezvous points at the spa. You can drink or dine al fresco (maybe a combination of both) at one of the tables placed in front of the large main building. Antiques and typical furnishings of the region have been used, and the place has a lot of rustic character. It's also a very good bargain: singles range in price from 35 DM ($11.55) to 45 DM ($14.85), depending on the plumbing, and doubles cost from 64 DM ($21.12) to 76 DM ($25.08). These tariffs include breakfast, and the staff is most helpful.

The **Hotel-Restaurant Cristall,** 15 Langemarckstrasse (tel. 30-34), stands across from the Kurpark. It has some very comfortable and reasonably priced rooms, and it costs only 55 DM ($18.15) per person to stay here, ordering breakfast and dinner with the room included as well. The food is good and plentiful downstairs in the café, which draws a lot of local patronage.

For meals, most guests dine at their hotel. However, there is one good independent eatery. It's **La Camargue,** 12 Brunnenallee (tel. 23-23), a specialty restaurant and rôtisserie-grill, serving both classical dishes and those of the nouvelle cuisine repertoire. Whenever possible, these specialties are reasonably prepared from authentically fresh ingredients. Food is temptingly displayed on your plate, and there's a large wine list. A choice of ten wisely selected main courses is offered, along with fixed-price menus which range from 18 DM ($5.94) to 45 DM ($14.85). The restaurant is open from noon to 2 p.m. and 6 p.m. to midnight daily exept on Monday.

3. Wiesbaden

This health resort has been firmly entrenched in a sheltered valley between the Rhine and the Taunus Mountains since it was first settled in Roman times. Part of its success as a spa is due, of course, to the 26 hot springs whose temperature ranges from 117° to 150°F, but its proximity to Germany's largest cities and transportation centers, such as Frankfurt, is what has made Wiesbaden the most international of spas. It lies only 20 minutes away by car from the Frankfurt International Airport, or a 30-minute run by frequent train service. Wiesbaden competes with Baden-Baden as Germany's most fashionable resort. It is also one of the most important cultural centers in the country. Every May it plays host to the **International Festival of Music, Ballet, and Drama,** when the best foreign companies perform operatic and dramatic works in German, French, and English.

There is still much of the turn-of-the-century splendor. In the Bath Quarter of Wiesbaden, around the Kurhaus and Brunnenkolonnade, most of the cultural activities of the theater and concert season take place. The **Brunnenkolonnade** is a pillared structure housing fountains fed by two of the spa's best known springs, the Kochbrunnen and Faulbrunnen. Concert and exhibition halls are also enclosed within its walls. The major concert halls are in the **Kurhaus,** a big, lively structure centering around a cupola-crowned hall which opens into rooms in all directions.

If you prefer the outdoors, Wiesbaden offers horseback riding, golf courses, swimming, tennis, and hiking. The streets of the city are enjoyable if you like to ramble about. The spa part is attractive, with old shade trees surrounding a lake. It is especially beautiful at night when the lights of the spa and the huge fountain in the lake are reflected in the water.

THE TOP HOTELS: Schwarzer Bock (Black Ram), 12 Kranzplatz (tel. 38-21), is a tradition in the area, tracing its history back to 1486. Most of its public rooms are a treasure house of Teutonic architecture and filled with antiques—Empire, Biedermeier, and Louis XVI. It's a world of wood paneling, gilt, and crystal. If you like cozy nooks, then this is your hotel. For example, the oak-paneled drinking salon lies under an ornate wood ceiling. Then there's the Chinese tea room, with screens, lanterns, vases, and a teak dragon table, plus a rustic tavern with an open grill. Le Capricorne is more elegant.

The bedrooms have private bath or shower, color TV, direct-dial phone, mini-bar, and radio. The most sought-after accommodations are those opening onto views of the sunpocket patio. On the whole, the bedroom furnishings are traditionally Germanic and comfortable. Singles go for 155 DM ($51.15) to 185 DM ($61.05), doubles for 250 DM ($82.50) to 290 DM ($95.70), and apartments (single/double) for 205 DM ($67.65) to 620 DM ($204.60). These rates include a buffet breakfast. Behind the scenes is a thermal bathhouse, with a Japanese swimming pool. In addition, there's an indoor pool, plus the usual spa facilities, including an exercise room, massage parlor, and thermal tub baths. To wind down after all this strenuous activity, guests retreat to the roof-garden terrace.

Nassauer Hof, 3-4 Kaiser-Friedrich-Platz (tel. 133-0), is an old favorite with up-to-date conveniences. In 1897, renovations preserved the baroque facade, and the interior was completely modernized in 1973. With the addition of two restaurants, this hotel now ranks with the most appealing in Germany. Die Pfanne features local German specialties in a rustic atmosphere at moderate prices, while Die Ente vom Lehel boasts the finest deluxe fare in Wiesbaden. The cozy Kamin Bar features an open fireplace and piano entertainment. The staff provides cordial service in understandable English, and the spacious rooms feature bath, TV, stocked mini-bar, and soundproof windows. Singles range from 220 DM ($72.60) to 285 DM ($94.05) and twins cost from 280 DM ($92.40) to 400 DM ($132), including service and tax. The hotel stands in the city center, within walking distance of Kurhaus gambling casino, State Opera and Theatre, spa, and the shopping area.

Wiesbaden Penta Hotel, 15 Auguste-Viktoria-Strasse (tel. 37-70-41), can't be beat at the spa for up-to-date amenities. A Penta chain member, it stands in the heart of Weisbaden, opposite Rhein-Main-Halle, a five-minute walk from the main station. Glamorously modern, it offers 200 well-furnished and soundproof rooms, each with private bath and individual balcony, many of which overlook the gardens that surround the hotel. Direct-dial phone, color TV, radio, and mini-bar are some of the equipment found inside each chamber. The cost in a single ranges from 165 DM ($54.45) to 205 DM ($67.65) daily; a double goes for 200 DM ($66) to 225 DM ($74.25).

A buffet is served in the split-level restaurant and coffeeshop, overflowing in summer to the terrace for al fresco meals. German beer and snacks are the feature of the hotel's Bierstube. Recreation is important here, with a health club, sauna, plunge pool, and tanning studio.

MEDIUM-PRICED AND BUDGET HOTELS: The Hotel Bären, 3 Bärenstrasse (tel. 30-10-21), is standard modern, lying only a three-minute walk from the Schloss and the Marktkirche (Market Church), as well as the Kurhaus. The bedrooms are clean, efficiently appointed, and comfortable. A bathless single costs 70 DM ($23.10); with private bath or shower, 100 DM ($33). Two persons pay

110 DM ($36.30) in a bathless double, 150 DM ($49.50) in a double with private bath. All these tariffs include breakfast, service, and the use of the thermal swimming pool. The cocktail bar and the restaurant, König im Bären, take care of your material well-being.

Hotel Klee am Park, 4 Parkstrasse (tel. 30-50-61), is a square, modern hotel set in a tranquil position at the edge of a park, surrounded by its own informal gardens. The theater is nearby as are the Casino and shopping area. All of the hotel's bedrooms have french doors opening onto balconies. Most of the accommodations have color TV and a sitting area large enough for entertaining. The baths are tiled, many containing double sinks. Singles range in price from 95 DM ($31.35) to 140 DM ($46.20); twin-bedded rooms, from 135 DM ($44.55) to 180 DM ($59.40); and three-bedded rooms, for 215 DM ($70.95) to 230 DM ($75.90). Breakfast is 16.50 DM ($5.45) per person. Guests will find a pleasantly decorated café and restaurant, where French cuisine is served. A comfortable bar in the English style offers a fine ambience for an evening drink. The hotel is highly recommended for those who find the older, super-luxurious hotels a bit too monumental.

Aukamm-Hotel, 31 Aukamm-Allee (tel. 57-60), built in 1970, is one of the leading first-class, 300-bed hotels in Wiesbaden. In a quiet, fashionable area beside the spa park, it has 160 comfortable rooms and luxury suites and apartments. All rooms have balcony, bath and shower, direct-dial phone, radio, in-house video in English, and color TV. The rate for a single room is 200 DM ($66), and for a double 230 DM ($75.90), including tax, service, and breakfast. The hotel lies only 30 minutes by car from the Frankfurt airport and 15 minutes from the Rhine Steamer pier.

Forum Hotel, 17 Abraham-Lincoln-Strasse (tel. 7-78-11), lies in a new office development area and is sleekly modern. Its comfortably furnished guest rooms can shelter one to four guests, each with private bath, mini-bar, and direct-dial phone, along with air conditioning when needed. A single rents for 170 DM ($56.10), rising to 200 DM ($66) in a double. These rates include a large breakfast buffet, plus free use of their indoor swimming pool and sauna, along with service and tax. Lots of business people like to stay here instead of Frankfurt, as it lies only 20 minutes form the airport. Its restaurant, Friesenstuben, offers three meals a day, blending regional dishes with those of the continent. Try a glass of Mosel wine or draft beer in the Bierpumpe Bar, perhaps a snack on the terrace bordering the indoor pool.

Hotel Am Kochbrunnen, 15 Taunusstrasse (tel. 51-20-01), is my own little "home in Wiesbaden," long a favorite of mine because of its town-housey atmosphere. Cozy and snug, it will fit you into one of its comfortable and attractively furnished bedrooms if you reserve in advance. Direct your problems to the director, K. D. Rogall, who speaks English. A double with shower and toilet, along with TV and mini-bar, costs 130 DM ($42.90), dropping to 85 DM ($28.05) in a single. These tariffs include the breakfast buffet. In fair weather, tables are set out in the courtyard.

Hotel Am Landeshaus, 51 Moritzstrasse (tel. 37-30-41), is under the same management as the previously recommended Am Kochbrunnen. In a central part of Wiesbaden, within walking distance of the station, this hotel opened in the spring of 1984. Within its short life span it has become recognized as one of the best of the moderately priced hotels at the spa. Completely modernized, it has been furnished in part with antiques. The hotel is warm, cozy, and inviting, a choice for the traditionalist. Rooms are well kept, equipped with shower, or a shower/toilet or complete bath, along with direct-dial phone. There is also an elevator. Singles with shower only rent for 85 DM ($28.05). Doubles, depending on the plumbing, range from 115 DM ($37.95) to 165 DM ($54.45). These tariffs include a breakfast buffet, service, and taxes. Guests can enjoy drinks in a rustic ale tavern.

Hansa Hotel, 23 Bahnhofstrasse (tel. 3-99-55), is like a big town house, near the Rhein-Main-Halle, and offering 130 beds in small, compact, but comfortable rooms, each with a shower (or bath) and toilet, along with phone (a few have TV and mini-bar). Singles cost from 80 DM ($26.40) to 95 DM ($31.35), with doubles going for 130 DM ($42.90) to 150 DM ($49.50). A real German pub, dark and mellow, serves good beer and continental food.

Fürstenhof-Esplanade, 30–32 Sonnenberger Strasse (tel. 52-20-91), is one of the warmest, most inviting, and most traditional of the hotels of the spa. The Eierdanz family, who own and run it, have a healthy respect for the past, as reflected by their furnishings. The 120-bed hotel in a quiet part of town stands close to the Casino, spa park, theater, and shopping center. It's central and convenient, and most important, reasonable. A single room without bath costs 65 DM ($21.45), going up to 120 DM ($39.60) with bath or shower. Doubles start at 110 DM ($36.30), climbing to 180 DM ($59.40) depending on the plumbing. If you want to take both breakfast and lunch or dinner in the hotel's quite good restaurant, you'll pay another 18 DM ($5.94) per person, a real enticement.

Hotel Oranien (VCH), 2 Platter Strasse (tel. 52-50-25), is a 110-bed hotel belonging to a nationwide hospiz organization. Right in the center of the spa, near a shopping center and surrounded by a small park, it offers rooms that are immaculate and rather plainly furnished with modern pieces. Singles with shower bath, toilet, and telephone cost 75 DM ($24.75); doubles 115 DM ($37.95). Breakfast and taxes are included.

READERS' HOTEL SELECTION: "We came across an outstanding small bed-and-breakfast (hotel garni) accommodation, **Hotel Im Park,** 104 Danziger Strasse (tel. 54-11096). It's next to the Café Hahn in Wiesbaden-Sonnenberg. Since 1982 it has been run by hotelier Christian Kollman, who speaks a little English. Each of the 12 bedrooms has a wash basin. Singles rent for 55 DM ($18.15) to 65 DM ($21.45), and doubles go for 80 DM ($26.40), which includes a spendid breakfast with homemade breads and rolls. The place is friendly and in impeccably good taste from the bed linens to the spotless showers, bathrooms, and toilets. It abuts the lovely Kurpark, making it ideal for the unrepentant traveler-jogger, and it's on a main bus route. Mr. Kollman's hotel is an experience" (Pip Theodor and Veronica Anderson-Theodor, Pittsburgh, Penna.).

WHERE TO DINE: **Die Ente vom Lehel,** 3-4 Kaiser-Friedrich-Platz (tel. 30-15-16). The innovative Hans-Peter Wodarz has found a fortunate culinary platform in the kitchens of the already-recommended Hotel Nassauer Hof. His cookery is as pleasing to the eye as to the palate. Often he combines the pulp of the freshest fruits with various meats and fish. An example of this would be a mousse of pike with tree tomatoes. One of his most unusual dishes is a calf's head with blue carp in a Riesling sauce. Lamb with lobster is another rare combination, as is breast of woodcock with goose liver sauce.

Winner of many German culinary awards, this intimate restaurant seats 85 on two levels. A wine boutique, delicatessen, and sandwich bistro are attached. The bistro offers some two dozen menu choices, served from 10 a.m. till midnight Tuesday to Saturday, with dishes costing 40 DM ($13.20) to 65 DM ($21.45). In the main restaurant, one of the most interesting desserts I've ever seen is a so-called Dialogue of Fruits, served elegantly in an octagonal dish. It's a melange of different fruit purees in a champagne sauce, the colors deftly swirled into one another in random patterns. The ultimate look is like an abstract painting by Jasper Johns. The effect is, and I'm not joking, too beautiful to eat. It's the only time in my life I ever wanted to photograph a dessert.

The main restaurant is open from noon to 3 p.m. and 7 p.m. till 1 a.m.

except on Sunday and Monday. It's closed from July 20 to August 10. At noon, fixed-price meals cost from 100 DM ($33), and dinner can go up to 160 DM ($52.80).

Le Gourmet, 42 Bahnhofstrasse (tel. 30-16-54), is elegantly modern, a setting for this restaurant that is unusual in that it specializes in both French and Turkish cookery. Although the combination may sound bizarre, the citadel of good food achieves harmony between the cuisines. Full of Oriental charm, this restaurant is run by Akin Soykandar. The Turkish coffee is divine, natch, as is their eggplant kebab over grilled lambsteak. They also specialize in lotte de mer, an extremely ugly fish that is rescued by being served in a Pommery mustard sauce. Mr. Soykandar is proud of his large wine and champagne list. Expect to spend 50 DM ($16.50) to 75 DM ($24.75) for a meal, maybe a lot more. Hours are 11:30 a.m. to 2:30 p.m. and 5 to 10 p.m. The place is closed on Sunday and for two weeks during the Hessian summer festivals.

Le Capricorne, in the Schwarzer Bock Hotel, 12 Franzplatz (tel. 38-21), is renowned, a favorite of *le tout Wiesbaden*. As you enter, you're immediately dazzled by the museum-level interior, an incredible array of priceless 15th-century woodcarvings. This was the type of delicate work that made German craftsmen famous in Europe. With some justification, the restaurant could rely on its decor, but it doesn't. It's a gourmet dining room, where guests enjoy "the specialties of the season." A buffet of many delicacies rests on a Renaissance table. This cold buffet is famous throughout Wiesbaden. After you've had some of it, you'll have more time to take in the decor. You'll note that the high relief is polished to a ruddy glow, and the whole place is dark, warm, and intimate, with albino-white table linens. Some 500 years of tradition went into this place, where stained-glass windows light the tables. The restaurant serves from noon to 2 p.m. and 6 to 11 p.m. Menus range in price from 42 DM ($13.86) to 110 DM ($36.30).

Restaurant de Franace, 49 Taunusstrasse (tel. 5-12-51), is Boris Keller's daringly innovative restaurant in a city that for decades stood as a reminder of the past. It hasn't lost any time in becoming one of the most popular dining spots in Wiesbaden. The decor is Norman, elegant, tasteful, and rich. The color scheme could be called earth-tone warm, with sienna, orange, terracotta, and cream. If I'm correct in judging the quality of the nouvelle cuisine here, the restaurant should be around for a long time. Try the navarin of salmon, turbot, and lobster, or a host of other delicacies. Specialties are fish and shellfish, with menus costing 65 DM ($19.80) to 105 DM ($34.65). More than 180 French wines make up the wine carte. Reservations are essential, and hours are noon to 2 p.m. and dinner from 6 p.m. (till closing). It's closed Sunday, Saturday at noon, and in July.

Lanterna, 3 Westendstrasse (tel. 40-25-22), is rustic and elegant both, featuring a nuova cucina (Italian) and nouvelle cuisine (French). Signor Carmine Carvelli concocts these light dishes, such as seafood salad with lemon sauce. Wild game, especially woodcock and pheasant, are a specialty in season. For dessert, ask for the campari sorbet. A big wine list accommodates a selection of at least 15 main dishes from which to choose. Expect to spend from 45 DM ($14.85) to 75 DM ($24.75) for a complete meal here. Hours are noon till 2 p.m. and 6 to 11 p.m.; closed Friday. As there are only a dozen tables, reservations are necessary. In summer, request a table on the fully planted terrace, which seats another 20 diners.

Alt-Prag, 41 Taunusstrasse (tel. 52-04-02), is for Bohemian specialties. Three salons and two different restaurants comprise the architecture of this country baroque-style place, which features and pays homage to the culinary specialties of "Old Prague," as its name suggests. The two rooms are called the

Bauernstube and the Moldaustube. A daily menu changes frequently, offering three fixed-price meals costing from 25 DM ($8.25) to 40 DM ($13.20). During Bohemian and German festivals, very elaborate specialties are offered. Examples of this would be "bear meat goulash" and roast goose. The restaurant serves daily except Monday from noon to 3 p.m. and 6 p.m. to midnight. You can also attend a piano bar nightclub, Charles, on the second floor, which is open from 10 p.m. to 4 a.m.

The **Ratskeller,** 7 Markstrasse (tel. 30-13-13), is like a vaulted temple cellar, with tables set in recesses. You dine in high-backed chairs or on wooden settles. The cellar is informal, serving good basic food that makes it an outstanding choice for those on a limited budget. The restaurant is popular with families, shoppers, and business people. The service is somewhat helter-skelter. You're served soup practically before you sit down at lunch—even if you never eat soup! A large choice of dishes is offered, international in scope. Veal piccata often appears on the menu. A more economical dish is bauern bratwursten with sauerkraut, as is chopped steak. Beer accompanies most dishes. Meals begin as low as 25 DM ($8.25), ranging upward to some 50 DM ($16.50).

ENTERTAINMENT: *"Rien ne va plus"* is the call when the ball starts to roll on the gaming table at the Wiesbaden casino, the **Spielbank Wiesbaden,** Im Kurhaus (tel. 52-69-54), which is open daily at 3 p.m. Roulette and baccarat are the featured games. It was here that the great Russian writer, Feodor Dostoyevsky, attempted to win a fortune, which he figured was an easier way to do it than writing *Crime and Punishment.*

On a more cultural note, the greatest event, as already mentioned, is the International May Festival. But music and theater flourish at Wiesbaden throughout the year. For information on what performances are available at the time of your visit (plus the availability of tickets), check at the **Wiesbaden Tourist Office,** 15 Rheinstrasse/Ecke Wilhelmstrasse (tel. 31-28-47 or 37-43-53). Its hours are Monday to Friday from 8 a.m. to 1 p.m. and 2 to 5 p.m. There's another office at the main railway station (tel. 31-28-48), open Tuesday to Friday from 8 a.m. to 9 p.m. and on Monday from 1 to 9 p.m. It's also open on weekends and holidays as well: from 9 a.m. to 1 p.m. and 5 to 9 p.m.

Perhaps among other offerings you'll get to visit the **Hesse State Theater,** known as the Staatstheatre, which, like the Casino, is part of the Kurhaus compound. It presents a program of operas, musicals, and plays, as well as ballets, with its own ensembles in this theater which was built in 1894.

For information about any facility within the Kurhaus compound, such as the casino or the theater, telephone 31-28-33.

At the **Brunnenkolonnade,** dating from 1825, you'll find not only thermal waters, but concerts given. Music is played for dancing, and you can enjoy a café there.

If you're in Wiesbaden on a summer night, you can wander in the **Kurpark,** enjoying the concerts and garden festivals with illumination and a fireworks display. That beats any after-dark activity likely to be going on within the walls of anything.

Wiesbaden even has its own version of the Via Veneto. Here it's called the **Wilhelmstrasse.** On this street you can find a café that looks good, where you can stake out a post to people-watch, a favorite pastime of both locals and visitors.

4. Bad Nauheim

Like many similar spas throughout Germany, Bad Nauheim grew popular in the early part of this century when the railroad became a convenient and inexpensive means of transportation. Still going strong today, the resort at the northern edge of the Taunus Mountains is a center for golf, tennis, and water sports, as well as the beginning point for energetic hikers to scale the 773-foot Johannisberg, towering over the town.

The warm carbonic acid springs of the spa are said to be beneficial in the treatment of heart and circulatory disorders. The Kurpark is attractive, well-maintained, and filled with promenaders all summer long.

In accommodations, Bad Nauheim offers a number of hotels that sprouted up in an era gone by to cater to the turn-of-the-century crowds who flocked to "take the waters."

THE UPPER-BRACKET HOTEL: Hotel Am Hochwald, 9 Carl-Oelemann-Weg (tel. 34-80), has attractive modern styling, enjoying a quiet location near woodlands which tempt you to go on walks. It's a hotel with much style and facilities, ranging from a swimming pool with a bar, to a sauna, solarium, massage room, and table tennis. The 124 bedrooms, each comfortably furnished, contain private bath or shower, balcony, self-dial phone, radio, TV (on request), and many other thoughtful touches. Singles cost from 100 DM ($33) to 150 DM ($49.50), with doubles beginning at 118 DM ($38.94) to 156 DM ($51.48), and peaking at 300 DM ($99) to 400 DM ($132) for a penthouse accommodation. The hotel offers interesting dining possibilities at its Hessenstube and its Terrassen-Restaurant.

MEDIUM-PRICED HOTELS: Blumes Hotel am Kurhaus, 3 Auguste-Viktoria-Strasse (tel. 20-72), is a huge classic-style villa, recommended for its tranquil setting in a residential district at the edge of the spa gardens. The furnishings are a mixture of modern and traditional. Many of the rooms have terraces, but those with the best views go quickly and are usually reserved in advance. Singles range from 55 DM ($18.15) to 95 DM ($31.35), and doubles cost from 105 DM ($34.65) to 130 DM ($42.90). Interesting food is served in the dining room, which has a baronial fireplace straight out of a castle.

Hotel Grunewald, 10 Terrassenstrasse (tel. 22-30), is a baroque pink confection of a building, not imposingly large, but on a human scale reflecting its probable use as a private house when it was built. It sits close to the street, with potted palms flanking the entryway to the lobby, which leads to the public rooms of the hotel. These lounges are decorated in an eclectic style, with a collection of 19th- and 20th-century furniture. One of the pier mirrors, where Wilhelminian ladies probably checked their hemlines, stretches almost to the ceiling. Framed needlepoint in pinks and beiges show idealized French huntresses chasing deer through a forest. Of particular interest is an elaborate Dresden vase, covered with ceramic fruit and flowers, almost four feet tall, sitting imposingly before a large window. The dining room is appropriately somber, with Jacobean chairs flanking the full-size leaded-glass breakfront cabinet covering an entire wall. The bedrooms are charmingly furnished, often with crystal chandeliers and swag draperies. A single with breakfast rents for 78 DM ($25.74), rising to 128 DM ($42.24) in a double. Some apartments are also rented to two persons at a cost beginning at 300 DM ($99).

Hotel Inter-Europa, 13 Bahnhofsallee (tel. 20-36), is a lively modern hotel, with a restaurant and a café that enjoys lots of patronage by Bad Nauheimers themselves. Rooms are compact, clean, and comfortable, each with shower, toilet, color TV, and phone. A double ranges from 130 DM ($42.90) to 155 DM ($51.15), and a single goes for 100 DM ($33) to 125 DM ($41.25), including a breakfast buffet. Oriental carpets and some antique paintings add warmth to some of the public rooms. The restaurant and grill room of the hotel serve many international specialties. There's also a weinstube.

BUDGET LIVING: Hotel-Restaurant Gaudes, 6 Haupstrasse (tel. 25-08), is known mainly for its restaurant, but it offers eight rooms (no baths) at a cost of 40 DM ($13.20) in a single, from 68 DM ($22.44) to 80 DM (26.40) in a double, breakfast included. Even if you don't stay here, you might want to patronize the dining room.

WHERE TO DINE: Restaurant Gaudesberger, 6 Hauptstrasse (tel. 25-08), has a good, large menu of well-chosen items which the chef prepares exceedingly well. You can stick to the tried-and-true specialties, such as a chateaubriand with a béarnaise sauce or a mixed grill. Or else you can dip into the international specialties, including, for example, pork in a curry cream sauce or perhaps ox tongue in a madeira sauce. At lunch you can order set menus costing from 15 DM ($4.95) to 28 DM ($9.24). At night the charge for the table d'hôte meals range from 28 DM ($9.24) to 65 DM ($21.45). The restaurant, part of the Hotel Gaudes, is closed on Wednesday and shuts down annually between November 6 and 25. The manager, Kurt Berger, is most cooperative and courteous to guests (he also speaks English).

Diessner's Kerzen-Stüberl, 3–5 Mittelstrasse (tel. 20-12), has not been touched by the inroads of urban trendiness, a fact that is probably viewed with relief by its conservative clients. The ambience is pleasantly woodsy, in a Teutonic fantasy of country-style details. You can select from an array of prime Argentine beefsteaks to accompany your wine or beer, or from about a dozen varieties of locally inspired house specialties. Meals cost from 35 DM ($11.55). The establishment is open only for dinner from 6 p.m. to 1 a.m. daily, except Tuesday, for three weeks in summer, and from Christmas Eve to the middle of January.

Am Hochwald, 9 Carl-Oelemann-Weg (tel. 34-80), offers friendly service amid a decor that's a combination of modern lines with country-cousin accents. The menu includes all the typical German dishes, as well as a selection of international specialties. Fixed-price meals begin around 23 DM ($7.59), although depending on what you order the tab can run to almost three times that. You can be served a beer and a cold snack or salad throughout the day. Warm food is served from 11:30 a.m. to 2:30 p.m. and 6:30 to 11:30 p.m. The restaurant is in one of the town's larger hotels, which has 140 rooms costing from 110 DM ($36.30) in a single and from 125 DM ($41.25) in a double.

5. Bad Homburg

Ten miles north of Frankfurt lies one of Germany's most attractive spas, still basking in the grandeur of turn-of-the-century Europe. Actually, Bad Homburg has been a popular watering spot since Roman times. Royalty from all over the world have visited the spa and left their mark. King Chulalongkorn, immortalized in *The King and I,* was so impressed by it that he built a Siamese temple in the Kurpark. Czar Nicholas erected an onion-domed Russian chapel nearby. The name of the town was popularized by Edward VII of England when, as Prince of Wales, he visited the spa and introduced a new hat style, which he called the homburg.

The spa park is an oasis in the middle of a large, rather commercial town. The spa's saline springs are used in the treatment of various disorders, especially heart and circulatory diseases. The Kurpark extends into the foothills of the Taunus Mountains, stretching in front of the Kurhaus (resort center). The gardens are filled with brooks, ponds, and arbors.

The town became the gaming capital of Europe when the Blanc brothers opened the **Casino** in the Kurpark in 1841. Predating its offspring by 25 years, the "Mother of Monte Carlo" is especially popular in summer with white-suited Frankfurt industrialists. From 3 p.m., roulette and baccarat are the games people play here. Entrance fee is 6 DM ($1.98).

The **Bad Homburg Palace,** Schlossverwaltung (tel. 2-60-91), a few short blocks from the spa gardens, was the residence of the landgraves of Hesse-Homburg from its construction in 1680 until the mid-19th century. Its builder, Prince Friedrich II von Homburg, preserved the still-standing White Tower of the medieval castle which had stood on that site, and incorporated it into the structure of the baroque palace. In the late 19th century the palace became a summer residence for Prussian kings and later German emperors who used it as a summer residence. After World War I the state assumed ownership.

The interior of the palace contains furniture and paintings of the 18th century, including a bust of Prince Friedrich II by Andreas Schluter, Germany's greatest baroque sculptor. The former "telephone room of the empress" includes a *Cleopatra* by Pellegrini. The palace and formal gardens are open daily from 10 a.m. to 4 p.m. in season, with guided tours every 40 minutes. Admission is 2 DM (66¢).

WHERE TO STAY: For such a world-famous spa, Bad Homburg has, with one exception, surprisingly modest hotels, but within that range some good ones, previewed below.

Maritim Kurhaus-Hotel, Kurpark, Ludwigstrasse (tel. 2-80-51), has ultra-modern spa facilities and an adjacent hotel, constructed in 1984. Visitors are treated to plushly comfortable accommodations, many illuminated with tall bay windows. Each unit has a balcony or terrace, permitting wide-angle views over the greenery of the surrounding park. The hotel's big-windowed indoor swimming pool tempts guests with the opportunity to exercise away any weight they might gain in either of the well-managed restaurants or at the café-terrace. There's a sauna for additional relaxation. Copious buffet breakfasts are a part of the many offerings at this attractive place. Prices range from 165 DM ($54.45) to 250 DM ($82.50) for a single, from 240 DM ($79.20) to 360 DM ($118.80) for a double.

Geheimrat Trapp, 55-57 Kaiser-Friedrich-Promenade (tel. 2-60-47), stands opposite the widely known Kurpark. It's a quiet and modern facility, noted for its individualized service. Rooms are attractively furnished and most comfortable. They rent more singles than doubles. A single costs 85 DM ($28.05) to 110 DM ($36.30), and a double goes for 130 DM ($42.90) to 190 DM ($62.70). These tariffs include breakfast. Units have showers, toilets, phones, and mini-bars. On the premises is a Chinese restaurant.

Hardtwald Hotel, Philosophenweg (tel. 2-50-16), is like a chalet set in a forest. Run by the Scheller-Kurze family since 1868, the hotel is an ideal retreat near the spa gardens. The modestly furnished rooms were built to overlook the forest. Prices are reasonable, ranging from as little as 80 DM ($26.40) for a bathless single to 85 DM ($28.05) with complete bath. Doubles with bath or shower cost from 120 DM ($39.60) to 138 DM ($45.54). Full board is available for 28 DM ($9.24) per person per day extra. And that may be the best bargain, as the hotel is noted for its fine food. The dining room, heavily planted with flowers, seems to do as much business as the hotel. In summer tables are set outdoors on the large patio.

Haus Daheim, 42 Elisabethenstrasse (tel. 2-00-98), is a pinkish corner building with good beds and much comfort. The innkeeper, Horst Stiegmann, sees to your needs, and his is one of the finest of the small hotels of the spa. A few singles have no baths, and naturally these are the cheapest, costing only 50 DM ($16.50) nightly. With bath, a single rises in price to 75 DM ($24.75). Peaking at 95 DM ($31.35) is a double with bath (or shower), toilet, phone, and radio. These tariffs include breakfast, taxes, and service. The location is only a short stroll from the Kurhaus.

Villa Kisseleff, 19 Kisseleffstrasse (tel. 2-15-40), lies in the Kurpark of Bad Homburg, close to the curative springs. It's a symmetrical, four-story baroque villa, a "gemütlich hotel garni," run by Frau Helena Klein. This quiet and restful villa was erected by Grafin Kisseleff, and tastefully renovated in 1976. A personal atmosphere pervades the place, and the rooms are comfortable, some with bath, shower, and toilet. A bathless single costs 50 DM ($16.50), going up to 75 DM ($24.75) with shower or bath. A bathless double is 75 DM ($24.75), climbing to 95 DM ($31.35) with shower or bath. The service is perfect, beginning with breakfast in your room to your final good night from the reception.

WHERE TO DINE: The Bad Homburg restaurant outlook has much improved in recent years. Diners are demanding and getting better food.

It's called simply **"Table,"** 85 Kaiser-Friedrich-Promenade (tel. 2-44-25), and it clearly outclasses every other restaurant at the spa. Hans Schweitzer, a man of vision, talent, and imagination, is the guiding force behind the success of the place. Well-made sauces and excellent, fresh ingredients are just part of the secret of "Table."

I'm so fond of the appetizers I have trouble getting to the main course. For openers you are faced with, say, a parfait of Bresse chicken with foie gras, a salad composed of sauteed veal liver slices, or quenelles in a crayfish sauce, or a wild crayfish bisque laced with champagne. For a main course, try the fresh salmon poached in champagne, or perhaps a composition of sweetbreads, liver, and veal kidney. Wild hare in a rose-hip sauce with fresh figs is one of the innovative nouvelle cuisine dishes, or a whole Barbarie duck (the breast served with peach, the legs with pink peppercorns). A roast rack of venison is made with cranberries, and turbans of sole are filled with pike mousse and presented with two sauces. For dessert, why not an almond soufflé with poached apricots or a mango sorbet with marinated cherries? Germany is clearly in a culinary Renaissance!

The "Table" is set Tuesday to Sunday from 6:30 p.m., and closes yearly from January 1 to 9 and from April 22 to May 6. I've saved the worst news for last, your final tab. It will likely be from 75 DM ($24.75), and I do mean "from."

Casino-Restaurant, im Kurpark (tel. 2-00-41). It is generally acknowledged that Bad Homburg's casino is neither the most glamorous nor the largest in the country. However, its restaurant competently maintains a traditional style of decor and service, with a good array of nouvelle and classical dishes. The daily-changing fixed-price meals cost from 35 DM ($11.55) to 50 DM ($16.50), with both seasonal and daily specialties.

Head chef Günther Schwanitz begins each workday with an examination of Bad Homburg's freshest produce, fish, and meats. He returns to the kitchen to turn out such outstanding dishes as sauteed chicken with sweetbreads in a mushroom cream sauce with a dandelion salad. Hot food is served from 6 to 11 p.m., and it's necessary to reserve a table.

Friedrichshof, 66 Saalburgstrasse (tel. 35-86-4), is a familiar, friendly, and tranquil choice. Its food is reliable and cooked to quite acceptable standards. You are likely to spend anywhere from 22 DM ($7.26) to 50 DM ($16.50). Tasty, competent selections include the soups, appetizers, standard main dishes, and often quite rich desserts. Hours are daily except Monday from 11:30 a.m. to 2:30 p.m. and 5:30 p.m. to midnight. It closes for three weeks sometime in summer.

If you're driving, you can patronize a restaurant in the environs. It's called **Darmstadter Hof mit Schoppe-Stübche,** 77 Frankfurter Landstrasse, at Gonzenheim (tel. 4-13-47). Reservations are suggested before heading here. It's a rustic grill restaurant with a large menu of many specialties, including (if you're there at the right time of year) trout, venison, and pheasant. This is a popular gathering place in the evening for the locals. It serves from 11 a.m. till 2 p.m. and 6 p.m. to midnight, with meals costing from 30 DM ($9.90) to 58 DM ($19.14). For some odd reason, it shuts down on weekends.

AFTER DARK: The **Tennis Bar,** im Kurpark, close to the Spielbank (tel. 2-60-41), is the most famous spot. Many Frankfurters visit it just for the evening. The kitchen stays open until 4 a.m., and meals begin at 35 DM ($11.55) and going up. It's closed on Monday in the off-season.

6. Bad Wiessee

If you've always believed that the best medicine is the worst tasting, you should feel right at home in Bad Wiessee—the mineral springs of this popular spa on the Tegernsee are saturated with iodine and sulfur. But the other attractions of this small town more than make up for this discomfort. Just 30 miles south of Munich, this spa, with a huge lake at its feet and towering Alps rising behind it, is a year-round resort. In summer, swimming and boating are popular pastimes; in winter, you can ski on the slopes or skate on the lake.

The springs are used for the treatment of many diseases, including rheumatism and heart and respiratory conditions. In spite of its tiny size, Bad Wiessee is sophisticated in its medicinal facilities as well as in accommodations and restaurants. There's even a small gambling casino.

The main season begins in May and ends in October. Bad Wiessee in recent years has become increasingly popular, mainly with holiday-makers from Munich itself, and if you're considering going there during these busy times, you should definitely make a reservation. Because of lack of business, many hotels are likely to close abruptly in winter, so be duly warned if you're an off-season visitor.

WHERE TO STAY: **Hotel Lederer am See,** 9-11 Bodenschneidstrasse (tel. 82-91), is clearly the most distinguished choice in the whole town. It's a spa and holiday hotel, and from the balcony of your room you'll most likely look out onto Tegernsee and the Lower Alps of Bavaria. The hotel has a pleasant atmosphere; warm, friendly service; and comfortable rooms. Singles range from 80 DM ($26.40) to 130 DM ($42.90) daily, and doubles cost from 130 DM ($42.90) to 230 DM ($75.90). The hotel stands in a large park, and there's a dock for bathing and a meadow for sunbathing. However, if the weather is bad, they also have an indoor swimming pool. Sometimes they barbecue meats on the terrace facing the lake. Later, you can enjoy entertainment or dancing in the Martinsklause. The hotel has its own medical staff and "beauty farm." The kitchen turns out an international cuisine of good standard, a set meal costing from 30 DM ($9.90) to 75 DM ($24.75).

Kurhotel Rex, 25 Münchnerstrasse (tel. 8-20-91), is a modern hotel of much charm and character, set against a backdrop of the Lower Alps of Bavaria. Run by a family, it's one of the nicer choices at the spa. There is a lavish use of wood and discreet lighting, and some decorator tried to make it as warm and inviting as possible, an ideal choice for a holiday by the lake. Single rooms range from 60 DM ($19.80) to 88 DM ($29.04), and doubles run from 110 DM ($36.30) to 155 DM ($51.15). Even more expensive apartments are rented. The hotel, open April to October, has good food and also caters to special dieters. Its Bierstüberl is often a lively gathering place for holiday-makers, many of whom have had quite a few liters.

Hotel Marina, 9 Furtwänglerstrasse (tel. 8-11-25), run by the Wagner family, is a typical Bavarian house with encircling balconies and a roof overhang. Potted plants in summer grace the balconies, making it even more colorful in keeping with the character of the region.Every guest here (well, almost) seems on a fitness campaign, swimming in the indoor pool or patronizing the solarium and sauna (no one shrieks at a little nudity around here). In summer the place has a lovely garden-like setting, and in winter it's a blaze of lights on a cold winter's night. The service is friendly and personal. Bavarian touches, such as tile stoves and wooden chairs, prevail throughout. The place gets quite festive at times. On the half-board plan, the single rate ranges from 70 DM ($23.10) to 100 DM ($33) nightly, the double costing from 85 DM ($28.05) per person.

Landhaus Hotel Sapplfeld, 8 im Sapplfeld (tel. 8-20-67), is another typical Bavarian-style inn, with geranium-filled balconies and a roof overhang. It's a real alpine resort, and people come here to have a good time when they're not involved in a fitness program, swimming in the indoor pool or working out with some of the gym equipment. Men go nude with their women into the sauna, sprawling out on the hot wooden benches. The hotel is biseasonal, attracting scenic-gulpers in summer, skiers in winter. Rooms are completely modern and up-to-date. A single with breakfast costs from 100 DM ($33) to 160 DM ($52.80), and a double goes for 160 DM ($52.80) to 200 DM ($66), with off-season reductions granted. Rooms contain private bath, balcony, radio, and TV.

Hotel Terrassenhof, 50 Adrian-Stoop-Strasse (tel. 8-27-61), run by the Gericke family, is exceptional in many ways. Attracting a largely German clientele, it delivers a lot for what it charges. A hotel "for all seasons," it has attractively furnished rooms, both public and private. Its lakeside setting makes it an idyllic retreat. High-season rates in a double or single range from 85 DM ($28.05) to 135 DM ($44.55) per person, including a breakfast buffet. Guests in summer enjoy a tree-shaded terrace overlooking the lake.

Hotel Resi von der Post, 14 Zilcherstrasse (tel. 8-27-88), has been an enduring favorite, and it's been around much longer than many of its fast-rising competitors. The Kamhuber family continue to offer good value. The hotel has much character, and has been considerably modernized. Inside, the atmosphere is often bustling, as diners who live nearby fill up the place. Many show up in Bavarian costumes. They know they can get fresh fish from the lake, and good, hearty Bavarian fare. Ask for a special cheese of the Tegernsee district, Miesbacher. The hotel rents out 50 beds, each unit with bath, phone, and many thoughtful amenities. Singles range in price from 35 DM ($11.55) to 62 DM ($20.46), while doubles go for 80 DM ($26.40) to 130 DM ($42.90). These tariffs include breakfast. This hotel has long been a special retreat of mine, because I like the hearty, fun-loving spirit of the place.

Wiesseer Hof, 46 Sanktjohanserstrasse (tel. 8-20-61). Most of the rooms in this modern hotel look out over balconies which in summertime are festooned with boxes of geraniums. The style of the place is like an overgrown chalet, with four floors of rooms, many with views over a lawn dotted with greenery, leading up to the blue expanse of the Tegernsee. The units are cheerfully up to date, and the stuccoed wooden walls of the public rooms create a gemütlich warmth. The family running the Wiesseer Hof has a healthy respect for traditional styles. The kitchen features many Bavarian specialties, and an elevator comes in handy when you've overindulged in them. Singles cost from 70 DM ($23.10) to 85 DM ($28.05), and doubles range from 136 DM ($44.88) to 154 DM ($50.82).

St. Georg, 20 Jägerstrasse (tel. 8-27-14), is a hotel garnis, which allows you to take lunch and dinner outside, adding variety to your holiday. This well-constructed chalet offers three stories of comfort to guests who, behind masses of geraniums in the window boxes, nestle in rooms under the heavy overhang of the timbered eaves. The interior is modern and designed in a comfortably rustic style. Everything is kept spotlessly clean, and many of the units open onto views of the Tegernsee. A single or double room rents for 70 DM ($23.10) per person daily.

Landhaus Rehbichl, 8 Adalbert-Stifter-Weg (tel. 8-10-29), is set in a wooded area. This family-run guest house offers personal service and the diligent attention of its small staff. They serve a big breakfast to guests who arrive in Bad Wiessee to wander through the woods near the Tegernsee. Some of the rooms overlook the hills around the spa, and a sun terrace is an attractive place for writing journals or letters. Singles rent for 70 DM ($23.10) to 85 DM ($28.05), and doubles go for 136 DM ($44.88) to 154 DM ($50.82).

Kurhotel Edelweiss, 21 Münchnerstrasse (tel. 8-12-87). The main body of this chalet-style guest house is beautifully decorated with painted detailing around its doors and windows, and skillfully ornamented with wooden balconies and trim. Additional units are available in the motel-like outbuildings, stretching beside the main structure, affording comfortable and clean lodging for guests in summer and winter. The public rooms are modern, with a certain German kitsch and vaguely Teutonic new furniture with cheerful colors and designs. The charges in single rooms range from 49 DM ($16.17) to 62 DM ($20.46). Doubles cost 84 DM ($27.72) to 109 DM ($35.97).

7. Bad Reichenhall

Only the most excellent German spas can call themselves Staatsbad, denoting supreme state approval. Bad Reichenhall bears that title with pride. This old salt town is the most important curative spa in the Bavarian Alps. Mountain chains surround it, protecting it from the winds; the town's brine springs, with a salt content of as much as 24%, are the most powerful saline springs in Europe. The combination of the waters and the pure air has made Bad Reichenhall a recognized spa for centuries, and it has been a source of salt for much longer, more than 2400 years.

In 1848 King Maximilian of Bavaria stayed here, doing much to popularize Bad Reichenhall as a fashionable resort. Today visitors come from all over the world to take the waters of the salt springs, which are supposedly effective in the treatment of asthma and other respiratory ailments. Treatment sessions are almost exclusively in the morning at the seven resort institutes, the therapy ranging from simply drinking the water to pneumato-therapy, and even electronic lungs for the most serious cases. But although Bad Reichenhall takes the medical side of the cure seriously, spa authorities encourage visitors to enjoy the many attractions in and around the town as well.

There's a wide choice of activities: from symphony concerts to folklore presentations. The State Gaming Rooms are popular, and the ideal climate permits a complete whirl of outdoor events, from hikes into the mountains to tennis tournaments. Incidentally, the spa gardens are unusual in that the sheltered location of the town amid the lofty Alps permits the growth of several varieties of tropical plants, giving the gardens a lush, exotic appearance.

WHAT TO SEE: The **Alte Saline** (Old Salt Works), just a short walk from the Kurgarten, is the home of the ancient industry responsible for the growth and prosperity of Bad Reichenhall from Celtic times to the present. Parts of the old plant still stand today, but most of it was reconstructed in the mid-19th century in the troubadour style by Ludwig I of Bavaria. The large pumps and huge marble caverns are impressive. Tours are provided daily from April 1 to October 31. Hours are 10 to 11:30 a.m. and 2 to 4 p.m. Admission is 5 DM ($1.65) for adults, 2.50 DM (83¢) for children.

The great fire of 1834 destroyed much of the town, but many of the impressive churches survived. One outstanding memorial is **St. Zeno,** a 12th-century Gothic church showing a later baroque influence. Its most remarkable feature is the painted interior, centering on the carved altarpiece of the *Coronation of the Virgin.*

THE TOP HOTELS: Steigenberger Hotel Axelmannstein, 2-6 Salzburger Strasse (tel. 40-01), occupies an excellent position in its own 7½-acre garden, complete with swimming pools, in- and outdoor. A first-class hotel attracting a mature clientele, it offers many rooms with views of the encircling Bavarian Alps. Each of the 153 well-furnished accommodations contains a private bath, color TV, radio, direct-dial phone, and a mini-bar. Single rooms cost from 130 DM ($42.90) to 168 DM ($55.44). Double rooms are 185 DM ($61.05) to 250 DM ($82.50). In July, August, and September the single room charge is 142 DM ($46.86) to 184 DM ($60.72), and doubles cost 205 DM ($67.65) to 285 DM ($94.05).

The dining room, opening onto a garden, attracts many nonresidents. The public rooms are traditionally furnished with antiques and reproductions, including some Gobelin tapestries. The most popular gathering point is the cozy wood-paneled Axel-Bar, with live entertainment daily. The hotel offers a cure department, sauna, solarium, fitness center, cosmetic studio, hairdressers, mini-golf, fitness path, tennis courts, and boccia.

Luisenbad, 33 Ludwigstrasse (tel. 50-11), is a world unto itself. It's an older hotel with a newer bedroom wing placed in a garden setting. Its most outstanding feature is its indoor swimming pool, with a glass wall bringing the outdoors inside. The lounges and atmosphere are invitingly home-like; nothing is austere here, as the emphasis is placed on informality and comfort. The new bedrooms are quite handsome, with bold colors and tasteful furnishings; most contain shower and bath. A single ranges in price from 90 DM ($29.70) to 130 DM ($42.90). A double with bath costs from 170 DM ($56.10) to 240 DM ($79.20). There are facilities for thermal baths, inhalations, massages, and mud baths, plus a Finnish sauna.

Hotel Panorama, 6 Baderstrasse (tel. 6-10-01), is in a pristine modern style, overlooking the spa with a scenic mountain backdrop. The hotel is for those who demand the latest in spa facilities. Accommodations are compact and sleekly contemporary, and they're divided into category "A" and category "B." Naturally, the most expensive category would be the chambers with the better view. The 126-bed hotel offers rooms with balcony, private bath, toilet, and radio. Singles cost from 112 DM ($36.96) to 125 DM ($41.25), and doubles go for 190 DM ($62.70) to 220 DM ($72.60). The hotel serves good meals in an attractive setting, and has many facilities to keep you fit, ranging from a large swimming pool to a sauna. The hotel also offers cure facilities, along with a café and bar you can enjoy when you've recovered.

MEDIUM-PRICED HOTELS: Salzburger Hof, 7 Mozartstrasse (tel. 20-62), is one of the best buys if you're shopping for a moderately priced hotel. Recently built and architecturally contemporary, most of the public rooms have been given an overlay of old Bavarian charm. Public lounges are sacrificed to make room for unique dining rooms and nooks. Best of all are the compact and refreshingly furnished bedrooms, most of which contain streamlined sofas, window desks, beds with built-in headboards, and armchairs placed around a breakfast table. All of the accommodations open onto tiny balconies, and all have bath, telephone, and mini-bar. Single rooms with half board range in price from 87 DM ($28.71) to 107 DM ($35.31); doubles, from 144 DM ($47.52) to 184 DM ($60.72). Your hosts, the Helmut Herkommer family, speak English.

Hotel Bayerischer, 14 Bahnhofsplatz (tel. 50-84), is also run by the Helmut Kerkommer family, who own the previously recommended Salzburger Hof. Their second hotel is of a fine international standard, standing all modern and inviting in the center of the spa. The staff is well trained, and the reception is helpful in arranging excursions to such places as Obersalzberg, Berchtesgadener Land, and Salzburg. If you're there in winter, they'll provide help in arranging such sports as long-distance and downhill skiing.

They rent out 45 single rooms and 18 two- and three-room apartments, each fitted out with elegant Bavarian furniture. A single room rents for 75 DM ($24.75) to 100 DM ($33), the more expensive units containing private balconies. Likewise, the double rate goes from 92 DM ($30.36) to 150 DM ($49.50). All units contain private bath, mini-bar, radio, and phone. The hotel is well equipped with facilities, including a roof-garden indoor swimming pool with Finnish sauna, plus another salon for massage and cosmetic treatment. In addition to its three restaurants, the hotel has a nightclub with international acts and Das Wiener Café, the Vienna café where Viennese and Swiss pastries are made by the hotel confectioners themselves.

Tiroler Hof, 12 Tiroler Strasse (tel. 20-55), is a pumpkin-colored building lying within "ten minutes of everything." It has a gray annex on the corner of the Tiroler Strasse, near where the ancient tollhouse once stood. There has been an eating place on this spot ever since 1634. Affiliated with Germany's Ringhotels, the Tiroler Hof is run in a personal way. It is warm and friendly, with a swimming pool and a colorful, wood-beamed restaurant on the premises. A single rents for 60 DM ($19.80) to 90 DM ($29.70), and a double goes for 115 DM ($37.95) to 150 DM ($49.50). The most expensive units contain complete private baths and balconies.

Hotel Garni Alfons Maria, 19 Schillerstrasse (tel. 20-88), lies about two blocks from the railway station, offering breakfast only. The modernity of this elongated, three-story building is relieved by the skillful use of weathered wood on the balcony railings, and the rows of geraniums in window boxes along the length of the building's facade. Inside, guests will find clean, comfortable rooms, many with a balcony or small terrace. You meet your fellow visitors in a warm, friendly room, the Bauernstube, with a small bar, handsome wooden ceiling, and rustic tables and chairs. In addition, there's a communal sun terrace and an informal breakfast room. They close the place from November 1 to February 1. Singles range in price from 40 DM ($13.20), and doubles cost from 80 DM ($26.40).

BUDGET HOTELS: The ornate facade at **Brauerei Bürgerbräu,** 2 Waaggasse (tel. 24-11), features groups of dancers. Inside, much use is made of wood and stone, and the vaulted dining rooms have an ambience typical of the popular breweries of Bavaria. The food is good, copious, and inexpensive. A range of menus, costing from 20 DM ($6.60) to 45 DM ($14.85), is offered. An elevator whisks you to immaculate modern and functional bedrooms with up-to-date plumbing. The hotel charges 40 DM ($13.20) in a single without bath, increasing to 55 DM ($18.15) with shower and toilet. Depending on the plumbing, doubles range from 72 DM ($23.76) to 105 DM ($34.65), including breakfast. The reception is on the second floor.

Hotel Hansi am Kurpark, 3 Rinckstrasse (tel. 31-08), is a late-19th-century building with a tiled mansard roof and flowering verandas. The pleasing symmetry of the structure welcomes guests from the corner of Rinckstrasse where it sits. The owners, Mr. and Mrs. Willi Bachmann, run a well-maintained establishment with a good cuisine prepared by Mr. Bachmann himself. Their room charges depend on the size and comfort of the unit, the rate going from 81 DM ($26.73) to 91 DM ($30.03) per person for full board. The same family also runs the **Appartementhaus Waldfrieden,** 100 yards above the town of Bad Reichenhall, offering apartment living (sans kitchen) to guests who prefer that way of traveling. Most of these units contain balconies with southern exposure and chaise lounges for sunning. They are fully equipped with private bath.

Hotel Kurfürst, 11 Kurfürstenstrasse (tel. 27-10), is under the personal management of its conscientious owner, Renate Voitz. Hers is a 20-bed, family-run hotel slightly on the outskirts of Bad Reichenhall, near the river and about a 20-minute walk to anywhere else in town. A trim and well-maintained modern facade in white stucco opens to a lobby with Oriental rugs and a skillfully crafted curved staircase going up to the upper floors. The rooms are spacious and sunny, some of them opening onto a terrace with tables and chairs. Lunch can be served here if a client prefers it. The price for a single or double bedroom with breakfast is either 40 DM ($13.20) or 46 DM ($15.18).

Excelsior, 12 Paepkestrasse (tel. 25-48). Frau Magdalena Klein keeps her small 26-room hotel open year round, and many visitors find their favorite time here is in winter. Across from the Kurpark, this 19th-century building has a red-tile mansard roof, green shutters, and encircling double verandas. If you want a calm, comfortable lodging, at a good price, the rather pretentiously named Excelsior might be a good bet. A single with shower or private bath and balcony ranges in price from 68 DM ($22.44) to 86 DM ($23.38); a double goes for 112 DM ($36.96) to 170 DM ($56.10).

Hotel-Pension Sonnenbichl, 2 Adolf-Schmid-Strasse (tel. 6-10-19). The interior of this modern hotel is almost overwhelmingly paneled in wood, especially the public rooms. The owners rent out clean, sunny rooms, often with views of the hills, and guests in summer enjoy the Bavarian sunshine from flower-filled balconies. The location is convenient too, only two blocks from the railroad station and very close to the Kurpark. Singles cost 60 DM ($19.80) to 80 DM ($26.40); doubles, from 100 DM ($33) to 140 DM ($46.20).

Bergfried, 8 Adolf-Schmid-Strasse (tel. 43-98), is a six-story balconied villa, which offers stunning views from its top floors. Close to the Kurgarten and Axelmannstein Park, it lies about a ten-minute walk from the railroad station. Your hosts offer clean, comfortable rooms, with modern conveniences, to their guests, whom they charge from 80 DM ($26.40) to 110 DM ($36.30) per person nightly for full board. In summer, guests can enjoy their little garden. If they can't accommodate you at the Bergfried, they have two other villas, the Villa Schönblick and the Pension Dora.

Hotel-Pension Erika, 3 Adolf-Schmid-Strasse (tel. 6-10-11), is a 19th-century villa of red brick and gingerbread splendor. This four-story, very grand edifice welcomes guests into the high-ceilinged splendor of a renovated palace, now updated to a modern hotel. The rooms are warm and comfortably furnished, and the hotel has many flowers that bloom profusely in summer. Singles in a unit with shower and toilet pay 53 DM ($17.49) to 70 DM ($23.10). Two persons are charged from 96 DM ($31.68) to 130 DM ($42.90).

If you have a car, you'll find some of the most engaging accommodations—

and some of the best food—in the environs. The choice spot to seek out is **Neu-Meran** at Nonn (tel. 40-78), a little satellite of Bad Reichenhall. This modern rendezvous point for visitors is composed of two beflowered and balconied wings stretching off at right angles to one another. The hotel nestles at the foot of a wooded mountain, with a view of the Lower Alps in the distance. Each of the windows is oversize, even the ones in the bedrooms. The comfortable bedrooms are tastefully appointed in pleasing earth tones. The hotel boasts a swimming pool where you wear your bathing suit and a sauna where you do not. It also has a "sun studio" and a whirlpool bath.

Single rooms range in price from 48 DM ($15.84) to 74 DM ($24.42), and doubles cost from 70 DM ($23.10). For half board, add another 25 DM ($8.25) per person daily. Guests register in the lobby surrounded by hand-carved massive balustrades before beginning a tour of the public rooms which show a skilled use of wood. The cuisine is Bavarian and international, prepared by head chef Franz Weber, who has won many coveted culinary awards. The Weber family has been running this hotel for three generations. Even if you're not staying there, perhaps you'd like to drive out for a meal, costing from 22 DM ($7.26) to 65 DM ($21.45).

WHERE TO DINE: Bad Reichenhall doesn't have any distinguished restaurants outside of the hotel dining rooms, except for one or two places I have discovered. Most guests here dine on "en pension" terms. However, if you can slip away for one meal, perhaps you'll try one of the following selections.

The **Parkrestaurant** and the **Axel-Stüberl** are in the Steigenberger Hotel Axelmannstein, 2-6 Salzburger Strasse (tel. 40-01), previewed above. The Parkrestaurant is known for international specialties, while the Axel-Stüberl features original Bavarian and Austrian cooking. The head chef, Adolf Payer, uses his skills to prepare nouvelle cuisine specialties—tasty and of low calorie count. The fish served in both restaurants is particularly good, as is the standing rack of lamb provençal, with fresh herbs and homemade bread. A gourmet menu, known as *feinschmeckermenu,* costs around 95 DM ($31.35). Otherwise, most meals are served for 44 DM ($14.52) to 55 DM ($18.15). Hot food is served at the Parkrestaurant from noon to 2 p.m. and 6:30 to 9 p.m., and at the Axel-Stüberl from noon to 2 p.m. and 6 to 11 p.m.

Luisenbad, 33 Ludwigstrasse (tel. 50-81), serves some of the best food at the resort. Its old-fashioned tradition and service have always had a seductive pull on me. It's a place where you can watch the flowers bloom and enjoy a world-class cuisine, with many diet-conscious selections. Try, for example, many original recipes developed here in the famous kitchens, and named after the spa or the hotel itself. Among these, I'd recommend marinated and roasted medallions of venison, Königen Luise, served with bacon, chanterelles (mushrooms), and whortleberries. The hotel restaurant is open from noon to 2 p.m. and 6:30 to 10 p.m., offering fixed-price menus costing from 35 DM ($11.55). With no imagination at all, you can also easily spend 60 DM ($19.80).

Schweizer Stuben, 8 Nonnerstrasse (tel. 27-60). If you want to throw a party, this is the place to do it. The cook will feed "any number of guests," or so he promises. However, if your "party" is confined just to yourself or one or two others, you can also drop in and be well taken care of. Messrs. Schwab and Anfang will open to you the delights of what is known as Bad Reichenhall's "rendezvous point for gourmets." They feature a light nouvelle cuisine, along with specialties from Bavaria and the Berchtesgaden region. The decor is appropriately rustic, the ambience gemütlich, and the choice of food attractively poised between international and regional. The restaurant serves from 11 a.m. to 2:30 p.m. and 5:30 to 11 p.m. It's closed on Friday and for three weeks in July.

Fixed-price menus begin at 35 DM ($11.55), while a seven-course gourmet menu costs 70 DM ($23.10).

8. Bad Neuenahr

Lying in the foothills of the Eifel Mountains, near the confluence of the Ahr and Rhine Rivers, this modern spa has a mild climate and wide range of facilities suitable to the international clientele who gather here. Twenty miles south of Bonn, Bad Neuenahr attracts a diplomatic crowd from the capital to its fashionable gambling casino, the largest in Germany. Roulette, American roulette, baccarat, and blackjack are played here daily from 2 p.m. till 2 a.m. It's called the **Spielbank Bad Neuenahr,** at 1 Felix-Rütten-Strasse (tel. 22-41). The entrance fee is 5 DM ($1.65).

Besides the spa installations, including facilities for the Kneipp hydrotherapy, Bad Neuenahr is a popular gathering spot for relaxation and sport. Business people often hold conferences here, combining decisions with golf, entertainment, fine food, and wines. The spa is also a good starting point for day trips and hiking expeditions into the Ahr Valley, one of the Rhine's most attractive tributaries. The river is lined with old wine villages, crumbling castles, and wooded hills.

UPPER-BRACKET HOTELS: **Steigenberger Kurhotel,** 1 Kurgartenstrasse (tel. 22-91), is a Wilhelmian hotel with a modern extension. When the newer wing was added, an interior decorator was given a free hand to create a completely contemporary look. This is especially reflected in the spacious bedrooms, containing adequate living space, plus sitting areas. A single room with shower or bath ranges in price from 125 DM ($41.25) to 155 DM ($51.15). Doubles with bath go for anywhere from 186 DM ($61.38) to a paralyzing peak of 425 DM ($140.25) for the super-deluxe accommodations. The chain hotel is right in the heart of the spa, 550 yards from the main station.

Guests are given a choice of dining places, including the Kupferkessel (Copper Kettle). The Pfeffermühle (Peppermill) is also a target, as are the Kurhaus Restaurant and the gambling casino. (The chef specializes in diets for diabetics, by the way.) Elaborate meals are offered, a three-course lunch going for 35 DM ($11.55), a dinner for 45 DM ($14.85).

The spa facilities here are exceptional, including therapeutic installations, plus an indoor swimming pool with thermal water. Either in the lounge with a fireplace, or in the large awning-shaded sun terrace, the living at the Steigenberger is easy.

Dorint Hotel, am Dahliengarten (tel. 23-25), is a modern, first-class hotel surrounded by parks and situated in a quiet location on the River Ahr. All year round it's lively with activities. The bedrooms are comfortably and attractively furnished, containing balconies. Each unit has a private bath/shower, toilet, radio, and color TV. Including breakfast, service, and tax, a single room rents for 125 DM ($41.25), and a double goes for 186 DM ($61.38). If you're traveling with a child, an extra bed will be placed in your room for 25 DM ($8.25). As a guest here, you'll also have use of the hotel's swimming pool and sauna.

MIDDLE-RANGE HOTELS: **Giffels' Goldener Anker,** 14 Mittelstrasse (tel. 23-85), a Ringhotel, lies on a quiet street only 100 yards from the Kurpark. Founded in 1869, it's still managed by the Giffels family, and the present operators, the fourth generation, carry on with the same friendly and personalized manner that has always been a hallmark of the hotel. On one recent occasion, one of their "repeaters" admitted to having patronized the establishment for 47 years. The bedrooms are nicely furnished, and some of the rear accommodations feature little private balconies. For overnight stays, bathless singles range in price from 69 DM ($22.77), increasing to 90 DM ($29.70) with some sort of plumbing. Doubles cost from 120 DM ($39.60) to 180 DM ($59.40), the higher price for a complete bath. Full-board terms are reasonable as well.

Hotel Fürstenberg, 4-6 Mittelstrasse (tel. 23-17). The most prominent feature of this four-story hotel is the brightly lit restaurant jutting onto the sidewalk, welcoming visitors in for a good meal and a comfortable room on the floors above. The overflow from the main building spills into the Beethovenhaus annex, an older structure next door. The strollers from the neighboring public gardens sometimes eat in the restaurant, with its coffered wooden ceiling, parquet floors, and Oriental rugs adding a colorful ambience. The Wilhelminian touches of the lobby show in the 19th-century moldings and the gold-and-black striped wallpaper. The rooms are tastefully and comfortably furnished, costing from 90 DM ($29.70) in a bathless double, rising to 113 DM ($37.29) in a double with bath. Singles with shower cost 60 DM ($19.80).

Hotel Elisabeth, 11 Georg-Kreuzberg-Strasse (tel. 2-60-74), has a modern boxy exterior whose white facade is relieved only by cement balconies and colorful awnings stretching over the ground-level sun terrace. The public rooms of the interior are warmly decorated, with comfortably upholstered armchairs in the sitting room and in 1983 gemütlich-rustic in the weinstube, with its red brick walls, wooden ceilings, and chalet-style furniture. The restaurant has one of those panoramic photographs of an autumn forest splashed across a windowless wall, and red medallion chairs under tables with spotlessly white linens. Many of the attractive bedrooms come with sun terraces. You can stay here for 75 DM ($24.75) to 90 DM ($29.70) in a single, 155 DM ($51.15) to 175 DM ($57.75) in a double, depending on your room assignment. Special features of the hotel include an indoor swimming pool, sauna bath, and solarium.

Hotel Pfäffle, 7 Lindenstrasse (tel. 2-42-35). The exterior of this six-story hotel could be considered interesting architecturally. Is it Bauhaus or is it German contemporary? The facade is broken into an intriguing interplay of surfaces, breaking up the light into patterns which change according to the direction of the sunlight. What matters is that the interior is warmly decorated with Oriental rugs and comfortable armchairs. The bedrooms are sunny (on a good day), tasteful, and inviting. The Kohler-Fresen family, who run the place, are proud of their good service and their location near the Kurhaus and Casino. In a single, with breakfast included, they charge from 50 DM ($16.50) to 85 DM ($28.05), depending on the plumbing. Doubles with shower or complete bath range in price from 135 DM ($44.55) to 165 DM ($54.45).

BUDGET HOTELS: Hotel Aurora Martha, 8–10 Georg-Kreuzberg-Strasse (tel. 2-60-20). The double columns of the entrance to this twin hotel show a healthy mind toward preservation of architectural detail. The family that owns and runs the hotel is not just concerned about facades either, but about the care and coddling of guests. The public rooms are an adaptation of the salons of this former private house, with high ceilings and windows opening onto views of a well-maintained garden. Many of the rooms are fairly new, added, it seems, onto the roof of the Wilhelminian structures. All are comfortably furnished, and on the right day, sunny. Depending on the plumbing, singles range from 45 DM ($14.85) to 85 DM ($28.05), and doubles cost from 137 DM ($45.21) to 165 DM ($54.45).

Haus Ernsing, 30 Telegrafenstrasse (tel. 22-21), is a modern, five-story hotel, painted white and decorated with flowerpots. It has a wide and welcoming sun terrace, and is situated in a quiet neighborhood. A popular place for breakfast is an al fresco terrace shaded by colorful parasols. The hotel has good food, and plenty of it, served in a white and green dining room. Rooms are simply but attractively furnished. Some open onto private balconies. Many guests opt to stay here on the halfboard plan, costing from 63 DM ($20.79) to 84 DM ($27.72) per person.

Hotel und Kurpension Krupp, 2–4 Poststrasse (tel. 22-73), is a baroque "great house," one of the most charming buildings in Bad Neuenahr, with a modern annex. Depending on your choice, it offers convenient comfort to some 50 guests. The hotel has been in the same family since 1883, offering friendly service and individualized cookery for every taste, including dieters. The location is only a block from the Kurpark. The price range depends on plumbing, room size, and whether or not you request a private balcony. Singles begin at 45 DM ($14.85), climbing to 70 DM ($23.10); doubles cost from a low of 110 DM ($36.30) to a high of 130 DM ($42.90). These prices include breakfast, and for only another 18 DM ($5.94) to 40 DM ($13.20) you can order lunch or dinner.

Hotel Garni Rieck, 45 Hauptstrasse (tel. 2-69-99), is a quiet and friendly guest house, with a small, above-ground swimming pool and a high-ceilinged arched lobby. The rooms are compact and simply furnished. Doubles cost 88 DM ($29.04), and singles go for 50 DM ($16.50) to 60 DM ($19.80). The place has a homey, comfortable feeling, and the price is right.

WHERE TO DINE: For an elegant and rarefied cuisine, you have to head for the environs to **Gourmet im Teufenbach** (tel. 3-41-98), about a kilometer south heading toward Im Stadtteil Walporzheim. There you'll meet the culinary genius Ivo Ivancic, who, in his own words, defines his cookery as "psychosomatic." You'll have to see the menu before you'll understand what that means, and even then you won't be sure. Herr Ivancic is one of those rare individuals who, like the old Chez Denis in Paris, picked the wrong era. He might have found the mid-19th century a more fitting time to live. He believes in those who abandon themselves to the gourmet rites.

This restaurant has an original and romantic decor, a backdrop for imaginative specialties that include all the good things—lamb, lobster, goose liver pâté, and truffles, of course. The wines are worthy of the food. Mr. Ivancic rightly feels that his services should be rewarded, and you therefore face a bill averaging from 45 DM ($14.85) to 80 DM ($26.40). He is closed Sunday. It is imperative to call for a reservation.

While in the neighborhood, you might also seek out the **Romantik-Restaurant Weinhaus St. Peter,** 134 Walporzheimer Strasse (Route B 267; tel. 3-40-31). Some restaurants give off a sense of history in addition to savory odors from the kitchen. This winehouse, whose walls date from 1246, is one of them. The exterior is white stucco, with a steeply tiled roof, jutting dormers, and the traditional window boxes of geraniums. The menu revolves around whatever fresh products are available at the time. Fish is imported, frequently from the North Sea, the Mediterranean, or the Atlantic, and turned into delicately seasoned specialties. The wine list, as befits the restaurant's name, is wide ranging. Fixed-price meals begin at 40 DM ($13.20), but could cost as much as 100 DM ($33). You pay for this romance and glamor. Luncheon service is from noon to 2:30 p.m. and dinner from 6 to 10 p.m. daily. It is closed from mid-December until the end of February every year.

Back in the center of the spa, the **Ratskeller,** 8 Casinostrasse (tel. 2-54-66), is about your best bet. An attractive bar area greets the visitor who enters this well-decorated restaurant, with paneled walls and porcelain china. The head chef is Rolf Hanssen, and his wife, Helga, helps service the tables. This husband/wife team have maintained a seven-year tradition of feeding visitors and locals alike, serving them such delicacies as fish soup with dill or baby turbot in cider. Another specialty is tournedos du chef, either veal or beef. Classic specialties and nouvelle cuisine entrees are both served. An average meal will cost about 60 DM ($19.80), with selections made from a handwritten menu. Service is from noon to 2 p.m. and 7 to 10:30 p.m. daily except Tuesday and Wednesday lunch. The Ratskeller shuts down in summer for three weeks. Check before going there.

Restaurant Pfeffermühle (Pepper Mill), Steigenberger Kurhotel, 1 Kurgartenstrasse (tel. 22-91), is a multilingual establishment with a competence in international dishes. The chef, Dieter Jochmann, is young and works only with ingredients fresh from the marketplace. With them, he fashions homemade terrines, loup de mer (sea bass) in a champagne sauce, and vegetables that taste as if they were only recently plucked from the gardens. His dessert wagon is truly impressive. The decor of this elegant place in a first-class hotel is a striking black and gold, with off-white accents and a row of windows against one wall. Fixed-price meals cost from 35 DM ($11.55) to 45 DM ($14.85), and it takes no talent to spend a lot more. Call to reserve a table and go between noon and 2:30 p.m. or from 7 to 10:30 p.m.

The **Casinobar im Kurhaus,** 1 Felix-Rutten-Strasse (tel. 22-41), is a place to "make an evening of it." You can alternate eating with dancing. This nighttime rendezvous lies inside the Kurhaus, and offers a tempting array of international specialties. Yet in spite of its chic, it isn't overpriced. Meals begin at 35 DM ($11.55). Except for Monday, it's open from 7 p.m. till 2 a.m. (on Saturday from 3 p.m. till closing).

Kurpark, 8 Oberstrasse (tel. 2-61-81), is probably the single most popular gathering point for a Bad Neuenahr evening. Brightly lit, its café and restaurant make a good choice for either drinks or complete meals, whatever fits your mood. A family runs this fine establishment, offering a large menu of Germanic specialties that include Hungarian goulash soup or herring filets to get you started. One of their specialties is "mixed grill American." The familiar filet steak is served with béarnaise sauce, or you can order rumpsteak in at least three different ways. Their pork dishes are particularly tasty. The dessert menu is wickedly long. Meals cost 22 DM ($7.26) to 60 DM ($19.80). The establishment usually opens at 10 a.m., closing at midnight, but there are seasonal variations. It's closed Thursday and from December through March.

Zum Deubel, 2 Sebastianstrasse (tel. 2-50-14), is one of my favorite spots for drinking and dining. Outside it looks somewhat like a German roadhouse, but inside the atmosphere is warm and inviting, with many rustic touches and lots of wood. It's both a restaurant and a weinstube, popular with the locals themselves. You get good value here, beginning with the tasty fish soups, onion soup, quiche Lorraine, and main dishes such as roast pork stuffed with plums, breast of turkey in fine mushroom cream sauce, filet goulash Stroganoff with homemade spätzle, and many other good dishes. For dessert, I suggest mousse au chocolat, homemade ice-cream parfait with oranges and Grand Marnier, or with fresh bananas, raisins, and rum. Expect to pay from 25 DM ($8.25) to 40 DM ($13.20) for a meal here. The restaurant is closed Wednesday and for three weeks in January.

9. Bad Oeynhausen

The Jordan spring at Bad Oeynhausen is considered the world's greatest carbonic acid thermal salt spring, said to be beneficial for heart and vascular diseases, as well as rheumatism and certain female ailments. Lying between the Wiehen and Weser Mountains at the northern edge of the Teutoburger Wald, the resort contains attractive spa gardens, although much of the town is industrial and commercial.

A MIDDLE-BRACKET HOTEL: Kur-und-Badehotel "Wittekind," 10 am Kur-park (tel. 2-10-96), stands like a sunny Italian villa overlooking the spa gardens. The emphasis is more on comfort than on stylized decor, and the rooms, some of them quite large, are furnished in a mixture of traditional or contemporary styles. It's all quite homey. Prices vary according to size and location of the rooms. All rooms have private toilet and bath or shower. With continental breakfast, taxes, and service included, a room will cost from 60 DM ($19.80) to 90 DM ($29.70) per person. The hotel's restaurant, the Wittekindstuben, serves some of the best food in town.

BUDGET HOTELS: Westfälischer Hof, 14–16 Herforder Strasse (tel. 2-29-10), is a straightforward, recently constructed four-story landhaus-type building, with clean rooms decorated for the most part in shades of terracottas and sien-nas. The hotel has been under the direction of the same family for more than a century, and the new establishment was built in 1975. Your present-day host, Martin Kleissmayer, welcomes you, charging from 36 DM ($11.88) to 60 DM ($19.80) in a single room, and from 90 DM ($29.70) to 110 DM ($36.30) in a double, including breakfast. The hotel also has a pleasant little bierstube.

Hotel Stickdorn, 17 Wilhelmstrasse (tel. 2-11-41). The sunny bar area of this three-story hotel is a popular rendezvous point for many of Bad Oeyn-hausen's local citizens, who drink beer as light streams in through a yellow-tinged picture window. The restaurant serves good, filling meals in a high-ceilinged, modern room, with warmly tinted Oriental rugs and large ex-panses of glass along one wall. Each of its 26 bedrooms has many modern conveniences—phone, toilet, bath or shower. Breakfast, included in the tariffs, is served either in the dining room, or in fair weather, on a white flagstone ter-race. The charge is 84 DM ($27.72) to 104 DM ($34.32) in a double, 50 DM ($16.50) to 62 DM ($20.46) in a single.

Hotel Bosse, 40 Hertforder Strasse (tel. 2-80-61). The unadorned facade of this modern hotel is built on the acute angle of a street corner, centrally located between the Kurpark and the Kaiser-Wilhelm-Platz. The pleasant but simple rooms are in fresh colors. The hotel has a little bar and restaurant, the Friesen-stübchen, on the premises. Singles begin at 55 DM ($18.15) with shower, rising to 58 DM ($19.14) with shower and toilet. Doubles with shower and toilet cost 92 DM ($30.36), climbing to 100 DM ($33) with complete private bath. Each room has a phone.

WHERE TO DINE: The Wittekindstuben, 10 am Kurpark, in the Kurhotel Wit-tekind (tel. 2-10-96), has, as mentioned, the best food in town, so superior in fact that many Germans drive for 50 miles or more just to dine here. You enter the building through a tunneled red awning. Once seated in the restaurant, you face the specialty of the house. The chef, Boris Schalk, has an unusual reper-toire in that he's fascinated with snails and knows how to prepare them in an infinite number of ways. My latest surprise, for example, came with artichoke hearts and was sauteed in chablis and surrounded by puff pastry. If you feel that snails are best left uneaten, then you might be tempted by oysters, lobster, and trout which come fresh to the table, each prepared in temptingly tasteful ways. For all this good service and excellent food, you pay of course, from 45 DM ($14.85) to 80 DM ($26.40) for a typical repast. The restaurant is open from 11:30 a.m. to 2 p.m. and 6 to 9:30 p.m. It's closed Sunday and Monday for lunch, and has various short closings throughout the year (always call to make sure it's open and to reserve a table).

On the outskirts of town, a distance of some 2.5 kilometers, you'll also find good food at another hotel, Romantik Hotel Hahnenkamp, 4 Alte Reichsstrasse (tel. 50-41). This hotel dining room stands on Route B 61, the road to Minden. The restaurant, typical of a "romantik" hotel, is decorated in a rustic mixture of woods, many of them hand-carved. Ample use is made of well-polished paneling. Food is well prepared and handsomely presented by a helpful staff. The cheapest way to dine here is to order the fixed-price menu, costing from 25 DM ($8.25) to 40 DM ($13.20). If you're feeling ravenously hungry and have a well-stuffed wallet, you can order the gourmet menu at 55 DM ($18.15), which, as the chef assures me, is "adjusted seasonally," depending on the available ingredients. The restaurant serves from noon to 2 p.m. and 6 to 10 p.m. year round. It also rents about two dozen bedrooms: a single goes for 100 DM ($33); a double costs 150 DM ($49.50).

10. Bad Kissingen

Of the many spas in the Franconian basin north of Bavaria, Bad Kissingen stands out as the most attractive and most popular. Aside from its modern cure installations for the treatment of liver and stomach disorders, the town is a major attraction. It's a quiet village, nestled in the valley of the Saale River. The sleepy little marketplace is flanked by old shops and the medieval Rathaus. Parks and gardens surround the town, including the Kurgarten with its palms, extensive walks, and the Rosengarten.

The huge Kurhaus is one of the most impressive buildings in the town, with arcades stretching to the mineral springs and the huge promenade hall. In summer there is always plenty to do besides taking the cure—tennis, golf, chess. This is probably the only place where chess is as much a test of the body as the mind—the board is nearly 35 feet square, with huge pieces that must be picked up and carried to the next square. For the less energetic, spectator games include horse racing at the track. At night, the track receives heavy competition from the gambling casino and the paneled concert hall.

THE TOP HOTELS: **Steigenberger Kurhaushotel,** 3 am Kurgarten (tel. 30-31), is the leading hotel at the spa, with direct access to the baths. Built in 1850, it was once a meeting place for some of the VIPs of Europe, including Bismarck, Leo Tolstoy, the czar of Russia, and the empress of Austria. The public rooms are serene, offering maximum comfort to well-seasoned spa habitués who gather in comfortably upholstered chairs to exchange notes on cures. The bedrooms are pleasant, with color TV and such homey touches as chintz draperies. Most of the accommodations are spacious enough to have sitting areas. A single with bath goes from 91 DM ($30.03) to 177 DM ($58.41), increasing to anywhere from 148 DM ($48.84) to 260 DM ($85.80) in a double, prices based on the size and situation of a room.

In the intimate bar, guests gather to drink and relax; breakfast is served in a private enclosed garden at the rear of the hotel. Afterward, guests take a morning stroll by the pond with its musical fountain. A meal at the hotel is elegant, enhanced by an elevated garden in the center of the two dining rooms. Meals are also served on the balconies which overlook the park and are bordered with flowers. The specialty of the executive chef is French haute cuisine, but he's quite used to some of the most esoteric dietary requests. There is a choice of five menus, including a diet one, beginning at 38 DM ($12.54).

Kurotel 2002, 18 Von-der-Tann-Strasse (tel. 50-11), is a big, efficiently run hotel on a size and scale familiar to many Americans. The facade is imposingly multileveled, with balconies and glass walls. But that doesn't keep the service inside from being personalized and the decor unusually appealing. In fact, the decorator worked hard to render this place as stimulating as possible, making ample use of gray marble flooring, geometric Oriental carpets, wood paneling, and recessed lighting. The gamut of health facilities and pastimes includes facial and body massages, sports facilities, a swimming pool, archery, tennis, horseback riding, and on special request, glider rentals with a pilot. The hotel is an entertainment complex in its own right, with dining and musical diversions. A single with bath rents for 130 DM ($42.90) to 140 DM ($46.20), and a double goes for 200 DM ($66) to 210 DM ($69.30). For half board, add another 35 DM ($11.55) per person. The Kurotel 2002 is an appealing choice in Bad Kissingen.

MIDDLE-BRACKET HOTELS: Das Ballinghaus, 3 Martin-Luther-Strasse (tel. 12-34), is favored by many over the larger and more expensive Kurhaushotel. A neoclassic building, it is prim and proper, lying only a few minutes from the Kurhaus Gardens and across the street from a row of boutiques. Actually, spa devotees who come here for liver and stomach cures need never leave the grounds, as Das Ballinghaus has its own gardens and indoor swimming pool with medical baths. Behind the sedate town-house look lies a classic interior. Semimodern furnishings enhance the air of quiet dignity. The rooms are comfortable and immaculately kept. A bathless single with toilet ranges in price from 85 DM ($28.05) to 95 DM ($31.35), going up to 90 DM ($29.70) to 105 DM ($34.65) with private bath or shower. All double accommodations have been equipped with private bath or shower, costing 93 DM ($30.69) to 95 DM ($31.35) per person, including tax, service charge, and a buffet breakfast.

Dorint Hotel, 1 Frühlingstrasse (tel. 30-50), stands two minutes away from the Kurpark. A quiet hotel, it looks a bit like an American Holiday Inn, but with a row of international flags flying out front. A host of domestic and foreign visitors stop in here for "the cure," everybody defining it differently. The decor is modern and as attractive as you might wish. There's also a wide range of health and sports facilities, including a sauna, whirlpool, solarium, and other equipment. The kitchen turns out French and other international dishes (including German ones too). Units contain private bath, phone, balcony, TV/radio, and mini-bar. In addition to the restaurant, there is a gemütliche Bitstube. Including a breakfast buffet, a single rents for 85 DM ($28.05) daily, a double going for 150 DM ($49.50), a reasonable price considering what you get.

Kurhaus Tanneck, 6 Altenbergweg (tel. 40-36), is a real Germanic type of institution, a health-spa hotel, again emphasizing "the cure" that clients can take for health problems, real or imagined. Modern, efficient, and businesslike, the hotel has a long wing of rooms, rising three stories, where guests have their own balconies with a view of the garden. Diet specialties are featured in the dining room, which also has a perpetually laden buffet table. With cuisine like that served here, you might not lose weight unless you can resist temptation. The philosophy is to relax, breathe deeply, and enjoy it here. An incredible array of massages are available, all of them priced separately from the room charge. You might have an underwater massage or an electrogalvanizing bath, whatever. There's a large indoor swimming pool and many other winning features, including the good-size and pleasant bedrooms. Christian and Lilo Zoll charge from 102 DM ($33.66) to 125 DM ($41.25) in a single and from 95 DM ($31.35) to 120 DM ($39.60) per person in a double for full board.

Hotel Diana, 40 Bismarckstrasse (tel. 40-61), enjoys a woodland setting that would have made even its namesake, the mythical huntress, feel at home. On the side of a hill, it opens onto a view over the valley of Bad Kissingen. The hotel is as warm and appealing as its owner, Maria Baunach. The lobby/sitting room has about half a dozen boldly patterned Oriental rugs scattered about, and the glass walls of the tasteful dining room give a panoramic view of the hillside greenery. On the edge of Luitpoldpark, the hotel has a swimming pool, sun terrace, and bar area for meeting other clients. Room prices are based on plumbing, the cheapest containing a toilet but no private shower or bath. Singles range from 75 DM ($24.75) to 125 DM ($41.25); doubles, 140 DM ($46.20) to 195 DM ($64.35).

Arkadenhof, 9 Von-Humboldt-Strasse (tel. 6-11-11), is a family-run hotel with gemütlich service and a formally rustic ambience in a four-story balconied hotel where there should be a room for every taste. My favorites are the wood-ceilinged, white-walled smaller units up under the eaves, where illumination comes from a slanted skylight which still gives a view of the forest and the hills in the distance. Short-term apartments at terms ranging from 60 DM ($19.80) to 80 DM ($26.40) are also available, containing living rooms, bedrooms, kitchens, and baths with separate entryways. Eduard Hahn runs one of the better small hotels of Bad Kissingen. The wide differences in the rental units are reflected in the tariffs. Singles range from 50 DM ($16.50) to 70 DM ($23.10); doubles, from 55 DM ($18.15) to 90 DM ($29.70) per person nightly. For half board, you are charged another 20 DM ($6.60) per person, 30 DM ($9.90) per person for full board.

BUDGET HOTELS: **Kurhotel Fürst Bismarck,** 4 Euerdorfer Strasse (tel. 12-77), has been in the same family for more than 40 years. This spa hotel, near the park, is a tastefully renovated villa with a modern motel annex extension. It possesses all of the medical and curative facilities of a well-equipped "bad hotel." Fritz Lang, the manager, does everything he can to see to your comfort. He speaks English and will give you tips on sightseeing in the area. His accommodations contain shower, toilet, TV, phone, and refrigerator, and the most expensive units also include a private balcony. The cost ranges from 65 DM ($21.45) to 75 DM ($24.75) per person nightly. These rates include breakfast, and for lunch and dinner you pay only another 32 DM ($10.56).

Hotel Garni Hanseat, 27 Salinenstrasse (tel. 43-45). The flowered balconies of this hotel rise out of the lawn like a many-tiered birthday cake, sheltering guests inside in cozy comfort. Owners Fritz and Ilse Eckhardt welcome guests into their breakfast room, and in fair weather, invite them to sun themselves on the manicured expanse of the lawn. The most desirable units contain balcony, bath (or shower), and toilet, and all are comfortably and pleasantly decorated with much home-like comfort. A double ranges from 75 DM ($24.75) to 90 DM ($29.70), and singles go for 42 DM ($13.86) to 55 DM ($18.15). Only breakfast is served.

WHERE TO DINE: **"le jeton,"** im Luitpold-Park (tel. 40-81), is the casino restaurant or Spielbank dining room. International cookery and a risqué, devil-may-care attitude on the part of the other diners could contribute to an interesting evening. The bartender knows how to make a good, stiff drink, and the wine list is far above average. The elegant rendezvous is open daily except Tuesday from 6 p.m. till the last call for the roulette wheel. It's also the hottest after-dark diversion (well, almost), as dancing begins at 7 p.m. A good and proper dinner costs from 25 DM ($8.25) to 50 DM ($16.50), which I find very reasonable considering the setting. The restaurant closes from mid-November until Christmas. The café is a pleasant place at which to spend a summer afternoon, and it opens at 2 p.m.

Restaurant Schubert and **Weinstuben,** 2 Kirchgasse (tel. 26-24), has more antique charm and rustic ambience than any other dining spot in Bad Kissingen. Since the beginning of the 19th century it has been run by the Schubert family. Local Franconian specialties and classics of the French cuisine are harmoniously blended here. Service is polite and friendly, but they'll also let you alone if you want to sit and drink a while. Once, on what must have been its busiest night, I counted at least 150 patrons. Chances are, you'll find far fewer enjoying the good food and wine. Fixed-price menus begin at 22 DM ($7.26), but you might find your meal costing 50 DM ($16.50), as mine recently did. In season, it is open from 2 p.m. until midnight (otherwise, 5 p.m. till midnight). On weekends, however, it's open from 10 a.m. to 2:30 p.m. and 5 p.m. till midnight.

Bratwurstglöckle, 6 Grabengasse (tel. 44-06), is your best bargain. Franconia is famous for its sausages, and you'll find several varieties here, along with ten kinds of beer. The restaurant has a comfortably rustic decor, and you can come here either to drink or dine. You can eat for as little as 10 DM ($3.30), but chances are you'll spend around 25 DM ($8.25). The place is small, with only 12 tables, and everybody is friendly, at least they were on my last visit. It's closed every Wednesday and from December 1 to March 1.

The **Ratskeller,** 1 Rathausplatz (tel. 25-50), is one of the most enchanting in Germany, containing several dining rooms on two levels. Decorations include a liberal mixture of pewter and antlers. Semiprivate areas are separated by ornately carved dark-wood partitions. You discover Old Germany here while enjoying some of the most savory (and least expensive) dishes in the spa. The townspeople, with good reason, are proud of their Ratskeller and its specialties. Among the selections are eels cooked in Riesling wine. Set dinners cost from 30 DM ($9.90). Closed Sunday.

After a well-deserved rest at a spa, we're ready to face the Lorelei.

Chapter V

THE RHINELAND

1. Bonn
2. Bad Godesberg
3. Cologne (Köln)
4. Aachen
5. Düsseldorf
6. Koblenz
7. Mainz
8. Worms
9. The Rheingau
10. Speyer
11. Idar-Oberstein

FEW RIVERS OF THE WORLD claim or deserve as important a role in the growth of a nation as does the Rhine. It is the greatest single contributor to the history, legend, wealth—even the art—of Germany, parading along its banks a capsule version of the past, present, and future of Western Europe.

The Rhine begins in Switzerland (as a trickling mountain stream), and eventually passes through the Netherlands in its search for the sea, but most of its 850 miles snake and stretch through the mountains and plains of West Germany. For more than 2000 years it has been the chief route of trade within the continent, its deep waters enabling the most modern of sea vessels to travel upstream from the North Sea as far as Cologne.

Trade was not the only commodity carried along the waters of the Rhine. From the earliest times, it was also the route and magnet for the intellectual, artistic, and religious minds of Europe. It has been called "a triumphal avenue of the muses," and a trip along its banks today reveals historic and artistic treasures. Cathedrals and castles, huge modern cities, and sleepy little wine villages dot the landscape. Legends and history seem to wait around every bend of the river, or on each little mound or ruin along the banks.

From Mainz to Koblenz stretches the most scenic section of the Rhine Valley, taking in the winding portion of the river, which cuts through steep vine-covered hillsides dotted with towns whose names are synonymous with fine German wines. In this section is the most symbolic formation in the Rhineland, the legendary Lorelei, written and sung about for centuries as the rock from which the siren lured men to their doom.

The saga of the Nibelungen is, however, the best known of the Rhine legends, associated with much of the topography along the Rhine, from the Seven

Mountains near Bonn where Siegfried slew the dragon, to the city of Worms where Brünhilde plotted against the dragon-slayer.

The Rhine is also the home of many of Germany's largest and most modern cities. Cologne and Düsseldorf vie for the prestige of trade and tourism; Bonn continues as the provisional capital of West Germany.

RHINE CRUISES: The best way to get a really intimate look at the Rhine Valley is by taking a boat along the Rhine River. A wide range of cruises is offered by several shipping lines, from a 500-mile tour of the river in the luxury of a liner complete with cabins, restaurant, deck, and swimming pool, to one-day cruises between selected scenic points via smaller tour boats. The KD German Rhine Line runs its liners all year (less frequently in winter, of course) between Rotterdam at the North Sea and Basel, Switzerland, with all the elegance of a tropical island cruise. These tours usually last five days (one way) and vary in price according to the ship and season.

For the visitor to Germany, however, the popular tours are the one-day cruises between Mainz and Cologne, also operated by the KD German Rhine Line. This short trip takes in the most scenic portion of the Rhine, including the Lorelei, the best of the Rhine castles, and the most interesting of the wine villages. Cruise tours are also available between almost any two major points along the full length of the Rhine. Special tickets are sold enabling you to leave or join a cruise at any of these points.

KD has operated for more than 150 years, and has a fleet of 22 vessels. To give you an example of fares, the five-day Rotterdam-Basel cruise goes from $689 to $624; a four-day Düsseldorf–Basel trip costs from $499 to $551. However, one of the shorter trips, such as Cologne to Koblenz, costs only 55.60 DM ($18.35) for a single one-way fare. On this method, you can decide which stretch of the Rhine you find the most beautiful, enjoy it by boat, and then return by train. Traveling this way is surprisingly cheap. For travel on the more luxurious fast ships, there is a surcharge of 40% except upstream sailings between Cologne and Koblenz. Children up to 4 years of age travel free on all KD excursion boats, and older children, up to 14 years of age, pay only half the passage fare. These cruises are free to holders of a Eurailpass.

Travel agents will book you on any of these cruises, or else you'll find the main headquarters of the **KD German Rhine Line** at 15 Frankenwerft, 5000 Cologne 1 (tel. 0221/2-08-80).

BY CAR: The best alternative for sightseeing on the Rhine is by car. The advantage of automobile travel is that you're free from the tour guides herding you in and out of castles, museums, and cathedrals. You will not be pressured to leave behind some sight unseen or some village unexplored. If your schedule can possibly accommodate the time, allow at least a week. Know then that you will have only scratched the surface, and promise yourself a return whenever possible.

If you wish, you can settle yourself in one of the big towns, such as Düsseldorf or Cologne, with its wide range of accommodations. But you may infinitely prefer to seek out a central, yet seemingly isolated, village with an old inn where the pace is less frenetic, the food worthy of the finest tables in Germany.

1. Bonn

Until 1949 Bonn was a sleepy little university town, basking in its glorious 2000 years of history. Suddenly it was shaken out of this quiet life and made the provisional capital of the Federal Republic of Germany. The city has adjusted to its important new position in the country's affairs, but many of the older citizens still long for the relaxed and unhurried days before the war.

Within sight of the Seven Mountains, the home of the Nibelungen legends, Bonn has been a strategic city since Roman times. In the 13th century it was the capital of the electors of Cologne. More than any other heritage, however, the city is proud of its intellectual and musical history. Beethoven was born here; Schumann lived here; Karl Marx and Heinrich Heine studied in Bonn's university.

Today the capital is a bustling city of civil servants, lobbyists, secretaries, diplomats, newspaper reporters, university students, and politicians. The population and physical size of Bonn have more than doubled since the war.

In addition to political goings-on, visitors are attracted to Bonn from all over the world for the Beethoven Festival, held every two years in Beethovenhalle, a modern concert hall renowned for its acoustics.

THE SIGHTS: The best way to become oriented to what Bonn has to offer is to take a guided sightseeing tour, leaving daily from May until October at 10 a.m. and 12:30 p.m. The meeting point is Stadthaus, 2 Berliner Platz, which is the Bonn **Tourist Information** office (tel. 77-34-66). It's open Monday to Saturday from 8 a.m. to 9 p.m. and on Sunday from 9:30 a.m. to 12:30 p.m. For those who prefer to explore on their own, the city has a number of fine attractions.

The **Beethoven House,** Bonn's pride and joy, is in the old section of town, just north of the marketplace, 20 Bonngasse. Beethoven was born in 1770 in the small house in back, which opens onto a little garden. On the second floor is a simple marble bust of the composer, the only decoration in the room where he was born. Within the house are many personal possessions of Beethoven, including manuscripts and musical instruments. In the Vienna Room, in the front of the house, overlooking the street, is Beethoven's last piano. The instrument was custom-made, with a special sounding board meant to amplify the sound enough so that the composer might possibly hear it in spite of his deafness. The house is open daily in summer from 9 a.m. to 1 p.m. and 3 to 6 p.m. (on Sunday from 9 a.m. to 1 p.m. only). Winter hours are 9:30 a.m. to 1 p.m. and 3 to 5 p.m. (from 9:30 a.m. to 1 p.m. on Sunday). Admission is 3 DM (99¢).

The **Government Quarter,** along the west bank of the Rhine, is a complex of modern white buildings, rather nondescript when compared to the architecture of the Old Town. The two most impressive structures, both along Koblenzerstrasse, are the President's Residence and the Chancellery of the prime minister. These villas are more reminiscent of Old Bonn, long before it became an international center of diplomatic activity. Running north along the Rhine from the government buildings is a promenade, lined with trees and flowers as far as the **Alter Zoll,** an ancient fortress whose ruins make a good viewing point from which visitors can see across the Rhine to the Seven Mountains and the old village of Beuel.

The **Rhineland Museum,** 14-16 Colmantstrasse, contains a fine collection of art and artifacts from the Rhine Valley, including the skull of the famous Neanderthal man, found in 1856 a few miles east of Düsseldorf. The most interesting collection, however, is in the department devoted to the Roman period, with altars, stones, glass, and artifacts found in the Roman settlements in the Rhineland. The most fascinating exhibit is the altar to the Aufanic Matrons, a group of deities worshipped by the landowners of the Rhine. The galleries continue with findings of the Frankish period and with the art and applied arts of the Middle Ages till modern times, containing paintings of noted German, Dutch, and Flemish artists, furniture, earthenware, glass, goldsmiths' art, and sculpture. Ten galleries exhibit contemporary Rhineland art. The museum is open Tuesday through Friday from 9 a.m. to 5 p.m. (on Wednesday to 8 p.m.), on Saturday and Sunday from 10 a.m. to 5 p.m. Admission is 2 DM (66¢).

From Bonn, if you're driving, it's easy to take an excursion to the German version of Disney World. It's called **Phantasialand** (tel. 02232/3-20-84), and it's at Brühl-Süd, northwest of Bonn on Route A 553. It's open daily at 9 a.m. between April 1 and November 1. Most rides start at 10 a.m., closing down at 5 p.m. And compared to the U.S.A.'s Disney rides, these are much cheaper. The fantasyland takes up some 280,000 square yards, making it the biggest "wonderland" in Europe, lying directly on Route B 51 between Brühl and Euskirchen (many road signs point the way—it's hard to miss). Admission is 15 DM ($4.95) for adults, 13 DM ($4.29) for children up to 11 years.

You can also plan to have lunch there, as there are five restaurants on the grounds, seating 2000 holiday makers. My favorite part is Alt-Berlin, a designer's rendition of what Berlin was like at the turn of the century, complete with horse tram and hurdy-gurdy man. The Water-Flume Ride is the biggest in Europe, and the monorail system is the major attraction of the park. There's even a "Chinatown." It's a great place to take the kids who may not be too turned on to the Beethoven House in Bonn.

THE TOP HOTELS: Steigenberger Hotel, am Bundeskanzlerplatz (tel. 202-91), is in a modern business complex on the outskirts of Bonn, opposite the government building and the Palais Schaumburg, the residence of the federal chancellor. It's in the heart of an area that is, in fact, a city within a city. Downtown Bonn couldn't possibly handle this type of hotel, with its high-rise accommodations. Everything has a sophisticated and somewhat lavish touch, perfect for visiting diplomats. (You might spot foreign ministers, or even presidents, around the lounge fireplace.) The bedrooms are on the five upper floors; each has a private bath, TV, radio, and self-dial phone. Rates include a continental breakfast. Singles range from 190 DM ($62.70) to 270 DM ($89.10); doubles go for 270 DM ($89.10) to 340 DM ($112.20). Designers and decorators were hired to make the 160 bedrooms stylish and to provide comfort. Grained woods are combined with pure colors, and sofas convert into beds at night, for studio-style living.

The 18th-floor dining room, adjoined by an intimate armchair lounge, opens onto a panoramic view. But the pièce de résistance is the top-floor swimming pool with its wall of glass providing views of the Rhine. In a stylized Swiss chalet atmosphere, the Juliette offers disco dancing. A sun terrace on the front plaza provides outside tables. Parking is available.

Königshof, 9 Adenauerallee (tel. 2-60-10), is a modern building, with wide terraces, occupying spacious grounds across the boulevard from the park. It is often filled with government officials from other nations. The Königshof is a sound and reliable haven. A twin-bedded room with private bath overlooking the Rhine costs from 210 DM ($69.30) to 240 DM ($79.20). Singles with bath go from 150 DM ($49.50) to 200 DM ($66).

Bristol, Poppelsdorfer Allee/Prinz-Albert-Strasse (tel. 2-01-11), is one of the leading hotels of Bonn, perched right in the heart of the capital near the railway station. A popular sun terrace and an elegantly tiled indoor pool are just two of its attractions. All 200 of its attractive and up-to-date units are air-conditioned, with their own phone, toilet, and private bath or shower. Windows are soundproofed. Regular singles range from 205 DM ($67.65) to 260 DM ($85.80), and doubles cost from 260 DM ($85.80) to 340 DM ($112.20).

Schlosspark Hotel, 27-31 Venusbergweg (tel. 21-70-36), lies a few minutes by car from downtown Bonn, just off the autobahn B9. There you'll find a quiet and elegantly modern hotel set across the street from the meticulous greenery of Bonn's botanical gardens which surround the Poppelsorfer Schloss. The innkeeper, Herr Eichholz, sees that his 70 bedrooms are clean, crisp, and contemporary. Singles range from 95 DM ($31.35) to 115 DM ($37.95), and doubles cost 135 DM ($44.55) to 185 DM ($61.05). A newly built guest house nearby offers singles for 90 DM ($29.70) and doubles for 140 DM ($46.20). It's open from Monday to Friday. The hotel has a swimming pool, sauna, and solarium, as well as a garage.

MEDIUM-PRICED HOTELS: Sternhotel, 8 Markt (tel. 65-44-55), is one of the best of Bonn's hotels in the moderately priced category. It's right in the heart of town, next door to Bonn's most colorful building, the baroque town hall. The Stern has been in the hands of the Haupt family for more than 80 years, and they offer an informal, homey place for guests. A reception lounge has been combined with a cafeteria, the furnishings harmoniously blending traditional and contemporary. Equally home-like are the bedrooms, the larger of which have sitting areas. A single with shower and toilet costs from 98 DM ($32.34), from 146 DM ($48.18) with complete bath. A twin-bedded room with shower runs from 122 DM ($40.26), increasing to 155 DM ($51.15) with complete bath. Meals are graciously served in the dining room.

Astoria, 105-113 Hausdorffstrasse (tel. 23-95-07), is a 50-room hotel frequented by traveling business people, members of Parliament, and diplomats. The hotel lies in the heart of "Greater Bonn," about a ten-minute walk from Parliament Center. Each unit is well furnished, containing private shower, tub bath, toilet, radio, and TV. Singles with shower cost 95 DM ($31.35) nightly, going up to 105 DM ($34.65) with complete bath. Doubles with shower go for 140 DM ($46.20), 160 DM ($52.80) with complete bath. Breakfast, a continental one, is included in the tariffs quoted. In the evening some hot meals are served.

Hotel Beethoven, 24-26 Rheingasse (tel. 63-14-11), stands across the street from the Stadttheatre, with one of its wings facing the Rhine. Its main attraction is a panoramic view of the river traffic from the high-ceilinged dining room, where first-class meals are served, supervised by the owner himself, Karl Heinz Lipper. Double-glazed windows prevent any urban noises from disturbing the calm in this hotel's clean, comfortable bedrooms, which go for anywhere from 65 DM ($21.45) to 135 DM ($44.55) in a single, depending on the plumbing, and from 138 DM ($45.54) to 158 DM ($52.14) in a double. Triple units with private toilet and shower are available for 158 DM ($52.14) also. The location is ten minutes from the main station.

Hotel Continental, am Hauptbahnhof (tel. 63-53-60), is refreshing for a railway station hotel. Of modern construction, it has gone out of its way to appear to have some soul and character, with the use of objects of art and an occasional Oriental rug. The rooms are attractively styled and well kept, costing from 130 DM ($42.90) to 150 DM ($49.50) in a single and from 190 DM ($62.70) to 215 DM ($70.95) in a double with bath or shower, these tariffs including breakfast, service, and tax. From its panoramic terrace there's a view of Bonn's forested skyline.

Hotel Auerberg, 362 Kölnstrasse (tel. 67-10-31), lies in North Bonn, easily reached by car by exiting at the Bonn-Nord exit of the Köln-Frankfurt autobahn. The hotel is attractively decorated. The charming hostess, Marieanne Tapper, welcomes you at the reception area. Her rooms are comfortable and clean, with lots of light from the oversize windows. Singles with shower and toilet rent for 79 DM ($26.07), and doubles cost from 116 DM ($38.28), including breakfast. Guests have the use of a swimming pool.

BUDGET HOTELS: In the precincts of the Hofgarten and within walking distance of the Rhine are hotels offering modest accommodation at moderate tariffs.

Haus Hofgarten, 7 Fritz-Tillmann-Strasse (tel. 22-34-82), is one of these. A friendly couple presides over this unique establishment, furnished with antiques. The look is slightly cluttered in places, but it's ideal if you appreciate the charm of another era. A good-size breakfast room makes it a bit like living in a private home. A wide dark mahogany staircase leads to the 15 bedrooms. Large doubles with bath go for 140 DM ($46.20); if bathless, 85 DM ($28.05). Singles with bath are 90 DM ($29.70), 55 DM ($18.15) if bathless.

Eden, 6 Am Hofgarten (tel. 22-40-77), right on the Hofgarten, is a modest place with a pleasant family management. A good breakfast is provided in the combination sitting room, lounge, and office. The decor is a bit fussy and cluttered, but clean and homey. Depending on the plumbing, singles range from 50 DM ($16.50) to 80 DM ($26.40), and doubles cost from 105 DM ($34.65) to 120 DM ($39.60).

Schwan, 24 Mozartstrasse (tel. 63-41-08), is a bourgeois-style house on a quiet street about six minutes by foot from the railway station. Not exactly an exciting choice, it is nevertheless clean, sternly furnished in a modern idiom. With bathless doubles going for 95 DM ($31.35). A single with shower ranges from 85 DM ($28.05), and doubles with shower or private bath go from 120 DM ($39.60).

Römerhof, 20 Römerstrasse (tel. 63-47-96), is not known to many travelers, but it's a suitable accommodation on a busy street close to the northern exit of the autobahn to Cologne. In reality it's a gasthof-type inn, where the friendly owner puts up overnight guests. The rooms are kept in good shape. Prices, including a continental breakfast, are 60 DM ($19.80) to 102 DM ($33.66) in a single with shower, rising to 90 DM ($29.70) to 148 DM ($48.84) in a double with shower or bath. At the Römerhof's restaurant, you can order hearty meals in the 18-DM ($5.94) to 50-DM ($16.50) range. The dining room is shut on Monday.

Rheinland Bonn, 11 Berliner Freiheit (tel. 65-80-96), is centrally located, near the Stadttheatre and the Beethovenhale. It's a modern, efficiently run hotel, whose friendly owner, Wolfgang Seiler, serves a fortifying breakfast every day. The cost on weekends and in July and August is 65 DM ($21.45) in a single and 110 DM ($36.30) in a double. Weekdays the prices are 85 DM ($28.05) in a single and 125 DM ($41.25) in a double. Units have private shower/bath, toilet, mini-bar, and phone. Breakfast is included.

Bergischer Hof, 23 Münsterplatz (tel. 63-34-41), is directly opposite Bonn's cathedral, a centrally located hotel which is reached via a pedestrian walkway, 300 yards from the central railway station. It offers a terrace, a café, and a substantial breakfast to visitors, and also has access to a parking garage only two minutes away. Rooms are clean, comfortable, and tranquil, renting for 45 DM ($14.85) to 75 DM ($24.75) in a single, depending on the plumbing, and from 89 DM ($29.37) to 110 DM ($36.30) in a double.

Hotel Weiland, 98a Breite Strasse (tel. 65-50-57), is great for a tight budget —a guest house not far from the Kölnstrasse. It's as clean as fresh violets, and the welcome from the Weiland family, who run it, is also warm. The decor is uninspired, but the rates, including breakfast, are compensatingly low: singles from 48 DM ($15.84) to 73 DM ($24.09); doubles, as little as 80 DM ($26.40) if bathless, increasing to 105 DM ($34.65) with a private shower. The receptionist on the first floor speaks English.

WHERE TO DINE: **Em Höttche,** 4 Markt (tel. 65-85-96), has a long and colorful history, tracing its origin back to the year 1389. Situated next to the baroque town hall, it has been restored by the Fassbender family, with carved wood paneling and columns, natural brick, old beamed ceilings, decoratively painted plaster, grandfather clocks, nooks for handholding by candlelight, and curlicue chandeliers. Favored as a dining spot are the tables set inside the walk-in fireplace, with its heavy wooden supporting posts. The front room is mostly for drinks. Set lunches range in price from 16 DM ($5.28) to 32 DM ($10.56). On the à la carte list, you'll find filet goulasch Stroganoff and specialties for two persons, including entrecôte. Fresh salmon often is available. You can complement your meal with a carafe of local wine—the best buy of the house. If you order à la carte, you're likely to spend from 30 DM ($9.90) to 70 DM ($23.10). The restaurant serves daily except Sunday from noon to 2:30 p.m. and 6 p.m. to midnight.

Im Stiefel, 30 Bonngasse (tel. 63-48-06), is a holdout to the past, representing antiquity, but in a completely up-to-date setting. A few doors down the street from Beethoven's House, this atmospheric restaurant is a favorite with students. Dining is at bare bleached tables in one of several rooms. The decor is rich in butterscotch and brown shades, with wood paneling, pewter plates, and stained glass. There's even a standup bar for mugs of beer. Try oxtail soup, along with typical German specialties, including hirschragoût (venison) and eisbein (pig's knuckles) with sauerkraut. Menus range in price from 12 DM ($3.96) to 25 DM ($8.25), and *everybody* finds those tariffs reasonable. It's closed on Sunday.

Restaurant Schaarschmidt, 14 Brüdergasse (tel. 65-44-07), is a desirable international rendezvous for dining. Run by the Schaarschmidt family, the restaurant does a flourishing business and enjoys an enviable reputation for its kitchen. Such specialties are offered as sweetbreads and Bresse chicken. In season, pheasant from Normandy is presented, and you can order veal filet in a tarragon-flavored cream sauce. When available, sea bass is also served to satisfied diners, who can enjoy it inside or at one of the sidewalk café tables. Since the place is popular, it's best to phone ahead for a table. Meals are served from 11:30 a.m. to 2:30 p.m. and 6 p.m. to midnight, except Sunday. At noon, luncheons cost from 40 DM ($13.20) to 60 DM ($19.80). Dinner can get quite expensive, especially if you order the seven-course banquet at 105 DM ($34.65). The restaurant closes from mid-August to mid-September.

Restaurant am Tulpenfeld, 2-10 Heussallee (tel. 21-90-81), lies in a hotel already recommended. This first-class restaurant is popular with journalists and government officials who frequently lessen the burdens of West Germany's newspaper coverage to savor the specialties served here. The restaurant is open daily from noon to 3 p.m. and 6:30 to 11 p.m. (closes at 3 p.m. on Saturday). A typical dinner will begin at 35 DM ($11.55), but could range as high as 85 DM ($28.05). You might begin your meal with white herring, perhaps a soup made with morels. The chef makes the famed boiled beef dish of Vienna, tafelspitz, exceedingly well. Saddle of venison is often featured.

Petit Poisson, 23a Wilhelmstrasse (tel. 63-38-83), is relaxed and friendly, reflecting the personality of the couple who own it. Herr Ludwig Reinarz and his wife, Johanna, have decorated this place in elegantly warm colors, and have done everything they can to see that clients enjoy themselves while ordering good food. They don't get frantic about the nouvelle cuisine, but that way of cookery has made itself felt here. All ingredients, for example, are fresh, and many of their concoctions are temptingly light. Try their cream of fish and mushroom soup. Some savory meat and game dishes are usually available, including a pot au feu for two persons. Fixed-price menus cost from 65 DM ($21.45) to 105 DM ($34.65), and you could spend around 50 DM ($16.50) ordering à la carte.

They're open from 11 a.m. to 3 p.m. and 6 p.m. till midnight every day except Sunday and Monday. Closed during all of July. Call for one of their 11 tables and seat yourself in friendly intimacy.

Im Bären, 1-3 Acherstrasse (tel. 63-32-00), is a very historic and very old gasthaus dating from 1385. The present management, in control since 1970, has maintained the quality of the good, hearty food and the antique atmosphere, which is in keeping with the style of the building. It's one of the best bargains of Bonn, with fixed-price menus costing from 12 DM ($3.96) to 30 DM ($9.90). It's open daily from 10 a.m. till midnight.

Weinhaus Jacobs, 18 Friedrichstrasse (tel. 63-73-53), is a traditional wine house serving an unusual array of local cheeses, and many recipes that date from the days of the Palatinate electors. The food and drink are reasonable in price as well, costing from 30 DM ($9.90) for a meal. It's open every evening from 5 p.m., but closed Sunday and in August. Lots of handcarving helped form its decor.

Le Marron, 35 Provinzialstrasse at Lengsdorf (tel. 25-32-61), outside Bonn. Reservations are strongly recommended because of the popularity of this place. It's a warmly rustic restaurant where in wintertime an open fireplace burns in the intimate dining room. It's directed by Hans-Josef Schlösser. A favorite dish is fresh mussels in a truffle butter sauce or with chervil and wild mushrooms, or Norwegian salmon in a Riesling wine sauce. Meals range from 50 DM ($16.50) to 85 DM ($28.05). Service is from noon to 2 p.m. and 7 to 10 p.m. The restaurant is closed on Saturday and on Sunday for lunch.

Zur Lese, 37 Adenauerallee (tel. 22-33-22), is a wine restaurant with a terrace café, one of the finest in Bonn, attracting the diplomatic corps. Hartmut Wicht, your English-speaking host, believes that care and precision should go into a cuisine, and he's imbued that feeling into his staff. Zur Lese opens at 10 a.m. for morning coffee and serves throughout the day. It's especially popular in the afternoon when visitors drop in for coffee and cakes. On a summer night the view of the Rhine is dramatic from the terrace. A carte of international specialties is presented (with very rough English translations). You might begin your meal with French onion soup or smoked salmon from Norway (my favorite is crayfish soup laced with cognac). Among the specialties, pork is served with curry sauce, and the chef prepares a superb filet goulash Lese. Meals cost from 35 DM ($11.55) to 65 DM ($21.45). Herr Wicht shuts down on Monday.

Ristorante Grand'Italia, 1 Bischofsplatz (tel. 63-83-33), right off the old market square, is rightly considered one of the best Italian restaurants along the Rhine. It's an excellent change of pace, and the service is good. Fish soup is a savory offering, and spaghetti is prepared with a number of sauces. Another pasta specialty is tagliatelle verde. The pizza oven turns out many different, sizzling pies. In season, the chef buys the white truffle of Piedmont to use in a variety of ways and also prepares pheasant. For dessert, you may want to sample the classic Italian zabaglione. Meals cost from 35 DM ($11.55) to 60 DM ($19.80). Hours are noon to 3 p.m. and 6 p.m. to 1 a.m.

WINE SAMPLING ACROSS THE RHINE: About 12½ miles from Bonn on the opposite bank of the Rhine in the town of Rheinbreitbach, I always like to go to **Im Hütchen,** 2 Burgstrasse (tel. 7-30-30), a little wine house where the proprietor, Heinz Rechmann, happily dispenses French, Italian, and German wines, the latter including some of the most celebrated output from the Rhine district as well as Franconia and Mosel. The structure housing Rechmann's establishment, built in 1790, has limited seating (three tables) but boundless hospitality. Two log fires add to the ambience when the weather indicates their use. Perhaps you'll be lucky enough to be here when some of the musicians of the district perform. A glass of wine costs from 4 DM ($1.32) to 6 DM ($1.98), and it can be accompanied by ham, cheese, bread, and sometimes soup.

2. Bad Godesberg

Bonn's diplomatic suburb four miles to the south is a modern town built around one of the Rhine's oldest resorts. Just opposite the Siebengebirge (Seven Mountains), it has a view of the crag, Drachenfel (Dragon's Rock), where Siegfried slew the dragon. The dragons are gone from the Rhine, but you can still see some ancient castle ruins on the hills. The most interesting is the Godesberg castle, built in the 13th century by the electors of Cologne. Its ruins have been incorporated into a hotel (see recommendations below). From the promenade along the Rhine, you can watch a constant flow of boats and barges wending their way up and down the river.

Most of the spa's activity centers around the Redoute Palace, a small but elegant 18th-century castle. Beethoven Hall, the main ballroom, was the scene of the meeting between the young Beethoven and Haydn. Although the town is mainly a residential center for the representatives of many nations in Bonn, including the United States, there is seemingly no end to the entertainment and cultural facilities here. Theaters, concerts, and social functions offer a constant whirl of events.

THE TOP HOTELS: Zum Adler, 60 Koblenzerstrasse (tel. 36-40-71), provides a 19th-century, cultural atmosphere. This oldtime prestige hotel, going back to 1860, is modest for the caliber of guests who have either stayed or dined here, but proud nevertheless.

The Zum Adler was once a private villa, built right on the street, with a small rear garden. It is furnished with good antiques—many inlaid desks and carved mirrors—but it contains a minimum of salons. Rates include a continental breakfast. The plumbing has been completely renewed and improved, although a few bathless singles still remain, for 75 DM ($24.75). With shower or bath, the single tariff rises to 110 DM ($36.30). Doubles with shower or complete bath are 140 DM ($46.20) to 160 DM ($52.80). A substantial breakfast is included in the price, but no other meals are served.

Rheinhotel Dreesen, 45-49 Rheinstrasse (tel. 8-20-20), enjoys a superior position, next to the Diplomatic Corps, directly on the Rhine, with its own gardens and terraces. Sliding glass roofs and infrared heating provide a sense of being outdoors, whatever the weather. A sentimental favorite of oldtimers, it is also frequented by travel groups and business people, as well as vacationing German families who make it a holiday resort center. Practically every dining table offers a panoramic view of the river boats. The furnishings of the bedrooms are elegant, the size generous, and the prices based on plumbing and view. The renovated accommodations have the following rates: singles with shower, 115 DM ($37.95); with private bath, from 185 DM ($61.05); doubles with shower or private bath, from 162 DM ($53.46) to 200 DM ($66). Breakfast is included.

Insel Hotel, 5-7 Theaterplatz (tel. 36-40-82), run by the same management as the Zum Adler, is a comfortable, medium-priced establishment right in the heart of this spa city. If you perch here, you'll be but a short car ride from the Rhine. The hotel has 70 pleasantly furnished rooms, each with private bath or shower. A single rents for 100 DM ($33) to 110 DM ($36.30), and a double goes for 155 DM ($51.15) to 75 DM ($57.75). In the restaurant or at the sidewalk café terrace, you can find both German dishes and international specialties, served with a fine selection of Rhine wines. There are ample free parking facilities.

Godesberg Castlehotel, 5 Auf dem Berg (tel. 31-60-71), is a comfortable place to stay. A winding road leads up to this hilltop castle ruin, converted into a hotel. It's distinctive and highly recommended. Its tall tower and many of its rugged stone walls were erected in 1210 by the archbishop of Cologne and are still intact. A lounge was built against one of the stone walls, providing a sunny perch and a view of the spa and the river. There's also a roof terrace, with tables for drinks. The bedrooms have been designed with zigzag picture windows, allowing for views. Various kinds of woods have been used in the units, each of which has a shower and bath. Singles range in price from 90 DM ($29.70) to 130 DM ($42.90), the difference based on your view or lack of it. Doubles with shower or complete bath go for anywhere from 120 DM ($39.60) to 160 DM ($52.80), breakfast included. The food is especially good here (see my restaurant recommendations).

WHERE TO DINE: Wirtshaus St. Michael, 26 Brunnenallee (tel. 36-47-65). The beautifully coffered ceiling of this elegant restaurant is painted white, and its look is stunningly effective when set against the forest-green walls. Century-old antiques and intimate lighting are part of the charm of this revered place, which serves the best cuisine in Bad Godesberg. A grandfather clock looks down on visitors, who regale themselves with lobster, shrimp, and homemade goose liver pâté, perhaps Norwegian salmon on a bed of freshly picked spinach leaves. The savory rack of lamb is tempting. Joint owners Jürgen Martin and Friedrich Braunbarth are present every night from 7 p.m. (except Sunday) to see to the comfort of their guests. You can spend 50 DM ($16.50) to 90 DM ($29.70) ordering à la carte. Reservations are necessary, and the restaurant closes for three weeks every summer.

Cäcilienhöhe, 17 Goldbergweg (tel. 32-10-01). Besides a panoramic view, this restaurant offers an array of classic German dishes along with specialties of Tuscany, and fish from both the Atlantic and Mediterranean. Natural and fresh, the ingredients used in the kitchen here are of top quality. Meals begin at 40 DM ($13.20), but most diners will probably spend a lot more. It's open from noon to 2:30 p.m. and 6:30 to 11 p.m., but closed Saturday at noon, Sunday, and for the first two weeks in August. Call for one of a dozen tables. The hotel also has 11 pleasantly furnished rooms attached, renting for 120 DM ($39.60) to 140 DM ($36.20) in a double.

La Redoute-"Claire Fontaine," 1 Kurfürstenallee (tel. 36-40-41). Arriving at this restaurant is about as much a festive occasion as the actual dining experience that will take place later. The location is on the first floor of a baroque "lustschloss" or pleasure palace. The accessories are elegant, including gilded service tables supported by rococo renderings of griffins and dolphins. You dine under high sculptured ceilings in immaculate white plaster. An array of nouvelle cuisine delicacies makes for an unusual and appetizing meal. An à la carte regalia would cost you from 50 DM ($16.50) to 95 DM ($31.35), while a fixed-price menu of six imaginative courses costs 100 DM ($33). The restaurant is open from noon to 2:30 p.m. and 6:30 to 11 p.m. every day but Sunday. It is closed from mid-July to mid-August. Always reserve a table.

Zur Korkeiche, 104 Lyngsbergstrasse (tel. 34-78-97), lies outside Bad Godesberg in the village of Lannesdorf, but it's such a tranquil and satisfying choice that it's worth arming yourself with a road map to find. It is a well-maintained half-timbered house with two stories of gemütlich comfort and tradition. It's advertised as a wine and sherry house, and its decor is rustic in a country-elegant way. Head chef Rainer-Maria Halbedel prepares a light nouvelle cuisine, among other dishes, including a delicately seasoned filet of veal in a mustard cream sauce. Menus range from 45 DM ($14.85) to 105 DM ($34.65), depending on your selection of items and your appetite, of course. Service is daily except Monday from 6 p.m. to midnight. Sometime in the summer there is a four-week shutdown—so always call first before heading here.

Weinhaus Maternus, 3 Löberstrasse (tel. 36-28-51), attracts a diplomatic crowd to its plush tavern atmosphere and has ever since 1950. The cuisine and service are excellent. There are some excellent à la carte suggestions: onion soup, deer steak (in season), and piccata Milanaise. For your dessert, a splashy crêpes suzette for two is luring. Menus begin at 30 DM ($9.90), rising to 55 DM ($18.15). Service is daily from noon to 3 p.m. and 6 p.m. to midnight, except Sunday. The wine house is easy to find—opposite the railway station, with sidewalk canopy tables in warmer weather. Unquestionably, Weinhaus Maternus offers some of the best food in the spa.

Godesberg Castlehotel Restaurant, 5 Auf dem Berg (tel. 31-60-71), offers excellent meals in a romantic situation. It's a part of the previously recommended 13th-century castle which was turned into a hotel. You dine in elegant style in a room nestled into the castle ruins. The former knight's hall has been converted into a spacious dining room with picture-window views—the true eagle's-nest style. The adjoining Weinstube is warmer in tone, with its inner wall paneled in grainy wood. Set lunches range in price from 28 DM ($9.24) to 45 DM ($14.85). The international menu appeals to the widest possible tastes. Even American fried chicken is featured. Hours are noon to 2 p.m. and 6 to 9 p.m.

3. Cologne (Köln)

The largest city in the Rhineland is so rich in antiquity that every time a new foundation is dug for a modern office building or the new subway, the excavators come up with another relic from its past. Tragic though the World War II devastation of Cologne was—nearly all the buildings of the Old Town were damaged —it helped to reveal a period of Cologne's history that had been steeped in mystery for centuries. When the rubble was cleared away after the bombings, evidence was found proving that Cologne was as important and powerful a city during the early Christian era as it was during Roman times and the Middle Ages.

Cologne (spelled Köln in German) traces its beginning back to 38 B.C., when Roman legions set up camp here. As early as A.D. 50 it was given municipal rights as a capital of a Roman province. It still retains part of its original name today, an eternal tie to its strong Roman heritage as a colony of that vast empire.

Historical findings since the war have proved what an important town Cologne also was during the early Christian era. It became a city of martyrs and saints, including the patron of the city, St. Ursula, murdered by the Huns. During the prosperous Middle Ages, churches were built with the gold of the zealous merchants, as Cologne became a center for international trade. Visitors come from all over the world just to visit the medieval churches of Cologne, and rightly so, but there is much to see from every period of the city's 2000-year history—from the old Roman towers to the ultramodern opera house.

The city was the birthplace of Jacques Offenbach, and the large square in front of the Cologne Opera commemorates that fact. It is named "Offenbachplatz." Offenbach was born on June 20, 1819, at 1 Grosser Griechenmarkt, and a plaque on the building there honors that occasion.

The very word, Cologne, has become a part of the common language, since the introduction to the world many years ago of the scented water called

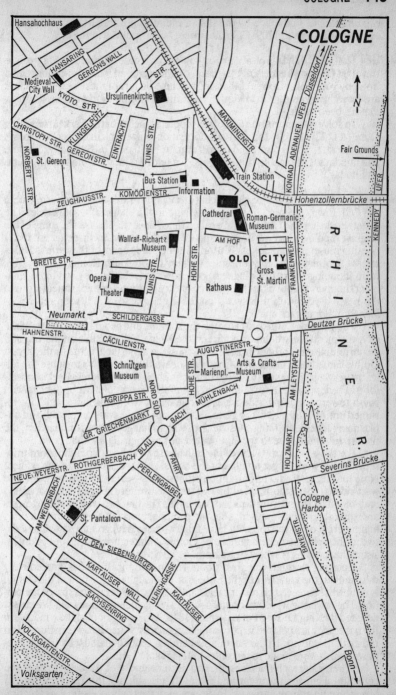

COLOGNE

Hansahochhaus

HANSARING

GEREONS WALL

Medieval
City Wall

KYOTO STR.

Ursulinenkirche

STR.

MAXIMINENSTR.

KONRAD ADENAUER UFER Düsseldorf

Fair Grounds

N

KENNEDY

UFER

CHRISTOPH STR.

KLINGELPÜTZ

GEREONSTR.

EINTRACHT

TUNIS STR.

NORBERT
STR.

St. Gereon

ZEUGHAUSSTR.

KOMÖDIENSTR.

Bus Station

Information

Train Station

Hohenzollernbrücke

Cathedral

Roman-Germanic
Museum

R
H
I
N
E

Wallraf-Richartz
Museum

AM HOF

OLD CITY

HOHE STR.

Gross
St. Martin

FRANKENWERFT

BREITE STR.

TUNIS STR.

Opera

Theater

Rathaus

Neumarkt

SCHILDERGASSE

Deutzer Brücke

HAHNENSTR.

CÄCILIENSTR.

AUGUSTINERSTR.

Schnütgen
Museum

HOHE STR.

Marienpl.

Arts & Crafts
Museum

AM LEYSTAPEL

AGRIPPA STR.

MÜHLENBACH

NORD SÜD

BACH

R.

GR. GRIECHENMARKT

HOLZMARKT

Severins Brücke

BLAU

FAHRT

NEUE. WEYERSTR. ROTHGERBERBACH

AM WEIDENBACH

St. Pantaleon

PERLENGRABEN

Cologne
Harbor

BAYENSTR.

VOR DEN SIEBENBURGEN

KARTÄUSER WALL

SACHSENRING

ULRICHGASSE

KARTÄUSER

Bonn

VOLKSGARTENSTR.

Volksgarten

eau de cologne, first made by the Italian chemist Giovanni Maria Farina, who settled in Cologne in 1709. Cologne water is still produced in the city.

GETTING AROUND: For about 60¢ you can purchase a ticket allowing you to travel on Cologne's excellent bus, tram, or underground (subway) connections. You buy your ticket from a dispensing machine on any of these vessels. Tickets are interchangeable. You stick the ticket into a cancellation machine to show that it's been used.

To solve transportation and other problems, head for the **Verkehrsamt,** am Dom (tel. 221-33-45), the tourist information office which is open weekdays from 8 a.m. to 10:30 p.m., and from 9 a.m. to 10:30 p.m. on Saturday, Sunday, and holidays. Off-season, this office is open until 9 p.m. weekdays, until 7 p.m. on Sunday.

THE SIGHTS: The major sightseeing attractions of this ancient city lie within the Old Town, the section along the Rhine in the shape of a semicircle. The streets enclosing the Old Town are called rings, since they follow the route of the original medieval city wall, remnants of which remain in three gates, today housing museums and depots. Cutting through the center of the town is **Hohestrasse,** a straight street connecting the north and south Roman Gates. This main shopping artery of Cologne is so narrow that vehicles are prohibited, enabling shoppers to move freely from one luxury boutique or department store to the next. If you walk northward on the Hohestrasse, you'll soon reach Cologne's major attraction.

The **Cologne Cathedral** (Dom) is the spiritual and geographical heart of the city, the most overwhelming edifice in the Rhine Valley. Built on the site of a pagan temple and earlier Christian churches, the majestic structure is the largest Gothic cathedral in Germany. Construction was begun in 1248 to house the relics of the Magi brought to Cologne by Archbishop Reinald von Dassel, chancellor of Frederick Barbarossa in 1164, but after the completion of the chancel, south tower, and north side aisles (about 1500), work was halted and not resumed until 1842. In 1880 the great 632-year enterprise was completed, and unlike many time-consuming constructions which change styles in mid-stream, the final result was as true to the Gothic style as the original plans had been.

For the best overall view of the cathedral, stand back from the south transept, where you can get an idea of the actual size and splendor of the edifice. Note that there are no important horizontal lines—everything is vertical. The west side (front) is dominated by two towering spires, perfectly proportioned and joined by the narrow facade of the nave. The first two stories of the towers are square, gradually merging into the octagonal form of the top three stories and tapering off at the top with huge finials. There is no great rose window between the spires, so characteristic of Gothic architecture, as the designers insisted that nothing was to detract from the lofty vertical lines.

Entering through the west doors (main entrance), one is immediately caught up in the grandeur of the cathedral. Although this portion of the church is somewhat bare, the clerestory and vaulting give an idea of the size of the edifice. The towering windows on the south aisles include the Bavarian Windows, donated by King Ludwig I of Bavaria in 1848. Typical of most of the windows in the nave, they are colored in portrait-like pigments, which have been burned on rather than stained. In the north aisles are the stained-glass Renaissance windows, which were made in the years 1507–1509.

When you reach the transept, you become aware of the actual size of the cathedral. Here are the organ and choir loft, just south of the Treasury, with its liturgical gold and silver pieces. In the center of the transept—and the cathedral

—is an elegant bronze and marble altar, which can be seen from all parts of the cathedral. This was to have been the site of the Shrine of the Three Kings, but the reliquary actually stands behind the high altar in the chancel.

The *Shrine of the Three Magi* is the most important and most valuable object in the cathedral. Designed in gold and silver in the form of a triple-naved basilica, it is decorated with relief figures depicting the life of Christ, the Apostles, and various Old Testament prophets. Across the front of the chancel are two rows of choir stalls divided into richly carved partitions. The unpainted oak choir dates from 1310 and is the largest still extant in Germany.

Surrounding the chancel are nine chapels, each containing important works of religious art. The Chapel of the Cross, beneath the organ loft, shelters the painted, carved oak cross of Archbishop Gero (969–976), the oldest full-size cross in the Occident. Behind the altar in Our Lady's Chapel, directly across the chancel from the Chapel of the Cross, is the famous triptych masterpiece painted by Stephan Lochner (1400–1451). When closed, the Dombild, as it is called, shows the Annunciation, and when opened, it reveals the Adoration of the Magi in the center, flanked by the patron saints of Cologne, St. Ursula and St. Gereon.

The cathedral welcomes visitors at any time till 7:30 p.m., except during religious services. Daily tours take place at 10 and 11 a.m., and 2:30, 3:30, and 4:30 p.m. Visitors are welcome to visit the Treasury and Cathedral Tower daily from 9 a.m. to 5 p.m. in summer (closes at 4 p.m. off-season). On Sunday and holidays they open at noon. Admission to each is 2 DM (66¢).

The **Dionysos-Mosaik,** from the third century, was discovered in 1941 when workmen were digging an air-raid shelter. Near the cathedral, this mosaic once was the decorative floor of the oecus (main room) of a large Roman villa. It was named Dionysos because most of the octagons and squares within the elaborately decorated and colored work are pictures dealing with the Roman god Bacchus, god of wine and dispeller of care. The mosaic is housed in the **Roman-Germanic Museum** (tel. 221-23-01). On the second floor is an unusual collection of Roman antiquities found in the Rhine Valley, including Roman glass from the third and fourth centuries, as well as pottery, marble busts, and jewelry. The museum and mosaic are open daily from 10 a.m. to 5 p.m. Admission is 3 DM (99¢).

The **Wallraf-Richartz Museum/Museum Ludwig** (tel. 221-23-79), just a short walk from the Domplatz, is Cologne's oldest museum, begun in the 19th century with a collection of Gothic works by Cologne artists. The group of works is still one of the main attractions, although today the Wallraf-Richartz shows art from 1300 to 1900, and the Ludwig, art from 1900 until today. Representative of the Gothic style in Germany is Stephan Lochner, best shown in his *Madonna in the Rose Garden,* painted in 1445. Several cathedral works are exhibited here, including the triptych of the *Madonna with the Vetch Flower* (1410). The museum is proud of its collection of German artists, spanning more than 500 years. It houses Germany's largest collection of works by Wilhelm Leibl, as well as paintings by Max Ernst, Paul Klee, and Ernst Ludwig Kirchner. There is also a representative collection of nearly every period and school of painting, from the Dutch and Flemish masters to the French impressionists to American art of the '60s and '70s (the famous Ludwig Donation). It is open daily from 10 a.m. to 5 p.m., on Tuesday and Thursday from 10 a.m. to 8 p.m.; closed Monday. Inquire at the Tourist Office about the museum's status, as plans to move were announced for 1986.

The **Schnütgen Museum** is a curator's dream: beautiful works of art displayed in their original surroundings. Cologne's best collection of religious art and sculpture is housed in the Church of St. Cecilia, a fine example of Rhenish

Romanic architecture. The works displayed here include several medieval tapestries, especially one showing rosy-cheeked Magi bringing gifts to the Christ child (1470). There is naturally an abundance of Madonnas, of all sizes and descriptions, carved in stone, wood, and metal. The museum is open Thursday to Sunday from 10 a.m. to 5 p.m. (on the first Wednesday of every month until 8 p.m.). Admission is 3 DM (99¢).

ORGANIZED TOURS: The easiest way to get a comprehensive look at Cologne's many attractions is to take one of the tours departing from the Tourist Office opposite the cathedral. Two-hour tours are offered daily at 10 a.m., noon, and 2 p.m. (from October 15 through April 30 daily departures are at 11 a.m. and 2 p.m.), and cover the major sights of the Old Town, including a large number of Gothic and Romanesque churches, a Roman tower, the medieval city gates, the Gothic (15th-century) town hall, Roman Praetorium, and the modern opera house. The tour also includes a stop at one of the major museums. The cost for either tour is 17 DM ($5.61).

From July 1 through August 31, evening tours of the city are offered every Friday and Saturday, departing from the Tourist Office at 8 p.m.

THE TOP HOTELS: Excelsior Hotel Ernst, 1-5 Trankgasse (tel. 27-01), is, from several points of view, Cologne's most prestigious hotel. Its position alone, facing the cathedral square, should be sufficiently commanding. But its tasteful and old-world ambience is also first rate. Add to this an outstanding Hanse Stuben restaurant on the premises, and you emerge with a winning combination. The bedrooms are spacious, with many facilities for comfort, including built-in wardrobes, bedside reading lamps, and traditional furnishings intermixed with reproductions, telephone, mini-bar, color TV, and radio. Doubles are priced according to size and position: 380 DM ($125.40) to 425 DM ($140.25) overlooking the cathedral. Singles range from 260 DM ($85.80) to 300 DM ($99). Tariffs include service, taxes, and a continental breakfast.

Inter-Continental, 14 Helenenstrasse (tel. 26-51). The enormous scale of this inner-city hotel, a 12-minute walk from the heart of town, will be familiar to many American urbanites. Its 292 rooms are unique, however, in the views that many offer of Cologne Cathedral. The first-class hotel offers dozens of diversions that only a big hotel can, including a climate-controlled indoor swimming pool, and the rooftop Belvedere Club, with nightly music and dancing, looking out onto a view of the city. Bars, and health clubs with sauna, massage, and manicure (also pedicure), round out the amenities. The Bergische Stube restaurant offers the latest in a well-prepared classic cuisine in a modern chain-hotel kind of ambience. Rooms are attractively furnished and decorated, costing from 190 DM ($62.70) to 300 DM ($99) in a single, from 230 DM ($75.90) to 350 DM ($115.50) in a double. Reservations are often hard to come by at certain times of the year.

Dom-Hotel Köln, 2a Domkloster (tel. 23-37-51), is opposite the cathedral, standing in a famous area tucked away from the bustle of traffic. It is ten minutes by car from the Cologne-Bonn Airport, and the railway station is close by. One of Europe's finest, the hotel has a pleasant, comfortable atmosphere. It is one of the few hotels in Germany to be regularly awarded five stars. In every room and in every detail, discernment, harmony, and culture can be seen and felt. There's an excellent French restaurant, inviting bar, and an open-air terrace. A public underground garage provides direct admittance to the hotel. There are 135 bedrooms, all with private bath. A single room runs from 205 DM ($67.65) to 290 DM ($95.70), and a double costs from 265 DM ($87.45) to 400 DM ($132), including a breakfast buffet, service, and tax.

Eden, 18 Am Hof (tel. 23-61-23), stands opposite the Dom, bringing a light, airy note to the old section of the city, with its sun-mad colors and architectural design. More than half of its bedrooms overlook the cathedral; each has its own bath, telephone, radio, mini-bar, and TV (on request). The accommodations are well conceived, with twin couches that convert to beds at night. Rates here include breakfast, taxes, and service. The largest doubles, with sitting and sleeping room, go for 235 DM ($77.50); other doubles cost 190 DM ($62.70). Singles range from 158 DM ($52.14) to 220 DM ($72.60). When you first walk in, you think you're in a tasteful and dramatic living room in a private home. Room and breakfast only are provided, although there's a Herren Bar for drinks.

MEDIUM-PRICED HOTELS: Haus Lyskirchen Ring hotel, 26-32 Filzengraben (tel. 23-48-91), is an unusual establishment in that it offers a rustic country decor in a 130-bed inner-city hotel, only four city blocks from the cathedral. The facade has one of those baroque yellow-stuccoed step-gabled rooflines. The units, with unfinished wood planking on parts of the ceilings and walls, look more like something from an unheated chalet in the Alps than a room in downtown Cologne. Rusticity aside, the hotel has a 19-foot by 37-foot heated swimming pool, along with an attractively masculine wood-paneled pub, as well as two warmly decorated restaurants. A single rents for 98 DM ($32.34) to 140 DM ($46.20), and a double costs 160 DM ($52.80) to 200 DM ($66).

Hotel Mondial, 10 Bechergasse (tel. 21-96-71), is a modern, large-scale international hotel across the street from the Roman-Germanic Museum. A short walk from the cathedral, the Mondial offers efficient service to many of Germany's business community on corporate trips to Cologne. Its 204 rooms are decorated in a clean but rather impersonal hotel-chain style, and the public rooms are a bland international modern. Still, its units are comfortable and clean, and its restaurant offers well-prepared meals with good service. Singles rent for 155 DM ($51.15) to 185 DM ($61.05); doubles cost 200 DM ($66) to 225 DM ($74.25).

Hotel Savoy, 9 Turiner Strasse (tel. 12-04-66). Residents of this recently renovated hotel need walk only a short distance to either the railway station or the Dom. The hotel, designed in an angular format of strong horizontal lines and sweeping bands of glass, includes 70 comfortably furnished bedrooms, each with a modern tile bath. The decor includes warmly monochromatic color schemes and a streamlined but plush assortment of simple lines and elegant materials, such as brass, black accents, French-style armchairs, and green plants. The Intermezzo Bar offers a warmly wood-lined hideaway for a drink, and lunch and dinner are served in a restaurant decorated with artworks. A sauna and solarium are available for the use of hotel guests. Singles range in price from 105 DM ($34.65) to 155 DM ($51.15), while doubles cost 145 DM ($47.85) to 230 DM ($75.90), including a breakfast buffet.

Hotel Bristol, 48 Kaiser-Wilhelm-Ring (tel. 12-01-95), is unusual and exceptional in that each of its 44 rooms is furnished with genuine antiques, either regal or rustic. There is a different antique bed in almost every room, ranging from French baroque and rococo to something reminiscent of High Rhenish ecclesiastical art. The oldest four-poster dates from 1742. Mrs. Duforet helps run this place, and does so exceedingly well. It is conveniently located near an underground stop, within walking distance of the cathedral. She charges 100 DM ($33) in a single and from 150 DM ($49.50) in a double, each with bath or shower, breakfast included.

Senats Hotel, 9 Unter Goldschmied (tel. 23-38-61), lies in a secluded corner within the heart of the city shopping center, five minutes' walk from the cathedral, the Rhinegardens, and the romantic Old Town. The rooms are attractive and comfortable. Rates are 145 DM ($47.85) for a single and 220 DM ($72.60) for a double room, including breakfast and service charges. All rooms have bath, toilet, phone, and radio. The color scheme throughout is brown, beige, and other natural colors. The restaurant is known for its cuisine and wide range of European wines and beverages.

Hotel PLM Baseler Hof, 2 Breslauer Platz (tel. 1-65-40), lies directly opposite the main station and the famous Dom, offering 108 comfortably furnished rooms, all with private bath, phone, radio, and TV. Including a buffet breakfast, the single tariff is 145 DM ($47.85) to 165 DM ($54.45), rising to 180 DM ($59.40) to 210 DM ($69.30) in a double. On the premises are a French-style restaurant and a bar.

Alstadt-Hotel, Salzgasse (tel. 23-41-87), is a retreat hotel in the old section, just two minutes from the Rhine‐boat-landing dock. Guests of this 24-room hotel have passed the word along to their friends, making it a big success. Herr Olbrich learned about catering to international guests while a steward on the German-America Line, and he has furnished his little hotel beguilingly. Each of his rooms is immaculate, individually decorated, a restful haven. Each room has a telephone and a refrigerator, with radio and television available on request. Rates are 60 DM ($19.80) for bathless singles, 85 DM ($28.05) with shower. Doubles without bath are 90 DM ($23.10); with shower, 120 DM ($39.60); with complete bath, 130 DM ($42.90). All rates include breakfast, service charge, and tax. A sauna is on the premises. Space is not easy to obtain, and reservations are recommended.

Hotel Ludwig, 24 Brandenburgerstrasse (tel. 12-30-31), has been much improved and upgraded in recent years by the Ahles family. It enjoys a central location, directly by the north entrance of the main station and only 100 yards from the cathedral. Rooms are pleasantly and attractively furnished, and the plumbing has been brought up-to-date. In a single with shower, the overnight charge is 105 DM ($34.65) to 175 DM ($57.75). Doubles with private baths peak at 250 DM ($82.50), but some cheaper units go for 175 DM ($57.75), including a breakfast buffet. If you're traveling with a child, he or she can be sheltered in your room for another 35 DM ($11.55).

Kommerz-Hotel, Breslauer Platz (tel. 12-40-86), is downtown, near the cathedral and main train station. A tangerine-colored modern hotel, it looks glaringly conspicuous when viewed with the Dom in the background. But despite this juxtaposition of the old with the new, the rooms are convenient, with full-length windows illuminating utilitarian furnishings. The sunny wood-paneled bar has an attractive U-shaped serving area where you're likely to meet anyone in Cologne. All units contain bath or shower, along with a toilet, and tariffs include breakfast: singles from 105 DM ($34.65) to 155 DM ($51.15) and doubles from 160 DM ($52.80) to 190 DM ($62.70). An additional bed costs another 30 DM ($9.90).

Hotel am Augustinerplatz, 30 Hohestrasse (tel. 23-67-17), stands in a shopping center between the cathedral and the main train station. It is internationally modern, with some effort at gemütlichkeit in the breakfast room where the staff will cook, within reason, anything you want. The rooms are clean and comfortable, with large beds and chairs upholstered in rich, dark fabrics. The cost of all units includes breakfast, and depends on the amount of plumbing contained within. Singles rent from a low of 95 DM ($31.35), climbing to 175 DM ($57.75); doubles, 130 DM ($42.90) to 225 DM ($74.25).

BUDGET INNS: **Hotel City,** 26 Ursulagartenstrasse (tel. 13-36-46), lies on a narrow, quiet street behind St. Ursula Church, near the center of town. The hotel offers quite a lot, mainly the hearty welcome of its owner, Mr. Taeschner, who knows well what a tired traveler yearns for: comfort and a friendly atmosphere at a reasonable price. His rooms are rather small, but sufficient. The ambience is not unlike that of the home of a friend. Some accommodations have their own shower, but in others you'll have to rely on the corridor facilities. Furnishings are standard. Doubles with shower go for 75 DM ($24.75), and the rates include breakfast served in an intimate lounge.

Breslauer Hof, 56 Johannisstrasse (tel. 12-30-09), is a minimal little 20-room hotel directly across from the Dom and the railway station. The furnishings are in the eternal oak functional type, the floors of plastic tile. However, all is kept immaculate in true Germanic tradition by its manager, Klaus Heinz. Singles cost 70 DM ($23.10); doubles, 90 DM ($29.70). All rooms contain showers. Included in the tariff is breakfast served in a café-style room with small tables opening directly onto the street. An elevator serves all floors, and the receptionist who sits at a corridor desk speaks a little English. The welcome's good.

Hotel Thielen, 1-5 Brandenburgerstrasse (tel. 12-33-33), is a pleasant, family-run hotel with good-size rooms that lies only a block in back of the main railway terminus for Cologne. The guest list is definitely international. The best and most economical way to stay here is in a room with no private bath. That way, a single costs only 45 DM ($14.85); a double, 60 DM ($19.80). Guests can shower free in one of the hallway facilities. With a shower, a twin-bedded room goes up in price to 85 DM ($28.05) and a triple-bedded unit rents for 100 DM ($33). In all, there are 100 good clean beds up for grabs.

Brandenburger Hof, 2 Brandenburgerstrasse (tel. 12-28-89), is a modest, family-style hotel where you can get cheaper rates in accommodations sheltering three or four persons. A room for three goes for 78 DM ($25.74). A regular single costs 30 DM ($9.90) to 40 DM ($13.20), and doubles (depending on the size) are yours for 52 DM ($17.16) to 58 DM ($19.14). A few doubles have both shower and toilet, going for 78 DM ($25.74) nightly. Breakfast with orange juice and eggs, included in the price, is served in a homey room with a big central table around which all the guests sit. The hotel is in back of the railway station, about three blocks from the river and within walking distance of the cathedral. The furnishings are in the dark wood mode. All the rooms are small, warm, and equipped with running water; there's a bath on each floor.

Hotel Lenz, 9 Ursulaplatz (tel. 12-00-55), advertises itself as "your home in Cologne," and for many overnight guests it's just that. The hotel was totally renovated in 1982, and now is better than ever with more up-to-date facilities. Most of the rooms have private bath. The Lenz is convenient to the railway station, the cathedral, and other major points of interest. Rooms are pleasantly and comfortably furnished. The doubles remaining that have only hot and cold running water rent for a low of 75 DM ($24.75). Doubles with private bath or shower cost from 165 DM ($54.45); singles, 55 DM ($18.15) to 105 DM ($34.65). The hotel also contains one of the most colorfully decorated wine houses in Cologne, with intricate woodcarvings, almost a Black Forest fantasy, everything brightened by panels of red.

THE TOP RESTAURANTS: Goldener Pflug, 421 Olpener Strasse (tel. 89-55-09), on the outskirts in the suburb of Merheim, should be visited for "that special occasion." Owned by Ludwig and Eleonore Robertz, it's one of the very top restaurants in all of Germany. The chef, Herbert Schönberner, appreciates impossibly demanding clients with jaded palates, and takes pleasure in sending them away satisfied. Top-quality ingredients are used in his imaginative blend of classical repertoires. Try, for example, any of his truffled specialties, ranging from soups down to a wide choice of delicately seasoned main courses. On the night I visited it was poached halibut in a saffron sauce. For dessert, the most exciting choices were an apple cake flambé or a soufflé à la Rothschild with strawberries.

The decor of what was a former tavern is surprisingly simple, with a golden motif repeated in the walls, draperies, and upholstery. Each dish is cooked to the specific requirements of the guests, who usually say that the food, service, and quality are worth the price. A fixed-price gourmet "surprise" menu costs 165 DM ($54.45) for eight courses. If you order à la carte, expect to spend from 95 DM ($31.35) or more for a meal. Hours are noon to 3 p.m. and 6 p.m. to midnight. Closed Sunday and for three weeks in summer. Always call for a reservation and ask for directions.

Chez Alex, 1 Mühlengasse (tel. 23-05-60), is the finest restaurant in the city itself. A festive vista of pink linen greets guests who enter this elegant "Maison du Champagne." It's the pink known in the '60s as "hot," and it contrasts beautifully with the elaborate paneling of the walls and the dark velvet of the banquettes. The decor is belle époque, with a few costly 18th-century paintings scattered about.

Established in 1978, it quickly moved to the foreground of Cologne restaurants, staying in the vanguard of the nouvelle cuisine devotees. The menu is in French with German subtitles. Among the offerings, you're likely to find coquilles St. Jacques en feuilletage or a mousse of smoked salmon with caviar. A nine-course *menu gastronomique* goes for 130 DM ($42.90). In season you can order a suckling lamb marinated in Pauillac. Dinners begin at 65 DM ($21.45). Hours are noon to 2:30 p.m. and 7 to 11 p.m., every day except Saturday for lunch, Sunday, and holidays.

Hanse-Stube, Domplatz/Bahnhofstrasse (tel. 27-01), on the ground floor of the Excelsior Hotel Ernst, is rightly considered one of the best restaurants in Cologne. The cuisine and service are top-drawer. The setting is that of a tavern, which you can enter through the hotel. In case you check into your hotel at a late hour, the restaurant provides a warm kitchen until midnight. Menus start at 40 DM ($13.20) to 90 DM ($29.70). The à la carte selections are international. To begin, try the bouillabaisse, and you may not want much more, it's so satisfying. Main-dish specialties include a mixed grill of seafood and a filet Singapore. The star dessert is the Salzburger nockerl.

La Poêle d'Or, 52 Komödienstrasse (tel. 13-41-00). The idea of a new philosophy in French cookery is nothing new to the chefs of this elegant restaurant. Roland and Jean-Claude Bado have used fresh ingredients and a lighter approach to classical French recipes for years. Cologne's sophisticated diners swear by their skill. Try their fresh mussels in lemon sauce or their goose salad with wild mushrooms, perhaps filet of turbot in a champagne sauce. Meals cost from 60 DM ($19.80) to 100 DM ($33). The decor is elegantly simple and the service is impeccable. Hours are noon to 2 p.m. and 6:30 to 10:30 p.m. daily except Sunday, holidays, and Monday lunch. The 12-table restaurant shuts down in July.

Bei Rino, 3 Ebertplatz (tel. 72-11-08). The trappings of this elegant restaurant are rich and old world, with a stunning replica of a Flemish tapestry on the wall. The cuisine is light and nouvelle, the entire show orchestrated with flair and panache by Guerino Casati, who diligently supervises the service and advises clients on the freshest delicacies available on his seasonally adjusted menu. Bei Rino lies across the street from the Baukunst Galleries, one of the well-known galleries of Cologne. Dining here is like an evening's entertainment, and "the production" isn't cheap—from 90 DM ($29.70) to 125 DM ($41.25) for a meal. But local gourmets insist that the price is worth it. Hours are noon till 2:30

p.m. and 6 to 10 p.m. except Sunday (closes for several weeks in summer). Always call for a reservation.

Die Bastei, 80 Konrad-Adenauer-Ufer (tel. 12-28-25), is the favored spot for your watch on the Rhine. The trick here is to aim for a window table. The split-level dining room is on the second floor of this circular tower-type building jutting out into the river, and the view from here is dramatic. The restaurant is as high class as its prices, no meals under 40 DM ($13.20), some reaching heavenward to 120 DM ($39.60), the latter for the seven-course gourmet menu. In addition to German specialties, many dishes are presented from neighboring Switzerland, Austria, and France. Dinner and dance music is played on Saturday evening.

OTHER LEADING RESTAURANTS: St. Georg, 3 Magnusstrasse (tel. 21-84-

18), offers nouvelle cuisine well prepared and served with style in this restaurant run by Karl-Heinz Steinbüchel. Between courses you might shop at the cookery boutique. Established in 1981, the boutique is only one of many attractions offered by head chef Klaus Zimmer. His specialties include a filet of turbot, stuffed with spinach and sauteed, and served in a champagne cream sauce. A fixed-price lunch of four courses costs 45 DM ($14.85), going up to 105 DM ($34.65) for a six-course evening repast. The handwritten menus are changed every two weeks. The decor is an elegant pastiche of modern and antique furniture, with much attention paid to small details. Service is from 11:30 a.m. to 2 p.m. and 6 to 10 p.m. Call for a table, but never on Sunday or a holiday.

Franz Kellers Restaurant, 21 Aachener Strasse (tel. 21-95-49). Franz Keller, Jr., runs this place, and it rates a superlative. Herr Keller is a remarkable chef who early in his career worked with Paul Bocuse and later Michel Guérard, the master chef who created cuisine minceur. Chef Keller is both a master of the Lyonnaise school of grande cuisine and of regional specialties as well.

As in any great restaurant, "fresh" is the essential byword. Try his breast of Bresse chicken with fresh herbs, côte de boeuf from Angus beef with red wine sauce, or turbot poached in white butter sauce, and for dessert, a kiwi salad in crème fraîche which, if the chef feels particularly inspired, will come with basil too. A fixed-price lunch will cost from 70 DM ($23.10) to 90 DM ($29.70); a set dinner, from 105 DM ($34.65) to 150 DM ($49.50). Service is from 7 p.m. to midnight. The weinstube on the premises, appropriately called Keller's Keller, will feed you at lesser tariffs, and you might end up enjoying it even more.

MIDDLE-BRACKET DINING: Bistro 1900, 1a Kettengasse (tel. 21-28-83), is

decorated in a turn-of-the-century style, with bentwood chairs and art nouveau accessories. A comfortable, classy place, it's the creation of Gerry Zoethout. Many of the tables (at least when I was there) carry the floral symbol of Holland, the tulip. At noon the cuisine is uncompromisingly *gutbürgerlichen* (traditional), but becomes tantalizingly French at night. The noontime menu, served till 2:30 p.m., could consist of any one of a dozen or so Germanic specialties, costing 18 DM ($5.94) and up. The evening menu, beginning at around 50 DM ($16.50) and ranging upward, is prepared with subtle blends of seasonings by chef Willi Heinen. Try, for example, his chicken stuffed with shrimp and covered with a delicately seasoned lobster and crab sauce. Dinner is served from 6 p.m. till midnight except Tuesday. Most intimate, the restaurant holds only six tables.

Auberge de la Charrue d'Or, 18-20 Habsburgerring (tel. 21-76-10), is a small, family-run restaurant that can rightfully claim to have been one of the first restaurants in Cologne to try the nouvelle cuisine (or *neuen kuchen,* as it's known here). Owners Erhard and Gertrud Lüdecke prepare a light and nourishing blend of the freshest ingredients with an intelligent choice of seasonings. Try, for example, lobster à la nage. Meals begin at 40 DM ($13.20), but could cost far more, of course. The restaurant serves five nights a week after 6 p.m. but is closed Sunday, Monday, and in July.

Börsen Restaurant, 10-26 Unter Sachsenhausen (tel. 13-56-26), near the stock exchange, is also not too far from the cathedral. This busy place welcomes the clerks, clients, and administrators of Cologne's financial community. It offers not only good value, but a glimpse of everyday Cologne life, particularly at noon. Seasonally adjusted fixed-price menus begin at 45 DM ($14.85). You get classic and conservative cookery from noon to 3 p.m. and 6 to 10 p.m. (there's no dinner served on Sunday).

Spezialitäten-restaurant Balduinklause, 10 Balduinstrasse (tel. 23-80-98). Visitors from anywhere will feel at home with the multilingual menu and the internationally modern decor. Colors are bright, the furnishings stylish, and the chef has a healthy respect for culinary delicacies around the world. Try his grilled shrimp or grilled Norwegian salmon. The location near the Rudolfplatz is open from noon to 3 p.m. and 6 to 11 p.m. every day except Sunday (it also takes a summer vacation). Fixed-price menus begin at 40 DM ($13.20).

"baguettchen," 35 Hochstadenstrasse (tel. 21-57-24). If you are looking for a good little French restaurant with an interesting menu, the "baguettchen," owned by Ursula Wegener, should be on your itinerary for Cologne. In a rustic, cozy atmosphere, the maître de cuisine, Petr Gryc from Prague, concocts what might be called a country-style nouvelle cuisine. You will find delicacies to satisfy even the fastidious gourmet, as well as savory provincial dishes, all served on white damask tablecloths. The three complete, fixed-price meals cost from 60 DM ($19.80) to 100 DM ($33). You can, of course, order à la carte. Service is from 7 to 11 p.m. except Sunday. Reservations are required.

Keller's Tomate, 11 Aachener Strasse (tel. 21-16-61), might be considered a cross between the back seat of your uncle's old Studebaker and gemütlichrustic. The place is amusingly bizarre with a pop art decor. A jukebox plays songs your Uncle Eddie used to sing, and clients seat themselves bistro fashion at wooden tables and kitchen chairs. Neon signs flash reminders of subway graffiti on New York's IRT. The food is surprisingly good in spite of the gimmicky decor. Try the goulash or lasagne or whatever looks good on your neighbor's plate. It's called Teutonic radical chic. Depending on what the chef found fresh that day at the market, meals begin at 35 DM ($11.55). The place is open from noon till 3 p.m. and 7 to 11 p.m. (closed Sunday and for Monday lunch).

Sigi's Bistro, 23 Kleiner Griechenmarkt (tel. 21-45-12), is like the kind you dream about. The ambience is modern, the crowd usually congenial, and you'll find yourself rubbing elbows with your neighbors (who could be in any of the industries that make Cologne tick). The food is good and the place is so popular it isn't always easy to get a table. Reserve early, and when you go, try, if featured, the leek tart, followed by veal steak with ratatouille. If you're in the mood, the vanilla custard Grand Marnier is a tempting dessert. Prices range from 35 DM ($11.55) to 55 DM ($18.15) for dinner. The place is open from 6 p.m. to midnight, but closed weekends and during parts of July and August.

DINING IN THE OLD TOWN: Weinhaus in Walfisch, 13 Salzgasse (tel. 21-95-75), is a step-gabled inn in the Old Town dating back to 1626. Behind its black-and-white timbered facade you'll find the leading atmospheric choice for dining. More important, it serves some of the best food in the city. Not too easy to find, it's on a narrow street set back from the Rhine. For an appetizer, try the Hamburger krebssuppe (crab soup). There are many main dishes, including a wide variety of fluffy omelets. Chef's specials include sole meunière and venison for two. Your final bill is likely to be anywhere from 35 DM ($11.55) to 65 DM ($21.45) per person. Hours are noon to 3 and 6 to 11 p.m., except on Sunday.

Im Stapelhäuschen, 1-3 Fischmarkt (tel. 21-30-43), is one of the finest wine taverns in Cologne. Just a few minutes from the cathedral, it's housed in an office building, opening onto the old fish market platz and the Rhine. The two-story-high dining room and service bar are antique in style, and provincial cabinets hold a superb wine collection behind the service bar. A carved Madonna attached to the wall, brass objects hanging against paneled wainscoting, a copper coffee urn—everything here is rustic. A wide, wooden, cantilevered staircase leads to mezzanine tables. While wine is the main reason for coming here (it's that special), the cuisine is excellent. Proof of that is how quickly the dining room becomes crowded. Soups are hearty and full of flavor, and main dishes such as medallions of veal in a creamy sauce are well prepared. A specialty is rumpsteak in the Balkan style (stuffed with cheese and ham). Desserts are appropriately luscious. A complete meal costs from 35 DM ($11.55).

THE BEER TAVERNS: Früh, 12 Am Hof (tel. 21-26-21), is a local beer tavern-restaurant within the cathedral precincts. It's the best all-around choice for economy and hearty portions. The denizens of Cologne congregate here for well-cooked meals served on scrubbed wooden tables. A different German specialty is offered every day of the week, ranging in price from 9 DM ($2.97) to 25 DM ($8.25). To make things easier, the menu is in English. You'll find the following dishes: soup of the day, bockwurst with sauerkraut and mashed potatoes, Hungarian goulash with boiled potatoes and a salad. Hot meals are served until 10 p.m.

Alt-Köln Stockheim, 7-9 Trankgasse (tel. 13-44-71), seemingly can feed half the visitors to Cologne on any busy day. Its location across from the cathedral and the railway station, right in the heart of the city, is hard to miss. It has a mechanical clock on its face; when it chimes the hour, a parade of figures emerges and disappears, a restive reminder of Old Germany. Alt Köln is a re-creation of a group of old taverns, including one done in the Gothic style. You can come here either for a beer or a good hot meal. Some of the upper-floor tables provide box-seat views of the Dom. The favorite main dishes include wienerschnitzel, schweinehaxe (pork knuckle), and a platter of sausage specialties with spicy mustard. Try also the braised leg of hare and braised beef Rhineland style. Meals begin at 18 DM ($5.94), going upward.

Brauhaus Sion, 5 Unter Taschenmacher (tel. 21-42-03). If you want a traditional local brauhaus, where the wood paneling is a little smoky with time and frequent polishings, where the portions are inexpensive and generous, where you can sit alone or with friends and enjoy a few tankards, this is the place. It's an institution that has been around for a long time, and will change only under great pressure. Traditional and filling fixed-price menus range from 10 DM ($3.30) to 22 DM ($7.26). You'll get such hearty fare as pig knuckles with sauerkraut or the inevitable bratwurst with spaetzle. It's open every day of the year except Christmas Eve from 10 a.m. to midnight.

DINING IN THE ENVIRONS: Remise, 48 Wendelinstrasse (tel. 49-18-81), lies in the suburb of Müngersdorf. It's a historic villa, with an apéritif bar where, if you feel like it, you can stop in just for a drink. The fixed-price menus change weekly, according to what was at the market and what's in season. Dinners range from 35 DM ($11.55) to 75 DM ($24.75). Nine tables seat some two dozen diners in friendly intimacy (or at least I hope so). Hours are noon to 3 p.m. and 6 p.m. till midnight, except Saturday lunch and all day Sunday.

Zur Krone, 58 Graf-Adolf-Strasse (tel. 61-42-30), on the outskirts at Mül-
heim, has a tasteful interior with lots of candlelight, half paneling on the walls,
and windows to let in the evening breeze on a fair night. The place is the statement of its head chef and owner, who features certain specialties depending on
the season. Should your visit happen to be in November, for example, you'll
find goose in all its manifestations on the menu. Hunting season brings out wild
game in all its varieties, including, perhaps, wild boar on Christmas Eve. Tasteful and intimate, it's a nice place to spend an evening in Cologne. Meals begin
modestly at 30 DM ($9.90), going up to 65 DM ($21.45). The restaurant is open
from 11 a.m. to 2:30 p.m. and 5 p.m. till midnight every day but Monday and
Saturday lunch.

Haus Marienbild, 561 Aachener Strasse (tel. 49-31-66), at Braunsfeld.
Some restaurants pride themselves on not bending to the demands of nouvelle
cuisine. At this staunchly conservative garden restaurant, the kitchen has determined the menus for some 20 years, and they still produce some of the finest
classic dishes served in Cologne. Here, in season, you can order venison, pheasant, woodcock, or, if available, thrush, cooked in a method perfected by experience and time. The decor is high ceilinged, a well-lit room with 50 tables divided
by wrought iron. Service is efficient and polite, and meals cost from 30 DM
($9.90) to 60 DM ($19.80). Hours are noon to 2:45 p.m. and 6 to 10 p.m. except
Thursday.

4. Aachen

Just 40 miles west of Cologne, where the frontiers of Germany, Belgium,
and Holland meet, is the ancient Imperial City of Aachen (Aix-la-Chapelle). It
is inseparably associated with Charlemagne, who selected this natural spa as the
center of his vast Frankish empire.

THE SIGHTS: About A.D. 800 the emperor built the octagon, the core of the
Imperial Cathedral. Within the cathedral stands the marble "Königsstuhl,"
Charlemagne's throne, considered one of the most venerable monuments in
Germany. For 600 years the kings of Germany were crowned here, until Frank-
furt became the country's coronation city in the mid-16th century.

The cathedral stands today an unusual mixture of Carolingian (the well-
preserved dome), Gothic (the choir, completed in 1414), and baroque (the
roof), all united into a magnificent upward sweep of architecture. The **Treasury,**
in the adjoining treasure house, is the most valuable and celebrated ecclesiastical treasure store north of the Alps. But the cathedral holds its own share of
wealth. The elaborate gold shrine in the chancel contains the relics of the Emperor Charlemagne. The pulpit of Henry II is copper studded with precious
gems. Visitors to the cathedral can view the throne of Charlemagne only with a
guide (request one at the Treasury). The Cathedral Treasury may be visited
daily except Monday from 9 a.m. to 1 p.m. and 2 to 5 p.m. (from April 15 to
October 15, until 6 p.m.; on Sunday from 10:30 a.m. to 1 p.m. and 2 to 5 p.m.).
Admission: 3 DM (99¢) for adults, 2 DM (66¢) for students.

The 14th-century **Rathaus** (Town Hall; tel. 432-73-10) was built on the original site of Charlemagne's palace. Part of the old structure can still be seen in the
so-called Granus Tower at the east side of the hall. The richly decorated facade
of the Town Hall facing the marketplace is adorned with the statues of 50
German rulers, 31 of them crowned in Aachen. In the center are the two most
important men in the Holy Roman Empire, Charlemagne and Pope Leo III, the
Majestas Domini, standing in relief above the main entrance.

On the second floor of the Rathaus is the double-naved and crossbeamed

Imperial Hall, dating from 1330, the scene of German coronation meals from 1349 to 1531, built as the successor to the Carolingian Royal Hall. This hall today contains exact replicas of the Imperial Crown Jewels, true in size and material to the originals, presently in the Vienna Secular Treasury. On the walls are the Charlemagne frescoes, painted in the 19th century by Alfred Rethel, illustrating the victory of the Christian Franks over the Germanic heathens. The hall is open weekdays from 9 a.m. to 1 p.m. and 2 to 5 p.m. Admission is 1 DM (33¢).

As a spa, Aachen has an even longer history than it does as an Imperial City. Roman legionnaires established a military bath here in the first century A.D. At the end of the 17th century it became known as the Spa of Kings, attracting royalty from all over Europe. In 1742 Frederick the Great took the cure here, and in 1818 the "Congress of Monarchs" brought Czar Alexander from Russia. After World War II, which badly damaged the whole town, the spa was rebuilt and today enjoys a mild reputation as a remedial center.

Its springs are among the hottest in Europe. The treatment includes baths and the *trinkkur* (drinking of water). The spa gardens are the center of the resort activity, with attractive ponds, fountains, and shade trees.

Most travelers visit Aachen on a day trip from Cologne, via the Cologne-Aachen autobahn, usually having dinner at the Ratskeller before returning to the larger city on the Rhine. However, those interested in the spa facilities can stay at one of the hotels described below.

Additional information on the sights is available at the **Tourist Office Aachen,** 39-41 Markt (tel. 3-27-50).

THE TOP SPA HOTEL: Steinberger Parkhotel Quellenhof, 52 Monheimsallee (tel. 15-20-81), is a palace-like structure in a tranquil setting. Architecturally neoclassic, it's furnished with a combination of antique reproductions and modern pieces. True to spa tradition, it is stately and dignified, with an impressive indoor swimming pool. Picture windows allow a view of the garden while guests swim in thermal water. In addition there are treatment rooms for chronic rheumatic diseases, gout, and skin diseases. Rates here include breakfast. Singles with full bath cost 155 DM ($51.15) to 215 DM ($70.95). Twin-bedded rooms with bath range from 230 DM ($75.90) to 320 DM ($105.60). Most of the accommodations are large scale.

The hotel's large restaurant seats more than 100 guests, and space between the tables allows for easy and intimate conversations. Both classic and nouvelle cuisine dishes are featured, along with a complete wine list. Nonresidents are welcome to dine here, but should make a reservation first. A meal costs from 40 DM ($13.20) to 85 DM ($28.05). There is modern elegance and a refined service aimed at satisfying the upper-class demands made here. The restaurant is open at noon, taking its last orders shortly before midnight.

UPPER BRACKET HOTELS: Aquis Grana, Büchel/32 Buchkremerstrasse (tel. 4-43-0), rises like a good piece of urban architecture from a downtown street corner in Aachen. A well-decorated establishment, it offers all the modern amenities of a large city hotel. Rooms are warm, comfortable, and inviting, with elegantly modern bathrooms and quilts in autumnal colors on the single or twin beds. All units contain complete bath or shower, and rent for 125 DM ($41.25) to 145 DM ($47.85) in a single, 195 DM ($64.35) to 210 DM ($69.30) in a double, including a buffet breakfast. Children up to 10 years stay free in the same room as their parents.

Novotel, am Europaplatz, Joseph-von-Görres-Strasse (tel. 16-40-91), has up-to-date comfort and amenities. It offers 119 well-furnished rooms with private bath, phone, radio, color TV, and mini-bar. The charge is 138 DM ($45.54) in a single, rising to 160 DM ($52.80) in a double, including a buffet breakfast. The hotel's swimming pool is open from May to September, and it also has a flower garden and a terrace.

MIDDLE-BRACKET HOTELS: Central Hotel, 5-9 Römerstrasse (tel. 2-68-73), lies about five minutes on foot from the center of town. It offers friendly and personalized service in clean, comfortable bedrooms, some of them with panoramic wall-size photographs of forest scenes above the beds. All rooms have toilet and either a bath or shower, renting for 115 DM ($37.95) in a single and from 170 DM ($56.10) in a double, breakfast included. On the premises is an Italian restaurant if you don't want to go out for the evening.

Hotel Krott, 16 Wirichsbongardstrasse (tel. 4-83-73), is built of brown brick with insulated climate-resistant windows. The face of this family-run hotel looks onto a quiet street within walking distance of the historic center of Aachen. The rooms might be called "cozy," with lots of places to sit, usually on upholstered or overstuffed armchairs. Single rooms, depending on the plumbing accessories, run anywhere from 95 DM ($31.35) to 120 DM ($39.60), and doubles rent for 130 DM ($42.90) to 160 DM ($52.80), with breakfast included. An extra bed can be added to most rooms for another 35 DM ($11.55).

Hotel Buschhausen, 215 Adenauerallee (tel. 6-30-71), can easily be reached by car from the center of Aachen (get off the autobahn at the Lichtenbusch exit in the direction of Aix-la-Chapelle). The innkeeper, Walter Homburg, rents rooms that are peaceful and quiet, owing to the double-glazed windows and the surrounding woods. The hotel has a swimming pool and two saunas, and its rooms are immaculate, decorated in an anonymous modern style. Breakfast is included in the rates, which depend on the plumbing: from 65 DM ($21.45) for the cheapest single, climbing to 115 DM ($37.95). Doubles begin at 100 DM ($33), rising to 145 DM ($47.85).

Hotel Royal, 1 Jülicher Strasse (tel. 1-50-61), is modern, its brick facade curving slightly to follow the contour of one of Aachen's peripheral ringed streets. The hotel offers cozy comfort within 200 yards of the casino. Rooms are carpeted, with colorfully tiled baths and a lobby with Oriental rugs. A double room with shower and toilet costs 150 DM ($49.50) to 160 DM ($52.80) nightly, and singles on the same arrangement rent for 99 DM ($32.67) to 108 DM ($35.64), including breakfast. Triple glazing on the windows keeps out the noise. In the attractive bar of the Royal, you can order a drink or a light meal.

BUDGET HOTELS: Hotel Benelux, 21 Franzstrasse (tel. 2-23-43), is warm, inviting, tastefully decorated, and personalized. It's a small, family-run hotel, my personal favorite for those watching their marks. The rooms fit gracefully together, leading eventually to the lobby/reception area where Americans from the West will feel at home. It has probably the only cactus collection in Aachen! Antiques are scattered throughout the corridors, and the rooms are streamlined in a contemporary style, each with bathroom tiled in pleasing earth tones. The Benelux is centrally located within walking distance "of everything." The hotel is also reasonably priced: from 95 DM ($31.35) in a single and from 118 DM ($38.94) to 155 DM ($51.15) in a double, each with shower or bath and toilet, and breakfast is included as well. On the premises is a Chinese restaurant.

Hotel Baccara, 174 Turmstrasse (tel. 8-30-05), is relaxed and friendly, lying a few minutes from central Aachen. Rooms are contemporary, clean, and comfortable, with blond-wood furniture and a predominant use of black and white. Some of the units contain private balconies, and all of them have toilets and showers (or complete baths). Parking is available. Singles rent for 75 DM ($24.75) nightly, and doubles go for 110 DM ($36.30), breakfast included.

Hotel Danica, 38 Franzstrasse (tel. 3-49-91), is a "breakfast only" hotel that is modern, efficient, clean, and centrally located. Everything is a little impersonal, but the price is right: 70 DM ($23.10) to 95 DM ($31.35) in a single, 110 DM ($36.30) to 120 DM ($39.60) in a double, and 140 DM ($46.20) in a triple, these rates including breakfast, service, and tax. If no room is available at the Danica, the same Adang family also owns the very similar **Hotel Danmark,** 21 Lagerhausstrasse (tel. 3-44-14), with almost the same prices.

Am Marschiertor, 1-7 Wallstrasse (tel. 3-19-41), stands in the center of Aachen, not far from the main station and next to the medieval town gate, Marschiertor, a beautiful and historical part of town. It has 45 recently furnished rooms in a cozy atmosphere. Parking facilities are available and, in addition, buses stop in front of the hotel. Singles without shower cost 60 DM ($19.80), going up to 95 DM ($31.35) with shower. Doubles without shower rent for 95 DM ($31.35), rising to 130 DM ($42.90) with complete bath. All these tariffs include a large buffet breakfast.

WHERE TO DINE: **Restaurant Gala,** 44 Monheimsallee (tel. 15-30-13), is one of the best in Germany. Light plays merrily through the crystal-draped decor onto the oak-paneled walls of this elegant restaurant, which is loosely linked to one of the country's busier casinos. Some of the paintings are by Salvador Dali. The Gala, owned by Gerhard Gartner, is reputed to be able to soothe the frayed nerves of even the heaviest gamblers, particularly when the concerned ministrations of the kitchen turns out such frequently updated menus as gamecock in a Calvados and mustard sauce or filet of venison in bloodsauce. Cookery here is a "reformed regional style," with many specialties from the nouvelle cuisine school. Other good dishes are likely to include a lobster parfait or turbot cooked in champagne. The food is trucked in daily from Rungis in Paris. The wine list is impressive, the confections French and delicious. A dinner is likely to cost from 100 DM ($33). The Gala serves from 7 p.m. till midnight, except Monday. Pretty frauleins in black dresses and frilly white aprons give attentive service.

Ratskeller, am Markt (tel. 3-50-01), is a charming place to dine, with its rustic atmosphere of brick and stone, oak benches and tables, hammered metal lanterns, decorative bronze and wood sculpture, and oil paintings. There are three major dining rooms. Most intimate and attractive is an extension, containing a pub where patrons gather to drink and play cards. Little drinking nooks upstairs are for other games. Soups might include a Viennese consommé with little bits of chopped meat or a pepper soup Madagascar with pineapple and cream. Main dishes include such chef's specialties as pork filet chasseur, with mushrooms, potatoes, and a fresh salad; veal fricassee; or a beef filet with a béarnaise sauce, mushrooms, grilled tomatoes, and fried potatoes. A dessert specialty—quite elaborate—is a cream of hot sour cherries flambé with kirsch. Meals range in price from 30 DM ($9.90) to 65 DM ($21.45).

Le Bécasse, 1 Hanbrucher Strasse (tel. 7-44-44), is a modern restaurant with much greenery, serving a pleasing combination of traditional German dishes with nouvelle cuisine specialties. Daily and seasonal specialties are served on a rotating basis of changing gourmet menus. Christof Lang, realizing early his "calling" toward reproducing the fine foods of France, has been the owner since 1981. The food is imported daily from the wholesale market at Rungis, outside Paris. Try, for example, his ragoût of fish or his cassoulet. Meals begin at 40 DM ($13.20). La Bécasse is open for lunch from 11 a.m. to 3 p.m. and for dinner from 6 to 11 p.m., except Sunday and Saturday lunch.

Elisenbrunnen, 13A Friedrich-Wilhelm-Platz (tel. 2-13-83), belongs to one of Germany's biggest concerns, offering a large and well-maintained terrace for summertime dining. The menu boasts more than 50 items, with complete meals costing from 25 DM ($8.25) to 40 DM ($13.20). Many of them will appeal to those who are vegetarian or calorie-conscious. On a warm day, it is said that a diner can sit in the shade of the Kaiserdom and the historic Rathaus and dream of the splendors of the old city. Once you've left the terrace, the interior is modern, albeit rustic. In the kitchen you'll find Hans Holland, whipping up the latest in nouvelle cuisine. Service is from 9 a.m. to 10:30 p.m.

On the outskirts, **Restaurant Schloss Friesenrath,** 46 Pannekoogweg (tel. 73-07), stands at Friesenrath, about 12 kilometers southeast of Aachen. There's plenty of atmosphere, as this was a castle with a garden terrace. Reservations are highly recommended, especially on weekends, when it's very popular with local residents. Specialties are deer (in season) and fish, and here one can enjoy the culinary arts with visual pleasure. You can dine here for around 38 DM ($12.54) if you really watch it, or else you could go wild at 120 DM ($39.60) by ordering some of the upper-grade specialties. Try the loup de mer (sea bass) in champagne sauce. Service is from noon to 2 p.m. and 6 to 9 p.m. except Monday. The Schloss is closed annually for about three weeks in January.

Restaurant St. Benedikt, 12 Benediktusplatz (tel. 28-88), is found in Kornelimünster, about ten kilometers (six miles) from Aachen. Owners Gisela and Hans Joachim welcome their guests into the intimate town-house facade, painted a terracotta red with blue-gray trim. The restaurant is actually a baroque-style house, with a wrought-iron sign discreetly announcing the entrance to this intimate, family-run restaurant. They offer attentive service and a thoughtful preparation of nouvelle and classical dishes. Reservations are essential, as they only have half a dozen tables. A varied menu of six meat dishes and four fish selections is offered, with an additional choice of two menus featuring ever-changing specials. Try, for example, salmon in champagne sauce, the filet of veal, or in season, pheasant. A spectacular dessert tray features sherbet mousses, pastries, and exotic fruits. In the kitchen, Gisela Kreus devotes herself to her work with zeal, soul, and fire, and is known throughout the town for her confections. Menus range from 65 DM ($21.45) to 90 DM ($29.70). It's also possible to dine for 45 DM ($14.85).

5. Düsseldorf
After 85% of this large city on the right bank of the Rhine was destroyed in World War II, it could easily have grown into just another ugly manufacturing town. Instead, Düsseldorf followed a modern trend in reconstruction, and today it is the most elegant metropolis in the Rhine Valley.

THE SIGHTS: As in all German cities, there is the Old Town, **Altstadt,** with its marketplace, a Gothic town hall, and a few old buildings and churches such as the twisted-towered St. Lambert's.

But in Düsseldorf it's the present that is important. A walk up the **Königsalle,** affectionately called the "Kö" by Düsseldorfers, will give the outsider a quick look at what the city and its residents are like. This street flanks an ornamental canal, shaded by trees and crossed by bridges. While one bank is lined with office buildings and financial centers, the other is filled with elegant shops, cafés, and restaurants. Here you'll see women dressed in the latest styles, as Düsseldorf is also the fashion center of Germany. It is known for its Fashion Weeks, attracting designers and buyers from all over Europe. Retail shops, incidentally, are generally open Monday to Friday from 9 a.m. to 6:30 p.m., on Saturday from 9 a.m. to 2 p.m. On the first Saturday in every month, shops stay open until 6 p.m.

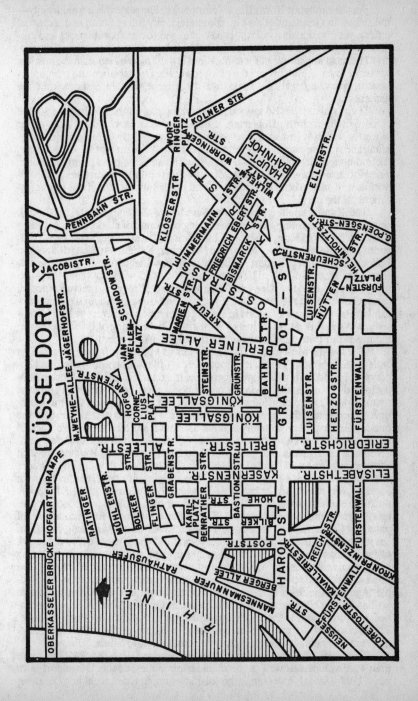

As the capital of North Rhine-Westphalia, Düsseldorf is a wealthy city—the richest in Germany. It's a big, commercial city full of banks and industrial offices, yet it's suprisingly clean. It has managed to incorporate parks and gardens throughout the city, some of them wedged comfortably between skyscrapers. The most impressive of these buildings is the **Thyssen House,** in the bustling center of town. Residents call the office tower the *Dreischeibenhaus* (three slice house), because it actually looks like three huge monoliths sandwiched together.

If you walk up the Kö toward the triton fountain at the northern end of the canal, you'll reach the **Hofgarten,** a huge rambling park. You could wander along the walks or just sit and relax for hours amid shade trees, gardens, fountains, and statues, almost forgetting you're in the very center of the city. Among the monuments is one to Düsseldorf's favorite son, the poet Heinrich Heine. The Hofgarten is a good central point for seeing the major attractions of Düsseldorf as well as nearly all the museums and other cultural attractions on the perimeter of the park.

The **Kunstsammlung Nordrhein-Westfalen,** 5 Grabbeplatz (tel. 13-39-61), opposite the Kunsthalle, has an outstanding collection of modern art, including works by Picasso, Georges Braque, Juan Gris, Fernand Léger, Max Ernst, Salvador Dali, René Magritte, Joan Miró, Kirchner, Kandinsky, Chagall, Jackson Pollock, Mark Tobey, Robert Rauschenberg, Roy Lichtenstein, Andy Warhol, Frank Stella, and others. The museum also has 92 works by Paul Klee—so many, in fact, that the Klee exhibition is rotated at regular intervals since all cannot be shown at the same time. Furthermore, there are about six temporary exhibitions of contemporary art in the large exhibition hall every year. The museum was scheduled to open in its new quarters in the spring of 1986. Therefore, inquire at the Tourist Office about hours and admission prices.

The **Goethe Museum,** in the Hofgarten, is housed in Jägerhof Castle, an 18th-century hunting lodge. It is sponsored by the Anton and Katharina Kippenberg Foundation. Mr. Kippenberg was the owner of the Insel-Verlag publishing house in Leipzig, and as a young bookseller, began collecting Goethe memorabilia. Düsseldorf joins Frankfurt and Weimar in having Goethe museums. Opened in 1956, this museum contains about 35,000 items relating to the famous German poet, so many that not all can be exhibited because of lack of space. Among such important documents as the first draft of Goethe's poem, "Noble be man, helpful and good . . ." and the first edition of *Werther,* are such esoteric items as a collection of glasses from spas frequented by Goethe. There's even a special room devoted to *Faust.* The museum is open Tuesday through Sunday from 10 a.m. to 5 p.m. (closed on Monday). Admission is 1 DM (33¢).

The **Kunstmuseum,** 5 Am Ehrenhof, is one of the largest and most comprehensive museums in the Rhineland. The museum is famous for its collection of paintings (Rubens, C. D. Friedrich, Brücke, Blaue-Reiter) and sculpture from the late Middle Ages to the 20th century and for its print room with a collection of Italian drawings. It is also a focal point for glass, and, naturally, a collecting area and research center for Düsseldorf art from the time of Schadow to the present day. On display are sculptures, paintings, and crafts from the late Middle Ages to the 18th century in the Kreuzherrenkirche, Ratinger Strasse (Altstadt); the glass collection in the Tonhalle, Grünes Gewölbe, 1 am Ehrenhof; the print room with the drawing collection at 50-52 Pempelforter Strasse. The Düsseldorf art can only be shown in sporadic exhibitions. The Kunstmuseum is open daily (except Monday) from 10 a.m. to 5 p.m.

The **Heinrich-Heine-Institut,** 14 Bilker Strasse (tel. 899-5574), has more than 4000 volumes as well as the manuscript bequest of this Düsseldorf-born poet (1797–1856). He was the author of many famous lyrics, including *Die Lore-*

lei and several anticonservative Sketchbooks. Forced to leave Germany because of his liberal political convictions, he was born Jewish, but converted to Christianity. The institute is open to the public Tuesday through Sunday from 10 a.m. to 5 p.m., charging a small admission. In the Altstadt you can visit the house where the poet was born. It's at 53 Bolker Strasse and is marked by a plaque.

On a different and more relaxing vein, you might want to visit one of Düsseldorf's breweries.

The biggest beer breweries in the city, both lying on the periphery of town, are **Schlösser,** 4 Huttenstrasse (tel. 38-981), and **Gatzweilers,** 52 Viersener Strasse (tel. 50-631). These two are very informal, and don't at all compare with the famous brewery tours of Europe such as those offered in Copenhagen. Since tours are not offered with any frequency or set pattern, you'll have to call first and take a chance.

TOURS: Rhine boats leave from the Rathausufer, on the periphery of Altstadt. As the most interesting jaunt, I recommend a trip to **Zons,** the only place on the lower Rhine that is still completely surrounded by walls and city towers, as in olden days. You can walk the ramparts, take in a tower or a windmill, and immerse yourself in a place that has been called the Rhenish Rothenburg.

Vessels depart from 1:30 to 5:30 p.m., leaving every hour. The trip takes about an hour and a half (one way), and costs $6.50 (U.S.) for a round-trip fare.

If you're in Düsseldorf from the end of June until mid-August, I'd also recommend a hydrofoil trip to **Mainz** (see Section 7 in this chapter). You've got to get up early, however, to make the 7:45 a.m. departure. Arrival time in Mainz is about 1 p.m. Along the way you'll cruise past medieval Rhenish castles, wine villages, and the celebrated Lorelei Rock. A one-way trip, as of this writing, costs $85 (U.S.) but that fare is subject to change.

If time remains, I suggest a 12-minute tram ride south of Düsseldorf to **Benrath Castle,** erected between 1755 and 1770 on the foundations of a fortress surrounded by a moat. After visiting the baroque castle, guests are allowed to explore the park with its mirror lake and the English- and French-style gardens. Visiting hours are 10 a.m. to 5 p.m. Tuesday through Sunday. Winter hours are noon to 3:30 p.m. weekdays, from 10 a.m. to 3:30 p.m. on Sunday. The house, the former residence of Elector Carl Theodor, charges an admission fee of 5 DM ($1.65).

Tram 701 leaves from Jan-Wellem-Platz in Düsseldorf, heading for Benrath.

THE TOP HOTELS: Inter-Continental, 5 Karl-Arnold-Platz (tel. 4-55-30), is one of the star hotels in Düsseldorf, a pace-setting establishment. Other German hotel designers could learn from this deluxe hostelry. Placed at the edge of the city, across from the Hilton, it's an attractive, high-rise building with its own entrance plaza and open swimming pool terrace. The service is efficient. Its rooftop restaurant offers set dinner-dances. The Brasserie is in the old Germanic tavern style, offering moderately priced lunches and dinners. The Herald Bar and lounge is one of the main social centers of the city, set against a background of heraldic shields, lanterns, and antiques. In addition to the three restaurants, there is a sauna with a massage service. The bedrooms, created by an internationally known designer, have coordinated colors with traditional furnishings. Most singles range in price from 205 DM ($67.65) to 345 DM ($113.85); doubles, 235 DM ($77.50) to 375 DM ($123.75).

Düsseldorf Hilton, 20 Georg-Glock-Strasse (tel. 43-49-63), and its adjoining congress centers are between the Kennedy Damm and the Rhine, close to the city, airport, and fairgrounds. It is exactly what you would expect from a

Hilton. Well-designed and streamlined bedrooms are offered, each with a handsomely equipped tile bath. Single rooms cost from 180 DM ($59.40), although they may go as high as 335 DM ($110.55). Doubles start at 230 DM ($75.90), going up to 410 DM ($135.20). The most expensive rooms are on the upper floors. But no matter what you pay, the view is good and the rooms attractively styled. Those added conveniences are there too: the color TV outlets, radios, direct-dial phones, mini-bars, whatever. The public lounges reflect a progressively ultramodern decor, utilizing free-form sculpture and contemporary paintings. Most popular is Neptune's Club, with its swimming pool, sauna, and massage facilities, as well as a fitness center and solarium. The San Francisco Restaurant is known for its creative cuisine, and at the Club 1001 it's disco time every night from 10 p.m. until 4 a.m. Most agreeable is the Hofgarten-Restaurant, a glassed-in garden room for informal dining. Late in the afternoon, there's a Happy Hour, with recorded music.

Breidenbacher Hof, 36 Heinrich-Heine-Allee (tel. 86-01), seems to have been designed to coddle the well-heeled German. Dating back to 1806 (alhough rebuilt when it was partially destroyed in World War II), it is Düsseldorf's leading traditional hotel, bordering on the luxurious. It was the leader long before the Hilton and the Inter-Continental came along. Everything for plush living is to be found here, including a nightclub and a grill room with orchestral background music during the cocktail hour. The Breidenbacher Eck, with its intimate atmosphere, is also a magnet. The main drawing rooms and lounges have traditional furnishings, somewhat glamorized by a sprinkling of antiques, gilt mirrors, paintings, and bronze chandeliers. The service is good. All bedrooms have private bath, telephone, radio, TV, and traditional furnishings. You pay from 240 DM ($79.20) to 270 DM ($89.10) in a single, from 320 DM ($105.60) to 380 DM ($125.40) in a double.

Steigenberger Park-Hotel, 1 Corneliusplatz (tel. 86-51), is one of the first-class traditional German hotels that survived World War II. Completely modernized and reequipped to meet modern demands, it is a prestige hotel maintaining a high service level in the true old-world style. The lounges were renewed in 1982. All bedrooms, refitted to the latest standards with private bath, are cozy and comfortable. Singles rent for 230 DM ($75.90) to 310 DM ($102.30) and doubles go for 280 DM ($92.40) to 400 DM ($132) per person. Both prices include breakfast, service, and tax. The Rôtisserie attracts gourmets from all over the world, drawn to its modern French-style cuisine. Before-dinner drinks are served in the Étoile Bar. In summer, a terrace overlooking the parks and gardens of Düsseldorf invites you for leisurely meals.

Nikko, 41 Immermannstrasse (tel. 86-61), is a five-star hotel located in the German-Japanese Centre in the heart of Düsseldorf. Opened in 1978, it is elegantly modern, with an imaginative use of Space Age materials in the almost endless series of public rooms. Affiliated with Japan Airlines, it often attracts as guests corporate visitors attending trade fairs. The exterior is an attractive steel-alloy gray, and the rooms inside are tastefully simple, with good color choices and streamlined, attractively grained modern furniture. Singles range in price from 200 DM ($66) to 290 DM ($95.70), and with doubles cost from 250 DM ($82.50) to 340 DM ($112.20). Good German food is to be found in one of the restaurants, and even better Japanese food in another, a diplomatic concession to both countries. A major attraction is the penthouse pool, with a fitness center, solarium, sauna, and massage parlor.

UPPER-BRACKET HOTELS: Günnewig Savoy Hotel, 128 Oststrasse (tel. 36-03-36). Its facade is of heavily sculpted white limestone, and its bar and restaurant are a rendezvous point for many members of the prominent business community of Düsseldorf. Owned by one of Germany's largest hotel chains, the Savoy gives personalized service in a gracious setting. In addition to the richly upholstered bar, it has dining rooms, a swimming pool, and bedrooms that are totally satisfactory, with all the modern conveniences. A single ranges from 180 DM ($59.40) to 240 DM ($79.20), while a double rents for 250 DM ($82.50) to 315 DM ($104). Breakfast and color TV come with all units. Bierhoff, the court confectioners in the Savoy, are more than 125 years old. When the old Savoy had to make way for the new underground, this famous city café was relocated in the Oststrasse. Today, in its reincarnation, the Bierhoff konditorei has reemerged with most of its old splendor.

Hotel Excelsior, 1 Kapellstrasse (tel. 48-60-06). Finally, here's a hotel with an imaginative classical color scheme. Bathrooms are decorated with refreshingly natural colors (forest green with pink fixtures, for example), and some of the rooms are beautifully carpeted and wallpapered with olive-green and pure-white accessories. Even the lobby is royal blue with gold and a few antiques, enough so that the hotel can advertise itself as a place "for the discerning guest." At the corner of the Kaiserstrasse and Kapellstrasse, the building offers six floors of air-conditioned comfort to travel-tired guests for anywhere from 145 DM ($47.85) to 155 DM ($51.15) in a single and from 220 DM ($72.60) to 255 DM ($84.15) in a double. Tariffs include breakfast.

Börsenhotel, 19 Kreuzstrasse (tel. 36-30-71), in the heart of Düsseldorf, stands almost at the front door of the stock exchange. It is surprisingly reasonable, considering how attractively furnished it is. The marble floor of the lobby and the bar, popular with stockbrokers, might appeal to you, and the high-ceilinged bedrooms are clean, comfortable, and well proportioned. Thermopane windows keep out the noise of the city. A single ranges in price from 130 DM ($42.90) to 160 DM ($52.80); a double goes for 190 DM ($62.70) to 220 DM ($72.60).

Holiday Inn, Graf-Adolf-Platz (tel. 37-70-53), stands at the very center of Königsallee, offering 120 attractively furnished, air-conditioned rooms, with large beds, private baths, radios, color TVs, direct-dial phones, and double-glazed windows. A single rents for 205 DM ($67.65) and a double costs 250 DM ($82.50). La Rhenane is a French restaurant, and Suppentopf serves soups, salads, homemade food, and draft beer. The inn also has an indoor swimming pool, sauna, and fitness center. Children up to 18 stay free in their parents' room.

Hotel Esplanade, 17 Fürstenplatz (tel. 37-50-10), is near the main shopping and business area, but it faces the Fürstenplatz, a quiet park area. The Esplanade has an excellent restaurant, the Rib-Room, and a hotel bar. All the public rooms are air-conditioned. The large heated indoor swimming pool with solarium and the original Finnish sauna can be reached from each floor by elevators. Rooms are comfortably furnished, with direct-dial phone, radio, color TV, private bathroom, and soundproof windows. Singles, depending on the plumbing, cost 170 DM ($56.10) to 210 DM ($69.30). Doubles are 220 DM ($72.60) to 280 DM ($92.40). Prices include a buffet breakfast, service, and taxes. You'll find the rooms comfortable and pleasant.

MEDIUM-PRICED HOTELS: Eden, 29-31 Aderstrasse (tel. 38-10-60), is a first-class hotel, catering to a business clientele. In spite of its name, it's more solid than lush. A lot of care has gone into making the bedrooms comfortable. But the baths, in most of the rooms, are more luxurious—tiled and spacious, with two basins and large fluffy towels. Singles are 110 DM ($36.30) with shower and 145 DM ($47.85) with complete bath. Double rooms with bath are from 230

DM ($75.90), and all these rates include a buffet breakfast as well. A high level of cleanliness is maintained throughout. The position of the Eden is fairly central, with private parking in a rear courtyard. The reception area is small, but adequate, leading to a combination grill-restaurant-bar.

Hotel Fürstenhof, 3 Fürstenplatz (tel. 37-05-45), has been totally revamped and renamed. It opens onto an attractive, tree-filled square, and is modern, but not glaringly so. All the attractively furnished bedrooms are equipped with private shower or bath, toilet, color TV, radio, mini-bar, and phone. A double room rents for 175 DM ($57.75) to 208 DM ($68.64), while a single goes for 115 DM ($37.95) to 150 DM ($49.50), these tariffs including a buffet breakfast. At different seasons, special reductions are granted. R. P. Marquigny, the manager, has employed an efficient and helpful staff who will ease your adjustment in Düsseldorf. It's a good, comfortable, safe choice.

Lindenhof, 124 Oststrasse (tel. 36-09-63), has been around for more crises than you or I could imagine for the past 80 years, and if the competent administration of Manfred Vossen continues, it should last another 80. On a tree-shaded street, it has five stories, lying within walking distance of central Düsseldorf. All rooms have shower/bath and toilet, and breakfast is included in the rates, which run anywhere from 130 DM ($42.90) to 155 DM ($51.15) in a single and from 170 DM ($56.10) to 195 DM ($64.35) in a double. Children are lodged in their parents' room free.

The **Hotel Am Rhein Schnellenburg,** 120 Rotterdamer Strasse (tel. 43-41-33), on the outskirts, was built on the ruins of a medieval castle opening directly onto the Rhine. In a traditional style, with window boxes of flowers in summer, it is an engaging choice, lying about 2½ miles from Düsseldorf's international airport and within walking distance of both the Convention Center and the Japanese Garden. All rooms are completely modern, with such amenities as refrigerator-bars, direct-dial phones, color TVs, and good-size bathrooms with showers. Rates are 130 DM ($42.90) in a single, rising to 200 DM ($66) in a double. The hotel has a good restaurant with a terrace overlooking the river. Sightseeing boats leave from the hotel's own pier. The hotel manages to be both sophisticated and cosmopolitan, yet still comfortably informal. English is spoken.

Lancaster, 166 Oststrasse (tel. 35-10-66), is attractively situated in the center of town. The mirrored reception area efficiently registers guests before packing them off to clean, comfortable, and often sunny rooms (albeit a bit anonymous in decor). Breakfast is included in the rates, with an assortment of sausage that might make a wurst fan of you. Singles go for 130 DM ($42.90) to 140 DM ($46.20); doubles, 170 DM ($56.10) to 180 DM ($59.40). Breakfast and private plumbing are included.

Central, 42 Luisenstrasse (tel. 37-90-01), has a plain tulip-yellow facade like a four-story urban brownstone in Baltimore, with black awnings and a yellow illuminated sign saying simply "Hotel." These are the identifying features of this well-located hotel which lies near the Königsallee. Rooms are modern and clean, with phone, TV, bath (or shower), and toilet. Including breakfast, units rent for 140 DM ($46.20) to 180 DM ($59.40) in a single and 200 DM ($66) to 220 DM ($72.60) in a double.

Hotel National, 16 Schwerinstrasse (tel. 49-90-62), lies 1½ miles from the downtown section. It's modern and efficient, and was pleasantly renovated a few years ago. Often you can find a room here when all other accommodations are booked, particularly during those busy trade fairs. All the comfortably furnished units are equipped with private bath, color TV, radio (English channel available), direct-dial phone, mini-bar, and balcony. There's a multistory car park available without charge. The regular rates are 115 DM ($37.95) to 165 DM ($54.45) in a single and 160 DM ($52.80) to 215 DM ($70.95) in a double. However, in July and August, tariffs are reduced to 95 DM ($31.35) in a single and 140 DM ($46.20) in a double.

BUDGET HOTELS: **Graf Adolf Hospiz,** 1 Stresemannplatz (tel. 36-05-91), is one of the better links in the Deutsche Verband Hospiz chain. The Düsseldorf sister offers you a super-clean, reasonably priced accommodation well situated about three blocks from the railway station. You can relax in the nice reception lounge, then take an elevator to one of the 100 good-size rooms, furnished in a trim contemporary manner. Because of the odd shape of the building, baths are present, but usually as an afterthought in design. Singles run from 95 DM ($31.35) to 123 DM ($40.59). The most expensive doubles, those with bath and toilet, cost from 155 DM ($51.15) to 172 DM ($56.76). All units have either private bath or shower. The atmosphere is fine, the rooms facing the street equipped with soundproof windows. The breakfast room on the first floor offers you a fair view of the morning crowd rushing to work. Breakfast is included in the rate.

Wurms, 23 Scheurenstrasse (tel. 37-50-01), offers 30 bedrooms that are most recommendable. It's in a five-story stucco building, close to the Graf-Adolf-Strasse, leading to the Rhine and about four blocks from the railway station. The accommodations are honestly furnished in dark wood that has been personalized with brightly colored bedspreads and curtains. Bathless singles are 70 DM ($23.10), increasing to 85 DM ($28.05) to 105 DM ($34.65) with shower. Doubles come only with bath or shower, costing from 130 DM ($42.90) to 150 DM ($49.50).

Hotel Grosser Kurfürst, 18 Kufürsterstrasse (tel. 35-76-47), is housed in a modern building. The rooms are well organized, but there's no furniture to spare. Rates include breakfast, and singles with private bath or shower range in price from 95 DM ($31.35) to 105 DM ($34.65); doubles go for 135 DM ($44.55) to 155 DM ($51.15). Accommodations are equipped with phone, mini-bar, and radio (in some cases, TV).

Rheinpark, 13 Bankstrasse (tel. 49-91-86), is a 30-room, antiseptically modern little hotel, about three blocks from the Rhine. You are quite far away from the center, but a streetcar stopping nearby will quickly bring you to the Königsallee. The hotel's in a colorless concrete building, with no proper reception area, but rooms are comfortable, the furnishings oakwood, the walls nicely decorated with old pictures. All rooms have running water, and there's a shower on each floor. Singles cost from 58 DM ($19.14) to 85 DM ($28.05); doubles, from 95 DM ($31.35) to 115 DM ($37.95).

THE TOP RESTAURANTS: **Orangerie,** 30 Bilker Strasse (tel. 37-37-33), now ranks as the most outstanding restaurant in the city, although some gourmets give the honor to the San Francisco in the Hilton Hotel. For elegant dining and high prices, the haute cuisine of the Orangerie is, in my opinion, without equal. Inviolately aristocratic, it draws the fashion moguls of the city on the see-and-be-seen circuit. Everything here is of the highest quality, including the service. The chef, Horst Weigandt, specializes in such dishes as a gratin of crayfish and suprême de turbot. Try especially his medallion de veau à la périgourdine—that is, veal with a garnish of truffles to which foie gras has been added. The French culinary masterpieces are pleasing both to eye and palate. The establishment's

well-deserved reputation for gourmetry is perpetuated by its exclusivity—
generated, to a large extent, by the rarefied prices, where a complete dinner can
cost from 55 DM ($18.15) to 120 DM ($39.60), and a lot more if you select an
expensive wine. Closed Sunday. This place gets very busy at the time of the
I.G.E.D.O., the international fashion trade fair held four times a year. It's open
from noon to 2:30 p.m. and 6:30 to 11 p.m. daily except Sunday. Reservations
are absolutely necessary.

Schneider-Wibbel-Stuben, 5 Schneider-Wibbel-Gasse (tel. 8-00-00), is in
Düsseldorf's Alstadt alleyway, with boutiques, a theater, and a museum, just off
the Rhine. You get some of the finest fish dinners in Düsseldorf, and this attractive restaurant, which avoids any gimmicky decor, is dedicated to the expert
preparation of fish. One of its three dining rooms honors the lobster, priced according to weight of course, and prepared in practically any style. You can also
dine at a counter, as in a New England oyster bar, or at one of the cozy booths.
Appetizers include a cocktail of Greenland crayfish or a cream soup. House specialties include blue carp and Nordland salmon. A meal costs from 50 DM
($16.50) to 90 DM ($29.70). The restaurant is closed Sunday.

San Francisco, 20 Georg-Glock-Strasse, in the Düsseldorf Hilton (tel. 43-
49-63). Whoever designed this international restaurant must have lost his heart
somewhere on the West Coast of the United States, because the decor is vaguely
"San Francisco," circa turn of the century. Victorian globe lights and handwritten menus create only part of the ambience here. Head chef Günter Scherrer,
besides using the best produce Düsseldorf can offer, imports his beef directly
from Hilton slaughterhouses in the U.S. He produces steaks with a distinctive
taste in Germany. But they do much more than that, including a lot of elegant
dishes such as mussels in champagne sauce or a navarin of turbot with wild rice.
Prepare to pay from 60 DM ($19.80) to 100 DM ($33) to dine here. Service is
daily from noon to 3 p.m. and 7 to 11 p.m.

Restaurant Frickhöfer, 47 Stromstrasse (tel. 39-39-31). A graduate of the
Bocuse school runs this rustically elegant gathering place, where residents of
Düsseldorf go for an unadulterated French cuisine. While the cuisine is strictly
classical, the decor is not. It might be called "nostalgic," with sunflower walls,
tastefully striped banquettes, and pumpkin-colored tablecloths. Karl-Horst
Frickhöfer does everything he can to see that his produce is as fresh as the local
markets will provide, and that the service is personalized and attentive. Try such
time-honored delicacies as Bresse chicken in a tarragon sauce or filet of veal
with wild mushrooms. Fixed-price specialties cost around 95 DM ($31.35). Oth-
erwise, à la carte orders average around 50 DM ($16.50). There are only ten
tables, so you must reserve, anytime from noon to 2:30 p.m. and 6 p.m. to 1
a.m. daily except Sunday and holidays.

De'Medici, 3 Ambosstrasse (tel. 59-41-51), on the outskirts at Oberkassel,
is elegantly modern, serving two culinary traditions that won't go out of style—
French and Italian. The oversize menu reflects the constant array of tried-
and-true dishes, with concessions to whatever was available in the market
that day. An unusual choice might be marinated sweetbreads over sauteed
eggplant, or medallions of veal in puff pastry. A tab of 50 DM ($16.50) is
about the cheapest you can do it, anytime from noon to 3 p.m. and 6 p.m. to
midnight, except Sunday. It closes for three weeks some time in June and
July.

Landhaus Werth, 11 Sankt-Göres-Strasse (tel. 40-12-27), in the historical
suburb of Kaiserwerth, holds 40 guests in country-style elegance. People come
here for the food, but the decor is inviting too, with tiled floors, colorful rugs,

hidden lighting, and enough space between tables. This well-known restaurant is viewed as a status symbol among the people who live nearby. Visitors who find the interior too confining on a summer night can have their nouvelle or classical dishes brought to them on a flowery terrace, which holds 30 in sylvan beauty. Salmon, snails, and roasted breast of goose in a red wine sauce are only a few of the delicacies presented here. Fixed-price menus cost from 75 DM ($24.75) to 100 DM ($33), and the Landhaus is open from noon to 2:30 p.m. and 6 to 10 p.m. every day except Tuesday.

Im Schiffchen, 9 Kaiserwerther Markt (tel. 40-10-50), on the outskirts at Kaiserwerth, offers what many gourmets consider the finest food in Düsseldorf, if you don't mind the journey out to enjoy it. The featured piece of decor here is the steering wheel from an old Rhine cruiser, now probably sunk to Lorelei's caves. One has the feeling of being in a boat here, looking past the steering wheel through the large windows beyond, savoring the ambience of the wooden walls of this 18th-century house.

The menu, written in German and French, features such nouvelle cuisine delights as homemade goose liver pâté with green peppercorns, Norwegian salmon in a Vouvray sauce, lobster cooked in camomile tea, and pike or perch in puff pastry, along with filet of baby veal in a crayfish sauce. For dessert, you might try a granulated fruit melange with almond cream.

For a complete meal, expect to spend from 65 DM ($21.45) to 175 DM ($57.75). Hours are 6 p.m. till 1 a.m. every day but Sunday and holidays. The restaurant is closed from mid-July to mid-August.

Robert's Restaurant, 100 Oberkasseler (tel. 57-56-72), on the outskirts at Kaiserwerth, across the river, is the domain of the *wunderkinder* chef of Düsseldorf, Robert Hülsmann. He trained for years in first-class hotels of Europe before launching his independent eatery. He patterned it in an elegant, light-filled art nouveau style, a proper background for his amazing cuisine. He blends a nouvelle and a classical repertoire. Try his fresh steamed mussels in a crabmeat vinaigrette sauce, his salmon terrine, or his "terrine of dove" with blood-orange marmalade. His specialty—and few have ever had it before—is a consommé of woodcock giblets en croûte. Your best bet might be to order his *menu de dégustation,* which changes daily. Prices, as you would expect them to, range from 65 DM ($21.45) to 120 DM ($39.60). Hours are 7 till 11 p.m., daily except Sunday and holidays and for three weeks in summer.

MEDIUM-PRICED DINING: Zum Schiffchen, 5 Hafenstrasse (tel. 32-71-76), has plenty of atmosphere. A golden model ship on top of the step-gabled building reminds you of its location, only a block from the Rhine. The interior of the 1628 structure relies heavily on the Germanic tavern tradition of scrubbed wooden tables and rustic artifacts. Good, hefty portions are the rule of the kitchen, open from noon to 3 p.m. and from 5 p.m. till 1 a.m. The Schiffchen roast plate is served for two. To eat here, expect to spend from 25 DM ($8.25) to 60 DM ($19.80) per person. The menu's large, the service rather hectic, the clientele friendly. Zum Schiffchen is the perfect place to sample Düsseldorf's own beer.

Zur Auster, 9 Berger Strasse (tel. 32-44-04), is a 150-year-old landmark restaurant that seems to have a lifespan as long as the oysters it proudly serves. Its name, in fact, means oyster, and it's decorated with oyster-colored walls, brown paneling, and checkerboard floors. It's about the closest thing to a New England oyster bar to be found in Germany. In addition, it specializes in fish of all kinds, including rare varieties for which you'll need an unabridged German dictionary to translate their names. Carl Maassen is the owner.

Zur Auster has a faithful list of habitués who know many of the waiters, and who insist on a unique blend of ingredients which go into, for example, the ragoût of squid. The broiled salmon might be more appealing to you, however. Oysters are, of course, prepared in about a dozen different ways.

The restaurant is open from noon to 12:30 a.m. daily, except Sunday and holidays. A fixed-price meal cost from 18 DM ($5.94) to 25 DM ($8.25), but chances are, you'll spend far more. And if you're in your hotel room feeling particularly extravagant, Zur Auster will send your choice of lobster or caviar by taxi to you anytime between 10 a.m. and midnight!

BUDGET DINING WITH ATMOSPHERE: Zum Schlüssel, Gatzweilers house-brewery, 43-47 Bolkerstrasse (tel. 32-61-55), is the original site of the famous Gatzweilers Alt brewery. The style is that of a classic German gasthaus, with an abundance of wood, ceramics, and pictures, capturing the aura of a country inn. The service, proffered by courteous, shirt-sleeved waiters, is swift. This establishment is as Germanic as the Rhine. Set lunches, running from 7 DM ($2.31) to 30 DM ($9.90), are featured. Actually, there are more than 30 meals to choose from. The aroma and taste are good, and there's plenty to eat. The eisbein (pig knuckles) is both filling and tasty. A huge bowl of soup might fill you up. If you want only to drink, there's a side bar. Try a quarter of a liter of the house beer, Gatzweilers Alt.

Im Alten Bierhause, 75 Alt-Niederkasseler-Strasse, at Alt-Niederkassel (tel. 5-12-72), on the outskirts. The centuries-old look of this guest house dates from 1641, when much of the place was built. Connoisseurs of German handicrafts will recognize the style of the Rhine's left bank (as opposed to the right). Typical German specialties, many of them sauteed, are served here, where meals cost around 30 DM ($9.90). This is actually more a weinstube than a restaurant: the karte is a "kleinekarte." It's open from 3 p.m. till 11 p.m. daily except Monday (it also closes for four weeks in summer). On Sunday, however, the beer drinkers pile in at 11 a.m.

When you tire of Germanic cookery, Zum Csikos, 9 Andreastrasse (tel. 32-97-71), is a refreshing change-of-pace with its Hungarian cuisine. The structure dates from 1697, and food is served on three different levels. Candlelight gives the place (and the diners) a mellow glow. The home-style Hungarian food is well prepared and the portions are hefty. The beef goulash is excellent, as is the chopped liver. Meals begin at 35 DM ($11.55). Strolling musicians take you back to Old Budapest. Always call ahead and make a reservation, as this place has a tendency to get crowded on certain nights. Hours are 6 p.m. until 2 a.m.

AFTER DARK: The Altstadt ("Old Town") is the place to go. Between the Königsallee and the Rhine River, this half a square mile of narrow streets and alleyways is jam-packed with restaurants, discos, art galleries, boutiques, night-clubs, restaurants, and some 200 song-filled beer taverns. If Düsseldorfers are going to spend a night cruising Old Town, they refer to the experience as *Altstadtbummel.*

A lot of beer is drunk every night in Alstadt, and my favorite place is Uerige Brewery, 1 Bergerstrasse, with half a dozen hearty drinking rooms, often filled with young people. Nearly 10,000 mugs of Uerige are tossed across the counter every day. This unique beer can only be purchased at this brewery-operated tavern. It's also possible at certain times to go on a tour of the brewery during working hours. Some people make an appointment the night before at the tavern (or else telephone 84-455). On rare occasions, Josef Schnitzler, head of the family who owns the brewery, will show you around himself.

In the other dozens of taverns, you can sample the leading beers of the city. I especially recommend that you try Schlösser and Frankenheim, two personal favorites.

Often, instead of going to a restaurant and spending a lot of marks, you can put together a decent meal right on the street (especially Flingerstrasse and Bölkerstrasse). *Reibekuchen* is a tasty potato pancake popular with Düsseldorfers. It's very, very fattening, filling, and good, and always inexpensive. Most Americans shun the blutwurst, a black (blood) pudding accompanied by raw onions. However, the bratwurst with one of those savory German mustards is delectable, as is *spanferkel brötchen,* a hefty slice of tender roast suckling pig, often served on rye bread. In the winter, mussels are offered at several little *intime* restaurants (where you stand up to eat). Sometimes they've been cooked in a Rhine wine sauce. I've easily put together a meal this way for no more than $3 (U.S.), plus the beer you've ordered to drink, of course. But even that's relatively cheap too. In the drinking halls the charge is about 85¢, although you can easily spend $1.35 or more in a better class restaurant for your good brew.

On the nightlife circuit, **Bei Fatty,** 13 Hunsrückstrasse, is a sentimental favorite. Housed in a building from 1648, it's been the traditional dining and drinking spot for Düsseldorf artists. Nowadays the alley out front is bombarded with discos at every door, but the pub tenaciously holds onto its atmosphere of nostalgic Bohemia. Artist-guests have contributed the paintings on the walls, and the decor remains cluttered and charming, with gingham cloths, lots of copper kettles and pots, ornate pumpkin-shaped glass lanterns, and frosted lights shining softly on pewter plates. At a horseshoe-shaped bar, you can drink up, ordering everything from good beer to an Irish coffee. Drinks cost from 5 DM ($1.65).

Düsseldorf has class too. The **Deutsche Oper am Rhein,** 16a Heinrich-Heine-Allee, is rated as one of the most outstanding opera companies in Europe. The season usually closes the last week in June, reopening again by about mid-September. Tickets range from $5 to $25 (telephone 89-081 for more information).

If you're in a classical mood, you might also want to hear a concert by the **Düsseldorf Symphony Orchestra,** which stages concerts in the Tonhalle. This first-class orchestra, said to be among the top dozen or so in Germany, usually sells out. Concerts cost from $5 to $12.

For a posh side of Düsseldorf nightlife, you have to patronize some of the hotels already described. And be prepared to pay from 15 DM ($4.95) for your libations.

There are also many cinemas in Düsseldorf. All foreign films are shown in German. Evening performances start at 8 or 8:30 p.m.

6. Koblenz

Just 55 miles southeast of Cologne, Koblenz has stood at the confluence of the Rhine and Mosel Rivers for more than 2000 years. Its strategic point in the mid-Rhine region has made the city a vital link in the international river trade routes of Europe. Visitors often find themselves here at either the start or finish of a steamer excursion through the Rhine Valley. Right in the heart of the wine country, Koblenz is surrounded by vine-covered hills dotted with castles and fortresses.

THE SIGHTS: The town was heavily bombed during World War II, but many of the historic buildings have been restored. For the best overall view of the town, go to the point where the two rivers meet. This is called **Deutsches Eck** (corner of Germany). From the top of the base, where a huge statue of Wilhelm I once stood, you can see the Old Town and across the Rhine to the Ehrenbreitstein Fortress.

The focal point of the Old Town is the **Liebfrauenkirche** (Church of Our Lady), a 13th-century Gothic basilica built on a Romanesque foundation. Of interest are the onion-shaped spires on the top of the church's twin towers. The early 18th-century **Town Hall** was formerly a Jesuit college. In the courtyard behind the hall is a fountain dedicated to the youth of Koblenz and called *The Spitting Boy,* and that's just what he does. At the edge of the Old Town, near the Deutsches Eck, is Koblenz's oldest and most attractive church, **St. Castor's,** dating from 836. This twin-towered Romanesque basilica was the site of the Treaty of Verdun in the ninth century, dividing Charlemagne's empire.

The **Ehrenbreitstein Fortress,** across the Rhine from Koblenz, can be reached by chair lift, but if you have a fear of heights, you can drive via the Pfaffendorfer Bridge just south of the Old Town. The fortress was built on a rock, towering 400 feet above the Rhine. The present walls were built in the 19th century by the Prussians, on the site of the 10th-century fortress of the archbishops of Trier. It was the headquarters of the American Occupation Army following World War I. From the stone terrace you can see for miles up and down the Rhine, a view that includes not only Koblenz, but also several castles along the Rhine and the terraced vineyards of the region.

UPPER-BRACKET HOTELS: **Diehls,** am Rhein, Ehrenbreitstein (tel. 7-20-10), is the most important hotel in Koblenz, built right on the banks of the Rhine across the river from the town. All of its public rooms, lounges, dining rooms, and bedrooms face the river directly. You can watch the sun set on the water from your bedroom. It's an old-style hotel, which often accommodates groups. Nearly all the rooms have been newly furnished and contain color TV; all have either a private bath or shower and toilet. Another advantage, besides the magnificent views, is the sliding scale of room prices. A single with shower or bath goes for 85 DM ($28.05) to 130 DM ($42.90). Doubles with shower or private bath range in price from 120 DM ($39.60) to 170 DM ($56.10). Tariffs quoted include a continental breakfast, but for another 30 DM ($9.90) you'll be served either lunch or dinner.

Hotel Brenner, 20-22 Rizzastrasse (tel. 3-20-60), close to the Kurfürstl Schloss (castle), and perhaps five city blocks from either the Rhine or Mosel, is a leading contender for top honors in Koblenz. It might vaguely remind you of the famed institution of Baden-Baden with the same name. It's run by Marelis von Rossen-Ruminski, who offers four floors of gilt detailing on white walls, with lots of little tables and chairs. Everything looks Louis XIV½. The garden retreat is a nice place to get back to nature. A single with shower or bath ranges from 120 DM ($39.60) to 145 DM ($47.85), and a double costs 175 DM ($57.75) to 230 DM ($75.90). These tariffs include breakfast, service, and taxes.

MIDDLE-RANGE HOTELS: **Kleiner Riesen,** 18 Rheinanlagen (tel. 3-20-77), is one of the few city hotels lodged right on the banks of the Rhine. In fact, its dining room terrace and most of its bedrooms are close enough to wave at the boats as they go by. The hotel is a large, overgrown chalet, informal, with several living rooms and comfortable, clean bedrooms. A double with bath costs 130 DM ($42.90); a single with bath, 80 DM ($26.40). Nicely situated away from the town traffic, it has a peaceful small-town quietness.

Hotel Höhmann, 5 Bahnhofplatz (tel. 3-50-11), stands across from the railway terminal, attracting train passengers who've traversed both the Mosel and the Rhine. The massively symmetrical facade of this high-ceilinged hotel rises to meet newly arriving visitors. Guests can take the elevator to their rooms, which have good, solid comfort, with private bath or shower. A double rents for 130 DM ($42.90) to 170 DM ($56.10), while a single goes for 70 DM ($23.10) to 95 DM ($31.35), including breakfast, service, and taxes. Heinrich Schade, the owner, employs a friendly, helpful staff.

BUDGET HOTELS: **Sophienhöhe,** 3 Lehrohl (tel. 7-20-96), is a gracious hillside home which has been converted by Marianne Vogt to accommodate paying guests. It's across the river from Koblenz, but so are several of the better hotels. Lodged off a steep, winding road, it sits on a ledge, providing a romantic view of the Rhine (be there at sundown). All its family-size bedrooms seem to have a share in this particular panorama, as does the dining room, with its projected tower room—a place where breakfast becomes a memorable meal. Hardworking women keep everything immaculate. The furnishings throughout are adequate, with generous helpings of comfort. Bathless doubles cost 100 DM ($33), increasing to 120 DM ($39.60) with bath. Singles without bath are only 60 DM ($19.80). Breakfast's included.

Trierer Hof, 1 Deinhardplatz (tel. 3-10-60), a private hotel built back in 1786 and converted into a gasthof as early as 1789, was considered "revolutionary" at the time of its conversion. It is behind the schloss in the midst of gardens and only a quarter of a mile from the Deutsches Eck where the Rhine meets the Mosel. Most of the bedrooms and lounges are overscale, and the furnishings are simple and most adequate. A bathless single room rents for 55 DM ($18.15), rising to 75 DM ($24.75) to 89 DM ($29.37) with shower. A bathless double costs 85 DM ($28.05), going up to 120 DM ($39.60) to 135 DM ($44.55) with shower and toilet. Some triple units are also rented for 135 DM ($44.55) to 150 DM ($49.50) nightly. On the premises is the Restaurant Dalmatia, serving good food and drink. The hotel is easy to spot, next to the Koblenz Theatre.

Gasthaus Christ, 32 Schützenstrasse (tel. 3-77-02), is a modest little inn which has been run by the same family for 60 years. Today, Maria Müller is in charge, and she does a fine job of offering home-like comfort. Life here is informal and friendly. Rooms are simple, clean, and comfortable. A single room with breakfast and shower costs only 40 DM ($13.20) per day; a double under the same arrangement goes for 60 DM ($19.80). The hotel stands about 15 minutes from the station.

Hotel Hamm, 32 St.-Josef-Strasse (tel. 3-45-46). Cozy and informal, the lobby of this family-run hotel looks a lot like the den where the foreman of your college construction crew used to watch football games. Rather anonymously modern in the public rooms, the bedrooms in contrast are comfortable and appropriate for an overnight stopover on your Rhineland exploration. A single, depending on the plumbing, ranges from 55 DM ($18.15) to 75 DM ($24.75), and a double with shower or bath costs from 95 DM ($31.35) to 125 DM ($41.25), including a buffet breakfast. The Hamm is run by the English-speaking Volker-Dick family, and it lies near the railway station, a five-minute walk from the Rhine.

Hotel Scholz, 121 Moselweisser Strasse (tel. 4-24-88), is small and personal, a family-run hotel under the same management for half a century. Only a five-minute bus ride to the town center, it offers units that are clean and sparsely furnished. It makes for a comfortable, reasonably priced overnight stopover: singles rent for 50 DM ($16.50); doubles go for 85 DM ($28.05), with shower and toilet. Breakfast is also included.

Hotel Union, 73 Löhrstrasse (tel. 33-00-3), and the **Gästehaus Victoria,** 25 Stegemannstrasse (tel. 33-0-27), are affiliated with one another, charging the same prices. Since they're close together, they'll offer you a room at the other place should one be full. The hotel makes an attractive use of fieldstone detailing, and has a popular restaurant and café on its ground floor. Singles range in price from 55 DM ($18.15) to 85 DM ($28.05), and doubles go for 86 DM ($28.38) to 120 DM ($39.60).

WHERE TO DINE: Weinhaus Hubertus, 54 Florinsmarkt (tel. 3-11-77), across from the Old Rathaus Museum, offers both rooms and meals in the Old Town. It looks like a timbered country inn, with boxes of red geraniums at the windows. The furnishings and the decor of the rooms are family style, providing a homey atmosphere. Family antiques are placed throughout. The owner welcomes guests to his large, warm, and friendly dining room. Wooden chairs and tables covered with white napkins provide an intimate setting, enhanced by candlelight. Game specialties in season are a feature. You get good substantial cookery here, and plenty of it, at a cost beginning at 30 DM ($9.90).

WINE-TASTING: Weindorf, at the foot of the Pfaffendorfer Bridge, right on the Rhine, is the center for tasting the wines of the vineyards of the Mosel and Rhine regions. It's a timbered wine village where everyone gathers on festive evenings. In fair weather you'll prefer to do your sampling in the open courtyard or on the river-view terrace. Let someone else do the driving afterward.

A SIDE TRIP TO HÖHR-GRENZHAUSEN: Just 12 miles from Koblenz, in the Westerwald, lies this little town where pottery has been produced since the 16th century. The gray-bodied, salt-glazed ceramics for which the town is known is still hand-molded and some is fired in woodburning kilns although most of the potters have changed to gas fires. The salt glazing of the products results in a strong, shiny finish on the pots and other items made here. To reach Höhr-Grenzhausen, take the no. 8 bus from Koblenz and change at Vallendar to the no. 7A bus.

At the **Keramik-Museum Westerwald,** 131 Rathausstrasse, you can see examples of local pottery from the Roman era to the present day, as well as a display of ceramics made all over the world. The processing of the gray Westerwald clay and the glazing work are shown. The museum is open daily except Monday from 10 a.m. to 5 p.m. Admission is 3 DM (99¢) for adults, 1.50 DM (50¢) for children. Guided tours are given only in German, but some members of the museum staff will answer questions put to them in English.

If you're here just for the day, a fine place to have lunch is the museum restaurant, where good, simple food is served on local ceramic dishes. For less than 15 DM ($4.95) you can have an assortment of cheese, sausages, and Westphalian ham, with black bread. For a beverage, nothing will beat the tangy apfelwein—which packs a wallop.

The shops of several of the potters can be visited, some of them following the time-honored method of molding and firing, others with innovative processes and use of colors. **Otto Blum's,** 64 Hermann-Geisenstrasse (tel. 71-63), is the only place where you can see a woodburning kiln still in use. The shop is open from 9 a.m. to noon and 1 to 5 p.m. Monday to Thursday, from 9 a.m. to noon on Friday. There are no guided tours except for groups that have made prior arrangements, but if you're there at the right time, no one seems to object if you tag along with a group.

Other workshops open to visitors are:

Mühlendycks, 39 Lindenstrasse, open Monday to Friday from 8:30 to 11:45

a.m. and 1:30 to 6 p.m., and on Saturday from 9:30 a.m. to 2:30 p.m. You'll find many gift items here, and they'll ship things home for you.

Peltners, 4 Kleine Emserstrasse, open Monday to Saturday from 9 a.m. to noon and 2 to 5 p.m., and on Sunday from 1 to 5 p.m. The Peltners have a small shop and a museum where they display pottery from Silesia, their home province (now part of Poland).

Heine Balzar, 84 Rheinstrasse (tel. 38-66), is a leader in contemporary pottery design. There are no regular hours here, so inquire before you go.

Food and Lodging

Kurhotel Heinz, 77 Bergstrasse (tel. 30-33). From certain perspectives the five stories of bay windows, terraces, balconies, and loggias make this sprawling hotel look almost like the stern of an ocean liner. The ensemble is capped by a red-tile roof whose many embellishments were mostly completed around 1920. Today this is a comfortable hotel with an adjacent spa facility. Peace and quiet are encouraged, even strictly enforced. A buffet breakfast is included in the daily rates of 55 DM ($18.15) to 90 DM ($29.70) for a single and 92 DM ($30.36) to 140 DM ($46.20) for a double, depending on the accommodation and the season. Each room contains a TV, phone, and refrigerator, and has a private balcony. There are two restaurants on the premises, ranging in style from a country inn to a more formal dining room splashed with sunlight from the soaring windows. Meals cost from 25 DM ($8.25) to 55 DM ($18.15). The aperitif bar serves drinks throughout the day.

A SIDE TRIP TO OBERWESEL: Hardly known to the average American visitor, Oberwesel is a small village on the Rhine's left bank, lying about 26 miles south from Koblenz, or 45 minutes by train from Frankfurt. You can cross on the ferry at Kaub to Oberwesel. The town, dominated by Burg Schönburg, still boasts 18 watchtowers. While in the area, try to visit **Liebfrauenkirche** (the Church of Our Lady). Lying to the south of the village, the reddish church is Gothic, and is known for its altarpieces, including one built in 1506 and dedicated to St. Nicholas.

Auf Schönburg (tel. 70-27) is a 1000-year-old castle where Wolfgang and Barbara Hüttl have restored rooms in the "romantik" German style and now shelter and feed paying guests. They have 18 double and three single rooms, all with bath (or shower) and toilet. A single rents for 90 DM ($29.70), and a double goes for 120 DM ($39.60) to 180 DM ($59.40), the latter a particularly spacious chamber with a view. Half board is another 45 DM ($14.85) per person in addition to the room rate, which always includes breakfast and tax.

They have opened three small restaurants, each seating about 30 diners (closed on Monday). The food is innovative and good, with many nouvelle cuisine adaptations, including "pepper soup" (made with pink peppercorns) and a fresh soup of white mushrooms. Main dishes are likely to include a veal steak flavored with whisky or fresh salmon in a saffron sauce, perhaps Barbarie duckling breast in a sherry cream sauce. For dessert you'll perhaps have my favorite, plum sherbert with plum brandy. Their special before-dinner drink is a glass of 1976 Sieben Jungfrauen. Meals cost 40 DM ($13.20) to 75 DM ($24.75).

Even if you don't stay here, you can stop in throughout the day, beginning at breakfast. They serve lunch, afternoon tea or coffee, and dinner. Lunch is served from noon to 2 p.m. and dinner from 6:30 to 9 p.m. The Burghotel shuts down from December 1 to March 1 when it gets too drafty around here.

A SIDE TRIP TO BACHARACH: From Koblenz, a journey of 31 miles will take you to the small town of Bacharach, that old wine town on the Rhine that still looks as if it basks in medieval romanticism. It's surrounded by vine slopes and steep slate rocks, having a pleasant charm set against a backdrop of the typical Rhineland landscape. A highway bypass keeps all the unwelcome traffic noises away, and once inside the walls of Bacharach you can forget the 20th century.

The town is ideally situated for Rhine steamer excursions, as well as daily excursions by train with frequent departures to Koblenz, Mainz, and Wiesbaden. The Rhine trip down from Koblenz is one of the most famous sections in the valley, known for its castles and Lorelei Rock. Often visitors find that even in the height of the season they don't have to fight the crowds if they venture into Bacharach.

If you're driving, park your car outside the ramparts near the river and across from the landing dock. Bacharach is approached through a gateway, and it blooms best at a square known simply as the **Markt.** Here you'll see the finest collection of old houses built in the half-timbered style. You might also seek out the **Peterskirche** (St. Peter's Church), which is open only in season from 9 a.m. to 6 p.m. (sometimes it closes earlier). Its Romanesque nave was one of the last known to have been erected in the country. Before leaving Bacharach, head for the antique fortress, **Burg Stahleck,** with its belvedere tower which offers a panoramic sweep of the Rhine Valley.

All accommodations in Bacharach are appropriately modest. The best is **Altkölnischer Hof,** 2 Blücherstrasse (tel. 13-39). This is a comfortable establishment with a good cuisine presided over by Gernot Scherschlicht. A half-timbered house, the hotel has an Old Rhineland dining room with lots of wooden paneling. The kitchen is first rate, and you may want to sample more than one bottle in the old German wine room. You might also request Bitburger beer. The modestly furnished guest rooms are clean and reasonably priced, costing from 46 DM ($15.18) to 78 DM ($25.74) in a single, from 70 DM ($23.10) to 100 DM ($33) in a double. Of course you'll want to take your meals here, with menus beginning at 22 DM ($7.26) and rising to 55 DM ($18.15) if you decide to get really extravagant. On weekends music is played for dancing.

7. Mainz

This 2000-year-old city at the confluence of the Rhine and Main Rivers remains very much the provincial wine town. Since the Romans brought the first vine stalks to Mainz in 38 B.C., it has been the center of the wine-producing regions of the Rheingau and Rheinhessen. It's a festive city, with its annual Wine Fair taking place each August and September. The most celebrated merrymaking is at the All Fools capers at Carnival each spring, broadcast throughout Germany like an annual Macy's parade. In June each year, the Gutenberg Festival sponsors a cultural season, a living memorial to the city's favorite son, the inventor of the movable-type printing press.

THE SIGHTS: Above the roofs of the half-timbered houses in the old section of town rise the six towers of **St. Martin's Cathedral.** The Romanesque basilica, dating from A.D. 975, has been constantly rebuilt and restored, until its present form, dating mainly from the 13th and 14th centuries. It is a medley of nearly every period of European architecture. Below the largest dome, a combination of Romanesque and baroque, is the transept, separating the west chancel from the nave and smaller east chancel. Many of the supporting pillars along the aisles of the nave are decorated with carved and painted statues of French and German saints. One of Germany's best collections of religious art is housed in the cathedral's **Diocesan Museum.** Within it are exhibitions of reliquaries and medieval sculpture, including works by the Master of Naumburg. In the 1000-year-old cathedral crypt is a contemporary gold reliquary of the saints of Mainz.

Among the most impressive furnishings in the sanctuary are the rococo choir stalls and a pewter baptismal font from the early 14th century.

The **Gutenberg Museum,** opposite the east towers of the cathedral, is a unique memorial to the city's favorite son. In the modern display rooms, visitors can trace the history of printing from Gutenberg's hand press on which he printed the 42-lined Bible from 1452 to 1455, to the most advanced typesetting processes. The collections cover the entire spectrum of the graphic arts as well as phases of books and printing, illustration, and binding in all countries, past and present. The most popular and valuable exhibit is the Gutenberg Bible. The museum is open Tuesday through Saturday from 10 a.m. to 6 p.m., on Sunday from 10 a.m. to 1 p.m. Closed on Monday.

The **Mittelrheinische Landesmuseum** (Provincial Museum of the Central Rhineland), 49-51 Grosse Bleiche (tel. 23-29-55), is worth a visit to get a pictorial history of Mainz and the middle Rhine, from prehistoric times to the present. The most impressive exhibits are the Roman marble head of the Emperor Augustus (or his nephew, Caius Caesar), about A.D. 14, and the towering Column of Jupiter, erected in Mainz by the Romans in A.D. 67. Although the original is in the museum, you may, if you are pressed for time, see the true-to-life replica in front of the Parliament building. Also of interest is the gallery of the museum with paintings from the 15th through the 20th centuries. The Lapidarium shows one of the most important collections of Roman monuments in Europe. The museum is open Tuesday through Sunday from 10 a.m. to 5 p.m. Closed Monday. Admission is free.

UPPER-BRACKET HOTELS: Many people visit Mainz on a day trip from Frankfurt, 25 miles away. The Rhine-Main International Airport is a 20-minute taxi ride from the center of the city. If you plan to stay over, however, be advised that reservations are needed during the spring and autumn festival seasons.

Mainz Hilton, 68 Rheinstrasse (tel. 24-50). Yes, there is a Hilton on the Rhine. Its exterior is all glass and marble, and the public rooms are attractive, especially the Beer Stube and the Roman Weinstube. The Rheinbar is more elegant and the Rheingrill simulates dining aboard a luxurious Rhine River yacht. The 435 bedrooms are tastefully appointed and color coordinated, with a unified theme. The higher up you go for your overnighting, the higher the price. A single room with bath begins at a basic low of 155 DM ($51.15), ranging upward to 290 DM ($95.70). Doubles start at 200 DM ($66), peaking at 370 DM ($122.10). A top-floor panoramic dining room and open terrace provide a view of the river boats. The hotel has a small, French-style restaurant, Le Bistro, and the Atriumbar cocktail lounge. The Hilton is connected to the Rheingoldhalle, one of the largest assembly halls in Europe.

The **Europahotel,** 7 Kaiserstrasse (tel. 67-10-91), is downtown near the railway station, its bright lights making it easy to find. Its bar and restaurant serve as attractive meeting places. The hotel offers 87 bedrooms, with color TV, video programs, and phone. You'll find all the up-to-date appurtenances here you are likely to need. A single room ranges in price from 120 DM ($39.60) to 190 DM ($62.70), and a double goes for 190 DM ($62.70) to 220 DM ($72.60). A breakfast buffet is included in the room rate. If the place is full, they'll shelter you at another hotel they own, the Mainzer Hof (see below).

MIDDLE-BRACKET HOTELS: Mainzer Hof, 98 Kaiserstrasse (tel. 23-37-71), is six floors of modernity directly on the river, almost at the point where some of the Rhine boats dock. It's a clean-cut, convenient stopover hotel on your journey down the Rhine. The rooms were completely renovated in 1985 and equipped with direct-dial telephones, TVs, radios, and mini-bars. The rate in a single with a bath or shower is 148 DM ($48.84), rising to 200 DM ($66) in a double, breakfast included. The dining room, with its sweeping view of the Rhine, is attractive.

Schottenhof, 6 Schottstrasse (tel. 23-29-68), is nice and modern. Off a busy avenue, it manages to have a warm atmosphere. The actual position is on a dead-end street, leading to the railroad and transit pedestrian plaza. The furnishings and carpeting are sometimes a little dark, but the comfort inside the room is real. Singles with shower or bath cost from 89 DM ($29.37) to 99 DM ($32.67), and doubles with the same plumbing go from 95 DM ($31.35) to 120 DM ($39.60). The hotel was renovated in 1978. It now offers a total of 38 rooms with shower, toilet, phone, and TV. Windows are soundproof. On the premises is a mini-bar.

Central Hotel Eden, 8 Bahnhofsplatz (tel. 67-40-01), is housed in a very grand building with reddish neoclassical pediments on many of its windows, plus two modern floors added on top of the four existing ones. Mainzers are fond of the café-restaurant on the ground floor, L'échalote, which has some of the best food in the city. The bedrooms are high ceilinged and comfortably appointed, with a vague nostalgia for a past era. Because of the thickness of the walls and the soundproof windows, you've got a better chance to catch up on your sleep. Singles rent from 88 DM ($29.04) to 135 DM ($44.55), and doubles cost from 130 DM ($42.90) to 200 DM ($66).

Grünewald, 14 Frauenlobstrasse (tel. 67-40-84), lies two blocks from the train station. A "breakfast-only" hotel, it is done in a severe modern style, and is in fact an unadorned rectangle with lots of glass, lying on a quiet residential street about ten minutes from the center of town. The cost for a double with shower and toilet is 140 DM ($46.20), dropping to 95 DM ($31.35) in a similar single. Prices include a generous buffet breakfast.

BUDGET HOTELS: Hotel am Römerwall, 53 Römerwall (tel. 23-21-35), near the university grounds, is two villas, pleasantly positioned in a garden. It attracts not only bargain seekers, but guests wanting to avoid the sterile atmosphere of the typical hotel. Here the accent is on home-like comfort, as reflected in the public living room and breakfast salon (the only meal served, incidentally). Each of the bedrooms is comfortably appointed, with heavy use made of all-white furnishings and bright, contrasting fabrics. A double with private bath and shower costs from 105 DM ($34.65) to 130 DM ($42.90), and a few singles with shower or bath go from 80 DM ($26.40) to 100 DM ($33). A few cheaper bathless doubles rent for anywhere from 85 DM ($28.05) to 95 DM ($31.35); bathless singles cost 60 DM ($19.80) to 75 DM ($24.75). Breakfast is included in all tariffs. The owner, Frau R. Flaschl, has a good staff who keep the bedrooms immaculate.

Hammer, 6 Bahnhofplatz (tel. 61-10-61), has been completely renewed. The furnishings are modern, and the reception is bright. The rooms are comfortable and of good size. All accommodations come with private shower, bath, toilet, radio, color TV, and mini-bar. The rates are 79 DM ($26.07) to 95 DM ($31.35) for a single, 108 DM ($35.64) to 130 DM ($42.90) for a double or twin. A buffet breakfast is included, as well as taxes and service.

Richter Eisenbahn, 6 Alicentstrasse (tel. 2-76-30), close to the station, looks more like a pension. The decoration may not always be dazzling, although the furniture often achieves an unexpected style. However, the accommodation is fair and comfortable, the prices a good bargain. Bathless singles are in the 35-DM ($11.55) to 44-DM ($14.52) range, rising to 46 DM ($15.18) with shower. Bathless doubles are priced from 65 DM ($21.45), increasing to 68 DM ($22.44) with shower, breakfast included.

Hotel Mira, 4 Bonifaziusstrasse (tel. 61-30-87). The delicate pink of the facade of this hotel is repeated in the pink tiles in the bathrooms inside. If you like pink (and many psychologists think it has a calming effect), you'll love it here. The Mira beckons warmly to tourists from its location near the Hauptbahnhof. Alfred Kohl is your host, providing maps, if available, and lots of useful information. He rents singles, doubles, or triple rooms, some with shower or bath. Self-dial phones are found in all units, and there is elevator service. A single begins at 55 DM ($18.15), going up to 65 DM ($21.45), and a double costs from 92 DM ($30.36) to 110 DM ($36.30), including a continental breakfast.

WHERE TO DINE: Drei Lilien, 2 Ballplatz (tel. 22-50-68). Head chef H. J.
Stuhlmiller practices a form of nouvelle cuisine that he has dubbed (in French) *cuisine du marché,* which means that a lot of imaginative flair is practiced every morning while stocking up on the day's meat and produce. Everything is cooked here with imagination and concern. Some of the chef's recipes were developed (with some foresight) by whatever was at hand that day at the greengrocers. The decor of this wood-beamed, chandeliered eatery could be called "graciously rustic," and the linens are always impeccably clean and the service politely deferential. Try the grilled steak with wild trumpet mushrooms in a cognac sauce with grape leaves, or a delicately poached baby turbot in mushroom sauce. At lunch, fixed-price meals go for 55 DM ($18.15), and dinner table d'hôte meals are available at 65 DM ($21.45) and 95 DM ($31.35). It is open from noon till 2:30 p.m. and 6 to 10:30 p.m. daily except Tuesday and Saturday lunch.

Schmüser, 16 Frankfurter Strasse (tel. 66-66), at Mainz-Kastel, on the outskirts, serves the best food in the Mainz area, at least in my opinion. You must phone for a reservation from your hotel in Mainz, and any gourmet will happily spend the extra money to savor the imaginative cuisine of Axel Schmüser. He stirs up a fury of creativity to produce, for example, an array of fresh salads dotted with goose liver, or warm goose liver pâté with sabayon of grapes, perhaps sweetbreads with a crab sauce, or snails in puff pastry with fresh tomatoes. Try also his breast of Barbary goose with an olive sauce. Frau Veronique Schmüser attends to the myriad details of running the city's most perfect restaurant, overseeing what residents of Mainz have called "impeccably attentive service." At noon a luncheon costs around 60 DM ($19.80), going up to 90 DM ($29.70) to 105 DM ($34.65) for an evening meal. Hours are noon to 2 p.m. and 6:30 to 10 p.m., daily except Sunday.

L'échalote, 8 Bahnhofsplatz (tel. 61-43-31), lies on the ground floor of the city's "grande dame of hotels," the Central Hotel Eden, previously recommended. The restaurant has a vivid awning in front, shading the big windows from the public square near the train station. Head chefs Günther Bornheimer and Michael Dimakakos head a surprisingly large staff to produce both nouvelle and classic dishes. The soups are a delight, everything from lamb consommé to saffron soup, followed by, say, fish, which is brought in twice a week from Rungis, the centralized food market of Paris. As in all nouvelle cuisine kitchens, nobody skimps on the raspberry vinegar. You'll find it here, for example, in the sauteed breast of Bresse hen with tomato noodles and "baby" vegetables. Fixed-price menus range from 50 DM ($16.50) to 100 DM ($33). Hours are 11 a.m. till 3 p.m. and 6 p.m. till "closing."

Panorama Restaurant, 98 Kaiserstrasse (tel. 23-37-71), in the Mainzer Hof, offers a panoramic view of the Rhine's traffic. Try the wild game with pistachios or escargot in a brandy sauce, perhaps an array of Atlantic fish cooked in the savory tradition of the classical Rhineland cuisine, or with the flair and imagination of the nouvelle cuisine. Meals range from 25 DM ($8.25) to 65 DM ($21.45), and hours are noon to 2:30 p.m. and 6:30 to 10:30 p.m.

Walderdorff, 4 Karmeliterplatz (tel. 22-25-15). Clients sit at rows of tables set next to one another, bistro style, in this restaurant established in 1982 by Gerhard and Eva Heymann. Everything is fresh in this upper-price, elegant place, where people-watching is as much fun as eating the classic French dishes prepared by the owner himself. Try, for example, his wurst in champagne with caramelized pears, or his fennel and sweetbread salad, or his veal shank in an oxtail ragoût. Dessert might be a cream strudel with a caramel sauce, accompanied by fresh raspberries with raspberry ice cream (and covered with whipped cream!). It will cost 50 DM ($16.50) to 85 DM ($28.05) to dine here, which you can do from noon to 3 p.m. and 6:30 p.m. till midnight. It's closed Sunday evening, all day Monday, and some time in June.

Gebert's Weinstuben, 94 Frauenlobstrasse (tel. 61-16-19), is a traditional weinstube, housed in one of the oldest buildings of Mainz, with a decor that is almost spartan when compared to the opulence of some of the city's other restaurants. But decor is not the reason people come here, and they patronize it in great numbers, so you'll have to call to reserve one of the dozen or so tables. Once seated, you are treated to a traditional meal of game, fish, or regional specialties such as goose à l'orange. Meals cost from 25 DM ($8.25) to 55 DM ($18.15), and they're served from 11:30 a.m. to 2 p.m. and 6 to 10 p.m. The weinstuben is closed all day Saturday and Sunday and from mid-July to mid-August.

Zum Augustiner, 8 Augustinerstrasse (tel. 23-17-37), was a popular beerhall before the imaginative entrepreneur, Michael Müller, took charge. Today, all of Mainz knows that its fish (trucked in from Rungis) and its French vegetables are among the best in town. Go here for such nouvelle cuisine dishes as breast of Bresse hen in either raspberry vinegar or flamed in cognac, or the pork filet in puff pastry. Herr Müller is a master of the classic cuisine as well, using lots of truffles, cream, and champagne, enough to make Escoffier proud. A simple meal will cost from 35 DM ($11.55), but chances are you'll spend far more. Save room for one of his tempting desserts or pastries, made fresh daily. Hours are for dinner only, served from 6 p.m. till closing.

Zum Löwen, 2 Mainzer Strasse (tel. 4-36-05), in Gonsenheim. There's plenty to see in this suburb of Mainz besides this restaurant, but for delicious dishes, both regional and nouvelle, it makes an attractive stopping place. Hans and Gisela Klapps work to bring the best gastronomy to your table, with lobster cooked in many different ways. Or you may be tempted by their seasoned mixture of salmon and turbot in puff pastry, or possibly their filet of veal with wild mushrooms and fresh plums. And only if it's to your taste, their suckling baby lamb, served for two persons. Many of the specialties change so frequently they aren't even on the menu. Fixed-price menus cost from 75 DM ($24.75) to 100 DM ($33). Zum Löwen is open for lunch from noon to 2 p.m. and for dinner from 6 to 10 p.m. It's closed on Sunday evening and all day Monday, and the annual closing is the month of September.

Löschs Weinstube, 9 Jakobsbergstrasse (tel. 22-03-83), is an old-fashioned weinstube, popular with generations of Mainzers and rich in tradition and gemütlichkeit. Menus, costing around 30 DM ($9.90), offer both hot and cold dishes, plus lots of Rhine wine. There are only 12 tables, but they seat some 85 guests who can visit anytime between 4 p.m. and 1 a.m., except Wednesday and in the month of July. Now that the Jakobsbergstrasse has been changed into a pedestrian mall, the weinstube places six additional tables out front in summer.

Haus des Deutschen Weines, 3 Gutenbergplatz (tel. 22-86-76), is a good wine restaurant. The shields outside represent the German wine districts, and the cellar inside stocks the finest bottles from the Rheingau. An easy walk from the Dom and the Gutenberg Museum, the House of German Wines makes a fine luncheon choice, offering set meals from 25 DM ($8.25). On the à la carte menu, game is featured in season. A recent repast began with a tasty onion soup with croutons and was topped by a smooth peach Melba. At dinner you can spend from 55 DM ($18.15) if you partake of the expensive specialties. Because the restaurant is affiliated with both the city of Mainz and the German Wine Institute, you can find a cross section of wines from the 11 leading wine regions of Germany. Hours are 10 a.m. to midnight daily, except on Sunday and holidays.

8. Worms

This ancient city traces its beginnings back to the earliest civilizations. Before the Romans settled here, Germanic tribes had made Worms their capital. Siegfried began his legendary adventures, recorded in the Nibelungenlied, when he visited here. The town's most famous visitor, Martin Luther, arrived under less desirable circumstances. He was "invited" to appear before the Imperial Diet at Worms, and after refusing to retract his grievance against the Church of Rome, he was excommunicated. Now that the majority of Worms is Protestant, it has erected a huge monument to Luther and other giants of the Reformation.

Worms also has one of the oldest Jewish communities in Germany, with a synagogue dating back to the 11th century. The Hebrew cemetery is much more interesting, however, with hundreds of tombstones, some going back more than 800 years.

Towering physically and historically above all the other ancient buildings of the city is the majestic **St. Peter's Cathedral** (Dom St. Peter), 9 Lutherring (tel. 61-15), considered the purest Romanesque basilica in the Rhine Valley. The east choir, with a flat facade and semicircular interior, is the oldest section, dating from 1110. This was designed as the sanctuary, where the clergy performed the rites of the divine service. Lavishly decorated in baroque style during the 18th century by the famous architect Balthasar Neumann, the chancel glows with the gold and marble of the pillared enclosure for the high altar. This opulent workmanship was so large that there was no place for a proper transept. In Gothic times the choir stalls stood in the apse, but now they had to build them into the transept. The west choir, dedicated in 1811, is more traditionally Romanesque, with a polygon-shaped exterior protruding between two round old towers. The interior has a quiet elegance, with little decoration other than the rosette window and several memorial slabs and monuments to the dead buried beneath the cathedral. Between these two extremes, which symbolize the coordination of ecclesiastical and secular power, is the nave. A new organ built like a bird's nest has been placed where an organ was situated until its destruction in 1689. Well worth seeing is the highly decorated 14th- or 15th-century side Chapel of St. Nicholas, with its Gothic baptismal font and new stained-glass windows. The cathedral is open for visitors daily in summer from 8 a.m. to 6 p.m. (in winter from 9 a.m. to 5 p.m.). A voluntary gift of .50 DM (17¢) is used to help maintain the grand old edifice.

MIDDLE-BRACKET HOTELS: Nibelungen Hotel, 8–16 Martinsgasse (tel. 69-77), is the newest and most luxuriously appointed hotel in Worms. In the center of town, it is named after the heroic Germanic legend. It offers modern comfort behind a yellow and mustard-colored facade. Each of its rooms has a bath with shower or tub, radio, phone, and mini-bar. The price for a single is 95 DM ($31.35), rising to 135 DM ($44.55) in a twin, including the buffet breakfast.

Dom-Hotel, 10 Am Obermarkt (tel. 69-13), is an all-purpose hotel, about a block from the cathedral. It's a postwar structure recently renovated, built in a complex of shops and boutiques. The glass-walled bedrooms have an assortment of contemporary furnishings, and they offer adequate comfort. All units contain bath or shower, phone, and radio (TV on request). Singles range from 72 DM ($23.76) to 80 DM ($26.40), and doubles go for 110 DM ($36.30) to 125 DM ($41.25). The guest lounge is a good place for relaxation. In the wood-paneled dining room, a breakfast buffet is spread out in the morning and, later, a French cuisine is served. Altogether, it's an ideal little hotel for the in-and-out traveler.

BUDGET LIVING: **Central,** 5 Kammererstrasse (tel. 64-57). The rooms are not too big, but Agnes Labidi has furnished them with a certain degree of comfort and warmth. All rooms have private shower, and some have a toilet as well. The single rate ranges from 52 DM ($17.16) to 56 DM ($18.48), and doubles run from 82 DM ($27.06) to 94 DM ($31.02), including a big breakfast and tax. The dining room of the hotel is pleasantly furnished. The reception staff speaks English fluently.

WHERE TO DINE: **Rôtisserie Dubs,** 6 Kirchstrasse (tel. 20-23). Despite the rustic beams on the ceiling and the massive stonework of the fireplace here, one still gets a feeling of elegant lightness. The decalorized nouvelle cuisine only adds to that impression. After traveling through France, the owners decided to feature nouvelle cuisine, including such dishes as salmon in a champagne marinade or a delicately seasoned pike and cabbage soup. A fixed-price meal will cost 85 DM ($28.05) to 125 DM ($41.25), and service is from noon to 2 p.m. and 6 to 11 p.m. A la carte meals begin at 45 DM ($14.85). They're closed for Saturday lunch and on Tuesday.

9. The Rheingau

When God was looking for a place to set up His Paradise, so goes the story. He once considered the sunny slopes between the Taunus Mountains and the Rhine. Even though He obviously changed His mind, the Rheingau today is the kingdom of another god, Bacchus, who reigns supreme here. Nearly every town and village from Wiesbaden to Assmanshausen, no matter how small, is a major wine-producer. The names suddenly seem familiar—Bingen, Johannisberg, Rüdesheim, Oestrich—because we have seen them on the labels of many favorite wines.

The Rheingau is also rich in old churches and castles, as well as landmarks. The **Niederwald Monument,** on a hill halfway between Rüdesheim and Assmanshausen—it can be reached by cable car from either town—is a huge statue of Germania, the *Watch on the Rhine,* erected by Bismarck in 1883 to commemorate the reunification of Germany. Below it, on a small island at the bend of the Rhine, is the infamous Mäuseturm (Mouse Tower), where, according to legend, the harsh bishop of Mainz was devoured by a swarm of hungry mice. But the real attraction of the Rheingau is the cheerful character of the wine villages and their friendly people.

In the heart of the Rheingau is the epitome of the Rhine Wine towns:

RÜDESHEIM: With its old courtyards and winding alleyways lined with timbered houses, Rüdesheim is everything that a wine town should be: festive and terribly serious about its wines. The vineyards around the village date back to the Roman Emperor Probus. Besides the full-bodied Riesling, brandy and champagne are also produced here. Rüdesheim is the scene of the annual September wine festival, when the old taverns on the narrow Drosselgasse are filled with jovial tasters from all over the world. To prove how seriously Rüdesheimers take their wines, they have opened a wine museum in Bromserburg Castle, which traces the history of the grape with an exhibition of wine presses, glasses, goblets, and drinking utensils dating from Roman times to the present.

Where to Stay

Rüdesheimer Hof, 1 Geisenheimer Strasse (tel. 20-11), is a village inn, set back from the Rhine, with a side garden and terrace where wine tasters gather at rustic tables. The atmosphere is informal; you can dine here and spend the night. All rooms have shower and bath. Singles cost 55 DM ($18.15) to 75 DM ($24.75), and doubles go for 80 DM ($26.40) to 120 DM ($39.60). Most of the accommodations are roomy and comfortably furnished. Antiques are used generously throughout.

Staying here is like sampling the pulse of a Rhine village—seeing the townspeople mingling with visitors, eating the regional food, and drinking the Rheingau wines. The inn opens in mid-February, closing in mid-November. If you're stopping by just to eat, you'll find set meals from 18 DM ($5.94) to 45 DM ($14.85). Guests dine at café tables placed under a willow tree.

Zum Bären, 31 Schmidtstrasse (tel. 2667), is a well-run, recently redecorated hotel presided over by Karl-Heinz Willig, a gracious host who has shown kindness to readers of this book. He offers both singles and doubles, all with shower and private toilet. There's also a sauna on the premises. The rate is 85 DM ($28.05) to 105 DM ($34.65) in a double, dropping to 60 DM ($19.80) in a single, including a continental breakfast, service, and tax. The restaurant offers good plain cooking. Guests enjoy sitting out on the cozy terrace and like the central, in-town location.

Gasthof Krancher, 4 Eibinger-Oberstrasse (tel. 27-62), is run by Herbert Krancher, and has been in his family for four generations. The location is about a ten-minute walk from the town center, standing next to Herr Krancher's own vineyards. Naturally, they make their own wines here, and they'll gladly show you their cellar, where they store bottles that have won gold and silver medals. The cuisine is first class, and certainly the wines are. Everything is decorated in a regional motif. The two-building complex contains 100 beds. The cost is 38 DM ($12.54) per person nightly, including breakfast. All rooms have shower. For half board, add another 18 DM ($5.94) to the rate quoted. From your bedroom window, you can look out at the vineyards. Perhaps you'll be there when the grapes are harvested.

Haus Dries, 1 Kaiserstrasse (tel. 24-20). In this wine-producing region of Germany, it seems appropriate for a tastefully decorated weinstuben to carve *"In Vino Veritas"* into one of the rustic beams. This, plus a tastefully sculpted ceiling and sea-green exterior balconies, identifies this friendly and cozy modern establishment, run by the Dries family. The hotel has its own swimming pool, along with a sun terrace decorated with flowerpots. Naturally there's a wide choice of local wines. Singles with shower and toilet rent for 55 DM ($18.15), a double goes for 95 DM ($31.35), breakfast included.

Hotel und Weinhaus Felsenkeller, 39 Oberstrasse (tel. 26-46). The beautifully carved timbers on the facade of this popular guest house and weinhaus suggest the kind of traditional aura you can expect inside. Since 1898 it's been run by the Rolz family. Inside, the weinhaus completes the rustic Teutonic theme implied by the facade. The establishment dates from 1613, and in 1982 an addition was added, but it was constructed in the half-timbered style, in keeping with the architecture of the building. A sampling of Rhine wine can be enjoyed in a room of vaulted ceilings stuccoed and muraled with vine leaves and pithy pieces of folk wisdom. In fair weather, guests are served on the terrace. Rooms, all with shower and toilet, are attractively modern and freshly painted, opening onto views of the vineyards surrounding the house. Singles go for 80 DM ($26.40), while doubles cost from 120 DM ($39.60).

Hotel Rheinstein, 20 Rheinstrasse (tel. 20-04). The elongated terrace facing the street is one of the most popular gathering places in Rüdesheim. Many locals drop in in the afternoon to enjoy the excellent cakes, all baked on the premises. Irene Gehrig has employed a friendly, helpful staff, and she offers 80 beds, all in units with phone (nearly all with a private bath or shower and a toilet). Singles range in price from 60 DM ($19.80) to 90 DM ($29.70), while doubles cost from 70 DM ($23.10) to 160 DM ($52.80), including breakfast. Some rooms have a balcony with a view of the Rhine.

Evening Entertainment

Rüdesheimer Schloss, Drosselgasse (tel. 20-31), is one of the most colorful restaurants along the Rhine. The intricately carved timbers of this castle date from 1729. There is no cover charge for entrance here, where a live band often plays the Rüdesheimer Polonaise (conga!). The restaurant offers well-prepared traditional foods in a wide price range, served by smiling fräuleins in colorful aprons, and the cellars hold gigantic barrels of aging wines (you can tour them). Every vintage since 1929 is available, plus some older rare ones including a 1893 Rheingau wine. Food service is open from 10 a.m. until the small hours of the morning, anytime from March to November. Heinrich and Susanne Breuer certainly run the liveliest place along the river. A three-course "musical meal" with a large bottle of the local wine costs 55 DM ($18.15). Dishes are likely to include sauerbraten or roast wild boar, perhaps stuffed suckling pig. In summer the revelry spills into the garden.

A Hunting Lodge at Niederwald

Waldhotel Jagdschloss Niederwald, auf dem Niederwald (tel. 06722/10-04), is perched high in the hills, three miles from the center of Rüdesheim. It's a world apart, attracting visitors for romantic weekends along with families on holiday. Part of the compound was the former hunting lodge of the dukes of Hesse. That tone is reflected in the entrance hall, with its hunting museum decor.

A wide-view terrace has been enclosed, allowing for a panoramic sweep over the Rhine Valley. Depending on the plumbing and room size (and the room's location), singles cost from 108 DM ($35.64) to 125 DM ($41.25), and doubles go for 170 DM ($56.10) to 200 DM ($66). Even more expensive suites are available. Half board costs an extra 35 DM ($11.55) per person. The management has added an elegant indoor swimming pool, with a steambath and solarium, plus two tennis courts.

Off the main travel route, the schloss is restful and rewarding. From Rüdesheim, drive toward Presberg (the Jagdschloss signs will appear).

ASSMANSHAUSEN: At the northern edge of the Rheingau, this old village is
built on the slopes on the east bank of the Rhine. The half-timbered houses and vineyards seem precariously perched on the steep hillsides, and the view of the Rhine Valley from here is awe-inspiring. Assmanshausen is known for its fine red burgundy-style wine.

Where to Stay

Krone, 10 Rheinstrasse (tel. 20-36), is one of a few inns in Germany with so distinguished a pedigree. Built right on the banks of the Rhine, surrounded by lawns, gardens, and swimming pool, it traces its origins back 400 years. The inn is overscale, a great big gingerbread fantasy. A small second-floor lounge is virtually a museum, with framed letters and manuscripts of some of the more celebrated personages who have stayed here—Goethe, for one. There's a stack of 37 autograph books, signed by writers, painters, diplomats, and composers.

Your bedroom may either be in a building from the Middle Ages, a Renaissance structure, or a postwar house. The bedrooms have an old-inn character, spacious with traditional furnishings. A single room, bathless, ranges in price from 50 DM ($16.50) to 60 DM ($19.80); singles with bath, 105 DM ($34.65). Bathless doubles are priced at 90 DM ($29.70) to 100 DM ($33); doubles with bath, 120 DM ($39.60) to 210 DM ($69.30). Breakfast is another 14 DM ($4.62).

The public rooms are time-seasoned, with a preponderance of antiques, old oak paneling, antlers, photographs, antique clocks, and oil paintings, all heavy Teutonic.

Even if you're not overnighting, you may want to stop over to sample one of the finest meals you're likely to be served on the Rhine, costing from 40 DM ($13.20) to 80 DM ($26.40). For example, you might begin with real turtle soup or a half-dozen snails, and follow with fresh salmon or broiled Rhine eel with dill. In season, the house specialty is a saddle of venison for two persons. For dessert, try the eisbecher Krone. Stocked in the rock-hewn cellars is one of the finest assortments of Rhine wines in the world.

Alte Bauernschänke (tel. 23-13) is owned by wine-growers. They have completely renovated two of the oldest mansions of the town, turning them into a hotel and restaurant. The interior decor is luxurious, with tapestries, carpeting, and ornate furniture. The comfort is fine, and the welcome hearty. Near the church inside the village, the hotel is not far from the Rhine, about a quarter of a mile. A bathless double costs 79 DM ($26.07), increasing to anywhere from 109 DM ($35.97) with bath. Singles range from 53 DM ($17.49) to 68 DM ($22.44). These prices include breakfast. The restaurant of the hotel provides a folkloric experience, with musicians playing every night. A goulash soup, a peppersteak with fresh green beans and french fries, plus a half bottle of their red wine, will cost a maximum of 40 DM ($13.20) per person. If you select from the menu less lavishly, you can get away for 23 DM ($7.59).

Unter den Linden, 1 Rheinallee (tel. 22-88), is a converted Rhine-fronting villa, which places emphasis on its cuisine and terrace wine drinking. A building was added at the rear, offering units for overnight. If there is a choice of rooms, avoid the rear location because of heavy railroad traffic (the line runs 30 yards from your window, and a train passes by every three minutes). Up front, the dining room overflows onto part of an open terrace. There's a minimum of public lounges as the space is eaten up primarily by tables. In front is a wide terrace shaded by a grape arbor and linden trees. In summer revelers fill up every table. English is spoken, the food is good, and the wine is superb. All bedrooms are pleasantly decorated and comfortable. Doubles cost 130 DM ($42.90), increasing to 160 DM ($52.80) with complete bath. A bathless single begins at 60 DM ($19.80), going up to 95 DM ($31.35) with bath. A dish of the day is featured in the dining room. On one recent occasion I enjoyed filet of smoked Black Forest trout. Meals in the 22-DM ($7.26) to 55-DM ($18.15) range are offered.

Schön, 3 Rheinuferstrasse (tel. 22-25), is a family-run hotel on the banks of the Rhine, offering comfortable rooms, all with bath or shower, and a café-terrace fronting the river. It spills over graciously from its original home in an olive-green baroque house to another building next door, painted harmoniously in the same color scheme. Room rates include breakfast. Singles range from 55 DM ($18.15) to 70 DM ($23.10), while doubles begin at 100 DM ($33), rising to

130 DM ($42.90). You can take all your meals here; half board costs 75 DM ($24.75) to 95 DM ($31.35) per person nightly. The hotel has an excellent restaurant with one of the best kitchens in Assmannshausen. It has had its own winery since 1752, and guests can visit the wine cellar.

Hotel-Café Post, 2 Rheinuferstrasse (tel. 23-26), is a country landhaus type of establishment, with an invitingly rustic ocher facade with dormers, a black roof, and a sun terrace. This cozy place, known for its Rhine-fronting terrace, is run by the Hötger family, who fly a West German flag in front of their establishment every sunny day. They do everything they can to make you feel at home. Their tastefully simple rooms provide a good resting place during your sojourn along the Rhineland. Single rooms cost from 50 DM ($16.50) to 70 DM ($23.10), and doubles begin at 75 DM ($24.75), climbing to 110 DM ($36.30). Their kitchen is widely known for its good cooking, with meals costing from 22 DM ($7.26) to 50 DM ($16.50).

Anker, 5 Rheinuferstrasse (tel. 29-12), was already old when Bismarck stayed here in 1842. Constructed in baroque yellow stucco in 1660, the building served as a guest house for the passengers and crews of the horse teams that pulled the barges, Erie Canal style, along this section of the Rhine. Today it's a gloriously renovated guest house, with an arbor-covered Rhine terrace fronting the river. Many of the rooms have views of the Rhine, along with high ceilings and Oriental rugs. A double costs from 80 DM ($26.40) to 110 DM ($36.30), and singles range from 70 DM ($23.10) to 90 DM ($29.70). The restaurant is decorated charmingly with old porcelain, brass tankards, and copper pots, serving meals that begin as low as 18 DM ($5.94) and climb to 45 DM ($14.85).

Pension Haus Resi-Ewige Lampe, 17 Niederwaldstrasse (tel. 24-17). You'll find a lot to do in this wine-producing center. You're within a few kilometers of some historic vineyards and from woodland trails through Rhenish forests. Engelbert Url and his family are your hosts, welcoming you to their cozy, tastefully furnished guest house. Many of their rooms have wooden ceilings, and all of them are impeccably clean, with colorfully tiled baths in some units. The cost, depending on the room assigned, ranges from 40 DM ($13.20) to 85 DM ($28.05) in a single, from 60 DM ($19.80) to 130 DM ($42.90) in a double. A fortifying breakfast is often served on a sun terrace under colorful parasols.

SAMPLING THE HOSPITALITY OF THE RHEINGAU: Everywhere you turn in this vine-laden region, you come upon little village inns, or massive castles converted into hotels. Here are two of the most unusual and enjoyable.

Romantik Hotel Schwan, 5-7 Rheinallee (tel. 30-01), in Oestrich, is one of the most celebrated inns in Germany. You might spend the night in the favored tower room with its seven windows overlooking the Rhine, descend the cantilevered wooden staircase built in 1628, or taste the Rheingau wine, Oestricher Lenchen, while sitting on a Rhine-fronting terrace. The innkeeping family, the Winkel-Wenckstern, keeps their Swan preening proud, hospitable and friendly. This is an inn of Renaissance gables and a half-timbered facade. It opens onto the little front garden facing a boat landing dock from which Rhine cruises depart.

The bedrooms have been brought up-to-date with modern plumbing and comfortable furnishings. Doubles with private bath, including tax and service, go for 220 DM ($72.60), and singles cost 120 DM ($39.60). Dining here is genuinely excellent, with menus in the 35-DM ($11.55) to 55-DM ($18.15) range. You'll also find a historical wine cellar here, with racks of rare vintages and huge wooden casks of "open wines."

Gutsschänke Burg Schwarzenstein, at Geisenheim-Johannisberg (tel. 88-50), is a restaurant installed in a fort and surrounded by vineyards in this old monastery town. The establishment nestles in the ruins of a turreted tower, with dining tables on a 100-foot terrace overlooking the valley. The patio is covered with bearing grapes. For colder weather, there's an indoor dining room affording a panoramic view. Some people come here to sample the wine. The food is good too, with menus priced from 18 DM ($5.94) to 60 DM ($19.80). Service is daily in summer from 10 a.m. to midnight, except Monday. Johannisberg is reached from Rüdesheim by taking the road to Winkel (from there, proceed on a northwestern route for approximately 1½ miles).

10. Speyer

As one of the oldest Rhine cities of the Holy Roman Empire, Speyer early became an important religious center, culminating in the Diet of Speyer, which in 1529 united the followers of Luther in a protest against the Church of Rome. Nothing recalls this medieval German empire as much as the **Imperial Cathedral** (Domkapitel), 3 Domplatz (tel. 10-22-59), in Speyer, perhaps the greatest building of its time.

The cathedral, begun in the early 11th century, is the largest Romanesque edifice in Germany. After several restorations in former times, the cathedral having weathered the damage of fires and wars, the silhouette of the cathedral (roofs and gables) was restored to its original shape from 1957 to 1969. Only the huge dome over the transept has kept its curved sweep. Entering the church through the single west door set in a stepped arch, you are immediately caught up in the vastness of the proportions, as the whole length of the nave and east chancel opens up before you. Lit by the muted daylight from above, it contains the royal tombs of four emperors and four kings of the Holy Roman Empire, as well as a row of bishops' tombs. The cathedral is open April 1 to September 30 on weekdays from 9 a.m. to 6 p.m., on Saturday till 4 p.m., and on Sunday from 1:30 to 4:30 p.m. Off-season weekday hours are 9 a.m. to noon and 1:30 to 5 p.m., till 4 p.m. on Saturday and from 1:30 to 4:30 p.m. on Sunday. Entrance to the crypt is 1 DM (33¢). A guided tour costs 2 DM (66¢) per person.

A MIDDLE-BRACKET HOTEL: Rhein-Hotel Luxhof, at the Rhine Bridge, just outside the town (tel. 06205/3-23-33), is a hotel of unusual character. It's modern in style, with many private bathrooms, but somehow the spirit of a rambling country inn has been retained. The dining rooms are charming and colorful, using ladderback chairs, long pine benches, a tall porcelain stove, deer antlers, and hanging copper lamps. There is an outdoor swimming pool. The bedrooms are clean, well designed, and compact, often including a small sitting area opening onto a tiny balcony. Price for a single bathless room ranges from 45 DM ($14.85); with bath, 85 DM ($28.05). Bathless doubles are in the 80-DM ($26.40) range, increasing to 130 DM ($42.90) with bath. A breakfast buffet is always included, plus a sauna, solarium, and other fitness facilities.

BUDGET HOTELS: Kurpfalz, 5 Mühlturmstrasse (tel. 2-41-68), is a little hotel, more like a guest house, run by the Schimsheimer-Fuchs family. English is spoken here. Their rooms are comfortably furnished. A single with bath costs 80 DM ($26.40), and a double goes for 108 DM ($35.64), with breakfast included.

Am Wartturm, 30 Landwehrstrasse (tel. 40-68), is a modern little guest house of 13 rooms, with immediate parking for guests. Owner Herr Koithahn rents out comfortably but simple furnished units, and will arrange for an evening meal if you request it. He charges from 58 DM ($19.14) in a single and 90 DM ($29.70) in a double, both with shower and toilet.

Trutzpfaff, 5 Webergasse (tel. 7-83-99), is conveniently located near the town cathedral. This family-run guest house offers a personalized service from the friendly, English-speaking owner, Edgar Ulses. His rooms are furnished pleasantly and comfortably. He charges from 75 DM ($24.75) in a single and from 100 DM ($33) in a double, with breakfast included.

Gaststätte Löwengarten, 14 Schwerdstrasse (tel. 7-10-51). Entrepreneur Karl-Heinz Graf is your host at this well-known hotel and restaurant, lying several blocks from the cathedral. He has a total capacity of 70 beds, and many of his units contain phone, TV, and balcony. A nourishing breakfast is included in the room tariffs: 75 DM ($24.75) to 130 DM ($42.90) in a single and 100 DM ($33) to 150 DM ($49.50) in a double.

WHERE TO DINE: **Backmulde,** 11 Karmeliterstrasse (tel. 7-15-77). Owner Gunter Schmidt has researched the centuries-old recipes of the Palatinate, added a touch of nouvelle cuisine zip, and come up with a combination that has made Backmulde the most important restaurant in Speyer. He is located unpretentiously in what used to be a former bakery, with a storefront entrance where you can imagine yesterday's hausfrau hauling off her household's daily bread. At the Backmulde, you can savor such unusual delicacies as a gratinée of oysters in a champagne sabayon, quail stuffed with well-seasoned sweetbreads, or roast baby lamb with freshly picked spinach. A meal ranges from 40 DM ($13.20) to 75 DM ($24.75), and service is from 11:30 a.m. to 2 p.m. and 6:30 to 10 p.m. It is closed on Sunday and for a three-week vacation in summer.

11. Idar-Oberstein

Idar-Oberstein, medieval twin cities, has long been considered the lapidary center of Europe, with many workshops, stores, and museums of rough and cut stones from all over the world. The **Deutsch Gemmologische Gesellschaft,** which is the principal German school for training gemologists, is there, and the city has a diamond and precious stones exchange, one of fewer than 20 diamond exchanges in the world, and the only precious stones exchange.

WHERE TO STAY: **Merian,** 34 Mainzer Strasse (tel. 48-11). Rising 20 stories abruptly out of a surrounding forest, this steel-and-concrete box houses many visitors to Idar-Oberstein from the international gem-trading companies. The Spiessbraten Restaurant offers well-prepared meals in a warmly decorated ambience, while the breakfast buffet is served in copious amounts in a top-floor aerie with a panoramic view. Rooms are freshly decorated in natural colors, usually forest green, and depending on the floor you're on, you might be able to see for miles around. Double rooms with bath cost 120 DM ($39.60), and singles rent for 90 DM ($29.70).

Zum Schwan, 25 Hauptstrasse (tel. 4-30-81), is a hotel-restaurant in a building of classic architecture, run by Herr Bierenfeld, who offers a really personal atmosphere. Rooms are modern, and most of them are quite spacious. A double without bath goes for 75 DM ($24.75), increasing to 105 DM ($34.65) with your own plumbing. Singles cost 43 DM ($14.19) to 58 DM ($19.14). All rates include a big buffet breakfast.

WHERE TO DINE: **Zum Schwan,** 25 Hauptstrasse (tel. 4-30-81), was previously recommended as a hotel, and it's also your best bet for dining. International cookery finds a place in this renowned diamond-trading town, and at this restaurant an open fireplace welcomes visitors on a nippy night to gutbürgerlich cookery and gemütlich charm. Regional dishes might include the chef's original recipe, an Idar-Obersteiner spiessbraten (ask the waiter to explain it). Or you might partake of a filet of veal in a cognac cream sauce with green pepper and homemade spätzle or lamb chops with baby cabbage leaves and a champagne mustard sauce. Fixed-price menus cost from 20 DM ($6.60) to 45 DM ($14.85). Hours are 11 a.m. to 2 p.m. and 6 to 10 p.m. daily except Friday.

———————

Germany's castle-studded river, the Neckar, is traveled in the upcoming chapter.

Chapter VI

HEIDELBERG, STUTTGART, AND THE NECKAR VALLEY

ANCIENT CASTLE RUINS in the midst of thick woodlands, quiet university towns, busy manufacturing centers—all this truly belongs to the countryside of southwestern Germany, extending along the Neckar River from Heidelberg past medieval towns and modern cities as far as Tübingen. Although the river is open to commercial shipping vessels as far as Stuttgart, much of the valley has remained unspoiled, its medieval privacy uninvaded.

Flowing between the Black Forest and the Swabian Alb, the Neckar has been the cradle of German royal families for centuries. The castles which lie around every bend in the river were once homes of the imperial families of Hohenstaufen and Hohenzollern. Many of the ruins were the summer palaces of kings and emperors. In the midst of all this baronial splendor, many castles and country palaces offer bed and board to travelers weary from their treks through the hills and woodlands along the river.

But before we embark on a tour of the countryside, we should visit the most fascinating city on the Neckar. . . .

1. Heidelberg

Summertime in Heidelberg, according to the song from the popular operetta *The Student Prince,* is a time for music and romance. Today it's also a time when droves of visitors invade this city on the Neckar—and with just cause. Heidelberg is one of the few large German cities not leveled by the air raids of World War II, and many of its important buildings date from the latter part of the Middle Ages and the early Renaissance.

Heidelberg is, above all, a university town and has been since 1386. Nearly 10% of the current population is made up of the huge student body. The colorful atmosphere that university life imparts to the town is felt nowhere more than in the old student quarter, with its narrow streets and lively inns.

There is a modern Heidelberg as well, centered around the green of Bismarck Square at the foot of the Theodore Heuss Bridge. The skyscrapers and shopping plazas contrast dramatically with the Old Town nearby. In the new city you will find many of the best hotels and restaurants. Across the Neckar are sports grounds, a zoo, and a large botanical garden. But before exploring the sights of Heidelberg, however, let's survey the range of accommodations and restaurants.

THE TOP HOTELS: **Der Europäische Hof-Hotel Europa,** 1 Friedrich-Ebert-Anlage (tel. 2-71-01), is Heidelberg's glamor hotel. Fronting the city park, with a quiet inside garden, it's in the heart of the town, within walking distance of the castle, the university, and the old part of town with its student inns. Its interior is like a gracious home, with a liberal sprinkling of antiques, crystal chandeliers, bas-relief walls in the salons, and Oriental rugs. The hotel has added 50 new units facing the quiet inside garden, some of them apartments with separate bedrooms and sitting rooms. The rooms are pleasantly traditional, done with rich taste. Each chamber is individually decorated and has a bath or shower, self-dial telephone, radio, television, and refrigerator. The rates depend on the season, the size of the room, and the location. Singles range from 139 DM ($45.87) to 159 DM ($52.47) with shower and toilet, from 183 DM ($60.39) to 219 DM ($72.27) with bath and toilet. Double- or twin-bedded rooms with complete bath rent for 250 DM ($82.50) to 310 DM ($102.30). A continental breakfast, service, and taxes are included in the rates. Meals are served in the Louis XVI restaurant, on the garden terrace where windows can be lowered to floor level, or in the finely paneled Kurfürstenstube. Before dinner, guests congregate around the curved bar in the wood-paneled drinking lounge. An elegant shopping arcade, a fitness center, swimming pool, massage room, and sun terrace, plus an underground parking garage, are on the premises.

The **Prinzhotel Heidelberg,** 5 Neuenheimer Landstrasse (tel. 4-03-20), in the town center and near the congress hall, has been totally renovated and turned into a first-class hotel which provides such amenities as private bath and toilet in all rooms, direct-dial phone, mini-bar, TV/video, and safe. Many of them have views of the Neckar Valley and the castle. Single rooms cost from 180 DM ($59.40) to 190 DM ($62.70), and doubles run 220 DM ($72.60) to 235 DM ($77.50). The hotel has a coffeeshop where you can enjoy a wide selection from the buffet for 30 DM ($9.90). In the Riverside, an à la carte restaurant overlooking the Neckar, you can have meals from 10 a.m. to midnight that have been described as culinary works of art.

MIDDLE-BRACKET HOTELS: **Romantik-Hotel Zum Ritter,** 178 Hauptstrasse (tel. 2-42-72), is a well-preserved rarity, a glorious old inn right out of the German Renaissance. Built in 1592 by the Frenchman Charles Bélier, it is now listed among the major sightseeing attractions of this university town, having survived the destruction of 1693. Deep in the heart of the student area of drinking houses and nightclubs, Zum Ritter holds its own. There are no public lounges; the bedrooms play second fiddle to the fine restaurant downstairs. Bathless doubles cost 95 DM ($31.35), increasing to 250 DM ($82.50) with bath. Singles cost 69 DM ($22.44) to 210 DM ($69.30), depending on the plumbing. The bedrooms are completely functional in style.

Hotel Hirschgasse, 3 Hirschgasse (tel. 4-99-21), is a historic guest house dating from 1472. Its spacious "Saal" is still used by students for fencing and dueling. Today it is a handsome restored hotel, with an excellent gourmet restaurant and comfortably modern rooms for its guests. The accommodations have been remodeled, but an attempt has been made to preserve the feeling of the old character. The most expensive doubles with private bath rent for 205 DM ($67.65), and some cheaper ones go for 170 DM ($56.10). Singles cost 140 DM ($46.20) to 170 DM ($56.10). All units have private bath and toilet.

The hotel lies on the side of the Neckar opposite the Altstadt (the antique central sector of the city). Furnishings are traditional. On a tree-shaded terrace, guests can order a leisurely breakfast or a before-dinner glass of wine. The English-speaking Kraft family also welcome you to their restaurant, serving fine meals and giving good service.

Hotel Monpti, 57 Friedrich-Ebert-Anlage (tel. 2-34-83), is just what Heidelberg has always needed: a small hotel with sophisticated charm, run on a personal basis and moderately priced. The owner, Peter Mack, was born in this stately little town house in 1939. After traveling extensively, especially in Spain, he returned to his native town, intending to convert his home into a super guest house. That he has done, utilizing both his inherent and acquired taste. Built in the neoclassic style, the Monpti is a charmer, painted an olive green with a distinctive architectural trim in gleaming white. Each bedroom has color and freshness. All of the practical items are behind doors, and your chamber is furnished like a little salon. All of the 14 double rooms have private shower and toilet, as well as phone and bar refrigerator. Two persons pay from 100 DM ($33) to 125 DM ($41.25), and a single is charged 89 DM ($29.37), including breakfast and taxes. There's a petite breakfast room where guests gather over morning coffee. The owner has transformed the lower level (it's built on a hillside) into the bodega Vinothek, where he, his wife, and friends gather in the evening to enjoy paella. It's practically become a youth center. Perhaps a Spanish guitarist will provide background music when you are there. The restaurant is open until 1 a.m. Free parking is on the open terrace.

Schrieder, an der Kurfürstenanlage (tel. 1-50-37), is a target center of activity in Heidelberg, three blocks from the Neckar, opening onto a wide boulevard. The Schrieder, with its small garden of trees and flowers, is one of the leading second-class choices. The interior may lack élan, but there's plenty of comfort. The 85 rooms are in the modern idiom and come in varying sizes. A bathless double costs 90 DM ($29.70), increasing to anywhere from 120 DM ($39.60) to 160 DM ($52.80) with private bath. Depending on the plumbing and the season, singles go for anywhere from 77 DM ($25.41) to 130 DM ($42.90). The English-speaking Patriarca family are most hospitable. Public rooms include a lounge, dining room, plus a breakfast salon opening onto a small rear garden. All prices include breakfast.

Acor, 55 Friedrich-Ebert-Anlage (tel. 2-41-30), is a recommendable 19-bedroom hotel that was converted from an old patrician house. An elevator has been installed and the furnishings updated. Most of the rooms are compact (although a few are large) and quite comfortable. Doubles with bath or shower are 130 DM ($42.90) to 150 DM ($49.50). Singles with bath or shower cost 80 DM ($26.40) to 110 DM ($36.30). These tabs include a continental breakfast, served in a little room overlooking a small rear garden. The street is busy with traffic, but soundproof windows have been installed.

Hotel Alt Heidelberg, 29 Rohrbacher Strasse (tel. 1-50-91). Arriving at night here is like a scene from Grimm's fairy tales, where a well-lit mini-palace welcomes wayfaring visitors to its portals. There are five floors of baroque embellishments, and the public rooms are elegantly decorated with Oriental rugs and half paneling. This is one of the nicest hotels in town, conveniently located in the center. Rooms are modern, with sparkling tiled baths, and cost from 135 DM ($44.55) in a single and from 175 DM ($57.75) in a double, breakfast included.

Hotel Schönberger Hof, 54 Untere Neckarstrasse (tel. 2-26-15). Renovated in 1970, this baroque villa offers today a hint of the grandeur of former times. It is attractively situated across from the Town Hall and Montpellier Park, and it lies only a short walk from the Neckar. The public rooms are rustically decorated, making use of original stonework and rough-hewn timbers. The limited number of bedrooms have high ceilings and comfortable beds. A popular weinstube fills the ground floor, where you'll probably want to stop in, if only for a beer. Singles rent for 80 DM ($26.40) to 90 DM ($29.70), while doubles go for 140 DM ($46.20), including breakfast.

Parkhotel Atlantic, 23 Schloss-Weolfsbrunnenweg (tel. 2-45-45), lies on the wooded outskirts of Heidelberg, near the Heidelberger Schloss. This rather grand hotel offers modern comfort in annexes built around the core of an older villa. The surrounding park is full of trees, and visitors are assured of calm and comfort. Often they take advantage of the many woodland trails extending through the Neckar Valley. The rooms, decorated in circa 1965 modern, go for 95 DM ($31.35) to 140 DM ($46.20) in a single and from 150 DM ($16.50) to 190 DM ($62.70) in a double, including breakfast.

Neckar-Hotel Heidelberg, 19 Bismarckstrasse (tel. 2-32-60), enjoys an enviable position, right on the Neckar River near the center of the university town. There is no garden, but a superb view. The facilities are substantial and comfortable. The bedrooms, 35 in all, are fitted with Germanic-modern pieces. A double- or twin-bedded room with bath or shower runs from 130 DM ($42.90) to 170 DM ($56.10). Singles, also with shower or bath, range from 95 DM ($31.35) to 110 DM ($36.30). These rates include breakfast, tax, and service. Breakfast is the only meal served; parking is available in the tiny lot.

Hotel Vier Jahreszeiten, 2 Haspelgasse (tel. 2-41-64), lives up to its name and is a worthy choice in any of the "four seasons." The location is by the Old Bridge in the heart of Heidelberg, the starting point for many interesting walks. You can walk not only to the castle, but you're convenient to many old student inns. The hotel has been much improved over the years, and rooms are comfortable and perhaps a bit dated. Depending on the plumbing, singles range from 55 DM ($18.15) to 125 DM ($41.25), while doubles go for 100 DM ($33) to 165 DM ($54.45). These tariffs include a continental breakfast. From the hotel there's a good view over the Neckar.

A BUDGET HOTEL: Hotel zum Pfalzgrafen, 21 Kettengasse (tel. 2-04-89), is a simple town inn, with good clean rooms. The hotel is in the heart of Old Heidelberg, only 15 minutes' walking distance to most major sights. Parking is available, and there are also garages. The best rooms contain private shower, and these are priced accordingly. The best bargains, however, are the rooms with hot and cold running water only. Public showers are on the same floor. Doubles or twins without shower cost 70 DM ($23.10) to 73 DM ($24.09); with shower, from 85 DM ($28.05). Singles cost 42 DM ($13.86) without shower, 55 DM ($18.15) to 60 DM ($19.80) with shower or bath. Triples cost 96 DM ($31.68). All rates include service, taxes, and a good breakfast.

THE TOP RESTAURANT: The Kurfürstenstube, Der Europäische Hof-Hotel Europa, 1 Friedrich-Ebert-Anlage (tel. 2-71-01), is the best restaurant in Heidelberg. Occupying a ground-floor wing of this outstanding hotel, the wine stuben is attractively decorated with provincial furnishings, pewter plates, and a stein collection. The menu is in English. Specialties include homemade tureen of quail with mushrooms and pumpkin sauce, homemade goose liver pâté with Campari sauce, lobster soup "chef style" with salmon quenelles, consommé of lamb, fresh Odenwald brook trout, filet of sole in a leaf of Savoy cabbage braised with nut sauce, filet of saddle of venison with red currant sauce, and filet of charolais beef with marrow sauce, shallots, mushrooms, and vegetables. Rounding out the meal might be flamed pancakes with bananas and maple sauce. The wine list is very impressive indeed, and a complete meal ranges from 62 DM ($20.46) to 95 DM ($31.35). Hours are noon to 3 p.m. and 6:30 p.m. to midnight.

MEDIUM-PRICED DINING: Kurpfälzische Wein Restaurant, 97 Hauptstrasse (tel. 2-40-50), is a quiet culinary oasis in the precincts of the Kurpfälzisches Museum. Housed in a baroque palace, the museum makes an interesting stopover before lunch. The restaurant's prices are moderate, the food good. Set meals cost from 18 DM ($5.94) to 38 DM ($12.54). From the à la carte menu, you can order such dishes as rump steak Madagascar (with green pepper). From your table, you can enjoy the little garden and splashing fountain. Hours are from 11 a.m. to midnight. Closed Monday.

Romantik-Hotel Zum Ritter, 178 Hauptstrasse (tel. 2-42-72), is popular with both students and professors, for they know they can get not only good German cooking here, but delectable Dortmunder Actien-Brauerei beer as well. You dine either in the first-class Great Hall (the Ritter Saal) or in the smaller Councillors' Chamber. I like the larger room, most elegant with sepia ceilings, wainscoting, woodcarvings, and Oriental rugs. Set meals range in price from a low of 25 DM ($8.25) to a high of 75 DM ($24.75). The house specialty in season is saddle of venison for two. The large international menu includes such selections as veal steak with cream sauce. A good beginning might be game soup St. Hubertus with brandy foam, followed by crêpes suzette.

Merian-Stuben, 24 Neckarstaden (tel. 2-73-81), is housed in the Kongresshaus Stadthalle. One of the best restaurants in Heidelberg, it offers attentive service and good food, with complete dinners beginning at 25 DM ($8.25), ranging upward to around 50 DM ($16.50). The menu is printed in English. You might begin with Alsatian snails cooked in a pan with onions, mushrooms, and fresh herbs, or frog legs sauteed in light garlic butter with glazed onions and tomatoes, or perhaps freshly smoked trout with a cranberry cream sauce. For a fish selection, poached pike comes in a creamy mustard sauce, and you can also order pork filet à la Dijon (spit broiled, basted with a mustard sauce, and served with onions, cucumber cubes, green beans, and potato croquettes). The ice cream is very good, especially the cherry-flavored one served with slivered chocolate and whipped cream.

BUDGET DINING: Heidelberg Castle Weinstube, Schloss Heidelberg (tel. 2-00-81), is a recreation of a wine tavern, tastefully and attractively done. You'll find antique ceramic stones, natural wood trestle tables, and many framed engravings under a ceiling of ornate paneling. Tables are shared freely, and many are arranged to provide the best view of Heidelberg Castle. The weinstube is entered through the inner courtyard, reached by steep stone steps. Three-course lunches range in price from 25 DM ($8.25). An elaborate dinner costs 50 DM ($16.50). The weinstube is open from 11 a.m. to 9:30 p.m. daily except Tuesday.

Schönberger Hof, 54 Untere Neckarstrasse (tel. 2-26-15). Tranquil would perhaps be a good word to describe this gaily painted old German weinstube, where Bavarian and French wines fill the carte. From the outside, you'll notice a charming house with art nouveau window frames. But once inside, you'll find a room where tradition and hearty Germanic cookery prevail. It's conveniently located between Montpellier Park on the Neckar and the Stadthalle. The establishment is closed for two weeks in summer, but open from 5 p.m. till midnight Monday to Friday, charging from 40 DM ($13.20) to 60 DM ($19.80).

Conditorei-Café Schafheutle, 94 Hauptstrasse (tel. 2-13-16). Rain need never ruin your summer afternoon outing in this café-garden for it's partially roofed over in case of such an eventuality. Food, costing around 25 DM ($8.25) for a good meal, is presented with attentive service. You face a large choice of items, including a formidable collection of desserts on the wagon. It's open from 9 a.m. till 6:30 p.m. (until 6 p.m. on Saturday), but closed on Sunday and holidays.

STUDENT DRINKING CLUBS: Zum Roten Ochsen (Red Ox Inn), 217 Hauptstrasse (tel. 2-09-77), created in 1703, in Heidelberg's most famous and revered student tavern. For six generations it's been in the Spengel family, who have welcomed everybody from Bismarck to Mark Twain. It seems that every student who has attended the university has left his mark on the walls—or at least his initials. Revelers sit at long oak tables under smoke-blackened ceilings. Distinguished patrons of yore have left mementos, often framed photographs of themselves. The series of rooms is arranged in horseshoe fashion. The "U" part has a pianist who sets the musical pace. As the evening progresses, the songs become more festive and vigorous. By midnight the sounds are heard from blocks away. Motherly looking waitresses bring in huge steins of beer and plates of heavy, basic food. A mug of beer costs around 4 DM ($1.32). Goulasch soup will get you going, and main dishes include such specialties as sauerbraten Rhineland style and veal steak Cordon Bleu. Menus cost from 14 DM ($4.62) to 25 DM ($8.25). Service is from 5 p.m. to midnight except on Sunday.

Schnookeloch, 8 Haspelgasse (tel. 2-27-33), is another ancient building, dating back to 1407. Right at the Old Bridge, the tavern attracts students who come nightly to drink and raise the rafters. During the days of the "new wine," the tempo picks up considerably. Meals cost from 18 DM ($5.94) to 30 DM ($9.90).

THE SIGHTS: All the important sights of Heidelberg lie on or near the south bank of the Neckar and you must cross the river (via the 18th-century Karl Theodore Bridge) for the best overall view of the Old Town. **Philosophen Weg** (Philosopher's Way), halfway up the mountain on the north bank, is best for viewing. And towering above the brown roofs of the town on the opposite bank is the rose-pink major attraction of Heidelberg, the castle.

Heidelberg Castle

In its magnificent setting of woodland and terraced gardens, the huge red sandstone castle is reached from the town below by several routes. The quickest way is the two-minute cable-car ride from the platform near the Kornmarkt (Corn Market) in the Old Town. The round trip costs 3.50 DM ($1.16). You may also drive to the winding Neue Schlosstrasse, past the old houses perched on the hillside. This is also a rewarding walking route because of the constantly changing view of the town and surrounding countryside. For a shorter walk, you may climb the steep Burgweg from the Corn Market, or take the more gradual walk from the Klingentor.

The castle is only a dignified ruin today; it was plundered and burned by the French in the latter part of the 17th century. Parts of the huge tower still lie in the moat where they fell after being blown up in 1693 at the command of Louis

XIV. Lightning added to the destruction by striking the castle twice in the mid-18th century. But at least the magnificent structure was spared the ultimate destruction of World War II bombs, and even in its deteriorated state, it's considered one of the finest Gothic-Renaissance castles in Germany.

Entering the castle walls at the main gate, you first come upon the huge **Gun Park** to your left from which you can gaze down upon Heidelberg and the Neckar Valley. Straight ahead is the Thick Tower, or what remains of it after its 25-foot walls were blown up by the French. Leaving the Gun Park via Elizabeth's Gate, erected by Friedrich V in 1615 for his English wife, Elizabeth Stuart, daughter of James I, you come to the Bridge House and the bridge crossing the site of the former moat.

Through the entrance tower lies the **castle courtyard,** the heart of the complex of structures. Surrounding it are buildings dating from the 13th to the 17th centuries. You'll notice that nature has done its best to repair the ravages of war, by covering the gaping holes and roofless sections with ivy and shrubbery. Walking around the courtyard in a clockwise fashion, you come first to the Gothic **Ruprecht Building,** built about 1400. Adjacent is the **Library,** with a Gothic oriel window dating from the early 16th century. It once housed the library of Ludwig V.

The **Frauenzimmer** (Women's Rooms) was originally a three-story Gothic-Renaissance building housing the ladies of the court, but today only the ground level, the King's Hall, remains.

Along the north side of the courtyard stretches the stern palace of Friedrich IV, erected from 1601 to 1607. Less damaged than other parts of the castle, it has been almost completely restored, including the gallery of princes and kings of the German Empire from the time of Charlemagne. The palace has its own terrace, the Altan, which offers a splendid view of the plain of the Neckar as well as the Old Town. The ancient Bell Tower, at the northeast end of the Altan, dates from the early 1500s.

At the west end of the terrace, in the cellars of the castle, is the Wine Vat Building, built in the late 16th century and worth a visit for a look at the **Great Cask,** symbol of the abundant and exuberant life of the Rhineland-Palatinate. This huge barrel-like monstrosity, built in 1751, is capable of holding more than 55,000 gallons of wine.

On the east, connecting the palace of Friedrich IV to the **Ottheinrich Building,** itself an outstanding example of German Renaissance architecture, is the **Hall of Mirrors Building,** constructed in 1549—a Renaissance masterpiece of its time. Only the shell of the original building remains, enough to give you an idea of its former glory, with its arcades and steep gables decorated with cherubs and sirens.

Next to Ottheinrich's palace is the Chemist's Tower, housing the **Pharmaceutical Museum.** Entrance fee: 1.50 DM (50¢). The museum, on the tower's ground floor, shows a chemist's shop with utensils and laboratory equipment from the 18th and 19th centuries. It is open during the usual castle visiting hours.

Returning to the Castle Gate, you will pass the old barracks for the soldiers of the garrison. Next to the barracks is the former well house, its roof supported by ancient Roman columns. Some of the household buildings, such as the bakery, kitchen, smithshop, and butchery nearby, have been restored.

In summer you can enjoy serenades and concerts in the large castle courtyard. But the biggest spectacle is the **castle illumination,** commemorating the battles of the 17th century. Several times throughout the summer, at dates rescheduled yearly, the castle is floodlit and fireworks are set off above it.

You can visit the castle grounds at any time during the day, free. If you wish to visit the interior of the castle, you must take one of the one-hour guided tours.

The fee is 4 DM ($1.32) for adults, 2 DM (66¢) for children. A visit to the Great Cask without the tour costs adults 1 DM (33¢); children, .50 DM (17¢).

Other Sights

Back in the town itself, a tour of the main attractions begins with the **Marketplace** in front of the Rathaus. On market days the square is filled with stalls of fresh flowers, fish, and vegetables. At the opposite end of the square is the late-Gothic **Church of the Holy Ghost,** built about 1400. For nearly 300 years the church was the burial place of the electors, but most of the graves were destroyed in the French invasion late in the 17th century. In 1706 a wall was erected dividing the church, giving both Catholics and Protestants a portion in which to worship. The wall has since been removed and the church restored to its original plan.

Around the corner from the church is the famous old mansion, **Zum Ritter,** recommended in the hotel listings above. If you follow the Hauptstrasse past the Hotel zum Ritter, you'll arrive at the **Kurpfälzisches Museum,** 97 Hauptstrasse, the Museum of the Palatinate, housed in a baroque palace. The museum presents a large collection of paintings and sculptures from six centuries, among them the Riemenschneider Altar from Windsheim (1509) with Christ and the Twelve Apostles. There is also a cast of the jawbone of the Heidelberg Man, 500,000 years old; an archeological collection; examples of history and culture of the Palatinate; and paintings from the Romantic period. The museum is open daily except Monday from 10 a.m. to 1 p.m. and 2 to 5 p.m. Admission is 2 DM (66¢).

The Hauptstrasse also runs through the old student quarter of Heidelberg, with its inns. Of special interest is the **Student Jail,** at 2 Augustinergasse. The walls and even the ceilings of the prison are covered with graffiti and drawings, including portraits and silhouettes. The last prisoners were housed here in 1914. Visiting hours are 9 a.m. to 5 p.m. except on Sunday and holidays. Ring the bell of the caretaker (same address) for admission, which is .60 DM (20¢) for adults, .40 DM (13¢) for students.

In the Environs

The Palatine electors in the 18th century journeyed to **Schwetzingen,** seven miles west of Heidelberg, which was their summer residence. Along this route came Voltaire and a host of other famous visitors.

Schwetzingen is home to the world-famous castle gardens which are open to the public April to September from 8 a.m. to 8 p.m. (otherwise, from 9 a.m. to 5 p.m.), charging an admission of 3 DM (99¢). The gardens are laid out in the spirit of Versailles, but with more rococo detail. Busts, urns, ancient gods, temples, and "ruins" everywhere conjure up romantic idylls. A mosque suggests the charm of the Orient, and watercourses, fountains, live animals, and flowerbeds complete the picture which the electors found "a paradise on earth."

The castle was formerly a low-lying fort surrounded by water. Later it became the hunting lodge and then the summer residence of Carl Theodor, the last Palatine elector. Productions are still staged at a rococo theater, and in the early summer of every year an international festival is held.

Gourmets flock to Schwetzingen in the spring (from the middle of April until the end of June) to enjoy the celebrated asparagus grown here.

2. The Neckar Valley

Heidelberg is a good point from which to begin an exploration of the Neckar Valley. During the summer you can take one of the **boat tours** along the river as far as Neckarsteinach and back; a three-hour round trip costs 13.50 DM

($4.46) per person. You can get a good meal and a drink on the boat for a price under 12.50 DM ($4.13). There are usually four or five round trips daily. Boats are operated by the **Rhein-Neckar-Fahrgastschiffahrt GMBH,** Stadthalle, Heidelberg (tel. 2-01-81). Some of the people who take you on this pleasant trip may be descended from the Neckar fishermen who helped Mark Twain when he rafted down from Hirschhorn. Boat people have been working the Neckar since the early 1600s.

The best way to get a close look at the many attractions along the banks of the Neckar is by car. Leaving Heidelberg, drive eastward along the right bank of the river (the same as Heidelberg's Old Town) and you'll soon arrive at the medieval town of:

HIRSCHHORN: Called the gem of the Neckar Valley, this old town still carries an aura of the past. It obtained its municipal rights in 1396. Overlooking the town and the Neckar from its fortified promontory is the 18th-century **Hirschhorn Castle.** The castle was erected on the site of an earlier Renaissance palace built by Ludwig von Hirschhorn in the late 16th century. The castle defenses are from the 14th century, and wall paintings from that period can be seen in the chapel. Although the castle is a hotel and restaurant, you can also visit it as a sightseeing attraction. For a view of the sharp bend of the Neckar below the town, climb to the top of the tower. Admission is 1.20 DM (40¢).

Hotel Burg Hirschhorn (tel. 13-73), on Highway B37 (Heidelberg-Eberbach), provides an opportunity to stay in a hilltop castle. After a stormy career, the castle settled down to serving as a hotel or dining room for wayfarers. The accommodations are divided between a palace and a guest-house annex. The bedrooms are furnished in modern, with a bathroom provided on each floor. Central heating and an elevator have been installed as well. Rates are cheaper in the guest house. A bathless single, with breakfast, service, and tax included, costs 40 DM ($13.20). Bathless doubles are in the 80-DM ($26.40) range in the guest house, rising to 170 DM ($56.10) in the castle. The food is good, particularly the veal dishes, the service is excellent, and the terrace dining views of the Neckar are superb. Meals cost from 22 DM ($7.26) to 50 DM ($16.50).

EBERBACH: Just 20 miles along the Neckar from Heidelberg is the ancient Imperial City of Eberbach, which traces its municipal rights back to 1227. Its castle is even older, dating from 1012. The fortress was destroyed in the 15th century, but its ivy-covered ruins attract many visitors today, as does the old Deutscher Hof, the medieval center of the town within the city walls.

Food and Lodging

Hotel Kettenboot, 1 Friedrichstrasse (tel. 24-70), is one of the better known hotels in town—the kind of place where practically everybody has been for at least one meal. Its 15 bedrooms, comfortably and conservatively furnished, are priced at 45 DM ($14.85) to 60 DM ($19.80) in a single, 84 DM ($27.72) to 110 DM ($36.30) in a double. It closes from October 20 to November 10. The in-house restaurant is a trustworthy place to get a well-cooked meal, with Germanic, French, and international specialties, costing from 25 DM ($8.25) to 55 DM ($18.15) for a meal. The restaurant is closed Friday.

Hotel Zum Karpfen, 1 Am Alten Markt (tel. 23-16), is one of the most colorful and authentically ancient hotels in town. Built more than two centuries ago near the river, it still welcomes guests into its darkly paneled interior. It contains a full-fledged restaurant, where you can have well-prepared meals in an old-world setting, as well as an informal weinstube where tasty specialties are served in generous portions. The 44 bedrooms rent for 40 DM ($13.20) to 70 DM ($23.10) in a single and 85 DM ($28.05) to 110 DM ($36.30) in a double, with breakfast included.

Haus Talblick, 5 Gaisbergweg, Brombach (tel. 14-51). Anyone who admires 19th-century craftsmanship as well as a well-prepared cuisine will enjoy this attractive restaurant. In warm weather the outdoor terrace is popular. If you eat indoors, there's plenty to admire and appreciate. Reservations are a good idea, especially on busy weekends, when some of the best heeled residents of the town show up for meals. These cost from 55 DM ($18.15) to 90 DM ($29.70) and include fresh wild game and a full array of fish dishes. The availability of individual specialties changes with the supply of the ingredients in the local markets. You can choose from such dishes as calf liver Berlin style with apples, bacon, and sauteed onions; grilled pheasant with pineapple; ragoût of venison with wild mushrooms, cranberries, and freshly made spätzle; and beef with mushrooms, cabbage, and grilled tomatoes. Meals are served daily except Thursday from noon to 2 p.m. and 6 to 11 p.m. The restaurant closes every year for the last three weeks in January and the last two weeks in July.

BAD FRIEDRICHSHALL: This small town, just north of Heilbronn, is noted for its old salt mines and brine spa. At the town, two rivers, the Jagst and the Kocher, flow into the Neckar. The surrounding countryside is excellent for hiking and camping. A few miles up the Jagst River from the town is the hunting castle of Götzenburg, now a hotel.

Burghotel Götzenburg Hornberg, Neckarzimmern (tel. 22-22). In this hilltop castle overlooking the Neckar, you can climb into a great, wooden antique bed and drop all your cares. Dating from the 11th century, the castle was once owned by Götz von Berlichingen, "The Knight with the Iron Hand," who died there in 1562. His grandson sold Hornberg in 1612 to Frieherr von Gemmingen, whose descendants own it today.

Hundreds of tourists pass through the hotel portion of the castle, but, fortunately, the quarters for guests are private. The interior is handsome and colorful—somewhat like an inn, more informal than grandiose. The public rooms have beamed ceilings, thick walls, decorative paintings, an antique tin collection, engravings and forge works, and wrought-iron objects. Within a recess is a framed portrait of the castle's former owner.

Surprisingly, the castle is inexpensive for an overnight stay. Bathless singles rent for 60 DM ($19.80), increasing to 65 DM ($21.45) with shower. Bathless doubles rent for 85 DM ($28.05) to 95 DM ($31.35). For a room with private bath, two persons pay 120 DM ($39.60) to 165 DM ($54.45). Breakfast is included in all the rates. If you want full board, add 50 DM ($16.50) per person. In the old horse stable of Knight Götz, a restaurant, Im Alten Marstall, was built. Charcoal meats are a specialty of the Götzen Grill.

Arrangements can be made for horseback riding, tennis, and swimming within an area of three miles. You'll enjoy walks through the hillside vineyards belonging to the castle. Best of all are the quiet, relaxing periods spent at the end of the day in front of the open fireplace.

HEILBRONN: This city on the Neckar, 33 miles north of Stuttgart, owes its name to the holy spring (Heiligbronn) that bubbled up from beneath the high altar of **St. Kilian's Church.** The church, begun in 1020 and completed in 1529, is a combination of Gothic and Renaissance styles. The tower is nearly 210 feet high and is considered the earliest example of Renaissance architecture in Germany. Inside are some excellent woodcarvings, including the elaborate choir and altar.

Heilbronn is mainly a thriving industrial community, noted for its manufacture of everything from machinery and automobiles to paper and soap. But its most popular product is its wine, harvested from the vineyards in the surrounding hills of Baden-Württemberg. In fact, Heilbronn is the largest producer of wine in the Neckar.

Where to Stay

Insel, Friedrich-Ebert-Brücke (tel. 63-00), is a completely modern hotel, built on an oasis island in the middle of the river, right in the heart of Heilbronn. Rebuilt in 1978, it now contains up to 120 rooms with 180 beds. Most of the bedrooms have balconies opening onto weeping willows and the park belonging to the hotel. The rooms are well designed and comfortable. All have private bath or shower, toilet, radio, and color TV. A twin-bedded room costs 178 DM ($58.74), rising to 238 DM ($78.54). A single goes for 104 DM ($34.32), rising to 188 DM ($62.04). All the tariffs include breakfast from a buffet which offers cheese, sausages, juices, cereals, and fruits. The front terrace is the beer and gossip center of town, a beehive of a place. Within, there's a cozy Swabian Restaurant where you can have homemade spätzle and other well-known specialties. The Insel also has a nightclub, an indoor swimming pool, a sauna, and a solarium.

Hotel Götz, 52 Moltkestrasse (tel. 1-80-01), is in a modern complex of business-related inner-city buildings. Many of the establishment's clients are connected with conventions and come here for annual meetings and policy discussions. Any individual visitor will receive comfortable and well-designed accommodations for 95 DM ($31.35) to 125 DM ($41.25) in a single, 155 DM ($51.15) to 175 ($57.75) in a double, with breakfast included. Each of the 86 rooms has a shower or bath, toilet, phone, and radio. There's a plushly furnished dining room, as well as a bierstube restaurant on the premises.

Where to Dine

Ratskeller, im Rathaus, Marktplatz (tel. 8-46-28), is one of your best bets for dining in Heilbronn. It's a true ratskeller, unlike so many others. However, it's been given the modern treatment, with upholstered banquettes and wrought-iron grillwork. Tables are set on two levels. The prices are modest and the cuisine is regional. Typical main dishes include a goulash, peppersteak with french fries and a salad, and grilled sole. There's an impressive wine list, but don't ignore the wine of the cellar. Meals cost from 30 DM ($9.90) to 55 DM ($18.15). The restaurant is open from 8 a.m. to midnight daily except Monday.

3. Stuttgart

Unlike many large, prosperous industrial centers, Stuttgart is not a concrete city. On the contrary, within the city limits two-thirds of the land is devoted to parks, gardens, and woodlands. Yet Stuttgart is one of Germany's largest manufacturing cities, the home of Mercedes and Porsche automobiles, Zeiss optical equipment, and many other industrial concerns. As a city interested in export and trade, it is also the home of many international trade fairs and congresses.

As a cultural center, Stuttgart is without peer in southwestern Germany. The Stuttgart Ballet performs throughout the world, highly acclaimed wherever it appears. Its State Opera and Philharmonic Orchestra are also well received at home or abroad. In addition, Stuttgart has an abundance of theater groups, cultural festivals, and museums.

Stuttgart is the capital of the southwest German Federal State of Baden-Württemberg. The city produced the philosopher Hegel, who in turn inspired

Marx and Engels. It also is the third-largest wine-growing community in Germany.

ACCOMMODATIONS: No matter when you come to Stuttgart, you will probably find an international trade fair in progress, from the January glass and ceramics exposition to the December book exhibition (Stuttgart is also southern Germany's most important publishing center). Because of this, suitable accommodations may be difficult to find unless you reserve in advance.

The Top Hotels

Steigenberger Hotel Graf Zeppelin, 7 Arnulf-Klett-Platz (tel. 29-98-81), is the best hotel for those who want to wheel and deal with Stuttgart business people. Although right at the railway station, it's not only attractive, but possesses dignity and style, setting a splashy pace. It has a sauna and an indoor swimming pool with a wood-paneled waterside lounge. The soundproof bedrooms are warmly and colorfully decorated and come complete with bath or shower, plus dial telephone, color TV, and mini-bar. Basic singles with shower begin at 200 DM ($66), going up to 310 DM ($102.30) with complete bath and a king-size bed. Doubles with complete bath range in price from 320 DM ($105.60) to 380 DM ($125.40). A full American breakfast is included. Guests congregate in the Aperitif-Bar before making their way to the Restaurant Graf Zeppelin with its French cuisine, the Zeppelin-Stüble serving Swabian dishes, or the Maukenescht (the Swabian wine corner). Later in the evening there is dancing in the Scotch-Club.

Hotel am Schlossgarten, 1 Schillerstrasse (tel. 29-99-11), is the tasteful bargain of the top contenders, where you get much more comfort for your mark. Totally renovated in 1985, it's not splashy, but offers conveniences in a dignified manner. It stands ten floors high on the railway station plaza. Most of its 125 bedrooms and apartments have their own bath, with shower or tub. The rooms skirt the line between modern and traditional. Singles with shower or bath cost from 185 DM ($61.05) to 220 DM ($72.60), and a double peaks at 270 DM ($72.60) to 290 DM ($95.70). Included in these rates is an American breakfast. The public rooms are consistently decorative and sedate. The main dining room has three walls of rich walnut paneling, an Oriental carpet, a tall brass lamp, 19th-century paintings, brown armchairs, and a wall of filmy white curtains. The lounge has the same fine theme, and the hotel bar is warm and cozy. Most intimate is the Zirbelstube, all woodsy with knotty pine on the walls and ceiling and birch armchairs. You dine by candlelight in this tavern atmosphere. Note: There's a 400-car garage.

Park Hotel Stuttgart, 21 Villastrasse (tel. 28-01-61), is the choice for those who seek a first-class accommodation in a secluded and quiet area. It's out of dead center, in the midst of the gardens of the Villa Berg, within walking distance of the mineral-water swimming pool surrounded by a park. Here the service is personalized. The decor is handsome and rather rich. For example, the dining room is created with wood paneling and fabric screens to provide semi-privacy. Roses adorn the white tables; molded white plastic armchairs and copper bowl droplights make for a colorful setting. The clubroom is just that, with dignified modern furnishings and a grand piano for background music. The bedrooms are also well designed, with a decidedly personal aura. A single goes for 160 DM ($52.80) to 190 DM ($62.70) with shower or full bath. Doubles with shower or bath range in price from 195 DM ($64.35) to 240 DM ($79.20). These rates include a buffet breakfast. If you arrive in time for dinner, there is a set meal for 40 DM ($13.20), besides many French and German specialties.

Hotel Royal, 35 Sophienstrasse (tel. 62-50-50). An uneventful facade opens to a well-designed interior, with attractive geometric carpets whose design is repeated in the glass of some of the wall dividers. Rooms are warmly lit and attractively decorated, with lots of wood in the elegantly upholstered chairs. An octagonal-shaped bar, finished in wood and sheltered by marble-covered walls, could serve as a rendezvous point for you and your partner. The dining room serves good-quality meals. Centrally located, the Royal lies a few paces off a major pedestrian walkway. A single begins at a low of 100 DM ($33), going up to 200 DM ($66); a double costs from 230 DM ($75.90) to 270 DM ($89.10).

Middle-Bracket Hotels

Kronen Hotel, 48 Kronenstrasse (tel. 29-96-61), stands slightly beyond the city limits, with a view over the vineyards which are surprisingly close to Stuttgart. This better-than-usual hotel offers spacious and elegant rooms furnished with upholstered armchairs in a variety of styles, along with Oriental rugs. The public rooms have a cozy gemütlichkeit, with even a grand piano for anyone wishing to practice before bedtime. The hotel has 90 rooms, with different levels of plumbing, which naturally affect the room rate. Singles range from 90 DM ($29.70) to 120 DM ($39.60), and doubles cost from 120 DM ($39.60) to 175 DM ($57.75). The hotel has an interior patio, a sauna, a whirlpool, and solar facilities, plus an elevator designed to accommodate wheelchairs.

Rieker, 3 Friedrichstrasse (tel. 22-13-11), across the street from the Hauptbahnhof, is an elegantly furnished, modern hotel. Its public rooms have lots of comfortably upholstered and matching armchairs, along with tastefully chosen Oriental rugs scattered over the parquet or terrazzo floors. Some of the bedrooms, most of which are different, are designed with sleeping alcoves and draw curtains. The units are virtually soundproof from the traffic outside. All accommodations have toilet and private bath (or shower), and many contain radio and TV. You'll be only a one-minute walk from Stuttgart's city air terminal, where buses leave frequently for Echterdingen Airport. The bilingual management charges from 95 DM ($31.35) to 125 DM ($41.25) in a single and from 145 DM ($47.85) to 165 DM ($54.45) in a double.

Hotel Ruff, 21 Friedhofstrasse (tel. 25-01-61). Some of the side benefits of this modern hotel make it all the more worthwhile to stay here. They include subtly lit tiled bathrooms, an attractively tiled indoor pool with a sauna, and a manicured garden where a waiter will take your drink order. The service, much of which is performed by Frida and Kurt Ruff, is friendly and helpful, and the dining room is an attractive place in which to eat if you're tired after a long trip. Singles, depending on whether or not there is a private bath, cost 89 DM ($29.37) to 111 DM ($36.63), and doubles range from 134 DM ($44.22) to 148 DM ($48.84), including breakfast, the only meal served.

Hotel Wartburg, 49 Lange Strasse (tel. 22-19-91), lies one block off the main thoroughfare of the Theodor-Heuss-Strasse. This boxy modern hotel has some flowers scattered through its balconies and a row of glass windows on the ground floor. The comfortable bedrooms, for the most part, are in earth tones. In the spacious lobby area, guests register for rooms, costing from 55 DM ($18.15) to 120 DM ($39.60) in a single and from 95 DM ($31.35) to 145 DM ($47.85) in a double, depending on the plumbing.

Hotel Unger, 17 Kronenstrasse (tel. 29-40-41), lies about a block away from the main train station. The blank facade of this modern hotel welcomes visitors with its simple but fairly distinguished decor and friendly reception. It's within walking distance of the shopping center, Königstrasse. Single rooms cost 110 DM ($36.30) to 152 DM ($50.16), and doubles range from 163 DM ($53.79) to 200 DM ($66), including breakfast.

The Budget Hotels

Hotel Mack, 7 Kriegerstrasse (tel. 29-19-27), is a fairly modern little hotel on a hillside ledge, an eight-minute walk from the railway station. Home-like and cozy, it offers up-to-date bedrooms that are small and basic, but quite adequate. Bathless singles go for 60 DM ($19.80), 105 DM ($34.65) with shower. A double with shower costs 150 DM ($49.50), dropping to 108 DM ($35.64) without bath. An elevator has been installed and there's a telephone in each room.

Hotel Pflieger, 9-11 Kriegerstrasse (tel. 22-18-78), is a tiny economy hotel, just eight minutes from the railway station. The Lehr family, who run it, also own the previously recommended Mack. Its lobby is miniature, but the bedrooms are well equipped and comfortable. There is a place to park your car, plus an elevator to take you to your room. In a double with shower or bath, the charge ranges from 130 DM ($42.90) to 160 DM ($52.80). A bathless single costs 60 DM ($19.80), going up to 105 DM ($34.65) with bath. The Pflieger is in a good area, central to sights you can set out for after having breakfast (included in the room price) in the pleasant modern salon.

Hotel Wörtz-Zur Weinsteige, 30 Hohenheimer Strasse (tel. 24-06-81). The amber lights of a weinstube welcome visitors to this, one of my favorite hotels in Stuttgart. Paneling covers parts of the walls of the bedrooms, which are practically furnished, sometimes with massive hand-carved armoires. All rooms are soundproof and air-conditioned. The weinstube is perfect for relaxing with a beer or a glass of wine after a long trip. It evokes the feeling that you're in some remote corner in Swabia. Depending on the plumbing, single rooms range from 60 DM ($19.80) to 130 DM ($42.90), and doubles cost 90 DM ($29.70) to 155 DM ($51.15).

WHERE TO DINE: **Alte Post,** 43 Friedrichstrasse (tel. 29-30-79), is most recommendable, both for its cuisine and high standards of service. Featuring an old tavern ambience, it provides the finest cuisine in Stuttgart. The hors d'oeuvres are superb, including coquilles St-Jacques à la Nantaise. A clear oxtail soup might get you going. Among fish dishes, I'd suggest the marvelous sole soufflé Alte Post. A special dish is rehschnitzel (venison) Waidmannsheil with spätzle. Desserts include an apple cake with vanilla sauce. Luncheon menus range from 45 DM ($14.85) to 60 DM ($19.80), and the cost of an à la carte dinner could go from 50 DM ($16.50) to 90 DM ($29.70). Hours are noon to 2:30 p.m. and 6 to 11 p.m. daily except Sunday. Stuttgart is modern, but this mellow inn, with its antique interior, provides a comfortable link with the Germany of old.

Zeppelin-Stüble, in the Steigenberger Hotel Graf Zeppelin, 7 Arnulf-Klett-Platz (tel. 29-98-81), is furnished with Swabian antiques and concentrates on local specialties, such as Schwäbisches Vesper (a variety of Swabian cold meats), along with such classic local fare as Schwäbischer rostbraten and apfelküchle. In all, eight daily dishes are offered, with menus ranging from 18 DM ($5.94) to 32 DM ($10.56). Service is continuous from 11 a.m. to midnight. And on the same premises you can patronize the elegantly appointed **Restaurant Graf Zeppelin,** where each dish is individually prepared from fresh ingredients. The menu is constantly changed according to the season. Gourmets ask for lobsters and coquilles St-Jacques in puff pastry, along with veal liver in cassis sauce with leeks, and a Viennese tafelspitz, among other delicacies. Twice a week, duck, lamb, and fresh herbs are delivered direct from Paris markets. The cheese selection is stunning—40 different types (the oldest from 1891). They offer about 75 types of German wines. Menus cost from 55 DM ($18.15). Hours are noon to 2:30 p.m. and 6 to 10:30 p.m. except Saturday and Sunday.

Fernsehturm Restaurant, in the Degerloch suburb of Stuttgart (tel. 24-61-

04), is for dining high in the sky. A tourist novelty, it simultaneously gives you good food and a panoramic orientation to Stuttgart. For 4 DM ($1.32) you'll be whisked to the top and can choose between two restaurants (the lower one is more expensive). The menu is à la carte, with most meals costing from 50 DM ($16.50). Hours are 9 a.m. to midnight daily. On a higher level is a coffeeshop, where you can order both lunch and bar snacks, with tourist menus priced from 22 DM ($7.26). At the bottom of the tower there are two restaurants, one in a Black Forest motif, with a garden terrace in the midst of an old forest. The tower is ten minutes by car from the city center and the airport, up a steep, winding road. (For a more detailed description, refer to the sightseeing section, coming up.)

Guts-Stuben, 11 Kernerstrasse (tel. 43-37-77), is a well-run weinhaus and restaurant that lies in the vicinity of the railway station and the city center. The proprietors, Gabriele and Benno Oberle, provide a personal service from their large and varied menu. The regional specialties are recommended. Meals cost from 35 DM ($11.55). It is open Monday to Friday from 11 a.m. to 2 p.m. and 5 p.m. to midnight, until 5 p.m. on Saturday; closed Sunday.

Oxie's Restaurant, 5 Karl-Schurz-Strasse (tel. 26-16-31). A gastronomic experience at this elegant restaurant might include some of the most time-tested dishes in the German repertoire as well as an array of nouvelle cuisine specialties made with very fresh ingredients. Martin Öxle, the owner, named his establishment after a nickname his friends have for him. His menu is almost rewritten at the beginning of each week, allowing his creative touch to manifest itself in his array of game, shellfish, fish, and truffles, along with both the red and white meats his clients consume with much gusto. The dozen or so beautifully set tables require an advance reservation. Fixed-price meals cost between 75 DM ($24.75) and 115 DM ($37.95), while à la carte dinners range between 60 DM ($19.80) and 135 DM ($44.55). The establishment serves lunch from noon to 2 p.m. and dinner from 6:30 p.m. to midnight every day except Sunday and holidays. On Monday, only dinner is served.

Zur Weinsteige, 30 Hohenheimer Strasse (tel. 24-53-96), in the Hotel Wörtz, was previously recommended as a hotel. The interior of this place might be called a celebration of German handicrafts. Everything looks handmade, from the hand-blown leaded glass in the small-paned windows to the carved columns and tables and chairs. As for gastronomy, the chef painstakingly prepares a wholesome, international cuisine, with numerous regional specialties. In summer you'll be tempted to sit among the grape vines stretching over the sun terrace. Fixed-price meals begin as low as 15 DM ($4.95), ranging upward to 45 DM ($14.85). The weinstube is open from 7 a.m. till midnight, although warm food is available from noon to 2 p.m. and 6 to 10 p.m. It is closed on weekends and holidays.

Alter Simpl, 64 Hohenheimer Strasse (tel. 24-08-21). Rustic and cozy warmth are the trademarks of this Germanic enclave of gemütlichkeit. From the filtered light streaming in through the bull's-eye glass in the leaded windows to the sympathetic chatter of the other guests, this place has much charm. Your host, Jürgen Lausterer, prepares predominantly Swabian specialties, with some nouvelle cuisine entries. Because all the ingredients used are likely to be very fresh and expensive, the menu is costly, ranging from 70 DM ($23.10) to 135 DM ($44.55), the latter a *menu gastronomique* of gourmet specialties. Hours are 6 p.m. till 1 a.m. daily.

Mövenpick Restaurant, 11 Kleiner Schlossplatz (tel. 22-00-34), part of the Swiss chain, has an unbelievably varied menu, including roast sirloin of Angus beef. There's nothing impersonal about this place, even though it's part of a chain. The food is consistently superior, the service friendly and professional.

Dinners cost from 35 DM ($11.55) to 70 DM ($23.10). The restaurant serves from 10 a.m. till midnight, and a café on the premises opens for breakfast at 7:30 a.m. Here meals served throughout the day cost from 22 DM ($7.26). There's also a pub.

Dining in the Environs of Stuttgart

Hotel Traube, 2 Brabandtgasse, Plieningen (tel. 45-48-33). By now an experienced mistress of her craft, the head chef of this establishment, Marianne Recknagel, after 30 years is still in charge of the delectable concoctions coming from the kitchens of this restaurant established in 1720. Her cookery could consist of, for example, Breton lobster, delicately seasoned Atlantic fish imported from France, fresh salads with wild mushrooms, and in season, just about any variety of fresh game found in Germany. Note: If arranged in advance and if your appetite is big enough, Chef Recknagel will serve you a crackling and succulent young pig, cooked in its own juices, for you and your party. Menus cost around 120 DM ($46.80) for a gourmet feast at this rustically paneled and cozy restaurant. Simpler meals are served from 18 DM ($7.02) to 60 DM ($23.40). It's open throughout the day until midnight, but closed on weekends.

Gasthaus Lamm, 24 Mühlstrasse (tel. 85-36-15), at Feuerbach, lies in a suburb of Stuttgart. The residents there have known for years about the good food available at this guest house. Nouvelle cuisine is served here, with a few regional dishes too, but overall the cookery looks westward to France. Try a clear truffled broth, dubbed "Paul Bocuse," or a sweetbread soup flavored with cream and basil, perhaps goose liver steeped in cider, or a filet of loup de mer (sea bass) in a saffron-flavored sauce. "Gala menus" range in price from a low of 50 DM ($16.50) to a high of 90 DM ($29.70). The restaurant has only six tables so reservations are imperative. It serves from noon to 2 p.m. and 7 to 9 p.m., but is closed all day on Saturday.

Gasthof Zum Löwen, 2 Veitstrasse (tel. 53-22-26), at Mühlhausen, has been under the same management for three generations. The current owners, Friedrich Nagel and his family, serve frequently changing menus, costing from 35 DM ($11.55) to 65 DM ($21.45). Cooking consists of both regional and French specialties, the repertoire including such delectable items as fresh asparagus in season, goose, crayfish, pheasant, and many kinds of fish. Service is from 11 a.m. to 2:30 p.m. and 5:30 to 11 p.m. It is closed Sunday and Monday and from July 10 to August 10 every year.

Waldhotel Schatten, 2 Im Gewandschatten (tel. 68-10-51), in Vaihingen-Büsnau. In winter here, meals are served around a blazing open hearth, while in summer they're most often taken on the outdoor terrace. Food in this suburban location is rustically Swabian, with regional specialties featuring the inevitable fish and game specialties. Continually open, the kitchen offers fixed-price menus costing from 25 DM ($8.25) to 45 DM ($14.85).

Hirsch-Weinstuben, 9 Maierstrasse (tel. 71-13-75), in Möhringen, is attractively rustic, with forest-green curtains, a wooden ceiling, and lots of hand-painted plates hanging on the walls. This popular restaurant is run by Martin and Heiderose Frietsch, who prepare with small-town gusto the kinds of Swabian specialties the local diners prefer. These are likely to include a ragoût of oxtail, perhaps rostbraten with cabbage, and in season, an array of game dishes. Reservations are suggested, especially since the suburb of Möhringen is a few kilometers outside of Stuttgart. Meals begin at 40 DM ($13.20), ranging upward, and they're served from noon to 2 p.m. and 6 to 10 p.m. except Sunday and holidays (and for three weeks at some point in summer).

THE SIGHTS: Many of the most remarkable structures in today's Stuttgart are of advanced technological design, created by such architects as Mies van der Rohe, Gropius, Scharoun, and Le Corbusier. There is another side to the city, however. Clustered around the Schillerplatz and the 19th-century statue of that German poet and dramatist is the Old Town. But it is to the modern buildings that visitors are attracted; the **Liederhalle,** constructed in 1956 of concrete, glass, and glazed brick, is fascinating inside and out. The hall contains three auditoriums so acoustically perfect that all can stage concerts at the same time and not disturb the others. The ultramodern **City Hall** faces the old Marketplace where flowers, fruits, and vegetables are still sold in open stalls.

For the best view of the city, you can climb to the top of the 1680-foot **Birkenkopf** to the west of the city. The hill is composed of the debris of Stuttgart gathered after the air raids of World War II. The 20-minute walk to the top will be rewarded by a view of Stuttgart and the surrounding Swabian Hills, covered with vineyards and woods.

The **Television Tower** (Fernsehturm), south of the city (just off Route 3), offers an outstanding view of Stuttgart from a unique location. The 712-foot tower was considered an innovative design when it was constructed in 1956. You can take the elevator up 492 feet to the restaurant and observation platforms for 4 DM ($1.32).

The **castle,** in the old town facing the Schillerplatz, is one of Stuttgart's oldest standing structures. The huge ducal palace was originally built in the 13th century as a moated castle, but was renovated in the 16th century to a more comfortable Renaissance style and now houses the **Württembergisches Landesmuseum** (State of Württemberg Museum), which traces the art and culture of Swabia from the Stone Age to the present day. The richest pieces are displayed in the Dürnitzbau, including a survey of handicrafts in Europe, the ducal art chamber, and the Württemberg Crown Treasure, the latter containing the biggest collection of Swabian sculpture. Look also for an exhibition of costumes and musical instruments. A Roman Lapidarium is on view in the Stiftsfruchtkasten. Also on display is one of the biggest collections of the Early Middle Ages in Germany, comprising the third to the eighth centuries A.D., the Merovingian period. The museum is open daily except Monday from 10 a.m. to 5 p.m. (on Wednesday till 7 p.m.), charging no admission.

The **State Gallery of Stuttgart,** 30-32 Konrad-Adenauer-Strasse (tel. 08-50-50), is the city's finest art museum, exhibiting works spanning some 700 years. However, the best collection is from the 19th and 20th centuries, especially the works of the modern German expressionists—Kirchner, Barlach, and Beckmann—as well as representatives of the Bauhaus movement, Klee and Feininger. The largest collection of non-German painters is the group of works by French artists of the 19th and 20th centuries, including Manet, Cézanne, Gauguin, Renoir, Picasso, Braque, and Léger, and by the European and American avant garde after World War II. The museum is open daily except Monday from 10 a.m. to 5 p.m. (on Tuesday and Thursday until 8 p.m.). Admission is free.

4. Tübingen

Often compared to Heidelberg, this quiet old university town on the upper Neckar has a look and personality all its own. The gabled medieval houses are crowded up against the ancient town wall at the bank of the river. In the summer the only movement to break this peaceful picture are the students poling gondola-like boats up and down the river. This far upstream, 25 miles south of Stuttgart, the Neckar is too shallow for commercial vessels, and Tübingen has been spared the industrial look of a trading community.

Progress has not passed the city by, however. In spite of its medieval look, it has a new residential and science suburb in the shadow of the Schoenbuch Forest north of the city, with medical facilities, research institutes, and lecture halls affiliated with the university. North of the botanical gardens stand the buildings of the old university, founded in 1477. Most of the buildings are in a functional neoclassical design, but they fit right in with the old city around them.

A unique feature of Tübingen is the man-made island in the Neckar, with its promenade lined with plane trees. This street, known as the **Platanenallee,** is always alive with summer strollers who cross from the main town via the wide Eberhardt Bridge. The island also offers the best view of the town, with its willows and houses reflected in the river. Towering above the roofs is the Renaissance castle, used by departments of the university. Visitors to Tübingen should go to the castle, at least for the dramatic view from the terraces.

The narrow streets of the Old Town wind up and down the hillside, but they all seem to lead to the **Marketplace,** where festive markets are still held today. You'll feel like you're stepping into the past when you come upon the scene of country women selling their fruits and vegetables in the open square. In the center of all this activity stands the softly murmuring Renaissance fountain of the god Neptune. Facing the square is the Rathaus, dating from the 15th century, but with more recent additions, including the 19th-century painted designs on the facade overlooking the Marketplace.

On the hillside above the Marketplace stands **St. George's Church,** the former monastery church of the Stift, an Augustinian monastery. The monastery became a Protestant seminary in 1548 and its church the Collegiate church. Worth seeing inside are the tombs of the dukes of Württemberg in the chancel and the French Gothic pulpit and rood screen, dating from the 15th century.

FOOD AND LODGING: Krone Hotel, 1 Uhlandstrasse (tel. 3-10-36). The university town's most tasteful and prestigious hotel is right off the river, in the heart of Tübingen. The hotel, dating from 1885, is both traditional and conservative. The interior has a home-like atmosphere with a liberal use of antiques or good reproductions. The dining salon has white Louis XVI–style chairs, red velvet draperies, and a niche with an antique statue. The Uhlandstube, on the other hand, is more informal, with an old tavern atmosphere of beamed ceilings, leaded-glass windows, ladderback chairs, and paneled wainscoting. There is yet another provincial dining room with paneled booths and country chairs.

The bedrooms are consistent with the public rooms, all personalized with a well-planned arrangement of furniture. Many of the baths are decoratively tiled, with stall showers, and nearly all rooms have private facilities. Singles cost from 85 DM ($28.05) to 150 DM ($49.50) and doubles run 145 DM ($47.85) to 230 DM ($75.90). The owners, Karl and Erika Schlagenhauff, provide some of the best meals in town (recommendable even if you're not an overnighter). The menu is international. Typical dishes include filet of sole fried in butter, wienerschnitzel, and tournedos Rossini. Meals cost from 32 DM ($10.56) to 65 DM ($21.45). Service is from noon to 2:15 p.m. and 6 to 10:30 p.m.

Hotel Stadt Tübingen, 97 Stuttgartner Strasse (tel. 3-10-71), with shrubbery burgeoning on the balconies, looks almost like something you'd find in a subtropical climate. Nonetheless, the well-managed staff and the competent director, Hans Sammet, convince you that the place is pure German, and generous doses of warm, up-to-date comfort are applied. The hotel was renovated in 1985, and a section was built around a sunny atrium accented with live plants. Each accommodation includes a private bath, TV, phone, and mini-bar, and a buffet breakfast is included in the rates. Single rooms rent for 85 DM ($28.05) to 130 DM ($42.90), while doubles cost from 120 DM ($39.60) to 150 DM ($49.50).

Hotel Hospiz, 2 Neckarhalde (tel. 2-60-02), is comfortably furnished and subtly lit from the outside, its large windows overlooking the cobblestone pavement in front. This is a delightfully old-fashioned hotel, with single rooms beginning at a low of 45 DM ($14.85), climbing to 90 DM ($29.70). Doubles, depending on the plumbing, cost 85 DM ($28.05) to 130 DM ($42.90). The Hospiz is in the old section, and you'll be within walking distance of most of the major sights.

Hotel Am Bad, 2 am Freibad (tel. 7-30-71). Lying in the center of one of Tübingen's well-maintained public parks, this hotel has the added advantage of containing an Olympic-size public swimming pool practically at its back door. The yellow exterior of this rambling hotel contrasts vividly with the masses of red flowers planted on the sun terrace. Inside, the comfortable rooms offer woodland calm not far from the city center. Singles rent for anywhere from 54 DM ($17.82) to 75 DM ($24.75), depending on the bath facilities, and doubles cost 90 DM ($29.70) to 105 DM ($34.65), a breakfast buffet included.

Outside of the hotel dining rooms, the **Restaurant Museum,** 3 Wilhelmstrasse (tel. 2-28-28), is the best independent eatery. The set meal it serves for 32 DM ($10.56) is considered by many locals, including students, not only to be the best meal in town, but the best value as well. The restaurant is rustically sympathetic, a pleasant place to dine on international specialties such as Marseille snail soup or a regional dish such as Swabian medallions of veal. It is open daily from 10 a.m. to midnight except Monday.

Landgasthof Rosenau, Beim Neuen Botanischen Garten (tel. 6-64-66), in the Botanical Gardens, is like a roadhouse with a café-annex. Ernst Fischer, the owner, serves superb Swabian specialties along with dishes from the repertoire of nouvelle cuisine. In fair weather, guests can order drinks outside in the sun. The typical regional fare is listed under the gutbürgerliches selections. Among these, for example, is a tasty and filling beef goulash Stroganoff. Under the section of the menu "reserved for gourmets," you might prefer veal steak with morels. Desserts are often elaborate concoctions, and prices range from 25 DM ($8.95) to 62 DM ($20.46) for a meal. The restaurant serves daily except Tuesday.

Weinstube Forelle, 8 Kronenstrasse (tel. 2-29-38), is one of the most reasonably priced restaurants in town. It serves both lunch and dinner daily except Tuesday and from mid-August to mid-September. Max Rohrer, the owner, offers a wide array of German specialties, many of which include trout (forelle) in one form or another. Other dishes feature omelets, several kinds of beef, pork, veal, and steak. Desserts include the simple but flavorful vanilla ice cream with raspberry sauce. Full meals cost from 18 DM ($5.94) to 35 DM ($11.55).

5. Schwäbisch Hall

Technically, this medieval town is not in the Neckar Valley, but if you skip it in your travels through this region, you will have missed one of the treasures of southwestern Germany. Lying in the heart of the forests of the Swabian Alb, 40 miles east of Heilbronn, the town clings to the steep banks of the Kocher River, a tributary of the Neckar. The houses of the Old Town are set on terraces built into the hillside, and from the opposite bank they appear to be arranged in steps, overlooking the old wooden bridges on the river.

The **Marketplace** is possibly the most attractive in all of Germany. Flanking the square are fine timbered patrician houses and at the lower end of the sloping square, the baroque Rathaus (Town Hall). In the center of the square is a 16th-century Gothic fountain, decorated with statues of St. George and St. Michael. Behind the fountain is a decorative wall holding the pillory, where offenders in days gone by were left to be jeered at by the townspeople. Today the square is the scene of festive occasions, such as the annual Kuchenfest (Salt Maker's Festival), celebrating the ancient industry which grew up around the springs in Schwäbisch Hall.

On the northern side of the Market Square, facing the Town Hall, are the imposing 54 large stone steps, delicately curved, leading up to **St. Michael's Cathedral.** The cathedral is a 15th-century Gothic Hallenkirche with a 12th-century Romanic tower. Many of the pews date from the 15th century, plus St. Michael's altarpiece in the side chapel. The church is open daily from 9 a.m. to noon and 1:30 to 5 p.m. Admission is 1 DM (33¢).

FOOD AND LODGING: Ratskeller, 12 am Markt (tel. 61-81), right on the Market Square, is an attractive stone building, much of it dating from 1400. The hotel has been completely renewed, and its rooms are now of a good standard. A heated swimming pool is a further lure. Singles with toilet and shower cost 77 DM ($25.41) to 104 DM ($34.32), and doubles go for 115 DM ($37.95) to 220 DM ($72.60), breakfast included. A sauna bath is extra. Downstairs, the restaurant serves some of the best food in town, with set meals ranging in price from 32 DM ($10.56) to 65 DM ($21.45).

Hotel Hohenlohe, 14 Weilertor (tel. 61-16), is a modern hotel, built beside the Kocher River in the historic Freie Reichsstadt district. From its bedroom floors a dramatic view unfolds. The accommodations are comfortable and compact, with bright color accents. All of them contain private bath as well. A single rents for 89 DM ($29.37) to 108 DM ($35.64), and a double for 146 DM ($48.18) to 250 DM ($82.50). These rates include breakfast on an open-view roofdeck. The hotel's restaurant offers set meals for 28 DM ($9.24) to 64 DM ($21.12), the latter including, on one recent occasion, crab cocktail and roast pheasant. The family of Theo Dürr is most hospitable. On the premises is a swimming pool, both indoor and outdoor, and in addition to the restaurant there are a cafeteria and bar. Other facilities include a sauna, solarium, and massage parlor.

Hotel Simon, 25 Schweickerweg (tel. 27-37). The facade of this modern concrete hotel is relieved somewhat by the skillful use of planting and the flowers that someone has placed in boxes on the balconies. Ten minutes by car from the center of town, it has a public swimming pool within easy reach. All rooms have private toilet along with a bath (or shower), costing 65 DM ($21.45) in a single, rising to 108 DM ($35.64) in a double, with breakfast included.

Café Scholl, 3 Klosterstrasse (tel. 67-95), is beautifully located on the medieval square to the side of Michaeliskirche. This hotel is made up of the union of two very old half-timbered houses, one pumpkin colored, the other in olive green. You'll find plenty of visitors enjoying the café's sun terrace in front, overlooking the Marketplace. Doubles, including breakfast, shower, and toilet, rent for 98 DM ($32.34), while singles cost 68 DM ($22.44) on the same arrangement.

From the Neckar, we travel to another major river of tourist interest, the Mosel.

Chapter VII

THE MOSEL VALLEY

1. Trier (Trèves)
2. Zell
3. Traben-Trarbach
4. Bernkastel-Kues
5. Beilstein
6. Cochem
7. Eltz Castle

THOSE RETURNING from Germany singing the praises of the Rhine as the most scenic of German rivers have definitely not taken the short trip up the Mosel River. Weaving its snake-like path through the mountains west of the Rhineland, the Mosel (Moselle) encounters town after town whose sole purpose seems to be to beautify the banks of the river. Nearly every village and every hill has its own castle or fortress, surrounded by vineyards where young, green grapes are grown for the popular wines.

Many of the Mosel wines are superior to those of the Rhine Valley, and in spite of their lightness, they are rich and full-bodied wines. Mosel wines have the lowest alcoholic content, only about 9%, of any white wine in the world. Because of this, they are best enjoyed in their youth. Their freshness deteriorates with age.

The Mosel begins in the hills of France, and its most colorful portion is the last 120 miles before it flows into the Rhine at Koblenz. Along these banks, the visitor enjoys the liveliest landscapes, the most legend-rich countryside, and of course the best wines. In recent years, locks have been built at strategic points along the river to enable vessels to sail the waters that once transported Roman ships. The locks have been incorporated into the landscape, and thus far have not hurt the appearance of the river.

If you enter Germany via France or Luxembourg, the Mosel is a good route by which to begin your tour of the German countryside. By following its path through the mountains, you'll first arrive at the major city of . . .

1. Trier (Trèves)
As the Romans spread out over Europe, they established satellite capitals and imperial residences for ruling their distant colonies. Of all the subcapitals, only August Treverorum (Trier) became known as Roma Secunda (the second

Rome). For nearly five centuries, well into the Christian era it remained one of Europe's most powerful cities, politically, culturally, and religiously.

Officially founded by the Romans under Augustus in 16 B.C., the history of Germany's oldest city actually dates back much further. In 2000 B.C., according to legend, the Assyrians established a colony here, and archeological findings indicate an even earlier civilization. Most of the buildings and monuments still standing today, however, date from Roman and later periods.

Trier is an important gateway, lying on the western frontier of Germany. Just six miles from the Luxembourg border, it is the first major city on the Mosel, a very German city, rich in art, festivities, and tradition. It became an important market city in 958, a fact commemorated by the Market Cross placed in the old Hauptmarkt by the archbishop. Because of its location, it is one of Germany's largest exporters of wine, as a visit to the huge wine vaults beneath the city will confirm. Tours of the vaults and special wine tastings (from 10 a.m. to 6 p.m.) can be arranged through the **city tourist office** at An der Porta Nigra (tel. 4-80-71). There you can also purchase a "Go-as-You-Please" ticket for one day, which is valid for use on all public transport in the central zone of Trier. The cost is 5 DM ($1.65) for adults, 2.50 DM (83¢) for children 6 to 15 years of age.

BOAT TRIPS ON THE MOSEL: In summer there are regular cruises and occasional excursions by boat starting from the town port, Zurlauben. The boats go from Trier to Koblenz, a two-day tour, stopping at little Mosel villages along the way. The tourist office has all the details about these excursions, which fluctuate from season to season and vary widely in price.

THE SIGHTS: When the last Roman prefect departed Trier in about 400, he left behind a vast collection of monuments to the centuries of Roman domination. The **Porta Nigra** (Black Gate) is the best preserved Roman relic in Germany, the only survivor of the great wall that once surrounded Trier. The huge sandstone blocks, assembled without mortar, were held together with iron clamps, the marks of which can still be seen in the blackened stones. From the outside of the gate, the structure appeared to be simply two arched entrances between rounded towers leading directly into the town, but intruders soon discovered that the arches only opened into an inner courtyard where they were at the mercy of the protectors of the town.

During the Middle Ages the Greek hermit Simeon, later canonized, chose the east tower as his retreat. After his death the archbishop turned the gate into a huge double church. When Napoleon invaded the Mosel, however, he ordered all the architectural changes to be removed and the original Roman core restored. The Porta Nigra is open daily from 9 a.m. to 1 p.m. and 2 to 6 p.m. in summer (closes at 5 p.m. off-season). It is also closed on Monday off-season. Admission is 1 DM (33¢).

The **Imperial Palace** district, stretching along the site of the former eastern wall of the city, begins with the huge Roman palace known today as the **Basilica.** Although much of the original structure, built in A.D. 310, has been demolished, the huge hall that remains gives some idea of the grandeur of the original palace. Believed to be the throne room, its hall is 220 feet long, 90 feet wide, and 98 feet high. The windows are arranged in two tiers within high-rising arches in which fragments of some of the original wall paintings can be seen. The unique method of Roman central heating through ducts beneath the floor was used to warm this hall from five large heating chambers outside the walls. Today the parish church of the Protestant community is housed within the northern end.

Adjacent to the Basilica is the **Kurfürstliches Palais** (Electoral Palace) built in the 17th century as the residence for the archbishops and electors. Originally designed in the style of the German Renaissance, the rebuilding in the 18th century created a more baroque appearance with the addition of a rococo wing facing the **Palace Gardens.** The formal gardens, full of ponds and flowers, are decorated with rococo statues.

The **Imperial Baths,** at the south end of the Palace Gardens, were erected in the early fourth century by Constantine I. Of the huge complex more than 284 yards wide, only the ruins of the hot baths remain. These baths were among the largest in the Roman Empire, and although never completed, were used in connection with the Imperial Palace, and built about the same time.

The **Amphitheater,** just outside the site of the old Roman walls, is the oldest Roman construction in Trier, dating from A.D. 100. The stone seats, arranged in three circles separated by broad promenades, held a capacity of nearly 20,000 people.

St. **Peter's Cathedral,** north of the Palace Gardens and Basilica, incorporated part of the former palace (fourth century) of the Empress Helena, mother of Constantine, into its precincts. This structure influenced the style adopted by the archbishop when he added the Romanesque facade in the 11th century. The Gothic and baroque additions in later centuries only helped to pull the ecclesiastical architecture into a timeless unity. The interior is also unique, combining baroque furnishings with the Gothic vaulting and archways. The treasury contains many important works of art, including the tenth-century St. Andrew's altar, an unusual portable altar, if you could lift it, made of gold. But the most valuable treasure is the Holy Robe, alleged to be the seamless garment of Christ, brought to Trier by the Empress Helena. The relic is so fragile that it is only displayed every 30 years (last shown in 1959).

The **Liebfrauenkirche** (Church of Our Lady), separated from the cathedral by a narrow passageway, is the parish church of Trier and is more pleasing esthetically than its older sister. The first example of French Gothic in Germany, it was begun in 1235. The ground plan is in the shape of a Greek cross, creating a circular effect with all points equidistant from the central high altar. The structure is supported by 12 circular columns, rather than the typical open buttresses. The interior is bathed in sunlight, which streams through the high transoms. Although the restoration after the war changed some of the effect of the central construction, the edifice is still unique among German churches. Most of the important works of art have been placed in the city's museum; the sepulchre of Bishop Karl von Metternich is among the most interesting of those remaining. The black marble sarcophagus is a sculptured likeness of the canon, who represented the archbishopric during the Thirty Years' War.

The **Rheinisches Landesmuseum,** 44 Ostallee, between the Imperial Roman Baths and the audience hall (Basilica), at the edge of the Palace Gardens behind the medieval city wall, is one of the outstanding museums of Roman antiquities north of the Alps. Numerous reliefs from funerary monuments show daily life in Roman times. The museum's most popular exhibit is the *Mosel Ship,* a sculpture of a wine-bearing vessel crowning a big funerary monument of the third century A.D. Many ornamental and figurative mosaics and frescoes, ceramics, an outstanding numismatic collection, and prehistoric and medieval art and sculpture are also exhibited. The museum is open daily from 9:30 a.m. to 4 p.m., on Saturday to 2 p.m., and on Sunday from 9 a.m. to 1 p.m. Admission is free.

The **Episcopal Museum** (Bischöfliches Museum), 6 Banthusstrasse (tel. 71-05), also near the Palace Gardens, contains valuable pieces of religious art from the Trier diocese. Among the most important is the ceiling painting from Constantine's imperial palace, recently discovered under the cathedral. Also included are medieval sculptures and other works of art from the treasures of the churches of Trier. The museum is open Monday to Friday from 10 a.m. to noon and 2 to 5 p.m., on Saturday and Sunday to 1 p.m. Admission is 1 DM (33¢) for adults, .50 DM (17¢) for children.

UPPER-BRACKET HOTELS: Dorint Porta Nigra, Porta-Nigra-Platz (tel. 2-70-10), offers a desirable accommodation that combines style, comfort, and position. Across from the Roman ruins, it is a six-story modern building whose interior is decorated with primitive colors and contemporary furnishings. However, the grill room is in the old style, with ladderback chairs and wood paneling. The bedrooms are refreshing, particularly those with bright-red sofas, panels of blue draperies, and bone-white walls. Usually, a sitting area is provided. The baths are ornately tiled. Rates depend on the view and size, with singles priced at 108 DM ($35.64) to 133 DM ($43.89); doubles run from 156 DM ($51.48) to 270 DM ($89.10). Guests enjoy drinks in the intimate bar before dining in the traditional restaurant, ablaze with red. A café with an entire wall of glass provides a semipanoramic view of the Roman ruins.

Europa Parkhotel Mövenpick, 29 Kaiserstrasse (tel. 4-00-11). An unusual facade of curved concrete with soundproof windows greets visitors to this ultramodern hotel. Maximum use is made of full-grained and natural building supplies in the public rooms (the modern bar and the rustic weinstube are among my favorites). Bedrooms are international, with all the conveniences of a first-class establishment. Singles rent for 119 DM ($39.27) to 139 DM ($45.87) per day, while doubles cost 163 DM ($53.79) to 178 DM ($58.74), breakfast included.

Holiday Inn, 164 Zurmaienerstrasse (tel. 2-30-91). The establishment makes every effort to reflect local ambience in its restaurants and public rooms, while containing 200 comfortable bedrooms designed in the predictably Holiday Inn international fashion. On the banks of the Mosel, it lies near the autobahn exit labeled "Koblenz–Köln–Trier," some five minutes by car from the city center of Trier. It offers a swimming pool, sauna, free parking, a French restaurant (La Brochette), and a panoramic bar on the 14th floor. Children under 18 can share their parents' room free. Rates are 149 DM ($49.17) to 205 DM ($67.25) in a double room, 113 DM ($37.29) to 123 DM ($40.59) in a single, breakfast included.

MIDDLE-RANGE HOTELS: Petrisberg, 11 Sickingenstrasse (tel. 4-11-81), is beautifully situated at a point where a forest, a vineyard, and a private park meet, with a view over the city of Trier. This intelligently designed four-story hotel offers rooms which contain almost one wall of glass, opening onto a refreshing view of the greenery outside. Furnishings include, for example, full-grained seven-foot armoires and reproductions of slant-topped antique desks. The weinstube on the ground floor is the gathering place for many residents who live nearby, particularly on weekends. Singles go for 75 DM ($24.75), and doubles rent for 85 DM ($28.05) to 105 DM ($34.65), depending on the plumbing. Breakfast is included, and some apartments, suitable for three persons, are available at 155 DM ($51.15) per night.

Am Hügel, 14 Bernhardstrasse (tel. 3-30-66). All the views from the windows of this lovely white house overlook either a private garden with old trees or the city of Trier. You can order food and beverage while sitting on a panoramic terrace. The sitting room/lobby area is decorated with masonry detailing and Oriental rugs, while the bedrooms, in keeping with the age of the house, are spacious and high-ceilinged. The Schütt family are your hosts, renting singles for 60 DM ($19.80) to 70 DM ($23.10) and doubles for 100 DM ($33) to 110 DM

($36.30). All rooms contain bath, toilet, and phone, and a nourishing breakfast is included in the tariffs.

BUDGET HOTELS: Hotel Monopol, 7 Bahnhofsplatz (tel. 7-47-55), is one of your best lodging possibilities if you're seeking a reasonably priced accommodation directly across from the railroad station. The rooms are well kept and of good size, and are reached by elevator. Singles range in price from 48 DM ($15.84) for a bathless room, going up to 61 DM ($20.13) for a unit with more elaborate plumbing. In a double without bath the tariff is 80 DM ($26.40), increasing to 105 DM ($34.65) with shower. Some three-bedded rooms, with shower and toilet, are rented for 130 DM ($42.90). The management has employed a helpful staff.

Hotel Kurfürst Balduin, 22 Theodor-Heuss (tel. 2-56-10), lies only one block from the railway station. It is most convenient, yet far enough away to escape the noise coming from the station. The bedrooms have been remodeled, and each unit is neat, clean, and comfortable. The most expensive doubles (those with shower and toilet) range in price from 95 DM ($31.35) to 108 DM ($35.64). Even cheaper doubles, containing only a shower, cost from 80 DM ($26.40) to 90 DM ($29.70). The bargain specials are the bathless doubles, costing 75 DM ($24.75) to 85 DM ($28.05). Single units with hot and cold running water rent for 55 DM ($18.15), going up to 70 DM ($24.75) with private bath. These tariffs include a continental breakfast, service, and taxes. The innkeeper's wife, Hella Schwarz, just can't seem to do enough for you to make your stay enjoyable. She'll give recommendations and directions for shops, restaurants, and sightseeing, and is in general a warm, friendly person. Readers have liked the old-fashioned charm of the hotel. Guests who don't seem to mind the lack of an elevator gather in the lounge-coffee room to watch television.

Deutschherrenhof, 32 Deutschherrenstrasse (tel. 4-83-08), is identified by an elegantly discreet entrance with an olive-drab awning over the door. The bedrooms are modern and comfortable, and the hotel stands in the middle of town, with an attractive bar and dining area in simple lines. Double rooms cost 78 DM ($25.74) to 88 DM ($29.04) and singles run 45 DM ($14.85) to 60 DM ($19.80), depending on the floor you're on and the plumbing.

Kessler, 23 Brückenstrasse (tel. 7-35-61). Because of its position on an acute angle of a downtown street corner, this modern hotel has direct sunlight from three sides. It offers attractively maintained single rooms for 55 DM ($18.15) to 90 DM ($29.70) and doubles for 90 DM ($29.70) to 130 DM ($42.90), breakfast included. The hotel is under the friendly administration of Jörg Mueller, who speaks some English, and does everything he can to make your stay pleasant. Most of the rooms have a private shower, toilet, and phone. Guests gather in the evening in the hotel's cozy bar.

WHERE TO DINE: Zum Domstein, 5 Hauptmarkt und Dom (tel. 7-44-90), overlooking the flowerstands and the fountain on the Hauptmarkt, is my preferred choice for dining. Opening onto an inner courtyard, it features authentic local cuisine and sets a high culinary standard. The three dining rooms have a true gemütlich atmosphere, in the best of the Germanic tavern tradition. English is spoken. No matter what you order, it's traditional to test the Mosel, Saar, and Ruwer wines. For 10 DM ($3.30) you're given six different wines of the local region, lined up so that you can drink them in proper order. In addition, 14 open wines and about 200 bottled ones are in the cellar awaiting your selection. No matter what you decide to eat, the dish at the next table will appear more tempting. A typical Germanic offering is Rheinischer sauerbraten, kartoffelklosse, and apfelkompott. The restaurant opens at 8 a.m., closing at midnight. Expect to spend from 20 DM ($6.60) to 50 DM ($16.50) to dine here. In winter you'll want to find a spot near a huge tile stove. You can also have a look at the Römischer Weinkeller. The room is in the area of the double cathedral (from A.D. 326), excavated in 1970. Original Roman artifacts, many of them connected with food and cooking, decorate the cellar room. In the Römischer Weinkeller you are served dishes prepared according to recipes attributed to Marcus Gavius Apicius, said to have been the foremost chef at the court of the Roman Emperor Tiberius.

Pfeffermühle, 76 Zurlaubener Ufer (tel. 4-13-33), in Zurlauben. How do you make a successful restaurant in Trier? Siegbert and Angelika use fresh ingredients, work long hours at skillfully crafting a reputation for a delectable French cuisine, and welcome diners to a friendly, well-decorated room with a beamed ceiling and lots of light. At least that's what has worked for this "Peppermill," a high-quality restaurant (many critics consider it "the best" in Trier). Charging 45 DM ($14.85) to 80 DM ($26.40) for dinner, it's open from noon to 2 p.m. and 6 to 10 p.m. daily, except Sunday and holidays (closed for three weeks from mid-July).

Lenz Weinstuben, 4-5 Vichmarkt-Platz (tel. 4-53-10), is located near the city's slaughterhouse and stockyards. It attracts clients familiar with quality meats. The maître d'hôtel encourages clients to order one of the excellent daily fixed-price specials which vary, naturally, according to the season. Count on spending around 50 DM ($16.50). Everything served is wholeheartedly German, with such local specialties as Trierer meat pie or a medallion of lamb in white wine with onion and potato disks. Service is from 11 a.m. to 1 a.m. daily except Monday.

Brasserie, 12 Fleischstrasse (tel. 7-52-31), is on the bottom floor of a beautifully maintained art nouveau house near the Hauptmarkt. A pub-style restaurant, it serves the finest fish and wild-game dishes in its price range in Trier. Fixed-price menus cost 32 DM ($10.56) to 55 DM ($18.15). Everything is superfresh here. Recipes feature international dishes at night, but at lunch there's a special emphasis on seasonal cookery. Try, for example, filet of doe in a wild mushroom cream sauce or ham served in a variety of ways, perhaps a filet of veal in a white wine sauce, and certainly marinated pork cooked by a special recipe. Food is served daily, except Sunday and holidays, from 10:30 a.m. till 1 a.m.

Im Simeonstift Brunnenhof, at the Porta Nigra (tel. 4-85-84), is nestled in historic ruins, occupying a portion of an old cloister and providing an excellent place at which to dine. You select a table in what was once a great hall, or in fair weather you may prefer the courtyard, where you can enjoy the splashing fountain and the purity of line of the Roman arches. The food is somewhat standardized, but good. Set meals in the 18-DM ($5.94) to 45-DM ($14.85) range are offered from 11:30 a.m. to 2:30 p.m.

Leaving Trier, you may want to consider the following stopover on the route to Zell.

WINTRICH: This is an attractive little Mosel wine village extending along the river. It lies at a half-moon curve of the Mosel, and in the distance you can see slopes planted with vineyards on sunny wine terraces. Don't come here seeking much excitement: it's mainly for relaxation.

However, if you lodge overnight you can go for a walk through nearby vineyards the next day. From the village, you can also branch out on a number of excursions—to the Hunsrück hills, including Idar-Oberstein, to the Eifel Mountains with their volcanic lakes, and to the castles along the Mosel.

For a combination weinstube/hotel/pension, I'd recommend **St. Michael** (tel. 233), run by the friendly, English-speaking Quint family on a spot that traces its history back to 1602. Next to the river, the old house presents a view not only of the Mosel with a dam, but of the wine hills in the distance. Rooms are in the contemporary style, and some of them are equipped with shower and bath. It costs 42 DM ($13.86) to 58 DM ($19.14) per person for half board.

The owners are outstanding vintners in these parts, and they process and mature wine in the old wooden vats in the cellars. Homemade beverages are distilled from the family's old established recipes. During your stay, they'll take you on a guided tour of the caves, and you can "slurp" and sample glasses of wine from different casks the way connoisseurs do. They have their own stock of wines, *eaux de vie,* and other drinks for sale by the bottle.

Facilities include not only a large sun terrace, but a gym as well, along with a sauna and solarium. Motorists will find a good-size car park. In the old German-style tavern, meals, costing from 25 DM ($8.25), and their fine wines are presented. The public rooms are decorated in a regional style, and on nippy nights guests gather in the lounge around the fireplace.

2. Zell

This old village, stretching along the east bank of the Mosel, is best known for its excellent wine, Schwarze Katz (Black Cat). The grape is king here, as you'll realize if you come to Zell during the annual wine festival.

Nowhere does the wine and the festivity of Zell rule more than at the **Schloss Zell,** 8 Schlossstrasse (tel. 40-84), one of the very special places in all of Germany. Installed in a 14th-century castle-like bastion, it is run by a family. Right in the heart of Zell, its twin domed towers are a village landmark. Because of high taxes and the ever-constant need for maintenance, the family now receives paying guests (try for the ornate bedroom used by Kaiser Maximilian, the last cavalier, in 1512, or the honeymooners' special in the tower).

The salons and the drawing room are filled with antiques—a flamboyant use of gilt, ornate inlaid woods, stained glass, bronze, and crystal. Be sure to see the settee given to Josephine by Napoleon. Favored guests who stay more than one night are invited into the private drawing rooms, in themselves museums of antiquity. For an accommodation here, you pay 80 DM ($26.40) to 100 DM ($33) in a single, 130 DM ($42.90) to 180 DM ($59.40) in a double. Taxes are included.

Dining at Schloss Zell is a gastronomic event worth crossing the Mosel for—or even the Rhine. One woman makes a weekly pilgrimage here just to sample the vineyard snails in garlic and tarragon. Specialties include freshwater trout, caught in the nearby streams, prepared in Mosel wine. The Mosel eel, also cooked in Mosel wine, is famous. Meals range from 40 DM ($13.20) to 80 DM ($26.40). A special treat: The family is the owner of the original Schwarze Katz (Black Cat) Mosel wine.

Zur Post, 21 Schlossstrasse (tel. 42-17). Painted a delightful shade of canary yellow, this beflowered hotel sits directly on the river. Its sun terrace is the kind of inviting space where you can catch up on your reading or gossip with a friend. The warmly decorated weinstube is the kind of place where you'll meet a new one. Rooms are carpeted, with french doors opening onto the balconies. All units have shower (or bath), and are priced at 39 DM ($12.87) per person daily, breakfast included, regardless of whether you stay in a single or double.

Weinhaus Mayer, 15 Balduinstrasse (tel. 45-30), is named after its founder.

This is a rustic, balconied, five-story hotel offering personalized comfort, usually in a room with a view over the Mosel. A single rents for 35 DM ($11.55) to 50 DM ($16.50), while a double goes for anywhere from 65 DM ($21.25) to 85 DM ($28.05), including breakfast.

On the left bank of the Mosel, 5 miles from Zell and 20 from Cochem, stands the little wine village of **Alf.** The surroundings are idyllic, especially if you climb up to the Marienburg. From there, you get a fine view overlooking the Mosel and the vineyards of Zell.

3. Traben-Trarbach

Thanks to their central location on the Mosel, halfway between Koblenz and Trier, the twin cities of Traben and Trarbach have become the wine capitals of the Mosel Valley. The garden-like promenades on both banks of the river are viewpoints for the annual international speedboat and waterskiing competitions on the Mosel. The July wine festival attracts visitors from all over Europe to the old wine cellars and taverns of the towns. But behind all the bustle and activity, Traben-Trarbach is proud of its attractions, especially its thermal springs and health resort, **Bad Wildstein,** just south of town.

Above Trarbach, on the east bank of the river, stands the 14th-century **Grevenburg Castle,** which, with five other now-in-ruins castles in the vicinity, was the scene of hard-fought battles to gain control of this strategic spot on the Mosel. On the opposite bank, above Traben, are the ruins of **Mont Royal,** a fortress built in the late 17th century by the invading Louis XIV.

FOOD AND LODGING: If you plan to stay over, you might try **Clauss-Feist,** am Moselufer (tel. 64-31), in Traben, a heavily Germanic structure right on the banks of the Mosel. It was created in an ornamental style around 1900 by the architect Moehring, and utilizes such adornments as elaborate timberwork, a domed tower, a highly pitched roof, gables, and dormers. A special feature is the ivy-covered terrace, where you can dine. Inside, stained-glass windows are set in ecclesiastical frames, and overstuffed chairs are drawn up around Victorian fringed "parlor tables," resting under vaulted ceilings. The accommodations are warmly decorated. A bathless single goes for 34 DM ($11.22), increasing to 45 DM ($14.85) with shower or bath and toilet. A bathless double is in the 58-DM ($19.14) to 68-DM ($22.44) range. With shower, you'll pay from 68 DM ($22.44), and up to 88 DM ($29.04) in a double with complete bath. For half board, expect to pay another 20 DM ($6.60) per person daily. It's an architectural hodgepodge, but fun if you're in the mood.

Zur Post, 17 Gestade (tel. 30-01), is a pleasant village inn, with a colorful exterior—shutters, window boxes for summer flowers, tiny windows inserted in the small bedrooms under the eaves, and tubs of flowers on the sidewalk. The Rössling family, your hosts, charge from 42 DM ($13.86) in a single without bath, and from 62 DM ($20.46) to 80 DM ($26.40) in a double, depending on the plumbing. The cuisine is hearty, and the wines are excellent with more than 100 selections. In season, eel is recommended. Zur Post is open from February through November only. It's within walking distance of the town, right below the castle.

Hotel Krone, 93 An der Mosel (tel. 63-63). Only a narrow country lane separates the sun terrace of this attractive hotel from the waters of the Mosel. The architecture might be that of a ski chalet in Aspen, with big glass windows and a modern roofline above the flowers scattered across the balconies. Your helpful host is Kurt Metzger, who sees that the rooms are immaculately maintained and that the service in the dining room is meticulous. All units contain private bath, mini-bar, radio, and TV. Singles rent for 75 DM ($24.75) to 80

DM ($26.40), and doubles cost 106 DM ($34.98) to 112 DM ($36.96), breakfast included.

Altes Gasthaus Moseltor, 1 Moselstrasse (tel. 65-51), on the outskirts, is at Im Ortsteil Trarbach. The exterior of this four-story rectangular building is a masterpiece of fieldstone masonry from another era. Inside, a charming combination of new construction with antique elements from the original building creates a warm mixture of comfort and convenience. The Bauer family runs this hotel, which dates from 1838. They rent singles at a cost of 60 DM ($19.80), and doubles for 45 DM ($14.85) to 60 DM ($19.80) per person, including breakfast. The light nouvelle cuisine food is prepared by chef Friedheinz Eggensperger, whose reputation has spread to such a degree that German urbanites come here for a "gastronomic weekend." The restaurant is small—only 11 tables—with fixed-price menus costing from 45 DM ($14.85) to 85 DM ($28.05) per meal. Hours are daily, except Tuesday, from noon to 2 p.m. and 6 to 9 p.m.

Bisenius, 56 An der Mosel (tel. 68-10), is a family-run modern country-villa-style hotel, with balconies, flowers, a sun terrace with a view of the Mosel, and an indoor swimming pool. The Bisenius family are your hosts here, as the name indicates. They serve breakfast only, allowing you to "cellar-hop" at night. Doubles go for 75 DM ($24.75) to 100 DM ($33), while singles cost 45 DM ($14.85) to 68 DM ($22.44).

Zum Anker, 3 Rissbacher Strasse (tel. 15-64), is attractively decorated with comfortably rustic furniture, sometimes with blond oversize armoires in the bedrooms. This riverfront hotel is efficiently run by the Ningel family. Many of their bedrooms have a riverfront balcony, and if yours doesn't, you can still enjoy sitting at the café/sun terrace, ordering a cup of coffee or a late-night beer. Prices, including breakfast, range from 55 DM ($18.15) to 75 DM ($24.75) in a double and from 45 DM ($14.85) to 55 DM ($18.15) in a single, depending on the plumbing and the time of year. Half board is available for another 25 DM ($8.25) per person.

Central, 43 Bahnstrasse (tel. 62-38), is a five-story, unembellished modern building, in a vaguely rustic shape, which opens to a reproduced gemütlich decor, with bright fabrics and wooden ceilings and benches in one of the dining rooms. Centrally located, as its name implies, it charges from 36 DM ($11.88) to 45 DM ($14.85) in a single and from 62 DM ($20.46) to 75 DM ($24.75) in a double, depending on the plumbing. Your host is Ernest Ochs.

4. Bernkastel-Kues

Like Traben-Trarbach, this town is split into twin villages on opposite banks of the Mosel. In a valley of wine towns, Bernkastel stands out as the most colorful, with its old Marktplatz surrounded by half-timbered buildings in good condition, dating from as early as 1608. In the center of the square stands **St. Michael's fountain** (17th century), which flows with wine during the annual September wine festival. Above the town stand the ruins of the 11th-century **Landshut Castle,** worth a visit for the view of the Mosel from the promontory on which it stands. During the wine festival the castle is lit by floodlights and fireworks.

FOOD AND LODGING: **Drei Könige** (Three Kings), 1 Bahnhofstrasse (tel. 23-27), is an ornate gingerbread relic, standing on the banks of the Mosel at Orsteil Kues. Its architecture is characterized by gables, bay windows, and a timbered tower. In all, there are 41 comfortable bedrooms, many of which contain private bath. To stay here costs 85 DM ($28.05) to 95 DM ($31.35) in a single, 125 DM ($41.25) to 150 DM ($49.50) in a double, depending on the accommodation you select. In the wine cellar you can sample Mosel wine.

Doctor Weinstuben, 5 Hebegasse (tel. 60-81). This intricately half-timbered building wasn't as popular with local residents when it was constructed in 1652 (then it was the headquarters of the tax collector). Today it's perhaps the most visually interesting hotel in Bernkastel. Transformed into a tavern back in 1830, it still has many of its original woodcarvings, including an elaborate double balustrade (the motif in vines and fruits) leading to the upper floors. The rooms are what is called "cozy," and they would serve you well. Doubles go for 98 DM ($32.34), including breakfast. Singles cost from 75 DM ($24.75). The Doctor serves some of the most savory viands in town. Fixed-price menus are offered for 22 DM ($7.26) and 60 DM ($19.80), and are made available from 11:30 a.m. to 2:30 p.m. and 6 to 10 p.m. The kitchen takes a vacation from mid-February to mid-March.

Römischer Kaiser, 29 Markt (tel. 30-38). The peach-colored facade of this hotel covers the angle of two downtown streets, and there's a view of the Mosel from many of the upper floors. Inside, the public rooms are decorated almost like a private home, with paintings, Oriental rugs, and, naturally, lots of tables with elegantly rustic wooden chairs. Including breakfast, a double room goes for 75 DM ($24.75) to 105 DM ($34.65), depending on the plumbing, and singles for 48 DM ($15.84) to 70 DM ($23.10). Many visitors come here just to dine, because the hotel is well known in the region for its gutbürgerlich cookery, using fresh ingredients only (if at all possible). Like any good restaurant along the Mosel, it features the wines of the region. A separate menu lists all the things anyone could possibly do with prawns. Meals cost 20 DM ($6.60) to 60 DM ($19.80). The place is open from 11 a.m. to 9:30 p.m., and closes annually from mid-November to mid-December.

Zur Post, 17 Gestade (tel. 30-01). Constructed as a stopover point for men and their horses on the local postal routes in 1827, this hotel is today directed by Bernhard Rössling. He maintains the pastel yellow and mustard-colored facade in good condition. A view of the interior will reveal an elegantly crafted stairwell flanked by half-timbered walls and a paneled and beamed dining room where excellent regional cookery is served, with 100 varieties of Mosel wine. Even some of the cozy bedrooms have half-timbers. Single rooms go for 45 DM ($14.85) to 60 DM ($19.80), and doubles, depending on the plumbing, range from 66 DM ($21.78) to 78 DM ($25.74). The restaurant, which is open to the "public at large," serves from 11 a.m. to 2:30 p.m. and 5:30 to 10:30 p.m. Fixed-price menus cost from 22 DM ($7.26) to 60 DM ($19.80).

Burg Landshut, 11 Gestade (tel. 30-19). The white neoclassical facade, with its triangular pediment and disciplined windows, seems strangely out of place in this town of rustic dwellings. However, a tour of the downstairs weinstube will eventually reveal heavy beams and a half-timbered bar. Parts of the rest of the hotel contain painstakingly handcrafted herringbone floors and high-ceilinged bedrooms in clear colors. Singles cost 46 DM ($15.18) to 90 DM ($29.70), and doubles go for 75 DM ($24.75) to 135 DM ($44.55). Additional meals go for 25 DM ($8.25) to 60 DM ($19.80).

Gasthof Moselblümchen, 10 Schwanenstrasse (tel. 23-35), lies on a narrow cobblestone street for pedestrians only. A small guest house, it is within walking distance of everything in Bernkastel. It's identified by a wrought-iron sign fastened to the corner of the building. They rent clean and charmingly appointed rooms here, many in irregular shapes. Visitors pay 40 DM ($13.20) to 60 DM ($19.80) in a single, 68 DM ($22.44) to 84 DM ($27.72) in a double. Breakfast is included in the tariffs, and it's also possible to order meals, at 20 DM ($6.60) to 55 DM ($18.15).

Rôtisserie Royale, 19 Burgstrasse (tel. 65-72), is a charmingly embellished half-timbered house whose four narrow stories are sandwiched between its neighbors. In summer geraniums festoon the spaces below the leaded-glass windows which are set on either side of the black-and-gilt sign hanging above the street outside. Hugo König is the owner, who, with his wife, Anita, prepares an imaginative fixed-price menu which changes almost every day. Many of the specialties are grilled by Hugo himself at the charcoal grill which occupies a corner of the intimate, warmly decorated dining room. You might enjoy such specialties as a terrine of pheasant in a madeira-flavored gelatin, a vol-au-vent of seafood with a lobster sauce, and tournedos "royale" with a fennel and tomato sauce. A super-fresh salad, an array of cheeses, and freshly prepared raspberries might accompany your meal, which is likely to cost from 75 DM ($24.75) with some wine included. Reservations are suggested. Only dinner is served, from 6 p.m. till midnight most of the year (from 7 p.m. to 1 a.m. in high season). From mid-November until the end of April the rôtisserie is closed on Tuesday.

5. Beilstein

On the east bank of the Mosel, this ancient wine town has an unusual marketplace hewn right into the rocky hillside. Above the town stands the former cloister church and the ruins of the 12th-century Metternich Castle.

You can sample the wines that made Beilstein famous at its favorite inn, **Haus Lipmann** (tel. 15-73). The centuries pass by, and time has been more than kind to this 1795 timbered inn, in one of the oldest and most unspoiled villages along the Mosel. For six generations the same family has tended the vast riverside vineyards that have won them acclaim. Try either their Ellenzer Goldbäumchen or Beilsteiner Schlossberg.

The spots for drinking and dining are so tempting that it's difficult making a decision. Most popular in summer, however, is the vine-covered terrace, with a statue of Bacchus, overlooking the Mosel. Of course, there's the antique-filled tavern or the wood-paneled Rittersaal, with its collection of old firearms and pewter. Candles are lit at night; in the cooler months, fires burn in either the tall walk-in fireplace or the tiny open hearth, with its copper kettle on a crane. Meals cost from 22 DM ($7.26) to 50 DM ($16.50). The Mosel eel in dill sauce is classic, but especially delectable is the fresh wild trout.

Lucky is the person who can spend the night. Bathless doubles cost only 62 DM ($20.46). A few doubles with shower go for 85 DM ($28.05). Singles rent for 38 DM ($12.54) to 55 DM ($18.15). These rates include breakfast. The bedrooms are furnished in a homey manner—some old pieces, some new, much of undetermined origin. Activities get hectic at grape harvest time. The hotel closes from mid-November to mid-March.

Klapperburg, 34 Marktplatz (tel. 14-37), is imaginatively built into the side of a hill. The masonry and stucco facade of this rustic hotel opens into a series of public rooms decorated in a typically Teutonic style, with rows of antique kitchen utensils, brass and pewter pots, and more than 100 hand-operated coffee grinders. Overnight rates are attractively set at 38 DM ($12.54) to 55 DM ($18.15) in a single, 62 DM ($20.46) to 75 DM ($24.75) in a double, depending on the plumbing. If the Klapperburg is full, the same rates apply at another pension not far away. Called the **Zur Guten Quelle,** it has the same ownership and houses guests in a rustically attractive half-timbered structure.

Burgfrieden, 63 im Mühlental (tel. 14-32). More a complex of buildings than a single hotel, this establishment has proved popular with locals and visitors alike for more than 25 years. It is maintained by Martha Sprenger, who has made ample use of the beamed ceilings and warm-toned fabrics. Comfortable rooms rent here for anywhere from 32 DM ($10.36) to 50 DM ($16.50) per person, including breakfast.

6. Cochem

In one of the best wine regions of the Mosel Valley, this medieval town is crowded against the left bank of the river by a huge vineyard-covered hill. The town is a typical wine village, with its tastings and festivals. But the biggest attraction is **Reichsburg Cochem** (tel. 17-87), a huge castle at the top of the mound behind the town. Originally built in 1027, it was almost completely destroyed by the army of Louis XIV in 1689. It has since been restored after the original ground plans, and its medieval ramparts and turrets create a dramatic backdrop for the town. To reach the castle, follow the steep footpath from the center of town. The 15-minute walk is well worth it for the views of the town below and the Mosel. Although you can visit anytime, the interior of the castle is open from 9 a.m. to 6 p.m. daily. Guided tours are conducted at regular intervals. Admission is 3 DM (99¢) for adults, 2.50 DM (66¢) for children and students. It is open from mid-March to mid-November.

WHERE TO STAY: Alte Thorschenke, 3 Brückenstrasse (tel. 70-59), is both a hotel and a wine/restaurant, one of the oldest, best known, and most colorful along either side of the Mosel. Innkeeping has been refined to its ultimate here, in a romantically conceived building with timbers, towers, and many antiques, including some bedrooms with four-posters. Built originally in 1332, it was remade into a hotel in 1960, when a modern wing was added, offering rooms with private bath. Most of the accommodations have old wooden beds, chests, and armoires. You reach them via a cantilevered wooden staircase that has creaked for centuries—and probably will for a few more. Of course, there is an elevator in the rear if you want to make it easy on yourself. Depending on the plumbing, the single rate ranges from 48 DM ($15.84) to 75 DM ($24.75); the double, from 80 DM ($26.40) to 165 DM ($54.45). If you want a room with one of the old-fashioned beds, ask for the *himmelbetten* (heaven beds). Not to be ignored are meals in the tavern, accompanied by Mosel wines. In the summer guests often take their lunch at one of the sidewalk tables. Meals range in price from 28 DM ($9.24) to 60 DM ($19.80). The castle closes January 5 to March 10.

The 500-year-old castle of Baron von Landenberg in Eller is seven kilometers from Cochem. Guests of the hotel can visit the old cellars and enjoy tasting the wines.

Germania, 1 Moselpromenade (tel. 2-61), is a big, old resort-style hotel, complete with dormers and balconies, as well as dining terraces surrounded by red geraniums. Best of all, it's right on the Mosel, with a view of Cochem Castle. The interior oozes with charm, leaning heavily on traditional wood paneling, provincial antiques, and lots of Teutonic artifacts. Part of the hotel dates back to 1749, but modernization has erased much antiquity. A bathless single ranges in price from 65 DM ($21.45); singles with shower or bath, 85 DM ($28.05). Bathless doubles go from 100 DM ($33), from 130 DM ($42.90) with bath or shower.

Burg Hotel, 23 Moselpromenade (tel. 71-17), is the happy domain of the Müller family, who offer guests a warm and friendly welcome. The family has renovated the inn, providing more private baths, showers, and toilets for the bedrooms. The furnishings are traditional, with a few antiques lending added style, and some rooms have balconies, opening onto views of the Mosel. Bathless singles cost 40 DM ($13.20), increasing to anywhere from 45 DM ($14.85) to 55 DM ($18.15) with bath. Bathless doubles go for 60 DM ($19.80) rising to 100 DM ($33) for the most expensive rooms with private bath. However, the bargain of the house is a double with bath, sans river view, costing only 80 DM ($26.40).

The food is still among the best you may expect in town. Meals begin at 35 DM ($11.55). Specialties include game fricassee with bits of asparagus and rice; trout meunière; and rumpsteak with mushrooms, french fried potatoes, and a salad. A large selection of the best Mosel wines is available to accompany your meal. The hotel offers an indoor swimming pool, sauna, solarium, and TV room.

Lohspeicher, 1 Obergasse (tel. 39-76). A former warehouse for supplies for the local tannery, this generously proportioned building was constructed with lots of hand-hewn beams in 1832. Completely renovated in 1979, it's now a delightfully furnished hotel, serving excellent meals and offering lodging in well-furnished rooms. Bed and breakfast costs from 50 DM ($16.50) per person, and a gourmet meal—considered by many as the best table in town—will cost from 25 DM ($8.25) to 60 DM ($19.80). Specialties include onion or snail soup, followed by all kinds of fish and game specialties (try the filet of venison with wild mushrooms in a cream sauce). The restaurant, open to the public daily except Tuesday, serves from noon to 2 p.m. and 6 to 11 p.m. Manfred Schmidt is your charming host at this hotel, now classified as a historical monument by the German Republic.

Haus Erholung, 65 Moselpromenade (tel. 75-99). The restaurant of this pension is gaily decorated in hanging pink and white lamps, pink and white tablecloths, lots of green plants, and rustic wooden beams supporting the ceiling. The dormers and mansard roof of the house itself indicate that it was probably a private villa before the addition of the sun terrace below it. Many of the double rooms are sunny, with large windows exposing views of the countryside. Your hostess is Hildegunde Lehmann, who will indicate the direction of the sauna and swimming pool, and serve you a wholesome breakfast included in your room rate, which, incidentally, is 74 DM ($24.42) in a double with private toilet and shower. Overflow guests are housed in an annex, which opens onto a view of the river and castle.

Triton, 10 Uferstrasse (tel. 2-18), is the best hotel in Cochem-Cond. One of the finest things about this small balconied hotel is the view of the baroque buildings and the fortified castle that you'll get from your river-view windows. Across the Mosel from the rest of Cochem, the hotel offers single rooms at 63 DM ($20.79) and doubles for 98 DM ($32.34) to 118 DM ($38.94). Units are modern, with glass-topped tables and barrel-shaped armchairs. In keeping with the symbol of the hotel (Neptune's Triton), the hotel also offers an indoor swimming pool with a sauna, plus a waterside café/sun terrace built almost on the banks of the river. The owner's name is Paul Kirstgen.

Am Hafen, 14 Uferstrasse (tel. 84-74), also across the river in Cochem-Cond, stands on the banks of the Mosel. It is a family-run hotel run by the Laux family, who offer comfortable rooms priced at 50 DM ($16.50) per person in a double room with shower and toilet. The four-story, generously proportioned building has terraces and a café on the ground floor. Meals cost from 18 DM ($5.94) to 45 DM ($14.85).

Am Rosenhügel, 57 Valwiger Strasse (tel. 13-96). The Goebel family are the hosts here, in an attractively decorated, big-windowed hotel with balconies and a sun terrace overlooking the Mosel. Some of the rooms offer spectacular views of the castle on the hill, and are decorated in soothing shades of wheat, cream, and brown. Singles rent from 42 DM ($13.86) to 48 DM ($15.84), and doubles cost 80 DM ($26.40) to 90 DM ($29.70), depending on the plumbing and the view.

Moselromantik Hotel-Café Thul, 27 Brauselaystrasse (tel. 71-34), also stands across the river in Cochem-Cond. Comfortably modern, this recently built hotel offers clean rooms and reproduction gemütlichkeit to guests who pay from 40 DM ($13.20) to 60 DM ($19.80) per person in a single or double, break-fast included. Many of the public rooms are somewhat lighter in scale than other hotels in the region, although a few massive pieces of old furniture fill nooks and crannies. The dining room serves good food in a pleasant, comfortable setting.

WHERE TO DINE: Hotel Brixiade, 13 Uferstrasse (tel. 30-15), in Cochem-Cond. The heyday of this hotel was in the period just preceding World War I, when it was a favorite of the poet Joseph von Lauff and of Kaiser Wilhelm II. This place takes itself and its illustrious tradition seriously. Service is friendly, and you can sit either in the weinstube or in the garden. A fixed-price menu begins at 22 DM ($7.26). Order Mosel wine here and you'll get the best of the region. It's open from 7 a.m., and warm food is served 11:30 a.m. to 2:30 p.m. and 6 to 9:30 p.m.

Parkhotel Landenberg, 1 Sehler Anlagen (tel. 71-10), is in Cochem-Sehl, offering a panoramic view of Cochem and the Mosel from its garden terrace. This wine restaurant and café offers some of the best Mosel wine in the region. My favorite dish is a "Landenbergische Jagdherrenplatte," which consists of medallions of doe, stag, and wild boar, served with glazed chestnuts and wild mushrooms. You might also order the pheasant which has been broiled with Calvados and served with sour cream. Meals begin at 25 DM ($8.25), but could climb to 60 DM ($19.80) if you order the specialties. Service is from noon to 2:30 p.m. and 5:30 to 10 p.m.

Weissmühle (tel. 89-55) is in Enterttal, an idyllic hamlet outside of Cochem. It's the home of the "White Mill," which is rustically decorated with comfortably upholstered chairs and beautifully decorated tables. Many of the specialties on the menu are unique culinary inventions of the restaurant, and include a series of wurst dishes, trout, or spiessbraten grilled to perfection over an open fire. Before or after your meal, you'll enjoy a walk through the romantic hamlet. Menus are attractively priced from 20 DM ($6.60) to 50 DM ($16.50), and food is served from 10 a.m. to 9 p.m.

7. Eltz Castle

This magnificent castle, completely surrounded by woodlands, can be reached in about 40 minutes from **Moselkern,** or, more conveniently, in about 15 minutes if you arrive via **Münstermaifeld** (with a remarkably beautiful Gothic abbey church) and **Wierschem.** The original structure, built from the 12th to 17th centuries, has been preserved in all its medieval glory. The romance of the Middle Ages really comes alive here, with no modern conveniences nearby to distract you from your dalliance in history. Completely surrounding a large inner court, the castle houses four separate residences, furnished with pieces from the Gothic period, including some fine old paintings. From April to November 1 the castle is open daily from 9 a.m. to 5:30 p.m. (from 10 a.m. on Sunday). Admission is 5.50 DM ($1.82) for adults, 3.50 DM ($1.16) for children. A romantic wine-tasting cellar and a treasury containing work by gold-smiths and silversmiths, armor, weapons, and other objects of value acquired by the family through the centuries, is open to the public at an extra charge. If you want to fortify yourself before the trek back to town, two small restaurants lie within the castle walls.

After the Mosel, the Black Forest is explored in the next chapter.

Chapter VIII

THE BLACK FOREST

1. Baden-Baden
2. Badenweiler
3. Freiburg
4. Wildbad
5. Triberg
6. Freudenstadt
7. Titisee

WHEN YOU VISIT this region in southwestern Germany, don't expect to come upon a little elf working on a cuckoo clock in his tiny gingerbread shop. What you will find, however, is nearly as exciting and altogether more enjoyable. The Black Forest is full of charming people and hospitable little villages that have retained their traditional flavor.

This region of Germany (called Schwarzwald) covers a triangular section of the large province of Baden-Württemberg roughly 90 miles long and 25 miles wide. The pine- and birch-studded mountains are alive with fairytale villages, sophisticated spas, and modern ski resorts, but, sad to say, pollution now threatens one of the most beautiful parts of Germany. The peaks in the southern part of the forest reach as high as 5000 feet, excellent for skiing in winter and hiking or mountain climbing in summer. The little lakes of Titisee and Schluchsee are popular for boating, swimming—and of course winter skating. Fish abound in the streams and lakes, and deer romp through the groves of pine.

Besides the cuckoo clock and the many toys manufactured in the Black Forest, this region is noted for another product—*kirschwasser,* an unsweetened cherry brandy derived from the fruit of its black, twisted cherry trees. This, along with Black Forest bacon and provincial-style rye bread, constitutes a memorable meal.

The ideal way to explore the Schwarzwald is on foot, but your time and energy would probably run out before the many scenic attractions did. So motoring is the best alternative. The roads through the forest are excellent, especially the **Schwarzwald Hochstrasse** (Black Forest High Road), running from Baden-Baden to Freudenstadt. This scenic route offers many opportunities to park your car and explore the countryside. Many of the side roads leading off the High Road are in good condition as well and take you to little villages, ancient castles, and rolling farmlands.

The adventure of the Black Forest begins at its gateway city:

1. Baden-Baden

In the 19th century the nobility of Europe discovered Baden-Baden, where the bath-conscious Roman Emperor Caracalla had taken the waters more than 1500 years before. Most of the titles and crowns are merely dust collectors today, but the legacy left by these Romans and Romanovs has made the resort on the edge of the Black Forest the most elegant and sophisticated playground in Germany. The clientele may have changed, but Baden-Baden still evokes an aura of 19th-century aristocracy, combined with the most up-to-date facilities.

THE SIGHTS: The center of activity is the **Lichtentaler Allee**, the park-promenade lining the bank of the Oosbach River (affectionately called the Oos —pronounced "Ohs"), which runs through the center of town. As you stroll along this promenade, you'll be amazed at the variety of exotic shrubs and trees, the colorful patches of rhododendrons, azaleas, roses, and zinnias. At the north end of the park, on the banks of the babbling stream, are the buildings of the Kurgarten, including the classical Kurhaus. Behind its sparkling white columns and facade is the oldest casino (**Spielbank**) in Germany where for more than 200 years everyone from Dostoievsky's Alexei Ivanovich to the Prince of Wales has tested his or her luck at the roulette wheel or the baccarat tables. The various rooms of the casino were designed more than 130 years ago in the style of an elegant French château, not unlike Versailles. In all this splendor, you can gamble year round, using real gold and silver chips. The minimum stake is 5 DM ($1.65), but visitors are not obliged to play. The historic gaming rooms may be viewed daily from 10 a.m. to noon on a conducted tour costing 2 DM (66¢). If visitors want to gamble later, a full day's ticket is available for 5 DM ($1.65). A jacket and necktie are mandatory for male visitors. To enter the casino during gambling time, you must possess a valid passport or identification card and be at least 21 years of age.

Most of the bathing establishments, including the old Friedrichsbad and the ultramodern Neues Augustabad, are on the opposite side of the Oos, in the heart of the Old Town. The spa gardens contain the **Pump Room** (Trinkhalle), where visitors can sip the radioactive chloride water. Built in the 19th century, the loggia of the hall is decorated with frescoes of Black Forest legends. The springs of Baden-Baden have been recognized for more than 2000 years, and yet their composition is almost the same today as when the Romans built their baths here in the third century. The remains can still be seen beneath the Römerplatz in the old section of the city.

Above the Römerplatz stands the Renaissance castle **Neues Schloss** (New Castle), built in the 16th century by the margraves of Baden to replace their 12th-century castle. The terraces offer an excellent view of the entire city. The castle houses the **Zähringer Museum,** containing historical living rooms from the 19th century when the New Castle was the summer residence of the grand dukes of Baden and documentation of the Grand Duchy of Baden. For a visit to the museum, call 2-55-93 for an appointment.

Baden-Baden is the ideal choice for sports and outdoor enthusiasts who would like to settle in for a few days of golf, tennis, or horseback riding. Horse-lovers will also enjoy the international racing season each August at Iffezheim Track. The surrounding countryside is good for hiking and mountain climbing. During the winter months Baden-Baden is still very active. As the gateway to the Black Forest, it is a convenient center for numerous ski resorts—and after a day on the slopes, you can return to a soothing swim in the thermal pools of the baths before a night out at the casino.

THE TOP HOTELS: Brenner's Park-Hotel, an der Lichtentaler Allee (tel. 35-30), is the Rolls-Royce resort hotel of Baden-Baden. A distinguished hotel, it lies in a large, private park facing the River Oos and Lichtentaler Allee. Some of its international habitués wouldn't dare let a year go by without making an appearance here for the cure. It's a glamorous place at which to stay. Rooms have good taste and offer much comfort. Singles range in price from 200 DM ($66) to 340 DM ($112.20), and a twin with bath costs from 260 DM ($85.80) to 500 DM ($165).

A pianist plays every afternoon at the lounge and in the evening at the new Oleander-Piano-Bar for dancing. There is gourmet dining in the main restaurant or in the Schwarzwald-Stube. The public rooms are fashionably conceived, each providing a rich background for the chic attire of guests.

One almost overlooks the fact that interwoven into the hotel life are extensive health facilities. Adjoining the swimming pool in the basement are a sauna, solarium, and massage and fitness studio. The staff includes a well-equipped team of beauticians and masseurs. Other installations feature modern facilities for diagnosis and therapeutics. If you want them to, the staff can arrange golf, tennis, riding, climbing, and walking on marked footpaths and promenades.

Steigenberger Hotel Badischer Hof, 47 Lange Strasse (tel. 2-28-27), with its colonnaded facade, is on a busy street in the center of town, but its rear opens onto an elegant garden with a wide balustraded terrace, flower beds, and a lawn around a stone fountain. Once a Capuchin monastery stood on this site, but gave way to a spa hotel in 1807. Then the hotel began its career as a social center for famous personalities who spent "the season" there, taking the cure. One of its most distinguished guests, composer Carl Maria von Weber, wrote: "The beautiful dining room with its high ceiling, the tastefully decorated casino, and the fine stone-encased bathing facilities will make this guest house more and more popular with the years." And so they have. You'll look in amazement at the colonnaded, four-story-high hallway, with its great staircase and encircling balustraded balconies. Giant bronze torchiers stand at the base of the staircase, and antiques are tastefully used. Other public rooms are attractive and old-world. The well-furnished bedrooms are priced according to size and view, as well as season. All the accommodations have private bath. Singles range from 149 DM ($49.17) to 199 DM ($65.67); doubles, from 200 DM ($66) to 330 DM ($108.90). A buffet breakfast is included. Many rooms have a private balcony, and all those in the monastery building have thermal water piped into the private bath. The hotel has a thermal-spring swimming pool, an open-air swimming pool, and a low-level garage. A magnificent park-restaurant is open in the monastery building, and next to it is a bar room connecting the two buildings.

Steigenberger Hotel Europäischer Hof, 2 Kaiseralle (tel. 2-35-61), stands opposite the Kurgarten and the casino, adjacent to the Oos River which runs at the edge of the Kurpark. Actually, it's a pair of hotels joined together that were built when it was considered important to provide dramatic living facilities. Its colonnaded, classic central hallway is stunning, and many of its suites and bedrooms open off balconies. Some 150 well-furnished rooms are offered, equipped with radio, phone, and, for the most part, color television. The atmosphere is one of elegance in this distinguished hotel. Single rooms with bath cost from 160 DM ($52.80) to 210 DM ($69.30), and doubles go for 260 DM ($85.80) to 320 DM ($105.60). All these tariffs include a large buffet breakfast.

You may want to dine in the restaurant even if you're not a guest. It has been called "elegant and noble," with meals costing from 45 DM ($14.85) to 80 DM ($26.40). It features a buffet set up in the middle of the restaurant, which is high-ceilinged, with a light-filled ambience of grays, greens, and beiges. The chef specializes in French and Swiss dishes, and there is light and friendly service, perhaps a lingering nostalgia for yesteryear. Windows overlook a park and sweep across one entire wall of the restaurant, open daily from noon to 2 p.m. and 6:45 to 10 p.m.

Der Quellenhof, 27 Sofienstrasse (tel. 2-21-34). This large, modern hotel complex could be your resting point in Baden-Baden, where your breakfast would be enjoyed in a plaid-carpeted room decorated with enlarged photographs of Baden-Baden and its royal patrons in the 19th century, and where dinner would be prolonged in the shelter of the all-wood walls of Im Süsses Löchel, the hotel's evening restaurant. Views of the spa's Wilhelminian architecture are generally spectacular from the balconies of the bedrooms, which have all the modern conveniences and are soundproof. Singles rent for 137 DM ($45.21) to 152 DM ($50.16), and doubles go for 180 DM ($59.40) to 210 DM ($69.30), with a breakfast buffet included.

Kurhotel Quisisana, 21 Bismarckstrasse (tel. 34-46). Radiating from the core of a 19th-century villa, the annexes of this hotel contain some of the most up-to-date health facilities anywhere in the Black Forest. Any of the individual elements considered separately would be worth traveling some distances for, but when grouped into one elegant health spa, they're compelling. You can spend an early morning in group calisthenics, for example, followed by a dozen different skin and muscle-toning techniques administered by an army of masseurs and beauticians. An evening could be spent savoring the sophisticated array of cuisine available from the world-class kitchens before retiring to your spacious and well-appointed bedroom. One of the staff will direct you to the center of the spa, eight minutes away by foot. Rates go from 150 DM ($49.50) to 190 DM ($62.70) a day in a single, and from 220 DM ($72.60) to 280 DM ($92.40) in a double, with breakfast included.

Golf-Hotel, 113 Fremersbergstrasse (tel. 2-36-91). Even if you don't play golf, you're still in luck if you choose this elegantly rambling hotel as your address in the Black Forest. You'll find, in addition to one of the finest golf courses in Germany, two swimming pools, a sauna, a gym, tennis courts, color TV in the rooms, and in winter, a fire burning almost constantly in the entrance area. Efficiently run by Paul Ortlieb, the hotel offers a panoramic view of Baden-Baden and the Black Forest from nearly every room, as well as a dining room serving excellent meals. Singles rent for 108 DM ($35.64); a double costs from 150 DM ($49.50) to 240 DM ($79.20). A buffet breakfast is included in the rates.

Holiday Inn Sporthotel, 2 Falkenstrasse (tel. 3-30-11). Lying pleasantly in a forest, this hotel rises futuristically in a series of irregularly shaped rectangles and triangles. This branch of the American hotel chain offers 121 comfortable rooms in a style you've come to expect from Holiday Inn. Doubles cost 220 DM ($72.60) to 300 DM ($99) a night, while singles go for 180 DM ($39.40) to 210 DM ($69.30), including a rich buffet breakfast and unlimited use of the hotel's sauna and swimming pool. Someone at the reception desk will tell you how you can borrow a bicycle from the hotel's collection, and the additional charges you'll pay for facial and body massages. All of this is within five blocks of the casino.

MIDDLE-BRACKET HOTELS: **Bad-Hotel zum Hirsch,** 1 Hirschstrasse (tel. 2-38-96), had been operated as a hotel by the same family since 1689, but in 1982 this beautiful, old-fashioned hotel was sold to the famed Steigenberger chain. It's a tranquil compound of several buildings, and throughout the centuries constant modernization has taken place. In spite of the physical improvements, the antique furnishings have been retained, making the hotel a living museum of the fine period pieces. The more formal dining room is dominated by crystal chandeliers and paneled walls. The Blauer Salon is equally attractive, with blue velvet provincial armchairs, classic draperies, and much crystal. There are several sitting and drawing rooms, each tastefully furnished. A breakfast terrace rests under a glycinia arbor, and an inner courtyard garden is an oasis. Consistently interesting are the old-style bedrooms, each individually furnished as in a country home. Singles with bath cost from 105 DM ($34.65) to 206 DM ($67.98). Twin-bedded rooms with bath run 196 DM ($64.68) to 250 DM ($82.50). A breakfast buffet is included. All the rooms have thermal water piped in. One of the special advantages of staying here is the abundant spa facilities at reasonable fees.

Holland, 14 Sofienstrasse (tel. 2-55-95). Kings and princes, along with a well-known composer or two (among them Franz Liszt), have frequented this hotel during its 240-year history. Today you can get that old-fashioned feeling, and the added benefit of a modern swimming pool and bowling alley, for anywhere from 57 DM ($18.81) to 138 DM ($45.54) in a single and from 88 DM ($29.04) to 154 DM ($50.82) in a double, a breakfast buffet included. Public rooms are richly decorated, although few of the furnishings are original.

Der Kleine Prinz, 36 Lichtentaler Strasse (tel. 34-64). Housed in a turreted Victorian building at least a century old, this well-run hotel offers beautifully furnished rooms to guests who pay 250 DM ($82.50) in a triple, 215 DM ($70.95) in a double, and 110 DM ($36.30) in a single. Most rooms have their own bath and toilet, and an elegant breakfast is served. Units often have well-polished handmade pine reproductions of antique desks, tables, and headboards. Norbert and Edeltraud Rademacher are the proprietors. He has had 22 years of experience in the United States at the Waldorf-Astoria and the New York Hilton as director of food and beverage operations.

Haus Reichert, 4 Sofienstrasse 9 (tel. 2-41-91). The angle of this 19th-century five-floor hotel meets in a round tower extending vertically from the ground to the top of the roofline, where it is capped by a funnel-shaped "witch's cap." Inside, the rooms are high-ceilinged and comfortable, although practically none of the original furniture or detailing has survived the many renovations. Exercise equipment, a pool, and a sauna are all at your disposal here, along with a central location not far from the casino. Owned by the same family since 1860, the hotel charges from 90 DM ($29.70) to 100 DM ($33) in a single, and from 140 DM ($46.20) to 170 DM ($56.10) in a double, breakfast included.

BUDGET LIVING: Hotel Am Markt, 18 Marktplatz (tel. 2-27-47), sits like a pleasant country inn on the old marketplace, far removed from the grandeur of the upper-bracket social life of Baden-Baden. It's a gem of a situation, with a tiny terrace café in front with window boxes of petunias. Best of all is the quietness, interrupted only by the chimes from the church across the square. There is no lounge to speak of, rather a tavern-style dining room with deep-toned wooden dado, deeply set small-paned windows, and straight-back country armchairs —in all, a relaxed and informal atmosphere. Innkeeper Herr Bogner has set the following prices for the upper-level bedrooms, each comfortably but simply furnished. Bathless singles are 38 DM ($12.54); bathless doubles, 72 DM ($23.76). A single with a private bath (shower) costs 52 DM ($17.16); a double with shower or bath, 80 DM ($26.40) to 88 DM ($29.04). Breakfast is included.

Hotel-Restaurant Zur Alten Laterne, 10 Gernsbacher Strasse (tel. 2-73-18). The present owner maintains the 300-year-old facade of this attractive hotel in impeccable condition. In summer masses of pink flowers add even more color to the already eye-stopping extravaganza of forest-green walls, crimson-colored shutters, and gilded embellishments. A sunflower-colored awning shelters the pink napery of the sidewalk café, which offers meals and drinks to passersby. The establishment is the personal domain of Mike Brandau who, in addition to his work as a restaurateur, maintains eight country-style bedrooms. Each is simply but comfortably furnished with colorful accents that mirror the tones used on the building's exterior. Singles cost between 60 DM ($19.80) and 85 DM ($28.05), while doubles go for 115 DM ($37.95) to 155 DM ($51.15). The restaurant contains only 19 tables, at any of which a visitor can talk comfortably while enjoying an array of regional specialties which the kitchen prepares with gusto. Meals are served from 11 a.m. to 3 p.m. and 5:30 p.m. to midnight, costing around 30 DM ($9.90).

THE TOP RESTAURANTS: Mirabell, 1 Kaiserallee (tel. 2-27-17), in the Kurhaus complex, is a fine place to dine in Baden-Baden. It's especially dramatic when the musicians play in the shell bandstand at the edge of the park. The cuisine is French. Your meal might begin with green pepper soup or salade nouvelle, then follow with one of these tempting main dishes: scallops, duckling with oranges, or filet of veal with spinach. The restaurant is open from 6 p.m., but closed on Monday. In addition to the formal dining room, the Boulevard, on a covered portico with floor-to-ceiling windows opening onto the esplanade, is open all day from 11 a.m. The cuisine is international, and a meal will cost between 40 DM ($13.20) and 75 DM ($24.75).

Stahlbad, 2 Augustaplatz (tel. 2-45-69), is a luxury restaurant with a stunning decor, providing dining in the French manner. And what a production it is! Mrs. Elisabeth Schwank does the cooking, as she has for some 30 years, and her daughter, Mrs. Ursula Monch, welcomes you in the dining room. The atmosphere evokes a tavern, chock-full of culinary memorabilia. Every square inch is covered with a colorful collection of framed prints, copper cooking and serving equipment, antique pewter plates, mugs and engravings. An open kitchen whets your appetite for the good food being prepared here. Some of the specialties are peppersteak and venison steak. Two other dishes that have won esteem are fresh mung fish and lobster thermidor, priced according to weight and lethally expensive. Their homemade fettuccine Alfredo is as good as—or better than—any you'll have in Rome. Meals range from 55 DM ($18.15) to 100 DM ($33), and hours are 11:30 a.m. to 3 p.m. and 5:30 to 10 p.m. daily; closed Sunday for dinner and all day Monday.

Schwarzwald-Grill, at Brenner's Park Hotel, 6 Schillerstrasse (tel. 35-30), it is generally conceded, serves the best food within Baden-Baden itself. At the corner of Lichtenaler Allee and Schillerstrasse, this is one of the renowned spa dining rooms of Europe. This grande dame of Baden-Baden, through skillful publicity, is attracting a younger and more attractive crowd than in years gone by. This noble restaurant is definitely worth its expensive price, with meals costing from 60 DM ($19.80) to 100 DM ($33). The cuisine here reaches the peak of international standards, as does the service. Fish and crustaceans are the specialties, and many dishes emerge from the kitchen as spectacular events. It's open daily from noon to 2 p.m. and 6:30 to 11 p.m.

A BUDGET RESTAURANT: Pavel's Schenke, 36 Lichtenaler Allee (tel. 2-36-87), offers well-prepared food and efficient service in a pleasant tavernstyle atmosphere. The Czech-born chef, Pavel Pospisil, is the owner, and is better known for his Pospisil's Restaurant Merkurius at Varnhalt (see below). His staff prepares a seasonally adjusted menu of relatively light German and Middle European food at reasonable prices. Fixed-price meals range from 35 DM ($11.55). There's even a smattering of nouvelle cuisine recipes for the more adventurous diner. The establishment is open daily except Monday for lunch, served from noon to 2 p.m. Dinner is presented nightly except Sunday and Monday from 6 to 10 p.m.

DINING AT NEUWEIER: It's traditional for the people of Baden-Baden to visit the satellite resort of Neuweier, ten kilometers (six miles) to the southwest, to dine. Here are some suggestions.

Schloss Neuweier, Mauerbergstrasse (tel. 5-79-44), is a small 12th-century castle entirely surrounded by its defensive water fortifications and vineyards belonging to the estate. You are welcomed by the Beck family. Its restaurant is not large but it offers impeccable service and a decor of tiled walls with paintings of its former inhabitants. The house proudly produces its local wines, including an excellent Riesling, and practices international cookery with flair. Food is fresh, with meals beginning at 35 DM ($11.55), going up to 80 DM ($26.40). The dessert menu is wide ranging and sinful. Hours are daily except Tuesday from noon to "closing." The staff takes a holiday in January.

Zum Alde Gott, 10 Weinstrasse (tel. 55-13), is a very old wine cellar with a terrace restaurant, specializing in Badische foods. Wild game in season is prepared to a fine art here. There are only 12 tables, in soft reds and clear white, a bright and cheerful ambience. Try the Black Forest trout or the sea bass. The cost of a meal ranges from 40 DM ($13.20) to 70 DM ($23.10), and service is daily (except Thursday and lunch Friday) from noon to 3 p.m. and 6 to 11 p.m.

Zur Traube, 107 Mauerbergstrasse (tel. 5-72-16), is a gutbürgerlich restaurant that offers wines from the Black Forest and very economical meals, costing from 22 DM ($7.26) to 45 DM ($14.85). The name of the restaurant means "bunch of grapes," and on a summer day guests drink a lot and eat even more. It's open from noon to 2 p.m. and 6 to 9:30 p.m. except Monday (it also closes January 20 to March 10).

DINING AT VARNHALT: In the same southwesterly direction from Baden-Baden, but only 3½ miles from the center of the spa, Varnhalt is another dining goal of many a visitor.

Pospisil's Restaurant Merkurius, 2 Klosterbergstrasse (tel. 54-74), is a family-run restaurant in a landhaus-style building. This three-story modern structure has blue awnings, a brown roof, and white stucco walls. Pavel Pospisil is an international type of man, importing his produce and meats every day from culinary-conscious Strasbourg. The food is an unusual blend of Czech and French specialties wedded harmoniously to dishes of the Black Forest. You might opt for an eight-course "surprise menu," selected by the chef, who guarantees you a gastronomic thrill. The cost of such good food isn't low—from 80 DM ($26.40) to 135 DM ($44.55) for a meal. The restaurant serves daily from noon to 2 p.m. and 7 to 10 p.m. except Monday (also no lunch on Tuesday).

Gasthaus Zum Adler, 15 Klosterbergstrasse (tel. 5-72-41). Baden-Baden can be intimidatingly chic, so if you're in the mood for an informal, relaxed, and getmütlich experience, you'll appreciate the rusticity of this country-style inn. It's cozy, decent, and proper, with original home-cookery reasonably priced, costing from 30 DM ($9.90) for a good meal. If you order some of the most expensive specialties you'll end up paying from 50 DM ($16.50). A choice of 12 daily specialties is offered, including much fish and game (in season). Perhaps it'll be carp, maybe roast hare or pheasant, possibly poached salmon or trout in Riesling. The house offers inexpensive wines. It's open from noon to 2:30 p.m. and 6 to 9 p.m. every day except Thursday. It closes annually in January. The inn also rents out reasonably priced rooms: a single goes for 55 DM ($18.15), and a double with shower or private bath for 82 DM ($27.06) to 90 DM ($29.70).

2. Badenweiler

Halfway between Freiburg and Basel, near the Swiss border, is the tiny spa of Badenweiler. The town authorities are so intent on keeping their community spotless that you will be required to park your car at the entrance. The designers of the Kurpark used the natural hillside setting to its best advantage by planting the cypress and cedar trees in groves around the walks and buildings. The springs of the spa have been known since Roman times. In fact the well-preserved Roman baths still stand today within the spa gardens.

In spite of its appearance of a sleepy little German village, Badenweiler offers its visitors a wide range of entertainment and activity, from summer concerts in open-air pavilions to winter skiing.

For another attraction of this area, you'll have to leave the city and drive about 12 miles south to **Schloss Bürgeln** (tel. 7626/237). Built in 1764 by order of the abbott of St. Blasien, the castle sits on an extension of the Blauen, the southernmost reaches of the Black Forest. The castle offers a view of the surrounding countryside as far as the Swiss Alps. On a clear day you can see Basel and the bend in the Rhine as it flows into Switzerland. The gardens around the castle are a delight in summer. Guided tours are conducted through the baroque palace daily, except Tuesday, at regular intervals between 10:15 a.m. and 5 p.m. (at 2 p.m. only on Sunday). Admission for adults is 3 DM (99¢); children, 1.50 DM (50¢).

THE TOP HOTELS: **Römerbad,** 1 Schlossplatz (tel. 700), is a stylish Victorian wedding cake, where discerning guests find a proper setting for resort living in addition to taking the cure. It's been family owned since the early 19th century. Over the years it's attracted everybody from Thomas Mann to Andy Warhol, from Nietzsche to the Yale Alley Cats. It's a bone-white structure, with domes, balconies, a mansard roof, plus an open-air swimming pool set in a woodland, amid lawns and flower beds. The interior has opera-house grandeur with rooms opening off its elegant reception hall ringed with a white balustraded balcony. Furnishings are discretely high fashion, employing antiques and tones of gold balanced with white or Wedgwood blue in the small dining room. Provincial furniture, a medallion collection, and bird prints make for an interesting decor. A wood-paneled drinking lounge is a draw in the evening, and there's a stately dining room as well, which contrasts sharply with an informal outdoor barbecue. The most recent addition is an enclosed swimming pool, with walls of glass to allow views of the neighboring park. In addition, there are numerous spa facilities and massage rooms.

Rates, including continental breakfast, are 170 DM ($56.10) to 220 DM ($72.60) for a single with bath, 260 DM ($85.80) to 320 DM ($105.60) for a double with similar plumbing. Two tennis courts with pro are reserved for guests.

Park, 6 Ernst-Eisenlohr-Strasse (tel. 7-10), is like a pair of Italian palaces on the side of the hill with a pastoral view. Within, traditional furnishings give a country estate look to the main living room. An enclosed thermal swimming pool makes the Park even more tempting. Bedrooms vary greatly in size and style, but each is nicely appointed and comfortable. Most have good views. The price of a single with bath goes from 140 DM ($46.20) to 200 DM ($66). A double with bath costs 210 DM ($69.30) to 250 DM ($82.50). The management is reluctant to rent rooms without meals. The cost of full board ranges from 190 DM ($62.70) to 210 DM ($69.30) per person daily. The Park is open March to November 10.

Weisses Haus, 6 Wilhelmstrasse (tel. 50-41). A three-gabled white house with awnings is the 19th-century core of this hotel complex on a forested hillside near Badenweiler. Guests take advantage of the sunny lawn to socialize in the chaise longues provided by the hotel. An attractively furnished single room rents for 85 DM ($28.05) to 115 DM ($37.95), while a double costs 165 DM ($54.45) to 215 DM ($70.95). Full board runs 125 DM ($41.25) to 155 DM ($51.15) per person daily. Axel Thiele is your thoughtful host here, and does what he can to be informative and helpful.

MIDDLE-BRACKET HOTELS: **Ritter,** 2 Friedrichstrasse (tel. 50-74), is an informal chalet building, with its own gardens and an annex with modern apartments. Its main building contains many traditional, but attractive, bedrooms, most with private bath. Bathless singles cost 65 DM ($21.45); doubles, 120 DM ($39.60). With private bath, singles rent for 100 DM ($33); doubles, 160 DM ($52.80). Rates include breakfast. The public rooms have a pleasant informality. The grillroom restaurant, for example, has a rustic theme, with a beamed ceiling and many trailing vines and plants. At the swimming pool one glass wall opens onto the lawn and woods. The Ritter lies just a short walk to the Kurpark and town social center.

Schlossberg, 3 Schlossbergstrasse (tel. 50-16). A tastefully modern hotel run by Rudolf Schwenn, this establishment blends discreetly with the flowering trees and the landscaping around it. Guests enjoy the manicured garden near the sun terrace, and the wrought-iron balconies attached to most rooms. Units are pleasantly and comfortably furnished, costing 80 DM ($26.40) to 110 DM ($36.30) in a single and 140 DM ($46.20) to 170 DM ($56.10) in a double, breakfast included. The management is helpful in directing you to interesting sights in the environs of Badenweiler. Closed mid-November to mid-February.

Romantik Hotel Sonne, 4 Moltkestrasse (tel. 50-53). The roof of this rambling 100-year-old building is covered in weathered terracotta tiles, the kind they don't make anymore. The interior is warmly and comfortably furnished in the kind of pieces that make you want to read three or four newspapers before dinner. The Fischer family runs this inviting complex, where an outdoor pool is surrounded by palms, giving the impression more of the Caribbean than of Deutschland. Singles go for 78 DM ($25.74) to 100 DM ($33), and doubles cost 125 DM ($41.25) to 170 DM ($56.10), including breakfast. Units contain either a private shower or bath and a toilet. The hotel is closed from mid-November to mid-February.

Hotel Post, 1 Sofienstrasse (tel. 50-51). The facade of this hotel is ornamented in a rich design of cream-colored walls and heavy window frames. Inside it benefits from an array of modern additions and improvements. There's a tile swimming pool on the premises, along with a sauna, a bath in each bedroom, a sun terrace, a rustic dining room whose arched wooden ceiling is supported by ornate wooden columns, and a warmly intimate weinstube. Guests enjoy the hotel's nearness to the many outdoor beauty spots, as well as the personalized attention of the Grathwol family. Any overflow from the main building is directed to a guest-house annex, the Gästehaus Grathwol, whose rambling horizontal lines, flowered balconies, and comfortably furnished country-rustic interior offer additional accommodations, as well as its own heated indoor swimming pool. Singles range from 65 DM ($21.45) to 105 DM ($34.65), and doubles cost between 120 DM ($39.60) and 185 DM ($61.05), including breakfast. Full board is available at a cost of 95 DM ($31.35) to 135 DM ($44.55) per person daily.

BUDGET LIVING: **Haus Christine,** 1 Glasbachweg (tel. 60-04). This is a modern, rambling hotel, where most of the rooms have their own balcony or sun terrace. You get the feeling of being in some apartment complex where you will get to know your neighbors nearby. The rooms are comfortable, furnished in browns and yellows for the most part, with big windows to let in the light. Breakfast is included in the price, which ranges from 50 DM ($16.50) to 58 DM ($19.14) in a single and from 50 DM ($16.50) to 65 DM ($21.45) per person in a double.

WHERE TO DINE: Grill Restaurant **Parkstüble,** Park Hotel, 6 Ernst-Eisenlohr-Strasse (tel. 7-10), is the gathering spot for those who want to dine out in Badenweiler. Although separate, it is within the Park Hotel. The interior is rustic. One room, for example, has wood-paneled walls adorned with primitive paintings, provincial furniture, and a coved ceiling. Best of all, the atmosphere is friendly and the food is good. On the à la carte menu, you can order lobster soup, sole Nantua, or ox tongue in madeira. The special dessert is crêpes suzette for two. Dinners range from 40 DM ($13.20) to 70 DM ($23.10), and the Stüble is open only from March to mid-November, daily except Monday.

Romantik-Hotel Sonne, 4 Moltkestrasse (tel. 50-53), is a historic building with a flowered courtyard dating from 1620. For five generations the Fischer family has run this Black Forest guest house. They have a weinstube, with high ceilings, and a wooden-ceilinged restaurant, giving friendly, attentive service. Some of the Fischer family's personal antiques are used. Inexpensive meals begin at 30 DM ($9.90), going up, of course. They are open from 11 a.m. to midnight, except Wednesday. They are also closed from mid-November to mid-February.

Kurhaus Restaurant, 1 Schlossplatz (tel. 7-21-60), is a gutbürgerlich or traditional food restaurant in the park, with a terrace and a café. Many specialties of the Black Forest, including rich desserts, appear on its weekly changing menu, ranging in price from 25 DM ($8.25) to 50 DM ($16.50). It serves from 10:30 a.m. till midnight daily except Tuesday. It's closed in November and for part of December.

Hotel Post, 1 Sofienstrasse (tel. 50-51), is a Swiss-style restaurant with an economical array of specialties—meals cost 20 DM ($6.60) to 55 DM ($18.15). The house specialty is a veal steak Badische and pig knuckles with sauerkraut. Three versions of grilled filets are offered, including Indian style. Hours are 11 a.m. to 2 p.m. and 6 p.m. to midnight. It's closed from November until the first of March.

3. Freiburg

This, the largest city in the Black Forest region, is often overlooked by visitors because it is off the beaten track. But those who go to Freiburg will be rewarded with one of the most scenic and interesting cities in southwestern Germany. Its strategic location at the southern edge of the Black Forest brought the town under the rule of the Austrian Habsburgs in 1368, and it remained theirs for more than 400 years. This same location is an awe-inspiring sight when you first arrive in Freiburg today. If you enter from the Rhine plain on the west, you are faced with the town silhouetted against huge mountain peaks towering more than 3000 feet. Within an hour you can reach most of these peaks by car, or in less time by funicular.

One of the most interesting facts about Freiburg's situation is its remarkable climate. In early spring the town is usually bursting into bloom while the mountain peaks are still covered with snow. In the fall the smell of new wine fills the narrow streets while reports of snowfalls on the nearby peaks are already reaching the ears of the townfolk. The reason for this unusual weather is that

Freiburg lies in the path of warm air currents which come up from the Mediterranean through the Burgundy Gap, balanced by the winds from the Black Forest hillsides. The two forces join together to make Freiburg a year-round attraction.

The winter "call of the slopes" makes Freiburg a sports center. No matter what the weather, it's easy to get to this city via the efficient German Federal Railway, whose fastest trains stop at this junction en route to the Swiss Alps. It's also the home of a 400-year-old university, which has claimed among its faculty and alumni great scholars, scientists, and humanists such as Erasmus, Zasius, and Waldseemüller (the first geographer to put America on the map).

THE SIGHTS: A town of historical interest and significance—Marie Antoinette "slept here" on her way to marry Louis XVI—Freiburg offers a number of well-preserved monuments, beginning with . . .

Freiburg Cathedral

Towering over the Münsterplatz (Minister Square), where the busy weekly market is still carried on today, the cathedral forms a grand sight with its unique spire of filigree-like stonework. This steeple sits on an octagonal belfry, whose historic bells include a five-ton wonder dating from 1258. Although construction on the church was begun in 1200 in Romanesque style, the builders had incorporated the styles of every Gothic period, as well as a bit of Renaissance, by the time it was completed in 1620. The overall look, however, is mainly Gothic, with heavy buttresses above the north and south walls, which are decorated with statues of biblical characters.

Entering the cathedral through the south door, you're in the transept facing an early 16th-century sculpture of the Adoration of the Christ Child by the Magi. Turning left into the nave, you'll see at the far end of the aisle, at the entrance to the tower, a 13th-century statue of the Virgin flanked by two adoring angels, a fine example of French Gothic art. Resting against one of the Renaissance pillars along the aisle is a carved 16th-century pulpit, with stairs winding around the curve of the column. The figures below the stairs are likenesses of the townspeople of the period, including the sculptor.

Of interest throughout the cathedral are the stained-glass windows, many of which are hundreds of years old. The oldest are the small round windows in the south transept, which date from the 13th century. Some of these, however, have been removed to the Augustinian Museum and replaced by more recent panels.

The vaulted chancel is the real treasure house of art within the cathedral. Most impressive is the painted altarpiece by Hans Baldung Grien, dating from 1516, above the high altar. If you follow the aisle around behind the choir, you can also see the reverse side of the work, depicting the Crucifixion. Each of the 12 chapels around the choir has its own important works of art, including the elaborate rococo font in the Stürzel Chapel and a 16th-century altarpiece by Sixth von Staufen in the Locher Chapel.

The cathedral can be visited at any time between 9 a.m. and 6 p.m. (in winter it closes at 4 p.m.).

Around the Old Town

Across the Münsterplatz from the cathedral is the **Kaufhaus,** the most colorful building in Freiburg. The Gothic structure, with oriel windows at each end, was originally an ancient emporium to which a balcony was added in 1550. Above the massive supporting arches, the facade is decorated with the statues of four emperors of the Habsburg dynasty, all but one of whom visited Freiburg during their reigns. The red-painted building is still used as the town's official reception hall.

The **City Hall,** on the attractively planted Rathausplatz just west of the Münsterplatz, became a happy marriage of two 16th-century merchants' houses when an arcade was built between them in 1900. The Renaissance houses are in suitable condition, and among the decorations on the oriel windows and facades, the one most commented upon is the relief of *The Maiden and the Unicorn.*

The **Augustiner Museum** is housed in the former church and monastery of the Order of St. Augustine and contains the town's finest collection of art, including religious art spanning more than 1000 years. Among the treasures are some of the original stained-glass windows from the cathedral and the most important part of its medieval gold and silver treasure, brought here for safekeeping. The best works, in the collection of medieval art, include the painting by Grünewald of the *Snow Miracle,* as well as works of Hans Baldung Grien (the best pupil of Albrecht Dürer). Besides, there is a rich collection of fine *oberrheinische* late-Gothic wooden sculpture. The folk art from the Black Forest in the upper story is well presented. The museum is open daily, except Monday, from 10 a.m. to 5 p.m. (on Wednesday from 10 a.m. to 8 p.m.). Admission is 1.50 DM (50¢) for adults, .75 DM (25¢) for children. On Wednesday and Sunday entrance is free; guided tours are conducted on Wednesday at 6 p.m. and on Thursday at 3:30 p.m. There is also an important collection of paintings of the 19th and 20th centuries, which concentrate on this area of southwest Germany, as well as special exhibitions of modern art.

AN UPPER-BRACKET HOTEL: Colombi Hotel, 16 Rotteckring (tel. 3-14-15).

The snow-white walls and angular lines of this inner-city hotel are easily recognizable. Despite its location, the rooms are quiet and peaceful, usually with views over the stately trees around the hotel. Many of its visitors are likely to be part of one of the many business conferences taking place here, but the Colombi caters to independent travelers as well. This is by all accounts the best hotel in town, and its restaurant (see below) is also the most outstanding in Freiburg. The hotel's 102 accommodations, well furnished and comfortably appointed, cost between 170 DM ($56.10) and 190 DM ($62.70) in a single and between 235 DM ($77.50) and 260 DM ($85.80) in a double, including breakfast. There is a hairstylist on the premises.

MIDDLE-RANGE HOTELS: Novotel Freiburg, am Karlsplatz (tel. 3-12-95).

Belonging to one of the most modern international hotel chains, this product of late-20th-century finance offers comfortable lodgings with all the amenities at a spot less than a block from the cathedral. Sports facilities are well developed, with a tennis court, swimming pool, sauna, and squash courts. Singles rent for 145 DM ($47.85), and doubles cost 165 DM ($54.45), plus another 14 DM ($4.62) for a buffet breakfast.

Victoria, 54 Eisenbahnstrasse (tel. 3-18-81). Situated less than 400 feet from the Hauptbahnhof, this hotel is, nevertheless, peaceful thanks to its frontage on Colombi Park. The facade is one of those elegantly symmetrical 19th-century rectangles, with big windows and dentil work, as well as a wrought-iron balcony stretched over the front door. The interior is lavishly paneled throughout the public rooms. Bedrooms are pleasantly furnished, costing anywhere from 70 DM ($23.10) to 115 DM ($37.95) in a single and 95 DM ($31.35) to 165 DM ($54.45) in a double, a breakfast buffet included.

Zum Roten Bären, 12 Oberlinden (tel. 3-69-13). A modern wing has been added, pleasantly blending in. The hotel is filled with antiques, and in the courtyard is a collection of exotic plants. This is in fact one of the oldest buildings in Freiburg, since parts of it date from 1120. The interior is delightfully decorated, emphasizing a few of the original construction elements between scattered antique pieces of furniture. Rooms are pleasantly styled and furnished, costing from 130 DM ($42.90) to 180 DM ($59.40) in a double, while singles go for 105 DM ($34.65), including breakfast. Have at least a glass of wine or beer on the weinstube's terrace in summertime.

Park Hotel Post, am Colombipark, 35 Eisenbahnstrasse (tel. 3-16-83). A marvelously baroque hotel, with an elaborate zinc cap on its octagonal turret, the Park Hotel Post is centrally located within walking distance of everything in Freiburg. The interior has been entirely renovated, with hardly a stick left of the old furniture. Reliable modern comfort with up-to-date amenities is the emphasis today. Breakfast is included in the room price of 95 DM ($34.35) in a single and 150 DM ($49.50) in a double. All units have a private toilet and a shower or bath.

Central Hotel, 6 Wasserstrasse (tel. 3-18-31), near the pedestrian zone, is a modern hotel imaginatively designed with skylights, marble floors, and a pleasantly furnished lobby. All bedrooms come with breakfast included in the rates, served in a wood-ceilinged dining room. Singles rent for 85 DM ($27.72) to 90 DM ($29.70), and doubles cost from 130 DM ($42.90) to 136 DM ($44.88). Each unit has an attractively tiled bathroom. An extra bed can be added for 35 DM ($11.55). Children under 6 are accommodated free in their parents' rooms.

Rappen, 13 Münsterplatz (tel. 3-13-53), is a charming, typical Black Forest inn, with a wrought-iron hanging sign, little dormer windows in its steep roof, and window boxes and shutters. Try to get a room overlooking the Gothic cathedral. There are three dining rooms on the street, all with beamed ceilings, leaded-glass windows, coach lanterns, and a collection of decorative plates and prints. Units contain telephone, color TV, and mini-bar. Doubles with shower are 150 DM ($49.50); with complete bath, 160 DM ($52.80). Breakfast is included. Whether you dine on the sidewalk terrace or inside, the cuisine is commendable for local dishes, with meals costing from 25 DM ($8.25) to 55 DM ($18.15).

WHERE TO DINE: **Falken- und Zirbelstuben,** Colombi Hotel, 16 Rotteckring (tel. 3-14-15). You'll probably find your table discreetly separated from that of your neighbors here by a leaded-glass and wood dividing wall. That kind of personalized attentiveness has made this the most desirable restaurant in Freiburg. Its food is unquestionably the finest served. Accenting the room is a ceramic stove composed of white tiles, similar to the ones used to heat mountain chalets of 100 years ago. The chef de cuisine, Alfred Klink, prepares a light nouvelle cuisine here, a deliciously flavored six-course menu going for 75 DM ($24.75). It might include a terrine of turbot, chanterelles over a filet of venison, or an array of Atlantic fish dishes sumptuously prepared and impeccably served. The restaurant is open from noon to 3 p.m. and 6 to 11 p.m.

Oberkirchs Weinstuben, 22 Münsterplatz (tel. 3-10-11), is where you'll be saturated with old Freiburg and love it. Innkeeper Frau Johner-Oberkirch provides excellent regional cooking and comfortable rooms. In the cellar are dozens of six-foot-high wooden kegs of wines. The setting is pure picture postcard, on a little square, with step-gabled roofs. A wrought-iron sign hangs over the entrance, and red and white tables are set out front for wine sampling or meals.

The main weinstube is old, with dark paneled walls holding framed engravings and prints, plus a monumental ceiling-high ceramic stove made with ornate decorative tiles. Crude country chairs are set around the tables. You get good old-fashioned food here, including tasty soups, meat dishes, poultry, and plenty of everything. In season you might try the young pheasant. Meals cost from 25 DM ($8.25) to 60 DM ($19.80). In the rear is a modern complex, fronting an open patio with a fish pond.

The weinstube also has some of the best rooms in town, most of which contain private bath or shower. Depending on the plumbing, doubles cost from 100 DM ($33) to 190 DM ($62.70), and singles rent for 70 DM ($23.10) to 130 DM ($42.90), breakfast included.

Ratskeller, 11 am Münsterplatz (tel. 3-14-15). It's hard to improve upon a good thing, but that's what the directors of this municipal town hall cellar did when they renovated the old establishment in 1981. Now crowned with a modern adaptation of the traditional Teutonic wooden ceiling, the place no longer radiates the medieval ambience of other ratskellers, but the attentive service and the elevated quality of the regional cookery make up for it. A three-course menu of the day costs between 25 DM ($8.25) and 40 DM ($13.20), with a selection of fish or meat entrees varied enough to please most diners. The cellar serves from noon to 2:30 p.m. and 6 p.m. to midnight.

Restaurant Eichhalde, 91 Stadtstrasse (tel. 5-48-17). Perhaps as a symbol of how aware he is of the international appeal of his cross-cultural menu, Hubert Freund has labeled the entrance to his establishment with a single word emblazoned on the doorway's red awning. That word is "restaurant," and it's that kind of self-effacing charm that makes this a memorable place. Cuisines from southern France, Italy, Switzerland, and Bavaria are all beautifully prepared here, and all of them have undergone a delicate change. They are lighter, contain less cholesterol, and all are fresh. This is, then, a nouvelle cuisine establishment par excellence, where the menu is too long to list, but would include a culinary specialty of practically every region in Europe. A fixed-price menu goes for 32 DM ($10.56) to 70 DM ($23.10). The restaurant serves from noon to 10 p.m. daily except Tuesday.

Weinstube Zur Traube, 17 Schusterstrasse (tel. 3-21-90). If your grandmother happens to be with you during this trip to Germany, and if she happens to be of German extraction, she will love this 600-year-old weinstube in Old Freiburg. The pewter and earthenware dinner services decorating the walls are art objects in their own right, and even the ceramic stove is 300 years old. Cooking here is regional and well prepared, emphasizing game, meat, and fish. Complete meals are priced at 20 DM ($6.60) to 45 DM ($14.85). The weinstube is open from 11:30 a.m. to 2 p.m. and 5 to 11 p.m. daily, except Sunday and for three weeks in summer.

Greiffenegg-Schlössle, 3 Schlossbergring (tel. 3-27-28). Head chef Engelbert Ortlieb cooks up a storm, turning out regional and international dishes at this family restaurant named after a former president of Austria. The most expensive fixed-price meal on the menu costs 42 DM ($13.86), although a selection of simpler meals is available, ranging from 14 DM ($4.62) to 28 DM ($9.24). Hours are daily except Monday from noon to 11 p.m.

On the Outskirts

Kühler Krug, 1 Torplatz, at Günterstal (tel. 2-91-03). Clients sit bistro style along a banquette here, except that instead of Gallic decor the furnishings are unmistakably Teutonic, with ceiling-level armoires, primitive Caucasian rugs, and rustic country chairs. The menu is international, with regional specialties offered when they become available in the marketplace. Your dinner could consist, for example, of a pâté of goose liver or standing rack of roast venison (served for two persons), or perhaps pheasant, hunter's style, in a mushroom sauce. The restaurant serves the most exceptional 32-DM ($10.56) menu I have ever eaten in the environs of Freiburg. But if you order à la carte, sampling some of the expensive specialties, your tab might run as high as 70 DM ($23.10). The restaurant is open from 11:30 a.m. to 3 p.m. and 5:30 p.m. to midnight. It's closed all day Thursday and on Friday until 6 p.m. (also closed for one week in February and two weeks in June).

Schwärs Hotel Löwen, 120 Kappeler Strasse, at Littenweiler (tel. 6-30-41). Local residents have told me that the adroit service here comes "from the heart" of the concerned family of Heinrich Schwär, who runs it. It's in a wooded area where you'll hear birds twittering in the branches of the tall trees. The restaurant serves daily menus, ranging from a reasonable 18 DM ($5.94) to 40 DM ($13.20). Food items, in keeping with the rustic decor, emphasize the regional. However, international selections are also offered and beautifully prepared. Your waitress will probably wear a dirndl as she hurries with your food and drink out onto the sun terrace. The restaurant is open from 11:30 a.m. to 2 p.m. and 6 to 10 p.m.; closed Monday. If you'd like to spend the night, the inn has comfortably furnished bedrooms. Singles cost from 42 DM ($13.86), and doubles go for 65 DM ($21.45) to 82 DM ($27.06).

Gasthof Adler, 3 Im Schulerdobel, at Kappel (tel. 6-54-13). This is a big, generous, family-style gemütlich kind of place, where wine comes in pitchers and where hotel rooms are available for any patron who decides he or she needs to sleep over. A children's menu is available for the toddlers you're likely to encounter here (or bring with you), along with an above-average list of international food items. A fixed-price meal ranges in price from 25 DM ($8.25) to 40 DM ($13.20). Service is from noon to 2 p.m. and 6:30 to 9:30 p.m. every day but Thursday and for two weeks in summertime. Those rooms I referred to rent for 42 DM ($13.86) in a single, from 65 DM ($21.45) in a double.

AFTER DARK IN FREIBURG: Freiburg, contrary to the popular impression (that is, from anyone who's never been there), is no sleepy little town hidden away in the Black Forest. For openers, it has a large cultural life centering around the **Städtischen Bühnen,** 46 Bertoldstrasse (tel. 3-48-74). Many "off-Broadway" theaters abound, but in these you must know German, of course, to appreciate the presentation. The Freiburg Symphony orchestra is distinguished, and there are many concerts presented at the **Freiburger Stadthallen,** 80 Schwarzwaldstrasse (tel. 7-10-20), their congress hall. Ask at the tourist office for details about "what's on."

If you're not into culture, the weinstuben that abound throughout the town, attracting the university student at night, might be a potent lure. Bars, cabarets, and (believe it or not) some nightclubs exist. Except in the most expensive places, drinks are cheap: a half liter of beer rarely costs more than 4 DM ($1.32).

As of this writing, the **Landhaus,** 3 Humboldstrasse (tel. 3-65-36), is currently the in-vogue disco (remember disco?). There's even a **Playboy Club,** at 3 Moltkerstrasse (tel. 3-2034), where you should bring your skimpy bikini, as it has a swimming pool and lots of young "bunnies."

The top cabaret shows in town are at **Regina-Cabarett,** 251 Kaiser-Joseph-Strasse (tel. 2-61-65), which is closed on Sunday, and there's more cabaret at **Traber-Bar,** 9 Adelhauserstrasse (tel. 2-69-61). Cabaret translates as "take it off."

When everything else shuts down (and you're still not sleepy), you can always stop in for a drink at the **Red Saloon,** 9 Adelhauserstrasse (tel. 2-69-61).

STAYING IN HINTERZARTEN: Instead of stopping over in Freiburg, you might prefer the following accommodations in Hinterzarten, less than 17 miles away.

Parkhotel Adler (tel. 711). When Marie Antoinette was on her way from Vienna to Paris for her wedding with Louis XVI, she spent a night in the oldest section of this hotel. Since then, an array of other prominent personages traveling between the German- and French-speaking worlds have consistently made this their temporary home. Today the 15th generation of the Riesterer family are the owners, and they do everything they can to treat modern-day guests with some of the style of an earlier century. You'll find the palatial lemon- and white-painted facade within its own gardens a few steps from the onion dome of the village church. The original core of the hotel dates from 1447, but there have been many 19th- and even late-20th-century additions.

The well-heeled and conservatively dressed clients make the most of the establishment's six different bars and restaurants. The older section offers an array of woodburning fireplaces, as well as scores of intimate hideaways which offer good drinks, good food, and good service. Clients who prefer apartment living opt for the chalet-cozy format of the nearby Adler Residenz, whose thick carpets and modernized comfort provide well-upholstered summer and winter accommodations. Live dance music is offered every evening in one of the bars, and guests can divert themselves at the hotel's spa facilities. A full range of sports is offered, including indoor and outdoor tennis, as well as horseback riding. A hairdresser and beauty parlor offer complete facials and other treatments.

Singles with bath cost between 130 DM ($42.90) and 240 DM ($79.20); doubles are priced between 230 DM ($75.90) and 310 DM ($102.30). Half board can be arranged for another 45 DM ($14.85) to 70 DM ($23.10) per person daily.

Weisses Rössle, 38 Freiburger Strasse (tel. 14-11). The "White Horse Inn" is only a half-hour drive from Freiburg. Many of the rooms, including those in a new "rustic"-style wing, are actually suites, with separate living and sleeping accommodations. Lots of dark rosewood was used in the furnishings. Baths are beautifully tiled and well lit. The living area includes a large sofa, bar, and refrigerator, leading out to a sun terrace. A single goes for 70 DM ($23.10) to 160 DM ($52.80), while doubles cost 125 DM ($41.25) to 265 DM ($87.45). Even more expensive apartments are available.

To vary your breakfast, you can order a smoked Black Forest trout (it'll cost extra). Karl-Heinz Zimmerman takes great pride in the food and beverages served here, and has also studied "dietary science." Menus range from 35 DM ($11.55) to 75 DM ($24.75).

The hotel has many facilities, such as an indoor pool, sauna, massage, and tennis court.

Sassenhof, 17 Adlerweg (tel. 15-15). Set into an impeccably maintained lawn and garden, this stylish contemporary chalet is accented with long horizontal rows of geraniums which bring out the reddish tones in the establishment's wooden siding. The hotel has an indoor swimming pool and a sauna, and in the vicinity are many walking paths for nature-oriented visitors. Most clients check into one of the dozen or so well-furnished bedrooms, or else ask for a full apartment with a kitchen if they're interested in a self-catering holiday. Singles cost between 60 DM ($19.80) and 72 DM ($23.76), while doubles range from 125 DM ($41.25) to 145 DM ($47.85), including breakfast. The six apartments are priced from 160 DM ($52.80) to 180 DM ($59.40) per day.

4. Wildbad

This tiny town in the valley of the Enz River is one of the best known spas in the Black Forest. Although not as elegant as nearby Baden-Baden, Wildbad lacks none of its important facilities and attracts visitors from all over Germany and Europe to its own promenades and thermal springs. The river that flows through the town divides the colonnaded shopping streets and the spa center.

The thermal springs in the spa gardens are popular for both drinking and bathing. Among the many unusual baths is the **Graf-Eberhard Bath,** dating from the 19th century and decorated in a Moorish style, with sunken baths and colorful tiles. In contrast, the newer **Kurhaus** is terraced with glass walls opening onto lush greenery and thermal pools where you can bathe year round.

One of the biggest attractions of Wildbad is its scenery. The paths and roads in the surrounding woodlands are always alive with strollers, the streams teeming with fish and fishermen. A cable railway runs from the town to the top of the **Sommerberg,** a 1000-foot peak overlooking Wildbad and visited by skiers and sightseers alike.

UPPER-BRACKET HOTELS: Sommerberg Hotel, auf dem Sommerberg (tel. 17-40). The accommodations in this 90-room hotel are scattered over four balconied stories of glass and concrete which curve in a gentle arc around a panoramic view of the surrounding forest. Many of the public rooms of the interior were stylishly designed behind sweeping expanses of glass; inside, an appealing mixture of open fireplaces and conservatively modern furnishings offers dozens of places for relaxation. You'll find an array of differently decorated sitting areas, dining rooms, and café terraces to choose from, ranging from rustic to streamlined and elegant. There's a hexagon-shaped indoor swimming pool on the premises, whose large windows take in the outdoors, plus a well-trained staff willing to initiate you into the benefits of Teutonic-style hydrotherapy. The Jägerstüble restaurant serves a mixture of nouvelle cuisine with regional specialties. Singles cost between 85 DM ($28.05) and 170 DM ($56.10), while doubles go for 210 DM ($69.30) to 270 DM ($89.10), including a breakfast buffet. If ordered separately, meals range from around 30 DM ($9.90) to 50 DM ($16.50). A ski lift is a short walk from the hotel, which in winter attracts sports lovers.

Badhotel Wildbad, 5 Am Kurplatz (tel. 13-95). Many guests of this alluring hotel make full use of the balcony that comes with their well-furnished bedroom. The hotel was completely renovated in 1984 in an imaginative format, including views of a nearby stream, an array of painstakingly set mosaics, and an attractive integration of an old and a new building. The in-house restaurant serves well-prepared dishes from the classic German repertoire. Both the forest and a heated indoor swimming pool are within a short distance of the building. Single rooms cost 48 DM ($15.85) to 145 DM ($47.85), and doubles range between 210 DM ($69.30) and 240 DM ($79.20), including breakfast. A TV and radio are standard equipment in each of the rooms, but private plumbing varies.

MIDDLE-BRACKET HOTELS: Kurhotel Post, 2 Am Kurplatz (tel. 16-11), is a beguiling inn, right in the heart of everything. In fact, its open dining terrace, with flower boxes and plants, is suspended bridge-like across a river wending its way through the spa.

Once the Post was a humble guest house, but as the years passed by it was enlarged. In 1827 it became known as a gastronomic center, and in 1921 it came under the wings of the Fritzsches, who provided plumbing for most of the bedrooms (more than a third have a bath with either shower or tub).

Bathless singles cost around 35 DM ($11.55), rising to 90 DM ($29.70) with bath. Doubles go for 105 DM ($34.65) to 160 DM ($52.80). If you can't dine on the terrace, there is a garden room with an informal atmosphere of Windsor chairs and mile-long vines. In addition, an attractive tavern-like weinstube grill also serves meals, offering vegetarian and nouvelle cuisine specialties as well as regional dishes.

Hotel Bären, 4 Am Kurplatz (tel. 16-81). Approaching the building, you'd think you were heading toward a Renaissance palazzo in Naples. However, a quick survey of the sun terrace will reveal a wonderfully Teutonic scene of fair-haired people sunning themselves in the midst of masses of flowers. The management tells me that there has been an inn of some sort here since the 16th century. With that tradition in mind, they have successfully recreated in a modern style the kind of wood-ceilinged gemütlichkeit that has made the Black Forest so famous. The Schreiner family are your genteel hosts, charging 60 DM ($19.80) to 90 DM ($29.70) in a single and 70 DM ($23.10) to 87 DM ($28.71) per person in a double, including breakfast.

Traube, 31 König-Karl-Strasse (tel. 20-66). Owned and operated by the Wentz family for many years, this elegant modern hotel has installed an attractive collection of reproduction furniture to create a warm ambience appreciated by German urbanites who stay here in large numbers. The attractively decorated dining rooms serve well-prepared international and regional specialties. On a breakfast-only plan, singles rent for 65 DM ($21.45) to 120 DM ($39.60), while doubles go for 136 DM ($44.88) to 152 DM ($50.16). Full-board plans are available for 100 DM ($33) to 140 DM ($46.20) per person.

BUDGET HOTELS: **Gästehaus Rothfuss,** 47 Olgastrasse (tel. 33-68), is a chalet-like, family-run hotel, built on the side of the hill, a virtual sun magnet. It's a steep walk from the center of town, and benches for resting are placed all along the way. Wide balconies surround the house, allowing private areas for sunbathing and breakfasts. The garden has abundant roses and geraniums, tended by Frau Richter. She and her husband, Heinz, keep a family staff busy seeing that everything is highly polished. The little sitting room is personalized, cluttered, and intimate. The dining room seems to be all tables and glass windows, providing one with a woodland view. Prices are quite low. Bathless singles are 35 DM ($11.55), though a few with toilet and shower go for 50 DM ($16.50). Doubles with shower and toilet cost 70 DM ($23.10) to 80 DM ($26.40). For the tariffs quoted, a breakfast is offered, usually featuring soft-boiled eggs, sausage, and cheese. There is free parking on the grounds, and in 1979 the hotel opened a medical treatment center, only a three-minute walk from the main building.

Parkhotel Windhof, 206 Kernerstrasse (tel. 13-55). Set into an idyllic spot which is partly meadow and partly forest, this multilevel modern hotel offers a spacious lawn area for clients to relax in the sun. It would be invigorating to walk to areas where miniature golf, tennis, or thermal baths can be enjoyed. The interior is warmly decorated in sunny colors with lots of Oriental rugs. The family of Kurt Schmid are your friendly, helpful hosts. Full board ranges from 100 DM ($33) to 115 DM ($37.95) per person daily.

WHERE TO DINE: **Sommerberghotel,** auf dem Sommerberg (tel. 16-41), three kilometers (two miles) from Wildbad, is the most scenic spot for dining. It also serves some of the best food in the area in its restaurant, Jägerstüble. Chef Gerd Pflug turns out a delectable nouvelle cuisine among other dishes. This is a special restaurant, attracting a largely German clientele, seemingly unknown to most North Americans. To dine here costs from 35 DM ($11.55) to 75 DM ($24.75), and you can do so from noon to 2 p.m. and 6:30 to 9 p.m.

Hotel Birkenhof, 50 Wildbader Strasse (tel. 33-87), is also on the outskirts at Calmbach, a distance of about four kilometers from Wildbad. For many years this gutbürgerlich (traditional) restaurant has been owned by the same family. The kitchen staff turns out an array of tasty specialties, especially from Swabia. Fixed-price menus range from 18 DM ($5.94) to 32 DM ($10.56), most reasonable, and they serve from 11:30 a.m. to 2 p.m. and 6 to 9 p.m., except Friday. They also close from January 10 to February 20.

5. Triberg

This town, deep in the heart of the Black Forest, claims to be the home of the cuckoo clock, and is also visited because it has the highest waterfall in the country.

THE SIGHTS: The **Wasserfall** (waterfall) is exceptional, but be prepared to walk an hour or so to reach it. You park your car in a designated area near the Gutach Bridge and walk along a marked trail anytime from 7 a.m. to 7 p.m. in summer for a cost of 2 DM (66¢). The Gutach Falls drop some 530 feet, spilling down in seven stages. At the bottom of the falls is a summer café serving the famed Black Forest cake which, by then, you will have worked up an appetite for.

The **Heimatmuseum** (history museum) of Triberg is open from the first of May until the end of September from 8 a.m. to 6 p.m. (off-season from 9 a.m. to noon and 2 to 5 p.m.), charging an admission of 3.50 DM ($1.16). Here, life in the olden days of the Black Forest comes vividly alive with displays of dresses, handicrafts, furnishings, and of course, several exhibitions of clockmaking. You can also see examples of Black Forest woodcarving, and children take delight in a model of the famed Schwarzwaldbahn railway (it works).

One of the most beautiful churches in the Black Forest, **Wallfahrtskirche Maria in der Tannen** ("Church of Our Lady of the Fir Trees") is within easy reach. It was built in the early years of the 18th century, and has a superb collection of elaborate baroque furnishings, including a remarkable pulpit.

In the little shops you'll find woodcarvings, music boxes, and other traditional crafts. If you're determined to return from Germany with a cuckoo clock or some other Black Forest timepiece, you may want to visit the **Haus der 1000 Uhren** ("House of 1000 Clocks") (tel. 5581), at Triberg-Gremmelsbach, along the B33 between Triberg and Hornberg. You'll recognize it immediately, with its giant cuckoo clock and waterwheel in front of the house. A painter of clock faces, Josef Weisser, launched the business in 1824. He was the great-great-grandfather of the present owner. For five generations patrons have been flocking to this shop, with its special clocks and souvenirs. They ship to the U.S. and take all major credit cards.

After a visit here, you may want to drive to **Vogtsbauerhof,** a little village containing original Black Forest homes, some dating back as much as six centuries. In the museum you can see artifacts of the old way of life in the forest. In summer guides will help demonstrate some of the looms and other skills. Visits are possible from April to October daily from 8:30 a.m. to 5 p.m. for an admission of 3 DM (99¢).

WHERE TO STAY: **Parkhotel Wehrle,** Markplatz (tel. 40-81). Its lemon-yellow walls and gabled mansard roof occupy one of the most prominent street corners in town. It was built in the early 1600s and, around 1730, was acquired by a family who has held onto it ever since. Today ivy trails across its facade, and its interior contains an array of antiques which are fully appreciated by the loyal clientele, many of whom wouldn't think of staying anywhere else. The main house offers an old-world atmosphere, but forest-loving vacationers often request an accommodation in the chalet-style villa, lying in a separate location near the woods. There, a swimming pool and breeze-filled balconies create a modern sylvan retreat. For either branch of this establishment, there is ample parking. Singles rent for 60 DM ($19.80) to 115 DM ($37.95), and doubles cost between 125 DM ($41.25) and 240 DM ($79.20).

Römischer Kaiser, 35 Sommerauer Strasse (tel. 44-18), at Nussbach, outside of Triberg, is a comfortable hotel which has been owned by several generations of the same family since 1840. It rents out about two dozen pleasantly furnished bedrooms. The exterior is a charmingly preserved Black Forest hotel, with lots of exposed wood, and the in-house restaurant is recommended separately. Singles cost from 48 DM ($15.84), while doubles run between 85 DM ($28.05) and 100 DM ($33), depending on the accommodation. The inn is closed from mid-November to December 20.

WHERE TO DINE: Parkhotel Wehrle, Marktplatz (tel. 40-81). On sunny days a sort of golden glow seems to emanate from the parquet floor of the hotel's elegantly proportioned restaurant. Accompanied by the ticking of a stately grandfather clock, full meals are served to a clientele who relax in the cane-bottomed comfort of French-style armchairs. Some of the wild game specialties served here are prepared for two persons. There is also an array of veal, fish, and regional specialties. If you like trout, it is prepared in about two dozen different ways. Fixed-price meals range from 50 DM ($16.50) to 110 DM ($36.30), while à la carte dinners cost 30 DM ($9.90) to 60 DM ($19.80). Food is served between noon and 2 p.m. and from 7 to 10 p.m. every day.

Römischer Kaiser, 35 Sommerauer Strasse (tel. 44-18), along route B33, at Nussbach, was previously recommended as a hotel. Some guests consider one of the best views in the area to be the one from a comfortable chair in this in-house restaurant. The mountains of distant Switzerland are visible on a clear day. Of more interest, however, is the well-prepared nouvelle cuisine repertoire which has made this restaurant so popular. An array of super-fresh fish is available throughout the year. Examples include lake trout served with a watercress mousse and wild salmon with a lobster cream sauce and fresh asparagus. Meals range from 25 DM ($8.25) to 55 DM ($18.15). Food is served from noon to 1:30 p.m. and 6 to 9 p.m. every day of the week but Thursday. The establishment is closed from mid-November until about ten days before Christmas.

6. Freudenstadt

This sunny resort has no castle overshadowing it as many German villages do, but it certainly has an enormous castle square. This plot of land, the largest marketplace in Germany, was laid out in the 16th century for a castle that was never built. But history's loss is today's gain, because the market square that greets the visitor to Freudenstadt is a maze of lawns and concrete, broken by patches of flowers and kiosks. The buildings surrounding the square are mainly postwar, since the air raids of World War II almost completely destroyed the city. A few of the old Renaissance structures on the square have been reconstructed, up to their neat little archways and gabled roofs.

Originally founded by Protestants, the town takes pride in its **Stadtkirche,** dating from the 17th century. The unusual L-shaped architecture of the church brings the two main aisles together at right angles. Over the entrances stand identical towers, topped with rounded domes and narrow spires. The church's most important treasure is the reading desk from the 12th century. The desk is supported by carved and painted likenesses of the writers of the four Gospels.

Freudenstadt's attraction springs not from the town itself, but from its ideal location in the midst of the best hiking and camping country in the Black Forest. Trails wind for hundreds of miles in the nearby hills, and in winter the snow-covered paths become ski trails.

AN UPPER-BRACKET HOTEL: Steigenberger Park-Hostellerie, 129 Karl-von-Hahn-Strasse (tel. 8-10-71). Looking like a modern steel-and-glass cube rising abruptly from the forest around it, this well-directed chain hotel offers clean and comfortable rooms to guests, costing from 180 DM ($59.40) to 235 DM ($77.50) in a double and from 108 DM ($35.64) to 148 DM ($48.84) in a single, depending on the season and the location of the room. A variety of board plans are also offered, as well as a special gourmet program. I was impressed by the imaginatively warm decor of the public rooms (there are a lot of them!) and by the size of the swimming pool. Bedrooms are comfortably carpeted, padded, and upholstered in pleasing autumnal tones. The manager here will see that things run smoothly during your visit.

MIDDLE-BRACKET HOTELS: Luz Posthotel, 5 Stuttgarter Strasse (tel. 24-21). Claire Luz is your host in this downtown hotel, established in 1809, which today has at least 50 years of ivy growing over it. Rooms inside are comfortably furnished in upholstered easy chairs and love seats, while the dining room has Oriental rugs over the well-polished floors, and, unusual for a hotel in Germany, Queen Anne chairs. With breakfast, a single rents for 75 DM ($24.75) to 110 DM ($36.30), a double goes for 125 DM ($41.25) to 150 DM ($49.50). The sun terrace and café in front appear to be popular with local residents.

Kurhotel Sonne am Kurpark, 63 Turnhallestrasse (tel. 60-44). The streamlined electric candelabra lighting the path to this modern hotel promise an attractively imaginative interior, and that's just what you'll get at this family-franchised chain hotel. Many of the ceilings are made of rustic wood paneling, with pink and mauve peacock designs set into panels in the dining room. The Espenlaub family charges 58 DM ($19.14) in a bathless single, the price rising to 130 DM ($42.90) in a deluxe single with all the plumbing needed and a private balcony. Doubles range in price from 102 DM ($33.66) to 188 DM ($62.04), with breakfast included. Half board is also available at another 30 DM ($9.90) per person daily.

Hotel Bären, 33 Langestrasse (tel. 27-29). The pleasing proportions of this rustic country house promise a sympathetic visit, thanks to the thoughtful administration of Louis Montigel. The interior is warmly decorated in a mixture of white stucco and exposed beams, with lots of wooden accessories highlighting key conversational areas. An attractively subdued dining room serves a first-class cuisine. Singles with breakfast rent from 50 DM ($16.50) to 65 DM ($21.45) apiece, while doubles run from 102 DM ($33.66) to 120 DM ($39.60). If the Hotel Bären is full, the management will direct you to their other establishment, the Landhaus Montigel, where rooms with breakfast are slightly less expensive.

Kur- und Sporthotel Eden, 5 Im Nickentäle (tel. 70-37), is a sprawling complex of concrete, glass, and wood detailing in a style vaguely reminiscent of an overblown chalet, but aesthetically pleasing nonetheless. You'll find a complete array of sports facilities here, including an indoor pool, a sauna, tennis, and golf. Prices, which include breakfast, range from 142 DM ($46.86) to 154 DM ($50.82) per person in a double and from 95 DM ($31.35) to 130 DM ($42.90) in a single. Herr Stollberg, the considerate manager, offers much help in making your stay here a memorable one.

Hotel Hohenried, 5 Zeppelinstrasse (tel. 24-14), is a beautifully constructed chalet-style building, with three floors of beflowered balconies and a modern annex stretching off to the side. This tasteful establishment is directed by Olivier Schrikker. Only 15 minutes by foot from the center of town, the hotel has a spacious interior, with much skillfully crafted detailing in the public rooms. The bedrooms are usually sunny and always well furnished. There is an indoor swimming pool and a well-maintained lawn with trees. You'll find a complete regimen of beauty treatments available from the licensed cosmetician, Frau Bärbel Kögel. Twice weekly a gym session is supervised every morning, followed by a massage. Prices in a single go from 95 DM ($31.35) to 100 DM ($33), and in a double from 85 DM ($28.05) to 90 DM ($29.70) per person. Half board is also available, costing another 22 DM ($7.26) per person daily.

A BUDGET HOTEL: Gasthof Schwanen, 65 Herrenfelder Strasse (tel. 27-71). This lemon-colored, four-story building has been owned by members of the same family since around 1900. Today its red-tile roof and steep gables shelter one of the most attractive and reasonably priced hotels in town. Guests climb to their bedrooms via a well-polished stairwell, whose balustrade curves toward a stone fireplace. There is an array of paneled public rooms, including a TV salon, a comfortable breakfast room capped by an arched wooden ceiling, and a country-rustic weinstube, plus a formal dining room. Most guests prefer to take full board here, a bargain at prices ranging between 55 DM ($18.15) and 63 DM ($20.79) per person daily, depending on the accommodation. The Schmutz family members are your congenial hosts.

WHERE TO DINE: Ratskeller, 8 Marktplatz (tel. 26-93), is a small inn directly on the marketplace. It's charmingly old world in style: the lower rooms are set back with three Romanesque colonnades, and the other levels have windows with shutters and windowboxes of red geraniums. The Ratskeller's manager disarmingly says, "We are a little house, but a fine house." The main dining room is traditional, with its dark paneled walls and ceiling. Tables are arranged around a tiled stove. Down below is the antique wine cellar, all bricked, even its steep coved ceiling. The Ratskeller has a distinguished cuisine, with many international specialties. Try, for example, the sole meunière, medallion of veal, or tournedos sauté Tour d'Argent. Meals cost from 32 DM ($10.56) to 70 DM ($23.10). Closed Tuesday.

    Steigenberger Park-Hostellerie, 129 Karl-von-Hahn-Strasse (tel. 8-10-71). The Restaurant "Im Schnokeloch," located on the premises of the most prestigious hotel in Freudenstadt, serves a savory and pungent array of grilled meats and Black Forest specialties such as trout in Riesling and wild game (in season). A complete meal here will cost from 35 DM ($11.55) to 60 DM ($19.80). Service is from noon to 2 p.m. and 6 to 9 p.m. Many of the guests at the restaurant are vacationing hikers who have spent the day traversing the myriad forest trails around the hotel.

    Kurhotel Sonne am Kurpark, 63 Turnhallestrasse (tel. 60-44). At this elegant Black Forest hotel, classical French cuisine in the grand style is served. Vegetarian dishes are also available. Everything is carefully organized and carried through under the direction of Elisabeth Espenlaub, from the moment you sit down until the arrival of the dessert buffet which puts the capstone on your culinary experience. Meals begin at 30 DM ($9.90), going up to 90 DM ($29.70) for a surprise banquet of eight courses. In this previously recommended hotel, the restaurant serves from noon to 2 p.m. and 6 to 10 p.m. It's closed in November and from mid-December until Christmas.

    Kurhotel Schwarzwaldhof, 74 Hohenrieder Strasse (tel. 74-21). In wintertime, a blazing fireplace welcomes guests to the dining room, which is part of the complete health complex of this international spa hotel. The hotel's restaurant is known in the Black Forest as a "watering hole" for devotees of nouvelle cuisine, which is reasonably priced for such a fine establishment. A dinner costs from 35 DM ($11.55), going up to 60 DM ($19.80) for the more elaborate specialties. You might try the suprême of capon or the veal in a saffron bouillon sauce. Service is from noon to 2 p.m. and 6 to 9 p.m.

Weinstuben Bären, 33 Lange Strasse (tel. 65-85), is part of a hotel previously recommended. Catering to a festive crowd of winter sports enthusiasts and summer vacationers, this gemütlich hotel shelters a wood-covered restaurant, with the predictably rustic furnishings that warm the heart of anyone who is tired of inner-city chrome and concrete. Serving a cuisine in keeping with its decor, the restaurant prepares Swabian specialties, offering more than half a dozen fixed-price menus, ranging from 26 DM ($8.58), which I found the best meal in Freudenstadt for the price, up to 65 DM ($21.45) if you want to go the whole piggie. Specialties include trout and game dishes, plus there is an array of wurst. The chef does a delightful sauerbraten as well. The weinstube is open from 10 a.m. to midnight, but closed Sunday after 3 p.m. and all day Monday. It also closed from mid-January until the first of February.

7. Titisee

After a brisk session of ice skating on the lake or horseback riding through the hills, you can return to your homey inn in this tiny resort. The hospitality of Titisee knows no hour nor season. This year-round resort on the banks of Lake Titisee, 20 miles southeast of Freiburg, is as popular for winter sleigh rides and skiing as it is for summer swimming, boating, and fishing. The surrounding mountains, including the **Feldberg,** the highest point in the Black Forest (5000 feet), are ideal for hiking and mountain climbing.

The town of Titisee is a well-staffed spa, with therapeutic thermal baths, and various treatments for cardiac and vascular disorders, as well as for rheumatism and intestinal diseases. It has all the other facilities of a resort town too, including concerts in the open-air pavilion, tennis courts, and various social events.

Shoppers gravitate to the waterfront stores where they find good buys in Bavarian enamelware and Hummel figurines.

At night a Bavarian marching band plays, its members going from one hotel to another.

THE TOP HOTELS: Treschers Schwartzwaldhotel am See, 12 Seestrasse (tel. 81-11), reigns supreme in Titisee as the most fashionable hotel. It gets "A" for position, in the heart of the village, right on the lakeside, with an unimpaired view. Most of its life centers around its waterside courtyard. Plants and garden furniture make for an easy life on the wide sun terrace. The dining room is provincial in style, the sun room a multitude of vines and plants (the latter is an ideal spot for breakfast). Also inviting is a rustic weinstube for drinks before or after your meal. Its decor has a barn theme, with horseshoes, brasses, alpine chairs, and wrought-iron lamps. A large enclosed swimming pool has an all-glass wall on the lakeside. It's fun to swim here. Accommodations are wide ranging, going from spacious to closet-sized. A bathless single in high season costs 110 DM ($36.30), rising to 160 DM ($52.80) with complete bath. A double without bath is 130 DM ($42.90), increasing to 230 DM ($75.90) with complete bath in high season. If you're not on the full-board plan, you can order a three-course dinner for anywhere from 35 DM ($11.55) to 70 DM ($23.10).

Seehotel Wiesler, Strandbadstrasse (tel. 83-30), may well be the most attractive place to stay around the lake. It's built in a chalet style, long and low, with three floors of bedrooms, each with its own balcony. Bedrooms are country style, with traditional furnishings. A bathless single costs from 80 DM ($26.40); with shower or bath, 102 DM ($33.66). Doubles with shower or bath go for 140 DM ($46.20) to 180 DM ($59.40).

Kurhotel Brugger am See, Strandbadstrasse (tel. 82-39), is one of the leading hotels around the waterfront. It's a modified chalet, with balconies and an all-window dining room. Its café and konditorei have an open-beamed ceiling and country-style chairs. The interior is contemporary, done in harmonious colors. On the premises are several cure baths and an indoor pool. Bedrooms are fair-sized. With a complete bath, the single tariff ranges from 110 DM ($36.30) to 140 DM ($46.20). In a double with bath, the charge goes from 150 DM ($49.50) to 240 DM ($79.20), depending on the quality of the room.

MEDIUM-PRICE HOTELS: Waldeck, 6 Parkstrasse (tel. 82-27). This country hotel is popular in both winter and summer, and an elegant crowd often shows up for some of the formal dinners the Franz family gives during the winter holidays. The exterior is sheltered against a pine-covered hillock, which attractively sets off the blunted ends of the gabled slate roof. The interior is richly decorated with Oriental rugs, hexagonal floor tiles, and a beamed and paneled wooden ceiling with full-grained molding and doorways. For activities, try the indoor pool, or the miles of forest trails around the hotel. Singles cost 58 DM ($19.14) to 73 DM ($24.09), breakfast included, while doubles go for 96 DM ($31.68) to 132 DM ($43.56) daily. Don't be surprised if you meet the owners in the sauna —they have to relax too!

Romantik Hotel Adler Post, Titisee-Neustadt (tel. 50-66). Many residents of town praise this attractive restaurant and hotel, a historic coaching inn dating from 1576. In the subsequent centuries it was a relay station on the postal route between Innsbruck and Strasbourg. Today it is run by Werner Ketterer, whose great-great-grandfather purchased it. The building rises an imposing four stories from a street-corner location in the center of town. It has stone corner mullions, a red gabled roof, and sunflower-colored walls. The 32 bedrooms are usually furnished with hand-painted Schwarzwald-style furniture, as well as complete bath, phone, radio, and mini-bar. My favorite rooms are up under the eaves in an exposed-beam format of woodsy charm and rustic accents. With breakfast included, the per-person rate ranges from 55 DM ($18.15) to 80 DM ($26.40), based on double occupancy. Singles cost between 65 DM ($21.45) and 90 DM ($29.70), depending on the plumbing and the season. Half board can be arranged for 35 DM ($11.55) per person extra per day. There's an indoor swimming pool on the premises. Clients arriving by train should get off at the Neustadt/Schwarzwald train station instead of at Titisee.

BUDGET LODGING: Rauchfang, 2 Bärenhofweg (tel. 85-55). One of the most pleasant pension-hotels in the upper Black Forest region, this modern auberge is one of the most convincingly authentic of all the reproduction chalet-style buildings. This is mainly because of its gently curving roofline capped with slates, and the masses of flowers on the wooden balconies. You'll find the interior of the public rooms covered in pine, and although the bedrooms appear somewhat stark, you'll probably spend a very pleasant evening here. Guests can enjoy the indoor pool or the miles of forest walks stretching in all directions. The Edlefsens are your hosts here, and they charge from 55 DM ($18.15) to 70 DM ($23.10) in a single and 96 DM ($31.68) to 136 DM ($44.88) in a double, including breakfast. For half board, you pay another 22 DM ($7.26) per person daily.

Rheinland, 25 Jägerstrasse (tel. 84-74). Pleasingly proportioned, with three well-constructed floors of oversize windows and wooden balconies, this recently built hotel is the property of the Kelletat family. They offer clean rooms with predictably modern furniture, costing anywhere from 45 DM ($14.85) to 65 DM ($21.45) in a single, and 100 DM ($33) to 105 DM ($34.65) in a double, breakfast included. The hotel also has a sauna.

WHERE TO DINE: **Treschers Schwarzwald Hotel,** 12 Seestrasse (tel. 81-11), was previously recommended as the featured hotel of Titisee. Even if you're not staying there (and aren't on the board plan somewhere else), you might want to escape your hotel dining room for a meal here in a tranquil setting. The menu is written in three languages, reflecting the international cuisine available here. Many of the chef's specialties are regional and prepared from scratch. The red-carpeted dining room offers a panoramic view of the Titisee a few yards away. One of the most popular selections on the menu here is a hunter's plate, a selection of game meats served with potato croquettes and cranberries, or a filet of venison with peaches and mashed potatoes. Meals range from 35 DM ($11.55) to 70 DM ($23.10). Hours are 7 a.m. (for the breakfast trade) to 11 p.m. It is closed from the beginning of November until December 20.

Titisee Hotel, 16 Seestrasse (tel. 81-52), stands near the just-previewed Treschers Schwarzwald Hotel. Many guests consider the Titisee equally as good, in both hotel amenities and food. Certainly it has an established restaurant, popular with both visitors and locals. The chef specializes in regional and French dishes against a backdrop of a Bavarian decor. A dinner here will cost from 30 DM ($9.90), and on some nights ravenous diners have spent as much as 70 DM ($23.10), but that would be sheer gluttony. Clients who prefer can serve themselves from the elegant buffet set up most nights at one end of the restaurant. The establishment is attractively intimate, and hours are 12:30 to 2:30 p.m. and 6:30 to 9:30 p.m.

The **Romantik Hotel Adler-Post,** 16 Hauptstrasse (tel. 50-66), at Neustadt, in the environs, is one of the most famous establishments in the Black Forest. You'll find it usually crowded with local residents on holiday outings, who savor the fresh trout, game dishes, and charcoal-grilled steaks, along with such specialties of the season as fresh asparagus, fresh herring filets, and fresh mushrooms such as chanterelles from the forest, plus mussels, oysters, and several varieties of fish from local rivers and lakes. Fixed-price menus begin at 30 DM ($9.90), and you could spend as much as 65 DM ($21.45) if you order the gourmet menu.

Coming up, more romantic scenery.

Chapter IX

LAKE CONSTANCE

1. Constance (Konstanz)
2. Meersburg
3. Lindau

EVEN THOUGH THREE NATIONS—Austria, Germany, and Switzerland—share the 162-mile shoreline of this large inland sea, the area around Lake Constance is united in a common cultural and historical heritage. The hillsides sloping down to the water's edge are covered with vineyards and orchards and dotted with colorful hamlets and busy tourist centers. The mild climate and plentiful sunshine make Lake Constance a vacation spot for lovers of sun and sand, as well as for sightseers and spa-hoppers. A well-organized network of cruise ships and ferries links every major center around the lake.

Lake Constance is divided into three lakes, although the name is frequently applied only to the largest of these, the **Bodensee.** The western end of the Bodensee separates into two distinct branches, including the **Überlingersee,** a long fjord. On the other hand, the **Untersee** is more irregular, jutting in and out of the marshlands and low-lying woodlands. It is connected to the larger lake by only a narrow channel of water—actually, the young Rhine, whose current flows right through the Bodensee. Tip: The blue felchen, a pike-like fish found only in Lake Constance, furnishes the district with a tasty and renowned specialty.

Our exploration of Lake Constance begins with the city on the Rhine which bears the same name.

1. Constance (Konstanz)

Crowded against the shores of Lake Constance by the borders of Switzerland, this medieval town had nowhere to grow but northward across the river. The resort city lies on both banks of the infant Rhine as it begins its long journey from the Bodensee to the North Sea. This strategic position has made Constance the most important city on the lake since a Roman fortification was established here under Claudius in A.D. 41.

The city's claim to historical fame is because it was the chosen site of the Christian Reform Council, held here from 1414 to 1418, when the delegates from the entire Christian world temporarily increased the population by 600%. During this period the Catholic church resolved its quarrel over the claims of three rivals for the papacy by electing a fourth individual, Martin V, as pope.

THE SIGHTS: The best way to see Constance is from the water. Several pleasure ships offer tours across the lake to Meersburg, or just along the shoreline of the city. (Ferries to Meersburg leave every ten minutes, day or night, the price depending on the size of your car. For the average compact car and two passengers, expect to pay 15 DM, or $4.95.) The water's edge is the most fascinating part of Constance, as the little inlets weave in and out of the land, around ancient buildings and the city gardens where concerts are presented outdoors during the summer.

Below the gardens is the **Council Building,** originally constructed as a storehouse in 1388, but used for many meetings during its early years. None was so important, however, as the meeting here in November 1417 of the Roman Conclave that elected Cardinal Otto of Colonna as Pope Martin V. The hall was restored in 1911 and decorated with murals depicting the history of the town. On the harbor in front of the building is an obelisk erected in memory of Count Ferdinand Zeppelin, a citizen of Constance who invented the first dirigible airship in the late 19th century.

From the water you can also see the towers of the Romanesque **basilica** rising behind the city garden. Begun in 1052 on the foundation of an even older cathedral, the church took centuries to complete. The neo-Gothic spire was added only in 1856. During the Council of Constance, the members of the synod met here. From the top of the tower, a view opens onto the lake and the city.

An Excursion to Mainau Island

Four miles north of Constance, in the arm of the Bodensee known as the Überlingersee, is the unusual island of Mainau, a tropical paradise. Here palms and orange trees grow in profusion and fragrant flowers bloom all year, practically in the shadow of the snow-covered Alps. In the center of this botanical oasis is an ancient castle, once a residence of the Knights of the Teutonic Order. Both the castle and the island are owned by a Swedish count, but can be visited by the public. You can get to the island either by tour boat from Constance, or by walking across the small footbridge connecting Mainau to the mainland north of the city. Admission is 7 DM ($2.31). The gardens are open Easter to October until dusk.

AN UPPER-BRACKET HOTEL: Steigenberger Hotel Insel, 1 Auf der Insel (tel. 2-50-11), is a successful example of the transformation of a lakeside 13th-century Dominican monastery into a first-class hotel. Its situation is prime for the area—on an island, with its own lakeside gardens and dock (the hotel has a private yacht for use of guests). The step-gabled building is white, with an inner Romanesque cloister. The informal dining room has Windsor chairs, wood-paneled walls, and planters of flowers, not to mention ecclesiastical arches and pillars. The bedrooms are well coordinated, with homey patterned fabrics. The furnishings are fine, and most doubles have a living room look with sofas, armchairs, and coffee tables. All rooms have their own bath. The cost ranges from 135 DM ($44.55) to 200 DM ($66) in a single and from 205 DM ($67.65) to 250 DM ($82.50) in a double.

At twilight, guests gather at the intimate Zeppelin Bar. Very club-like, its walls are cluttered with framed letters and documents. (The man who pioneered the airship also turned this abbey into a hotel.) A gemütlich spirit prevails in the Weinstube, with its knotty-pine bar, pine chairs and tables, parquet floors, ceramic collection, and decorative green and white eight-foot-high tiled stove in the corner. Here guests order wine, beer, and light snacks.

MIDDLE-BRACKET HOTELS: Mago Hotel, 4 Bahnhofplatz (tel. 2-70-01). The entrance to this hotel is one of those elegantly and rigidly narrow archways with an ornate paneled and wrought-iron door set into it. The interior is boldly decorated, in red and black plaid carpeting, op-art, and modern chandeliers. Rooms are sunny, comfortable, and warm, and come with plumbing, phone, TV, and a mini-bar which you stock yourself. Singles go for 85 DM ($28.05) to 115 DM ($37.95), while doubles cost 140 DM ($46.20) to 190 DM ($62.70), breakfast included. You're just a two-minute walk from the Bahnnof here, and within view of the lake.

Buchner Hof, 6 Buchnerstrasse (tel. 5-10-35). A well-proportioned and elegantly simple white facade greets guests of this 25-bed hotel in Petershausen, across the river from Constance. Nonetheless, you'll find the hotel a short walk to most points of interest. Owners Niko and Stefan Ott do everything they can to explain the diversions of the lake district. The hotel, incidentally, is named after the composer Hans Buchner, who became the organist of the town cathedral in 1510 and is said to have been one of the first musicians to arrange and catalogue the wealth of Gregorian chants he found in the region. Rooms are pleasantly and comfortably furnished, renting for 70 DM ($23.10) to 95 DM ($31.35) in a single and 90 DM ($29.70) to 145 DM ($47.85) in a double, including breakfast. The hotel has a sauna and a solarium.

Seeblick, 14 Neuhauser Strasse (tel. 5-40-18). In summer you'll probably want to spend a lot of time beside the pool of this modern balconied hotel, with a low annex and a landscaped sun terrace. Directed by Friedrich Ganter, the hotel rents clean, comfortable rooms with breakfast included. Singles cost from 62 DM ($20.46) to 130 DM ($42.90), and doubles go for 112 DM ($36.96) to 162 DM ($53.46). The hotel also has a good restaurant where meals cost from 28 DM ($9.24).

Eden, 4 Bahnhofstrasse (tel. 2-30-93), is close to the train station but still enjoys a quiet central location. This inconspicuous family-run guest house could be a comfortable lodging place during your holiday in Constance. Whether you prefer to stay at the hotel all day playing bridge, or perhaps go boating, the staff will do all they can to make your stay comfortable. They rent their cozy rooms for 75 DM ($24.75) in a single and from 130 DM ($42.90) in a double, breakfast included.

BUDGET LODGING: Deutsches Haus, 15 Marktstätte (tel. 2-70-65). You might find some of the neighbors gossiping on the two wrought-iron benches in front of this hotel, and you might even find that before the end of your stay you've joined them. This six-story hotel of 42 rooms offers clean, quiet, comfortably furnished units behind a modern facade. Twin-bedded rooms rent for 120 DM ($39.60) to 140 DM ($46.20), while singles go for 55 DM ($18.15) to 70 DM ($23.10), breakfast included.

Goldener Sternen, 1 Bodanplatz (tel. 2-52-28). The owner maintains a friendly atmosphere and tasteful decorations. The color of the dozens of healthy green plants is reflected in the pleasing tones of green throughout the Goldener Sternen. The rooms are comfortable and spotlessly maintained, costing from 45 DM ($14.85) to 55 DM ($18.15) in a single and from 80 DM ($26.40) to 90 DM ($31.35) per person in a double.

WHERE TO DINE: Seehotel Siber, 25 Seestrasse (tel. 6-30-44), is an outstanding choice for food, the best in Constance, and it's run by Berthold Siber, a celebrated chef in the area. He operates this place, which also has rooms, at a location near the casino overlooking the lake. Earlier in his career Herr Siber studied with Paul Bocuse and Roger Verge, the famous French chefs. Today his establishment occupies an art nouveau–style villa, whose rich decor has been modernized.

Here specialties border on a conservative dosage of nouvelle cuisine. The menu changes daily, based on the seasonal availability of certain ingredients. Your meal might begin with a lobster terrine with a butter and red basil seasoning, or freshly caught lake trout with an array of seasonings. You might also prefer, if featured, his roast Barbary goose with a beaujolais sauce or his stuffed turbot with lobster (served with freshly picked leaf lettuce). Most guests opt for one of three fixed-price menus, one of which is reasonably priced at 40 DM ($13.20). However, the tab could easily go as high as 125 DM ($41.25). The establishment takes its last dinner order at 11 p.m.

The Seehotel Siber is mostly acclaimed as a restaurant, but it also rents out 11 handsomely furnished rooms in an adjacent hotel, costing between 200 DM ($66) and 260 DM ($85.80) in a double and from 160 DM ($52.80) to 210 DM ($69.30) in a single.

Ratsstube, 16 Kanzleistrasse (tel. 2-24-44). Fortunately for the view, this "rat" is not housed in a cellar, so you can enjoy the sunlight while eating in this white and gold room with pink napery. Chef Gerhard Waskan prepares regional gutbürgerlich specialties such as trout from the nearby lake or a half quail, roasted and basted in its own juices. If, however, you yearn for the lighter fare of the neuen kuchen, you can request that your quail be served with an aspic of sauterne and a salad of baby lettuce, or perhaps you'd enjoy a salad made from local freshwater fish in a warm cabbage sauce. This could be followed by Black Forest cake or an appropriately nouvelle cuisine fruity dessert. A fixed-price meal begins at 18.50 DM ($6.11), but more likely you'll spend around 55 DM ($18.15), or even more if you order some specialties. Hours are 11 a.m. to 3 p.m. and 5 to 11 p.m.

Casino Restaurant am See, 21 Seestrasse (tel. 6-36-15). If you happen to be losing at French or American roulette on one of your casino outings in Constance, you can revive your spirits (and drink a few too) on the lakeside terrace of this casino restaurant. The view is lovely, the food first rate. You'll need a break anyway from the intensity of the gaming tables. Meals cost 28 DM ($9.24) to 40 DM ($13.20). The restaurant offers a good choice of dishes, especially fresh fish. Everything is backed up by a good wine cellar. Hours are daily from 5:30 p.m. to 2 a.m. (on Sunday from 3 p.m. to 2 a.m.).

Schwedenschenke, on Mainau Island (tel. 3-13-62). Local holiday-makers sometimes make a pilgrimage to this island in Lake Constance for a gourmet meal in a country villa housing an old-fashioned restaurant in a comfortable setting. Meals can easily run as high as 45 DM ($14.85), depending on what you order. Hours are 8:30 a.m. to midnight. The restaurant is closed on Monday in November and December, and from the first of the year until mid-March.

2. Meersburg

Like the towns of the lake district of Italy, this village on the northern shores of Lake Constance cascades in terraces down the hillside until it touches the water. You can drive into town as far as the New Castle, but it's best to leave your car at the northern edge and explore on foot. In the center, the streets become nothing but narrow promenades and steps wandering up and down the hillside.

THE SIGHTS: Entering the town through the ancient **Obertor** (upper gate), you're in the Marketplace and facing the 16th-century Rathaus (Town Hall), containing a typical German Ratskeller. Leading off from this is **Steigstrasse,** the most interesting artery, passing between rows of half-timbered houses whose arcades serve as covered walkways above the street. Nearby is the **Old Castle** (Alte Schloss), with its Dagobert's Tower dating from 628, the oldest German castle still standing. The interior contains exhibits of medieval weapons and armor, as well as a group of furnished rooms where the German poetess Annette von Droste-Hülshoff lived and died. Adjoining is the **Castle Mill**

(1620), with a 28-foot wooden water wheel, the oldest of its kind in Germany. The castle is open March 1 until the end of October from 9 a.m. to 6 p.m. (November until the end of February from 10:30 a.m. to noon and 1 to 4:30 p.m.), charging an admission of 5 DM ($1.65).

Even more interesting is the **New Castle,** a masterpiece by the leading German baroque architect, Balthasar Neumann. Erected in 1750, the castle was the residence of the prince-bishops of Constance. The chapel in the left wing is worthy. Note also the huge double staircase, with rococo grillwork alternated with baroque statuary. Perched on the crest of the steep hill which plunges to the lake below, the castle affords a view.

On the promenade below stands the **Great House,** dating from 1505 and housing ticket offices for the railway and for steamer lines on Lake Constance. Regular ferry service to Constance leaves from the dock on the outskirts of town.

A 15-minute drive from Meersburg will take you to the famous **Wallfahrtskirche,** the pilgrimage basilica at Birnau, three miles southeast of Überlingen. It dates from the mid-18th century and was built in the rococo style, with rose, blue, and beige marble predominating. One statuette here is celebrated. The Germans call it a *honigschlecker* or "honey-taster." It shows a baby sucking its finger as he's yanked out of a nest of bees. It's found to the right of the St. Bernard altarpiece. The 15th-century *Mother and Child* above the tabernacle on the main altar is an object of worship among the devout who flock here.

MIDDLE-BRACKET HOTELS: Villa Bellevue, 5 Am Rosenhag (tel. 97-70).

The generous and homey spirit of Fritz Brandner is reflected in the furnishings he chose for his modern chalet-style hotel whose balconies look over the lake. Every square foot of this place seems to be overstuffed with Wilhelminian gemütlichkeit, Oriental rugs, and heraldic emblems. In winter, however, he often has a fire burning in the sitting room, which changes everything into a heart-warming Teutonic kitsch. Single rooms go for 80 DM ($26.40) to 90 DM ($29.70), while doubles rent for 145 DM ($47.85) to 185 DM ($61.05), including breakfast. The hotel is closed from the end of October until March.

Wilder Mann, 2 Bismarckplatz (tel. 90-11). Built just beyond a stone embankment which defines the edge of the lake, the facade of this country baroque building is the backdrop for a painted illustration of a local version of the abominable snowman (der Wilde Mann) contemplating whether he'll have a stag or a unicorn for supper. Even the roofline's step-gabled design evokes another era in building construction. Rooms, available with or without private shower, range from a low of 55 DM ($18.15) per person to a high of 87 DM ($28.71), based on either single or double occupancy. It is open from March to October.

Terrassenhotel Weisshaar, 24 Stefan-Lochner-Strasse (tel. 90-06). Separated from the lake by a few weeping willows and a slight elevation, the panoramic windows of this hotel with their orange awnings can be seen from far away. The establishment is proud of its genteel traditions and entertains guests in spacious and sunny public rooms without any of the ponderous clutter of so many other hotels. The owner charges from 55 DM ($18.15) in a single and from 130 DM ($42.90) to 190 DM ($62.20) in a double, including breakfast.

Hotel 3 Stuben, 1–3 Winzergasse (tel. 60-19), is a Hansel and Gretel timbered weinhaus-restaurant-hotel. Potted trees stand at the doorway, along with window boxes of red geraniums. It's in the heart of the village—known not only for its old-world dining rooms, but for its modernized bedrooms. Innkeeper Peter Nicolaus knows his job well. He offers his guests immaculate rooms that are colorful and attractive, well appointed and not overpriced. All rooms contain shower or complete bath. Doubles range in price from a low of 108 DM ($35.64) to a high of 130 DM ($42.90), and singles cost from 80 DM ($26.40). If you come here to eat, the average set meal is 25 DM ($8.25). From the à la carte menu, try trout amandine or trout Konstanz. Filet of hare and pork steak with cherries are just some of the chef's specialties.

Weinstube Löwen, 2 Marktplatz (tel. 60-13), is an old inn, right on the market square, colorful for such a village. Its facade is a raspberry pink with green shutters, window boxes filled with red geraniums, and vines reaching the upper windows under the steep roof. For more than 50 years it's been run by the Stadelhofer-Langeder family, who have updated its interior, especially the bedrooms, which are almost all modernized. All rooms have a bath of some sort. Singles with shower rent for 65 DM ($21.45) to 70 DM ($23.10). Doubles with shower cost from 110 DM ($36.30), peaking at 138 DM ($45.54) with bath. The family has made everything home-like. For example, in the entry, with its provincial furnishings, are subtropical plants, a cage of canaries, a spinning wheel, and a mandolin on the wall. The Weinstube is wood paneled with a white ceramic stove in the corner. On the shelves are hunting and farming artifacts.

BUDGET HOTELS: **Seehotel zur Münz,** 7 Seestrasse (tel. 90-90). Only a pedestrian walkway and an iron railing separate this hotel from the tree-lined lakefront, and the management certainly capitalizes on the fact with the business they do at their lakeside café. The hotel is balconied and dotted with parasols, offering a kind of relaxed and sleepy ambience where you can forget urban bustle. Bernd Knaus and his family are your hosts, charging 60 DM ($19.80) in a single and from 92 DM ($30.36) to 116 DM ($38.28) in a double (without and with the lake view, respectively). All units have a shower and toilet, and tariffs include breakfast.

Hotel Zum Schiff, 5 Bismarckplatz (tel. 60-25). The sun terrace of this sprawling, oversize hotel, with a red tile roof and a single square tower, is built directly on the water, which will certainly improve your suntan if you choose to spend your morning idling over coffee. The ambience is pleasant here, and the interior is warm and comfortable. Lothar Gröer and his family rent clean and carpeted bedrooms for 40 DM ($13.20) in a single and from 75 DM ($24.75) in a double. If you want a shower and toilet, the prices go up to 75 DM ($24.75) in a single and 120 DM ($39.60) in a double. The hotel is open from April to October.

Gasthof zum Bären, 11 Marktplatz (tel. 60-44), is a picture-book inn right in the heart of the village, a delightful place to stay. A five-story corner building with step gables, it has window boxes overflowing with red geraniums, an ornately decorated corner tower with steeple, plus a tangle of purple wisteria crawling over most of the facade. The innkeepers are the Gilowsky-Karrer family, who speak English and open their guest house from March to November. They treasure Zum Bären, which was built in the year 1510 and has been owned by their family since 1851. It is furnished with tavern pieces and alpine stools, all resting under beamed ceilings. The two dining rooms are colorfully primitive, and the bedrooms are most attractive. The cost for a single room is 50 DM ($16.50), and a double with shower goes for 86 DM ($28.38) to 96 DM ($31.68). These tariffs include a continental breakfast.

WHERE TO DINE: **Weinstube zum Becher,** 4 Höllgasse (tel. 90-09). If you've come to Germany with images of a handcrafted weinstube that radiates a kind of gemütlich warmth, then this is a place where you should dine. From a corner, a pea-green tile oven provides heat in winter and is merely decorative at other times. The chairs are not all that comfortable, as they are designed with a heart-shaped single splat, but the Teutonic comfort of the rest of the beflowered, paneled, and happily cluttered room will guarantee you a pleasant evening. The specialty of the chef is an onion-flavored Swabian rostbraten with spätzle, along with a host of other regional specialties. Be sure to reserve a table here for the meals, served between 10 a.m. and midnight every day except Monday and Tuesday (on Tuesday it opens at 5 p.m.). It's closed from December 1 to mid-January. A superb 32-DM ($10.56) set dinner is offered, which I always select, although you can spend far more ordering à la carte.

3. Lindau

Its unique setting on an island at the eastern end of the Bodensee made Lindau such a tourist attraction that it outgrew its boundaries and spread to the shores of the mainland. The garden city, stretching for five miles along the shoreline, caters to your every whim, from bathing to baccarat. The island also offers a look into the past of the former Free Imperial City.

Connected to the mainland by a road bridge and a causeway for walkers and trains, Lindau is easy to reach. It lies just at the edge of the Austrian frontier and is a transportation link between the western part of Lake Constance and the towns of Austria and Switzerland, which lie directly across the water.

THE SIGHTS: Whether you arrive at Lindau by boat or train, a tour of the Ferieninsel (Holiday Island) begins with the **old harbor,** seen from the lakeside promenade. The Mangturm, the old lighthouse, stands on the promenade as a reminder of the heavy fortifications that once surrounded the city. It also marks the point where Lindau was once divided into two islands (now filled in). The entrance to the harbor is marked by two silhouettes, the 108-foot **New Lighthouse** (19th century) and the **Bavarian Lion,** standing guard as yachts and commercial ships pass by below. From the promenade, you can gaze out past these monuments over the water to the Alps on the opposite side of the lake.

In the center of the town, the **Hauptstrasse** is the main street of the Altstadt. The most easily recognized building is the **Old Rathaus,** erected in 1422 on the site of a vineyard. The stepped gables are typical of the period, but the building's facade also combines many later styles of architecture. The interior, once used by the Imperial Diet as a Council Hall, is the town library.

Just north of the Hauptstrasse, with its half-timbered houses, is the town's most familiar landmark, the round **Diebsturm** (Thieves' Tower), with its turreted roof. Next to it is the oldest building in Lindau, **St. Peter's Church** (11th century), which houses a war memorial chapel. In the church is a group of frescoes painted by Hans Holbein the Elder.

Returning to the Hauptstrasse, which cuts through the exact center of the island, follow the street eastward to the **Haus zum Cavazzen,** considered the handsomest patrician's house on Lake Constance. Rebuilt in 1730 in the style of a baroque country mansion, it houses the municipal art collections. Included are exhibits of sculpture and painting from the Gothic, Renaissance, and baroque periods. Some of the rooms are furnished with period pieces showing how wealthy citizens lived in the 15th and 16th centuries. The 18th-century murals on the facade have been restored. It is open weekdays from 9 a.m. to noon and 2 to 5 p.m. (on Sunday from 10 a.m. to noon only). It is closed Monday and from January to March; admission is 3 DM (99¢).

Passing across the Marketplace and by the Collegiate Church and St. Stephen's Church, both baroque, you come to the strange pile of rocks known as **Heathen's Wall,** dating from Roman times. Beyond this is the solitude of the **Stadtgarten** (Town Gardens), which, although peaceful during the day, livens up at night when the wheels of the town's casino begin to whirl and spin.

UPPER-BRACKET HOTELS: Two hotels, under the same ownership and management, have taken over the best lakeside estate. They are right on the promenade facing the small harbor, with its monuments, a stone sphinx, and lighthouse. The twosome is appropriate for two budget levels. The more expensive is the Bayerischer Hof, followed by the middle-income Reutemann und Seegarten. A framed family tree in the Bayerischer Hof traces the lineage of the owners (the Spaeth family) back to the year 1660. The Reutemann and Seegarten has a special dining and dancing restaurant shared by all three hotels (closed in winter)—Zum Lieber Augustin, a romantic tavern, where spirits fly high under a beamed ceiling. Tyrolean chairs and tables are set on two levels, and a small orchestra plays in the background.

Bayerischer Hof, an der Seepromenade (tel. 50-55), is first class in atmosphere and service. It rises five stories high, one side facing the railway station plaza, the other the lake. Three-quarters of its rooms have a good view. The lesser chambers overlook a narrow thoroughfare. The dining room has dignity, with wide screened windows to allow a view for everyone. The lounges are tastefully decorated in traditional fashion, with antiques and reproductions, and Oriental rugs on parquet floors. A single with private bath costs 110 DM ($36.30) to 168 DM ($55.44). Doubles with private bath are 180 DM ($59.40) to 300 DM ($99). Breakfast is included.

Reutemann und Seegarten, an der Seepromenade (tel. 50-55, the same switchboard as the Bayerischer Hof), are two villas joined together to make one hotel. Standing next door to their parent, the Bayerischer Hof, the hotels, though one, are different. The Reutemann section has its own waterfront garden, with outdoor furniture amid the lemon trees and wisteria vines. Open all year, it is un-self-consciously and traditionally furnished in fine style. Most rooms are large, and some have tile bath, along with heated towel racks, huge tub, and endless hot water. It has a glassed-in dining room, where good meals are served. The Seegarten has the more attractive facade. It's built like a Bavarian villa, with little flower-filled balconies and trailing vines. It too has an informal lakefront garden with flowerbeds and furniture for sunbathing. The public rooms are modest and traditional, but attractive. The bedrooms are spacious and handsome, especially the lake-view ones (at higher rates, naturally). Singles begin modestly at 86 DM ($28.38), climbing to 120 DM ($39.60). Doubles range in price from 125 DM ($41.25) to 222 DM ($73.26).

MIDDLE-BRACKET HOTELS: **Lindauer Hof,** an der Seepromenade (tel. 40-64), is right in the center of activity, close to the boat docks and harbor, yet only a five-minute walk from the railway station plaza. An eye-catching, shuttered and gabled building, it faces a square, with a second-floor water-view terrace. Here you can dine under a flourishing wisteria vine. The lounge has an attractive collection of Empire and Biedermeier furniture. The bedrooms are nicely decorated, each in a unique fashion. Try for one with a view of the plaza and lake. Depending on the plumbing and the view, singles range from 60 DM ($19.80) to 88 DM ($29.04); doubles, 126 DM ($41.58) to 148 DM ($48.84), the latter tariff for accommodations with private bath, overlooking the lake. Facilities include an indoor swimming pool and sauna. It's open from March 15 to the end of November.

Helvetia, an der Seepromenade (tel. 59-98). In the evening the rows of lights below the eaves of this symmetrical building with striped sidewalk awnings give an effect like that of a carousel. The management tells me that a dye shop occupied the site of this hotel in the 12th century, but today the coloring vats have been replaced by barrels of beer and wine, which flow freely to the patrons of this establishment's busy sidewalk café. The interior is warmly decorated, with fabric-covered hanging lamps and an open fireplace, along with colorful carpets and big windows. Single rooms go for 85 DM ($28.05) to 115 DM ($37.95), while double rooms rent for 140 DM ($46.20) to 200 DM ($66), breakfast included.

BUDGET HOTELS: Insel, 42 Maximilianstrasse (tel. 50-17), only a quarter of a mile from the lake, is a completely renovated accommodation, with a bit of a reception room, plus an elevator. The upstairs rooms are comfortable and furnished with modern pieces. The breakfast room opens onto the traffic-free Maximilianstrasse (described under "Sights"). Singles rent for 80 DM ($26.40) with shower and toilet. A double with private bath rents from 130 DM ($42.90). Mr. and Mrs. Hans Grättinger provide a warm welcome.

Hotel-Pension Brugger, 11 Bei der Heidenmauer (tel. 2-64-64). Named after its owners, this hotel is pleasingly proportioned, with a gabled attic and expansive French doors opening onto the balconies in the back. Rooms are up-to-date, with toilet and shower, and lots of light. With breakfast included in the price, a single rents for 64 DM ($21.12) to 70 DM ($23.10); a double costs from 100 DM ($33) to 126 DM ($41.58). The same family owns an older building nearby where rates are roughly half those charged in their newer accommodation.

WHERE TO DINE: Hoyerberg Schlössle, 64 Hoyerbergstrasse, at Lindau-Aeschach (tel. 2-52-95), presents some of the finest food on Lake Constance. The location is in a building constructed as a private palace, then turned into an elegant bourgeois residence. Eventually the schloss was purchased by the city of Lindau and renovated. Since 1979 the inhabitants of the palace have been a team of dedicated chefs who have come closer than anyone else to recreating the ambience of the former lustschloss. A beautifully decorated inner room with a view of the mountains or lake, or one of two terraces, could be your choice of places to sample the delicacies produced by head chef Friedbert Lang. These include, for example, a terrine of shrimp, cream of scampi soup, fresh salad of homemade pâté de foie gras, Bodensee trout with a sauce of Pinot Blanc, and fresh suckling pig with baby cabbage. Dessert could be an impressive array of fruited sherbets. The café sections are open every day but Monday from noon to midnight, while warm food is served only from noon to 2 p.m. and 6:30 to 11 p.m. Count on spending from 40 DM ($13.20) to 85 DM ($28.05).

Walliser Stube, 7 Ludwigstrasse (tel. 64-49). Horst Bosselmann has gained a reputation as a gastronome since he established this cheerfully rustic restaurant and set out to become one of the most celebrated chefs on Lake Constance. He calls his art form "cuisine of the market," which emphasizes his zeal for fresh fish and meats. Of special note would be his terrine of goose liver, meat, poultry, and fish and also a new "variation of goose liver." Another hit is his creation of breast of poultry filled with mushrooms and roasted in cabbage. I recommend the selection of different fish in their own juice with fresh vegetables, game and wildfowl dishes, and the steak, rack of veal with a morel cream sauce, and homemade spätzle. Herr Bosselmann's charming wife, Hildegard, will see that everything runs smoothly in the dining room during your visit. She is also responsible for the wine recommendations (all the wines offered are from the small vintners in the lake region). The restaurant is open daily from 6 p.m. and on Saturday also from noon to 2 p.m. The stube is closed Sunday, for two weeks in November, and for two weeks in February. Reservations are recommended.

Spielbank Restaurant, 2 Oskar-Groll-Anlage (tel. 52-00), is one of the most prestigious restaurants in Lindau, perfect for a celebration meal. It is, in reality, a pavilion right on the lake, with scenic views. Surprisingly, you won't have to break the bank at the casino to dine here. For example, set lunches range from 35 DM ($11.55) up. In the evening, an à la carte dinner could cost as much as 70 DM ($23.10). It is closed on Tuesday and from November through March.

Gasthaus Zum Sünfzen, 1 Maximilianstrasse (tel. 58-65), is owned by the same family as the Insel. In an old arched house/restaurant, all wooded with windows in the antique glass style, it offers pleasant groups of tables covered with napkins. The food is good, the cost low. Meals begin at 22 DM ($7.26), climbing to 45 DM ($14.85). The restaurant closes from mid-January to mid-February.

———

In the following chapter, we head inland to the most romantic strasse in Germany.

Chapter X

THE ROMANTIC ROAD

1. Bad Mergentheim
2. Rothenburg
3. Dinkelsbühl
4. Nördlingen
5. Augsburg
6. Füssen
7. The Royal Castles

NO AREA OF GERMANY is more aptly named than this. Even if the road that runs through central Bavaria isn't romantic itself, the medieval villages and 2000-year-old towns through which it passes certainly are. The Romantic Road (Romantische Strasse) stretches for 180 miles between the cities of Würzburg, in the north, and Füssen, in the foothills of the Bavarian Alps.

You may, if you wish, take the regular bus tour, accompanied by an English-speaking guide, which traverses the entire route each day. But the best way to see this stretch of Germany is by car, stopping whenever the mood suggests and then driving on through miles of vineyards and over streams until you arrive at the alpine passes in the south.

If you begin your tour of the scenic route at the north, you'll find yourself, after leaving the Franconian city of Würzburg, in Bad Mergentheim.

1. Bad Mergentheim

From the name you can guess that this little town along the northern stretches of the Romantic Road is a spa resort community, but that is only one of the faces of Bad Mergentheim. In fact, it was only as recently as 1826 that the healing springs of the town were accidentally rediscovered (archeological evidence indicates that they had been known in the Bronze and Iron Ages). Perhaps the spa side of the town is the one that will interest you most, since after a few weeks of German beer and sausages you may wish to shed a few pounds. Bad Mergentheim, among its various treatments, offers a cure for obesity.

But a more pleasant cure for the overweight visitor would be a walking tour through the crooked, narrow streets to the old **Marketplace** with the **Town Hall,** the town's major sightseeing attraction, and the **Mergentheim Palace** (the Deutschordensschloss), on the opposite bank of the Tauber from the spa facilities. The palace was the seat of the Knights of the Teutonic Order from 1527 until their dispossession by Napoleon in 1809. During its residence in this Renaissance castle, the order was a politically influential one, straying from its original purpose as a religious and military order founded during the Crusades. Especially interesting is the palace church, redesigned in the 18th century by Balthasar Neumann and François Cuvilliés in a rich baroque style with frescoes and rococo altars. Tours are conducted on Saturday, Sunday, and holidays from 10 a.m. to noon and 2:30 to 5:30 p.m. There are also tours Tuesday through Friday from 2:30 to 5:30 p.m. between March and October. Admission is 3 DM (99¢). There are possibilities for excursions to Markelsheim for wine tests or to see the *Stuppacher Madonna,* a beautiful medieval painting in Stuppach by Matthias Gruenewald.

AN UPPER-BRACKET HOTEL: Kurhotel Victoria, 2 Poststrasse (tel. 59-30). One wing of this spa hotel looks like a modern version of a medieval watchtower, with the added benefit of a heated swimming pool on top that can be closed to the elements or open to the summer sunlight. What's even better is the view of the old city you'll get from the top. The public rooms are darkly paneled in handcrafted pine, with deer antlers and ceramic tile stoves. There are massage facilities, and if you want to shed pounds, you can order special low-calorie meals in the wood-beamed dining room. Breakfast is included in the room prices. Singles with sinks cost 70 DM ($23.10), and those with the latest plumbing and lots of space cost 130 DM ($42.90). Doubles rent for 140 DM ($46.20) in the cheapest units, 210 DM ($69.30) in the more elaborate rooms. Some of the units have glassed-in balconies. Fixed-price lunches and dinners range from 25 DM ($8.25) to 60 DM ($19.80).

A MIDDLE-BRACKET HOTEL: Deutschmeister, 7 Ochsengasse (tel. 72-85). A short 60 yards from the Rathaus, this 32-room hotel is directed and maintained by the Siebold family. You'll recognize the building by its sunflower-yellow, four-story facade with a gabled attic and elegant white highlights painted in symmetrical bands around each of the windows. Inside, you'll find a two-lane bowling alley, public rooms decorated in a gemütlich style, and a friendly reception and service. The somewhat anonymous rooms are spotlessly clean with toilet and shower, costing 62 DM ($20.46) in a single, 102 DM ($33.66) in a double. It closes in January.

A BUDGET HOTEL: Garni am Markt, 40 H.-H.-Ehrler-Platz (tel. 61-01), is an immaculate little hotel. Far removed from the life of a typical spa hotel, it sits right off the marketplace. There are only 32 bedrooms, most of which have private bath with shower. The pleasant Scandinavian furnishings are restful to the eye and body. A bathless single costs 40 DM ($8.25), rising to 55 DM ($18.15) with shower. Bathless doubles run 72 DM ($23.76); doubles with bath, 100 DM ($33).

WHERE TO DINE: Kettler's Altfränkische Weinstube, 12 Krumme Gasse (tel. 73-08). This is another of those wood-paneled weinstuben that seem to correspond so accurately to everyone's fantasy of what such an establishment should look like. Built in 1823, and doing a popular business ever since, the restaurant serves more than 120 kinds of wine, along with gutbürgerlich cookery, priced from 18 DM ($5.94) to 40 DM ($13.20) for a meal. Service is from 10:30 a.m. to 1 p.m. and 6 p.m. till midnight. It is closed Friday and from Christmas until mid-January.

Tiroler Stuben, in the Kurhotel Victoria, 2 Poststrasse (tel. 70-36). Catering to the tastes of an international clientele, who come here for "the cure," this hotel has a number of places to dine. Among them are the Blaue Terrasse. However, you may prefer the Tiroler Stuben, a Tyrolean stube restaurant with Austrian and international foods, each deliciously prepared, including one of my favorites, goulash with bacon noodles. You might also like the Frankish bratwurst and cabbage. You can dance in the hotel bar, and eat from 11 a.m. to midnight. Fixed-price menus cost 25 DM ($8.25) to 75 DM ($24.75).

2. Rothenburg

Admittedly, if you arrive at Rothenburg's bahnhof (railway station) at the northeast corner of town, you may find it hard to believe that this is actually the finest medieval city in Europe. Contemporary life and industry have made an impact here too, and the first sights to greet your eyes as you leave the station are factories and office buildings. But don't be discouraged—inside those undamaged 13th-century city walls is a completely preserved medieval town, relatively untouched by the centuries that have passed by outside.

THE SIGHTS: The only way to see Rothenburg properly is to wander through the town on foot, beginning at the typical hub of any old German village, the **Rathaus.** Set in the center of the Old Town, Rothenburg's Rathaus consists of an older Gothic section from 1240 and a newer Renaissance structure facing the marketplace. From the 165-foot tower of the Gothic hall you can get an overview of the town below. The belfry has quite a history. Fire destroyed the Gothic hall's twin (where the Renaissance hall now stands) in 1501. Prior to that, the tower was used as a lookout for enemy forces, but from that time on it became a watchtower for fire. The guards had to ring the bell every quarter hour to show that they were wide awake and on the job.

The new Rathaus, built in 1572 to replace the portion destroyed in the fire, is decorated with intricate friezes, an oriel extending the full height of the building, and a large stone portico opening onto the square. The octagonal tower at the center of the side facing the square contains the grand staircase, leading to the upper hall. On the main floor is the large Court Room, the scene of the annual Whitsuntide Festival, *der Meistertrunk,* commemorating the preservation of the city by the heroic Burgermeister Nusch, who accepted the challenge from the conquering Commander Tilly in 1631 to drink a goblet of wine in one draught. This sounds like a simple achievement until you see the actual tankard on display at the Reichstadt museum (see below). It holds almost 3½ quarts (3¼ liters)! Visiting hours are 9:30 a.m. to 12:30 p.m. and 1 to 5 p.m., for an admission of 1 DM (33¢).

On the north side of the marketplace, across from the Rathaus, is the town council's **drinking hall** (1406), where only the patrician families were allowed to drink. The most interesting feature of the tavern is the old clock on the facade facing the square. At 11 a.m., noon, and 1, 2, 3, 9, and 10 p.m. daily the clock chimes and the windows on either side open to expose Commander Tilly on the left standing in amazement while Burgermeister Nusch downs the massive goblet of wine.

Leaving the marketplace, walk north on the street that opens off the square between the Rathaus and the tavern. This will lead you to the Klingengasse, a narrow old street that passes directly under **St. Jakobskirche** (Church of St. James). This church is a completely vertical Gothic edifice with three naves; the east choir, dating from 1336, is the oldest section of the church. The altar was a gift of Burgermeister Toppler, the town leader during Rothenburg's most prosperous period. The fine painted-glass windows in the choir date from the same period. To the left is the tabernacle, from 1448, which was recognized as the "free place," where condemned criminals could not be touched. The church's most important work is the Altar of the Holy Blood, created by Tilman Riemenschneider in 1504. A relic claimed to be the blood of Christ is kept in a piece of crystal in the Romanesque cross above the altarpiece. The most interesting work on the altar is a carving of the Last Supper, in which all the figures, save one, were carved from one piece of lime-tree. Judas, the betrayer, was carved from a separate chunk of wood. On the eastern side of the north nave are two more Riemenschneider altars. Hours are 9 a.m. to 5 p.m. from the first of April until the end of October (on Sunday it opens at 10:30 a.m.). From November until the end of March it's open only from 10 a.m. to noon and 2 to 4 p.m. (from 10:30 a.m. on Sunday), charging an admission of only 1.50 DM (50¢).

For a look at one of the old ramparts, follow the Klingengasse northward, from the church to the **Klingentor,** its top portion adorned with four oriels and a ball lantern. You can wander along the covered ramparts of this portion of the wall, and to continue your tour of the town, walk on the wall west and south to the 13th-century Dominican nunnery, housing the **Reichsstadtmuseum,** with the historical collection of Rothenburg. The cloisters are well preserved, and you can visit the convent hall, kitchen, and apothecary, and view the ancient frescoes and antiques. The museum collection includes period furniture and art from Rothenburg's more prosperous periods, plus the famous goblet that saved the town. Among the exhibits is the work of Martinus Schwarz, the 1494 *Rothenburg Passion* series, 12 pictures depicting scenes from suffering of Christ. In the gallery you can also see the works of the English painter Arthur Wasse (1854–1930), whose pictures managed to capture the many moods of the city in a romantic way. The original glazed "Elector's Tankard" around which the story of the Meistertrunk (see above) is woven is displayed. The museum is open daily from 10 a.m. to 5 p.m. in summer, from 1 to 5 p.m. in winter. Admission is 2.50 DM (83¢) for adults, 1.50 DM (50¢) for children.

From the museum it's just a short walk to the **Herrengasse,** which leads back to the marketplace. This street was once the most exclusive in the Old Town, and many of its half-timbered houses have been converted into shops. On one side of the street is the 13th-century Gothic **Franciscan Church,** with an unusual rood screen separating the east choir from the naves. The church is most notable for its numerous tombs, decorated with sculptures.

At the opposite end of the Herrengasse from the marketplace is the **Burgtor,** the tower that originally led to the Castle of the Hohenstaufen (destroyed in 1425). The tower once had a drawbridge, and although the moat and castle are both gone now, you can still see the holes where the ropes once raised and lowered the bridge and the huge hole, called the peat, through which hot oil or tar was poured on the enemy.

The gardens where the castle once stood jut out from the rest of the town toward the Tauber River. Across the river from the Burggarten is the **Toppler Castle,** actually a small tower built in 1908 to commemorate the 500th anniversary of the death of the town's greatest mayor.

Take the Burggasse for a short distance east and you'll come to the **Kriminal Museum** (Medieval Crime Museum), 3 Burggasse (tel. 53-59), the only one of its kind in Europe. It's housed in a structure built in 1395 for the Order of the Johanniter, who cared for the sick. It was rebuilt in 1718 in the baroque style, the only edifice of this style still standing in Rothenburg. To give an insight into the life, laws, and punishments of medieval days, on four floors of the building the museum shows the legal history of seven centuries. You'll see chastity belts, women's shame masks, a shame flute for bad musicians, a cage for bakers who baked bread too small or too light, and other mementos of crime and punishment. The museum is open from 9:30 a.m. to 6 p.m. April to October, 2 to 4 p.m. November to March. Admission is 2.50 DM (83¢) for adults, 1.50 DM (50¢) for children.

From here, it's just a few steps east to the Schmiedgasse. Turn down this street and you'll arrive at the **Baumeisterhaus,** home of Leonard Weidmann, who built the Renaissance Rathaus. The facade is decorated with 14 carved stone figures representing the seven vices and virtues. The interior houses a restaurant, about which more later.

UPPER-BRACKET HOTELS: Eisenhut (The Iron Helmet), 3–5 Herrengasse

(tel. 20-41), is the most celebrated inn on the Romantic Road. Attracting an international crowd, it is perhaps the finest small hotel in Germany. Four medieval patrician houses, dating from the 12th century, were joined to make this colorful and distinctive inn. It's a virtual museum of antiquity. Most impressive is the three-story galleried dining hall, with ornate classic wood paneling, balconies, and a collection of ceramic mugs on display. There are additional places to dine as well, each richly decorated and furnished, although in sunny weather they're all deserted in favor of the multitiered flagstone terrace on the Tauber. Meals are à la carte, costing from 35 DM ($11.55) to 75 DM ($24.75). The specialty of the house is filet of lamb in tarragon or pike dumplings in crayfish sauce.

The main living room has a beamed ceiling, Oriental carpets, ecclesiastical sculpture, and grandfather clock. The reception lounge continues the theme, with a wooden ceiling, wide staircase, statuary, and ancestral chairs. The bedrooms are individualized—no two are alike—and antiques of distinction are used unsparingly. Your bedroom may contain hand-carved and monumental pieces, or be given a Hollywood touch with a tufted satin headboard. Regardless, you are assured of charm, comfort, and personality. Because of the wide range of rooms, prices tend to be complicated. The highest rates are in effect from mid-April to October 31. At that time a single with bath goes for 170 DM ($56.10) to 176 DM ($58.08). Twins with bath are in the 195-DM ($64.35) to 290-DM ($95.70) bracket. These prices include breakfast. The Iron Helmet is easy to find, just across the street from the Town Hall.

Goldener Hirsch, 16-25 Untere Schmiedgasse (tel. 20-51), is a first-class hotel, a remake of an inn that dated from 1600. In the heart of town, it's housed in a rustic building, with a Blue Terrace for dining that offers a panoramic view of the Tauber and the surrounding hills. Or you may prefer to take your dinner in the blue and white Regency salon. So popular has this hostelry become that it's annexed another patrician house across the street. The bedrooms are comfortable and home-like, showing a respect for traditional taste. Prices are based on the time of year and the type of bath you request. Bathless singles are 82 DM ($27.06); with bath or shower, from 190 DM ($62.70). Bathless doubles rent for 150 DM ($49.50), increasing to 260 DM ($85.80) with bath. Breakfast is included. The hotel is closed December and January.

MIDDLE-BRACKET HOTELS: Romantik Hotel Markusturm, 1 Rödergasse

(tel. 23-70). An integral part of the Rothenburg defense system was used as one of the walls of this hotel when it was built back in 1264. Today that defense wall has been torn down, except for the section built into the hotel, which is still doing a lively business next to St. Mark's Tower. The interior is a Teutonic fantasy of wood beams, paneling, and massive furniture. All the rooms have private bath, and one has an antique bed that might be strong enough to support the entire hotel! Singles with breakfast go for anywhere from 120 DM ($39.60) to 130 DM ($42.90), and doubles cost 170 DM ($56.10) to 220 DM ($72.60).

Mittermeier, 9 Vorm Würzburger Tor (tel. 22-59). Because of its long veranda, flanked with big trees, and its pleasing horizontal lines, the facade of this hotel could as easily be found in the American Midwest as it could in Rothenburg. The interior is spaciously designed, with a free-standing fireplace in the sunny reception area, plus an indoor swimming pool that's quite beautiful. Rooms are contemporary and comfortable. Doubles rent for anywhere from 150 DM ($49.50) to 190 DM ($62.70), while singles rent for 90 DM ($29.70) to 110 DM ($36.30), breakfast included. It's closed in January.

Burg-Hotel, 1–3 Klostergasse (tel. 50-37), built right on top of the old town wall, is a large timbered house with a high pitched roof, flower garden, window boxes of geraniums, and a picket fence. The dining terrace provides a panoramic view of the Tauber River and the surrounding fields. The interior was rebuilt by Gabrielle Berger, who has good, reliable taste. Each bedroom is different, with tile bath. One room, for example, may have swagged and draped beds; another may be filled with antiques; yet another could be done in sleek contemporary style. All rooms have private bath and toilet. Singles cost from 125 DM ($41.25), and doubles go for 150 DM ($49.50) to 175 DM ($24.75). Some apartments are available, costing from 200 DM ($66) for two persons. Breakfast is served in an attractive room, with a view. The little sitting room also has nice touches, such as ecclesiastical sculpture, crystal chandeliers, and antiques combined with good reproductions.

Hotel Bären, 9 Hofbronnengasse (tel. 30-31), is one of the leading old inns of town, dating back to 1577, and it's centrally located. Modernized by the Müller family, it still has 15-inch oak beams and ornate wainscoting. The rooms are all styled differently, with coordinated colors. The rebuilt rooms are quite elaborate. For quiet moments, there is a reading and writing room with an open fireplace. Rates for a single with bath or shower run from 90 DM ($29.70) to 120 DM ($39.60). For a twin with bath or shower, the price range is 130 DM ($42.90) to 260 DM ($85.80). Triples cost 210 DM ($69.30) to 300 DM ($99). Children up to the age of 6 stay free. These rates include all taxes, a buffet breakfast, and the use of the indoor swimming pool. There's an extra charge for use of the sauna and solarium.

Hotel Gasthof Glocke, 1 Am Plönlein (tel. 30-25). The designer of this comfortable hotel took pains to recreate a country-rustic kind of farmer's decor inside. Most of your meals, drinks, and entertainment take place beneath heavily beamed ceilings and big windows framed with frilly curtains and well-polished paneling. The Thürauf family, the owners, are justifiably proud of their in-house restaurant. There lies the reputation of this establishment, as its wine cellar is very complete. Unknown to many revelers, it also rents out comfortably modern bedrooms, where singles cost between 45 DM ($14.85) and 85DM ($28.05), and doubles go for 75 DM ($24.75) to 130 DM ($42.90), with breakfast included. Each accommodation contains its own bath, phone, radio, and often a private balcony.

Hotel Reichs-Küchenmeister, 8 Kirchplatz (tel. 24-06), is one of the oldest buildings in Rothenburg. It was the seat of a chief steward for Rothenburg's nobility. The house is on different levels. You wander down the corridors to nicely furnished bedrooms with regionally painted wooden furniture. However, the plumbing is first rate. A single without bath is 45 DM ($14.85), rising to 75 DM ($24.75) with bath. A bathless double rents for 80 DM ($26.40), peaking at 110 DM ($36.30) with bath. In the restaurant the food is good, the choice wide. I recommend the Reichs-Küchen "master plate," including a choice of filet of pork, beef, and veal with fresh vegetables. In season, you may prefer a leg of roebuck with mushrooms, potatoes, and cranberries.

BUDGET INNS AND GUEST HOUSES: Greifen, 5 Obere Schmiedgasse (tel. 22-81), is one of the better little inns that not only offers well-cooked meals at modest prices, but has 22 bedrooms to rent as well. Just off the marketplace, it is next door to the prestigious Baumeisterhaus, recommended below. It too is a patrician house, dating back to the 14th century. It contains a sun-pocket garden, and here you can order your morning coffee in the midst of roses and geraniums. The bedrooms are simple, but offer good comfort, soft eiderdowns, and hot and cold running water (a few contain private bath). Singles are 35 DM ($11.55) to 50 DM ($16.50). The rate in a double ranges from 65 DM ($21.45) to 95 DM ($31.35). The dining room is closed Monday.

Bayerischer Hof, 21 Ansbacherstrasse (tel. 34-57), is a good and reasonably priced hotel, standing midway between the railway station and the medieval walled city. Willi and Katharina Schellhaas welcome guests, housing them in one of their clean, well-furnished rooms. The hotel has been recently renovated, offering eight double rooms and one single, with shower and toilet. The price in a double is 40 DM ($13.20) per person, 45 DM ($14.85) in a single, including a breakfast of orange juice, eggs, cheese, and sausage. The food is very good, with many international and Bavarian specialties. For that reason, you may want to take the full-board rate, costing yet another 30 DM ($9.90) per person in addition to the room tariffs.

Gästehaus Gernert, 4 Winterbachstrasse (tel. 46-72), stands outside the historic sector of Rothenburg, but an invigorating 15-minute walk to its center. This modern, unpretentious building offers sheetrocked rooms, wallpapered and tiled in geometric patterns, to guests who prefer its quiet location. Singles rent for 26 DM ($8.58) to 36 DM ($11.88), while doubles cost 48 DM ($15.84) to 60 DM ($19.80). The house is run by Helga Gernert.

WHERE TO DINE: **Baumeisterhaus,** 3 Obere Schmiedgasse (tel. 34-04), is housed in an ancient patrician residence right off the marketplace. Built in 1596, it contains what is universally considered the most beautiful courtyard in Rothenburg (which, incidentally, can be visited only by guests). You must reserve well ahead in the day if you want a good table in the courtyard in the evening. The patio has colorful murals, draped serenely by vines. Even though the cuisine is good, the prices are kept low. Try, for a starter, the soup of the day. Main dishes are well prepared and attractively served, and desserts are rich and luscious. Meals begin at 25 DM ($8.25), climbing up to 54 DM ($17.82).

Ratsstube, 6 Marktplatz (tel. 34-04), enjoys a position right on the marketplace, one of the most photographed spots in Germany. The Ratsstube is a bustling center of activity throughout the day—a day which begins, incidentally, when practically every Rothenburger stops by for a cup of morning coffee, perhaps a beer. Inside, a true tavern atmosphere prevails, with hardwood chairs and tables, vaulted ceilings, pierced copper lanterns, and decorative swords. On the à la carte menu are many regional dishes, such as homemade soups. Main dishes include blood sausages with sauerkraut or Franconian meat kebabs. Meals cost from 25 DM ($8.25). The Ratsstube is closed Wednesday.

Romantik Hotel Markusturm, 1 Rödergasse (tel. 23-70). Decorated with hand-painted Teutonic designs on the plaster walls, this old-fashioned establishment offers good Frankish wines and wholesome regional cookery. A quick inspection of the kitchens reveals about a dozen different aquariums, which are used to keep different species of fish alive until the last minute. They include trout, eel, carp, and sole. The restaurant is open every day except in February, charging from 30 DM ($9.90) to 55 DM ($18.15) for a complete meal.

The **Goldener Hirsch,** 16 Untere Schmiedgasse (tel. 20-51), was previously recommended as one of the top hotels of Rothenburg. Its dining facilities (see the description under "Upper-Bracket Hotels") have made it a preferred choice for many nonresidents. The cuisine is Frankish and international, and fixed-price meals cost from 30 DM ($9.90) to 75 DM ($24.75). The menu changes every season as different produce becomes available. The inn is closed in December and January, but open otherwise from noon to 2 p.m. and 6 to 9 p.m.

Hotel Gasthof Glocke, 1 Am Plönlein (tel. 30-25), is a traditional hotel and guest house, serving regional specialties along with a vast collection of Frankish wines. Meals begin at 25 DM ($8.25), climbing to 50 DM ($16.50), with a heavy emphasis on regional and seasonal specialties. It serves daily from 11 a.m. to 2 p.m. and 6 to 9 p.m.

Tilman Riemenschneider, 11 Georgengasse (tel. 50-61). In a town as rich in historic buildings as Rothenburg, you'll find a lot of traditional old weinstuben, and this one is no exception. The cook here shows an elevated respect for old-fashioned regional cookery served with a rustic gemütlichkeit. You can have dinner for as little as 25 DM ($8.25), although some tabs climb to 55 DM ($18.15). The food is well prepared and served in generous portions. Hours are 11 a.m. to 2 p.m. and 6 to 10 p.m.

Reichs-Küchenmeister, 8 Kirchplatz (tel. 30-46). This might be called an old-fashioned entertainment complex. This hotel certainly offers a wide range of gastronomic choices. These might include such dishes as trout bleu, white herring with potatoes, carp bleu, roast goose with potato dumplings and red cabbage, sauerbraten, Bavarian liver dumplings with sauerkraut and potatoes, and game stew with noodles and cranberries. You'll find a conservatively decorated weinstube, with the prerequisite wood beams and paneling, a garden terrace, a konditorei, and traditionally helpful service. A meal begins at 18 DM ($5.94), going up to 45 DM ($14.85). It's open daily except Tuesday from 7 a.m. to midnight, and it's closed from mid-November to December.

TOURING IN THE ENVIRONS: Using Rothenburg as your base, there are several interesting excursions that can be made from there, beginning with—

Ansbach

With one toe still left in the Middle Ages and another toe dripping with baroque, this small Frankish town is the site of a well-attended Bach Festival staged every other year. It grew in prestige and influence under the Hohenzollerns, and under Frederick the Great the Ansbach-Bayreuth Dragoons won fame throughout Europe. The court life that held sway here in the 18th century was known for its brilliance and pomp under the margravines.

The seat of this splendor was the **Ansbach Residenz,** or castle, which dates from the 14th century. Gabrieli, the architect to the Court of Vienna, greatly embellished it much later in what is called the Franconian baroque style. It knew its greatest influence under the reign of the Margrave Wilhelm-Friedrich. Inside you can visit a porcelain gallery, with nearly 3000 pieces, along with a salon of mirrors which is dazzling. In the red gallery you can stare eye-to-eye with the Hohenzollerns (at least their portraits), and you can also see the apartments once inhabited by the princes. Beautiful parks surround the place. Summer visiting hours are 9 a.m. to noon and 2 to 5 p.m. (off-season from 10 a.m. to noon and 2 to 4 p.m.), costing an admission of 4 DM ($1.32). It is closed on Monday.

Afterward, save time for a visit to **St. Gumpert-Kirche,** a church that has a 15th century Gothic chancel, but was much transformed over the centuries. In back of the main altar, a door to your left leads to the Schwanenritterorden-kapelle, or "Chapel of the Knights of the Order of the Swan."

What time remains should not be devoted to any more specific sights, but to the Old Town of Ansbach itself, which suffered no war damage. The town has many old structures, and as you walk along narrow lanes paved with cobblestones you'll see a number of shops specializing in German handicrafts.

FOOD AND LODGING: Am Drechselsgarten, 1 Am Drechselsgarten (tel. 8-50-91). This cozy hotel has benefitted from an extensive renovation, which has made its 58 rooms even better than before. Each contains a private balcony, TV, radio, and phone, and many are filled with unusual, individually chosen furnishings. Guests find a pleasant dining room, a weinstube, and a morning breakfast buffet whose wake-up foods are included in the price of a hotel room. Singles rent for 100 DM ($33) to 140 DM ($46.20), and doubles go for 130 DM ($42.90) to 200 DM ($66), depending on the accommodation and the season.

Platengarten, 30 Promenade (tel. 32-17). You can leave your comfortable bedroom and find yourself in the mainstream of summertime strollers, as this hotel is surrounded by the trees of one of the town's parks. French specialties are served in a stylish dining room, where meals range in price from 18 DM ($5.94) to 45 DM ($14.85). The dining room is closed on Saturday. The 18 bedrooms rent for 42 DM ($13.86) to 78 DM ($25.74) in a single, and 78 DM ($25.74) to 125 DM ($41.25) in a double, including breakfast.

Leutershausen

About ten miles east of Ansbach, the old walled city of Leutershausen struck reader William J. O'Dwyer of Fairfield, Connecticut, as a place "where houses appear to be made of candy for a Hansel and Gretel playlet, where ponds burst with trout." Actually, Leutershausen had to be rebuilt at the close of World War II because it was hit by incendiary bombs dropped by the American air force, because of some insane last-ditch defense effort by a dozen fleeing SS troops.

The town is ancient, tracing its origin back to the year 1000 and the reign of Kaiser Otto III. The gate tower contains a museum of local relics, and the friendly burgermeisters meet at the new Rathaus (Town Hall). Across from this municipal structure was the birthplace of the mother and maternal grandparents of Henry Kissinger. Kissinger's parents fled in the 1930s to escape persecution, but upon their triumphant return in 1976, they were honored by the town. The former secretary of state under Nixon has also paid Leutershausen a visit.

Another famous local son, Gustav Weisskopf, is credited by some with having flown in powered aircraft even before the Wright brothers took off at Kitty Hawk, North Carolina. A small museum in town named after him displays photographs of his early experiments in aviation.

Colmberg

Schloss Colmberg (tel. 262) is perhaps the most romantic stopover in the area, and in fact many couples come here to get married atop a medieval fortress. A hillside setting has been turned into a zoo, and the strutting peacocks are always a delight. The location of this castle, with its 12th-century stone walls, is some four miles from Leutershausen, in the direction of Rothenburg.

The castle rents out some two dozen handsomely furnished bedrooms, costing 42 DM ($13.86) to 60 DM ($19.80) in a single and between 78 DM ($25.74) and 130 DM ($42.90) in a double. The adjoining restaurant features in wild-game dishes and local specialties, served in medieval and panoramic splendor guaranteed to evoke a nostalgia for the "good old days" of the Middle Ages. Full meals are served throughout the day from 8 a.m. to midnight, except Tuesday. The cost ranges from 20 DM ($6.60) to 40 DM ($13.20).

3. Dinkelsbühl

Still surrounded by medieval walls and towers, this town is straight out of a story by the Grimm Brothers, even down to the gingerbread, which is one of its main products. Behind the ancient walls, originally built in the tenth century, is a dreamy village which seems to awaken only once a year for the **Kinderzeche** (Children's Festival), commemorating the saving of the village by the children. According to the story, they pleaded with the conquering Swedish troops to leave their town without pillaging and destroying it, and got their wish. The pageant includes concerts given by the local boys' band dressed in historic military costumes.

In spite of the great hordes of tourists who come here, Dinkelsbühl retains its quiet, provincial attitude. The cobblestone streets of the town are lined with fine 16th-century houses, many with carvings and paintings depicting biblical and mythological themes. In the center of the town is the late-Gothic **St. George's Church,** from 1450, containing a carved "Holy Cross Altar" from the same period. Many of the pillar sculptures were done by the pupils of the Gothic master Tilman Riemenschneider.

BED AND BOARD AT OLD-WORLD INNS: Eisenkrug, 1 Dr.-Martin-Luther-Strasse (tel. 34-29). The sienna-colored walls of this centrally located hotel were originally built in 1620. Today its forest-green shutters are easily familiar to practically everyone in town, many of whom celebrate family occasions at the in-house restaurant. There's even a café, which in warm weather spills out onto the sidewalk with al fresco tables. The stylish rooms are sometimes wallpapered with flowery prints and often filled with an engaging series of pieces of old furniture. With breakfast included, singles cost from 70 DM ($23.10), while doubles go for 100 DM ($33) to 115 DM ($37.95). Each unit contains a phone, TV, and radio. The hotel also serves good food, and plenty of it, at costs ranging from 22 DM ($7.26) and 27 DM ($8.91).

Goldene Rose, 4 Marktplatz (tel. 8-31), is a landmark in the heart of this village. Intricately timbered, it rises six stories high, with a steeply pitched roof and window boxes overflowing with geraniums and petunias. It's one of the leading inns of Dinkelsbühl, tracing its history back to 1450. Don't expect liveried attendants, but rather a rustic, homey atmosphere. In the style of a country inn, the dining rooms are more important than the lounges. Adding to the ambience is a wealth of oak, antiques, and portraits of sovereigns (that's Queen Victoria at the bottom of the steps). The à la carte menu offers such tempting items as French onion soup, lobster and crab with dill, or rumpsteak Goldene Rose. A good variety of tasty desserts includes fresh raspberries flambé. Meals cost from 25 DM ($8.25) to 55 DM ($18.15). The bedrooms are modernized, each with shower or bath and good, soft beds. Singles cost from 50 DM ($16.50); doubles, from 79 DM ($26.07) to 99 DM ($32.67); and triples, from 99 DM ($32.67) to 109 DM ($35.97). All tariffs include breakfast. At the wine restaurant, Alte Nagelschmiede, about 300 feet from the hotel, you can have a hot and cold buffet lunch or dinner, as well as steaks done over the open fire grill. There's live entertainment in the evening. The inn is closed from January 6 to the first of March.

Deutsches Haus, 3 Weinmarkt (tel. 23-46), hides behind a facade dating from 1440 and rich in painted designs and festive woodcarvings. In a niche on the second floor of the arched entrance is a 17th-century Madonna. Casually run, Deutsches Haus features a dining room with an elaborately decorated ceiling, inset niches with primitive scenic pictures, parquet floors, and provincial chairs. The bedrooms are unique. You may find yourself in one with a ceramic stove or in another with a Biedermeier desk. A single costs 45 DM ($14.85) with bath. A double without bath is rented for 65 DM ($21.45), going up to 100 DM ($33) with bath, breakfast included.

Even if you're a nonresident, you may want to come here to dine in its Altdeutsches Restaurant, one of the finest in Dinkelsbühl. It is intimate, convivial, and an attractive rendezvous point. Fixed-price meals cost from 18 DM ($5.94) to 45 DM ($14.85). The restaurant serves Frankish and regional specialties from 8 a.m. to midnight. It's closed from December until the end of February.

Hotel Restaurant Hecht, 1 Schweinemarkt (tel. 8-11), dates from the 17th century. An elegant ochre building, it offers three hand-built stories of stucco, stone, and tile to guests who pay 62 DM ($20.46) to 70 DM ($23.10) in a single and from 90 DM ($29.70) to 100 DM ($33) in a double. Half board in the high-ceilinged dining room goes for another 20 DM ($6.60) per person. The rooms are sunny, large, and comfortable, at least most of them, and they come in a variety of color schemes you may or may not love, according to your tastes. If you adore violet, ask for the purple room; otherwise, stick to the brick and wheat-colored ones.

4. Nördlingen

One of the most irresistible medieval towns along the Romantic Road, Nördlingen is still encircled by the well-preserved city fortifications from the 14th and 15th centuries. You can walk completely around the town on the covered parapet, which passes 18 towers and fortified gates set into the walls.

At the center of the circular-shaped Old Town formed by these walls is the **Rübenmarkt.** If you stand in this square on market day, you will be swept into a world of the past—still alive today. The country people have preserved many medieval customs and costumes here, which, along with the ancient houses, create a living medieval city. Around the square stand a number of buildings, including the Gothic **Rathaus** (Town Hall), with a Renaissance outside staircase and a collection of antiquities in the **Reichsstadt Museum** inside. Tours are conducted every hour from 9 a.m. to noon and 2 to 5 p.m. (on Sunday and holidays from 10 a.m. to noon and 2 to 4 p.m.). It is closed on Monday and during the month of November. Admission is 2 DM (66¢) per visit.

St. George's Church, on the northern side of the square, is the town's most interesting sight, and one of its oldest buildings. The Gothic hallenkirche is from the 15th century. The fan-vaulted interior is decorated with plaques and epitaphs commemorating the town's more illustrious residents of the 16th and 17th centuries. Although the original Gothic altarpiece by Friedrich Herlin (1470) has been placed in the Reichsstadt Museum, a portion of it, depicting the Crucifixion, remains in the church. Above the high altar today stands a more elaborate baroque altarpiece. The most prominent feature of the church, however, is the 295-foot French Gothic tower, called the "Daniel." At night the town watchman calls out from the steeple, his voice ringing through the streets of the town.

FOOD AND LODGING: Sonne, 3 Marktplatz (tel. 50-67), is in a bull's-eye position—next to the cathedral and the Rathaus. It's practically heady from having entertained so many illustrious personalities since it opened as an inn in 1405. It has counted emperors, kings, and princes among its guests, including Frederick III, Maximilian I, and Charles V; even Goethe came this way. Also the American astronauts from Apollo 14 and Apollo 17 have stayed here. The Sonne is owned by the Madlener family, who perpetuate the tradition of hospitality. The interior has been completely modernized, providing tasteful accommodations with comfort. In a choice of dining rooms, you can order the soup of the day, main courses such as rumpsteak Mirabeau, and good, fattening German desserts. Meals range from 18 DM ($5.94) to 45 DM ($14.85). It's quite casual; the waitresses even urge you to finish the food on your plate. The bedrooms are well planned, with two price levels, depending on the plumbing you get. Bathless doubles go for 68 DM ($22.44), increasing to 105 DM ($34.65) with private bath and toilet. Singles cost 40 DM ($13.20) to 75 DM ($24.75). Breakfast, service, and taxes are included.

Am Ring, 14 Bürgermeister-Reiger Strasse (tel. 40-29), is a hotel based on modern amenities. It should appeal especially to business people, with its location near the Hauptbahnhof and its masculine, dignified rooms decorated in a kind of executive modern style. Bedrooms, for the most part, are high-ceilinged, with tiled bath and lots of light. The Mammel family rents singles for 52 DM ($17.16) to 60 DM ($19.80), and doubles for 95 DM ($31.35) to 100 DM ($33), breakfast included.

5. Augsburg

The 2000 years that have gone into the creation of this, the largest city on the Romantic Road, also have made it one of the major sightseeing attractions in southern Germany. Little remains from its early Roman period (it was founded under Tiberius in 15 B.C.), but the wealth of art and architecture from the Renaissance is staggering in quantity and scope. Over the years Augsburg has been host to many famous visitors and has an array of famous native sons. These have included Bertolt Brecht, whose Marxist proclivities infuriated the Augsburgers, to Martin Luther, who was summoned here in 1518 to recant his 95 Theses before a papal emissary.

THE SIGHTS: Augsburg has been an important city throughout its history but during the 15th and 16th centuries it was the wealthiest city in Europe, mainly because of its textile industry, and the political and financial power of its two banking families, the Welsers and the Fuggers. The Welsers, who once owned nearly all of Venezuela among other things, have long since faded from the minds of Augsburgers. But the founders of the powerful Fugger family have established themselves forever in the hearts of the townsfolk by an unusual legacy, the **Fuggerei,** actually a miniature town established in 1519 by the Fugger family to house the poorer of the townsfolk. The quarter consists of several streets lined with well-maintained Renaissance houses, as well as a church and administrative offices, all enclosed within its own walls. As the oldest social housing project in the world, it charges its tenants a rent of only 1.71 DM per year, a rate that has not changed in more than 450 years. But the tenants must pay the balance of their debt in an unusual form of payment—each night, when the gates of the Fuggerei are closed, they are obligated to pray for the souls of their patrons.

The **High Cathedral,** or Dom, of Augsburg has the distinction of containing the oldest stained-glass windows in the entire world. The Romanesque windows, from the 12th century, are younger than the cathedral itself, however, which was begun in 944 on the foundation walls of an early Christian baptismal church. The ruins of the original basilica are found in the crypt beneath the west chancel. Partially Gothicized in the 14th century, it stands on the edge of the park which also fronts the Episcopal Palace, where the basic creed of the Lutheran Reformation was presented at the Diet of Augsburg in 1530. The cathedral remains the episcopal see of the Catholic bishop to this day. The 11th-century bronze doors, leading into the three-aisled nave, are adorned with bas reliefs of a mixture of biblical and mythological characters, including a scene of Adam and Eve. The interior of the cathedral, restored in 1934, contains side altars with altar pieces by Hans Holbein and Christoph Amberger. The windows in the south transept are the oldest, depicting prophets of the Old Testament in a severe, but colorful, Romanesque style.

The third most artistically significant church in Augsburg is **St. Anne's,** opening onto Annastrasse, a short walk from the Rathaus. Its most celebrated visitor was Martin Luther who, it is said, did not put much faith in his imperial letter of safe conduct and slipped "out the back way" in the middle of the night. Still, his visit must have been powerful, because St. Anne's became Protestant some seven years afterward. Luther's visit, as mentioned, was in 1518. Up to then St. Anne's had formed part of a Carmelite monastery. It has rich decorations in both the flamboyant Gothic style and the rococo, the latter reflected in its richly adorned frescoes and stucco work. Dating from the time of Luther's visit, the Fuggerkapelle, or Fugger funeral chapel, is called the first example of the Italian Renaissance style that made its way into Germany from the south. Dürer designed two of the reliefs on the sepulcher. The church owns two works of art by Lucas Cranach the Elder, including a portrait of Luther. On the second floor, overlooking the cloisters, is a book-lined cell in which Luther found refuge.

From the cathedral, follow the Hoher Weg southward past the **Rathaus** (Town Hall) built by Elias Holl in 1620. It was visited by Napoleon in 1805 and 1809. Regrettably, it was also visited by an air raid in 1944 (the flyers were trying to knock out a Diesel engine factory), leaving it gutted, a mere shell of a building that had once been known as a palatial eight-story monument to the glory of the Renaissance. The destruction by air left its celebrated "golden chamber" in shambles. Now after much restoration and the spending of $6 million in funds raised by Augsburgers, the Rathaus can be visited by the public—daily from 10 a.m. to 6 p.m. Admission is free. In front of the Town Hall is the **Augustus fountain,** forged in bronze by the Dutch sculptor Hubert Gerhard in 1594 to commemorate the founding of Augsburg.

At this point, the main street of Augsburg's Old Town begins. Extending southward from the Town Hall is the wide **Maximilianstrasse,** lined with old burghers' houses and studded with fountains by the Renaissance Dutch sculptor Adrien de Vries. Near the southern end of the street is the **Hercules Fountain,** and behind it, the most attractive church in Augsburg, the **Church of St. Ulrich and St. Afra,** which was constructed between 1476 and 1500 on the site of a Roman temple. As a tribute to the 1555 Peace of Augsburg, which recognized two denominations, the Catholics and the Lutherans, this church contains a Catholic and a Protestant church within its walls. The church is 15th-century Gothic, but many of the furnishings, including the three altars representing the birth and resurrection of Christ and the baptism of the Church by the Holy Spirit, are done in the later baroque style. The large pulpit looks almost like a pagoda, with decorative angels dressed in Chinese red and gold. The crypt of the church contains the tombs of the Swabian saints Ulrich and Afra, and the lance and saddle of St. Ulrich are on display in the sacristy. The church honors both Saints Ulrich and Afra. He was an Augsburg bishop who died in 973 and she was a Roman girl who was sacrificed because she refused to recant her Christian beliefs.

The **Schaezlerpalais,** 46 Maximilianstrasse (tel. 324-21-71), facing the Hercules Fountain, contains the city's art galleries—and what a collection is on display here. Constructed as a 60-room mansion between 1765 and 1770, it was willed to Augsburg after World War II. If only the works of artists who lived in Augsburg during the Renaissance were exhibited, it would be an imposing sight. (Regrettably, however, there is no painting by Titian in all the town, although he was here twice, in 1548 and again in 1551.) Works by local artists are displayed, including Hans Burgkmair and Hans Holbein the Elder (his even greater son, represented by a fine drawing, was born in a house nearby). Non-German European masters are represented by such greats as Rubens, Veronese, and Tiepolo. However, the larger number of paintings are by German artists of the Renaissance and baroque periods. One of the most famous of these is Dürer's portrait of Jakob Fugger the Rich, founder of the dynasty that once elected the heads of the Holy Roman Empire. Besides the art collections, the palace-gallery contains a rococo ballroom, with gilded and mirrored wall panels and a ceiling fresco of the *Four Continents*. Here Marie Antoinette danced the night away on April 28, 1770. The galleries are open daily, except Monday, from 10 a.m. to 5 p.m. (in winter from 10 a.m. to 4 p.m.). Admission is free.

The town's major collection of sculpture is displayed at the **Maximilian-Museum,** 24 Philippine-Welser-Strasse, together with works of art, highly important silver and gold pieces, as well as scientific instruments. It is open from May 1 until the end of September from 10 a.m. to 5 p.m. (off-season until 4 p.m.). It's closed on Monday.

Roman figures, monuments, and sepulchral finds are found in the **Römisches Museum,** 15 Dominikanergasse. The museum is housed in a former Dominican church. Seek out a gilded horse's head from the second century, all that remains of an equestrian statue of Roman emperor Marcus Aurelius.

Augsburg is the native town of the Mozart family. Leopold Mozart was born in Augsburg in 1719. He not only became the father of the world's greatest musical genius, but also founded the first violin school. The **Mozarthaus,** lying north of the Dom, is open Monday to Friday from 10 a.m. to noon and 2 to 5 p.m. (until 4 p.m. on Friday and until noon on Saturday and Sunday). It is closed on weekends and also on Tuesday. It contains a 1785 pianoforte which was built by Johann Andreas Stein, an organ- and piano-maker whose instruments were not only eagerly sought by the young Mozart but by Beethoven. The magenta-colored house is at 30 Frauentorstrasse, and for information, telephone 3-24-21-96).

AN UPPER-BRACKET HOTEL: Steigenberger Drei Mohren Palasthotel, 40 Maximilianstrasse (tel. 51-00-31), was one of the most renowned hotels in Germany before its destruction in 1944 in an air raid. Before that it had been a hotel since 1723, and was known to diplomats, composers, and artists. Former guests include such names as the Duke of Wellington, Mozart, Goethe, Mascagni, Paganini, and Franklin D. Roosevelt. In 1956 it was rebuilt in a modern style. The interior treatment of the "Three Moors" incorporates stylish contemporary pieces with traditional furnishings. For example, the drawing room contains a slatted natural-wood ceiling and wall, contrasting warmly against a room-wide mural of Old Augsburg. In the formal dining room, an international cuisine is offered. More winning is the breakfast terrace, where rainbow-hued umbrellas and white garden chairs are set in view of the flowerbeds and three free-form splashing fountains. The bedrooms are restrained and restful, handsomely proportioned. Singles go for 145 DM ($47.85) to 210 DM ($69.30). Doubles with bath cost 210 DM ($69.30) to 240 DM ($79.20). Breakfast from the buffet is included.

A MIDDLE-BRACKET HOTEL: Holiday Inn-Turmhotel, Wittelsbacher Park (tel. 57-70-87). Students of architectural history might immediately recognize Chicago's Marina City in the facade of this rounded and balconied concrete tower thrusting itself skyward. This is a true skyscraper (it's advertised as the tallest tower hotel in Europe, with 35 floors). You'll find a swimming pool, a sauna, and an ultramodern Space Age dining room with what look like orange plastic stalactites hanging at random lengths from the ceiling. Children up to 18 years stay free in their parents' rooms, which are comfortable, tasteful, and sunny, with rounded terraces. The hotel is only ten minutes from the heart of

Augsburg. A single rents for 165 DM ($54.45), and a double costs from 210 DM ($69.30). Breakfast is yet another 16 DM ($5.28) per person.

BUDGET HOTELS: **Hotel Riegele,** 4 Viktoriastrasse (tel. 3-90-39). Offering only 27 rooms to its guests, this is a respected business person's hotel, used frequently by Augsburgers for their meetings and conferences. Modern and efficient, it offers comfortable rooms and friendly service. Singles rent for 89 DM ($29.37) to 99 DM ($32.67), while doubles go for 130 DM ($42.70) to 145 DM ($47.85), breakfast and plumbing included.

Dom Hotel, 8 Frauentorstrasse (tel. 15-30-31). To arrive at this 65-bed hotel, you can take trolley line no. 2 from the Hauptbahnhof (direction Lechhausen), and get out at the first stop to catch trolley line no. 2 (direction Kriegshaber). Get out at the third stop, the Mozart House, and the hotel is 200 yards away. From your windows you'll have an interesting view of parts of the old city. You'll reach your room via a grand winding staircase with wrought-iron balustrades. Units have been starkly renovated, sometimes exposing knotty-pine boards set horizontally onto the walls. Singles with breakfast range from 55 DM ($18.15) to 70 DM ($23.10); doubles rent for 83 DM ($27.39) to 118 DM ($38.94). Breakfast is included in all rents. All rooms contain private bath or shower with toilet.

Alpenhof, 233 Donauwörther (tel. 41-30-51), lies less than a mile off the autobahn (take the Augsburg West exit), and as such might be ideal for motorists unwilling to negotiate the old streets of town. Quiet and peaceful, the hotel offers some 135 modernized bedrooms, each with radio, phone, TV, and other amenities. A generous breakfast buffet is included in the price of the well-furnished rooms, which range between 85 DM ($28.05) and 115 DM ($37.95) in a single and from 125 DM ($41.25) to 265 DM ($87.45) in a double. There's a bar as well as a pleasant restaurant on the premises, along with plenty of parking space.

One of the least expensive and best budget accommodations in the area is about three kilometers from the heart of Augsburg, along the Augsburger Strasse in the western sector. It's the **Hotel Garni Weinberger,** 55 Bismarckstrasse (tel. 52-30-61) at Stadtbergen. The owner rents out large, light, and airy double rooms with complete private bath for 85 DM ($28.05) nightly. Singles go for 45 DM ($14.85). The place is well patronized by Germans, who know a good bargain, and its café is one of the most popular in the area for dinner and snacks.

WHERE TO DINE: **Ratskeller Augsburg,** 2 Rathausplatz (tel. 51-78-48). This restaurant is set in the basement of a Renaissance building, with original oil paintings, sculpture, and good gutbürgerlich cookery. The restored Town Hall itself is one of the principal secular buildings of the Renaissance north of the Alps. The weinstube can seat nearly 100 guests. You'd expect the food in such a historic place to be very expensive, but all items are reasonably priced. Menus cost from 18 DM ($5.94) to 40 DM ($13.20). The keller is open daily except Sunday and Monday from 11 a.m. to midnight.

Welser Kuche, 83 Maximilianstrasse (tel. 3-39-30). Seven tables seat up to 80 guests here in long, informal rows. You just might be rubbing elbows with the bürgermeister of Augsburg, or any of the local residents, because this is a historic place, having survived intact since the 15th and 16th centuries. A traditional menu of Schwäbish cookery is served nightly by the knechte and mägde, the "knaves" and "wenches" in 16th-century costumes, as the waiters and waitresses are called. A six- or a ten-course menu, called a "Welser feast," is served, costing between 55 DM ($18.15) and 75 DM ($24.75). For smaller appetites, four-course meals are also served, beginning at 28 DM ($9.24). A dagger and fingers are used as utensils. Stone walls, knotty-pine paneling, and stucco arches frame the wooden tables with their earthenware pitchers, and the friendly hubbub of neighbors reminiscing about the old days. Many of the recipes served here were found in a cookbook that belonged to Freiin von Zinnenburg, the wife of the Habsburg Archduke Ferdinand II. Discovered in 1970, the cookbook serves as a culinary guide for some of the dishes. It takes about three hours to have an average meal here. Guests are expected to arrive promptly at 7:30 p.m. (on Sunday, at 6:30 p.m.). Sometimes parties of two or four can be fitted in at the last minute, but reservations should be made as far in advance as possible (call 08231/2020).

Sieben-Schwaben-Stuben, 12 Bürgermeister-Fischer-Strasse (tel. 31-45-63), specializes in Swabian dishes, and does so exceedingly well. This unusual restaurant has a high barrel-vaulted ceiling, with half-moon windows, the brainchild of the owner Willy Ost. Early in the history of this restaurant Mr. Ost conceived of the idea of printing the establishment's menu in English, German, and French, and mailing it regularly to his best clients. Your best bet here is to order the fixed-price menu, called Schwäbische Lakkeln; it costs around 45 DM ($14.85) and features seven courses. Actually, prices vary according to the food served that day, and each day a different menu is written out. The restaurant is open from 11 a.m. to 1 a.m.

Hotel Riegele mit Bräustüberl, 4 Viktoriastrasse (tel. 3-90-39). Behind a rather plain exterior lies a house with gutbürgerlich (traditional) cookery, and a cozy interior, with minutely carved wooden benches evoking fables from the Black Forest, and a stenciled scroll winding in lyrical curves across the top section of the walls. These contain pithy folkloric wisdom amid heraldic signs, leaves, and branches. Swabian specialties, including country-style buffets, lure hungry diners here. The wide variety of appealing local specialties is coupled with kind and attentive service, along with reasonable prices. About 25 dishes a day are offered, costing as little as 18 DM ($5.94), rising to 55 DM ($18.15) if you decide to go whole-hog. The stube serves from 8 a.m. till midnight.

Zum Alten Fischertor, 14 Pfärrle (tel. 51-86-62), is a small restaurant with eight tables smack in the center of Augsburg, on a quiet street near in the cathedral. A six-course dinner menu is presented for 80 DM ($26.40), featuring daily and seasonal specialties such as baby turbot. Lunches begin at 40 DM ($13.20). Much of the cookery is in the nouvelle cuisine style. The restaurant is open from 11:30 a.m. to 2 p.m. and 6 to 11 p.m. It's closed around the end of June and for part of July, and on Sunday and Monday.

Hotel Gregor, 62 Landsberger Strasse (tel. 8-30-10), lies five miles south of Augsburg, a rustic country restaurant that retains an antique flavor in spite of new construction. Swabian and Bavarian dishes are offered here, with some French classics. Soups are important, along with such rare treats as wild boar (in season). On a lighter side, they make a Waldorf salad with orange segments. Menus are cheap, costing from 18 DM ($5.94) to 25 DM ($8.25). It's also possible to stay here in one of the pleasantly furnished bedrooms. Singles cost from 80 DM ($26.40) to 90 DM ($29.70), while doubles go for 105 DM ($34.65) to 150 DM ($49.50), including breakfast.

Ecke-Stuben, 2 Elias-Holl-Platz (tel. 51-06-00). If you decide to dine here, your name can join the roster of distinguished clients who have also experienced the establishment's charms. Since it was founded in the year Columbus sighted the New World, its guests have included Hans Holbein the Elder, Wolfgang Amadeus Mozart, and in more recent times, Rudolf Diesel of engine fame and Bertold Brecht (Brecht, it is reported, often showed sharp-tongued irreverence, which tended to irritate the bourgeois diners of more conservative political leanings).

The decor is an alluring blend of very old paneling and a weinstube kind of ambience that belies the very sophisticated cuisine concocted by the chef, Ralf Koczut. Both Gallic and Swabian cuisine is given an array of nouvelle touches which make for the kind of dining where reservations are imperative. A gourmet six-course fixed-price dinner is served for 95 DM ($31.35). Less elaborate fixed-price meals cost as little as 30 DM ($9.90). À la carte meals range between 22 DM ($7.26) and 38 DM ($12.54) on an average, and are served every evening from 5 p.m. to 1 a.m. Your meal might include such elegant fare as breast of duckling, preceded by a pâté of pheasant, or perhaps a saddle of hare in tarragon sauce. If you're not in a fowl or gamey mood, you might enjoy the filet of sole in Riesling sauce, and most definitely some of the lobster and shellfish dishes the chef prepares.

6. Füssen

Depending on which direction you take, Füssen is the beginning or end of the Romantic Road. The town has a number of attractive buildings, including a 15th-century castle once used by the bishops of Augsburg as a summer palace. Füssen's popularity lies in its ideal location as a starting point for excursions into the surrounding countryside.

Besides being the terminus of the Romantic Road, Füssen is in the foothills of the Bavarian Alps, making it equally enjoyable for winter and summer vacationers. An added attraction to sightseers is its proximity to the royal castles of Neuschwanstein and Hohenschwangau.

MIDDLE-BRACKET HOTELS: Hotel Christine, 31 Weidachstrasse (tel. 72-29), is run by the helpful, English-speaking Mrs. Ruppert, who seems to have always been a "favorite landlady" with our readers. The long winter months are spent refurbishing her rooms so that they'll be fresh and sparkling to greet spring visitors. She charges from 80 DM ($26.40) to 100 DM ($33) in a single, and from 130 DM ($42.90) to 160 DM ($52.80) in a double. Breakfast, included in the tariffs, is served on beautiful regional china, as Mozart or some other classical composer is played in the background. Units contain shower or bath. Her rooms are quite spacious, with balconies, plus sitting areas in the lobby. If her place is too much for your wallet, she'll suggest others in Füssen.

Fürstenhof, 23 Kemptener Strasse (tel. 70-06). The setting is crisply alpine, and the conifers around this hotel radiate a kind of good health. Something about this hotel calls its guests to shed their ailments and breathe more deeply, which they usually do in the beautifully crafted public rooms. Here the ceilings are of massively exposed paneling, the full-grained beams set into the modern stucco with taste and craftsmanship. Singles go for 55 DM ($18.15), and doubles cost 105 DM ($34.65), with shower and toilet. Each unit also has a phone and TV. Breakfast, included in the rates, is served by your hosts, the von Langendorff family.

Alpenblick, 10 Uferstrasse (tel. 70-18), is found at Hopfen am See, three miles from Füssen. It is an attractively designed mountain chalet whose encircling balconies are edged with borders of flowers. From the windows of many of the bedrooms, a guest can see the lake and the far-away Alps. The premises are impeccably maintained in a kind of rustic ambience of exposed wood and an occasional piece of hand-painted furniture. On a chilly evening you might seek out a quiet corner beside the open fireplace in the hotel bar. There's both an indoor and an outdoor swimming pool within walking distance, as well as a panoramic sun terrace where drinks and snacks are served to residents and roadside visitors as well. The 30 comfortably furnished bedrooms rent for 70 DM

($23.10) in a single and between 70 DM ($23.10) and 155 DM ($51.15) in a double, depending on the room and the season. Each unit contains its own balcony, TV, radio, phone, and refrigerator.

BUDGET HOTELS: Sailers Kurhotel, 14 Bildhauer-Sturm-Strasse (tel. 70-89). This is a well-proportioned adaptation of a chalet, with four floors of modern comfort rising starkly from a meadow. Many of the rooms have balconies and large windows, with comfortable armchairs and draw curtains separating the bed from the rest of the room. Health facilities include a dramatically crafted swimming pool, with a wood-paneled roof angled over it, and thermal baths staffed by professionals. Accommodations are usually in twin-bedded rooms. Their cost, depending on the exposure of the room, runs from 65 DM ($21.45) to 75 DM ($24.75) in a single, from 88 DM ($29.04) to 132 DM ($43.56) in a double, breakfast included. The hotel is closed from November 25 through December.

Gasthof Weissensee (tel. 70-95), at Füssen-Weissensee, along the B310, about four miles from Füssen. The fish that your obliging hosts serve you during dinner might have been caught in the ice-blue waters of the nearby lake, whose far shore you can see from the dining room. You'll find this chalet-style building filled with 22 bedrooms, each paneled with full-grained pine, containing sliding glass doors opening onto a private balcony overlooking the lake. Each accommodation contains a mini-bar stocked with beer, wine, and champagne. Breakfast is an appetizing and generous meal of cheese, marmalade, cold cuts, breads, pastries, eggs, and beverages served buffet style. Singles cost from 60 DM ($19.80), and doubles run between 105 DM ($34.65) and 150 DM ($49.50). The hotel is open all year except from November 20 until sometime in December.

Hotel-Gasthof Zum Hechten, 6 Ritterstrasse (tel. 79-06). The Pfeiffers have maintained this impeccable guest house in their family for generations. Its white-walled facade comes directly to the edge of the centrally located street where it sits. It is said to be one of the oldest guest houses in town, but it has been unpretentiously and tastefully modernized into a functional format with its own kind of charm. It's laden with a conservative sense of peace and quiet. With breakfast included, bathless doubles rent for 65 DM ($21.45), going up to 85 DM ($28.05) with bath. Bathless singles go for 40 DM ($13.20), rising to 50 DM ($16.50) with bath. Half board is another 15 DM ($4.95) per person daily.

WHERE TO DINE: Zum Schwanen, 4 Brotmarkt (tel. 61-74). A conservatively flavorful blend of Swabian and Bavarian specialties is served to loyal clients of this attractively old-fashioned restaurant. The staff is amicable, and the ingredients strictly fresh. Desserts are freshly prepared, tastefully caloric, and very tempting. Fixed-price menus cost between 18 DM ($5.94) and 35 DM ($11.55), and à la carte averages about the same. There are only about half a dozen tables in the entire restaurant, so a meal is fairly intimate. Food is served between 11:30 a.m. and 1:30 p.m. and from 6 to 9 p.m. every day but Sunday and Monday.

READER'S PENSION SELECTION AT FÜSSEN-WEISSENSEE: "Pension Garni Haus Steigmühle (tel. 73-73) is run by Josef and Guste Buhmann. This is an absolutely beautiful chalet-type pension with a view of the lake and mountains. I had a large, comfortable room with bath, a balcony, and a sitting area. Singles cost 35 DM ($11.55) to 50 DM ($16.50), and doubles cost 62 DM ($20.46) to 68 DM ($22.44). You'll want to stay longer here because of the comfort, beauty, and location. It's close to Füssen and the two royal castles, and within easy driving distance of the Kirche an der Wies, as well as Oberammergau and Linderhof. There is also ample parking" (Mrs. Glenn Rehn, Olmsted Township, Ohio).

7. The Royal Castles

The 19th century saw a great classical revival in Germany, especially in Bavaria. This was mainly because of the enthusiasm of the Bavarian kings for ancient art forms. Beginning with King Ludwig I (1786–1868), who was responsible for many of the neo-Greek buildings in Munich, this royal house ran the gamut of ancient architecture in just three short decades. It culminated in the remarkable flights of fancy of Ludwig II, often called "Mad King Ludwig," who died under mysterious circumstances in 1886. In spite of his rather lonely life and controversial alliances, personal and political, he was a great patron of the arts.

THE SIGHTS: Although the name "Royal Castles" is limited to the castles of **Hohenschwangau** (built by Ludwig's father, Maximilian II), and **Neuschwanstein,** the extravagant king was responsible for the creation of three magnificent castles. The remaining two, described in other parts of the book, are Linderhof (near Oberammergau) and Herrenchiemsee (Chiemsee). These pet projects were so close to the king's heart that, when his ministers sought to check his extravagance, he became violent.

In 1868, after a visit to the great castle of Warburg, Ludwig wrote to his good friend, Richard Wagner: "I have the intention to rebuild the ancient castle ruins of Hohenschwangau . . . in the true style of the ancient German knight's castle." The following year, construction began on the first of a series of fantastic castles, a series that stopped only with Ludwig's untimely death in 1886, only five days after he was deposed because of alleged insanity.

Neuschwanstein Castle

Neuschwanstein was the fairytale castle of Ludwig II. Until the king's death, construction had taken 17 years. After his death, all work stopped, leaving a part of the interior not completed. In the years from 1884 to 1886 Ludwig lived in the rooms on and off for a total of only about six months.

Neuschwanstein was his most ambitious project, set in its isolated location atop a rock ledge high above the Pöllat Gorge. The ledge served as the foundation of the castle, and because of its unusual configuration, supported portions of the third floor as well as the first. This is obvious in the oddly shaped vestibule on the third floor, at the top of the main staircase of Untersberg marble. This hall, with its colorfully painted Romanesque vaults, is trapezoidal in shape, the walls decorated with scenes from the primitive version of the Siegfried saga.

The doorway off the left side of the vestibule leads to the king's apartments. The study, like most of the rooms, is decorated with wall paintings showing scenes from the Nordic legends (which also inspired Wagner's operas). The theme of the study is the Tannhäuser saga, painted by J. Aigner. The only fabric in the room is that used in the hand-embroidered silk curtains and chair coverings, all designed with the gold and silver Bavarian coat-of-arms.

From the vestibule, you enter the throne room through the doorway at the opposite end. This hall, designed in a Byzantine style by J. Hofmann, was never completed. The floor of the hall is a mosaic design, depicting the animals of the world. The columns in the main hall are the deep copper red of porphyry. The circular apse where the king's throne was to have stood is reached by a stairway of white Carrara marble. The walls and ceiling are decorated with paintings of Christ in heaven looking down on the twelve Apostles and six canonized kings of Europe.

The king's bedroom is the most richly carved in the entire castle. It took

4½ years to complete this room alone, which, aside from the wall painting depicting the legend of Tristan und Isolde, is completely covered in oakwood carvings. The walls are decorated with panels carved to look like Gothic windows. In the center is a large wooden pillar completely encircled with gilded brass sconces. The bed, on its raised platform, is the most ornate furnishing in the room. The elaborately carved canopy blends into a simple Gothic design at the foot. Through the balcony window you can see the 150-foot waterfall in the Pöllat Gorge, with the mountains in the distance.

Passing through the winter garden and a grotto with artificial stalactites, you come to the great parlor, whose theme is the Lohengrin saga, expressed in the paintings of Heckel and Hauschild. Note the heavy chandelier, holding 48 candles and studded with pieces of colored Bohemian glass.

The fourth floor of the castle is almost entirely given over to the Singer's Hall, the pride of Ludwig II and all of Bavaria. Modeled after the hall at Wartburg where incidents from the saga of Tannhäuser were supposed to have occurred, this hall is decorated with marble columns and elaborately painted designs interspersed with frescoes depicting the life of Parsifal.

The castle can be visited year round, and in September visitors have the additional treat of hearing Wagnerian concerts in the Singer's Hall. For information and reservations, contact the Verkehrsamt (tourist office) Schwangau. The rooms are open daily from 8:30 a.m. to 5:30 p.m. (in winter from 10 a.m. to 4 p.m.). Admission is 6 DM ($1.98). Before returning down the slope, more energetic visitors can follow the winding path to the **Marienbrücke,** named for the mother of Ludwig II. This bridge crosses over the Pöllat Gorge at a height of 305 feet. From that vantage point you, like Ludwig, can stand and meditate on the glories of the castle and its surroundings.

To reach that magnificence, however, you must climb a steep hill, a 25-minute walk for the energetic, an eternity for anybody else. However, buses will take you up to Marienbrücke for 3.50 DM ($1.16). The descent costs 2 DM (66¢). Even so, you're not transported directly to the castle, but must add on a ten-minute hike to reach it. This footpath is very steep and not easy for elderly people to negotiate—or for anyone who has trouble walking up or down precipitous hills. However, the most romantic way to go is by carriage, costing 5 DM ($1.65) for the ascent, 3 DM (99¢) for the descent. (Note: Carriages require a minimum of 30 DM or $9.90, so round up some extra people.) However, some readers have objected to the buggy rides, complaining that too many people are crowded in. It should be pointed out that the buggy ride doesn't bring you all the way to the top. As you get out, you're faced with a steep path leading to the castle. You still have to walk uphill to the castle on a convenient road. The walk takes about ten minutes. For information, phone 8-10-35.

Hohenschwangau Castle

Not as glamorous or spectacular as Neuschwanstein, this neo-Gothic castle nevertheless has a much richer history. The original structure dates back to the Knights of Schwangau of the 12th century. When the knights faded away, the castle began to do so too, helped along by the Napoleonic War in 1809. When Ludwig II's father, Crown Prince Maximilian (later King Maximilian II), saw the castle in 1832, he purchased it, and in four years had it completely restored. Ludwig II spent the first 17 years of his life here, and later received Richard Wagner in its chambers, although Wagner never visited Neuschwanstein on the hill above.

The rooms of Hohenschwangau are styled and furnished in a much heavier Gothic mood than the castle built by Ludwig. Many are typical of the halls of knights' castles of the Middle Ages in both England and Germany. There is no doubt that the style greatly influenced young Ludwig and encouraged his fanciful boyhood dreams which formed his later tastes and character. Unlike Neuschwanstein, however, this castle has a comfortable look about it, as if it actually were a home at one time, not just a museum. The small chapel, once a drinking hall, is still the scene of Sunday mass. The suits of armor and Gothic arches here set the stage for the rest of the room.

Among the most attractive chambers is the Hall of the Swan Knight, named for the wall paintings depicting the saga of Lohengrin—pre-Wagner and pre-Ludwig II. Note the Gothic grillwork on the ceiling with the open spaces studded with stars. The furniture in the room, once reserved for dining, is a mixture of period Gothic, overdecorative gifts from admiring subjects, and cherry or maple Biedermeier pieces from the 19th century.

Probably the most authentically Gothic room is the Hall of Heroes. The paintings lining the walls depict the old German saga of Dietrich of Berne. On the long banquet table are centerpieces of hot-gilded bronze decorated with scenes from the Nibelungen saga.

From Ludwig's bedroom on the third floor the young king could keep an eye on his castle on the hillside above. As in other rooms, the ceiling of the bedroom was decorated with the typically Gothic stars—with one difference. Here they lit up at night.

Nearby is the music room where Ludwig and Wagner spent long hours entertaining one another at the maple piano. The small chapel in the alcove off the music room was executed by Ludwig. The room also contains an exhibit of emotional letters sent by the king to Wagner, expressing his great admiration for him.

Hohenschwangau is open daily from 8:30 a.m. to 5 p.m. (in winter, 10 a.m. to 4 p.m.). Admission is 6 DM ($1.98). Several parking lots nearby enable you to leave your car here while visiting both castles.

STAYING IN THE TOWN OF HOHENSCHWANGAU: Hotel Lisl und Jägerhaus, 1–3 Neuschwansteinstrasse (tel. 8-10-06), is a graciously styled villa with an annex across the street. It was seemingly made to order to provide views as well as comfort. Both houses sit in a narrow valley, surrounded by their own gardens. In the main house, two well-styled dining rooms serve good meals, including Hungarian goulash, and averaging around 30 DM ($9.90). The restaurant features an international as well as local cuisine. If you're staying over, you'll find comfortably furnished and attractive bedrooms renting for widely varying prices. In a bathless single, the rate is 40 DM ($13.20), rising to 78 DM ($25.74) with bath. In a bathless double, the charge is 58 DM ($19.14) per room, increasing to 170 DM ($56.10) in a double with complete bath.

Hotel Müller, 14–16 Alpseestrasse (tel. 8-10-56), is a small-town inn with many colorful elements. In the hub of village activity, its facade is adorned with dormers, flower boxes, and balconies. The dining room is in the country style, with blue fabric and natural woods, and it forms the chief social center. The stube is also popular, decorated in a provincial vein, with leather-backed chairs, beamed ceilings, and plate rails of pewter. In case you're just passing through, you can order good-tasting food here, a meal averaging around 30 DM ($9.90). Singles cost 80 DM ($26.40) to 110 DM ($36.30). Doubles go for 120 DM ($39.60) to 170 DM ($56.10), and some apartments are rented, ranging from 220 DM ($72.60) to 270 DM ($89.10). The prices for the latter rooms depend on the views of the castles.

READERS' GUEST HOUSE SELECTION: "We stayed at the immaculate and exquisitely furnished **Gästehaus Brückner,** 37 Schwangauer Strasse (tel. 8-11-52). The three of us paid

82 DM ($27.06) for two designer-decorated rooms and a private bath. Gästehaus Brückner overlooks King Ludwig II's Neuschwanstein Castle. From the Brückner house, one can walk up to the castle to go inside. The fairytale atmosphere and surroundings are absolutely majestic. You'll never want to leave this dreamland—not to mention Mrs. Brückner's outstanding command of English and her superb breakfasts, which include juice, coffee, tea, eggs, cheese, meats, jam, and homemade rolls and bread. Also, at cocktail hour you can relax in the beautiful Oriental-carpeted and antique-filled drawing room to imbibe" (The Rovert C. Bentleys, Sewickley, Penna.).

The most popular tourist section of Germany unfolds in the upcoming chapter.

Chapter XI

THE BAVARIAN ALPS

1. Berchtesgaden
2. Garmisch-Partenkirchen
3. Chiemsee
4. Oberammergau
5. Mittenwald
6. Starnberger See
7. Tegernsee

IF YOU WALK into a rustic alpine inn along the German-Austrian frontier and ask the innkeeper if he's German, you'll most likely get the indignant response, "Of course not! I'm Bavarian." And he is undoubtedly right, because even though Bavaria is politically a part of Germany, many of its older folk can still remember the kingdom of Bavaria, which did not become part of the German Reich until 1918.

The huge province includes not only the Alps, but Franconia, Lake Constance, and the capital city of Munich as well. However, we will take this opportunity to explore separately the mountains along the Austrian frontier, a world unto itself. The hospitality of the people of this area is world famous. The picture of the plump rosy-cheeked innkeeper with a constant smile on his face is no myth.

Many travelers think of the Alps as a winter vacationland, but you'll find that nearly all of the Bavarian resorts and villages boast year-round attractions.

I'll begin our exploration of the Bavarian Alps with . . .

1. Berchtesgaden

Ever since Ludwig I of Bavaria chose this resort as one of his favorite hideaways—his first choice was Lola Montez's—the tourist business in Berchtesgaden has been booming. Its setting below the many summits of the Watzmann Mountain is among the most outstanding in Bavaria. According to legend, the peaks of the mountain were once a king and his family who were so evil that God punished them by turning them into rocks. The king has evidently not been completely silenced, however, because even in recent years the Watzmann has been responsible for the deaths of several mountain climbers who have endeavored to scale the one-mile-high cliff on its eastern wall.

THE SIGHTS: Berchtesgaden grew up in the Middle Ages around the powerful

Augustine monastery, whose monks introduced the art of woodcarving for which the town is noted to this day. When the town became part of Bavaria in 1809, the abbey was secularized and eventually converted to a palace for the royal family of Wittelsbach. The **castle** has been turned into a museum, exhibiting the collections of furniture and art owned by the royal family. More interesting is the adjacent **Stiftskirche** (Abbey Church), from 1122. The church is mainly Romanesque, with Gothic additions. One of its ancient twin steeples was destroyed by lightning and rebuilt in 1866. The interior of the church contains many fine works of art, including the high altar with a painting by Zott dating from 1669. In the vestry is a small silver altar donated by the Empress Maria Theresa of Austria.

The **Schlossplatz** (Castle Square), partially enclosed by the castle and Stiftskirche, is the most attractive plaza in town. On the opposite side of the square from the church is a 16th-century arcade which leads to the Marketplace with its typically alpine houses and a wooden fountain from 1677 (restored by Ludwig I in 1860). Some of the oldest inns and houses in Berchtesgaden line this square. Extending from the Marketplace is the **Nonntal,** lined with more old houses, some of which have been built into the rocks of the Lockstein Mountain that towers above.

Berchtesgaden is less a sightseeing center than it is a jumping-off place for excursions into the surrounding mountains, but there is one attraction: the **Salt Mines** (Salzbergwerk), at the eastern edge of town, once owned by the monastery for many years after operations began here in 1517. The mines contain two types of salt, one of which is suitable only for "salt licks" for cattle and other animals. The deposits are more than 990 feet thick and are still processed today from four galleries or "hills." Visitors on guided tours enter the mine on a small wagon-like train after donning the protective costume of the miner. After nearly a half-mile ride, they leave the train and explore the rest of the mine on foot (even taking a "wild slide"), and enjoy a ride on the salt lake in a small boat. The highlight of the tour is the "chapel," a grotto containing unusually shaped salt formations illuminated to create an eerie effect. The best thing about the 1½-hour tour is that you can take it any time of year, in any weather. Hours are 8 a.m. till 5 p.m., May 1 to October 15. Off-season it is open weekdays from 12:30 to 3:30 p.m. The price of admission is 6 DM ($1.98) for children and 11 DM ($3.63) for adults.

THE TOP HOTEL: Geiger Hotel, 111 Berchtesgadenstrasse (tel. 50-55), is a genuine antique. It's an ornate chalet-style inn on the upper fringes of Berchtesgaden. From its terraces (one with an open-air swimming pool), bedrooms, or breakfast rooms, one can enjoy fantastic views of the mountaintops named the Watzmann Family—mother, father, and seven children—by the local people. The "why" of this remarkable retreat is the Geiger family, who created the hotel more than a century ago.

Bedrooms, dining and living rooms are furnished with antiques. Biedermeier enthusiasts will revel over the several sitting rooms completely furnished in that period. Any member of the Geiger family will give you the history of any of the furnishings, especially the painting in the paneled drawing room of *Silent Night* (it upset everyone by depicting Mary as awaiting the birth of Jesus on a Bavarian farm). Guests like to gather in the drawing room for after-dinner coffee and cognac in front of the fireplace. Dining rooms have the requisite deer horns and wooden dado holding pewter plates. Dining is a true event here. Be sure to try the alpine river trout. The menu of the day is 35 DM ($11.55) to 45 DM ($14.85). Have a drink of water before you depart, from the fountain where Bach drank.

The Geiger's bedrooms are comfortable, and furnished with antiques, although the plumbing may strike you as having that same characteristic too. Prices include breakfast, and are gauged on whatever bath facilities you request, plus your view—i.e., if you have a balcony or not. Rooms with showers range in price from 65 DM ($21.45) to 85 DM ($28.05) per person, from 85 DM ($28.05) to 140 DM ($46.20) per person with bath. Half-board terms are 35 DM ($11.55) per person daily, in addition to the room rates. The hotel also has an indoor swimming pool.

MIDDLE-RANGE HOTELS: Vier Jahreszeiten, 20 Maximilianstrasse (tel. 50-26), is an old inn with modern extensions that has been in the hands of the Miller family since 1876. It's in the heart of the village and has a colorful and distinguished restaurant (see my dining recommendations). The inn has been remodeled and improved over the years and now brings a good level of comfort to its guests. The newer units have been furnished with many wooden pieces, and some of them are like suites with tiny sitting rooms and balconies. In addition to the main dining room, there's a terrace for summer dining and viewing. Depending on the plumbing, singles range from 85 DM ($28.05) to 98 DM ($32.34), and doubles go for anywhere from 130 DM ($42.90) to 200 DM ($66).

Wittelsbach, 16 Maximilianstrasse (tel. 50-61), has been modernized stylishly, now offering well-furnished bedrooms in the heart of Berchtesgaden. It represents a connection of tradition and modern comfort. The rooms and apartments are quiet and sunny, with shower or bath and toilet, mini-bar, and phone. Most have balconies from which you have fine views of the mountains. The rates are 90 DM ($29.70) to 100 DM ($33) in a single, 150 DM ($49.50) to 170 DM ($76.10) in a double, while an apartment costs 220 DM ($72.60) to 300 DM ($99). The rates include a buffet breakfast and tax.

Demming, 2 Sunklerg (tel. 50-21), looks like a chalet, but on closer inspection the hotel is massive, with four floors of balconied rooms and an annex extending at right angles to the main building, containing an attractive decor in a regional motif. The entire complex is nestled in a depression between two forested hills, which offer good views in both summer and winter. The bedrooms are clean, comfortable, and delightfully furnished with reproduction alpine pieces and autumnal colors. You may be interested in some of the artifacts in the reception area, among them two wine presses, their wooden screws somewhat weakened by time but still tinged with the color of the grape. All units have plumbing facilities, and a breakfast buffet is included in the tariffs, costing from 84 DM ($27.72) in a single and from 158 DM ($52.14) in a double. Half board is another 15 DM ($4.95) per person. You will also have the use of an indoor swimming pool. Under separate administration, a skin-care studio offers a regime of skin- and muscle-toning sessions.

Sporthotel Seimier, 4 Maria am Berg (tel. 50-31), outside of the center. You'll get the feeling of lots of light in this place, which is decorated in a traditional motif of beamed ceilings and panelings. Public rooms are spacious and airy. There's even a bowling alley if you're interested, along with a wood-paneled swimming pool. In the basement is a rustically decorated disco, with a 19th-century device that looks like a plow hanging from the ceiling. The hotel is beautifully situated with a view of the Alps from many of its rooms, which rent for 104 DM ($34.32) to 110 DM ($36.30) in a double and 67 DM ($22.11) to 72 DM ($25.41) in a single, including breakfast. The Brandner family are your conscientious hosts. They close the hotel from mid-November to mid-December.

BUDGET INNS: Watzmann, 2 Franziskanerplatz (tel. 20-55), is a country-town inn on the square opposite the church. It's Bavarian, with shuttered windows, window boxes of red geraniums, and a wide front terrace with dining tables. Everyone seems to stop by here day or night for a beer, coffee, or lunch. Inside, the Watzmann contains huge carved wooden pillars, oak ceilings, wrought-iron light fixtures, and a circular, antler-horn chandelier in the hunt dining room. Evenings there is folk singing and yodeling, with mountain musicians performing. The Piscantors do the innkeeping. Bathless singles are 40 DM ($13.20); doubles, 65 DM ($21.45). Doubles with shower or bath and toilet are 100 DM ($33). Breakfast is included. Simply furnished bedrooms, with an occasional antique, are kept immaculate; the beds are downy-soft. The inn is closed from November 1 through December 20.

Grassl Hotel, 15 Maximilianstrasse (tel. 40-71), is a hillside villa run by the Lipp family, with one side opening onto the main street of town and the other upon the valley below, with a view of the Alps beyond. It's an old building with overhanging balconies. Inside it has caught up to today's taste by use of simple furnishings and lots of splashes of color. There is no proper restaurant but rather a breakfast terrace and a pleasant café for snacks, with wide-view windows. Bedrooms are personalized, zinging with color, and most have plenty of space. Important: Ask for rooms with a view, which are away from the noises of the street. Prices quoted are for high season (generally in the low season there is a drop of about 10% per person). The bathless single rate (including breakfast, taxes, and service) on the street side is 40 DM ($13.20), 70 DM ($23.10) with shower. The rate in a bathless double on the street side is 70 DM ($23.10); on the view side, a double with private bath costs 126 DM ($41.58). For one or two nights, there is an extra 5-DM ($1.65) charge per person.

WHERE TO DINE: **Hubertusstuben,** in the Hotel Vier Jahreszeiten, 29 Maximilianstrasse (tel. 50-26), has been owned and directed by the Miller family since 1876. It has one of the most elaborate menus in Berchtesgaden. The dining room is decorated in a traditional style, and it's warm and intimate. The wine list is also distinguished. Among the soups, a fresh fish soup is presented, and you may enjoy frog legs as an appetizer. Specialties include banana steak Bombay and deer steak with vegetables and homemade noodles (along with almond balls). For dessert, I'd suggest the apple fritters on walnut ice cream. Meals cost from 18 DM ($5.94) to 45 DM ($14.85).

The **Hotel Geiger,** 111 Berchtesgadener Strasse (tel. 50-55), is a gabled and extravagantly ornate hotel that looks like what every tourist imagines a German hotel to be. It was previously recommended, but even if you don't stay there, you may want to visit for a meal. Its owner, Hugo Geiger, makes his guests feel happy and well cared for in a cultivated atmosphere surrounded by Bavarian antiques. Meals—good, hearty regional cookery along with international specialties—range from 30 DM ($9.90) to 55 DM ($18.15), and are served daily from noon to 2 p.m. and 6:30 to 9 p.m.

Demming-Restaurant Le Gourmet, 2 Sunklerg (tel. 50-21), was previously recommended as a hotel, but it also houses one of the best restaurants in town. The copious proportions of what used to be a wealthy private house look out over a panoramic view of mountains and forests. Reservations are necessary for dining here, which many local residents regard as something of an event. Only fresh ingredients are used in the well-prepared dishes, including such hearty mountain fare as roast beef with chive sauce, plus an array of veal and fish dishes. Fixed-price meals cost between 22 DM ($7.26) and 60 DM ($19.80). The restaurant is open every day from 6 p.m. to midnight.

THE ENVIRONS: Time may not permit you to take every excursion through the mountains and valleys around the town, but the two most popular sights make it well worth spending an extra night here.

Königssee

This "jewel in the necklace" of Berchtesgaden is very likely one of the most scenic bodies of water in Europe. Its waters appear to be a dark green because of the steep mountains which jut upward from its shores. The northern edge of the lake borders enough low-lying land to contain a car park and a few charming inns and bathing facilities, and the rest of the lake is enclosed by mountains, making it impossible to walk along the shoreline. The only way to explore the waters, unless you're one of the mountain goats you may see on cliffs above, is by boat. **Electric motorboats**—no noisy gas-powered launches allowed—carry passengers on tours around the lake throughout the summer and occasionally even in winter. The favorite spot on the Königssee is the tiny peninsula on the western bank. It's the only flat area surrounding the lake, and was the site of a monastery as early as the 12th century. Today the Catholic chapel of **St. Bartholomae** is still used for services (except in winter). The clergy must arrive by boat since there is no other way to approach the peninsula. The adjacent buildings include a fisherman's house and a restaurant, where you can sample trout and salmon caught in the crisp, clean waters. At the southern end of the lake you come to the "Salet-Alm," where the tour boat makes a short stop near a thundering waterfall. If you follow the footpath up the hillside, you'll reach the summer pastures used by the cattle of Berchtesgaden Land.

Just over the hill is **Lake Obersee,** part of Königssee until an avalanche separated them eight centuries ago. The complete tour of the Königssee lasts about two hours. If you prefer a shorter trip, you can take the boat as far as St. Bartholomae and back. To reach the lake from Berchtesgaden by car, follow the signs south from the town (only three miles). It's also a pleasant hour walk, or a short ride by electric train or bus from the center of town.

Obersalzberg

The drive from Berchtesgaden to Obersalzberg is along one of the most scenic routes in Bavaria, reaching a height of 3300 feet by the time you arrive at the bus station at the Hintereck Restaurant. Here you may park your car and take the thrilling ride by bus up the 4½-mile-long mountain road, blasted out of solid rock and considered an outstanding feat of construction and engineering when it was begun in 1937. At the end of the journey, after winding around numerous curves and through five tunnels, you'll arrive at your destination, the "Eagle's Nest," which was not, as its name suggests, a heavily defended military installation. Hitler, reportedly, visited this site only about half a dozen times. As a young man, he lived in Obersalzberg, completing his book, *Mein Kampf.* To reach the house, you must enter the tunnel and take the 400-foot elevator ride through a shaft in the Kehlstein Mountain to its summit. The building, with its solid granite walls and huge picture windows, houses an inn and a restaurant, the Kehlsteinhaus. The modest house belies the fact that the entire project cost in the neighborhood of $10 million!

From this eagle's-eye view you can observe the Obersalzberg area below, where Hitler's Berghof once stood, and nearby, the site of the house of Martin Bormann and the SS barracks, all destroyed. To the north you can see as far as Salzburg, Austria, and just below the mountain, to the west, Berchtesgaden, with its rivers dwindling off into threads in the distance.

The bunkers and air raid shelter were built by Hitler in 1943. Three thousand laborers completed the work in nine months, connecting all the major Nazi buildings of the Obersalzberg area to the underground rooms.

The tours of the mountain, the Eagle's Nest, and the Obersalzberg area are conducted daily (lasting about two hours) at half-hour intervals between 9 a.m. and 5:30 p.m. Because the roads become treacherous in winter, no tours are conducted between November and April.

Back at Kehlstein, you can walk around the ruins of the dictator's famed Berghof and its surrounding bunkers. If you climb a steep, brush-studded hill, you'll even see the shell of his garage. The Berghof was destroyed in 1952 by the Bavarian government authorities at the "request" of the U.S. Army. The only fully remaining structure from the Nazi compound is a guest house, which is behind the General Walker Hotel, used by U.S. troops stationed in the area. Wear good walking shoes and be prepared to run into some "Verboten!" signs.

It is important to stress that the Berghof was destroyed. Many readers have expressed their disappointment when reaching this site, apparently thinking they were going to be taken on a tour of Hitler's sumptuously decorated private apartments which he shared with his mistress, Eva Braun. The Americans didn't want to create a "monument" to Hitler—hence the destruction of the Berghof, which, incidentally, is where the Nazi dictator vacationed and, as such, is not to be confused with the so-called "Eagle's Nest." Therefore go up the mountain for the magnificent view, not to see the faded retreat of the hierarchy of the Third Reich.

In Obersalzberg, the **Hotel Zum Türken** (tel. 24-28) is legendary. It stands today in the alpine style, with terraces and views for everyone. On its facade is a large painted sign of the "the Turk," and the foundation is stone, the windows framed in shutters. A large handmade sign is written across the hillside, with a rather ominous pronouncement, pointing the way to the "Bunker."

The story goes that it was erected by a Turkish war vet. At the turn of the century it was acquired by Karl Schuster, who turned it into a well-known restaurant that drew many celebrities of the day, including Brahms and Crown Prince Wilhelm of Prussia. However, anti-Nazi remarks in the '30s led to trouble for Mr. Schuster, who was arrested. In time, Bormann used the building as a Gestapo headquarters, a role that came to an end when Allied forces captured Obersalzberg. Air raids and looting in April of 1945 led to much destruction of the Türken.

Mr. Schuster's daughter, Therese Partner, petitioned for the Türken back in 1946 and started to rebuild it. However, the U.S. government forced her out, which led to more looting. It wasn't until the spring of 1949 that she was able to get her property back. She opened a café, and soon started to attract visitors again. Many tourists erroneously think the Türken was Hitler's famed Berghof.

Fourteen pleasantly furnished bedrooms are rented out, costing 35 DM ($11.55) to 55 DM ($18.15) per person nightly. For half board, you pay another 25 DM ($8.25) per person.

2. Garmisch-Partenkirchen

The charm of the village that became Germany's top alpine resort is still there, even though Garmisch-Partenkirchen has grown into the largest city in the Bavarian Alps. Even today you occasionally see country folk in their traditional costumes, and you may be held up in traffic while the cattle are led from their mountain grazing grounds down through the streets of town.

THE SIGHTS: The symbol of the city's growth and modernity is the **Olympic Ice Stadium,** built for the Winter Olympics of 1936 and capable of holding nearly 12,000 people. On the slopes at the edge of town is the much larger **Ski Stadium,** with two ski runs and slalom course. In 1936 more than 100,000 people watched the events in this stadium. Today it is still an integral part of winter life in Garmisch, as many of the events in the annual winter competitions are held here.

Garmisch-Partenkirchen is more a center for winter sports and for summer hiking and mountain climbing than for sightseeing. In addition the town and its environs offer some of the most exciting views and colorful buildings in Bavaria. The pilgrimage chapel of **St. Anton,** on a pinewood path at the edge of Partenkirchen, is all pink and silver, inside and out. Its graceful lines are characteristic of the 18th century, when it was built. The adjoining monastery pays tribute to the local men who died in the two world wars. The strange memorial consists of a collection of hundreds of photographs of the local boys who never returned from the wars.

The Philosopher's Walk in the park surrounding the chapel is a delightful spot to wander, just to enjoy the views of the mountains around the low-lying town. See especially the tallest peak of them all, the **Zugspitze,** at the frontier of Austria and Germany, the highest mountain in Germany, its summit towering more than 9700 feet above sea level. Its slopes for skiers begin at the **Hotel Schneefernerhaus** at a height of 8700 feet. For a spectacular view of both the Bavarian and Tyrolean (Austrian) Alps, go all the way to the peak. To get to the Zugspitze summit, you have a variety of transportation choices. I will concentrate only on those from the German side, but there are also means of access from the Austrian side.

From Garmisch, you drive to Eibsee, a small lake at the foot of the mountain, and then take the underground railway leading up to the hotel. From the hotel you board the short cable-car lift to the peak. Or you may take the one-hour train ride from Garmisch, which merges with the underground railway. An alternative route is the funicular from Eibsee directly to the summit.

The cogwheel train to the Schneefernerhaus Hotel at the Zugspitzplatt leaves every hour between 8 a.m. and 4 p.m. The travel time from Garmisch is 75 minutes.

The Eibsee cable car (Eibsee-Seilbahn) leaves from Eibsee directly, going to the Zugspitz summit at nearly 10,000 feet. It runs at least every half hour from 8:15 a.m. to 5:45 p.m. (in July and August till 6:15 p.m.), a ten-minute ride.

The cable car to the Zugspitz summit (Gipfelseilbahn) departs from Schneefernerhaus to the Zugspitz summit at least every half hour during the operating hours of the cogwheel train and the Eibsee cable car. This latter one is only a four-minute ride.

The Zugspitz summit and return or the Zugspitz round trip is 45 DM ($14.85), with reductions for children.

The **Alpspitz** region can also be explored. It's a paradise for hikers and nature lovers in general. From early spring until late fall its meadows and flowers are a delight, and its rocks evoke a prehistoric world. At altitudes of 4600 to 6300 feet, the Alps present themselves in a storybook fantasy. Those who want to explore the northern foot of the Alpspitz can take the Alpspitz round trip by going up with the Osterfelder cable car, over the Hochalm, and back down with the Kreuzeck or Hausberg cable car, allowing time in between for hikes lasting from half an hour to an hour and a half. Snacks are served at the top station of the Osterfelder cable car or at the more rustic Hochalm Chalet.

The Osterfelder cable car to Osterfelderkopf, at a height of 6300 feet runs at least every hour from 8 a.m. to 5 p.m., a nine-minute ride. The round-trip cost is 25 DM ($8.25) for adults, 15 DM ($4.95) for children 4 to 14.

The Hochalm cable car from the Hochalm to Osterfelderkopf runs at least every hour during the operating hours of the Osterfelder cable car, a four-minute ride. A single ride costs adults 7 DM ($2.31); children, 5 DM ($1.65).

The Alpspitz round trip with the Osterfelder cable car, the Hochalm cable car, and the Kruezeck or Kreuzwankl/Hausberg cable car is 30 DM ($9.90) for adults and 18 DM ($5.94) for children.

These fares and times of departure can fluctuate from season to season. Therefore, for the latest details, check with the tourist office, **Kurverwaltung,** at 35 Bahnhofstrasse (tel. 25-70), open from 8 a.m. to 6 p.m. Monday to Saturday and on Sunday from 10 a.m. to noon only.

From Garmisch-Partenkirchen, many other peaks of the Witterstein range are accessible as well, via the ten funiculars ascending from the borders of the town. From the top of the **Wank** (5850 feet) to the east, you get the best view of the plateau on which the twin villages of Garmisch and Partenkirchen have grown up. This summit is also a favorite with the patrons of Garmisch's spa facilities, because the plentiful sunshine makes it ideal for the *liegekur* (deck-chair cure).

Another excursion from the town is a hike through the **Partnachklamm Gorge,** lying between the Graseck and Hausberg peaks. After taking the cable car to the first station on the Graseck route, follow the paths along the sides of the slope to the right and trail the river as it cascades over the rocks. The path circles around by crossing the gorge, and returns you to the point where you entered. Many readers have found this one of their most memorable sightseeing adventures in Bavaria. The experience of walking along a rocky ledge just above the rushing river and often behind small waterfalls, while looking up at 1200 feet of rocky cliffs, always fills me with awe.

THE TOP HOTELS: **Posthotel Partenkirchen,** 49 Ludwigstrasse (tel. 5-10-67), was a posting inn, and after many different stages in its development has emerged as one of the most prestigious hotels in town, especially when you consider the added asset of its unusually fine restaurant (refer to my dining suggestions). The bedrooms are stylish with antiques and hand-decorated or elaborately carved furnishings. You feel apart from conventional hotel life here. It's old-world living, and the owners bring a personalized service.

Its facade is studded with window boxes of red geraniums, and around the front entrance are decorative murals and designs. There are two dining rooms, the larger known for its wooden beamed ceiling, wrought-iron chandeliers, and natural-wood chairs. Huge arches divide the room, making it more intimate. In the arched, rustic Weinlokal Barbarossa, there are nooks for quiet before- or after-dinner drinks. Musicians provide background music.

Bedrooms are U-shaped, overlooking a garden and parking for your car. Bedroom balconies are sun traps, and from them you'll have a view of the Alps. Singles with complete bath range in price from 90 DM ($29.70) to 170 DM ($56.10), and doubles go for 120 DM ($39.60) to 190 DM ($62.70).

Alpina Hotel, 12 Alpspitzstrasse (tel. 5-50-31), is a Bavarian hostelry where guests have all sorts of luxury facilities. It's a large chalet done in a tasteful manner. Only three minutes from the Hausberg ski lifts, it has its own covered swimming pool with a recreational terrace alongside, a garden with wide lawns and trees, and a large open patio, with an open-air swimming pool and surrounding terrace for sunning.

Its facade is graced with a wide overhanging roof and Tyrolean-style entranceway and windows. A decorating job has given the rooms a sophisticated but rustic decor, with beamed ceilings, provincial chairs, Oriental rugs, gilt sconce lights, and handmade chests. The open tavern dining room has two levels, and there is an extensive brick wine cellar, offering a wide and excellent choice.

Each bedroom is personalized, with its own color scheme and restrained furnishings. Your room may have snow-white sofa, chairs, walls, and lamps, an olive carpet, and original colorful paintings as an accent; or you may be assigned a room with sloped pine ceilings, a Spanish bedspread, and matching armchairs. Meals are served in the beamed, rustic dining room and on the sun terrace, all warmly accented by geranium red.

You pay 68 DM ($22.44) in a bathless single, 90 DM ($29.70) with bath. Doubles cost from 170 DM ($26.10) bathless to 190 DM ($62.70) with bath. The hotel is open from December 20 to October 1.

Grand Hotel Sonnenbichl, 97 Burgstrasse (tel. 5-20-52), is on the hillside overlooking Garmisch-Partenkirchen, with views of the Wetterstein mountain range and the Zugspitze. The 100 rooms have all been renovated and offer all the modern amenities, including private bath, mini-bar, color TV, video, radio alarm clock, and direct-dial phone. Doubles rent for 200 DM ($66) to 260 DM ($85.80), and singles run 140 DM ($46.20) to 165 DM ($54.45). The hotel boasts an excellent cuisine. You can have nouvelle cuisine in the elegant Gourmet Restaurant or Bavarian specialties in the Zirbelstube. Afternoon coffee and fresh homemade cakes are served in the lobby or on the terrace, which lies in the sun. You can enjoy a cocktail in the Peacock Bar. A swimming pool, sauna, solarium, and fitness and massage rooms are here for the use of guests, and entertainment is offered on the premises.

Holiday Inn, 2 Mittenwalder Strasse (tel. 75-61), made an interesting adaptation of its traditional style when it built this hotel in Garmisch-Partenkirchen. The entrance looks like a discreetly designed branch of a private bank. It doesn't interfere with the small scale of the rest of the architecture at the resort. Yet the inn offers 117 fairly luxuriously appointed bedrooms in a quiet park just 15 minutes from the railway station. Once there, you'll find a swimming pool and all the accessories, such as a sauna. Not only that, but you have a choice of two restaurants and an apéritif bar. Children up to 18 stay free in their parents' room, which costs 166 DM ($54.78) to 216 DM ($71.28) for a single, 212 DM ($69.96) to 270 DM ($89.10) for a double. You might also check out the nightclub bar and disco.

Obermühle, 22 Mühlstrasse (tel. 70-40). The Wolf family, the owners of this hotel, come from a 300-year-old line of hoteliers. Although their present building was constructed in 1969, they still maintain the traditional hospitality that has characterized their family for so long. Most of their rooms have a balcony with a view of the Alps. You'll also have access to the hotel's indoor pool, set below a wooden roof shaped like a modified Gothic arch (at least it's pointed). Nearby are miles of woodland trails crisscrossing through the nearby foothills. The garden and cozy weinstube might be places you'll choose to wander through also. In a single, prices range from 78 DM ($25.74) to 175 DM ($57.75), and from 170 DM ($56.10) to 290 DM ($95.70) in a double, breakfast included.

Partenkircher Hof, 15 Bahnhofstrasse (tel. 5-80-25), owes its fine reputation to innkeeper Karl Reindl and his family, who have made it a special Bavarian retreat. They're also known for their much-honored restaurant, the Reindl-Grill, considered one of the best restaurants in all of Bavaria. The guestbook lists a glittering array of celebrated people, ranging from the Rothschilds to princesses to American governors and senators. There are balconied additions, but the main building has wrap-around verandas, giving each room an unobstructed view of the mountains and the town. Most bedrooms have been recently redecorated, complete with bath and balcony. Rates vary according to the facilities. Singles with bath and toilet cost 80 DM ($26.40) to 120 DM ($39.60). Doubles with bath, toilet, radio, and color TV rent for 120 DM ($39.60) to 160 DM ($52.80). From January 6 to February 5, April 1 to July 10, and October 1 to November 10, the room prices are reduced by 20%. For half board, add 35 DM ($11.55) per person to the room rates. The hotel's facilities include a covered swimming pool, sauna, sun room, fitness room, and a beauty farm with a slimming gourmet menu. An open terrace for snacks, two attractive gardens, a large garage, and private parking are also provided.

Clausing's Posthotel, 12 Marienplatz (tel. 5-80-71), is all Bavarian, in a colorful way. In operation more than 350 years as a hotel, it offers village-center accommodations under delightful circumstances. Its elaborate pink facade is decorated with baroque statues, and a long awning shades sidewalk tables for refreshments and dining, from which you can look out across the central square. All the bedrooms have bath/shower and toilet. Singles rent from 110 DM ($36.30), and doubles, from 160 DM ($52.80). The hotel contains many genuine antiques, contributing to an intimate atmosphere enjoyed by guests. Four eating places are maintained by the hotel. From the roofed, glassed-in Terrasse, you can watch the world go by while you munch on homemade baked goods or order from the à la carte menu. It is open from 7 a.m. to 11 p.m. Coffeehouse music is played in the afternoon. The Stüberl, open from 11:30 a.m. to 2 p.m. and 6:30 to 11:30 p.m., is a cozy place where gourmet food is served. The elegance of Upper Bavaria surrounds you in the Klause, open the same hours as the Stüberl and also offering a special gourmet menu. For typical Bavarian food and entertainment, there's the Post-Hörndl, a beer garden open from 11:30 a.m. to midnight.

MIDDLE-RANGE HOTELS: **Garmischer Hof,** 51 Bahnhofstrasse (tel. 5-10-91), couldn't be more dead center, right in the hotel and shopping section, but its encircling balconies and small rear garden where guests sunbathe give it country Bavarian character. Bedrooms are small and comfortable for sleeping. In high season, bathless singles are 53 DM ($17.49); with bath, 74 DM ($24.42). Bathless doubles are 85 DM ($28.05); with private bath, 110 DM ($36.30). Prices include a buffet breakfast and the service charge.

Vier Jahreszeiten Hotel, 23 Bahnhofstrasse (tel. 5-80-84), is a first-class hotel with a city touch, perfect for those who are not attracted to village quaintness. Actually, looking at its rather formal modern lounge and dining room, you would never think you were in the Garmisch area. Nevertheless, there are numerous comfort-ensuring amenities: an elevator, balconies, many private bathrooms with shower and a cozy Bavarian beer cellar, the Bierstuben. Singles without bath are 65 DM ($21.45); with bath, 80 DM ($26.40). Doubles without bath are 110 DM ($36.30); with private bath, 130 DM ($42.90). Off-season there is a 10% reduction (January 8 to 31, April 1 to June 30, and October 1 to December 15).

Bernriederhof, 12 von-Müller-Strasse (tel. 7-10-74). The exterior is elegantly decorated with brown shutters, stag horns, a statue of the Madonna, and lots of seasonal flowers spilling over the balconies. The rustic motif is skillfully carried into the interior as well, where massive arched beams support the painstakingly crafted timbered ceilings and tile floors. Rooms are bright and sunny, and you'll find comfortable armchairs and, in winter, an open fire burning in the living room hearth. The hotel is run by Katja Haupt. The bedrooms could be called nothing less than plush, and open into bathrooms which are covered from floor to ceiling in striated black-and-white marble. Singles rent for 90 DM ($29.70) to 120 DM ($39.60), depending on the season, while doubles go for anywhere from 130 DM ($42.90) to 210 DM ($69.30). Breakfast is included.

Boddenberg, 21 Wildenauer Strasse (tel. 5-10-89). If you happen to arrive by private plane, the roof of this hotel is the same green as the lawns and trees around it. If you use a more conventional form of transportation, you'll recognize it by its boxy shape, its balconies, and its location near the ski jump of the Olympic Ski Stadium. If you're on foot, you can catch a bus at a nearby stop which will take you quickly into town. The comfortable, sunny rooms, many of them with lots of wooden furniture and wood paneling, rent for 75 DM ($24.75) in a single and 110 DM ($36.30) to 135 DM ($44.55) in a double, including a buffet breakfast. All units have a shower or bath and a toilet. Guests have unrestricted use of the pool nearby.

Wittelsbach, 24 Von-Brug-Strasse (tel. 5-30-96). A rocky outcrop of the mountain chains Wetterstein and Zugspitze frames a visitor's view of the front of this fine hotel, with green and white verandas, and depending on the season, cascades of flowers or a covering of snow. The Obexer family manages this idyllic spot, maintaining the covered swimming pool in near-Olympic condition, overseeing the dining room's sumptuous buffets, and caring for the needs of clients who peacefully vow to return year after year. Doubles rent for 160 DM ($52.80) to 190 DM ($62.70), depending on the season, while singles cost 104 DM ($34.32) to 124 DM ($40.92), breakfast included.

Hotel Königshof, 4 St.-Martin-Strasse (tel. 5-30-71). This is a holiday resort hotel with a lot of activity going on inside and out. The exterior is a massive rectangular solid broken by large windows and a triple-peaked roofline evoking a chalet. The spectacular alpine backdrop helps with that impression, but so does the range of sports available. You'll find a sauna, a swimming pool, massage therapy, a collection of bars, boutiques, and nightclubs, along with live musicians and a hairdressing salon, plus a bowling alley and an underground garage for 50 cars. The dining room is large and sunny, with oversize windows and a view. Bedrooms are spacious enough to feel comfortable in, renting for 110 DM ($36.30) to 130 DM ($42.90) in a single and for 170 DM ($56.10) to 196 DM ($64.68) in a double.

BUDGET LODGINGS: **Haus Erika,** 45 Wettersteinstrasse (tel. 48-09), a five-minute walk from the railway station, offers not rooms, but low-cost apartments with kitchens and shower baths. However, you must book one for at least three days. The tariff for one day is 80 DM ($26.40) in a single apartment, 120 DM ($39.60) in an apartment for four persons, each for short stays. The apartments contain balconies, opening onto beautiful mountain views. The personable owner, Henriette Teufl, speaks English fluently.

Gästehaus Villa Maunz, 42 Mittenwalderstrasse (tel. 504-66), is a cluster of completely furnished apartments in a Tyrolean-style building at the edge of town where Mr. and Mrs. Maunz rent apartments by the week or month. Their apartment house villa is white, with a blue overhanging roof and shutters. Decorative murals adorn the facade. In a fine residential section, the apartments come in various sizes and are especially good bargains for families. You have every home comfort, as well as private balconies and personalized furnishings with complete kitchens. The rooms cost 50 DM ($16.50) per person per day, including breakfast. An apartment for two to three persons is 95 DM ($31.35) per day, and the one for four to six persons costs 130 DM ($42.90) daily.

Hotel-Pension Therese, 41 Wettersteinstrasse (tel. 27-73), is one of the better pensions, and it's run by the Anuschewski family. They have a large garden, a reception, a TV room, a breakfast room, plus a small bar. Most of their comfortably furnished units contain a private balcony. Their North American guests seem to like it here. The hospitality extended by the English-speaking hosts has won the praise of many a reader. Rates depend on the room assignment and the plumbing. Some of the accommodations have a private balcony. Singles range in price from 43 DM ($14.19) to 58 DM ($19.14), while doubles cost 48 DM ($15.84) to 66 DM ($21.78). The tariffs include breakfast, service, and tax.

Gasthof Fraundorfer, 24 Ludwigstrasse (tel. 21-76), in Partenkirchen, is a family-owned inn, directly on the main street of the town, just a five-minute walk from the old church. Its original style has not been updated, and it retains the character of another day. Altogether there are three floors under a sloping roof, with a facade brightly decorated with window boxes of red geraniums and decorative murals depicting a family feast. You'll be in the midst of village center activities, near interesting shops and restaurants. The bedrooms are pleasant, comfortable, and adequately furnished. Owners Josef and Bärbel Fraundorfer are proud of their country-style meals. In rooms with shower and toilet, rates range from 45 DM ($14.85) to 58 DM ($19.14) per person, including a continental breakfast.

Hotel Hilleprandt, 17 Riffelstrasse (tel. 28-61). This cozy chalet is close to the Zugspitz rail station and the Olympic ice stadium. Its cutout wooden balconies, its attractive garden, and its backdrop of forest-covered mountains give the impression of an oldtimey alpine building. However, it was completely renovated in the 1970s into a streamlined format of modern comfort. Guests enjoy a fitness room, a sauna, a solarium, a pleasant breakfast room, and the personality of the accommodating owner, Klaus Hilleprandt. Each comfortably furnished bedroom contains a private balcony, private bath, phone, TV, and a collection of Bavarian folksy furniture. Singles rent for 65 DM ($21.45), and doubles go for 100 DM ($33), including breakfast.

Zur Schönen Aussicht, 36 Gsteigstrasse (tel. 24-74), is a beautiful fairly new hotel above Garmisch-Partenkirchen, with a spectacular view of the mountains and the Olympic ski area from most bedrooms. Right across the road are the start of several mountain paths. Having a car would help, but it can be reached by bus and a short walk from the bus line. Prices are 35 DM ($11.55) in a single, 65 DM ($21.45) in a double, and 85 DM ($28.05) in a double with a bath and a balcony. Breakfast is included in all the rates. Herr and Frau Maurer provide good food in their terrace restaurant.

Haus Lilly, 20a Zugspitzstrasse (tel. 5-26-00). Many visitors appreciate this spotlessly clean guest house lying near the rail station. It wins prizes for its copious breakfasts and the personality of its smiling owner, Maria Lechner, whose English is limited but whose hospitality is universal. Each of her clean and cozy bedrooms includes free access to a kitchen, so that in-house preparation of meals is an option for guests wanting to save money. Breakfasts include a combination of cold cuts, rolls, cheese, eggs (either soft boiled or in omelet form), pastries, and coffee, tea, or chocolate. Bathless singles begin at 35 DM ($11.55), whereas an apartment with a full kitchen goes for 80 DM ($26.40), double occupancy.

READER'S GUEST HOUSE SELECTION: "In four weeks of traveling in southern Germany, our best bargain in accommodations was the **Gästehaus zur Linde,** 11 Badgasse, in Partenkirchen (tel. 26-83). We had a lovely, large corner room with tastefully coordinated furnishings, two flower-filled balconies, a tile private bath, and breakfast for 80 DM ($26.40) for the two of us. It is run by young, charming Frau Ursula Mangold, whose family has been in the hotel business for more than 50 years. A short block and a half away is Ludwigstrasse, whose painted facades we found more varied and attractive than those in Mittenwald and Oberammergau. At that intersection there is a theater presenting live Bavarian folk plays and entertainment. Anyone planning to be in Germany in August should plan the visit to coincide with the annual Partenkirchen Festwoche, a delightful series of folklife events the residents put on for themselves" (Betty P. Crislip, Tampa, Fla.).

WHERE TO DINE: Reindl's Drei Mohren, 65 Ludwigstrasse, Partenkirchen (tel. 20-75), is one of the best places to eat, and offers an outstanding choice of Bavarian dishes. The restaurant was built in 1873 and is created in a cozy, rustic style, where you can rub shoulders with the local characters. Each day a specialty is offered, made after Bavarian recipes from the 19th century. There is a wide choice of fish and game dishes. Meals range from 20 DM ($6.60) to 38 DM ($12.54), and hours are 10:30 a.m. to 2:30 p.m. and 5:30 to 9:30 p.m., daily except Monday. They are closed from mid-April until the first of May.

Posthotel Partenkirchen, 49 Ludwigstrasse in Partenkirchen (tel. 5-10-67), is renowned for its distinguished cuisine—in fact, its reputation is known throughout Bavaria. The interior dining rooms are rustic with lots of mellow, old-fashioned atmosphere. You could imagine meeting Dürer here. Everything seems comfortably subdued, including the guests. Perhaps the best way to dine here is to order one of the set menus, costing 30 DM ($9.90) to 35 DM ($11.55). These table d'hôte selections change daily, depending on the availability of seasonal produce. The à la carte menu is long and extensive, featuring such products of the season as game in the autumn. Among the selections, you can order soups such as fresh cauliflower, followed by such main dishes as veal schnitzel Cordon Bleu or a mixed grill St. James. The wienerschnitzel served here with a large salad is the best I've had in the resort. Or you may prefer the entrecôte Café de Paris, another fine dish. Hours are noon to 2 p.m. and 6 to 9 p.m.

Reindl Grill, in the Partenkirchner Hof, 15 Bahnhofstrasse (tel. 5-80-25), pleases many vacationing diners who have memories of lingering after dinner on its terrace in the warmth of a summer evening. Knowledgeable locals eat here too, and have done so for years. The grill is a first-class restaurant in every sense of the word. The whole atmosphere is pleasant and the service commendable.

The menu is international, not just regional Bavarian dishes. The cuisines of France, England, and Switzerland, even Spain, are also represented. Karl Reindl apprenticed in the Walterspiel kitchens at the Vier Jahreszeiten and also worked at such famous places as Claridge's in London, Horchers in Madrid, and Maxim's in Paris. The grill is known for honoring each "food season" in Europe. Therefore, if you're here in asparagus season (the spring), a menu will appear allowing you to sample the dish in all its best known varieties.

For a good opening to a fine repast, I suggest the salade Niçoise or the hors d'oeuvres Reindl Grill, a tasty selection. Or perhaps you'll go for the Lady Curzon soup. Among main dishes, I recommend fondue bourguignonne for two or half a grilled chicken Diable. Among the fish dishes, try fried scampi with remoulade sauce or sole meunière. I'm also fond of the filet goulash Stroganoff. For dessert, you can select a peach Melba or something more spectacular, a Salzburger nockerl for two. Simple menus range from 23 DM ($7.59) to 32 DM ($10.56), whereas gourmet dinners are in the 90-DM ($29.70) to 110-DM ($36.30) bracket. The restaurant is closed from mid-November to mid-December.

Obermühle, 22 Mühlstrasse (tel. 70-40). The decor is not strikingly noteworthy, but nonetheless there is an ambience radiating from the golden light of the hanging lamps and the immaculate napery covering some 40-odd tables. Part of a hotel recommended previously, the restaurant offers one of the finest 30-DM ($9.90) table d'hôte meals at the resort, and you may want to stick to it since it's so good. The menu includes some delectable "fruits of the sea." If you're in the mood, you can request a special gourmet menu of seasonal specialties, which will cost a great deal more. It might expand both your culinary consciousness and probably your waistline too. The restaurant serves daily from noon to 2 p.m. and 6:30 to 10:30 p.m.

Flösserstuben, 2 Schmiedstrasse (tel. 28-88). Regardless of the season, a bit of the Bavarian Alps always seems to flower amid the wood-trimmed nostalgia of this intimate restaurant. You'll find it around the corner from the Goldener Engle Hotel, near the center of town. In the evening the weathered beams above the dining tables are likely to reverberate from the evergreen music an orchestra is likely to be playing. You can select a seat at one of the colorfully set wooden tables or on one of the ox-yoke-inspired stools in front of the spliced saplings decorating the bar. A loyal crowd of local residents is attracted to the cuisine, which is not only German, but Greek and international. Full meals cost between 18 DM ($5.94) and 35 DM ($11.55).

Restaurant-Café Föhrenhof, 2 Frickenstrasse (tel. 66-40) at Farchant. You'll find that the five-kilometer drive north from Garmisch to Farchant well worth the effort. This unpretentious and friendly establishment serves some of the best food in the area. It's presented in copious portions in an appetizing array of homemade specialties. One of these is called a kellermeister toast and includes a juicy portion of rumpsteak along with bacon, mushrooms, hollandaise sauce, and salad. If you're in the mood for game (and it's in season), you might enjoy a filet of venison Hubertus with homemade spätzle, cranberries, and salad. The goulash-style filet Stroganoff is an undeniable favorite as well. The restaurant thoughtfully provides a trio of children's specialties, as well as extra-thick portions of entrecôte or chateaubriand for two persons. Cheese might follow your main course, then a cream- or chocolate-covered portion of homemade ice cream. If you're in the mood for the blarney, you might order a cup of Irish coffee. Full meals, costing around 35 DM ($11.72), are served only in the evening from 5:30 to 9 p.m.

THE CASINO: At the **Spielbank Garmisch-Partenkirchen,** 13 Marienplatz (tel. 5-30-99), you can play such games as roulette, baccarat, or blackjack from 3 in the afternoon.

ON THE OUTSKIRTS AT MURNAU: Alpenhof Murnau, 8 Ramsachstrasse (tel. 10-45), is a deluxe hotel and restaurant lying halfway between Munich and Innsbruck, off the autobahn leading to Garmisch-Partenkirchen, 15 miles to the south. Set in hilly terrain, the hotel lies in a large, pasture-like park. It's built chalet style with a widely spread, overhanging roof. Bowers of red geraniums are placed at the windows in summer. Its bedrooms are built like a motel-style Spanish hacienda, forming a courtyard. Each unit has a generous covered balcony. The view from every room is beautiful and restful.

The Alpenhof is a member of the highly selective Relais de Campagne, which means that it pampers its guests in style. The bedrooms are highly individualized, some with modern canopy beds, Oriental rugs, and a spacious bedsitting room combination area. Singles range from 125 DM ($41.25) to 185 DM ($61.05); doubles, 175 DM ($57.75) to 260 DM ($85.80). Tariffs include breakfast as well.

The restaurant is the best in the area. The cuisine is inspired, and the service is attentive, informal yet courteous. The dining room is in a stylized chalet style, with white plaster walls, a decorative wooden-beamed ceiling, and highback Windsor chairs. Adjoining is a weinstube created in an idealized tavern style, reminiscent of Spanish paradors.

You can order the gourmet menu at 125 DM ($41.25) or make selections from the à la carte menu. I'd definitely recommend the chef's specialty, a soup of mussels. For a main course, I suggest the veal fricassee or the lammsattel fines herbes with gratin Dauphinois. For dessert, the specialty is soufflé glacé Grand Marnier.

The Alpenhof Murnau can be used as a break on the trip from Munich to Austria. In fact, it's possible to check in after a transatlantic flight from North America. Just pick up a rental car at the airport, get on the autobahn, and before you know it you're enveloped in peace and beauty. Have a swim in the garden pool, an exquisite lunch, and a nap on your balcony with its view of the Alps.

3. Chiemsee

THE SIGHTS: Many resorts line the shores of Bavaria's largest lake, but the main attractions of Chiemsee are on its two islands, Herrenchiemsee and Frauenchiemsee. From the liveliest resort, **Prien,** on the west shore, you can reach either or both of the islands via the lake steamers which make regular trips throughout the spring and summer. The round-trip fare is 6 DM ($1.98) for Herrenchiemsee, 8 DM ($2.64) for both islands.

Frauenchiemsee

Frauenchiemsee, also called Fraueninsel, is the smaller of the two islands. Along its sandy shore stands a fishing village, whose 60 boats drag the lake for its pike and salmon. At the festival of Corpus Christi these boats are covered with flowers and streamers while the fishermen are dressed in Bavarian garb. The girls of the village are dressed as brides as the boats circle the island, stopping at each corner to sing the Gospels. The island is also the home of a Benedictine nunnery, originally founded in 782. The convent is known for a product called Kloster Likör—literally translated, that's cloister liqueur. Sold by nuns in black cowls with white-winged headgarb, it's supposed to be an "agreeable stomach elixir."

Herrenchiemsee

Herrenchiemsee, also called Herreninsel, is the most popular tourist attraction on the lake because of the fantastic castle, **Neues Schloss,** begun by Ludwig II here in 1878. Although never completed because of the king's death in 1886, the castle was to have been a replica of the grand palace of Versailles, which Ludwig so greatly admired. A German journalist once wrote: "The Palace, a monument to uncreative megalomania and as superfluous as the artificial castle ruins of the 19th century, is an imposing postlude of feudal architectural grandeur nonetheless." One of the architects of Herrenchiemsee was Julius Hofmann, whom the king had also employed for the construction of his fantastic alpine castle, Neuschwanstein. When the work was halted in 1885, only the center of the enormous palace had been completed. Surrounded by woodlands of beech and fir, the palace and its formal gardens remain one of the most fascinating of Ludwig's adventures, in spite of their unfinished state.

The entrance to the palace is lit by a huge skylight over the sumptuously decorated state staircase. Symbolic frescoes personifying the four states of man's existence are alternated with Greek and Roman statues set in niches on the staircase and in the gallery above. The vestibule is adorned with a pair of enameled peacocks, the favorite bird of Louis XIV.

The **State Bedroom** is brilliant to the point of gaudiness, as practically every inch of the room is covered with gilt. On the dais, instead of a throne, stands the richly decorated state bed, its purple velvet draperies weighing more than 300 pounds. Separating the dais from the rest of the room is a carved wooden balustrade covered with gold leaf. On the ceiling is a huge fresco depicting the descent of Apollo, surrounded by the other gods of Olympus. The sun god's features bear a strong resemblance to Louis XIV.

The **Great Hall of Mirrors** is unquestionably the most splendid hall in the palace, and probably the most authentic replica of Versailles. The 17 door panels contain enormous mirrors reflecting the 33 crystal chandeliers and the 44 gilded candelabra. The vaulted ceiling is covered with 25 paintings depicting the life of Louis XIV. At the entrance to what would have been the private apartments of the king (Ludwig spent less than three weeks in the palace) is a small hall of mirrors, with mirrored panels set into the marble walls.

The **Dining Room** is a popular attraction for visitors because of the table nicknamed "the little table that lays itself." A mechanism in the floor permitted the table to go down to the room below to be cleaned and relaid between each course of the meal. Over the table hangs the largest porcelain chandelier·in the world, produced by Meissen, the most valuable single item in the whole palace.

The **Royal Bedroom** is the only room in the palace to make use of rich solid colors on the walls. Set in gilded panels, royal blue silk which matches the fabric of the draperies and canopy over the bed offsets the gilded ceiling and furnishings of the room. Separating the bed from the rest of the room is a gilded balustrade like that in the throne room.

You can visit Herrenchiemsee at any time of the year. In summer, tour hours are 9 a.m. to 5 p.m., and in winter, 10 a.m. to 4 p.m. Admission (in addition to the round-trip boat fare) is 5 DM ($1.65) for adults. Students and children pay 2.50 DM (83¢).

HOTELS AT PRIEN AM CHIEMSEE: **Bayerischer Hof,** 3 Bernauer Strasse (tel. 10-95). The decorator must have applied extraordinary care to produce rustic touches which at times create the illusion that this relatively severe modern hotel is indeed older and more mellow than it is. Of particular note is the painted ceiling in the dining room, which, while not looking authentically baroque, at least comes close. The rest of the hotel is more streamlined—modern, efficient, and quite appealing. The Estermann family are your hosts, charging 50 DM ($16.50) to 60 DM ($19.80) in a single and 45 DM ($14.85) to 54 DM ($17.82) per person in a double. Closed mid-November to December 10.

Reinhart, 117 Seestrasse (tel. 10-45). This pleasant hotel borders directly on the lake, offering rustic charm in three well-appointed floors of wooden beams, utilitarian artifacts, and polished paneling. You'll find a heated indoor swimming pool, a family-run sauna, and a series of public rooms beautifully decorated with Oriental rugs, warm colors, and chalet chairs. Double rooms with bath or shower cost 130 DM ($42.90) to 140 DM ($46.20), while singles with the same appointments rent for 75 DM ($24.75). A breakfast buffet comes with a generous portion of yogurt, cheese, and cold cuts. You'll also have access to a nearby golf course. The hotel is closed in November and January 8 to mid-April.

4. Oberammergau

If you were an actor in this alpine village, you'd be wise to find another trade to occupy you since the only theatrical production presented here is the world-famous Passion Play, with performances generally ten years apart. Surely the world's longest running show (in more ways than one), it began in 1634 as the result of a vow taken by the town's citizens after they were spared from the devastating plague of 1633. Lasting about eight hours, the play is divided into episodes, each of which is introduced by an Old Testament tableau connecting the incidents of Christ's suffering to the predictions of the great Prophets.

THE SIGHTS: If you visit Oberammergau on an "off" year, you can still see the modern theater, at the edge of town. The roofed auditorium holds only 5200 spectators, but the open-air stage is a wonder of engineering, with a curtained center stage flanked by gates opening onto the so-called streets of Jerusalem. The theater and production methods are of today, but the spirit of the play is marked by the medieval tradition of involving the entire community in its production. The 124 speaking parts are taken by amateur actors from the surrounding villages. The rest of the community seems to be included in the crowd scenes. The impressive array of scenery, props, and costumes is open to the public daily.

Aside from the actors, Oberammergau's most respected citizens include another unusual group, the woodcarvers, many of whom have been trained in the woodcarvers' school in the village. You'll see many examples of this art form throughout the town, on the painted cottages and inns, in the churchyard and in the **Museum on the Dorfstrasse,** which has a notable collection of Christmas crèches, all hand-carved and painted, from the 18th through the 20th centuries. Also worth seeing on a walk through the village are the houses painted with frescoes by Franz Zwink (18th century) and named after fairytale cottages, such as the "Hansel and Gretel House" and the "Little Red Riding Hood House."

THE TOP INN: Alois Lang, 15 St.-Lukas-Strasse (tel. 41-41), is a name that brings memories to seasoned travelers who have made pilgrimages to the Passion Play in Oberammergau. It was in 1929 that handsome, long-haired Alois Lang was elected by the village to play the role of Christ in the pageant. Long ago the custom originated of the players having as paying guests in their homes visitors who came to see the now-famous production.

Within walking distance of the village center, the site of his rustic home, run by the Lang family, was built chalet style, with long bedroom extensions. The accommodations are modern Bavarian style, the beds are soft, and all is kept immaculately. Meals are elaborate, including international specialties in addition to local dishes. Be sure to try the onion soup. Equally tasty is the saddle of venison in cream sauce. And to show how sophisticated this once-simple place has become, it now offers crêpes Alois Lang. You may want to dine in the inner tavern, or on the open sun terrace, where you can enjoy a view of the mountains.

All rooms have private bath. For a single, the rate is from 130 DM ($42.90); for a twin-bedded room, from 210 DM ($69.30). During the height of the season, board rates are required. Half board costs an additional 35 DM ($11.55) per person. The inn has a sauna, fitness center, and the biggest private hotel park in the whole area.

MIDDLE-BRACKET HOTELS: Wolf Hotel-Restaurant, 1 Dorfstrasse (tel. 69-71), is an overgrown Bavarian chalet right in the heart of village life. Its facade is consistent for the area, with an encircling balcony, heavy timbering, and window boxes spilling cascades of red and pink geraniums. Inside it has some of the local flavor, although certain concessions have been made: an elevator, conservative bedroom furnishings, a dining hall with zigzag paneled ceiling, and spoke chairs. The Keller is a regional rustic place for beer drinking as well as light meals.

Only five singles are available, renting from 65 DM ($21.45) to 80 DM ($26.40). Doubles 100 DM ($33) to 130 DM ($42.90). All accommodations contain private bath or shower.

Dining here can be both economical and gracious, with menus ranging from 22 DM ($7.26) to 30 DM ($9.90). There's always a freshly made soup of the day, followed by a main course such as roast pork with dumplings and cabbage or wienerschnitzel. The helpings are generous.

Alte Post, 19 Dorfstrasse (tel. 66-91), is a provincial inn, right in the heart of the village, with lots of Bavarian character. It is chalet style, with a wide, overhanging roof, green shuttered windows painted with decorative trim, a large carved crucifix on the facade, and tables set on a sidewalk under a long awning. It's the social hub of the village. The interior has storybook charm, with a beamed ceiling, tavern-style decor, a ceiling-high green ceramic stove, alpine chairs, and shelves of pewter plates.

Bedrooms are rustic, with beamed wooden ceilings, wide beds with giant posts, and, from most rooms, a view. Bathless singles are 40 DM ($13.20). Bathless doubles are 75 DM ($24.75), 95 DM ($31.35) with full bath. Breakfast is included. A main dining room is equally rustic, with a collection of hunting memorabilia. There is an intimate drinking bar. The restaurant provides excellent dishes. On the à la carte menu, meals average 22 DM ($7.26) to 40 DM ($13.20). Closed the last two weeks in October and in December.

Hotel Schilcherhof, 17 Bahnhofstrasse (tel. 47-40), is an enlarged chalet with surrounding gardens and a modern wing which provides excellent rooms. There's even a small group of apartments. In the summertime the terrace overflows with festive living and lots of beer. Five minutes away lies the Passion Theater, and also nearby, the Ammer River flows through the village. In the high season it's not easy to get a room here unless you make reservations well in advance. Singles cost 40 DM ($13.20) to 52 DM ($17.16), and doubles go for 70 DM ($23.10) to 90 DM ($29.70). Tariffs include breakfast. Although the house is built in the old style, with wooden front balconies and tiers of flower boxes, it has a fresh, new look to it. The hotel is closed December and January.

Parkhotel Sonnenhof, 12 König-Ludwig-Strasse (tel. 9-71), is surrounded by conifers bigger than the hotel itself. The four-story chalet with weathered balconies offers clean, comfortable, and attractively furnished rooms with up-to-date bath. The cost, including breakfast, ranges from 65 DM ($21.45) to 85 DM ($28.05) per person in a double. Singles pay a nightly supplement of 15 DM ($4.95). Half board costs another 22 DM ($7.26) per person, and you can enjoy your meal in the rustically beamed and paneled dining room with decorative stucco arches. Walter Rauguth is the friendly host here.

Böld, 10 König-Ludwig-Strasse (tel. 5-20). Only a stone's throw from the river, this well-designed chalet-style hotel offers comfortable public rooms in its central core and well-furnished bedrooms (some of which contain four-poster beds) in its contemporary annex. The Böld could serve as an attractive base for either your summer or winter sports programs, which might include skiing, mini-golf, tennis, or just a peaceful walk in the country. The in-house sauna is offered for guests' relaxation. The restaurant offers European and American cuisine. In the cellar bar you'll find a peaceful atmosphere, plus well-prepared cocktails and attentive service. Raimund Hans and his family are the hosts. The price range for rooms is 80 DM ($26.40) to 105 DM ($34.65) in a single, 100 DM ($33) to 130 DM ($42.90) in a double.

Turm Wirt, 2 Ettaler Strasse (tel. 42-91), is a cozy, small hotel in the Bavarian style, many of its rooms containing a private balcony opening onto views of the Ammer mountains. A lodging house stood on this spot in 1742, and the present building was constructed in 1889. It has received many alterations and renovations over the past few decades. It's a homey, intricately painted, green-shuttered country house, with hints of baroque embellishments on the doors and window frames. The interior is well maintained, with chintz-covered armchairs, wooden banquettes, Oriental rugs, beamed ceilings, and handcrafted cubbyholes with tables and chairs. It's an invigorating 12-minute walk to the village up a slight incline. Including a breakfast buffet, doubles with private bath rent for 95 DM ($31.35) to 140 DM ($46.20), while singles go for 55 DM ($18.15) to 90 DM ($29.70). The owners are three generations of the Glas family. Closed November 15 through December.

Friedenshöhe, 31 König-Ludwig-Strasse (tel. 5-98), is set in an alpine meadow with huge conifers towering over parts of it. From the compact core, which at one time might have been a private home, there sprawl two modern wings decorated in rural gemütlichkeit. You'll find villagers taking morning coffee on the parasol-covered sun terrace. The owners, Erich and Gretel Schmid, see that everyone gets attentive service. They lived for eight years in the U.S. before taking over this place from Mr. Schmid's parents in 1979. Singles rent for 55 DM ($18.15) to 85 DM ($28.05), while doubles cost 106 DM ($34.98) to 136 DM ($44.88), depending on the season. All units have balcony, toilet, and bath or shower. Breakfast is included in the prices.

BUDGET ACCOMMODATIONS: There are more than 100 private homes in Oberammergau that have bedrooms set aside for visitors. They are inexpensive and provide an opportunity to meet the villagers. A full list, with details such as prices and bath facilities, is available by going to or writing to the **Tourist Office,** 6–8 Schnitzlergasse (tel. 49-21), 8103 Oberammergau, West Germany. A reservation form can be secured in advance. Usually the accommodation is in a rustic chalet (often newly built) with flower boxes at the windows, scrubbed and polished rooms, and soft beds with fluffy eiderdowns. Prices generally include a home-style breakfast, taxes, and service.

There are no private baths, and occasionally you are charged for use of a bath or shower in the corridor. All the houses have central heating; many contain balconies and offer TV in the living room, plus parking space.

Among the leading economy hotels, I prefer the **Wittelsbach,** 21 Dorfstrasse (tel. 45-45). Elisabeth and Julius Streibl own this family-run place, which sprawls over a village street corner. It has light-brown shutters, a red metal roof with ice catchers on the edges, prominent gables, and yards of balconies with flowers virtually spilling over the edges. They offer 75 beds, all of them comfortable, in units that are clean, sunny, and cozy. Regardless of the season, the dining room has a kind of "aprés-ski" ambience where diners feel relaxed and low key as they linger over drinks. Singles rent for 75 DM ($24.75), and doubles cost 60 DM ($19.80) per person, including a buffet breakfast. Half board costs another 22 DM ($7.26) per person daily. All of the units contain private bath or shower and toilet. They have been recently renovated.

ABC Hotel, 21 Ludwig-Lang Strasse (tel. 45-50), a modern chalet-style hotel, with balconies and a quiet location, is directed by Peter Müller, who thoughtfully does everything he can to make your visit comfortable. Singles with private bath cost 65 DM ($21.45); without bath, 46 DM ($15.18). Doubles with private bath go for 85 DM ($28.05) to 95 DM·($31.35).

SIGHTS IN THE ENVIRONS: Outside Oberammergau King Ludwig displayed another kind of "passion" at Schloss Linderhof. You can visit his creation and the Ettal Abbey as well.

Schloss Linderhof

Eight miles west of the village, until the late 19th century, stood a modest hunting lodge on a large piece of land owned by the Bavarian royal family. In 1869 "Mad Ludwig" struck again, this time creating in the Ammergau Mountains a French rococo palace. Unlike Ludwig's palace at Chiemsee, the Linderhof was not meant to be a copy of any other structure of the past. And unlike his castle at Neuschwanstein, its concentration of fanciful projects and designs was not limited to the interior of the palace. In fact the gardens and smaller buildings at Linderhof are, if anything, more elaborate than the two-story main structure.

As you stand on the steps in front of the castle's white stone facade, you'll note that the ground floor is rather plain, with almost a complete lack of decoration, while the upper story is adorned with relief columns altered with niches occupied by statues of mythological figures. In the center, over the three arched portals, is a large statue of Victory. Towering above the gable with its oval windows is a huge statue of Atlas supporting a world that seems just a bit too much for even him.

The most interesting rooms inside the palace are on the second floor, where ceilings are much higher because of the unusual roof plan. Ascending the winged staircase of Carrara marble, you'll find yourself at the West Gobelin Room (Music Room), with carved and gilded paneling and richly colored tapestries. This leads directly into the **Hall of Mirrors.** The mirrors are set in white and gold panels, decorated with gilded woodcarvings. The ceiling of this room is festooned with frescoes depicting mythological scenes, including the birth of Venus and the judgment of Paris.

The two side rooms are oval in design, each having a smaller, horseshoe-shaped anteroom. The eastern room is the **dining room,** mirrored and decorated with marble fireplaces, mythological sculptures, and an elaborately carved and gilded sideboard. The table, like that at Chiemsee, could be raised and lowered through the floor to permit the servants in the room below to reset the various courses without intruding on the shy king's privacy.

The **king's bedchamber** is the largest room in the palace, and placed in the back, overlooking the Fountain of Neptune and the cascades in the gardens. In the tradition of Louis XIV, who often received visitors in his bedchamber, the king's bed is closed off by a carved and gilded balustrade.

In the popular style of the previous century, Ludwig laid out the gardens in formal parterres with geometrical shapes, baroque sculptures, and elegant fountains. The front of the palace opens onto a large pool with a piece of gilded statuary in its center. From the statue grouping a jet of water sprays 105 feet into the air.

The steep slopes behind the palace lent themselves well to the arrangement of a long cascade, made up of 32 marble steps and adorned with vases and cherubs. At the base of the cascade is the Fountain of Neptune, surrounded by a bed of flowers. Around these formal terrace and garden designs is a large English Garden, merging almost imperceptibly into the thick forests of the Ammergau.

The park also contains several other small but fascinating buildings, including the **Moorish Kiosk,** where Ludwig often spent hours, smoking chibouk and dreaming of himself as an Oriental prince. The **magic grotto** is unique, built of artificial rock with stalagmites and stalactites dividing the cave-like room into three chambers. One wall of the grotto is painted with a scene of the Venus Mountain from *Tannhäuser*. The main chamber is occupied by an artificial lake illuminated from below, and has an artificial current produced by 24 dynamo engines. A shell-shaped boat, completely gilded, is tied to the platform called the Lorelei Rock.

The fantasy and grandeur of Linderhof is open to the public throughout the year and makes a day trip from Munich, as well as Oberammergau. During the summer, hours are 9 a.m. to noon and 1 to 5 p.m. In winter, the time is from 9 a.m. to noon and 1 to 4 p.m. Admission is 6 DM ($1.98) in summer, 4 DM ($1.32) in winter. The Moorish Kiosk and magic grotto are open only from April 1 till September 30 because of snow.

A short drive from Oberammergau leads to:

Ettal Abbey

In a valley sheltered by the steep hills of the Ammergau, the Ettal Abbey was founded by the Emperor Ludwig the Bavarian in 1330. Monks, knights, and their ladies shared the honor of guarding the statue of the Virgin, attributed to Giovanni Pisano. In the 18th century, the golden age of the abbey, there were about 70,000 pilgrims every year. The Minster of Our Lady in Ettal is one of the finest examples of Bavarian rococo architecture in existence. Around the polygonal core of the church is a two-story gallery. An impressive baroque facade was built from a plan based on designs of Enrico Zuccali. Inside, visitors stand under a vast dome, admiring the fresco painted by Joh. Jacob Zeiller in the summers of 1751 and 1752.

5. Mittenwald

Seeming straight out of *The Sound of Music,* the year-round resort of Mittenwald lies in a pass in the Karwendel Range through which heavy commercial traffic once passed. The roads to the village are kept busy today as well, but the traffic now is mainly tourists who flock here with cameras and walking shoes.

Before setting out for the 60 some miles of paths winding up and down the mountains around the village, you will want to take a look at the old market town. Especially noteworthy and photogenic are the painted Bavarian houses with their overhanging eaves. Even the tower of the baroque church is covered with frescoes. On the square stands a monument to Mathias Klotz, who introduced the town's major industry, violin making, to Mittenwald in 1684. The town's museum has exhibits devoted to violins and other stringed instruments, from their conception through the various stages of their evolution.

Mittenwald also has good spa facilities, in large gardens landscaped with tree-lined streams and trout pools. Concerts are given during the summer in the music pavilion.

On daily excursions into the countryside, you are constantly exposed to changes in the scenery of the Wetterstein and Karwendel ranges. Besides hiking through the hills on your own, you can take part in mountain-climbing expeditions, trips by horse and carriage, or coach tours from Mittenwald to the nearby villages of Bavaria. In the evening you are treated to typical Bavarian entertainment, often consisting of folk dancing or singing, zither playing, and yodeling, but you also have your choice of spa concerts, dance bands, and cinemas.

THE INNS: **Alpenrose,** 1 Obermarkt (tel. 50-55), has about everything one could hope for in an alpine village inn. It's in the center of the village, at the foot of a rugged mountain. The facade of the hotel is covered with decorative designs, with window boxes holding flowering vines. The basic structure of the inn is 14th century, although refinements, additions, and improvements have been made over the years. The present inn is truly comfortable, with suitable plumbing facilities.

Its tavern room, overlooking the street, has many ingratiating features, including coved ceilings (one decoratively painted), handmade chairs, flagstone floors, and a square tile stove in the center where one huddles during the winter months. In the cellar is the Josefkeller, where beer is served in giant steins and in the evening musicians gather to entertain guests. The dining room provides many excellent meals, including Bavarian specialties.

Just as winning as the public rooms are the attractive bedrooms, with wood ceilings and a few antique reproductions, which are decoratively painted. In a single room, the rate is from 90 DM ($29.70) nightly. The per-person rate in a double runs from 85 DM ($28.05), these tariffs including breakfast. The half-board rate begins at 52 DM ($17.16) per person, going up to 110 DM ($36.30).

Berghotel Latscheneck Café, 1 Kaffeefeld (tel. 14-19). Set against a craggy backdrop of rock and forest, this pleasant chalet is ringed with green shutters, wrap-around balconies, and a flagstone-covered sun terrace. Guests are never far from a vista, since large expanses of the exterior walls are devoted to rows of weatherproof windows that flood the wood-trimmed interior with sunlight. During chilly weather an open fireplace is likely to illuminate the knickknack-covered walls of one of the heavily beamed eating areas. The Neuner-Klaus family are the owners of this place which you'll find in a forest a short walk above the center of town. The Kranzberg ski lift is nearby, making the place attractive to skiers. A covered swimming pool and an in-house sauna sometimes allow guests a relaxing prelude before a well-prepared dinner. Singles cost between 100 DM ($33) and 110 DM ($36.30), while doubles go for 190 DM ($62.70) to 210 DM ($69.30), including breakfast. The hotel's restaurant is open only to guests, and the establishment is closed from mid-October to mid-December.

Rieger Hotel, 28 Dekan-Karl-Platz (tel. 50-71), is an attractive Bavarian hotel, whether snow is piled up outside or the window boxes are cascading with petunias. It's authentic, with overhanging roof, balconies, shutter-framed windows, and murals on its facade. There are two reasons for its popularity: one is the family-style living room with beamed ceiling, wide arches, and table and armchair groupings around a three-sided open fireplace. The other attractive feature is the indoor swimming pool with a picture-window wall. Add to this a room for sauna and massages (segregated except on Monday, family time, when both sexes join the crowd).

Prices are modest for room and breakfast only. Singles begin at 52 DM ($17.16), climbing to 110 DM ($36.30), and doubles cost 103 DM ($33.49) to 148 DM ($48.84). Fashionably decorated, the bedrooms are pleasant and comfortable. The dining room has a view of the Alps.

Post Hotel, 9 Obermarkt (tel. 10-94), is one of the more seasoned, established chalet hotels, housing guests all year. It dates from 1632. It captures much of the charm required for a successful inn (the competition is high). It's delightful to have breakfast here on the sun terrace (or on a balcony), with a view of the Alps. Although the lobby is basic and simple Bavarian, the tavern and dining room go all out with mountain-chalet decor—black-and-white beams, a collection of deer antlers, and wood paneling. The bedrooms are furnished in a standard way. A single, depending on the plumbing, ranges in price from 50 DM ($16.50) to 95 DM ($31.35), and a double goes for 80 DM ($26.40) to 180 DM ($59.40). Menus begin at 18 DM ($5.94), going up to 35 DM ($11.55). An indoor swimming pool, massage, and sauna are available.

Gästehaus Sonnenbichl, 32 Klausnerweg (tel. 50-41). Set pleasantly into a hillside, this adaption of a chalet is pleasingly painted in brown and white, where some of the doorways are half-rounded apertures going into the restaurant on the ground floor. From the balconies there's a view of the village set against a backdrop of the Alps. All rooms are freshly decorated in vivid natural colors, with impeccably clean sheets and furnishings. The hotel is often completely booked, so reservations would be a good idea. Single rooms rent for 52 DM ($17.16) to 60 DM ($19.80) a night, while doubles cost 86 DM ($23.83) to 112 DM ($36.96), depending on the season. Breakfast is included, and all units contain private bath (or shower). Closed November 15 through December.

Gästehaus Franziska, 24 Innsbruckerstrasse (tel. 50-51). When Olaf Grothe built this guest house, he named it after the most important person in his life, his wife, Franziska. Both of them have labored to make it the most personalized guest house in town, by furnishing it with clear-grained furniture upholstered in bright, tasteful colors, and by giving their sympathetic attention to the needs of their guests. The ceilings are made of polished wood paneling, intricately crafted, and although the building is relatively new, there is nonetheless a green tile oven against a wall of one of the public rooms. Singles with shower go for 45 DM ($14.85) to 60 DM ($19.80), while doubles cost 40 DM ($13.20) to 60 DM ($19.80) per person, depending on the accessories (balcony, private bath) and the season.

READER'S GUEST HOUSE SELECTION: "I can't say enough when it comes to the **Gasthof Zur Brucke,** 38 Innsbrucker Strasse (tel. 13-88). The proprietor, Max Hoffman, speaks good English and offers pleasant surroundings. You can reach the hotel by car, or if you come by train, the hotel is just a short walk outside the heart of town. We had a superb double room with balcony and bath for 120 DM ($39.60), breakfast included. Meals cost from 22 DM ($7.26). The proprietor has a good sense of humor, in true Bavarian style—and if you ask for a beer, don't be surprised if he mentions Miller" (Diane Patterson, Hillsborough, Calif.).

WHERE TO DINE: Arnspitze, 68 Innsbruckerstrasse (tel. 24-25), is the finest dining room in Mittenwald, housed in a chalet-style modern hotel on the outskirts of the town. The restaurant is decorated in the old style with alpine features. The feeling that you can rely on the food turns out to be entirely justified. The cookery is honest and good—solid, satisfying, and wholesome. You might order sole with homemade noodles or veal steak in a creamy smooth sauce, topped off by the dessert specialty, guglhupf-parfait Wipfelder. For a meal composed of soup or hors d'oeuvres, a main dish with vegetables, plus a dessert, you are likely to pay anywhere from 35 DM ($11.55) to 60 DM ($19.80). The restaurant shuts down from October 20 to December 20, on Tuesday, and Wednesday lunch.

6. Starnberger See

Less than 20 miles southwest of the capital of Bavaria, this large lake is a favorite with Münchners on holiday. From the water—steamer cruises are frequent on the lake in summer—you can observe the change in terrain from the low-lying marshlands on the north to the alpine ranges towering above the lake in the south. Around the 40-mile shoreline you can see no fewer than six castles, including the Schloss Berg, where Ludwig II was sent after he was certified insane in 1886. It was in the Starnberger See that Ludwig was drowned, along with his doctor, just a few days after he was deposed. The mysterious circumstances of his death have never been explained, and many historians have suggested that he was murdered. A cross on the water marks the spot where his body was found.

FOOD AND LODGING AT BERG: Schloss Berg, 17 Seestrasse (tel. 56-21). In summer residents from the surrounding hamlets come here for the daily dance music accompanying the sunshine and beer on the outdoor terrace. Many of the comfortably modernized bedrooms offer lake views. Some 30 bedrooms are rented at a cost ranging from 60 DM ($19.80) to 90 DM ($29.70) in a single, and between 90 DM ($29.70) and 175 DM ($57.75) in a double. Meals in the well-appointed dining room include fixed-priced repasts costing from 18 DM ($5.94) to 38 DM ($12.54). You can also order a light snack in the café. Tennis lovers can arrange a game nearby, and boats can be rented at a nearby marina.

Dorint-Seehotel Leoni, 44 Assenbucher Strasse (tel. 59-11). Its many balconies look out over the lakeside, where sailboats and bathers make the most of the clear waters of the Tegernsee. On sunny days the colorful awnings shield sun-sensitive visitors from the reflected glare of the water, which laps almost to the foundations of the terraces in front. There's a biergarten near the boat docks, along with a café, an accommodating bar, and a well-prepared cuisine served in a panoramic dining room. Each of the some 75 bedrooms contains a private balcony, as well as a phone, TV, radio, and mini-bar. Singles range from 115 DM ($37.95) to 130 DM ($42.90), while doubles cost 175 DM ($57.75) to 200 DM ($66).

7. Tegernsee

Lying 30 miles southeast of Munich, this alpine lake and the resort town on its eastern shore have the same name. Although small, this is one of the loveliest of the Bavarian lakes, with huge peaks seemingly rising right out of the water. The lake and its string of resort towns (the finest, I think, is Rottach-Egern) are popular year round. Because of the size of the lake, it freezes over early in winter, making it an attraction for skaters.

In the town of Tegernsee, the two major sights span some 12 centuries. The oldest of these is the Benedictine monastery, turned into a castle and village church. The other attraction is a contemporary church, one of the finest examples of German architecture, designed by Olaf Gulbransson of Munich.

HOTELS IN ROTTACH-EGERN: Bachmair Hotel am See, 47 Seestrasse (tel. 64-44), is perhaps the most attractive, all-around resort establishment in the entire area. A world unto itself, with every conceivable recreational facility at your disposal, it is rich in the Bavarian spirit. The complex of nine buildings is on the lake, surrounded by lawns and park, with wide terraces under linden trees, umbrellaed tables, a covered garden room with wall-to-wall windows, white wrought-iron furniture, and garlands of vines trailing over the ceiling. Outdoors is a large, free-form swimming pool, edged by lawns for sunbathing, and there's also a beautiful, covered pool where you can swim in any weather, enjoying the view of snow-capped mountains. Extensive buildings house facilities for the cure—saunas, special baths, and massage rooms. Additional attractions are a nightclub, mini-golf, skiing, boating and water sports, bowling, ice skating, and shuffleboard on ice during winter months.

The Bachmair's interior is stylized rustic, but done with sophistication. Baroque gilt carvings, ecclesiastical paintings, and country-style furniture are mixed with antiques and reproductions, including Louis XV, Directoire, and Biedermeier. Each of the many sitting rooms, lounges, cafés, and restaurants has its own particular style. In the evening the Bavarian beer hall has local dances, yodeling, and zither playing, as well as conventional music.

Bedrooms are often dramatically conceived, again combining antiques, smart decorating devices, and an eclectic combination of furnishings. All rooms have private bath. Depending on the location, singles cost from 185 DM ($61.05) to 270 DM ($89.10), and doubles rent anywhere from 250 DM ($82.50) to 375 DM ($123.75). High season is December 20 to January 7, February 10 to March 25, and June 1 to October 31, plus three days at Easter.

Seehotel Überfahrt, 7 Überfahrt (tel. 2-60-01), is a medium-size chalet resort, facing the lake and surrounded by a view of the Alps. It is in fact more than a resort, also having fine spa facilities. It is a joining together of rusticity and modern facilities. The facade is characterized by balconies (big enough for sunbathing and breakfast) and window boxes with a profusion of flowers. The interior is attractive, upper level rustic, with stylish comfort. The living room has clusters of armchairs and sofas placed to allow a view of the lake through roomwide windows. For dining, you can use the room with booths set against view windows, or choose a more formal room, with a stage and a dance floor for weekend entertainment. The tavern, with pine stools, a slat-wood ceiling, and farm artifacts, is popular in the evening.

Bedrooms show the touch of a decorator's flair. Some rooms have terraces, some balconies, others sitting-room areas. According to the size and exposure of your room, you pay the following: singles with a shower bath rent for 140 DM ($46.20), peaking at 180 DM ($59.10) with complete bath and a view of the lake. Again, depending on the view and the plumbing, doubles range in price from 200 DM ($66) to 260 DM ($85.80). Use of the indoor swimming pool and parking space is free to guests.

Hotel Franzen and **Pfeffermühle,** 2a Karl-Theodor-Strasse (tel. 60-87). The outside of the building looks like lots of other chalet-style hotels in Bavaria, except the detailing is a little more elaborate, the flowers a little fresher. Inside, however, you'll be greeted with beautifully decorated public rooms, warmly patterned red plaid carpeting, and a profusion of provincial antiques. The whole effect is pleasing, particularly since the antiques lead right up to the bedrooms. Some of the private rooms are furnished with painted country baroque armoires and headboards, and others with grained late-19th-century pieces. Singles cost 85 DM ($28.05) to 130 DM ($42.90), and doubles rent for 130 DM ($42.90) to 205 DM ($67.05). All rates include breakfast, and units are equipped with a private shower or bath and a balcony. The Pfeffermühle restaurant on the premises attracts a large following to its meals, which range in price from 40 DM ($13.20) to 65 DM ($21.45). In the grill corner of the restaurant, guests broil their own steaks and vegetables on an individual grill built into the specially constructed wooden tables. The owners of this hotel and their manager speak fluent English. Pfeffermühle is the German word for peppermill.

Gästehaus Maier-Kirschner, 23 Seestrasse (tel. 2-60-75). For anyone who ever dreamed of making an entrance on an elegantly carved marble-covered staircase with wrought-iron railings, this is the place to do it. That, of course, would take place in the central hall of this lakeside hotel. The preambles to that entrance would be in the paneled and rustically decorated public rooms, all of which invite guests to linger over their newspaper or coffee. The bedrooms, for the most part, are furnished with voluptuously carved neobaroque headboards with comfortable armchairs. Singles rent for 55 DM ($18.15) to 70 DM ($23.10) per day, while doubles cost 110 DM ($36.30) to 160 DM ($52.80) per day, breakfast included.

Gasthof zur Post, 17 Nördliche Hauptstrasse (tel. 2-60-85). Four stories of elaborate decoration and flowered balconies contribute to the facade of this chalet-style building in the heart of the resort. The interior is beautifully crafted, with a soft patina glowing from the crossbeams and diagonal supports of the wooden ceilings found in many forms throughout the public rooms. Bedrooms are furnished with large armoires made of natural-grained white pine. Some of the windows are a little undersize, but the accommodations are clean and comfortable. It charges, on the breakfast-only plan, anywhere from 100 DM ($33) to 150 DM ($49.50) per person in a double and 65 DM ($21.45) to 85 DM ($28.05) in a single. Prices depend, of course, on plumbing accessories and the season.

WHERE TO DINE: La Cuisine, 2 Südliche Hauptstrasse (tel. 2-47-64), is an elegant art nouveau restaurant, serving the finest cuisine in the area. Soft colors and turn-of-the-century accessories, all chosen by owner Erwin Schnitzler, are the setting for the most imaginative classic and nouvelle cuisine of the region. Every menu is "overhauled" daily, a bevy of fanciful combinations culminating in the popular menu du jour priced at 90 DM ($29.70), which is served every evening after 9 p.m. and adjusted daily to account for the availability of local ingredients. Some recent items served here (although I don't know what new creative statements will be made by the time of your visit) are filet of pork in a green pepper sauce with kohlrabi, and a rack of veal in a mushroom cream sauce with a spinach soufflé. Dessert might be a fresh passionfruit sorbet or a choice from a formidable tray, such as the colorful Assiette La Cuisine. Regular dinners cost 42 DM ($13.86) to 72 DM ($24.75), and are served daily from 6:30 to 10 p.m. except Monday.

Coming up next: a relatively unexplored section of Germany.

Chapter XII

FRANCONIA AND THE GERMAN DANUBE

1. Ulm
2. Aschaffenburg
3. Bamberg
4. Coburg
5. Nürnberg (Nuremberg)
6. Würzburg
7. Bayreuth
8. Regensburg
9. Passau

WHEN THE GOLDEN AGE of the Renaissance swept across Germany, it seemed to concentrate its full forces on the part of northern Bavaria which had once been a Frankish kingdom. In spite of history's tendency to destroy the past through progress and war, Franconia still holds some of Germany's greatest medieval and Renaissance treasures. From its feudal cities sprang some of the greatest artists the world has seen—Albrecht Dürer, Lucas Cranach, Veit Stoss, Adam Krafft, and many others. As a center for cultural events, Franconia draws music lovers from all over to its annual Mozart Festival in Würzburg and Wagner Festival in Bayreuth.

The hillsides of Franconia are dotted with well-preserved medieval castles, monasteries, and churches. Part of the architecture of the region owes its beauty to the limestone range along the southern edge of the province. And between these hills and the edge of the Bavarian Forest is Germany's "other" river, the young Danube. It gradually builds up its force from the many smaller streams flowing out of the Alps and Swabian Jura until by the time it reached the Austrian border at Passau, it is powerful enough to carry commercial ships and barges. Although not as important to the German economy as the Rhine, the Danube was responsible for the growth of several influential centers in centuries past, including . . .

1. Ulm

Ulm, lying at the strategic point on the Danube where the young stream begins to take on the form of a navigable river, has been a prosperous city since the Middle Ages. Its most famous son was Albert Einstein.

THE SIGHTS: If you approach the town from the Stuttgart-Munich autobahn, you'll miss the best view. So sometime during your visit, cross the Danube into Neu Ulm for a look at the gables and turrets of the Old Town lining the north bank of the river. Here is the **Fishermen's Quarter,** with its little medieval houses and tree-shaded squares. Nearby are the more elaborate Renaissance patrician houses and the Gothic-Renaissance Town Hall. But the skyline and the spirit of the whole town are dominated by its major attraction:

Ulm Cathedral (Münster)

Before you even reach the city, you'll recognize the skyline of Ulm by its towering cathedral, the landmark of the medieval town. Its steeple, at 528 feet is the tallest in the world, and the Münster is second only to the Cologne Cathedral among the huge Gothic structures of Christendom. Without the pews, the nave of the church could hold nearly 20,000 people, more than twice the population of Ulm at the time the cathedral was built in 1377. When Ulm joined the Protestant movement in the early 16th century, work was suspended after 151 years of continuous building. It was not resumed until 1844, and lasted until 1890. Miraculously, the cathedral escaped serious damage during the air raids of World War II.

The exterior is almost pure German Gothic, even though bricks were often used in the walls along with the more typical stone blocks. The unique feature of Ulm's Münster, however, is that the architects placed as much emphasis on the horizontal lines as the usual Gothic vertical look. Before entering, stop to admire the main porch, whose three massive arches lead to two Renaissance doors. This section dates from the 14th and 15th centuries and contains a wealth of statues and reliefs. At the pillar between the two doors is the finest sculpture on the outside of the church, *Our Lord of Dolours,* by Hans Multscher (1429).

On the inside, you can climb the tower as far as the third gallery, all 768 steps, where you can look out on the town and surrounding countryside over the Danube plain as far as the Alps.

The five aisles of the cathedral lead directly from the hall below the tower through the nave to the east chancel. The conspicuous absence of a transept heightens the emphasis on the chancel and also increases the length of the nave. Each of the five aisles is enclosed by huge pillars towering into steep arches. Above them, the ceiling is swept into net-vaults so high that many of Germany's church steeples could sit comfortably beneath them. The nave is so large that, even with the pews, it can accommodate more than 11,000 people at one service.

Up the central aisle toward the chancel, you come to the 15th-century pulpit, carved with prophets, apostles and martyrs. Above the canopy is a second pulpit, symbolizing the Holy Spirit. Just to the left is a handsomely decorated tabernacle, containing the elements of the Eucharist. The wood panels, carved with figures, date from 1470.

The chancel is entered through baroque iron gates set in the "triumph arch." Above the arch is a fresco depicting the *Day of Judgment* (1471). The other treasures are diminished by the grand choir stalls carved by Jörg Syrlin the Elder between 1469 and 1474. The 89 seats of dark oak are divided into sections, marked by busts of biblical and heathen characters. The stalls on the north side of the chancel are adorned with figures of men; those on the south, of women. The panels behind the stalls are decorated with elaborate tracery, containing figures from the Old and New Testaments, as well as several saints.

The most attractive stained-glass windows of the chancel are in the little Besserer Chapel, on the south side behind the women's choir. The five windows in this room are from the 15th century and depict scenes from the Old and New Testaments. The main south window, from the same period, represents the Day of Judgment in striking colors and figures. Although most of the windows in the side aisles of the nave were destroyed in the war, the tall Gothic windows behind the chancel were preserved.

The Ulm cathedral is open daily, except during services on Sunday mornings. From October through February the hours are 9 a.m. to 4:45 p.m.; in March, to 5:45 p.m.; in April, until 6:45 p.m. Beginning in May, hours begin at 7 a.m., and in the busy months of July and August the cathedral remains open until 7:45 p.m. Admission is .50 DM (17¢); to visit both the cathedral and the tower, you pay an admission price of 1 DM (33¢).

Other Sights Around Town

The **Town Hall** (Rathaus) was built in 1370 as a warehouse, but it has been the Town Hall since 1419. A Gothic and Renaissance building, it has ornate murals dating from the mid-16th century and allegorical decorations. On the south gable are the coats-of-arms of the cities and countries with which Ulm is linked by trade and commerce. On the east gable is the astronomical clock dating from 1520. Above the interior staircase is a replica of the flying machine constructed by A. L. Berblinger, "the tailor of Ulm." He was the first man (or at least one of the first) who ever seriously attempted to fly.

The **Ulm Museum,** on Neue Strasse, in the vicinity of the cathedral, contains an important collection of creative art and crafts produced in Ulm and Upper Swabia from medieval times onward. There are also successive exhibitions of both ancient and modern art, including those of the masters of Ulm. It is open from July 1 until the end of September from 10 a.m. to 5 p.m. (during the rest of the year only from 10 a.m. to noon and 2 to 5 p.m., from 1 p.m. on Sunday). It's always closed on Monday.

UPPER-BRACKET HOTELS: Intercity Hotel, 1 Bahnhofsplatz (tel. 6-12-21). Although the walls of this inner-city hotel are emblazoned with heraldic emblems of the late 20th century (beer and Coca-Cola advertisements), the interior is comfortable, hospitable, and quiet, thanks to the hermetically sealed windows. You're only a step from the railway station here, and because of the hotel's convenience, you'll find lots of business people making use of the rooms, many of which contain Oriental rugs along with tile baths. Including breakfast, a single rents for 90 DM ($29.70) and a double goes for 150 DM ($49.50).

Neutor Hospiz, 23 Neuer Graben (tel. 1-51-60). Smack in the center of town, this hotel blends harmoniously into the old city, yet opens to reveal a startlingly modern interior. The lobby has one wall covered with an abstract mural crafted from slabs of dramatically colored stone, with Oriental rugs, gray marble floors, and hospitable leather armchairs so low you might need help in getting up. Singles rent for 94 DM ($31.02) without private bath, costing from 115 DM ($37.95) with bath. Doubles are priced 103 DM ($33.99) to 155 DM ($51.15), including breakfast.

MIDDLE-RANGE HOTELS: Ulmer Spatz, 27 Münsterplatz (tel. 6-80-81). This corner stucco hotel-and-restaurant combination has an "impudent" position, right at the side of the cathedral, with most of its bedrooms overlooking the tower. The decor here may be slightly overdone, but one exception is the little Weinstube, where tasty meals are served in a mellowed setting of wood paneling and a collection of "things." The bedrooms are fairly priced. Bathless singles begin at 40 DM ($13.20); singles with bath, 70 DM ($23.10); bathless doubles, 80 DM ($26.40); and doubles with bath, 106 DM ($34.98). Set meals cost 18 DM ($5.94) to 50 DM ($16.50), and the à la carte menu has good main dishes, such as roast pork Schwäbisch.

Stern, 17 Sterngasse (tel. 6-30-91). Less than three blocks from both the railroad station and the cathedral, this modern hotel shows a cheerful yellow facade with rows of evenly spaced windows to visitors who arrive exhausted after a day's journey. The hotel is bigger than it looks from the outside, offering 90 beds in units with bath. There is also an elevator, plus a sauna. Comfortably furnished singles rent from 85 DM ($28.05) to 95 DM ($31.35), while doubles cost 120 DM ($39.60) to 150 DM ($49.50), a filling breakfast buffet included.

Hotel und Rasthaus Seligweiler, at Ulm-Seligweiler, an der B19 (tel. 2-60-80). From across the meadow, the first thing you'll see is the gold lettering of the word "Hotel" splashed across the top floor of this 44-room hotel. All accommodations have modern bathrooms, air conditioning, and soundproof windows and walls. There is also a swimming pool, equipped with whirlpool jets, and three bowling alleys. The hotel, suitable for motorists, lies a few miles, about a six-minute car ride, from the center of Ulm. Singles with breakfast go for 74 DM ($24.42), while doubles run from 114 DM ($37.62), and triples, from 133 DM ($43.89).

BUDGET HOTELS: Goldenes Rad, 65 Neue Strasse (tel. 6-70-48). Because of its location directly on the Münsterplatz, you'll have a view of the cathedral from many of the soundproof windows of this hotel. The rooms are clean and hospitable, with color-coordinated wallpaper and curtains along with tile-coated bathrooms. Singles range in price from 52 DM ($17.16) to 88 DM ($29.04), while doubles cost from 80 DM ($26.40) without bath, 110 DM ($36.30) with bath, breakfast included.

Schwarzer Adler, 20 Frauenstrasse (tel. 2-10-93), is one of the best of the budget hotels of Ulm. Run by a pleasant and hospitable family, it lies a short walk from the Ulm cathedral. The accommodations are well maintained and immaculately kept, and the showers are large with a consistent supply of hot water. The prices are right too: from 40 DM ($13.20) to 48 DM ($15.84) in a single and from 68 DM ($22.44) to 78 DM ($25.74) in a double, depending on your room assignment. Meals are good and plentiful, attracting local residents, a good sign. You can dine as cheaply as 18 DM ($5.94) or more elaborately at 45 DM ($14.85). The restaurant is closed on Friday.

WHERE TO DINE: Ratskeller, 1 Marktplatz (tel. 6-07-22), offers dining on almost any budget level. It's central, close to the cathedral, and features varied menus in a pleasing and restful atmosphere. It's fairly recently renovated, with comfortable leather chairs, among other things. There is no mad rush here— just dignified dining with self service. Set meals range from 18 DM ($5.94) to 38 DM ($12.54). You can order a wienerschnitzel, which is very good here. Wines are inexpensively priced, and desserts are excellent.

Zum Pflugmerzler, 6 Pfluggasse (tel. 6-80-61). Small and intimate, and open later than most restaurants in Ulm, this place might be perfect for an after-concert supper in an old-world setting. Herbert Wagner (no relation) is your host here, and he cooks a variety of Swabian, Bavarian, and international meat and fish dishes. He offers an exceptional set meal at 30 DM ($9.90) that I have found the best in town for value and taste. Hours are 11 a.m. to 11:30 p.m.

weekdays. On Saturday, he opens at 2:30 p.m., and he's closed on Sunday and holidays.

Zur Forelle, 25 Fischergasse (tel. 6-39-24). Only ten tables can accommodate the kinds of delicacies that the lessees of this space keep inventing. The owners have created a sympathetic and cozy environment where Swabian specialties and nouvelle cuisine share equal billing. They offer such fare as homemade parfait of eel, lobster, goose, and stag, perhaps filet of trout (forelle) in a puff pastry with mushrooms and slices of smoked ham. Dinners cost from 28 DM ($9.24) to 60 DM ($19.80). They are open from noon to 2 p.m. and 6 to 9:30 p.m. daily except Sunday.

2. Aschaffenburg

Industry in recent years has not destroyed the pastoral illusion created by the parks and shady lanes in and around this city on the Main. Just 26 miles southeast of Frankfurt, it is the gateway to the streams and woodlands of the Spessart Hills. With 250 garment manufacturers in the city, it has become the production center for men's clothing in West Germany. Yet it has remained a peaceful, provincial town, where weekly fairs are held on the square and seafood is sold directly from the buckets of the fishermen along the banks of the river. The traditional shopping streets are in a pedestrian zone, made peaceful by lamps, fountains, and flowers. You are invited to stroll and to chat, as you look into store windows.

THE SIGHTS: The favorite park in Aschaffenburg is the **Schönbusch Park,** where you can ramble along shaded paths through groves of old trees. It is across the Main (two miles on foot or by car), a marvel of planning, using the natural surroundings as a setting for formal 18th-century gardens, wandering lanes, temples, and gazebos. At the edge of the mirror-smooth lake is a small neoclassic castle, really a country house, once used by the electors of Mainz. The house is open from April 1 to September 30 from 8 a.m. to 1 p.m. and 2 to 5 p.m., charging 1.50 DM (50¢) for admission. In summer it's possible to rent small boats to go on the lake, and the café-restaurant is open each day from 8 a.m. to 8 p.m.

The most impressive castle in Aschaffenburg is the huge Renaissance **St. Johannisburg castle,** 4 Schlossplatz (tel. 2-24-17), reflected in the waters of the Main. Erected in 1605–1614 by Archbishop Johann Schweickard von Kronberg to replace an earlier structure, the red sandstone castle is almost perfectly symmetrical, with four massive lantern towers surrounding an inner courtyard. The interior is open from April 1 to September 30 from 9 a.m. to noon and 1 to 5 p.m. Admission is 2.50 DM (83¢). Off-season, its hours are 10 a.m. to noon and 1 to 4 p.m. A few treasures remain, but most of the works of art have been removed to the Town Museum. From the gardens of the castle you reach the **Pompeianum,** built by the Bavarian King Ludwig I as a replica of the Castor and Pollux palace discovered among the ruins of Pompeii.

The abbey **Church of Sts. Peter and Alexander** (Stiftskirche) has stood on its hill overlooking the town for 1000 years. Its architecture has changed over the centuries, however, as it was remodeled and reconstructed, until today it stands as a combination of Romanesque, Gothic, and baroque. Its most precious treasure is the painted retable, *The Lamentation of Christ,* by the court painter Grünewald. The interior is decorated with several paintings of the school of Lucas Cranach, as well as a marble-alabaster pulpit by Hans Juncker. One of the oldest pieces is a Roman-style crucifix from 1150. Adjacent to the north side of the church is a Romanesque cloister from the 13th century. The church is open to the public throughout the day, but to view the treasury and the cloisters, you must request admission through the sacristan at 1 Stiftsgasse. The charge is 1 DM (33¢).

AN UPPER-BRACKET HOTEL: Romantik Hotel Post, 19 Goldbacherstrasse (tel. 2-13-33), is an all-around hotel, and it certainly serves some of the best food in Aschaffenburg. Close to the heart of the town, its exterior may be conventional, but there is drama inside. The focus of attention is the dining room, a stylized version of an old posting inn, including an original mail coach, timbering on the walls and ceiling, leaded-glass windows, and tavern chairs. Even the breakfast room has charm, with its corner fireplace of decorative tile and its raffia-seated chairs. A miniature sitting room is equally rustic, almost New England in character, with natural pine chairs, café curtains, and hanging oil lamps, plus lots of decorative copper.

All rooms have bath or shower. Singles with shower start at 75 DM ($24.75), peaking at 102 DM ($33.66) with private bath. Doubles rent from 145 DM ($47.85). Each accommodation is uniquely furnished and comfortable.

MIDDLE-BRACKET HOTELS: Wilder Mann, 51 Loeherstrasse (tel. 2-15-55), at the edge of town, is a stylized, overgrown inn, with an electric modern interior. The breakfast room is decorated with blue and white bentwood chairs and bronze chandeliers. The inviting entry lounge is in tones of orange and yellow, with sleek back chairs. Most treasured is a fine baroque carved wood statue of a Madonna and Child. The namesake of the inn (wild man) is the wrought-iron sculpture sign on the facade that pictures a man who may remind you of the Wizard of Oz. Depending on the plumbing, singles range in price from 55 DM ($18.15) to 57 DM ($18.81). Likewise, doubles go from 75 DM ($24.75) to a high of 110 DM ($36.30).

Aschaffenburger Hof, 20 Weissenburgerstrasse (tel. 2-14-41), is housed in a tall yellow building with a single balcony on each floor. It was built in an area four blocks from the castle with lots of trees. This establishment offers the kind of thoughtful details that turn a good hotel into an exceptional one. The hotel is popular in town, especially with a local branch of the Rotary Club, which uses it for meetings, enjoying its nouvelle cuisine selection of fresh food. Rooms are pleasantly and comfortably furnished, costing from 80 DM ($26.40) to 98 DM ($32.34) in a single and 100 DM ($33) to 158 DM ($52.14) in a double, breakfast included. The hotel is 40 minutes' drive from Frankfurt on the autobahn. Turn off at the Aschaffenburg-Ost exit.

Syndikus, 35 Löherstrasse (tel. 2-35-88). An unpretentious three-story facade, with a vertical sign announcing "hotel," is what greets visitors to this modern but traditional hotel, a few blocks from the basilica. The bar area is rustically decorated with timbered ceilings, wheel chandeliers, and old pieces of salt-glazed pottery and pewter. The bedroom furniture, for the most part, is richly upholstered in autumnal floral designs, while all units have large baths and up-to-date fixtures and wooden ceilings. Doubles rent for 99 DM ($32.67) to 150 DM ($49.50), while singles cost 63 DM ($20.79) to 98 DM ($32.34).

A BUDGET HOTEL: Kolping, 26 Treibgasse (tel. 2-88-82). Designed to look like an almost perfect cube of concrete and glass, this 33-room hotel is only about two blocks from the castle. Clean and modern rooms rent for 57 DM ($18.81) to 73 DM ($24.09) in a single and from 76 DM ($25.08) to 102 DM ($33.66) in a double, all with shower and toilet. Breakfast is included in the rates. It is run by Peter Seifert.

WHERE TO DINE: Hotel Syndikus, 35 Löhrstrasse (tel. 2-35-88). Good service and traditional cookery are the trademarks of this limited-menu restaurant, serving two versions of a table d'hôte daily. Of the two, the emphasis is on fresh fish and shellfish. There's also a bar. The competent chef, Wolfgang Weilharter, uses only the freshest of ingredients. The choice of his menus is determined by what's in season, and what's currently contained in the enormous saltwater aquarium which keeps ocean fish alive until the very last minute. Specialties include fresh crayfish grilled in an envelope of bacon. If you like meat, you can order his goose liver pâté or a rack of lamb with fresh baby cabbage. Meal prices range from 35 DM ($11.55) to 85 DM ($28.05). It's open from 5 p.m. till 1 a.m., but closed on Sunday and in August.

Romantik-Hotel Post, 19-21 Goldbacher Strasse (tel. 2-13-33). Dining here is a special event, both to the townspeople and the Americans stationed nearby. Even diet and vegetarian meals are offered. In season, quail, venison, and stag are featured. This restaurant is architecturally divided into several sections by low wooden partitions. The overall effect is one of white stuccoed walls and heavy wood beams supporting the ceiling. Meals cost from 35 DM ($11.55) to 100 DM ($33) if you're being extravagant. The most noticeable part of the decor is the original post coach which made the frequent run through Bavaria in 1880. Now it sits like a museum piece, which it is, in one corner of the 50-table restaurant. Service is from 6 a.m. to midnight, and the menu is so long, more than 70 items, that it may take much of the night to decide on your selection. Many international dishes are served, but mainly the cook concentrates on regional dishes such as pork tongue, Swabian style, and a very delicious beef consommé with liver dumplings which would make a fine beginning for your meal.

Wilder Mann, 51 Loeherstrasse (tel. 2-15-55), which was previously recommended as a hotel, also serves good food. The place has existed in one form or another since 1558. Highly traditional in cookery, it specializes in trout along with wild game. You face a choice of 12 main courses. The restaurant opens early, serving breakfast from 9 a.m. until the last dinner orders are taken at midnight. The colors are brown, ocher, and pink, with painted bentwood chairs. The dessert table holds a cornucopia of breadstuffs and desserts. To have dinner here will cost from 25 DM ($8.25) to 52 DM ($17.16). It closes around Christmas, reopening after the first week of January.

Aschaffenburger Hof, 20 Weissenburgerstrasse (tel. 2-14-41), is a modern hotel with a restaurant popular with locals who concentrate on the solid, good, honest, filling, unfrilly gutbürgerlich food. The menu offers at least ten main courses, with set meals ranging in price from 25 DM ($8.25) to 60 DM ($19.80). The emphasis is on natural ingredients, and diet dishes are also available. Lunch is served daily, except Saturday, from noon to 2 p.m. and dinner from 6 to 10 p.m.

Schlossweinstuben, Schloss Johannisburg (tel. 1-24-40). One of the most alluring corners of this historic castle is its popular wine cellar. You'll find a wide variety of German wines to complement anything that might strike your fancy among the conservative but well-prepared menu items. A meal might begin with liver noodle soup, then follow with a game specialty (depending on the season and availability, of course). A list of very fresh fish is likely to include trout and pike, as well as several Frankish specialties. Several fixed-price meals are offered. Count on spending from 13 DM ($4.29) to 30 DM ($9.90). The stube is open daily except Monday from 11 a.m. to midnight.

3. Bamberg

Bamberg and beer go together like barley and hops. It's been called "a beer drinker's Eden," outranking Munich in the number of breweries concentrated within its city limits. The average Bamberger drinks 50 gallons of beer a year, making the rest of the German people look like teetotalers by comparison. Many brew fanciers journey all the way to Bamberg just to sample Rauchbier, a smoked beer dating from 1536.

THE SIGHTS: Handsomely positioned on seven hills, Bamberg is a cathedral city, just 39 miles north of Nürnberg. It is considered the greatest medieval city of Germany, a powerful ecclesiastical center whose roots go back 1000 years. The **Domplatz** (Cathedral Square), the most harmonious in Germany, is dominated by **Alte Hofhaltung,** the Renaissance imperial and episcopal palace, with a courtyard surrounded by late-Gothic framework buildings. Within the palace are the remains of the original Diet hall, built in the 11th century. Opposite is the **New Residence** (tel. 5-63-51), the much larger palace of the prince-bishops, from the 17th century. Its buildings show the influence of both Renaissance and baroque. It is open between April 1 and September 30 from 9 a.m. to noon and 1:30 to 5 p.m. (closes at 4 p.m. the rest of the year). Admission is 2.50 DM (83¢).

On the Domplatz sits the **Imperial Cathedral,** erected in the 11th century, but rebuilt in 1237 in a Romanesque and early-Gothic style. Resting on a hillside, the cathedral is a basilica with a double chancel, the eastern one raised on a terrace to compensate for the slope. The massive towers at the four corners of the church dominate the skyline of the city. The interior of the cathedral contains some of the most noted religious art in Christendom. The best known is the *Bamberg Rider,* an equestrian statue from the 13th century representing the idealized Christian king of the Middle Ages. Among the many tombs is that of Emperor Heinrich II, who erected the original cathedral. Tilman Riemenschneider labored more than a decade over this masterpiece and that of the king's wife, Kunigunda, who was suspected of adultery—a fact actually commemorated in one of the scenes on the tomb. The only papal tomb in Germany —in fact, the only one north of the Alps—contains the remains of Pope Clement II, who died in 1047. He is buried in the western chancel. The cathedral may be visited at any time during daylight hours, except between noon and 2 p.m. (and during services, of course). The Cathedral Treasury, a rich collection, may be seen in the **Diozesanmuseum,** Kapitelshaus, 5 Domplatz. It can be visited April to November Tuesday through Friday from 10 a.m. to 5 p.m., on Saturday and Sunday from 10 a.m. to 3 p.m.; closed Monday. Admission is 2 DM (66¢).

Among the other places of interest is the **Altes Rathaus,** considered the strangest town hall in Germany. Determined not to play favorites between the ecclesiastical and secular sections of the city, the town authorities built this Gothic structure (with more recent rococo overtones) on its own little island in the middle of the Regnitz River—halfway between the two factions—a true middle-of-the-road (or river) political stand. From the island you get the best view of the old fishermen's houses along the river in the section fancifully called "Little Venice."

The **E.T.A. Hoffman House,** 26 Schillerplatz, was the home of the writer, poet, and critic from 1809 to 1813. The little narrow-fronted house is filled with mementos and memorabilia of the storyteller whose strange tales formed the basis of Offenbach's famous opera, *Tales of Hoffman.* The house is open from April through October; admission is 2 DM (66¢).

Excursions in the Environs

The most interesting excursion from Bamberg is to **Schloss Weissenstein** (also called Pommersfelden Castle), lying about 13 miles from the heart of Bamburg, and reached by taking the Würzburg highway. After some five miles, take a left-hand turn onto Route 22 heading toward Oberndorf. Signs point the way.

Considered a treasure of the secular baroque, one of the finest examples in the country, the schloss was built between 1711 and 1718. One of its most stunning architectural achievements is called the well, a spectacular three-story staircase. Apollo's chariot races across the ceiling. As was popular in Renaissance days, a ground-floor room has a grotto effect with elaborate shell decorations. A detailed tour takes in the apartments of the bishops of Bamberg, along with a painting salon and a hall of mirrors. Guided tours go through the castle from 9 a.m. to noon and 2 to 5 p.m. for a cost of 6 DM ($1.98).

The pilgrimage **Vierzehnheiligen Church** lies to the northeast of Bamberg. A gem of the rococo era, it was constructed by Balthasar Neumann in 1743. It overlooks Banz Abbey (see below). In the mid-15th century a herdsman reportedly saw visions of the "Fourteen Saints of Intercession," the last of which was identified as being the Christ Child. Over the years the site attracted thousands of pilgrims to a chapel here which eventually gave way to a sumptuous rococo church, showing that Neumann was indeed a master of baroque architecture. One reader wrote, "The interior is so dazzling I walked around as if in a trance."

Built of ocher-colored stone, the church is characterized by its domed towers. Inside, in addition to enjoying the elaborate but also subtle decoration, seek out the Nothelfer Altar, dating from 1764. The altar, a rococo pyramid, stands on the spot where the alleged visions were said to have taken place. The saints of the intercession are depicted, including St. Acacius, the "agony of death."

After viewing Vierzehnheiligen, it is but a short distance to **Banz Abbey,** which lies 19 miles north of Bamberg. This baroque church, celebrated for its astonishing beauty, was built on the opposite slope from Vierzehnheiligen on what is called "the holy mountain of Franconia." This cluster of baroque buildings, part of which now house a colony of Germany's senior citizens, was constructed between 1698 and 1772. The Klosterkirche or abbey church, the work on which was finished in 1719 to the designs of Johann Dientzenhofer, is open to the public from 8:30 to 11:30 a.m. and 1 to 5:30 p.m. In winter it closes at 4:30 p.m., and on Sunday and holidays it opens at 10 a.m. One of the statues decorating the front of the abbey depicts St. Denis, whom the Franks once made a cult figure. From the terrace you'll have a stunning panoramic sweep of the Main Valley and the just-visited Vierzehnheiligen Church.

AN UPPER-BRACKET HOTEL: **National,** 37 Luitpoldstrasse (tel. 2-41-12). This very grand-looking hotel could as easily be found in Paris as in Bamberg. With its black mansard roof, iron balconies, and combination baroque and classical detailing, you'll quickly understand why. Public rooms are appropriately opulent, and the bedrooms are whimsically decorated in light-colored floral prints. Singles rent for 80 DM ($26.40) to 120 DM ($39.60), and doubles cost 105 DM ($34.65) to 190 DM ($62.70). All units have shower or bath and toilet, and a breakfast buffet is included in the rates.

MIDDLE-BRACKET HOTELS: **Barock Hotel am Dom,** 4 Vorderer Bach (tel. 5-40-31). The owners of this symmetrical confection of a hotel have retained every detail of the original ornamented facade, and renovated key areas of the interior. The result is a winning combination of baroque elements in a well-painted, well-lit modernized building, where singles rent for a reasonable 58 DM ($19.14) to 64 DM ($21.12), and doubles cost 95 DM ($31.35) to 105 DM ($34.65). A few triple rooms, ideal for families, are rented for 125 DM ($41.25). Tariffs include a nourishing breakfast of everything you'd expect, plus wurst and cheese. The breakfast room is located near the foundations of the house which predate the American Revolution. The management has set up tables with colorful napery under the plastered stone vaulting of the cellar, added a new floor, new lighting, fresh paint, and *voilà!* They've created about the most unusual breakfast room in Bamberg.

Brudermühle, 1 Schranne (tel. 5-40-91). My favorite ornament on the facade of this white and terracotta building is a corner statue of a saint being protected by two cherubs. I can't guess the age of the statue, but the building itself dates from 1314 when it was constructed as a mill powered by the Regnitz River lapping at its foundations. The interior is a carefully crafted network of beams supporting the second floor and the whimsically carved balustrade for the stairwell. The hotel couldn't be more centrally located, within a few blocks of the cathedral. Rooms are attractively furnished and immaculately kept, costing 98 DM ($22.44) to 102 DM ($33.66) in a double and 68 DM ($22.44) to 78 DM ($25.74) in a single.

Altenburgblick, 59 Panzerleite (tel. 5-40-23). Surrounded by majestic deciduous trees, which don't interrupt the fine view from the balconied windows, this modern hotel charges 46 DM ($15.18) to 65 DM ($21.45) in a single and 86 DM ($28.38) to 100 DM ($33) in a double. Rooms are comfortably appointed and well maintained, with carpeting and lots of light. All units have private bath. You'll discover a panoramic view from the wine terrace near the hotel, and probably a lot of Bambergers too, drinking and eating on a summer day.

Romantik-Hotel and **Weinhaus Messerschmitt,** 41 Lange Strasse (tel. 2-78-66), is mainly visited because of its reputation as a restaurant, considered by many locals as the finest in the city. But, unknown to many, it also rents rooms, 12 in all. The exterior is a gabled expanse of pale blue and yellow, with intricate baroque patterns carved into the window frames of the second and third floors. Once you're inside, the dozens of windows make the heavy paneling seem elegantly appropriate. That, coupled with the ceramic ovens and the antiques, makes for a mellow sojourn in Bamberg. Many of the beds upstairs have meticulously crafted headboards. Single rooms cost from 60 DM ($19.80) to 90 DM ($29.70); doubles, from 108 DM ($35.64) to 145 DM ($47.85). Breakfast is included. Otto Pschorn is in charge of this complex, and does everything he can, with the assistance of his staff, to be helpful.

Bamberger Hof Bellevue, 4 Schönleinsplatz (tel. 2-22-16), is a great old palace of stone, crowned by a tower and facing a little park, was renovated in 1984 but the old style was retained. All the comfortably furnished bedrooms now have private bath or shower, toilet, TV, radio, mini-bar, and phone. Try to get one of the bedrooms that are large enough to contain several sitting areas. Prices for accommodations depend on the placement and size. Doubles range in price from 150 DM ($49.50) to 160 DM ($52.80), and singles run from 95 DM ($31.25) to 105 DM ($34.65). All tariffs include a large buffet breakfast. There is a first-class restaurant. The service is by helpful and attentive people, who give tips on the best dishes of the day. You can have set meals for 30 DM ($9.90) and up.

BUDGET HOTELS: Die Alte Post, 1 Heiliggrabstrasse (tel. 2-78-48), is one of the most reasonably priced hotels in Bamberg, dating from 1920. The helpful hosts do much to make a guest's stay comfortable. Double rooms cost 84 DM ($27.72) to 115 DM ($37.95), and singles run 56 DM ($18.48) to 75 DM ($24.75). The units are well maintained with flowery wallpaper. All rooms have showers, telephones, and TVs. For the price quoted, you're given a good breakfast with orange juice, fresh cheese, and sausage. There's also a restaurant on the premises.

Hotel Garni Graupner, 5 Lange Strasse (tel. 2-60-56). Many residents of town know this establishment by its big-windowed café and pastry shop occupying its ground floor. Much renovated, rebuilt, and overhauled over the years, it has a tradition of accepting overnight guests dating from the 14th century. The café is open daily from 8 a.m. to 7 p.m. You can get a room here—space available—at any time. Each of the accommodations contains a phone, while many have private bath and views over the old city. Depending on the plumbing, singles in the main hotel cost between 45 DM ($14.85) and 54 DM ($17.82), while doubles range between 60 DM ($19.80) and 85 DM ($28.05), with breakfast included. If the main hotel is full, guests are directed to their guest house at 21a Kapellenstrasse, about eight blocks away across the canal. Constructed in the late '60s, it offers ten comfortably modern rooms for about the same price charged in the main hotel. The same family also owns a rose-garden café in yet another part of town, a stone's throw from the cathedral.

WHERE TO DINE: Würzburger Weinstube, 6 Zinkenwörth (tel. 2-26-67), is an old, attractive, half-timbered inn on a secluded street near the river, with a courtyard in front for warm-weather dining. The bottled wines available from the owner, Hans Krebs, will keep you smiling, but don't hesitate to drink the open wine of the house. The set meal at 25 DM ($8.25) is one of the most outstanding values in the city. On the à la carte listing you'll find toast Nizza, rainbow trout from nearby streams, and tenderloin of pork cooked in a cream sauce. If you order à la carte you can spend as much as 50 DM ($16.50). The weinstube is closed from the end of August to mid-September.

Romantik Restaurant-Weinhaus Messerschmitt, 41 Lange Strasse (tel. 2-78-66), is a comfortable and pleasant restaurant, with mainly Franconian specialties. The restaurant is 150 years old, and the sixth generation of the same family runs it. It's known through Bamberg for its "Romantik-Menu," a complete meal costing from 32 DM ($10.56) to 60 DM ($19.80). The dishes offered depend on seasonal shopping; in spring you get fresh white asparagus. Freshwater fish, kept in an aquarium, are also available. Game is another specialty, and the veal and lamb dishes are prepared with exquisite care. The weinhaus is open from 9 a.m. to 11 p.m.

Böttingerhouse, 14 Judenstrasse (tel. 5-40-74). The baroque ornamentation of this restaurant's facade stands in sharp contrast to the deliciously light-textured nouvelle cuisine served inside. Visitors are amply rewarded after climbing the flight of steps leading to the second-floor dining room. There the Orsenne family, Victor and Maria, maintain a daytime coffeehouse as well as an evening restaurant where some of the best food in town is served as a matter of course. You might enjoy such specialties as veal goulash, mussels in a saffron-flavored sauce, many fish delicacies, and an array of such mouthwatering desserts as raspberry Charlotte. You can order a pastry and coffee throughout the day in one of several rooms. Hot meals are served between noon and 2 p.m.; dinner, from 6 to 10 p.m. Full meals cost between 30 DM ($9.90) and 60 DM ($19.80).

The restaurant also owns the well-recommended Gästehaus Steinmühle (same phone). The reception desk is part of the restaurant, and the rooms are located just around the corner ("38 meters away"). Comfortably furnished singles cost between 85 DM ($28.05) and 100 DM ($33), while doubles range between 135 DM ($44.55) and 150 DM ($49.50). Some of the rooms overlook the Regnitz River. Free parking is available.

Michels Küche, 13 Markusstrasse (tel. 2-61-99), is a restaurant with a decidedly pleasant atmosphere, offering nouvelle cuisine and regional specialties. A small à la carte menu is supplemented by daily specialties. One, for example, is filets of stag or lamb à la provençale baked en croûte. Venison is also offered in season, augmented by a wholesome collection of soups and desserts such as pastries with cognac cream or pistachios and rum sauce. Formerly a brewery established in 1670, since 1895 the site has belonged to the Michel family, who maintain the old tradition with a dedication. The food is served against a backdrop of saffron-colored walls, with Windsor chairs and white lace curtains framing a view. The restaurant serves an exceptional set meal for just 33 DM ($10.89), or you might spend as much as 55 DM ($18.15) ordering à la carte. Hours are daily except Sunday and Monday from 6 p.m. till 1 a.m. There are ten tables seating guests in friendly conviviality.

Historischer Brauereiausschank Schlenkerla, 6 Dominikanerstrasse (tel. 5-60-60). Clients sit here much as they did in 1678 when the brewery (which is what this used to be) was established. The decor is predictably rustic, with long wooden tables and smallish chairs more suited to anatomies of the 17th century than of today. The price is right, however, and the gemütlich atmosphere genuine. Wholesome German food is served, costing from 10 DM ($3.30) to 22 DM ($7.26) for a meal. It is open from 9:30 a.m. to 11 p.m. daily, except Tuesday, and closes for around two weeks in January every year.

4. Coburg

This town, about 30 miles north of Bamberg near the East German border, is forever linked to the Saxe-Coburgs. In their day they were called a "royal stud farm," as they provided queens, kings, and consorts for some of the ruling families of Europe, including England, Portugal, Bulgaria, and Belgium. At the zenith of their power they were said to "rule over half the globe." One of the most notable members of this family was Prince Albert, Queen Victoria's "beloved Albert." The queen herself was also descended from this same aristocratic family.

THE SIGHTS: In the **Market Square** visitors can compare the statue of Prince Albert here with the famous one in London. Here one can see the **Stadthaus,** in the Renaissance style, and the **Rathaus** (Town Hall), which was first constructed in the 1500s but later reconstructed, with its Great Hall remaining intact during the rebuilding. The greatest Renaissance structure, however, is the **Gymnasium Casimirianum** or Casimir School. Constructed in 1605, it is considered the most magnificent secular Renaissance building in town. It faces the Church of St. Maurice.

One can also visit **Ehrenburg Castle,** which is the schloss where Prince Albert lived as a boy. A Renaissance structure, it saw much rebuilding in the 19th century. Guests wander through the baroque throne room, inspecting the Hall of the Giants, later admiring the Gobelin salon with its many tapestries. The baroque chapel is also of interest. Hours are daily except Monday from 9 a.m. to noon and 1 to 4 p.m. Admission costs 2.50 DM (83¢).

Seen from a great distance, the **Veste** or fortress is one of the largest castles in Germany. Originally dating from the 12th century, it has a double ring of heavily fortified walls. With its high roofs and dormers, it is an impressive sight, and the government has filled it with museums that will take several hours to explore if you can afford the time. The present fortress dates mainly from the 16th century. The **Fürstenbau** or palace of the princes is open from the first of April until the end of October, daily except Monday, from 9 a.m. to noon and 2 to 4 p.m. (from 2 to 3:30 p.m. off-season), charging an admission of 5 DM ($1.65). Luther stayed here in 1530. The palace is built in the half-timbered style, and has many art treasures, including a quartet of paintings by Lucas Cranach the Elder. More pictures by Cranach, along with other treasures, such as antiques, can be inspected at the **Kunstsammlungen** (arts museum), which is open the same hours, charging another 3 DM (99¢) for admission. Other exhibits include antique carriages, armor, weapons, sculpture, porcelain, silver, and more paintings, including works by such old masters as Dürer and Rembrandt, along with the "Golden Virgin of Bamberg." Wedding carriages from the 17th century and sledges from the same period are on view in the **Herzoginbau** or duchess' building, which keeps the same visiting hours as the Kunstammlungen.

Between the fortress and the Ehrenburg Castle is the Hofgarten, where you will find the **Naturwissenschaftliches Museum** (natural history museum), open from 9 a.m. to 6 p.m. (until 5 p.m. off-season), charging an admission of 2 DM (66¢). Its bird collection, with some 7500 specimens, is reputed to be one of the biggest on the continent.

WHERE TO STAY: Schloss Neuhof, 10 Neuhofer Strasse (tel. 2-51), at Neu-Neershof. Many of the residents of this hamlet, about four miles from Coburg, come to this establishment to enjoy its attractive beer garden. There, shaded by the massive stone walls of this castle, dating from the 14th century, they can enjoy an array of international specialties in pleasant surroundings. Of course there's a bierstube inside, along with a more formal dining room and an amply stocked wine cellar. Meals range in price from 30 DM ($9.90) to 60 DM ($19.80). The management also rents out 20 stylishly decorated bedrooms for 55 DM ($18.15) to 90 DM ($29.70) in a single, and 100 DM ($33) to 160 DM ($52.80) in a double, including a breakfast buffet.

Goldene Traube, 2 Am Viktoriabrunnen (tel. 98-33). If you're looking for a location central to everything in town, consider this bay-windowed, white-walled hotel whose facade is partially screened in summer with colorful awnings. Breakfasts are served from an amply stocked buffet, and evening meals are well prepared, generous, and reasonably priced, ranging from 18 DM ($5.94) to 45 DM ($14.85). Singles cost between 42 DM ($13.86) and 95 DM ($31.35), the latter with private bath. Likewise, doubles, depending on the room, run from a low of 75 DM ($24.75) to a high of 175 DM ($57.75), including breakfast.

WHERE TO DINE: Coberger Tor–Restaurant Schaller, 22 Ketschendorfer Strasse (tel. 2-50-74). The plushly elegant restaurant contained within this medium-sized hotel is the personal fiefdom of chef Ulrich Schaller. You'll find it, along with practically every other gourmet in town, in a residential neighborhood on the town's outskirts. Advance reservations are important. Someone will usher you to a comfortable banquette in an easy-on-the-eyes decor of soft beiges and moss greens. Intimate corners are illuminated with spotlighting from hanging lamps.

Menu specialties depend on fresh ingredients, and their availability changes with the seasons. Examples include an array of homemade terrines, several kinds of fish in puff pastry, and wild game with seasonal mushrooms. It would be unfortunate to miss one of the establishment's desserts, since much of the effort of the chef is devoted to his pastry trolley. Have you ever enjoyed three flavors of chocolate mousse, all served on the same platter?

Lunchtime fixed-price meals cost between 18 DM ($5.94) and 45 DM ($14.85). Many evening visitors choose the fixed-price six-course meal, which will regale its consumers for 75 DM ($24.75) per person. The restaurant is open from 11 a.m. to 2 p.m. and 5:30 to 10 p.m. It's closed on Friday at dinnertime and on Saturday at lunchtime. It also shuts down for two weeks in January and about ten days in midsummer.

Single rooms in the adjoining hotel cost between 55 DM ($18.15) and 60 DM ($19.80). Doubles go for 90 DM ($29.70) to 120 DM ($39.60).

Künstler-Klause, 4a Theaterplatz (tel. 7-52-61). If you plan on an evening at the theater, you'll find everyone from some of the performers to members of the audience at this stylish bistro a few steps from the stage. It serves late suppers until midnight every night but Monday. If the culinary tastes of your companions range from nouvelle cuisine to classic Teutonic specialties, the accommodating chefs are happy to provide.

Fred Raab is the owner, and in some ways he is a celebrity in his own right. One of the evening fixed-price meals, ranging from 35 DM ($11.55) to 95 DM ($31.35), might include lobster with mango, medallions of venison with potato puffs, an internationally derived cheese platter, or a campari parfait with amaretto mousse. Noonday menus cost 18 DM ($5.94) to 40 DM ($13.20). Warm food is served daily except Monday and Saturday from 11:30 a.m. to 2 p.m. and 6 p.m. to midnight. The restaurant closes for the first two weeks of January. There are only about ten tables, so reservations are important.

5. Nürnberg (Nuremberg)

When this, the largest city in Franconia, celebrated its 900th birthday in 1950, the scars of World War II were still fresh in its memory. It was once considered the ideal of medieval splendor, but that legacy was lost in the ashes of World War II. With the exception of Dresden, no other German city suffered such devastation in a single air raid as did Nürnberg. On the night of January 2, 1945, 525 British Lancaster bombers rained fire and destruction on Nürnberg, which up to then had been considered the ideological epicenter of the Third Reich. Since the war, many of the most important buildings have been restored.

Visitors in Nürnberg today can see not only the ruins of the ramparts that once surrounded the city, but also the **Justice Palace** where the War Crimes Tribunal sat in 1946. You can visit some of the most important churches in Germany and also the huge amphitheater where Hitler staged his dramatic rallies on the southeastern edge of Nürnberg. Here, Hitler's armaments minister, Albert Speer, constructed what has been called a "concrete mecca," in which a million uniformed and jack-booted S.A. and S.S. troopers could goose-step in review. Today the grounds that once rang with the shouts of the S.S. pledging allegiance to their hysterically ranting Führer have been turned into a park, with apartment blocks, a trade fair, and a concert hall.

Speer's Congress Hall, larger than the Colosseum in Rome, is today a recording studio and warehouse. But what of the Nazi leader's "Grand Avenue"? It is now a parking lot. The Zeppelinfeld arena, in which all those jack-booted men goose-stepped, is an athletic field for American soldiers and also is the setting for local rock festivals.

Centuries of art and architecture went to make Nürnberg a little treasure chest of Germany.

THE SIGHTS: Nearly all the attractions of the city are within the medieval fortifications that enclose the Old Town on both banks of the little Pegnitz River. Between the main wall with rampart walks and the secondary wall once ran the waters of a protective moat. Set at the "corners" of the town are the massive stone towers of the city gates, but the remains of dozens of towers still exist along the ramparts as well.

Within these walls the Renaissance was given its greatest impetus in Germany. The flourishing artists' workshops of Nürnberg boasted such talent as Albrecht Dürer, Veit Stoss, Peter Vischer, and Michael Wolgemut. The unparalleled Meistersingers of Nürnberg made great strides in the 14th and 15th centuries in the evolution of German music. You can still visit the Martha Church,

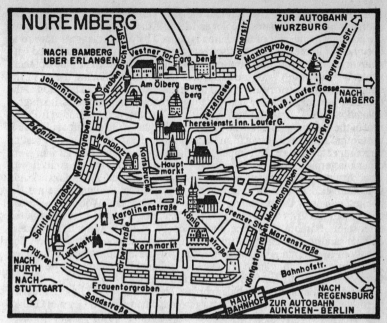

which served as their singing school. Advanced humanistically as well as artisti-cally, Nürnberg established its **Holy Ghost Hospital** as early as 1331. The build-ing is supported on arches spanning one branch of the Pegnitz River. Possibly the best example of Nürnberg's passion for beauty is the **"Beautiful Fountain"** on the Marketplace. The stone pyramid, 60 feet high, dates from 1396 and is adorned with 30 figures arranged in four tiers. Within it is enclosed the symbol of Nürnberg, the journeyman's ring.

The town's most popular shrine is the **Albrecht Dürer House,** am Tiergartnertor, 39 Albrecht-Dürer-strasse (tel. 16-22-71), just up the cobble-stone Burgstrasse from the Dürer Monument and St. Sebald's Church. It was the home of the greatest German Renaissance artist during the last 19 years of his life. Aside from the historical and artistic contents inside, the house is well worth the short walk up the hill. Typical of the half-timbered burghers' houses of the 15th century, the structure is the only completely preserved Gothic house in Nürnberg. The first floors are sandstone, surmounted by two half-timbered stories and a gabled roof with a view of the town below. Dürer bought this house near the medieval city walls in 1509 and painted many of his masterpieces here before his death in 1528. The building houses a museum devoted to the life and works of the multifaceted individual who established Nürnberg as a flourishing cultural center. Many of the rooms are furnished with important historical pieces as well as copies of many of Dürer's paintings mixed with original etch-ings and woodcuts. The house is open daily from 10 a.m. to 5 p.m. (to 9 p.m. on Saturday). Closed Monday. Admission for adults is 2 DM (66¢); for children and students, 1 DM (33¢).

St. Lorenz Church, Königstrasse (tel. 20-92-87), across the Pegnitz River from most of the sights of the Old Town, is the largest and stateliest church in Nürnberg. Begun in 1260, it took more than 200 years to complete, but the final result is one of Gothic purity, inside and out. The twin towers flank the west portal, with its profusion of sculptures depicting the whole theme of Redemption, from Adam and Eve through the Last Judgment. Upon entering the church, you can appreciate the color and detail in the stained-glass rosette above the portal. The interior of the church is defined by pillars that soar upward to become lost in the vaulting shafts above the nave. Each pillar is adorned with sculptures carrying on the theme introduced at the entrance. The oldest of these works is *Mary with Child*, created about 1285. The continuing theme of the sculptures urges you forward toward the single east choir, the last portion of the church to be completed (1477). Separating the choir from the nave is the *Angelic Salutation* (1517), carved in linden wood by Veit Stoss and suspended from the roof of the church just behind the Madonna Chandelier. To the left of the altar is the Gothic Tabernacle, hewn from stone by Adam Krafft (1496), its upthrusting turret repeating the vertical emphasis of the church. Above the high altar is another masterpiece by Veit Stoss, a carved crucifix. The church is filled with woodcarvings, paintings, and reliefs, seemingly utilizing every artists' workshop that flourished in Nürnberg during the Renaissance. Among these are the painted panels at the beginning of the choir by Michael Wolgemut, Dürer's teacher. In the first chapel on the left off the nave is a sandstone relief of the three saints, Barbara, Catharine, and Agnes (1420). Halfway up the right side is another sandstone relief by Adam Krafft, the strangulation of St. Beatrice. The beauty of the church is heightened by the well-preserved stained and painted glass, much of it dating from pre-Dürer Nürnberg. The church can be viewed from 9 a.m. to 5 p.m. (on Sunday from 2 to 4 p.m.).

St. Sebald's Church, Sebaldkirchplatz, consecrated in 1273, is a fine example of the transition in the 13th century from Romanesque to German Gothic. The nave and west choir are late Romanesque, with a narrow chancel containing a simple altar and an ancient bronze baptismal font. The larger east choir, consecrated in 1379, is pure Gothic, and contains the most important treasures of the church. Between the two east pillars is a huge 16th-century Crucifixion group dominated by a life-size crucifix by Veit Stoss. Just behind the altar is the elaborate shrine of St. Sebald, whose remains are encased in a monument cast in brass by Peter Vischer in 1519. The nave of the church also holds several important works of art, including 14th-century statues of St. Catharine and St. Sebald and a Madonna with a Halo (1440). On the outside wall of the east choir is the tomb of the Schreyer-Landauer family, decorated with scenes of the Passion and Resurrection of Christ. The church is open daily April to September from 9 a.m. to 6 p.m., October to March from 10 a.m. to 4 p.m.

The **Kaiserburg** (Castle of Nürnberg) on Burgstrasse (tel. 22-57-26) looms above the city from its hilltop at the northern edge of the Old Town. For more than 500 years, from 1050 to 1571, it was the official residence of the German kings and emperors, including the zealous Crusader, Frederick Barbarossa, who entertained such exotic guests as the emperor of Byzantium and the sultan of Tyre within its walls. The castle is divided into three complexes of buildings, indicating its main periods of architecture and history: the **Imperial Castle,** the **Burgraves' Castle,** and the **Municipal Buildings of the Free City.**

The oldest portion of the complex is the Pentagonal Tower (1050). It probably dates from the previous palace of the Salian Kings, over which the Burgraves' Castle was constructed. Although the Burgraves' Castle has been in ruins since it was destroyed by fire in 1420, it offers the visitor an interesting look into the layout of a feudal castle. The heavy ramparts with the parapet walks and secret passages were used by the watchmen and guards who protected not only the burgraves, but the emperors as well, who lived in the inner core of the castle complex.

The Imperial Castle, grouped around the Inner Court within the ramparts of the Burgraves' Castle, was the residence of the kings and emperors of Germany. Most of the buildings were constructed during the 12th century, centering around the once-magnificent "Palas" built by Konrad III in 1138. The great Knights' Hall on the ground floor, and the Imperial Hall on the floor above look much as they did when King Frederick III rebuilt them in the 15th century, with heavy oak beams and painted ceilings. The rooms are decorated with period Gothic furnishings. Adjoining the Palas is the **Imperial Chapel,** the most important building in the castle complex. It consists of two chapels, one above the other in cross section, but united at the center by an open bay. Thus the emperor could worship with his court in the upper chapel to the same liturgy as the lesser members of his retinue in the lower chapel.

The third set of buildings on the Castle Hill, built outside the Burgraves' Castle, was erected by the council of Nürnberg in the 14th and 15th centuries when it took over the responsibility of protecting the emperor. This section includes the Imperial Stables, now housing a youth hostel, the massive bastions of the fortress, and the Castle Gardens.

From April to September, the castle is open daily from 9 a.m. to noon and 12:45 to 5 p.m.; from October to March the hours are 9:30 a.m. to noon and 12:45 to 4 p.m. Admission for all parts of the castle is 3 DM (99¢) for adults, 2 DM (66¢) for children; for the Palas only, 2.50 DM (83¢) for adults, 1.50 DM (50¢) for children. Even more impressive than the fortress, however, is the view of the rooms and towers of Nürnberg from its terraces.

The **Germanic National Museum** (Germanisches Nationalmuseum), Kornmarkt (tel. 20-39-71), the most comprehensive collection of German art and culture, is just inside the south section of the medieval city walls (near the main railway station). Its setting, incorporating the buildings of the former Carthusian monastery into its complex, covers the entire spectrum of German craftsmanship and fine arts, from its beginning to the 20th century. The pre- and early historical section contains finds from the Stone Age to the burial sites of the Merovingians. The extensive painting and sculpture sections include works by two of the city's most important artists, Albrecht Dürer and Veit Stoss. The demonstrations of the boundless variety and richness of German handicraft play a major role in the museum's orientation toward cultural history. In this area, medieval bronze casting and tapestries, works of goldsmithery, scientific instruments, costumes, arms, armor, and toys are well represented. During the last few years the folk art section and the section devoted to historical musical instruments have been greatly expanded. The Print Room and the Numismatic Collection are among the most comprehensive of the German-speaking world. Many original parchment documents from important families are housed in the Archive. The active and broad-based scholarly programs of the museum would not be possible without its library of more than 500,000 volumes, including manuscripts, incunabula, engraved and illustrated works. Hours are Tuesday through Sunday from 9 a.m. to 5 p.m.; Thursday also 8 p.m. to 9:30 p.m. Closed Monday year round. Admission: 2.50 DM (83¢) for adults; 1 DM (33¢) for students. No one pays admission on Sunday or public holidays.

The **Tucher Castle** (Tucherschlösschen), 9 Hirschelgasse, was the summer residence of the most famous and still existing patrician family, Tucher, known for beer. The structure was built in 1534 by Peter Flötner, and it contains a small but precious collection of artworks which had been commissioned by the Tuchers since the days of the Renaissance. Tours Monday through Friday are at 2, 3, and 4 p.m.; at 10 a.m. and 11 a.m. on Sunday. Closed Saturday. The entrance fee is 2 DM (66¢) for adults, 1 DM (33¢) for children.

Spielzeugmuseum (Toy Museum), 13 Karlstrasse. Nürnberg is recognized as the toy capital of the world. It is only fitting that the city devote a museum to this industry, containing toys not only made in Nürnberg, but from around the world. Some date back to medieval times. The collection of old dollhouses is vastly amusing, as is a mechanical ferris wheel. In one of the dollhouse kitchens, every utensil is created in miniature, as it was for the world's most famous doll-house, Queen Mary's Dollhouse displayed at Windsor Castle. Toys, both hand- and machine-made, fill three floors. You'll often see adults (without children) enjoying this museum. Hours are 10 a.m. to 5 p.m. Tuesday through Sunday. On Wednesday it stays open until 9 p.m. It is closed Monday, otherwise charg- ing an admission of 2 DM (66¢). The museum occupies a restored Renaissance house.

The **Handwerker Hof,** Königstor from Königstrasse, is like a walk back into the past where you find yourself in a land of half-timbered houses. Craftspeople can be seen at work making handicrafts, which you can purchase as souvenirs. You can also eat many local specialties such as small pork sau- sages, röstbratwurst, which the law says must be served the same day they are made. The section is open from the last week of March until right before Christ- mas from 10 a.m. to 6:30 p.m. Monday to Friday. On Saturday it is open from 10 a.m. to 2 p.m. Normally it is closed on Sunday, except during Advent when it is open from 10 a.m. to 6:30 p.m.

Lochgenfängniss, under the Altes Rathaus (Old Town Hall), is a medieval prison with cells, including torture chambers, where the hapless victims were taken. This gruesome attraction is open from the first of May until the end of September from 10 a.m. to 4 p.m. Monday through Friday (on Saturday and Sunday from 10 a.m. to 1 p.m.), charging an admission of 2 DM (66¢).

The **Verkehrsmuseum,** 6 Lessingstrasse, lies just outside the wall. It is the transport and communications museum of Nürnberg. Its major exhibit is a re- construction of the famous train that ran between Nürnberg and Fürth in 1835. Philatelists will be delighted to know (if they don't already) that the museum has one of the largest postage stamp collections anywhere. You can also see stage- coaches and early railroad cars. It is open daily from 10 a.m. to 4 p.m. April through September. Admission is 2 DM (66¢).

THE TOP HOTELS: Grand Hotel, 1 Bahnhofstrasse (tel. 20-36-21), is Nürnberg's grand old hotel. It's a solid six-floor blockbuster, built when "hotels were really hotels"—that is, before the First World War. Across from the rail- way station, its convenience of location may be an asset or a curse, but all rooms have soundproof windows. The restaurant provides dignified dining, and the cuisine is international-Germanic. The cozy pub is restful. The best beers and wines by the glass are served, accompanied by local specialties and light snacks.

The Grand Hotel's 187 bedrooms are well furnished and mostly spacious containing private bath and shower as well. Most of the double rooms are twin bedded. Singles with bath cost 180 DM ($59.40); twins with bath, 225 DM ($74.25).

Carlton Hotel Nürnberg, 13-15 Eilgustrasse (tel. 20-35-35), is a first-class hotel, considered by some the best in Nürnberg. It's on a quiet street a block from the railway station. The most formal restaurant is done in red and white, and many prefer luncheons on an outdoor stone terrace, with umbrella-shaded tables and flower garden. All of the bedrooms have private bath or shower. The accommodations are well conceived, with many modern built-in pieces. Some doubles have a pair of L-shaped sofas with coffee tables, making them com- bined living-sleeping rooms. Rates are based on size. A single with shower costs 125 DM ($41.25) to 145 DM ($47.85), peaking at 165 DM ($54.45) with full bath and toilet. Doubles with shower cost 186 DM ($61.38) to 220 DM ($72.60), in- creasing to 320 DM ($105.60) for two persons in an apartment with bath/shower and toilet.

Atrium Hotel, 25 Münchener Strasse (tel. 4-90-11). Whoever designed this hotel was concerned with the distribution of natural light, and did everything he could to pierce windows through to the greenery beyond the concrete walls. One of the newest hotels in Nürnberg (and some say the very best accommodation in town), the hotel lies five minutes by car from the city center, set in a landscaped park on a manicured lawn. It looks like a four-story collection of concrete cubes set up on stilts, of course with many windows angled toward the sun. Rooms are spacious, elegantly modern, with all the conveniences you'd expect. The single rooms come with double beds big enough to sleep two persons, and cost 155 DM ($51.15) to 165 DM ($54.45) for one. The regular doubles (where children under 12 can stay free) go for 172 DM ($56.76) to 216 DM ($71.28). Breakfast is included, along with the use of an indoor pool. The hotel accommodates handicapped clients in three specially designed rooms, and is directly connected to the Meistersingerhalle, used by Nürnbergers for concerts and conventions.

MIDDLE-BRACKET HOTELS: Loew's Hotel Merkur, 1 Pillenreuther Strasse (tel. 44-02-91), lies directly across from the south entrance of the railroad station, within three minutes' walking distance of the old city. Behind the neobaroque facade of this family-run hotel are 160 comfortable rooms. Units for the most part are large, high-ceilinged, and well furnished, with plush carpeting or well-chosen Oriental rugs. Friedrich Loew and his staff are your conscientious hosts, charging 160 DM ($52.80) to 270 DM ($89.10) in a double and 105 DM ($34.65) to 145 DM ($47.85) in a single, including private bath, TV, mini-bar, and breakfast. The hotel also has an indoor swimming pool, a sauna, and a solarium.

Deutscher Hof, 29 Frauentorgraben (tel. 20-38-21). Just two blocks from the railroad station, this is probably one of the most imaginatively decorated modern hotels in Nürnberg. If you're looking for a weinstube, the one here is appropriately conservative, but the rest of the hotel makes a bold, rustic statement in the use of plaids, natural colors, full-grained paneling, and sophisticated lighting. Bedrooms are spacious, bright, clean, and furnished with chrome and velvet armchairs. Breakfast is included in the rates, which are 115 DM ($37.95) to 135 DM ($44.55) in a single and 150 DM ($49.50) to 170 DM ($56.10) in a double.

Reichshof, 16 Johannesgasse (tel. 20-37-17). Two blocks from the Lorenzkirche, one of the landmark churches of Nürnberg, this hotel offers quiet and well-appointed rooms, usually soundproof. In traditional styling, singles cost 60 DM ($19.80) to 105 DM ($34.65), depending on the plumbing, and doubles go for anywhere from 110 DM ($36.30) to 170 DM ($56.10). The restaurant is illuminated with enormous half-rounded windows, while the bedrooms are romantically lit. Since 1914 the Reichshof has been in the hands of the same family, and has always been known as a hotel of high standard and solid character.

Victoria, 80 Königstrasse (tel. 20-38-01). In a historic section not far from the Lorenzkirche, the entrance to this hotel is identified by the restrained carving on the stonework of the rounded front. The sandstone facade of the hotel actually dates back to the 19th century. In 1976 the Victoria was completely renovated and equipped with soundproof windows and doors, direct-dial phone, private bath (or shower), and toilet in each unit. The interior is modernized, but still high-ceilinged, with an elegantly curved staircase leading to bright rooms on the second floor. Singles rent for 60 DM ($19.80) to 89 DM ($29.37), and doubles cost 110 DM ($36.30) to 140 DM ($46.20), with breakfast included.

Weinhaus Steichele, 2 Knorrstrasse (tel. 20-43-78). The overflow from the original building spills into a modern annex next door which still blends harmoniously with the more antique structure. The central core is a beautifully balanced and handcrafted building made of heavy stone blocks with a curved slope for a roofline supporting one half-timbered gable. The rooms are perfectly satisfactory, with a bright, big-windowed feeling. Singles rent for 62 DM ($20.46) to 72 DM ($23.76). Doubles range from 98 DM ($32.34) to 114 DM ($37.62). Breakfast is included in all these rates.

Drei Linden, 1 Aussere Suizbacher Strasse (tel. 53-36-20). The 100th anniversary of this establishment was celebrated in 1977 by the third generation of the Zeuner family to welcome guests to this renovated guest house. Inside, you'll find big-windowed comfort in 30 rooms, all with private bath and comfortably tufted chairs. The public rooms are attractively decorated in a sort of international modern. Including breakfast, a single costs 90 DM ($29.70) to 105 DM ($34.65), and a double goes for 140 DM ($46.20) to 160 DM ($52.80).

Burghotel-Grosses Haus, 3 Lammsgasse (tel. 20-44-14). This unusual hotel offers, among other attractions, the luxury of a heated indoor swimming pool opening onto a tile bar area furnished with plants, antiques, and bar stools, where you can sip your favorite drink and pretend you're in the Caribbean. Even better, your door will practically open into one of the most historic parts of the old city of Nürnberg. The public rooms are in the rustic modern style so popular in Germany, with the heavy beams you've come to expect, along with gaily striped green-and-red upholstery and intricately crafted wrought-iron dividers separating one area from another. Carefully chosen colors augment the bedrooms, which rent for 85 DM ($28.05) in a single and 120 DM ($39.60) to 170 DM ($56.10) in a double, breakfast included.

Novotel Nürnberg-Süd, 340 Münchener Strasse (tel. 8-67-91), part of a chain, offers 117 comfortable and spacious rooms, each with bath or shower, along with extra-wide French beds, toilet, phone, radio, color TV, an alarm clock, and mini-bar. The rooms, quietly positioned in the gardens, are fully air-conditioned and soundproof. The cost is about 150 DM ($49.50) for a double room, plus a 16-DM ($5.28) surcharge for breakfast. Singles rent for 140 DM ($46.20). The restaurant starts serving breakfast at 6 a.m., and will also provide special menus for children. The bar has a fine atmosphere, and recreational activities include a heated outdoor swimming pool and a big sun terrace, along with a sauna and solarium. There is also a children's playground. The hotel is easily reached from all motorways, and an underground train will take you into the heart of Nürnberg in about five minutes. Parking is provided free.

Hotel am Sterntor, 8-14 Tafelhofstrasse (tel. 23-58-1), is one of the railway station hotels that has been reconstructed and freshly decorated. Most important, it's not too noisy. The front lobby, with its contemporary elegance, sets the example for the nicely furnished bedrooms. Considering everything, am Sterntor is a good bet for your marks. Bathless singles cost 65 DM ($21.45), ranging upward to 95 DM ($31.35) with shower to a peak 100 DM ($33) with bath. Bathless doubles rent for 95 DM ($31.35), up to 190 DM ($62.70) with bath. Breakfast is included.

Deutscher Kaiser, 55 Königstrasse (tel. 20-33-41), has one of the most attractive old-world exteriors of any of the Nürnberg hostelries. At the top of a vehicle-free pedestrian mall, it is built of gray stone, with step gables and a highly pitched roof studded with dormers. Three Romanesque-style arches lead into the main lobby. For more than 60 years the Deutscher Kaiser has been managed and owned by the same family. Its lounges are at a minimum; the dining room is rather simple, but fresh and clean; the bedrooms decorated with matching modern. The general effect is one of comfort in immaculate surroundings. Bathless doubles are 75 DM ($24.75); with shower or bath, 100 DM ($33). Singles with hot and cold running water cost 45 DM ($14.85); singles with bath, 70 DM

($23.10). It's difficult getting in during June, July, August, and February, as German tourists reserve then, knowing this one's a good bargain. Parking is available. In the basement is one of the Wienerwald restaurants.

BUDGET HOTELS: Drei Raben, 63 Königstrasse (tel. 20-45-83), is a good place to consider. It offers a comfortable bed in a clean room. This modest little establishment with 41 beds is owned and run by Herr and Frau Deibel. One block from the station, it's entered from a side street. A three-passenger elevator takes you to the bedrooms upstairs. All bedrooms have color TV, radio/alarm, mini-bar, and direct-dial phone. Singles rent for 95 DM ($31.35) with bath/shower and toilet, while doubles go for 105 DM ($34.65) to 140 DM ($46.20) with the same plumbing. Breakfast is included in the tariffs. English is spoken. About 60 yards from the hotel is a parking lot.

The **Bavarian-American Hotel,** on the Bahnhofplatz, 3 Bahnhofstrasse, directly opposite the main train station, accommodates persons carrying a United States armed services ID card. Priority is to military personnel on permanent change-of-duty orders, then to personnel on temporary-duty orders, and others involved in travel for such service-connected matters as hospital appointments and leave. Requests may be made to be placed on a stand-by waiting list, but no guarantee can be made until the day of arrival at the hotel. Rates, payable only in American dollars, are $18 to $25 per person, depending on the room. An American buffet breakfast is included in the prices. Advance payment of room rates is mandatory. There is a full-service restaurant and bar, laundry facilities, and a small convenience store. Correspondence may be addressed to: Bavarian American Hotel, Nürnberg, APO New York 09696, or 3 Bahnhofstrasse, 8500 Nürnberg, W. Germany. Telephones are: Country Code (49) 0911-23440; military, 2621-7249. Space is limited during the peak summer months.

THE TOP RESTAURANTS: Essigbrätlein, 3 Weinmarkt (tel. 22-51-31), is one of the outstanding gourmet restaurants in Germany, and is actually the number one in Nürnberg. It's owned by a distinguished restaurateur, Heinzrolf M. Schmitt, who for many years operated the famous Goldenes Posthorn. All the German magazines and newspapers have written about Herr Schmitt's wife, Claudia Simone Schmitt, who is hailed as Germany's most outstanding young female chef de cuisine. She has made frequent appearances on TV and radio.

Mr. and Mrs. Schmitt serve nightly from 7 p.m. to 1 a.m., offering guests a gourmet menu likely to cost from 60 DM ($19.80) to 110 DM ($36.30), including many small courses. Everything is cooked to order, and only the best and freshest produce from the market is used.

At the entrance level is room for only 25 diners. Up a flight, the next floor is a library and cocktail lounge with a private gastronomic museum. You'll find many antiques and decorations, unique in a restaurant in Germany. In summer a small garden restaurant is opened in front of the house, right in the Old Town. The house dates back to 1550, when it was mentioned for the first time in a chronicle of the city. It is the oldest original restaurant in Nürnberg, and was a favorite meeting place of wine merchants. The cuisine today harmoniously blends local and regional recipes with exciting offerings from the nouvelle cuisine. Reservations are imperative, incidentally. The place is closed Sunday. In the cellar is a wine bistro with small dishes, which also come from the kitchen of Claudia Simone Schmitt. You can order wine or champagne in this historic former meeting place of the wine merchants of Nürnberg.

Goldenes Posthorn, 2 Glöckleinsgasse (tel. 22-51-53), is lodged in a building whose history goes back to 1498. However, the present structure was rebuilt after destruction in 1960. Once one of Germany's most famous restaurants, it today offers an Egyptian-Oriental cuisine. The restaurant is run by Nosshi A. Malak. He and his head chef have received many medals and awards from different culinary experts all over Europe. Specialties of their kitchen are an Egyptian lamb filet flamed in date liqueur and an unusually good sheetfish flavored with saffron-truffles and served with gourmet rice. Two gourmet menus and a Patrician Feast (a typical menu from the time of Hans Sachs and Albrecht Dürer) are offered. There is a fine wine list with vintages dating back to 1886. A waiter will explain this and other specialties of the house for your consideration. Meals range in price from about 42 DM ($13.86) to 100 DM ($33). The restaurant is open all week from 11 a.m. to 2:30 p.m. and 6 to 11:30 p.m. It's closed Sunday. At the attractive cocktail bar on the second floor you can enjoy soft music and dancing.

Nassauer Keller, 2 Karolinenstrasse (tel. 22-59-67), occupies the cellar of one of the most romantic buildings in Nürnberg, opposite the Church of St. Lorenz. It features an original cuisine, specializing in trout and game in season. Main dishes include wienerschnitzel Cordon Bleu or filet of venison with mushrooms and cranberries. Meals range from 25 DM ($8.25) to 45 DM ($14.85). Closed Sunday.

MIDDLE-BRACKET DINING: Zum Waffenschmied, 22 Obere Schmiedgasse
(tel. 22-58-59), is attractively decorated with naturally aged paneling, mustard-colored walls, and bright napery. This restaurant serves traditional Franconian food to the dozens of local Nürnbergers who show up regularly. Chef Herman Schiller can cook an entire roast pig as easily as he can concoct, for example, Norwegian trout served with a sauce of wild mushrooms and cream, grilled scampi, roast Aberdeen steer, Bresse hen with fresh vegetables, and a rack of lamb with rosemary. Food is served from 11 a.m. to midnight, and a complete meal costs from 35 DM ($11.55) to 75 DM ($24.75). The restaurant lies conveniently between Albrecht Dürer house and the Kaiserburg.

BUDGET DINING: Bimbala vo Laff, 24-26 Bergstrasse (tel. 22-59-41), stands
next to the old Nürnberg Castle. Here you will find a very charming and typical old Franconian restaurant, serving such local specialties as potato pancakes, Nürnberg sausages, homemade cheese, and many more delicacies. For my money, it has the best beer in town: Arnold Bier Pils and Dunkel fresh from the barrel. Expect to spend anywhere from 18 DM ($5.94). The owner, Werner Becker, will entertain you with his guitar and by singing folk songs.

Weinhaus Steichele, 2 Knorrstrasse (tel. 20-43-78), was previously recommended as a hotel. But it also has the finest and tastiest 26-DM ($8.58) set dinner in all of Nürnberg. That's reason enough to visit, even if you're not staying in one of its bedrooms. The walls are covered with polished copper pots. Antique display cases are lit from within, and the weathered paneling is burnished to a ruddy glow. Hanging chandeliers carved into double-tailed sea monsters, salty mariners, and mythical beasts evoke some Teutonic legend. The Franconian specialties are a delight, backed up by a superb wine list.

Böhms Herrenkeller, 19 Theatergasse (tel. 22-44-65). Parts of this weinstube date from 1499, with later additions completed in 1948. You'll get a feeling of history here as you sample the well-rounded collection of wines and the straightforward gutbürgerlich cookery. A fixed-price menu begins at 20 DM ($6.60) going up to 50 DM ($16.50). The cellar is open from 11:30 a.m. to 2 p.m. and 5:30 to 10 p.m., although drinks and cold plates are served until midnight. It's closed on Sunday evening.

Heilig-Geist-Spital, 12 Spitalgasse (tel. 22-17-61), is an old tavern of dark woods, entered through an arcade near the river. It is Nürnberg's largest historical wine house. Carp, often prepared french-fried, is a specialty, and it's priced according to weight. The wine is abundant and excellent, with more than 100 different vintages to go with the typically Franconian specialties. Main dishes are hearty and filling, and not too expensive. In season you can order a leg of venison with noodles and berries. Everything goes down easier with a pitcher of wine. Meals cost from 18 DM ($5.94) to 60 DM ($19.80).

Historische Bratwurstküche, im Handwerkerhof (tel. 22-76-25), lies in the "village" of crafts people. If you want to try bratwurst in all its variations before leaving Nürnberg, this is the place to do it. The kitchen prepares a six-course meal of bratwurst as a main course, with traditional side dishes, for a surprisingly low price of 8.50 DM ($2.81). It's served on a tin plate. Since wurst is the perfect food to eat with beer, you'll enjoy sampling some of the brews on tap here, while admiring the craftsmanship of the room around you which dates from the Middle Ages. More expensive fixed-price meals are available as well, costing from 20 DM ($6.60). Be careful that you don't spend your entire afternoon on the sun terrace here—it's that tempting.

Bratwurst-Häusle, 1 Rathausplatz (tel. 22-76-95). Because it's opposite the Town Hall, you might want to visit this sausage restaurant on a luncheon stopover as you explore historic Nürnberg. In winter, you'll find an open hearth to warm you from the Franconian snows, and in summer, a refreshingly cool retreat from the heat. Fixed-price menus here begin at only 10 DM ($3.30), going up to 22 DM ($7.26), including a host of regional specialties, although most diners prefer a platter of bratwurst and beer, especially its large student clientele. The place is open from 9 a.m. to 9 p.m. every day except Sunday.

THE BEST CUISINE IN THE ENVIRONS: With one or two exceptions, you get your best food, not within the city center of Nürnberg, but in one of the rapidly developing suburbs.

Romantik-Restaurant Rottner, 15 Winterstrasse (tel. 61-20-32), at Grossreuth bei Schweinau, lies just a few kilometers outside Nürnberg. This half-timbered house with a garden terrace has green and red shutters and a chevron design carved into the door. It's one of the area's most popular and idyllic dining locales. Regional cookery is featured here, and specialties include wild game in season, all kinds of local fish (with other seafood flown in from the Mediterranean), and asparagus in the spring. Fixed-price menus, served in an ambience of wood paneling and colorful napery, cost from 40 DM ($13.20) to 80 DM ($26.40), the latter for a gourmet repast. They serve from 10 a.m. to 1 a.m. but are closed Saturday for lunch and all day on Sunday. They also shut down for four weeks in August and for a very long Christmas and New Year's holiday.

Lutzgarten, 113 Grossreuther Strasse (tel. 35-80-00), at Grossreuth. Every three weeks the menu here changes completely, so don't expect to find anything you read in this review. What doesn't change, however, is the historical ambience of this very old restaurant, where the chef prepares a few traditional dishes along with a delectable choice of nouvelle cuisine specialties, including a rack of lamb in a peppered puff pastry and homemade pâté of goose liver with an essence of fresh tomatoes. Be prepared to spend from 40 DM ($13.20) to 75 DM ($24.75) for a complete meal. Since there are only 13 tables, it is imperative to reserve a table. The restaurant closes annually sometime in January. Otherwise, it serves from noon to 2:30 p.m. and 6 to 10 p.m. every day except Sunday and holidays.

Gasthof Bammes, 63 Bucher Hauptstrasse (tel. 39-13-03), at Nürnberg 90-Buch. Residents of the city often select the fashionable address of this honest and straightforward establishment, decorated, as you would expect, in rustic colors with lots of wood paneling. Noonday meals are traditional gutbürgerlich, although the chefs take some imaginative risks at night by experimenting with nouvelle cuisine in an appealing combination of fresh produce with low-calorie ingredients. Sample dishes might include trout, mussels with wild rice, a gratinée of pike, among many specialties. Your bill is likely to run from 48 DM ($15.84) to 85 DM ($28.05). The restaurant is open from 11 a.m. to 2:30 p.m. and 5:30 to 9:30 p.m.; however, you can drink anytime from 11 a.m. to 10 p.m. It's closed on Sunday.

Alte Post, 164 Kraftshofer Hauptstrasse (tel. 39-10-63), at Kraftshof. If you're lucky enough to visit in summer, you'll find masses of flowers clustered in vases around the traditional wood-paneled decor of this gemütlich restaurant. There is where you join the Nürnberg housewife and her husband for specialties from the Franconian region—"just like grandmother made." These might include bratwurst in vinegar with onions, a "farmer's plate," or an assortment of sausages and meats sauteed together. Try, for example, a whole leg of veal with noodles and a salad, or if you're feeling elegant, asparagus (in spring), carp, or venison. Service is friendly, and the food is moderately priced, with meals beginning at 25 DM ($8.25), although you could spend far more of course. Hours are 11 a.m. to 2 p.m. and 5 p.m. to midnight; closed Wednesday and in October.

6. Würzburg

For the German, the South begins at Würzburg, the loveliest baroque city in all the country. It has been called a "rococo jewel box." Würzburg is the starting point for the Romantic Road, and is also at the junction of the most important motorways in Germany. The location is only 60 miles from Frankfurt.

THE SIGHTS: Remaining faithful to the Catholic church throughout the Reformation, this city on the Main has been called "the town of Madonnas" because of the more than 300 statues of its patron saint that adorn many of the house fronts. The best known statue of the Virgin is the *Patrona Franconiae,* a sweeping baroque Madonna which stands with the statues of other Franconian saints along the buttresses of the **Alt Mainbrüke,** Germany's second-oldest stone bridge, from the 15th century.

During the last few weeks of World War II, Würzburg was shattered by a series of bombing raids. In a miraculous rebuilding program, every major structure has been restored. Much of the original splendor of the city was because of the efforts of one man—the greatest master of the German baroque, Balthasar Neumann (1687–1753). As court architect to the prince-bishop of Würzburg, his major accomplishment is the pride of the entire baroque world, the Residence.

The Residence

Begun in 1720 to satisfy the passion for elegance and splendor of the Prince-Bishop Johann Philipp Franz von Schönborn, this palace is the last and finest of a long line of baroque castles built in Bavaria in the 17th and 18th centuries. Completed within 24 years, the great horseshoe-shaped edifice was the joint effort of the best Viennese, French, and German architects working under the leadership of Neumann. Because it was built in such a short time, the castle shows a unity of purpose and design not usually evident in buildings of such size.

Leading upward from the vestibule at the center of the castle is the **Treppenhaus** (staircase), standing detached in the lower hall and branching into twin stairways at a landing halfway to the second floor. This masterful creation by Neumann is the largest staircase in German baroque art. The high, rounded ceiling above it is decorated with a huge fresco by Tiepolo. At the center, Apollo is seen ascending to the zenith of the vault. The surrounding themes represent the four corners of the world, the seasons, and the signs of the zodiac. The illusion of the painting is so thorough it appears to be overflowing onto the walls of the upper hall.

At the top of the staircase you enter the White Hall, whose deliberate absence of color provides the ideal transition between the elaborate staircase and the connecting **Imperial Hall** (Kaisersaal), the culmination of the splendor of the entire castle. Based on Neumann's design, Tiepolo worked on this room in conjunction with the accomplished sculptor and stucco artist, Antonio Bossi. The walls of the hall are adorned with three-quarter marble pillars with gilded capitals. In the niches between the columns are original sculptures of Poseidon, Juno, Flora, and Apollo by Bossi. The highlight of the hall, however, is in the graceful combination of the white and gold stucco work, and the brilliantly colored paintings on the upper walls and ceiling. The work is so well done that it is difficult to tell where the paintings leave off and the relief work begins. On the flat part of the ceiling Tiepolo has depicted an allegorical scene of Apollo escorting the bride of Frederick Barbarossa to the emperor. The paintings between the upper, rounded windows glamorize important incidents in the history of Würzburg.

The other important attraction in the Residence is the **Court Chapel,** in the southwest section. Neumann placed the window-arches at oblique angles to coordinate the windows with the oval sections, thus creating a muted effect. The rectangular room is divided into five oval sections, three with domed ceilings. Colored marble columns define the sections, their guilded capitals enriching the ceiling frescoes by Byss. Bossi trimmed the vaulting and arches with intricate gilded stucco work. At the side altars, Tiepolo painted two important works— *The Fall of the Angels* on the left and *The Assumption of the Virgin* on the right.

The **Court Gardens,** at the south and east sides of the Residence, are entered through the gate next to the Court Chapel. The terraces are connected by walks and stairways and end in a large orangerie on the south side. The various gardens are laid out in geometric designs and studded with little statues by Johann Peter Wagner, plus several fountains spouting from sunken parterres.

In the 1945 bombings the roofs of such buildings as the Imperial Hall were pierced. Rain could easily have damaged the magnificent Tiepolo ceiling. And it would have had not Lt. John D. Skilton, a U.S. Army officer, intervened. He arranged for lumber to be shipped down the Main, and at Heidingsfeld he set up a sawmill, which turned out the planking needed to cover the roofs. The lieutenant also personally financed the whole operation, and anyone who goes to Würzburg today can be grateful for his foresight and generosity.

From April through September you can visit the Residence daily from 9 a.m. to 5 p.m. During the winter, hours are reduced to 10 a.m. to 4 p.m. Closed Monday throughout the year. Admission is 4 DM ($1.32). During the summer the Mozart Festival is held in the upper halls. (For information, phone 5-27-43).

The Marienberg Fortress

The Marienberg Fortress, over the stone bridge from the Old Town, was the residence of the prince-bishops from 1253 to 1720, when the transition was made to the more elegant "Residence." Although portions of the stronghold have been restored, the combination of age and wartime destruction has taken a serious toll on its thick walls and once impenetrable ramparts. But what remains is worth a visit. One of the oldest churches in Germany, the **Marienkirche,** from the eighth century, stands within its walls. In the former arsenal and Echter bulwark, to the right of the first courtyard, is the **Main-Franconian Museum,** housed here since 1946. A treasure house, the museum contains a history of Würzburg in art, from marble epitaphs of the prince-bishops to a carved wood model of the town in 1525. Works by the greatest artists engaged by patrons of Würzburg art are included here—a well-known collection of sculptures by Tilman Riemenschneider, including his *Adam and Eve,* paintings by Tiepolo, sculptures by Peter Wagner, and sandstone figures from the rococo gardens of the prince-bishops' summer palace. A further tribute to one of the few industries of the city, that of winemaking, is paid in the presshouse, the former vaults of the fortress. Historic casks and carved cask bases and a large collection of glasses and goblets make a conclusion to the museum and castle tour. The fortress is open daily, except Monday, from 9 a.m. to 5 p.m. (from 10 a.m. to 4 p.m. in winter). Admission is 1.50 DM (50¢). The museum, entered separately, is open from 10 a.m. to 5 p.m. (from 10 a.m. to 4 p.m. in winter). The charge here is 2.50 DM (83¢).

Other Sights

The **Cathedral of St. Kilian** (Dom) was begun in 1045, and it was the fourth-largest Romanesque church in Germany. The east towers dated from 1237, and the interior was adorned with High Baroque stucco work after 1700. The Dom is dedicated to St. Kilian, who was the Irish missionary to Franconia in the seventh century. Destroyed in the early spring bombings of 1945, the Dom has been rebuilt, as it was formerly. The baroque stucco work in the cross aisle and the choir has been preserved. The imposing row of bishops' tombs begins with Gottfried von Spitzenberg (circa 1190). Look for such Franconian works of art as tombstones by Riemenschneider.

Few visitors leave Würzburg without making the drive up to the baroque hilltop church, the bulb-topped **Käppele.** Often visited by pilgrims, this church was erected by Neumann in the mid-18th century. It has splendid interior stucco work by J. M. Feichtmayr, along with frescoes by Matthäus Günther. But it isn't to see the church so much that foreign visitors come here. It's for the view over the town of Würzburg, with its vine-covered hills and, in the far distance, the Marienberg Fortress.

The most interesting excursion in the area is to **Veitschöchheim,** a distance of about five miles. You can take a Main River excursion to this summer retreat of the prince-archbishops of the 18th century. The trip lasts about 30 minutes. The park, like Würzburg itself, is a rococo jewel box. The Parnassus group, carved in the mid-18th century, stands in the center of the lake, depicting Apollo and the Muses. It is open in summer from 9 a.m. to noon and 1 to 5:30 p.m. daily except Monday, charging 2 DM (66¢) for admission.

THE TOP HOTEL: Rebstock, 7 Neubaustrasse (tel. 5-00-75), is unique and impressive, worth a detour for a stopover for a night or two. Housed in a palace, it is decorated with style and flair. The facade is attractive, with its neoclassic pilasters, baroque plaster window trim, and a steep roof studded with tiny dormers. Through a classic doorway, you enter a wide foyer adorned with carved wooden doors and an old Spanish sea chest. A red carpet guides the way to the reception area.

The interior is splashy in a tasteful way, using ingenuity. Some of the best of contemporary furnishings have been well coordinated with the old. The main parquet-floor restaurant has been entirely redecorated. The wooden ceiling, hand-painted, is indirectly lighted. The gourmet is served here from delicate dishes prepared by master cooks. The Fränkische Weinstube comes with oak beams, stark-white walls, wooden chairs matching the ceiling, wooden tables, and a gilded baroque painting along with a carved Madonna. Here, guests gather for local wine and meals.

The bedrooms are equipped with wall-to-wall draperies and matching sofas, a pair of deep armchairs, along with a bare wood coffee table. Baths are colorfully tiled. Singles range in price from 125 DM ($41.25) to 164 DM ($54.12); twin-bedded rooms, 195 DM ($64.35) to 277 DM ($91.41). A breakfast buffet, included, is served in the courtyard under a trellis, next to a splashing fountain.

MIDDLE-BRACKET HOTELS: Amberger, 17 Ludwigstrasse (tel. 5-01-79). The color scheme on the outside of this family-run hotel is cream and coffee, and if you like that combination you'll enjoy drinking the real thing in the comfortable public rooms inside. They are high-ceilinged, with wood moldings set prominently into the corners. The bedrooms on the upper floors usually have one inwardly sloping wall. They are comfortable, with tiles in the modern baths and earth colors predominating. The hotel is named after the family that owns it. They charge from 90 DM ($29.70) to 115 DM ($37.95) in a single and from 120 DM ($39.60) to 195 DM ($64.35) in a double, breakfast included. You'll be close to the center of town, near the Berliner Ring.

Hotel and Weinrestaurant Schloss Steinburg, auf den Steinburg (tel. 9-30-61). This turreted castle sprawls, with its outbuildings, amid a cluster of trees, standing high on a hill overlooking Würzburg, about four miles away. From the sun terrace guests appreciate the view of the Main River, the acres of vineyards surrounding the property, and the web of rail lines carrying their cargoes far into the distance. The foundations of this schloss date from the 13th century, but the castle as you see it now was largely rebuilt around 1900. Today the Bavarian furnishings include several wall tapestries, Oriental rugs, and a scattering of 19th-century antiques. The comfortable bedrooms sometimes have parquet floors and a country nostalgia. With breakfast included, the single rate ranges from 85 DM ($28.05) to 105 DM ($34.65), while doubles go for 120 DM ($39.60) to 150 DM ($49.50). Half board can be arranged for another 30 DM ($9.90) per person daily. The hotel has a sauna, as well as an open-air pool covered with a canopy. The competent staff is directed by Franz Bezold.

Schönleber, 5 Theaterstrasse (tel. 1-20-68). Thirty-four rooms lie behind the salmon-colored facade of this family hotel in the central part of historic Würzburg. The ground floor is rented to boutiques, which monopolize the two enormous arched windows facing the sidewalk. But the upper floors are completely devoted to the hotel, which offers smallish but comfortable rooms with a variety of plumbing options. Singles rent for 44 DM ($14.52) to 65 DM ($21.45), while doubles cost 80 DM ($26.40) to 110 DM ($36.30).

Walfisch, 5 am Pleidenturm (tel. 5-00-55). The logo of this appealing guest house is a smiling whale with a laughing cherub on its back. The cherub is holding a bunch of grapes, which is an appropriate reminder that the weinstube here serves a good selection of wines and generous portions of traditional Germanic food in its timbered but modern dining room. You'll be able to gaze across the Main from the windows of your bedroom, seeing much of the old town as far as Marienberg Castle high on the opposite hill. Singles rent for 95 DM ($31.35) to 120 DM ($39.60), and doubles cost 130 DM ($42.90) to 170 DM ($56.10), breakfast included.

Würzburger Hof, 2 Barbarossaplatz (tel. 5-38-14), lies in the center of town. You'll recognize it by the gabled roofline which gracefully curves inward, and the enormous half-round windows on the ground floor. You'll move from the austere lobby area, the floor of which is covered with blue tiles, to one of the high-ceilinged bedrooms. Some of these units are carpeted and contain elegant white headboards and armoires, and many are decorated with garlands of fruit and flowers. The Heinen family are your hosts, and they will direct you to the central station, only a five-minute walk. Single rooms, depending on plumbing and other accessories, rent for 55 DM ($18.15) to 70 DM ($23.10), while doubles cost 90 DM ($29.70) to 170 DM ($56.10), breakfast included.

Franziskaner, 2 Franziskanerplatz (tel. 5-03-60). Sleek and internationally modern, this hotel has an illuminated sign in blue neon, identifying the sidewalk parapet leading to the door of your waiting car. However, even if you're on foot, you'll still receive a hearty welcome from Frau Lisl Englert-Stecher, who will charge you from 60 DM ($19.80) to 85 DM ($28.05) in a single and from 90 DM ($29.70) to 120 DM ($39.60) in a double, breakfast included. The lobby is attractively covered with black panels surrounded with natural wood, while the dining room has fine large windows looking out to the greenery beyond.

Central, 1 Koellikerstrasse (tel. 5-69-52). Five minutes from the rail station, this hotel is aptly named. It stands across the street from the Juliusspital. Although it presents an undistinguished facade to the street, it nonetheless offers quiet, clean, and comfortable rooms to visitors for 55 DM ($18.15) to 70 DM ($23.10) in a single and 85 DM ($28.05) to 110 DM ($36.30) in a double. Rooms have soundproof windows, and are pleasantly decorated in neutral colors with angular wooden furniture. The owners are helpful.

Bahnhof Hotel Excelsior, 2–3 Haugerring (tel. 5-04-84). Each of the rooms of this imposing hotel is differently designed, sometimes accessible via a labyrinthine series of upper hallways. The central core of the place contains a grandly proportioned garden courtyard awash with potted shrubs and flowers, visible through the fan-shaped windows of the attractive dining room. The management and staff are friendly and helpful, offering advice on how best to park on the traffic-clogged streets in the neighborhood. The hotel is near the railway station, behind a classically inspired five-story facade. Most of the comfortable bedrooms contain a private bath, phone, mini-bar, and TV. Singles range from 55 DM ($18.15) to 110 DM ($36.30), while doubles cost between 110 DM ($33) and 190 DM ($62.70), including a breakfast buffet.

Hotel Alter Kranen, 11 Kärrnergasse (tel. 5-00-39), occupies one of a long row of five-story houses set on the quay next to the river. Its yellow facade is highlighted with country-style stencils that are set like shutters between each of the snugly weatherproof windows. Inside you'll find a warmly comfortable contemporary environment filled with thick upholstery and gleaming exposed wood. Each of the accommodations has a private bath, radio, TV connection, and self-dial phone. With breakfast included, singles cost from 70 DM ($23.10), and doubles going for 120 DM ($39.60). This hotel appreciates advance reservations.

A BUDGET HOTEL: **Gasthof Greifenstein,** 1 Häfnergasse (tel. 5-16-65), is recommendable if you want the good simple life. It's a true tavern, abounding in village atmosphere, just off the Marienkapelle with its colorful food market. The dining room tavern is stage center, and the upper-floor bedrooms have a private entrance. The Greifenstein is easy to spot, with its shutters and window boxes dropping with bright geraniums. All rooms have basins with hot and cold running water, and some contain private bath. Singles cost from 50 DM ($16.50). Doubles run from 70 DM ($23.10), priced according to size and location. If you prefer more modern accommodations, you can ask to be booked into the new wing, offering some of the most comfortable rooms in Würzburg. Forty-five of these contain complete private bath, and rent for 110 DM ($36.30) to 135 DM ($44.55), including breakfast. An underground parking garage provides space for the cars of hotel guests. For a hearty Germanic cuisine, the restaurant is economical. A city parking space is nearby. The innkeeper is Adolf Schraud.

St. Josef, 28 Semmelstrasse (tel. 5-31-41), has long been recognized as one of the best of the budget accommodations in the Old Town. Its owner, Karl Siedler, has been successful in bringing it up to date. Of its 38 pleasantly and comfortably furnished bedrooms, a total of 22 contain private bath or shower along with a toilet. Singles, depending on the plumbing, begin at a low of 50 DM ($16.50), climbing to 70 DM ($23.10). Likewise, doubles range from a low of 80 DM ($26.40) to a high of 110 DM ($36.30). The rooms are well maintained, and breakfast is served in a large room—it's a good one, but the only meal offered. You'll be directed to the many weinstuben nearby, or you can pick a dining choice from the reviews coming up. If you're driving, you can park in a garage nearby, but it'll cost you. Fresh flowers add a personalized touch to this well-run establishment.

WHERE TO DINE: The town has numerous weinstuben, where most of the nightlife occurs. Try a local specialty, zwiebelkuchen, which is like a quiche Lorraine, and you should also look for a fish specialty, meefischle. The white Franconian wines go well with the local sausages.

Wein-und-Fischhaus Schiffbäuerin, 7 Katzengasse (tel. 4-24-87), is one of the best restaurants in the region. A combined wine house and fish restaurant, it is across the river in an old half-timbered building on a narrow street. The situation is about one minute from the old bridge. The house specializes in pike, carp, char, tench, trout, wels, and eel (blue grilled or frite). Most of these dishes are priced per 100 grams. Soup specialties are fish, snail, lobster, and french onion. Food is served from 11 a.m. to 2:30 p.m. and 5:30 p.m. to 9:30 p.m. Meals cost around 30 DM ($9.90) and up. The restaurant is closed Sunday evening and all day Monday, and from mid-July to mid-August.

The **Ratskeller,** 1 Langgasse (tel. 1-30-21), is not only an interesting place to visit, but it also serves tasty Franconian specialties at reasonable prices. Country cookery is an art here. Mr. and Mrs. Messer, your English-speaking hosts, will help you with menu selections, which in season might be game. They also specialize in the local beer and the famous Franconian white wines. Meals range in price from 22 DM ($7.26) to 45 DM ($14.85). They are closed from mid-January until after the first week in February. The cellar is part of the Town Hall in downtown Würzburg, near the old stone bridge.

Bürgerspital-Weinstuben, 19 Theaterstrasse (tel. 1-38-61), near the Stadtheatre, is a high-ceilinged restaurant which is wide and long enough for echoes to reverberate when it's empty, which it almost never is. The floors are gleaming blond wood, and the arched plasterwork on the ceiling is painted a clear white. The overall effect is lovely, and the diners chattering intimately together certainly give the impression of a fun time in Old Würzburg. Wines here are superb, and the chef specializes in typically Franconian dishes, a meal costing a modest 15 DM ($4.95), going up to 30 DM ($9.90). Hours are 9 a.m. till midnight every day but Tuesday. It's closed mid-July to mid-August.

Weinstuben Juliusspital, 19 Juliuspromenade (tel. 5-40-80), is one of the best known of the Franconian wine taverns of Würzburg. It is traditionally decorated with paneling and the beamed ceiling you've come to expect. The place is distinguished by its friendly service and the wide range of its regional dishes. A good meal can be ordered here for only 15 DM ($4.95), and even if you're being extravagant, it's unlikely that you'll spend more than 35 DM ($11.55). Service is friendly if rushed, and they open the doors early in the morning and keep them that way until late at night—that is, except Wednesday and all of February when the staff takes a much-needed break.

Backöfele, 2 Ursulinergasse (tel. 5-90-59). There has been a tavern at this address for the past 500 years, and since it's a short walk to both the Residenz and the Rathaus, you'll probably include it for at least one of your meals in

Würzburg. Even the locals don't really know whether to call it a beer hall, a wine cellar, or a restaurant. The family that owns it doesn't worry about the label. All that matters to them is that traditional food is served, that it's well prepared, and that it's dished up in copious quantities. Menu items include all kinds of bratwurst with cabbage and onions, ham casseroles, blue pike, pig knuckles, and ribs with sauteed cabbage. A fixed menu of the day will cost from 12 DM ($3.96) to 25 DM ($8.25). They're open for drinks from 4 p.m. to 12:30 a.m. Grilled food is offered between 6 and 11 p.m.

Mühlenhof-Daxbaude, 205 Frankenstrasse (tel. 2-10-01), on the outskirts at Versbach, is so ancient that historians have traced the names of other weinstuben which have stood on this site since the Middle Ages. (They've already counted three.) Menus, beginning at 30 DM ($9.90), are offered in the paneled and beamed dining room. The cuisine usually consists of traditional Franconian specialties, including dishes of game, veal, pork, and fish. Service is from 7 a.m. until midnight every day except for Monday lunch. They also rent out 34 bedrooms, ranging in price from 70 DM ($23.10) to 125 DM ($41.25) in a single, 95 DM ($31.35) to 155 DM ($51.15) in a double, including breakfast.

Zur Stadt Mainz, 39 Semmelstrasse (tel. 5-31-55). The facade of this 500-year-old guest house looks like an elaborately iced wedding cake, with garlands of flowers, stucco bunting, and turquoise medallions containing portraits of elegant ladies and the mustachioed pirates waiting to ravish them. With a facade that elaborate (the only color used is lilac), the owners probably decided that a sign wasn't necessary. All that identifies this establishment is a discreet "39" and a small but elaborate hook holding a red-and-white heraldic shield over the street. Since 1430 local residents have come here to savor such delights as their legendary oxtail stew or roasted spare ribs. They offer the best table d'hôte meal in town, costing 25 DM ($8.25), an exceptional bargain for what you get. The restaurant is open from 6:30 a.m. to midnight every day except Monday and holidays. It shuts down from December 20 to January 20. The Stadt Mainz also offers one of the best bargain accommodations in Würzburg, with 20 rooms renting for 35 DM ($11.55) to 40 DM ($13.20) in a single, 55 DM ($18.15) to 65 DM ($21.45) in a double.

Weinhaus zum Stachel, 1 Gressengasse (tel. 5-27-70). There are dozens of wine houses in Würzburg—many of them with integrity and character—but none of them is as old as this one, constructed in 1413. The seats and walls have been burnished by the homespun clothing of the hundreds of drinkers and diners who have sated their appetites here for the past 500 years, in a setting of heavy timbers, polished paneling, and conservative Franconian cookery. Meals, costing from 25 DM ($8.25) to 40 DM ($13.20), are served from 4 p.m. till 1 a.m. every day but Sunday (and from mid-August to mid-September). The portions are copious.

7. Bayreuth

If you arrive in this city on the Main during the late summer months, you may think the whole town has turned out to pay homage to the great operatic composer who once lived (and died) here. Indeed, for one month each year, everything else in Bayreuth stops for the **Wagner Festival.** Stores that usually display their own commercial items place recordings of Wagnerian operas in the windows. Landladies become so concerned that guests will be late for the evening's performance that they may offer to press a tuxedo or wash and iron a shirt.

THE SIGHTS: The operas of Wagner are dispensed like a musical Eucharist from the **Festspielhaus** at the northern edge of town. Pilgrims from all over the world gather here for performances in the theater, designed by the composer himself as the perfect setting for his epic operas. Although the opera house is far from perfect in appearance, it is an ideal Wagnerian theater, with a huge stage capable of swallowing up Valhalla, and beautifully balanced acoustics throughout the auditorium. When the festival was opened here in 1876 with the epic *Ring* cycle, it was so well received that the annual tradition has been carried on ever since. When the composer died, his wife, Cosima, daughter of Franz Liszt (who also is buried in Bayreuth), took over. Today Wagner's grandchildren produce the operas, with exciting staging and musicians brought here from all over.

The **Markgräfliches Opernhaus** (Margraves' Opera House), although not as large or as acoustically perfect as the house that Wagner built, is certainly a more glamorous structure from an architectural point of view. Considered the oldest and finest baroque theater in Germany, it was opened in 1748 by Bayreuth's patron of the arts, the Margravine Wilhelmine, sister of Frederick the Great. Behind its weathered wooden doors is a world of gilded canopies and columns, ornate sconces and chandeliers, and staircases leading to plush boxes. Today the opera house, which seats only 500 people, is used for Bayreuth's "second" festival, the **Franconian Weeks' Festival** usually held in late May. The greatest of the baroque composers—Mozart, Rameau, and Handel—would be pleased to see their works performed in such surroundings. If you don't catch a performance, you may visit the opera house April through September from 9 to 11:30 a.m. and 1:30 to 4:30 p.m., and October through March from 10 to 11:30 a.m. and 1:30 to 3 p.m. Guided tours, in German only, are conducted daily, except Monday, for 2 DM (66¢).

The **New Castle** (Neues Schloss), in the center of town a few blocks from the Margraves' Opera House, also shows the influence and enlightened taste of the talented and cultured Wilhelmine. Built in the mid-18th century after fire nearly destroyed the Old Palace, the castle has been well preserved in a baroque style, with a definite French touch. The apartments of Wilhelmine and her husband, the Margrave Friedrich, are decorated in a late rococo style, with period furnishings. The castle also contains the **Regional Historical Museum** and **Bavarian Art Gallery,** with paintings. The various museums and apartments of the castle can be visited daily, except Monday. Hours, April through September, are 10 a.m. to 5 p.m.; October through March, from 10 a.m. to noon and 1:30 to 3:30 p.m. Admission is 2 DM (66¢). While touring the rooms, you should take the opportunity to wander through the adjacent court garden, planned in a natural, English style.

The margraves of Bayreuth also had a pleasure palace outside the city, the **Hermitage** (Schloss Eremitage), just three miles northeast of Bayreuth, reached via a road lined with chestnut trees planted in honor of Frederick the Great. This summer palace was built in 1718 as a retreat by Margrave Georg Wilhelm. The structure almost looks as if it were hewn out of a rock, but the interior again felt the baroque touch of Margravine Wilhelmine. Seek out the Japanese salon and the rococo music room. The castle is set in a park, full of formal as well as English-style gardens. The palace and gardens are open daily, except Monday, from 9 to 11:30 a.m. and 1 to 4:30 p.m. (in winter, from 10 to 11:30 a.m. and 1 to 2:30 p.m.). Admission is 1.50 DM (50¢). Telephone 9-25-61 for information.

UPPER-BRACKET HOTELS: Bayerischer Hof, 14 Bahnhofstrasse (tel. 2-20-81), is the leading Bayreuth hotel. It's near the railway station yet on a quiet street, with a small garden of weeping willows and a swimming pool. An elevator takes you on the fifth-floor roof-garden restaurant, overlooking the Festival House and the environs of Bayreuth. All in all, "The Hof" is a substantial hotel, combining contemporary furnishings with traditional. Some bedrooms have

French pieces; others are in Nordic modern. Bathless singles cost 55 DM ($18.15); with shower or bath, from 65 DM ($21.45) to 95 DM ($31.35). Bathless doubles go for 110 DM ($34.65), and doubles with shower or tub for 110 DM ($36.30) to 170 DM ($56.10). Breakfast is included. The Bayerischer Hof also has a hotel bar, indoor pool, sauna, and solarium.

Hotel Königshof, 23 Bahnhofstrasse (tel. 2-40-94). The stylish opulence of this hotel's gilded, paneled, and rococo interior hints at the kind of grandeur that might have appealed to Frederick the Great. The hotel's reverence for the decor of the 18th century appeals to the masses of Wagnerian opera lovers who flock to the establishment's formal dining room, where crystal chandeliers, gilt trim, and French-style armchairs complement the well-prepared meals and elaborate desserts. Fixed-price meals in the restaurant, where reservations are suggested, range between 30 DM ($9.90) and 95 DM ($31.35), depending on the seasonal availability of ingredients. Each of the 45 bedrooms is individually decorated, sometimes with a scattering of fine carpets and antique furniture. A breakfast buffet is included in the room prices: between 55 DM ($18.15) and 130 DM ($42.90) in a single, and 75 DM ($24.75) to 180 DM ($59.40) in a double.

BUDGET HOTELS: Am Hofgarten, 6 Lisztstrasse (tel. 6-90-06), is a private home on a residential street, with a rear garden opening onto the castle grounds. From some of the windows you can look down the street at Richard Wagner's former home and across the street at the former home of Franz Liszt. Ingeniously rebuilt, it provides personalized accommodations at attractive prices. The Bauernstube for drinks has a country theme, with alpine chairs and a wooden ceiling; the dining room is pine paneled, with a trio of picture windows. But best of all is the garden in the back, with its little terrace, lawn, and flowerbeds. The small bedrooms are decorated attractively. For example, one may be all white and pink, with Louis XV–style furniture, including a crystal chandelier; or an accommodation might be provincial, with a postered bed and a painted armoire. Bathless singles start as low as 55 DM ($18.15). With bath or shower, a single rents for 80 DM ($26.40). Bathless doubles run 85 DM ($28.05), rising to 130 DM ($42.90) with bath, breakfast included. The English-speaking manager, Irene Bettermann, will help you find your way around the town. Interest note: Look at a plaque on the house opposite am Hofgarten. It says that Franz Liszt lived there, and the street is named after him.

Goldener Anker, 6 Opernstrasse (tel. 6-55-00), is the unquestioned choice for opera enthusiasts, especially Wagner buffs. Next door to the Opera House, it has been "the hotel" for distinguished composers, singers, operatic stars, even maestros for more than 200 years. Framed photographs on the time-seasoned, oak-paneled walls are museum treasures. The guestbook includes such signatures as Richard Strauss, Elisabeth Schwarzkopf, Toscanini, Thomas Mann, Fritz Kreisler, Bruno Walter, William Saroyan, Patrice Chereau, and Lauritz Melchior. The inn is furnished with fine antiques and Oriental rugs. Your bed may be a towering wooden structure, or an elaborate brass. In rooms with private bath or shower, singles cost from 65 DM ($21.45), and doubles, from 105 DM ($34.65), these tariffs including breakfast, taxes, and the service charge. There are 28 bedrooms in all, each one different.

WHERE TO DINE: "Annecy," 11 Gabelsbergerstrasse (tel. 2-62-79), is a youthful-style restaurant with French wines and French specialties. They offer a choice of about a dozen main dishes every day, with three fixed-price menus ranging from 35 DM ($11.55) to 85 DM ($28.05). The food is good, the service attentive, and hours are 6 p.m. till midnight every day except Sunday.

Hotel Bayerischer Hof, 14 Bahnhofstrasse (tel. 2-20-81), already recommended as a hotel, is the major place to eat in town, offering you a selection of dining spots, with both French and international cooking. The Hans Sachs Stube, for example, is an air-conditioned replica of an old inn, with small private boxes. On the wall are pictures of famous singers who have performed in Bayreuth. The kitchen also turns out Franconian specialties, with nine daily specialties offered. Set meals are in the 30-DM ($9.90) to 55-DM ($18.15) bracket. Service is from 11:30 a.m. to 2 p.m. and 6 till 11 p.m. daily except Sunday.

GERMANY'S OLDEST CASTLE: Burghotel auf Burg Lauenstein, Lauenstein, near Ludwigsstadt (tel. 256), is a fairytale castle, the oldest in Germany, dating back to 915 when it was built as a sprawling fortress. Approached by a narrow and winding road, it stands like a crown on the mountain, often veiled by clouds. The location near the East German border is private, although it lies only 47 miles north of Bayreuth and 18½ miles from Kronach.

Acquired by the State of Bavaria and run by the Wagner family, the castle has a central core with stone towers, turrets, and a narrow moat. This is unused. The hotel is in the manor house which partially encircles the castle. The part in active use has recently been modernized, turning it into a simple yet comfortable hotel.

Its 22 bedrooms vary in size and character. Some have reproductions of provincial furniture and other hand-decorated pieces of the region. All rooms have good views. Several of the accommodations contain private bath; others share tower bathrooms with monumental tubs. Bathless singles cost 35 DM ($11.55), rising to 50 DM ($16.50) with shower. Bathless doubles are tabbed at 35 DM ($11.55) per person, rising to 48 DM ($15.84) per person with shower. Meals are regional and well prepared. Half board costs another 18 DM ($5.94) per person daily.

There is no grand hall or lounge with coats of armor. But there is a dining room, with mountain-style furnishings. Weather permitting, meals are served on a covered veranda with a panoramic view of the neighboring Franconian woods. The castle shuts down in February.

8. Regensburg

The architecture that remains from its 2000 years of history testifies to the past grandeur of the city on the Danube which, by the beginning of the Gothic era, had already reached its peak. Fortunately, the wars of this century did not touch Regensburg, and its buildings and towers offer an unspoiled look into history. Of its ancient structures many are not just museum pieces, but are actually in use today. The best example of this is the **Stone Bridge,** built in 1146 on 16 huge arches, in continuous service for more than 800 years.

THE SIGHTS: Regensburg is a city of churches—and for good reason. When Christianity was introduced into Germany, this city became the focal point from which the religion spread throughout the country and even into Central Europe via the Danube. The most majestic of these churches is the towering **St. Peter's Cathedral,** on the Domplatz. Begun in the 13th century on the site of an earlier Carolingian church, it was inspired by the French Gothic style. Because of its construction of easily corroded limestone and green sandstone, the edifice is constantly being renewed and renovated. The massive spires of the two western towers, only added in the mid-19th century, were almost completely replaced in 1955 with a more durable material. Most impressive are the well-preserved stained-glass windows in the high choir (14th century) and south transept (13th century). Most of the pillar sculptures on the aisles of the nave were made in the cathedral workshop in the mid-14th century. The two little sculptures in the niches on opposite sides of the main entrance (inside the cathedral) are called "The Devil" and "The Devil's Grandmother's" by the townsfolk.

You can also visit the treasures of the cathedral, the **Domschatzmuseum,** 3 Krauterermarkt (tel. 59-66-199), which shows goldsmith works and splendid textiles from the 11th to the 19th centuries. Entrance is through a portal at the northern nave in the cathedral. It is open April to October on Tuesday through Saturday, 10 a.m. to 5 p.m.; on Sunday from 11:30 a.m. to 5 p.m.; closed Monday. During the winter months it is generally open only on Friday and Saturday from 10 a.m. to 4 p.m. and on Sunday from 11:30 to 4 p.m. It's closed in November. The charge is 2 DM (66¢).

A museum of the Diocese of Regensburg, **Diözesanmuseum,** 1 Emmeramsplatz (tel. 5-10-68), occupies the ancient outlying buildings of the chapter of Obermünster, dating from about 1470. Here is shown religious art, including sculptures, paintings, goldsmith works, and textiles from the 12th to the 19th centuries. The museum is open April to October on Tuesday through Sunday from 10 a.m. to 5 p.m.; closed Monday. During the winter months it's generally open only on weekends from 10 a.m. to 4 p.m. The charge is 2 DM (66¢).

Crossing the cathedral garden, you enter the **Cloister,** with its Romanesque All Saints' Chapel and St. Stephen's Church. The ancient frescoes on the walls of the chapel depict liturgical scenes from All Saints' Day. The 11th-century Ottonian church of St. Stephen contains an altar made of a hollowed limestone rock with openings connecting to a martyr's tomb. Although the cathedral is open during the day, you may visit the cloisters and St. Stephen's Church only with the regular guides. Visiting hours are mid-May until the end of September at 10 and 11 a.m., and 2 and 3 p.m. From October to March, tours are at 11 a.m. and 1 p.m. From April to mid-May, tours leave at 11 a.m. and 2 p.m. The charge is 3 DM (99¢).

Among the remnants of the Roman occupation of Regensburg, the ancient **Porta Praetoria,** behind the cathedral, is the most impressive, with its huge stones piled in the form of an arched gateway. Through the grille beside the eastern tower you can see the original level of the Roman street nearly ten feet below (which is why you often step down into the churches of Regensburg).

The city's **Municipal Museum** at Dachauplatz contains other relics of the Roman period, including the stone tablet marking the establishment of the garrison here in the second century, several Christian tombstones from that period, and a stone altar to the Roman god Mercury. It is open from 10 a.m. to 1 p.m. and 2 to 5 p.m. (until 4 p.m. off-season), charging an admission of 2 DM (66¢). It's closed on Sunday and Monday.

No town hall in Germany has been preserved better than Regensburg's **Altes Rathaus.** The Gothic structure, begun in the 13th century, contains a **Reichssaal** (Imperial Diet Hall), where the Perpetual Diet sat from 1663 to 1806. In the basement of the Town Hall are the dungeons, with the only torture chamber in Germany preserved in its original setting. The rooms and dungeons of the Rathaus are open daily. Admission is 2 DM (66¢). Guided tours are conducted weekdays at 9:30, 10:30, and 11:30 a.m., and 2, 3, and 4 p.m., costing 2 DM (66¢).

UPPER-BRACKET HOTELS: Parkhotel Maximilian, 28 Maximilianstrasse

(tel. 56-10-11). The next best thing to staying in one of Ludwig's palaces would be to anchor into this exquisitely renovated neorococo building, the facade and public rooms of which have been classified as a public monument. The day café inside is a Bavarian fantasy in soft colors, crystal chandeliers suspended high above the tables, and elaborate plaster detailing, sometimes illuminated with gilt paint. The main salon, with a ceiling that is supported by columns of polished red stone, continues the elegant theme of 18th-century opulence with 20th-century convenience. You'll find the steaks you've been missing in the Arizona steakhouse, where you can abandon the Bavarian theme and chow down on midwestern beef. There are also two weinstuben and a French restaurant serving a classical cuisine. Rooms are attractively furnished, with modern plumbing added, renting for 128 DM ($42.24) in a single and from 168 DM ($55.44) in a double, including breakfast.

Avia Hotel, 1 Frankenstrasse (tel. 4-20-93). The old city of Regensburg offers some strikingly modern hotels, of which the Avia is the leader. Composed of at least three architectural units, the hotel offers balconied rooms with views over a manicured garden, comfortable beds, Oriental rugs, and up-to-date plumbing. Singles go for 85 DM ($28.05) to 90 DM ($29.70), and doubles cost 110 DM ($36.30) to 130 DM ($42.90). Business persons tend to like it here, enjoying the restrained decor of earth colors with black accents and ample use of wood on the walls and ceilings.

MIDDLE-RANGE HOTELS: **Bischofshof am Dom,** 3 Krauteremarkt (tel. 5-90-86). Constructed as their ecclesiastical academy by the bishops of Regensburg in 1810, this building still gives off the vaguely monastic smell of a cloister. The vaulted ceiling in the dining room is supported by a single Romanesque column which dwarfs the modern wood chairs pulled up to the dozens of covered tables. The weinstube has a green tile oven, and the rest of the establishment looks like the unusual blend it is of 19th-century monastic with modern secular updates. One of Regensburg's most popular sun terraces lies behind this place, and you might want to sit at one of its checkered tablecloths enjoying a beer. Bedrooms are comfortable and attractively furnished, costing from 72 DM ($23.76) in a single and from 105 DM ($34.65) in a double, including breakfast.

St. Georg, 8 Karl-Stieler-Strasse (tel. 9-68-01). Slightly outside the city limits, this hotel lies between the autobahn and the historic center. You'll find this a family-run hotel of 59 rooms, where guests lodge in various parts of a compound, all of which are connected (but probably erected at different eras). The interior is decorated in a no-nonsense functional way, with some attempt to recreate gemütlichkeit in the shallow half timbers visible through the distressed stucco wall of the dining room. Singles go for 61 DM ($20.13) to 85 DM ($28.05), while doubles cost 102 DM ($33.66) to 140 DM ($46.20), breakfast included.

Kaiserhof am Dom, 10 Kramgasse (tel. 5-40-27), is housed in an old building with deep windows set at irregular intervals below the gabled roof with iron ice-catchers. The interior is nothing short of elegant. The beams supporting the dining room ceiling run a long distance between their exposed stone and stucco supports, and the fieldstone masonry of the weinkeller hints at the number of guests who have dined here over the centuries. From the sun terrace and from many of the hotel's windows, you'll have a view of the cathedral. The rooms, all of which contain shower and toilet, are soothingly lit and decorated in good taste. Including breakfast, rates are 112 DM ($36.96) in a double and 80 DM ($24.60) in a single. My favorite spot is the reading room with carved sandstone ribs supporting the plaster vaulted ceiling. The restaurant has earned more than a dozen gold medals. The owners have patented their special recipe for herb and cream sauce, which, if you ask for it, will be served with dozens of specialties they prepare from all over Germany. Meals range in price from 20 DM ($6.60) to 50 DM ($16.50), and service is from 10 a.m. to midnight.

Karmeliten, 1 Dachauplatz (tel. 5-43-08), is a hotel with 125 years of tradition, yet with a young, modern look. It's set on a square about three blocks from the river and a four-minute walk to the Dom, reached via an open-air fruit and vegetable market. The bedrooms, the public lounges, and the breakfast rooms are in a family style, renovated and comfortable. The restaurant, open from 6 p.m. to midnight, is in the 16th-century monastery cellars of the house, serving Spanish and German specialties. Set meals range in price from 20 DM ($6.60) to 30 DM ($9.90), and extensive à la carte listings are offered as well. Bathless singles cost 60 DM ($19.80), and those with bath rent for 85 DM ($28.05) to 96 DM ($31.60). Doubles cost 92 DM ($30.36) to 130 DM ($42.90), depending on the plumbing. Rates include breakfast, service, and tax.

A BUDGET HOTEL: Straubinger Hof, 33 Adolf-Schmetzer-Strasse (tel. 5-90-75). On a street corner at the eastern edge of Regensburg, this attractively unpretentious hotel has been in the same family for 60 years. The rooms are perfectly satisfactory, with lots of sunlight, unadorned wood-grained armoires, and pleasing color schemes. Inexpensive and satisfying meals are served in the dining room by the Schmid and the Rolf families. Breakfast is included in the room price. The more expensive units have self-contained bath, while the cheaper ones have only a sink. Singles rent for 40 DM ($13.20) to 65 DM ($21.45), while doubles cost 80 DM ($24.60) to 98 DM ($32.34). Triples go for 100 DM ($33) to 115 DM ($37.95).

WHERE TO DINE: Ratskeller, 1 Rathausplatz (tel. 5-17-77), is traditional and unspoiled. Here, you get some of the best meals for your money in Regensburg. Just five minutes from the Dom, this comfortable, middle-class establishment consists of two dining rooms, with vaulted ceilings, paneled walls, and painted crests. The cooking is good, in the Germanic tradition, although internationally inspired offerings are introduced to give added variety and flair. At your adjoining table you'll likely find a Regensburg matron taking time out between shopping sprees. The best buy is the set luncheon, ranging in price from 18 DM ($5.94) to 28 DM ($9.24). If you order à la carte, you might pay around 35 DM ($11.55) or more. Good, hearty Franconian soups are made here, followed by such offerings as veal schnitzel Cordon Bleu or perhaps, as an exotic touch, an Indonesian nasi-goreng. Or you can opt for the always-reliable entrecôte with french fries.

Historische Wurstküche, 3 Thundorfer Strasse (tel. 56-18-10). The owners here will tell you that this is one of the oldest bratwurst-stubes in Europe, and considering the age of Regensburg, that's not too far-fetched. Much of the decor here is original, so dining might be somewhat of a lesson in social history. The specialties of the house are potato soup, pork bratwurst, grilled meats over a wood fire, and other delicacies. You'll find three times as many seats on the ⁄sun terrace outside. The restaurant is inexpensive: meals average around 22 DM ($7.26). Hours are 8 a.m. to 7 p.m. every day except Sunday.

9. Passau

One reason for visiting this *Dreiflüssetadt* (town of three rivers) on the Austrian frontier is to take one of the numerous boat tours along the Danube and its tributaries, the Inn and Ilz Rivers, which join the Danube at Passau. The trips range from a one-hour, three-river tour to a steamer cruise downriver to Vienna. If you hold a Eurailpass, you can travel free on the **Erste Donau Dampfschiffahrts steamer,** which makes the run between Passau and Vienna. Your auto can't be carried, and food and drink are served on board. In Passau, call 33-0-35 for information. But before you wander off from this medieval city, you'll find it worthwhile to stop to see—

THE SIGHTS: The Old Town is built on a rocky spur of land formed by the confluence of the Inn and Danube, 75 miles downstream from Regensburg. To best appreciate its setting, cross the Danube to the **Veste Oberhaus,** a medieval episcopal fortress towering over the town and the river. Note how many of the houses are joined together by arches, giving them a unity of appearance. As you view the town, you can sense in its architecture that it is more closely allied to northern Italy and the Tyrolean Alps than to its sister cities to the north.

Dominating the scene are the twin towers of **St. Stephen's Cathedral.** The original Gothic plan of the church is still obvious in spite of its reconstruction in the 17th century in the style of grand baroque. Its most unusual feature is the octagonal dome over the intersection of the nave and transept. The interior of the cathedral is mainly Italian baroque—almost gaudy, with its many decorations and paintings. Of particular interest is the east wing, which remains from the Gothic period. The cathedral's newest addition is a huge organ, possibly the largest in the world, built in 1928 and placed in an 18th-century casing. Concerts are given every day at noon during the summer.

Below the cathedral, on the bank of the Danube, is the attractive Marketplace with its **Rathaus.** Dating from the 13th century, Passau's Town Hall is a colorful structure, its facade decorated with painted murals depicting the history of the town. Inside, the huge Knights' Hall contains two large 19th-century frescoes depicting incidents from the German epic, the legend of the Niebelungen.

WHERE TO STAY: **Passauer Wolf,** 6 Rindermarkt (tel. 3-40-46). The elegantly crafted baroque facade of this hotel on the banks of the Danube alternates a shell design with a motif of flowers on the rococo windows, which open onto an 18th-century church. The opposite side of the hotel is newer, but still designed to look like a watchtower, rising six stories above the pavement. Inside, you'll find modern and comfortable bedrooms, decorated in upholstered wood furniture and up-to-date plumbing, along with friendly service. Singles cost 80 DM ($26.40) a night, while doubles go for 120 DM ($39.60) to 150 DM ($49.50), with breakfast included. Units contain radio, TV, phone, and minibar.

Zum König, 2 Rindermarkt (tel. 3-40-98). The front of this mustard-colored, six-story hotel faces an asphalt street and an unlandscaped parking lot, but once you're inside, you'll find that the rear opens onto a manicured lawn with trees, a sun terrace, and a view of the Danube. The interior is warmly decorated in wood paneling and heavy timbers, and the bedrooms are clean, a bit sterile, but warm and comfortable nevertheless. Breakfast is included in the price of 60 DM ($19.80) in a single and 100 DM ($33) in a double. From the hotel it's only a five-minute walk to the Residenz and the cathedral.

Weisser Hase, 23 Ludwigstrasse (tel. 3-40-66), has been completely rebuilt. One would never know that it traces its history back to 1512. The only clue would be a pair of antique family portraits hanging over a tufted Victorian sofa in a little salon. The Weisser Hase is in the heart of Passau, off Ludwigsplatz, halfway between the Dom and the railway station. It straddles the peninsula, between the Danube and the Inn Rivers. The Weinstube has a Bavarian-Austrian decor, with much woodcarving, red table coverings, and provincial chairs. The accommodations are clean and comfortable, with modern furnishings. Bathless singles range in price from 45 DM ($14.85); bathless doubles go for 75 DM ($24.75). Singles with bath or shower cost from 78 DM ($25.74), while doubles with private bath or shower are 125 DM ($41.25), breakfast included.

Altstadthotel, 27–29 Bräugasse (tel. 3-34-51). The waters of the Danube, the Ilz, and the Inn converge at a point a few steps from the foundations of this lime- and cream-colored hotel. It's built in two interconnected sections, each of which merges tastefully with the surrounding buildings of the Old Town. Inside, guests find a well-maintained and plushly upholstered environment of white plaster accented with dark wood trim. Each of the comfortably furnished bedrooms has a private bath, phone, TV connection, and often a ceiling covered with well-polished planking crafted from knotty pine. Singles cost between 75 DM ($24.75) and 87 DM ($28.71), while doubles go for 125 DM ($41.25) to 140 DM ($46.20). Residents need only walk a few feet to reach the in-house pub, a popular gathering spot for locals. The hotel has two restaurants, and motorists can use the underground garage.

Schloss Ort, 11 Ort, am Dreiflusseck (tel. 3-40-73), is a remake of a 1250 castle, standing right on the banks of the Inn River, rising five stories directly from the water's edge. The most dramatic feature of the bedrooms is that they provide views of where the rivers converge. All is modern inside; chrome and plastic set the tone. But the situation is decidedly glamorous, the rooms fresh. Singles with shower cost 60 DM ($19.80). Doubles rise to 100 DM ($33) with private bath. Your morning meal is best when taken on the open terrace overlooking the Inn River. Riverboat excursions begin at the dock right at the foot of the schloss.

WHERE TO DINE: **Heilig-Geist-Stift-Schenke,** 4 Heiliggeistgasse (tel. 26-07), is a little inn born in 1358. It's easily found, across from the Hotel Weisser Hase, previously recommended. Many good and low-cost regional dishes emerge from its ancient kitchen, including Serbian bean soup. Typical main dishes include sirloin steak with french fries or a grilled pork cutlet. The Salzburger nockerl is definitely worth sampling for dessert. Menus range in price from 16 DM ($5.28) to 45 DM ($14.85), and hours are 10 a.m. to 1 p.m. and 5 p.m. till 1 a.m. It's closed Wednesday and in November.

LOWER SAXONY AND NORTH HESSE

THE WIDE EXPANSE between Frankfurt and Hamburg is probably Germany's most neglected tourist area, and yet it holds some of the most pleasant surprises for sightseeing. Some of the best preserved medieval timbered towns stand in the flatlands and rolling hills of Lower Saxony and North Hesse, as well as many of the major spas.

Extending from the Netherlands to the East German border, this area includes a wide variety in its landscape, from the busy port of Bremen to the isolation of the Lüneburg Heath. It even contains one of Germany's best winter resort areas, the **Harz Mountains.** These mountains and the flatlands around the Weser River nearby gave rise to some of the most familiar legends and fairy tales in Western literature.

I'll begin our tour of Lower Saxony and North Hesse with its most famous city, the Free and Hanseatic City of Bremen.

1. Bremen

Whether you arrive at "this ancient town by the gray river" by land, sea, or air, you are instantly aware that Bremen is closely tied to the sea. The sights and smells of coffee, cocoa, tropical fruit, lumber, and tobacco give this port city an international flavor. In the days of the transatlantic ocean crossing, most travelers disembarked at Bremerhaven, Bremen's sister port 40 miles up the Weser

River. Many visitors rush immediately off in all directions from the port, ignoring the treasure right under their noses—Bremen, second only to Hamburg among German ports.

Germany's oldest coastal city was already a significant port when it was made an episcopal see in 787. In the 11th century, under the progressive influence of Archbishop Adalbert, Bremen became known as the "Rome of the North." During the Middle Ages it was one of the strongest members of the Hanseatic League and remains one of Europe's most important port cities.

GETTING AROUND BREMEN: Tram tickets cost 2.80 DM (92¢) for a normal fare. You can also purchase a "go-as-you-please" ticket for 6 DM ($1.98), giving you ten trips. The basic taxi charge starts at 4 DM ($1.32).

Sightseeing tours of the city, in both English and German, depart from the central railway station, costing 13 DM ($4.29) for adults and 7 DM ($2.31) for children. From the beginning of May until the end of October they leave at 3 p.m. on weekdays, at 10 a.m. on Sunday. From November to April they leave only at 10:30 a.m. on Sunday. Tickets must be obtained at the tourist information kiosk, Verkehrsverein (tel. 36-36-1), opposite the central railway station. Its hours are 8 a.m. to 8 p.m. Monday to Thursday, to 10 p.m. on Friday, to 6 p.m. on Saturday, and from 9:30 a.m. to 3:30 p.m. on Sunday.

You can also ask at the tourist office about trips around the harbor, departing from the Martini Church jetty (a three-minute walk from the Marketplace along Böttcherstrasse), lasting 1¼ hours. From the end of March until the end of October they leave at 10 and 11:30 a.m., and at 1:30, 3:10, and 4:30 p.m.

ACCOMMODATIONS: Before we explore the impressive array of sights, let's see what Bremen holds in the way of accommodations.

A Deluxe Choice

Park Hotel Bremen, in Bürgerpark (tel. 34-08-555), is a peaceful world only five minutes by taxi from the heart of the city. Its situation is in a park setting where the life is restrained. The bedrooms vary from impressive suites to cozy singles, but all offer comfort, and many have a lake view. Single rooms with shower and toilet go for 170 DM ($56.10) to 235 DM ($77.50); doubles with bath and toilet range from 250 DM ($82.50) to 270 DM ($89.10). You can enjoy well-prepared meals in any of several dining rooms, including a New England-style grill. Many French dishes are included in the menu. The Halali Bar, with its open terrace in summer, is a good spot for drinks and relaxation. The English-speaking staff is noted for hospitable service.

The First-Class Bracket

Columbus, 5–7 Bahnhofsplatz (tel. 1-41-61), is an updated building across from the railway station. In the reading and cocktail lounge, a room-wide mural honors the hotel's namesake. The bedrooms, as well as the public rooms, combine reproductions of traditional furniture with good modern. A liberal decorative use of paintings, tapestries, and Oriental rugs gives a warm colorful touch. Soundproofing in the rooms cuts down the busy traffic noise on the street outside. A single with bath or shower costs 140 DM ($46.20) to 200 DM ($66). Doubles with bath and toilet go for 200 DM ($66) to 260 DM ($85.80). Breakfast is included.

The Middle Range

Hotel zur Post, 11 Bahnhofsplatz (tel. 1-80-31), may well be a close contender for Bremen's leading modern hotel. The present structure has had four ancestors, the first built in 1889. The latest renovation has created up-to-date accommodations. Singles with bath or shower cost 150 DM ($49.50) to 185 DM ($61.05) and doubles with bath are also 185 DM ($61.05). It's an ideal choice for train passengers, who can refresh themselves after their journey in the hotel's free swimming pool.

Überseehotel, 27 Wachtstrasse (tel. 32-01-97), doesn't look like a hotel, but it is, and a practical and efficient one at that. It occupies the top four floors of a business building a short block from the city center. Adjoining the Böttcherstrasse, it is a satisfactory combination of the new and the old. The bedrooms are efficient, and immaculate, many with sofas as well as desks. All rooms are equipped with bath or shower and toilet, mini-bar, and TV. The cost is 90 DM ($29.70) to 110 DM ($36.30) in a single, 115 DM ($37.95) to 150 DM ($49.50) in a double, all tariffs including a big buffet breakfast.

Bremer Hospiz, 18 Löningstrasse (tel. 32-16-68). This hotel is one of a long row of buildings a few blocks from the Hauptbahnhof. All of them are painted a dazzling white, which accentuates the low relief of the arched and ornamented windows. The hotel is identified by a double staircase welcoming guests from the sidewalk. Once inside, those guests find modern public rooms and a sun terrace overlooking a flowering garden. Singles rent for 95 DM ($31.35) to 105 DM ($34.65), while doubles cost 135 DM ($44.55) to 155 DM ($51.15). All units have bath or shower and toilet, and contain functional chairs, tables, and headboards. Breakfast is included in the rates.

Hotel Munte, am Stadtwald (tel. 21-20-63). You'll think you're in the country here, because this brick hotel fronts directly onto one of Bremen's biggest parks, the Burgerpark (an invigorating walk through the park will eventually lead to the Town Hall). Inside the hotel, you'll find a wood-ceilinged swimming pool with a sauna and massage table, a sympathetic weinstube (the Fox), a sunny dining room with a panoramic view of the woods, and clean and comfortable bedrooms decorated with woodland colors. Singles rent for 75 DM ($24.75) on the ground floor, 115 DM ($37.95) on the upper floors; and doubles cost 108 DM ($35.64) on the ground floor, 170 DM ($56.10) on the upper floors. All units contain private bath and come with a big breakfast.

The Budget Range

Residence, 42 Hohenlohestrasse (tel. 34-10-20). Advertised as a hotel with a Flemish ambience, the public rooms here are elegantly high-ceilinged, with polished and crisscrossed timbers supporting the chandeliered ceiling of the main salon. The building was probably at one time a private home, with half-timbering and the kind of recessed balconies where children and grandparents used to hold long conversations. You'll find a sunny breakfast room, a Nordic sauna, and singles renting for 55 DM ($18.15) to 75 DM ($24.75) and doubles going for 90 DM ($29.70) to 120 DM ($39.60). Not all of the units contain a private bath, however. Herman and Brigitte Straten are your hosts here, and are fluent in English.

DINING IN BREMEN: As a seaport, Bremen has developed its own style of cooking, concentrating much of its effort, naturally, on seafood from Scandinavia and the North Sea.

Deutsches Haus-Ratsstuben, 1 Am Markt (tel. 32-10-48), combines pure local color on a comfortable level with some of the best food in town. The six-story, high-gabled patrician building sits on the Marketplace, opposite the Ratskeller, directly facing the square. You dine on either of two levels, including the second-floor Ratsstuben. If the time is right, you may catch festive group singing, especially on Saturday night. The food is excellent, from the mock turtle soup to the creamy desserts. Meat dishes are usually fine. For seafood, try the sole meunière, priced according to weight. Meals range from 25 DM ($8.25) to 50 DM ($16.50). This restaurant is highly recommended for cuisine, atmosphere, and location.

The **Ratskeller,** am Markt, in the 500-year-old Rathaus (tel. 32-09-36), is one of Germany's most celebrated dining halls—and certainly one of the best. It's filled, especially on Saturday night, with the townspeople, who have adopted it as a social club. The wine list is outstanding, probably the longest list of German wines in the world. Some of the decorative wine kegs have actually contained wine for nearly 200 years. It's traditional for friends to gather in the evening over a good bottle of Mosel or Rhine wine. Beer is not served in the Ratskeller. Set lunches are served daily in the 18-DM ($5.94) to 25-DM ($8.25) range. The starred items on the menu are available at night only. You may prefer the Hubertus topf or the game ragoût with orange and vegetables. Rumpsteak is another favorite dish, as is the soup of the day. If you order à la carte at dinner, expect to spend from 25 DM ($8.25) to 60 DM ($19.80). Hours are 10 a.m. to midnight.

Martini Grill-Restaurant, 2 Böttcherstrasse (tel. 32-60-06), in keeping with the mood of the street where every building is an original, is as contemporary as the avant-garde theater next door (it lies just off the theater's lobby). The imaginative decor consists of a ceiling of crisscrossed sticks and a wall of pressed natural pebbles. Balloon lights hang above the tables. Halfway between the Marketplace and the Weser River, the restaurant is convenient to all the major sights, shopping, and of course, the theater. Fresh fish, much of it from Norway, is the specialty. The fresh North Sea plaice is priced according to weight; the heilbuttschnitte (halibut steak) is always available. The mock turtle soup is a delicious introduction to Bremenese cooking. Lighter eaters may prefer the bauern omelet with french fries. For a complete meal, expect to pay from 28 DM ($9.24) to 50 DM ($16.50). Closed Sunday.

Alte Gilde, 24 Ansgaritorstrasse (tel. 17-17-12), is housed in one of the most ornately decorated houses in Bremen. In spite of the new buildings surrounding it, the structure, with its gilt gargoyles and sea serpents, clings tenaciously to the past. The restaurant (entrance on Hutfilterstrasse) is in the vaulted cellar of the 17th-century structure. The house specialty is "Alte-Hanse Platte," reminiscent of Old Bremen, for two persons. For a safe, but typically German, choice, try the pork steak à la Kempinski with poached eggs and béarnaise sauce. The cost is 28 DM ($9.24) to 60 DM ($19.80) to dine here. Closed Sunday and May to September.

Grashoff's Bistro & Weinbar, 80 Contrescarpe, Hillmann Passage (tel. 1-47-49), is an intimate French restaurant serving many delicacies produced from ingredients imported every day from Paris. Two men, Rüdiger König and Jürgen Schmidt, are responsible for the wealth of good food prepared here. Their attention to the wine list is also conscientious. Their favorite dishes include roast beef Italian style, fresh she-crab soup, a gratinée of spinach with mushrooms, filet of turbot in a champagne sauce, and goose à l'orange. The walls are covered with shelves containing practically every known variety of liquor or liqueur. Fixed-priced menus range from 52 DM ($17.16) to 80 DM ($26.40), and are served from noon till 6 p.m. The gentlemen, after all that work, want the evening off. You can sit at the bar, sampling "one of everything," anytime from 10 a.m. to 6:30 p.m. every day except Sunday. Saturday hours, however, are 10 a.m. to 2 p.m.

Restaurant Flett, 3 Böttcherstrasse (tel. 32-09-95). The immaculate napery of this warmly decorated place often reflects the amber tones of the dozens of stained-glass windows that serve as this restaurant's room dividers. Clients seat themselves on modified Windsor chairs set onto intricately patterned Oriental carpets before beginning full meals priced between 25 DM ($8.25) and 55 DM ($18.15). Fresh seafood is a specialty of the house, and you can also order a full array of classic German dishes. Meals are served every day between noon and 3 p.m. and from 6 to 11 p.m.

Comturei, 31 Ostertorstrasse (tel. 32-50-50). If ever a restaurant in Europe should harbor a resident ghost, this one should. The building itself goes back to the 13th century when it was a church. Then it was the headquarters of a branch of German knighthood, where Teutonic warriors initiated new members into their order, and later a city mint. The feasts of the knights of yesterday can be repeated, however, in the restaurant of today that much of Bremen talks about. An international regime of traditional Bremer cookery—sometimes jazzed up with nouvelle cuisine—is offered here, including crab, trout, halibut, and marinated herring, all delectably seasoned and beautifully served. Other meat dishes include bratwurst, roast goose, and bacon served with roast potatoes. Menus begin at 35 DM ($11.55) and go way, way up from there. The restaurant serves from noon to 3 p.m. and 5 p.m. till midnight every day except Sunday.

Beck's in'n Snoor, 35–36 Schnoor (tel. 32-31-30), stands in one of the oldest sections of the Hanseatic city. You'll be escorted politely to whichever one of three rooms you'll feel most comfortable in. The Unner Deck is the friendly bar area, ruggedly masculine but entirely hospitable to women. De Schinken-Deel is the less formal of the two restaurants, specializing in ham and wurst, along with North Atlantic fish and cold fish salads of all kinds. Finally, De Goode Stuub serves North Germanic specialties in a more elaborate format, tantalizingly prepared. You'll probably wash everything down with copious quantities of the dark beer produced in Bremen. Fixed-price meals in either restaurant cost from 18 DM ($5.94) to 35 DM ($11.55), with an ever-changing list of daily specials, which might include crab and eel along with ham prepared in no fewer than ten different ways. The restaurant serves from 11 a.m. to midnight, although the bar (opening at 6 p.m.) serves drinks until 2 a.m.

La Villa, 4 Goetheplatz (tel. 32-79-63), is an attractively contemporary restaurant whose specialty is hearty Italian food. There's a flower-dotted garden terrace, ideal for conjuring up images of Italy in springtime. The friendly staff is well versed in Mediterranean charm. You can order any of the typical dishes, including pasta, veal, or fish. Interesting dishes include a ragoût of snails or a paper-thin carpaccio with forest-fresh mushrooms. Full meals, ranging from 25 DM ($8.25) to 40 DM ($13.20), are served between noon and 2:30 p.m. and from 6 p.m. to midnight. The restaurant is closed Saturday night and all day Sunday.

Jan Tabac, 93 Weserstrasse (tel. 66-22-72), in Vegesack, somewhat to the northwest of the city, is for anyone who's partial to romantically lit paneled rooms, with deep-red wall coverings, lots of green plants, and amusing artwork. In fact this may be about the most appealing restaurant in Bremen. The service is impeccable and the tableware sparkles. So does the price: from 70 DM ($23.10) to 110 DM ($36.30). You get such nouvelle cuisine delicacies as "three-fish" terrine, crab bisque, trout with crab sauteed together in a butter sauce, or filet of turbot with grated vegetables in Noilly Prat. Dessert might be a champagned lemon sorbet. Menus change daily. Service is from noon to 3 p.m. and from 7 p.m. till midnight. They're closed for Saturday lunch and all day

Sunday, taking a vacation in September and again at Christmas until mid-January.

THE TOP SIGHTS: The most practical way to see Bremen is on foot. If you don't like to explore on your own, guides are available for walking tours, as well as motorcoach tours.

The Major Sights

The main sights center around the **Marktplatz,** the "parlor" of Bremen life for more than 1000 years. The 30-foot statue of the city's protector, **Roland,** erected in 1404, still stands today, his sword raised toward the cathedral, symbolizing Bremen's declaration of freedom against the Church. Shortly after the statue was put up, Bremen became Germany's first Protestant state.

The **Rathaus** (Town Hall) has stood for some 560 years on the Marketplace and has seen several periods of transformation. The original Gothic foundations remain basically unchanged, but the upper section reflects the 17th-century Weser Renaissance style in the facade; the tall windows alternate with relief statues of Charlemagne and the electors of the Holy Roman Empire. The Upper Hall, part of the original structure, contains a beautifully carved oak staircase dating from the early 17th century and a mural (1537) depicting *The Judgment of Solomon* and typifying the hall's original character as a council chamber and courtroom. In the Lower Hall are oak pillars and beams supporting the building, and below, the historic wine cellar, the previously recommended "good Ratskeller of Bremen." At the west end of the Rathaus is one of the most recent additions, a sculpture of Bremen's visitors from the land of Grimm—the Bremen Town Musicians. The donkey, dog, cat, and cock are stacked, pyramid style, in a constant pose for the ever-present cameras. For tours of the Town Hall, inquire at the information booth at the **New Town Hall** (entrance opposite the cathedral). When there is no session of the city fathers, tours generally depart at 10 a.m. (but not on Sunday), at 11 a.m., and again at noon. It's closed Sunday in the off-season.

St. Peter's Cathedral (Dom St. Petri) is set back from the square, but towers majestically over all the other buildings in the Altstadt (Old Town). Originally designed in 1043 as the archbishop's church, it has since been rebuilt twice, in the 16th and 19th centuries. Dating from the early church, however, is the Romanesque **East Crypt,** containing the tomb of St. Adalbert and an organ on which Bach once played. The West Crypt, from the same period, houses a bronze baptismal font, a fine example of 12th-century workmanship. There is a collection of mummies in the chapel in the cathedral cellar. The cellar is open May to September from 9 a.m. to around noon and from 2 to 5 p.m. (closed Saturday afternoon, Sunday, and holidays). Admission is 2 DM (66¢).

Across the square from the Rathaus stands another example of a happy merger of Gothic and Renaissance architecture, the **Schütting,** a 16th-century guildhall used by the Chamber of Commerce. In direct contrast to these ancient masterpieces is the **Haus der Bürgerschaft,** home of Bremen's Parliament, constructed in 1966. The structure was scaled down to fit in with its surroundings. Even though the architecture is a maze of glass, concrete, and steel, it does not look entirely out of place.

Other Sights

The **Böttcherstrasse,** running from the Marketplace to the Weser River, is a brick-paved reproduction of a medieval alley, complete with shops, restaurants, museum, and galleries. The street was the brainchild of a wealthy Bremen merchant, Ludwig Roselius, and designed to present a picture of Bremen life, past and present. Dedicated in 1926 and rebuilt after World War II, the artery is one of Bremen's biggest attractions. Try to visit around noon, 3 p.m., or 6 p.m., when the Meissen bells strung between two gables set up a chorus of chimes for a full 15 minutes. Besides the fine handicraft and pottery shops, the street also contains buildings of historical significance. The **Paula Modersohn-Becker House,** at no. 8, is dedicated to Bremen's most outstanding contemporary painter and contains many of her best works, including several self-portraits and some still lifes. The **Roselius House,** next door, is a 16th-century-style merchant's manor housing Roselius's collection of medieval objets d'art and furniture. These houses are open weekdays from 10 a.m. to 4 p.m., to 7 p.m. on Saturday, and from 11 a.m. to 1 p.m. and 3 to 7 p.m. on Sunday, charging 2 DM (66¢) for admission.

The **Schnoor,** the old quarter of Bremen, has undergone restoration by the custodian of ancient monuments. The cottages of this east end district, once the homes of simple fishermen, have been rented to artists and artisans in an effort to revive many old arts and crafts. Sightseers visit not only for the atmosphere but for the unusual restaurants, shops, and art galleries.

The **Rampart Walk** is a green park where the ramparts protecting the Hanseatic city used to stand. The gardens divide the Old Town from the newer extensions of the city. Extending along the canal (once Bremen's crown-shaped moat), the park is a peaceful promenade just a few short blocks from the Marktplatz. Its major attraction is an ancient windmill, still functioning.

2. Hannover

Every student of English history is aware of the role that the House of Hannover played in the political history of Great Britain. For more than 100 years, until a woman named Victoria split the alliance, Britain and Hannover were ruled simultaneously by German monarchs, some of whom preferred to live in their native state (much to the annoyance of the British).

The city of Hannover today has lost much of its political influence, although it is the capital of the province of Lower Saxony. It has instead become one of Germany's hubs of industry, transportation, and commerce. The annual industry trade fair is a magnet. Held the last ten days in April, the Hannover Fair has grown to be the largest trade fair in the world. Producers and buyers from around the globe meet en masse. Thanks to its central location in West Germany, the city has become a major railway terminus. Its international airport is a convenient shuttle point for flights to Berlin.

The Green Metropolis is a masterpiece of advanced planning, combining parks and tree-lined streets with bold and imaginative solutions to a large city's traffic problems. Before we explore the treasures these streets hold, however, let's check into a hotel.

ACCOMMODATIONS: Hannover is a business person's city, and the hotel accommodations reflect this in the super-abundance of deluxe and first-class hotels which are big on comfort but short on romantic architecture.

Deluxe Hotels

Hotel Inter-Continental, 11 Friedrichswall (tel. 1-69-11), opposite the Rathaus, is one of the finest hotels in northern Germany. It's a splendid contemporary palace of comfort, with built-in style, where you get the most for your money. Heavily patronized by American, German, and Japanese business people, the hotel has many fine public facilities, including a garage, shopping center, beauty salon, currency exchange, barbershop, drugstore, and a large international newsstand. Each of the 285 ultramodern rooms has its own tile bath and shower, a radio, color TV, direct-dial telephone, and a mini-bar. In the widest possible price range, single rooms begin at 80 DM ($59.40) and spiral upward to 350 DM ($115.50). Double rooms begin at 240 DM ($79.20) and range upward to 380 DM ($125.40). Prices include tax and service.

The Inter-Continental's spacious but intimate Prinz Taverne is one of Hannover's most popular restaurants. The food and service are both outstanding. Two à la carte specials on the dinner menu: filet of sole "belle vue" and filet de veau au citron (marinated sirloin of veal with lemon-pepper). For cocktails before dinner, or for an evening of live entertainment and dancing afterward, stop in at the Grenadier Lounge, a disco. There's usually a combo for dancing, or you may prefer just to relax and sip your drink. And you only pay for what you drink here—no admission or cover charge. Besides the Prinz Taverne, the Inter-Continental has two other restaurants, for lighter and less expensive meals: the Bierstube, for beer and snacks, and the Brasserie, opening onto a view of the Rathaus, for snacks, breakfast, and full-course meals.

Maritim Hotel, 34–40 Hildesheimer Strasse (tel. 1-65-31). One of the city's newest hotels was built in an ideal location in 1984. An oasis of verdant plants separates the colorful awnings of the front portico from the street. Many of the comfortably up-to-date accommodations contain narrow private terraces thanks to the architect's plan of indenting some of the floors in receding layers. The casino, the old city, and the commercial center are all nearby. On the premises is a plant-filled restaurant staffed by a polite and uniformed crew of well-trained personnel. There are a café, a bar, and about 275 well-furnished bedrooms, each with private bath, phone, radio, TV, and mini-bar. Singles cost 150 DM ($49.50) to 235 DM ($77.50), while doubles range between 210 DM ($69.30) and 335 DM ($110.55), including a breakfast buffet.

First-Class Hotels

Kastens Hotel Luisenhof, 2 Luisenstrasse (tel. 1-61-51), just 300 yards from the main railway station and a few minutes by car from the airport, is one of Hannover's leading hotels. For many, however, it remains the traditional favorite, having been in the same family since it was established by Heinrich Kasten in 1856. The 220 extensively modernized rooms are agreeable and well maintained. Singles with bath or shower range from 150 DM ($49.50) to 210 DM ($69.30). All doubles have private bath, and rent for from 210 DM ($69.30) to 270 DM ($89.10). The hotel has several dining facilities, including a restaurant, grill-room, and a cozy bar. There is a parking garage for 100 cars. The English-speaking staff is helpful and efficient.

Am Stadtpark, 6 Clausewitzstrasse (tel. 2-80-50), stands next to the City Hall, near the main railway station. This upper-bracket hotel contains 255 rooms and suites, along with an array of facilities, including hairdressers, boutiques, an indoor pool, a sauna, massage facilities, and a bicycle-rental center. Strikingly modern, the hotel is made up of three wings arranged at equal distances around a central core which rises high into the Hannoverian skies. The rooms are spacious, and decorated with chrome furniture which is usually upholstered in black. Singles rent for 140 DM ($46.20) to 192 DM ($63.36), while doubles cost 218 DM ($71.94) to 250 DM ($82.50), including an elegant buffet. The Bristol Grill at the hotel is one of the best in Hannover, charging from 35 DM ($11.55) to 70 DM ($23.10) for a meal.

Crest Hotel Hannover, 117 Tiergartenstrasse (tel. 5-20-30), in the suburb of Kirchrode, is an excellent choice, about four miles from the center of town. The ultramodern rooms, often decorated in sunflower gold and chocolate brown, all contain private bath or shower, mini-bar, trouser press, radio, and direct-dial telephone. The filmy white curtains at the windows are drawn back to look out on a deer park and woodland. A double room rents for 170 DM ($56.10) to 210 DM ($69.30), a single for 100 DM ($33) to 200 DM ($66). An international breakfast buffet is included. Hearty fare and good wines and beer are served in a semirustic restaurant. The attractive Bierstube has a warm and inviting atmosphere. The hotel can easily be reached from the Hannover-Anderten exit (just a mile away) of the Hamburg-Kassel motorway.

Grand Hotel Mussmann, 7 Ernst-August-Platz (tel. 32-79-71), stands right in the heart of Hannover, opposite the air terminal and the railroad station. A pleasant, top-rate establishment, it offers 100 comfortable and soundproof rooms, costing from 128 DM ($42.24) to 260 DM ($85.80) in a single and from 200 DM ($66) to 320 DM ($105.60) in a double, including a copiously stocked breakfast buffet. Everything about this place is friendly, efficient, and predictably modern. All the attractively furnished rooms have phone, TV, a large bathroom (some with window), and a digital alarm clock built right into the woodwork.

The Medium and Budget Range

Hotel am Leineschloss, 12 Am Markt (tel. 32-71-45), across from the City Hall, is a surprise discovery, one of the best for value in Hannover. It's the preferred hotel for those who want to be in the heart of the old section, yet it's quiet despite its central location. It's like being snuggled warmly in contemporary comfort in old-world surroundings. The generously sized rooms, with their bright colors, are housed in an avant-garde structure. Most units have sitting areas big enough for a leisurely breakfast. Every room has either a bath or shower as well as toilet. Singles with shower rent for 160 DM ($52.80); doubles with bath, 190 DM ($62.70) to 210 DM ($69.30). The individual service and good comfort may make you want to prolong your stay. There is a garage, or you can park in the space in front of the hotel. The only meal served is breakfast, included in the rates.

Thüringer Hof, 37 Osterstrasse (tel. 32-64-37), lies just a few blocks from the rail station. It presents a somewhat grim facade of white brick and unadorned windows to passersby. However, all those windows open onto sunny bedrooms, all of which have private bath, chintz wallpaper, patterned rugs, and reproductions of 19th-century furniture. The lobby area boasts a magnificent red Oriental rug which is reflected in the polished paneling on the walls. Singles rent for 65 DM ($21.45) to 145 DM ($47.85), while doubles cost 100 DM ($33) to 210 DM ($69.30), with breakfast included. Peter Neitz is your English-speaking host here.

Hotel Königshof, 12 Königstrasse (tel. 31-20-71). Both the skylights and the modernized crenellations on this hotel's mansard-style roof make it look like an updated version of a feudal fortress. The hotel was built in 1984 above a glass-and-steel shopping arcade in the center of town, not far from the railway station. The rigidity of the glistening marble in the strictly contemporary public rooms is softened by the ornately baroque chandeliers and the soft contours of the French-inspired armchairs. Upstairs, each of the plushly carpeted accommodations has a mixture of contemporary furniture with reproduction antiques, as well as an eye-stopping white- and turquoise-colored tile bath. The couch in each of the rooms converts to a bed, permitting visitors under 16 to pay half price when accompanied by their parents. The Czako family, the owners, have installed a pair of bars on the premises. They charge from 108 DM ($35.64) in a single and from 158 DM ($52.14) in a double, with breakfast included.

Hospiz Loccumer Hof, 16 Kurt-Schumacher-Strasse (tel. 32-60-51), a short walk from the station, is one of the best economy finds in the city. The rates are reasonable, considering the general comfort and amenities offered. The utilitarian rooms are small, the service and frills minimal, but it's a good stopover. With private bath, the price in a single is 80 DM ($26.40) to 115 DM ($37.95); a double, 110 DM ($36.30) to 170 DM ($56.10). Prices include service and tax, plus breakfast. The standard Germanic fare in the hotel's dining room is quite good.

Am Rathaus, 21 Friedrichswall (tel. 32-62-68), is a hotel directly facing the Town Hall. It offers a good choice of small, comfortable rooms, well furnished with oak pieces. The hotel is immaculately kept as well. The reception is tiny, but the welcome is big. An elevator takes you to one of the guest bedrooms. All rooms have private bath or shower. The price in a single runs from 90 DM ($29.70) to 170 DM ($56.10), increasing to 150 DM ($49.50) to 230 DM ($75.90) in a double.

Hotel Am Funkturm, 34 Hallerstrasse (tel. 31-70-33). Sabine Czako is the vivacious owner of this 40-room hotel in the center of Hannover. Her rooms all have private, marble-floored bath, with antiques scattered throughout. It's one of the best accommodations for value in Hannover, if you can get in. Breakfast is served for an additional 12 DM ($3.96), although an Italian restaurant and disco under separate management are housed under the same roof. Singles, all attractively furnished, rent for 100 DM ($33), while doubles cost 140 DM ($46.20).

A Country Retreat Near the Herrenhausen Gardens

Georgenhof, 20 Herrenhäuser Kirchweg (tel. 70-22-44), is a country inn positioned within the city. Sitting in a private park near the Herrenhausen Gardens, the hotel is the quietest, most secluded retreat in Hannover. Single rooms range from 75 DM ($24.75) to 155 DM ($51.15), depending on the plumbing and the location. Doubles range from 120 DM ($39.60) to 190 DM ($62.70). The rooms are clean and pleasant, furnished with a mixture of antiques and traditional furniture, often hand-painted pieces.

The Georgenhof's restaurant is among the finest in Hannover, and you may want to call for a table reservation even if you're not staying there. All selections are à la carte and rather expensive, but well worth the price. The difficulty in choosing the main course is that they're all tempting. The specialties include deep-fried prawns and breast of chicken suprême. A selection of international dishes is also featured, including Valencian paella. Seafood and fresh fish, prepared in the nouvelle cuisine style, will tempt the diner, as will the game dishes. A dinner costs from 50 DM ($16.50) to 110 DM ($36.30). In summer tables are set out on the terrace, overlooking a restful garden and pond. The Georgenhof is highly recommended for both food and lodging.

DINING IN HANNOVER: Besides the fine food served in many of the hotels' dining rooms and restaurants, including the Hotel Inter-Continental, Kastens, and the Georgenhof, Hannover enjoys a wide variety of cuisine in its numerous restaurants. You can find anything from a hamburger to chop suey to nouvelle cuisine if you wish.

Witten's Hop, 4 Gernsstrasse (tel. 64-88-44), on the outskirts at Hannover 51-Bothfeld. Three hundred years ago this served as a prosperous farmer's home, and today the hand-hewn ceiling timbers and the glowing patina of the antiques are evidence of that. Decorated in a Dutch country style, this is an upper-level restaurant. Specialties are pâté of calf sweetbreads, goose liver, and black truffles, fresh salads with poultry of Lower Saxony or seafood, and cassolette of lobster and dorade royal. The owner, Andreas Lüssenhop, is an unabashed Francophile (he spent a lot of time in Alsace) when it comes to cuisine. Meals cost 65 DM ($21.45) to 110 DM ($36.30). The wine list contains about 450 great and famous wines from the best vineyards of France, Italy,

Spain, and Germany. The place is filled with classical music, masses of flowers, and candlelight. The restaurant is open Monday to Saturday from 6 p.m. till "closing." On Sunday and holidays it is open for lunch from noon to 2 p.m., reopening for dinner at 7 p.m.

Wichmann, 230 Hildesheimer Strasse, at Hannover 81-Döhren (tel. 83-16-71), on the eastern edge of Hannover. A family-owned establishment, this white-walled, shuttered inn, with slate walks and carefully tended flowerbeds, is an oasis of Teutonic comfort. Guests have a choice of five rooms in which to dine. Cooking is gutbürgerlich—wholesome, hearty, and one of the best samplings of such specialties as fish terrine, rack of lamb, homemade noodles, and an array of wines and cheeses from all over Germany. A full meal here would average about 30 DM ($9.90) to 60 DM ($19.80). It's open from noon to 3 p.m. and 6 p.m. to midnight (closed Sunday, Monday, and holidays).

Steuerndieb, 1 Steuerndieb (tel. 69-09-58). The food is very good at this rustic restaurant on the edge of a public forest to the east of Hannover. Many of the specialties are cooked over an open fire, and some of the chef's dishes enjoy quite a reputation, including the house special, a Hausteller Herrenhauser, medallions of three kinds of meat in a mustard-cream sauce. Other specialties include wild duck in an orange sauce and medallions of venison. Fixed-price menus, in generous quantities, cost from 32 DM ($10.56) to 60 DM ($19.80). The restaurant serves daily from 11 a.m. to 11 p.m., on Sunday to 6 p.m.

Hindenburg Klassik, 55 Gneisenaustrasse (tel. 85-85-88). The decor of this restaurant runs a fine line between the classic and the modern. The walls are white, the Oriental rugs intricate and well chosen, and the walls look like some extension of an art gallery. The wooden chairs are elegantly upholstered in a simple white fabric. The owners call their menu nouvelle Italian, and this means impeccably fresh ingredients (fish from all the European seas is a specialty), served with unusual variations. Whoever created the dessert menu, I suspect, must have foraged through the tropics to discover such unusual fruits which the chef uses so lavishly. Meals start around 60 DM ($19.80), but could range far higher of course. There's a good choice of wines from the best Italian vineyards. The restaurant is open from 4 p.m. till 2 a.m., although the kitchen closes at 11:30 p.m. It is closed on Sunday and for a few weeks in summer. Always call ahead for a reservation.

Mövenpick Café Kröpcke-Baron de la Mouette, 35 Georgstrasse (tel. 32-62-85), is a double-barreled chain threat in Hannover. It is open from 8 a.m. till midnight, and you can order some delectable Swiss specialties here. I recently enjoyed Zürcher geschnetzeltes with rösti (sliced veal in white wine crème sauce with Swiss rösti potatoes), and on another occasion, scampi. Desserts are so elaborate you'll think you're in Old Wien. It's cheaper to dine in the café, where a meal begins at 18 DM ($5.94), going up to 28 DM ($9.24). In the Baron, expect to spend from 25 DM ($8.25) to 40 DM ($13.20).

Mövenpick im Casino am Maschsee, 3 Arthur-Menge-Ufer (tel. 80-10-20). This elegant second-floor restaurant sits at the end of the squared-off lines of the Machsee, with direct access to the fashionable casino of Hannover. The decor is restrained, and the service excellent. You'll find that the fish selections include the freshest available at the market that day, including Norwegian salmon and trout. Delectably prepared meals begin at 40 DM ($13.20), going up to 75 DM ($24.75). You can always have a drink here, but warm food is served only between noon and 2:30 p.m. and from 6 p.m. till midnight.

à la lune, 41 Marktstrasse (tel. 1-24-29). The cuisine, as implied in the title, will "send you to the moon." At least, that's what the chef claims. When you arrive, a waiter will seat you in the beflowered dining room and present you with an oversize menu with lots of daily specialties listed. Meals begin at 45 DM

($14.85) and go up from there. Try such delicacies as roast beef with Provençal herbs or a fresh goose liver pâté. A superb dish I recently enjoyed was the fresh pigeon stuffed with grapes and mushrooms, while a companion raved about medallions of lamb in mustard butter. Another delight is the filet of pork in an apple cream sauce. It'll take two to order the roast goose with cranberries, crème fraîche, and green peppercorns served piping hot from the kitchen's scented oven. Food is presented, like a showcase, from 6 to 11 p.m. except Sunday, holidays, and during all of August.

Clichy, 31 Weissekreuzstrasse (tel. 31-24-47). If you befriend a native of Hannover, he or she might confide one of the city's better kept secrets: the address of this elegantly decorated restaurant a few blocks northeast of the Hauptbahnhof. You'll see lots of gold and cream, with an appealing combination of art nouveau and art deco (unfortunately, none of the sculpture is for sale). The cuisine is a sophisticated preparation of nouvelle cuisine. Meals, ranging in price from 45 DM ($14.85) to 85 DM ($28.05), the latter the price of "the great menu," could include a pâté of goose liver in port, a fricassée of shellfish in a champagne sauce, Barbary goose in cognac, and "seawolf" in a Pernod sabayon. Owner and chef Ekkehard Reimann and his partner, Peter Bücken, open their establishment from noon to 3 p.m. and 6:30 p.m. to midnight every day but Sunday. On Saturday the restaurant serves dinner only.

Alte Mühle, 3 Hermann-Löns-Park (tel. 55-94-80). This half-timbered building, on the outskirts of the city at Hannover 71-Kleefeld, has gained many additions and new wings since its construction as a mill back in the 16th century. It sits today in a manicured park (which certainly didn't look that good 500 years ago). Greatly modernized, it's like the clubhouse of an elegant country club. Wild game is a specialty in season, and a number of Dutch specialties are prepared with flair and beautifully served. Fixed-price menus, including a mixed grill, range from 30 DM ($9.90) to 65 DM ($21.45). The mill is open every day except Thursday from 10 a.m. to 11 p.m.

Altdeutsche Bierstube, 4 Lärchenstrasse (tel. 34-49-21), is pleasantly decorated and old-fashioned, a bierstube with many of the original elements still left over from generations ago. The food is hearty, wholesome, and filling, also unpretentious. Fixed-price meals begin at 18 DM ($5.94), ranging upward. The regular fare is augmented by seasonal specialties. They are open from midmorning until midnight for drinks, and hot food is served from 11:30 a.m. to 2:30 p.m. and 5 p.m. till 11 p.m. They're closed on Sunday and holidays, and during all of July.

The **Ratskeller,** in the historic old Town Hall, 60 Köbelingerstrasse (tel. 1-53-63), as in most German cities, is one of the most popular dining spots for townspeople and visitors alike. Patrons dine in two rooms at tables set under vaulted brick arches. The lunches are among the best bargains in town. From noon to 3 p.m., a complete luncheon, including soup, main course, and dessert, ranges from 24 DM ($7.92). The à la carte appetizers in the evening begin with soups. Main-dish specialties include veal steak Hannovera, venison, fresh fish dishes, and wienerschnitzel. For a complete meal in the evening, expect to spend 35 DM ($11.55) to 60 DM ($26.40). Service is from noon to 1 a.m.

THE SIGHTS: No matter where you go in Hannover, you will not be far from a park or garden. But if you have time to explore only one of these, it might be the **Herrenhausen Gardens,** the only surviving example of Dutch/Low German early baroque-style gardening. Designers from France, the Netherlands, England, and Italy, as well as Germany, worked together to create this masterpiece of living art. The **Grosser Garten,** from 1666, is the largest, consisting of a rectangle surrounded by a moat. Within the maze of walks and trees are examples of French baroque, rococo, and Low German rose and flower gardens. The Grosser Garten also contains the highest fountain in Europe, shooting jets of water 270 feet into the air, and the world's only existing baroque hedge-theater (1692), where Shakespeare, Molière, and Brecht are still performed today, along with ballets and jazz concerts. The smaller 17th-century **Berggarten,** across the Herrenhauserstrasse from the Grosser Garten, is a botanical garden with several houses containing rare orchids and other tropical flowers. The gardens are open daily, in season, from 8 a.m. to dusk. The Grosser Garten is illuminated on Wednesday, Saturday, and Sunday from May 1 to October 1.

The **Market Church,** on the Market Square, is one of Hannover's oldest structures, built in the mid-14th century. Its Gothic brick basilica houses several religious works, including a 15th-century carved altarpiece and a bronze baptismal font. The **Rathaus** (Old Town Hall), facing the square, is from 1425. Badly damaged during the war, it has been restored and houses a museum and the civic archives.

The "new" **City Hall** is a large structure dating from 1901. It is a good place to visit for a panoramic view of Hannover from its 100-meter tower. You can ascend by elevator from April to October every hour from 9:30 a.m. to noon and 2 to 5 p.m., for a ticket which costs only 2 DM (66¢). The building is made more attractive because it sits in the **Machpark,** reflected in a small lake, just a short distance from the extensive **Machsee,** a man-made lake frequented by Hannoverians for its beach, boating, and restaurants.

The **Kestner Museum,** 3 Trammplatz (tel. 168-27-30), next to the City Hall, contains treasures representing 6000 years of history. Its four departments (Egyptian Art, Greek and Roman Art, Decorative Art, and Numismatics) show objects of the finest quality. The museum is open from 10 a.m. to 4 p.m. Tuesday, Thursday, and Friday; from 10 a.m. to 8 p.m. on Wednesday; and from 10 a.m. to 6 p.m. on Saturday and Sunday. Admission is free.

3. Celle

The well-preserved town of Celle stands at the edge of a silent expanse of moorland, looking like something out of a picture book. Its ancient half-timbered houses were spared in the air raids of the war, and the legends carved on their beams seem to live on today. Most of the houses date from the 16th and 17th centuries—the oldest was built in 1526—but they are in such good condition that they could have been built in this century.

One of the landmarks of the town is the **Palace of the Dukes of Brunswick and Lüneburg,** a square Renaissance castle with towers at each corner. The palace's bizarre 16th-century Renaissance chapel was designed by Martin de Vos, with galleries and elaborate ornamentation. But the pride of the castle, and of the town, is its baroque theater, the oldest in Germany (1674) and still in regular use today. The Ducal Palace is open daily for guided tours only, from 9 a.m. to noon and 2 to 4 p.m. Admission is 2 DM (66¢) for adults and 1.50 DM (50¢) for children.

For a picture of life as lived from the 16th to the 20th centuries in Celle, visit the **Bomann Museum,** one of Germany's finest regional museums, with extensive exhibits illustrating the life in the country and in the town. Included is a complete 16th-century farmhouse, as well as rooms from old cottages, period costumes, and Hannoverian uniforms from 1803 to 1866. In the portrait gallery of Brunswick-Lüneburg dukes, you can see pictures of the electors, later kings of England and Hannover.

ACCOMMODATIONS: If you're stopping over, either for lodgings or meals, you might consider one of the following.

The Upper Bracket

Fürstenhof Celle, 55 Hannoverschestrasse (tel. 20-10), far superior to any other accommodation, is surprisingly sophisticated for such a provincial town. Standing at the edge of Celle, it is a small-scale manor house flanked with timbered wings which house beauty parlors, shops, and a bierstube. The brick courtyard in front of the salmon-colored mansion is shaded by a towering chestnut tree. The hotel's interior has formal neoclassic paneling and a collection of antiques, many of them removed from castles—almost high-fashion furnishings. A modern annex beyond the rear courtyard contrasts with the main building in its use of daring and refreshing colors in the rooms and apartments. On the lower level is a tile swimming pool. All rooms have toilet facilities, and depending on whether you prefer bath or shower, the price of a single room ranges from 110 DM ($36.30) to 200 DM ($66). Doubles range from 170 DM ($56.10) to 310 DM ($102.30), which includes breakfast, use of the hotel's indoor swimming pool, service, and taxes. All the doubles have been refurnished, and further amenities include color TV sets and mini-bars. Besides the heated swimming pool, the hotel also has a sauna and massage rooms for guests.

Fürstenhof's restaurant, Endtenfang, is warmly formal, done in autumnal colors. The elegant dining room is decorated with painted tapestries. It is known for its ducal duck, after an old recipe from the court of Celle. The bar room is in the ancient vaults of the mansion. Fine food and wines are the order of the day here, with meals costing from 40 DM ($13.20) to 85 DM ($28.05). The beer tavern built into the old coach house is more informal, with its old wooden tables and farm artifacts.

The Medium Range

Hotel Celler Hof, 11 Stechbahn (tel. 2-80-61), is on the street where tournaments of knights were once held. Considering the old-world architecture of the hotel and its neighboring timbered houses, the interior furnishings are incongruously modern, but quite pleasing. The Celler Hof's advertisement of "internationaler komfort" holds true for all the guest rooms. Bathless singles rent for 55 DM ($18.15). With bath or shower, the price in a single is 158 DM ($52.14); in a double, 210 DM ($69.30). Prices include breakfast, service, and taxes.

Borchers, 52 Schuhstrasse (tel. 70-61), is elegantly half-timbered, with a red tile gabled roof. A family-run establishment, it lies about 90 yards from the Rathaus. Guests here benefit from the gravel-slabbed sun terrace, and from the big-windowed, tastefully furnished bedrooms which rent for 89 DM ($29.37) to 140 DM ($46.20) in a single and 150 DM ($49.50) to 180 DM ($59.40) in a double, including breakfast.

Hotel Schifferkrug, 9 Speicherstrasse (tel. 70-15). The brick and timber walls of this elegantly comfortable hotel have witnessed more than three centuries of innkeeping tradition. It's peaceful, with a garden. The very clean bedrooms are warmly furnished in conservative Teutonic grace, sometimes with lace curtains and eiderdown quilts. There are only about a dozen rooms, most of which are doubles. The limited number of singles rent for 85 DM ($28.05), while doubles range from 110 DM ($36.30) to 150 DM ($49.50), including a breakfast buffet. The doubles contain phone, TV, and radio. There's a bar on the premises, along with a country-rustic weinstube and a more formal restaurant with a conservative but tasty German menu.

WHERE TO DINE: **Historischer Ratskeller,** 14 Markt (tel. 2-23-97), is a plusher version of the typical German town hall dining room. The food, as well, is superior to the usual ratskeller fare. The attentive waiters are constantly passing by, carrying silver platters heaped with spicy, flavorful dishes. Complete lunches, including soup and dessert, range in price from 18 DM ($5.94). At night, the à la carte menu is varied, with meals costing as much as 55 DM ($18.15). Hours are 10 a.m. to midnight. Closed Tuesday.

Städische Union Celle, 1 Albrecht-Thaer-Platz (tel. 60-96). The view from the terrace of this attractively art nouveau restaurant encompasses the walls of the town castle. Most guests find the menu easily as interesting as the architecture around them. The cuisine is imaginatively contrived from fresh ingredients to create a frequently changing array of daily seasonal specialties. Your meal might include a terrine of trout, a three-fish platter of local grilled delicacies swimming in an aromatic dill-flavored sauce, and delectably tempting desserts awash in pungently textured flavors. Fixed-price menus range from 34 DM ($11.22) to 45 DM ($14.85), and are served from noon to 11 p.m. except on Monday.

Hotel Celler Tor, 13 Celler Strasse, at Gross-Hehlen (tel. 5-10-11), is about two miles outside of town. You'd never guess that this comfortable hotel with a red tile roof, five gables, stucco walls, and banks of geraniums was a secret haven for a Brazilian and Javanese restaurant—but that's exactly what it is. You can get some good shrimp and rice dishes here. Chef Horst Niebuhr also knows how to prepare gutbürgerlich specialties, including wild game in season, perhaps a ragoût of stag with mushrooms. Fixed-price menus begin at a reasonable 28 DM ($9.24), going up to 60 DM ($19.80). Service is from 6 a.m. to 1 a.m. Closed Sunday evening and for a few weeks in August. Celler Tor has some of the most desirable and well-furnished bedrooms in the area, 58 in all, costing from 82 DM ($27.06) to 94 DM ($31.02) in a single and from 146 DM ($48.18) to 164 DM ($54.12) in a double.

4. Lüneburg and the Heath

Motorists driving south from Scandinavia through the Baltic port of Lübeck often find themselves on the Old Salt Road leading to the Hanseatic city of Lüneburg. The road was so named because it was the route by which the heavy salt deposits of Lüneburg were delivered to the countries of Scandinavia during the Middle Ages. Most of the buildings of the Salt City are from its most prosperous period, the 15th and 16th centuries. Although the medieval brick buildings are the most prevalent, seven centuries of architecture are represented in this 1000-year-old city. The rising gables of the once-patrician houses range from Gothic to Renaissance to baroque.

THE SIGHTS: The **Rathaus** (Town Hall) is a perfect example of several trends in architecture and design. You'll enter through a Gothic doorway into a Renaissance hall, then find yourself in a baroque chamber. The Great Council Room is its most outstanding feature, with sculptures and bas-reliefs by Albert von Soest (1578). From the painted beamed ceiling in the Fürstensaal, chandeliers made of antlers hang down, adding a festive touch. Guided tours are conducted from May to October beginning at 10 a.m., then again at 11 a.m., noon, 2 p.m., and 3 p.m. on weekdays (on weekends at 10 a.m., 11 a.m., 2 p.m., and 3 p.m.). In the off-season, tours are at 10 a.m., 11:15 a.m., 2 p.m., and 3 p.m. (on weekends at 10 a.m., 11 a.m., 2 p.m., and 3 p.m.). No tours are conducted on Monday, and the cost is 3.50 DM ($1.16).

Because of its heavy salt deposits, Lüneburg remains a spa even today. In the Kurpark is a bathing house where visitors take brine mud baths. In the spa gardens there are also indoor swimming pools, sauna baths, and tennis courts.

Lüneburg is the ideal starting point for excursions into the **Lüneburg**

Heath. The soil of the heath is sandy and is mainly covered with brush and heather, although there are a few oak and beech forests in the northern valleys. The heath covers nearly 300 square miles and includes many beauty spots for the outdoors person. The **Wilsede National Park** is a 100-square-mile sanctuary for plants and wildlife, and for people as well. Strict laws enforce the maintaining of the thatched houses and rural atmosphere. The heath is beautiful in late summer and early autumn, when the heather turns shades of deep purple. The pastoral scene of shepherds, sheep, and undulating hills is peaceful.

ACCOMMODATIONS: You may wish to return to Lüneburg to spend the night, or at least for a meal before continuing on to Hamburg, Hannover, or some other destination.

The Upper Bracket

Seminaris, 3 Soltauer Strasse (tel. 20-81). This is a 165-room modern hotel complex in a spa park. The exterior is white with a buff-colored trim, while the inside provides the latest in glass-walled elegance, attracting the business-minded client. There's a cozy fireplace den, as well as tennis courts, a gymnasium, a saltwater simulated-surf swimming pool, a freshwater indoor pool, a solarium, a massage room, and a sauna, all of which will let you work off the weight gained in the inviting bar and the intimately lit restaurant. Room rentals are administered by Brigitte Steiner, who speaks English. She charges 85 DM ($28.05) in a single and from 150 DM ($49.50) in a double, including breakfast. Half board is available for a relatively modest 20 DM ($6.60) per person extra.

The Middle Bracket

Residenz am Kurpark, 8 Munstermannskamp (tel. 4-50-47). Each of the buff and brown units of this tasteful hotel are so separated from one another that it will remind you almost of an apartment building rather than a hotel. Since the establishment is right inside the city's Kurpark, you'll get enough shade to pretend you're in a forest. Inside, you'll find an inviting bar and an up-to-date restaurant, serving both international and regional specialties. Rooms are elegant, comfortable, and chic, and many of them are covered in plush white carpeting. The rooms also have tile baths with lots of mirrors, and everything is designed to make for a comfortable stay. Singles rent for 85 DM ($28.05) to 95 DM ($31.35) while doubles cost from 140 DM ($46.20). Breakfast is included.

Wellenkamp's Hotel, 9 Am Sande (tel. 4-30-26). A building this unusual could only have been designed for public use, and that's exactly what it was. This hotel used to be a post office, but not an ordinary one. It was a station on the postal run between Kurfurst and Hannover more than a century ago. Today the bins that held the coal in the cellar now contain some of the finest wines in the region, attracting locals from far and wide to the delectable cuisine offered in the restaurant, where meals begin at 32 DM ($10.56). The hotel welcomes guests into its attractive singles with modern plumbing for 52 DM ($17.16) to 75 DM ($24.75), and into its doubles for 83 DM ($27.39) to 128 DM ($42.24). The exterior is crafted out of reddish bricks arranged in a generously proportioned style that could be described as 19th-century neofortification, with small Gothic arches set into the country-baroque step arrangement of its roofline. One of the public rooms is entirely furnished in vintage Biedermeier. Bedrooms are usually sunny, modern, and comfortable.

The Budget Range

Bremer Hof, 13 Lüner Strasse (tel. 3-60-77). The logo of this hotel is an illustration for the animals of Bremen, who, with their braying, frightened away the men who were about to eat them for supper. You could glance at the facade of this family-run hotel and imagine that it would have been an appropriate setting for such a legend, because it looks like something straight out of the 16th century. You'll be only two minutes on foot from the Marktplatz, and in spite of the old-fashioned facade your room will be modern, up-to-date, and sunny. Albert Brakel or his family have owned this place since 1889, charging from 56 DM ($18.48) to 64 DM ($21.12) in a single, 84 DM ($27.72) to 98 DM ($32.34) in a double, including breakfast. The Brakels also own two other establishments.

WHERE TO DINE: The **Ratskeller,** 1 Marktplatz (tel. 3-17-57), is a good dining choice. Right on the marketplace the town's dining hall offers a varied menu, including game (in season). Regional specialties are served according to the season. Always you can count on good home-style cooking in a pleasant setting, backed up by a fine wine list. The cheapest meal costs around 25 DM ($8.25), but your tab might climb to 50 DM ($16.50) by ordering some of the specialties. The cellar is closed on Wednesday.

5. Braunschweig (Brunswick)

Between the Harz Mountains and Lüneburg Heath, Braunschweig (Brunswick in English) is the second-largest town in Lower Saxony. Henry the Lion fortified and improved the town, making it his residence. Brunswick was one of the chief cities of the Hanseatic League.

Brunswick is a main stopover on the Hannover-Berlin route. Motorists nearing the East German border in the late afternoon or early evening might want to stop at Brunswick to spend the night.

Up until 1918 the city was a German duchy. Brunswick was virtually destroyed in World War II, but it has been rebuilt. The "isles of tradition"—that is, the castle square and the old town market—were restored authentically.

The castle square or **Burgplatz** is in the Romanesque style. In the center is a lion monument, **Löwendenkmal,** the emblem of Brunswick. The sculpture was erected by Henry the Lion in 1166.

Dominating the square is the cathedral of Brunswick, **St. Blasius,** from 1173. The chancel contains the tombs of the Dom's founder, Henry the Lion, and his consort, Mathilda of England. Emperor Otto IV is also entombed here. The remains of the Guelphs of the Brunswick line from 1681 are in the vaulting beneath. The most outstanding artwork is a triumphal cross carved by Master Imerward in the mid-12th century. Visiting hours are 10 a.m. to 1 p.m. and 3 to 5 p.m.

The **Burg Dankwarderode,** also at Burgplatz, a 19th-century reconstruction of the 12th-century palace of Henry the Lion, houses the important collection of medieval art of the **Herzog Anton Ulrich-Museum,** 1 Museumstrasse (tel. 484-24-00), founded in 1754 by Carl I, Duke of Braunschweig. It is now housed in this neoclassical building designed in 1886, and includes on the first floor the art library and print room with drawings by Cranach, Dürer, Holbein, Rembrandt, Rubens, and prints from the 15th century to the 20th century. On the second floor, the picture gallery has paintings by Cranach, Van Dyck, Tintoretto, Rubens, Rembrandt, Vermeer, Holbein, Palma Vecchio, and a noble self-portrait by Giorgione, among others. An antique collection containing the Mantuan Onyx Vase together with a large collection of Renaissance and baroque minor artworks are on the third floor. The museum received a great deal of press when it acquired an early medieval manuscript known as Henry the Lion's gospel book for a record-breaking price of $11.9 million. Hours are 10 a.m. to 5 p.m. Tuesday through Sunday, 10 a.m. to 8 p.m. on Wednesday; closed Monday. Admission is free.

At the **Altstadtmarkt** is the old **Town Hall,** a gem of Gothic architecture from the 13th century. From there you can walk to the **Gewandhaus,** the cloth merchant's hall, characterized by its richly ornamented Renaissance facade. Nearby is **St. Martin's Church,** from 1180. Originally a Romanesque basilica, it was enlarged in the 13th century in the Gothic style. Its Annenkapelle is from 1434 and is the first chapel in the south aisle. The church is open daily except Monday from 10:30 a.m. to 12:30 p.m.

AN UPPER-BRACKET HOTEL: Hotel **Atrium,** 3 Berliner Platz (tel. 7-30-01), was constructed in 1967 and completely renovated in 1976, making it the most prestigious hotel in Brunswick, outclassing its nearest competitor, the Mövenpick. The management has thoughtfully provided a pedestrian bridge over the road separating the hotel from the Hauptbahnhof. The atrium in the center (hence the name) shelters a three-tiered lit fountain, surrounded by a landscaped collection of flowering shrubs. Most of the activity of the hotel centers around this central courtyard. The restaurant is dramatically lit by dozens of pin spots shining on the black-and-red op-art carpet. Rooms are spacious and handsome, with all the modern conveniences. Axel Schuldt, the manager of the complex, charges from 125 DM ($41.25) to 200 DM ($66) in a single and from 175 DM ($57.75) to 320 DM ($105.60) in a double, including breakfast. Children can stay free in their parents' room. In addition to its prestigious Atrium Restaurant, serving a French cuisine, the hotel also has a number of other places to dine, as well as a bar. You can also bowl in the in-house lanes, later sweating away your cares in a sauna.

MIDDLE-RANGE HOTELS: Deutsches Haus, 1 Ruhfäutchenplatz (tel. 4-44-22). The pleasing symmetrical facade of this hotel sits directly on the Burgplatz, giving views of the cathedral from many of its rooms. The pink-and-brown brick fronting is attractively embellished with an arched portico (the columns and arches of which are repeated on the interior stairwells), Renaissance-style bay windows, and stone corner mullions. The interior is high-ceilinged, richly appointed, and detailed as only a 19th-century building can be. The bedrooms have been stripped of their former embellishments and replaced with big patterned modern wallpaper and carpeting. They are clean, comfortable, and spacious, for the most part. Singles rent for 85 DM ($28.05) to 103 DM ($33.99), while doubles cost 116 DM ($38.28) to 152 DM ($50.16). All units contain shower or bath and come with breakfast.

Fürstenhof, 12 Campestrasse (tel. 79-10-61). The swimming pool of this family-run guest house is guarded at the edges by two cement statues of hobgoblins. The rest of this comfortable establishment is cozily decorated with Oriental rugs, hanging lamps, and warm autumnal colors. Each of the pleasant rooms has its own bath (or shower), costing from 80 DM ($26.40) to 100 DM ($33) in a single and from 130 DM ($42.90) to 160 DM ($52.80) in a double, including breakfast. The location here is only three minutes from the railway station.

Lessing-Hof, 13 Okerstrasse (tel. 4-54-55). Irma Sterdt is the genteel owner of two guest houses located across the street from one another a few blocks from the Andreas-Kirche in the center of Brunswick. Both establishments are clean and comfortable, and rooms include breakfast in the rates. A restaurant on the premises serves unpretentious food between 5:30 and 11:30 p.m. Monday to Saturday. Single rooms in either hotel, depending on the plumbing, range from 50 DM ($16.50) to 85 DM ($28.05), while doubles cost from 89 DM ($29.37) to 125 DM ($41.25).

Forsthaus, 72 Hamburger Strasse (tel. 3-28-01). The management is the primary reason for staying in this hotel which is comfortable and modern, with all the conveniences. It has been under the rule of the Hampe Michels family for the past 90 years. They have a boxy building with a low-lying extension containing a glass-walled restaurant. The location is within walking distance of an inner-city lake, the Olpersee. Pleasantly furnished singles rent for 75 DM ($24.75) with shower and toilet, while doubles cost 92 DM ($30.36) to 105 DM ($34.65), including breakfast.

A BUDGET HOTEL: Frühlings Hotel, 7 Bankplatz (tel. 4-93-17), may not win style awards, but it does excel at comfort. It's a substantial, 66-bedroom corner hotel, with a modern Germanic look. There is a respectable dining room, plus a cozy bar and lounge. Most of the adequately furnished bedrooms have tile private bath. Bathless doubles go for 95 DM ($31.35) increasing to 115 DM ($37.95) with a private bath. Singles cost 56 DM ($18.48) to 95 DM ($31.35). Taxes, service, and breakfast are included in these tariffs. Nearby is a community parking garage.

WHERE TO DINE: Gewandhauskeller, 1 Altstadtmarkt (tel. 4-44-41), is a stone building dating from 1352 and located on the most beautiful square of Brunswick. Once it was a guildhouse for sailmakers, and later it acquired an elegant Renaissance facade. Its fine wines are kept in a 1000-year-old cellar. Rhine and Mosel wines are a specialty. In the midst of this antiquity, well-prepared international dishes are served. Specialties include tournedos Monte Carlo and sole Ceylon. Menus range from 28 DM ($9.24) to 70 DM ($23.10), and hours are 11 a.m. to midnight, except on Sunday.

Haus zur Hanse, 7 Güldenstrasse (tel. 4-61-54), is another historic restaurant. Built in 1567, it lies behind a half-timbered structure with the most interesting facade in Brunswick. Plan to make an evening of it. For openers, I'd recommend onion soup, followed by snails French style and veal steak with young spinach. Another specialty is king-size prawns flambé with Pernod. The ice sorbet made from kiwi fruit makes a good finish. Menus begin at 18 DM ($5.94), climbing to 60 DM ($19.80). Hours are 11 a.m. to 3 p.m. and 5 p.m. till closing (likely to vary).

Hotel Deutsches Haus, 1 Burgplatz (tel. 4-44-22). The location of this restaurant, in a hotel previously recommended, might suit anyone making a tour of the city, as it stands next door to the cathedral. And because it has specialties from practically every region of the country, the menu might be called "Pan-Germanic." Also featured is a series of Dutch specialties as well. The restaurant is open from 6 a.m. to 1 a.m. every day of the week, charging from 18 DM ($5.94) to 55 DM ($18.15) for a satisfying meal.

6. Hildesheim

Just 15 miles southeast of Hannover, the town of Hildesheim basks in the glory of its more than 1150 years. It was considered the capital of Ottonian Romanesque art, but many of its treasures were lost to Allied bombing missions in the spring of 1945. The history of the community is closely tied to a romantic tale about the rose tree, still flourishing today, which supposedly marked the spot for the founding of the seat of the bishopric. As with most episcopal sees, Hildesheim became a free city and prospered as a center, not only for the church, but for art and industry as well.

THE SIGHTS: Some of the original ramparts, built by the bishop about A.D. 1000, are standing around the Old Town. The streets are lined with many houses with overhanging upper stories and elaborately adorned wooden facades. The

Rathaus, or Town Hall (tel. 30-11), from the 15th century, contains frescoes illustrating the history of the city. Visiting hours are 9 a.m. to 4 p.m.

The chief attraction, however, remains the **cathedral** (Dom) (tel. 3-20-21), which, although badly bombed, has been restored. The present structure, built in the 11th century, occupies the site of the original building of the early 9th century. The basilica is Romanesque in design, but the side chapels are Gothic and the dome is classical. The 11th-century bronze bas-relief doors were turned out by local artisans under St. Bernward, bishop of Hildesheim. The cathedral also contains a treasury full of valuable works, including the intricately designed bishop's staff. Within the church are also many works of art, and last but not least, the Romanesque cloister at the end of the cathedral houses the town's most valuable possession, the rose tree.

The **Pelizaeus Museum,** 1-2 Am Stein (tel. 3-29-83), is unique in Germany, containing one of the world's most impressive collections of Egyptian antiquities, including sarcophagi, statues, and even the chapel of a 4500-year-old coffin-tomb of one Egyptian official. The museum is open daily (except Monday) from 10 a.m. to 4:30 p.m. Admission is 3 DM (99¢).

Other than the Dom, a remarkable ecclesiastical building in Hildesheim is **St. Michaelis Kirche,** which was first constructed in the early part of the 11th century. Gutted by those spring bombers of 1945, it has since been rebuilt in the early Romanesque Ottonian style, as was typical of the region. The decor and architectural plans of Old Saxony were respected here, and today you can see two apses and a nave with a restored painted ceiling which was originally done in the 1200s. In the transept you will see two-tiered galleries in the Romanesque style. An "angel screen," seen to the right of the west chancel, is what remains of the kirche's original embellishments.

WHERE TO STAY: **Gollart's Hotel Deutsches Haus,** 5 Carl-Peters-Strasse (tel. 1-59-71). Rising seven floors above the pavement a few blocks from the Hauptbahnhof, the modern exterior of this recently constructed hotel is tastefully built of polished concrete and darkly enameled aluminum. The interior is attractively decorated in blues or browns, with a pleasantly rustic bierstube and a swimming pool almost 40 feet long. All of the comfortable bedrooms have bath, color TV, phone, and radio. They rent for 86 DM ($28.38) to 99 DM ($33.67) in a single and 120 DM ($39.60) to 135 DM ($44.55) in a double. You'll be able to release the tension of traveling in the hotel's fitness room followed by a session in the sauna.

Bürgermeisterkapelle, 8 Rauthausstrasse (tel. 1-40-21). You can identify this establishment by the vertical "hotel" sign ("Bürgermeisterkapelle" was probably too long to write in neon), and the cement rib and brick construction capped by the reproduction half-timbered tile roof. The interior is clean, comfortable, and sunny, and some of the units are snuggled under the eaves near the triangular window just under the roofline. You'll find a wide range of plumbing accessories in the rooms, which rent for 50 DM ($16.50) to 100 DM ($33) in a single and 87 DM ($28.71) to 130 DM ($42.90) in a double. The most elaborate rooms have private shower and toilet; for the others, a bathroom is on each hall. Breakfast is included. Richard Strohmeyer is the manager and owner.

Hotel Rose, 7 Am Markt (tel. 1-59-55), across the Marketplace from the historic Town Hall, is completely modern with most attractive accommodations. Many people stay here during the Hannover Fair (just a six-minute drive from the autobahn) when the hotels of Hannover are fully booked. All rooms contain private bath or shower. Many have a terrace overlooking the Marketplace. Single rooms rent for 70 DM ($23.10) to 105 DM ($34.65), and doubles go for 100 DM ($33) to 130 DM ($42.90). Patrons and guests of the hotel and restaurant (see my dining recommendations) may park in either the parking lot or the subterranean garages.

WHERE TO DINE: The **Ratskeller,** 1 Markt (tel. 1-44-41), is an attractive dining room under a vaulted ceiling in the cellar of the old Rathaus. Every attempt has been made to create a cozy atmosphere. Main courses are reasonably priced and consist of both regional and international specialties. Menus begin at 28 DM ($9.24), going up to 65 DM ($21.45). With every meal, you have a free selection from 40 freshly prepared salads, which they claim is the biggest choice in north Germany.

Romantik-Restaurant Kupferschmiede, 6 Steinberg (tel. 26-23-51), stands outside town some 3½ miles, at Ausserhalb. Built at least a century ago as a rendezvous point for gourmets, this family-run establishment still serves that purpose for the hundreds of locals who prefer it above any other eatery. Owner Wolfgang Bleckmann encourages his staff to prepare an original interpretation of nouvelle cuisine, with such specialties as loup de mer (sea bass) in a basil sauce, or according to the preference of a client, in puff pastry. Or perhaps you might be offered breast of Barbary goose in a peppermint sauce, or a gratinée of baby piglet in a spicy ratatouille. The desserts run the gamut from nouvelle low-cal to traditional Germanic sumptuous. Fixed-price meals cost between a reasonable 33 DM ($10.89) and a staggering 110 DM ($36.30). The restaurant is open from noon to 2:30 p.m. and 6:30 to 9:30 p.m. It's closed all day Sunday.

The **Restaurant Knochenhauer,** on the premises of the Hotel Rose, 7 Am Markt (tel. 1-59-55), offers selections from a wide-ranging international menu, with dinners costing from 28 DM ($9.24) to 55 DM ($18.15). A well-chosen selection of wines rounds out the menu. Patrons and guests of the restaurant may park in the hotel parking lot or suberannean garages.

7. Minden

Also in the "Land" of North Rhine-Westphalia, Minden is just 44 miles from Hannover, so it's included in this chapter for convenient touring purposes. On the left bank of the Weser, the old Hanseatic city made its mark in history as the site of the Battle of Minden, fought in 1759, at which time the British infantry defeated the French cavalry in the Seven Years' War.

Minden's best known building is its cathedral, in the center of town. Characterized by a Romanesque facade, the Dom has somewhat the look of a fortress. Inside, its most valued art treasure is a Romanesque crucifix from the 11th century.

The **Mittellandkanal** merits a visit too. It crosses the Weser by means of a 1200-foot-long bridge, allowing the canal to go from the Münster to Hannover without benefit of locks.

In the environs, **Porta Westfalica,** or the Westphalian Gap, is a natural geological attraction. From either the Bismarck Tower or the monument to Kaiser Wilhelm across the river, there is a panoramic view of the Weser as it enters the plains of North Germany.

WHERE TO STAY: Hotel **Exquisit** and **Gaststätte Zum Bären,** 2A In den Bärenkämpen (tel. 4-30-55), form a unified complex in a quiet wooded area a few miles from the center of town. Tennis lovers will enjoy the use of three illuminated indoor courts about a mile from the hotel, and after the game they can relax in the hotel pool and sauna. The rooms are clean and unpretentious, but attractively styled, renting for 108 DM ($35.64) to 125 DM ($41.25) in a double and 85 DM ($28.05) to 125 DM ($41.25) in a single. The more expensive accommodations are in the main house, and the cheapest rooms, which are still most satisfactory, are in the guest house across the street. All units are furnished with shower and toilet, and breakfast is included in the rates. You might want to take some of your meals in the attractive dining room, which is decorated with a stylized mural of medieval horsemen and bordered with wood trim.

Kruses Park Hotel, 108 Marienstrasse (tel. 4-60-33). My favorite part of this gemütlich hotel is the covered terrace where meals and drinks are served until late at night in summer. The rest of the hotel welcomes guests in any season with warm yellow light coming from the big modern windows, and with a gracious reception given by your host, Horst Kruse. Rooms are spacious and decorated in pleasing shades of lemon yellow and cream. Since the establishment is part of the Ringhotel chain, you can be assured of a better-than-average quality. Accommodations rent for 55 DM ($18.15) to 95 DM ($31.35) in a single (with a wide range of plumbing possibilities) and from 94 DM ($31.02) to 146 DM ($48.18) in a double. The hotel lies at the northern edge of the city, and many residents of the town come to the restaurant/konditorei for its gutbürgerlich and international specialties. Something you might want to try is a combination of ham, pickles, and cranberries, seasoned in "a secret way" known only to the chefs. Meals cost from 25 DM ($8.25) to 50 DM ($16.50). The two-part restaurant, comprising the Blue Salon and the Hunter's Lodge, is open from noon to 3 p.m. and 6 to 10 p.m. every day.

Silke, 21 Fischerglacis (tel. 2-37-36), is a modern hotel raised on concrete stilts above a well-tended lawn with potted geraniums. Rooms are bright, big-windowed, and sunny, as well as tastefully furnished. They cost from 96 DM ($31.68) in a single and from 145 DM ($47.85) in a double, containing a private shower and toilet. The spot is somewhat isolated from downtown, and should appeal to those seeking a tranquil location.

Hotel Bad Minden, 36 Portastrasse (tel. 5-10-49). The low-slung brick facade of this comfortably furnished modern hotel is within one of the town's most spacious public parks. The trees, thanks to dozens of metal pots, extend right up to the blue neon sign and the sweeping modern portico of the reception area. Inside, the decor includes lots of warmly textured brick, wall-length murals of autumn forests, and lots of plants, sometimes skillfully illuminated. The hotel's kitchen turns out a well-prepared cuisine, and facilities include massage, sauna, and hydrotherapy treatments. Accommodations are sunny, spacious, clean, and generally pleasant: singles cost from 90 DM ($29.70), and doubles go for 160 DM ($52.80).

Victoria Hotel, 11 Markt (tel. 2-22-40), is a good and reliable choice, lying in the center of this historic town, opening onto a view of the 1000-year-old Marketplace and the cathedral. Ideal as a center for your excursions, it offers 44 comfortably furnished, very modern bedrooms, some with bath, shower, and toilet. An elevator services all floors. A double room with bath goes for 105 DM ($34.65), although you can stay here in a unit without bath for only 82 DM ($27.06). Again, depending on the plumbing, a single ranges from a low of 48 DM ($15.84) to a high of 68 DM ($22.44). English is spoken, and facilities include a sauna. The Victoria also has a small restaurant, serving quite good food. Underground parking garages are available nearby.

WHERE TO DINE: Ratskeller, 1 Markt (tel. 2-58-00), is known for its bierkeller Tonne. A nicely vaulted cellar from the Middle Ages, its original stones intact, the Ratskeller features set lunches and dinners from 18 DM ($5.94). A specialty is leg of veal Ratskeller, with potatoes Lyonnaise and a hollandaise sauce. Other dishes include steak tartare and a medallion of veal with mushrooms. Dinners cost from 35 DM ($11.55). Hours are daily except Monday from 11 a.m. to midnight.

Laterne, 38 Hahler Strasse (tel. 2-22-08). This is one of those comfortably cluttered restaurants where the primary colors give off a sort of autumnal warmth, and where the chef will probably come out of his lair to inquire about his cuisine after the meal is through. Open from 11 a.m. till 1 a.m. every day but Tuesday, the restaurant serves such specialties as flambé meats, fresh trout from its aquarium, marinated snails, and wild game dishes grilled over an open fire. Klaus Kothe is the owner and the chef, offering meals which range in price from 25 DM ($8.25) to 55 DM ($18.15).

8. Detmold

Detmold was the capital of Lippe, a former "Land" of the German Reich. After World War II it was incorporated into North Rhine-Westphalia and is included in this chapter for convenient touring purposes, not geographical designations.

Until 1918 Detmold was the center of the family of Prince Bernard of Holland when Lippe was a principality.

About ten miles from Bad Pyrmont, Detmold is a center for many tours. Following are several examples: **Teutoburger Forest,** where visitors travel a distance of four miles to the **Hermannsdenkmal** (Arminius Monument), to commemorate the victory of native tribes against the Roman legions in A.D. 9. With the dawn of German nationalism, the monument was completed in 1875. Armed with a sword, the copper statue of hero Arminius stands more than 50 feet high. In summer you can visit from 8 a.m. to 6 p.m., providing you don't mind climbing 75 steps for a panoramic view. Admission is 2 DM (66¢).

Another three miles and you're at **Externsteine,** the collection of limestone rocks (known in English as the Extern Stones). Beside a lake, this was a place of pagan worship, turned into a pilgrimage site for Christians in the Middle Ages. A remarkable bas-relief, the *Descent from the Cross,* was carved into the rock in the 12th century.

Back in Detmold, you can visit the **Palace of Detmold** (Detmold Schloss), a Renaissance building from the 16th century, with interior decoration from the 18th and 19th centuries. The front wing of the inner courtyard is exceptional, in the Weser Renaissance style. Tapestries of the 17th century, most of them woven in Belgium, were based on cartoons by Rubens and Le Brun. Hours are 9:30 a.m. to noon and 2 to 5 p.m. daily April 1 till October 31. From November 1 till March 31, guided tours are at 10 and 11 a.m. and 2, 3, and 4 p.m. Admission is 4 DM ($1.32).

FOOD AND LODGING: **Detmolder Hof,** 19 Langestrasse (tel. 2-82-44), was a 16th-century hostelry, with a handsome landmark gable. Tradition still prevails, as reflected by the sumptuous hall, with its marble and luxurious carpeting not to mention the deluxe dining room, with bright silver settings and antiques. The large bedrooms, all with bath, are also tastefully furnished. With all of this, the cost is still not exorbitant: singles run 80 DM ($26.40) to 100 DM ($33); doubles, 108 DM ($35.64) to 150 DM ($49.50). Breakfast is included. The culinary reputation is high, and the wine cellar is excellent.

Hotel Lippischer Hof and **Restaurant Le Gourmet,** 2 Allee (tel. 3-10-41). This elegantly decorated restaurant, in one of Detmold's most historic houses, a hotel dating from 1724, serves a light nouvelle cuisine of such specialties as green dill soup with fresh lobster, or pike presented in unusual and imaginative ways. Meals range in price from 40 DM ($13.20) to 65 DM ($21.45). The garden terrace welcomes you in summertime with its masses of flowers. Chef Gottfried Schusters is in charge of the kitchen, preparing everything to the wishes of his patrons. Food is offered from noon to 2 p.m. and 6 p.m. to midnight every day except on Saturday for lunch. They are closed for about two weeks sometime during the summer. Their accommodations are attractively and comfortably furnished, about the best in town. Singles range in price from 70 DM ($23.10) to 90 DM ($29.70), while doubles cost 128 DM ($42.24) to 150 DM ($49.50).

Gästehaus am Wall, 8 Wall (tel. 2-43-94). The mulberry-colored exterior of this attractive guest house is pierced with symmetrical rows of rectangular windows and accented in summer with flowers. Heinz Stratmann, the owner, charges guests from 55 DM ($18.15) in a bathless single, the price going up to 110 DM ($36.30) to 160 DM ($52.80) in doubles with private bath or shower. Rooms are simply but comfortably furnished, and breakfast is included in the price. The hotel is conveniently close to the center of town.

Hirschsprung, 212 Paderborner Strasse, at Berlebeck (tel. 49-11), lies in a suburb a few miles from the center of Detmold. You'll find an elegantly decorated restaurant that looks somewhat like a wealthy gentleman's private hunting lodge. The cuisine is an assemblage of regional specialties from throughout Germany, with a special emphasis on game. Dinners cost 35 DM ($11.55) to 75 DM ($24.75), and children's menus are also available. Lunch is served from 11 a.m. to 2 p.m. and 6 to 10 p.m. every day except Thursday. You'd be wise to phone ahead, as there are only 11 tables. The inn also has ten comfortably and pleasantly furnished bedrooms, costing from 60 DM ($19.80) to 85 DM ($28.05) in a single, 90 DM ($29.70) to 120 DM ($39.60) in a double.

Parkhotel Berkenhoff, 48 Stoddartstrasse, at Pivitsheide (tel. 81-20). You'll need to make a small expedition six miles west of town to dine here, but the warm decor of Oriental rugs and antique armoires, coupled with the well-prepared cuisine, might make the trip more than worthwhile. Trout seems to be the specialty that everybody in the region orders, and you'll find it prepared in many different ways. Dinners average around a reasonable 35 DM ($11.55). The restaurant is open from 7 a.m. for breakfast, serving lunch until 3 p.m. It reopens at 5:30 p.m. for dinner, staying open until 11 p.m. (closed Monday). The hotel rents out three single rooms at a cost of 40 DM ($13.20) to 55 DM ($18.15), and eight doubles going for 62 DM ($20.46) to 80 DM ($26.40). All are comfortable and well furnished.

Falkenberger Hof, 14 Am Krugplatz, Heiligenkirchen (tel. 4-74-47). Both the restaurant and its owner/chef have had many years of experience at feeding large groups of people. The restaurant has a 200-year-old history, but parts of it have been rebuilt, and the chef worked for some time as a ship's cook at sea. His occupation today is considerably more elegant than serving meals to rotating shifts of sailors, although his nautical past is reflected in the dozens of fish specialties he almost effortlessly sends from his kitchen. Examples would be filets of grilled carp with cabbage hollandaise and fresh mushrooms, fresh green eel in dill sauce, pike in a cabbage cream sauce, and as a change of pace, marinated filet of wild boar Russian style, served with apple sauce, rosemary sauce, baby cabbage, and mushrooms. Try to get a seat in one of the intimate niches below the balcony. Meals are modest in price: 18 DM ($5.94) to 40 DM ($13.20). They're served from 11:30 a.m. to 2:30 p.m. and 5 to 10:30 p.m. The restaurant is closed on Monday in winter and during all of November.

9. Hameln

Halfway from Hannover to Bad Pyrmont or Detmold lies Hameln (Hamelin in English), most notorious for its folklore history. It was the town of that famous ratcatcher, the Pied Piper, immortalized by both Goethe and Robert Browning.

The legend is that in 1284 the town was infested by rats. There appeared a piper who, for a fee, offered to lure the vermin into the Weser River. The ratcatcher kept his bargain; the stingy denizens of Hameln did not, claiming he was a sorcerer. He reappeared the next Sunday and played a tune that lured all the children, except one lame boy, into a mysterious door in a hill. The children and the Pied Piper were never heard from again. The story is retold every summer Sunday at noon in a special performance at Town Hall. In the shops of the town, you can buy rats made of every conceivable material, even candy ones.

In Lower Saxony, Hameln traces its history back to the 11th century. The most interesting buildings include the **Münster,** dedicated to St. Boniface and built in the Gothic style; the **Rattenfängerhaus** (ratcatcher's house), with frescoes illustrating the Pied Piper legend; and the **Hochzeitshaus** (wedding house), with its trio of attractive gables. The finest houses in the town are built in what is known as the "Weser Renaissance" style, from the late 16th century. You can admire these nicely sculpted houses as you stroll along pedestrian streets.

WHERE TO STAY: Zur Krone, 30 Osterstrasse (tel. 74-11), is an old house with antique furniture, comfortable and very clean, in the center of the historic town. A lot of copper utensils are placed all around, giving it a rustic aura. The dining rooms and breakfast salons are small, but numerous. Bathless singles go for 70 DM ($23.10), rising to 105 DM ($34.65) with shower. A bathless double is priced at 123 DM ($40.59), going up to 163 DM ($53.79) with shower, those tariffs including a continental breakfast.

Dorint Hotel Weserbergland, 3 von-Dingelstedt-Strasse (tel. 79-20), stands in a park with lots of trees, but is within walking distance of the heart of the old city. This comfortable modern hotel rises like a futuristic collection of building blocks, its oversize glass walls aimed toward the sunlight. All the attractively furnished units contain private bath or shower, and guests have access to the pool, sauna, solarium, and massage facilities. Singles, with breakfast included, rent for 95 DM ($31.35) to 105 DM ($34.65), while doubles cost 166 DM ($54.78).

Hotel Zur Börse, 41a Osterstrasse (tel. 70-80), lies within the walls of the old city. This balconied and mustard-colored hotel can be identified by the four peaks of the modern roofline and by the green parasols set up on the garden terrace. The interior is refreshingly uncluttered, tastefully painted in different shades of white. Rooms are spacious and sunny, renting for 42 DM ($13.86) to 52 DM ($17.16) in a single and 75 DM ($24.75) to 95 DM ($31.35) in a double, breakfast included. Most units have shower or toilet.

WHERE TO DINE: Rattenfängerhaus, 28 Osterstrasse (tel. 38-88), is the Renaissance building from 1603 referred to earlier as the "ratcatcher's house." The outside is well preserved and inviting. The inside is also historical looking, with small wood windows, antiques, and pictures. It's practically like eating in a museum. The house specialty is rumpsteak Madagascar with green pepper, potato croquettes, and green beans. Another specialty is rattenschwanze Balireis with salad and a "mousecatcher" plate, a pork filet. Menus range in price from 22 DM ($7.26) to 55 DM ($18.15), and service is daily except Tuesday from 9:30 a.m. to 1 a.m.

Seehof, 3 Tönebönweg (tel. 4-17-22). Visitors to this setting have called it idyllic, and everything about it seems to contribute to such a description. Set on the edge of a lake and surrounded by greenery, the restaurant serves such time-honored specialties as filet of trout, filet of gander in crab sauce, fresh eel delicately seasoned in brown butter, wursts, and peppered hamsteak, plus the usual array of wild game. There is also a generous expanse of salad bar. Meals cost from 25 DM ($8.25) to 60 DM ($19.80), and are served daily from noon to 2:30 p.m. and 6 to 10 p.m.

Weinstuben am Kamin, 12 Pyrmonter Strasse (tel. 6-21-22). Town gossips made much of the fact that in 1962 members of the Franke family redesigned and rebuilt a historical building in the center of town. Critics have since contended that the renovations are tasteful and appropriately centered around an open fireplace, the flames from which illuminate the dozens of regular patrons, many of whom have made this their favorite restaurant. The specialty of the house is Russian-style roast beef, which is served from 7 p.m. till 1 a.m. every day but Monday. Complete meals average from 20 DM ($6.60) to 50 DM ($16.50).

Hotel Sintermann-Restaurant Merlin, 2 Bahnhofsplatz (tel. 1-42-48). You won't have far to walk if you're hungry as soon as you get off the train at the Hauptbahnhof. Across the square, you'll find an enclave of Teutonic decor and hospitality, serving reasonably priced meals costing 22 DM ($7.26) to 40 DM ($13.20). Food tends to be international, but you can still get pig knuckles and bratwurst if you want them. They serve from noon to 2:30 p.m. and 6 to 10:30 p.m. every day of the week. The restaurant is attached to a hotel which charges from 50 DM ($16.50) to 80 DM ($26.40) in a single and from 75 DM ($24.75) to 120 DM ($39.60) in a double. It has been directed for several generations by the same family.

Café-Restaurant Klütturm, auf der Klütberg (tel. 6-16-44). Although lovely, the traditional decor of this restaurant takes second place to the panoramic view of the old city you'll get once you're inside. Meals are traditional German, costing 22 DM ($7.26) to 50 DM ($16.50), with special care lavished on the dessert wagon whose confections are changed every day. In season the cook will prepare game dishes, and throughout the year rack of baby lamb with fresh vegetables or perhaps entrecôte of beef with escargots. Service is from 11 a.m. to 10 p.m. However, hot food is served only from noon to 2:30 p.m. and 6 to 9 p.m. They are closed Tuesday and in January.

10. Upper Weser Valley

Running for 273 miles, the Weser River winds along Germany's "fairytale country." Sleeping Beauty, the characters in the Grimm Brothers' fairy tales, and the tall tales of Baron Münchausen were created here.

This most interesting day tour traditionally begins at Hannoversch Münden. At this point the Fulda and Werra Rivers meet. Many end their jaunt in the Pied Piper town of Hameln in the north. The most romantic way to see the river is on a paddle-steamer in summer.

HANNOVERSCH MÜNDEN: In the center of town are hundreds of half-timbered houses built in many styles. At the confluence of the Werra and Fulda Rivers, the Weserstein (stone) commemorates the joining. In the medieval town you can park your car and begin your exploration of Hannoversch Münden by going inside **St. Blaise's Church.** In the nave is the tomb of William of Brunswick, who died in 1503. With its trio of gables, the **Town Hall** is also interesting. The facade is a good example of the style known as Weser Renaissance. From here you can branch out and tour the already-mentioned medieval houses. The tombstone of the much maligned Doctor Eisenbart is also in Hannoversch Münden. He is honored every year at a folk festival.

Food and Lodging
Hotel Eberburg, 14 Tillyschanzenweg (tel. 44-53). This is an attractively decorated guest house set in a forest not far from the center of town. You won't be alone if you choose to dine on the sun terrace or inside the restaurant, because many locals from the city often decide to do just that. Attractively styled

and comfortably furnished singles rent for 45 DM ($14.85) to 70 DM ($23.10), while doubles cost 80 DM ($26.40) to 112 DM ($36.96), including a generous breakfast buffet. Fixed-price meals go for anywhere from 18 DM ($5.94) to 45 DM ($14.85).

Jagdhaus Heede, 81 Hermannshäger Strasse (tel. 23-95). Thanks to its location inside the town's nature preserve, this hotel offers peaceful accommodations. It originated as a conservatively designed house. Over the years, the owners added a sprawling three-story modern wing filled with sunwashed bedrooms and lots of comfort. Each of the accommodations contains a private balcony, phone, and a view of the forest. Closed every November, the hotel charges from 50 DM ($16.50) in a single and from 90 DM ($29.70) in a double. There's a café-style sun terrace on the premises, as well as a children's playground. In the dining room a conservative German cuisine is prepared with flavor and served in generous portions.

Ratskeller, 1 Am Markt (tel. 10-00). The Rathaus (Town Hall) of Münden, dating from 1605, is one of the best examples of a Renaissance public building north of the Alps. Its keller is no less an architectural curiosity. Much of the original decor is still intact, although new kitchens have been added which permit the Strasbourg-born chef, Henri Fleck, to create his imaginative nouvelle cuisine. Examples of this are venison pâté in Waldorf salad, veal chops in a mustard madeira sauce, breast of goose with red cranberries, or rack of lamb provençal cooked with lots of garlic and fresh beans. Food is served from 11 a.m. to 2:30 p.m. and 6 to 10:30 p.m. every day of the week but Monday. Meals range from 30 DM ($9.90) to 75 DM ($24.75).

After leaving Hannoversch Münden, you have to detour west of the river at a marked turnoff to reach—

SABABURG: Across forest roads you arrive at **Sababurg Castle** where Sleeping Beauty supposedly slumbered. This castle has had a long and turbulent history since it was first built in 1334 by the archbishop of Mainz. It eventually fell to ruin. However, between 1490 and 1492 Count Wilhelm I constructed a hunting lodge on the ruins, and in time it became known for its banquets of the hunt. He also laid out a zoological garden on the 500-acre estate, making it what is reportedly the oldest zoological garden in the world. Since 1971 it has again become a home for rare animals, including bison and reindeer. Troops plundered the castle during the Thirty Years' War, and the French caused further damage during the Seven Years' War. Friedrich II in 1765 turned the castle back into a hunting castle, but that too was allowed to go to seed. New life began on the castle in 1961. In summer you generally have to park down below and walk up, as the limited space at the top is almost always filled. This castle is in Hesse, and it's partially in ruins, but it is believed to have inspired the Grimm Brothers. For 2 DM (66¢) you can explore it. To the west of the castle lie 70 acres of wild forest which has not been cultivated for more than a century. The wilderness of ancient oak and beech trees, along with tall ferns, suggest to many a "fairytale forest."

Food and Lodging

The **Burghotel Sababurg** (tel. 10-52) occupies a wing of the castle in Hofgeismar-Sababurg, 8½ miles north from Kassel. The hotel, run by Mr. Koseck, is beautifully furnished with antique reproductions. He rents out 16 bedrooms, a dozen of which contain private bath. Nearly all of the well-furnished units open onto views. Depending on the plumbing, singles range in price from 60 DM ($19.80) to 100 DM ($33), and doubles are priced from 90

DM ($29.70) to 170 DM ($56.10). Each of the luxurious, period-style bedrooms has its own original name, such as "Das Einhorn" (The Unicorn), "Im Wildt" (The Game), and "In der wilden Sau" (The Wild Sow). Half board (breakfast and dinner) costs an extra 35 DM ($11.55) per person daily. The inn shuts down from January 5 to February 25. If you're stopping by to dine, expect to pay from 25 DM ($8.25) to 45 DM ($14.85) for a meal. Summer feasts, announced by blowing horns, are staged in the fortress ruins, with wild pig or spitted bullock, a glass of wine at fireside, or a dance by torchlight. Game and fish dishes, along with spit-grilled items, are also offered. There is also a private guest house near-by called Sababurger Mühle, offering 30 beds.

Again, you have to traverse the Reinhardswald, an oak forest, to reach the main route along the Weser.

The next recommended stopover is at—

BAD KARLSHAFEN: This is a baroque town founded in 1699 by the Huguenots and lying at the confluence of the Diemel and the Weser. In the town is one of the most interesting stopovers for both food and lodgings along the Weser River, previewed below.

Hotel zum Schwan, 3–4 Conradistrasse (tel. 10-44), is an elegant although miniature spa, situated beside the main bathhouse and opposite the town pond on which swans float. Built in 1765, it has the baroque facade of a small palace, with an entrance terrace overlooking the river. Life is informal here, and the rococo dining salon is rather grand, with its paneled walls and monumental ceramic stove. The living room is modern, and in the rear is an attractive courtyard garden. Breakfast is served in a period-piece room, with beaded hanging lampshades and lace curtains. Doubles go for 42 DM ($13.86) to 80 DM ($46.20). All prices include breakfast. If you stop only for a meal, expect to pay 25 DM ($8.25) to 35 DM ($11.55). English is spoken. The hotel is closed from December 15 to February 15.

Continuing north along the river, you reach—

FÜRSTENBURG: On a hill overlooking the right bank, a castle-factory has been making a famous porcelain since 1747.

From there, the approach is easy to—

HÖXTER: This town is filled with Renaissance and baroque buildings. The most visited is called **Dechanei,** or the deanery, and it stands to the right of St. Nicholas's Church. The house is twin gabled and dates from 1561. A walk down the **Westerbachstrasse** reveals many half-timbered medieval buildings. The 11th-century **St. Kilian's Church** contains an outstanding Renaissance pulpit decorated with motifs in alabaster.

Take the Corveyer Allee from Höxter for about two miles to **Corvey,** where the abbey stands. The oldest part of the abbey, and the only section still left from the original structure, is the west facade. The lower parts are examples of Romanesque art from the ninth century. Guided tours are conducted through the abbey from April 1 to October 31 from 9 a.m. to 5 p.m. for an admission of 3.80 DM ($1.25).

You can also dine within the castle precincts at **Schloss-Restaurant,** Schloss Corvey (tel. 83-23). In summer ask for a table on the garden terrace. This restaurant is installed in the former living quarters of the castle. It's surrounded on two sides by well-trimmed linden trees. The great hall is used mainly for special events, and the tavern-style dining room offers luncheons and dinners with a fairly large international repertoire of dishes. The waiters are cordial, and the food is well prepared. The restaurant, really a weinstube, is open only from April to December. It is closed Monday. The least expensive meal here will cost about 20 DM ($6.60), but it's also possible to spend 55 DM ($18.15). Hours are 8:30 a.m. to 10 p.m.

Continuing on, we reach our final goal at—

BODENWERDER: Thirteen miles south of Pied Piper's Hameln lived Baron Münchausen and his son. The Münchausen name has gone down in literary history. A hunting lodge owned by the baron is a pilgrimage site for dreamy souls. Münchausen's narrative about his "travels and campaigns" in Russia increased in renown and was translated into many languages. The original author was Rudolf Erich Raspe, who apparently became acquainted with Freiherr von Münchausen upon his retirement in 1760 in Russian service against the Turks. He was widely known for his tall tales about his prowess as a sportsman and a soldier. Many of the stories for which Münchausen is celebrated were actually inspired by other tellers of tall tales and were included in subsequent editions.

Deutsches Haus, 4 Münchhausenplatz (tel. 39-25). Its location on one of the town's most prominent squares makes this modern hotel easy to find. Its bedrooms are clean, styled in a streamlined up-to-date comfort, with a buffet breakfast included in the price of the room. The 40 bedrooms rent for 38 DM ($12.54) to 60 DM ($19.80) in a single and between 75 DM ($24.75) and 110 DM ($36.30) in a double. All accommodations have phone and radio, while the doubles contain a TV set. An in-house restaurant provides tasty and generous meals. A public swimming pool and options for various promenades are all within walking distance.

11. Goslar

In spite of the progress and growth of Goslar, the old portion of the town looks just as it did hundreds of years ago. This ancient Hanseatic town lies at the foot of the Harz Mountains. The 600-year-old streets are still in use today and the carved, half-timbered houses are more than just monuments to the past. Many of them are used as homes or as offices of various organizations.

Goslar owes its early prosperity to the mines in the Harz Mountains, from which silver was drawn as early as 968. The town works the lead and zinc mines in nearby Rammelsberg.

THE SIGHTS: To best explore this 1000-year-old town, park your car, put on a pair of comfortable shoes, and set out on foot. That way you won't miss any of the numerous attractions that await you, beginning with the **Rathaus** (Town Hall), one of the oldest and perhaps the most impressive town halls in Germany. Begun in the 12th century, the main section was not constructed until 1450. This part of the structure consists of an open portico with Gothic crossvaulting, topped by the burghers' hall. The open arcade on the ground level was used for centuries as a market by the townspeople. The open gallery on the second floor was closed up with stained-glass windows in the 17th century. In the early 1500s the original assembly hall in the Rathaus was turned into a **Hall of Homage,** and lavishly decorated with a cycle of 55 paintings called *The Incarnation of God in Jesus Christ.* The paintings, which cover the walls and ceilings of the room, include not only works depicting the life of Christ, but other biblical characters as well. Many of the faces are actually the portraits of townspeople of the period. It is open from 9:30 a.m. to 5:30 a.m. June to September, and from 10 a.m. to 4 p.m. October to May, charging an admission of 2.50 DM (83¢).

The **Marketplace,** in front of the Rathaus, was for a long time the town's hub of activity. In the center of the large square is a 13th-century fountain with two bronze basins and the German Imperial Eagle at the top. Townspeople and visitors alike gather in the square at 6 o'clock each evening to hear the clock concert and to watch the parade, including the zinc miners, returning home from the Rammelsberg mines.

The churches of Goslar provide a look into the architectural history of the area. Many of the oldest churches—five had already been built by 1200—have been expanded and altered from their original Romanesque style to their current Gothic appearance. The Romanesque **Market Church,** opposite the Rathaus, still has its 700-year-old stained-glass windows and a 16th-century bronze baptismal font. The **Neuwerk Church** has retained its purely Romanesque basilica, and its well-preserved sanctuary contains a richly decorated choir and stucco reliefs. The **Jakobikirche,** from the 11th century, has been transformed into a Gothic masterpiece, complete with baroque altars. The church contains the *Pietà* by Hans Witten (1520).

The **Frankenberg Church** is from the 12th century, but was completely remodeled in the 1700s. Over the elaborate baroque pulpit and altars hangs the intricately carved "Nun's Choir Gallery," bedecked with little gilded saints and symbols.

One of the reminders that Goslar was once a free Imperial and Hanseatic city is the **Breites Tor** (Wide Gate), a fortress with 23-foot-thick walls and ramparts stretching to the **Kaiserpfalz** (Imperial Palace). The palace, rebuilt in the 19th century along the lines of its 11th-century original, is a Romanesque hall. Within its walls is the 12th-century twin-storied chapel of St. Ulrich, containing the sarcophagus of Emperor Henry III. It's open May 1 until the end of September from 9 a.m. to 5:30 p.m., from 10 a.m. to 4 p.m. in March, April, and October, and from 10 a.m. to 3 p.m. November to February, charging an admission of 2.50 DM (83¢).

For a quick and less exhausting look at the history of Goslar, visit the **Civic Museum** (Goslarer Museum), which has displays of the early town, models of the architecture, and several relics of the past. The museum also contains an exhibition of 1000 years of mining, including a large geological collection from the Harz Mountains. It's open from 9 a.m. to 5 p.m. June to September (from 10 a.m. to 1 p.m. on Sunday); the rest of the year, from 10 a.m. to 1 p.m., and again from 3 to 5 p.m. (from 10 a.m. to 1 p.m. on Sunday). Admission is 2.50 DM (83¢).

Incidentally, for hikers and other outdoor enthusiasts, Goslar is a suitable starting point for day trips and excursions into the Harz Mountains. Not only are these hills known for their minerals and Harz canaries, but they also contain some of Germany's best skiing resorts and several spas.

For the demonology expert, the Harz is rich in tales of witchcraft and other folklore. Walpurgis Eve (Witches' Sabbath) is still celebrated in the hills each year.

WHERE TO STAY: **Kaiserworth,** 3 Markt (tel. 2-11-11), right in the heart of town, is a big old-fashioned Germanic hotel. The building dates from 1494 and is considered a sightseeing attraction. Below the eaves are carved baroque statues of the German emperors. The hotel's exterior is Gothic, with an arched arcade across the front of the structure, topped by a turreted oriel window facing the Marketplace. The rooms are large; in fact, the corner rooms are big enough to be suites. Room 21 (a corner room) offers the best view of the Marketplace and the 6 o'clock concert by the clock on the square. With bath, the price is 85 DM ($28.05) to 115 DM ($37.95) in a single and 140 DM ($46.20) to 175 DM ($57.75) in a double. The rooms are designed with an accent on comfort. On the ground floor the hotel has a sedate, wood-paneled breakfast room and a vaulted-ceilinged dining room, Die Worth. Step through a 1000-year-old cistern and you are in the cellar restaurant, the Dukatenkeller, with its vaulted ceilings, stone pillars, and ecclesiastical chairs.

Der Achtermann, 20 Rosentorstrasse (tel. 2-10-01), was completely gutted and has been restored. The reputation of this historic structure has spread throughout the Harz region. The 140 rooms—enough for 200 guests—are completely modernized, each with private bath, TV, and radio. Singles cost from 85 DM ($28.05) to 135 DM ($44.55), and doubles go for 148 DM ($48.84) to 200 DM ($66). In addition to the major dining room, the hotel also has an intimate bar and a bierstube. The latter is housed in a circular medieval tower for which the hotel is named. Incorporating the tower into the structure, the hotel has created an old-world atmosphere in the bierstube, with time-blackened oak and snug nooks for drinking.

Hotel Restaurant das Brusttuch, 1 Hoher Weg (tel. 2-10-81), sits like a dunce's cap on a narrow street corner in the old city, with a sharply peaked roof rising as high as the main body of the building itself. The ground floor is made of rough-hewn stone, above which a half-timbered second story is gaily decorated with sea dragons, nymphs, and flowers. Inside is an elaborately decorated restaurant/wine cellar, with so many unusual artifacts below the soaring ceiling that it's difficult to concentrate on the menu. Aside from the restaurant, you'll find 13 rooms with modern bath renting for 90 DM ($29.70) to 100 DM ($33) in a single and from 150 DM ($49.50) in a double, including breakfast.

Schwarzer Adler, 25 Rosentorstrasse (tel. 2-40-01). Wolfgang Schmidt is your gracious host at this modern, 31-room hotel which benefits from a long tradition of good food, hospitality, and comfort. Singles rent for 55 DM ($18.15) to 85 DM ($28.05), while doubles cost 80 DM ($26.40) to 120 DM ($39.60). Half board is an extra 18 DM ($5.94) per person. You'll enjoy the botanical sun terrace.

Goldene Krone, 46 Breite Strasse (tel. 2-27-92), near the Breites Tor (Wide Gate), is a village inn, complete with a friendly innkeeper and his wife who attend to the rooms and the meals. The intricately timbered building sits on a busy street along with other old structures. If you enjoy local color, this hotel is a real find. Singles without bath rent for 40 DM ($13.20), 70 DM ($23.10) with bath. Doubles without bath cost 65 DM ($21.45); with shower, 100 DM ($33). Breakfast and taxes are included. The rooms are simple, but home-like and clean. The food and drink available are good and inexpensive. Set lunches cost from 19 DM ($6.27), including soup and dessert. The restaurant is closed Wednesday.

WHERE TO DINE: Die Worth, 3 Markt (tel. 2-11-11), is the most rustic and also the most attractive dining room in Goslar. Right in the heart of town, in the Hotel Kaiserworth, the restaurant is a Gothic stone crypt with vaulted ceilings and arches, stained-glass windows, wrought-iron lanterns, and trestle tables. The food is good, if uninspired, and the portions are hearty. The menu consists of heavy Germanic cooking. In season, roast game is featured with wild mushrooms, mashed apples, and berries. A set lunch goes for 30 DM ($9.90), but you could spend as much as 55 DM ($18.15) at night if you order the à la carte specialties. The restaurant closes on Monday in winter.

Mamma Rosa, 4 Mauerstrasse (tel. 4-02-07), is one of the most popular dining rooms in town. Its decor is undeniably Italian, similiar to something you'd find much farther south, and its sophisticated kitchen offers Italian specialties, as is to be expected, but with a nouvelle cuisine culinary flair. Reservations are essential at one of the immaculately set tables. Seasonal specialties change with the availability of fare—lobster, oysters, mussels, fowl, and game—which the chefs use with style and abandon. One of the best values is the 70-DM

($23.10) gourmet menu. Meals are served from noon to 2 p.m. and 6 to 11 p.m. every day except Thursday and during June.

Harzhotel Bären, 11a Krugwiese (tel. 78-20). Music and dancing often accompany a meal at this modern hotel decorated with light-grained wood and frequented by dozens of partying locals. The comfortably rustic bierstube could provide a suitable spot for a beer or some schnapps before moving into the main restaurant where meals cost anywhere from 18 DM ($5.94) to 45 DM ($14.85). Specialties of the house include grilled goose, roast piglet, or a shank of either pork or veal. They also serve "Kentucky ham" with buttered corn. Service is every day from 5 p.m. till 1 a.m. (the kitchen closes at 11 p.m.).

Goldene Krone, 46 Breite Strasse (tel. 2-27-92). Everyone in town seemingly knows about this historic weinstube on the eastern edge of Goslar, which features an international menu with meals costing from 20 DM ($6.60) to 45 DM ($14.85). It's open from 7 a.m. to midnight every day. Hot food is offered between 11 a.m. and 2 p.m. and from 6 to 10 p.m. The decor is rustic and cozy, and you'll surely feel at home with the friendly service.

Grauhof Restaurant Quellschänke, am Grauhof-Brunnen (tel. 8-40-01). If summertime is your favorite season, you'll love the approach to this country restaurant north of Goslar. A low-lying modern building with a red tile roof, it has a sun terrace near an elaborately planted garden. The interior boasts a ceramic-tile oven and lots of windows looking out onto the flowers. International specialties include game and asparagus dishes in season, each beautifully prepared. Meals cost from a modest 18 DM ($5.94) to 35 DM ($11.55), and are served from 10 a.m. till 11 p.m. every day of the week.

Harzhotel Kreuzeck Dorint, 1 Kreuzeck, at Hahnenklee (tel. 7-41), lies in a wooded area south of Goslar. This rustic villa serves a nouvelle cuisine in its restaurant, Bergkanne, with menus costing between 35 DM ($11.55) and 65 DM ($21.45). All the products used are the freshest available, and many are imported directly from France. Some of the specialties include fried filet of smoked salmon, filet of turbot with fresh mushrooms, juicy steaks poached in butter, sauteed medallions of Charmoise lamb with fresh vegetables and grain dauphinoise, and a complete list of fresh salads. Music and dancing often accompany the meal, which could be terminated with a tempting array of fresh sqrbets. The restaurant is open from noon to 2:30 p.m. and 6 to 11 p.m.

12. Göttingen

A city in Lower Saxony, Göttingen was pronounced "famous for its sausages and university" by Heinrich Heine. The university in this Gothic town is one of the most respected and oldest in Germany, and it suffered little damage during World War II.

Medieval romanticism and the vivacity of student life, particularly as lived in the numerous taverns, make Göttingen worth a day's visit. By making a slight detour, you can explore the university town before dipping into the fairytale country of the Upper Weser Valley. Göttingen is halfway between Bonn and Berlin.

In 1737 George II, king of Great Britain and Ireland and elector of Hannover, opened the Georgia Augusta University, and in time Göttingen became the most popular university town in Europe. The university granted absolute freedom in doctrine and research. For the first time, female as well as Jewish students were admitted.

The **Town Hall,** from 1369, wasn't completed until 1443. Before the structure is a modern fountain of a goose-girl, around which students congregate. Around the Town Hall, the **Marktplatz** is the most interesting section of Göttingen. A visit here is traditionally capped by going to one of the student taverns, such as **Alte Krone,** 13 Weenderstrasse (tel. 5-66-40), which has long been a cellar attracting students in the evening. Its "University Room" is adorned with old drawings.

In the center of Göttingen are some old churches. **St. Alban's** is the church of the "old village," and is said to have been founded by St. Boniface. The present structure dates from 1423. **St. John's** is characterized by two octagonal towers, and **St. James's** is graced by a tower rising 243 feet, the tallest in town.

In the center of Göttingen you can wander down narrow streets, looking at wide-eaved, half-timbered houses. Some of the facades are carved and painted.

WHERE TO STAY: Gebhards Hotel, 22 Goethe-Allee (tel. 5-61-33), stands in front of the station. Housed in a grand building that reminds me of a Tuscan villa, this comfortable hotel has a modern balconied annex built onto the back. The renovated interior offers high-ceilinged public rooms, a pleasant bar area, a swimming pool, and several restaurants. Singles go for 75 DM ($24.75) to 115 DM ($37.95), the latter with private shower and bath, while doubles rent for 140 DM ($46.20) to 165 DM ($54.45). The cheapest doubles have a toilet and shower; the most expensive contain a complete private bath. The Albes family are your hosts, bringing solid experience to the management of their hotel.

The attached restaurant has gained international fame as a place where a king of Denmark and a few German presidents have dined, along with a smattering of scientists and writers. The dining room prepares an array of good-tasting food, beautifully served. The menu is likely to feature homemade pâtés in aspic, fresh fish and fresh fish terrines, turbot poached in cider, medallions of quail, and Swabian pork with apple compote. Thursday is buffet night, in a style more elaborate than you might think. Meals range from 30 DM ($9.90) to 60 DM ($19.80), and are served from noon to 2:30 p.m. and 6 p.m. to midnight daily.

Central Hotel, 12 Judenstrasse (tel. 5-71-57). Although this quiet hotel is centrally located, as its name indicates, on a pedestrian walkway near the university, its best feature is the imaginative care the designers used to decorate the bedrooms. One is flamboyantly wallpapered and curtained with vivid yellow and white paper, while another seems to be covered in pink silk, or at least something very close to it. All the attractively furnished bedrooms contain private bath, color TV, and phone, renting for 75 DM ($24.75) to 90 DM ($29.70) in a single and from 145 DM ($47.85) to 155 DM ($51.15) in a double, with breakfast included. Albert Fette and his wife, Ingeborg, are your hosts here.

Sporthotel Göttingen, 3 Dransfelder Strasse (tel. 9-20-51), lies only 400 yards from the autobahn. You'll notice a modern glass-and-concrete hotel with a collection of low-lying slope-roofed buildings scattered around it. These low buildings contain the tennis court, squash courts, swimming pool, and exercise facilities, which represent some of the best athletic equipment in town. Rooms are not neglected either. They are comfortably furnished, renting from 65 DM ($21.45) to 75 DM ($24.75) in a single and from 85 DM ($28.05) to 95 DM ($31.35) in a double.

Hotel zur Sonne, 10 Paulinerstrasse (tel. 5-67-38), is in the core of Göttingen, at the rear of the Gothic Town Hall. The hotel sleeps 120 guests, mostly in rooms with private bath or shower. Good comfort and convenience are bought at moderate prices; singles are in the 65-DM ($21.45) to 80-DM ($26.40) range; doubles run from 95 DM ($31.35) to 112 DM ($36.96). Breakfast is included. A guarded car park is opposite the hotel, or you can park in the hotel's underground garage.

WHERE TO DINE: Junkernschänke, 5 Barfürsserstrasse (tel. 5-73-20), is a traditional restaurant steeped in ancient traditions. Dating from 1503, it is a black-and-white timbered corner building with ornate carvings. Inside this atmospheric hostelry are three dining rooms with beamed ceilings and wood-carvings. Set dinners range from 35 DM ($11.55) to 65 DM ($21.45).

Zum Schwarzen Bären, 12 Kurzestrasse (tel. 5-82-84), is a fine restaurant, also housed in a black-and-white timbered circa-1500 building. It still has the original stained-glass leaded windows. The facade has name plates of well-known guests. Inside, the ambience is tavern style, with a ceramic stove in the corner and dining rooms with intimate booths. Service is courteous and friendly. The innkeeper suggests Puzsta schinken or nasi-goreng. Wienerschnitzel is also offered. The restaurant serves complete meals for 28 DM ($9.24) to 60 DM ($19.80). It's closed on Monday.

13. Kassel

Much of Kassel's 1000-year history went down in ruins in World War II, but the city that rose from the rubble holds its own culturally and industrially. Known as a city of gardens, Kassel has been designed with traffic-free promenades and pedestrian tunnels. Public parks and sports grounds offer residents and visitors relaxation and entertainment.

THE SIGHTS: Culturally, Kassel has earned fame as the home of the **Documenta,** possibly the world's most important international art exhibition. Its State Theater sets the stage for operatic and dramatic productions. Long a center for drama and the arts, Kassel also boasts the **Ottoneum,** the oldest permanent theater building in Germany (1604), housing the **Natural Science Museum.**

Visitors to Kassel are drawn here for a variety of reasons—for the art exhibitions, for individual and trade conferences, or for the theatrical productions. But no matter why they come, everyone eventually visits Kassel's biggest attraction:

Schloss Wilhelmshöhe

Built on a small wooded slope where a monastery once stood, this 18th-century classic castle was the summer residence of the landgraves and electors of Hessen-Cassel. For seven years it became the residence of Napoleon's brother, the king of Westphalia, during the Napoleonic era and later became the summer palace of Kaiser Wilhelm II. The apartments are richly and lavishly furnished with good period pieces, and art lovers go to Kassel just to see the fine collection of Dutch, Flemish, Italian, and German old masters in the castle. There is one of the most important Rembrandt collections in the world, including three self-portraits of the artist. The collection also includes works by Dürer, Lucas Cranach, Rubens, Van Dyck, and Frans Hals, as well as Titian, Piazzetta, Jan Liss, and others. In addition to the picture gallery of old masters, the castle also houses a collection of Greek and Roman sculpture, gold, and pottery.

Also interesting is the huge **castle park,** unique in Europe because of its layout across the slopes of Habichtwald. The crowning feature of the park is the massive **Hercules Monument,** constructed in the early 18th century to a height of 250 feet. From the foot of the monument, a series of waterfalls cascades down the slope of the 800-foot hill. The park also contains the **Löwenburg Castle,** a romantic imitation of a ruined English castle, built at the same time as the Wilhelmshöhe. The park and castles are open Tuesday to Sunday from 10 a.m. to 5 p.m. (slightly shorter hours in winter). It is closed on Monday. Admission to Schloss Wilhelmshöhe, Löwenburg Castle, and the Hercules Monument is 3 DM (99¢) each. The castle grounds are open free to the public during the same hours indicated above.

Other Sights

The Waldeck Region, the Reinhards Forest, and Kassel were responsible for the birth of many legends and tales about witches, sleeping princesses, strange beasts, and magic spells. These tales had a profound influence on the Brothers Grimm, who lived in Kassel from 1798 to 1830. The **Brüder Grimm-Museum,** 2 Schöne Aussicht (tel. 787-40-59), contains letters, portraits, and mementos of the famous brothers and their relatives. The most interesting exhibit is a collection of editions of their fairy tales from the first copy to the present day. Admission to the museum is free. It's open from 10 a.m. to 1 p.m. and 2 to 5 p.m. (until 1 p.m. only on weekends), but closed on Monday.

Nearby is Kassel's second-largest park, the **Karlsaue,** extending along the bank of the Fulda River. The park contains the ruins of the orangerie, flanked by the **Marble Pavilion,** worth a visit to look at the 12 statues of mythological characters.

The **Hessisches Landesmuseum,** 5 Brüder-Grimm-Platz (tel. 1-27-87), and **Neue Galeries,** 1 Schöne Aussicht (tel. 1-52-66), contain exhibits of interest. In the former, there are four departments: prehistory; Hessian folk art; European arts and crafts, including French and Germanic art nouveau, armories, glassware, and medieval triptychs and sculpture; and for the science buff, there is the astronomy and physics collection, containing priceless scientific instruments dating as far back as Copernicus.

The New Gallery, on the green terrace high above the River Fulda, houses German and international paintings, sculpture, and objects from 1750 to today. There are many works of the Tischbein family and the elder Kassel school. Modern artists such as Lovis Corinth, Max Ernst, Paul Klee, Ernst Ludwig Kirchner, Joseph Beuys, Richard Hamilton, and Claes Oldenburg are also represented.

Admission to the Landesmuseum and the gallery is free. They are open from 10 a.m. to 5 p.m. daily except Monday.

ACCOMMODATIONS: In Kassel, you have a choice of living in fine hotels within the city proper or in comfort on the outskirts.

Schloss Hotel Wilhelmshöhe, 2 Schlosspark (tel. 3-08-80), is misnamed. It's not an old castle at all, but completely modern in the tradition of an American motel. Built directly across the street from the palace, and next to what were once the imperial stables, the hotel has many private terraces with views of the rolling castle park and its buildings. The bedrooms are comfortable and decorated in a bright, airy style. The rooms are of a high standard and equipped with bath or shower, toilet, telephone, radio, color TV, and mini-bar. Single rooms cost 95 DM ($31.35) to 125 DM ($41.25). Doubles go for 170 DM ($56.10) to 230 DM ($75.90), including a breakfast buffet. Adjoining the hotel is an excellent restaurant-café. There are also a swimming pool and a bowling alley. In fair weather you can dine at a café table on the terrace, listening to band music and enjoying the panorama of Kassel.

Park Hotel Hessenland, 2 Obere Königstrasse (tel. 1-49-74), near the Town Hall, couldn't be more convenient for viewing the Flemish masterpieces in the museum across the street. It's one of the leading hotels within the city proper, and its success has brought about another addition, in which most of the rooms have a balcony overlooking the museum gardens. The bedrooms are standard modern, fairly large, with built-in conveniences. One person in a room with hot and cold running water pays 50 DM ($16.50); with shower, the price goes up to 105 DM ($34.65). With full bath, doubles cost 145 DM ($56.55). The hotel is also convenient to the town's best restaurants, or if you prefer, it has its own dining facilities as well as a grillroom. Heinrich Mess is the owner of this popular hotel, which he has almost single-handedly turned into a comfortable and attractive oasis since it was rebuilt in 1947. The staff here is friendly and efficient, and seem to take a personal interest in each guest.

Dorint Hotel Reiss, 24 Werner-Hilpert-Strasse at Am Hauptbahnhof (tel. 7-88-30), rises from a downtown street corner close to the railway station. This 102-room hotel welcomes guests with comfortable, clean rooms (decorated in autumnal colors, wood and leather chairs, and lots of light). Windows are soundproof. Singles begin at 60 DM ($19.80) if bathless, going up to 108 DM ($35.64) with bath. Doubles, each with private bath, range from 150 DM ($49.50) to 160 DM ($52.80). Breakfast is included in the room price. The restaurant evokes a forest theme, with dark-wood paneling and green leather upholstery on the Empire chairs. Monochromatic illustrations of military life in the early 19th century illuminate the walls. International foods are served. These might include broiled steaks and sauteed meats of all kinds, each delicately seasoned and properly cooked. The restaurant is open from noon to 2 p.m. and 6 to 9 p.m. every day, charging from 30 DM ($9.90) to 45 DM ($14.85) for an average meal.

Hotel Domus, 1–5 Erzberger Strasse (tel. 10-23-85), was built around 1900. This four-story brick hotel near the Hauptbahnhof was the former headquarters for a trading house until it became one of the most popular hotels in Kassel. The canopy over the entrance is crafted from an art nouveau metal frame with glass insets (a style repeated in the hanging lamps throughout the hotel). Every detail of the facade of the hotel and many of the appointments inside evoke a sense of the turn of the century. Bedrooms are sunny and decorated tastefully, with graceful curves in the woodworking of the furniture and doorways. Singles cost 95 DM ($31.35) to 105 DM ($34.65), while doubles rent for 140 DM ($46.20) to 160 DM ($52.80). Breakfast is included, and all of the units contain private bath.

Schweizer Hof, 288 Wilhelmshöher Allee (tel. 3-40-48). The bierstube/restaurant attached to this unpretentious hotel is rustically decorated with Swiss-style curtains, small-paned windows, and checkered curtains, while the rest of the establishment is as modern and efficient as a Swiss watch. Rooms are decorated in unembellished furniture, frequently upholstered in paprika red. All units contain private bath, radio, phone, and TV. Guests have free access to the bowling alley, a bar area dramatically tiled in black, and a heated swimming pool elegantly landscaped with a slate-covered island connected by a bridge to the mainland. Singles rent for 60 DM ($19.80) to 95 DM ($31.35), while doubles go for 90 DM ($29.70) to 140 DM ($46.20).

Hotel Seidel, 29 Holländische Strasse (tel. 8-60-47), is comfortably perched in the center of town on a tree-lined street with a popular bar and café on the ground floor. This five-story modern hotel offers clean, sunny, and carpeted rooms to guests, charging 56 DM ($18.48) to 85 DM ($28.05) in a single and 76 DM ($25.08) to 112 DM ($36.96) in a double. The hotel is under the careful supervision of Hellfried Beiling. Meals are taken in a dining room with a wood-paneled ceiling and upholstered pink chairs.

WHERE TO DINE: The **Ratskeller,** 8 Obere Königstrasse (tel. 1-59-28), is seemingly everyone's favorite place for dining. The attractive, semirustic atmosphere makes people forget their troubles and helps them relax and enjoy their meals. You can find the tables shared by a diverse clientele, from white-haired matrons to young people, from business people to Kassel's students and their professors. The Ratskeller serves both international specialties and regional dishes such as ratsherrentopf and altdeutsches schnitzel. Among the international dishes you will find medallions of turkey, fried in egg and cheese, garnished with tomatoes and served with macaroni and green salad; medallions of pork Alsatian style; and pork steak in spicy beer sauce with bacon, onions, sausages, and green beans. At lunchtime there is a special menu prepared for clients in a hurry. The extraordinary ice-cream menu is well known. Meals begin at 18 DM ($5.94), going up to 40 DM ($13.20). Hours are 11 a.m. to 11:30 p.m.

Bei Henkel, im Hauptbahnhof (tel. 1-45-11), is in an annex of the main railroad station, and is, surprisingly, considered by many critics to be the finest dining room in Kassel. This comfortably decorated restaurant serves carefully prepared specialties to an international clientele. Menu items include such specialties of the chef as henkel-platte, three different filets with mushrooms, vegetables, and.Berner rösti, or filets of lamb provençal with onions, tomatoes, olives, and hollandaise sauce, garnished with string beans and roast potatoes. Meals average around 30 DM ($9.90) and are served daily from 9:30 a.m. to 11 p.m.

Landhaus Meister, 140 Fuldatalstrasse (tel. 87-50-50). The ground-floor café here serves elegant pastries and coffee Viennese style, as well as a heavenly apple strudel. The main restaurant offers such foods as oysters on the half-shell, oyster cream soup with truffles and wine, and a tempting array of fish and meat dishes. Sunday is a special day here, when the most outstanding fare is presented. Meals range from 35 DM ($11.55) to 70 DM ($23.10). The restaurant is open from 11 a.m. to 11 p.m. for drinks and pastries, and the restaurant serves hot food from noon to 2 p.m. and 6 to 10 p.m.

Hotel Gude-Restaurant Pfeffermühle, 229 Frankfurter Strasse (tel. 4-20-35). There are so many comfortably intimate cubbyholes within this establishment that choosing one is a minor accomplishment. Many of the local residents come here in groups, filling the upholstered banquettes and making the heavily beamed ceiling reverberate with conversation and bantering. On the premises is a walk-in grill ringed with a large stone mantelpiece. From a vantage point nearby, a uniformed chef prepares succulent roasts and grills. A specialty of the house is rumpsteak Strindberg, served with a mustard sauce and lightly glazed onions. Full meals begin at 18 DM ($5.94), going up. They are served from 11 a.m. to 2 p.m. and 5 p.m. to 1 a.m. A series of well-furnished and very comfortable rooms, some of them furnished alpine style with painted furniture and flowery wallpaper, are rented to overnight guests. These cost between 65 DM ($21.45) and 90 DM ($29.70) in a single, and from 110 DM ($36.30) to 140 DM ($46.20) in a double, with breakfast included. On the premises you'll find a fitness center, indoor swimming pool, and hydrotherapy facilities.

LIVING IN A CASTLE: Burg Hotel Trendelburg, Trendelburg (tel. 1021), lies
21 miles from Kassel. Some of the trees that grow within the 15-foot-thick stone walls of this brooding medieval fortress are ancient in their own right. The fortress was built seven centuries ago on a hillock overlooking the surrounding countryside. The current owners have added tennis courts and a swimming pool, but there's still plenty on hand to impart a feeling of medieval history. Access to the stone-floored courtyard takes you over a dried-out moat beneath narrow overhead slits which an earlier generation of inhabitants used to pour boiling oil onto unwelcome guests.

Today the von Stockhausen family opens their castle to paying guests between mid-February and December, allowing visitors to explore the building's myriad passageways, as well as the array of stone and wooden staircases. Some of these lead into mysterious corners and baronial halls, many of which are furnished with antique halberds, swords, and oversize armoires.

Some of the bedrooms contain four-poster beds, perfect for sleeping away the aches left over from an afternoon of horseback riding (there's a stable nearby). Most of the well-furnished rooms contain a private bath. The accommodations in the main house are supplemented by a handful of units in an outlying building. Each contains a phone, radio, and mini-bar, and costs 85 DM ($28.05) to 120 DM ($39.60) in a single and between 170 DM ($56.10) and 190 DM ($62.70) in a double. Fixed-price meals in the dining room range between 30 DM ($9.90) and 70 DM ($23.10).

Chapter XIV

HAMBURG

1. Hotels
2. Restaurants
3. Sights
4. Hamburg After Dark

HAMBURG IS A CITY with many faces. A trip through the canals makes you realize why it has been called "the Venice of the North." A walk down the neon-lit Reeperbahn at night assures you that it is the "wickedest city in Europe." A ride around the Alster Lake in the center of the city reveals the elegance of its finest parks and buildings. A view from the old tower of the baroque church of St. Michael opens on the steel-and-glass buildings of modern Hamburg. A Sunday-morning visit to the Altona fish market gives you a good look at the stout, Wagnerian housewives mingling with the late-nighters from the Reeperbahn.

Above all, Hamburg has a unique and versatile personality. It's a flexible city—it has had to be to recover from the many disasters during its 1100-year history. Not the least of these was the almost total destruction of this North Sea port during World War II. But the industrious Hamburgers seized this as an opportunity to rebuild a larger and more beautiful city, with huge parks, impressive buildings, and cultural institutions.

GETTING AROUND HAMBURG: A word to the wise—park your car and use the public transportation in this busy and at times frantic city. Hamburg's **U-Bahn** is one of the best subway systems in Germany, serving the entire downtown area, and connecting with the **S-Bahn's** surface trains in the suburbs. This train network is the fastest means of getting around, but if you refuse to go underground, the slower **streetcars** and **buses** offer a good alternative. The advantage of surface travel, of course, is that you get to see more of the city. Fares range between 2 DM (66¢) and 3.50 DM ($1.16), depending on the distance you go.

A **Day Ticket** is recommended, as it allows you to use, within the central zone, several methods of transportation (buses, trams, U- and S-Bahn underground services). It is valid between 9 a.m. and 4:30 a.m. the following morning and costs 6.50 DM ($2.15). You can travel by express (Schnell) or S-Bahn first class for an additional 2 DM (66¢). Day tickets are obtainable at the U- and S-Bahn ticket offices, on buses, trams, boats, and at automatic machines.

Taxis are available at all hours by telephoning 4-10-11 or 44-11-81. Basic fare is 4 DM ($1.32).

HELPFUL INFORMATION CENTERS: Tourist Information, Bieberhaus, near the railway station at Hachmannplatz (tel. 24-87-00), is open Monday through Friday from 7:30 a.m. to 6 p.m., on Saturday from 8 a.m. to 3 p.m. At the airport arrival hall (tel. 50-84-57) is another tourist information counter, open Monday to Friday from 8 a.m. to 11 p.m. Both of these centers will assist with maps, accommodation reservations, and inquiries by telephone, plus give tips and advise of local tours by bus and boat.

1. Hotels

With thousands of hotel beds in Hamburg, the visitor has a wide selection of accommodations to choose from, ranging from luxurious living overlooking the Alster, to friendly, clean boarding houses in the suburbs. Hamburg is an expensive city, and you'll find an abundance of first-class hotels, but a limited number of budget accommodations, especially in the city proper. During a busy convention period, you may have trouble finding a room on your own. In such a case, go to the hotel information desk at the airport or the main railway station. But if you reserve in advance, there are excellent choices available to you.

THE DELUXE HOTELS: Vier Jahreszeiten (Four Seasons), 9 Neuer Jungfernstieg (tel. 3-49-41), is a warm, mellowed hotel, one of the leading hotels of the world and, some critics say, the finest in Germany. Its position is ideal, right on the Binnenalster. Built in the baronial style, with rich wood paneling, it evokes a memory of the grand hotels of 1910. Ancestral paintings, ecclesiastical woodcarvings, tapestries, and antiques are everywhere mixed with comfortable upholstered pieces. The large rooms are handsomely furnished and immaculately kept, and despite the large size of the hotel (175 rooms), personal service is a hallmark. Single rooms with bath range from 235 DM ($77.50) to 300 DM ($99). Double rooms with bath go from 330 DM ($108.90) to 410 DM ($135.20). The inclusive prices vary with the view and size of accommodations. A continental breakfast is an additional 22 DM ($7.26). All rooms contain color TV and direct-dial telephone.

The hotel's dining room, bedecked with garlands and four large porcelain cherubs, is an attractive setting for the excellent international cuisine. There's also an informal country-style grill room. The tea room, Condi, furnished in Biedermeier style, is a favorite afternoon rendezvous point. International bands play in the hotel's own nightclub. Garage and parking facilities are available for guests. The Simbari Cocktail Bar is of more recent vintage, and there is also a wine shop as well as a confectioner's shop, selling the chef's own pastry.

Atlantic Hotel, Kempinski, 72-79 An der Alster (tel. 24-80-01), is Hamburg's other prestige hotel, its glistening neoclassic facade opening onto the lake. The Atlantic made its debut in 1909 as a grand hotel for passengers of the luxury liners then playing the ocean. The interior is conservative and traditional, with a definite formal aura. Emphasis is on service and comfort, and the staff contributes to the smooth-running operation. The lounges are spacious and comfortable, as are most of the rooms. Many decorator touches, such as flowery fabrics and subtle prints, add to the warmth of the 303 rooms, all of which have bath or shower, radio, color TV, direct-dial phone, and mini-bar. Try to get one of the accommodations overlooking the Alster, where you can breakfast while watching the boats sailing on the smooth water. A single with shower costs 235 DM ($77.50), rising to 285 DM ($94.05) with bath. Doubles with bath cost 330 DM ($108.90) to 380 DM ($125.40). Prices include service, taxes, and breakfast.

The hotel's facilities include the Atlantic Rendezvous, a drinking lounge with clusters of deep armchairs where you can meet for drinks. Lobster is a specialty in the Atlantic-Grill, the hotel's restaurant, but a wide variety of international cuisine is also served. You can also eat in the pub restaurant, Atlantic Mühle, and there's dancing in the Atlantic Bar (except on Monday and in July and August). The hotel provides one-day laundry and dry cleaning service, and 24-hour room service. It has a beauty salon, barbershop, currency exchange, newsstand, souvenir shop, flower shop, heated swimming pool, sauna, massage parlor, solarium, and fitness room.

CP Hamburg Plaza, 2 Marseiller Strasse (tel. 35-02-0), thrusts itself elegantly into the Hamburg skyline in Planten un Blomen Park. This hotel, a Canadian Pacific chain member, looks like a collection of narrow black lines banded vertically together to give an impression of real architectural interest. Opened some 15 years ago, this skyscraper offers beautifully appointed rooms, many with handsomely paneled walls and soaring stairways, along with dramatically decorated corners for eating and drinking. All 570 units come with bath, individually controlled air conditioning, color TV, radio, and direct-dial phone. Singles rent for 190 DM ($62.70) to 260 DM ($85.80), while doubles cost 230 DM ($75.90) to 310 DM ($102.30). A buffet breakfast is another 22 DM ($7.26). Substantial weekend discounts are likely to be offered. The hotel stands near the international railway station, Dammtor, a 20-minute taxi ride from the airport. The disco, Blauer Satellit, on the 26th floor offers a view over Hamburg and its harbor. On the premises are a heated pool, sauna, solarium, and "keep-fit" rooms.

Inter-Continental, 10 Fontenay (tel. 41-41-5-0). If you're in a ferryboat on Alster Lake, you'll be able to see this hotel rising majestically above the trees. The massive construction of the outside doesn't affect the ambience of the interior, because every effort has been expended to create a classically elegant series of public rooms. Lavish use has been made of rich leathers, embroidered fabrics, brass lamps, and live plants, all of which combine to form Inter-Continental "cozy." The bierstube, the rooftop Fontenay Grill, the Brasserie, and an attractively masculine bar with live music and dancing could all be sympathetic rendezvous points. You can even celebrate your wins, or forget your losses, at the in-house casino with a swim and a sauna in the hotel's sports department. Rooms are color coordinated and handsomely appointed, costing from 235 DM ($77.50) to 285 DM ($94.05) in a single and from 265 DM ($87.45) to 330 DM ($108.90) in a double.

Ramada Renaissance, Grosse Bleichen (tel. 34-91-80). You're greeted at the entrance of this palace by a uniformed doorman below a protective canopy, and from there you enter a glass-and-hardwood empire of subtle lighting and comfort. From the elegant lobby to the carpeted bar area where the primary impact is one of warm brass and polished wood, you'll be fêted and serenaded by an army of waiters and a resident pianist. Accommodations range from a well-appointed double-bedded room to a sumptuously upholstered series of suites. My favorite has a carpet in pale violet with turbulent swirls of purple and rust-colored waves painted onto the walls. You can relax in the whirlpool or sauna before drinks in the lounge bar and dinner at the Noblesse restaurant. The hotel was built into the facade of a historic 19th-century building, and the entire complex was designed with connections to Hanse-Viertel, Europe's longest shopping arcade. Singles rent for 230 DM ($75.90) to 330 DM ($108.90), and doubles go for 270 DM ($89.10) to 360 DM ($118.80). Substantial reductions are sometimes granted for weekend visits.

FIRST-CLASS HOTELS: Hotel Berlin, 1 Borgfelderstrasse (tel. 25-16-40), about one-half mile from the central railway station, at the intersection of main thoroughfares, is a convenient hotel, particularly for motorists. Its conservative and restful restaurant serves an excellent French cuisine. It's a modern hotel with a wide range of amenities; the rooms, in contemporary style, emphasize comfort. Singles with bath go from 150 DM ($49.50). Doubles with bath cost 200 DM ($66) to 220 DM ($72.60). Depending on their size, rooms are classified as cabinet (meaning small), standard (medium size), and studio (large). Each unit has a color TV, radio, mini-bar, and phone. There's an intimate bar with a fireplace in the lobby, convenient for the thirsty traveler. You can park in the 100-car garage. The English-speaking staff is cooperative.

Crest Hotel Hamburg, 1 Mexicoring (tel. 630-50-51), overlooks the Stadtpark, just 15 minutes from the heart of Hamburg, five minutes from the airport. Each of the 185 attractively furnished guest rooms has its own bath or shower, as well as bedside radio, direct-dial telephone, mini-bar, electric trouser presser, and color TV. A single goes for 160 DM ($52.80) to 187 DM ($61.71). Twins cost 205 DM ($67.65) to 225 DM ($74.25). No charge is made for children up to 12 sharing rooms with adults.

Hanseatic dishes and international fare are offered in both the Windsor Restaurant and the Friesenstube. The hotel also houses a cocktail lounge and intimate bierstube. The hotel offers a swimming pool and sauna in a fitness center across the street, bicycles to rent, and table tennis. To reach the hotel, follow the signs to Geschäftsstadt Nord (City North) from the autobahn exit. It's about 6½ miles from the Elbe Bridges exit of the Hannover–Bremen–Hamburg autobahn and 3½ miles from the Hamburg–Horn exit of the Lübeck–Hamburg autobahn.

Reichshof, 34 Kirchenallee (tel. 24-83-30), lies only a few blocks from the parks near Alster Lake. This huge hotel—one of the biggest in Hamburg, with 350 rooms—offers acres of public rooms decorated in an upgraded 1930s art deco chic, with classical elements of gemütlich wood paneling and Wilhelminian gilt. You're close to the railway station here, and you'll have everything you need to stay fed for a week without getting bored. Rooms are attractively furnished and most comfortable, costing from 138 DM ($45.54) to 185 DM ($61.05) in a single and from 196 DM ($64.68) to 238 DM ($78.54) in a double, with the breakfast buffet included. The Reichshof is certainly one of the Hamburger grande dames.

Europäischer Hof, 45 Kirchenallee (tel. 24-81-71). The management here claims that, being family directed and not corporate owned, this presents an advantage in terms of service and gemütlichkeit. The public rooms are comfortable, and you're likely to enjoy the musician in the hotel bar. The rooms are furnished in a sort of international modern, and the hotel attracts many persons in Hamburg on business. Singles begin at a low of 150 DM ($49.50) and go all the way to 200 DM ($66); doubles cost 180 DM ($59.40) to 260 DM ($85.80), plus 16 DM ($5.28) per person for a buffet breakfast.

Ambassador, 34 Heidenkampsweg (tel. 23-40-41). Seven floors of modern architectural design greet visitors to this 123-room, inner-city hotel, which is affiliated with Best Western. The bar, restaurant, swimming pool, and bedrooms are all attractive and pleasant places to spend time in, and the management is an interesting blend of chain-hotel efficiency and personal service. Singles range in price from 95 DM ($31.35) to 160 DM ($52.80), while doubles cost 190 DM ($62.70) to 200 DM ($66), breakfast included.

MEDIUM-PRICED HOTELS: The **Prem Hotel,** 9 An der Alster (tel. 24-54-54), is a favorite rendezvous in Hamburg. An attractive and sophisticated clientele makes this "white house on the Alster" its home in Hamburg during frequent trips to the city. Originally a mansion, the hotel has been in the possession of the Prem family since it was first established in 1912. The glistening white facade overlooks the Alster, and the rear faces a quiet garden with umbrella-covered tables. The interior shows off a personalized collection of French-style antiques and reproductions, many of them Louis XV. The reception salons are dignified but not at all austere. Everywhere there are interesting accessories, such as the tall inlaid clock in the lobby and 18th-century porcelain figurines in some of the rooms. Most of the bedrooms are furnished with white and gold Louis XV-style pieces. The hotel is the best value in town in the middle-bracket category. Doubles rent for 220 DM ($72.60) to 280 DM ($92.40). Singles cost 160 DM ($52.80) to 250 DM ($82.50). All the rooms are sunlit and cheery, but the garden-facing accommodations are much quieter than the front rooms on the Alster. You can enjoy a pleasant breakfast in the white and gold dining room jutting out into the garden. The restaurant also serves well-prepared lunches and dinners.

Hotel Bellevue, 14 An der Alster (tel. 24-80-11), just a short ride from the central station, opens onto the Alster. The building is like a glistening town house with some ornate Venetian touches on its facade, and it has been considerably modernized. Some of the larger rooms contain traditional furnishings, but the newer singles are modern, often in the Scandinavian style. Many theatrical celebrities make this their Hamburg choice. The front windows open onto the lake, but the back rooms are quieter. Bathless singles rent for 69 DM ($22.77). Singles with private bath go for 125 DM ($41.25). Bathless doubles cost from 100 DM ($33); doubles with bath or shower, from 155 DM ($51.15) to 175 DM ($57.75). Prices include service and taxes, plus a buffet breakfast. All rooms contain a self-dial phone, and most have color TV and mini-bar. The Alster Restaurant on the ground floor serves as a breakfast room, and you can enjoy international cuisine as well as regional specialties in the cozy Pilsner Urquell Stuben. Live organ music is played in the INA bar after 8 p.m. Guests may leave their cars in the hotel parking lot or in the underground garage.

Alster-Hof, 12 Esplanade (tel. 35-00-70), is a serviceable, efficient hotel on a quiet street near the Binnenalster. Most of the decor, especially in the public rooms and lounges, is in modern German taste. Bathless singles rent for 75 DM ($24.75); with shower and toilet, the price goes up to 160 DM ($52.80) to 190 DM ($62.70). Doubles range from depending on bath and location. One of the better known middle-bracket hotels of Hamburg, the Alster-Hof is well recommended.

Fürst Bismarck, 49 Kirchenallee (tel. 280-10-91). This building looks best when it's approached through one of Hamburg's frequent mists, when it rises abruptly from a narrow corner lot in all its black, white, and gilded splendor. The interior has been carefully renovated to keep the personalized feeling of being in a special place. Sabine Müller is the friendly and helpful manager who sees that everything about your pleasantly simple room is up to standards. Accommodations here rent for 130 DM ($42.90) to 160 DM ($52.80) in a double with shower and toilet, dropping to 85 DM ($28.05) to 130 DM ($42.90) in a single.

Hafen Hamburg, 9 Seewartenstrasse (tel. 31-15-25). Constructed years ago in the Wilhelminian style, this Hamburg landmark offers splendid views of the river and harbor traffic from the windows of its usually spacious rooms. The accommodations are simply furnished with vaguely nautical pieces, and the grand staircase is an elaborately twisting wrought-iron fantasy "like they'll never make again." Singles go for 95 DM ($31.35) to 120 DM ($39.60), while doubles rent for 137 DM ($45.21) to 160 DM ($52.80), breakfast included. If you can possibly afford the more expensive harbor-view room, take it.

St. Raphael, 41 Adenauerallee (tel. 24-11-91). This well-administered hotel on the famous Adenauerallee is constructed of white brick, with modern soundproof windows to guarantee a good night's sleep. The interior has the kind of uncluttered simplicity that soothes and relaxes you after a decadent night on the Reeperbahn. Hans Gerst is the manager here, and he charges from 105 DM ($34.65) to 130 DM ($42.90) in a single and from 150 DM ($49.50) to 170 DM ($56.10) in a double. An extra bed will be placed in your room for another 30 DM ($9.90). A buffet breakfast is included in the rates.

BUDGET CHOICES: Wedina Hotel, 23 Gurlittstrasse (tel. 24-30-11), is a friendly little family-style hotel just a minute from the lake and a five-minute walk from the railway station. Most of the bedrooms open onto a small, informal rear garden. It's a pleasant, quiet retreat, owned and run by an English-speaking family. Bathless singles rent for 55 DM ($18.15) to 62 DM ($20.46). With bath, the price in a single is 75 DM ($24.75) to 90 DM ($29.70); in a double, 106 DM ($34.98) to 125 DM ($41.25). Breakfast is included, and these tariffs also cover the use of a swimming pool. No parking facilities are available other than metered spaces in front of the hotel.

Hotel Alt Nürnberg, 15 Steintorweg (tel. 24-60-24), lies right near the main station for Hamburg's rail lines, yet in spite of its central location, its interior has the mellow atmosphere of a country inn. That's because the hotel was decorated with stylish furnishings in the old Franconian style. Don't expect an elevator, but once you reach the accommodations on the top floors you'll find each unit equipped with oak or brightly colored rustic furniture. The owners over the years have collected paintings and ceramics to give the hotel style. In a bathless room, they charge 50 DM ($16.50), the price rising to 100 DM ($33) with shower or complete bath. A double room without bath is only 85 DM ($28.05), the tariff going up to 130 DM ($42.90) with complete bath. These charges include tax and service. To complement the antique styling, the rooms contain all the modern conveniences such as radio, phone, or TV if required. A large breakfast includes Franconian sausage, cheese, jam, and honey.

Süderelbe, 29 Grosser Schippsee (tel. 77-32-14). Only breakfast is served in this modern hotel which was built next to one of Hamburg's outlying parking garages. The hotel lies in the Harburg district, away from the center of town. Many guests save money by staying here and reaching the heart of Hamburg by public transportation. Each of the rooms is quiet, pleasant, and filled with a contemporary collection of comfortable furniture. The 30 bedrooms rent for 90 DM ($29.70) in a single and from 120 DM ($39.60) in a double. Each accommodation contains a private bath, phone, and radio.

READER'S HOTEL SELECTION: "The Hotel-Pension Bergunde, 5 Eppendorfer Baum (tel. 48-22-14), is run by Frau Bergunde in a lovely section of Hamburg—the upper-class residential and shopping district called Eppendorfer. The immaculate and nicely decorated pension is on the second floor of a building sandwiched between a konditorei and an appliance store. Many of the six rooms have beds to accommodate three persons and are large enough to provide sitting areas, armoire, chairs, and nightstands with lamps for reading. Our room overlooked the boulevard and a flower stand at the doorstep of the pension. Also at the doorstep is the entrance to the U-Bahn, the Klosterstern station, which transports you to the shopping district Jungfernstieg station in ten minutes. Bus service also stops at the curb outside the door of the building and a taxi stand is half a block away. In the area are delicatessens, banks, clothing stores, and a dry cleaner, as well as a small park. Our stay with Frau Bergunde was the highlight of the trip. Although she does not speak English, she makes herself understood and is utterly charming. She helped us with phone calls and hovered over us. Best of all, her rates are affordable in expensive Hamburg. We paid 65 DM ($21.45) per night in a bathless room which had a large basin with hot and cold water. This was a reduced rate offered for three nights or longer. Breakfast is available for an extra 9 DM ($2.97) per person" (Mrs. R. P. Belluomini, San Francisco, Calif.).

2. Restaurants

Hamburg life is eternally tied to the sea, and nothing reflects this more than the cuisine. Lobster from Helgoland, shrimp from Büsum, turbot, plaice, and sole from the North Sea, and fresh oysters in huge quantities, make up the Hamburger's diet. Of course there's also the traditional meat dish, Hamburger steak, called stubenküchen, and the favorite sailor's dish, labskaus, made with cured meat, potatoes, herring, and gherkins. The eel soup is probably the best known of all Hamburg's typical dishes. The sweet-and-sour eel soup is said to contain more than 75 different ingredients. The cuisine of Hamburg was commented upon by Heinrich Heine, who knew the city in his youth. He called it "the best Republic: Its manners are from England and its food is from Heaven."

HAUTE CUISINE: Le Canard, 11 Martinstrasse (tel. 460-48-30). Its reputation as one of the best restaurants in Germany has made advance reservations essential. Virtually every major restaurant critic in the Federal Republic has lauded the unusual nouvelle cuisine of its handsome and imaginative owner-chef, Josef Viehhauser. You'll dine amid an unpretentiously simple decor of arranged flowers, framed lithographs, and contemporary accents, each made more alluring by the softly discreet lighting. Meals are a culinary event, beginning at noon for lunch and at 6 p.m. for dinner. The restaurant is closed on Sunday and during most of December.

Your elegant repast might include a set of seasonally adjusted dishes, including medallions of lobster garnished with mussels and leaf spinach, sauteed frog legs with fresh tomatoes, a suprême of seawolf with a cabbage-flavored sabayon, a medley of turbot and lobster simmered in a champagne sauce, and Barbary duckling stuffed with goose liver, perhaps calf sweetbreads garnished with meaty chunks of lobster. For dessert you are faced with a wide choice each night, including, as an example, a melon-flavored cake garnished with strawberry cream or a mocha-flavored parfait with mango segments. A fixed-price "quick lunch" can cost as little as 60 DM ($19.80), but be prepared to pay between 100 DM ($33) and 125 DM ($41.25) in the evening.

THE UPPER BRACKET: Peter Lembcke, 49 Holzdamm (tel. 24-32-90), is not only one of Hamburg's leading restaurants with truly good food, but also one of the friendliest places in town. In its unprepossessing location on the second floor of an old town house, it attracts a widely diverse clientele, from sculptors to bankers. The good-hearted, helter-skelter service adds to the charm of the restaurant, but the food is the real attraction here. Lembcke specializes in the cuisine of northern Germany, including the most local dish of all, labskaus. A house specialty that may not please everybody, but attracts a loyal following of gourmets, is the eel soup, with dill and fruit swimming in the broth along with the eel. Possibly a more appealing dish to the foreign palate is the house-style bouillabaisse. Besides the best rau kalbs filet, the restaurant also serves excellent steaks. There seems to be no end to the menu. For dessert I recommend the strawberry gelatin dish with whipped cream. It's so fantastic that the waiters sometimes congratulate you on your good judgment in ordering it. Lembcke's is invariably crowded, and late arrivals without reservations must wait it out in the foyer—so phone ahead. Dinners range in price from 42 DM ($13.86) to 85 DM ($28.05). Meals are served from noon to 11 p.m. daily, except Sunday and from July 20 to August 10.

W. Schumann's Austernkeller, 34 Jungfernstieg (tel. 34-62-65), is admittedly one of the most expensive restaurants in the city, but this one is really worth it. You'll pay dearly for a dozen oysters at this "oyster cellar," but what a treat for those who can afford it. Available September through April, the oysters are selected by the chef as if he were buying pearls. You enter this belle époque restaurant, which was founded in 1884, and you are instantly transported back into the grand, elegant world of the kaisers.

You can dine "in state" here, with your own waiter in formal attire in one of the tiny private dining salons on the long passageway. Each salon is decorated differently, ranging from intimate rustic to Empire, with silk damask wall coverings, paneled dado, doors with large brass handles, and gilt mirrors. There are even a few Biedermeier-style salons. The restaurant, suitably situated in the Heinrich Heine house, has been in the same family for around a century. Service is among the finest in Hamburg.

The Hamburger crab soup might be a good beginning unless you prefer the oysters. The best of fresh fish is served here, and the chef knows how to prepare a platter just right. Meals begin at 50 DM ($16.50), but could easily go up to 130 DM ($42.90). It is closed Sunday.

Alsterpavillon, 54 Am Jungfernstieg (tel. 34-50-52), is a pavilion built right on the Binnenalster. Café tables are placed outside in summer when the lake takes on a festive air. The food isn't ignored, however, just because of the dramatic location. Both service and cuisine make this one of the finest dining choices in Hamburg. The sole meunière in chive butter is a superb selection. Other specialties include Strasbourg sauerkraut with pork. A good beginning for any meal is Matjes herring. Set lunches are also served daily from 30 DM ($9.90). An average à la carte meal will cost from 50 DM ($16.50). A concert is given daily from 3 to 10 p.m. Food is served from 10 a.m. to 11 p.m. daily.

Restaurant im Finnlandhaus, 41 Esplanade (tel. 34-41-33), is a panoramic restaurant, close to the heart of the city. The setting is Finnish, with warm autumnal colors and stylish molded armchairs, and the cuisine is Finnish as well, along with international recipes. It's a chic place to dine, in the modern glass Finland House near the Binnenalster. Take the elevator to the top, where the restaurant opens on three sides to spectacular views of the city. On the à la carte menu, a good beginning is the Brazil avocado with crabmeat. Specialties include Finnish salmon soup, cured salmon, and moose prepared several different ways. The restaurant is open daily and serves meals from noon to 10 p.m., costing from 38 DM ($12.54) to 72 DM ($23.76).

Landhaus Scherrer, 130 Elbchaussee (tel. 880-13-25), was, in its previous incarnation, a brewery, but that is all gone now. It is a citadel of gastronomy, lying on the banks of the Elbe River at Altona outside the heart of Hamburg. The lighting fixtures are covered with small pink shades, and the wall paneling was intricately joined together long ago by a master carpenter. Armin Scherrer has gained a reputation in Hamburg for correct service and imaginatively prepared food in an amiable and genteel setting. Specialties are fresh fish and shellfish, excellent meats, and mushrooms imported in winter from Morocco. An unusual variation might be roast goose with rhubarb in a cassis sauce. Dessert might be a praline cream or one of 30 types of pastries loading down the sweet trolley. Because of the restaurant's location in a country house surrounded by trees, it's popular with local residents for wedding receptions. An à la carte meal will cost about 50 DM ($16.50) to 75 DM ($24.75), and service is from noon to midnight every day but Sunday.

Restaurant Ehmke, 14 Grimm (tel. 32-71-32), is a traditional restaurant, one of the finest in Hamburg. It is elegantly decorated, with many of the original antiques still there. Dieter Parsch is the conscientious owner, and Myko Hluschok is chief of the kitchen. Specialties include fresh oysters, delicately seasoned lobster taken fresh from an aquarium on the premises, as well as eel, trout, crab, filet of turbot, and rack of lamb with mint sauce. An average meal ranges from 35 DM ($11.55) to 70 DM ($23.10). The restaurant is open daily except Sunday from noon to midnight.

Le Délice, 9 Klosterwall (tel. 32-77-27), is one of the greatest restaurants of Hamburg, right at the Markthalle, in the very heart of the city. The restaurant is a chic enclave of neon script, potted palms, rattan walls, and a checkered black-and-white op-art floor. The tablecloths and chairs are of a dazzling white, an attractive contrast to the buff-colored walls and the bouquets of flowers that add life to a streamlined, fun, and whimsical ambience. Werner Henssler and Alex Henkel run the place, charging an average price of 110 DM ($36.30) for a six-course gourmet meal (sometimes far more, depending on the rarity of the food presented). Specialties might include salmon, a clear fish soup with turbot and mushrooms, filet of lamb with homemade noodles, followed by fresh raspberries with homemade ice cream. You can also dine less elaborately for 50 DM ($16.50). The restaurant is open from 7 to 11 p.m. It's closed on Sunday.

THE MIDDLE BRACKET: Ratsweinkeller, 2 Grosse Johannisstrasse (tel. 36-41-53), is one of the most impressive and distinguished ratskellers in northern Germany. The theme is suggested at the entrance, where you'll find a stone statue of Bacchus. The main dining hall has high vaulted ceilings; wood-paneled columns and antique ship models add to the decor. Medieval scenes are depicted on the three large stained-glass windows. The city takes pride, and deservingly so, in the culinary offerings of its Ratskeller. One excellent dish is the halibut steak in a curry sauce. The fresh sole bonne femme is heavenly and served in large portions. Try the Hamburg crab soup. Luncheon specials are offered daily from 11:30 a.m. to 3 p.m., including soup and dessert. Dinners begin at 25 DM ($8.25), going up to 85 DM ($28.05) and beyond. The service is smooth. Listen for the great-grandfather clock to chime the quarter hour, resounding throughout the chambers. They serve from 10 a.m. to 11 p.m. Closed on Sunday and holidays.

Fernsehturm Hamburg Restaurant, 2–8 Lagerstrasse (tel. 43-80-24), has been totally renovated and is an elegant place to eat, with a warm atmosphere. The food is as good as the view you get from this restaurant halfway up Hamburg's 900-foot television tower in the suburb of Rotherbaum. You dine as the fully air-conditioned room revolves (one complete turn each hour). One of Hamburg's best known chefs is in charge, and English-speaking waiters are available. Meals range from 25 DM ($8.25) to 45 DM ($14.85). The restaurant is open daily from noon to 11 p.m. During the afternoon, you can have coffee and cake for 8.50 DM ($2.81). Visitors must have a 4-DM ($1.32) ticket to go up in the tower.

Alte Mühle, 34 Alte Mühle, in Bergstedt (tel. 6-04-91-71), is a restaurant in a residential quarter, near a waterfall with an old mill. Home-style Germanic fare is featured, including pig trotters with sauerkraut and potatoes. Many Hamburgers make the journey out here just to enjoy the fresh carp with melted butter, horseradish, and potatoes. Blue trout is another feature. However, the chef delivers his peak performance when he serves venison with red cabbage. An average meal will cost from 28 DM ($9.24) to 60 DM ($19.80). After an opulent meal, you can take a walk through the pond-filled woods and watch the horses nearby. It is closed Wednesday.

Alsterpark, 12C Brombeerweg (tel. 59-65-34). My first impression of this restaurant was elegantly set tables with masses of flowers, run by Jaap Niermeijer. It's a gemütlich place near a canal leading into the Alstersee. While summertime patrons usually prefer to sit on the terrace, the interior is decorated with taste and flair. Weekly specials change frequently, and a typical meal would begin at 55 DM ($18.15), going up to 90 DM ($29.70). The cuisine is a mixture of classical French and nouvelle cuisine, including such specialties as tournedos with crushed peppercorns, breast of hen sauteed with green peppercorns, pike mousse in fresh crab sauce, rack of wild hare, and mussels cooked "in the style of the house." It's open from noon to 2:30 p.m. and 6 to 9:30 p.m. every day but Saturday and for a few weeks' vacation (the exact dates change yearly).

Johann Cölln-Austernstuben, 1–5 Brodschrangen (tel. 33-07-22). You're reminded of what a seafaring town Hamburg really is as soon as you step into this 1833 restaurant which specializes in oysters and seafood. Oysters are priced by the dozen, lobsters by the half kilo, and the kitchen will prepare and serve them in practically any way you can imagine. A full meal here begins at 55 DM ($18.15), but could cost a small fortune if you order lobster or some of the most expensive dishes. A glance around the paneled room offers glimpses of nocturnal life in this most international of German seaports. The restaurant serves from 11 a.m. to 9:30 p.m. daily except Sunday. Reservations are strongly recommended.

Deichgraf, 23 Deichstrasse (tel. 36-42-08), is an elegant restaurant filled with an unusual collection of antiques, one of which is a four-foot model of a many-sailed schooner. You'll recognize the building by its five-story town-house structure sandwiched into a centrally located city block. Amid gilded mirrors, floor-to-ceiling windows, and a uniformed staff, guests enjoy such northern German specialties as salmon in a mustard-flavored dill sauce and flavorfully grilled meats and fish. You can also order several kinds of fondue here. One of the restaurant's separate menus devotes itself to just about everything a chef can compose from fresh seasonal lobster. You can also enjoy a juicy filet of lamb in a herb-flavored sauce, oysters, and several varieties of well-marinated steaks. Many of the shellfish specialties are sold by weight. You can get a filling meal for around 40 DM ($13.20), but your tab will run far more, of course, if you order lobster. The establishment is open daily except Sunday and holidays from 11 a.m. to 11 p.m.; on Saturday only lunch is served. The restaurant is dedicated to the thousands of builders who maintained the area's dikes, which on many occasions prevented parts of the city from being flooded.

Dimanche, Karl-Muck-Platz (tel. 34-45-11), gives off a sense of order, dignity, and well-being, with its cream-colored walls half covered by dark paneling, its white tablecloths, and the massive round pillars supporting the high-beamed ceiling. Some nouvelle cuisine dishes are prepared here by the two chefs, Udo Sonntag and Jacques Mazouaud. However, their specialties fall into the category of the wholesome and savory new generation German cookery. Meals, costing from 30 DM ($9.90) to 45 DM ($14.85), are served Tuesday to Friday from noon to 2:30 p.m. and 6 to 11 p.m., from 6 to 11 p.m. on Saturday and Sunday. You can linger over coffee until shortly before midnight.

Don Camillo e Peppone, 50 Im Soll (tel. 642-90-21), is at Hamburg-Bramfeld, outside the center of town. The Mediterranean feeling of this intimate restaurant is reflected both by the Tuscan cuisine and by the Italian antiques scattered attractively about. Sergio Camerini is the owner of this elegant place, serving specialties such as homemade ravioli in a sage cream sauce, fresh salmon in vermouth, as well as a savory regime of game, lamb, and fresh Mediterranean fish. A full meal will cost 32 DM ($10.56) to 75 DM ($24.75). The restaurant is open from 6 to 11 p.m. daily. Call first.

Old Commercial Room, 10 Englische Planke (tel. 36-63-19), founded in 1643, is so tied into maritime life in Hamburg that many residents consider it the premier sailor's stopover. It is, in my opinion, the best place in town to order labskaus, which is still avidly consumed just as it was by Hamburg's Hanseatic forebears. It is prepared with devotion by Paul Rauch, owner of the restaurant.

The name of his place, along with the street, Englische Planke, speak of the historic mercantile links between Hamburg and England.

In Mr. Rauch's labskaus, fish such as herring is definitely not added to the concoction. It's actually a kind of North Sea hash, a mixture of beef, onions, pickles, and beets. If you order a plate of it, you're given a numbered certificate proclaiming you as a genuine labskaus-eater. The list long ago toppled the million mark. You'll also be given a baptismal certificate promising protection during your voyages at sea by Poseidon. You can also order such dishes as Hamburger-style sour soup, filet of herring with new potatoes, smoked spare ribs, and many other traditional North German dishes. Fixed-price meals cost from 48 DM ($15.84). The establishment, at the foot of St. Michaelis Church, the sailors' church, is open from 11 a.m. to 1 a.m. every day of the week.

THE BUDGET RANGE: Vegetarische Gaststätte, 13 Neuerwall (tel. 34-47-03), a refreshing change of pace, is the oldest vegetarian restaurant in the world—and certainly the best known. The restaurant is on the second floor. There are two folding chairs halfway up the two flights for the older vegetarians who have trouble navigating the steps all at once. The restaurant, which has been around since 1892, consists of three generous rooms, one of them terrace-style surrounded by windows. Care is taken in the preparation of the vegetables, which are often overcooked in Germany. Yogurt fans will find the product here among the best. The restaurant is open daily from 11:15 a.m. to 7 p.m., until 3:30 p.m. on Saturday. It is closed Sunday. Get your check as you enter. Meals cost 10 DM ($3.30) to 25 DM ($8.25).

Destille, 1 Steintorplatz (tel. 280-33-54), is sheltered within one of Hamburg's museums, Das Museum für Kunst und Gewerbe. This art nouveau restaurant has been called a rendezvous point for entrepreneurs, art dealers, minor celebrities, and the merely curious. Aside from the social contacts that the clientele seems to cultivate here, the food is uncompromisingly good, including an array of salads, cold marinated meats, and an enormous cheese board. Every day at lunch a portion of the steaming "hot pot" will cost a reasonable 6 DM ($1.98). An enormous salad plate can make your lunch at only 18 DM ($5.94). For 22 DM ($7.26) you can have a meal large enough to sate your appetite for hours. They are open daily except Sunday and Monday from 10 a.m. to 5 p.m.

Hotel Norge with **Kon-Tiki Grill,** 49 Schäferkampsallee (tel. 44-17-21). Scandinavian specialties are featured at this hotel dining room with a modern decor. The cold buffet is something you'd otherwise have to go to Oslo for, and the other specialties include fish, meats, and both hot and cold vegetables dishes. It's open from noon to 3 p.m. and 6 to 11 p.m. A fixed-price menu begins at 23 DM ($7.59), but you can spend far more of course, unless you're careful.

Flic Flac Bistro, 29 Blankeneser Landstrasse (tel. 86-53-45), is an attractive bistro awash with unusual lithographs and fresh flowers. It's the personal statement of its owner, Iris Seybold. After it opened a few years ago, its garden-style terrace quickly became popular with a young professional crowd of people. Menu items include a full repertoire of French and German nouvelle cuisine, with a strict emphasis on fresh vegetables and light-textured sauces. Greenery lovers will appreciate the amply supplied salad bar. Only dinner is served, offered nightly except Monday at 6 p.m., finishing around midnight. Full meals begin as low as 20 DM ($6.60), but could go as high as 40 DM ($13.20). The annual closing stretches from mid-March to mid-April.

Zum Wattkorn, 230 Tangstedter Landstrasse (tel. 520-37-97). This old-fashioned guest house offers a handful of bedrooms, as well as a popular biergarten where an Austrian cuisine is served in generous portions. It's outside the commercial core of the city in a green oasis of nesting birds and flowering plants. The menu changes each week, making good use of seasonally available fruits and vegetables. Your dinner might include a ragoût of veal, pike-perch with a chive sauce, duckling in a red wine sauce, or roebuck with port. Alfred Hillen, the owner, welcomes guests for coffee and snacks every day (except Monday) from 8 a.m. to 11 p.m. Lunch begins at noon, dinner at 6 p.m. Fixed-price menus begin at 30 DM ($9.90). The adjoining hotel rents singles costing 48 DM ($15.84) to 60 DM ($19.80), and doubles go for 78 DM ($25.74) to 110 DM ($36.30).

Nikolaikeller, 36 Cremon (tel. 36-61-13). You can see the sprawling maritime facilities of Hamburg from the windows of this place, filled with a no-nonsense crowd of local business people and workers. The menu includes more than two dozen varieties of herring, including all the traditional preparations and a few that may be new to you (for instance, with avocadoes and garlic cloves). Many of the dishes taste better when washed down with ample quantities of local beer, which the staff provides in oversize mugs. Full meals begin at a low of 25 DM ($8.25), and are served from noon until midnight every day but Sunday.

DINING IN THE ENVIRONS: Sagebiels Fährhaus, 107 Blankeneser Haupt-strasse (tel. 86-15-14), is a restaurant in an old house on a terrace above the Elbe River, with a clear view of ships going up and down the stream. One of the most popular eating places in northern Germany, the Fährhaus has undergone changes—from a facility for the ferry and its passengers to a farmhouse and now a restaurant. In the glassed-in dining room, you can enjoy traditional German food, served attractively and capably. Try to get a seat on the garden terrace if the weather is fine. Meals cost 30 DM ($9.90) to 80 DM ($26.40). In the off-season the restaurant is closed on Monday. Blankenese is ten miles from the heart of Hamburg.

3. Sights

Hamburg was subject to several severe bombings in the summer of 1943, and more than half the city, including 295,000 houses, was completely destroyed. Thousands more structures were badly damaged. Instead of restoring many of the completely demolished buildings, the city fathers decided on a creative plan of action, and today Hamburg is Germany's showplace of ultramodern architecture. Many historic structures stand today, side by side with towering steel-and-glass buildings. The 4½ square miles of parks and gardens are a vital part of the city. Hamburgers are proud of their 22 square miles of rivers and lakes as well.

The **Alster** is the perfect starting point for a pleasurable exploration of Hamburg. This lake, rimmed by the city's most significant and attractive buildings, sparkles with the white sails of small boats and ripples with the movement of motor launches. The lake is divided by the Lombard and John F. Kennedy Bridges into the **Binnenalster** (Inner Alster) and the larger **Aussenalster** (Outer Alster). The Binnenalster is flanked on the south and west by the **Jungfernstieg,** one of Europe's best known streets, and Hamburg's most vital artery, and also its best shopping district. For landlubbers, the best view of the Alster is from this "maiden's path."

The **Port of Hamburg** is the world's fifth-largest harbor, stretching for nearly 25 miles along the Elbe River. More than 1500 ships call at this important port each month, connecting it with 1000 other cities throughout the world. Since 1189 the stretch of water has been one of the busiest centers for trade on the continent, making Hamburg one of Germany's wealthiest cities.

Before you tour the harbor, however, get a good overall view from the tower of the nearby **St. Michael's Church,** Hamburg's favorite landmark. It is considered the finest baroque church in the north of Germany. And the view from the top of the hammered copper tower (1762) is magnificent. Church and tower are open weekdays from 9 a.m. to 5:30 p.m., on Sunday from 11:30 a.m. to 5:30 p.m. (in winter from 10 a.m. to 4 p.m. weekdays, 11:30 a.m. to 4 p.m. on Sunday). Take the elevator or climb the 449 steps.

Then, for a closer look at the river's activity, join one of the tours conducted every half hour in summer by the **Hadag Line,** from 10 a.m. to 4 p.m. Running commentaries are given by the guides in German. Departure is from St. Pauli landing stage at Entrance 3.

The **Alstadt** actually has little left of the old architecture, but there are a few sights among the canals (fleets) that run through this section from the Alster to the Elbe. The largest of the older buildings is the **Rathaus,** which is actually modern compared with many of German's town halls. Hamburg's City Hall is a Renaissance-style structure, built in the late 19th century on a foundation of 4000 oak piles. Its 160-foot clock tower overlooks the **Rathausmarkt** and the **Alster Fleet,** the city's largest canal. A few blocks away is **St. Petri Cathedral,** built in the 12th century and renovated in 1842. The lionhead knocker on the main door is the oldest piece of art in Hamburg, dating from 1342. The nearby 14th-century church of **St. Jacobi** was destroyed in the last war, but its tower and the Arp-Schnittger organ were rebuilt.

The **Hamburger Kunsthalle,** Glockengiesserwall, containing the works of the world's greatest painters and sculptors, is the leading art museum in northern Germany. One of the most outstanding works is the Grabow Altarpiece, painted for the St. Petri-Kirche in 1379 by Master Bertram, Hamburg's first painter known by name, and the leading master of 14th-century Germany. The 24 scenes on the wing-panels are a free adaptation of the medieval text "The Mirror of Human Salvation," and depict the story of mankind from the Creation to the Flight into Egypt. Particularly interesting is the creation of the animals, in which a primitive Christ-like figure is surrounded by the animals of his creation, from the fish of the sea to the fowl of the air. As a sardonic note, or possibly prophetic, one little fox is already chewing the neck of the lamb next to it. In the center panel of the Crucifixion, Master Bertram has depicted prophets, apostles, and saints; in a band above, more prophets appear in medallions. The wise and foolish virgins are lined up above the center shrine.

The museum also contains works by Master Francke, a Dominican monk, including the altar of St. Thomas of Canterbury (1424) with the first representation of the murder in the cathedral. There is a remarkable collection of Dutch and local paintings of the 17th century. Van Dyck, Rubens, Rembrandt, Claude Lorrain, de Champaigne, Tiepolo, Goya, Boucher, and Fragonard are well represented, and the German school particularly by Mengs, Denner, and Tischbein. Emphasis is laid on 19th-century art, beginning with Wilson, Reynolds, and Fuseli. Friedrich's landscapes and Runge's visions are hardly to be seen better anywhere else where work of the Romantic movement is to be viewed. The Nazarenes (Overbeck, Cornelius) are followed by the British Pre-Raphaelites (Rossetti, Burne-Jones, Dyce). Later trends are marked by Leibl, Menzel, Meissonier, Corot, Daubigny, Courbet, Millet, Böcklin, Feuerbach, and von Marées. Notable works by French impressionists are the *Nana* by Manet and paintings by Cézanne, Degas, Monet, Renoir, and Sisley. Twentieth-century artists are represented by Kirchner, Picasso, Chagall, Kandinsky, Klee *(Golden Fish* and *Revolution of the Viaduct),* Ernst, Magritte, Léger. Examples of constructivism and recent Western art trends are displayed. Sculpture of the 19th and 20th centuries—by Rodin, Maillol, Renoir, Matisse, Marini, Moore, Calder, Segal, Graesel, Luginbuehl, Nachi, and Caro—is shown. Hours are 10 a.m. to 5 p.m. Tuesday to Sunday. In addition, seven or eight exhibitions are staged every year, some of international prominence. Admission is 3 DM (99¢).

The **Hagenbeck Zoo,** at Stellingen (tel. 540-00-10), in the northwest suburbs, was the first of its kind. It was founded in 1848 by Carl Hagenback, a pioneer of the "natural environment" theory of exhibiting animals, and has animals roaming free in terrains resembling their native homes. The U-Bahn takes you from the main station almost directly to the entrance, marked by bronze elephants, in about 20 minutes. The zoo has about 2100 animals. Its unfenced paddocks and the well-tended park are famous. This is considered one of the three top zoos in the world. The zoo has a troparium, sea lion and dolphin shows, rides on elephants and camels, a rail trip through "fairyland," and a children's playground. The zoo is open daily from 8 a.m. Admission is 10.50 DM ($3.47) for adults, 5.25 DM ($1.73) for children.

SOME NOTES ON SHOPPING: A stroll through the city center is like taking a look at one large international shop window. Hamburg is a city of merchants. In general, stores are open Monday to Friday from 9 a.m. to 6:30 p.m. (on Saturday from 9 a.m. to 2 p.m.). Unfortunately, the interesting shops are not concentrated in just one location. Two of the oldest and most important shopping streets, **Grosse Bleichen** and **Neuer Wall,** run parallel to the canals, connected transversely by Jungfernstieg and Ufer Strasse on the Binnenalster.

Seek out, in particular, **Harry Rosenthal's** bazaar cellar on Bernhard-Nocht-Strasse, where you can purchase curios from all over the world. Most of the merchandise was brought here by sailors seeking a little extra cash after the clip joints of St. Pauli had taken their money.

Mainly, Hamburg is a city of shopping malls, nine major ones. Even on the grayest, rainiest day in winter, you can shop in Hamburg in relative comfort. These include the glass-roofed **Hanse Viertel Galerie Passage,** which is some 220 yards long.

A SIDE TRIP TO WILLKOMM-HÖFT: By car you leave the center of Hamburg via the Elbchaussee or the Osdorfer Landstrasse, heading for Wedel, the trip taking about half an hour. From there you can follow the signs to Willkomm-Höft, or "welcome point." Ships of various nations go past this point, and they're welcomed in their own language, as well as German, and their national anthem is played as a salute. You can also reach the point by taking the S-Bahn up to Wedel. A bus will take you from the station, or you can enjoy the 15-minute walk. In summer the best way to go is to take a **Hadag** riverboat, leaving from St. Pauli Landungsbrücken in Hamburg, the ferry taking more than an hour.

The station was founded in the late spring of 1952. It was at this point that the sailor first catches sight of the soaring cranes and slipways of the Port of Hamburg. As a vessel comes in, you'll see the Hamburg flag on a 130-foot-high mast lowered in salute. The ship replies by dipping her own flag. More than 50 arriving ships, and as many departing ones, pass Welcome Point within 24 hours.

If you're planning a visit there, you can have lunch at **Schulauer Fährhaus,** 29 Parnasstrasse (tel. 23-03), in Wedel. Attractively situated on the wide lower Elbe, the place is run by Otto Friedrich Behnke, who founded Welcome Point. A respected merchant and well-known gastronomer, he runs this restaurant with a large enclosed veranda, a big open veranda, and a spacious tea garden. Guests are welcomed for breakfast, lunch, teatime, or dinner.

Fish dishes are a specialty of the kitchen, and seasonal German specialties are offered as well. The wine list is modest but interesting. For example, I recently enjoyed a tasty platter of sauerbraten. The restaurant has its own bakery, turning out a tempting array of goodies. Meals cost from 28 DM ($9.24) to 75 DM ($24.75).

4. Hamburg After Dark

THE CULTURAL SCENE: Hamburg is the cultural center of northern Germany. Its state opera, **Staatsoper,** 28 Dammtorstrasse (tel. 35-15-55), is known throughout the world, with an international repertoire of operas and ballet presented during its season. The opera house is also one of the most modern in the world.

The city's three symphony orchestras and several chamber groups have produced some of the finest recordings of classical works, and give frequent and varied concerts throughout the year. At the **Musikhalle,** Karl-Muck-Platz (tel. 34-69-20), you can hear performances of the Hamburg Philharmonic, the Hamburg Symphony, and the NDR Symphony.

Hamburg is blessed with more than 15 theaters, but for most of these a good knowledge of German is necessary. Plays in English, however, are presented at the **English Theater,** 14 Lerchenfel (tel. 22-55-43).

If you speak German, then you may want to attend a performance at the **Deutsches Schauspielhaus,** 39 Kirchenallee (tel. 31-11-76). It is recognized as one of the outstanding theaters in the German-speaking world, performing both the classics and the avant-garde.

Some of the greatest stars of the German-speaking stage perform at the **Thalia Theater,** 67 Raboisen (tel. 33-04-44).

And for children, where language is often not a problem, there is the **Theater für Kinder,** 76 Max-Brauer-Allee (tel. 38-25-38).

The **Hansa Theatre,** 17 Steindamm (tel. 24-14-14), is a North German variety show which claims that it's intelligible to all foreigners. The humor is so broad that that's surely true. The acts include Spanish flamenco dancers, magicians pulling rabbits out of hats, and aerialists balancing on wires above the stage. Each show usually has about 40 performers. There are special tables for smoking and drinking. Two shows are performed daily, one at 4 p.m. and another at 8 p.m. If you go to the 8 o'clock show, you're out by 11 p.m. On Sunday the first show starts at 3 p.m. and the second at 7 p.m. Prices range from 13 DM ($4.29) to 19 DM ($6.27) for the afternoon show, increasing to 19 DM ($6.27) to 23 DM ($7.59) on weekends. For the night show, tickets range from 21 DM ($6.93) to 27 DM ($8.91), increasing to 26 DM ($8.58) to 31 DM ($10.23) on Saturday.

THE "INFAMOUS" REEPERBAHN: For the true nightlife of Hamburg, you have to go where the action is, on the Reeperbahn in the St. Pauli quarter of the city. The hottest spots are on a tawdry little side street called Grosse Freiheit, meaning Great Freedom. St. Pauli is the sailors' quarter. Sailors, in fact, have more experience in taking care of themselves than the innocent abroad, so be on guard.

The streets are lined with pornography shops, interspersed with clubs with names such as Las Vegas and San Francisco. A word of warning: German law requires restaurants and nightclubs to display their price list. Know the cost of your drinks before ordering. If the management refuses to give you a price list, get up and leave, unless you've already fallen in love with someone and are prepared to risk anything. And a final bit of advice: This section is *not* for women traveling alone.

The **Colibri,** 34 Grosse Freiheit (tel. 31-31-25), is not for prudes. Its shows, depicting the most lurid forms of sexual intercourse between man, woman, beast, or whatever, are among the most erotic you'll see in Germany, but this is the main attraction of Reeperbahn nightlife. For the sake of delicacy, I won't go into any detailed description of the acts, but by now you probably get the gist. You'll pay 15 DM ($4.95) for beer, plus 30 DM ($9.90) to enter. But don't expect to make one beer last for the whole show. The shows are long, seemingly endless, and 80 attractions are advertised each night. Go between 8 p.m. and 4 a.m.

Other clubs on the same street impose about the same prices, but always exercise caution. Stick to beer. *Avoid ordering whisky or especially "champagne."*

The farmer from the environs, in the old seaport without his wife, wants to go on a **"Safari."** That's the name of a club at 24 Grosse Freiheit (tel. 31-54-00). This is what is known as a *kabaret d'amour.* It offers live sex on the stage, in some actions and forms perhaps unfamiliar to you. It's open from 8 p.m. to 4 a.m.

Tabu, 14 Grosse Freiheit (tel. 31-55-96), also presents live sex shows on stage, but with a difference. Its cabaret shows are often relieved by humor. Hours are 8 p.m. to 4 a.m.

The Beatles got their start at **Salambo,** 11 Grosse Freiheit (tel. 31-56-22), but not as a strip act. Many fans go there to seek it out, but instead of the Beatles, they get a live sex show. Incidentally, the Salambo was the first club to present live sexual intercourse between members of the opposite sex.

Another major tourist attraction is not in a club at all, but on the street. It's the famous **Herbertstrasse,** which every sailor in town visits when he's in port. For years it's been celebrated as the "street of harlots." These working girls sit in windows on this little alleyway, hustling men to come inside. Naturally, the windows are lit in red. When the curtains are closed, the occupant of the cage is "engaged." Exhibitions and "special requests" are catered to in the second and third stories of these little houses.

JAZZ: Hamburg has become firmly established as the number one jazz city in Germany. Stars in the music field also make appearances here.

A good spot I'm fond of is **Dennis' Swing Club,** 25 Papenhuderstrasse (tel. 2-29-91-92), which lies in a residential part of Hamburg. Here you are usually charged no minimum and no admission. It's a completely informal atmosphere for jazz, and it's operated by Dennis Busby, who is not only the owner and manager, but the piano player and bartender as well. He's been an accompanist to some of the finest Stateside jazz talents, and old friends who remember him from those days are always passing through Hamburg. About 80 people can show up here on a good night anytime after 8 p.m. When a name artist turns up (often unannounced), Dennis may suddenly decide to impose a door charge of about 20 DM ($6.60) per person. But he assures you that you'll hear something good for that.

Cotton Club, 10 Alter Steinweg (tel. 34-38-78), is legendary. A jazz cellar, it has a motto: *"Wo Jazz noch Jazz ist."* The oldest jazz house in Hamburg, it consists of one long room, and its prices are cheap. You can drink and also smoke here (the latter forbidden when the band is playing). It's open from 8 p.m. to 1 a.m. (on Friday and Saturday until 2 a.m.). Depending on "what's happening," the entrance could range from 8 DM ($2.64) to 20 DM ($6.60).

Onkel Pö's Carnegie Hall, 44 Lehmweg (tel. 48-26-84), is another of the famous places in Hamburg for jazz, and also for rock. Helen Schneider and Al Jarreau got their start here. It often draws what used to be called a "mixed bag" of people, from chicly dressed Hamburgers on the town to students in jeans. Since it's always overcrowded, go early—and be prepared to stand in line. Its repertoire of stars include the "Who's Who of Jazz/Rock," and the entrance fee ranges from 8 DM ($2.64) to 20 DM ($6.60). Hours are 8 p.m. to 2 a.m.

FOR DANCING: Bayrisch Zell, 110 Reeperbahn (tel. 31-42-81), may be on the Reeperbahn, but you could take your great-aunt there, especially if she likes to dance the polka. It's really a way to spend a Bavarian night in Hamburg. Clearly an imitation of Munich's famed Hofbräuhaus, Bayrisch Zell attracts couples young and old, and it has plenty of seats for all of them, 1200 in all. One of the most popular places in the St. Pauli district, it has good cookery, with meals costing from 18 DM ($5.94). If you see someone whom you find attractive, you can call him or her from your table. That's what those phones are for.

Zillertal, 27 Spielbudenplatz, off the Reeperbahn (tel. 31-46-03), is much the same thing as Bayrisch Zell, and it can also seat some 1200 revelers on a busy night. It's open from 7 p.m. to 2 a.m. weekdays and until 4 a.m. on weekends. Here you can order a simple meal for 18 DM ($5.94), and you'll pay another 1 DM (33¢) to enter. King George once visited here, a fact the management has never forgotten. It's very touristy, and a lot of fun if you're in the mood. Locally it's known as the "Bavarian Embassy," and has been an enduring Hamburg tradition, since it existed before the war.

Café Keese, 19–21 Reeperbahn (tel. 31-08-05), features a "Ball Paradox." That means, the women can choose the men as dance partners. The doorman tries to keep out hustlers. Actually, the place is legitimate, even though it wouldn't let Jayne Mansfield in back in the '50s (she refused to surrender her fur coat at the door). Live bands entertain, and ladies (hopefully, 20 to 50) go there to look for a man, ordering sandwiches at around 7 DM ($2.31) and beer from 7 DM also.

Boccaccio, 49 Kirchenallee (tel. 24-94-44), is where you go when you're straight and looking for a partner. Many Hamburg couples first met in this middle-brow place and still come back for sentimental reasons. Guests dance, often in the afternoon. It's open from 4:45 to 6:30 p.m. and again from 8:30 p.m. to 1 a.m. (on Friday and Saturday nights until 3 a.m.). It serves food until 1 a.m., with simple meals costing around 18 DM ($5.94). Today many guest workers, usually Yugoslavs and Turks, show up looking for bored Hamburg women, single or otherwise. Closed Monday.

Zigeunerkeller, 48 Reeperbahn (tel. 31-48-07), can also be fun if you're in the mood. This is a large cellar restaurant with a gypsy band and good cookery like they do it in Budapest. To the throbbing, soulful strings of a Hungarian violinist, you can order tasty specialties that cost from 22 DM ($7.26) to 35 ($11.55).

WINE DRINKING: Schwenders, 1 Am Grossen Markt (tel. 34-54-23), is one of Hamburg's most venerated wine houses. In modern times it has been spruced up, and is now as good as ever. The namesake Schwenders came from Vienna, bringing their style and charm to this old Hanseatic city. Apparently they made a lasting impression, as the place today often attracts some 400 or more patrons, even though there is room for only 200 to sit down to drink. Local musicians, usually the amateur or "out of work," drop in to entertain, and spontaneous concerts are common. Deli-type cold cuts and excellent cheese will do if you want something to eat with your wine. But most people come here to drink and be entertained in a belle époque setting filled with nooks and crannies.

DRAG SHOWS: Pulverfass, 12 Pulverteich (tel. 24-97-91), is the best known.

It's usually featured on the "Hamburg by Night" tours. This place is not for the timid. The shows can get downright vulgar, especially if you know German. Three shows are presented nightly, usually at 8:30 p.m., 11:15 p.m., and 2 a.m. Female impersonators from all over Europe appear here, and you can order steaks if you're hungry. The entrance fee is 25 DM ($8.25), and your first drink goes for 18 DM ($5.94).

DISCO: One of the best is **Chesa**, 15 Beim Schlump (tel. 45-88-11), which is open from 9 p.m. to 4 a.m., drawing a chic crowd, usually 25 years of age or more. The cookery is good in case you're hungry, and beer costs from 7 DM ($2.31).

ROCK: **Markthalle**, 9–21 Klosterwall, near the Central Station (tel. 33-94-91), has one of the best programs in Germany. It often provides a forum for up-and-coming English groups who like to play here. It's a series of boutiques and dining areas set in a marketplace. For an admission fee ranging from 12 DM ($3.96) to 20 DM ($6.60), you are admitted to the performing area, which is an indoor amphitheater with a stage and a large central section. You can listen to the artists in concert fashion or else view them in the theater-in-the-round style. Seats are really backless benches. You're allowed to bring beer or other drinks into the hall as you listen to the music.

    Trinity, 5 Eimsbütteler Chaussee (tel. 439-80-94), was the first copy in Europe of New York's Studio 54. The owners spent some 3 million marks to create, in the words of *Billboard* magazine, "the best light effects in the world." Hamburg's super-disco is now into rock, on Friday and Saturday night after 9—and it's still got those light effects. Entrance is 12 DM ($3.96).

    After Shave, 7 Spielbundenplatz (tel. 319-32-15), features rock, but also jazz. Many clients go there to listen to music and perhaps talk. It draws an age group around 20 to 45. The location may be in a sleazy area, frequented by prostitutes, but that's not why one goes to After Shave. Beer is from 7 DM ($2.31); long drinks, from 15 DM ($4.95).

    Logo, 5 Grindelallee (tel. 410-56-58), near the university, is one of the most popular clubs with young college-age visitors who meet Hamburgers of the same type. It's a small show place, which often features rock bands. Sometimes well-known singers appear here in concert. It's not chic; you often sit on the floor. Simple meals are served, costing from 10 DM ($3.30).

    Fabrik, 36 Barnerstrasse, five minutes from Bahnhof Altona (tel. 39-15-63), is a cultural center, along the same style as Markthalle. Originally it was an old ammunition depot (circa 1830), until it was burnt down. It was rebuilt in the same style. Children often come here in the afternoon with their parents (its hours then are noon to 6 p.m.). But after 7:30 p.m. and until midnight or later on weekends, it's a nightclub, offering a mixed program, rock, perhaps classical. The entrance fee ranges from 5 DM ($1.65) to 18 DM ($5.94), and beer and snacks cost 3.50 DM ($1.16) to 10 DM ($3.30). The club is in a district peopled, in part, by Turkish and Greek workers flooding into Hamburg.

GAY HAMBURG: Hamburg, like Berlin, is one of the major homosexual havens of Europe. Nightlife in the city reflects that. Some of the so-called gay places are often frequented by straights, for reasons known only to the latter. **Spundloch**, 19 Paulinenstrasse (tel. 31-07-98), is like that. It's been known to be patronized by men and their fraus, perhaps curiosity seekers. It's the oldest and most famous so-called "homo bar" (the German designation) in Hamburg. It's open from 9 p.m. to 4 a.m. (closed Monday). On some nights there's amateur cabaret, and it's also a small disco.

Pit Club, 17 Pulverteich, near the Hauptbahnhof, is currently the hottest gay disco in town, catering to all ages, with an accent on the young. Downstairs is "**Toms,**" the most famous leather bar in Hamburg, with back rooms. **Chaps,** behind Martkhalle, near the main station, is another well-known leather bar.

A BROTHEL: Hamburg has one of the most famous brothels in Europe, the so-called **Palais d'Amour,** 138 Reeperbahn. It lies on the north side of the Reeperbahn (often you'll see men lined up outside, waiting their turns). This is commercial sex on a scale rarely seen in a major city. The place has been called a "cattle ranch." The girls give an initial quote, but once in the stalls they occupy, they charge more to take off their clothes. At the "Palace of Love" medical authorities check the "inmates" (some of whom are very young) at least once a week. One commentator once wrote, "Imagine you are visiting the playground of an all-girl high school at recess."

From Hamburg, we strike out for Germany's northernmost province, Schleswig-Holstein.

Chapter XV

SCHLESWIG-HOLSTEIN

1. Lübeck
2. Kiel
3. Schleswig
4. Westerland (Sylt)
5. Helgoland

YOU WALK ALONG THE DUNES and hear the roaring waves breaking fiercely on the rocks. Or perhaps you lie on a tranquil beach while tiny waves lap at your feet. Sounds inconsistent, doesn't it? But not in Schleswig-Holstein. This northernmost province of Germany borders both the turbulent and chilly North Sea and the smooth, gentle Baltic. And between these two bodies of water are rolling groves and meadows, lakes and ponds, and little fishing villages with thatched cottages. But there's more to life in this part of Germany than peaceful country living. Fashionable seaside resorts line the North and Baltic Seas. Even in the coldest weather you can swim in heated seawater at the resorts of Westerland and Helgoland. In Kiel you can wander around the harbor and explore Schleswig with its Viking ghosts.

But let's begin our tour of Germany's north country with a visit to the Queen of the Hanseatic Cities, Lübeck.

1. Lübeck

It is said that nothing testifies to the wealth of an old European city as much as the size and number of its church spires. If this is so, Lübeck is rich indeed, for no fewer than seven towering steeples make up the skyline of this Hanseatic city. It has prospered since it was made a Free Imperial City in 1226 by the Emperor Frederick II. Lübeck held this position for 711 years, until 1937. In addition, it was the capital and Queen City of the Hanseatic League for centuries, and retains the title even though the economic and political importance of the league dissolved with its last meeting in 1630.

Lübeck is a city of high-gabled houses, massive gates, and strong towers. The Hanseatic merchants decorated their churches with art treasures and gilded their spires to show off their wealth. Many of these survivors of nearly 900 years of history stand side by side today with postwar housing developments, and the neon lights of the business district shine out on the streets and narrow passageways of bygone days. West Germany's top custodian of national monuments has called Lübeck "richer in antiquities than any other German city."

Lübeck has two famous sons: Thomas Mann and Willy Brandt. As a young man, Brandt, who was later the West German chancellor and Nobel Peace Prize winner, opposed the Nazis so stubbornly he fled his hometown on a boat to Norway. Mann too won a Nobel Prize. However, his was for literature. His novel,

Buddenbrooks, was set in his hometown and catapulted the 27-year-old author to international fame in 1902.

The city is the capital of marzipan. According to legend, Lübeckers, riding out a long siege, ran out of flour and started grinding up almonds to make bread. So delighted were they with the results, they've been doing it ever since. To sample a marzipan on home turf, go to the Niederegger shop across from the Rathaus.

THE SIGHTS: The Old Town of Lübeck is surrounded by the Trave River and its connecting canals, giving it an island-like appearance. It suffered heavily during World War II and it is estimated that one-third of the city was leveled. Today most of the damaged buildings have been repaired or reconstructed. Now Lübeck stands, as always, with a wealth of historic attractions.

The **Holstentor** (Holsten Gate), just across the south bridge from the Altstadt (Old Town), is the first greeting for visitors entering from the railway station. At one time it was the main entrance, built in the 15th century as much to awe visitors with the power and prestige of Lübeck as to defend it against intruders. To the outside world the towers look simple and defiant, rather like part of a great palace. But on the city side they contain a wealth of decoration, with windows, arcades, and rich terracotta friezes. Within the gate is the municipal museum, **Museum in Holstentor** (tel. 2-41-29), housing a model of Lübeck as it appeared in the mid-17th century. It is open daily except Monday from 10 a.m. to 5 p.m. (until 4 p.m. off-season), charging 2 DM (66¢) for admission.

The **Salt Lofts,** if viewed from the river side near the Holstentor, are among the most attractive buildings in Lübeck. These buildings, dating from as early as the 16th century, were once used to store the salt brought here from Lüneburg before it was exported to Scandinavia. Each of the five buildings is slightly different, reflecting several trends in Renaissance gabled architecture.

The **Rathaus** (Town Hall) traces its origins back to 1230. It has been rebuilt several times, but there are remains of the original structure in the vaulting and Romanesque pillars in the cellar and the Gothic south wall. The towering walls have been made with open-air medallions to relieve the pressure on the Gothic-arcaded ground floor and foundations.

It is estimated that within an area of two square miles around the city hall stand 600 medieval houses. Nearby is **Petersgrube,** the finest street in Lübeck, lined with some of the best preserved structures in Europe, one from 1363.

St. Mary's Church (Marienkirche), across the Marketplace from the Town Hall, is the most outstanding church in Lübeck, possibly in northern Germany. Built on the highest point in the Old Town, its flying buttresses and towering windows leave the rest of the city's rooftops at its feet. St. Mary's is undoubtedly one of the finest examples of Gothic brick churches, and the largest of its kind in the world. Originally planned as a Romanesque basilica, it was somehow switched to a Gothic style and designed as a Westphalian hall-church instead. Some of its greatest art treasures were destroyed in a fire in 1942. After the fire, the original painted decoration on the walls and clerestory was discovered. The bells from the original tower were struck in a World War II air raid, fell, and embedded themselves in the floor of the church, where they remain to this day. Organ concerts have been revived during the summer months, carrying on the tradition of St. Mary's best known organist, Dietrich Buxtehude (1668–1707).

Other Sights

Many of the art treasures of old Lübeck have been preserved in **St. Anne's Museum** (tel. 2-41-37), a former convent built in 1502. The museum is devoted mainly to religious works and statues, many of which had been removed from the bombed churches of the city. A major art treasure here is Memling's 1491 *Passion Altarpiece.* The museum is open daily, except Monday, from 10 a.m. to 5 p.m. (to 4 p.m. off-season), charging 2 DM (66¢) for admission.

Among the other important churches of Lübeck, the **cathedral,** built in the early 13th century, is the oldest church in the town. Badly damaged in 1942, it has not yet been completely repaired, but the slender twin spires again tower over the quiet south end of the Altstadt. The 14th-century **St. Catherine's** is the only monastic church within the city, built by the Franciscan order with a light spaciousness and severe, clean lines.

The **Seamen's Guild House** (Haus der Schiffergesellschaft) is one of the last of the elaborate guild houses of Hanseatic Lübeck, built in 1535 in Renaissance style, with stepped gables and High Gothic blind windows. It's worth seeing just for the medieval furnishings and beamed ceilings in the main hall, now a restaurant (see my recommendation below). A walk through the old streets of Lübeck reveals a constant use of brick as the local building material (the city insisted on this after fires in the 13th century). The effect is one of unity among all the houses, churches, shops, and guildhalls.

You can take an excursion boat around **Lübeck Harbor,** departing from Trave Landing, right in front of the Hotel Jensen. In season, departures are every half hour, anytime between 10 a.m. and 6 p.m.

THE TOP HOTEL: Lysia Hotel-Mövenpick, auf der Wallhalbinsel (tel. 1-50-40), enjoys a garden setting opening onto a canal. The accommodations in back are more desirable, as the front bedrooms open onto railway tracks. The Lysia is right at the entrance to Old Lübeck. The well-designed chambers are colorful and compact, almost motel-like. A single with shower and toilet ranges in price from 150 DM ($49.50) to 180 DM ($59.40). A twin-bedded room with shower or tub and toilet is in the 170-DM ($56.10) to 200-DM ($66) bracket. On the premises is a café-konditorei, as well as a bierstube. Tables outside are hedged in by boxes of geraniums. The Mövenpick Restaurant serves tasty specialties, with meals costing 28 DM ($9.24) to 60 DM ($19.80).

MIDDLE-BRACKET HOTELS: Jensen, 4-5 An der Obertrave (tel. 7-16-46), is one of the best in the medium-priced field. Right on a canal, near Holstentor, it offers the finest views from its bedroom windows of any hotel in the city. The view is of the Hanseatic brick architecture across the canal. The rooms are furnished in modern style—modest, but comfortable, as befits a town inn. For a double with bath, two persons pay 140 DM ($46.20) to 170 DM ($56.10). Singles cost 80 DM ($26.40) to 115 DM ($37.95) with bath. Breakfast is served in a room with picture windows overlooking the old canal, a delightful way to begin your day. Either lunch or dinner is good in the warmly decorated tavern-style restaurant. Menus cost 28 DM ($9.24) to 55 DM ($18.15).

Kaiserhof, 13 Kronsforder Allee (tel. 7-91-011), is a successful remodeling of a patrician town house as a hotel. Outside the center, it sits on a tree-lined boulevard. Since she fled from East Germany with her family, the gracious owner, Ruth Klemm, has created a fashionable home-like environment here for her guests. Every room is uniquely furnished, combining period pieces with modern. An elevator takes guests to all floors. An elaborate and authentic Scandinavian sauna opens off the rear garden. With her two annexes, Mrs. Klemm now has a total of 100 beds, all in rooms with private shower or bath. The single rate, depending on the placement of the room, ranges from 75 DM ($24.75) to 125 DM ($41.25). A double costs 105 DM ($34.65) to 170 DM ($56.10).

Hotel am ZOB, 3 Hansestrasse (tel. 8-26-26). The splendid proportions of this symmetrical baroque building give the impression that the interior will be in the same style. But as you climb the stairs leading to the lobby, you'll soon learn that everything has been entirely renovated and modernized. The hotel is comfortable and clean, and it is located near the Lindenplatz. Singles with shower and toilet rent for 80 DM ($26.40) to 145 DM ($47.85), while doubles go for 105 DM ($34.65) to 180 DM ($59.40), breakfast included.

WHERE TO DINE: Schabbelhaus, 48-52 Mengstrasse (tel. 7-20-11), is like the informal wing of a palace. On a medieval street, you make your way to this classic example of Hanseatic architecture. (The old Schabbelhaus was destroyed by a 1942 air raid. The new Schabbelhaus was installed in two patrician buildings dating from the 16th and 17th centuries.) Inside, in an atmosphere of German baroque (note the painted ceilings), you get attentive service and some of the best food in Lübeck. In the restaurant, ceiling-high studio windows overlook the small gardens; a pair of 15-foot-high armoires hold linen and glassware which are eventually placed on scrubbed wooden tables with pewter candlesticks. Lunches are 38 DM ($12.54). The fare includes such tempting items as Lübecker crab soup, fresh items from the sea, and steaks. Set dinners begin at 75 DM ($24.75), going up to 110 DM ($36.30) for the most elaborate specialties. Hours are noon to 3 p.m. daily and 6 to 11 p.m., except Sunday. A wooden staircase and balcony lead to two rooms devoted to memorabilia of Thomas Mann.

    Haus der Schiffergesellschaft, 2 Breitestrasse (tel. 7-67-76), opposite the Church of St. Jakobi, basks in the Hanseatic tradition. Memorabilia such as ship models hang from the ceiling and decorate the walls. Dining in this mellowed Baltic atmosphere is like entering a museum of Hanseatic architecture. The restaurant was once patronized exclusively by sailors and other men of the sea. Today good food (and large portions) is served on scrubbed-oak plank tables as you sit in a carved high-backed wooden booth, showing coats-of-arms from Baltic merchants. Often you must share a table here. Meals, including soup and dessert, are in the 35-DM ($11.55) to 50-DM ($16.50) range. The more expensive price includes such elaborate dishes as sole meunière (one pound) with a salad. You should have a drink in a cocktail bar in an historical cellar, called the Gotteskeller, open 6 p.m. to 2 a.m. (closed Sunday). The restaurant is open from 10 a.m. to 1 a.m. daily except Monday.

    Stadtrestaurant, 2-4 am Bahnhof (tel. 8-40-44). Close to everything in the heart of town, the enormous expanse of this elegant dining room in the railway station offers well-prepared meals to travelers and locals alike. The restaurant is on the first floor of the station and parking facilities are available in front. The rooms are furnished in Venetian, Empire, Baroque, and English style. Many critics consider it the best restaurant in Lübeck. Under the same roof you'll also find a café and several private salons, usually for conferences. Specialties include saltimbocca (a Roman dish of veal and ham, literally meaning "jump-in-your-mouth"), and leckerbissen, a Swiss recipe made of veal, ham, marsala, risotto, tomato paste, and hearts of lettuce. In season, the chef prepares medallions of baby stag in red wine, served "Romantik style." Meals range in price from 24 DM ($7.92) to 65 DM ($21.45), and are served daily from 10:30 a.m. to 11 p.m.

    La Nouvelle Etoile, 8 Grosse Petersgrube (tel. 7-64-40). After years of experience in another restaurant, Michael and Margitta Schünzel decided to open their own establishment inside this art nouveau home they lived in. Today their prospering bistro is laden with turn-of-the-century artifacts which include hand-painted tiles and an array of other handcrafted touches. The menu changes twice a month, but at the time of your visit might include such items as a Greek-style carpaccio with lemon sauce, venison pâté, Barbary duckling in a Cassis sauce, and such temptingly rich desserts as a pistachio parfait with a fresh fruit topping. Fixed-price meals range from 60 DM ($19.80) to 75 DM ($24.75), while à la carte dinners cost about 20 DM ($6.60) higher. Lunch is served from noon to 2 p.m., and dinner is between 6 and 10:30 p.m. The restaurant is closed on Sunday and holidays.

Lübecker Hanse, 3 Am Kolk (tel. 7-80-54), is one of the more expensive restaurants of Lübeck, but many locals "swear by it." The exterior is authentically weathered, and dark paneling graces much of the interior. The aquarium in the kitchen keeps much of the seafood fresh (to say the least) until the last minute, and there's also an elaborate salad buffet which is most popular. Specialties of the chef include a seafood terrine, bouillabaisse, wild game, and a never-ending series of plats du jour. Meals begin at 40 DM ($13.20) but could climb to 70 DM ($23.10) if you order the more expensive specialties. They serve from 11:30 a.m. to 2:30 p.m. and 6 to 11:30 p.m. every day but Sunday.

Historische Weinstuben, Heiligen-Geist-Hospital, 8 Koberg (tel. 7-62-34). In the basement of one of Lübeck's monuments (Holy Ghost Hospital), you'll find this first-class restaurant and 12th-century wine cellar. Specialties are likely to include half a dozen snails prepared Alsace style, followed by roast curried prawns Bombay style in a delicate sauce of mustard and fresh fruits. If you want something simpler, I'd recommend a grilled entrecôte, served on a wooden platter with all the trimmings. Full meals here average about 50 DM ($16.50), but perhaps you'll do it for less. Service is from 11 a.m. to 3 p.m. and 5 p.m. to 1 a.m., every day except Tuesday.

The **Ratskeller,** 13 Markt (tel. 7-20-44), is one of the finest town hall dining cellars in Germany. You make your way through the flower vendors on the square outside to enjoy the offerings of an ambitious chef. High standards and excellent food are the order of the day. The menu is backed up by a good wine list. As befits a seaport, fish is the house specialty. Wide-ranging delicacies are offered, including some high-priced lobster and caviar. Depending on your selection, expect to spend 25 DM ($8.25) to 70 DM ($23.10) here. The cellar is open from 10 a.m. to midnight, except Sunday.

J. G. Niederegger, 89 Breite Strasse (tel. 7-10-36), sells that "sweetest of all sweetmeats," the famous marzipan, with which the culinary reputation of Lübeck is linked. I suggest that you skip dessert at the restaurant where you've dined and head here to this pastry shop, dating from 1806. It's right across from the main entrance to the Town Hall. On the ground floor you can purchase these pastries (perhaps to savor later), or you can go upstairs to a pleasant café where you can order dessert and excellently brewed coffee (the best in Lübeck). Ask for their pastry specialty, a nut torte resting under a huge slab of fresh marzipan. Then swear off pastries for life!

2. Kiel

Even the name of this port and fishing city—it means "haven for ships" in old Anglo-Saxon—shows the importance of the sea to the growth and prosperity of Kiel. The perfect natural harbor at the end of the seven-mile-long extension of the Baltic Sea made Kiel a center for commerce with other northern European countries. The opening of the Kiel Canal in 1895 connected the Baltic Sea with the North Sea and western trade.

Kiel Week, held each June, is a further example of the port's close ties with the sea. This week of special events, held each summer for the past 85 years, includes a spectacular regatta in which hundreds of yachts race on the waters of the Roadstead. In 1972 the Olympic yacht races were held on the waters at Schilksee. Stretches of sandy beaches in the nearby resorts make the port a Baltic vacation spot as well.

Although Kiel is nearly 1000 years old, there is little in the way of streets or building to make the casual visitor believe that the town ever was anything other than a city of today. Almost all of its buildings were destroyed in World War II, and in their place is an admirable example of town planning. Kielers are proud of their broad streets, spacious squares, and green parks in the heart of town.

THE SIGHTS: Most of the attractions of Kiel center in and around the harbor. For the best overall look at the city and the Roadstead, go to the top of the Town Hall's 350-foot tower. Guided tours are at 10:30 and 11:30 a.m. from May to mid-October. For a closer view, wander the **Hindenburg Embankment** (Hindenburgufer) stretching for two miles along the west side of the fjord, opposite the shipyards. It's also one of the best spots from which to watch the regatta.

The **Sea Fish Market,** on the east bank of the fjord, is one of the largest in the world, and a fascinating place to visit, if the smell doesn't turn you off. You'll see a wide variety of sea life here.

If you have the time, take a short steamer trip to one of the nearby Baltic towns, such as Laboe with its sandy beach. Steamers and ferries also connect Kiel with Baltic ports in Denmark, Norway, and Sweden.

In the environs, the **Schleswig-Holstein Open-Air Museum** (called Freilichtmuseum in German) lies four miles outside Kiel. Go on the B4 highway to Neumünster. Farms and rustic country homes, dating from the 16th to the 19th centuries, have been assembled here in a sylvan setting. Local crafts people operate the shops, and working animals have been brought in. A half-timbered inn serves tasty lunches. The park is open from April 1 to mid-November on weekdays from 9 a.m. to 5 p.m. and on Sunday from 10 a.m. to 6 p.m. In the off-season it's open only on Sunday from 10 a.m. to dusk. It's always closed on Monday, and admission is 5 DM ($1.65).

WHERE TO STAY: Maritim-Bellevue, 2 Bismarckallee (tel. 3-50-50), built in 1972, and rated "superior first class," is a convention hotel opening onto the shore promenade of the Baltic, a few steps from the Düsternbrooker Seebad and the Kieler Yacht Club's marina (a ten-minute drive to Olympic Harbor). This well-appointed hotel offers attractively styled and well-furnished bedrooms, many of them with good views of the sea. Singles begin at 130 DM ($42.90), rising to 220 DM ($72.60) for the most superior units, and doubles, likewise, range from a low of 205 DM ($67.65) to 360 DM ($118.80) for the luxurious corner accommodations. All tariffs include a breakfast buffet. The rooms contain baths and balconies, along with radios and TVs, and you'll have access to the hotel's swimming pool, sauna, fitness room, solarium, bar, restaurant, and nightclub.

The **Hotel Conti-Hansa,** 7 Am Schlossgarten (tel. 5-11-50), is only a three-minute walk from the pedestrian shopping area. Half the bedrooms overlook the Oslo Kai; the other half, the Palace Park with its pond, the Kleine Kiel. There are 167 bedrooms, each one with bath/shower, toilet, color TV, video, radio, self-dial phone, trouser press, hairdryer, and mini-bar. You can snuggle into your bedroom or the Conti-Bar after you encounter the pleasures of the hotel's cuisine. You can choose between two dining rooms: the international Hansa-Pavillon and the well-known evening restaurant, Fayence. Singles range in price from 155 DM ($51.15) to 215 DM ($70.95); doubles run from 200 DM ($66) to 260 DM ($85.80).

Kieler Yacht Club, 70 Hindenburgufer (tel. 8-50-55), is exactly what its name implies—a yacht club with unusually fine guest facilities. It's an old classic building, standing back from the harbor, with an adjoining motel-style annex of contemporary design. It's the most spirited and ideal accommodation in Kiel. Prices are lower in the older portion. For example, in the old building, doubles with bath are 155 DM ($51.15), increasing to 195 DM ($64.35) in the annex. Singles with bath are 115 DM ($37.95) in the old part, 135 DM ($44.55) in the new. All tariffs include breakfast and service. The newer rooms are designed yacht-cabin style; the older rooms have more space and are pleasantly furnished and decorated. There is a multi-tiered restaurant where the tables are staggered to provide the best views. The Mastenkeller in the basement is for beer drinking. Note: The front rooms with water views are preferred, although the accommodations in the back open onto greenery. On the waterside, chairs and sidewalk tables are placed on terraces surrounded by planters of roses.

Hotel Astor, 1 Holstenplatz (tel. 9-30-17) stands within a short walk of both the ferryboat station and the Hauptbahnhof. The hotel shares a modern office building with several other corporations, although when you're admiring the view from the ninth and tenth floors, you'd think you were the only person in the hotel. The 60 bedrooms, each well appointed and with toilet and shower or bath, rent for 55 DM ($18.15) to 80 DM ($26.40), while doubles cost 100 DM ($33) to 160 DM ($52.80). A buffet breakfast is an additional 12 DM ($3.96) per person. The hotel restaurant is considered one of the best in Kiel, serving an international array of foodstuff, a fixed-price menu beginning at 22 DM ($7.26). The restaurant serves every day, except Sunday, from 7 a.m. to 11 p.m. It's decorated with Scandinavian-style furnishings, offering an impressive view from its big windows.

Hotel Wiking, 1-3 Schutzenwall (tel. 67-30-51), has a name that always reminds me of how far north I am, and how close to the Scandinavian countries. The facade of this modern hotel is ornamented with heavy walled balconies, painted white in vivid contrast to the dark walls of their background. The interior is attractively decorated with lots of taste, with dramatic contrasts between the dark and light areas of the sunny bedrooms. In the center of Kiel, the Wiking offers prices that vary according to the season (but with small differences). Singles rent for 80 DM ($26.40), doubles for 110 DM ($36.30), including breakfast. The bar and breakfast rooms are especially attractive, with a warm Nordic ambience.

WHERE TO DINE: Restaurant im Schloss, 80 Wall (tel. 9-11-58), is one of the finest and most elegant restaurants in Kiel, as well as the most expensive and formal. The service is superb, as are the food and choice of wine. It's a modern restaurant, across from the embarkation point for boats to Scandinavian countries. In a stone building overlooking the harbor, the Schloss looks like a museum set in a park. If you reserve, you can get one of the window tables opening onto the water. Set menus are offered for 28 DM ($9.24), but tabs can run as high as 70 DM ($23.10). The staff here keeps a long day: from 9 a.m. to midnight. However, only lunch is served on Sunday—the kitchen's got to take a break sometime.

Restaurant Kieler Yacht Club, 70 Hindenburgufer (tel. 8-50-55). The bar here is one of the most sophisticated hangouts in the north of Germany, attracting the yachting set from Newport to St. Tropez. The specialty is, naturally, seafood, with a menu beginning at 35 DM ($11.55) and going up to 80 DM ($26.40). The decor predictably has a nautical flavor. The food is good and attractively served.

Restaurant Drathenhof, Hamburger Landstrasse, am Molfsee (tel. 6-58-89). North German specialties are cooked with respect and attention to detail at this restaurant whose walls and ceilings are entirely covered with rustically grained wood. You'll see a small model of a 19th-century buggy next to one of the service tables. Some of the chef's specialties include herring filet with green beans, bacon, and potatoes with parsley; and marinated roast goose accompanied by salty pickles and red beets. Menus begin at 18 DM ($5.94), climbing to 45 DM ($14.85). Service is from 10 a.m. till midnight except Monday (it's also shut in January). The location is south of the center of the city.

Claudio's Weinkeller, 46 Königsweg (tel. 67-68-67), is considered one of the most attractive restaurants in town. Claudio Berlese is the effusive chef, preparing a tempting array of all kinds of light-textured Italian dishes for his highly responsive clientele. Specialties are concocted from the day's inventory of lobster, mussels, oysters, game fowl, and super-fresh vegetables which have made this country-modern establishment so popular. You might enjoy eggplant stuffed with mozzarella and tomatoes, spaghetti with mussels, oven-cooked salmon with fresh basil, and an array of other fish plates prepared in light sauces. The choice of wines is appropriately tempting. The establishment is open only for dinner, beginning every night (except Sunday) at 7 p.m. Last orders are taken at midnight. Fixed-price meals cost between 50 DM ($16.50) and 75 DM ($24.74).

Landkrug Stampe, 31-35 Alte Landstrasse (tel. 3-50), at Quarnbek-Stampe, makes for a pleasant outing if you don't mind the 6½-mile drive west of Kiel. You'll come upon a well-built country house, circa 1900, where the same family has maintained a restaurant for more than 80 years. Specialties include such traditional favorites as savory wursts, well-seasoned ham, and all the game dishes available in season. You might want to try their well-known grünkohlplatte of bacon, wurst, cheese, and roasted potatoes, which will probably be washed down by a stein of North German beer. Complete meals cost 25 DM ($8.25) to 60 DM ($19.80), and are served between noon and 2:30 p.m. and 5 to 10 p.m. every day but Monday (also closed for some part of the summer).

3. Schleswig

This one-time Viking stronghold on the Schlei (an arm of the Baltic Sea) is Schleswig-Holstein's oldest town, and it is steeped in all the myths and legends that go with such a long history. Even the seagulls, whose eggs are a delicacy here, have a legend of their own. According to tradition, the birds nesting on Seagull Island in the middle of the Schlei are actually the fellow conspirators of Duke Abel, who in 1250 murdered the duke's brother, King Eric. The crime was discovered when the king's body, weighted with chains, washed ashore from the Schlei. The duke went mad and eventually died and was impaled and buried in the Tiergarten. But his followers, according to the story, were doomed to nest forever on Seagull Island.

Fortunately, legends are not the only survivors in this ancient city. The bombing raids of World War II did not touch Schleswig, and it stands today a witness to 1200 years of history.

THE SIGHTS: A tour of the attractions usually begins in the **Altstadt** (Old Town), with a visit to the jewel of Schleswig—

St. Peter's Cathedral is a brick Romanesque-Gothic hall-church begun in the 11th century. The towering spire makes the rest of the Old Town seem like so many dollhouses by comparison. Inside is the outstanding Bordesholm Altarpiece, a powerful work, carved in oak by Hans Brüggemann (1514-1521) for the convent at Bordesholm. It was brought to the cathedral in 1666. Its elaborately carved Gothic panels contain nearly 400 figures. The cathedral and cloisters also contain art treasures, including the *Blue Madonna* by J. Ovens, and 13th-century frescoes on the walls and ceilings. The cathedral is open daily from 9 a.m. to 5 p.m., except Sunday when visiting hours begin at the close of the morning service. Winter hours are slightly shorter. There is no charge for admission.

Schloss Gottorf lies on a small island in the Burgsee, a bay at the west end of the Schlei. A dam and a bridge connect the island with the town. As you walk around the harbor, the panorama of the Old Town and the widening bay open up behind you. The castle is the largest in Schleswig-Holstein. The foundations date from the original 13th-century ducal palace, and the present structure was built mainly in the 16th and 17th centuries, and reconditioned since 1948 to house two museums and the State Archives.

The **Provincial Museum for Prehistoric and Early Times** (tel. 81-33-00) is one of the two museums housed in Schloss Gottorf. Exhibitions include displays of Stone Age reindeer hunters and artifacts from the Bronze Age to medieval times. Housed in a separate building is the most remarkable exhibit, the Nydam Boat, a fourth-century ship found in the Nydam marshes in 1863. In glass cases in the same room are artifacts and weapons found with the ship and moor-corpses, all adding up to the major archeological finds in northern Germany. Admission is 3 DM (99¢) for adults, 1.50 DM (50¢) for children.

About 1½ miles from Schleswig at Haithabu is a new **Viking Museum,** opened in 1985, showing the results of archeological excavations of the Viking-age town of Haithabu with all aspects of daily life including a Viking ship.

The **Schleswig-Holstein State Museum** (tel. 81-32-22), also housed in the castle, contains an exceptional collection of fine and applied arts from medieval times to the 20th century (paintings, sculpture, furniture, textiles, weapons, and arms, plus folk art). Outstanding are the Late Gothic "King's Hall," the 17th-century ducal living rooms with rich stucco ceilings, and the Renaissance chapel with a private pew for the ducal family decorated with intricate and elaborate carving and inlays. Two separate buildings east of the castle contain the collections of contemporary art in Schleswig-Holstein and the ethnological collections with extensive displays of implements and tools representing the rural life of farmers, artisans, and fishermen in Schleswig-Holstein. The same 4-DM ($1.32) ticket admits you to both museums. From April through October the museums are open Tuesday through Sunday from 9 a.m. to 5 p.m. On Monday only the "Nydamhalle" and the Middle Ages collection are open to the public. From November through March the museums are open Tuesday through Sunday from 9:30 a.m. to 4 p.m.; closed on Monday.

WHERE TO STAY: Strandhalle, 2 Strandweg (tel. 2-20-21), is the best hotel in Schleswig, and has been a family-run business since 1905. Actually it's more of a holiday resort—right on the water with rowboats, its own swimming pool in a beautiful garden, a natatorium with steam bath, and alpine sun. The owners set the informal atmosphere in the homey and comfortable rooms. You should ask for a room opening onto the water, with a view of the yacht harbor. Bathless singles range in price from 58 DM ($19.14); with shower, from 88 DM ($29.04). Doubles with shower or complete bath and toilet cost from 110 DM ($36.30) to 118 DM ($38.94). Menus cost 25 DM ($8.25) to 60 DM ($19.80). The wine list contains more than 250 different kinds of wine. You can bake out in the sauna, or take a cool dip in the pool.

Waldhotel am Schloss Gottorf, 1 An der Stampmühle (tel. 2-32-88), is a brick mansion lodged on a grassy plateau surrounded by a park and pine trees. It's on the outskirts of Schleswig, en route to the castle and approached by a winding driveway. A secluded holiday retreat, it's a fine bargain. There are no lounges to speak of, but the emphasis is placed on the sunny dining room and the bedrooms (large enough to have breakfast in, unless you prefer your morning coffee on the front terrace). Only two singles are rented, costing 45 DM ($14.85) to 60 DM ($19.80). The eight doubles rent for 92 DM ($30.36) to 106 DM ($34.98). All prices include breakfast, and you can also get moderately priced luncheons and dinners in the range of 25 DM ($8.25) to 50 DM ($16.50).

Hotel Waldschlösschen, 152 Kolonnenweg (tel. 3-20-26), at Schleswig-Pulverholz, 1½ kilometers to the southwest. This elegant country hotel is equipped with every convenience to make your stay here interesting and comfortable. You'll notice a rock garden, a gabled house, an elongated annex, and lots of green trees before you enter the hotel's public rooms, which are intimately lit and covered with tasteful carpeting, warm brick detailing, and wood paneling. The swimming pool is centrally heated year round, and the bowling alley is one of the most modern I've seen. Rooms are carpeted, with private bath, and are completely satisfactory in every way. The English-speaking owner, Hans-Werner Behmer, charges 85 DM ($28.05) to 100 DM ($33) in a double and 55 DM ($18.15) to 70 DM ($23.10) in a single, each unit with private bath and phone. A generous breakfast is included in the tariffs, and for 25 DM ($8.25) per person extra you can book in here on half-board terms.

Hotel and Restaurant Skandia, 89 Lollfuss (tel. 2-41-90), is a modern building owned by Hermann Meurer, without much external adornment other than some pleasing proportions. It opens to reveal a collection of banqueting halls and high-ceilinged public rooms, along with small bedrooms decorated in modern wood-grained pieces. All units have tile bath, TV, radio, and phone. With breakfast, the rate is 40 DM ($13.20) to 55 DM ($18.15) in a single and 90 DM ($29.70) to 110 DM ($36.30) in a double. The hotel has an excellent kitchen, turning out northern specialties, with meals costing 25 DM ($8.25) to 55 DM ($18.15).

WHERE TO DINE: Schloss Keller, Schloss Gottorf, 1 Stampfmühle (tel. 2-32-88), on the lower level of the already-recommended castle, is a fine choice for dining. There's also a café for light snacks and refreshments. Meals in the restaurant (which include soup of the day) are in the 20-DM ($6.60) to 45-DM ($14.85) range. The cuisine is typically and reliably Germanic, with dishes such as wienerschnitzel, rumpsteak, and sole. The dining room is pleasant, the cooking good.

4. Westerland (Sylt)

The mineral spas are a favorite summer spot for vacationing Germans, and others prefer to "take the waters" at the seacoast or in the crisp freshness of the Frisian Islands in the North Sea. The long, narrow island of Sylt and its capital, Westerland, attract northern Europeans drawn here by the invigorating sea air. Sylt is Germany's northernmost point, lying west of Germany's border with Denmark.

Salty air and pounding surf are not the only attractions of Westerland. It's a fashionable, chic resort with first-class hotels, fine restaurants, a promenade overlooking the sea, and a gambling casino. In addition it has some of the best therapeutic facilities of any seaside spa. The basic therapy here is sunshine, pure air, and seawater, but in recent years mud baths have also become a method of treatment. The spa has facilities for the treatment of everything from heart disease to skin irritations.

Some of the more remote sections of the dunes have been turned into nudist beaches for purists in the art of sunshine therapy. In addition to bathing, there are facilities in and around Westerland for horseback riding, along with surf, golf, and tennis, as well as more sedentary entertainment such as the theater and concerts.

When the sunlight begins to fade at the end of each day, the Casino (Spielbank) becomes the center of activity. In the center of town, it is in the same building as the town hall. All major games are played here: baccarat, roulette, and blackjack. The Casino bar serves the best drinks in town and is open daily from 5 p.m.

The only link between the mainland and Sylt, other than car-ferry, is the causeway running from the town of Neibüll. However, this causeway is only a railroad track, so if you wish to bring your car to the island, you'll have to load it on the train at Niebüll for the long slow ride. No advance booking is necessary. You just arrive and take your chances. Passengers are carried free.

The other way to go is by car-ferry, with boats going between Havneby on the Danish island of Römö, which can be reached by highway from West Germany, and List, at the northern tip of Sylt. There are at least a dozen crossings in summer, with a much-reduced schedule in winter. Unlike the railway, the car-ferries accept reservations. Call Havneby in Denmark (00454/75-53-03); or in West Germany, the Haus der Reise, 154 Grosse Bergstrasse in Hamburg at (040/38-18-21). In List itself, you can dial 04-652/475.

WHERE TO STAY: The most hotels are found at Westerland. Scattered accommodations are found at other spots on the island as well, including Sylt Ost, Kampen, and Wenningstedt.

The Top Hotel at Westerland

Stadt Hamburg, 2 Strandstrasse (tel. 85-80), is the superior hotel on the island. It's more like a well-appointed country home than a hotel, its gleaming white entrance reached through a white picket fence with street lanterns. It's built close to the street, next to the Casino, and its rear windows overlook a well-kept lawn. The interior is bright and cheerful, with country-estate furnishings (antiques intermixed with good reproductions), including wing-backed chairs and floral-covered armchairs. Each of the 75 bedrooms is individually furnished, with home-like touches. In high season, bathless singles go from 65 DM ($21.45) to 78 DM ($25.74); with shower or bathtub, from 114 DM ($37.62) to 150 DM ($49.50). The rate per person in a double without bath ranges from 54 DM ($17.82); with shower or bathtub, from 82 DM ($27.06) to 155 DM ($51.15). Half board costs 60 DM ($19.80) per person in addition to the room rate. You'll want to take your morning meal in the breakfast room, with its blue-and-white ceramic stove. Guests gather on cooler evenings around the open fireplace. For what it offers, the Stadt Hamburg is a bargain. It has all this and style too. And the hotel's restaurant serves some of the best cookery at the resort (see below).

Middle-Range Hotels at Westerland

Wünschmann Hotel, 4 Andreas-Dirks-Strasse (tel. 50-25), is the second choice for accommodations. This hotel may be in the core of a modern building plaza (with more than two dozen boutiques), but its inner aura is one of comfortable old-world tranquility. Breakfast is the only meal served, and it's offered in a woodsy and informal room, a pleasant place to begin the day. The bedrooms are one of a kind—all with strong colors, all cheerful, each with its own bath or shower. The high-season rates are as follows: singles range from 126 DM ($41.58) to 151 DM ($49.83), doubles, from 210 DM ($69.30) to 305 DM ($100.70). All rooms have private shower or bath. Breakfast is included, as are taxes and service. The hotel is in the heart of the tourist belt of Westerland, yet only minutes from the sand dunes.

Dünenburg, 9 Elisabethstrasse (tel. 60-06), is standard modern, set a block from the town center and beach. All its front bedrooms face the water and contain balconies (the higher up you go, the better the accommodation). Every bedroom is immaculate, comfortable, nicely furnished, and each has its own shower and toilet, color TV, and mini-bar. High-season rates are charged from June 1 to September 30. Singles with shower and toilet range in price from 90 DM ($29.70) to 130 DM ($42.90); doubles with bath and balcony, from 170 DM ($56.10) to 240 DM ($79.20).

Vier Jahreszeiten, 40 Johann-Möller-Strasse (tel. 2-30-28), is like an informal country inn, practically in the sand dunes, although right in the heart of the resort activity, about a five-minute walk to the Casino and swimming pool. Most of its bedrooms embrace the sea, and the lifestyle here is informal. It's easy to spot, bone white with red tile roof. In high season, depending on the plumbing, it charges from 80 DM ($26.40) to 130 DM ($42.90) in a single room and from 140 DM ($46.20) in a double, although some suite-like accommodations could cost as much as 240 DM ($79.20).

Hotel Roth, 31 Strandstrasse (tel. 50-91), is at the edge of the sea. This modern balconied hotel would look as much at home in southern Florida as it does in northern Germany. The inside opens to reveal carpeted rooms, many of them with exposed masonry walls. Rates are complicated and depend on the season. They begin at 126 DM ($41.58) for the most modest off-season single, climbing to 220 DM ($72.60) at the peak of the season. Off-season, you can stay here in a small, simple double for 232 DM ($76.56); however, for the best double room at the height of the summer season you might pay as much as 320 DM ($105.60).

Hotel Miramar, 43 Friedrichstrasse (tel. 85-50). My favorite room here is the comfortable sitting salon illuminated from above by an octagonal light, a construction detail left over from techniques used by the builders in 1903. The rest of the hotel sits on a bluff just above the beach, surrounded by an arched veranda and painted in contrasting tones of beige and barnyard red. The public rooms are graced with enormous arched windows with views of the sea beyond, and with pink napery on the tables in the pleasant dining room. Regardless of the season, you'll be able to go swimming—in winter in the sunny wood-paneled indoor pool near the sauna and fitness room. The high-ceilinged bedrooms, all of which contain bath, phone, and TV, as well as a toilet, rent for 140 DM ($46.20) to 230 DM ($75.90) in a single and for 240 DM ($79.20) to 350 DM ($115.50) in a double. Keep in mind that the wide price differences are caused by the fact that Sylt hotels double or triple their rates in the peak weeks of July and August. Breakfast is included in the tariffs.

Hotel Hanseat, 1 Maybachstrasse (tel. 2-30-23), is centrally located in the middle of town on a pedestrian walkway. The owner of this family-run establishment offers spacious, light-colored public rooms and clean and comfortable bedrooms to guests wishing to breathe in the salt air of Sylt. Singles rent for 120 DM ($39.60) to 180 DM ($59.40), and doubles go for 170 DM ($56.10) to 280 DM ($92.40), depending on the season. Units are equipped with TV, bath (or shower), toilet, and phone.

WHERE TO DINE AT WESTERLAND: Stadt Hamburg Stuben, 2 Strandstrasse, at Westerland (tel. 85-80), offers top-rate cuisine in an attractive setting. The menu is so wide ranging it makes selection difficult. Even if you aren't a guest at the hotel, you're welcome to drop in, either for lunch or dinner. Set meals range in price from 32 DM ($10.56) to 45 DM ($14.85). On the à la carte listings, the smoothest beginning is cream of lobster soup with cognac. There are many seafood specialties, such as filet of fresh North Sea plaice baked in egg, with béarnaise sauce, parsley potatoes, and lettuce salad; or an elegant sole Col-

bert, the price varying daily. By request, the chef will make you a special apple pancake. Meals are served from noon to 2 p.m. and 6 to 10 p.m.

Hardy auf Sylt, 65 Norderstrasse (tel. 2-27-75), is a round, thatched restaurant with a nostalgic interior, run by French gastronomer André Speisser since 1984. The decor features furniture dating back to about 1890. Finely worked columns and an intricate veneer adorn the dining area, and there are some imposing old oil portraits. Beautiful glass lamps and skillfully wrought candlesticks combine to create a relaxed, intimate dinner, with candlelight, soft music, the best of wines, and good food. Mr. Speisser, a master chef, came to the island from Alsace, which is reflected in the menu here. For example, you'll find listed such dishes as quiche Lorraine, langostinos à la Provence, and southern French tomato soup. There is also a fine selection of French and German wines. A full meal costs from 35 DM ($11.55) to 62 DM ($20.46), including wine. The restaurant is open daily from Easter to the first of January. The kitchen serves from 6 p.m. to midnight.

Käpt'n Hahn, 10 Trift (tel. 5461). Chef Dieter Holterbusch's adaptation of fresh salmon is said to be one of the island's main tourist attractions. Other culinary attractions include imaginative and flavorful preparation of lobster, oysters, freshwater fish (including crabs prepared "Berlin style"), and several regional specialties, some of which were based on "grandmother's recipes." Of the latter, you might be served a tasty version of sweetbreads in white wine. All of this regional nostalgia can be sampled inside the nautically decorated dining room of an old Frisian house where table reservations are important. A fixed-price meal costs between 80 DM ($26.40) and 130 DM ($42.90). The establishment is open from 6 p.m. to 1 a.m. every day but Monday during the winter. Annual vacation time is between early November until just before Christmas.

Alte Friesenstube, 4 Gaadt (tel. 12-28). This thatched building housing this "stube" was first constructed in the mid-1600s. The restaurant serves northern German and Frisian specialties in a warmly old-fashioned kind of style. The menus are written on the wall, but in a dialect of low German that might be difficult to translate. Someone will gladly assist you in deciphering some of the specialties, which include an array of regional pork, fish, and beef dishes. The establishment is open daily except Monday for dinner only, which begins at 6, lasting until 10 p.m. Full dinners cost between 25 DM ($8.25) and 40 DM ($13.20).

Das Kleine Restaurant, 8 Strandstrasse (tel. 2-29-70), is in a passage. The ten tables in this small, expensive restaurant almost always fill to capacity. Care has been taken to decorate the walls with original paintings and a gemütlich decor. Nouvelle cuisine has taken hold here at this little citadel, as witnessed by the specialties concocted by the chef: mousse of coquilles St. Jacques, goose liver pâté in port wine and vinegar garnished with red onions, and breast of Bresse hen stuffed with scampi mousse. A meal will begin at 85 DM ($28.05), and is served from 6 p.m. to 1 a.m. They're closed on Sunday and from September 15 to March 15.

"Die Seekiste," 9 Kapt'n-Christiansen-Strasse (tel. 2-25-75). If you're into boating, you'll love the maritime theme of this intimate restaurant and beer tavern. House specialties include all the seafood you'd expect, such as shrimp, lobster, and mussels, along with homemade soups, wursts, ham, and cheese. Everything is accompanied by beer, and meals cost 22 DM ($7.26) to 55 DM ($18.15).

WHERE TO DINE AT MORSUM NÖSSESTIG: Nösse (tel. 422). One of the

most alluring restaurants on the island is housed under the hip-roofed design of this Frisian-style house. The view from its panoramic windows encompasses an isolated stretch of the sandy soil whose tough grasses slope gently down to the sea. In this place, the chef and owner, Jörg Müller, prepares a sophisticated blend of nouvelle cuisine with many imaginative variations of French recipes. The menu changes frequently, according to his inspiration. Guests are assured of a savory blend of the freshest of local fish, shellfish, meat, cheese, and an impeccable selection from a well-stocked dessert trolley. Many guests reserve several days in advance, and then order one of the gourmet fixed-price menus. These cost between 115 DM ($37.95) and 150 DM ($49.50), depending on the number of courses (either five or seven). Less expensive meals can be ordered à la carte. A bare-bone minimum might be 40 DM ($13.20).

The bar is open before and after meal service, but hot meals are served between noon and 2:30 p.m. and between 6 and 10:30 p.m. every day of the week. Annual closings stretch from early November till just before Christmas and from mid-January to mid-March.

Nösse-Bistro (tel. 422). Even visitors not concerned with keeping a budget sometimes head for the warmly intimate ambience of this attractive bistro. It's contained in a separate section of the same house as the more formal restaurant Nösse. In true bistro style, only a limited number of well-prepared dishes are available, each listed on a handwritten menu changed frequently. Your meal might include a mussel salad in a spicy herb sauce, ragoût of marinated salmon with fresh bib lettuce, followed by a fresh fruit salad garnished with a scoop of homemade vanilla ice cream. Full meals range between 28 DM ($9.24) and 40 DM ($13.20). Meals are served from noon to 2:30 p.m. and 6 to 10:30 p.m. The room is so small that only about a half dozen tables can fit in, so always call for a reservation.

5. Helgoland

You may remember the North Sea island of Helgoland if you're a devotee of late-night movies about World War II on TV. Helgoland (also Heligoland) lies about 42 miles from the mouth of the Elbe River. It can be visited on a day trip (most often from Hamburg) or else you can spend time there staying at one of its modern hotels or seeking bed-and-breakfast accommodations among the islanders.

Tourist officials are fond of pointing out that Helgoland attracts more summer visitors than, say, Capri. But don't get the wrong idea. Most of its visitors, nearly all of whom are German, flock to Helgoland because of its status as a duty-free haven. Cigarettes, whisky, and such staples are sold at about half the price charged on the mainland. Many visitors from Hamburg call a visit here a "butter fahrt," meaning butter ride, as they're allowed to take back five kilos of butter. Some try to get away with more, but visitors are subjected to random inspection by Customs officials.

It takes about two hours to cross the sea to Helgoland, where some 2700 persons live. Excursion ships arrive en masse, especially in the summer months, but these vessels can't dock. Passengers are transferred to a flottila of small boats, piloted by Frisian sailors, for the ride into town. One way to reach this traffic-free island is to take a train to Cuxhaven where you can board a ship to Helgoland. Another way to go is by a Hadag vessel leaving from stage 9 at the St. Pauli boat station in Hamburg. One of these day excursions, operated in summer, will give you about four hours on Helgoland. You leave at 7:30 a.m., and you're back on the Reeperbahn in Hamburg by 11 p.m.

Helgoland is ancient, its origins going back to the eighth century when it was an ecclesiastical center. In fact its name means "holy land," from the German "heilige land." In time it became a haven for smugglers, attracting pirates who menaced North Sea shipping. Over the years it has been ruled by

Britain and Denmark, as well as Germany, because of its strategic position. In 1890 Kaiser Wilhelm II wanted Helgoland back so badly that he gave up Zanzibar in East Africa to gain Helgoland's release from British forces.

Even before Victoria became queen of England, Helgoland had been turned into a spa, attracting artists and writers, and later wealthy visitors who gambled at the casino and attended summer theater, after feasting on a supper of Helgoland lobster (which is quite expensive and much rarer these days).

Helgoland had a more ominous role to play in both world wars, as it was turned into a submarine base. Britain reclaimed the island at the end of World War II and attempted to blow it up, not wanting it to become another base in the event of some future war with Germany. The sandstone of Helgoland resisted the attempts of the RAF. In 1952 the island was returned to West Germany, but John Kennedy had already been elected president in America before most of the population started to drift back. The population had fled to the mainland in the closing months of World War II to escape Allied bombing raids. Even today it's possible to go on a tour of the bunkers and underground tunnels where Helgolanders hid out during those bombing attacks.

Therefore don't come here looking for quaint Hansel and Gretel architecture. Every building, including the pastel-washed homes of the islanders, is new.

After landing at the pier, you can stroll along the main street of town, Lung Wai or "long way." Actually it's not all that long, and the street is flanked with shops hawking duty-free wares for those day-trippers mentioned. When they're gone, Helgoland takes on a much more peaceful air.

The town is made up of two parts, Oberland and Unterland. You can walk a stairway of 180 steps or else take an elevator to the upper level. Many Germans take the scenic walk around the island, taking in the bird rocks, tall red cliffs, and dramatic North Sea scenery. At some point you can take a ferryboat over to Dune, which is the sister island of Helgoland. These islands were joined until a storm in the 18th century split them apart. Many come here for the beaches, paying for the rental of a hooded wicker chair, so typical of North Sea resorts. Others seek out a section of the beach reserved for nudists. You can also visit an aquarium on the island, filled with North Sea fauna.

For those who'd like to spend time here, I have a sampling of suggestions for—

FOOD AND LODGING: Kurhotel, 27 Lung Wai (tel. 595). The modern-style bedrooms of this sunny hotel are one of its best features. Each contains a private balcony, phone, TV, and many up-to-date conveniences. Most residents choose to stay here on the half-board plan, costing between 65 DM ($21.45) and 100 DM ($33) in a single and from 210 DM ($69.30) for both occupants in a double. The view from many of the windows encompasses the sea and the marshlands around it, each teeming with birdlife. Unlike some of its neighbors, this hotel receives guests all year. Some visit just to head for its big-windowed restaurant, where French specialties are served in a contemporary setting. Menu specialties include a wide array of lobster and fish dishes, many coming from the restaurant's aquarium. Try the salmon in a Riesling and watercress cream sauce or rolled filet of sole in a herb-flavored snail sauce. Meals are served between 11:30 a.m. and 2:30 p.m. and from 6 to 10 p.m., costing between 35 DM ($11.55) and 55 DM ($18.15).

Hanseat, 21 Südstrand (tel. 663). Many of this charming hotel's accommodations are individually decorated and filled with several modern comforts. Each benefits from its own private balcony, TV, and easy access to an indoor swimming pool a short distance from the hotel. It's closed every year between

November and February, but open otherwise, charging between 60 DM ($19.80) and 85 DM ($28.05) in a single and 95 DM ($31.35) to 150 DM ($49.50) in a double. A generous breakfast, included in the price, is served.

Villa Augusta, 16 Südstrand (tel. 220), is a contemporary-style hotel whose four floors of white-painted balconies run the entire horizontal length of the building. There's a sea view from each of the bedrooms, plus a café terrace for midafternoon drinks or tea. About a dozen comfortably conservative bedrooms are rented, costing between 60 DM ($19.80) and 70 DM ($23.10) in a single and 120 DM ($39.60) to 145 DM ($47.85) in a double, with breakfast included. The hotel is closed from early November until just after Christmas.

Fernsicht, 313 Am Falm (tel. 642). Although not on the sea, this hotel gives you a panoramic view of the shoreline and surrounding hills. This conservatively decorated house is a peaceful oasis, offering comfortably furnished rooms, 21 in all. The rate in a single ranges from 60 DM ($19.80) to 85 DM ($28.05), while doubles cost 95 DM ($31.35) to 150 DM ($49.50), with breakfast included. Specialties of the dining room, which is open only to hotel guests, include an array of fresh seafood prepared with skill and served in generous portions.

———————

Our tour of West Germany is over. The road now heads east to both Berlins.

Chapter XVI

WEST BERLIN

1. Hotels
2. Restaurants
3. Sights
4. West Berlin After Dark

IF YOU WERE ONE of the pilots engaged in bringing supplies to the people of Berlin in the great airlift of 1948 and 1949, you wouldn't recognize the city today. The same optimistic spirit and strength of will that caused the remarkable Berliners to survive the destruction of the war and the postwar Soviet blockade of the city have caused the creation of a new West Berlin, a metropolis unequaled in Germany. Structures of steel and glass now tower over streets where more than 40 years ago only a pile of rubble lay. Parks that were once reduced to muddy swamplands and battlefields are again lush forests and gardens. Children play in a quiet side street right within the shadow of the one thorn in the flesh of the city, the Berlin Wall.

The tragedy of the city is that it is no longer one Berlin, but two. Families and friends are divided by the concrete and barbed wire through the center of the metropolis. But most of them have adjusted to the fact, and life goes on from day to day in this, the most sophisticated, lively, friendly city in Germany.

From a legal standpoint, West Berlin seems to belong to no one. It is still occupied by the victorious Allies of World War II—the United States, Great Britain, and France—but it elects its own mayor. It also sends members to the West German Parliament in Bonn; however, they are nonvoting delegates.

To call West Berlin an "outpost" is almost an understatement. It is just that, lying completely surrounded by Communist-controlled East Germany and literally encircled by an almost astonishing array of Soviet divisions as if it posed some immediate military threat to the Soviet Union—which it doesn't, of course. It was Hitler's capital, and because of that dubious position, it was almost bombed out of existence.

The center of West Berlin activity is the 2½-mile-long street named the **Kurfürstendamm,** but called the Ku-damm by Berliners, who seem to have a habit of irreverently renaming every street and building in the city. Along this wide boulevard you'll find the best hotels, restaurants, theaters, cafés, nightclubs, shops, and department stores. As the showcase of West Berlin, it is the most elegant and fashionable spot in the city, but like the paradox that is West Berlin itself, the Ku-Damm combines chic with sleaze.

Before getting into the sights, sounds, and tastes of this exciting city, I'll survey the hotel situation. But even before this, a look at transportation.

GETTING TO BERLIN: You can reach West Berlin from the Federal Republic or other points in Western Europe by air, by car, or by train.

By Air

Several airlines make regular flights from Hannover, Hamburg, Frankfurt, Munich, and other cities, to the Tegel Airport right in West Berlin. Pan American, British Airways, and Air France fly from leading cities in the Federal Republic to West Berlin. (Lufthansa is not allowed to fly into West Berlin.) It is also possible to fly from such major cities as Paris, London, New York, and Zurich. It is cheaper to fly standby to London and then catch a flight into West Berlin, since the New York–London route is so much cheaper than New York–Berlin. From London, an APEX ticket, which carries certain restrictions, costs £150 ($193), while a straight one-way coach-class ticket from London to West Berlin is £149 ($192). From Frankfurt, the regular coach-class fare to West Berlin costs 223 DM ($73.59), although standby fares are available on certain flights for students aged 22 to 25, any passenger aged 12 to 22, or any passenger over 65. The standby fare, if it applies, is 128 DM ($42.24).

By Car

It is also accessible by car, bus, and train. The days of East German roadside inspections and endless delays seem at an end, since the signing of a treaty between the two countries in 1972.

There are three major points of entry for motorists traveling from West Germany to West Berlin. The shorter (approximately two hours) route is at the border town of Helmstedt, east of Hannover. You can also go east from Frankfurt in the direction of Bad Herzfeld toward the East German border. Finally, another autobahn is north of Nürnberg, with a crossing at Rudolphstein.

Customs is open 24 hours a day. You must carry the proper traveling papers for your car and your passport, of course; you'll have to cross the West German and East German checkpoints at the border. If you're the driver, you should possess an International Driver's License.

Road tolls for driving in the GDR are not collected from those driving cars with West German or West Berlin license plates. These are currently paid in a lump sum each year by the West German government and will continue, under current agreements, through 1986 (applicable only to those driving on the transit routes). This exemption also applies to such cars driven into East Berlin on a one-day visa. If you possess the International Green Card insurance, you will not need to purchase additional vehicular insurance while in the GDR.

You'll also have to declare your intention of visiting West Berlin to the East German border guards. You surrender your passport and pay a 5-DM ($1.65) visa fee. Rarely does any guard speak English, although cryptic words are sometimes understood. Under favorable circumstances, all the border formalities need take no more than 20 minutes. The trip itself from any point in West Germany is about 2½ hours.

Along the route you'll notice speed limits posted. They change frequently and with little warning, based on the condition of the often badly maintained autobahns. (The East Germans treat their ordinary autobahns much better than they do their transit routes.) Fleets of police cars patrol the autobahn. Many hide out in concealed places waiting for speeders. Occasionally cars are stopped indiscriminately, and all of a driver's luggage is tediously inspected. Members of the East German police patrolling this route have been called "cash-hungry comrades." The autobahn is filled with speed traps, so follow the posted speed limits religiously. Even if you go five kilometers above the speed limit, you can be arrested and fined. One newspaper reported of a businessman from Hannover who was fined as much as $2300! The *New York Times* reported that the East German police like to go for "capitalists in big cars." If driving in the left lane (which should be for passing only), keep your signals flashing. Otherwise you may be subjected to a heavy fine. One couple, apprehended on such a charge, wrote me: "Our fine was savage."

This brings up another point. Drinking and driving is a very serious offense in West Germany, but it is *an extremely serious offense* in East Germany. Therefore be sure to keep any alcoholic beverages in the trunk or some other storage area (even if you're only transporting them to West Berlin). The object is to avoid even the appearance of drinking alcohol while driving on the roads of the GDR.

Warning: Along the way you'll pass villages and towns. Do not be fooled into thinking you can leave the autobahn without police detection. If you venture into any of these towns without the proper documents, you are invariably subject to arrest.

Along the transit routes you will occasionally find rest stops specifically for buses in transit between West Germany and West Berlin. You are forbidden to use these if you're not riding on one of these buses.

Transit routes are clearly marked. The top of the signs will have yellow areas superimposed on the ordinary blue autobahn signs. "Transit-Westberlin," or "Transit-BRD," depending on the direction.

In case of a breakdown along the badly paved autobahns, boxes are placed at strategic points. However, if you seem to be a long way from a box, police cars will often find you and send a hauling truck if required.

Gasoline stations and restaurants intended for Western travelers are called "Inter-tank" and "Inter-shop." When stopping at an Inter-tank, bear in mind that many are self-service; however, others are full service. There are separate pump islands for persons using Western money and others for those with currency from the socialist countries. (At this point, the warning against carrying GDR marks or other Eastern bloc currencies cannot be emphasized too much). Use *only* Western (GDR lingo, "convertible") currency.

Although the use of West German marks is preferred for many reasons when engaged in transactions while in East Germany, in a pinch you can instead use U.S. dollars, pounds, francs, or whatever. You will probably receive change (if any) in West German marks. Not all stations are open around the clock, so pay close attention to your fuel supply. It's wise to begin the trip with a full tank.

Persons using the West German autobahns must keep their eyes open for signs pointing to Berlin, or in their absence, one of the East German cities located along the transit routes to Berlin. You will eventually see a sign indicating "Grenzkontrollstelle" (border control point), which is the West German checkpoint. Their main purpose is to assist and advise before continuing on into East Germany. After being allowed to proceed, continue on down the road. You will pass signs saying, "Halt! Hier Grenze!" (Stop! Here Is the Border!), and the GDR seal, indicating the actual border. After proceeding through the GDR checkpoint, signs will direct you toward the autobahn to Berlin. (While in the GDR checkpoint, don't be surprised if the border guards engage in staring "wars" or similar games.)

As you near West Berlin, you can begin to receive English-language broadcasts from either the American or British military FM stations in West Berlin. The American station's frequency is 88 MHz, and the British is located at (approximately) 96-98 MHz.

Eventually you'll reach the Berlin Ring Road, which encircles both Berlins. Be certain to take the sign to *West* Berlin, if that is your goal. Don't be misled! The East Germans call their Berlin simply "Berlin," as if West Berlin did not exist. Proceed to the border check, passing through East German Customs once again and across into West German lines, where the traffic laws of the Federal Republic once again apply.

By Train

Traveling by air to Tegel Airport in West Berlin is of course the simplest and easiest way, but the train isn't much harder. When taking the train, remember to pay only in Western money. The dining car may be operated by the Mitropa (East German) or DSG (West German) firms, but payment is required in West German DM. The issuance of transit visas on the train is now not much more than a formality. The visa forms aren't taken up when arriving either in West Germany or West Berlin (unlike automobile travel). Perhaps you'll want to keep yours as a souvenir. Keep them someplace other than in your passport since, chances are, you'll never need them again. But always hold onto them.

The rail trip from Frankfurt to West Berlin should take seven hours (sometimes a little more), and it costs $63 (U.S.) one way in first class and $43 in second class. Round-trip fares for the trip run $119 in first class, $80 in second.

Rail fares from Hamburg to Berlin are $34 one way in first class, $23 in second class. Round-trip fares are $64 in first and $43 in second. This trip requires three hours one way.

Warning: Eurailpasses are not valid in crossing through East Germany.

TRANSPORTATION IN THE CITY: The bus and subway (underground lines) of West Berlin are operated by an efficient organization known as the **Berliner Verkehrs-Betriebe (BVG),** 188 Potsdamer Strasse (tel. 2-56-1).

Tegel Airport, lies within the city limits, about five miles to the north of West Berlin. Economically, this is a great boon to the visitor, since public transportation is convenient to all points. For example, the 30-minute ride from Tegel Airport to the center of the city via bus A9 costs only 2.10 DM (69¢). In contrast, a taxi from Tegel Airport to a hotel on the Kurfürstendamm is likely to cost 30 DM ($9.90) or even more. Telephone the airport's information office at 4-10-11 for updates about incoming or departing flights.

The famed Tempelhof Airport of Berlin Airlift legend has been closed to civilian flights for many years now.

In the unlikely event you should land at **Schönefeld Airport** in the GDR, just outside the city limits of East Berlin, there is a bus service available between that airport and the Funkturm in West Berlin. The transit visa costs 5 DM ($1.65) or the equivalent in some other hard currency, and the one-way bus fare is 8 DM ($2.64).

The Berlin transportation system consists of **buses,** the underground **(U-Bahn),** and the **S-Bahn** (surface trains). Fares for the U-Bahn, S-Bahn, and buses, which operate only from about 4:30 a.m. to 1 a.m. (except for a few additional night buses), run 2.70 DM (89¢) for a single fare. Both the U-Bahn and S-Bahn run in both West and East Berlin. One U-Bahn and one S-Bahn line have been established for frontier-crossing traffic. Another U-Bahn line goes through East Berlin without a stop.

In 1984 the BVG took over the running of the S-Bahn train system in West Berlin. For some visitors to West Berlin, the location of certain S-Bahn stations may make its use more convenient than the U-Bahn or a bus. Under the operation of the BVG the service has been extended and former lines reopened.

The U-Bahn and S-Bahn line stop at the Friedrichstrasse station in East

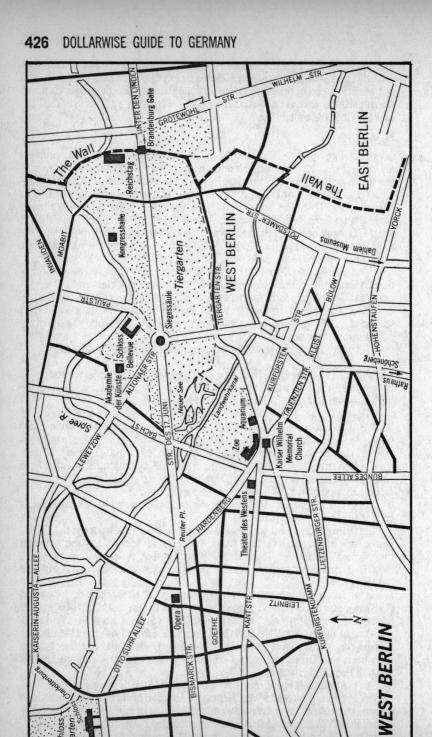

Berlin. There is an additional S-Bahn line which stops at the Friedrichstrasse, the so-called partly underground Nordsudbahn, which travels between the northern and southern parts of West Berlin. They all use the same border-crossing point (Grenzübergangstelle).

The train station for West Berlin is known as the **Bahnhof Zoologischer Garten** (called Bahnhof Zoo for short). It lies near the Zoo (also the Kurfür-stendamm). Trains to West Berlin, of course, run through the East German Zone, and passengers are subject to checks. For information about train sched-ules or whatever, telephone 312-10-42.

A special service to tourists is the **Touristenkarte,** a ticket good for unlim-ited travel on the U-Bahn, S-Bahn, and buses. These tickets can be purchased at the **BVG information booth** across from the bahn-hof (railway station), in front of the zoo. A ticket with a two-day validity costs 18 DM ($5.94), going up to 36 DM ($11.88) for four days. The ticket is also good for ferryboats on Wannsee Lake. At the booth, you can also purchase a **Sammelkarte,** which is valid for five rides, costing 9.50 DM ($3.14). These passes are good for two hours of transport in one direction. You are allowed to switch from underground to bus and S-Bahn. Keep your ticket to the end of your journey; otherwise, you may be subject to a fine of 40 DM ($13.20).

Special **excursion buses,** marked with a small triangular symbol, provide fast and convenient access from the center of the city (the Zoo Railway Station) to the recreation areas at Schildhorn, the Grunewald Tower, and Pfaueninsel, from Wannsee station to Pfaueninsel and the Krumme Lanke subway station to Wannsee Beach during the summer months only (fare is 1 DM, or 33¢; no trans-fer).

Taxis are readily available throughout Berlin as well, either by hailing them on the street or by calling 69-02. The average fare is about 15 DM ($4.95), and the meter drops at 3 DM (99¢) before you've gone one foot. You are usually charged 1 DM (33¢) for each suitcase.

BERLIN BOATING: You might not think of a boat as a means of traveling in Berlin, but many operate here, and a boat ride can become quite an outing when you tire of museums and the cafés along the Kurfürstendamm. The lakes of Wannsee (known as "Kleiner" and "Grosser," depending on their size) are the major targets in summer.

Sand is imported from some of the North Sea beaches and on a hot day the **Wannsee Strandbad** is packed. Many visitors like to come here to "cruise" mem-bers of both sexes, as the Prussians traditionally have been considered among the best-looking people of Europe. And in summer many are scantily clad. The lake fills with sailboats, and, hopefully, the "captains" know where they're going. Some parts of the Wannsee or Havel belong to the GDR, and East German police have been known to seize craft venturing into their territorial waters!

I'd suggest you take a **water bus** ride, departing from the Wilden-bruchbrücke, adjacent to the Rathaus Neukölln, an underground station of the U-Bahn. The water bus goes to Pfaueninsel (the so-called peacock island) in Wannsee. Allow about three hours or more for the trip and pay a modest 7 DM ($2.31) for the pleasure. The elevated train (S-Bahn) back to the train station in West Berlin costs only 2.20 DM (73¢). Ask at the tourist information office about departure times.

While there, also ask about a popular water excursion on the pleasure steamer *Moby Dick,* which tours the Havel lakes daily beginning in April. The ship is shaped like a whale, and sails from the Wannsee jetty up north to Tegel Airport.

PRACTICAL FACTS: For tourist information and possibly hotel bookings, head for the **Berlin Tourist Information Office,** Europa-Center (on the Budapester Strasse side) (tel. 262-60-31). It's open daily from 7:30 a.m. to 10:30 p.m. There's a branch office in the main lobby of Tegel Airport (tel. 41-01-37-45), which is open daily from 8 a.m. to 10:30 p.m.

The offices of **American Express,** on the other hand, are at 11 Kurfürstendamm (tel. 882-75-75), a second-floor location. Hours are Monday to Friday from 8:30 a.m. to 5:30 p.m. (on Saturday, only from 9 a.m. to noon). If you have mail sent here and don't possess an American Express gold or green card or some Am Ex traveler's checks, you must pay 2 DM (66¢) just to inquire if you have any mail.

Another useful address (and hopefully you won't need it) is the **U.S. Consulate,** 170 Clayallee (tel. 832-40-87). The **Canadian Embassy** is in the Europa-Center (tel. 261-11-61).

The **post office** is open 24 hours a day at the main rail terminal, the Bahnhof Zoo. If you have mail sent there, have it marked "Poste Restante." You can also make long-distance telephone calls at night.

In a **medical emergency,** telephone 25-85. However, if you need a **drugstore** (called *Apotheken)* at night, go to any one on any corner. There you'll find a sign in the window giving the address of the nearest drugstore open at night. This is required by law.

There is a **currency exchange** at the Bahnhof Zoo open from 8 a.m. to 9 p.m. weekdays and from 10 a.m. to 6 p.m. on Sunday.

1. Hotels

The day of *Grand Hotel,* when the lives of gamblers, ballerinas, noblemen, and stenographers became intertwined behind those revolving doors, is no more. The prewar ideal of luxury has been replaced by ultramodern comfort and conveniences. In many of Berlin's newest hotels, electric eyes and pushbuttons have made doormen and elevator operators obsolete. If you're still looking for that personal touch, Berlin has that too, in the many small hotels and pensions in the vicinity of the "Ku-damm."

Since Berlin is the scene of frequent trade fairs and conferences, it's wise to make reservations in advance, especially at the deluxe and first-class hotels. However, you should have no problem finding accommodations to suit both your taste and your pocketbook. I'll survey some of the best choices in all price categories below.

ON OR OFF THE KURFÜRSTENDAMM: Here are the most central hotels in Berlin, in all price ranges.

Deluxe Choices

Bristol Hotel Kempinski Berlin, 27 Kurfürstendamm (tel. 88-10-91), is a legend in Berlin. A century ago Kempinski was the name of one of the most renowned restaurants in Germany. In 1952 it rose out of the debris of World War II to become a landmark hotel, enjoying a position in the "island city" similar to that of the Waldorf-Astoria in New York. Business people who want to conclude international deals select the Kempinski as their base of operation, knowing they will be assured of a dignified ambience, attentive service, and a dramatic setting in the center of the city.

The decor is conservatively traditional, although everything, from tapestries to antiques to Persian carpets, seems special. The lobby sets the relaxed mood, with its fine and comfortable groupings of furniture. A high-level cuisine is served in the Restaurant Kempinski, which opens onto a Kurfürstendamm terrace. Other discriminating diners prefer the grillroom, with its open hearth. The Bristol Bar is low key, with patent-leather chairs and a pianist playing soft background music. An outstanding feature is the Kempinski pool, a recreation center with an inside swimming pool (24 by 48 feet), sauna, massage, solarium, fitness center, and pool bar.

The bedrooms—358 in all, with marble bathrooms, full air conditioning, color TV, direct-dial telephone, and fully stocked mini-bar—match the taste level of the public rooms. The accommodations are richly carpeted, the furnishings a selection of antique reproductions combined with modern. A single room with complete bath ranges in price from 205 DM ($67.65) to 300 DM ($99). Doubles with complete bath range from 265 DM ($87.45) to 360 DM ($118.80).

If you'd like to experience an added touch of class, try the Kempinski Luxury Limousine Service. You can use it for transportation from and to the airport, or for a sightseeing tour, in an old-fashioned, chauffeur-driven Daimler limousine.

Steigenberger Berlin, 30 Rankestrasse (tel. 2-10-80). No expense seems to have been spared during the 1979 construction of my preferred choice among the expensive modern hostelries of Berlin. The facade boasts a double level of panoramic windows on the ground floor, overlooking the landscaped expanse of the front garden. The reception and the second-floor sitting areas make extravagant use of a well-decorated space, using much wood, brass, and leather. The private bedrooms have all of the modern conveniences, and are handsomely appointed in warm, subdued colors. A kind of lemon light often suffuses the glass, marble, chrome, and plush upholstery. You'll be able to relax under the wood-ribbed dome of the swimming pool before entering the mixed sauna where au naturel seems to be the native dress. Singles rent for 210 DM ($69.30) to 290 DM ($95.70), while doubles cost 280 DM ($92.40) to 350 DM ($115.50).

The hotel's dining room is one of the best in Berlin. The primary elements are a gleaming decor of brass detailing over etched glass, vivid monochromatic paintings, enough waiters to serve the entire cast of a Wagnerian opera, and an elegant blend of both nouvelle and classical cuisines. The predominant color is one of those intriguing shades described as peach or russet or salmon. Fixed-price menus in the evening range from 55 DM ($18.15) to 105 DM ($34.65). It is open from noon to 3 p.m. and 6 p.m. to midnight every day of the week.

First-Class Hotels

Hotel Arosa Berlin, 79-81 Lietzenburger Strasse (tel. 88-00-50), still has the old deceivingly austere facade, giving no clue as to the charm, style, and flair of its interior. It's strongly recommended for many reasons, but most especially because it opens onto a rear courtyard and garden with a good-size open-air swimming pool and terrace for relaxation and refreshments. On the premises is a specialty restaurant, the Walliser Stuben, a successful re-creation of a country inn, with a rough wooden ceiling, heavy beams, alpine chairs, and pine tables, not to mention excellent provincial cuisine.

The main living room of the Arosa has a country flavor with a rounded open fireplace, pine ceiling, and groups of good armchairs arranged in clusters. The drinking lounge evokes the turn of the century, with its fringed hanging lamps, ornate cash register, and wood paneling. The bedrooms are skillfully styled as well, with TV set, comfortable furniture, telephone, radio, and private bath or shower. Singles rent for 118 DM ($38.94) to 140 DM ($46.20) nightly, and doubles run 180 DM ($59.40) to 220 DM ($72.60). All rates include a buffet breakfast, free use of the outdoor pool, and taxes.

arosa aparthotel Berlin, 82-84 Lietzenburger Strasse (tel. 88-28-81), stands just five minutes from the Kurfürstendamm, in a modern building near a group of boutiques, restaurants, and nightclubs. Elevators lead to an airy, spacious lounge. The rooms are modern in a nice way, quite attractive, with a picture window and glass door opening onto a balcony.

In the aparthotel, a regular single room with shower costs 125 DM ($41.25) to 150 DM ($49.50), while a double with bath ranges in price from 190 DM ($62.70) to 210 DM ($69.30). Two persons may be interested in renting one of the well-furnished apartments, complete with a living room and bedroom, costing 210 DM ($69.30) to 300 DM ($99) nightly for two to four guests. All tariffs include a buffet breakfast, service, and tax. For either lunch or dinner, you may want to dine in the provincial-style Walliser Stuben or Tell's Fass, which are open only to guests of the hotel.

The Medium-Priced Range

Hotel am Zoo, 25 Kufürstendamm (tel. 88-30-91), sits snugly on the main street of Berlin. Substantial and well maintained, it was built when bedrooms were expansive, so you'll have plenty of space to tuck away your overweight luggage. The rooms are well furnished, clean and comfortable. All units now have private bath, and singles range in price from 108 DM ($35.64) to 140 DM ($46.20), and doubles go for 170 DM ($56.10) to 180 DM ($59.40), depending on the type of plumbing. Breakfast is included. Dining is recommended at the old Germanic restaurant, where the atmosphere is authentic. Rooms have triple-glazed windows, which helps cut down the noise from the street. Incidentally, on his visit to Berlin in the 1930s, Thomas Wolfe, the author, stayed here.

Hotel Meineke, 10 Meinekestrasse (tel. 88-28-11), could become your *pied-à-terre* while in Berlin. Although greatly remodeled, this 60-room hotel was around before the war—World War I, that is. It stands in an apartment house on a pleasantly quiet street. It caters mainly to the increasing number of foreign visitors to Berlin, and you're likely to see French and Japanese, as well as Americans and Canadians. Bedrooms are simply furnished and comfortable. The price range is from 120 DM ($39.60) to 150 DM ($49.50) per person, based on double occupancy, and from 100 DM ($33) to 110 DM ($36.30) in a single.

Very similar in character, the **Domus Berlin,** 49 Uhlandstrasse (tel. 88-20-41), lies on a relatively quiet side street off the heartbeat Kurfürstendamm. Generally improved in recent years, it offers rooms that are adequate in size and fairly comfortable, with baths that have been modernized. The hotel is run with notable personal concern. You'll pay 98 DM ($32.34) in a single, 175 DM ($57.75) in a double. These tariffs include a buffet breakfast and tax. Although it's run by different managers, on the ground level is a friendly, bustling little brasserie-restaurant, where the action overflows onto a sidewalk café.

Hotel Bremen, 25 Bleibtreustrasse (tel. 881-40-76). You'll be in the center of the Kurfürstendamm if you stay here, which pleases most visitors to Berlin. The neighborhood isn't as noisy as you'd think, and the hotel has windows that are fairly soundproof. The lobby is graced with an elegant Oriental rug that any of us would like to take home, and the rest of the public rooms are comfortably furnished in a utilitarian modern. Rooms are simply but pleasantly furnished, costing from 120 DM ($39.60) to 130 DM ($42.90) in a single and from 155 DM ($51.15) to 200 DM ($66) in a double, including breakfast.

Hotel Kurfürstendamm am Adenauerplatz, 68 Kurfürstendamm (tel. 88-28-41). Recently this hotel was renovated in a refined way: it's modern, but the public rooms look distinguished and pleasing. In the dining room, where only breakfast is served, the light from the double-tiered windows is bordered by the charcoal-colored draperies which frame the view of the street beyond. You'll be close to everything here, and your room will be comfortable and well furnished. Singles rent for 69 DM ($22.77) to 96 DM ($31.68), while doubles cost 122 DM

($40.26) to 132 DM ($43.56), including breakfast. The staff here is interested and alert, and should prove most helpful.

Hotel Kronprinz Berlin, 1 Kronprinzendamm (tel. 89-60-30). The facade of this place has remained virtually unchanged since it was first constructed at the end of the 19th century. The owners have renovated the interior into a kind of art deco severity, which doesn't detract from the comfort of the well-appointed bedrooms. Many of the guests congregate in the cozy in-house bar before heading out to their various nighttime obligations. The approximately 50 bedrooms are each suitable for two persons, who pay between 120 DM ($39.60) and 180 DM ($59.40). If a single person wants to rent one of these doubles, the charge drops to 85 DM ($28.05) to 120 DM ($39.60). A buffet breakfast is included in the price. Each accommodation contains a balcony, radio, phone, TV, and mini-bar.

The Budget Hotels

Hotel Regina, 37 Kurfürstendamm (tel. 881-50-31), is solid, modern, and comfortable, lying in the center of town near the railroad station and zoo. Bus no. 9 stops nearby and takes you directly to Tegel Airport, and you can also make easy connections for most other points. If you're driving, you'll find an underground garage around the corner from the hotel. All rooms have hot and cold running water and phones; some have private shower or bath. An elevator takes you upstairs, and units also contain TV sets. Depending on the plumbing, singles range from 60 DM ($19.70) to 85 DM ($28.05); doubles, 92 DM ($30.36) to 125 DM ($41.25). These tariffs include breakfast as well.

Frühling am Zoo, 17 Kurfürstendamm (tel. 881-80-83). There is no elevator, but this hotel offers one of the best budget accommodations right in the heart of West Berlin. Just two minutes from the Memorial Church, it occupies the upper floors of a corner building, directly on the Kurfürstendamm. The reception area is tiny, but the old-fashioned, chandeliered bedrooms are spacious, comfortable, and well maintained. Singles with shower cost from 60 DM ($19.80), peaking at 105 DM ($34.65) with complete bath. Doubles with shower go for 100 DM ($33), rising to 140 DM ($46.20) with complete bath. Breakfast is included, served in a handsome, formal salon overlooking the busy boulevard.

Astoria, 2 Fasanenstrasse (tel. 312-40-67). This rebuilt and modernized hotel is just off the Kurfürstendamm, near the Bahnhof Zoo. Its exterior looks somewhat like a town house. You can stay here for a modest amount of money in a rather expensive section of Berlin, especially if you ask for a room without a private bath. A double-bedded accommodation ranges in price from 90 DM ($29.70) without bath to 150 DM ($49.50) with bath. Bathless singles go for 68 DM ($22.44), rising to 105 DM ($34.65) with bath. Breakfast is included in the rates. The bedrooms contain all the necessary comforts. The miniature dining room is restrained, with wood paneling and bright walls and chairs.

Bogotá, 15 Schlüterstrasse (tel. 881-50-01). Although you're just off the Kurfürstendamm, when you walk into the Bogotá you'll think you're in a small town on the northern coast of Spain. When you hear Spanish spoken, your impression will be confirmed. The lobby is Iberian in character, with a high beamed ceiling, an open wooden staircase leading through an arch to the bedrooms, a wooden balcony, and a heavy bronze chandelier. There are 124 bedrooms, some of which have private shower; otherwise, each room contains hot and cold running water. Singles go for 50 DM ($16.50) to 70 DM ($23.10), the latter price for one with shower. Bathless doubles are 80 DM ($26.40), increasing to 105 DM ($34.65) with shower. Rates include breakfast. The rooms are elbow-action clean. To economize, ask about staying here on a half- or full-board arrangement and taking your meals in the downstairs restaurant.

Cortina, 140 Kantstrasse (tel. 313-90-59), is a modest, well-maintained little pension just off the Kurfürstendamm. Its prices won't break the bank. Bathless singles cost 42 DM ($13.86); doubles, 68 DM ($22.44); and triples, 90 DM ($29.70). Rates include use of the corridor bath, as well as a continental breakfast. It's not fancy, yet there's a pleasant feeling of roominess and cleanliness. A friendly, English-speaking management helps out too. Hot and cold running water, as well as a telephone, are in every room. Many doubles have a little sitting area where you can have your morning meal.

NEAR THE MEMORIAL CHURCH AND ZOO: The bomb-flattened area between the Memorial Church and Zoo has become the major hotel belt of Berlin. Here was enough space to build and accommodate the luxurious hotels. The Kurfürstendamm changes character at the church and becomes less a promenade shopping street and more an avenue of first class hotels. It is the most prestigious place in Berlin to stay.

Deluxe Hotels

Hotel Inter-Continental Berlin, 2 Budapester Strasse (tel. 2-60-20), is a Berlin landmark, a world apart that is prestigious, tasteful, ingenious, and dramatic. It overlooks the Zoological Garden and is close to the Tiergarten park area, yet it lies only a five-minute walk from the center of Berlin. In the autumn of 1981 it revealed 600 attractively furnished bedrooms, including 70 apartments, costing from 215 DM ($70.95) to 275 DM ($90.75) in a single and 260 DM ($85.80) to 340 DM ($112.20) in a double. The hotel is fully air-conditioned.

Its facilities are vast, including a health center with an indoor swimming pool, saunas, and a fitness-room. An indoor garage has space for 100 cars. The Hugenotten is a French restaurant serving international dishes, and the Brasserie is more for moderately priced meals and snacks. The Lobby Bar is an informal meeting point for the business people of Berlin, and there is also a Roofgarden Supper Club with dancing. On a cool night in Berlin, you can also relax around the open fireplace in the Rooftopbar.

Hotel Palace Berlin, 42 Budapester Strasse (tel. 26-20-11). This luxurious modern hotel offers the double benefit of a recent renovation, as well as a convenient location at Berlin's city-within-a-city, the Europa-Center. Guests "disembark" under a massive canopy, under the illumination of hundreds of tiny lights which appear to be cascading from the glass-and-steel walls above. Inside, the designers included a commercially attractive blend of plushly colorful carpeting with live plants, a scattering of old tapestries, and both an autumnal-toned bar and an alluring modern restaurant. An indoor swimming pool, dozens of gleaming shops, a greenhouse-style café (the Tifanny), and a wood-paneled old-world weinstube (Alt Nürnberg) are contained within the corridors. You'll also find a casino and a health spa within the center. Well-furnished singles rent for 175 DM ($57.75), and doubles cost between 230 DM ($75.90) and 250 DM ($82.50).

First-Class Hotels

Hotel Ambassador Berlin, 42-43 Bayreuther Strasse (tel. 21-90-20), is an upper-grade contemporary hotel, whose dining rooms and lounges are among the best conceived and designed of any Berlin hotel in this price range. The main lounge sets the pace, with its sophisticated steel-and-leather chairs gathered around a spherical copper-and-glass open fireplace that looks something like a space capsule. One of the best places for fish dishes in town is the Conti-Fischstuben. One wall is decorated as a sea with sailboats, a wooden fish-scales panel, and one glass wall opening onto a maritime garden. The bar is also attractive, and in the pretty little restaurant, Küchenstube, tasty international and Berlin dishes are served. A lively crowd is drawn to the heated tropical pool on the eighth floor with its sun lounge on the roof. In addition, bodies from many nations are baked in a genuine log-cabin sauna before being massaged.

Bedrooms are excellent and well planned, with tasteful furnishings. Each has a shower or a private bath, a radio, color TV, mini-bar, and direct-dial telephone. A single with shower starts at 128 DM ($48.24), going up to 175 DM ($57.75) with private bath. A twin-bedded room with bath is between 210 DM ($69.30) and 280 DM ($92.40).

Berlin Excelsior, 14 Hardenbergstrasse (tel. 3-19-93). The name of the hotel is elaborately set into gray tiles near the entrance of this ultramodern establishment, a few blocks from the main railway station. The reception area and the high-ceilinged bar give the feeling of almost unlimited space, with modern partitions crafted of valuable hardwoods and blue-gray patterned carpeting muffling the footsteps of the hundreds of international guests who stay here every year. Even though one wing of this 320-room hotel faces the Kurfürstendamm, your sleep will be aided by the soundproof windows. All units have private bath, many of them tiled in dark colors, and a collection of electronic devices diverse enough to keep anyone happy. Rooms are well furnished and attractively styled, costing 155 DM ($51.15) in a single and from 185 DM ($61.05) in a double, including a buffet breakfast. The Peacock Restaurant, with elaborate representations of that bird in brilliant blues and greens, serves world-class meals in an aura of intimate simplicity.

Berlin Penta Hotel, 65 Nürnberger Strasse (tel. 24-00-11). The boxy shape of this 1980 hotel in the center of Berlin is relieved somewhat by the stone facade and the recessed windows on the ground floor. Following a hotel concept which has been fine-tuned by the Penta chain for many years, this gigantic hotel shelters more than 400 bedrooms, along with restaurants, a bierstube, a host of shops and service establishments such as a salon de coiffeur, plus a self-service breakfast buffet. All the attractively furnished units are equipped with private bath and modern fixtures, costing 210 DM ($69.30) in a single and 240 DM ($79.20) in a double, plus 19 DM ($6.27) for breakfast.

Schweizerhof, 21-31 Budapester Strasse (tel. 2-69-61), has brought honors and success to its Swiss owners. Built in a fashionable and convenient section, close to the Memorial Church and opposite the Zoo, it's clearly a winner in every department. The service, the amenities, and the comfort are first class. However, the overall effect is not one of lavishness—rather, dignified restraint. Increased patronage has led to a whole new wing of streamlined bedrooms, both substantial and comfortable. An Olympic-size swimming pool, even a whirlpool, suggests that the Schweizerhof is one of the leading first-class hotels of Berlin. The bedrooms are more traditional than daring, each containing a private bath (most with shower attachments). Singles range all the way from 125 DM ($41.25) to 195 DM ($64.35); doubles, from 180 DM ($59.40) to 230 DM ($75.90). The Schweizerhof Grill, offering a fine Helvetian cuisine backed by Swiss wines, is most recommendable. You can also dine in the Zunft-Stube and the Schützen-Stubli, after having had a before-dinner drink in the Lömmli-Bar.

Hotel Berlin, 62 Kurfürstenstrasse (tel. 26-92-91), is a true international hotel, built honeycomb modern, with its own grounds and gardens. Each of the 255 rooms has an inset balcony, just large enough for breakfast. This chain hotel is noted primarily for its Berlin-Grill, considered one of the finest dining rooms in the city. It also operates the Four Seasons Restaurant, but it has a claim to fame as a hotel as well. It is used primarily by travelers who want everything at their fingertips—not only a top restaurant, but consistently good service and up-to-date accommodations. The latter are especially good—rather cozy in style, each with a TV, private telephone, bath or shower, and toilet. Singles go for 115 DM ($37.95) to 165 DM ($54.45); doubles, 180 DM ($59.40) to 215 DM ($70.95).

The Savoy, 9-10 Fasanenstrasse (tel. 31-06-54), was the only Berlin hotel to survive World War II. Erected in the 1920s, it was once filled with Russian aristocrats, who stopped off here before going on to Cannes. Nowadays it attracts conservative travelers who appreciate a traditional ambience and setting, just minutes from the Kurfürstendamm. Persian carpets, crystal chandeliers, and contemporary upholstered pieces add a warm note. "Germanic modern" accommodations have private bath or shower—most rooms have sitting area with TV, couch, and desk. Rates, including tax, service, and continental breakfast, are as follows: singles with shower or tub bath range from 128 DM ($42.24) to 158 DM ($52.14); twins with shower or bath go for 170 DM ($56.10) to 320 DM ($105.60). A big buffet breakfast is included. The American Bar, dining room, and garden are most popular.

Sylter Hof, 116 Kurfürstenstrasse (tel. 2-12-00), is recently built, offering rich trappings at moderate prices. The main lounges are warmly decorated in an old-world style, with chandeliers, Louis XV-style and provincial chairs, and such antiques as an armoire and a grandfather clock. The bar-lounge serves drinks to guests seated in velvet armchairs nestling on Persian rugs. The dining room is more conservative, done in green. Although small, the bedrooms are warmly appointed, with compact, traditional furnishings, plus private tile bath. Singles rent for 125 DM ($41.25); doubles, for 195 DM ($64.35). Garage parking is available.

Medium-Priced Hotels

Hamburg, 4 Landgrafenstrasse (tel. 26-91-61), is one of the newer streamlined hotels, renovated in 1980, offering up-to-date accommodations at reasonable prices. The Hamburg, with its checkerboard facade of glass and two-tone marble, is a five-minute walk from the Kurfürstendamm. Each bedroom contains its own tile bath and shower, telephone, radio, and color TV. Singles are 118 DM ($38.94); a twin-bedded room is 144 DM ($47.52) to 168 DM ($55.44). An extra bed in your room costs an additional 26 DM ($8.58). A buffet breakfast is included.

The decor of the rooms is most satisfactory, a combination of Germanic modern with wall-wide draperies and comfortably upholstered armchairs. Other facilities include a cocktail lounge behind open white grillwork, where the bartender prides himself on international brews. Best of all is the living room, with its clusters of deep, well-styled, velvet-upholstered armchairs arranged around tables or the stone fireplace with copper slats.

President Hotel, 16 An der Urania (tel. 21-90-30). Its white marble facade and streamlined decor seem right in step. About a ten-minute walk from the Kurfürstendamm, this hotel rises seven floors, with bands of picture windows. An expansive roof garden with a panoramic view is its most winning feature; a Nordic sauna, its most restful. Bedrooms are geared more for efficiency than high style, with lots of swivel armchairs, and trim sofas that convert into extra beds. In addition, each room has its own bath, radio, TV, mini-bar, and direct-dial phone. Singles with shower are 100 DM ($33) to 170 DM ($56.10). Doubles cost 160 DM ($52.80) to 210 DM ($69.30).

Hotel Remter, 17 Marburger Strasse (tel. 24-60-61). A black-and-white awning extends over the sidewalk in front of this saffron-colored building, only two blocks from the Kaiser Wilhelm Memorial Church. Each of the hotel's 32 bedrooms is priced from 100 DM ($33) to 110 DM ($36.30) in a single and 130

DM ($42.90) to 140 DM ($46.20) in a double, with breakfast and color TV, radio, and phone included. The interior is clean and comfortable, decorated in a sort of Berlin Airlift modern (such as unframed hexagonal mirrors in the dining room). The location, however, is perfect, and in summer price reductions are often granted.

SOUTH OF THE KURFÜRSTENDAMM: This area has no special geographical boundaries except for its northern border. Only a few hotels are in this area, as it's mostly a residential and shopping section.

The Medium-Priced Range

Alsterhof, 5 Augsburger Strasse (tel. 21-99-60), is a relatively unknown hotel which is an excellent buy. Set back from the street, it rises seven stories. The lounges and reception area have walls of glass. There is a Grill-Room with bar. Each of the 139 bedchambers has its own private bath, radio, TV, mini-bar, and telephone, and is furnished with fine-grained wooden pieces. Many contain a sitting area as well. Singles with shower are 115 DM ($37.95); with complete bath, 150 DM ($49.50). A double-bedded room rents for 160 DM ($52.80) to 210 DM ($69.30).

Econtel, 24 Sömmeringstrasse (tel. 34-40-01), is for those who want streamlined modern efficiency—and few frills—and don't mind the location. If you find lodgings here, you'll be about halfway between the airport and the center of West Berlin, which is easily reached by public transportation. You're also convenient for visits to Charlottenburg Palace. The Econtel might be a good bet when the hotels in "downtown" West Berlin are full (as they often are), since it offers a total of 205 relatively small but comfortable bedrooms, housing nearly 500 guests at its peak capacity. The rate in a single ranges from 75 DM ($24.75) to 105 DM ($34.65), rising to 100 DM ($33) to 130 DM ($42.90) in a double. In its price range, it's one of the best buys around. Only breakfast is served.

The Budget Choice

Dom Hotel, 33 Hohenzollerndamm (tel. 87-97-80), is quite economical. This modern building, with its absolute minimum lobby, provides good sleeping rooms. Bathless singles range from 38 DM ($12.54) to 60 DM ($19.80), increasing to 70 DM ($23.10) with bath. Bathless doubles rent for 80 DM ($26.40); with private bath, from 95 DM ($31.35). A continental breakfast is extra. Meals are served in the friendly restaurant, the Dom Klause. Young visitors enjoy the Dom's proximity to the Riverboat disco.

IN CHARLOTTENBURG: This is an area combining private residences, apartment houses, and hotels, about a five- to ten-minute taxi drive from the Memorial Church and Kurfürstendamm. On its main artery, Bismarckstrasse, is where you'll find the Deutsche Opera and the Schiller Theatre.

A First-Class Choice

Seehof, 11 Lietzensee-Ufer (tel. 32-00-20), is one of the most attractive and enjoyable hotels in Berlin. It's comparatively unknown, as it lies in the residential section of Charlottenburg. Yet it's only five minutes from the center by taxi. The hotel borders Lake Lietzen. You start your day here with a swim in the rooftop, glassed-in pool, then order breakfast at one of the garden tables. The blue-and-white checkerboard facade opens onto a tree-shaded street. On the waterside stone terrace in the rear you can have refreshments, sunbathe, or take your lunch.

The living room is styled like a country house, with a natural stone wall, a planter, a window wall, and low couches for relaxed conversation. The main dining room is seductively designed; a pianist plays soft background music. Drinks are available in the rustic tavern bar. The bedrooms, while small, are well conceived, with splashes of color against stark-white walls. Most of the accommodations have slim-line sofas, armchairs, and cocktail tables. A single with shower costs from 165 DM ($54.45). Doubles with bath range from 200 DM ($66) to 230 DM ($75.90), including breakfast.

Medium-Priced Hotels

Hotel Ibis Berlin, 10 Messedamm (tel. 30-20-11), built in 1966, stands halfway between the Olympia Stadium and the Europa-Center, and adjacent to the Berlin Exhibition Grounds and the Congress Center, at the end of the Federal and Berlin City Highways. Its features are attractive and winning. Crowning its top floor is a garden-style terrace restaurant, the Bellvue, one of the most panoramic spots for luncheons in the city. Its bedrooms have full baths, with wall-wide glass windows. Radios, telephones, desks, and armchairs add to the comforts. Single rooms cost from 105 DM ($34.65) to 115 DM ($37.95); doubles, 130 DM ($42.90) to 140 DM ($46.20). Breakfast is included. For before dinner drinks, there's an intimate wood-paneled bar and cocktail lounge. It's a leader in the moderately priced field if you don't mind the long haul.

Hotel am Studio, 80-81 Kaiserdamm (tel. 30-20-81), is recommended to those seeking a bright and cheery accommodation at lower-than-usual prices for what you get. This 80-bedroom structure of bands of marble and glass windows is built in the Charlottenburg district, near the Olympic Stadium and next to the Radio and Television Center. Two subway stops are nearby. The bedrooms are pleasantly decorated and comfortable. Each of the rooms has its own private bath. Singles go for 80 DM ($26.40) to 85 DM ($28.05); twin-bedded units, anywhere from 105 DM ($34.65) to 125 DM ($41.25). A breakfast buffet, service, and taxes are included. Your morning meal will be served in a sun-filled salon.

Kanthotel, 111 Kantstrasse (tel. 32-30-26), has architecture that looks like something vaguely out of Bauhaus. The interior is spacious, high-ceilinged, and modern, with up-to-date bathrooms and color TVs in most of its 55 units. Conveniently located a few blocks north of the Kurfürstendamm, the hotel charges 100 DM ($33) to 130 DM ($42.90) in a single and 150 DM ($49.50) to 170 DM ($56.10) in a double, breakfast included.

IN KREUZBERG: Near the Tiergarten, a modern hotel is open which will put you into the heart of Berlin by taxi in just five minutes, or 15 minutes by bus.

Hervis Hotel International, 97 Stesemannstrasse (tel. 261-14-44), made its debut in 1968. The rear of this hotel, which is planted with lawn, looks somewhat like a U-shaped condo in Florida. All the rooms are sunny and spacious, and decorated with steel-and-wood contemporary furnishings along with patterned wall-to-wall carpeting. You'll be able to see the Brandenburg Gate from many of the private rooms, and from the top floors you can glimpse over "The Wall" into East Berlin. The hotel is within walking distance of Checkpoint Charlie, the National Galerie, and the Philharmonie, and stands across the street from the Martin Gropius building (the former arts and crafts museum). Including a breakfast buffet, singles rent for 98 DM ($32.34) to 132 DM ($43.56), while doubles cost 144 DM ($47.52) to 185 DM ($61.05). All units contain shower or bath along with toilet, color TV, radio, and mini-bar. An extra bed is another 30 DM ($9.90). Children up to 12 stay free in their parents' rooms.

IN GRÜNEWALD: The "Green Forest" of Berlin is the most pleasant residential section of the city, with tree-shaded streets and many town houses which were spared the destruction of war. It's ideal for a peaceful night's sleep.

Schlosshotel Gehrhus, 4-10 Brahmsstrasse (tel. 826-20-81), offers a rare opportunity to live in an Italian Renaissance-style palace in the Grünewald residential section of Berlin. It was created in 1912 by Dr. Pannwitz, personal attorney to Kaiser Wilhelm II, who was the hotel's first guest. The palace was built as a showcase to house the attorney's outstanding art and china collection. Gehrhus miraculously escaped destruction in World War II. Today it is owned by Regine Gehrhus. On a shady street—it is reached via a formal driveway—it is a 15-minute taxi ride from the center. Surrounding the estate are tranquil, park-like gardens.

Inside, the architectural grandeur remains the same. Gilt is used flamboyantly. The two-story grand hall contains an elaborate staircase and minstrel gallery. Glittering chandeliers glow in the French-style salons, with their brocaded walls.

The bedrooms vary greatly, ranging from grand to average. A bathless single costs 56 DM ($18.48) to 80 DM ($26.40), rising to 120 DM ($39.60) to 135 DM ($44.55) with bath. Bathless doubles begin at 120 DM ($39.60), going up to 165 DM ($54.45) to 185 DM ($61.05) with bath. Even though they're not guests of the hotel, many tradition-minded Berliners come here just to have coffee or tea—perhaps a nostalgic reminder of the past. Others use the Gehrhus for fashionable weddings, receptions, and cocktail parties.

AT KLADOW: **Havelhaus,** 33-35 Imchenalle (tel. 365-58-00), lies in the suburbs of West Berlin at Kladow, south from Spandau, about a 22-minute ride from the center. The location is near the East Berlin border. If you don't mind the commute, you can settle into this pension on the banks of the Havel River. It has its own bathing beach in summer, but may shut down for a month-long holiday right in the peak of the season (always call before heading out here). At times it's possible to rent a boat for a little cruise on the river, but stay out of East German waters! A tranquil choice, it offers 50 clean but small units, each with hot and cold running water. The price is right: from 45 DM ($14.85) in a single to 62 DM ($20.46) in a double.

2. Restaurants

If it's true that optimism and appetite go hand in hand, the West Berliners must be among the most optimistic people in Europe. In breads alone, the visitor is likely to be tempted by a dozen varieties, including brötchen, mohnbrötchen, milchbrötchen (all types of rolls), graubrot (rye), pumpernickel, and several others. If you're interested in local food, these breads go equally well with the "Berliner schlachteplatte" (cold plate), or pig trotters cooked with sauerkraut and pea puree.

But Berlin does not limit itself to German cuisine—nearly every major nation on the globe is represented here by a restaurant. Only the thickness (or thinness) of your wallet and the flexibility of your tastebuds need determine your choices. And don't think that an excellent dinner in Berlin has to be expensive. On the contrary, as you'll see in the recommendations below, you can have a memorable dinner in an unheralded wine restaurant or sidewalk café.

THE TOP RESTAURANTS: **Berlin-Grill,** Hotel Berlin, 62 Kurfürstenstrasse (tel. 26-92-91), is one of Berlin's leading candidates for in-depth preparation of haute cuisine. You feel absolutely coddled dining here as a train of serving carts with your choices is brought to your chair. Salads are made on the spot and pretested. Many of the dishes are prepared right at your table, for your closest scrutiny. After any finger food is served, you get hot, scented towels. Everything is top-grade—no substitutes, in the food, service, or atmosphere. Fresh flowers placed on the tables add yet another warming note. In the illustrated multilingual menu, you'll find weekly and seasonal specialties such as a terrine of stewed eel or a light soufflé of Breton turbot.

The cuisine is Germanic-international. Many of the soups are prepared and served right at your table, including consommé of lobster with parfait of turbot. Specialties of the house feature grilled scampi with English mustard and garlic butter; stuffed filet of beef with braised onions, green pepper, and garlic, and broccoli; and filet of veal in butter with medallion of lobster, sour cream sauce and morels, and homemade spinach noodles. Mousse au chocolate with peppermint sauce makes a delicious dessert. A complete meal will cost from 50 DM ($16.50) to 90 DM ($29.70). Hours are noon to 3 p.m. and 6 p.m. to midnight. Closed Saturday lunch and Sunday.

Maître, 31 Podbielskiallee (tel. 832-60-04). Classical music might be playing softly in the background of this plushly elegant restaurant whose color tones are based on pastel shades of creams, golds, and peaches. This is the latest home of one of Berlin's best established—and most expensive—restaurants. Part of the allure is the well-versed knowledge of the wine stewards, whose cellars include some very rare and very prestigious wines . . . for a price.

If your tastes run to grand fare, your meal might be one of the elegantly presented fixed-price menus. The petit menu includes five fanciful courses, costing from 130 DM ($42.90). The grand menu comprises seven courses, each a work of well-crafted art, at a cost of 180 DM ($59.40). Typical specialties include marinated salmon in a fennel-flavored cream sauce, a foie gras salad, seawolf with a beluga caviar sauce, and an array of wild game in season, including venison in red wine sauce. Cheese lovers will appreciate the unusual variety on the cheese board. Desserts might include a lemon cream sabayon, followed by homemade petits fours and coffee.

Almost no one is permitted entrance without a table reservation. Ordinarily, only dinner is served, beginning at 7 p.m. and lasting until midnight. The restaurant is closed on Monday. However, on Sunday the evening meal is replaced with a service lasting from noon to 3 p.m.

Ritz, 26 Rankestrasse (tel. 24-72-50), is one of the most celebrated restaurants of Germany, set against a backdrop of a Shangri-La setting. Mrs. Gisela Schnöke, owner of the small place (only 12 tables), directs a trained staff which prepares the foods of many nations. The key to the success of the Ritz is the choice ingredients imported from all over the world for use in dishes typical of both the East and the West. They offer French, Spanish, Italian, Russian, Japanese, Indian, and Chinese specialties. Menus cost from 45 DM ($14.85) to 150 DM ($49.50). The restaurant is open from noon to 2:30 p.m. and 6 to 10:30 p.m. except Sunday. It is also closed from July 15 to August 15.

Ristorante Anselmo, 17 Damaschkestrasse (tel. 323-30-94), is a modern restaurant, seating diners at 14 tables in a decor that might be called futuristic chic. People go here for good Italian food, expensively priced at 70 DM ($23.10) to 100 DM ($33) for dinner. The decor of pin lights, magenta walls, lots of chrome and light, along with stark tables and chairs, draws many theatrical personalities. The owner, who has spent long years in Germany, freely gives advice on the available selections in his kitchen. There are many good steak dishes. The restaurant serves from noon to midnight, but is closed Monday and for all of July.

Rockendorf's Restaurant, 1 Düsterhauptstrasse (tel. 402-30-99), occupies the primary position in an art nouveau villa near the Englischer Garten in north Berlin. The chef, whose name graces this elegant restaurant, often sticks to the classical French cuisine, which he prepares beautifully. However, he frequently sends his creativity into the uncharted waters of nouvelle cuisine, concocting some strikingly original dishes. Perhaps you'll try his paprika torte with freshwater crabmeat, or fresh jellied aspic with cucumber sauce; perhaps filet of turbot in a Ricard sauce, or goosemeat pâté in sauterne with cranberries. Ever had a fennel soufflé? Other lures are the saffron fish soup and venison Colbert flavored with vanilla.

The innovative thinking of S. M. Rockendorf also goes to the borders of China, with his bouillon of wild quail, served with breast of quail over fresh quail eggs. The furnishings of this restaurant are restrained. Noonday meals cost from 55 DM ($18.15) to 90 DM ($29.70), and dinner, at 115 DM ($37.95) to 150 DM ($49.50), attracts only the well-heeled. It's open from noon to 3 p.m. and 7 p.m. to midnight daily except Sunday, Monday, and holidays. It also closes for three weeks in February and two weeks in August.

Tessiner Stuben, 33 Bleibtreustrasse (tel. 881-36-11). As you enter this paneled restaurant, which sometimes is bathed in a golden light, you can almost imagine yourself in the Italian section of Switzerland. Raimund Karbowiak has carefully crafted that impression with comfortably cluttered walls and woodwork. For specialties of the Ticino region, be prepared to pay from 55 DM ($18.15) to 70 DM ($23.10) for an elaborate four-course meal. Food items might include raclette Valaisienne, a combination of melted cheeses, grilled veal steak with morels, and grilled lamb chops with green beans. Other specialties include calf brains with a white wine sauce, filet of pork in a mustard sauce, and black Angus filet steak with a pepper sauce. The wine list offers not only German wines, but bottles from California and Israel as well. They are closed Saturday all day and on Sunday for lunch. Otherwise, hours are noon to 3 p.m. and 6 p.m. to 1:30 a.m.

Conti-Fischstuben, 42 Bayreuther Strasse (tel. 21-90-20). In spite of its name, this is a hotel restaurant that specializes not only in fish but also in meat. It looks like a salon in an elegant yacht, with an aquamarine glow shining from the waters of a stunning fish tank in the center of the dining room. The furniture is modern, the walls are richly grained wood, lacquered to a shining smoothness, and the light a soothing blue-green. The fish is extremely fresh and delicately seasoned for the most part, and you face a staggering choice of wines from all over Europe. In the Hotel Ambassador Berlin, the restaurant charges from 60 DM ($19.80) to 90 DM ($29.70) for a complete meal, which it serves from noon to midnight every day except Sunday.

MEDIUM-PRICED DINING: In this category West Berlin has dozens of dining spots. Here are the best choices:

Mampes Gute Stube, 14 Kurfürstendamm (tel. 881-71-01), is a genuine Old Berlin restaurant. You expect the cast from *Grand Hotel* to walk in at any minute. Housed in a building that survived World War II, the "stube" couldn't be more traditional, although you'd never know it, judging by the modern glassed-in sidewalk tables outside on the Kurfürstendamm. Inside, the dining nooks are more atmospheric, with dark woods and leather, as well as tile tables. Try the chicken fricassée or the veal steak. The sole meunière is also good. For dessert, try the sour cherries with fresh cream. Menus begin as low as 18 DM ($5.94), going up to 35 DM ($11.55).

Kopenhagen, 203 Kurfürstendamm (tel. 883-25-03). The Danes are among the finest cooks in Europe. Just ask them! Their most famous specialty is smørrebrød (literally, bread and butter), on which they are likely to pile everything from a slice of Danish cheese to steak tartare crowned by a raw egg. These open-face sandwiches, when prepared correctly, are a delight. Copenhagen more than a quarter of a century ago invaded Berlin (not the other way around). The selection of smørrebrød is so huge that you may spend half your lunchtime deciding what to order. I favor the marinated herring and roast beef with remoulade sauce. However, the liver pâté is heartily recommended as well. A special smørrebrød is the aquavit cream cheese. Naturally, you'll want to accompany your meal with a Danish Carlsberg beer. Hot main dishes, Danish style, are featured as well, including lobster soup. A good main course is game pie, with Cumberland sauce and a Waldorf salad. A dinner will cost from a low of 30 DM ($9.90) to 55 DM ($18.15).

Zlata Práha, 4 Meinekestrasse (tel. 881-97-50), serves the best Eastern European cuisine of any restaurant in Berlin. Hungarian, Bulgarian, and Austrian wines are featured. However, the pièce de résistance is the special tap-drawn beer, Pilsner Urquell das Echte. Actually, if your palate isn't Slavic, you may want to steer clear of this brew; otherwise, it makes the perfect drink for toasting your Czech friends at the next table. Most of the food seems inspired by the Prague kitchen. Although many of the dishes may be esoteric to you, you'll recognize the Balkan salad and the bean soup. Among the main-dish specialties are the paprika schnitzel and the sauerbraten. Few can resist the topfer strudel. Go between noon and midnight and never on Sunday. Meals cost 25 DM ($8.25) to 55 DM ($18.15).

Bacco, 5 Marburger Strasse (tel. 211-86-87), is small and Tuscan, lying near the Europa-Center. Owner and head chef Massimo Manozzi practices a classical Italian cuisine. Fish comes from Rungis, the market outside Paris, where he flies three times weekly to buy only the freshest ingredients. A house specialty is the piccata, three little veal steaks with artichokes, mushrooms, tomatoes, and an aromatic pepper-flavored wine sauce. You get good service *con brio* (with flair). Meals cost 30 DM ($9.90) to 70 DM ($23.10), and they're served noon to 3 p.m. and 6 p.m. to midnight (closed Sunday and in July and August).

Rhumerie AVEC Restaurant, 42 Mommsenstrasse (tel. 323-79-25), offers a French cuisine with both nouvelle dishes and those from the classical repertoire. The place has a warm, rustic gemütlichkeit. Featured in the center of the room are two large millstones which now serve as hors d'oeuvres display tables. A daily fixed-price menu, ranging from three to seven courses, is available for 50 DM ($16.50). Fish and shellfish are the specialties. Head chef Udo Kämper is a Francophile, who uses only the freshest products. Two menus are presented, one a standardized à la carte, another listing the specialties of the day. Before dinner you might enjoy a drink in the apéritif bar. Service is from 7 p.m. to midnight daily except Sunday and holidays.

Alt-Berliner Schneckenhaus, 37 Kurfürstendamm (tel. 883-59-37). In the old Prussian style, this restaurant is reached by passing through a garden house. The interior reveals a high-ceilinged Wilhelminian delight. The German Victorian wooden furniture is a well-polished and well-oiled splendor. Paintings and portraits add to the decor, along with green-on-green wallpaper and wood and leather banquettes. The style is definitely 19th century, an informal and friendly atmosphere in which to dine. The menu is nostalgic, listing many delicacies from appetizers to desserts, with snails a specialty. Menus begin at 22 DM ($7.26), going up to 45 DM ($18.45). The restaurant serves daily from 6 p.m. to 1 a.m. The kitchen stops serving hot food at 11:30 p.m.

Borbone, 12 Windscheidstrasse (tel. 323-83-05), is Italian with a pleasant and original atmosphere. Small tables are discreetly separated from one another, and the service is friendly and efficient. The wine list is extensive, with some legendary expensive bottles, but they also contain many reasonable vintages from southern Italy. Notable dishes include a filetto al Pepe and fresh filet of beef in a cream sauce with green pepper and cognac. Pasta courses are invariably excellent. A meal will cost 45 DM ($14.85) to 60 DM ($19.80), and you can order from noon to midnight. The Borbone is closed on Sunday and from mid-July until the end of August.

Ernst-August, 16 Sybelstrasse (tel. 324-55-76), serves a French cuisine to an elite clientele in Berlin, in a room filled with antique art displayed against walls done in shades of brown. Samplings from the menu might be steaks or filets in one of the famous sauces perfected by the traditional school of French cuisine. A savory meal is likely to cost 40 DM ($13.20) to 110 DM ($36.30). The restaurant is open from 7 p.m. to 2 a.m. Monday to Friday; closed in July and August.

Grossbeerenkeller, 90 Grossbeerenstrasse (tel. 251-30-64), is an underground "keller" in a historic century-old restaurant which escaped the bombings. You'll see people here who have probably been mentioned in the Berlin newspapers in recent months, many of them prominent in politics and the arts. Dozens of beer steins hang from the rafters, their images dimly reflected in the polished paneling of the walls. The keller is open from 4 p.m. to 2 a.m. Monday to Friday, 6 p.m. to 2 a.m. on Saturday; closed Sunday and holidays. You'll find it most crowded for late-night suppers, when drama lovers savor such specialties as bacon or herring salad with scrambled eggs, a tempting selection of steaming-hot soups (homemade every day), steaks and schnitzels, and enough combinations of knockwurst (hot, cold, in all shapes and dishes, even salads) to make any Prussian happy. Meals here begin at a modest 12 DM ($3.96), going up to 32 DM ($10.56). Since 1984 the keller also has rooms to rent. A single with breakfast is priced modestly at 50 DM ($16.50), and a double goes for 80 DM ($26.40) to 100 DM ($33), depending on the plumbing. Reservations are strongly recommended.

Heinz Holl, 26 Damaschkestrasse (tel. 323-29-93), has gained a reputation in Berlin as one of those imperturbable and select dining spots which is somewhat of a social center as well. Call and reserve a table to savor the recipes that much of Berlin seems to want, including a roulade of marinated cabbage leaves, Yiddish gefilte fish, Argentine steak, and a host of other well-prepared international offerings. Meals cost 22 DM ($7.26) to 40 DM ($13.20). Many diners spend much time in the Whiskey Bar, since the restaurant is open from 7 p.m. to 2 a.m. with warm food served continuously until closing. It's closed on Sunday and holidays.

Weinrestaurant Heising, 32 Rankestrasse (tel. 213-39-52). You'll find copies of Gobelin tapestries upholstered onto the backs of the antique chairs here, and a festive atmosphere created partly by the open fireplace and partly by the music provided by the pianist in the corner. The chef is a specialist in a French-oriented international cuisine, which seems to find its best expression in the wide range of fresh fish dishes offered, depending on the shopping at the market that day. Fresh snails can be served either as a soup or as a main course with wild mushrooms; or perhaps you'll prefer the filet of lamb or filet of sole (braised or sauteed according to your choice). The wine list contains at least two dozen German wines, each reasonably priced. Excluding the wine, a meal will average around 32 DM ($10.56) to 45 DM ($14.85), and it's served from 6 p.m. till 1 a.m. every day.

Pullman-Restaurant im ICC, 11 Messedamm (tel. 303-839-46). You'll have to cross through the portals of one of the most popular convention centers in Europe (the Congress Center of Berlin) to arrive at this modern restaurant. It's decorated in a style vaguely reminiscent of its famous neighbor, the Kempinski. Here you'll meet internationally minded couples, such as the Japanese, each group savoring the warm buffet priced at a reasonable 35 DM ($11.55) per person and served every Saturday night from 6 to 11. Depending on the month, the à la carte selections might include crabmeat soup with fresh quenelles, a combination fish plate à la marseillaise, your choice of delicately flavored pike, salmon, trout, halibut, sole, or scampi, served with saffron cucumbers, dill potatoes, and vine-ripened tomatoes, and if you ask for it, sauce béarnaise. If you're not a fish fancier, try one of the pork or veal dishes, all served in generous portions. Fixed-price meals cost from a low of 32 DM ($10.56) to 55 DM ($18.15). Lunch is also served daily from noon to 3 p.m.

Zitadellen-Schänke, Strasse Am Juliusturm (tel. 334-21-06). You'll find a traditional Germanic decor embellishing this historic restaurant within the Citadel of Spandau, in the famous Berlin suburb, site of the internationally known prison. You won't be reminded of a prison in this restaurant in the citadel, however, in spite of the ancient stone walls. The soft candlelight and open fireplace provide a cozy and relaxing ambience. The chefs cook dozens of time-honored specialties, yet also experiment with neuen küchen too. Some of their better concoctions include wild boar pâté with St. Lucie cherry sauce, rippenpraten mit krusten (roast ribs with white cabbage salad), ground filet with steamed dumplings, and Wallenstein grill platter for two persons, consisting of stuffed quails, beef filet, and loin of pork. They're open from 10 a.m. to midnight, with warm food available at noon, every day except Monday. An average three-course meal will cost 50 DM ($16.50). The weekly special is called Spiesbratenessen, served as a fixed-price meal for 45 DM ($14.85) beginning at 6 p.m. every Sunday.

Zum lustigen Finken, 20 Alt Lübars (tel. 404-78-45). Berliners come here in winter for the kind of restaurant ambience their grandfathers enjoyed. Yet summer is even more popular, when everyone, including grandmother, sits on the 500-seat sun terrace, sipping schnapps, drinking beer, and watching the geraniums bloom. Both warm and cold specialties are available, costing from 24 DM ($7.92) to 40 DM ($13.20) for a meal. Hours are 10:30 a.m. to 8 p.m. every day except Friday, and they shut down in January.

Blockhaus Nikolskoe, Nikolskoer Weg (B-39) (tel. 805-29-14), at Am Wannsee und an der Havel, is a holdover from the Berlin of yesterday. The ancestors of present-day Berliners came here on a summer weekend to drink schnapps and beer on the terraces overlooking Lake Havel. The elaborate trim on the log cabin that gives this place its name dates from 1819. It's patterned in the Russian style. Historians tell me the house was a present from King Friedrich Wilhelm III to his daughter, Charlotte, on the occasion of her wedding to the man who was later to become Czar Nicholas I. Nicholas, after accepting the gift from his father-in-law, commissioned the construction of a Russian Orthodox church on a nearby hill, which still performs the sacraments today.

The restaurant is open from 10 a.m. to 10 p.m. from the first of May until the end of October, and from 10 a.m. to 8 p.m. the rest of the year. It's closed on Thursday, on holidays, and for a short time in January.

You can choose to sit either on the sun terrace or inside the wooden-walled dining room, with a ceramic stove at one end. Many come here just to order drinks, or salads, sandwiches, and wursts on the terrace, averaging about 12 DM ($3.96) for a snack. Or else you can order one of the regional meals, attractively priced at 22 DM ($7.26), going up to 50 DM ($16.50).

To get there, take the U-Bahn to the Berlin suburb of Wannsee, getting off at Pfaueninsel station. From there, follow the footpath for ten minutes in the direction of Peter-Pauls-Kirche.

Chalet Corniche, 56 Königsallee (tel. 892-85-97), in the Grünewald sector, has a gemütlich chalet atmosphere with an open fireplace and a view through the panoramic window overlooking the Halensee. The restaurant is in the

"Green Forest," an idyllic retreat. The most prominent artistic feature here is the wall motif of flowers, branches, and twigs painted around a giant book, for a rustic and charming ambience which is startingly original. A tree is erected beneath one of the wood-beamed ceilings. Head chef Ḥelmut Hacher writes his daily specials on a board. Portions are generous here, and the carte shows 100 varieties of wine. Full meals cost from 35 DM ($11.55) to 50 DM ($16.50). The chalet is open daily from 6 p.m. to 1 a.m.

Du Pont, 1 Budapester Strasse (tel. 261-88-11), is a restaurant-rôtisserie in the heart of Berlin, which is run by Messrs. Keuch and Losito. They offer a three-course meal ranging in price from 35 DM ($11.55) to 50 DM ($16.50). Since they use only seasonally fresh produce, their menus change frequently. The waiters give faultless service, and the food is carefully prepared, from sauces to meats, from appetizers to desserts. On one recent occasion I enjoyed a peppersteak with cognac, along with perfectly done pommes frites and the "salad of the season." They are open Monday to Friday from noon to midnight (on Saturday from 6 p.m. to midnight).

Funkturm, Messedamm (tel. 303-829-96). Dining in towers enjoys a vogue in Germany bordering on madness. West Berlin is not without its high-rise cuisine, and the Funkturm in the Charlottenburg district of West Berlin scores by serving good food. At this panoramic restaurant, the local Berlin dishes are notable. Try, for example, braised leg of beef, with mixed vegetables and potatoes. A more international offering is the sole meunière. Goulash soup makes a good beginning. Menus cost from 28 DM ($9.24), but chances are you'll spend far more of course, perhaps 35 DM ($11.55), anytime between 11 a.m. and 9 p.m.

BUDGET DINING: Of the many budget dining spots in West Berlin, here are the top choices:

Schultheiss Bräuhaus, 220 Kurfürstendamm (tel. 881-70-50), sits diagonally across from the deluxe Bristol-Kempinski Hotel. Ever since its appearance on the scene, it has fast gained admirers, making it one of the leading beer hall restaurants in West Berlin. You can dine on the terrace, in the midst of planters filled with greenery, or go inside to the dark and more mellowed tavern, gravitating to one of several rooms. Beer barrels have been converted to cozy dining nooks. Under the beams and against a background of rustic trimmings, large, hearty portions are served. The prices are low. A fresh soup is made daily. Typical dishes include a thick pork cutlet in brown gravy, with salad and freshly done french fries. A Sülze cotelet with potato salad makes a filling course, and a country breakfast (that is, an omelet with bacon) is also served. Meals cost from 22 DM ($7.26) to 30 DM ($9.90).

Hardtke's, 27 Meinekestrasse (tel. 881-98-27), right off the Kurfürstendamm, is the best all-around budget restaurant in Berlin. A traditional favorite, it was well known before the war. Restored after a bombing, it is in the old style, with dark beams and wood paneling, heavily Teutonic in flavor, along with Heidelberg steins, pewter, scrubbed wooden tables, and wrought-iron chandeliers. A copper-topped serving bar is always kept shiny clean. There are many cozy booths for pleasant, leisurely dining. The prices are low. If you want a most filling snack, order bockwurst with potato salad. A large schinkenhaxe is good, as are grosses eisbein (pig trotters). The restaurant is noted for its sausages. Set meals, served until 4 p.m., range in price from 22 DM ($7.26) to 24 DM ($7.92). Otherwise, count on spending 30 DM ($9.90) for dinner.

Hecker's Deele, 35 Grolmanstrasse (tel. 88-90-1), stands about a block from the Kurfürstendamm. For solid Germanic fare, it is one of the nuggets of Berlin. The restaurant zealously guards its time-tested recipes, such as its way of preparing venison and wild boar (available only during game season), and keeps its prices down. Meals cost from 12 DM ($3.96) to 35 DM ($11.55). With your main course, you are likely to order a stein of Bavarian dark draft beer (one of six different draft beers), or perhaps a martini made with Steinhaeger gin from Westphalia. Specialties include sauerbraten with potato dumplings and red cabbage, bratwurst (veal sausage), knacker (ham sausage), blutwurst, leberwurst, and Westphalian ham. The true devotee of the German kitchen will order boiled pork knuckles with sauerkraut and mashed peas, a classic favorite. The kitchen stays open until midnight. The restaurant is part of a modern 60-room hotel with all private facilities and a cozy hotel bar, Kutscherstube, which stays open until you've had your nightcap. The hotel is one of the best in the heart of Berlin, charging 105 DM ($34.65) in a single room and 155 DM ($51.15) in a double.

Hong Kong, 210 Kurfürstendamm (tel. 881-57-56), occupies space on the second floor of a building standing on this major artery. The Chinese food here, mostly specialties from the southern provinces, is of fine quality. Savory roast pork, pieces of chicken, soft noodles, appetizers, fried rice, seafood, whatever, your meal is likely to taste very good indeed. There is freshly brewed tea, all you can drink. Considering the quality of the food, the prices are fair. It's a fine spot for a dinner, which is likely to cost from 25 DM ($8.25) to 40 DM ($13.20) for the average repast.

Ratskeller Schöneberg, Schöneberg Rathaus, John-F.-Kennedy-Platz (tel. 71-01-41). This ratskeller is on the square that became famous when former President Kennedy made his now legendary *"Ich bin ein Berliner"* speech. Many Americans, when visiting the square and the Freedom Bell inside, like to stop off here for food. The wines are good, and they can be ordered to accompany one of the set luncheons. Among the à la carte items, the main dishes are fairly ambitious, including such offerings as steak Diane or veal schnitzel Cordon Bleu, with a fresh salad and french fries. The day's soup is invariably good. A meal averages around 30 DM ($9.90).

Restaurant Giraffe, 2 Klopstockstrasse (tel. 391-47-17). Your visit to Berlin's Tiergarten won't be complete without a beer at one of its restaurants. This might be as good a choice as anything else. A meal will cost from 22 DM ($7.26) up, and might run the gamut of international dishes, both meat and fish. All are well prepared. Meals are served in one of two inside rooms, or on one of two verandas. A blackboard near the front door indicates the daily specials. The Giraffe is open from 10 a.m. to half past midnight (12:30 a.m.) every day of the week.

Weissbierstuben, 14 Lindenstrasse (tel. 251-01-21). If you're a museum buff, you'll be able to combine a visit to the Berlin Museum with beer and pickles at this restaurant which is housed in the same building. Rollmop herring is a popular snack here for people who often wouldn't otherwise set foot inside a museum. The restaurant is designed in a way that any North German would quickly label "Berliner." In addition to many snacks, it serves a Sunday breakfast which is fairly elaborate, including such specialties as sauerbraten, sauteed wurst with vegetables "hunter's style," and a host of other well-prepared meat and fish dishes. Meals begin at 18 DM ($5.94). They serve beer, wine, and food from 11 a.m. to 6 p.m. (on weekends from 11 a.m. to 4 p.m.) every day of the week except Monday.

Schwejk-Prager Gasthaus, 4 Ansbacher Strasse (tel. 213-78-92). The taste of Eastern Europe is alive and flourishing at this Czech-style bistro where Bohemian specialties are served in generous portions. You'll find it about two blocks from the Memorial Church, in a kind of neighborhood-tavern ambience of well-scrubbed tables and regular clients. There's a small bar for drinking. Much of the food here tastes better when washed down with a mug of the local Pilsner, and wine is also available. Table reservations are a good idea, at least during the popular dining hour at 8 p.m. Full meals turn out to be one of the best bargains in town, priced between 12 DM ($3.96) and 25 DM ($8.25). A full range of Czechoslovakian liqueurs might round off a meal of such specialties as crackling broiled pork shanks (schweinhaxen) with salad and sauerkraut, good-sized bowls of thick borscht or liver-noodle soup, along with various kinds of "toasts" piled high with different kinds of meats and vegetables, served with flavorful sauces. The restaurant is open from 6 p.m. to 2 a.m. every night.

DINING AT EUROPA-CENTER: This 22-story skyscraper, crowned by a re-volving Mercedes star, is a virtual culinary United Nations. Many visitors take all their meals in Berlin here and enjoy a widely varied cuisine.

Alt Nürnberg (tel. 261-43-97), on the ground level, is successful in its an-tique theme. It handsomely and dramatically captures the old style of a German tavern, complete with copper lanterns and dark woods. It's not expensive ei-ther. The house specialty is a plate of Nürnberger rostbratwurst. Each day the chefs prepare a different specialty. You might begin with a typical Berlin pea soup with croûtons or a clear oxtail soup. The wienerschnitzel is always reliable, as is the herring salad and the pork filet in a pepper sauce with broccoli. You can order from the Berliner buffet at 35 DM ($11.55) per person or select one of the set meals, beginning at 22 DM ($7.26).

The **Daitokai,** 9 Tauentzienstrasse (tel. 261-80-99) on the second floor, is one of the best Japanese restaurants in Berlin. Festively decorated, it serves lunch from noon to 3 p.m. and dinner from 6 p.m. to 11:30 p.m., costing 35 DM ($11.55) to 60 DM ($19.80). One part of the menu is devoted to special Japa-nese drinks, ranging from sake to a Sayonara cocktail. Their appetizers are es-pecially appealing, and you may want to clear your palate with a clear Japanese soup before going on to one of their delicately prepared meat or fish courses.

3. Sights

In the midst of the daily whirl of working, shopping, dining, and entertain-ment, Berliners along the Kurfürstendamm often glance at the sobering re-minder of less happy days. At the end of the street stands the **Kaiser Wilhelm Memorial Church,** destroyed in World War II. Only the shell of the old neo-Romanesque tower (1895) remains, as a symbol of West Berlin after the war. In striking contrast to the ruins, a new church has been constructed west of the old tower seating 1200 people in its octagonal hall, and lit solely by the thousands of colored-glass windows set into the honeycomb framework. Dedicated in 1961, the church has an overall look best described by the nickname given it by Ber-liners, "the lipstick and powder box." You can wander through the ruins any day from 9 a.m. to 7:30 p.m. Ten-minute services are held in the church daily at 5:30 and 6 p.m. for those going home from work.

This remarkable combination of old and new is what Berlin is all about. Although there is much more new than old in this city, which suffered more than any other European metropolis during World War II (except perhaps Warsaw), Berlin offers a multitude of sights for the visitor.

MODERN BERLIN: In World War II, one out of every three Berliners lost his or her home. After the rubble was cleared away—a major problem in itself for this isolated city—the great task of rebuilding began. It took the united effort of many of the world's greatest architects to create the example of contemporary Berlin which lies just north of the Tiergarten. The **Hansa Quarter** (U-Bahn to Hansaplatz) was a direct result of the great Interbau (international builders' ex-hibition) of 1957, when architectural designers from 22 nations constructed homes and apartments in this district, along with shops, schools, churches, a cinema, library, and museum. The excitement here is in the variety: each of the nearly 50 architects, including Gropius, Niemeyer, and Düttman, was able to express himself in his own way. Even Le Corbusier submitted a design for an apartment house, but the structure would have been too gigantic for the quarter. You can see it today where it was built in the less congested western section of the city, near the Olympic Stadium. The **Corbusier House,** called Strahlende Stadt (radiant city) is Berlin's largest housing complex, and one of the biggest in Europe. Its 530 apartments (more than 1000 rooms) can house up to 1400 people. Typical of the architect's style, this tremendous building rests on stilts.

Berlin's tallest building sits in the heart of the city's activity. The 22-story **Europa-Center,** just across the plaza from the Kaiser Wilhelm Memorial Church, is the largest self-contained shopping center and entertainment complex in Europe. This town-within-a-town opened in 1965 and has been fascinating Berliners and outsiders alike ever since. Besides its three levels of shops, restaurants, nightclubs, bars, and movie houses, it contains hundreds of offices, a car park, and an observation roof from which you can view every part of the city.

At the Europa-Center, you can enjoy a multivision show which you might want to view before beginning your exploration of the city. It's like going into a time machine, Berlin in three dimensions. On six screens computers flash the saga of Berlin, everything from the Prussian drill to the Allied airlift. The show can be seen from 9 a.m. It lasts 90 minutes and costs 7 DM ($2.31). For information, telephone 261-79-07.

THE ZOO AND AQUARIUM: You wouldn't expect to find anything more than a handful of tiny animal cages in the center of a city where space is at such a premium. Yet in West Berlin, where the proportion of green parkland is surprisingly large in comparison to many of the large cities of Europe, you can see the oldest, and finest zoo in all of Germany. It's called the **Zoologischer Garten Berlin,** 8 Hardenbergplatz, and it was founded in 1844. Just a short walk north from the main street of town, the Ku-damm, it occupies almost the entire southwestern corner of the Tiergarten.

Until World War II the zoo boasted thousands of animals of every imaginable species and description, many of them familiar to Berliners by nicknames. The tragedy of the war struck here as well as in the human sections of Berlin, and by the end of 1945 only 91 animals had survived. For the past 40 years, however, the city has been rebuilding its large and unique collection until today there are more than 11,000 animals, some of them housed here to prevent their becoming extinct. The zoo has the most modern birdhouse in Europe, with more than 720 different species of birds. Furthermore, great and small cats from all over the world can be seen in a Carnivore House. The zoo's most valuable inhabitant is a giant panda. In the Nocturnal House the visitors can watch the way of life of nocturnal animals. The monkey center is a popular spot, and in the Berlin Zoo you can see breeding groups of apes (no fewer than five gorillas, 12 orangutans, and seven chimpanzees). There are also large open ranges where wild animals can roam in a simulated natural habitat.

In the center of the zoological gardens is a large restaurant where you can dine indoors or out. In summer you may have the added treat of music.

The Aquarium, on the edge of Budapester Strasse, is as impressive as the adjacent zoo. Its collection of more than 6000 fish, reptiles, amphibians, and other animals holds a fascination for every visitor. The second floor is devoted entirely to creatures that live exclusively under water, with one section for saltwater fish and one for those that live in lakes and streams. Benches are along the viewing promenade so you can sit and watch your favorite turtle or octopus for as long as you wish. But even more intriguing is the terrarium on the second floor, with a crocodile collection and a pair of komodo-monitors. You can even walk into the terrarium on a bridge over the reptile pit—but don't lose your balance. Around the outside are several glass cases containing a large collection of snakes, lizards, and turtles, and a large terrarium at the corner with giant tortoises, and on the third floor, you can watch the world of insects and amphibians.

The zoo (tel. 261-11-01) is open daily from 9 a.m. to 6:30 p.m. (it closes at dusk in winter), and charges 6 DM ($1.98) admission. The aquariaum, with its separate entrance, is open from 9 a.m. to 6 p.m. Admission is 5 DM ($1.65), but you can purchase a combined ticket for 9 DM ($2.97) which will admit you to both the aquarium and the zoo.

THE DAHLEM MUSEUM: War is no respecter of persons or objects, and the art collections of Berlin suffered tragically in 1945. Although many smaller paintings of the national museums of Berlin were stored in inoperative salt mines during the war, many larger works, including eight paintings by Rubens and three by van Dyck, were destroyed by fire. Some works that survived are now in East Berlin, where many of Berlin's finest galleries were located before the war. Of the paintings that were relegated to the West and passed from nation to nation in the late 1940s like so many decks of cards, most have now been returned to Berlin and are permanently ensconced in the Dahlem, 23/27 Arnimallee (tel. 83-01-1), making it one of Germany's finest galleries. Of the nearly 1500 paintings in its possession, more than 600 are on display.

The ground floor has several rooms devoted to early German masters, with panels from altarpieces dating from the 13th, 14th, and 15th centuries. Note the panel of *The Virgin Enthroned with Child* (1350), surrounded by angels which resemble the demons so popular in the later works of Hieronymus Bosch. Eight paintings make up the Dürer collection in the adjacent rooms, including several portraits and a Madonna, with a crown held above her head by two cherubs whose bodies fade into puffs of smoke.

Two contemporaries of Dürer, Albrecht Altdorfer and Lucas Cranach the Elder, are both represented by paintings of *The Rest on the Flight into Egypt*. Note the contrasts between the two works, the former in the Renaissance style, with a town as the background setting and tiny angels playing in an elegant fountain in the foreground. Cranach, on the other hand, chose a quiet pastoral setting and confined the colors and action to the characters themselves, seemingly ready to pose for a family portrait.

Another gallery on the ground floor is given over entirely to Italian painting. Here you'll find five Raphael Madonnas, works by Titian *(The Girl with a Bowl of Fruit)*, Fra Filippo Lippi, Botticelli, and Coreggio *(Leda with the Swan)*.

Furthermore, on the ground floor are early Netherlands paintings from the 15th and 16th centuries (van Eyck, van der Weyden, van der Goes, Bosch, and Bruegel).

The floor above is devoted mainly to Flemish and Dutch masters of the 17th century, with no fewer than 24 works by Rembrandt alone. Among the most famous of the great painter's works in the Dahlem are *The Man with the Golden Helmet*, and the warmly human *Head of Christ*. Several portraits and biblical scenes make up most of the balance of this excellent collection. In spite of the several works by Rubens that were burned after the war, you can still see 19 on display here, including the charming *Child with a Bird*, and one of his landscapes, showing milkmaids tending cattle.

In the not-too-distant future the Dahlem will be moving to newer and larger quarters in the southeastern part of the Tiergarten. But until then, we will remain deprived of the more than 800 works packed in the vaults of the museum. The rest of the building is occupied by several other museum exhibitions, including the **Department of Sculpture,** with its bas-relief in Carrara marble by Donatello of a serene Madonna and Child (1422). The **Prints and Drawings Collection** contains several pen-and-ink drawings by Dürer, including his signed (1511) sketch of the *Holy Family at Rest.* There's even a landscape sketch by Rembrandt.

The **Ethnographical Museum** houses arts and artifacts from Africa, the Far East, the South Seas, and South America. Many of the figures and ritualistic masks are grotesquely beautiful, presenting a striking contrast in art, especially after a visit to the gallery of paintings. In addition to all the above museums, the Dahlem also houses the **Museums of Far Eastern Art, Islamic Art, and Indian Art.**

You can visit any of the collections at the Dahlem Tuesday through Sunday from 9 a.m. to 5 p.m. Closed Monday. Admission to all departments is free. To get there, take bus 1, 10, or 68 or the U-Bahn to the Dahlem-Dorf stop.

The museum has a good restaurant where you can have hot meals, including meat, potatoes, and salads, from 11:30 a.m. to 2:30 p.m., as well as cold dishes the rest of the day during museum hours. Meals cost from 18 DM ($5.94), but you may be content with one of the excellent pastries.

CHARLOTTENBURG PALACE: Perhaps Napoleon exaggerated a bit in comparing this palace to the great Versailles when he invaded Berlin in 1806, but Charlottenburg (tel. 32-01-1) was, in its heyday, the most elegant residence for the Prussian rulers outside the castle in Potsdam. Begun in 1695 as a summer palace for the friend of the arts, Electress Sophie Charlotte, wife of King Frederick I (Elector Frederick III), the little residence got out of hand until it grew into the massive structure you see today, branching out in long narrow wings from the main building. When you visit the palace, you should plan on spending the day, since it contains not only the apartments of Prussian royalty, but several museums as well.

When you pass the heavy iron gates and enter the courtyard, you'll immediately encounter a baroque equestrian statue of the pompous Great Elector himself; by Andreas Schlüter. The main entrance to the palace is directly behind, marked by the 157-foot-high cupola capped by a gilded statue of Fortune. Inside you'll find a columned rotunda with stucco reliefs depicting the virtues of the Prussian princes in mythological terms.

From this vestibule, you can take guided tours of the **Historical Rooms** Tuesday to Sunday from 9 a.m. to 5 p.m. Tours leave every hour. Since they are in German only, you'll have to be content to appreciate the works of art without the running commentary unless you know the language. If you wish to prepare for what you'll be seeing, you can buy the English translation of the guide's lecture in book form at the ticket counter.

Parts of the palace were badly damaged during the war, but most of it has now been completely restored. Many of the furnishings were saved, especially the works of art, and are again on display. The main wing contains the apartments of Frederick I and his "philosopher queen." Of special interest in this section is the **Reception Chamber,** in the left projection of the wing. This large room is decorated with frieze panels, vaulted ceilings, and mirror-paneled niches. The tapestries on the walls (1730) depict men in the style of Plutarch's *Lives.* Included are scenes of Pericles in battle and the sacrifice of Theseus on Delos.

At the far end of the west wing is the **Porcelain Chamber,** which is decorated solely by various pieces of Oriental porcelain, hung on the walls, standing on pedestals, some even partly inserted into the walls or suspended by metal rings. The unusual effect is heightened by the profusion of mirrors.

The **New Wing** (Knobelsdorff Wing), built in 1740-1746, contains the apartments of Frederick the Great, which have in essence been converted into a museum of paintings, many of which were either collected or commissioned by the king. Most of the ground-floor apartments are galleries of portraits mixed with examples of period furniture, but the treasures are on the upper floor. Here you can see several works by Watteau, including *The Tradesign of the Artdealer Gersaint,* purchased by Frederick the Great in 1745 for the concert hall of the palace. Another room is devoted to Boucher tapestries depicting love affairs among the gods, including Bacchus and Ariadne on Naxos, and Venus seducing Vulcan at his forge. In addition to the fine works of art in this wing, it is interesting to notice the decoration on the walls and ceilings of the rooms. Of course, many rooms have been virtually reproduced since the war.

The Charlottenburg Museums

The **Egyptian Museum** is in the east guardhouse at the entrance to the palace. It's worth a trip just to see the bust of Nefertiti, dating from the Amarna period of Egypt (about 1400 B.C.). In addition, you can see seals and plaques that go back to the invention of writing, about 3000 B.C., and prehistoric implements that date back even further. The museum contains the monumental Kalabsha Gateway, dating back to 30 B.C., a gift from Egypt. Also to be seen are objects relating to the Egyptian belief in the afterlife, including a traveling boat, complete with all the necessities for the long journey. The museum is open daily, except Friday, from 9 a.m. to 5 p.m. There is no admission charge for this or any of the other museums.

The **Museum of Greek and Roman Antiquities,** 1 Ischlosstrasse, is housed in the west guardhouse, just opposite the Egyptian Museum. The collection includes some of the finest Greek vases of black- and red-figured style dating from the sixth to the fourth centuries B.C. Of the several excellent bronze statuettes, one, the *Zeus of Dodone* (470 B.C.), shows the god about to cast a bolt of lightning, which looks remarkably like a hero sandwich. The most unusual exhibits are a large collection of ancient jewelry and of funerary portraits from Egypt. Those from the first and second centuries A.D. are well preserved and realistic. Museum hours are 9 a.m. to 5 p.m. every day except Friday.

The **Museum of Pre- and Protohistory,** in the western extension of the palace facing the Klausener Platz, contains five rooms devoted to art and artifacts discovered mainly in Europe, with a few interesting pieces from the Near East and the Orient sandwiched in. The rooms have exhibits grouped into the ages of man, from 1,000,000 B.C. up to the first millennium A.D. You can visit any day except Friday from 9 a.m. to 5 p.m.

In addition to the exhaustive—and exhausting—collections in the interior of the palace buildings, you can enjoy a relaxing ramble through the palace gardens, where, just a few years ago, lay a field of mud and swampland created by the ravages of war. The gardens have been restored, however, and landscaped much as they were in the days of Friedrich-Wilhelm II. Boxing in the formal gardens are two rows of cypresses leading to a lake complete with swans and other waterfowl. To the west of the cypress grove, between the English Gardens and the Prehistory Museum, stands the **Mausoleum,** practically unharmed during the war. Beneath its small temple are the tombs of King Friedrich-Wilhelm II and Queen Louise, sculptured by Rauch, as well as several other interesting funerary monuments of the Prussian royal family.

Charlottenburg lies in the quarter of Berlin of the same name, just west of the Tiergarten. You can get there by a number of routes, including the U-Bahn to either Sophie-Charlotte-Platz or Richard-Wagner-Platz, or by bus 21, 54, 55, 62, 74, or 86.

A TOUR ALONG THE BERLIN WALL: The ideological rift between East and West Berlin, which grew out of the dissolution of the Kommandantura of the Big Four powers in 1948, became a stark reality in August 1961. Most West Berliners have adjusted to the fact that the wall marks the eastern end of their world, but for the visitor, the concrete and barbed-wire barrier still holds an awe-inspiring, sobering fascination.

After a bracing cocktail or cup of coffee at the Intercontinental Hotel we'll begin a tour of the area of West Berlin along the Wall. If you follow Budapester Strasse eastward from the hotel, you'll soon reach the entrance to the **Tiergarten,** Berlin's largest park. The road that enters the park at this point is called the Hofjäger (hunter's ground) Allee, reminding us of its 16th-century use by the electors of Brandenburg. When seen by those who trudged into Berlin in 1945, the park was a dreary battlefield laid waste. Children play safely here today amid the young trees planted since the war to replace the ancient forest cut down to supply fuel in the cold winters of 1945-1946. If you wander from the main roads, you'll come upon rustic bridges, fishponds, and peaceful, isolated paths and streams.

At the center of the park, where the Hofjäger Allee meets the wide avenue called the Strasse des 17 Juni (named in memory of those East Berliners who were killed in the unsuccessful uprising against the Soviets on June 17, 1953), is the highest point in the park, the **Victory Column** (Siegess'a'ule). This landmark of West Berlin sits on a traffic circle called the Grosser Stern (Big Star). Erected in 1873, the yellow sandstone column is hollow and you can climb the 290 steps to the observation platform at the top, 210 feet above the street. Towering above the platform is the gilded bronze statue of Victory, 27 feet high, commemorating the German military accomplishments in the Franco-Prussian Wars. The observation platform is open daily except Monday from 10 a.m. to 5 p.m. (till 4 p.m. in winter), and admission is 1 DM (33¢).

If you follow the Strasse des 17 Juni eastward from the Grosser Stern, it will take you directly to the Wall. As you proceed, however, you'll pass several attractions worth at least a quick visit. About halfway between the Victory Column and the Wall, set at the northern edge of the Tiergarten near the Spree River, is the **Kongresshalle,** built as the American contribution to the 1957 Interbau, when the world's greatest architects constructed several buildings in West Berlin. Given to the people of Berlin in the following year, this convention hall is irreverently, but affectionately and perhaps appropriately, called the "pregnant oyster," because of the spans of concrete that curve across the roof and end up in open arches on each side. The auditorium alone seats 1250, and is equipped with translation equipment and other facilities. In addition the building houses a 400-seat theater, conference rooms, a garden café, and a restaurant. So big is the hall that it has its own waterworks, which supply not only the building, but the pool and fountain below the wide outer staircases as well.

Back on the Strasse des 17 Juni, you'll next come to the **Soviet War Memorial,** lying on the left side of the street, on the wrong side (West Berlin side) of the Wall. Built in 1946 from the marble of Hitler's former Berlin headquarters, the semicircular colonnade is guarded night and day by Soviet soldiers. On top of the memorial is a large bronze statue of a soldier in battle uniform, holding a bayonet. Above the inscription are the dates 1941-1945, and a wreath enclosing a hammer and sickle. Once a popular spot for demonstrations against the Soviets, the memorial and its guards are also guarded by British soldiers and West German police.

At this point you can see the Wall and past it to the landmark of old Berlin, the **Brandenburg Gate,** and beyond it the former main street and promenade of Berlin, the **Unter den Linden.** The gate represents a unique combination of cooperation between the sectors of the divided city. When the Quadriga (a chariot drawn by four horses) atop the gate was destroyed during the war, and the gate badly damaged, the people of East and West Berlin were anxious to have it restored. The Senate of West Berlin had a new Quadriga hammered in copper and presented it to the administration of East Berlin to place on the newly repaired colonnade. Thus, even though West Berliners don't get to their beloved landmark often, they can still admire it through the barbed-wire barrier. On special occasions it is illuminated at night.

Just north of this point, along the West Berlin side of the Wall, lies the large square called the **Platz der Republik,** only a sand dune until it was developed as the home of the German Parliament in the 18th century. At the eastern side of the square, right next to the Wall, sits the 19th-century **Reichstag,** the neo-Renaissance Parliament building. The building was destroyed in a mysterious fire in 1933 and badly damaged by bombs in the closing days of World War II, as the Allies moved in on the beleaguered city. A pastiche of styles, mainly High Renaissance, it was opened in 1894 as the august body, the "Imperial Diet," was called to order. At Paul-Löbe-Strasse, you can enter the west wing of the building to see an exhibition devoted to German history since the early 19th century. It is open Tuesday to Sunday from 10 a.m. to 5 p.m. The Reichstag lies north of the Brandenburg Gate, at the eastern side of the Tiergarten. The Wall runs right next to the Reichstag, which is used today for political conclaves.

In one wing of this building, a restaurant has been installed, offered moderately priced Teutonic fare, with several regional specialties. It's usually not necessary to make a reservation, but you can do so by calling 397-721-72.

Turning to the west side of the square, make for the street called Umgehungs-Strasse, which cuts south through the Tiergarten. As you leave the park on the south side, you'll see the wavy roof of the **Philharmonie** (Philharmonic Hall), an outstanding example of functional design (1963). Its unusual layout allows the audience to sit on all sides of the orchestra, yet the technical and acoustical aspects of the hall permit you to hear and see well from any point. The Philharmonie is the home of the renowned Berlin Philharmonic Orchestra. You can purchase tickets for performances at the office in the main lobby of the hall Monday through Friday from 3:30 to 6 p.m., and on Saturday and Sunday from 11 a.m. to 2 p.m. If you wish to get to the hall directly from the center of Berlin's activity on the Ku-damm, take bus 29.

Opposite the Philharmonie is the **Kunstgewerbemuseum,** which has various translations. Some call it a museum of applied arts, others a museum of arts and crafts. Until 1985 it was housed at Charlottenburg, but now has been moved into its new home. Room after room is devoted to domestic and ecclesiastical art from the Middle Ages through the 18th century. Its most outstanding exhibition is the Guelph Treasure, a collection of medieval church treasures in gold and silver. More impressive than the precious metal is the reliquary made in Cologne in 1175. It is formed like a Byzantine church, in the shape of a cross with an umbrella-like cupola supported by carved biblical figures. In niches on either side of the Crucifixion scene at the base are carvings of the Apostles. The porcelain figurines are outstanding. Some of the treasures are most delicate, showing superb craftsmanship, including a translucent opal and enamel box by Eugene Feuillatre. The museum is open daily except Friday from 9 a.m. to 5 p.m.

From Kemper Platz in front of the Philharmonie, follow Bellevuestrasse southeast to **Potsdamer Platz,** a rather dreary square that was once the most active spot in all of Berlin. Along the street leading to the square, you can still see some of the streetlamps which added their nighttime charm to the old city. The square is referred to as the three-sector corner because it is the meeting place of the British, American, and Soviet sectors of the city. Cutting right through the middle of the square is the Wall. Because most of the buildings around the square have been destroyed, you can glimpse the Reichstag, the Brandenburg Gate, and other important buildings along the Wall from this vantage point. On the East Berlin side, buildings have been cleared away for about 100 yards, creating a deserted sector where a number of daring escapes from East Germany have been attempted, many of which have failed tragically. Raised high on the West Berlin side is an illuminated newspaper, emphasizing the contrast between Western freedom and Eastern suppression.

If you don't intend to visit East Berlin, but would still like at least a glimpse of it, you can get your best look from the observation platform near the Potsdamer Platz. A photomural here shows the square in its heyday in 1929 and as it looks today. Another mural depicts the near-massacre of the East Germans on June 17, 1953, when they began their unsuccessful revolt against the Soviet oppression of East Germany. A light note is added to the sobering scenes by the souvenir shops and ice-cream stands nearby.

In 1981 the **Martin-Gropius-Bau Gallery** opened, about a 12-minute stroll from the Tiergarten. The *New York Times* called it one of the "most dramatic museums in the world." However, it displays only temporary exhibits, and you may want to consult a copy of *Berlin Programm* (available at the tourist office) to see what it might be showing at the time of your visit. The building lies only a dozen or so feet from the infamous Berlin Wall, and the eastern part of the museum opens onto the leveled former Gestapo headquarters, which were adjoining. Even if nothing is being exhibited, it makes for a fascinating stroll to look at this building, whose exterior terracotta friezes were not restored. If they were damaged, destroyed, or left intact, that is how they remain today.

You can visit the "House at Checkpoint Charlie," the **Museum of the Wall.** This small building houses exhibits depicting the tragic events leading up to and following the erection of the Wall. You can see some of the instruments of escape used by East Germans, including chair lifts, false passports, even a minisub. Photos document the building of the Wall, the establishment of escape tunnels, and the postwar history of both parts of Berlin from 1945 until today, including the airlift. One of the most moving exhibits is the display on the staircase of drawings by schoolchildren in 1961–62 who were asked to depict both halves of Germany in one picture. You can also see works by well-known German painters. On the floor above, you can look out toward East Berlin from the observation platform. Visit the museum any day between 9 a.m. and 8 p.m. There is a 2.50 DM (83¢) admission fee.

NEW NATIONAL GALLERY (NATIONALGALERIE): In its ultramodern glass-and-steel home designed by Mies van der Rohe, this gallery is a sort of sequel to the art housed at the Dahlem. Here you'll find works of 19th- and 20th-century artists with a heavy concentration on the French impressionists, such as Manet, Renoir, Monet, and Pissarro. An adjoining room offers a comparison in style in the works of the German impressionists of the same period—Liebermann, Slevogt, and Corinth. Earlier 19th-century German artists are represented as well, including Leibl and Caspar David Friedrich (*A Man and Woman Contemplating the Moon*).

The 20th-century collection includes a number of works by Max Beckmann, Edvard Munch, and Kirchner—*Brandenburger Tor* (1929) is among the most popular—as well as a few paintings by Francis Bacon, Dufy, Picasso, Max Ernst, and of course, Paul Klee.

The National Gallery has a continuously growing collection of contemporary art, European as well as American, including such artists as Barnett Newman, Joseph Beuys, and Edward Kienholz.

Small exhibitions on the second floor are free, although you'll have to pay changing fees for the larger shows. Admission to the downstairs gallery is free. The gallery is open Tuesday through Sunday from 9 a.m. to 5 p.m.; closed Monday. The museum is at 50 Potsdamerstrasse (tel. 266-6) just south of the Tiergarten and near the Wall. You can get there by taking bus 24, 29, 48, 75, or 83.

SCHÖNEBERG RATHAUS: Of special interest to Americans, this political center of West Berlin administration and parliamentary life since 1948 was the scene of John F. Kennedy's memorable *"Ich bin ein Berliner"* speech on June 26, 1963, just a few months before he was assassinated. Berliners, taking the speech literally as well as symbolically, have renamed the square around the building the John-F.-Kennedy-Platz. Built in 1911, the facade of the hall is not as outstanding as the interior. Here you'll find many paintings, especially portraits of political leaders of the past, and an exhibition of the history of the Schöneberg quarter of Berlin. Note the eight tinted-glass panels in the vestibule with scenes of various sections of Berlin, each with its own coat-of-arms.

From the 237-foot-high tower of the hall, a replica of the Liberty Bell is rung every day at noon. A gift from the American people in 1950, the Freedom Bell, as it is called, symbolizes U.S. support in the determination of West Berliners to preserve their freedom. The document chamber contains a testimonial presented with the bell bearing the signatures of 17 million Americans who gave their moral support in the struggle. You can visit the Liberty shrine on Wednesday and Sunday between 10 a.m. and 3:30 p.m.

BOTANICAL GARDEN: In the Dahlem quarter of West Berlin, 6-8 Königin-Luise-Strasse (tel. 831-40-41), near the Dahlem Museum, the huge Botanischer Garten contains vast collections of European and exotic plants in the open and in 15 greenhouses, among which the most popular ones are: the big palm house, one of the largest in the world, with its palms, bamboos, and tropical flowers; and the Victoria house, where *Victoria amazonica* and *Victoria cruziana* are in bloom in late summer. In the open, the plant geographical section representing the vegetation of the temperate regions of the northern hemisphere is most noteworthy. There are also a large Arboretum and several special collections such as a garden for the blind, water plants, and protected plants of Germany. During the summer the garden is open from 9 a.m. to 8 p.m. In winter the garden is closed at dusk. Admission is 2 DM (66¢).

A unique approach to botany is represented in the **Botanical Museum** near the entrance to the gardens. Here you can see dioramas and exhibit cases portraying the history and significant facts of plant life around the world. The museum is open Tuesday to Sunday from 10 a.m. to 5 p.m., on Wednesday to 7 p.m. Admission is free.

OLYMPIC STADIUM: Built in 1936 by Werner March for the 11th Olympic Games, this Olympia-Stadion seating 100,000 people was the first in Europe to supply all the facilities necessary for modern sports. Hitler expected to see the "master race" run off with all the awards in the 1936 Olympics, and you can imagine his disappointment when a black American named Jesse Owens took four gold medals for the U.S. team.

The stadium area covers a total of 330 acres, including a swimming stadium, a hockey arena, tennis courts, and riders' exhibition grounds. But the main attraction is the arena, so large that if the seats were laid end to end, they would stretch for more than 25 miles. The playing field in its center lies 47 feet below ground level. You can take the elevator to the top of the 260-foot platform where the Olympic bell hangs. From this point you have a panoramic view of Berlin to the east. It is open from 10 a.m. to 4 p.m., costing 1 DM (33¢). Since the Olympic Stadium lies northwest of the Radio Tower, you can reach it in a few minutes by a brisk walk. If you come directly via U-Bahn, take the train one stop past the Radio Tower stop to the Theodore-Heuss-Platz.

RADIO TOWER (FUNKTURM): Nearly every sizable town in Germany seems to have a television tower, but this steel-frame construction predates them all—in fact it predates television. Erected in 1924–1926, it sits on a base of porcelain pedestals. Popularly called the tall dwarf, the tower has been converted to a television transmitter, but if you visit here it will likely be either for the restaurant (at 170 feet) or for the view of Berlin and its environs (as far as Potsdam) from the observation platform at 457 feet. The elevator reaches the top in hardly more than half a minute. The elevator is in operation from 10 a.m. to 11 p.m., but if you wish you can climb the seemingly endless stairs to the restaurant. Admission to the platform is 3 DM (99¢). The tower sits in the fairgrounds in the western section of West Berlin. To get there, take the U-Bahn to the Kaiserdamm stop, or the S-Bahn to the closer Witzleben stop.

STEINSTÜCKEN: One of the curiosities of the Cold War of the postwar era in Berlin is this tiny enclave which is surrounded by East German borders. Steinstücken, only 31 acres, is one of a dozen satellite enclaves, small strips of land cut off from West Berlin, under terms of the Big Four agreements. It is under the guardianship of the American military police.

Road access to Steinstücken was once denied to the general public unless they were permanent inhabitants. The military police had to fly there in helicopters. That has changed ever since 1977. Any visitor to West Berlin can go there on the bus. The road to it is walled on both sides. A no. 18 double-decker bus (labeled "Steinstücken") will take you along the eerie run. If you sit on top, you can gaze over the wall.

Once daring helicopters rescued East Germans who had fled to the security of the enclave. The area even today is heavily patrolled by East German guards and their police dogs.

Once you get to Steinstücken there isn't much to see, except for a simple monument marking the site of the helicopter run that saved Steinstücken from being absorbed by East Germany. The excitement comes from being in such an unusual and bizarre piece of geography, which is enclosed within the general district of Potsdam. The East Germans have cleared an area around the little colony which is often referred to as a kind of no man's land. An East German watchtower looms high over the forbidding border wall.

SCHLOSS TEGEL: To the north of Berlin, Schloss Tegel is a two-story building constructed along classical lines with bas-reliefs by Friedrich Tieck on its four towers. It was visited by Goethe in 1778, who wrote of the "ghosts in Tegel." The white-painted castle was erected in 1558 in the reign of Elector Prince Joachim II. It was redesigned in 1822–1824 by Karl Friedrich Schinkel, one of the most outstanding architects of Prussia. The work was commissioned by Wilhelm von Humboldt, the philosopher and founder of Berlin University (his descendants own the castle to this day). In the interior, mementos of the family are exhibited, along with works of art. Visits are possible. The address is 19-21 Adelheidallee, and it's reached by taking bus 13, 14, 15, or 20. However, it is open only in summer. Therefore check with the tourist office about its hours before heading there.

BRÜCKE MUSEUM: At 9 Bussardsteig, a considerable proportion of the work of Schmitt-Rottluff is displayed, along with the works of a group of artists known as *Die Brücke* ("the Bridge"). These were a group of expressionists, which included one of my favorite German artists, Ernst Ludwig Kirchner, the leader of the "Bridge" expressionists who gathered in Dresden in 1905. His pictures were sharply patterned and colored, the figures distorted. The Nazi government burned many of his paintings, and before the outbreak of World War II he committed suicide. The one-story museum at the edge of the Grünewald is open from 11 a.m. to 5 p.m. daily except Tuesday, charging an admission of 3 DM (99¢).

BERLIN MUSEUM: This was once the Court of Justice, built in the late baroque style in 1735. These former law courts on the Kreuzberg are at 14 Lindenstrasse, and have been converted into a museum of the city of Berlin, with exhibits depicting the life of its citizenry from the 17th to the early 20th century. It is open from 11 a.m. to 6 p.m. daily except Monday, charging 3 DM (99¢) for admission.

BAUHAUS MUSEUM: The Bauhaus school of architecture and design was founded by Walter Gropius in 1919 at Weimar. (He was later to become a long-time resident of the U.S.) This school was largely responsible for revolutionizing the teaching of sculpture and painting, along with architecture and industrial arts, throughout the Western world. The Bauhaus artists were kicked out of Weimar in 1925, but still went on to glory. This museum, at 13-14 Klingelhöferstrasse, will bring you closer to the ideas and concepts of modern design and where they originated. Even if you're not a student of architecture or design, you should still be fascinated. The sculptures of Oskar Schlemmer are only one of the many exhibits, which are open daily except Tuesday from 11 a.m. to 5 p.m., charging an admission of 5 DM ($1.65).

SPANDAU CITADEL: One of the most popular day trips from the heart of Berlin is to Spandau. Head up Am Juliusturm and you'll eventually reach this suburb, which was incorporated into Berlin in 1920. It is one of the oldest parts of Altmark, receiving its city charter back in 1232. The Hohenzollern electors of Brandenburg turned it into a summer residence, and in time it became the chief military center of Prussia, housing the imperial war treasury.

The Spandauer Zitadelle or Spandau Citadel stands at the confluence of both Berlin's rivers, the Spree and Havel. The Julius Tower (Juliusturm) and the Palas are the oldest buildings still standing, the only remaining parts of the castle built in the 13th and 14th centuries. In the main building, accessible by footbridge, is a local history museum, open from 9 a.m. to 5 p.m. daily except Monday (from 10 a.m. on Saturday and Sunday), charging an admission of 1.50 DM (50¢).

The citadel has had a checkered past, and it's been beseiged by everybody from the French to the Prussians. It has also been a state prison. However, the remaining leader of the Nazi hierarchy, Rudolf Hess, is not housed there, but at Spandau Prison in Wilhelmstrasse, in the middle of Spandau. It obviously can't be visited by the public, even though it still occupies world attention.

Hess was appointed deputy Führer in 1933, but parachuted into Scotland where he was arrested and interned until the end of the war. He was sentenced to life imprisonment at Nürnberg in 1946, and thus began his lonely vigil at Spandau. He is guarded—at great expense to all countries—by the Americans, Russians, French, and British. Attempts by the son of the former war criminal to get him released have been unsuccessful. His age is among the major factors cited. You see, Hess was born in 1894.

TRANSPORT MUSEUM: The Verkehrsmuseum, at 15 An der Urania, occupies the same location as the Berlin Postal Museum. One commentator once wrote, "If it flies, rolls, or floats, you'll find it here." Not just for children, it holds an equal fascination for adults as well. It is open from 9 a.m. to 6 p.m. Tuesday to Friday (from 10 a.m. to 6 p.m. on Saturday and Sunday), charging an admission of 3.50 DM ($1.16), half price for children. The museum displays models of trains and trams, as well as spacecraft and even a copy of Columbus's *Santa Maria* which sailed to the New World. The early aeronautical pioneer, Berlin-born Otto Lilienthal who died in 1896, is also honored. His achievements in "flying models" were said to have been studied by the Wright brothers. Since this museum was bulging with displays, a second wing has opened. It took over the freightyard of the oldtime Anhalter Bahnhof, where the fictional Sally Bowles arrived in Isherwood's Berlin stories. If you want to go there, following in the footsteps of such famous characters as Herr Issyvoo, ask at the main museum for directions.

ORGANIZED TOURS: West Berlin and East Berlin can be difficult to navigate on your own. Many of the attractions of West Berlin are spread out, and the border formalities of East Berlin may intimidate the less adventurous. Therefore you may need the security of an organized tour. The best ones are operated by **Severin & Kühn,** 216 Kurfürstendamm (second floor; tel. 883-10-15). Across from the Bristol-Kempinski Hotel, this agency offers a host of tours, including some interesting excursions into East Germany.

Their big tour combines East and West Berlin, costs 45 DM ($14.85), and lasts six hours. There's an extra 16-DM ($5.28) guidance fee in East Berlin. If you prefer, you can take a 3½-hour tour of East Berlin on one day and a 3-hour tour of West Berlin on another. The tours cost 28 DM ($9.24), plus a guidance fee. If you go on the 10 a.m. tour of West Berlin, your visit will include a view of the New National Gallery. If you go on the 2:30 p.m. tour, it will include a visit to the Egyptian Museum, with its celebrated bust of Nefertiti. The tour of East Berlin requires the presentation of a passport and includes a visit to the important Pergamon Museum if you take the 2 p.m. tour. An earlier tour, leaving at 10 a.m., does not include the museum.

An even more exotic tour is the one to Potsdam and Sans Souci, leaving on Tuesday, Thursday, and Saturday from May 1 to October 31, beginning at 9:30 a.m. and lasting eight hours. The cost is 94 DM ($31.02), with lunch included. You go on a guided visit to the world-famous Sans Souci Palace, explore the Orangerie and the Chinese Tea House. On the full-day tour, you visit not only the New Palace, but also the ancient Palace of the Crown Prince, Cecilienhof, where the "Four Power Agreements" of 1945 were concluded. A lunch or coffee break is taken at the Interhotel Potsdam. An abbreviated five-hour tour is offered at 1 p.m., at a cost of 79 DM ($26.07) (instead of lunch, you get coffee and cake). This afternoon tour is available Wednesday, Friday, and Sunday from May 1 to October 31; a tour from 9:30 a.m. to 4 p.m., including lunch, leaves on Tuesday, Thursday, and Saturday from November 1 to March 31.

SOME NOTES ON SHOPPING: The central shopping destinations for all Berliners are Kurfürstendamm (its Fifth Avenue), Tauentzienstrasse, and am Zoo. Each quarter of Berlin has shopping centers as well. The show windows of the Ku-damm are in sparkling contrast to the drab stores of East Berlin.

The **Royal Porcelain Factory,** known as KPM, is at 1 Wegelystrasse (tel. 39-00-9), and it's been in existence since 1763. King Frederick the Great once purchased the factory, and today it's known as the State Porcelain Factory. Its products carry a distinctive official signature, an imperial orb and the letters "KPM." Guided tours let you look at the work of the employees, and you can buy beautiful pieces of porcelain here. Because of small defects—many visible only to experts—the prices of these "seconds" are quite reasonable.

Kaufhaus des Westens, 21-24 Tauentzienstrasse (tel. 24-01-71), known popularly as **KaDeWe,** is a luxury department store on Tauentzienstrasse, about two blocks from Kurfürstendamm. Of all the extravagant items on display, it is known mainly for its food department featuring delicatessen items of tempting originality. The finest in German sausages are displayed here. But not only that —delicacies from all over the world's continents are shipped in here. Sit-down counters are available for sipping Sekt or ordering tasty dishes and desserts. After proper fortification, you can explore the six floors of goodies.

Berlin is a fashion-conscious city, and you can look at a sample of what is au courant for chic women at **Horn's,** 213 Kurfürstendamm (tel. 881-40-55).

You might also want to check out the action at **Berlin's Flea Market** at the old U-Bahn station at Nollendorfplatz. Abandoned underground trains have been turned over to sellers who hawk their wares between 11 a.m. and 7:30 p.m. most days.

4. West Berlin After Dark

"A Teutonic determination to achieve offbeat gaiety." That's how one writer described Berlin nightlife. Berlineers certainly do try their best to keep their city going well after dark. The seductive, intriguing cabaret life of prewar Berlin may have faded, but the spirit and determination are still there. So get yourself together, and get ready for a night on the town, Berlin style.

There is such a variety of nightspots to choose from in Berlin—cabarets, saloons, cafés, discos, beer halls. But let's start on a higher note:

CULTURAL LIFE: On a cultural note, the Berlin Philharmonic Orchestra, under its permanent conductor Herbert von Karajan, enjoys world renown. If you're staying in a first-class or deluxe hotel, you can usually get the concierge to obtain seats for you. These seats begin at $3 (in back of the orchestra while seated on stage) and range up to $20 (even more for special performances). Of the 2218 seats, none is more than 100 feet from the rostrum. So for everything from a Brahms violin concerto to Wagner's *Idylls of Siegfried,* head for the **Berliner Philharmonisches Orchester,** 1 Matthäikirchstrasse (tel. 26-92-51). The location is in the Tiergarten sector.

The lighter muse of the operetta and the musical are at home at the **Theatre des Westens,** 12 Kantstrasse (tel. 312-10-22). This theater lies between the Zoo and Kurfürstendamm.

The city's most distinguished theater is the **Schiller-Theater,** 110 Bismarckstrasse (tel. 319-52-36), and its satellite, the **Schloss-Park-theatre,** 48 Schloss Strasse (tel. 791-12-13). Combined, they often present two dozen shows a year in Berlin. Here you are likely to see everything from *Othello* to *A Streetcar Named Desire.*

Peter Stein's **Schaubühne am Lehniner Platz,** 153 Kurfürstendamm (tel. 89-00-23), is considered by some to be the most important German-language theater in the country (which means the world, of course).

The **Deutsche Opera Berlin,** 34 Bismarckstrasse (tel. 341-44-49), in Charlottenburg, is one of the world's great opera houses. It was built on the site of the great prewar Opera House that enjoyed world fame. The present structure isn't as grand, of course (but then, what is?). In fact, Berliners call the modern edifice "Sing-Sing," as part of their habit of applying nicknames to structures. Architecture aside, the house books singers and an orchestra that attract opera lovers the world over. They are willing to tackle a Puccini rarity, the work of a "youthful genius," and most definitely Wagner whom they don't dare neglect. The ballet company performs once a week. Concerts, including "Leider evenings," are also performed on the opera stage.

CAFÉ LIFE: There is no better way to begin or end your evening than taking a table at the **Café Kranzler,** 18-19 Kurfürstendamm (tel. 881-80-26). At the turn of the century Berlin was famous for its cafés. Many survived until World War II. But after the war, the momentum of café life was never revived—some scattered to such points as Frankfurt, some never rose from the debris. However, the Kranzler continues in the old tradition and does so exceedingly well. Its bright, breezy decor lifts the fog from many a gray day in Berlin. You can anchor at a sidewalk table on the Kurfürstendamm in fair weather, or take a table inside when the cold winds blow, peering outside through the glass-fronted entrance. Many begin their day over breakfast, served till noon. Throughout the day and evening, those rich cakes begin at 4 DM ($1.32). The lager beer is 5 DM ($1.65). It is said that the best ice cream in Berlin is served here.

A CLASSIC WINE CELLAR: Historischer Weinkeller, 32 Alt-Pichelsdorf (tel. 361-80-56), might be your most interesting evening in Berlin if you've grown bored with nudity and drag shows. Not to mention inflated prices. Here Lilo Ruschin lights a sugarcone and performs an age-old ceremony of "burning the punch." The ceremony is performed on three nights a week: Wednesday, Thursday, and Sunday. Hours are daily except Monday from 5 p.m. to 1 a.m. The punch, her specialty, costs only 7 DM ($2.31) per glass. As the flame burns, you're supposed to make a wish. On other nights of the week you can select from more than 100 German wines, at prices that begin at 7 DM ($2.31) per glass. Frau Ruschin is a wine expert and will be happy to guide you in your choice. The 250-year-old cellar vaults are atmospheric, and this little squat inn on a cobbled street has survived wars and all sorts of disasters. Hopefully, it will go on forever.

MUSIC AND DANCE: Café Keese, 108 Bismarckstrasse (tel. 312-91-11), offers what the Germans call a ball paradox. This is a fancy way of saying that the women have a chance to ask the men to dance, instead of the other way around. It's an old-fashioned Teutonic atmosphere. People go here who actually like to dance the familiar way, holding each other in their arms. While this custom may seem quaint to readers of more advanced tastes, it still continues to pack them in at the Keese. Of course the management also encourages more "unconventional" dancing as well. The orchestra plays music quite slowly at times, and the place is often jammed, especially on Saturday night. If you're a lone male and fear the women will mob you if you make an appearance on the floor, you can remain perched at the bar. Incidentally, the management reserves the right to kick out any male patron who turns down a female request to dance! Actually, the Keese is something of a matrimonial bureau, always announcing new statistics about the number of people who have met and fallen in love on its premises and later gotten married. Men are requested to wear jackets and ties; women, anything seductive. No entrance fee is charged. Inside, you can order a beer at 7

DM ($2.31), the cheapest way to spend an evening here, incidentally, or most whiskies at 11 DM ($3.63) a shot. It's open until 4 a.m. daily.

Quartier Latin, 96 Potsdamer Strasse (tel. 261-37-07), in a refurbished movie theater not far from the Berlin Philharmonie on Mattäikirchstrasse, is a center for all kinds of music, including jazz, rock, folk, blues, and pop. It's open every day from 8:30 p.m. Prominent groups, both foreign and domestic, appear here. While you drink beer at 7 DM ($2.31) and smoke if you wish, you can listen to current developments in music. Admission ranges between 8 DM ($2.64) and 15 DM ($4.95), depending on who's appearing. In the balcony is a restaurant operated independently of the music club.

The **New Eden Saloon,** 71 Kurfürstendamm (tel. 323-41-15), is an outgrowth of the now-defunct Old Eden, but it's an entirely different "paradise." One newspaper writer termed this garden "too elegant and expensive for vagabond types." Essentially what you get here is dancing to smooth orchestra music and striptease. One lone male, sitting close to the scene of action, appraised the strippers as "advanced in their craft." Rolf Eden, who was the MC that night, corrected him. "It's an art," he said. Certainly the carefully selected girls strip with flair and style, each having a unique act. Shows, three nightly, begin at 10 p.m., midnight, and 2 a.m. The last acts are usually the liveliest. The entrance fee is 10 DM ($3.30). A double whisky costs 39 DM ($12.87), and you can order a pilsner at 10 DM ($3.30) as a second drink.

Big Eden, 202 Kurfürstendamm (tel. 323-20-16), bills itself as a dance paradise for 2000 people. It certainly is that and more! Boys dance with boys, by themselves, or occasionally even with a girl. The latest electronic gimmicks, all zany, decorate the place, the creation of the fertile mind of Rolf Eden. The strobe system alone may send you into a trance. Here, you'll find a wonderful melange of Berlin youth, in every conceivable form of dress (or lack of it), dancing to recorded music. As befits the means of most of the clientele, prices are kept low. Entrance is free Monday to Thursday. It costs 2 DM (66¢) on Friday, Saturday, and Sunday. Drinks run from 4 DM ($1.32).

Riverboat, 174 Hohenzollerndamm (tel. 87-84-76). The building is unprepossessing; you think you're taking an elevator to a floor in a warehouse. But once inside you feel you've boarded a Mississippi riverboat. The decor gives one the impression that he or she is on the largest boat ever known on the U.S. mother river. It's like wandering in a labyrinth, with galleyways, portholes, as well as photostat blow-ups of the actual craft that sailed the river. Some nights can be slow, but the Riverboat at its most active has been known to have a band and four disc jockeys. There are offshoot galleys, where a person can enjoy a quiet beer. If you're alone, you can cruise because you'll find many young Berliners in your same predicament. Should you bring someone, you stand a chance of losing him or her in the crowd, as the Riverboat really packs 'em in. Relief comes in summer when an open-air deck accommodates another 1000 guests. The boat doesn't navigate on Monday, but does so admirably on other nights of the week. The entrance fee is usually 3 DM (99¢), increasing to 4 DM ($1.32) on Friday, 5 DM ($1.65) on Saturday. Once inside, you'll pay 5 DM ($1.65) for beer. Take the U-Bahn to Fehrbelliner Platz.

Coupe 77, 177 Kurfürstendamm (tel. 881-35-46), is one of the chicest places in town. An elegant bar and disco, it looks like you're about to embark upon the *Orient Express:* the appointments were purchased from old German railways cars. Not only do you get atmosphere here, but (if the doorman will let you in), you'll meet some of the hottest guys and gals in town. Drinks cost from 25 DM ($8.25).

Metropol, 5 Nollendorfplatz (tel. 216-41-22), is one of the leading discos in town, happily blending straights and gays in what used to be a former cinema.

It's reached by underground: two stops from the Bahnhof Zoo. It's been called the Studio 54 of Berlin, and for sheer size it tops everything. Don't come here for an intimate beer with a friend. Facilities include a restaurant, theater, music hall, whatever. Entrance is 10 DM ($3.30), and beer costs another 4 DM ($1.32). It's open from 7 p.m. to whenever, but Wednesday to Sunday only.

In folk music, the best place to go is to **Go-In,** 17 Bleibtreustrasse (tel. 881-72-18), which is now well into its second decade. The stage is pint-sized, but folk artists from all over the world have occupied it.

Cheetah, 13 Hasenheide (tel. 691-35-40), is a totally plastic world. Taking the name of the famed New York disco of the '60s, it is a projection of the world of tomorrow, an architectural melange of lily-padded wonder. It's multitiered—you can perch high or low depending on your mood. An orange glow flatters everybody. Live groups are booked. The entrance fee is 6 DM ($1.98). Once inside, you can order a beer at 6 DM ($1.98).

Eierschale ("Eggshell"), 50 Podbielskialle (tel. 832-70-97), is a popular place to hear jazz. It draws a student audience who come here anytime from 7 p.m. to midnight, paying a cover charge of around 5 DM ($1.65). A student ID card might be asked for.

DRAG SHOWS: Ever since the 1920s when George Grosz was doing his savage caricatures and Greta Garbo, then unknown, was slipping around the town undetected, drag acts have been a staple of Berlin nightlife. Today's scene still goes on, the only problem being that it lacks a Christopher Isherwood to record it.

La Vie en Rose, Europa-Center, 22 Waitz-Strasse (tel. 323-60-06), is the country's only revue theater, to be found in the cellar of the Europa-Center. Dancing and drag are well combined here. On one visit "Josephine" welcomed the revelers, who had come to eye such transvestites as the inevitable drag queen impersonation of the legendary Marlene Dietrich, a favorite subject in postwar drag shows. Everything from disco to ballet is presented with flair. Drinks cost from 20 DM ($7.80).

The drag show at **Chez Nous,** 14 Marburger Strasse (tel. 213-18-10), has gone on to world fame. Show times are at 8:30 and 11 p.m. on weekdays, with a late show at 1 a.m. on weekends. The setting has been called merely-the-mock Louis XIV. If you like herren who become damen, then you too may think, as the Berliners do, that this club books some of the best transvestite acts in Europe, everything from a sultry, boa-draped striptease star from Rio de Janeiro to a drag queen who looks like a gun moll from the 1940s. Drinks cost from 25 DM ($8.25).

GAY BERLIN: The **Kleist-Casino** (nicknamed KC for short), 35 Kleiststrasse (tel. 24-74-96), is the leading gay male rendezvous in West Berlin, and it has been for a long, long time. Drinks cost from 15 DM ($4.95).

GAMBLING: One of the biggest attractions for visitors is the **Spielbank** or gambling casino (tel. 261-15-01) at the Europa-Center (entrance on Budapester Strasse). It's open daily from 3 p.m. to 3 a.m. Inside you'll find 14 roulette tables, in addition to tables for baccarat and blackjack. The bar is the longest in Berlin, and it's a watering spot between rounds at the tables. There's also a restaurant serving an expensive international cuisine. There's a 5-DM ($1.65) entrance fee, plus a minimum bet of 5 DM also.

BEER GARDENS: **Münchner Hofbräuhaus,** 29 Hardenbergstrasse (tel. 261-36-27), across from the Kaiser Wilhelm Memorial Church. This Berlin namesake has little to do with the celebrated Hofbräuhaus of Munich, but it does provide one of the most gemütlich evenings in Berlin. Near the center of the room, a seven-piece brass band plays Bavarian music. Dancers choose their partners to take them out to the large floor. Prussians, of course, are not Bavarians, and their dancing reflects this. But it's good fun nevertheless. The hall itself is attractively decorated, with carved wood chairs and pine tables—sort of half modern, half rustic. Beer is served in gray and blue ceramic steins at 8 DM ($2.64) for a half liter. You can also order food here, especially weisswürste, the white sausages of Munich. Meals cost from 20 DM ($6.60). The beer hall opens at 6 p.m., but it's best to go later. Admission is free on weekdays, 3 DM (99¢) on Friday and Saturday, and 2 DM (66¢) on Sunday.

Loretta im Garten, 89 Lietzenburgerstrasse (tel. 882-78-63), lies off Knesebeckstrasse, within walking distance of the Europa-Center. This beer garden, weather permitting, can get very lively at times, especially when amateur bands play. You can come here to eat, listen to the music, or just hang out. It's all in good fun.

FINDING A KNEIPE: It has long been the custom of a typical Berliner to find his favorite *kneipe* or bar in which he can relax after work, or meet sympathetic friends (or be introduced to new ones). A kneipe is the equivalent of a Londoner's local pub. Usually (but not always) these places are cozy rendezvous places. Sometimes they serve food, and often are attached to restaurants. There are hundreds upon hundreds of these kneipen in Berlin. I can only get you started by recommending a handful.

Ax-Bax, 34 Leibnizstrasse (tel. 313-85-94), is a hangout for a chic crowd who like to be seen here. The bar is well decorated, but there's no sign on the door. They like to keep it discreet here. The doors open at 9 p.m., and you can also order excellent food from a continental menu.

Zwiebelfisch, 7 Savignyplatz (tel. 31-73-63), has long been a favorite hangout of artists, writers, and newspaper people who find a communal drinking spirit here. Gossip is easily exchanged, and companions and friends easily met. There is a limited menu in case you want more than libations.

The oldest kneipe in Berlin is reputed to be **Wilhelm Hoeck,** 59 Wilmersdorferstrasse. It is also one of the most attractive if you prefer vintage Wilhelmian charm, 1892 style. The interior, incidentally, is authentic—it survived the war. A wide sampling of Berliners, including a number of artists and journalists, frequent this landmark building.

Paris Bar, 152 Kantstrasse (tel. 313-80-52) is one of the more sophisticated "watering holes" after dark in Berlin. It attracts a wide range of clients, especially actors and writers. Many prefer to come here to drink; others order from the continental menu, a meal costing about 55 DM ($18.15).

Lutter und Wegner, 55 Schlüterstrasse (tel. 881-34-40), is one of the best known of the Berlin kneipen. It attracts a lively crowd, who come here for a mixed drink, a beer, or a snack.

A SIDE TRIP TO EAST GERMANY (GDR)

THE SOVIETS CARVED this country out of their zone of occupation in 1949. Starting slow, its growth, known locally as an economic miracle, has indeed been phenomenal. It is roughly the size of Ohio, its population less than a third of the Federal Republic's, yet East Germany has become the number ten industrial power in the world. Among the Eastern bloc nations, it is second only to the Soviet Union. Its people have the highest standard of living in Eastern Europe.

Its boundaries are formed by the Baltic Sea in the north and Communist Poland in the east (East Germany after the war had to surrender parts of its territory to Poland). It also borders fellow Soviet bloc nation Czechoslovakia to the south, and to the south and west, West Germany, to which it was once united. Today the dream of a united Germany seems more distant than ever.

Before the infamous Berlin Wall was erected in 1961, some four million East Germans escaped to the West. Clichés are long in dying. East Germany isn't the concentration camp it so forebodingly appeared to be in the '50s and '60s. Beginning in the '70s it has had much more contact with the West. You still see barbed wire at the border (and you know there must be land mines), but the dismal gray image, so often depicted, has turned considerably whiter as economic conditions have improved.

Many of the young people I've talked to are right proud of their country, and aren't planning a hasty escape to the West. They seem pleased to live under a socialist regime. After all, they were born into it, unlike many of their parents, and have known no other system.

As everybody by now knows, Germany was split into four zones at the end of World War II, Russia taking the eastern sector (with the exception of West Berlin). The Soviet blockade of West Berlin in 1948 and 1949 (remember the Berlin airlift?) did not succeed. It led to the current separation of Germany into two distinct and individual states.

For years East Germany struggled for worldwide recognition. That breakthrough came in 1969 when its very existence was recognized by many nonaligned nations. Today the U.S. has diplomatic relations with the GDR, and East Germany is also a member of the United Nations. By the agreement formulated in Helsinki in 1975, its boundaries received international acceptance.

Americans are free to visit East Germany. The government, more and more, welcomes tourists, although it imposes massive restrictions. The reason is simple: the GDR needs hard Western currency, while at the same time fearing the "contamination" by Western influences.

Other than its much-visited capital of East Berlin, the GDR itself remains relatively undiscovered by Americans. It's a new frontier in travel, so to speak.

East Germany is a land of romantic mountainous scenery (one part, in fact, is called "Saxon Switzerland"), heavy forests, and gently rolling plains. But much more than physical geography, it offers a chance to see a slice of living history, a Communist nation right in the heart of Central Europe.

In many ways, rural traditions have lingered longer in East Germany than they have in the more modernized Federal Republic. There are no traffic jams on the roads of East Germany as you make your way through the Harz Mountains, the Thuringian Forest, or along the Elbe River. Gasoline stations are few and far between, and many of the back roads are in poor condition. Be careful if you run into Soviet-piloted military equipment. When they pass by, they like the road to themselves!

If you travel in East Germany, be prepared for lots of red tape, slow trains, and very delayed responses on occasion to your requests.

You'll visit cities that rose out of ashes, including Dresden. Many East German cities were bomb-blackened ruins and shell-pocked buildings in 1945. East Germany's factories were tangled masses of wrecked machinery, and even those were being dismantled for shipment to the Soviet Union. A remnant of once-powerful Prussia, and later a faded piece of real estate left over from the gaudy dream of the Hitlerian Reich, East Germany appeared to face a bleak future. Now, florid baroque palaces are being restored and modern high-rise hotels built.

There isn't much extreme in temperature. The overall average is about 40 to 50 degrees Fahrenheit.

In food, meals are hearty and heavy, a gluttony probably caused by the still-lingering memory of hunger suffered in the postwar era. Major hotels and restaurants offer an international cuisine that most often is inferior to that of the Federal Republic. The Eastern European influence in cookery is strongly felt.

Venison, wild fowl, and wild boar appear with some frequency, as do carp and trout, along with an infinite variety of wurst (sausages) and deli-type cold cuts. Among the specialties, local dishes include pork knuckle with sauerkraut, rolled stuffed meat, potato pancakes, eel, pot roast, baked ham, and sauerbraten, each accompanied by beer, which is the national drink, of course. Wines are served in the better restaurants (ever had Bulgarian wine?), and better yet are the Russian and Polish vodkas.

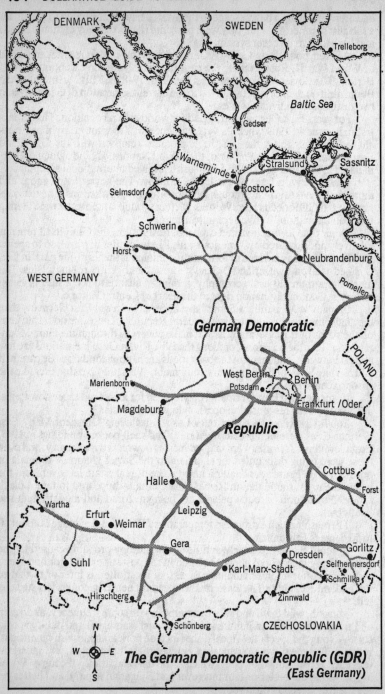

DENMARK

SWEDEN

Trelleborg

Baltic Sea

Gedser

Warnemünde · Stralsund · Sassnitz

Selmsdorf

Rostock

Schwerin

Horst

Neubrandenburg

WEST GERMANY

Pomellen

German Democratic

POLAND

West Berlin · Berlin

Marienborn

Potsdam

Magdeburg

Frankfurt /Oder

Republic

Cottbus

Halle

Forst

Wartha

Leipzig

Erfurt · Weimar

Gera

Görlitz

Suhl

Dresden

Seifhennersdorf

Karl-Marx-Stadt

Schmilka

Hirschberg

Zinnwald

Schönberg

CZECHOSLOVAKIA

N
W · E
S

The German Democratic Republic (GDR)
(East Germany)

WHAT'S IN A NAME: When conversing with East Germans, particularly officials, you'll get better results if you refer to East Berlin as "Berlin-Hauptstadt der DDR" (Berlin, capital of the GDR), or merely Berlin. Also, never use the terms "East Germany" or "East Berlin" if you can avoid them. The official name for the country is not East Germany, but the Deutschen Demokratischen Republik or "the German Democratic Republic."

The official position of the U.S. government is that East Berlin is not a part of the GDR (or its capital), but is instead a Soviet-occupied sector of Berlin under the Four-Power Occupation of the city. However, only those persons who are using official or diplomatic passports are bound to that protocol (as well as the U.S. military). Of course, it is at the individual's discretion to cater to an East German's preference for calling his or her country or capital by its officially designated labels, and no political inferences should be drawn concerning this.

THE FORMALITIES: To visit the GDR, or any Communist country for that matter, you must plan in advance to meet its requirements. (If you're planning only a day trip to East Berlin, that will be the easiest to arrange. Refer to the information in Section 1, below.)

If you want to tour East Germany, you must arrange hotel accommodations in advance. This should be done through a travel agent. You can, of course, book directly through the government travel bureau inside East Germany, but that's far more complicated and time-consuming. It's best to have all the arrangements made before you go.

In New York, **Koch Overseas Co.**, 157-161 E. 86th St., New York, NY 10028 (tel. 212/369-3800), specializes in East German travel, although the agency and its affiliates are a full-service outfit as well. Mr. Koch, however, is a specialist on East German tours, and is an authorized agent for the Travel Bureau of the German Democratic Republic. Born in Leipzig, he was the son of hoteliers there. So at an early age he learned to be sensitive to the needs of travelers.

For purposes of visa applications to the GDR, most tourists fall into one of two categories: those planning on staying in the homes of friends or relatives in the GDR, and those persons planning on staying exclusively in hotels. The entrance requirements are slightly different for each category, but Mr. Koch and his assistants can arrange things smoothly in either case.

If you plan to stay in private homes, you'll need an entrance permit (also called a provisional visa), which you should apply for at least seven to nine weeks in advance. Because of the paperwork involved, Mr. Koch charges $40 per application, and asks for a detailed list of your marital and occupational status, dates and duration of travel, the names and addresses of the friends and relatives (if any) you plan on visiting in the GDR, and your intended border-crossing point. An additional $15 is added to the $40 fee if you need your documents sooner, in which case it will take six instead of nine weeks. Upon receipt of your preliminary visa, which will be forwarded to you through Mr. Koch, you'll need to aply for a tourist visa when you arive at the East German border. This is almost always granted without delay—if the preliminary papers are in order—for an additional fee of 15 DM ($4.95), which must be paid in non–East German currency. This is a one-time-only entry permit. If you are staying in a relative's home, you'll need to register—and pay a fee of approximately $5 U.S.—at the local GDR police precinct, which will issue a permit for the desired length of stay as well as an exit visa for your eventual departure.

If you plan to stay in private houses during your travels in the GDR, you must exchange a minimum of 25 DM ($8.25) per person per day for each day that your visa allows you to stay in East Germany. The day of entrance and the day of departure will both be viewed as complete days. Children ages 6 to 15 must exchange 7.50 DM ($2.48) per day for each day of their sojourn in the GDR.

The entrance procedure is different for those tourists who choose to stay in hotels and will not contact friends or relatives in the GDR. In that case, you must select which hotels you want to stay in in the GDR (Mr. Koch will mail literature on the potential candidates, which usually tend to be little more than photographs of the exterior of the hotels with the ratings given them by the government tourist agencies). You must prepay in advance for a specified number of nights, and Mr. Koch will issue vouchers for funds exchanged. These vouchers replace the provisional visas required of tourists staying with relatives. Upon presentation of these vouchers at the frontier, a visa will be issued for 15 DM ($4.95). You then report for registration at your preselected hotel and present your vouchers, at which time the hotel will automatically register you with the local police precinct. Visas issued in this way, by the way, are valid only for the number of days for which you present prepaid hotel vouchers. *Warning: Never seek accommodations in any city of the GDR for which you have no visa.* Incidentally, Westerners cannot stay at hostels in East Germany, but they can obtain camping permits.

If you're driving to East Germany from West Germany, refer to the introductory section in Chapter XVI on West Berlin, which explains gasoline purchases and toll fees.

For information and assistance once you're in the GDR, you can contact the official East German travel organization, the **Reisebüro der DDR,** at their branch office, located at 5 Alexanderplatz, in East Berlin. If you want to write to them for information before you leave home, their address is: Reisebüro der DDR, Generaldirektion, Postschliessfach 77, DDR 1026 Berlin (tel. 215-44-02).

PRACTICAL FACTS: Do not attempt to bring in any **GDR currency** at the border. The police will confiscate it, and you will be turned back. However, you can bring in unlimited convertible currency (that is, any Western currency), provided it is declared.

Once inside East Germany you can **exchange foreign currency** at branches of the Staatsbank. The official exchange rate of the East German mark—called a Reichsmark (M)—is on a par value with the West German mark, known as a Deutsches Mark (DM). This one-to-one rate is inflated. The West German mark is far more valuable than the East German mark.

On the **black market** the DM-RM rate is anywhere from 3.60 to 4 (and sometimes 5) RM for 1 DM. *But currency dealings on the black market can get you a prison penalty in the GDR.* Don't fall into a trap. It isn't worth it. Agents provocateur are plentiful, especially in East Berlin. If you are approached, walk on by after politely *but firmly* turning down their offer to exchange your money.

It's always good to be very discreet when traveling in East Germany. One investigator reported that hotel rooms, and certainly hotel phones, are likely to be bugged.

When visiting East Germany, do not take Western periodicals, such as magazines, especially news magazines, and newspapers. However, this travel guide can usually make it across the border.

Remember—and this is most important—*hold onto your visa slip,* which is attached to your passport. You may have to produce it several times while visiting the GDR, and you will most definitely need it upon your return to the frontier with the West.

It is possible to pay bills in hotels, restaurants, and shops in foreign currency, where a notice to this effect is found.

CUSTOMS: Gifts worth up to M 200 ($66) for each day of your visit to a maximum of five days—that is, a maximum of M 1000 ($330)—may be brought in duty free. On leaving the country, gifts and articles purchased to the value of M 20 ($6.60) per day to a maximum of five days—that is, a maximum of M 100 ($33)—can be taken out duty free.

PRACTICAL FACTS: If your **automobile** does not have the "Blue Card" or "Green Card," **liability insurance** is compulsory. For private vehicles and mini-buses up to eight seats, for a stay of one to ten days, the cost is M 40 ($13.20); from 11 days, M 80 ($26.40). **Road tolls** are also assessed. For private cars and mini-buses up to eight seats (including driver), for a distance of up to 200 kilometers, M 5 ($1.65) is charged; for a distance of up to 300 kilometers, M 15 ($4.95); up to 400 kilometers, M 20 ($6.60); and up to 500 kilometers, M 25 ($8.25). Gas or motor oil can be paid for in U.S. dollars or Deutsche marks. The requisite coupons can be obtained at all branches of the Reisebüro der DDR, and at international service stations, in the following values: M 5 ($1.65); M 10 ($3.30), and M 20 ($6.60).

The **official language,** of course, is German, followed by Russian. After that, English is widely understood in Interhotels and major restaurants.

Public holidays are as follows: January 1 (New Year's); Good Friday and Easter Sunday; May 1; October 7 (founding date of the GDR); and Christmas (a two-day holiday, December 25 and 26).

Shopping hours vary. In general, shops are open from 10 a.m. to 7 p.m. in Berlin, on Thursday to 8 p.m. Outside Berlin, hours are 9 a.m. to 6 p.m. On Saturday morning, only large shops and department stores are open (closed Sunday).

Banks, in general, conduct business from 8 a.m. to 11:30 a.m., excluding Saturday and Sunday.

Most museums are open from 10 a.m. to 6 p.m., including Sunday. They are closed either Monday or Tuesday. Restaurants stagger their hours, and most bars open at 9 p.m., closing at 4 a.m.

The charge for local **telephone calls** is M .20 (7¢). Coin boxes take 20-pfennig coins. You can't make a long-distance call from a pay phone. For that, you must go through your hotel switchboard.

For a **medical care emergency,** inform the police or hospital directly. Expenses incurred have to be borne by the patient (unless special insurance has been taken out).

If you plan to do some **shopping,** popular souvenirs include gramophone records, books, pottery, woodcarvings from the Erzgebirge, glass from Thuringia, and Meissen porcelain. **Intershops,** which can be found at all frontier-crossing points and in Interhotels, offer these goods, for which you must pay in Western currency.

In East Berlin, the offices of the **U.S. Embassy** are at 4/5 Neustaedtische Kirchstrasse, 108 Berlin-Mitte (tel. 220-27-41). Canada has no representation in East Germany (in an emergency, you can telephone the Canadian Military Mission in West Berlin at 261-11-61).

Tipping is not officially sanctioned, but no one has ever complained to me when I followed the Western custom of leaving at least 10%.

In East Berlin, the main government **post office** stands on the corner of Strasse der Pariser and the Ostbahnhof. There you can send telegrams and small express items. It's open day and night.

Toilets are found in major hotels, bars, restaurants, nightclubs, and public buildings such as museums (that is, most museums).

The **electricity** is 220 volts **A.C.**

Camping, as mentioned, is possible with an entry visa. The fee for camping is $10 (U.S.) per person from the age of 16 ($4 for children 6 to 15). Entry into the GDR for camping can only take place at official frontier crossings, and camping equipment must be brought with you. Camping holidays can be booked directly upon entry at branches of the Reisebüro der DDR at the frontier-crossing points. Campsites are open from around mid-May until the end of September.

Incidentally, I urge anyone using the services of the **Deutsche Reichsbahn** (German State Railways of the GDR) to procure a first-class ticket and a seat reservation whenever possible. Second-class passenger trains are packed and accommodations are rather spartan, but of course the fares are correspondingly less.

Also, whenever you check into your hotel, don't be surprised when your passports are taken from you. You will receive a receipt for them while they are taken to the local police station for registration, in accordance with GDR law. Many times this registration can be accomplished at your first hotel stop for all the dates and places you have booked into the GDR without further inconvenience to you. Your passports will be ready to return to you by 8 a.m. of the following morning after you have surrendered them for registration.

NARROW-GAUGE RAILWAYS: Introduced as the first modern public conveyances in Germany 150 years ago, narrow-gauge railways today have both a certain nostalgia and a practical use. In the most beautiful parts of the GDR they link health and holiday resorts and serve as tourist attractions. Some of them even serve as a part of the railway network of the Deutsche Reichsbahn of the GDR.

Some routes start in Dresden, trains run into the Erzgebrge and Harz Mountains, and still others take passengers on trips in the Baltic coast region, one even serving the island of Rugen out at sea. All of the trains are pulled by steam locomotives, the newest of which was built in 1910. Each of the coaches has a small stove which the conductor will light up if it's cold outside.

The GDR Travel Agency offers ten tours on the trains, with visits to old track installations, machinery, railway repair and servicing shops, and railway stations included.

1. East Berlin

Even on a rushed visit to West Berlin, you should at least spend a half day in East Berlin, the cultural and political capital of one of the most important industrial countries of the world. For it was here, prior to World War II, that the real cultural center of Berlin lay: the best museums, the finest churches, the most important boulevards. Of course the city you see today on the opposite side of the Wall is not the exciting, lively city of prewar days, but it still has many attractions, especially its museums.

The old image of a war-torn East Berlin—ripped from the pages of John le Carré's *The Spy Who Came in from the Cold*—is now a bit of a cliché. In 40 years, much progress has been made. There are still many reminders of war, such as bullet-pocked buildings, but the blackened rubble of World War II for the most part has been long wiped away. Broad avenues radiate in several directions from the vast and impressive Alexanderplatz. These impersonal boulevards lead to massive housing blocks built for workers.

Actually, East Berliners have accomplished a near miracle since their city was destroyed by the ravages of war in 1945. After the shooting died down, they found nothing but ruins of faded glory about them. With incredible hard work, they have virtually eliminated unemployment and poverty (no one seems hungry, as they often were in the dark days of the late '40s and early '50s). They still don't have enough housing, but that is true virtually all over the world today.

East Berlin became the capital of Communist East Germany in 1949. It is today a metropolis of some one million industrious people. Believe it or not, it was the dreaded Wall that stabilized East Berlin by stopping the massive flow of talent and people power to the West, human energy needed to rebuild the devastated city.

Today the Iron Curtain is far more penetrable than it has been in years, especially on an easily arranged one-day visa, which most tourists use for a day in East Berlin (they have to be out by midnight). Since 1972 West Berliners can now more easily visit their friends and relatives in East Berlin. They bring plenty of hard-to-get luxury items from the West, reminding their more unfortunate relatives how much richer life is in a capitalist country.

You won't see as many people on the streets of East Berlin as you do in the West. But it isn't deserted either. There certainly aren't as many cars, and those they do have are often funny, with amusing names like Wartburg.

There are often curious juxtapositions of the aristocratic Prussian Berlin with the Communist Berlin of today. Many of the baroque wonders known to German emperors have been restored, and often, at least in the "fancy" restaurants, the maître d'hôtel will still seat you while clad in "tails." But the military presence is powerful, and you can feel it everywhere. Chances are, you'll customarily run into Russian soldiers. So don't be misled. The iron fist of the Soviet Union, in spite of some relaxation, still has a stranglehold on the city.

Yet in spite of their military control, the Soviet occupation forces have failed to prevent West German radio and TV from penetrating the Iron Curtain. It is estimated that at least 70% of East Berlin watches West German television at night, so they have a pretty good idea of what life must be like in the west.

TOURS: If you are of the "safety in numbers" school, perhaps one of the already-recommended tours (see "Organized Tours" in the preceding chapter) offered by the **Severin & Kühn Line**, at 216 Kurfürstendamm (tel. 883-10-15), is the best way for you to tour East Berlin. A four-hour tour of the major sights of East Berlin leaves each afternoon and costs an inclusive 30 DM ($9.90). This tour has the added advantage of cutting through the red tape of border crossing (but carry your passport). You, however, have the disadvantage of being almost completely confined to your bus seat except for a few quick museum stops. You don't have the opportunity to explore the city as you would on your own.

For a more realistic picture of life in East Berlin, I recommend a personal tour of the city, either by car or on foot. As of this writing, citizens of Western nations should have no problems in entering East Berlin—and more important, in returning to the West.

CROSSING THE BORDER: One of the control points for non-Socialist countries is **Checkpoint Charlie.** To reach it on West Berlin's U-Bahn, take the train from the Zoologischer Garten station to Hallesches Tor. At that station, board the train for Kochstrasse, which is only one stop away. This station is the exit point for the Wall crossing.

All you need to take with you is your passport, a few marks, and if you're driving, your "Green Card." If all goes well, you should be through the Customs inspection within 20 minutes—that is, if the person in front of you isn't carrying 35 copies of *Time* magazine. I've seen East German Customs officials tediously go through every page of a magazine before permitting access to its owner.

You must exchange the equivalent of 25 DM ($8.25) hard currency into East German marks, and pay a 5-DM ($1.65) fee for a one-day visa. And you might as well spend it because you can't bring it out again. Additional West German marks can be brought with you without restriction (you must declare them, however), and you can exchange them during your visit at the offices of the Bank of Industry and Commerce. You probably won't find this necessary, however, since many shops, restaurants, and hotels will accept foreign currency (including West German marks).

Before passing through Customs, visit the "House at Checkpoint Charlie," the Museum of the Wall described in the previous chapter.

East Germany is making attempts to brighten this so-called gateway to the Communist world of Eastern Europe, perhaps in time for the city's 750th anniversary celebrations in 1987. Perhaps they want to make the crossing appear more like an international frontier, but they may not be very successful, at least in making such an impression on the wartime allies manning the west side of the checkpoint. The U.S., Britain, and France feel that Checkpoint Charlie is only an inter-sector boundary and that Berlin is united, not divided by a frontier as the fourth ally, Russia, views it.

Visitors can also travel to East Berlin on the S-Bahn train. Reader Clayton A. Vieg writes: "I have used both Checkpoint Charlie and the Friedrichstrasse station when entering East Berlin, and based upon my experiences I must recommend using the Friedrichstrasse. I encountered much less hassle there compared to Checkpoint Charlie. Perhaps that's because a person with a car presents many more problems to GDR authorities than does a pedestrian or transit user."

The Friedrichstrasse checkpoint in East Berlin may be reached by taking the West Berlin U-Bahn line (marked "Tegel-Alt-Mariendorf –6") or by traveling the Nordsudbahn S-Bahn line, going between the Anhalter and Humboldthain stations in West Berlin.

Although you must use the same border-crossing point for entering and leaving East Berlin, you are not restricted from choosing which means of public transport you wish to use once you have passed through the checkpoint returning to West Berlin.

If you are using the S-Bahn to travel to East Berlin, you must buy a special ticket at the ticket window in West Berlin, paying 2 DM (66¢) for a one-way fare. Also, if you take the S-Bahn back to West Berlin, before entering the checkpoint area at the Friedrichstrasse, be sure to go to the S-Bahn ticket window in the station to buy the return ticket to West Berlin. The cost is M 2 (66¢). This way you can use up some of your East German marks if you have any left over. You can wait until you've passed through the border checkpoint to buy your ticket, but then you will have to pay in DM.

When you leave the train at the Friedrichstrasse going into East Berlin, follow the signs to the "Grenzübergangstelle" (border-crossing point). Once there, follow the signs saying "Bürger anderen Staaten" (citizens from other countries).

All that is necessary when you desire to enter East Berlin on a one-day visa is to give your passport to the border officer in the booth when you are in the line. After you've paid your visa fee, the officer will issue you the visa, hand you your passport, and permit you to pass on through the next stations.

First, you will encounter the currency exchange. For faster processing, it's best to have the 25 DM ($8.25) ready to hand to the exchange clerk, who will in turn give you East German currency. This is the only transaction possible at this station. Larger amounts may be changed at any branch of the Staatsbank der DDR. However, it's also possible to use any other Western currency in lieu of DM.

Once in East Berlin, Friedrichstrasse station is only a block from Unter den Linden. However, if you wish to begin your sightseeing on the main square, Alexanderplatz, you can take a taxi, one of which is usually found waiting outside the station exit. At the base of the tower on the square is a tourist information office, dispensing data in English.

Fares on the S-Bahn, bus system, or streetcar begin at M .20 (7¢) in East Berlin if you confine your visits to the downtown area. Tickets issued by one system are valid on the other systems as well. A one-day tourist card good for unlimited S-Bahn travel within East Berlin costs only M 1 (33¢) and is also available for all public transit in East Berlin for only M 2 (66¢).

To return to West Berlin, go back to the station on Friedrichstrasse. Proceed to the Customs offices which are in an annex to the station across from the taxi stand. Present your passport and card at the entrance marked "Entrance for Foreigners." At this point you'll be required to exchange any East German marks in your possession back into West German marks.

INFORMATION: A monthly guide to events in East Berlin is available at the Information Center in the TV tower and at many newsstands. Appropriately enough, it's called *Wohin in Berlin* (What's Going on in Berlin). You must be prepared to accept the fact that many museums, restaurants, and other places can be closed without prior notice on "technical grounds." The monthly *Wohin in Berlin* is very useful in this regard.

The Information Bureau is called **Informationszenturm am Fernsehturm,** and it's beneath the TV tower on the Alexanderplatz (tel. 212-46-75). It's open from 1 to 6 p.m. on Monday, from 8 a.m. to 6 p.m. Tuesday to Friday, and from 10 a.m. to 6 p.m. on weekends. In the summer months the staff also opens an information center near the Bahnhof on Friedrichstrasse at the crossing point. This latter one might be even more convenient.

Arranging to stay in East Berlin overnight on short notice (less than a week in advance) is best arranged through the Ausländerservice (foreigner's service) of the **Reisebüro der DDR** in the Reisebüro building at 5 Alexanderplatz and Hans-Beimler-Strasse (tel. 215-44-02). They're located at Window 13 on the second floor, and are open from 7 a.m. to 10 p.m. daily. The staff speaks English and can answer most questions.

Please note that—except on rare occasions—they can arrange short-notice accommodations only at the Palasthotel and the Hotel Metropol. The best thing to do is to reserve at least two months in advance directly through the Reisebüro der DDR (Generaldirektion, 1026 Berlin, 77 Postschliessfach) or through a travel agent as outlined in the introduction to East Germany. That way, you'll not only have a greater choice, but (probably) a better price.

If you're in East Berlin and need to call West Berlin, it will cost M .80 (26¢). From West Berlin, if you want to call East Berlin, the area code is 0372.

You cannot hail a taxi on the street in East Berlin; however, if you dial 229-27-17, one will come to you. Taxis cost from M .70 (23¢) to M 1.10 (36¢) per kilometer.

EXCHANGING MONEY: The lowest commissions for cashing traveler's checks are, believe it or not, at the **Staatsbank der DDR** (State Bank of the GDR). The branches at the Friedrichstrasse and Ostbahnhof stations are open around the clock daily. Well-known checks, such as American Express, VISA, and Thomas Cook, are accepted without hassles (as well as some not-so-well-known checks, albeit with some difficulty, which might be turned down at some banks in West Berlin). At the GDR state bank, checks can be turned into DM, U.S. dollars, and Mark der DDR. The largest commission I ever paid was M 1.

Remember that any and all East German marks you have left when you leave East Berlin above the minimum exchange rate will be exchanged into DM at the official rate of 1:1 when you leave (and remember, too, that people who have paid for hotel and/or camping accommodations in the GDR are exempt from the minimum exchange rate for the duration of their stay).

Also, American Express, MasterCard, VISA, and Diner's Club cards are being accepted at a growing number of locations in East Berlin.

THE SIGHTS: There is no better way to begin your tour of East Berlin than by walking down its world-famous street . . .

Unter den Linden

The linden trees for which this street was named have been replanted, and many of the old buildings have been restored, but the prewar gaiety and glamor of the Unter den Linden have never returned. The palaces that once lined this street have either been destroyed or turned into lecture halls for Humboldt University, which numbers among its former students the young Karl Marx.

The contrast between the prewar and postwar thoroughfares is obvious from the beginning of Unter den Linden at the **Marx-Engels-Platz.** This large "people's square," built in 1951, was once the site of the 16th-century Imperial Palace. Rather than restore the damaged structure after World War II, however, the Soviets, in their rebuilding program, chose to level it completely and create the square instead. Today it is the scene of staged demonstrations against capitalism.

Beginning at the square, walk down the left side of Unter den Linden, past the Palais Unter den Linden (restored in 1969) to the Opera Café. This former 18th-century palace, complete with gardens and fountains, is used as a nightclub, wine tavern, and concert café, especially popular with the crowds from the adjoining **Deutsche Staatsoper** (German State Opera) at 7 Unter den Linden. After 200 years of almost continuous performances, the State Opera Company was made homeless in 1941 when bombs almost completely destroyed the structure. In 1955 another opera house, built to the original (18th-century) plans of Knobelsdorff, opened with Wagner's *Die Meistersinger*. The neoclassic hall seats nearly 1500 persons in its three tiers and box stalls. In addition it contains smaller concert halls such as the Apollo Hall, a copy of a room in the Sans Souci Castle at Potsdam.

Directly behind the opera house, on Bebelplatz, is the once magnificent **St. Hedwig's Cathedral,** now the cathedral of the Berlin diocese. The entrance to the building is marked by a series of columns. The copper dome is designed after the Pantheon in Rome. Pictures outside show the Dom as it looked in 1905.

Facing the cathedral on the Bebelplatz is the **Royal Library,** part of Humboldt University. The facade of this building is worth a passing glance because of its rather unusual shape. (The curved wings of the structure have prompted irreverent Berliners to christen it the Kommode, chest of drawers.)

Continuing down the Unter den Linden, you'll pass the **Altes Palais** (Old Palace), once the residence of Kaiser Wilhelm, but currently in use by Humboldt University. Next are several buildings and administrative facilities of the East German government. Near the end of the street sits the Soviet Embassy, the first of the buildings on Unter den Linden to be restored after the war. The ground floor of this palace-like structure contains propaganda shops and travel agencies offering information about holidays within the Soviet Union.

The walking tour brings us within sight of the **Brandenburg Gate,** which forms not only the end of the Unter den Linden but also the end of East Berlin. From this angle, you get the best view of the gate, with its two classical gatehouses flanking the heavy Roman attica. From the East Berlin side you can also approach the Quadriga at its best, since the "best" side of the horses is not displayed to West Berliners.

The right side (on your left from Brandenburg Gate) of Unter den Linden is mainly taken up by embassies and buildings of **Humboldt University,** the largest university in East Germany since 1949. It dates from the mid-1700s, and in 1810 it became known as Friedrich Wilhelm University. Einstein and Hegel taught here, and famous alumni have included Marx and Engels.

The two sights worth crossing the street for, the Memorial and the Museum of German History, lie at the end of Marx-Engels Platz.

Memorial for the Victims of Fascism and Militarism

It's much less exhausting to call this classical temple by its older name, the **Neue Wache.** Previous to its current use, the building was a memorial to the dead of other German wars, including World War I. Today, however, it contains the ashes of an unknown soldier (placed there in 1969) to commemorate "the heroism of the resistance fighters who fought for the freedom of the German Democratic Republic" (East Germany). The main attraction here, for Westerners at least, is not the memorial but the changing-of-the-guard ceremony in front of the building every Wednesday at 2:30 p.m. The address is 4 Unter den Linden. Tourists cluster around for picture taking while the guards look on stoically. U.S. soldiers enjoy having their pictures taken while making faces at the unmoving guards. But when the clock strikes for the guard to change, the crowds scatter as the goose-stepping soldiers begin their ceremony. Anyone standing in the way is likely to get a great black boot on a tender spot, because nothing deters these guards from their rigid discipline.

The Museum of German History

In what must be the most beautiful arsenal of all time, the **Museum für Deutsche Geschicht** (Museum of German History), 2 Unter den Linden, gives a highly politicized view of the history of the German-speaking people. It offers you a chance to see a propaganda center in action. Grouped in exhibits representing various periods of German history from 1789 to 1949, the museum draws some rather far-fetched contrasts between the horrors of capitalism and the ideal socialist state. Military uniforms, photomurals, and models depict the German attempts at colonialism; and documents and photos show the social inequality—champagne parties of capitalists versus the squalid rooms of the working classes in 1900. In the room dealing with World War II you'll see photos of the Krupp armament factories, along with a profit chart for the heavy wartime production of guns and ammunition. In the same room are anti-Nazi posters and photos of Hiroshima. The section devoted to 1945–1949 includes pictures of the Nürnberg trials, along with many Communist propaganda posters of the critical point in Berlin's history.

The museum building is much easier to take than its contents. Originally constructed as an arsenal and war trophy museum in 1695 in a subdued baroque style, it is a perfectly square structure, with a large center courtyard, where chamber concerts are held in the summer. Above the windows are the most outstanding features of the facade, the sculpted heads of 22 dying warriors by Andreas Schlüter (1696). The museum is open weekdays from 9 a.m. to 7 p.m. (from 9 a.m. to 4 p.m. on Saturday and Sunday). Admission is M .50 (17¢);

students, M .30 (10¢). Built on the Spree, the history museum overlooks Museum Island.

ART MUSEUMS: The old Berlin of prewar days was proud of its fine museums, many of which came under East German control when the boundaries were set up for the divided city. On the island in the Spree, which marks the beginning of the Unter den Linden, you'll find the greatest concentration of these. One must remember in visiting the wealth of ancient art and treasures within some of the historical museums that German archeologists of the 19th and early 20th centuries led the way in the studies of ancient civilizations.

Pergamon Museum

A museum complex (tel. 220-03-83), this building houses several departments. But if you have time for only one exhibit, go straight to the central hall of the U-shaped building to see the **Pergamon Altar.** This Greek altar (180-160 B.C.) is so large that it has a huge room all to itself. Some 27 steps lead from the museum floor up to the colonnade. Most fascinating is the frieze around the base, tediously pieced together over a 20-year period. Depicting the struggle of the Greek gods against the giants as told in Hesiod's *Theogony,* the relief is strikingly alive, with its figures projected as much as six feet from the background. This, however, is only part of the attraction of the **Department of Greek and Roman Antiquities,** housed in the north wing of the museum. Here you'll also find a Roman market gate discovered in Miletus, sculptures from many Greek and Roman cities, including a statue of a goddess holding a pomegranate (575 B.C.), which was found in southern Attica where it had lain beneath the ground for 2000 years wrapped in lead. So well preserved was the goddess that you can still see flecks of the original paint on her garments.

The **Near East Museum,** in the south wing, contains one of the largest collections anywhere of antiquities discovered in the lands of ancient Babylonia, Persia, and Assyria. Among the exhibits is the Processional Way of Babylon with the **Ishtar Gate,** dating from 580 B.C.; these monuments and also the throne room of Nebuchadnezzar were decorated with glazed bricks. Cuneiform clay tablets document much of the civilization of the period which created ceramics, glass, and metal objects while Europe was still overrun with primitive tribes.

The museum's upper level is devoted to the Islamic Museum, the East Asiatic Collection, and the Museum of Ethnography. Although these suffered great losses during the war, the collections contain many noteworthy items. Of special interest are the miniatures, carpets, and woodcarvings in the Islamic Museum.

Hours may vary from day to day in the Pergamon Museum, so it's best to check in advance. Generally, hours are 9 a.m. to 6 p.m. every day (Monday and Tuesday only for the Near East Museum and the three halls of ancient architecture, including the Pergamon Altar). Admission is M 1.05 (35¢); students, M .50 (17¢).

The Bode Museum

According to East Berlin authorities, the West Berliners broke up a set when they allegedly stole the bust of Nefertiti from the Egyptian Museum. You see, the head of her husband, King Ikhnaton, still remains on the east side of the Wall. Even without the world-renowned queen, the Bode Museum contains tons of the most significant Egyptian collections in the world. Exhibits vary in size from the huge sphinx of Hatshepsut (1490 B.C.) to fragments of reliefs from Egyptian temples. Of special interest is the "Burial Cult Room," where coffins, mummies, and grave objects are displayed along with life-size x-ray photographs of the mummies of humans and animals.

Adjoining the Egyptian Museum is the **Papyrus Collection,** containing about 25,000 documents of papyrus, ostraca, parchment, limestone, wax, and wood in eight different languages. On the opposite side of the staircase is the **Collection of Early Christian and Byzantine Art,** with a rich display of early Christian sarcophagi, Coptic and Byzantine sculpture, icons, and even gravestones dating from the third through the 18th centuries. Also on the lower level is the **Sculpture Collection,** with several pieces from the churches and monasteries, including a sandstone pulpit support by Anton Pilgram (1490) carved in the shape of a medieval craftsman.

Upstairs you'll find the **Art Gallery,** devoted mainly to German and Dutch paintings of the 15th and 16th centuries and Italian, Flemish, Dutch, English, and French masters of the 14th through the 18th centuries, as well as contemporary German and Dutch paintings. There is also a collection of **Pre-Historic Art.** The museum is open daily, except Monday and Tuesday, from 9 a.m. to 6 p.m.; on Friday from 10 a.m. to 6 p.m. Admission is M 1.05 (35¢); students and children, M .50 (17¢).

Altes Museum (Old Museum)

This 19th-century building would be worth a visit even if it were empty. The facade is supported by 18 Ionic columns. The central vault room was restored in similar style while the rest of the building was modernized and air-conditioned to display more than 40,000 prints and drawings. Among the most valuable works here are about 135,000 illustrations by Botticelli for Dante's *La Divina Commedia.* Sketches, woodcuts, and engravings by Dutch, German, English, and French masters are supplemented with drawings by 19th- and 20th-century artists, including a number of works by Edvard Munch, whose art Hitler considered scandalous. Propaganda is present here too, in hundreds of pieces categorized as "GDR socialist art." But don't let that keep you away. The Botticellis and the old masters are worth wading through the hundreds of WPA-type drawings.

The Old Museum has the same hours as the Bode Museum (above); admission is M 1.05 (35¢) for adults, M .50 (17¢) for students. As you leave, note the Neues Museum (New Museum) directly behind this museum. This structure, although still in ruins, is scheduled for restoration.

The National Gallery (Nationalgalerie)

With an entrance on Bodestrasse, this gallery mainly contains 19th- and 20th-century paintings and sculpture. The Nazi campaign against degenerate art depleted this collection during World War II, but you can still see quite a few works by Cézanne, Rodin, Degas, Liebermann, Tischbein, and Corinth. Many of the German works of the 19th century show scenes of court life at Wilhelm I's "Königsberg." The best of these are by Adolph von Menzel (1815-1905), who also is represented in the numerous sketches and drawings included in the museum. You can also see several paintings by one of Germany's greatest portrait artists, Max Liebermann (1847-1935). On the top floor is a large collection of watercolors, many of them satirical. Hours and admission charges for the National Gallery are the same as those for the Old Museum (above).

At the **Otto Nagel House,** 16-18 Am Märkischen Ufer, about 1100 yards from Museum Island, the Nationalgalerie exhibits works of what the government calls "proletarian revolutionary and antifascist art." Here you get an exclusive "Marxist-Leninist truth."

OTHER MUSEUMS: The **Kunstgewerbemuseum** (Museum of Applied Art), at Schloss Köpenick, shows the history and development of applied art in Europe from the Middle Ages to the present day. In the 36 exhibition rooms, you'll see a wide range of glass, porcelain, faïence, and work by goldsmiths, as well as jewelry and antiques. The museum is open on Wednesday, Saturday, and Sunday from 9 a.m. to 5 p.m. and on Friday from 10 a.m. to 6 p.m. Admission is M 1 (33¢) for adults. To reach the museum, catch the S-Bahn to Köpenick. From there, go by tram 8.

At the **Märkisches Museum,** 5 Am Köllnischen Park, the full array of the cultural history of Berlin (maybe more than you want to know) is displayed in one of the most prominent buildings on the banks of the Spree. The museum is operated by the Municipal Council of the GDR government. The 42 rooms contain collections of artifacts from excavations, as well as art treasures, including Slav silver items and finds from the Bronze Age. The history of Berlin's theaters and literature, arts in Berlin and the March of Brandenburg, and sections dedicated to the life and work of Heinrich Zille, may be seen here. Most visitors like the array of mechanical musical instruments. The museum is open Wednesday to Saturday from 9 a.m. to 5 p.m., on Sunday to 6 p.m. Admission is M 1.05 (35¢) for adults, M .50 (17¢) for children.

The **Postmuseum der DDR** (Postal Museum), Leipziger Strasse and Ecke Mauerstrasse (tel. 231-22-02), provides insight into the historic development of postal service and communications, as shown by original letters that are thousands of years old, postal coaches used in the Middle Ages, modern methods of postal transport, and a modern TV studio, among the exhibits. Philatelists will be attracted to the large stamp collection. The museum also houses radio receivers made by prisoners in Nazi concentration camps with the aim of listening to Voice of Liberty broadcasts. Check on the status of the museum before you go, as it was closed for reconstruction in 1985 with a promised opening in 1986.

The **Museum für Naturkunde** (Museum of Natural History), 43 Invalidenstrasse (tel. 23-97-0), is attached to Humboldt University. Among the exhibits illustrating evolutionary phases is the original skeleton of the gigantic reptile, *Brachiosaurus brancai,* which terrified the world some 125 million years ago. The 25 million-plus natural science objects contained here make this one of the largest museums of its kind in the world. Displays trace the evolution of organic life and inorganic matter, including man. Mineralogical, zoological, and paleontological departments make up the vast collections. An arboretum is attached to the museum. You can visit from 9 a.m. to 5 p.m. Tuesday to Sunday (closed Monday). Admission is M 1.05 (35¢) for adults, M .50 (17¢) for children.

The **Hugenottenmuseum** (Huguenot Museum), on the Platz der Akademie (tel. 229-17-60), in the French Cathedral, has documents, maps, historic pictures, and objects relating to the spread and status of the Huguenots who were forced to flee France under Louis XIV and found new homes in Berlin and Brandenburg. This relatively small museum contains Huguenot archives and a Huguenot library. Check its hours with the tourist office.

OTHER ATTRACTIONS: Not to be outdone by the cities of western Germany, East Berlin has constructed a massive **Television Tower** (opened in 1969) which is the second-highest structure in Europe (1100 feet), second only to the tower in Moscow. It's worth the M 4 ($1.32), or M 2 (66¢) for students, you'll pay to take the 60-second elevator ride to the observation platform, 610 feet above the city. From this isolated vantage point you can clearly distinguish most of the landmarks of both cities. On the floor above you can enjoy a piece of cake and cup of coffee as the tele-café slowly revolves, making one complete turn every hour. By the time the revolution is completed, you'd better be on your way, however, or the guard will throw you out. The tower is open to visitors daily from 9 a.m. to 11 p.m.

At the foot of the tower stands one of Berlin's oldest churches, the brick Gothic **Marienkirche** (St. Mary's), opening onto Karl-Liebknecht-Strasse. Constructed in the 15th century, it is especially notable for the wall painting depicting the *Dance of Death* (1475), discovered beneath a layer of whitewash in the entrance hall of the church in 1860. Also worth seeing is the marble baroque pulpit carved by Andreas Schlüter (1703).

On the opposite side of the TV Tower stands the **Alexanderplatz,** center of East Berlin activity. Several modern buildings line the square, including an HO Department Store and the Congress Hall. Information and tickets pertaining to events in East Berlin are available at the Berolina House on the square, open from 9 a.m. to 7 p.m. Monday through Friday (on Saturday until 4 p.m.).

The **Sowjetisches Ehrenmal** (Soviet War Memorial) in Treptower Park, along the Spree, entered from Puschkinallee at the park, is the final resting place of more than 5000 Soviet soldiers. Entering the park, you pass between two huge red granite pylons in the form of stylized flags, each towering over a bronze sculpture of a kneeling Soviet soldier. The cemetery consists of five large communal graves flanked by 16 raised stone sarcophagi on which bas-reliefs portray the events of World War II. At the end of the "Grove of Honor" stands the Memorial Statue, atop the Mausoleum which contains the "Book of Honor," listing the 5000 victims of the war who are buried here. Much of this memorial was constructed from marble from Hitler's demolished Chancellery.

Incidentally, many readers have asked the way to the **Reichschancellery,** Hitler's bunker where on April 30, 1945, the Third Reich came to an end with the suicide of the German dictator. Hitler had proclaimed it would last 1000 years. Although the Reichschancellery once stood within walking distance of Checkpoint Charlie after one crosses into East Germany, it does not exist today. The Russians bombed the area totally, and what was left was bulldozed by the Soviets. The Communists did not want to create a memorial of any kind to Hitler. The site today is an open space. Only a mound of rubble marks the spot where the Nazi nerve center once stood. At one time the building of marble and glass was vast. Art adorned its great halls. The bunker was built 50 feet below ground following the bombing of Hitler's military headquarters. For persons wishing to visit the site, take the U-Bahn to Thälmannplatz, which is, incidentally, the last stop. The site of the building is at the northwest corner of Vossstrasse and Otto-Grotewohl-Strasse. The mound marking the Führer-bunker is located inside the so-called Death Strip. You can get an idea of the grandeur of the building by walking around the Thälmannplatz U-Bahn station or at the Soviet War Memorial in Treptower Park. The walls of the station are lined with red marble taken from the Chancellery.

Most tourists miss one of the delights of East Berlin, boat excursions on the Spree. For a scenic boat ride through the waterways of the city, check with **Weisse Flotte,** whose white-painted vessels dock at Treptower Park (tel. 2-71-20). They operate between April and September, usually leaving about eight times a day. I'd suggest you get off at the Mecklenburger Dorf in Köpenick, which is a reconstruction of a typical 19th-century village in the north of Germany. Here you can also obtain light meals, all Berlin specialties accompanied by the brew, of course.

Theater buffs may also want to seek out the house occupied by **Bertolt Brecht,** the German poet and playwright who lived in the U.S. during World War II but in East Germany thereafter. It was in East Germany that he created his own "epic theater" company, the Berliner Ensemble, in which he often expressed Marxist, antibourgeois, antimilitarist themes. East Berlin retains the Bertolt-Brecht-Haus as the Bertolt Brecht Center at 125 Chausseestrasse in an old tenement house not far from the Berlin-Friedrichstrasse station. This was where Brecht and his life companion, Helene Weigel, lived from 1953 until their deaths. The center contains the artists' living and working rooms and the Brecht and Weigel Archives containing 75,000 manuscripts, typescripts, collections of his printed works, press cuttings, playbills, and sound documents. It's open from 10 a.m. to noon on Tuesday and Friday, from 5 to 7 p.m. on Thursday, and from 9:30 a.m. to noon and 12:30 to 2 p.m. on Saturday.

A rustic cellar restaurant in the building is a good place to stop in for a bite to eat and a drink.

Kept as a reminder of the Nazis' death grip are the remains of a **Jewish synagogue** at 28 Oranienburgerstrasse, which was firebombed during Kristallnacht, November 10, 1938. That night, Jewish places of worship throughout the country were devastated by firebombs, and this one has been left standing as a memorial, untouched since the Nazi era. To find it, follow Friedrichstrasse away from Checkpoint Charlie to Oranienburgerstrasse, then turn right for about five blocks. The synagogue is on the left side of the street as you approach. *Warning:* It's a long walk from the checkpoint, across the river and past the railway station.

PREVIEW OF COMING ATTRACTIONS: Reconstruction is under way on the **Nicholas area,** a historic site in East Berlin. Here on the banks of the River Spree is where Berlin was born, and the present project will see many of the old buildings totally rebuilt under expert guidance to bring the area back to a place in the sun as a part of the architectural culture of the city. **St. Nicholas Church,** which was destroyed in the war, is being rebuilt and restored. It's the oldest building on the Olde Markt (later the Whey Market) and will be used for various cultural purposes. The **Gerichtslaube,** seat of early jurisdiction, and the 18th-century **Ephraim Palace** will also be rebuilt, as well as new structures being erected to house apartments, shops, boutiques, and cafés, all reflecting the memory of Old Berlin. The city will celebrate its 750th anniversary in 1987.

HOTELS: Because there is so much to see in East Berlin, you may want to spend more than a day's visit. If so, you can make arrangements with travel bureaus or the East German tourist office for a proper visa for overnight stopovers. What follows are the major hotels of East Berlin. Hotel prices are quoted in U.S. dollars. *Warning:* Because of fluctuating exchange rates, there could easily be a variance of $10 more or less in these prices during the life of this edition.

Palasthotel, 5 Karl Liebknecht (tel. 24-10), completed in 1979, is East Berlin's flagship hotel. It was built in cooperation with some Swedish firms. The location is near the Palace of the Republic and conveniently near the S-Bahnhof Marx-Engels-Platz and "Museum Island." It offers 600 fully air-conditioned rooms and apartments, with all the modern conveniences, including TV, radio, direct-dial phone, an alarm clock, a private bath, and a refrigerator with a minibar. A single room costs $58 (U.S.), and a double goes for $42 per person.

Its fitness center has a swimming pool, sauna, solarium, massage service, bowling alley, and club bar. There are a dozen restaurants, bars, and salons, and the kitchen turns out many culinary specialties, from French to Asian. On-site services include a rent-a-car service, a car park, an Interflug city office, an office of the Reisebüro for the GDR, a central box office, a hairdressing salon, a souvenir shop, and an Intershop.

The **Metropol,** 150-153 Friedrichstrasse (tel. 2-20-40), is the next best hotel in Berlin, also built with Swedish help and completed in 1977. It lies only a short walk from the Friedrichstrasse station and border checkpoint, and close to the Unter den Linden. Many business people choose to stay here because of its location opposite the International Trade Center in Friedrichstrasse. The 340 rooms are made up of both singles and doubles, along with apartments and suites. Many amenities are provided, including a refrigerator, direct-dial phone, TV, and mini-bar, along with private bath and toilet. A single costs from $58, and a double runs $42 per person.

The hotel also has a fitness center, with a swimming pool, saunas (unlike in West Germany, the sexes are segregated), solarium, massage service, and bar. There is a Panorama Sauna on the 12th floor, with a terrace attached. The Metropol Club on the premises offers dancing and entertainment. It also has good food in its specialty or grill restaurants.

Interhotel Stadt Berlin, Alexanderplatz (tel. 21-90), is a 2000-bed establishment with 37 floors standing to the side of the heartbeat Alexanderplatz. Its public facilities are modern and spacious, with lobbies overflowing with large groups of Russians and touring Eastern Europeans or business people. Luggage from group travel is often piled high. The architecture is self-described as *"des neuen sozialistischen Berlins."* A single room costs from $50, while the double rate goes from $70.

In the Rôtisserie, specialties are served. Facing the big plaza is a milk bar where you can order coffee and light meals from 11 a.m. to 11 p.m. If you go to the second-floor restaurant, the Zillestube, you'll find an ethnic decor and cuisine. Here the specialty is Berliner eisbein (pig trotters) with sauerkraut. In addition, other catering facilities include a Nachtbar and an international restaurant, where a complete meal might run $15. The Panoramic Restaurant on the top floor is open from 11 a.m. till midnight. Other facilities include a garage, barbershop, beauty parlor, and sauna.

Interhotel Berolina, Karl-Marx-Allee (tel. 21-095-41), is smaller than the nearby Interhotel Stadt Berlin. There are 677 beds in rooms furnished in "DDR modern." Each accommodation contains a private bath. The per-person rate in a single or double ranges from $39. The hotel's dining room provides an authentic German cuisine. The restaurant is open from 6 a.m. till midnight. A game specialty I recently enjoyed was accompanied by apple sauerkraut and potatoes. It's called "Wildschweinbraten in Sahne mit Apfelrotkraut und Schwenkkartoffeln bereits." On the lower level is a wine restaurant, Bodega, open from 6:30 p.m. till 2 a.m. Drinks, including not only wine but beer, are offered in addition to food. Another spot for drinks is the Nachtbar, which remains open till 2 a.m. In summer you can enjoy coffee on the garden terrace, perhaps request the "Theaterplatte Berolina," a variety of mixed cold meats.

Interhotel Unter den Linden, 14 Unter den Linden (tel. 22-003-11), stands on the most famous street of Berlin, within walking distance of the S-Bahn station. Handy for visiting the major museums of the capital, it is impersonally modern, containing 443 beds in generously proportioned rooms, all with private bath and soft beds. The rate per person ranges from $35. In the lounge is the Hallenbar and the Hallencafé, open from 10 a.m. till 3 a.m., where you can order international drinks. The pastries are good. The main restaurant, open until midnight, features international dishes, with a complete meal costing from $15.

RESTAURANTS: East Berlin is gaining a string of international restaurants, all of which reflect the cuisines of Communist countries. There's even a Nachtbar Havanna.

Gaststättenensemble Fernsehturm, Alexanderplatz (tel. 21-042-32), is housed in the previously recommended Television Tower. If you're visiting just for the view and coffee, see "Other Attractions." For more serious dining, the main restaurant is open from 10 a.m. till midnight. Regional specialties feature such dishes as herring filets in an apple cream sauce, pork cutlets with ham and cheese, and a fish platter. On the ground level, the Tagescafé is self-service. Featured is a Berliner hackepeter, a generous plate of chopped meat, with mix-it-yourself condiments, topped by an egg. You can also order pea soup with bockwurst, a typical dish of pig trotters with sauerkraut and potato salad. Meals cost less than $10. Young Berliners come here for evening dancing to contemporary music.

Operncafé, 5 Unter den Linden (tel. 20-002-56), is the leading café of East Berlin, a good choice if you're visiting the State Opera House next door. The building is a remodeled version of a former structure built for royalty in 1733. The atmosphere is historic, but the interior is of today. You have a choice of places at which to eat, drink, or dine. In the cellar is a bar, on the street floor a café, and upstairs two restaurants. The café has a modest opera theme, with red and white chairs grouped around a small dance floor with a bandstand. An orchestra plays in the evening until 9:30. Lots of green plants and framed theater prints add extra glamor. From 10 a.m., you can order light snacks, Berliner cakes, tea, or coffee. A dinner costs less than $15. The second-floor Weinrestaurant offers more formal dining. Here, specialties include curried pork and a porterhouse steak for two persons. On a lower level, the Nachtbar is open from 9:30 p.m. till 4:30 a.m. At least 70 varieties of drinks are offered. The restaurant is closed Sunday and Monday.

Restaurant Moskau, 34 Karl-Marx-Allee (tel. 27-940-52), is a restaurant and café devoted to Russian specialties. Soviet generals in long woolen coats often dine here, attesting to the authenticity of the recipes and the decor of the room, inspired by one of the "republics" of the Soviet Union. Specialties from the Russian kitchen include a Kiever cutlet, chicken Tabaka, and bauernteller (a Russian peasant's dish). A meal will cost up to $15. Of course you can order Russian vodka, even Russian champagne (listed as SU-Sekt). The restaurant is open Monday through Friday from 11 a.m. to 11 p.m. A coffee bar, Mokkabar, has an outside mural, evoking the WPA days, showing workers striving for the dignity of man. There are also a Tanzcafé, open from 3 p.m. till midnight, and a Nachtbar, serving from 9 p.m. till 4 a.m. On certain nights of the week shows are presented.

Lindencorso, 17 Unter den Linden (tel. 22-024-61), offers five areas for food, drinks, and entertainment. It is one of East Berlin's most fashionable cafés on a historic street, although its interior is plastic modern. It overlooks the previously recommended Hotel Unter den Linden. At Das Konzertcafé, open till midnight, you can dance to music. In summer Das Boulevard-café offers 180 guests a chance to sit out and absorb the unique atmosphere of the city. The major spot for dining is the Weinrestaurant, seating 116 guests. It is open from 11 a.m. till midnight. A three-course meal is featured for $10. Such regional dishes as fried liver with red cabbage and potatoes are offered. The restaurant is closed on Monday. On the Kaffeegedecke you can order pastries and espresso. Finally, the Nachtbar Havanna offers entertainment from 7:30 p.m. till 1 a.m. (on weekends, until 2 a.m.). International drinks and Cuban specialties are served.

Ermeler Haus, 10 Märkisches Ufer (tel. 27-940-36), is as close as you can come in the capital to dining in an old-world manner. Not only that, but many critics consider this the best place to eat in East Berlin. Behind the classic facade is an elegant rococo restaurant, where you can have a light meal for around $15. There are other restaurants on the premises, including a rustic cellar where you can order some of the cheapest food in East Berlin, and drink it down with Pilsner beer. The specialty is "einen Zeitungsfahrerschmaus," which is pork steak on toast with ham and mushrooms. It's open from 11 a.m. till midnight. On Saturday night East Berliners congregate in the upper room to dine and dance.

Weinstube Morava, 5 Rathausstrasse (tel. 21-232-92), offers a host of Czech specialties in a rustic restaurant opposite the Neptune fountains in front of the tall TV tower. In summer tables are set up on the terrace. The specialty here is a filling grillplatte Morava. In addition, you can order typical dishes and wine from Hungary, Rumania, and Bulgaria. The restaurant is open from noon to midnight. The average tab is about $10.

Ganymed, 5 Schiffbauerdamm (tel. 282-95-40), lies on the Spree, which runs into West Berlin, in the vicinity of the checkpoint station at Friedrichstrasse. It serves an international cuisine, and does so with a little flair. Dishes are well prepared and nicely served, a meal costing from $15. You should call for a reservation. You will also be presented with a good wine carte.

Offenbach Stuben, 8 Stubbenkammerstrasse (tel. 448-41-06), has a theatrical flair, honoring the creator of the grand opera *Tales of Hoffmann.* In fact this is an independently run eatery, reportedly subsidized by two of the leading theaters of the capital. It presents an array of international dishes and Berliner specialties at around $12 or less for dinner. You should call for a reservation, but never on Sunday or Monday.

Palast der Republik, Marx-Engels-Platz (tel. 23-80), is an avant-garde modern building erected on the site of the royal palace of the Prussian heyday. The Hohenzollerns lived here from the mid-15th century until the closing days of World War I. Today, in marked contrast, among other things it's the headquarters of the Parliament of the GDR. The East German government has allowed three restaurants to open in this showcase building: the Spree Restaurant (no service on Monday), the Palast Restaurant (a Tuesday shutdown), and the Linden Restaurant (no service on Wednesday). They cook both regional and international specialties. If you want something simple, try the wurst with potato salad (about the cheapest meal here). You can also enjoy more elaborate fare, such as tender veal in a mushroom and cream sauce. Meals cost around $7.

Want a really good East German bierstube? Try **Wernesgrüner Bierstuben,** 11 Karl-Liebknecht-Strasse (tel. 282-42-68). This cellar is an easy walk from the Alexanderplatz. Forget about nouvelle cuisine here. What you get is typical home-style Berliner cookery. That means knuckle of pork with pickled cabbage, thick pea soups, potato pancakes, various types of smoked wurst, and an occasional sauerbraten with dumplings. Prices are cheap. You might get away for around $7 unless you have a lot to drink. It's open daily, and reservations aren't usually necessary.

The **Budapest,** 90 Karl-Marx-Allee (tel. 436-21-89), is another leading national restaurant. Offering both a restaurant and keller, plus a Kleine Bar, it presents the outstanding cuisine of Hungary. However, the dishes lose something in translation from Budapest. The chicken paprika is generally good, and goulash is invariably offered. Prices range from $7 to $15.

The **Ratskeller,** in the basement of the Rathaus on Rathausstrasse (tel. 212-53-01), near the TV tower, offers a more traditional German atmosphere, replete with heavy red bricks, stained glass, and dark wood beams. Many an American who has never visited an East German restaurant must be prepared to accept somewhat different customs, such as the socially mandated use of the cloakroom in winter and the somewhat impatient attitudes and lack of patience on the part of the waiters. Surviving all that, you'll find hearty fare at a good price: about $8 for a big meal in the Bierstube, which has a traditional German atmosphere. On the opposite side of the building is the Weinstube, with a completely different and more formal setting. It's quieter with soft recorded music. The waiters are in uniform, and the service more courteous. The food here is excellent, and there is also a salad bar. For the same price you can enjoy such dishes as Ukrainian soup, rumpsteak Hungarian style with potatoes, your selection from the salad bar, and if you wish, a bottle of good Hungarian wine. The hours are 9 a.m. to midnight.

CULTURAL LIFE: The **German State Opera** (Deutsche Staatsoper), 7 Unter den Linden (tel. 200-04-91), was already previewed in our sightseeing attractions. If you can get a ticket for a performance, by all means go. It often presents some of the finest opera in the world, along with a regular repertoire of ballet and concerts. Tickets begin at M 4 ($1.32), going up to M 16 ($5.28). The box office in general sells tickets from noon to 6 p.m. on weekdays. However, if you visit near the end of summer, the opera will be closed.

A visit to another East Berlin performing house might be in order, the **Komische Oper** (Comic Opera), at 55-57 Behrensstrasse (tel. 229-25-55), lying between the S-Bahnhof Friedrichstrasse and the U-Bahnhof Stadtmitte.

East Berlin, as in legend, has a number of excellent theaters which still flourish under the Communist regime. One of the most famous is the **Berliner Ensemble,** am Bertolt-Brecht-Platz (tel. 282-58-71), which the late playwright, creator of *The Threepenny Opera,* founded in 1948. Tickets begin at M 2 (66¢), going up to M 15 ($4.95). The box office is open from 2 to 5 p.m. on Monday, from 2 to 7 p.m. Tuesday to Friday, and from 6 to 7 p.m. on Sunday. Again, it's closed in late summer.

Tickets to most performances can also be ordered at the government travel agency at 5 Alexanderplatz (tel. 215-44-10).

2. Potsdam

Of all the tours possible from both Berlins, the three-star attraction is the baroque town of Potsdam on the Havel River.

From the beginning of the 18th century it was the residence and garrison town of the Prussian kings. World attention focused on Potsdam from July 17 to August 2, 1945, when the Potsdam Conference took place here.

The town, 16 miles from East Berlin, can be reached by a short bus or train ride (two local rail lines service it). However, if you plan to spend the night, you must make arrangements in advance for a hotel and a proper visa. You can do this at the offices of American Express in West Berlin.

Warning: Do not attempt to go to Potsdam on your one-day visa granted to East Berlin. Many readers have reported doing this successfully, but you could get caught. Know that it is illegal, and it's wrong to take such risks with the grim-faced *Volkspolizei* (police), who are not noted as the most sympathetic and understanding souls in Europe. These boys follow the rule book, and so should you.

WHAT TO SEE: At Potsdam, a British air raid on April 14, 1945, destroyed much of the center of the old city, but the major attraction, **Sans Souci Park,** and its palace buildings, survived.

With its palaces and gardens, Sans Souci Park was the work of many architects and sculptors. The park covers an area of about one square mile. Arrangements for tours of the park can be made at the **Tourist Pavilion,** 15 Potsdam, Schopenhauerstrasse (tel. 238-19). The charge for admission is only M 2 (66¢)

per person. The length of the tour is about 1½ hours. Note: There is an extra charge to visit any historic buildings within the park. Also, at the pavilion you can make arrangements to tour the town for only M 1 (33¢).

Frederick II (called "The Great") chose Potsdam rather than Berlin as his permanent residence. The style of the buildings he ordered erected are called Potsdam rococo, an achievement primarily of Georg Wenzeslaus von Knobelsdorff.

Knobelsdorff built **Sans Souci Palace,** with its terraces and gardens, as a summer residence for Frederick II. The palace was inaugurated in 1747 and called Sans Souci, meaning "free from worry."

It is open throughout the year. From March to October hours are 9 a.m. to 5 p.m.; from November to February, 10 a.m. to 4 p.m. Guided tours, costing M 2 (66¢), last 40 minutes and are conducted frequently throughout the day.

The palace is a long, one-story building crowned by a dome and flanked by two round pavilions. Of all the rooms, the music salon is the supreme point of the rococo style. The elliptically shaped Marble Hall is the largest in the palace. As a guest of the king, Voltaire is said to have lived in the last general room from 1750 to 1752. A small bust of Voltaire commemorates that event.

The **Picture Gallery** (Bildergalerie) was built between 1755 and 1763. Its facade is similar to that of Sans Souci Palace. The interior is considered one of the most flamboyant rooms in the GDR. A collection of some 125 paintings is displayed, including works from both the Italian Renaissance and baroque periods. Dutch and Flemish masters are also exhibited. Such artists as Rubens, Terbrugghen, van Dyck, Vasari, and Guido Reni, as well as Caravaggio, are represented. Concerts at the Potsdam Park Festival take place here. In summer the hours are 10 a.m. till 5:30 p.m. with guided tours conducted every hour on the hour. The tour lasts 30 minutes. Admission to the museum is M 2 (66¢), plus another M 1 (33¢) for a guide.

To the west of Sans Souci is the **Orangerie,** built between 1851 and 1860. It was based on designs of Italian Renaissance palaces. Its purpose was to shelter southerly plants during the cold months. In the central core, with its twin towers, is the Raphael hall, with 47 copies of that master's paintings. In addition, you can visit five lavishly decorated salons. The Orangerie is open daily from 10 a.m. to 5:30 p.m. Guided tours are offered for M 1 (33¢). To ascend the tower, you pay a supplement of M .50 (17¢).

The largest building in the park is the **New Palace** or Neues Palais, built between 1763 and 1769, at the end of the Seven Years' War. Frederick II called it a *fanfaronade.* Crowning the center is a dome. The three Graces bear the crown on the lantern. The rooms inside were used as a residence for members of the royal family. Filled with paintings and antiques, they were decorated in the rococo style. The most notable chamber is the Hall of Shells, with its fossils and semiprecious stones. At the Palace Theater, also in the rococo style, concerts take place every year from April to November. The palace is open in summer from 9 a.m. to 5:15 p.m. and in winter from 10 a.m. to 4:15 p.m. You can either be admitted individually, or take a guided tour leaving every half hour in summer. The length of the tour is 50 minutes, and the admission is M 2 (66¢).

Reached by tram lines 1 and 4, **Charlottenhof Palace** stands south of Ökonomieweg. It was built between 1826 and 1829 to the designs of Karl Friedrich Schinkel, the greatest master of neoclassical architecture in Germany. He erected the palace in the style of a villa, and designed most of the furniture inside. The palace is open daily from 10 a.m. to 5:30 p.m., costing M 2 (66¢) for admission. The tour lasts 30 minutes.

Neighboring the palace, the **Roman Baths** are on the north of the artificial lake known as "machine pond" or Maschinenteich. This group of buildings was constructed between 1829 and 1835, based in part on designs by Schinkel. The baths were strictly for the romantic love of antiquity, having no practical purpose. They can be visited on guided tours at regular intervals in summer from 10 a.m. to 5:30 p.m. for an admission of M 1 (33¢).

With the proper visa, as mentioned, and with arrangements made at a travel bureau before you visit, you can spend the night at Cecilienhof Palace.

On the Heiliger See or "holy lake" in the northern parts of Potsdam lies the **New Garden** or Neuer Garten (tel. 2-31-41). It is about a mile northwest of Sans Souci. The nephew and successor to Frederick the Great, Friedrich-Wilhelm II, ordered the gardens laid out.

WHERE TO STAY: To the north of the 200-acre park, **Cecilienhof Palace** (tel. 2-31-41) was completed in the style of an English country house. It was ordered built by Kaiser Wilhelm II between 1913 and 1916. The 176-room mansion became the new residence of the then Crown Prince Wilhelm of Hohenzollern. It was occupied as a royal residence until March 1945 when the crown prince and his family fled to the West, taking many of their possessions with them.

Cecilienhof was the headquarters of the 1945 Potsdam Conference. For the conference, 36 rooms had to be quickly reconditioned. Truman represented the United States, and Stalin, of course, represented the Soviet Union. Churchill at first represented Great Britain, but at the time of the actual signing on August 2, 1945, Clement R. Attlee had replaced him. It is possible to visit the studies of the various delegations and see the large round table, made in Moscow, where the actual agreement was signed. Visiting hours are daily, from 9 a.m. to 5 p.m.

You can stay here in a room without bath at a cost of $22 per person. If you're visiting only for a luncheon, a set meal will run around $10.

Hotel Potsdam, Lange Brücke (tel. 46-31), is one of the best of the highrise Interhotels. At the entrance to Potsdam, on the route nearest Berlin, it rises over the water. It features a number of amenities, including a sauna and massage, and an Intershop where you can purchase souvenirs. Dancing and entertainment are provided by the nightclub, Bellevue. Its major restaurant is the Rouen. It also has a Russian teestube and a garden restaurant which is popular in summer. There is also a café on the premises. All of the 400 bedrooms are equipped with a private bathroom, along with radio and TV. The cost is from $31 per person in a double room, plus another $6 per set meal. Water-sports facilities are available as well.

READER'S DINING SELECTION: "If you don't want to dine in one of the major hotels, try the very nice **Klosterkeller** at the corner of Gutenbergstrasse and Friedrich-Ebert-Strasse. The food is well prepared, and a simple menu should cost no more than $5 per person" (Henry Peck, Los Angeles, Calif.).

3. Leipzig

Chances are, your visit to Leipzig will be at one of the annual Trade Fairs, held around March and again in September. The city is called the "metropolis of fairs," but it also enjoys renown as a center of music. Richard Wagner was born here in 1813, and Johann Sebastian Bach (you'll surely see a statue of him) is famously associated with Leipzig.

Known as "the secret capital of East Germany," Leipzig lies about 111 "rail miles" southwest of Berlin and some 70 miles northwest of Dresden. It stands above the junction of three tiny rivers, the Elster, the Parthe, and the Pleisse, all of which have names that will send you rushing to your geography books.

Because of its strategic value as a rail center, both the R.A.F. and the U.S.

Air Force bombed Leipzig heavily in 1943, 1944, and 1945, but it has been rebuilt, more or less well. Leipzig is once again a major rail terminus. From its railway station, the largest in Europe with 26 platforms, lines radiate to all the chief German cities, and from there to the rest of Europe.

Today Leipzig rivals Berlin as the economic and cultural center of the GDR. It still has some narrow streets and leftover houses from the 16th and 17th centuries. However, it's estimated that Allied bombs destroyed nearly a quarter of the city. The heart of Leipzig is encircled by a "ring road," as in Vienna.

For orientation purposes, such as finding your way around a city of more than half a million people, you should head first for the **Reisebüro der DDR,** 1-3 Katharinenstrasse, Alte Wagge (tel. 7-92-10). There you *may* be given a map pinpointing the major sights. This place becomes a beehive of activity at the time of the annual Trade Fairs. These fairs are hardly what they were when they rose to fame first under the margraves of Meissen and later under the electors of Saxony.

Revived by the Communists after the war, today they draw business representatives from more than 50 countries. A lot of people who come to them are concerned with the printing industry, as Leipzig is the principal center of GDR publishing. Because of that concentration, the city is also a literary center. Many German authors live in and around Leipzig.

Goethe, who was a student at Leipzig, called the city "Klein Paris" or Paris in miniature. The German Library, the **Deutsche Bücherei,** is the central archive of German literature, which can be visited only with special permission. It is reputed to possess every item of German literature ever published.

Founded in 1409, the University of Leipzig has contributed greatly to the cultural growth of the city. At the time of Hitler's ill-fated Third Reich, it was the largest university in Germany (today it's the largest in the GDR). The Führer would not have been at all pleased with its new name: **Karl Marx University.**

The **Musikinstrumentenmuseum** (Museum of Musical Instruments), 2 Eingang Täubchenweg (tel. 29-31-27), at Karl Marx University, collects, cares for, and exhibits treasures of musical culture, chiefly Italian, German, and French instruments of the 16th to the 19th centuries. The museum is open from 9 a.m. to 5 p.m. daily except Monday. Admission is M 2.05 (68¢). Perhaps you'll be able to attend one of the concerts sometimes played with historic instruments.

A towering figure in the history of music, master of contrapuntal style, Bach (1685-1750) lived in Leipzig from 1723 until his death. Unlike Wagner, he wasn't born in the city. However, he spent the most creative years of his life here. He was a choirmaster at St. Thomas Church **(Thomaskirche),** which has been handsomely restored after World War II damage. It has a high-pitched roof built originally in 1496. The church grew up on the site of a 13th-century monastery. The city's Thomaner Choir presents concerts (and they're free in this socialist state) every Sunday morning and Friday evening. That is, when they're in residence. The choir is popular all over the GDR, and often they are on the road touring, keeping alive the memory of Bach. Incidentally, Bach was buried at the eastern end of this kirche.

Contrary to popular belief, St. Thomas Church isn't the oldest in Leipzig. That distinction belongs to **Nikolaikirche,** erected in 1165. **Paulinerkirche** was erected in 1229 and restored in 1900. It has a grooved cloister, a curiosity, damaged after the Reformation (1556).

A landmark since the Middle Ages, **Thüringer Hof** stands near St. Thomas Church.

The Old Town Hall **(Rathaus)** dates from the 16th century, standing on the

Marketplace which dates from the 12th century. Again, Allied bombs rained down on it, but it has been restored.

A gateway in the Town Hall leads to **Nasch Market,** the city's best known square; and a short walk nearby takes you to **Königshaus,** which was for many centuries the headquarters of the Saxon monarchs who ruled over Leipzig.

The **New Town Hall** or Rathaus was erected on the site of the old Pleissenburg, the citadel where Martin Luther in 1519 held a momentous disputation.

On a cultural note, the **Gewandhaus Orchestra** of Leipzig was founded by Felix Mendelssohn who died in Leipzig in 1847. It's still going strong. Known to music lovers all over the world, the orchestra was founded originally in 1781. The **Neues Opernhaus** today is at Karl-Marx-Platz, although the chief box office is at 1 Sachsenplatz.

Going out the Strasse des 18 Oktober will take you to a memorial honoring the famed 1813 battle. Along the way, see a pre–World War I Russian Orthodox church, built in the Byzantine style as a monument to the 22,000 soldiers killed at Leipzig, and the fairgrounds which come alive at the time of the annual Trade Fairs. At the far end, the memorial, the **Völkerschlachtdenkmal,** was dedicated in 1913 to the combined German and Russian armies who defeated the Grande Armée. It rises some 300 feet in the air. Climb to the top for a view of Leipzig.

Nearby is a museum devoted to the history of Leipzig, including a diorama of the famous 1813 battle fought here. Some historians call this "The Battle of Leipzig," and others more pretentiously refer to it as "The Battle of Nations." At any rate, it's known in all European history books as the battle that led to the defeat of Napoleon and the destruction of his Grande Armée.

While in Leipzig, I'd suggest, if the weather is right, an outing to **Wörlitzer Park,** laid out in 1765.

WHERE TO STAY: Merkur, Gerberstrasse (tel. 79-90), is a silver-and-concrete skyscraper near the fairgrounds in the city center. Opened in 1981, it receives guests from all over the world, maintaining fine international standards. It also has a rent-a-car service available on the premises. Its 450 rooms and apartments are comfortably furnished and air-conditioned, each unit with a private bath, color TV, radio, and alarm clock, along with direct-dial phone, mini-bar, and refrigerator. If you're fitness-minded, you'll find a swimming pool, saunas for both men and women, a solarium, massage room, and a bowling alley. A single ranges in price from $54, and a double goes for $80. However, at the time of the Leipzig Fairs, tariffs go up. The hotel has many dining facilities, including the Brühl restaurant, the Sakura Japanese restaurant, the Arabeske restaurant, and the Milano restaurant, an international array. It will also entertain you in its nightclub, the Club Merkur. If you order drinks at Club 27, you can also enjoy a panoramic view. Also on the premises are a city office of Interflug, a branch office of the Reisebüro der DDR, a hairdressing salon, and many shops.

Astoria, Platz der Republik (tel. 7-17-10), stands across from one of the most famous railway stations in Europe. If you have a choice at all, try to get a room on one of the upper floors and not directly above the Astoria Bar on the ground floor. The hotel has a rent-a-car office on the premises, and some fairly good facilities. During the 19th century the hotel consisted of an elegant corner building with ornate window ledges and lunette windows. In the 20th century someone commissioned the construction of a dignified annex which extends the hotel another couple of hundred yards from the Platz der Republik. Today the entire mass looks solid, substantial, and very "de rigeur." From the street, you'll notice that most of the ground floor is occupied by the Astoria Bar and

Restaurant, two names well known in Leipzig. The public rooms are divided into a series of salons, conference rooms, cafés, and a nightclub with dancing. Sauna and massage are also available, and it's here that the myth of a middle-aged Valkyrie pummeling your sore muscles can come true. The cost is from $35 per person nightly with private bath or shower.

Stadt Leipzig, Richard-Wagner-Strasse (tel. 28-88-14), stands on a street honoring the famous "hometown boy." It too lies across from the railway station, built back from attractively landscaped grounds in downtown Leipzig, with rows of healthy trees setting off the blue-and-white facade. This hotel shelters almost 350 clean, well-maintained units, which cost about $35 per person nightly in a room with private bath or shower. The Stadt Leipzig also has two restaurants, a café, and a nightclub. And if you feel vaguely uncomfortable from the feeling of being watched too closely, you can relieve your frustrations in the fitness room.

Am Ring, Karl-Marx-Platz (tel. 7-95-20), an Interhotel, is big, wide, and boxy, with its monotonous facade of tile. In downtown Leipzig, it's not unlike a Holiday Inn in the Middle West. Its 278 rooms, costing from $35 per person nightly in a room with shower or private bath, are predictably furnished with modern pieces. In its favor, everything is clean, in working order, and the service is fairly good. The hotel boasts three restaurants, a café, a separate breakfast room, and a nightclub.

Hotel International, Tröndlinring (tel. 73-86), is set in a neighborhood which seemed to escape—at least partially—the war bombings. This green-and-white baroque style hotel welcomes you inside with the lights of its glassed-in restaurant extending onto the sidewalk in front. In Leipzig it is considered a moderately priced hotel, with rooms costing from $32 per person nightly. From the café on the ground floor to the rounded gables sticking out of the modified mansard roofline, the hotel has much to recommend it.

Zum Löwen, Rudolf-Breitscheid-Strasse (tel. 77-51), low on the totem pole, might do in an emergency. This downtown hotel is housed behind an eight-story buff-colored facade, with pairs of smallish windows grouped together in symmetrical rows. A somewhat forbidding expanse of asphalt extends a long distance in front of the hotel, but the service is fairly good and some of the staff seem genuinely friendly. Cost is from $29 per person nightly.

WHERE TO EAT: Most visitors to Leipzig eat at their hotels. However, I suggest that you escape for at least one night to dine at the most famous restaurant in the city, **Auerbachs Keller,** at Mädlerpassage (tel. 20-91-31). This is the restaurant and tavern where Goethe staged his debate between Faust and the Devil. In *Faust,* of course. It's still there, amazingly, after all that bombing. It lies off the market square, close to the old Rathaus. The cellar dates from 1530, and has a series of murals from the 16th century, representing the legend on which the play *Faust* was based. The food is good (much better than the service), and you can also order a fine selection of wine and beer. It is unlikely you'll spend more than $12 for dinner.

Also historic, **Zum Kaffebaum,** Fleischberg (tel. 2-0452), is the most famous and also the oldest coffeehouse in this university city. It dates from 1694, and everybody from Goethe to Wagner has patronized it. Leibnitz dined here. Robert and Clara Schumann lived here, and in 1848 Robert Blum organized the liberal revolution. The cuisine is simpler than the Auerbachs, but it's suitable nevertheless. It enjoys popularity among the students of Karl Marx University as well as all visiting foreigners. You can eat here for around $10 including service.

Students are also attracted to the cellar of the new Town Hall (Rathaus), but its **Ratskeller** (tel. 791-35-91) doesn't have either the charm or atmosphere of Auerbachs Keller and Kaffebaum.

If you're going to be in Leipzig for another day, you might pay a visit to **Paulaner,** 3 Klostergasse (tel. 28-19-85), installed in a former bank (you can read about the history of the restaurant on the menu). On a Saturday night, a three-piece band comes in to play romantic songs from the '40s and '50s. Soup, a main course, and a large glass of beer costs from $5 per person, including the tip. The menu is in German.

DAY TRIPS FROM LEIPZIG: While still based at Leipzig, you can branch out in several directions to explore some of the most interesting sights in East Germany. That way, you don't have to go through all the red tape of trying to book another hotel for the night, since you can easily explore the environs and return to Leipzig in time for dinner. Visitors interested in Martin Luther will especially find value in these tours.

You might want to check with local tourist offices about hours of any museum. They tend to vary, and are closed sometimes for no apparent reason.

Gohlis

This is a tiny suburb of Leipzig. At a small farmhouse here, Johann Christoph Friedrich von Schiller, a friend of Goethe's and, after him, the greatest name in German literature, wrote his *Ode to Joy* in 1785. This was the inspiration for Beethoven's Ninth Symphony. The house is open to the public.

Gohliser Schlösschen, once a gathering place for Leipzig literati, today houses the world's greatest collection of Bach archives and mementos.

Nearby are **Zoological Gardens** on Dr.-Kurt-Fischer-Strasse, where the animals—many wild ones, of course—are bred for export to zoos all over Europe and North America. The zoo was founded in 1878 and is internationally known for the breeding of lions. There's even an animal kindergarten here.

If you follow Martin-Luther-Strasse, you'll come to the **Georgi Dimitroff Museum** at Dimitroffplatz (tel. 3-30-32). Housed in a building constructed in 1888 as the home of the Supreme Court of the Reich and changed into a museum in 1952, it was given the name of Georgi Dimitroff, head of the Communist party in Bulgaria who was a target for Adolf Hitler. Hitler accused Dimitroff and other Communist leaders of responsibility for the Reichstag fire. They were tried in this building, in what Hitler thought would be a great blow against the Communists and a victory for the Nazis. The plan backfired, however, when the Leipzig jury acquitted the defendants. In the carefully preserved courtroom, tapes of the Reichstag trial are played, and you can also hear music in back of the museum. It's coming from the Gewandhaus music center, referred to earlier. The Museum of Fine Arts is also housed in this building. It's closed Monday.

Wittenberg

This is the city forever associated with Martin Luther, attracting pilgrims from all over the world. It was the center of the German Reformation. In the Halle district on the Elbe, Wittenberg lies 60 miles southwest of Berlin.

Wittenberg had not one, but two famous sons, and both men are honored with statues in front of the Rathaus. Its other celebrated son was Melanchthon (1497–1560), the German Protestant reformer and scholar, who was a friend of Luther's and later of Calvin's (but more humanistic than either).

Both Luther and Melanchthon were buried in the **Schlosskirche,** which dates from the 15th century (but was rebuilt in the 19th century). It was on the Schlosskirche doors that Luther nailed his 95 theses in 1517. The 1858 bronze doors bear the Latin text of the theses.

Part of an Augustinian monastery in which Luther lived has been turned into a **Luther Museum,** and the parish church in which Luther preached is from the 14th century. An oak tree marks the spot outside the Elster gate where Luther publicly burned the papal bull in 1520.

You can also visit the **Stadtkirche,** with an altar by Lucas Cranach the Elder, who used to be the bürgomeister of Wittenberg.

If you're planning to write a paper on Luther or stick around a while in Wittenberg, you'll find two very basic little hotels, the **Goldener Adler,** 7 Markt (tel. 20-53), and the **Wittenberger Hof,** 56 Collegienstrasse (tel. 25-90). Neither hotel has a room with a bath or shower. Of the two, the Goldener Adler is better, charging from $23 in a single and from $16 per person for a double. The Wittenberger Hof is cheaper, charging from $20 in a single and from $18 per person in a double.

Halle

The town of Halle lies about 21 miles northwest from Leipzig. U.S. forces, in bitter street fighting, destroyed much of the town in 1945. Today Halle is one of the leading industrial cities of the GDR, with a population of some 250,000 residents. It is also a major railway transportation hub.

George Frederick Handel, the English composer, was born here in 1685. His former home is the **Handel Museum,** displaying musical instruments, some as old as 500 years.

In the center of town is the **Market Square,** dating from the Middle Ages (but restored in the mid-1880s), and a Gothic **Marienkirche** from the 16th century (it has twin towers linked by a bridge). A statue in the square honors Handel.

The **St. Moritzkirche** from the 14th century is still standing, with many woodcarvings and sculpture. The **cathedral** from the 16th century is also worth seeing. All that is left of the **Castle of Moritzburg,** which used to be the headquarters of the archbishops of Magdeburg, is a wing. The rest was burned down at the time of the Thirty Years' War.

For food and lodging, the choice is obvious, the **Hotel Stadt Halle,** Emst-Thälmann-Platz (tel. 3-80-41). Almost deliberately designed to look forbiddingly massive, this product of state-directed architectural planning sprawls across hundreds of thousands of square yards in downtown Halle. The concrete-and-glass facade is relieved by a le Corbusier-style concrete parapet extending a welcoming shelter over the pavement in front of the hotel. You'll find 345 rooms inside, although all of them may not be in use at any one time. The cost is from $30 per person daily in a double unit with private bath or shower. Singles go for $33. The hotel also has a rather grand restaurant, a comfortable weinstube, a café, a sun terrace, and a nightclub.

Eisleben

The leader of the German Reformation, Martin Luther, was born and died in this old Prussian town, which lies on the southeastern spurs of the Harz Mountains, about 25 miles northwest of Halle. The town is divided into two parts, **Alstadt** (Old Town) and **Neustadt** (New Town).

The house at the end of Lutherstrasse, in which Luther was born in 1483, was damaged by fire in 1689 but was rebuilt in its present Gothic Franconian town-house style and used for a long time as a free school for homeless children. You can see the room in which he was born, as well as exhibits tracing his life story. You can see the woodcarving, the **Luther Swan,** inspired by the reference of Luther's reformer predecessor, John Hus, to the swan (Luther) who was to follow Hus.

At the end of his life the ailing Luther returned to his birthplace, and here he died in 1546, in a house near the market square where a memorial statue to him stands. A museum here contains his deathbed, death mask, and coffin shroud, and you can see the room where he died.

In Eisleben you can also see the font where Luther was baptized in the late-Gothic **Peter-Paul-Kirche,** as well as the gigantic statue of Lenin in working-man's clothes. It was presented to the town by the Soviet government when its troops came in in 1945.

Naumburg

If you have unlimited time for the GDR, you might seek out the old medie-val town of Naumburg, also in the Halle district. A former *land* of Saxony, it lies 29 miles southwest from Halle. In the tenth century it was a stronghold of the margraves of Meissen.

Built in the Romanesque Transition style, the **Cathedral of Sts. Peter and Paul** dates from the early 13th century and is known for its huge crypt and tow-ers. Look inside for the hand-carved folk figures. In the Town Hall, opening on Wilhelm Pieck Platz, is a good **Ratskeller,** serving beer, hearty food, and a local wine which is quite dry. Meals here cost around $5.

Altenburg

Some 30 miles south of Leipzig, Altenburg is known as the birthplace of the card game skat. A playing-card museum has been installed in a former ducal castle from the tenth century (much destroyed and rebuilt). Altenburg is still noted for turning out playing cards, which it exports all over the world. The Em-peror Barbarossa chose Altenburg as the site of his royal palace, and an Augus-tinian monastery was also founded here.

4. Dresden and Meissen

It was called "Florence on the Elbe." Throughout Europe, prewar Dres-den, 111 miles south of Berlin by rail, was celebrated for its architecture and art treasures. Then came the night of February 13, 1945. The Allies, presumably in an attempt to crush the morale of the German people, rained down phosphorus and high-explosive bombs on Dresden. It is estimated that some 35,000 Dres-deners were sucked into the devastating fire storm that engulfed the historic city. By morning the Dresden of legend was but a memory. The bombing of this great city of art is considered one of the major tragedies of World War II, and there are those, especially the Russians, who have compared its destruction to that of Hiroshima.

For many, many long and dreary years after the war, Dresden no longer resembled the city of baroque paintings on the Elbe, a scene immortalized by Canaletto. Most of it still doesn't, but much of the familiar silhouette has been belatedly restored. Bouncing back from disaster, Dresden, the third-largest city in the GDR, is, outside of Berlin, its major sightseeing target, especially its "centerpiece," the museum-clogged Zwinger (more about this later).

One of the major means of transport in Dresden is the tram, a modern, reliable, low-energy system for getting around. Also, you can take trips on the big paddle-steamers that ply the River Elbe from central moorings below the Brühl Terrace. You can take trips from April to October on one of the ships belonging to the Weisse Flotte (White Fleet). Even if you don't make a river trip, it's exciting to watch as the paddle-steamers lower their funnels to pass under a bridge. One of Dresden's most celebrated bridges is called Blaues Wunder (Blue Wonder), a tribute to the bridge-building genius applied here at the turn of the century. The funicular railway, the first of its kind in the world, takes passengers up to the viewing site at Loschwitzhöhe. The railway was built from 1898 to 1900. Dresden also has a **Transport Museum** which is worth visiting.

THE SIGHTS: Today a pedestrian mall, the Prager Strasse, once the fashionable Champs-Élysées of Dresden, cuts through the heart of the city that "rose from the ashes." The street is lined with modern heavy gray commercial buildings seemingly inspired by Moscow, but its severity is relieved by fountains and benches. On those benches you'll find many foreign tourists, usually those from the Eastern Communist nations, including Russia. "Prague Street" runs from the Old Market to the Hauptbahnhof.

However, Dresden isn't all concrete and glass. The restoration of old buildings in the "monumental zones" has been tremendous. Ruins from the war can still be seen, most notably in the baroque **Frauenkirche,** the Church of Our Lady, built between 1726 and 1743 and once known throughout Europe for its cupola. The blackened hulk remains, supposedly a deliberate decision on the part of the government to remind the passerby of "the horrors of modern warfare." It stands today, a ghostly reminder of what happened to this *Kunststadt,* or city of art.

Some of Dresden's famous churches have been restored, however. These include the **Sophienkirche** with its twin towers, a landmark rising from the Postplatz. The **Hofkirche,** built in the rococo style with a slender clock tower, rises some 300 feet. It was elevated to the status of cathedral by the Vatican following its restoration. The **Kreuzkirche** (Church of the Cross) stands at the Altmarkt. This church is the home of the Kreuzchor, the famous boys' choir of Dresden.

The **Altmarkt** itself is the historic hub of the city, with its Palace of Culture, built in 1969.

Dresden consists of both an **Alstadt** (Old Town) and a **Neustadt** (New Town). Actually, since the war both terms have been a misnomer. Since it was rebuilt the Altstadt is newer than the Neustadt. The Old and New Towns are connected by four road bridges and one railway bridge, of which the Dimitroff is the best known.

Of Dresden's many parks and gardens, the most visited is the **Grosser Garten,** which lies to the southeast of Altstadt. The park was mapped out in 1676, and today contains a zoo and a botanical garden. In the center is a lustschloss (pleasure palace) built in 1670.

Dresden's **Semper Opera House,** between the Elbe and the Zwinger, was originally designed by Gottfried Semper, the architect who mapped out the famous picture gallery of Dresden. The opera house, at which both Wagner and Weber conducted, was completed in 1878 in a Renaissance style. What you see today standing on the western side of Theaterplatz is the work of restorers who have brought the two-tiered facade and interior of the Italian Renaissance-style building back to life. Careful attention was paid to the replacement of the paintings and decorations used by Semper when the place was built, and the fine acoustics for which the opera house was known have been restored. The stage was altered somewhat to allow for use of modern technology, and fewer seats were designed to allow for more comfort (the old auditorium held 1700 persons; the new, 1400). The Semper Opera House was reopened in 1985.

The rulers of the Land of Saxony held sway in Dresden. Their **Zwinger** (palace complex) is a series of beautiful baroque buildings which have been restored and turned into a collection of museums, some 20 in all. As the court of the 17th-century princes of Saxony, Dresden enjoyed renown throughout Europe.

The Zwinger is a large quadrangle of pavilions and galleries. It was here that Augustus the Strong, the elector of Saxony (he was also the king of Poland) staged tournaments that dazzled the townfolk. He also kept dozens of concubines here, as he was reportedly something of a sexual athlete. His physique was called Herculean, his temperament Rabelaisian, but he had a great love of the arts. It was this monarch who started the collection of paintings, which in time was supplemented by his son.

The Zwinger was initially conceived by M. D. Pöppelmann as a forecourt of the castle. In its center are formal gardens, fountains, and promenades, forming a deep curving bay which is enclosed by pavilions. The Renaissance-style building is from 1846, and the exterior is decorated with sculptures of such celebrated figures as Goethe, Dante, and Michelangelo.

The most important museum is the **Gemäldegalerie Alte Meister** (Gallery of the Old Masters), open daily except Monday from 10 a.m. to 5 p.m. (to 4 p.m. in winter), charging an admission of DM 2.05 (68¢) for adults and DM 1.05 (35¢) for students. The gallery, considered one of the best on the continent, has as its showpiece Raphael's *Madonna di San Sisto,* which occupies one entire gallery by itself, and well it should. You'll also see works by Rembrandt, Vermeer, and Van Eyck, plus an array of others, including Correggio, Veronese, Rubens, and Titian. For a study in sensuality, seek out one of my favorites, Giorgione's *Sleeping Venus.*

The **History Museum** displays an ornamental collection of weaponry that is truly stunning if a bit frightening. Its hours are 9 a.m. to 5 p.m. daily except Wednesday.

In the **Pewter Museum** and the **Porcelain Museum** a vast array of two of the best known crafts of Dresden is exhibited. Visiting hours are 9 a.m. to 4 p.m. daily except Friday.

The glass-domed **Albertinum,** from 1559, is another complex, housing the state art collection. It's open daily except Tuesday from 9 a.m. to 6 p.m., charging an admission of M 2.05 (68¢) for adults and M 1.05 (35¢) for students. Its most famous attraction is the Green Vault, or Grünes Gewölbe, a dazzling exhibition of jewelry and other treasures from the 16th to the 18th centuries.

The museum complex also contains the **Galerie Neue Meister** (Gallery of the New Masters), with paintings by an array of artists going from Gauguin to Corot. It is open June through September from 9 a.m. to 6 p.m.; otherwise, from 10 a.m. to 5 p.m.

Before tackling Dresden, which is a virtual "museumland," you should head first to the **Information Center** at 10 Prager Strasse (tel. 4-40-31), open Monday to Saturday from 9 a.m. to 8 p.m. (on Sunday from 9 a.m. to 2 p.m.). It stands near the Hauptbahnhof and the Interhotel Newa. You can purchase a map which you'll definitely need. Ask about purchasing a *Sammelkarte,* which is good for half a dozen rides on the public transportation system and costs only M 1 (33¢), a great bargain. The **Central Post Office** is at 21 Otto-Buchwitz-Strasse (tel. 5-94-40).

In the environs, a major sightseeing target is **Schloss Moritzburg,** eight miles northwest of Dresden. It is surrounded by small lakes. Usually, it can be visited from 9 a.m. to 7 p.m. It's closed Monday and Tuesday. Always check with the tourist office before heading there to make sure it's open at the time of your visit. Admission is M 2.05 (68¢) for adults and M 1.05 (35¢) for students. Visitors cross over a bridge to enter this former royal hunting lodge of the Saxon rulers. The lodge is actually a palace. Augustus the Strong built this schloss in the 18th century, and in it is a collection of furnishings, hunting weaponry, and elegantly baroque porcelain.

A fascination for the American Old West and especially for the red Indians is present in all of Germany, and especially in **Radebeul,** about five miles west of

Dresden, where the German writer, Karl May, lived until his death in 1912. May wrote about prairies and Indians and frontier villains even though he never visited the United States until after his last book was written. However, even in his belated journeys he collected Indian artifacts and started the **Indianer Museum** in a log cabin built near his villa in Radebeul, a project completed by his widow in 1928 and opened to the public. Much of the material displayed came from later acquisitions, and today the museum contains peace pipes, tomahawks, totem poles, scalps, moccasins, and many other items of Indian lore. The museum is open from 9 a.m. to 5 p.m. Admission is 1 M (33¢). May's restored villa nearby was opened to the public in 1985. It houses many mementos of the writer's life.

LODGING IN DRESDEN: Hotel **Bellevue,** Kopckestrasse (tel. 5-39-27), which opened in the spring of 1985, is the top hotel of Dresden. It stands on the most attractive part of the bank of the Elbe, and a look out the hotel's windows and from its terraces to the opposite bank makes you feel as if this must be the spot from which Canaletto painted his magnificent scenes of the Old City. The new hotel building incorporates Dresden's only double court, which was formerly the Royal Chancellery. The court survived the bombing of 1945 and is now a protected monument, which has been carefully integrated into the hotel, giving a feeling of special elegance and style. Whether you stay in the old part of the hotel building or in the new section, you'll find such amenities as air conditioning, TV, and mini-bar in the well-appointed bedrooms, with carpeting, comfortable armchairs, and elegant bathrooms. Rents are $66 in a single and from $48 per person in a double, based on occupancy by two persons.

Five eating places offer a variety of cuisine, together with consistent good service. Restaurants are the Palace, the Polynesian, the Canaletto Specialty, and the Elbe Terrace, and there is also the Pöppelmann Foyer Café. Guests can enjoy drinks in the foyer bar, the special wine and beer cellar, or the Jupiter nightclub. Facilities include a fitness club, which has a swimming pool, a solarium, a "bronzarium," saunas, bowling alleys, and a massage room, with therapists to help ease any aches and pains. A shopping arcade contains a variety of boutiques and other interesting shops.

Hotel **Newa,** 34 Leningrader Strasse (tel. 49-62-71). Surrounded by a flat expanse of green lawn, with another high-rise building set immediately behind it, this buff-and-beige rectangle is supported by an even-larger one-story rectangle containing a popular glass-walled restaurant called the Leningrad. There is yet another restaurant, the Baltic, as well as a Café Newa, along with two salons, the Repin and Puschkin. You can dine here for as little as $6 a meal—that is, if you can get in (the tables are often assigned only to guests of the hotel). This Interhotel is across from the main station. Rooms are standard but fairly comfortable, costing from $38 nightly in a single with bath or shower. The rate in a double is $28 per person nightly. In all, the hotel is big, bustling, and fairly anonymous, often filled with tour groups from Eastern bloc countries. You'll find a flower shop and a sauna too. If you're assigned an accommodation on one of the upper floors, you'll have a spectacular view of the city.

Hotel **Königstein,** Prager Strasse (tel. 4-85-60), stands across from the Newa, also at the main station, of course. It was built near a pedestrian walkway planted with masses of flowers, which change seasonally. It's a big white monster of a building, offering 303 rooms, with an anonymous facade pierced by uninterrupted horizontal lines of glass. The rooms in fair weather are sunny and clean, and decorated in a predictably utilitarian modern, costing from $28 per person nightly in a room with private plumbing. Other facilities include a restaurant, a Dach garden, and a sauna. The restaurant, incidentally, is restricted to residents for most of the day. You'll have to wait for a table, and once you have one, you'll most often have to share it, perhaps with a couple visiting from the Soviet Union—which should lead to an interesting exchange, considering the language barrier!

Hotel Astoria, Ernst-Thälmann-Platz (tel. 4-41-71). You'll enjoy coffee on the beflowered sundeck of this five-story modern hotel whose inspiration was probably one of the dozens of private villas that once stood in the region. The windows are utilitarian and unadorned, and the facade is a buff-colored stucco, but the central building with its elongated wing still offers clean rooms and friendly, albeit cautious, service. Rates are from $28 per person in this 89-room hotel which has a restaurant, café, terrace, and bar, along with an Intershop selling souvenirs.

Motel Dresden, Münzmeisterstrasse (tel. 4-48-51), on the outskirts, is built on a more human scale than the monumental hotels within the city. This low-lying establishment is surrounded by green landscaping and a parasoled sun terrace near its glass-and-concrete modern facade. You'll be about two miles from the Dresden center here, but there's plenty of parking for your car in this motel-style arrangement. Rooms—clean, unimaginatively furnished—rent for $28 per person nightly with private plumbing. In all, 82 bedrooms are offered, along with a restaurant and a terrace, plus an Intershop selling souvenirs.

WHERE TO DINE: Chances are, you'll be eating in your hotel. If you dine out, Dresden also has some independent eateries, but not as many as are needed. One can only reflect nostalgically about all the restaurants, cafés, and beer gardens of yesterday.

Try the **Ratskeller,** in the cellar of the Rathaus (Town Hall; tel. 49-32-12). Here it's easy to strike up a conversation if there's no language problem. Tables are shared, and often your fellow diners are from Eastern Europe or the Soviet Union. My companions, a man and a woman from Berlin, spoke English, but we avoided politics, except for a grim reference to *darüber,* which I found out later means "over there," a common reference to the way East Germans refer to West Germany. You can get sauerbraten and wienerschnitzel here, along with plain roast beef and Hungarian goulash. Potatoes—boiled, fried, roasted, mashed, whatever—are always served. Desserts are simple, usually a fruit compote or ice cream. You'll spend about $8 for dinner, if that.

You can dine at **Am Gewandhaus,** 1 Ringstrasse (tel. 49-62-96), although the hotel of the same name in which it is housed is not open to Westerners. The restaurant specializes in excellent fish and meat dishes, served in what is reputed to be the finest dining room in the city. A meal costs around $6, but you must be sure to tip the headwaiter if you want a table.

Ungarische Gaststätte Szeged, on the second floor of a building at 6 Ernst-Thälmann-Platz, is the place to go for food cooked by recipes of the Austro-Hungarian Empire, as well as latter-day additions inspired by the cuisine of Budapest. If you're hungry for a little paprika, this is the restaurant for you. Expect to pay around $5.50 to $6 for a complete meal.

Sekundogenitur, Brühl Terrace (tel. 49-61-47), has a limited menu but a fine view. The terrace on which you dine is a fortified embankment on the other side of the Hofkirche, above the moorings of the paddle-steamers that ply the Elbe. Only one or two main courses are offered each day. Perhaps you'll be here when they serve their tasty sauerbraten. You might also get a good wienerschnitzel prepared in the authentic way (that is, with lard instead of butter). A goulash soup is a good beginning for a meal, and you can enjoy a wilted cucumber salad on the side. A complete meal will cost around $6.

Am Zwinger, the quadrangle of pavilions and galleries previewed above, is also a good place to go for food and drink. One of the buildings, just called **Am Zwinger,** has a lively beer cellar below and a more formal restaurant upstairs. Here you'll also find a konditorei where you can meet and perhaps chat with students of the technical university who come to linger over schnapps, which they take with a beer chaser. You can have a light lunch in the konditorei or in the beer cellar for around $3, while a complete meal in the restaurant will cost from $5.50 to $6, perhaps more.

For my final meal in Dresden—unless I am leaving on a weekend—I go to **Luisenhof,** 8 Bergbahnstrasse, where however good the food is, it takes second place to the magnificent view. Take the funicular railway up to the restaurant site, which has been called "the balcony of Dresden," high above the city. From here you can see the reemerging baroque skyline of the historic, carefully restored buildings and bridges. Try to avoid going here on weekends, when it is sure to be thronged with tourists, some of the five million persons who visit Dresden every year. A meal at Luisenhof will cost $6 and up.

A DAY TRIP TO MEISSEN: Few Western visitors overnight in Meissen, as accommodations are severely limited. The "city of porcelain" is most often visited on a day trip from Dresden. To reach it is very inexpensive, costing only M 1 (33¢) from the railway station in Dresden. If you're there in summer, the best way to go is to take a boat of the Weisse Flotte (White Fleet), leaving two times a day from Dresden's Brühl Terrace, that fortified embankment on the other side of the Hofkirche. The fare is only DM 1.50 (50¢), a great bargain in travel, as you get to enjoy the scenery along the Elbe.

Since 1710 Meissen has been known around the world as the center of the manufacture of Dresden china. The early makers of this so-called white gold were virtually held prisoner within Meissen. The princes who ruled the city didn't want the secret of the porcelain to escape. Of course it did, and other rivals imitated it.

Meissen lies on both banks of the Elbe, 15 miles northwest of Dresden. The **Altstadt** (Old Town) lies on the left bank.

Towering over the town is the **cathedral** on the Schlossberg. It's a marvelous early-Gothic building, whose bells are made of porcelain. It was actually built from 1200 to 1450 on the foundation of an even earlier structure. Meissen is very old, dating from 920. It became the seat of the Saxon bishops. Inside the cathedral you can see one of the works of Lucas Cranach the Elder. The Bishop's Castle is also on the hill.

Sharing the castle quarter with the cathedral and Bishop's Castle is **Albrechtsburg Castle** (tel. 29-20), where the first Meissen porcelain was made. The castle construction began in 1471 and went on intermittently until 1525, with restoration in the late 19th century. From 1710 to 1864 it was the site of the Meissen Porcelain Manufactory, and presently a museum tracing the production of the fine products is being set up on the fourth floor of the castle. Museum departments are already in existence; the history of the construction of this important monument of late-Gothic secular architecture is on the first floor. There is also an art collection with wooden effigies from the Middle Ages. The castle is open daily from 9 a.m. to 4 p.m.; closed in January and December 24, 25, 26, and 31. Admission is M 1.05 (35¢) for adults, M .55 (18¢) for children.

The city is known for its factories making pottery, porcelain, and glass. Guided tours go through the **Staatliche Porzellan-Manufaktur** April 1 to October 31 on Tuesday and Sunday from 8 a.m. to 4 p.m. You can see how the centuries-old manufacture of Dresden china is still carried on, many times using the same designs.

The terraces of the nearby vineyards in the Elbe valley produce a fine wine for which Meissen is also known, including the hard-to-obtain Meissner Domherr.

Most visitors in Meissen take lunch there, and there's no better place than one of the little cafés in the castle precincts. My favorite is the privately owned and run wine house of **Vincenz Richter,** at 12 An der Frauenkirche (tel. 32-85), just off the Market Square. It's run by Hannelore Müller. Here you can sample the famous wines of Meissen and get good, hearty food, a meal with wine costing around $8. The place dates from 1523.

5. Weimar and Buchenwald

It is with a certain irony that Weimar, which evokes German humanism, should be grouped with Buchenwald, the notorious concentration camp the Nazis built in the 1930s. But that is the nature of geography, as they stand near each other, demonstrating the best and worst of mankind.

Weimar itself, after Dresden and East Berlin, is the chief target in the GDR for the lover of German culture. The 1000-year-old town lies on the edge of the Thuringian forest. A 19th-century writer called it "one of the most walkable towns of Europe"—and so it is. The town can really name-drop: Goethe, Liszt, Bach, Schiller, Walter Gropius. These are just some of the famous names who have been linked to this city, a former Land of Thuringia in the Erfurt district, whose existence goes back to the ninth century.

The German national assembly met at Weimar on February 6, 1919, in the aftermath of World War I, and drafted a constitution a few months later, forming the "Weimar Republic." This led to a reestablishment of the German Reich, which was a democratic republic that was, regrettably, to dissolve into dictatorship 14 years later.

Unlike many of the cities of East Germany, Weimar still retains much of its old flavor, with its narrow winding streets left over from the Middle Ages and its high-pitched gables and roofs. There is no town in the GDR that has so many important monuments of German classical history that were spared from the bombings of World War II.

THE SIGHTS: You may want to head first for the government tourist agency, the **Weimar Informationscentrum,** at 4 Marktstrasse (tel. 21-73), which is open on Monday from 10 a.m. to 5 p.m., Tuesday to Friday from 9 a.m. to 5 p.m., and on Saturday from 8:30 a.m. to 1 p.m. and 1:30 to 4:30 p.m. You can purchase a map for M 1 (33¢), which will be most helpful in orientation. Ask at the Zentralkasse to purchase a wholesale museum ticket, entitling you to visit six of the most important cultural museums, including those associated with Goethe, for only M 3.05 ($1.01) for adults, M 1.25 (41¢) for children. Otherwise you must pay separate admissions: M 1.05 (35¢) for adults and M .50 (17¢) for children.

The museums of Weimar are all open from 9 a.m. to 5 p.m. (perhaps 4:30 p.m. in winter). Each museum shuts down for lunch, but there is always something open and always something to see if you've allowed, as most visitors do, only one day for exploring Weimar. Some museums shut down on Monday; others on Tuesday. Ask at the tourist office for museums likely to be closed during your visit.

The principal attraction of the town is the **Goethe National Museum,** 1 Am Frauenplan, where the poet lived from 1782 to 1832. It's an example of a German nobleman's house, a baroque structure built in 1709. There are 14 exhibition rooms, some of them pretty much as Goethe and his wife, Christiane Vulpius, left them. There is much original art in the house, and the library contains more than 5000 volumes. The writer's mineral collection is here also. At Weimar, Goethe held the post of minister of state, and although his reputation rests today on his writing, the rooms in which he lived reveal his diverse interest in science as well (he was an early advocate of the belief in the common origin of all animal life, for example). He died in Weimar on March 22, 1832. The crowning achievement of Goethe's life was, of course, the completion of *Faust,* and you might note with sardonic interest how the Communists treat this subject.

Goethe's **"Garden House"** (German name: Goethes Gartenhaus) stands in a park on the Ilm River. This is a plain wood cottage with a high-pitched roof, where the poet retreated for most of his summers to contemplate nature and anatomy. Goethe selected this house as his first residence when he came to Weimar. Even after he moved to other quarters, he still came here seeking peace and tranquility, describing the park around him as "infinitely beautiful."

The **Schillerhaus**, in Schillerstrasse, contains the rooms in which this great poet and philosopher lived. A friend of Goethe's, he was, after him, perhaps the greatest name in German literature. Schiller lived here with his family until his death in 1805. A museum has been installed, displaying mementos of his life and work. It also has a collection of costumes from dramas by Schiller. The attic rooms have been refurnished as they were believed to have been in Schiller's day. He wrote his last works here, including *Wilhelm Tell.*

The Schiller house is opposite the Gänsemännchen, which is named after the Germanic legend of the little boy who owned the goose that laid the golden egg.

The house of yet another famous artist, Franz Liszt (1811–1886), can also be visited, as it has been turned into a museum. The **Liszt House,** 17 Marienstrasse, is where the Hungarian composer and pianist spent time during the last period of his life. It is said that he "strove to express the deepest romantic emotion in his playing and compositions." His daughter, Cosima, was to become the wife of Richard Wagner. A two-story building, the Liszt House was once the home for the royal gardeners of Weimar. You'll find several mementos, both personal and musical, from the composer's life, including communications between Liszt and his son-in-law. You can also see pianos at which he played and taught his pupils.

The **Kunstsammlungen zu Weimar,** 4 Burgplatz (tel. 6-18-31), contains the state art collections, among other exhibits. Under the guidance of Goethe, the palace was erected in 1789 and completed in 1803 (the previous castle had burned down in 1774; only a tower survived). In one of the wings are a series of galleries dedicated not only to Schiller and Goethe, but to two other famous names also associated with Weimar: Herder (1744–1803), the German critic and philosopher who was a pioneer of the *Sturm and Drang* movement, and Wieland (1733–1813), the poet and critic who wrote the satirical romance *The Republic of Fools.* The second floor displays works by Lucas Cranach the Elder. On some of the upper floors you can see art of the famous Bauhaus movement, led by Walter Gropius, which once flourished in Weimar until it was expelled. The school of design, *Das Staatliche Bauhaus Weimar,* was principally responsible for revolutionizing the teaching of sculpture, painting, industrial arts, and architecture throughout the Western world. Followers around the globe may have been impressed, but not the good people of Weimar. They "tolerated" the school until 1925, bombarding it in the press, until it finally moved to Dessau, where it was to survive until the Nazis closed it in 1933, claiming it was a center of "Communist intellectualism."

Nearby, on the Marktplatz, you can view the **Lucas Cranach the Elder House,** which is decorated with bouquets and Neptunian adventures.

In the **cemetery,** you can see the controversial **Denkmal der Marz Gefallenen,** a monument to the revolutionaries slain in 1919 that hastened the exit of Gropius from Weimar, along with his Bauhaus followers. But most Germans visit the cemetery today to pause in tribute at the grand ducal family vault, where Goethe and Schiller, friends in life, also lie side by side in death.

The **Kirms-Krackow-Haus,** 10 Jakobstrasse, is one of the curiosities of Weimar. It's a residence with classical furnishings, which also contains exhibits of the *Sturm und Drang* movement of such "noblemen" as Goethe, but with a Communist overlay, the whole mixture a strange set of bedfellows.

Follow the Rittergasse until the end when you come upon the **Wittumspalais,** which was the residence of the Duchess Anna Amalia. The old ducal dowerhouse is devoted to mementos of the German classical Enlightenment.

On a more ecclesiastical vein, you can follow Vorwerksgasse to the Gothic church, the **Herderkirche,** with an alterpiece by Lucas Cranach the Elder. It may be visited daily from 10:30 to 11:30 a.m. and 2:30 to 3:30 p.m., short visiting hours indeed.

Other churches worth visiting (if they're open) include the Gothic **Stadtkirche,** dating from the early 1400s, with an interesting altarpiece triptych, and the **Hofkirche,** the court church, which is also ancient.

In the so-called Goethepark you can see the neoclassical summer residence of Carl August, the **Römisches Haus.** The location is near the Belvederer Allee on the other side of the Ilm River. The duke wanted to please Goethe, whose fondness for Roman architecture was well known.

Some two miles south from Weimar stands the baroque **Château of Belvedere,** with its open-air theater where stage productions were presented in Goethe's day. This was a favorite retreat of Anna Amalia and the "enlightened" Weimar set, including Carl August. It was a hunting seat and pleasure schloss in the 18th century. An orangerie was built, along with the open-air theater and an English-style park. A collection of historical coaches is here. In the château are displays of the daintiness of rococo art. It's open Wednesday to Sunday from 9 a.m. to 1 p.m. and 2 to 5:30 p.m. From the Goetheplatz, take the "Belvedere Express" bus, which leaves about every hour (more buses on weekends).

You can also visit **Tiefurt Palace,** on the outskirts of Weimar. This was formerly the site of another summer retreat for Duchess Anna Amalia. Guests today can wander through its pavilions and gardens. To reach it, go east along the Tiefurter Allee. It can also be visited by bus leaving from the main station close to the Schillerstrasse.

Buchenwald

The worst for last! A train from the Weimar Hauptbahnhof will take you to Buchenwald, Hitler's concentration camp and death chamber where both racial and political prisoners, including the Communist leader Ernst Thälmann, were confined and brutally murdered from 1937 until 1945 when the starving and diseased final prisoners, awaiting extermination, were released by the U.S. Army. On the Ettersberg, four miles northwest of Weimar, Buchenwald was the last site that some 56,000 unfortunate souls saw before their extermination. It is reminiscent of a similar camp, Dachau, outside Munich. You can safely skip the propaganda film shown. It seems to be an attack on the capitalist West, and there is a strong suggestion that Buchenwald existed as a camp to persecute Communists.

Buchenwald virtually eliminated the Jewish population of East Germany —that is, those who had not already fled. The attempt on the part of the Soviets to turn this into a propaganda forum against the West only continues the horror. It is estimated that a quarter of a million people were sent here during the camp's reign of infamy. A memorial with a cluster of "larger-than-life" people, victims of fascism, was created by Prof. Fritz Cremer to honor the victims of 32 nations who lost their lives at Buchenwald.

FOOD AND LODGING: Back in Weimar, if you've made the proper arrangements, you can check into the **Hotel Elephant,** am Markt (tel. 6-14-71). The elegant facade of this circa-1696 building is set off with stone corner mullions, a beautifully weathered terracotta roof, an elongated series of bay windows stretching from the second to the third floors, and best of all, a frontage onto the old marketplace containing a dried-up fountain dedicated to Neptune. Many celebrities have visited this hotel, including Tolstoy and Bach. Even Hitler was a guest. The Elephant became famous, however, through the Thomas Mann novel, *Lotte in Weimar* (published in English under the title *The Beloved Returns*). A state-run establishment, it has 120 rooms and apartments, some without bath. Singles rent for $42 nightly, and doubles cost from $33 per person. The Elephantkeller in the basement serves some of the best food in town, where you drink beer and enjoy hearty specialties, such as a zweibelmarkt salad (made with onions). Otherwise, you can dine in the more formal and expensive restaurant upstairs. A meal in the cellar costs $4, while in the restaurant you'll pay from $10 for a meal. The wine served here is likely to have come from Bulgaria or Rumania.

If you don't want to go with the Elephant, you'll find another historic place in Weimar, the **Zum Weissen Schwann,** on Frauentorstrasse, which was known to Goethe. A meal here isn't likely to cost more than $8, and for that you'll get some specialties of the region, perhaps Thüringer rotwurst (blood sausage), Thüringer klösse (dumplings), and Thüringer rostbrätl (roast joint).

At some point in your visit, you may want to take time out to visit a café. The most popular is the **Café Esplanade.** In the center of town, this café is loud and much favored by the local people.

If you want something more intimate, head to the **Goethecafé** on Wielandstrasse. Tables are freely shared, and many residents speak a bit of English.

6. Thuringia

One of the famous German Lands, this heavily forested district lies in the most southwesterly sector of the GDR. Thuringian forest covers most of it, and it also contains some of the most historic cities in the country, including Eisenbach. (Other cities in the area, such as Weimar and Erfurt, are previewed separately.)

Beerberg, at 3225 feet, is the chief elevation, and its principal river is the Saale. The history of the region is long. The fifth-century Thuringians, for example, were vassals to Attila the Hun.

For those rare Westerners who have time to explore it, this is one of the most unspoiled regions in both German countries. Not only are there forests and steep slopes, but clear mountain streams and unusual vegetation.

For motorists seeking individual destinations, we'll briefly explore its major centers, beginning with:

EISENACH: This historic town lies on the northwestern slopes of the Thuringian forest, at the confluence of the Nesse and Hörsel Rivers, some 30 miles west of Erfurt, which we'll visit later. This is the home of those funny-looking little Wartburg cars that you most likely saw during your visit to East Berlin.

It's best known as the site of **Wartburg Castle,** which stands on a hill 600 feet above the town. This ancient castle from 1400 belonged to the landgraves of Thuringia. It has now been turned into a regional museum. Once it was the home of the medieval Minnesänger poets, who were immortalized by Wagner in *Tannhaüser.* Students of Martin Luther will know that it was at this castle that, upon his return from the Diet of Worms in 1521, he hid out until he could complete his translation of the Bible. He is also said to have "fought the Devil with ink" at Wartburg.

Part of the castle has been turned into a hotel and restaurant, opening onto beautiful views of the city.

Eisenach is also famously associated with Johann Sebastian Bach, who was born here in 1685. The **Bach Haus** at 21 Am Frauenplat contains many mementos of the Bach family, along with a collection of musical instruments. It has been turned into a museum.

The house where Fritz Reuter lived from 1868 to 1874, known as the **Reuter House,** is also a museum, commemorating this German novelist who made Plattdeutsch a literary language. Although arrested for high treason in 1833 and condemned to death by the Prussian government, he was later set free by a general amnesty. He died in Eisenbach on July 12, 1874. The museum also has a Wagner collection.

You can also visit the **Lutherhaus** of the Cotta family where the famous reformer stayed as a schoolboy.

All Eisenach museums are generally open from 10 a.m. to 6 p.m., including Sunday. Each one is closed one day a week (either Monday or Tuesday). Ask at the city tourist office for specifics, and expect to pay from M 1.50 (50¢) for adults for admission.

While in the city you might also want to visit the Romanesque **Church of St. Nicholas,** which was restored in 1887, and **St. George's,** which was built in the late Gothic style (it has been restored many times).

It's unlikely that you'll spend the night in Eisenach. Most Westerners are booked into hotels in nearby towns such as Weimar. However, Eisenach does have two good hotels. The first is the **Stadt Eisenach,** 11–13 Luisenstrasse (tel. 36-82), which has modestly furnished rooms, 85 beds in all, costing from $22 per person in a bathless chamber. The hotel has a restaurant offering hearty Thuringian specialties, a simple meal costing $6.

Parkhotel, 2 Wartburg Allee (tel. 62-35-291), is the "second choice," and it's an extremely good buy, even though often filled with visitors from the Eastern bloc nations. The hotel has a restaurant, plus a state-run gift shop where you can make purchases. Rooms are simply furnished without private facilities and cost from $20 per person nightly.

SAALFELD: At the opposite extremity of the Thüringer Wald, Saalfeld is another historic city, visited chiefly because it has the most stunning stalactite caves in the GDR (ask at the tourist information office about guided tours).

It lies on the left bank of the previously mentioned Saale River, about 25 miles south from Weimar and some 75 "rail" miles from Leipzig. It seems a shame the town is so little known by Western tourists, although East Germans visit it.

Still partially encircled by its medieval bastions and walls, many of its old houses, spared from war damage, evoke the Middle Ages. A palace was constructed here in 1679 on the foundation of St. Peter's Abbey, a Benedictine order. Among its historic churches, St. John's was built at the beginning of the 13th century in the Gothic style, and so was the Rathaus, constructed in 1537. The Kitzerstein Palace, on an eminence above the Saale, is believed to have been originally constructed by Henry I, the German king. The present structure, however, dates from around the 16th century.

ARNSTADT: Arnstadt lies about 16 miles southwest of Erfurt (coming up) on the River Gera, at the northern sector of the Thüringer Wald. It is one of the oldest towns in Thuringia, first mentioned in records of the year 704. The most outstanding attraction is the famous "Mon Plaisir" doll collection in the **Neue Schloss** (New Castle) **Museum,** which also has on display East Asian, Meissen, and Thuringian porcelain as well as Brussels carpets. The town museum, also in the castle, traces the history of Arnstadt and its surroundings.

Two churches are of interest: the double-towered **Liebfrauenkirche,** dating from the 12th and 14th centuries and reflecting the transition from Romanesque to Gothic architecture, and **Bach Church,** which was called the Bonifatiuskirche when Johann Sebastian Bach was organist here from 1703 to 1707. See also the Renaissance **Rathaus** (Town Hall).

To the northwest of Arnstadt is **Drei Gleichen,** a trio of castles on both sides of the autobahn. Wachsenburg Castle, which has a museum and restaurant within its walls, was built around 900. It occupies a commanding position from the 1390-foot-high Keuperkegel near Holzhausen, allowing a panoramic view of the countryside of Thuringia. To the west is the Mühlburg, the oldest of the Thuringian castles, which has unfortunately been allowed to fall into decay, except for its tower. Opposite the Mühlburg, north of the autobahn, is the Schloss Gleichen ruin (Wanderslebener Gleiche) on a 1220-foot height.

GERA: In the region of the Weisse Elster (White Elster), a river in the Vogtland area, Gera merits a stopover. It stands on the banks of the river some 45 miles southwest of Leipzig. It was first mentioned in records of the year 995 and referred to as a town in 1237. Noted even in its medieval days for the manufacture of cloth and linen, Gera suffered much from invaders. It was sacked by the Bohemians in the mid-15th century and burned by the Swedes in 1639. Some buildings survived both of these assaults, with the **Rathaus** dating from the 16th century. There is also a chemist's shop from the 17th century. The **Gera Theatre,** still an important cultural institution of the town, has a 350-year-old tradition.

You can visit the orangerie, built between 1729 and 1732, the municipal museum, the Botanical Gardens, and other sites of historic interest and beauty, as well as the three old churches. They are **Marienkirche,** parts of which date from the 12th century, including a wooden carved altar; **Trinitatiskirche,** enlarged in 1611 by incorporating elements from 1323 and with a 1500 pulpit; and **Salvatorkirche,** dating from the 18th century.

A side trip from Gera worth taking is to **Wünschendorf** to see the old Wehrkirche (Defense Church) on the Veitsberg, one of the oldest East Thuringian edifices, as well as the 18th-century shingle-roofed wooden bridge and the Pramonstratenser Monastery of Mildenfurth, built in 1193.

Taking the road up the Elster from Gera, you come to Weida, a little town dominated by the 12th-century **Osterburg Castle,** which was once the residence of the princes of Reuss who took possession of Gera and had the castle built on the site of a ninth-century structure. The castle now houses the district museum and a youth hostel.

For overnight stopovers or for dining, you can patronize the **Hotel Gera,** Strasse der Republik (tel. 2-29-91). In season, you'll find masses of marigolds planted densely together on the flat lawn in front of this seven-story hotel. The sleek, streamlined architecture of the building itself may not seem inspired, but the windows are large, the rooms bright and clean, and you can enjoy the beer hall, the café, and the sun terrace, along with three restaurants clustered here which specialize in Thuringian specialties, a meal costing around $6. To stay here in a room with private facilities costs $31 per person nightly in a double. Singles cost from $33.

OBERHOF: Chances are, if you're a worker in Bulgaria, as a vacation destination Oberhof will be as glamorous as St. Moritz is for a West German. This is a resort attracting scenic gulpers who want to hike in the mountains in summer and winter-sports enthusiasts drawn to its skiing. It has toboggan runs, among many other outdoor activities.

You can also visit a botanical garden for alpine flora. There are a lot of "folkloric" restaurants in the mountains which the tourist office will direct you to. These include the Forsthaus Sattelbach. Many guests who stay at Oberhof take hiking tours along the Rennsteig ridgeway, enjoying the scenery of Thuringian Forest. The first stage from Oberhof to Frauenwald is a distance of some 12½ miles.

In your tour of Thuringia, you will most likely pass through Oberhof. For food and lodging, it offers the **Hotel Panorama,** Theodor-Neubauer-Strasse (tel. 5-01). The architect of this resort hotel courageously decided to construct two separate buildings and link them visually by sloping their rooflines in dramatically acute angles. The result here is a successful combination of triangles and rectangles, which forms one of the most attractive state-owned hotels in the GDR. The hotel offers 373 rooms and apartments, plus five restaurants (one of them is called Hanoi), along with a café, sun terrace, and nightclub. Sports facilities include a swimming pool, sauna, massage parlor, bowling alley, and minigolf. Bed and breakfast costs from $33 per person nightly, and meals begin at $6.

SUHL: This is considered the unofficial capital of the Thüringer Wald. Mainly in the 19th and 20th centuries, it became famous for manufacturing sporting guns. It is one of the most popular tourist regions in the GDR, often attracting many visitors from the Eastern bloc countries, including a lot of Soviet holiday makers.

The manufacture of hunting and sports guns continues to the present, and you can follow the history of small arms in the **Weapons Museum,** where exhibits and displays trace their development and manufacture from 1535. The museum is in the Malzhaus, a timber-frame structure dating from 1650, beside the River Lauter. The landmark of the city is a sculpture of an armorer on the top of a fountain.

Besides the Malzhaus, Suhl has a number of other timber-frame houses dating from the 16th and 17th centuries, as well as two historic churches. The **Hauptkirche,** originally built in late Gothic style but later extended by adding baroque elements, contains a beautiful rococo pulpit altar. The **Church of the Holy Cross** (Kreuzkirche) is a baroque structure.

From Suhl it's an easy trip to the city of **Meiningen** to see the **Elisabethenburg,** a 17th-century castle; to **Schleusingen,** which has an exhibition center tracing the history of the toy industry; and into the Thuringian Forest.

The **Hotel Thüringen Tourist,** Ernst-Thälmann-Platz (tel. 2-53-6), stands on a square named after the Communist leader martyred at Buchenwald, a gloomy note for a resort hotel to sound. Within the city limits, the entrance to this hotel is boldly announced in huge black letters on an aluminum background. The starkness of the sign is relieved somewhat by the parasols at the sun terrace. If you've forgotten your wristwatch, you can always tell what time it is by glancing at the begonias on the front lawn. There, a team of gardeners have laboriously planted a clockface ten feet across, growing out of miniature shrubs and flowers. Over 100 bedrooms are available inside, each decorated anonymously, but all clean and comfortable. The charge is from $28 per person nightly for bed and breakfast based on double occupancy. Singles cost $6. You can buy meal vouchers beginning at $6. The hotel has a restaurant with specialties of the Thüringen Wald, as well as a terrace café and nightclub. An Intershop on the premises sells GDR souvenirs.

7. Jena and Erfurt

In the vicinity of Weimar, two towns attract two very different types of visitors: Jena, the nostalgic-loving devotees of the German Romantic Period, and Erfurt, the disciples of Martin Luther.

ERFURT: After a half-hour train ride beginning at the Weimar Hauptbahnhof, you'll be delivered to 1200-year-old Erfurt. After arriving, head for the government-run information bureau at 37 Bahnhofstrasse (tel. 2-62-67), where you can obtain data about what's happening locally and what might be open on the occasion of your visit.

On the Gera River, the city, part of the Land (state) of Thuringia, lies right on the autobahn from Berlin to Frankfurt am Main.

The Augustinian monastery, where the reformer, Luther, was a monk for some five years, is now used as an orphanage. Beginning in these monasteries, gardens originally cultivated by monks just grew and grew until Erfurt today is world famous as a horticultural center, known for its wide variety of flowers and vegetables. An international horticultural exhibition is held in Cyriaksburg Park.

One of the curiosities of the town is the **Krämer Bridge,** from the 14th century, with houses on both sides, nearly three dozen in all. This Krämerbrücke (Shopkeepers' Bridge), spanning the Gera, is now filled with book stalls, cafés, and antique shops, and you'll certainly want to spend some time here browsing.

Well-preserved patrician mansions built in both the Gothic and Renaissance styles are the historic town's dominant features. Many of its narrow streets are lined with half-timbered houses. These houses, for the most part, stood before World War II. Miraculously, Erfurt was the only town of its size in East Germany that wasn't virtually leveled in the bombing raids. The American army liberated it in the spring of 1945 before turning it over to the Russians.

The ecclesiastical center of town is the **Domberg,** where two Catholic churches stand side by side, their 15th-century walls almost closing in on each other at one point. The **cathedral,** begun in the 12th century, was later rebuilt in the 13th century in the Gothic style. It contains many ecclesiastical treasures and some 15th-century stained glass. Its neighbor is the **Church of St. Severus.** The most beautiful churches of Erfurt, "rich in towers," are the Romanesque **Peterskirche,** dating from the 12th and 14th centuries; the **Predigerkirche,** a 13th-century house of worship of the Order of Mendicant Friars; and three churches from the early Middle Ages—**Ägidienkirche, Michaeliskirche,** and **Allerheiligengeistkirche.**

Of special interest is the **Steinerne Chronik** (chronical of stone) in Michaelisstrasse, a combination of architectural styles from different eras.

At the **Museum am Anger,** a splendid baroque structure, you can see exhibits relating to prehistoric times and on up through the Middle Ages, as well as displays regarding the town's history.

The **Museum of Thuringian Folk Art** gives an insight into the history of Thuringian crafts.

In the Renaissance building, Zum Stockfisch, dating from 1607, you'll find the **Natural Science Museum,** with illustrations of the flora and fauna as well as of the geological characteristics of the Erfurt region.

For food and lodging, try the **Erfurter Hof,** am Bahnhofsvorplatz (tel. 5-11-51), an Interhotel. This was at one time a very grand hotel, and over the years it has hosted many famous guests, among them the former chancellor of West Germany, Willy Brandt, who came here in 1970 seeking reconciliation with the GDR. The most expensive hotel in town, it has many eight-foot-tall windows, plus small wrought-iron balconies in front, the facade done in sculptured limestone. Recent renovations have added a covering and picture windows to the facade of the ground floor, although the original upper stories remain. Inside, you'll find four restaurants, along with two cafés, high-ceilinged rooms, a nightclub, and a flower shop. The hotel's rooms are among the best in the GDR, as reflected by the rather high price scale of $32 per person nightly for bed and breakfast in a double unit with private bath or shower. Singles cost $42. You can dine here for about $10 for a most satisfying meal.

Hotel Kosmos, Juri-Gagarin-Ring (tel. 5-51-0). The bronze-tinted glass of the low rectangle of the first floor will reflect your image as you try to locate the point where the skyscraper ends, hundreds of feet above you. This is one of the GDR's newest hotels, with a rarely used color, orange (not red), highlighting the vertical expanse of the tower. Its 332 rooms are modern, sunny, and clean, decorated in the sterile Interhotel format. The cost is from $28 per person nightly for bed and breakfast in a double with private bath or shower. Singles go for $38. Inside you'll find a café (called the Orbit), a restaurant, serving meals that begin at $8, a "dancebar," and a flowershop.

JENA: A 12-minute train ride from Weimar, 12 miles away, the university town of Jena conjures up the leaders of the German Romantic movement. Badly damaged during World War II, the town lies on both banks of the Saale River about 57 miles southwest of Leipzig. As a city, it dates back to the 13th century. The famous Battle of Jena in 1806, in which Napoleon defeated the Prussians, was fought to the north. In spite of war destruction, Jena still has a market square from the Middle Ages and many old patrician homes and narrow streets.

Today university buildings take over the site of the old ducal Jena Schloss, where Goethe wrote his *Hermann und Dorothea*. Martin Luther spent a night in the Hotel Schwarzer Bär, 2 Lutherplatz (tel. 2-25-43), after his flight from the Wartburg. The **University of Jena** dates from 1558, reaching the zenith of its fame when its teaching staff numbered among them such great men as Hegel, Schelling, Fichte, Schlegel, and Schiller. Karl Marx wrote his doctor's thesis here. Friedrich von Schlegel, the German poet, critic, and scholar, the younger brother of August Wilhelm von Schlegel, lectured at Jena as a *Privatdozent* (official but unpaid lecturer). His older brother completed his translation of Shakespeare at Jena (considered one of the best poetical translations in the world). At Jena, these famous brothers were leaders in the new romantic criticism.

In the heart of town, the **Weigel Haus** was the former home of an astronomer of the same name. The building has a deep shaft through which stars can be seen even in daytime.

The most interesting ecclesiastical structure is the Church of St. Michael from the 15th century. The Fuchs-Turm (or fox tower) was once notorious for its student orgies. Finally, the Zeiss firm of optical instrument makers has its headquarters in Jena, and they have opened a Planetarium.

For food and lodging (the latter arranged in advance), seek out the **Hotel International,** Ernst-Thalmänn-Ring (tel. 88-80). The facade curves around a street corner in the heart of town, and the garden in front is planted with seasonal flowers and graced with jets of water. The facade of the second floor is almost entirely made of glass, behind which you'll find three restaurants and a café, serving meals in the $5 to $8 range. Windows for the boxy bedrooms face the square and are airtight, offering good soundproofing. If you've gone through the formalities of reserving a room, you'll find units costing from $27 per person in a double, $29 in a single.

8. The Harz Mountains

Known for its folklore and traditions, the Harz Mountains, in the southwest sector of East Germany, are also extolled for their scenic beauty. As the last stronghold of paganism in Germany, this is still a land of legends and fanciful names. It is said that the last bear was killed in the Harz in 1705, the last lynx in 1817. The wolf has also become extinct, but there are wildcats, badgers, deer, and the sly fox. The beech tree that grows in the Harz range has an unusual size and great beauty, and walnut trees abound. The region is also pocked by limestone caves. Much of the Middle Ages, spared from war damage, remains in old towns with their churches and castles.

Of all the many charming towns and "townlets" in the Harz, one of my favorites is—

WERNIGERODE: A romantic hamlet with a castle perched on Agnesberg hill overlooking it, Wernigerode has many half-timbered houses in its narrow streets left over from medieval days. The town stands on the northern slopes of the Harz in the Magdeburg district. In its earliest days the town was ruled by the counts of Wernigerode, who date back to the early 12th century. They held sway until their downfall in 1429. Wernigerode was absorbed into Prussia in 1714.

Perhaps the most interesting structure in town is the framework **Rathaus,** dating from the 16th century and standing at the junction of Breitestrasse and Markt Strasse.

The castle referred to at **Agnesberg** contains a feudal museum, tracing the history of vassals and whatever, and open to the public from 10 a.m. to 6 p.m., charging an admission of M 1.50 (50¢).

For your most exciting adventure, you can take one of the many narrow-gauge steam railways that still exist in the GDR. For just M .50 (20¢), you can board the train and go up past Brocken, the highest peak in the mountains, which was immortalized by Goethe in the "Walpurgisnacht" section of *Faust.*

NORDHÄUSEN: The southern terminus of the rail trip from Wernigerode is this town, which lies on the Zorge to the south of the Harz range. A flight of steps connects the upper and lower parts of town. Near the Rathaus, which dates from the Middle Ages, is **Roland's Column,** an ancient landmark symbolizing free trade. Nordhäusen is known today because it has distilleries turning out **Korn Schnapps,** the best known schnapps in the GDR. Curiously, the drink is not readily available in town, as all of it seemingly is exported because of its popularity and the need to raise hard cash.

QUEDLINBURG: Quedlinburg Castle, near the Harz range, was for many centuries the residence of the abbesses of Quedlinburg, who ranked among the princes of the empire and had no church superior except the pope himself. They held sway until the secularization of the abbey in 1803.

Spared the destruction of war, the town still basks dreamily in the Middle Ages, with its framework houses, narrow little winding lanes, and Schlossberg, whose tiara is the **cathedral** of Quedlinburg, with towers from the 19th century rising out of a medieval structure. At the Marktplatz, the Rathaus is built in the Renaissance style.

Within the castle precincts, you can order a good lunch at the **Schlosskrug,** on Müllerstrasse (tel. 28-36), in the forecourt of the castle. The cost is rarely more than $8. Should you arrive too late for lunch, you can also stop over here for afternoon coffee and delicious little cakes.

Accommodations in all of the little towns and hamlets considered so far are extremely limited, and you might even be discouraged by the government to attempt to overnight there, unless you have relatives, of course.

For your base in the Harz mountains, I suggest the following city:

MAGDEBURG: Razed by Allied bombing in the last year of the war, Magdeburg has been rebuilt under the Communists. It is the largest inland port in East Germany, as well as the junction of many important rail lines and highways. Standing mainly on the left bank of the Elbe some 90 miles southwest of Berlin, Magdeburg was the capital of the former Prussian province of Saxony. Once a member of the Hanseatic League, the city became known for its *Magdeburger Recht,* or Magdeburg law, a type of municipal administration that was adopted all over Germany and in many parts of Eastern Europe.

The **cathedral** of Magdeburg is dedicated to St. Catherine and St. Maurice. The complex has two 345-foot-high towers, which first saw the light of day in 1209 but that were not completed until 1520. Over the years the Romanesque style gave way to Gothic. It has a three-nave basilica with a polygonal choir-gallery and a ring of chapels.

The oldest church in Magdeburg is the **Liebfrauenkirche,** a Romanesque structure from the 11th century which was completed two centuries later (the citizens of Magdeburg took a long time on their churches). The Prussians restored it in the closing years of the 19th century.

The **Rathaus** (Town Hall) was built in the Renaissance style in 1691 and expanded in 1866. A copy of the famous equestrian statue of Otto I, erected in 1290, stands on this square. The original, spared from the war, was moved to the **Civic Museum** on Otto-von-Guericke-Strasse.

For food and lodging, the **Hotel International,** a four-star selection, stands on Otto-von-Guericke-Strasse (tel. 38-40), named after the most famous citizen of Magdeburg, its former mayor who lived in the 17th century. Although gargantuan, this 358-room hotel breaks up the monotony of its facade with criss-cross ribs of concrete reinforcing the windows, giving the effect of a pleasing checkerboard. The expanses of green around the hotel are large enough to keep out the noise of traffic. The rooms themselves are without character, in the standardized "peas-in-a-pod" format common to GDR hostelries. However, each chamber is comfortably furnished, costing from $27 per person nightly in a double with private bath. Singles run $38. You'll certainly enjoy people-watching in the hotel restaurants, one of them called Moskwa, or taking coffee in the Café Wien, followed by after-dinner drinks in one of the two salons (the Magdeburg or, test your geography, the Donezk). There's also a nightclub on the premises, along with an Intershop.

9. The Erzgebirge

One of the least visited (by Western tourists) sections of the GDR, the Erzgebirge (ore mountains) section lies in the southeast, near the border with Czechoslovakia. Its roads, except for an occasional Soviet military vehicle, are virtually free of traffic, except around big cities such as Karl-Marx-Stadt.

It is a land of wooded hills and mountains, suitable for hiking or driving along badly kept roads, discovering some hamlets that seem little changed in 40 years. You'll come upon caves left over from mining days and the ruins of an occasional castle.

All in all, the Erzgebirge qualifies as an offbeat adventure in travel.

KARL-MARX-STADT: The district's chief city, Karl-Marx-Stadt was known as the old Saxon city of Chemnitz until 1953. On the River Chemnitz at the foot of the Erz mountain range, it was severely damaged in the Allied bombing raids of World War II, but has been rebuilt, albeit in a rather characterless way.

Originally it was a trading post on the salt route to Prague. Over the centuries it has always been connected to industry, as it is today. For example, it made the first German tools and the first German locomotives. Today its factories turn out everything from underwear to textiles, and are responsible for 15% of the gross GDR output. Because of the availability of its hotel accommodations, my suggestion is to use the city only as a base for exploring the southeastern part of the GDR.

You can walk from the Hauptbahnhof to the Market Plaza, along the "Street of Nations." At Schillerplatz, you'll see a memorial to Engels and Marx.

In the northwest, the **Schlossbergmuseum,** open from 10 a.m. to 6 p.m., charging M 1.50 (50¢) for admission, was formerly a Benedictine monastery established in 1136. Fortified as a castle in 1546, it today contains artifacts of the region, tracing the history of Chemnitz. Seek out the interesting sculpture collection in the Gothic church of the castle.

Once the city had two dozen medieval towers, of which only the **Rote Turm** (red tower) stands today (it was originally built as a courthouse).

Where to Stay

Kongress, Karl-Marx-Allee (tel. 68-30). Immediately next to the futuristic Stadthalle stands this ultramodern hotel complex. Towering over its neighbors, it encompasses more than 300 rooms between its concrete slabs, which are arranged in vertical lines to emphasize the building's height. Rooms are standardized, costing from $32 per person nightly for bed and breakfast in a double, $48 in a single. Meals in one of the hotel's four restaurants, carrying such exotic names as Pasardshik and Irkutsk, begin at $8. There is a wealth of other facilities as well, including two bars, two cafés, and a nightclub. The health facilities include an exercise room, sauna, solarium, and massage parlors.

Chemnitzer Hof, Theaterplatz (tel. 6-04-21), honors the old name of the city. Breathing an aura of solidity, the massive concrete blocks of the facade of this hotel allow ample room for the oversize windows of the ground-floor restaurants. The windows of the upper stories are rhythmically arranged below the five-foot orange letters announcing the name of the hotel. Once inside, however, you'll find that the hotel is only a third of the size of most of the government-run hotels of the GDR. It offers 106 comfortable bedrooms, costing from $27 per person nightly for bed and breakfast. The Chemnitzer has three restaurants, plus a bar and a nightclub popular with businessmen in Karl-Marx-Stadt.

TOURING IN THE ENVIRONS:

TOURING IN THE ENVIRONS: A number of interesting excursions are possible from Karl-Marx-Stadt, either on a day-trip basis or to stay overnight in one of the little towns in the Erzgebirge mountains. On the town's outskirts, visit **Burg Rabenstein,** a 12th-century castle, and the Rabenstein group of rocks, Felsendome.

At nearby **Pelzmühle,** you can take pleasure steamers for a trip along the river.

Zwickau, the town where composer Robert Schumann was born, has a number of architectural monuments of different eras.

An interesting tour is to the huge **Augustusburg,** a Renaissance castle built in 1572 as the hunting seat of the Saxon electors. It now houses the Erzgebirgian Zoological Museum and a motorcycle museum. The castle chapel has an altar painting by Lucas Cranach the Younger. The well house, which is architecturally interesting, has a 561-foot-deep well.

From the Augustusburg, it's an easy run to the scenically beautiful **Kriebstein Dam,** which is a paradise for lovers of water sports.

Oberwiesenthal is the highest town in the GDR, lying more than 3000 feet above sea level. This is an important mountain health resort and winter sports center, lying at the foot of the **Fichtelberg,** some 4000 feet high. At the summit you'll find an attractive restaurant. You can get good mountain food at quite reasonable prices—$5 to $6 for a complete meal. A suspension railway takes you up to the Fichtelberg. A magnificent panoramic view of the Upper Erzgebirge is possible from the 132-foot observation tower.

The most famous town in the Erzgebirge is probably little **Seiffen,** widely known for its woodcarving, its toy museum, and the display workshops of turners and joiners (woodworkers). The Seiffen Toy Museum will acquaint you with the development of Erzgebirge Mountain toys. Nearby in the Sehma Valley is the **Frohnauer Hammer,** an iron-processing center from the 15th and 16th centuries which has been rebuilt as a monument to the history of technology. You can dine here in a restaurant that was a former forge owner's house.

Klingenthal and **Markneukirchen** are known throughout the world for the musical instruments made here for centuries. You can see what may be Europe's largest collection of the instruments in the Markneukirchen museum.

One of the most impressive towns of the Obererzgebirge is **Annaberg-Buchholz,** about 2000 feet above sea level, some 22 miles south of Karl-Marx-Stadt and quite close to Oberwiesenthal, just visited. This was once an area known for silver mines. Towering above the town is St.-Annen-Kirche (St. Anne's Church), dedicated in 1520, with beautifully designed reticulated vaulting. Annaberg is known for its bobbin-lace making. The Erzgebirge Museum contains a wealth of information on the history of the Upper Erzgebirge and its folk art. Here also are two former homes of prosperous silver-mine owners of the Middle Ages. The mines were closed about 1600 because of low yields.

In the east Erzgebirge lies **Freiberg** (Freyberg), an old Saxon mining town 19 miles southwest of Dresden. Among the sights of interest here is Donats Tower, the remains of the medieval fortifications. You can also see old miners' houses in narrow, twisting little lanes. St. Nicholas Church, a baroque structure, stands on the Buttermarkt. You can also see the town theater, rebuilt from the house of a rich merchant, the Rathaus on the Obermarkt, along with attractive old burgher houses with their colorful painting and gilding. The gem of Freiberg is the late-Gothic cathedral, with wood sculptures on slender pillars and reticulated vaulting, ceiling paintings, a tulip pulpit, and a huge Silbermann organ from 1714. This is the oldest of the 31 organs made by the master hand of Silbermann which still exist. The Golden Door of the old Marienkirche (St. Mary's Church), from the 13th century, built into the south side of the cathedral, is worth seeing.

10. The Baltic

Part of the GDR opens onto the Baltic Sea, which the Germans call Ostsee. Swept by salty breezes, the atmosphere here is completely different from the rest of East Germany. On any summer day the place is overrun with Communist holiday-makers. Scandinavians often visit here too. In my frankest recommendation, I suggest the GDR Baltic coast not so much for its seaside resorts and beach facilities (there are far more exciting spots in Western Europe for that), but for the remnants that remain of its old Hanseatic towns. That is, what was spared from Allied bombing raids.

ROSTOCK: Largest of the GDR ports, Rostock lies on an estuary of the Warnow, a distance of some 175 miles northwest of Berlin by train and some 80 miles northeast of its more famous neighbor, Lübeck, the hometown of Thomas Mann. Copenhagen lies about 100 miles away to the north.

Rostock joined the Hanseatic League in the 14th century. Because it was the location of one of the largest Nazi aircraft factories, it was blasted by British bombers as early as 1942, which sent the townspeople fleeing to the countryside. Other bombings followed. Its principal street, Lange Strasse or "Long Street," was completely demolished, but has now been rebuilt and modernized. A row of buildings has been restored in the old style as a reminder of the past.

Some noteworthy historic buildings stand on Ernst Thalmann Square, including the Rathaus, a 13th- or 14th-century Gothic brick structure. Early 16th-century Walldiener House and Kerkhof House are also of interest. Among the buildings that survived war destruction is the **Marienkirche** (St. Mary's Church), one of the most outstanding ecclesiastical structures of the Baltic region. Dating from 1398, it is a Gothic building with two towers in the Romanesque style. Look for its clock.

Other churches to be seen are the **Heilig-Kreuz-Kirche** (Holy Cross Church), a three-nave Gothic brick hall church from the 14th century, and **Michaelis Monastery**, a one-nave house of worship of the Order of Mendicant Friars, built between 1480 and 1488.

Rostock also has Zoological Gardens, a sports forum, and Barnstord, with an open-air theater, an auditorium, and several restaurants.

You can tour the port of Rostock by boat.

The following hotel makes Rostock the best center for exploring the Baltic coast:

Hotel Warnow, Hermann-Duncker-Platz (tel. 3-73-81), has a boxy block-like shape with indented balconies. The entire building, the best hotel in Rostock, containing 338 rooms, is surrounded by an expanse of green lawn dotted with political statues of girls in heroic poses. Inside the hotel you'll find that the rooms are comfortably furnished and appointed, costing from $32 per person daily for bed and breakfast in a double, $46 in a single. You'll also find three restaurants which for the most part serve specialties of the Mecklenburg region. There's also the Café Riga (named for another Baltic capital), as well as a sun terrace, bar, nightclub, and the inevitable Intershop.

Touring in the Environs

Warnemünde is the largest seaside resort in the GDR, with a ferryboat harbor, a 585-yard long pier, a lighthouse, and the big Warnow shipyard on the water. It is about nine miles from Rostock. A ship serves as an exhibition and cultural center for the town. Teepott restaurant, directly on the beach, is a good place to stop for a meal and/or a drink. Warnemünde's beach is good to look at, but going in the water can be a chilling experience.

A little more than ten miles from Rostock is **Bad Doberan**, a spa town surrounded by forested hills. The main attractions are the Doberan Cathedral in a Lower German Gothic brick style; the Zisterziens (Cistercian) Monastery from the 13th to 14th centuries; and the Brewery and Brick House with a water mill dating from 1270.

Some three miles on from Bad Doberan lies **Heiligendamm**, the oldest sea resort of the Baltic, founded in 1793. It's called the White Seaside Town. You can go here on the Molli narrow-gauge railway train.

Greifswald, in the east of Rostock County, is the smallest university town in the GDR, known for learning and research, and rich in tradition. The university was founded in 1456. Interesting sights of the town include Kirche St. Marien, with art and historical monuments, such as the pulpit, which has fine marquetry work. It's the town's oldest house of worship. Two other churches worth seeing are Kirche St. Jakobi, started in the 13th century, and Kirche St. Nikolai, a cathedral with a panoramic view from its gallery. The brick burgher's house at 11 Platz der Freundschaft, built around 1430, is the best example of houses of this type in Greifswald.

Don't miss seeing the little fishing village of **Wieck,** which has been a part of Greifswald since 1939. You'll see typical fishermen's houses with thatched roofs, whitewashed walls, and tarred framework, all still in good condition. The village, including the wooden drawbridge over the River Ryck, has been taken over as a national monument. Although it has a medieval look, some of it was built as late as 1886.

STRALSUND: A seaport on the Baltic Strait of Bodden, across from Rügen Island, this town dates from the 13th century. Once it was rivaled only by Lübeck in its prominence in the Hanseatic League. Because of its vital importance, it was fought over and has known many masters. Its last conquerors arrived in 1945: they were Soviet troops, and they're still there, or at least the grandchildren of the original troops. Stralsund is about 21 miles from Greifswald, just visited.

Buildings of historic interest are mostly of Lower German Gothic brick construction. They include the **Rathaus,** the oldest parts of which date from the 13th century. This is considered one of the most imposing examples existing of the North German secular brick Gothic architecture. Ecclesiastical buildings predominate among points of interest. **Nikolaikirche** and **Marienkirche** are 14th-century churches with rich interior decoration. The **Jacobikirche** was transformed into a three-nave basilica in the 14th century. It has a high altar with baroque mounting and paintings by J. H. Tischbein, one of the foremost ecclesiastical artists of his day. The 15th-century **Katharinenkloster** is a significant monastery, and **Heiligengeistkirche** (Church of the Holy Ghost), not far from Katharinenkloster, is noteworthy for its inner courtyard with wooden galleries.

In the city center of this old maritime port are remnants of the town wall.

Stralsund has a **Cultural-Historical Museum,** which traces the story of the port and its region from the days of the Vikings to Hanseatic League power and to the present. There is also an **Oceanographic Museum,** the only one of its kind in the GDR.

The Weisse Flotte (White Fleet) not only serves the daily passenger shipping routes of the Baltic resorts with boats from Stralsund, but the harbor here is also the starting point of "Round Rügen" trips, all-day deep-sea excursions, and journeys to Swinoujscie in Poland.

The Baltic island of **Rügen,** opposite Stralsund, is not only the largest in Germany but arguably the most beautiful. It lies just 1½ miles off the northwest coast of what used to be Pomeranian Prussia. Its coastline is dotted with peninsulas and bays. From north to south at its greatest length, it stretches for 32 miles. An excursion from Stralsund takes visitors over the Rügen Dam. The chalk cliffs of Stubbenkammer with the Königstuhl rock, the Granitz hunting lodge, and Kap (Cape) Arkona, the most northerly point of the GDR, can be seen, as well as Spyker Castle with its old walls and dolmens. Try also to visit Jasmund, which is the most beautiful part of the island.

Planned excursions are offered, or you can go on your own, taking a ferryboat from Stralsund to Altefähr on Rügen. From there you can take a narrow-gauge railway train which traverses the island. The old capital of the barony of the princes of Putbus is here, named, appropriately, Putbus.

Another excursion offered by the White Fleet is to **Hiddensee Island,** about

11 miles long. Although it is geologically closely related to Rügen Island, it has a number of characteristics of its own that are worth seeing. It is accessible only by sea, so there are no cars and no streets of any appreciable width. In fact many of the roadways, such as they are, are not even paved. Botanists find this a good place to study Baltic island flora, and the island's native birds attract nature lovers, birdwatchers, and ornithologists. Parts of Hiddensee are nature reserves.

The former residence of dramatist Gerhart Hauptmann is open to visitors. The best place to stay in Stralsund is the **Hotel Baltic** (tel. 53-81), whose rooms are impersonal but well kept. Many Scandinavians, especially Swedes, favor this place for a holiday. Simply furnished singles cost $23 nightly, dropping to $21 per person in a double. The hotel also has the best dining facilities in town, with meals costing from $8. You can get good fresh fish here.

As a dining alternative, you can sample the fare at the **Zur Post,** a cellar restaurant in the Rathaus.

SCHWERIN: Lying inland, this town at the southwest corner of Lake Schwerin is set in a district of "lakelets." It is the industrial and cultural center of an important agricultural district, but it has more to recommend it to visitors than commerce. Once the seat of the ducal court of Mecklenburg, its history is ancient. There are not many historic buildings in Schwerin, however, as most of the old structures were destroyed by fire and replaced during the 19th century. Among these is the **Arsenal** by the Pfaffenteich, an artificial reservoir in the city center, the **Marstall** (royal stables), and the **Kollegiengebäude,** seat of government until 1945.

Schwerin Castle, the seat of the Mecklenburg dukes, was spared by the fire. It stands on Castle Island, a pentagonal structure of many towers and turrets, with characteristics of the Gothic, baroque, and Renaissance styles of architecture. While some of the structural elements are from the 15th to the 16th centuries, the castle's appearance today is in the French Renaissance style of the mid-19th century. It now accommodates a teachers' college and the Polytechnic Museum. Concerts are held in the castle garden, which has terraced waterfalls and a canal running through it. These grounds have been designated as a public park. The baroque castle garden contains valuable sculptures and arcades, and is considered a good example of 18th-century landscape gardening.

Two imposing buildings stand in the former Alter Garten (old gardens) parade grounds, the **Mecklenburgisches Staatstheater** (state theater) and the **Staatliches Museum Schwerin** (state museum) (tel. 75-81). The museum contains a collection of famous Dutch paintings including Rembrandt's *Portrait of an Old Man, Lot and His Daughters* by Rubens, and Willem von Aeist's *Breakfast Table and Nautilus Cup*. There are also 18th-century court paintings and prehistoric and historic ethnological collections. The museum is open from 9 a.m. to 1 p.m. and 2 to 5 p.m. in summer. Admission is M 1.25 (41¢).

Schwerin's Gothic **cathedral** is a fine example of medieval architecture. It dates from 1248, though the present building is in the Lübeck Baltic Gothic style. The Mecklenburgische Landesbibliothek (regional library) is housed in the cathedral's former cloister.

Several interesting trips are possible from Schwerin. You can take boat trips or hikes around the southern shore of Schwerin Lake, where the baths near Schwerin-Zippendorf and Schwerin-Meuss are situated. Of particular interest is the **Television Tower** near Zippendorf, 455 feet high, which offers a panoramic view of West Mecklenburg lakes and hills from its tower café.

Wismar is another seaport town in the county of Mecklenburg. It can be visited by taking a train from Schwerin, a trip of about 20 minutes. Wismar was once ruled by Sweden. World War II bombs wreaked tremendous damage on the town, but it has been largely rebuilt. However, its Marktplatz dates from the Middle Ages.

Staying in Schwerin

The town has a better-than-average hotel, **Stadt Schwerin,** 5 Grunthalplatz (tel. 52-61), which you can book in America and arrive with prepaid hotel vouchers. The rooms are pleasantly furnished, and often they fill up with tourists from Denmark who take the unbelievably cheap excursions by train, with car-ferry connections, to get a look at life on the Communist side of the sea. Each of the pleasantly furnished accommodations contains a private bath. Singles go for $27 nightly; doubles run $23 per person. The hotel has the best restaurant facilities in town.

GERMAN VOCABULARY

		Pronounced
Hello	Guten Tag	goo-ten-tahk
How are you?	Wie geht es ihnen?	vee gayt ess ee-nen
Very well	Sehr gut	zayr goot
Thank you	Danke Schön	dahn-keh-shern
Goodbye	Auf Wiedersehen	owf vee-dayr-zayn
Please	Bitte	bit-tuh
Yes	Ja	yah
No	Nein	nine
Excuse me	Entschuldigen Sie	en-shool-di-gen zee
Give me	Geben Sie mir	gay-ben zee meer
Where is?	Wo ist?	voh eest
—the station	—der Bahnhof	—dayr bahn-hohf
—a hotel	—ein Hotel	—ain hotel
—a restaurant	—ein Restaurant	—ain res-tow-rahng
—the toilet	—die Toilette	—dee twah-let-tuh
To the right	Nach rechts	nakh reshts
To the left	Nach links	nakh leenks
Straight ahead	Geradeaus	geh-rah-deh-ous
I would like	Ich möchte	ikh mersh-ta
—to eat	—essen	—ess-en
—a room	—ein Zimmer	—ain tzim-mer
—for one night	—für eine Nacht	—feer ai-neh nakht
How much is it?	Wieviel kostet?	vee-feel kaw-stet
The check, please	Zahlen, bitte	tzah-len bit-tuh
When?	Wann?	vahn
Yesterday	Gestern	geh-stern
Today	Heute	hoy-tuh
Tomorrow	Morgen	more-gen
Breakfast	Frühstück	free-shtick
Lunch	Mittagessen	mi-tahg-gess-en
Dinner	Abendessen	ah-bend-ess-en

1 **eins** (aintz)
2 **zwei** (tzvai)
3 **drei** (dry)
4 **vier** (feer)
5 **fünf** (fewnf)
6 **sechs** (zex)
7 **sieben** (zee-ben)
8 **acht** (ahkht)
9 **neun** (noyn)
10 **zehn** (tzayn)

11 **elf** (ellf)
12 **zwölf** (tzvuhlf) .
13 **dreizehn** (dry-tzayn)
14 **vierzehn** (feer-tzayn)
15 **fünfzehn** (fewnf-tzayn)
16 **sechzehn** (zex-tzayn)
17 **siebzehn** (zeeb-tzayn)
18 **achtzehn** (akh-tzayn)
19 **neunzehn** (noyn-tzayn)

20 **zwanzig** (tzvahn-tzik)
30 **dreissig** (dry-tzik)
40 **vierzig** (feer-tzik)
50 **fünfzig** (fewnf-tzik)
60 **sechzig** (zex-tzik)
70 **siebzig** (zeeb-tzik)
80 **achtzig** (akht-tzik)
90 **neunzig** (noyn-tzik)
100 **hundert** (hoon-dert)

GERMAN MENU TERMS

Soups

Erbsensuppe	pea soup	Linsensuppe	lentil soup
Gemüsesuppe	vegetable soup	Nudelsuppe	noodle soup
Hühnerbrühe	chicken soup	Ochsenschwanzsuppe	oxtail
Kartoffelsuppe	potato soup		soup
Königinsuppe	cream of chicken	Schildkrötensuppe	turtle soup
Kraftbrühe	consommé		

Meats

Aufschnitt	cold cuts	Kassler Rippchen	pork chops
Brathuhn	roast chicken	Lamm	lamb
Bratwurst	grilled sausage	Leber	liver
Deutsche Beefsteak	hamburger	Nieren	kidneys
	steak	Ragout	stew
Eisbein	pig's knuckles	Rinderbraten	roast beef
Ente	duck	Rindfleische	beef
Gans	goose	Sauerbraten	sauerbraten
Gefüllte Kalbsbrust	stuffed	Schinken	ham
	breast of veal	Schweinebraten	roast pork
Hammel	mutton	Taube	pigeon
Hirn	brains	Truthahn	turkey
Kalb	veal	Wienerschnitzel	veal cutlet
Kaltes Geflügel	cold poultry	Wurst	sausage

Fish

Aal	eel	Lachs	salmon
Forelle	trout	Makrele	mackerel
Hecht	pike	Rheinsalm	Rhine salmon
Karpfen	carp	Schellfisch	haddock
Krebs	crawfish	Seezunge	sole

Eggs

Eier in Schale	boiled eggs	mit Speck	with bacon
Rühreier	scrambled eggs	Verlorene Eier	poached eggs
Spiegeleier	fried eggs		

Sandwiches

Käsebrot	cheese sandwich	Schwarzbrot mit	
Schinkenbrot	ham sandwich	Butter	rye bread and butter
		Wurstbrot	sausage sandwich

Salads

Gemischter Salat	mixed salad	Kopfsalat	lettuce salad
Gurkensalat	cucumber salad	Rohkostplatte	vegetable salad

Vegetables

Artischocken	artichokes	Reis	rice
Blumenkohl	cauliflower	Rote Ruben	beets
Bohnen	beans	Rotkraut	red cabbage
Bratkartoffeln	fried potatoes	Salat	lettuce
Erbsen	peas	Salzkartoffeln	boiled potatoes
Grüne bohnen	string beans	Sauerkraut	sauerkraut
Gurken	cucumbers	Spargel	asparagus
Karotten	carrots	Spinat	spinach
Kartoffelbrei	mashed potatoes	Steinpilze	mushrooms
Kartoffelsalat	potato salad	Tomaten	tomatoes
Knödel	dumplings	Vorspeisen	hors d'oeuvres
Kohl	cabbage	Weisse Rüben	turnips

Desserts

Blatterteiggebäck	puff pastry	Obstsalat	fruit salad
Bratapfel	baked apple	Pfannkuchen	sugared pancakes
Käse	cheese	Pflaumenkompott	stewed plums
Klöss	dumpling	Teegebäck	tea cakes
Kompott	stewed fruit	Torten	pastries
Obstkuchen	fruit tart		

Fruits

Ananas	pineapples	Kirschen	cherries
Apfel	apples	Pfirsiche	peaches
Apfelsinen	oranges	Weintrauben	grapes
Bananen	bananas	Zitronen	lemons
Birnen	pears		

Beverages

Bier	beer	Eine Tasse Kaffee	a cup of coffee
Ein Dunkles	a dark beer		
Ein Helles	a light beer	Eine Tasse Tee	a cup of tea
Milch	milk	Tomatensaft	tomato juice
Rotwein	red wine	Wasser	water
Sahne	cream	Weinbrand	brandy
Schokolade	chocolate		

Condiments and Others

Brot	bread	Pfeffer	pepper
Brötchen	rolls	Salz	salt
Butter	butter	Senf	mustard
Eis	ice	Zitrone	lemon
Essig	vinegar	Zucker	sugar

Cooking Terms

Gebacken	baked	Geröstet	broiled
Gebraten	fried	Gut durchgebraten	well done
Gefüllt	stuffed	Nicht durchgebraten	rare
Gekocht	boiled	Paniert	breaded

NOW, SAVE MONEY ON ALL YOUR TRAVELS!
Join Arthur Frommer's $25-A-Day Travel Club

Saving money while traveling is never a simple matter, which is why, over 23 years ago, the **$25-A-Day Travel Club** was formed. Actually, the idea came from readers of the Arthur Frommer Publications who felt that such an organization could bring financial benefits, continuing travel information, and a sense of community to economy-minded travelers all over the world.

In keeping with the money-saving concept, the annual membership fee is low—$18 (U.S. residents) or $20 (Canadian, Mexican, and foreign residents)—and is immediately exceeded by the value of your benefits which include:

(1) The latest edition of any TWO of the books listed on the following page.

(2) An annual subscription to an 8-page quarterly newspaper *The Wonderful World of Budget Travel* which keeps you up-to-date on fastbreaking developments in low-cost travel in all parts of the world—bringing you the kind of information you'd have to pay over $25 a year to obtain elsewhere. This consumer-conscious publication also includes the following columns:

Hospitality Exchange—members all over the world who are willing to provide hospitality to other members as they pass through their home cities.

Share-a-Trip—requests from members for travel companions who can share costs and help avoid the burdensome single supplement.

Readers Ask . . . Readers Reply—travel questions from members to which other members reply with authentic firsthand information.

(3) A copy of *Arthur Frommer's Guide to New York*.

(4) Your personal membership card which entitles you to purchase through the Club all Arthur Frommer Publications for a third to a half off their regular retail prices during the term of your membership.

So why not join this hardy band of international budgeteers NOW and participate in its exchange of information and hospitality? Simply send $18 (U.S. residents) or $20 U.S. (Canadian, Mexican, and other foreign residents) along with your name and address to: $25-A-Day Travel Club, Inc., 1230 Avenue of the Americas, New York, NY 10020. Remember to specify which *two* of the books in section (1) above you wish to receive in your initial package of members' benefits. Or tear out this page, check off any two books on the opposite side and send it to us with your membership fee.

FROMMER/PASMANTIER PUBLISHERS   Date_____
1230 AVE. OF THE AMERICAS, NEW YORK, NY 10020

Friends, please send me the books checked below:

$-A-DAY GUIDES
(In-depth guides to low-cost tourist accommodations and facilities.)

☐ Europe on $25 a Day $11.95	☐ New Zealand on $25 a Day $10.95
☐ Australia on $25 a Day $10.95	☐ New York on $45 a Day............. $9.95
☐ England on $35 a Day............. $10.95	☐ Scandinavia on $35 a Day.......... $9.95
☐ Greece on $25 a Day............... $10.95	☐ Scotland and Wales on $35 a Day..... $10.95
☐ Hawaii on $35 a Day............... $10.95	☐ South America on $25 a Day $9.95
☐ India on $15 & $25 a Day........... $9.95	☐ Spain and Morocco (plus the Canary
☐ Ireland on $25 a Day............... $9.95	Is.) on $35 a Day $9.95
☐ Israel on $30 & $35 a Day $10.95	☐ Washington, D.C. on $40 a Day...... $10.95
☐ Mexico on $20 a Day $9.95	

DOLLARWISE GUIDES
(Guides to accommodations and facilities from budget to deluxe, with emphasis on the medium-priced.)

☐ Austria & Hungary $10.95	☐ Caribbean $12.95
☐ Egypt........................... $11.95	☐ Cruises (incl. Alaska, Carib, Mex,
☐ England & Scotland $10.95	Hawaii, Panama, Canada, & US) $10.95
☐ France.......................... $10.95	☐ California & Las Vegas $9.95
☐ Germany........................ $11.95	☐ Florida.......................... $10.95
☐ Italy............................ $10.95	☐ New England..................... $11.95
☐ Japan & Hong Kong (avail. Apr. '86) . $11.95	☐ Northwest $10.95
☐ Portugal (incl. Madeira & the Azores) . $11.95	☐ Skiing USA—East $10.95
☐ Switzerland & Liechtenstein $11.95	☐ Skiing USA—West $10.95
☐ Bermuda & The Bahamas........... $10.95	☐ Southeast & New Orleans........... $11.95
☐ Canada $12.95	☐ Southwest....................... $10.95

THE ARTHUR FROMMER GUIDES
(Pocket-size guides to tourist accommodations and facilities in all price ranges.)

☐ Amsterdam/Holland $4.95	☐ Mexico City/Acapulco $4.95
☐ Athens.......................... $4.95	☐ Montreal/Quebec City.............. $4.95
☐ Atlantic City/Cape May $4.95	☐ New Orleans $4.95
☐ Boston.......................... $4.95	☐ New York........................ $4.95
☐ Dublin/Ireland $4.95	☐ Orlando/Disney World/EPCOT $4.95
☐ Hawaii $4.95	☐ Paris $4.95
☐ Las Vegas $4.95	☐ Philadelphia...................... $4.95
☐ Lisbon/Madrid/Costa del Sol........ $4.95	☐ Rome $4.95
☐ London $4.95	☐ San Francisco $4.95
☐ Los Angeles $4.95	☐ Washington, D.C.................. $4.95

SPECIAL EDITIONS

☐ Bed & Breakfast—N. America $7.95	☐ Museums in New York $8.95
☐ Fast 'n' Easy Phrase Book	☐ Shopper's Guide to England, Scotland
(Fr/Ger/Ital/Sp in *one* vol.) $6.95	& Wales........................ $10.95
☐ Guide for the Disabled Traveler....... $10.95	☐ Swap and Go (Home Exchanging) $10.95
☐ How to Beat the High Cost of Travel ... $4.95	☐ Travel Diary and Record Book........ $5.95
☐ Marilyn Wood's Wonderful Weekends	☐ Urban Athlete (NYC sports guide) $9.95
(NY, Conn, Mass, RI, Vt, NJ, Pa) $9.95	☐ Where to Stay USA (Lodging from $3
	to $30 a night) $9.95

In U.S. include $1 post. & hdlg. for 1st book; 25¢ ea. add'l. book. Outside U.S. $2 and 50¢ respectively.

Enclosed is my check or money order for $_____

NAME_____

ADDRESS_____

CITY_____ STATE_____ ZIP_____